THE WRITINGS
כתובים
KETHUBIM

THE WRITINGS

כתובים

KETHUBIM

A new translation of
THE HOLY SCRIPTURES
according to the Masoretic text

THIRD SECTION

THE JEWISH PUBLICATION SOCIETY OF AMERICA
PHILADELPHIA

ISBN 0–8276–0202–2 (cloth-bound)
ISBN 0–8276–0203–0 (leather-bound)
Library of Congress Catalog Card No. 81–85106
Manufactured in the United States of America

PREFACE

The committee of translators for *The Writings–Kethubim*—the third part of the Hebrew Bible—was set up in 1966 by The Jewish Publication Society of America. It comprised professors Moshe Greenberg (now of the Hebrew University), Jonas C. Greenfield (now of the Hebrew University), and Nahum M. Sarna (of Brandeis University). Associated with them were rabbis Saul Leeman, Martin Rozenberg, and David Shapiro, representing the three sections of organized Jewish life in America. Chaim Potok served as secretary of the committee.

The Five Megilloth, which form a part of *The Writings,* have been translated by an earlier committee and were published separately, together with the Book of Jonah, in 1969. This translation was done by the following committee: H. L. Ginsberg as editor-in-chief, Harry M. Orlinsky as fellow editor, and associated with them, Max Arzt, Bernard J. Bamberger, Harry Freedman, and Solomon Grayzel.

The present English rendering of *The Writings* is a new version, not a revision of an earlier translation. It is based on the traditional Masoretic Hebrew text—its consonants, vowels, and syntactical divisions—although on occasion the traditional accentuation has been disregarded for an alternative construction of a verse that appeared to yield a better sense. Such departures from the traditional accentuation often were made by many earlier Jewish commentators and translators.

The entire gamut of biblical interpretation, ancient and modern, Jewish and non-Jewish, has been consulted, and whenever possible, the results of modern study of the languages and cultures of the ancient Near East have been brought to bear on the biblical word. In choosing between alternatives, however, just as antiquity was not in itself a disqualification, so modernity was not in itself a recommendation. When the present translation diverges from recent renderings (as it frequently does), this is due as much to our judgment that certain innovations, though interesting, are too speculative for adoption in the present state of knowledge as it is due to our commitment to the received Hebrew text, a commitment not made by most recent translations.

For many passages, our as yet imperfect understanding of the language of the Bible or what appears to be some disorder in the Hebrew text makes sure translation impossible. Our uncertainty is indicated in a note, where the Hebrew text permits, and alternative renderings sometimes have been offered. Emendations of the text are not proposed, however, and notes are kept to a minimum.

The style of the translation is modern literary English. An effort has been made to retain the imagery of the Hebrew rather than to render it by English equivalents and approximations alien to the biblical world. Consistency in rendering Hebrew terms was an aim but not a rule. Where its employment would have resulted in encumbered or awkward language, it was abandoned. Several passages in *The Writings* are very similar to passages in *The Torah* and *The Prophets*. The rendering of these passages in *The Writings* generally follows the wording in the earlier books. On occasion, owing to various considerations, divergences in style and translation will be found. For example, in the presentation of the poetry of the Psalms, it was deemed fitting, because of their liturgical use, to depart from the practice followed elsewhere in this work, and to indicate the thought units through appropriate indentation.

The interpretation of the text and meaning of *The Writings* presented us with extraordinary, and at times insuperable, difficulties. We know, too, that we have not conveyed the fullness of the Hebrew, with its ambiguities, its overtones, and the richness that it carries from centuries of use. Still, we hope to have transmitted something of the directness, the simplicity, and the uniquely Israelite expression of piety that are so essential to the sublimity of the Hebrew Bible.

We give thanks to God, who has enabled us to complete this sacred task.

מנחם אב תשל״ט
August 1979

CONTENTS

THE WRITINGS – KETHUBIM

תהילים

PSALMS

תהילים
PSALMS

BOOK ONE

1 Happy is the man who has not followed the counsel of the
  wicked,
  or taken the path of sinners,
  or joined the company of the insolent;
² rather, the teaching of the LORD is his delight,
  and he studies*a* that teaching day and night.
³ He is like a tree planted beside streams of water,
  that yields its fruit in season,
  whose foliage never fades,
  and whatever *b-*it produces thrives.*-b*

⁴ Not so the wicked;
  rather, they are like chaff that wind blows away.
⁵ Therefore the wicked will not survive judgment,
  nor will sinners, in the assembly of the righteous.
⁶ For the LORD cherishes the way of the righteous,
  but the way of the wicked is doomed.

2 Why do nations assemble,
  and peoples plot*a* vain things;
² kings of the earth take their stand,
  and regents intrigue together
  against the LORD and against His anointed?
³ "Let us break the cords of their yoke,
  shake off their ropes from us!"

---

a Or "recites"; lit. "utters."
b-b Or "he does prospers."

a Lit. "utter."

⁴ He who is enthroned in heaven laughs;
 the Lord mocks at them.
⁵ Then He speaks to them in anger,
 terrifying them in His rage,
⁶ "But I have installed My king
 on Zion, My holy mountain!"
⁷ Let me tell of the decree:
 the LORD said to me,
 ᵇ⁻"You are My son,
 I have fathered you this day.⁻ᵇ
⁸ Ask it of Me,
 and I will make the nations your domain;
 your estate, the limits of the earth.
⁹ You can smash them with an iron mace,
 shatter them like potter's ware."

¹⁰ So now, O kings, be prudent;
 accept discipline, you rulers of the earth!
¹¹ Serve the LORD in awe;
 ᶜ⁻tremble with fright,⁻ᶜ
¹² ᵈ⁻pay homage in good faith,⁻ᵈ
 lest He be angered, and your way be doomed
 in the mere flash of His anger.
 Happy are all who take refuge in Him.

3 A psalm of David when he fled from his son Absalom.

² O LORD, my foes are so many!
 Many are those who attack me;
³ many say of me,
 "There is no deliverance for him through
 God."   *Selah.*ᵃ

ᵇ⁻ᵇ *Compare II Sam. 7.14, and Ps. 89.27ff.*
ᶜ⁻ᶜ *Meaning of Heb. uncertain; others "rejoice with trembling."*
ᵈ⁻ᵈ *Meaning of Heb. uncertain.*

ᵃ *A liturgical direction of uncertain meaning.*

4 But You, O Lord, are a shield about me,
  my glory, He who holds my head high.
5 I cry aloud to the Lord,
  and He answers me from His holy mountain.   *Selah.*
6 I lie down and sleep and wake again,
  for the Lord sustains me.
7 I have no fear of the myriad forces
  arrayed against me on every side.

8 Rise, O Lord!
 Deliver me, O my God!
 For You slap all my enemies in the face;[b]
 You break the teeth of the wicked.
9 Deliverance is the Lord's;
  Your blessing be upon Your people!   *Selah.*

4 [a]For the leader; with instrumental music.[a] A psalm of David.

2 Answer me when I call,
  O God, my vindicator!
 You freed me from distress;
  have mercy on me and hear my prayer.
3 You men, how long will my glory be mocked,
  will you love illusions,
  have recourse to frauds?   *Selah.*
4 Know that the Lord singles out the faithful for Himself;
  the Lord hears when I call to Him.
5 So tremble, and sin no more;
  ponder it on your bed, and sigh.[b]
6 Offer sacrifices in righteousness
  and trust in the Lord.

7 Many say, "O for good days!"
  [c]Bestow Your favor on us,[c] O Lord.

---

[b] *Lit. "cheek."*

[a-a] *Meaning of Heb. uncertain.*
[b] *Others "be still."*
[c-c] *Lit. "Lift up the light of Your countenance upon us"; cf. Num. 6.25f.*

5

⁸ You put joy into my heart
    when their grain and wine show increase.
⁹ Safe and sound, I lie down and sleep,
    ᵈ-for You alone, O LORD, keep me secure.*ᵈ*

5   *ᵃ*-For the leader; on *nehiloth.*-*ᵃ* A psalm of David.

² Give ear to my speech, O LORD;
    consider my utterance.
³ Heed the sound of my cry,
    my king and God,
    for I pray to You.
⁴ Hear my voice, O LORD, at daybreak;
    at daybreak I plead before You, and wait.

⁵ For You are not a God who desires wickedness;
    evil cannot abide with You;
⁶   wanton men cannot endure in Your sight.
You detest all evildoers;
⁷   You doom those who speak lies;
    murderous, deceitful men the LORD abhors.

⁸ But I, through Your abundant love, enter Your house;
    I bow down in awe at Your holy temple.
⁹ O LORD, *ᵇ*-lead me along Your righteous [path]-*ᵇ*
    because of my watchful foes;
    make Your way straight before me.
¹⁰ For there is no sincerity on their lips;*ᶜ*
    their heart is [filled with] malice;
    their throat is an open grave;
    their tongue slippery.
¹¹ Condemn them, O God;
    let them fall by their own devices;
    cast them out for their many crimes,

ᵈ⁻ᵈ *Or "for You, O LORD, keep me alone and secure."*

ᵃ⁻ᵃ *Meaning of Heb. uncertain.*
ᵇ⁻ᵇ *Or "as You are righteous, lead me."*
ᶜ *Lit. "mouth."*

6

for they defy You.

12 But let all who take refuge in You rejoice,
ever jubilant as You shelter them;
and let those who love Your name exult in You.

13 For You surely bless the righteous man, O LORD,
encompassing him with favor like a shield.

6 *a*-For the leader; with instrumental music on the *sheminith.* -*a*
A psalm of David.

2 O LORD, do not punish me in anger,
do not chastise me in fury.

3 Have mercy on me, O LORD, for I languish;
heal me, O LORD, for my bones shake with terror.

4 My whole being is stricken with terror,
while You, LORD—O, how long!

5 O LORD, turn! Rescue me!
Deliver me as befits Your faithfulness.

6 For there is no praise of You among the dead;
in Sheol, who can acclaim You?

7 I am weary with groaning;
every night I drench my bed,
I melt my couch in tears.

8 My eyes are wasted by vexation,
worn out because of all my foes.

9 Away from me, all you evildoers,
for the LORD heeds the sound of my weeping.

10 The LORD heeds my plea,
the LORD accepts my prayer.

11 All my enemies will be frustrated and stricken with terror;
they will turn back in an instant, frustrated.

---

a-a Meaning of Heb. uncertain.

7 *ᵃ-Shiggaion* of David,*-ᵃ* which he sang to the LORD, concerning Cush, a Benjaminite.

² O LORD, my God, in You I seek refuge;
    deliver me from all my pursuers and save me,
³   lest, like a lion, they tear me apart,
    rending in pieces, and no one save me.
⁴ O LORD, my God, if I have done such things,
    if my hands bear the guilt of wrongdoing,
⁵   if I have dealt evil to my ally,
    —*ᵇ-*I who rescued my foe without reward*-ᵇ*—
⁶   then let the enemy pursue and overtake me;
    let him trample my life to the ground,
    and lay my body in the dust.   *Selah.*

⁷ Rise, O LORD, in Your anger;
    assert Yourself *ᶜ-*against the fury of my foes;*-ᶜ*
    bestir Yourself on my behalf;
    You have ordained judgment.
⁸ *ᵃ-*Let the assembly of peoples gather about You,
    with You enthroned above, on high.*-ᵃ*
⁹ The LORD judges the peoples;
    vindicate me, O LORD,
    for the righteousness and blamelessness that are mine.
¹⁰ Let the evil of the wicked come to an end,
    but establish the righteous;
    he who probes the mind and conscience*ᵈ* is God the
      righteous.
¹¹ *ᵉ-*I look to God to shield me;*-ᵉ*

ᵃ⁻ᵃ *Meaning of Heb. uncertain.*
ᵇ⁻ᵇ *Meaning of Heb. uncertain; others "or stripped my foe clean."*
ᶜ⁻ᶜ *Or "in Your fury against my foes."*
ᵈ *Lit. "kidneys."*
ᵉ⁻ᵉ *Cf. Ibn Ezra and Kimhi; lit. "My shield is upon God."*

the deliverer of the upright.

12 God vindicates the righteous;
God *f*-pronounces doom*-f* each day.

13 *g*-If one does not turn back, but whets his sword,
bends his bow and aims it,

14 then against himself he readies deadly weapons,
and makes his arrows sharp.*-g*

15 See, he hatches evil, conceives mischief,
and gives birth to fraud.

16 He has dug a pit and deepened it,
and will fall into the trap he made.

17 His mischief will recoil upon his own head;
his lawlessness will come down upon his skull.

18 I will praise the LORD for His righteousness,
and sing a hymn to the name of the LORD Most High.

8 *a*-For the leader; on the *gittith.*-*a* A psalm of David.

2 O LORD, our Lord,
How majestic is Your name throughout the earth,
b-You who have covered the heavens with Your
splendor!-*b*

3 *a*-From the mouths of infants and sucklings
You have founded strength on account of Your foes,
to put an end to enemy and avenger.-*a*

4 When I behold Your heavens, the work of Your fingers,
the moon and stars that You set in place,

5 what is man that You have been mindful of him,
mortal man that You have taken note of him,

6 that You have made him little less than divine,*c*

---

f-f Others *"has indignation."*

g-g *Meaning of vv. 13–14 uncertain; an alternate rendering, with God as the main subject, is:* [13] *If one does not turn back, He whets His sword, /bends His bow and aims it; /* [14] *deadly weapons He prepares for him, /and makes His arrows sharp.*

a-a *Meaning of Heb. uncertain.*

b-b *Meaning of Heb. uncertain; or "You whose splendor is celebrated all over the heavens!"*

c Or *"the angels."*

and adorned him with glory and majesty;
7 You have made him master over Your handiwork,
   laying the world at his feet,
8 sheep and oxen, all of them,
   and wild beasts, too;
9 the birds of the heavens, the fish of the sea,
   whatever travels the paths of the seas.
10 O LORD, our Lord, how majestic is Your name
   throughout the earth!

9 *a*-For the leader; *'almuth labben.*-*a* A psalm of David.

2 I will praise You, LORD, with all my heart;
   I will tell all Your wonders.
3 I will rejoice and exult in You,
   singing a hymn to Your name, O Most High.

4 When my enemies retreat,
   they stumble to their doom at Your presence.
5 For You uphold my right and claim,
   enthroned as righteous judge.
6 You blast the nations;
   You destroy the wicked;
   You blot out their name forever.
7 *b*-The enemy is no more—
   ruins everlasting;
   You have torn down their cities;
   their very names are lost.-*b*
8 But the LORD abides forever;
   He has set up His throne for judgment;
9 it is He who judges the world with righteousness,
   rules the peoples with equity.
10 The LORD is a haven for the oppressed,
   a haven in times of trouble.
11 Those who know Your name trust You,

a-a *Meaning of Heb. uncertain; some mss. and ancient versions,* 'al muth labben, *as though "over the death of the son."*
b-b *Meaning of Heb. uncertain.*

for You do not abandon those who turn to You, O LORD.

12 Sing a hymn to the LORD, ^cwho reigns in Zion;^{-c}
declare His deeds among the peoples.

13 ^dFor He does not ignore the cry of the afflicted;
He who requites bloodshed is mindful of them.^{-d}

14 Have mercy on me, O LORD;
see my affliction at the hands of my foes,
You who lift me from the gates of death,

15 so that in the gates of ^eFair Zion^{-e}
I might tell all Your praise,
I might exult in Your deliverance.

16 The nations sink in the pit they have made;
their own foot is caught in the net they have hidden.

17 The LORD has made Himself known:
He works judgment;
the wicked man is snared by his own
devices.   *Higgaion.*^b   *Selah.*

18 Let the wicked be^f in Sheol,
all the nations who ignore God!

19 Not always shall the needy be ignored,
nor the hope of the afflicted forever lost.

20 Rise, O LORD!
Let not men have power;
let the nations be judged in Your presence.

21 ^bStrike fear into them,^{-b} O LORD;
let the nations know they are only men.   *Selah.*

10 Why, O LORD, do You stand aloof,
heedless in times of trouble?

2 The wicked in his arrogance hounds the lowly—
^amay they be caught in the schemes they devise!^{-a}

---

^{c-c} *Or "O you who dwell in Zion."*
^{d-d} *Order of Hebrew clauses inverted for clarity.*
^{e-e} *Lit. "the Daughter of Zion."*
^f *Others "return to."*

^{a-a} *Or "they (i.e. the lowly) are caught by the schemes they devised."*

3 *b-*The wicked crows about his unbridled lusts;
   the grasping man reviles and scorns the LORD.
4 The wicked, arrogant as he is,
   in all his scheming [thinks],*-b*
   "He does not call to account;
   *c-*God does not care."*-c*
5 His ways prosper at all times;
   Your judgments are far beyond him;
   he snorts at all his foes.
6 He thinks, "I shall not be shaken,
   through all time never be in trouble."
7 His mouth is full of oaths, deceit, and fraud;
   mischief and evil are under his tongue.
8 He lurks in outlying places;
   from a covert he slays the innocent;
   his eyes spy out the hapless.
9 He waits in a covert like a lion in his lair;
   waits to seize the lowly;
   he seizes the lowly as he pulls his net shut;
10   he stoops, he crouches,
   *b-*and the hapless fall prey to his might.*-b*
11 He thinks, "God is not mindful,
   He hides His face, He never looks."
12 Rise, O LORD!
   *d-*Strike at him,*-d* O God!
   Do not forget the lowly.
13 Why should the wicked man scorn God,
   thinking You do not call to account?
14 You do look!
   You take note of mischief and vexation!
   *b-*To requite is in Your power.*-b*
   To You the hapless can entrust himself;
   You have ever been the orphan's help.
15 O break the power of the wicked and evil man,

---

b-b Meaning of Heb. uncertain.
c-c Lit. "There is no God."
d-d Lit. "Lift Your hand."

so that when You *-look for-* his wickedness
You will find it no more.

16 The LORD is king for ever and ever;
    the nations will perish from His land.
17 You will listen to the entreaty of the lowly, O LORD,
    You will make their hearts firm;
    You will incline Your ear
18 to champion the orphan and the downtrodden,
    -that men who are of the earth tyrannize no more.-

11 For the leader. Of David.

In the LORD I take refuge;
    how can you say to me,
    "Take to *-the hills like a bird!-*
2 For see, the wicked bend the bow,
    they set their arrow on the string
    to shoot from the shadows at the upright.
3 *-When the foundations are destroyed,
    what can the righteous man do?"-*

4 The LORD is in His holy palace;
    the LORD—His throne is in heaven;
    His eyes behold, His gaze searches mankind.
5 The LORD seeks out the righteous man,
    but loathes the wicked one who loves injustice.
6 He will rain down upon the wicked blazing coals and
        sulfur;
    a scorching wind shall be *-their lot.-*
7 For the LORD is righteous;
    He loves righteous deeds;
    the upright shall behold His face.

- A play on darash, *which in vv. 4, 13 means "to call to account."*

- *Meaning of Heb. uncertain; lit. "your hill, bird!"*
- *Or "For the foundations are destroyed; what has the Righteous One done?" Or "If the foundations are destroyed, what has the righteous man accomplished?"*
- *Lit. "the portion of their cup."*

13

12 For the leader; on the *sheminith*. A psalm of David.

² Help, O LORD!
For the faithful are no more;
the loyal have vanished from among men.
³ Men speak lies to one another;
their speech is smooth;
they talk with duplicity.
⁴ May the LORD cut off all flattering lips,
every tongue that speaks arrogance.
⁵ They say, "By our tongues we shall prevail;
with lips such as ours, who can be our master?"

⁶ "Because of the groans of the plundered poor and needy,
I will now act," says the LORD.
ᵃ-"I will give help," He affirms to him.*⁻ᵃ*
⁷ The words of the LORD are pure words,
silver purged in an earthen crucible,
refined sevenfold.
⁸ You, O LORD, will keep them,
guarding each *ᵃ*-from this age-*ᵃ* evermore.
⁹ On every side the wicked roam
ᵃ-when baseness is exalted among men.*⁻ᵃ*

13 For the leader. A psalm of David.

² How long, O LORD; will You ignore me forever?
How long will You hide Your face from me?
³ How long will I have cares on my mind,
grief in my heart all day?
How long will my enemy have the upper hand?
⁴ Look at me, answer me, O LORD, my God!

ᵃ⁻ᵃ *Meaning of Heb. uncertain.*

Restore the luster to my eyes,
>lest I sleep the sleep of death;
5 lest my enemy say, "I have overcome him,"
>my foes exult when I totter.
6 But I trust in Your faithfulness,
>my heart will exult in Your deliverance.
I will sing to the LORD,
>for He has been good to me.

14 *a*For the leader. Of David.

The benighted man thinks,
>*b*-"God does not care."-*b*
Man's deeds are corrupt and loathsome;
>no one does good.
2 The LORD looks down from heaven on mankind
>to find a man of understanding,
>a man mindful of God.
3 All have turned bad,
>altogether foul;
>there is none who does good,
>not even one.
4 Are they so witless, all those evildoers,
>who devour my people as they devour food,
>and do not invoke the LORD?
5 There they will be seized with fright,
>for God is present in the circle of the righteous.
6 You may set at naught the counsel of the lowly,
>but the LORD is his refuge.

7 O that the deliverance of Israel might come from Zion!
When the LORD restores the fortunes of His people,
>Jacob will exult, Israel will rejoice.

---

a *Cf. Ps. 53.*
b-b *Lit. "There is no God"; cf. Ps. 10.4.*

15 A psalm of David.

LORD, who may sojourn in Your tent,
    who may dwell on Your holy mountain?
2 He who lives without blame,
    who does what is right,
    and in his heart acknowledges the truth;
3   *a*-whose tongue is not given to evil;-*a*
    who has never done harm to his fellow,
    or borne reproach for [his acts toward] his neighbor;
4   for whom a contemptible man is abhorrent,
    but who honors those who fear the LORD;
    who stands by his oath even to his hurt;
5   who has never lent money at interest,
    or accepted a bribe against the innocent.
The man who acts thus shall never be shaken.

16 A *michtam*[a] of David.

Protect me, O God, for I seek refuge in You.
2 I say to the LORD,
    "You are my Lord, *b*-my benefactor;
    there is none above You."-*b*
3 *c*-As to the holy and mighty ones that are in the land,
    my whole desire concerning them is that
4   those who espouse another [god]
    may have many sorrows!-*c*
I will have no part of their bloody libations;
    their names will not pass my lips.

a-a *Meaning of Heb. uncertain; or "who has no slander upon his tongue."*

a *Meaning of Heb. uncertain.*
b-b *Others "I have no good but in You."*
c-c *Meaning of Heb. uncertain; "holy and mighty ones" taken as epithets for divine beings; cf. qedoshim in Ps. 89.6, 8, and 'addirim in I Sam. 4.8.*

⁵ The LORD is my allotted share and portion;*d*
  You control my fate.
⁶ Delightful country has fallen to my lot;
  lovely indeed is my estate.
⁷ I bless the LORD who has guided me;
  my conscience*e* admonishes me at night.
⁸ I am ever mindful of the LORD's presence;
  He is at my right hand; I shall never be shaken.
⁹ So my heart rejoices,
  my whole being exults,
  and my body rests secure.
¹⁰ For You will not abandon me to Sheol,
  or let Your faithful one see the Pit.
¹¹ You will teach me the path of life.
  In Your presence is perfect joy;
  delights are ever in Your right hand.

17 A prayer of David.

  Hear, O LORD, what is just;
  heed my cry, give ear to my prayer,
  uttered without guile.
² My vindication will come from You;
  Your eyes will behold what is right.
³ You have visited me at night, probed my mind,
  You have tested me and found nothing amiss;
  a-I determined that my mouth should not transgress.
⁴ As for man's dealings,
  in accord with the command of Your lips,-*a*
  I have kept in view the fate*b* of the lawless.
⁵ My feet have held to Your paths;
  my legs have not given way.

⁶ I call on You;
  You will answer me, God;

---

d Lit. "cup."
e Lit. "kidneys."

a-a Meaning of Heb. uncertain.
b Cf. Prov. 1.19; lit. "paths."

> turn Your ear to me,
> hear what I say.
> 7 Display Your faithfulness in wondrous deeds,
> You who deliver with Your right hand
> those who seek refuge from assailants.
> 8 Guard me like the apple of Your eye;
> hide me in the shadow of Your wings
> 9 from the wicked who despoil me,
> *c*-my mortal enemies who-*c* encircle me.
> 10 *a*-Their hearts are closed to pity;-*a*
> they mouth arrogance;
> 11 now they hem in our feet on every side;
> they set their eyes roaming over the land.
> 12 He is like a lion eager for prey,
> a king of beasts lying in wait.

> 13 Rise, O LORD! Go forth to meet him.
> Bring him down;
> rescue me from the wicked with Your sword,
> 14 *a*-from men, O LORD, with Your hand,
> from men whose share in life is fleeting.
> But as to Your treasured ones,
> fill their bellies.-*a*
> Their sons too shall be satisfied,
> and have something to leave over for their young.
> 15 Then I, justified, will behold Your face;
> awake, I am filled with the vision of You.

18 *a*For the leader. Of David, the servant of the LORD, who addressed the words of this song to the LORD after the LORD had saved him from the hands of all his enemies and from the clutches of Saul.

> 2 He said:
> *b*-I adore you, O LORD, my strength,-*b*

---

c-c Or "from my enemies who avidly."

a This poem occurs again at II Sam. 22, with a number of variations, some of which are cited in the following notes.

b-b Not in II Sam. 22.2.

3 O LORD, my crag, my fortress, my rescuer,
  my God, my rock in whom I seek refuge,
  my shield, my ^cmighty champion,^{-c} my haven.

4 ^{d-}All praise! I called on the LORD^{-d}
  and was delivered from my enemies.

5 Ropes^e of Death encompassed me;
  torrents of Belial^f terrified me;

6 ropes of Sheol encircled me;
  snares of Death confronted me.

7 In my distress I called on the LORD,
  cried out to my God;
  in His temple He heard my voice;
  my cry to Him reached His ears.

8 Then the earth rocked and quaked;
  the foundations of the mountains shook,
  rocked by His indignation;

9 smoke went up from His nostrils,
  from His mouth came devouring fire;
  live coals blazed forth from Him.

10 He bent the sky and came down,
  thick cloud beneath His feet.

11 He mounted a cherub and flew,
  gliding on the wings of the wind.

12 He made darkness His screen;
  dark thunderheads, dense clouds of the sky
  were His pavilion round about Him.

13 Out of the brilliance before Him,
  hail and fiery coals ^gpierced His clouds.^{-g}

14 Then the LORD thundered from heaven,
  the Most High gave forth His voice—
  ^{h-}hail and fiery coals.^{-h}

---

^{c-c} Lit. "horn of rescue."
^{d-d} Construction of Heb. uncertain.
^e II Sam. 22.5, "breakers."
^f I.e., the netherworld, like "Death" and "Sheol."
^{g-g} II Sam. 22.13, "blazed."
^{h-h} Not in II Sam. 22.14.

¹⁵ He let fly His shafts and scattered them;
He discharged lightning and routed them.
¹⁶ The ocean bed was exposed;
the foundations of the world were laid bare
by Your mighty roaring, O LORD,
at the blast of the breath of Your nostrils.
¹⁷ He reached down from on high, He took me;
He drew me out of the mighty waters;
¹⁸ He saved me from my fierce enemy,
from foes too strong for me.
¹⁹ They confronted me on the day of my calamity,
but the LORD was my support.
²⁰ He brought me out to freedom;
He rescued me because He was pleased with me.

²¹ The LORD rewarded me according to my merit;
He requited the cleanness of my hands;
²² for I have kept to the ways of the LORD,
and have not been guilty before my God;
²³ for I am mindful of all His rules;
I have not disregarded His laws.
²⁴ I have been blameless toward Him,
and have guarded myself against sinning;
²⁵ and the LORD has requited me according to my merit,
the cleanness of my hands in His sight.

²⁶ With the loyal, You deal loyally;
with the blameless man, blamelessly.
²⁷ With the pure, You act purely,
and with the perverse, You are wily.
²⁸ It is You who deliver lowly folk,
but haughty eyes You humble.
²⁹ It is You who light my lamp;
the LORD, my God, lights up my darkness.
³⁰ With You, I can rush a barrier;[i]

---

[i] *Cf. note to II Sam. 22.30; or "troop."*

with my God I can scale a wall;
31   the way of God is perfect;
the word of the LORD is pure;
He is a shield to all who seek refuge in Him.
32 Truly, who is a god except the LORD,
who is a rock but our God?—
33   the God who girded me with might,
who made my way perfect;
34   who made my legs like a deer's,
and let me stand firm on the[j] heights;
35   who trained my hands for battle;
my arms can bend a bow of bronze.
36 You have given me the shield of Your protection;
Your right hand has sustained me,
Your care[k] has made me great.
37 You have let me stride on freely;
my feet have not slipped.
38 I pursued my enemies and overtook them;
I did not turn back till I destroyed them.
39 I struck them down,
and they could rise no more;
they lay fallen at my feet.
40 You have girded me with strength for battle,
brought my adversaries low before me,
41   made my enemies turn tail before me;
I wiped out my foes.
42 They cried out, but there was none to deliver;
[cried] to the LORD, but He did not answer them.
43 I ground them fine as windswept dust;
I trod them flat as dirt of the streets.
44 You have rescued me from the strife of people;
You have set me at the head of nations;
peoples I knew not must serve me.
45 At the mere report of me they are submissive;
foreign peoples cower before me;

j *Taking* bamothai *as a poetic form of* bamoth; *cf. Hab. 3.19; others "my."*
k *Meaning of Heb. uncertain; others "condescension."*

46 foreign peoples lose courage,
   l-and come trembling out of their strongholds.-*l*

47 The LORD lives! Blessed is my rock!
   Exalted be God, my deliverer,
48   the God who has vindicated me
   and made peoples subject to me,
49   who rescued me from my enemies,
   who raised me clear of my adversaries,
   saved me from lawless men.
50 For this I sing Your praise among the nations, LORD,
   and hymn Your name:
51   *m*-He accords great victories-*m* to His king,
   keeps faith with His anointed,
   with David and his offspring forever.

19 For the leader. A psalm of David.

2 The heavens declare the glory of God,
   the sky proclaims His handiwork.
3 Day to day makes utterance,
   night to night speaks out.
4 There is no utterance,
   there are no words,
   a-whose sound goes unheard.-*a*
5 Their voice*b* carries throughout the earth,
   their words to the end of the world.
   He placed in them*c* a tent for the sun,
6   who is like a groom coming forth from the chamber,
   like a hero, eager to run his course.
7 His rising-place is at one end of heaven,
   and his circuit reaches the other;
   nothing escapes his heat.

---

l-l Meaning of Heb. uncertain.
m-m II Sam. 22.51, "Tower of victory."

a-a With Septuagint, Symmachus, and Vulgate; or "their sound is not heard."
b Cf. Septuagint, Symmachus, and Vulgate; Arabic qawwah, "to shout."
c Viz. the heavens.

8 The teaching of the LORD is perfect,
   renewing life;
   the decrees of the LORD are enduring,
   making the simple wise;
9 The precepts of the LORD are just,
   rejoicing the heart;
   the instruction of the LORD is lucid,
   making the eyes light up.
10 The fear of the LORD is pure,
   abiding forever;
   the judgments of the LORD are true,
   righteous altogether,
11 more desirable than gold,
   than much fine gold;
   sweeter than honey,
   than drippings of the comb.
12 Your servant pays them heed;
   in obeying them there is much reward.
13 Who can be aware of errors?
   Clear me of unperceived guilt,
14 and from *d*-willful sins-*d* keep Your servant;
   let them not dominate me;
   then shall I be blameless
   and clear of grave offense.
15 May the words of my mouth
   and the prayer of my heart*e*
   be acceptable to You,
   O LORD, my rock and my redeemer.

20 For the leader. A psalm of David.

2 May the LORD answer you in time of trouble,
   the name of Jacob's God keep you safe.
3 May He send you help from the sanctuary,

d-d *Or "arrogant men"; cf. Ps. 119.51.*
e *For* leb *as a source of speech, see note to Eccl. 5.1.*

and sustain you from Zion.

4 May He receive the tokens[a] of all your meal offerings,
    and approve[b] your burnt offerings.   *Selah.*

5 May He grant you your desire,
    and fulfill your every plan.

6 May we shout for joy in your victory,
    arrayed by standards in the name of our God.

May the Lord fulfill your every wish.

7 Now I know that the Lord will give victory to His
    anointed,
    will answer him from His heavenly sanctuary
    with the mighty victories of His right arm.

8 They [call] on chariots, they [call] on horses,
    but we call on the name of the Lord our God.

9 They collapse and lie fallen,
    but we rally and gather strength.

10 [c-]O Lord, grant victory!

May the King answer us when we call.[-c]

21 For the leader. A psalm of David.

2 O Lord, the king rejoices in Your strength;
    how greatly he exults in Your victory!

3 You have granted him the desire of his heart,
    have not denied the request of his lips.   *Selah.*

4 You have proffered him blessings of good things,
    have set upon his head a crown of fine gold.

5 He asked You for life; You granted it;
    a long life, everlasting.

6 Great is his glory through Your victory;
    You have endowed him with splendor and majesty.

7 You have made him blessed forever,

---

[a] *Reference to* azkara, *"token portion" of meal offering; Lev. 2.2, 9, 16, etc.*
[b] *Meaning of Heb. uncertain.*
[c-c] *Or, in the light of v. 7, "O Lord, grant victory to the king; may He answer us when we call."*

24

gladdened him with the joy of Your presence.
8 For the king trusts in the LORD;
Through the faithfulness of the Most High
he will not be shaken.
9 Your hand is equal to all Your enemies;
Your right hand overpowers Your foes.
10 You set them ablaze like a furnace
a-when You show Your presence.*-a*
The LORD in anger destroys them;
fire consumes them.
11 You wipe their offspring from the earth,
their issue from among men.
12 For they schemed against You;
they laid plans,
but could not succeed.
13 *b*-For You make them turn back*-b*
by Your bows aimed at their face.
14 Be exalted, O LORD, through Your strength;
we will sing and chant the praises of Your mighty deeds.

22 For the leader; on *a*-*ayyeleth ha-shahar.*-a* A psalm of David.

2 My God, my God,
why have You abandoned me;
why so far from delivering me
and from my anguished roaring?
3 My God,
I cry by day—You answer not;
by night, and have no respite.

4 *b*-But You are the Holy One,
enthroned,
the Praise of Israel.*-b*
5 In You our fathers trusted;

---

a-a Or, "at the time of Your anger."
b-b Meaning of Heb. uncertain.

a-a Meaning of Heb. uncertain.
b-b Or "But You are holy, enthroned upon the praises of Israel."

they trusted, and You rescued them.
6 To You they cried out
and they escaped;
in You they trusted
and were not disappointed.

7 But I am a worm, less than human;
scorned by men, despised by people.
8 All who see me mock me;
^{c}-they curl their lips,$^{-c}$
they shake their heads.
9 "Let him commit himself to the LORD;
let Him rescue him,
let Him save him,
for He is pleased with him."
10 You ^{a}-drew me-^{a} from the womb,
made me secure at my mother's breast.
11 I became Your charge at birth;
from my mother's womb You have been my God.
12 Do not be far from me,
for trouble is near,
and there is none to help.
13 Many bulls surround me,
mighty ones of Bashan encircle me.
14 They open their mouths at me
like tearing, roaring lions.
15 ^{d}-My life ebbs away:-^{d}
all my bones are disjointed;
my heart is like wax,
melting within me;
16   my vigor dries up like a shard;
my tongue cleaves to my palate;
You commit me to the dust of death.
17 Dogs surround me;
a pack of evil ones closes in on me,

$^{c-c}$ *Lit. "they open wide with a lip."*
$^{d-d}$ *Lit. "I am poured out like water."*

e-like lions [they maul] my hands and feet.*-e*

18 I take the count of all my bones
  while they look on and gloat.

19 They divide my clothes among themselves,
  casting lots for my garments.

20 But You, O LORD, be not far off;
  my strength, hasten to my aid.

21 Save my life from the sword,
  my precious life*f* from the clutches of a dog.

22 Deliver me from a lion's mouth;
  from the horns of wild oxen rescue*g* me.

23 Then will I proclaim Your fame to my brethren,
  praise You in the congregation.

24 You who fear the LORD, praise Him!
  All you offspring of Jacob, honor Him!
  Be in dread of Him, all you offspring of Israel!

25 For He did not scorn, He did not spurn
  the plea*h* of the lowly;
  He did not hide His face from him;
  when he cried out to Him, He listened.

26 *i*-Because of You I offer praise-*i* in the great congregation;
  I pay my vows in the presence of His worshipers.

27 Let the lowly eat and be satisfied;
  let all who seek the LORD praise Him.
  Always be of good cheer!

28 Let all the ends of the earth pay heed and turn to the LORD,
  and the peoples of all nations prostrate themselves before You;

29   for kingship is the LORD's

---

e-e With Rashi; cf. Isa. 38.13.
f Lit. "only one."
g Lit. "answer."
h Or "plight."
i-i Lit. "From You is my praise."

and He rules the nations.
30 *j-*All those in full vigor shall eat and prostrate themselves;
all those at death's door, whose spirits flag,
shall bend the knee before Him.*-j*
31 Offspring shall serve Him;
the LORD's fame shall be proclaimed to the generation
32 to come;
they shall tell of His beneficence
to people yet to be born,
for He has acted.

23 A psalm of David.

The LORD is my shepherd;
I lack nothing.
2 He makes me lie down in green pastures;
He leads me to *a-*water in places of repose;*-a*
3 He renews my life;
He guides me in right paths
as befits His name.
4 Though I walk through *b-*a valley of deepest darkness,*-b*
I fear no harm, for You are with me;
Your rod and Your staff—they comfort me.

5 You spread a table for me in full view of my enemies;
You anoint my head with oil;
my drink is abundant.
6 Only goodness and steadfast love shall pursue me
all the days of my life,
and I shall dwell in the house of the LORD
for many long years.

---

j-j Meaning of Heb. uncertain; others "All the fat ones of the earth shall eat and worship;/All they that go down to the dust shall kneel before Him,/Even he that cannot keep his soul alive."
a-a Others "still waters."
b-b Others "the valley of the shadow of death."

24 Of David. A psalm.

The earth is the LORD's and all that it holds,
　　the world and its inhabitants.
2 For He founded it upon the ocean,
　　set it on the nether-streams.

3 Who may ascend the mountain of the LORD?
　Who may stand in His holy place?—
4 He who has clean hands and a pure heart,
　　who has not taken a false oath by My[a] life
　　or sworn deceitfully.
5 He shall carry away a blessing from the LORD,
　　a just reward from God, his deliverer.
6 Such is the circle[b] of those who turn to Him,
　　Jacob, who seek Your presence.　　　　　　　　　*Selah.*

7 O gates, lift up your heads!
　Up high, you everlasting doors,
　　so the King of glory may come in!
8 Who is the King of glory?—
　　the LORD, mighty and valiant,
　　the LORD, valiant in battle.
9 O gates, lift up your heads!
　Lift them up, you everlasting doors,
　　so the King of glory may come in!
10 Who is the King of glory?—
　　the LORD of hosts,
　　He is the King of glory!　　　　　　　　　　　*Selah.*

[a] *Ancient versions and some mss. read "His."*
[b] *Lit. "generation."*

25 Of David.

א   O Lord, I set my hope on You;

ב   2   my God, in You I trust;
    may I not be disappointed,
    may my enemies not exult over me.

ג   3 O let none who look to You be disappointed;
    let the faithless be disappointed, empty-handed.

ד   4 Let me know Your paths, O Lord;
    teach me Your ways;

הו   5   guide me in Your true way and teach me,
    for You are God, my deliverer;
    it is You I look to at all times.

ז   6 O Lord, be mindful of Your compassion
    and Your faithfulness;
    they are old as time.

ח   7 Be not mindful of my youthful sins and transgressions;
    in keeping with Your faithfulness consider what is in my
      favor,
    as befits Your goodness, O Lord.

ט   8 Good and upright is the Lord;
    therefore He shows sinners the way.

י   9 He guides the lowly in the right path,
    and teaches the lowly His way.

כ   10 All the Lord's paths are steadfast love
    for those who keep the decrees of His covenant.

ל   11 As befits Your name, O Lord,
    pardon my iniquity though it be great.

מ   12 Whoever fears the Lord,
    he shall be shown what path to choose.

נ   13 He shall live a happy life,
    and his children shall inherit the land.

ס   14 The counsel[a] of the Lord is for those who fear Him;

   a *Or "secret."*

to them He makes known His covenant.

ע 15 My eyes are ever toward the LORD,
for He will loose my feet from the net.

פ 16 Turn to me, have mercy on me,
for I am alone and afflicted.

צ 17 *b*-My deep distress-*b* increases;
deliver me from my straits.

ר 18 Look at my affliction and suffering,
and forgive all my sins.

19 See how numerous my enemies are,
and how unjustly they hate me!

ש 20 Protect me and save me;
let me not be disappointed,
for I have sought refuge in You.

ת 21 May integrity and uprightness watch over me,
for I look to You.

22 O God, redeem Israel
from all its distress.

26 Of David.

Vindicate me, O LORD,
for I have walked without blame;
I have trusted in the LORD;
I have not faltered.

2 Probe me, O LORD, and try me,
test my *a*-heart and mind;-*a*

3 *b*-for my eyes are on Your steadfast love;
I have set my course by it.-*b*

4 I do not consort with scoundrels,
or mix with hypocrites;

5 I detest the company of evil men,
and do not consort with the wicked;

6 I wash my hands in innocence,

b-b *Lit. "The distress of my heart."*

a-a *Lit. "kidneys and heart."*

b-b *Or "I am aware of Your faithfulness, and always walk in Your true [path]."*

31

and walk around Your altar,
7 raising my voice in thanksgiving,
and telling all Your wonders.
8 O LORD, I love Your temple abode,
the dwelling-place of Your glory.
9 Do not sweep me away with sinners,
or [snuff out] my life with murderers,
10 who have schemes at their fingertips,
and hands full of bribes.
11 But I walk without blame;
redeem me, have mercy on me!
12 My feet are on level ground.
In assemblies I will bless the LORD.

27 Of David.

The LORD is my light and my help;
whom should I fear?
The LORD is the stronghold of my life,
whom should I dread?
2 When evil men assail me
a-to devour my flesh-*a*—
it is they, my foes and my enemies,
who stumble and fall.
3 Should an army besiege me,
my heart would have no fear;
should war beset me,
still would I be confident.

4 One thing I ask of the LORD,
only that do I seek:
to live in the house of the LORD
all the days of my life,
to gaze upon the beauty of the LORD,

---

a-a *Or "to slander me"; cf. Dan. 3.8; 6.25.*

b-to frequent-*b* His temple.
5 He will shelter me in His pavilion
on an evil day,
grant me the protection of His tent,
raise me high upon a rock.
6 Now is my head high
over my enemies roundabout;
I sacrifice in His tent with shouts of joy,
singing and chanting a hymn to the LORD.

7 Hear, O LORD, when I cry aloud;
have mercy on me, answer me.
8 *b*-In Your behalf-*b* my heart says:
"Seek My face!"
O LORD, I seek Your face.
9 Do not hide Your face from me;
do not thrust aside Your servant in anger;
You have ever been my help.
Do not forsake me, do not abandon me,
O God, my deliverer.
10 Though my father and mother abandon me,
the LORD will take me in.
11 Show me Your way, O LORD,
and lead me on a level path
because of my watchful foes.
12 Do not subject me to the will of my foes,
for false witnesses and unjust accusers
have appeared against me.
13 Had I not the assurance
that I would enjoy the goodness of the LORD
in the land of the living . . .

14 Look to the LORD;
be strong and of good courage!
O look to the LORD!

b-b *Meaning of Heb. uncertain.*

28 Of David.

O LORD, I call to You;
  my rock, do not disregard me,
  for if You hold aloof from me,
  I shall be like those gone down into the Pit.
2 Listen to my plea for mercy
  when I cry out to You,
  when I lift my hands
  toward Your inner sanctuary.
3 Do not *a*-count me-*a* with the wicked and evildoers
  who profess goodwill toward their fellows
  while malice is in their heart.
4 Pay them according to their deeds,
  their malicious acts;
  according to their handiwork pay them,
  give them their deserts.
5 For they do not consider the LORD's deeds,
  the work of His hands.
May He tear them down,
  never to rebuild them!
6 Blessed is the LORD,
  for He listens to my plea for mercy.
7 The LORD is my strength and my shield;
  my heart trusts in Him.
I was helped,*b* and my heart exulted,
  so I will glorify Him with my song.
8 The LORD is *c*-their strength;-*c*
  He is a stronghold for the deliverance of His anointed.
9 Deliver and bless Your very own people;
  tend them and sustain them forever.

---

a-a *Or "drag me off"; meaning of Heb. uncertain.*
b *Or "strengthened."*
c-c *Septuagint, Saadia, and others render, and some mss. read,* 'oz le'ammo, *"the strength of His people."*

29 A psalm of David.

Ascribe to the LORD, O divine beings,
  ascribe to the LORD glory and strength.
2 Ascribe to the LORD the glory of His name;
  bow down to the LORD, majestic in holiness.
3 The voice of the LORD is over the waters;
  the God of glory thunders,
  the LORD, over the mighty waters.
4 The voice of the LORD is power;
  the voice of the LORD is majesty;
5 the voice of the LORD breaks cedars;
  the LORD shatters the cedars of Lebanon.
6 a-He makes Lebanon skip like a calf,-a
  Sirion, like a young wild ox.
7 The voice of the LORD kindles flames of fire;
8 the voice of the LORD convulses the wilderness;
  the LORD convulses the wilderness of Kadesh;
9 the voice of the LORD causes hinds to calve,
  b-and strips forests bare;-b
  while in His temple all say "Glory!"
10 The LORD sat enthroned at the Flood;
  the LORD sits enthroned, king forever.

11 May the LORD grant strength to His people;
  may the LORD bestow on His people well-being.

30 A psalm of David. A song for the dedication of the House.a

2 I extol You, O LORD,
  for You have lifted me up,
  and not let my enemies rejoice over me.

a-a _Lit. "He makes them skip like a calf, Lebanon and Sirion, etc."_
b-b _Or "brings ewes to early birth."_

a _I.e. the Temple._

35

³ O Lord, my God,
  I cried out to You,
  and You healed me.
⁴ O Lord, You brought me up from Sheol,
  preserved me from going down into the Pit.

⁵ O you faithful of the Lord, sing to Him,
  and praise His holy name.
⁶ For He is angry but a moment,
  and when He is pleased there is life.
  ^{b-}One may lie down weeping at nightfall;^{-b}
  but at dawn there are shouts of joy.

⁷ When I was untroubled,
  I thought, "I shall never be shaken,"
⁸   for You, O Lord, when You were pleased,
  made [me]^c firm as a mighty mountain.
  When You hid Your face,
  I was terrified.
⁹ I called to You, O Lord;
  to my Lord I made appeal,
.¹⁰   "What is to be gained from my death,^d
  from my descent into the Pit?
  Can dust praise You?
  Can it declare Your faithfulness?
¹¹ Hear, O Lord, and have mercy on me;
  O Lord, be my help!"

¹² You turned my lament into dancing,
  you undid my sackcloth and girded me with joy,
¹³   that [my] whole being might sing hymns to You
    endlessly;
  O Lord my God, I will praise You forever.

---

^{b-b} *Or "Weeping may linger for the night."*
^c *Following Saadia, R. Isaiah of Trani; cf. Ibn Ezra.*
^d *Lit. "blood."*

31 For the leader. A psalm of David.

2 I seek refuge in You, O LORD;
  may I never be disappointed;
  as You are righteous, rescue me.
3 Incline Your ear to me;
  be quick to save me;
  be a rock, a stronghold for me,
  a citadel, for my deliverance.
4 For You are my rock and my fortress;
  You lead me and guide me as befits Your name.
5 You free me from the net laid for me,
  for You are my stronghold.
6 Into Your hand I entrust my spirit;
  You redeem me, O LORD, faithful God.
7 I detest those who rely on empty folly,
  but I trust in the LORD.
8 Let me exult and rejoice in Your faithfulness
  when You notice my affliction,
  are mindful of my deep distress,
9   and do not hand me over to my enemy,
  but *a*-grant me relief.*-a*

10 Have mercy on me, O LORD,
  for I am in distress;
  my eyes are wasted by vexation,
  b-my substance and body too.*-b*
11 My life is spent in sorrow,
  my years in groaning;
  my strength fails because of my iniquity,
  my limbs waste away.
12 Because of all my foes
  I am the particular butt of my neighbors,

---

a-a *Lit. "make my feet stand in a broad place."*
b-b *Meaning of Heb. uncertain.*

a horror to my friends;
those who see me on the street avoid me.

¹³ I am put out of mind like the dead;
I am like an object given up for lost.

¹⁴ I hear the whisperings of many,
intrigue ᶜ on every side,
as they scheme together against me,
plotting to take my life.

¹⁵ But I trust in You, O LORD;
I say, "You are my God!"

¹⁶ My fate is in Your hand;
save me from the hand of my enemies and pursuers.

¹⁷ Show favor to Your servant;
as You are faithful, deliver me.

¹⁸ O LORD, let me not be disappointed when I call You;
let the wicked be disappointed;
let them be silenced in Sheol;

¹⁹ let lying lips be stilled
that speak haughtily against the righteous
with arrogance and contempt.

²⁰ How abundant is the good
that You have in store for those who fear You,
that You do in the full view of men
for those who take refuge in You.

²¹ You grant them the protection of Your presence
ᵇ-against scheming men;⁻ᵇ
You shelter them in Your pavilion
from contentious tongues.

²² Blessed is the LORD,
for He has been wondrously faithful to me,
a veritable bastion.

²³ Alarmed, I had thought,
"I am thrust out of Your sight";
yet You listened to my plea for mercy
when I cried out to You.

ᶜ Others "terror."

38

²⁴ So love the LORD, all you faithful;
　the LORD guards the loyal,
　and more than requites
　him who acts arrogantly.
²⁵ Be strong and of good courage,
　all you who wait for the LORD.

32 Of David. ᵃ⁻A *maskil.*⁻ᵃ

Happy is he whose transgression is forgiven,
　whose sin is covered over.
² Happy the man whom the LORD does not hold guilty,
　and in whose spirit there is no deceit.

³ As long as I said nothing,
　my limbs wasted away
　from my anguished roaring all day long.
⁴ For night and day
　Your hand lay heavy on me;
　my vigor waned
　as in the summer drought.　　　　　　*Selah.*
⁵ Then I acknowledged my sin to You;
　I did not cover up my guilt;
　I resolved, "I will confess my transgressions to the
　　LORD,"
　and You forgave the guilt of my sin.　　*Selah.*
⁶ Therefore let every faithful man pray to You
　ᵇ⁻upon discovering [his sin],⁻ᵇ
　that the rushing mighty waters
　not overtake him.
⁷ You are my shelter;
　You preserve me from distress;
　You surround me with the joyous shouts of
　　deliverance.　　　　　　　　　　*Selah.*

ᵃ⁻ᵃ *Meaning of Heb. uncertain.*
ᵇ⁻ᵇ *Meaning of Heb. uncertain; others "in a time when You may be found."*

8 Let me enlighten you
and show you which way to go;
let me offer counsel; my eye is on you.
9 Be not like a senseless horse or mule
a-whose movement must be curbed by bit and bridle;-*a*
c-far be it from you!-*c*
10 Many are the torments of the wicked,
but he who trusts in the LORD
shall be surrounded with favor.
11 Rejoice in the LORD and exult, O you righteous;
shout for joy, all upright men!

33 Sing forth, O you righteous, to the LORD;
it is fit that the upright acclaim Him.
2 Praise the LORD with the lyre;
with the ten-stringed harp sing to Him;
3 sing Him a new song;
play sweetly with shouts of joy.
4 For the word of the LORD is right;
His every deed is faithful.
5 He loves what is right and just;
the earth is full of the LORD's faithful care.
6 By the word of the LORD the heavens were made,
by the breath of His mouth, all their host.
7 He heaps up the ocean waters like a mound,
stores the deep in vaults.

8 Let all the earth fear the LORD;
let all the inhabitants of the world dread Him.
9 For He spoke, and it was;
He commanded, and it endured.
10 The LORD frustrates the plans of nations,
brings to naught the designs of peoples.
11 What the LORD plans endures forever,
what He designs, for ages on end.

c-c *Meaning of Heb. uncertain; for this rendering cf. Ibn Ezra.*

12 Happy the nation whose God is the LORD,
the people He has chosen to be His own.
13 The LORD looks down from heaven;
He sees all mankind.
14 From His dwelling-place He gazes
on all the inhabitants of the earth—
15 He who fashions the hearts of them all,
who discerns all their doings.

16 Kings are not delivered by a large force;
warriors are not saved by great strength;
17 horses are a false hope for deliverance;
for all their great power they provide no escape.
18 Truly the eye of the LORD is on those who fear Him,
who wait for His faithful care
19 to save them from death,
to sustain them in famine.
20 We set our hope on the LORD,
He is our help and shield;
21 in Him our hearts rejoice,
for in His holy name we trust.
22 May we enjoy, O LORD, Your faithful care,
as we have put our hope in You.

34 Of David, *a*-when he feigned madness in the presence of Abimelech, who turned him out, and he left.-*a*

א 2 I bless the LORD at all times;
praise of Him is ever in my mouth.
ב 3 I glory in the LORD;
let the lowly hear it and rejoice.
ג 4 Exalt the LORD with me;
let us extol His name together.
ד 5 I turned to the LORD, and He answered me;
He saved me from all my terrors.

a-a *Cf. I Sam. 21.14ff.*

ה   ⁶ Men look to Him and are radiant;
ו   let their faces not be downcast.

ז   ⁷ Here was a lowly man who called,
      and the LORD listened,
      and delivered him from all his troubles.

ח   ⁸ The angel of the LORD camps around those who fear Him
      and rescues them.

ט   ⁹ Taste and see how good the LORD is;
      happy the man who takes refuge in Him!

י   ¹⁰ Fear the LORD, you His consecrated ones,
      for those who fear Him lack nothing.

כ   ¹¹ Lions have been reduced to starvation,
      but those who turn to the LORD shall not lack any good.

ל   ¹² Come, my sons, listen to me;
      I will teach you what it is to fear the LORD.

מ   ¹³ Who is the man who is eager for life,
      who desires years of good fortune?

נ   ¹⁴ Guard your tongue from evil,
      your lips from deceitful speech.

ס   ¹⁵ Shun evil and do good,
      seek amity[b] and pursue it.

ע   ¹⁶ The eyes of the LORD are on the righteous,
      His ears attentive to their cry.

פ   ¹⁷ The face of the LORD is set against evildoers,
      to erase their names from the earth.

צ   ¹⁸ They[c] cry out, and the LORD hears,
      and saves them from all their troubles.

ק   ¹⁹ The LORD is close to the brokenhearted;
      those crushed in spirit He delivers.

ר   ²⁰ Though the misfortunes of the righteous be many,
      the LORD will save him from them all,

ש   ²¹   keeping all his bones intact,
      not one of them being broken.

ת   ²² One misfortune is the deathblow of the wicked;
      the foes of the righteous shall be ruined.

[b] Or "integrity."
[c] Viz. the righteous of v. 16.

42

23 The LORD redeems the life of His servants;
all who take refuge in Him shall not be ruined.

35 Of David.

O LORD, strive with my adversaries,
give battle to my foes,
2 take up shield and buckler,
and come to my defense;
3 ready the spear and javelin
against my pursuers;
tell me, "I am your deliverance."
4 Let those who seek my life
be frustrated and put to shame;
let those who plan to harm me
fall back in disgrace.
5 Let them be as chaff in the wind,
the LORD's angel driving them on.
6 Let their path be dark and slippery,
with the LORD's angel in pursuit.
7 For without cause they hid a net to trap me;
without cause they dug a pit*a* for me.
8 Let disaster overtake them unawares;
let the net they hid catch them;
let them fall into it when disaster [strikes].
9 Then shall I exult in the LORD,
rejoice in His deliverance.
10 All my bones shall say,
"LORD, who is like You?
You save the poor from one stronger than he,
the poor and needy from his despoiler."

11 Malicious witnesses appear
who question me about things I do not know.
12 They repay me evil for good,

a Transferred from first clause for clarity.

43

[seeking] my bereavement.

13 Yet, when they were ill,
my dress was sackcloth,
I kept a fast—
b-may what I prayed for happen to me!-*b*

14 I walked about as though it were my friend or my brother;
I was bowed with gloom, like one mourning for his
mother.

15 But when I stumble, they gleefully gather;
wretches gather against me,
I know not why;
c-they tear at me without end.

16 With impious, mocking grimace-*c*
they gnash their teeth at me.

17 O Lord, how long will You look on?
Rescue me *c*-from their attacks,-*c*
my precious life, from the lions,

18 that I may praise You in a great congregation,
acclaim You in a mighty throng.

19 Let not my treacherous enemies rejoice over me,
or those who hate me without reason wink their eyes.

20 For they do not offer amity,
but devise fraudulent schemes against harmless folk.

21 They open wide their mouths at me,
saying, "Aha, aha, we have seen it!"

22 You have seen it, O LORD;
do not hold aloof!
O Lord, be not far from me!

23 Wake, rouse Yourself for my cause,
for my claim, O my God and my Lord!

24 Take up my cause, O LORD my God, as You are
beneficent,
and let them not rejoice over me.

b-b Meaning of Heb. uncertain; lit. "my prayer returns upon my bosom."
c-c Meaning of Heb. uncertain.

25 Let them not think,
"Aha, just what we wished!"
Let them not say,
"We have destroyed him!"
26 May those who rejoice at my misfortune
be frustrated and utterly disgraced;
may those who vaunt themselves over me
be clad in frustration and shame.
27 May those who desire my vindication
sing forth joyously;
may they always say,
"Extolled be the LORD
who desires the well-being of His servant,"
28 while my tongue shall recite Your beneficent acts,
Your praises all day long.

36 For the leader. Of the servant of the LORD, of David.

2 *a*-I know-*a* what Transgression says to the wicked;
he has no sense of the dread of God,
3 *b*-because its speech is seductive to him
till his iniquity be found out and he be hated.-*b*
4 His words are evil and deceitful;
he will not consider doing good.
5 In bed he plots mischief;
he is set on a path of no good,
he does not reject evil.

6 O LORD, Your faithfulness reaches to heaven;
Your steadfastness to the sky;
7 Your beneficence is like the high mountains;
Your justice like the great deep;
man and beast You deliver, O LORD.
8 How precious is Your faithful care, O God!

a-a *Lit. "In my heart is."*
b-b *Meaning of Heb. uncertain.*

45

Mankind shelters in the shadow of Your wings.
9 They feast on the rich fare of Your house;
　　You let them drink at Your refreshing stream.
10 With You is the fountain of life;
　　by Your light do we see light.
11 Bestow Your faithful care on those devoted to You,
　　and Your beneficence on upright men.
12 Let not the foot of the arrogant tread on me,
　　or the hand of the wicked drive me away.
13 There lie the evildoers, fallen,
　　thrust down, unable to rise.

37　Of David.

א　Do not be vexed by evil men;
　　do not be incensed by wrongdoers;
2　for they soon wither like grass,
　　like verdure fade away.

ב　3 Trust in the LORD and do good,
　　abide in the land and remain loyal.
4 Seek the favor of the LORD,
　　and He will grant you the desires of your heart.

ג　5 Leave all[a] to the LORD;
　　trust in Him; He will do it.
6 He will cause your vindication to shine forth like the light,
　　the justice of your case, like the noonday sun.

ד　7 Be patient and wait for the LORD,
　　do not be vexed by the prospering man
　　who carries out his schemes.

ה　8 Give up anger, abandon fury,
　　do not be vexed;
　　it can only do harm.
9 For evil men will be cut off,

---

[a] *Lit. "your way."*

46

but those who look to the LORD—
they shall inherit the land.

ו   10 A little longer and there will be no wicked man;
you will look at where he was—
he will be gone.

11 But the lowly shall inherit the land,
and delight in abundant well-being.

ז   12 The wicked man schemes against the righteous,
and gnashes his teeth at him.

13 The Lord laughs at him,
for He knows that his day will come.

ח   14 The wicked draw their swords, bend their bows,
to bring down the lowly and needy,
to slaughter *b*-upright men.-*b*

15 Their swords shall pierce their own hearts,
and their bows shall be broken.

ט   16 Better the little that the righteous man has
than the great abundance of the wicked.

17 For the arms of the wicked shall be broken,
but the LORD is the support of the righteous.

י   18 The LORD is concerned for the needs*c* of the blameless;
their portion lasts forever;

19   they shall not come to grief in bad times;
in famine, they shall eat their fill.

כ   20 But the wicked shall perish,
and the enemies of the LORD shall be consumed,
like meadow grass*d* consumed in smoke.

ל   21 The wicked man borrows and does not repay;
the righteous is generous and keeps giving.

22 Those blessed by Him shall inherit the land,
but those cursed by Him shall be cut off.

מ   23 The steps of a man are made firm by the LORD,
when He delights in his way.

24 Though he stumbles, he does not fall down,
for the LORD gives him support.

---

b-b *Lit. "those whose way is upright."*
c *Lit. "days."*
d *Meaning of Heb. uncertain.*

47

נ 25 I have been young and am now old,
      but I have never seen a righteous man abandoned,
      or his children seeking bread.
  26 He is always generous, and lends,
      and his children are held blessed.

ס 27 Shun evil and do good,
      and you shall abide forever.
  28 For the LORD loves what is right,
      He does not abandon His faithful ones.
  They are preserved forever,
      while the children of the wicked will be cut off.
  29 The righteous shall inherit the land,
      and abide forever in it.

פ 30 The mouth of the righteous utters wisdom,
      and his tongue speaks what is right.
  31 The teaching of his God is in his heart;
      his feet do not slip.

צ 32 The wicked watches for the righteous,
      seeking to put him to death;
  33 the LORD will not abandon him to his power;
      He will not let him be condemned in judgment.

ק 34 Look to the LORD and keep to His way,
      and He will raise you high that you may inherit the land;
      when the wicked are cut off, you shall see it.

ר 35 I saw a wicked man, powerful,
      well-rooted like a robust native tree.
  36 Suddenly he vanished and was gone;
      I sought him, but he was not to be found.

ש 37 Mark the blameless, note the upright,
      for there is a future for the man of integrity.
  38 But transgressors shall be utterly destroyed,
      the future of the wicked shall be cut off.

ת 39 The deliverance of the righteous comes from the LORD,
      their stronghold in time of trouble.
  40 The LORD helps them and rescues them,

rescues them from the wicked and delivers them,
for they seek refuge in Him.

38 A psalm of David. *Lehazkir.*[a]

2 O Lord, do not punish me in wrath;
  do not chastise me in fury.
3 For Your arrows have struck me;
  Your blows have fallen upon me.
4 There is no soundness in my flesh because of Your rage,
  no wholeness in my bones because of my sin.
5 For my iniquities have [b-overwhelmed me;-b]
  they are like a heavy burden, more than I can bear.
6 My wounds stink and fester
  because of my folly.
7 I am all bent and bowed;
  I walk about in gloom all day long.
8 For my sinews are full of fever;
  there is no soundness in my flesh.
9 I am all benumbed and crushed;
  I roar because of the turmoil in my mind.

10 O Lord, You are aware of all my entreaties;
  my groaning is not hidden from You.
11 My mind reels;
  my strength fails me;
  my eyes too have lost their luster.
12 My friends and companions stand back from my
    affliction;
  my kinsmen stand far off.
13 Those who seek my life lay traps;
  those who wish me harm speak malice;
  they utter deceit all the time.
14 But I am like a deaf man, unhearing,

---

[a] *Meaning of Heb. uncertain.*
[b-b] *Lit. "passed over my head."*

like a dumb man who cannot speak up;
15 I am like one who does not hear,
who has no retort on his lips.
16 But I wait for You, O LORD;
You will answer, O Lord, my God.
17 For I fear they will rejoice over me;
when my foot gives way they will vaunt themselves
against me.
18 For I am on the verge of collapse;
my pain is always with me.
19 I acknowledge my iniquity;
I am fearful over my sin;
20 for my mortal enemies are numerous;
my treacherous foes are many.
21 Those who repay evil for good
harass me for pursuing good.

22 Do not abandon me, O LORD;
my God, be not far from me;
23 hasten to my aid,
O Lord, my deliverance.

39 For the leader; for *Jeduthun*. A psalm of David.

2 I resolved I would watch my step
lest I offend by my speech;
I would keep my mouth muzzled
while the wicked man was in my presence.
3 I was dumb, silent;
I was very*a* still
while my pain was intense.
4 My mind was in a rage,
my thoughts were all aflame;
I spoke out:

ᵃ *Cf. use of* ṭwb *in Hos. 10.1; Jonah 4.4.*

50

5   Tell me, O Lord, what my term is,
    what is the measure of my days;
    I would know how fleeting my life is.
6 You have made my life just handbreadths long;
    its span is as nothing in Your sight;
    *b-*no man endures any longer than a breath.*-b*   *Selah.*
7 Man walks about as a mere shadow;
    mere futility is his hustle and bustle,
    amassing and not knowing who will gather in.
8 What, then, can I count on, O Lord?
    In You my hope lies.
9 Deliver me from all my transgressions;
    make me not the butt of the benighted.
10 I am dumb, I do not speak up,
    for it is Your doing.
11 Take away Your plague from me;
    I perish from Your blows.
12 You chastise a man in punishment for his sin,
    consuming like a moth what he treasures.
    No man is more than a breath.   *Selah.*

13 Hear my prayer, O Lord;
    give ear to my cry;
    do not disregard my tears;
    for like all my forebears
    I am an alien, resident with You.
14 Look away from me, *b-*that I may recover,*-b*
    before I pass away and am gone.

40 For the leader. A psalm of David.

2 I put my hope in the Lord;
    He inclined toward me,
    and heeded my cry.

b-b *Meaning of Heb. uncertain.*

3 He lifted me out of the miry pit,
  the slimy clay,
  and set my feet on a rock,
  steadied my legs.
4 He put a new song into my mouth,
  a hymn to our God.
May many see it and stand in awe,
  and trust in the LORD.
5 Happy is the man who makes the LORD his trust,
  who turns not to the arrogant or to followers of falsehood.
6 *a*-You, O LORD my God, have done many things;
  the wonders You have devised for us
  cannot be set out before You;-*a*
  I would rehearse the tale of them,
  but they are more than can be told.
7 *b*-You gave me to understand that-*b*
  You do not desire sacrifice and meal offering;
  You do not ask for burnt offering and sin offering.
8 Then I said,
  b-"See, I will bring a scroll recounting what befell
  me."-*b*
9 To do what pleases You, my God, is my desire;
  Your teaching is in my inmost parts.
10 I proclaimed [Your] righteousness in a great
   congregation;
   see, I did not withhold my words;
   O LORD, You must know it.
11 I did not keep Your beneficence to myself;
   I declared Your faithful deliverance;
   I did not fail to speak of Your steadfast love in a great
   congregation.
12 O LORD, You will not withhold from me Your
   compassion;
   Your steadfast love will protect me always.

---

a-a *Or "You, O LORD my God, have done many things—the wonders You have devised for us; none can equal You."*
b-b *Meaning of Heb. uncertain.*

¹³ For misfortunes without number envelop me;
　　my iniquities have caught up with me;
　　I cannot see;
　　they are more than the hairs of my head;
　　ᶜ-I am at my wits' end.-ᶜ
¹⁴ ᵈO favor me, LORD, and save me;
　　O LORD, hasten to my aid.
¹⁵ Let those who seek to destroy my life
　　be frustrated and disgraced;
　　let those who wish me harm
　　fall back in shame.
¹⁶ Let those who say "Aha! Aha!" over me
　　be desolate because of their frustration.
¹⁷ But let all who seek You be glad and rejoice in You;
　　let those who are eager for Your deliverance always say,
　　"Extolled be the LORD!"
¹⁸ But I am poor and needy;
　　may the Lord devise [deliverance] for me.
　You are my help and my rescuer;
　　my God, do not delay.

41 For the leader. A psalm of David.

² Happy is he who is thoughtful of the wretched;
　　in bad times may the LORD keep him from harm.
³ May the LORD guard him and preserve him;
　　and may he be thought happy in the land.
　Do not subject him to the will of his enemies.
⁴ The LORD will sustain him on his sickbed;
　　ᵃ-You shall wholly transform his bed of suffering.-ᵃ
⁵ I said, "O LORD, have mercy on me,
　　heal me, for I have sinned against You."
⁶ My enemies speak evilly of me,
　　"When will he die and his name perish?"

ᶜ⁻ᶜ *Or "my courage fails me."*
ᵈ *With vv. 14–18, cf. Ps. 70.*

ᵃ⁻ᵃ *Meaning of Heb. uncertain.*

7 If one comes to visit, he speaks falsely;
    his mind stores up evil thoughts;
    once outside, he speaks them.
8 All my enemies whisper together against me,
    imagining the worst for me.
9 "Something baneful has settled in him;
    he'll not rise from his bed again."
10 My ally in whom I trusted,
    even he who shares my bread,
    a-has been utterly false to me.-*a*
11 But You, O LORD, have mercy on me;
    let me rise again and repay them.
12 Then shall I know that You are pleased with me:
    when my enemy cannot shout in triumph over me.
13 You will support me because of my integrity,
    and let me abide in Your presence forever.

14 Blessed is the LORD, God of Israel,
    from eternity to eternity.
    Amen and Amen.

BOOK TWO

42 For the leader. A *maskil* of the Korahites.

2 Like a hind crying for water,*a*
    my soul cries for You, O God;
3   my soul thirsts for God, the living God;
    O when will I come to appear before God!
4 My tears have been my food day and night;
    I am ever taunted with, "Where is your God?"
5 When I think of this, I pour out my soul:
    how I *b*-walked with the crowd, moved with them,-*b*
    the festive throng, to the House of God

---

a *Lit. "watercourses."*
b-b *Meaning of Heb. uncertain.*

with joyous shouts of praise.

6 Why so downcast, my soul,
    why disquieted within me?
Have hope in God;
    I will yet praise Him
    c-for His saving presence.-*c*

7 O my God, my soul is downcast;
    therefore I think of You
    in this land of Jordan and Hermon,
    in Mount Mizar,

8   where deep calls to deep
    in the roar of *b*-Your cataracts;-*b*
    all Your breakers and billows have swept over me.

9 By day may the LORD vouchsafe His faithful care,
    so that at night a song to Him may be with me,
    a prayer to the God of my life.

10 I say to God, my rock,
    "Why have You forgotten me,
    why must I walk in gloom,
    oppressed by my enemy?"

11 *b*-Crushing my bones,-*b*
    my foes revile me,
    taunting me always with, "Where is your God?"

12 Why so downcast, my soul,
    why disquieted within me?
Have hope in God;
    I will yet praise Him,
    my ever-present help, my God.

43   *a*Vindicate me, O God,
    champion my cause
    against faithless people;
    rescue me from the treacherous, dishonest man.

---

*c-c Several ancient versions and Heb. mss. connect the first word in v. 7 with the end of 6,
reading* yeshu'ot panai we'Elohai, *"my ever-present help, my God," as in vv. 12 and
Ps. 43.5.*

a A continuation of Ps. 42.

2 For You are my God, my stronghold;
    why have You rejected me?
  Why must I walk in gloom,
    oppressed by the enemy?
3 Send forth Your light and Your truth;
    they will lead me;
    they will bring me to Your holy mountain,
    to Your dwelling-place,
4   that I may come to the altar of God,
    God, my delight, my joy;
    that I may praise You with the lyre,
    O God, my God.
5 Why so downcast, my soul,
    why disquieted within me?
  Have hope in God;
    I will yet praise Him,
    my ever-present help, my God.

44 For the leader. Of the Korahites. A *maskil.*

2 We have heard, O God,
    our fathers have told us
    the deeds You performed in their time,
    in days of old.
3 With Your hand You planted them,
    displacing nations;
    You brought misfortune on peoples,
    and drove them out.
4 It was not by their sword that they took the land,
    their arm did not give them victory,
    but Your right hand, Your arm, and Your goodwill,
    for You favored them.
5 You are my king, O God;
    decree victories for Jacob!

6 Through You we gore our foes;
    by Your name we trample our adversaries;
7   I do not trust in my bow;
    it is not my sword that gives me victory;-
8 You give us victory over our foes;
    You thwart those who hate us.
9 In God we glory at all times,
    and praise Your name unceasingly.   *Selah.*

10 Yet You have rejected and disgraced us;
    You do not go with our armies.
11 You make us retreat before our foe;
    our enemies plunder us at will.
12 You let them devour us like sheep;
    You disperse us among the nations.
13 You sell Your people for no fortune,
    You set no high price on them.
14 You make us the butt of our neighbors,
    the scorn and derision of those around us.
15 You make us a byword among the nations,
    a laughingstock[a] among the peoples.
16 I am always aware of my disgrace;
    I am wholly covered with shame
17   at the sound of taunting revilers,
    in the presence of the vengeful foe.

18 All this has come upon us,
    yet we have not forgotten You,
    or been false to Your covenant.
19 Our hearts have not gone astray,
    nor have our feet swerved from Your path,
20   though You cast us, crushed, to where the [b]sea
    monster[b] is,
    and covered us over with deepest darkness.
21 If we forgot the name of our God

---

[a] *Lit. "a wagging of the head."*
[b-b] *Heb.* tannim=tannin, *as in Ezek. 29.3 and 32.2.*

and spread forth our hands to a foreign god,
22 God would surely search it out,
    for He knows the secrets of the heart.
23 It is for Your sake that we are slain all day long,
    that we are regarded as sheep to be slaughtered.

24 Rouse Yourself; why do You sleep, O Lord?
    Awaken, do not reject us forever!
25 Why do You hide Your face,
    ignoring our affliction and distress?
26 We lie prostrate in the dust;
    our body clings to the ground.
27 Arise and help us,
    redeem us, as befits Your faithfulness.

45

For the leader; *a-*on *shoshannim.-a* Of the Korahites. A *maskil.*
A love song.

2 My heart is astir with gracious words;
    I speak my poem to a king;
    my tongue is the pen of an expert scribe.

3 You are fairer than all men;
    your speech is endowed with grace;
    rightly has God given you an eternal blessing.
4 Gird your sword upon your thigh, O hero,
    in your splendor and glory;
5 *a-*in your glory, win success;
    ride on in the cause of truth and meekness and right;
    and let your right hand lead you to awesome deeds.*-a*
6 Your arrows, sharpened,
    b-[pierce] the breast of the king's enemies;
    peoples fall at your feet.*-b*
7 Your *c-*divine throne*-c* is everlasting;

---

a-a *Meaning of Heb. uncertain.*
b-b *Order of Heb. clauses inverted for clarity.*
c-c *Cf. I Chron. 29.23.*

your royal scepter is a scepter of equity.
8 You love righteousness and hate wickedness;
    rightly has God, your God, chosen to anoint you
    with oil of gladness over all your peers.
9 All your robes [are fragrant] with
    myrrh and aloes and cassia;
    from ivoried palaces
    lutes entertain you.
10 Royal princesses are your favorites;
    the consort stands at your right hand,
    decked in gold of Ophir.

11 Take heed, lass, and note,
    incline your ear:
    forget your people and your father's house,
12   and let the king be aroused by your beauty;
    since he is your lord, bow to him.
13 O Tyrian lass,
    the wealthiest people will court your favor with gifts,
14   *a-*goods of all sorts.

The royal princess,
    her dress embroidered with golden mountings,
15   is led inside to the king;-*a*
    maidens in her train, her companions,
    are presented to you.
16 They are led in with joy and gladness;
    they enter the palace of the king.
17 Your sons will succeed your ancestors;
    you will appoint them princes throughout the land.

18 I commemorate your fame for all generations,
    so peoples will praise you forever and ever.

46 For the leader. Of the Korahites; *a-*on *alamoth.-a* A song.

² God is our refuge and stronghold,
  a help in trouble, very near.
³ Therefore we are not afraid
  though the earth reels,
  though mountains topple into the sea—
⁴   its waters rage and foam;
  in its swell mountains quake.   *Selah.*

⁵ There is a river whose streams gladden God's city,
  the holy dwelling-place of the Most High.
⁶ God is in its midst, it will not be toppled;
  by daybreak God will come to its aid.
⁷ Nations rage, kingdoms topple;
  at the sound of His thunder the earth dissolves.
⁸ The Lord of hosts is with us;
  the God of Jacob is our haven.   *Selah.*

⁹ Come and see what the Lord has done,
  how He has wrought desolation on the earth.
¹⁰ He puts a stop to wars throughout the earth,
  breaking the bow, snapping the spear,
  consigning wagons to the flames.
¹¹ "Desist! Realize that I am God!
  I dominate the nations;
  I dominate the earth."
¹² The Lord of hosts is with us;
  the God of Jacob is our haven.   *Selah.*

ᵃ⁻ᵃ *Meaning of Heb. uncertain.*

47 For the leader. Of the Korahites. A psalm.

2 All you peoples, clap your hands,
   raise a joyous shout for God.
3 For the LORD Most High is awesome,
   great king over all the earth;
4   He subjects peoples to us,
   sets nations at our feet.
5 He chose our heritage for us,
   the pride of Jacob whom He loved.   *Selah.*

6 God ascends midst acclamation;
   the LORD, to the blasts of the horn.
7 Sing, O sing to God;
   sing, O sing to our king;
8   for God is king over all the earth;
   sing a hymn.*a*
9 God reigns over the nations;
   God is seated on His holy throne.
10 The great of the peoples are gathered together,
   the retinue of Abraham's God;
   for the guardians of the earth belong to God;
   He is greatly exalted.

48 A song. A psalm of the Korahites.

2 The LORD is great and much acclaimed
   in the city of our God,
   His holy mountain—
3   fair-crested, joy of all the earth,
   Mount Zion, summit of Zaphon,*a*
   city of the great king.   ·

a Heb. maskil, *a musical term of uncertain meaning.*

a A term for the divine abode.

⁴ Through its citadels, God has made Himself known
    as a haven.
⁵ See, the kings joined forces;
    they advanced together.
⁶ At the mere sight of it they were stunned,
    they were terrified, they panicked;
⁷   they were seized there with a trembling,
    like a woman in the throes of labor,
⁸   as the Tarshish fleet was wrecked
    in an easterly gale.ᵇ
⁹ The likes of what we heard we have now witnessed
    in the city of the Lord of hosts,
    in the city of our God—
    may God preserve it forever!   *Selah.*

¹⁰ In Your temple, God,
    we meditate upon Your faithful care.
¹¹ The praise of You, God, like Your name,
    reaches to the ends of the earth;
    Your right hand is filled with beneficence.
¹² Let Mount Zion rejoice!
    Let the townsᶜ of Judah exult,
    because of Your judgments.

¹³ Walk around Zion,
    circle it;
    count its towers,
¹⁴   take note of its ramparts;
    ᵈ-go throughᵈ its citadels,
    that you may recount it to a future age.
¹⁵ For God—He is our God forever;
    He will lead us ᵈ-evermore.ᵈ

ᵇ *See I Kings 22.49.*
ᶜ *Or "women."*
ᵈ⁻ᵈ *Meaning of Heb. uncertain.*

49 For the leader. Of the Korahites. A psalm.

² Hear this, all you peoples;
   give ear, all inhabitants of the world,
³ men of all estates,
   rich and poor alike.
⁴ My mouth utters wisdom,
   my speech^a is full of insight.
⁵ I will turn my attention to a theme,
   set forth my lesson to the music of a lyre.

⁶ In time of trouble, why should I fear
   the encompassing evil of those who would
      supplant me—
⁷ men who trust in their riches,
   who glory in their great wealth?
⁸ ^b-Ah, it-^b cannot redeem a man,
   or pay his ransom to God;
⁹ the price of life is too high;
   and so one ceases to be, forever.
¹⁰ Shall he live eternally,
   and never see the grave?
¹¹ For one sees that the wise die,
   that the foolish and ignorant both perish,
   leaving their wealth to others.
¹² Their grave ^c is their eternal home,
   the dwelling-place for all generations
   of those once famous on earth.
¹³ Man does not abide in honor;
   he is like the beasts that perish.

¹⁴ Such is the fate of those who are self-confident,
   ^d-the end of those pleased with their own talk.-^d *Selah.*

---

^a *Lit. "utterance of my heart"; on* leb, *cf. Ps. 19.15.*
^{b-b} *Or "A brother."*
^c *Taken with ancient versions and medieval commentators as the equivalent of* qibram.
^{d-d} *Meaning of Heb. uncertain.*

¹⁵ Sheeplike they head for Sheol,
with Death as their shepherd.
The upright shall rule over them at daybreak,
^{d-}and their form shall waste away in Sheol
till its nobility be gone.^{-d}
¹⁶ But God will redeem my life from the clutches of Sheol,
for He will take me. *Selah.*

¹⁷ Do not be afraid when a man becomes rich,
when his household goods increase;
¹⁸ for when he dies he can take none of it along;
his goods cannot follow him down.
¹⁹ Though he congratulates himself in his lifetime
—^{d-}"They must admit that you did well by yourself"^{-d}—
²⁰ yet he must join the company of his ancestors,
who will never see daylight again.
²¹ Man does not understand honor;
he is like the beasts that perish.

50 A psalm of Asaph.

^{a-}God, the LORD God^{-a} spoke
and summoned the world from east to west.
² From Zion, perfect in beauty,
God appeared
³ —let our God come and not fail to act!
Devouring fire preceded Him;
it stormed around Him fiercely.
⁴ He summoned the heavens above,
and the earth, for the trial of His people.
⁵ "Bring in My devotees,
who made a covenant with Me over sacrifice!"

^{a-a} *Heb.* 'El 'Elohim YHWH.

⁶ Then the heavens proclaimed His righteousness,
   for He is a God who judges.   *Selah.*

⁷ "Pay heed, My people, and I will speak,
   O Israel, and I will arraign you.
I am God, your God.
⁸ I censure you not for your sacrifices,
   and your burnt offerings, made to Me daily;
⁹   I claim no bull from your estate,
   no he-goats from your pens.
¹⁰ For Mine is every animal of the forest,
   the beasts on ᵇ⁻a thousand mountains.⁻ᵇ
¹¹ I know every bird of the mountains,
   the creatures of the field are subject to Me.
¹² Were I hungry, I would not tell you,
   for Mine is the world and all it holds.
¹³ Do I eat the flesh of bulls,
   or drink the blood of he-goats?
¹⁴ Sacrifice a thank offering to God,
   and pay your vows to the Most High.
¹⁵ Call upon Me in time of trouble;
   I will rescue you, and you shall honor Me."

¹⁶ And to the wicked, God said:
   "Who are you to recite My laws,
   and mouth the terms of My covenant,
¹⁷   seeing that you spurn My discipline,
   and brush My words aside?
¹⁸ When you see a thief, you fall in with him,
   and throw in your lot with adulterers;
¹⁹   you devote your mouth to evil,
   and yoke your tongue to deceit;
²⁰   you are busy maligning your brother,
   defaming the son of your mother.

ᵇ⁻ᵇ *Meaning of Heb. uncertain.*

²¹ If I failed to act when you did these things,
  you would fancy that I was like you;
  so I censure you and confront you with charges.
²² Mark this, you who are unmindful of God,
  lest I tear you apart and no one save you.

²³ He who sacrifices a thank offering honors Me,
  ᵇ-and to him who improves his way-ᵇ ·
  I will show the salvation of God."

51 For the leader. A psalm of David, ² when Nathan the prophet came to him after he had come to Bathsheba.ᵃ

³ Have mercy upon me, O God,
  as befits Your faithfulness;
  in keeping with Your abundant compassion,
  blot out my transgressions.
⁴ Wash me thoroughly of my iniquity,
  and purify me of my sin;
⁵   for I recognize my transgressions,
  and am ever conscious of my sin.
⁶ Against You alone have I sinned,
  and done what is evil in Your sight;
  so You are just in Your sentence,
  and right in Your judgment.
⁷ Indeed I was born with iniquity;
  with sin my mother conceived me.
⁸ ᵇ-Indeed You desire truth about that which is hidden;
  teach me wisdom about secret things.-ᵇ

⁹ Purge me with hyssop till I am pure;
  wash me till I am whiter than snow.
¹⁰ Let me hear tidings of joy and gladness;
  let the bones You have crushed exult.

ᵃ *Cf. II Sam. 12.*
ᵇ⁻ᵇ *Meaning of Heb. uncertain.*

¹¹ Hide Your face from my sins;
  blot out all my iniquities.
¹² Fashion a pure heart for me, O God;
  create in me a steadfast spirit.
¹³ Do not cast me out of Your presence,
  or take Your holy spirit away from me.
¹⁴ Let me again rejoice in Your help;
  let a vigorous spirit sustain me.
¹⁵ I will teach transgressors Your ways,
  that sinners may return to You.

¹⁶ Save me from bloodguilt,
  O God, God, my deliverer,
  that I may sing forth Your beneficence.
¹⁷ O Lord, open my lips,
  and let my mouth declare Your praise.
¹⁸ You do not want me to bring sacrifices;
  You do not desire burnt offerings;
¹⁹ True sacrifice to God is a contrite spirit;
  God, You will not despise
  a contrite and crushed heart.

²⁰ May it please You to make Zion prosper;
  rebuild the walls of Jerusalem.
²¹ Then You will want sacrifices offered in righteousness,
  burnt and whole offerings;
  then bulls will be offered on Your altar.

52 For the leader. A *maskil* of David, ² when Doeg the Edomite came and informed Saul, telling him, "David came to Ahimelech's house."ᵃ

³ Why do you boast of your evil, brave fellow?
  God's faithfulness ᵇ‑never ceases.‑ᵇ

ᵃ *Cf. I Sam. 22.9 ff.*
ᵇ⁻ᵇ *Lit. "is all the day."*

⁴ Your tongue devises mischief,
like a sharpened razor that works treacherously.
⁵ You prefer evil to good,
the lie, to speaking truthfully.   *Selah.*
⁶ You love all pernicious words,
treacherous speech.
⁷ So God will tear you down for good,
will break you and pluck you from your tent,
and root you out of the land of the living.   *Selah.*
⁸ The righteous, seeing it, will be awestruck;
they will jibe at him, saying,
⁹   "Here was a fellow who did not make God his refuge,
but trusted in his great wealth,
relied upon his mischief."

¹⁰ But I am like a thriving olive tree in God's house;
I trust in the faithfulness of God forever and ever.
¹¹ I praise You forever, for You have acted;
c-I declare that Your name is good-*c*
in the presence of Your faithful ones.

53   *a*For the leader; on *mahalath.*ᵇ A *maskil* of David.

² The benighted man thinks,
c-"God does not care."-*c*
Man's wrongdoing is corrupt and loathsome;
no one does good.
³ The Lᴏʀᴅ looks down from heaven on mankind
to find a man of understanding,
a man mindful of God.
⁴ Everyone is dross,
altogether foul;
there is none who does good,
not even one.

---

c-c Meaning of Heb. uncertain; others "I will wait for Your name for it is good."
ᵃ *Cf. Ps. 14.*
ᵇ *Meaning of Heb. unknown.*
c-c Lit. "There is no God"; cf. Ps. 10.4.

⁵ Are they so witless, those evildoers,
  who devour my people as they devour food,
  and do not invoke God?
⁶ There they will be seized with fright
  —ᵈnever was there such a fright—
  for God has scattered the bones of your besiegers;
  you have put them to shame,ᵈ
  for God has rejected them.

⁷ O that the deliverance of Israel might come from Zion!
When God restores the fortunes of His people,
  Jacob will exult, Israel will rejoice.

54 For the leader; with instrumental music. A *maskil* of
David, ² when the Ziphites came and told Saul, "Know, David is
in hiding among us."ᵃ

³ O God, deliver me by Your name;
  by Your power vindicate me.
⁴ O God, hear my prayer;
  give ear to the words of my mouth.
⁵ For strangers have risen against me,
  and ruthless men seek my life;
  they are unmindful of God.   *Selah.*

⁶ See, God is my helper;
  the Lord is my support.
⁷ He will repay the evil of my watchful foes;
  by Your faithfulness, destroy them!
⁸ Then I will offer You a free-will sacrifice;
  I will praise Your name, Lord, for it is good,
⁹   for it has saved me from my foes,
  and let me gaze triumphant upon my enemies.

d-d *Meaning of Heb. uncertain.*

ᵃ *Cf. I Sam. 23.19.*

69

55 For the leader; with instrumental music. A *maskil* of David.

² Give ear, O God, to my prayer;
    do not ignore my plea;
³   pay heed to me and answer me.
  I am tossed about, complaining and moaning
⁴   at the clamor of the enemy,
    because of the oppression of the wicked;
    for they bring evil upon me
    and furiously harass me.
⁵ My heart is convulsed within me;
    terrors of death assail me.
⁶ Fear and trembling invade me;
    I am clothed with horror.
⁷ I said,
    "O that I had the wings of a dove!
  I would fly away and find rest;
⁸   surely, I would flee far off;
    I would lodge in the wilderness;   *Selah.*
⁹   I would soon find me a refuge
    from the sweeping wind,
    from the tempest."

¹⁰ O LORD, confound their speech, confuse it!
  For I see lawlessness and strife in the city;
¹¹   day and night they make their rounds on its walls;
    evil and mischief are inside it.
¹² Malice is within it;
    fraud and deceit never leave its square.

¹³ It is not an enemy who reviles me
    —I could bear that;
    it is not my foe who vaunts himself against me

—I could hide from him;
14 but it is you, my equal,
    my companion, my friend;
15 sweet was our fellowship;
    we walked together in God's house.
16 Let Him incite death against them;
    may they go down alive into Sheol!
For where they dwell,
    there evil is.

17 As for me, I call to God;
    the Lord will deliver me.
18 Evening, morning, and noon,
    I complain and moan,
    and He hears my voice.
19 He redeems me unharmed
    from the battle against me;
    -it is as though many are on my side.-a
20 God who has reigned from the first,
    who will have no successor,
    hears and humbles those who have no fear of
        God.   *Selah.*

21 He*b* harmed his ally,
    he broke his pact;
22 his talk was smoother than butter,
    yet his mind was on war;
    his words were more soothing than oil,
    yet they were drawn swords.

23 Cast your burden on the Lord and He will sustain you;
    He will never let the righteous man collapse.
24 For You, O God, will bring them down to the nethermost
        Pit—
    those murderous, treacherous men;

---

a-a *Meaning of Heb. uncertain.*
b *I.e. the friend of v. 14.*

· they shall not live out half their days;
    but I trust in You.

56 For the leader; *a*-on *jonath elem rehokim.*-a Of David. A *michtam;* when the Philistines seized him in Gath.

² Have mercy on me, O God,
    for men persecute me;
    all day long my adversary oppresses me.
³ My watchful foes persecute me all day long;
    many are my adversaries, O Exalted One.
⁴ When I am afraid, I trust in You,
⁵   in God, whose word I praise,
    in God I trust;
    I am not afraid;
    what can mortals*b* do to me?
⁶ All day long *a*-they cause me grief in my affairs,-*a*
    they plan only evil against me.
⁷ They plot, they lie in ambush;
    they watch my every move, hoping for my death.
⁸ Cast them out for their evil;
    subdue peoples in Your anger, O God.

⁹ *a*-You keep count of my wanderings;
    put my tears into Your flask,
    into Your record.-*a*
¹⁰ Then my enemies will retreat when I call on You;
    this I know, that God is for me.
¹¹ In God, whose word I praise,
    in the LORD, whose word I praise,
¹²   in God I trust;
    I am not afraid;
    what can man do to me?
¹³ I must pay my vows to You, O God;

---

a-a Meaning of Heb. uncertain.
b Lit. "flesh."

I will render thank offerings to You.
14 For You have saved me from death,
   my foot from stumbling,
   that I may walk before God in the light of life.

57 For the leader; *ᵃ-al tashheth.⁻ᵃ* Of David. A *michtam;* when he fled from Saul into a cave.

2 Have mercy on me, O God, have mercy on me,
   for I seek refuge in You,
   I seek refuge in the shadow of Your wings,
   until danger passes.
3 I call to God Most High,
   to God who is good to me.
4 He will reach down from heaven and deliver me:
   God will send down His steadfast love;
   my persecutor reviles.   *Selah.*

5 As for me, I lie down among man-eating lions
   whose teeth are spears and arrows,
   whose tongue is a sharp sword.
6 Exalt Yourself over the heavens, O God,
   let Your glory be over all the earth!
7 They prepared a net for my feet ᵇ⁻to ensnare me;⁻ᵇ
   they dug a pit for me,
   but they fell into it.   *Selah.*

8 ᶜMy heart is firm, O God;
   my heart is firm;
   I will sing, I will chant a hymn.
9 Awake, O my soul!
   Awake, O harp and lyre!
   I will wake the dawn.
10 I will praise You among the peoples, O LORD;

ᵃ⁻ᵃ *Meaning of Heb. uncertain.*
ᵇ⁻ᵇ *Cf. Mishnaic Heb.* kefifah, *a wicker basket used in fishing.*
ᶜ *With vv. 8–12, cf. Ps. 108.2–6.*

73

I will sing a hymn to You among the nations;
11   for Your faithfulness is as high as heaven;
Your steadfastness reaches to the sky.
12 Exalt Yourself over the heavens, O God,
let Your glory be over all the earth!

58 For the leader; *al tashheth*. Of David. A *michtam*.

2 *a*-O mighty ones,-*a* do you really decree what is just?
Do you judge mankind with equity?
3 In your minds you devise wrongdoing in the land;
a-with your hands you deal out lawlessness.-*a*
4 The wicked are defiant from birth;
the liars go astray from the womb.
5 Their venom is like that of a snake,
a deaf viper that stops its ears
6   so as not to hear the voice of charmers
or the expert mutterer of spells.

7 O God, smash their teeth in their mouth;
shatter the fangs of lions, O LORD;
8   let them melt, let them vanish like water;
let Him aim His arrows that they be cut down;
9   *a*-like a snail that melts away as it moves;-*a*
like a woman's stillbirth, may they never see the sun!
10 Before *a*-the thorns grow into a bramble,
may He whirl them away alive in fury.-*a*

11 The righteous man will rejoice when he sees revenge;
he will bathe his feet in the blood of the wicked.
12 Men will say,
"There is, then, a reward for the righteous;
there is, indeed, divine justice on earth."

a-a *Meaning of Heb. uncertain.*

59 For the leader; *al tashheth.* Of David. A *michtam;* when Saul sent men to watch his house in order to put him to death.[a]

2 Save me from my enemies, O my God;
    secure me against my assailants.
3 Save me from evildoers;
    deliver me from murderers.
4 For see, they lie in wait for me;
    fierce men plot against me
    for no offense of mine,
    for no transgression, O LORD;
5   for no guilt of mine
    do they rush to array themselves against me.
Look, rouse Yourself on my behalf!
6 You, O LORD God of hosts,
    God of Israel,
    bestir Yourself to bring all nations to account;
    have no mercy on any treacherous villain.   *Selah.*

7 They come each evening growling like dogs,
    roaming the city.
8 They rave with their mouths,
    [b]-sharp words-[b] are on their lips;
    [they think,] "Who hears?"
9 But You, O LORD, laugh at them;
    You mock all the nations.

10 O my[c] strength, I wait for You;
    for God is my haven.
11 My faithful God will come to aid me;
    God will let me gloat over my watchful foes.
12 Do not kill them lest my people be unmindful;
    with Your power make wanderers of them;

[a] *Cf. I Sam. 19.11.*
[b-b] *Lit. "swords."*
[c] *With several mss.; cf. v. 18; lit. "His."*

bring them low, O our shield, the Lord,
13 because of their sinful mouths,
   the words on their lips.
Let them be trapped by their pride,
   and by the imprecations and lies they utter.
14 In Your fury put an end to them;
   put an end to them that they be no more;
   that it may be known to the ends of the earth
   that God does rule over Jacob.   *Selah.*

15 They come each evening growling like dogs,
   roaming the city.
16 They wander in search of food;
   and whine if they are not satisfied.
17 But I will sing of Your strength,
   extol each morning Your faithfulness;
   for You have been my haven,
   a refuge in time of trouble.

18 O my strength, to You I sing hymns;
   for God is my haven, my faithful God.

60 For the leader; on *ᵃ-shushan eduth.⁻ᵃ* A *michtam* of David (to
be taught), 2 when he fought with Aram-Naharaim and Aram-
Zobah, and Joab returned and defeated Edom—[an army] of
twelve thousand men—in the Valley of Salt.ᵇ

3 O God, You have rejected us,
   You have made a breach in us;
   You have been angry;
   restore us!
4 You have made the land quake;
   You have torn it open.
   Mend its fissures,

ᵃ⁻ᵃ *Meaning of Heb. uncertain.*
ᵇ *Cf. II Sam. 8; I Chron. 18.*

for it is collapsing.

5 You have made Your people suffer hardship;
  ^{c-}You have given us wine that makes us reel.^{-c}

6 ^{a-}Give those who fear You because of Your truth
    a banner for rallying.^{-a}   *Selah.*

7 ^dThat those whom You love might be rescued,
    deliver with Your right hand and answer me.

8 God promised ^{e-}in His sanctuary^{-e}
    that I would exultingly divide up Shechem,
    and measure the Valley of Sukkoth;

9   Gilead and Manasseh would be mine,
    Ephraim my chief stronghold,
    Judah my scepter;

10 Moab would be my washbasin;
    on Edom I would cast my shoe;
    acclaim me, O Philistia!

11 Would that I were brought to the bastion!
   Would that I were led to Edom!

12 But You have rejected us, O God;
    God, You do not march with our armies.

13 Grant us Your aid against the foe,
    for the help of man is worthless.

14 With God we shall triumph;
    He will trample our foes.

61 For the leader; with instrumental music. Of David.

2 Hear my cry, O God,
    heed my prayer.

3 From the end of the earth I call to You;
    when my heart is faint,

---

^{c-c} *Or "You have sated Your people with a bitter draft."*
^d *Cf. Ps. 108.7–14.*
^{e-e} *Or "by His holiness."*

You lead me to a rock that is high above me.
4 For You have been my refuge,
  a tower of strength against the enemy.
5 O that I might dwell in Your tent forever,
  take refuge under Your protecting wings.   *Selah.*

6 O God, You have heard my vows;
  grant the request*ª* of those who fear Your name.
7 Add days to the days of the king;
  may his years extend through generations;
8   may he dwell in God's presence forever;
  appoint*ᵇ* steadfast love to guard him.
9 So I will sing hymns to Your name forever,
  as I fulfill my vows day after day.

62 For the leader; on *Jeduthun.* A psalm of David.

2 Truly my soul waits quietly for God;
  my deliverance comes from Him.
3 Truly He is my rock and deliverance,
  my haven; I shall never be shaken.
4 How long will all of you attack*ª* a man,
  to crush*ª* him, as though he were
  a leaning wall, a tottering fence?
5 They lay plans to topple him from his rank;
  they delight in falsehood;
  they bless with their mouths,
  while inwardly they curse.   *Selah.*

6 Truly, wait quietly for God, O my soul,
  for my hope comes from Him.
7 He is my rock and deliverance,
  my haven; I shall not be shaken.
8 I rely on God, my deliverance and glory,

ª *Taking the noun* yršt *as an alternate form of* 'ršt; *cf. Ps. 21.3.*
ᵇ *Meaning of Heb. uncertain.*

ª *Meaning of Heb. uncertain.*

   my rock of strength;
   in God is my refuge.
 9 Trust in Him at all times, O people;
   pour out your hearts before Him;
   God is our refuge.   *Selah.*

 10 Men are mere breath;
   mortals, illusion;
   placed on a scale all together,
   they weigh even less than a breath.
 11 Do not trust in violence,
   or put false hopes in robbery;
   if force bears fruit pay it no mind.
 12 One thing God has spoken;
   two things have I heard:
   that might belongs to God,
 13 and faithfulness is Yours, O Lord,
   to reward each man according to his deeds.

63   A psalm of David, when he was in the Wilderness of Judah.

 2 God, You are my God;
   I search for You,
   my soul thirsts for You,
   my body yearns for You,
   as a parched and thirsty land that has no water.
 3 I shall behold You in the sanctuary,
   and see Your might and glory,
 4 Truly Your faithfulness is better than life;
   my lips declare Your praise.
 ·5 I bless You all my life;
   I lift up my hands, invoking Your name.
 6 I am sated as with a *a-*rich feast,*-a*
   I sing praises with joyful lips

---

a-a *Lit. "suet and fat."*

7 when I call You to mind upon my bed,
when I think of You in the watches of the night;
8 for You are my help,
and in the shadow of Your wings
I shout for joy.
9 My soul is attached to You;
Your right hand supports me.

10 May those who seek to destroy my life
enter the depths of the earth.
11 May they be gutted by the sword;
may they be prey to jackals.
12 But the king shall rejoice in God;
all who swear by Him shall exult,
when the mouth of liars is stopped.

64 For the leader. A psalm of David.

2 Hear my voice, O God, when I plead;
guard my life from the enemy's terror.
3 Hide me from a band of evil men,
from a crowd of evildoers,
4 who whet their tongues like swords;
they aim their arrows—cruel words—
5 to shoot from hiding at the blameless man;
they shoot him suddenly and without fear.
6 *a*-They arm themselves with an evil word;
when they speak, it is to conceal traps;-*a*
they think, "Who will see them?"
7 *b*Let the wrongdoings they have concealed,*c*
each one inside him, his secret thoughts,
be wholly exposed.
8 God shall shoot them with arrows;
they shall be struck down suddenly.

a-a *Meaning of Heb. uncertain.*
b *Meaning of verse uncertain.*
c *Reading* tamnu *with some mss. (cf. Minhat Shai) and Rashi; most printed editions,* tamnu, *traditionally rendered "they have accomplished."*

⁹ Their tongue shall be their downfall;
　　all who see them shall recoil in horror;
¹⁰　all men shall stand in awe;
　　they shall proclaim the work of God
　　and His deed which they perceived.
¹¹ The righteous shall rejoice in the LORD,
　　and take refuge in Him;
　　all the upright shall exult.

65 For the leader. A psalm of David. A song.

² Praise befits You in Zion, O God;
　　vows are paid to You;
³　all mankind*ᵃ* comes to You,
　　You who hear prayer.
⁴ When all manner of sins overwhelm me,
　　it is You who forgive our iniquities.
⁵ Happy is the man You choose and bring near
　　to dwell in Your courts;
　　may we be sated with the blessings of Your house,
　　Your holy temple.

⁶ Answer us with victory through awesome deeds,
　　O God, our deliverer,
　　in whom all the ends of the earth
　　and the distant seas
　　put their trust;
⁷　who by His power fixed the mountains firmly,
　　who is girded with might,
⁸　who stills the raging seas,
　　the raging waves,
　　and tumultuous peoples.
⁹ Those who live at the ends of the earth are awed by Your
　　signs;

ᵃ *Lit. "flesh."*

You make the lands of sunrise and sunset shout for joy.
10 You take care of the earth and irrigate it;
  You enrich it greatly,
  with the channel of God full of water;
  You provide grain for men;
  for so do You prepare it.
11 Saturating its furrows,
  leveling its ridges,
  You soften it with showers,
  You bless its growth.
12 You crown the year with Your bounty;
  fatness is distilled in Your paths;
13   the pasturelands distill it;
  the hills are girded with joy.
14 The meadows are clothed with flocks,
  the valleys mantled with grain;
  they raise a shout, they break into song.

66 For the leader. A song. A psalm.

2 Raise a shout for God, all the earth;
  sing the glory of His name,
  make glorious His praise.
3 Say to God,
  "How awesome are Your deeds,
  Your enemies cower before Your great strength;
4   all the earth bows to You,
  and sings hymns to You;
  all sing hymns to Your name."   *Selah.*

5 Come and see the works of God,
  who is held in awe by men for His acts.
6 He turned the sea into dry land;

they crossed the river on foot;
  we therefore rejoice in Him.
⁷ He rules forever in His might;
  His eyes scan the nations;
  let the rebellious not assert themselves.   *Selah.*

⁸ O peoples, bless our God,
  celebrate His praises,
⁹   who has granted us life,
  and has not let our feet slip.

¹⁰ You have tried us, O God,
  refining us, as one refines silver.
¹¹ You have caught us in a net,
  ᵃ-caught us in trammels.-ᵃ
¹² You have let men ride over us;
  we have endured fire and water,
  and You have brought us through to prosperity.

¹³ I enter Your house with burnt offerings,
  I pay my vows to You,
¹⁴   [vows] that my lips pronounced,
  that my mouth uttered in my distress.
¹⁵ I offer up fatlings to You,
  with the odor of burning rams;
  I sacrifice bulls and he-goats.   *Selah.*

¹⁶ Come and hear, all God-fearing men,
  as I tell what He did for me.
¹⁷ I called aloud to Him,
  glorification on my tongue.
¹⁸ Had I an evil thought in my mind,
  the LORD would not have listened.
¹⁹ But God did listen;
  He paid heed to my prayer.

ᵃ⁻ᵃ *Lit. "put a trammel on our loins."*

20 Blessed is God who has not turned away my prayer,
   or His faithful care from me.

67 For the leader; with instrumental music. A psalm. A song.

2 May God be gracious to us and bless us;
   may He show us favor,   *Selah.*
3 that Your way be known on earth,
   Your deliverance among all nations.

4 Peoples will praise You, O God;
   all peoples will praise You.
5 Nations will exult and shout for joy,
   for You rule the peoples with equity,
   You guide the nations of the earth.   *Selah.*
6 The peoples will praise You, O God;
   all peoples will praise You.

7 May the earth yield its produce;
   may God, our God, bless us.
8 May God bless us,
   and be revered to the ends of the earth.

68 [a]For the leader. Of David. A psalm. A song.

2 God will arise,
   His enemies shall be scattered,
   His foes shall flee before Him.
3 Disperse them as smoke is dispersed;
   as wax melts at fire,
   so the wicked shall perish before God.
4 But the righteous shall rejoice;

[a] *The coherence of this psalm and the meaning of many of its passages are uncertain.*

84

they shall exult in the presence of God;
they shall be exceedingly joyful.

5 Sing to God, chant hymns to His name;
extol Him who rides the clouds;
the LORD is His name.
Exult in His presence—
6 the father of orphans, the champion of widows,
God, in His holy habitation.
7 God restores the lonely to their homes,
sets free the imprisoned, safe and sound,
while the rebellious must live in a parched land.

8 O God, when You went at the head of Your army,
when You marched through the desert, *Selah.*
9 the earth trembled, the sky rained because of God,
yon Sinai, because of God, the God of Israel.
10 You released a bountiful rain, O God;
when Your own land languished, You sustained it.
11 Your tribe dwells there;
O God, in Your goodness You provide for the needy.

12 The LORD gives a command;
the women who bring the news are a great host:
13 "The kings and their armies are in headlong flight;
housewives are sharing in the spoils;
14 even for those of you who lie among the sheepfolds
there are wings of a dove sheathed in silver,
its pinions in fine gold."
15 When Shaddai scattered the kings,
it seemed like a snowstorm in Zalmon.

16 O majestic mountain, Mount Bashan;
O jagged mountain, Mount Bashan;
17 why so hostile, O jagged mountains,

toward the mountain God desired as His dwelling?
The LORD shall abide there forever.

18 God's chariots are myriads upon myriads,
   thousands upon thousands;
   the Lord is among them as in Sinai in holiness.

19 You went up to the heights, having taken captives,
   having received tribute of men,
   even of those who rebel
   against the LORD God's abiding there.

20 Blessed is the LORD.
   Day by day He supports us,
   God, our deliverance.   *Selah.*

21 God is for us a God of deliverance;
   GOD the Lord provides an escape from death.

22 God will smash the heads of His enemies,
   the hairy crown of him who walks about in his guilt.

23 The LORD said, "I will retrieve from Bashan,
   I will retrieve from the depths of the sea;

24   that your feet may wade through blood;
   that the tongue of your dogs may have its portion of
      your enemies."

25 Men see Your processions, O God,
   the processions of my God, my king,
   into the sanctuary.

26 First come singers, then musicians,
   amidst maidens playing timbrels.

27 In assemblies bless God,
   the LORD, O you who are from the fountain of Israel.

28 There is little Benjamin who rules them,
   the princes of Judah who command them,
   the princes of Zebulon and Naphtali.

²⁹ Your God has ordained strength for you,
the strength, O God,
which You displayed for us
³⁰ from Your temple above Jerusalem.
The kings bring You tribute.
³¹ Blast the beast of the marsh,
the herd of bulls among the peoples, the calves,
till they come cringing with pieces of silver.
Scatter the peoples who delight in wars!
³² Tribute-bearers shall come from Egypt;
Cush shall hasten its gifts to God.

³³ O kingdoms of the earth,
sing to God;
chant hymns to the Lord,   *Selah.*
³⁴ to Him who rides the ancient highest heavens,
who thunders forth with His mighty voice.
³⁵ Ascribe might to God,
whose majesty is over Israel,
whose might is in the skies.
³⁶ You are awesome, O God, in Your holy places;
it is the God of Israel who gives might and power to the
people.
Blessed is God.

69 For the leader. On *shoshannim.ᵃ* Of David.

² Deliver me, O God,
for the waters have reached my neck;
³ I am sinking into the slimy deep
and find no foothold;
I have come into the watery depths;
the flood sweeps me away.
⁴ I am weary with calling;

ᵃ *Meaning of Heb. uncertain.*

my throat is dry;
my eyes fail
while I wait for God.
⁵ More numerous than the hairs of my head
are those who hate me without reason;
many are those who would destroy me,
my treacherous enemies.
Must I restore what I have not stolen?

⁶ God, You know my folly;
my guilty deeds are not hidden from You.
⁷ Let those who look to You,
O LORD, God of hosts,
not be disappointed on my account;
let those who seek You,
O God of Israel,
not be shamed because of me.
⁸ It is for Your sake that I have been reviled,
that shame covers my face;
⁹ I am a stranger to my brothers,
an alien to my kin.
¹⁰ My zeal for Your house has been my undoing;
the reproaches of those who revile You have fallen upon
me.
¹¹ When I wept and fasted,
I was reviled for it.
¹² I made sackcloth my garment;
I became a byword among them.
¹³ Those who sit in the gate talk about me;
I am the taunt of drunkards.

¹⁴ As for me, may my prayer come to You, O LORD,
at a favorable moment;
O God, in Your abundant faithfulness,
answer me with Your sure deliverance.

15 Rescue me from the mire;
    let me not sink;
    let me be rescued from my enemies,
    and from the watery depths.
16 Let the floodwaters not sweep me away;
    let the deep not swallow me;
    let the mouth of the Pit not close over me.
17 Answer me, O LORD,
    according to Your great steadfastness;
    in accordance with Your abundant mercy
    turn to me;
18   do not hide Your face from Your servant,
    for I am in distress;
    answer me quickly.
19 Come near to me and redeem me;
    free me from my enemies.

20 You know my reproach,
    my shame, my disgrace;
    You are aware of all my foes.
21 Reproach breaks my heart,
    I am in despair;[a]
    I hope for consolation, but there is none,
    for comforters, but find none.
22 They give me gall for food,
    vinegar to quench my thirst.
23 May their table be a trap for them,
    a snare for their allies.
24 May their eyes grow dim so that they cannot see;
    may their loins collapse continually.
25 Pour out Your wrath on them;
    may Your blazing anger overtake them;
26   may their encampments be desolate;
    may their tents stand empty.
27 For they persecute those You have struck;

they talk about the pain of those You have felled.
²⁸ Add that to their guilt;
    let them have no share of Your beneficence;
²⁹   may they be erased from the book of life,
    and not be inscribed with the righteous.

³⁰ But I am lowly and in pain;
    Your help, O God, keeps me safe.
³¹ I will extol God's name with song,
    and exalt Him with praise.
³² That will please the LORD more than oxen,
    than bulls with horns and hooves.
³³ The lowly will see and rejoice;
    you who are mindful of God, take heart!
³⁴ For the LORD listens to the needy,
    and does not spurn His captives.

³⁵ Heaven and earth shall extol Him,
    the seas, and all that moves in them.
³⁶ For God will deliver Zion
    and rebuild the cities of Judah;
    they shall live there and inherit it;
³⁷   the offspring of His servants shall possess it;
    those who cherish His name shall dwell there.

70

For the leader. Of David. *Lehazkir.*[a]

² [b]Hasten, O God, to save me;
    O LORD, to aid me!
³ Let those who seek my life
    be frustrated and disgraced;
    let those who wish me harm,
    fall back in shame.

[a] *Meaning of Heb. uncertain.*
[b] *Cf. Ps. 40. 14–18.*

⁴ Let those who say, "Aha! Aha!"
　　turn back because of their frustration.

⁵ But let all who seek You be glad and rejoice in You;
　　let those who are eager for Your deliverance always say,
　　"Extolled be God!"
⁶ But I am poor and needy;
　　O God, hasten to me!
　You are my help and my rescuer;
　　O LORD, do not delay.

71 I seek refuge in You, O LORD;
　　may I never be disappointed.
² As You are beneficent, save me and rescue me;
　　incline Your ear to me and deliver me.
³ Be a sheltering rock for me to which I may always repair;
　　decree my deliverance,
　　for You are my rock and my fortress.
⁴ My God, rescue me from the hand of the wicked,
　　from the grasp of the unjust and the lawless.

⁵ For You are my hope,
　　O Lord GOD,
　　my trust from my youth.
⁶ While yet unborn, I depended on You;
　　in the womb of my mother, You were my support;*ᵃ*
　　I sing Your praises always.
⁷ I have become an example for many,
　　since You are my mighty refuge.
⁸ My mouth is full of praise to You,
　　glorifying You all day long.
⁹ Do not cast me off in old age;
　　when my strength fails, do not forsake me!

ᵃ *Meaning of Heb. uncertain.*

10 For my enemies talk against me;
  those who wait for me are of one mind,
11   saying, "God has forsaken him;
  chase him and catch him,
  for no one will save him!"
12 O God, be not far from me;
  my God, hasten to my aid!
13 Let my accusers perish in frustration;
  let those who seek my ruin be clothed in reproach and
    disgrace!

14 As for me, I will hope always,
  and add to the many praises of You.
15 My mouth tells of Your beneficence,
  of Your deliverance all day long,
  though I know not how to tell it.
16 I come with praise of Your mighty acts, O Lord GOD;
  I celebrate Your beneficence, Yours alone.
17 You have let me experience it, God, from my youth;
  until now I have proclaimed Your wondrous deeds,
18   and even in hoary old age do not forsake me, God,
  until I proclaim Your strength to the next generation,
19   Your mighty acts, to all who are to come,
  Your beneficence, high as the heavens, O God,
  You who have done great things;
  O God, who is Your peer!
20 You who have made me undergo many troubles and mis-
    fortunes
  will revive me again,
  and raise me up from the depths of the earth.
21 You will grant me much greatness,
  You will turn and comfort me.
22 Then I will acclaim You to the music of the lyre
  for Your faithfulness, O my God;
  I will sing a hymn to You with a harp,

O Holy One of Israel.
23 My lips shall be jubilant, as I sing a hymn to You,
 my whole being, which You have redeemed.
24 All day long my tongue shall recite Your beneficent acts,
 how those who sought my ruin were frustrated and disgraced.

72 Of Solomon.

O God, endow the king with Your judgments,
 the king's son with Your righteousness;
2 that he may judge Your people rightly,
 Your lowly ones, justly.
3 Let the mountains produce well-being for the people,
 the hills, the reward of justice.
4 Let him champion the lowly among the people,
 deliver the needy folk,
 and crush those who wrong them.
5 Let them fear You as long as the sun shines,
 while the moon lasts, generations on end.
6 Let him be like rain that falls on a mown field,
 like a downpour of rain on the ground,
7 that the righteous may flourish in his time,
 and well-being abound, till the moon is no more.
8 Let him rule from sea to sea,
 from the river to the ends of the earth.
9 Let desert-dwellers kneel before him,
 and his enemies lick the dust.
10 Let kings of Tarshish and the islands pay tribute,
 kings of Sheba and Seba offer gifts.
11 Let all kings bow to him,
 and all nations serve him.

12 For he saves the needy who cry out,
 the lowly who have no helper.

13 He cares about the poor and the needy;
   He brings the needy deliverance.
14 He redeems them from fraud and lawlessness;
   a-the shedding of their blood weighs heavily
      upon him.-*a*

15 So let him live, and receive gold of Sheba;
   let prayers for him be said always,
   blessings on him invoked at all times.
16 *b*-Let abundant grain be in the land, to the tops of the
      mountains;
   let his crops thrive like the forest of Lebanon;
   and let men sprout up in towns like country grass.
17 May his name be eternal;
   while the sun lasts, may his name endure;-*b*
   let men invoke his blessedness upon themselves;
   let all nations count him happy.

18 Blessed is the LORD God, God of Israel,
   who alone does wondrous things;
19 Blessed is His glorious name forever;
   His glory fills the whole world.
   Amen and Amen.

20 End of the prayers of David son of Jesse.

BOOK THREE

73 A psalm of Asaph.

God is truly good to Israel,
   to those whose heart is pure.
2 As for me, my feet had almost strayed,
   my steps were nearly led off course,

a-a *Or "their life is precious in his sight."*
b-b *Meaning of some Heb. phrases in these verses uncertain.*

3 for I envied the wanton;
   I saw the wicked at ease.
4 Death has no pangs for them;
   their body is healthy.
5 They have no part in the travail of men;
   they are not afflicted like the rest of mankind.
6 So pride adorns their necks,
   lawlessness enwraps them as a mantle.
7 *a*-Fat shuts out their eyes;
   their fancies are extravagant.-*a*
8 They scoff and plan evil;
   from their eminence they plan wrongdoing.
9 They set their mouths against heaven,
   and their tongues range over the earth.
10 *a*-So they pound His people again and again,
   until they are drained of their very last tear.-*a*
11 Then they say, "How could God know?
   Is there knowledge with the Most High?"
12 Such are the wicked;
   ever tranquil, they amass wealth.

13 It was for nothing that I kept my heart pure
   and washed my hands in innocence,
14 seeing that I have been constantly afflicted,
   that each morning brings new punishments.
15 Had I decided to say these things,
   I should have been false to the circle of Your disciples.
16 So I applied myself to understand this,
   but it seemed a hopeless task
17 till I entered God's Sanctuary
   and reflected on their fate.

18 You surround them with flattery;
   You make them fall through blandishments.
19 How suddenly are they ruined,

a-a *Meaning of Heb. uncertain.*

wholly swept away by terrors.

20 *a*-When You are aroused You despise their image,
as one does a dream after waking, O LORD.*-a*

21 My mind was stripped of its reason,
b-my feelings were numbed.*-b*

22 I was a dolt, without knowledge;
I was brutish toward You.

23 Yet I was always with You,
You held my right hand;

24 You guided me by Your counsel
c-and led me toward honor.*-c*

25 Whom else have I in heaven?
And having You, I want no one on earth.

26 My body and mind fail;
but God is the stay*d* of my mind, my portion forever.

27 Those who keep far from You perish;
You annihilate all who are untrue to You.

28 As for me, nearness to God is good;
I have made the Lord GOD my refuge,
that I may recount all Your works.

74

A *maskil* of Asaph.

Why, O God, do You forever reject us,
do You fume in anger at the flock that You tend?

2 Remember the community You made Yours long ago,
Your very own tribe that You redeemed,
Mount Zion, where You dwell.

3 *a*-Bestir Yourself*-a* because of the *b*-perpetual tumult,*-b*
all the outrages of the enemy in the sanctuary.

4 Your foes roar inside Your meeting-place;
they take their signs for true signs.

b-b Lit. "I was pierced through in my kidneys."
c-c Meaning of Heb. uncertain; others "And afterward receive me with glory."
d Lit. "rock."

a-a Lit. "Lift up Your feet."
b-b Meaning of Heb. uncertain.

5 *b*-It is like men wielding axes
 against a gnarled tree;
6 with hatchet and pike
 they hacked away at its carved work.-*b*
7 They made Your sanctuary go up in flames;
 they brought low in dishonor the dwelling-place of
 Your presence.
8 They resolved, "Let us destroy them altogether!"
 They burned all God's tabernacles in the land.
9 No signs appear for us;
 there is no longer any prophet;
 no one among us knows for how long.

10 Till when, O God, will the foe blaspheme,
 will the enemy forever revile Your name?
11 Why do You hold back Your hand, Your right hand?
 b-Draw it out of Your bosom!-*b*

12 O God, my king from of old,
 who brings deliverance throughout the land;
13 it was You who drove back the sea with Your might,
 who smashed the heads of the monsters in the waters;
14 it was You who crushed the heads of Leviathan,
 who left him as food for *c*-the denizens of the desert;-*c*
15 it was You who released springs and torrents,
 who made mighty rivers run dry;
16 the day is Yours, the night also;
 it was You who set in place the orb of the sun;
17 You fixed all the boundaries of the earth;
 summer and winter—You made them.

18 Be mindful of how the enemy blasphemes the LORD,
 how base people revile Your name.
19 Do not deliver Your dove to the wild beast;
 do not ignore forever the band of Your lowly ones.
20 Look to the covenant!

c-c Or "seafaring men"; meaning of Heb. uncertain.

For the dark places of the land are full of the haunts of
  lawlessness.
21 Let not the downtrodden turn away disappointed;
  let the poor and needy praise Your name.
22 Rise, O God, champion Your cause;
  be mindful that You are blasphemed by base men all day
  long.
23 Do not ignore the shouts of Your foes,
  the din of Your adversaries that ascends all the time.

75 For the leader; *al tashheth.*
  A psalm of Asaph, a song.

2 We praise You, O God;
  we praise You;
  Your presence is near;
  men tell of Your wondrous deeds.

3 "At the time I choose,
  I will give judgment equitably.
4 Earth and all its inhabitants dissolve;
  it is I who keep its pillars firm. *Selah.*
5 To wanton men I say, 'Do not be wanton!'
  to the wicked, 'Do not lift up your horns!' "

6 Do not lift your horns up high
  a-in vainglorious bluster.-*a*
7 For what lifts a man comes not from the east
  or the west or the wilderness;*b*
8   for God it is who gives judgment;
  He brings down one man, He lifts up another.
9 There is a cup in the LORD's hand
  with foaming wine fully mixed;
  from this He pours;
  all the wicked of the earth drink,

a-a Lit. *"with arrogant neck you speak."*
b *Reading* midbār *with many mss.*

draining it to the very dregs.

¹⁰ As for me, I will declare forever,
   I will sing a hymn to the God of Jacob.

¹¹ "All the horns of the wicked I will cut;
   but the horns of the righteous shall be lifted up."

76 For the leader; with instrumental music.
A psalm of Asaph, a song.

² God has made Himself known in Judah,
   His name is great in Israel;
³ Salem became His abode;
   Zion, His den.
⁴ There He broke the fiery arrows of the bow,
   the shield and the sword of war.   *Selah.*

⁵ You were resplendent,
   glorious, on the mountains of prey.
⁶ The stout-hearted were despoiled;
   they were in a stupor;
   the bravest of men could not lift a hand.
⁷ At Your blast, O God of Jacob,
   horse and chariot lay stunned.
⁸ O You! You are awesome!
   Who can withstand You
   when You are enraged?
⁹ In heaven You pronounced sentence;
   the earth was numbed with fright
¹⁰   as God rose to execute judgment,
   to deliver all the lowly of the earth.   *Selah.*

¹¹ ᵃ-The fiercest of men shall acknowledge You,
   when You gird on the last bit of fury.⁻ᵃ

ᵃ⁻ᵃ *Meaning of Heb. uncertain.*

¹² Make vows and pay them to the LORD your God;
a-all who are around Him shall bring tribute to
the Awesome One.-*a*
¹³ He curbs the spirit of princes,
inspires awe in the kings of the earth.

77 For the leader; on *Jeduthun.* Of Asaph. A psalm.

² I cry aloud to God;
I cry to God that He may give ear to me.
³ In my time of distress I turn to the Lord,
a-with my hand [uplifted];
[my eyes] flow all night without respite;-*a*
I will not be comforted.
⁴ I call God to mind, I moan,
I complain, my spirit fails.   *Selah.*

⁵ You have held my eyelids open;
I am overwrought, I cannot speak.
⁶ My thoughts turn to days of old,
to years long past.
⁷ I recall at night their gibes at me;
I commune with myself;
my spirit inquires,
⁸   "Will the Lord reject forever
and never again show favor?
⁹ Has His faithfulness disappeared forever?
Will His promise be unfulfilled for all time?
¹⁰ Has God forgotten how to pity?
Has He in anger stifled His compassion?"   *Selah.*
¹¹ And I said, *a*-"It is my fault
that the right hand of the Most High has changed."-*a*

ᵃ⁻ᵃ *Meaning of Heb. uncertain.*
ᵃ⁻ᵃ *Meaning of Heb. uncertain.*

12 I recall the deeds of the LORD;
   yes, I recall Your wonders of old;
13 I recount all Your works;
   I speak of Your acts.
14 O God, Your ways are holiness;
   what god is as great as God?
15 You are the God who works wonders;
   You have manifested Your strength among the peoples.
16 By Your arm You redeemed Your people,
   the children of Jacob and Joseph.   *Selah.*
17 The waters saw You, O God,
   the waters saw You and were convulsed;
   the very deep quaked as well.
18 Clouds streamed water;
   the heavens rumbled;
   Your arrows flew about;
19 Your thunder rumbled like wheels;
   lightning lit up the world;
   the earth quaked and trembled.
20 Your way was through the sea,
   Your path, through the mighty waters;
   Your tracks could not be seen.
21 You led Your people like a flock
   in the care of Moses and Aaron.

78 A *maskil* of Asaph.

Give ear, my people, to my teaching,
   turn your ear to what I say.
2 I will expound a theme,
   hold forth on the lessons of the past,
3 things we have heard and known,
   that our fathers have told us.

⁴ We will not withhold them from their children,
   telling the coming generation
   the praises of the LORD and His might,
   and the wonders He performed.
⁵ He established a decree in Jacob,
   ordained a Teaching in Israel,
   charging our fathers
   to make them known to their children,
⁶   that a future generation might know
   —children yet to be born—
   and in turn tell their children
⁷   that they might put their confidence in God,
   and not forget God's great deeds,
   but observe His commandments,
⁸   and not be like their fathers,
   a wayward and defiant generation,
   a generation whose heart was inconstant,
   whose spirit was not true to God.

⁹ Like the Ephraimite bowmen
   who played false in the day of battle,
¹⁰   they did not keep God's covenant,
   they refused to follow His instruction;
¹¹   they forgot His deeds
   and the wonders that He showed them.
¹² He performed marvels in the sight of their fathers,
   in the land of Egypt, the plain of Zoan.
¹³ He split the sea and took them through it;
   He made the waters stand like a wall.
¹⁴ He led them with a cloud by day,
   and throughout the night by the light of fire.
¹⁵ He split rocks in the wilderness
   and gave them drink as if from the great deep.
¹⁶ He brought forth streams from a rock
   and made them flow down like a river.

17 But they went on sinning against Him,
  defying the Most High in the parched land.
18 To test God was in their mind
  when they demanded food for themselves.
19 They spoke against God, saying,
  "Can God spread a feast in the wilderness?
20 True, He struck the rock and waters flowed,
  streams gushed forth;
  but can He provide bread?
Can He supply His people with meat?"
21 The LORD heard and He raged;
  fire broke out against Jacob,
  anger flared up at Israel,
22 because they did not put their trust in God,
  did not rely on His deliverance.
23 So He commanded the skies above,
  He opened the doors of heaven
24 and rained manna upon them for food,
  giving them heavenly grain.
25 Each man ate a hero's meal;
  He sent them provision in plenty.
26 He set the east wind moving in heaven,
  and drove the south wind by His might.
27 He rained meat on them like dust,
  winged birds like the sands of the sea,
28 making them come down inside His camp,
  around His dwelling-place.
29 They ate till they were sated;
  He gave them what they craved.
30 They had not yet wearied of what they craved,
  the food was still in their mouths
31 when God's anger flared up at them.
He slew their sturdiest,
  struck down the youth of Israel.

³² Nonetheless, they went on sinning
and had no faith in His wonders.
³³ He made their days end in futility,
their years in sudden death.
³⁴ When He struck^a them, they turned to Him
and sought God once again.
³⁵ They remembered that God was their rock,
God Most High, their Redeemer.
³⁶ Yet they deceived Him with their speech,
lied to Him with their words;
³⁷ their hearts were inconstant toward Him;
they were untrue to His covenant.
³⁸ But He, being merciful, forgave iniquity
and would not destroy;
He restrained His wrath time and again
and did not give full vent to His fury;
³⁹ for He remembered that they were but flesh,
a passing breath that does not return.

⁴⁰ How often did they defy Him in the wilderness,
did they grieve Him in the wasteland!
⁴¹ Again and again they tested God,
vexed^b the Holy One of Israel.
⁴² They did not remember His strength,
or the day He redeemed them from the foe;
⁴³ how He displayed His signs in Egypt,
His wonders in the plain of Zoan.
⁴⁴ He turned their rivers into blood;
He made their waters undrinkable.
⁴⁵ He inflicted upon them swarms of insects to devour them,
frogs to destroy them.
⁴⁶ He gave their crops over to grubs,
their produce to locusts.
⁴⁷ He killed their vines with hail,
their sycamores ^{c-}with frost.^{-c}

---

^a *Lit. "killed."*
^b *Or "set a limit to."*
^{c-c} *Meaning of Heb. uncertain.*

48 He gave their beasts over to hail,
   their cattle to lightning bolts.
49 He inflicted His burning anger upon them,
   wrath, indignation, trouble,
   a band of deadly messengers.
50 He cleared a path for His anger;
   He did not stop short of slaying them,
   but gave them over to pestilence.
51 He struck every firstborn in Egypt,
   the first fruits of their vigor in the tents of Ham.
52 He set His people moving like sheep,
   drove them like a flock in the wilderness.
53 He led them in safety; they were unafraid;
   as for their enemies, the sea covered them.
54 He brought them to His holy realm,*d*
   the mountain His right hand had acquired.
55 He expelled nations before them,
   e-settled the tribes of Israel in their tents,
   allotting them their portion by the line.*-e*

56 Yet they defiantly tested God Most High,
   and did not observe His decrees.
57 They fell away, disloyal like their fathers;
   they played false like a treacherous bow.
58 They vexed Him with their high places;
   they incensed Him with their idols.
59 God heard it and was enraged;
   He utterly rejected Israel.
60 He forsook the tabernacle of Shiloh,
   the tent He had set among men.
61 He let His might *f* go into captivity,
   His glory into the hands of the foe.
62 He gave His people over to the sword;
   He was enraged at His very own.
63 Fire consumed their young men,

---

d Or "hill" with Septuagint and Saadia.
e-e Inverted for clarity.
f I.e. the Ark; cf. Ps. 132.8.

and their maidens *g*-remained unwed.*g*
64 Their priests fell by the sword,
and their widows could not weep.

65 The Lord awoke as from sleep,
like a warrior *c*-shaking off-*c* wine.
66 He beat back His foes,
dealing them lasting disgrace.
67 He rejected the clan of Joseph;
He did not choose the tribe of Ephraim.
68 He did choose the tribe of Judah,
Mount Zion, which He loved.
69 He built His sanctuary like the heavens,
like the earth that He established forever.
70 He chose David, His servant,
and took him from the sheepfolds.
71 He brought him from minding the nursing ewes
to tend His people Jacob, Israel, His very own.
72 He tended them with blameless heart;
with skillful hands he led them.

79   A psalm of Asaph.

O God, heathens have entered Your domain,
defiled Your holy temple,
and turned Jerusalem into ruins.
2 They have left Your servants' corpses
as food for the fowl of heaven,
and the flesh of Your faithful for the wild beasts.
3 Their blood was shed like water around Jerusalem,
with none to bury them.
4 We have become the butt of our neighbors,
the scorn and derision of those around us.

g-g Lit. "had no nuptial song."

5 How long, O LORD, will You be angry forever,
   will Your indignation blaze like fire?
6 Pour out Your fury on the nations that do not know You,
   upon the kingdoms that do not invoke Your name,
7 for they have devoured Jacob
   and desolated his home.
8 Do not hold our former iniquities against us;
   let Your compassion come swiftly toward us,
   for we have sunk very low.
9 Help us, O God, our deliverer,
   for the sake of the glory of Your name.
   Save us and forgive our sin,
   for the sake of Your name.
10 Let the nations not say, "Where is their God?"
   Before our eyes let it be known among the nations
   that You avenge the spilled blood of Your servants.
11 Let the groans of the prisoners reach You;
   reprieve those condemned to death,
   as befits Your great strength.
12 Pay back our neighbors sevenfold
   for the abuse they have flung at You, O LORD.
13 Then we, Your people,
   the flock You shepherd,
   shall glorify You forever;
   for all time we shall tell Your praises.

80 For the leader; on *shoshannim, eduth.* Of Asaph. A psalm.

2 Give ear, O shepherd of Israel
   who leads Joseph like a flock!
   Appear, You who are enthroned on the cherubim,
3   at the head of Ephraim, Benjamin, and Manasseh!
   Rouse Your might and come to our help!

⁴ Restore us, O God;
    show Your favor that we may be delivered.

⁵ O Lᴏʀᴅ, God of hosts,
    how long will You be wrathful
    toward the prayers of Your people?
⁶ You have fed them tears as their daily bread,
    made them drink great measures of tears.
⁷ You set us at strife with our neighbors;
    our enemies mock us at will.
⁸ O God of hosts, restore us;
    show Your favor that we may be delivered.

⁹ You plucked up a vine from Egypt;
    You expelled nations and planted it.
¹⁰ You cleared a place for it;
    it took deep root and filled the land.
¹¹ The mountains were covered by its shade,
    mighty cedars by its boughs.
¹² Its branches reached the sea,
    its shoots, the river.
¹³ Why did You breach its wall
    so that every passerby plucks its fruit,
¹⁴   wild boars gnaw at it,
    and creatures of the field feed on it?

¹⁵ O God of hosts, turn again,
    look down from heaven and see;
    take note of that vine,
¹⁶   the stock planted by Your right hand,
    the stem[a] you have taken as Your own.
¹⁷ For it is burned by fire and cut down,
    perishing before Your angry blast.
¹⁸ Grant Your help[b] to the man at Your right hand,
    the one You have taken as Your own.

[a] *Lit. "son."*
[b] *Lit. "hand."*

19 We will not turn away from You;
   preserve our life that we may invoke Your name.
20 O LORD, God of hosts, restore us;
   show Your favor that we may be delivered.

81   For the leader; on the *gittith.* Of Asaph.

2 Sing joyously to God, our strength;
   raise a shout for the God of Jacob.
3 Take up the song,
   sound the timbrel,
   the melodious lyre and harp.
4 Blow the horn on the new moon,
   on the full moon for our feast day.
5 For it is a law for Israel,
   a ruling of the God of Jacob;
6   He imposed it as a decree upon Joseph
   when *a-*he went forth from*-a* the land of Egypt;
   I heard a language that I knew not.

7 I relieved his shoulder of the burden,
   his hands were freed from the basket.
8 In distress you called and I rescued you;
   I answered you from the *b-*secret place of thunder*-b*
   I tested you at the waters of Meribah.   *Selah.*

9 Hear, My people, and I will admonish you;
   Israel, if you would but listen to Me!
10 You shall have no foreign god,
   you shall not bow to an alien god.
11 I the LORD am your God
   who brought you out of the land of Egypt;
   open your mouth wide and I will fill it.

a-a *Or "He went forth against."*
b-b *Meaning of Heb. uncertain.*

¹² But My people would not listen to Me,
   Israel would not obey Me.
¹³ So I let them go after their willful heart
   that they might follow their own devices.
¹⁴ If only My people would listen to Me,
   if Israel would follow My paths,
¹⁵   then would I subdue their enemies at once,
   strike their foes again and again.
¹⁶ Those who hate the LORD shall cower before Him;
   their doom shall be eternal.
¹⁷ He fed them*c* the finest wheat;
   I sated you with honey from the rock.

82 A psalm of Asaph.

God stands in the divine assembly;
   among the divine beings He pronounces judgment.
² How long will you judge perversely,
   showing favor to the wicked?   *Selah.*
³ Judge the wretched and the orphan,
   vindicate the lowly and the poor,
⁴   rescue the wretched and the needy;
   save them from the hand of the wicked.

⁵ They neither know nor understand,
   they go about in darkness;
   all the foundations of the earth totter.
⁶ I had taken you for divine beings,
   sons of the Most High, all of you;
⁷   but you shall die as men do,
   fall like any prince.

⁸ Arise, O God, judge the earth,
   for all the nations are Your possession.

c Lit. "him," i.e. Israel.

83 A song, a psalm of Asaph.

2 O God, do not be silent;
   do not hold aloof;
   do not be quiet, O God!
3 For Your enemies rage,
   Your foes *a-*assert themselves.*-a*
4 They plot craftily against Your people,
   take counsel against Your treasured ones.
5 They say, "Let us wipe them out as a nation;
   Israel's name will be mentioned no more."
6 Unanimous in their counsel
   they have made an alliance against You—
7   the clans of Edom and the Ishmaelites,
     Moab and the Hagrites,
8   Gebal, Ammon, and Amalek,
     Philistia with the inhabitants of Tyre;
9   Assyria too joins forces with them;
     they give support to the sons of Lot.   *Selah.*

10 Deal with them as You did with Midian,
    with Sisera, with Jabin,
    at the brook Kishon—
11   who were destroyed at En-dor,
      who became dung for the field.
12 Treat their great men like Oreb and Zeeb,
    all their princes like Zebah and Zalmunna,
13   who said, "Let us take the meadows of God
      as our possession."
14 O my God, make them like thistledown,
    like stubble driven by the wind.
15 As a fire burns a forest,
    as flames scorch the hills,
16   pursue them with Your tempest,

---

a-a Lit. *"lift up the head."*

terrify them with Your storm.
¹⁷ Cover^b their faces with shame
    so that they seek Your name, O LORD.
¹⁸ May they be frustrated and terrified,
    disgraced and doomed forever.
¹⁹ May they know
    that Your name, Yours alone, is the LORD,
    supreme over all the earth.

84

For the leader; on the *gittith*. Of the Korahites. A psalm.

² How lovely is Your dwelling-place,
    O LORD of hosts.
³ I long, I yearn for the courts of the LORD;
    my body and soul shout for joy to the living God.
⁴ Even the sparrow has found a home,
    and the swallow a nest for herself
    in which to set her young,
    near Your altar, O LORD of hosts,
    my king and my God.
⁵ Happy are those who dwell in Your house;
    they forever praise You.   *Selah.*

⁶ Happy is the man who finds refuge in You,
    whose mind is on the [pilgrim] highways.
⁷ They pass through the Valley of Baca,
    ^aregarding it as a place of springs,
    as if the early rain had covered it with blessing.^{-a}
⁸ They go from ^brampart to rampart,^{-b}
    appearing before God in Zion.
⁹ O LORD, God of hosts,
    hear my prayer;
    give ear, O God of Jacob.   *Selah.*

^b *Lit. "Fill."*

^{a-a} *Meaning of Heb. uncertain.*
^{b-b} *Others "strength to strength."*

¹⁰ O God, behold our shield,
   look upon the face of Your anointed.

¹¹ Better one day in Your courts than a thousand [anywhere
      else];
   I would rather stand at the threshold of God's house
   than dwell in the tents of the wicked.
¹² For the LORD God is sun[c] and shield;
   the LORD bestows grace and glory;
   He does not withhold His bounty from those who live
   without blame.

¹³ O LORD of hosts,
   happy is the man who trusts in You.

85 For the leader. Of the Korahites. A psalm.

² O LORD, You [a-]will favor[-a] Your land,
   restore[b] Jacob's fortune;
³ You [c-]will forgive[-c] Your people's iniquity,
   pardon[d] all their sins;   Selah.
⁴ You [e-]will withdraw[-e] all Your anger,
   turn[f] away from Your rage.
⁵ Turn again, O God, our helper,
   revoke Your displeasure with us.
⁶ Will You be angry with us forever,
   prolong Your wrath for all generations?
⁷ Surely You will revive us again,

[c] Or "bulwark," with Targum; cf. Isa. 54.12.

[a-a] Or "have favored."
[b] Or "have restored."
[c-c] Or "have forgiven."
[d] Or "have pardoned."
[e-e] Or "have withdrawn."
[f] Or "have turned."

so that Your people may rejoice in You.
⁸ Show us, O Lord, Your faithfulness;
grant us Your deliverance.

⁹ Let me hear what God, the Lord, will speak;
He will promise well-being to His people, His faithful
ones;
may they not turn to folly.
¹⁰ His help is very near those who fear Him,
to make His glory dwell in our land.
¹¹ Faithfulness and truth meet;
justice and well-being kiss.
¹² Truth springs up from the earth;
justice looks down from heaven.
¹³ The Lord also bestows His bounty;
our land yields its produce.
¹⁴ Justice goes before Him
as He sets out on His way.

86 A prayer of David.

Incline Your ear, O Lord,
answer me,
for I am poor and needy.
² Preserve my life, for I am steadfast;
O You, my God,
deliver Your servant who trusts in You.
³ Have mercy on me, O Lord,
for I call to You all day long;
⁴ bring joy to Your servant's life,
for on You, Lord, I set my hope.
⁵ For You, Lord, are good and forgiving,
abounding in steadfast love to all who call on You.
⁶ Give ear, O Lord, to my prayer;

heed my plea for mercy.
7 In my time of trouble I call You,
  for You will answer me.

8 There is none like You among the gods, O LORD,
  and there are no deeds like Yours.
9 All the nations You have made
  will come to bow down before You, O LORD,
  and they will pay honor to Your name.
10 For You are great and perform wonders;
  You alone are God.

11 Teach me Your way, O LORD;
  I will walk in Your truth;
  . let my heart be undivided in reverence for Your name.
12 I will praise You, O LORD, my God, with all my heart
  and pay honor to Your name forever.
13 For Your steadfast love toward me is great;
  You have saved me from the depths of Sheol.

14 O God, arrogant men have risen against me;
  a band of ruthless men seek my life;
  they are not mindful of You.
15 But You, O LORD, are a God
  compassionate and merciful,
  slow to anger, abounding in steadfast love and faithfulness.
16 Turn to me and have mercy on me;
  grant Your strength to Your servant
  and deliver the son of Your maidservant.
17 Show me a sign of Your favor,
  that my enemies may see and be frustrated
  because You, O LORD, have given me aid and comfort.

87 ^a1-2   Of the Korahites. A psalm. A song.

> ^bThe LORD loves the gates of Zion,
>> His foundation on the holy mountains,^{-b}
>> more than all the dwellings of Jacob.
> ³ Glorious things are spoken of you,
>> O city of God.   *Selah.*
> ⁴ I mention Rahab^c and Babylon among those who acknowl-
>> edge Me;
>> Philistia, and Tyre, and Cush—each was born there.
> ⁵ Indeed, it shall be said of Zion,
>> "Every man was born there."
> ^dHe, the Most High, will preserve it.^{-d}
> ⁶ The LORD will inscribe in the register of peoples
>> that each was born there.   *Selah.*
> ⁷ Singers and dancers alike [will say]:
>> "All my roots^e are in You."

88   A song. A psalm of the Korahites. For the leader; ^aon
mahalath leannoth.^{-a} A *maskil* of Heman the Ezrahite.

> ² O LORD, God of my deliverance,
>> ^bwhen I cry out in the night^{-b} before You,
> ³   let my prayer reach You;
>> incline Your ear to my cry.

---

^a *The meaning of many passages in this psalm is uncertain.*
^{b-b} *Order of lines inverted for clarity.*
^c *A primeval monster; here, a poetic term for Egypt; cf. Isa. 30.7.*
^{d-d} *Or "He will preserve it supreme."*
^e *Lit. "sources."*

^{a-a} *Meaning of Heb. uncertain.*
^{b-b} *Or "by day I cry out [and] by night."*

⁴ For I am sated with misfortune;
  I am at the brink of Sheol.
⁵ I am numbered with those who go down to the Pit;
  I am a helpless man
⁶   abandoned*ᶜ* among the dead,
  like bodies lying in the grave
  of whom You are mindful no more,
  and who are cut off from Your care.
⁷ You have put me at the bottom of the Pit,
  in the darkest places, in the depths.
⁸ Your fury lies heavy upon me;
  You afflict me with all Your breakers.   *Selah.*
⁹ You make my companions shun me;
  You make me abhorrent to them;
  I am shut in and do not go out.
¹⁰ My eyes pine away from affliction;
  I call to You, O LORD, each day;
  I stretch out my hands to You.

¹¹ Do You work wonders for the dead?
  Do the shades rise to praise You?   *Selah.*
¹² Is Your faithful care recounted in the grave,
  Your constancy in the place of perdition?
¹³ Are Your wonders made known in the netherworld,*ᵈ*
  Your beneficent deeds in the land of oblivion?

¹⁴ As for me, I cry out to You, O LORD;
  each morning my prayer greets You.
¹⁵ Why, O LORD, do You reject me,
  do You hide Your face from me?
¹⁶ From my youth I have been afflicted
  and near death;
  I suffer Your terrors *ᵉ*wherever I turn.*ᵉ*
¹⁷ Your fury overwhelms me;
  Your terrors destroy me.

ᶜ *Lit. "released."*
ᵈ *Lit. "darkness."*
ᵉ⁻ᵉ *Following Saadia; meaning of Heb. uncertain.*

¹⁸ They swirl about me like water all day long;
 they encircle me on every side.
¹⁹ You have put friend and neighbor far from me
 and my companions out of my sight.^f

89 A *maskil* of Ethan the Ezrahite.

² I will sing of the LORD's steadfast love forever;
 to all generations I will proclaim Your faithfulness with
  my mouth.
³ I declare, "Your steadfast love is confirmed forever;
 there in the heavens You establish Your faithfulness."

⁴ "I have made a covenant with My chosen one;
 I have sworn to My servant David:
⁵ I will establish your offspring forever,
 I will confirm your throne for all generations." *Selah.*

⁶ Your wonders, O LORD, are praised by the heavens,
 Your faithfulness, too, in the assembly of holy beings.
⁷ For who in the skies can equal the LORD,
 can compare with the LORD among the divine beings,
⁸ a God greatly dreaded in the council of holy beings,
 held in awe by all around Him?
⁹ O LORD, God of hosts,
 who is mighty like You, O LORD?
Your faithfulness surrounds You;
¹⁰ You rule the swelling of the sea;
 when its waves surge, You still them.
¹¹ You crushed Rahab; he was like a corpse;
 with Your powerful arm You scattered Your enemies.
¹² The heaven is Yours,
 the earth too;
 the world and all it holds—
 You established them.

^f *Lit. "into darkness."*

118

13 North and south—
     You created them;
     Tabor and Hermon sing forth Your name.
14 Yours is an arm endowed with might;
     Your hand is strong;
     Your right hand, exalted.
15 Righteousness and justice are the base of Your throne;
     steadfast love and faithfulness stand before You.

16 Happy is the people who know the joyful shout;
     O Lord, they walk in the light of Your presence.
17 They rejoice in Your name all day long;
     they are exalted through Your righteousness.
18 For You are their strength in which they glory;
     our horn is exalted through Your favor.
19 Truly our shield is of the Lord,
     our king, of the Holy One of Israel.

20 Then*a* You spoke to Your faithful ones in a vision
     and said, "I have conferred power upon a warrior;
     I have exalted one chosen out of the people.
21 I have found David, My servant;
     anointed him with My sacred oil.
22 My hand shall be constantly with him,
     and My arm shall strengthen him.
23 No enemy shall *b-*oppress him,*-b*
     no vile man afflict him.
24 I will crush his adversaries before him;
     I will strike down those who hate him.
25 My faithfulness and steadfast love shall be with him;
     his horn shall be exalted through My name.
26 I will set his hand upon the sea,
     his right hand upon the rivers.
27 He shall say to Me,
     'You are my father, my God, the rock of my deliverance.'
28 I will appoint him firstborn,

---

a *Referring to vv. 4–5; cf. II Sam. 7.1–17.*
b-b *Meaning of Heb. uncertain.*

highest of the kings of the earth.

29 I will maintain My steadfast love for him always;
My covenant with him shall endure.

30 I will establish his line forever,
his throne, as long as the heavens last.

31 If his sons forsake My teaching
and do not live by My rules;

32 if they violate My laws,
and do not observe My commands,

33 I will punish their transgression with the rod,
their iniquity with plagues.

34 But I will not take away My steadfast love from him;
I will not betray My faithfulness.

35 I will not violate My covenant,
or change what I have uttered.

36 I have sworn by My holiness, once and for all;
I will not be false to David.

37 His line shall continue forever,
his throne, as the sun before Me,

38 as the moon, established forever,
an enduring witness in the sky." *Selah.*

39 Yet You have rejected, spurned,
and become enraged at Your anointed.

40 You have repudiated the covenant with Your servant;
You have dragged his dignity in the dust.

41 You have breached all his defenses,
shattered his strongholds.

42 All who pass by plunder him;
he has become the butt of his neighbors.

43 You have exalted the right hand of his adversaries,
and made all his enemies rejoice.

44 You have turned back the blade of his sword,
and have not sustained him in battle.

45 You have brought *b*-his splendor-*b* to an end
and have hurled his throne to the ground.

⁴⁶ You have cut short the days of his youth;
   You have covered him with shame.   *Selah.*
⁴⁷ How long, O Lord; will You forever hide Your face,
   will Your fury blaze like fire?
⁴⁸ O remember ᵇ-how short my life is;-ᵇ
   why should You have created every man in vain?
⁴⁹ What man can live and not see death,
   can save himself from the clutches of Sheol?   *Selah.*
⁵⁰ O Lord, where is Your steadfast love of old
   which You swore to David in Your faithfulness?
⁵¹ Remember, O Lord, the abuse flung at Your servants
   ᵇ-that I have borne in my bosom [from]
      many peoples,-ᵇ
⁵² how Your enemies, O Lord, have flung abuse,
   abuse at Your anointed at every step.

⁵³ Blessed is the Lord forever.
   Amen and Amen.

BOOK FOUR

90 A prayer of Moses, the man of God.

O Lord, You have been our refuge in every generation.
² Before the mountains came into being,
   before You brought forth the earth and the world,
   from eternity to eternity You are God.

³ You return man to dust;ᵃ
   You decreed, "Return you mortals!"
⁴ ᵇ-For in Your sight a thousand years
   are like yesterday that has past,
   like a watch of the night.
⁵ You engulf men in sleep;-ᵇ
   at daybreak they are like grass that renews itself;

ᵃ *Or "contrition."*
ᵇ⁻ᵇ *Meaning of Heb. uncertain.*

⁶ at daybreak it flourishes anew;
 by dusk it withers and dries up.
⁷ So we are consumed by Your anger,
 terror-struck by Your fury.
⁸ You have set our iniquities before You,
 our hidden sins in the light of Your face.
⁹ All our days pass away in Your wrath;
 we spend our years like a sigh.
¹⁰ The span of our life is seventy years,
 or, given the strength, eighty years;
 but the ᵇ-best of them-ᵇ are trouble and sorrow.
 They pass by speedily, and we ᶜ-are in darkness.-ᶜ
¹¹ Who can know Your furious anger?
 Your wrath matches the fear of You.
¹² Teach us to count our days rightly,
 that we may obtain a wise heart.

¹³ Turn, O LORD!
 How long?
 Show mercy to Your servants.
¹⁴ Satisfy us at daybreak with Your steadfast love
 that we may sing for joy all our days.
¹⁵ Give us joy for as long as You have afflicted us,
 for the years we have suffered misfortune.
¹⁶ Let Your deeds be seen by Your servants,
 Your glory by their children.
¹⁷ May the favor of the LORD, our God, be upon us;
 let the work of our hands prosper,
 O prosper the work of our hands!

91 O you who dwell in the shelter of the Most High
 and abide in the protection of Shaddai—
² I say of the LORD, my refuge and stronghold,

ᶜ⁻ᶜ *Or "fly away."*

my God in whom I trust,

3 that He will save you from the fowler's trap,
from the destructive plague.

4 He will cover you with His pinions;
you will find refuge under His wings;
His fidelity is an encircling shield.

5 You need not fear the terror by night,
or the arrow that flies by day,

6 the plague that stalks in the darkness,
or the scourge that ravages at noon.

7 A thousand may fall at your left side,
ten thousand at your right,
but it shall not reach you.

8 You will see it with your eyes,
you will witness the punishment of the wicked.

9 Because you took the LORD—my refuge,
the Most High—as your haven,

10 no harm will befall you,
no disease touch your tent.

11 For He will order His angels
to guard you wherever you go.

12 They will carry you in their hands
lest you hurt your foot on a stone.

13 You will tread on cubs and vipers;
you will trample lions and asps.

14 "Because he is devoted to Me I will deliver him;
I will keep him safe, for he knows My name.

15 When he calls on Me, I will answer him;
I will be with him in distress;
I will rescue him and make him honored;

16 I will let him live to a ripe old age,
and show him My salvation."

92 A psalm. A song; for the sabbath day.

² It is good to praise the Lord,
    to sing hymns to Your name, O Most High,
³   to proclaim Your steadfast love at daybreak,
    Your faithfulness each night
⁴   with a ten-stringed harp,
    with voice and lyre together.

⁵ You have gladdened me by Your deeds, O Lord;
    I shout for joy at Your handiwork.
⁶ How great are Your works, O Lord,
    how very subtle *ᵃ* Your designs!
⁷ A brutish man cannot know,
    a fool cannot understand this:
⁸   though the wicked sprout like grass,
    though all evildoers blossom,
    it is only that they may be destroyed forever.

⁹ But You are exalted, O Lord, for all time.

¹⁰ Surely, Your enemies, O Lord,
    surely, Your enemies perish;
    all evildoers are scattered.
¹¹ You raise my horn high like that of a wild ox;
    I am soaked in freshening oil.
¹² I shall see the defeat of my watchful foes,
    hear of the downfall of the wicked who beset me.
¹³ The righteous bloom like a date-palm;
    they thrive like a cedar in Lebanon;
¹⁴   planted in the house of the Lord,
    they flourish in the courts of our God.
¹⁵ In old age they still produce fruit;

ᵃ *Or "profound."*

they are full of sap and freshness,
16 attesting that the LORD is upright,
my rock, in whom there is no wrong.

93 The LORD is king,
He is robed in grandeur;
the LORD is robed,
He is girded with strength.
The world stands firm;
it cannot be shaken.
2 Your throne stands firm from of old;
from eternity You have existed.
3 The ocean sounds, O LORD,
the ocean sounds its thunder,
the ocean sounds its pounding.
4 Above the thunder of the mighty waters,
more majestic than the breakers of the sea
is the LORD, majestic on high.
5 Your decrees are indeed enduring;
holiness befits Your house,
O LORD, for all times.

94 God of retribution, LORD,
God of retribution, appear!
2 Rise up, judge of the earth,
give the arrogant their deserts!
3 How long shall the wicked, O LORD,
how long shall the wicked exult,
4 shall they utter insolent speech,
shall all evildoers vaunt themselves?
5 They crush Your people, O LORD,
they afflict Your very own;
6 they kill the widow and the stranger;

they murder the fatherless,
7   thinking, "The Lord does not see it,
the God of Jacob does not pay heed."

8 Take heed, you most brutish people;
fools, when will you get wisdom?
9 Shall He who implants the ear not hear,
He who forms the eye not see?
10 Shall He who disciplines nations not punish,
He who instructs men in knowledge?
11 The Lord knows the designs of men to be futile.

12 Happy is the man whom You discipline, O Lord,
the man You instruct in Your teaching,
13   to give him tranquillity in times of misfortune,
until a pit be dug for the wicked.
14 For the Lord will not forsake His people;
He will not abandon His very own.
15 Judgment shall again accord with justice
and all the upright shall rally to it.

16 Who will take my part against evil men?
Who will stand up for me against wrongdoers?
17 Were not the Lord my help,
I should soon dwell in silence.
18 When I think my foot has given way,
Your faithfulness, O Lord, supports me.
19 When I am filled with cares,
Your assurance soothes my soul.

20 Shall the seat of injustice be Your partner,
that frames mischief by statute?
21 They band together to do away with the righteous;
they condemn the innocent to death.
22 But the Lord is my haven;
my God is my sheltering rock.

23 He will make their evil recoil upon them,
   annihilate them through their own wickedness;
   the Lord our God will annihilate them.

95 Come, let us sing joyously to the Lord,
      raise a shout for our rock and deliverer;
   2   let us come into His presence with praise;
      let us raise a shout for Him in song!
   3 For the Lord is a great God,
      the great king of all divine beings.
   4 In His hand are the depths of the earth;
      the peaks of the mountains are His.
   5 His is the sea, He made it;
      and the land, which His hands fashioned.

   6 Come, let us bow down and kneel,
      bend the knee before the Lord our maker,
   7   for He is our God,
      and we are the people He tends, the flock in His care.
   O, if you would but heed His charge this day:
   8   Do not be stubborn as at Meribah,
      as on the day of Massah, in the wilderness,
   9   when your fathers put Me to the test,
      tried Me, though they had seen My deeds.
   10 Forty years I was provoked by that generation.
   I thought, "They are a senseless people;
      they would not know My ways."
   11 Concerning them I swore in anger,
      "They shall never come to My resting-place!"

96 ªSing to the Lord a new song,
      sing to the Lord, all the earth.
   2 Sing to the Lord, bless His name,
      proclaim His victory day after day.

ª Cf. I Chron. 16.23–33.

³ Tell of His glory among the nations,
His wondrous deeds, among all peoples.
⁴ For the LORD is great and much acclaimed,
He is held in awe by all divine beings.
⁵ All the gods of the peoples are mere idols,
but the LORD made the heavens.
⁶ Glory and majesty are before Him;
strength and splendor are in His temple.

⁷ Ascribe to the LORD, O families of the peoples,
ascribe to the LORD glory and strength.
⁸ Ascribe to the LORD the glory of His name,
bring tribute and enter His courts.
⁹ Bow down to the LORD majestic in holiness;
tremble in His presence, all the earth!
¹⁰ Declare among the nations, "The LORD is king!"
the world stands firm; it cannot be shaken;
He judges the peoples with equity.
¹¹ Let the heavens rejoice and the earth exult;
let the sea and all within it thunder,
¹²   the fields and everything in them exult;
then shall all the trees of the forest shout for joy
¹³   at the presence of the LORD, for He is coming,
for He is coming to rule the earth;
He will rule the world justly
and its peoples in faithfulness.

97 The LORD is king!
Let the earth exult,
the many islands rejoice!
² Dense clouds are around Him,
righteousness and justice are the base of His throne.
³ Fire is His vanguard,
burning His foes on every side.

⁴ His lightnings light up the world;
    the earth is convulsed at the sight;
⁵   mountains melt like wax at the LORD's presence,
    at the presence of the Lord of all the earth.
⁶ The heavens proclaim His righteousness
    and all peoples see His glory.
⁷ All who worship images,
    who vaunt their idols,
    are dismayed;
    all divine beings bow down to Him.
⁸ Zion, hearing it, rejoices,
    the towns[a] of Judah exult,
    because of Your judgments, O LORD.
⁹ For You, LORD, are supreme over all the earth;
    You are exalted high above all divine beings.

¹⁰ O you who love the LORD, hate evil!
    He guards the lives of His loyal ones,
    saving them from the hand of the wicked.
¹¹ Light is sown for the righteous,
    radiance[b] for the upright.
¹² O you righteous, rejoice in the LORD
    and acclaim His holy name!

98 A psalm.

Sing to the LORD a new song,
    for He has worked wonders;
    His right hand, His holy arm,
    has won Him victory.
² The LORD has manifested His victory,
    has displayed His triumph in the sight of the nations.
³ He was mindful of His steadfast love and faithfulness
    toward the house of Israel;

[a] Or "women."
[b] Others "joy."

all the ends of the earth beheld the victory of our God.
⁴ Raise a shout to the LORD, all the earth,
    break into joyous songs of praise!
⁵ Sing praise to the LORD with the lyre,
    with the lyre and melodious song.
⁶ With trumpets and the blast of the horn
    raise a shout before the LORD, the king.
⁷ Let the sea and all within it thunder,
    the world and its inhabitants;
⁸   let the rivers clap their hands,
    the mountains sing joyously together
⁹   at the presence of the LORD,
    for He is coming to rule the earth;
    He will rule the world justly,
    and its peoples with equity.

99 *ᵃ*-The LORD, enthroned on cherubim, is king,
    peoples tremble, the earth quakes.-*ᵃ*
² The LORD is great in Zion,
    and exalted above all peoples.
³ They praise Your name as great and awesome;
    He is holy!

⁴ *ᵇ*-Mighty king-*ᵇ* who loves justice,
    it was You who established equity,
    You who worked righteous judgment in Jacob.
⁵ Exalt the LORD our God
    and bow down to His footstool;
    He is holy!

⁶ Moses and Aaron among His priests,
    Samuel, among those who call on His name—
    when they called to the LORD,
    He answered them.

ᵃ⁻ᵃ *Clauses transposed for clarity.*
ᵇ⁻ᵇ *Meaning of Heb. uncertain.*

⁷ He spoke to them in a pillar of cloud;
 they obeyed His decrees,
 the law He gave them.
⁸ O LORD our God, You answered them;
 You were a forgiving God for them,
 but You exacted retribution for their misdeeds.

⁹ Exalt the LORD our God,
 and bow toward His holy hill,
 for the LORD our God is holy.

100 A psalm *ª-for praise.*⁻ª

 Raise a shout for the LORD, all the earth;
² worship the LORD in gladness;
 come into His presence with shouts of joy.
³ Acknowledge that the LORD is God;
 He made us and *ᵇ-we are His,*⁻ᵇ
 His people, the flock He tends.
⁴ Enter His gates with praise,
 His courts with acclamation.
 Praise Him!
 Bless His name!
⁵ For the LORD is good;
 His steadfast love is eternal;
 His faithfulness is for all generations.

101 Of David. A psalm.

 I will sing of faithfulness and justice;
 I will chant a hymn to You, O LORD.
² I will study the way of the blameless;
 when shall I attain it?

ª⁻ª *Traditionally, "for the thanksgiving offering."*
ᵇ⁻ᵇ *So qere; kethib and some ancient versions "not we ourselves."*

I will live without blame within my house.
3 I will not set before my eyes anything base;
    I hate crooked dealing;
    I will have none of it.
4 Perverse thoughts will be far from me;
    I will know nothing of evil.
5 He who slanders his friend in secret I will destroy;
    I cannot endure the haughty and proud man.
6 My eyes are on the trusty men of the land,
    to have them at my side.
He who follows the way of the blameless
    shall be in my service.
7 He who deals deceitfully
    shall not live in my house;
    he who speaks untruth
    shall not stand before my eyes.
8 Each morning I will destroy
    all the wicked of the land,
    to rid the city of the LORD
    of all evildoers.

102 A prayer of the lowly man when he is faint and pours forth his plea before the LORD.

2 O LORD, hear my prayer;
    let my cry come before You.
3 Do not hide Your face from me
    in my time of trouble;
    turn Your ear to me;
    when I cry, answer me speedily.
4 For my days have vanished like smoke
    and my bones are charred like a hearth.
5 My body is stricken and withered like grass;
    a-too wasted-*a* to eat my food;

a-a *Others "I forget."*

132

6   on account of my vehement groaning
     my bones *b*-show through my skin.*-b*
7 I am like a great owl in the wilderness,
     an owl among the ruins.
8 I lie awake; I am like
     a lone bird upon a roof.
9 All day long my enemies revile me;
     my deriders use my name to curse.
10 For I have eaten ashes like bread
     and mixed my drink with tears,
11   because of Your wrath and Your fury;
     for You have cast me far away.
12 My days are like a lengthening shadow;
     I wither like grass.

13 But You, O LORD, are enthroned forever;
     Your fame endures throughout the ages.
14 You will surely arise and take pity on Zion,
     for it is time to be gracious to her;
     the appointed time has come.
15 Your servants take delight in its stones,
     and cherish its dust.
16 The nations will fear the name of the LORD,
     all the kings of the earth, Your glory.
17 For the LORD has built Zion;
     He has appeared in all His glory.
18 He has turned to the prayer *c*-of the destitute-*c*
     and has not spurned their prayer.
19 May this be written down for a coming generation,
     that people yet to be created may praise the LORD.
20 For He looks down from His holy height;
     the LORD beholds the earth from heaven
21   to hear the groans of the prisoner,
     to release those condemned to death;
22   that the fame of the LORD may be recounted in Zion,

b-b Lit. *"cling to my flesh."*
c-c Meaning of Heb. uncertain.

His praises in Jerusalem,
23 when the nations gather together,
the kingdoms, to serve the LORD.

24 He drained my strength in mid-course,
He shortened my days.
25 I say, "O my God, do not take me away
in the midst of my days,
You whose years go on for generations on end.
26 Of old You established the earth;
the heavens are the work of Your hands.
27 They shall perish, but You shall endure;
they shall all wear out like a garment;
You change them like clothing and they pass away.
28 But You are the same, and Your years never end.
29 May the children of Your servants dwell securely
and their offspring endure in Your presence."

103 Of David.

Bless the LORD, O my soul,
all my being, His holy name.
2 Bless the LORD, O my soul
and do not forget all His bounties.
3 He forgives all your sins,
heals all your diseases.
4 He redeems your life from the Pit,
surrounds you with steadfast love and mercy.
5 He satisfies you with good things in *the prime of life,*
so that your youth is renewed like the eagle's.

6 The LORD executes righteous acts
and judgments for all who are wronged.
7 He made known His ways to Moses,

---

a-a *Meaning of Heb. uncertain.*

His deeds to the children of Israel.
8 The Lord is compassionate and gracious,
   slow to anger, abounding in steadfast love.
9 He will not contend forever,
   or nurse His anger for all time.
10 He has not dealt with us according to our sins,
   nor has He requited us according to our iniquities.
11 For as the heavens are high above the earth,
   so great is His steadfast love toward those who fear Him.
12 As east is far from west,
   so far has He removed our sins from us.
13 As a father has compassion for his children,
   so the Lord has compassion for those who fear Him.
14 For He knows how we are formed;
   He is mindful that we are dust.

15 Man, his days are like those of grass;
   he blooms like a flower of the field;
16   a wind passes by and it is no more,
   its own place no longer knows it.
17 But the Lord's steadfast love is for all eternity
   toward those who fear Him,
   and His beneficence is for the children's children
18   of those who keep His covenant
   and remember to observe His precepts.
19 The Lord has established His throne in heaven,
   and His sovereign rule is over all.

20 Bless the Lord, O His angels,
   mighty creatures who do His bidding,
   ever obedient to His bidding;
21   bless the Lord, all His hosts,
   His servants who do His will;
22   bless the Lord, all His works,

through the length and breadth of His realm;
bless the LORD, O my soul.

104 Bless the LORD, O my soul;
O LORD, my God, You are very great;
You are clothed in glory and majesty,
² wrapped in a robe of light;
You spread the heavens like a tent cloth.
³ He sets the rafters of His lofts in the waters,
makes the clouds His chariot,
moves on the wings of the wind.
⁴ He makes the winds His messengers,
fiery flames His servants.
⁵ He established the earth on its foundations,
so that it shall never totter.
⁶ You made the deep cover it as a garment;
the waters stood above the mountains.
⁷ They fled at Your blast,
rushed away at the sound of Your thunder,
⁸ —mountains rising, valleys sinking—
to the place You established for them.
⁹ You set bounds they must not pass
so that they never again cover the earth.

¹⁰ You make springs gush forth in torrents;
they make their way between the hills,
¹¹ giving drink to all the wild beasts;
the wild asses slake their thirst.
¹² The birds of the sky dwell beside them
and sing among the foliage.
¹³ You water the mountains from Your ᵃ lofts;
the earth is sated from the fruit of Your work.
¹⁴ You make the grass grow for the cattle,
and herbage for man's labor

ᵃ *Lit. "His."*

that he may get food out of the earth—
15   wine that cheers the hearts of men
    b-oil that makes the face shine,-*b*
    and bread that sustains man's life.
16 The trees of the LORD drink their fill,
    the cedars of Lebanon, His own planting,
17   where birds make their nests;
    the stork has her home in the junipers.
18 The high mountains are for wild goats;
    the crags are a refuge for rock-badgers.

19 He made the moon to mark the seasons;
    the sun knows when to set.
20 You bring on darkness and it is night,
    when all the beasts of the forests stir.
21 The lions roar for prey,
    seeking their food from God.
22 When the sun rises, they come home
    and couch in their dens.
23 Man then goes out to his work,
    to his labor until the evening.

24 How many are the things You have made, O LORD;
    You have made them all with wisdom;
    the earth is full of Your creations.
25 There is the sea, vast and wide,
    with its creatures beyond number,
    living things, small and great.
26 There go the ships,
    and Leviathan that You formed to sport with.
27 All of them look to You
    to give them their food when it is due.
28 Give it to them, they gather it up;
    open Your hand, they are well satisfied;
29   hide Your face, they are terrified;

b-b Lit. "to make the face shine from oil."

take away their breath, they perish
and turn again into dust;
30 send back Your breath, they are created,
and You renew the face of the earth.

31 May the glory of the Lord endure forever;
may the Lord rejoice in His works!
32 He looks at the earth and it trembles;
He touches the mountains and they smoke.

33 I will sing to the Lord as long as I live;
all my life I will chant hymns to my God.
34 May my prayer be pleasing to Him;
I will rejoice in the Lord.
35 May sinners disappear from the earth,
and the wicked be no more.
Bless the Lord, O my soul.
Hallelujah.

105 Praise the Lord;
call on His name;
proclaim His deeds among the peoples.
2 Sing praises to Him;
speak of all His wondrous acts.
3 Exult in His holy name;
let all who seek the Lord rejoice.
4 Turn to the Lord, to His might;[a]
seek His presence constantly.
5 Remember the wonders He has done,
His portents and the judgments He has pronounced,
6 O offspring of Abraham, His servant,
O descendants of Jacob, His chosen ones.

7 He is the Lord our God;
His judgments are throughout the earth.

---

[a] *I.e. the Ark; cf. Ps. 78. 61; Ps. 132. 8.*

8 He is ever mindful of His covenant,
   the promise He gave for a thousand generations,
9 that He made with Abraham,
   swore to Isaac,
10 and confirmed in a decree for Jacob,
   for Israel, as an eternal covenant,
11 saying, "To you I will give the land of Canaan
   as your allotted heritage."

12 They were then few in number,
   a mere handful, sojourning there,
13 wandering from nation to nation,
   from one kingdom to another.
14 He allowed no one to oppress them;
   He reproved kings on their account,
15 "Do not touch My anointed ones;
   do not harm My prophets."

16 He called down a famine on the land,
   destroyed every staff of bread.
17 He sent ahead of them a man,
   Joseph, sold into slavery.
18 His feet were subjected to fetters;
   an iron collar was put on his neck.
19 Until his prediction came true
   the decree of the LORD purged him.
20 The king sent to have him freed;
   the ruler of nations released him.
21 He made him the lord of his household,
   empowered him over all his possessions,
22 to discipline his princes at will,
   to teach his elders wisdom.
23 Then Israel came to Egypt;
   Jacob sojourned in the land of Ham.

²⁴ He made His people very fruitful,
>   more numerous than their foes.
²⁵ ^{b-}He changed their heart^{-b} to hate His people,
>   to plot against His servants.
²⁶ He sent His servant Moses,
>   and Aaron, whom He had chosen.
²⁷ They performed His signs among them,
>   His wonders, against the land of Ham.
²⁸ He sent darkness; it was very dark;
>   ^{c-}did they not defy His word?^{-c}
²⁹ He turned their waters into blood
>   and killed their fish.
³⁰ Their land teemed with frogs,
>   even the rooms of their king.
³¹ Swarms of insects came at His command,
>   lice, throughout their country.
³² He gave them hail for rain,
>   and flaming fire in their land.
³³ He struck their vines and fig trees,
>   broke down the trees of their country.
³⁴ Locusts came at His command,
>   grasshoppers without number.
³⁵ They devoured every green thing in the land;
>   they consumed the produce of the soil.
³⁶ He struck down every firstborn in the land,
>   the first fruit of their vigor.
³⁷ He led Israel^d out with silver and gold;
>   none among their tribes faltered.
³⁸ Egypt rejoiced when they left,
>   for dread of Israel^d had fallen upon them.

³⁹ He spread a cloud for a cover,
>   and fire to light up the night.
⁴⁰ They asked and He brought them quail,
>   and satisfied them with food from heaven.

b-b *Or "Their heart changed."*
c-c *Meaning of Heb. uncertain.*
d *Lit. "them."*

⁴¹ He opened a rock so that water gushed forth;
   it flowed as a stream in the parched land.
⁴² Mindful of His sacred promise
   to His servant Abraham,
⁴³ He led His people out in gladness,
   His chosen ones with joyous song.
⁴⁴ He gave them the lands of nations;
   they inherited the wealth of peoples,
⁴⁵ that they might keep His laws
   and observe His teachings.
   Hallelujah.

106

Hallelujah.
Praise the LORD for He is good;
   His steadfast love is eternal.
² Who can tell the mighty acts of the LORD,
   proclaim all His praises?

³ Happy are those who act justly,
   who do right at all times.
⁴ Be mindful of me, O LORD, when You favor Your people;
   take note of me when You deliver them,
⁵ that I may enjoy the prosperity of Your chosen ones,
   share the joy of Your nation,
   glory in Your very own people.

⁶ We have sinned like our forefathers;
   we have gone astray, done evil.
⁷ Our forefathers in Egypt did not perceive Your wonders;
   they did not remember Your abundant love,
   but rebelled at the sea, at the Sea of Reeds.
⁸ Yet He saved them, as befits His name,
   to make known His might.
⁹ He sent His blast against the Sea of Reeds;

    it became dry;
      He led them through the deep as through a wilderness.
10 He delivered them from the foe,
      redeemed them from the enemy.
11 Water covered their adversaries;
      not one of them was left.
12 Then they believed His promise,
      and sang His praises.
13 But they soon forgot His deeds;
      they would not wait to learn His plan.
14 They were seized with craving in the wilderness,
      and put God to the test in the wasteland.
15 He gave them what they asked for,
      then made them waste away.
16 There was envy of Moses in the camp,
      and of Aaron, the holy one of the LORD.
17 The earth opened up and swallowed Dathan,
      closed over the party of Abiram.
18 A fire blazed among their party,
      a flame that consumed the wicked.
19 They made a calf at Horeb
      and bowed down to a molten image.
20 They exchanged their glory
      for the image of a bull that feeds on grass.
21 They forgot God who saved them,
      who performed great deeds in Egypt,
22   wondrous deeds in the land of Ham,
      awesome deeds at the Sea of Reeds.
23 He would have destroyed them
      had not Moses His chosen one
      confronted Him in the breach
      to avert His destructive wrath.
24 They rejected the desirable land,
      and put no faith in His promise.
25 They grumbled in their tents

and disobeyed the Lord.
²⁶ So He raised His hand in oath
　　to make them fall in the wilderness,
²⁷　　to disperse^a their offspring among the nations
　　and scatter them through the lands.
²⁸ They attached themselves to Baal Peor,
　　ate sacrifices offered to the dead.
²⁹ They provoked anger by their deeds,
　　and a plague broke out among them.
³⁰ Phinehas stepped forth and intervened,
　　and the plague ceased.
³¹ It was reckoned to his merit
　　for all generations, to eternity.
³² They provoked wrath at the waters of Meribah
　　and Moses suffered on their account,
³³　　because they rebelled against Him
　　and he spoke rashly.

³⁴ They did not destroy the nations
　　as the Lord had commanded them,
³⁵　　but mingled with the nations
　　and learned their ways.
³⁶ They worshiped their idols,
　　which became a snare for them.
³⁷ Their own sons and daughters
　　they sacrificed to demons.
³⁸ They shed innocent blood,
　　the blood of their sons and daughters,
　　whom they sacrificed to the idols of Canaan;
　　so the land was polluted with bloodguilt.
³⁹ Thus they became defiled by their acts,
　　debauched through their deeds.
⁴⁰ The Lord was angry with His people
　　and He abhorred His inheritance.
⁴¹ He handed them over to the nations;

^a *Cf. Targum, Kimhi.*

their foes ruled them.

42 Their enemies oppressed them
and they were subject to their power.
43 He saved them time and again,
but they were deliberately rebellious,
and so they were brought low by their iniquity.
44 When He saw that they were in distress,
when He heard their cry,
45 He was mindful of His covenant
and in His great faithfulness relented.
46 He made all their captors kindly disposed toward them.

47 Deliver us, O Lord our God,
and gather us from among the nations,
to acclaim Your holy name,
to glory in Your praise.

48 Blessed is the Lord, God of Israel,
From eternity to eternity.
Let all the people say, "Amen."
Hallelujah.

BOOK FIVE

107 "Praise the Lord, for He is good;
His steadfast love is eternal!"
2 Thus let the redeemed of the Lord say,
those He redeemed from adversity,
3 whom He gathered in from the lands,
from east and west,
from the north and from the sea.

4 Some lost their way in the wilderness,
in the wasteland;

they found no settled place.
5 Hungry and thirsty,
  their spirit failed.
6 In their adversity they cried to the LORD,
  and He rescued them from their troubles.
7 He showed them a direct way
  to reach a settled place.
8 Let them praise the LORD for His steadfast love,
  His wondrous deeds for mankind;
9   for He has satisfied the thirsty,
  filled the hungry with all good things.

10 Some lived in deepest darkness,
   bound in cruel irons,
11   because they defied the word of God,
   spurned the counsel of the Most High.
12 He humbled their hearts through suffering;
   they stumbled with no one to help.
13 In their adversity they cried to the LORD,
   and He rescued them from their troubles.
14 He brought them out of deepest darkness,
   broke their bonds asunder.
15 Let them praise the LORD for His steadfast love,
   His wondrous deeds for mankind,
16   For He shattered gates of bronze,
   He broke their iron bars.

17 There were fools who suffered for their sinful way,
   and for their iniquities.
18 All food was loathsome to them;
   they reached the gates of death.
19 In their adversity they cried to the LORD
   and He saved them from their troubles.
20 He gave an order and healed them;
   He delivered them from the pits.[a]

[a] *Viz. of death.*

²¹ Let them praise the LORD for His steadfast love,
His wondrous deeds for mankind.
²² Let them offer thanksgiving sacrifices,
and tell His deeds in joyful song.

²³ Others go down to the sea in ships,
ply their trade in the mighty waters;
²⁴ they have seen the works of the LORD
and His wonders in the deep.
²⁵ By His word He raised a storm wind
that made the waves surge.
²⁶ Mounting up to the heaven,
plunging down to the depths,
disgorging in their misery,
²⁷ they reeled and staggered like a drunken man,
all their skill to no avail.
²⁸ In their adversity they cried to the LORD,
and He saved them from their troubles.
²⁹ He reduced the storm to a whisper;
the waves were stilled.
³⁰ They rejoiced when all was quiet,
and He brought them to the port they desired.
³¹ Let them praise the LORD for His steadfast love,
His wondrous deeds for mankind.
³² Let them exalt Him in the congregation of the people,
acclaim Him in the assembly of the elders.

³³ He turns the rivers into a wilderness,
springs of water into thirsty land,
³⁴ fruitful land into a salt marsh,
because of the wickedness of its inhabitants.
³⁵ He turns the wilderness into pools,
parched land into springs of water.
³⁶ There He settles the hungry;
they build a place to settle in.

37 They sow fields and plant vineyards
   that yield a fruitful harvest.
38 He blesses them and they increase greatly;
   and He does not let their cattle decrease,
39   after they had been few and crushed
   by oppression, misery, and sorrow.
40 He pours contempt on great men
   and makes them lose their way in trackless deserts;
41   but the needy He secures from suffering,
   and increases their families like flocks.

42 The upright see it and rejoice;
   the mouth of all wrongdoers is stopped.
43 The wise man will take note of these things;
   he will consider the steadfast love of the LORD.

108   A song. A psalm of David.

2 ^aMy heart is firm, O God;
   I will sing and chant a hymn with all my soul.
3 Awake, O harp and lyre!
   I will wake the dawn.
4 I will praise You among the peoples, O LORD,
   sing a hymn to You among the nations;
5   for Your faithfulness is higher than the heavens;
   Your steadfastness reaches to the sky.
6 Exalt Yourself over the heavens, O God;
   let Your glory be over all the earth!
7 ^bThat those whom You love may be rescued,
   deliver with Your right hand and answer me.

8 God promised ^cin His sanctuary^{-c}
   that I would exultingly divide up Shechem,
   and measure the Valley of Sukkoth;

---

^a *With vv. 2–6, cf. Ps. 57.8–12.*
^b *With vv. 7–14, cf. Ps. 60.7–14.*
^{c-c} *Or "by His holiness."*

9 Gilead and Manasseh would be mine,
   Ephraim my chief stronghold,
   Judah my scepter;
10 Moab would be my washbasin;
   on Edom I would cast my shoe;
   I would raise a shout over Philistia.
11 Would that I were brought to the bastion!
   Would that I were led to Edom!

12 But You have rejected us, O God;
   God, You do not march with our armies.
13 Grant us Your aid against the foe,
   for the help of man is worthless.
14 With God we shall triumph;
   He will trample our foes.

109 For the leader. Of David. A psalm.

   O God of my praise,
      do not keep aloof,
2   for the wicked and the deceitful
      open their mouth against me;
      they speak to me with lying tongue.
3 They encircle me with words of hate;
      they attack me without cause.
4 They answer my love with accusation
      *-and I must stand judgment.-a
5 They repay me with evil for good,
      with hatred for my love.

6 Appoint a wicked man over him;
      may an accuser stand at his right side;
7   may he be tried and convicted;
      may he be judged and found guilty.

a-a *Or "but I am all prayer"; meaning of Heb. uncertain, but see v. 7.*

⁸ May his days be few;
    may another take over ᵇ-his position.-ᵇ
⁹ May his children be orphans,
    his wife a widow.
¹⁰ May his children wander from their hovels,
    begging in search of [bread].
¹¹ May his creditor seize all his possessions;
    may strangers plunder his wealth.
¹² May no one show him mercy;
    may none pity his orphans;
¹³   may his posterity be cut off;
    may their names be blotted out in the next generation.
¹⁴ May God be ever mindful of his father's iniquity,
    and may the sin of his mother not be blotted out.
¹⁵ May the Lord be aware of them always
    and cause their names to be cut off from the earth,
¹⁶   because he was not minded to act kindly,
    and hounded to death the poor and needy man,
    one crushed in spirit.
¹⁷ He loved to curse—may a curse come upon him!
He would not bless—may blessing be far from him!
¹⁸ May he be clothed in a curse like a garment,
    may it enter his body like water,
    his bones like oil.
¹⁹ Let it be like the cloak he wraps around him,
    like the belt he always wears.
²⁰ May the Lord thus repay my accusers,
    all those who speak evil against me.

²¹ Now You, O God, my Lord,
    act on my behalf as befits Your name.
Good and faithful as You are, save me.
²² For I am poor and needy,
    and my heart is pierced within me.
²³ I fade away like a lengthening shadow;

ᵇ⁻ᵇ *Meaning of Heb. uncertain.*

I am shaken off like locusts.
²⁴ My knees give way from fasting;
my flesh is lean, has lost its fat.
²⁵ I am the object of their scorn;
when they see me, they shake their head.
²⁶ Help me, O Lord, my God;
save me in accord with Your faithfulness,
²⁷ that men may know that it is Your hand,
that You, O Lord, have done it.
²⁸ Let them curse, but You bless;
let them rise up, but come to grief,
while Your servant rejoices.
²⁹ My accusers shall be clothed in shame,
wrapped in their disgrace as in a robe.

³⁰ My mouth shall sing much praise to the Lord;
I will acclaim Him in the midst of a throng,
³¹ because He stands at the right hand of the needy,
to save him from those who would condemn him.

110 Of David. A psalm.

The Lord said to my lord,
"Sit at My right hand
while I make your enemies your footstool."

² The Lord will stretch forth from Zion your mighty
scepter;
hold sway over your enemies!
³ ^{a-}Your people come forward willingly on your day of bat-
tle.
In majestic holiness, from the womb,
from the dawn, yours was the dew of youth.^{-a}

---

^{a-a} *Meaning of Heb. uncertain.*

⁴ The LORD has sworn and will not relent,
   "You are a priest forever, ᵇ⁻a rightful king by My
      decree."⁻ᵇ
⁵ The Lord is at your right hand.
   He crushes kings in the day of His anger.

⁶ He works judgment upon the nations,
      heaping up bodies,
      crushing heads far and wide.
⁷ He drinks from the stream on his way;
      therefore he holds his head high.

111 Hallelujah.

א   I praise the LORD with all my heart
ב   in the assembled congregation of the upright.
ג   ² The works of the LORD are great,
ד   ᵃ⁻within reach of all who desire them.⁻ᵃ
ה   ³ His deeds are splendid and glorious;
ו   His beneficence is everlasting;
ז   ⁴ He has won renown for His wonders.
ח   The LORD is gracious and compassionate;
ט   ⁵ He gives food to those who fear Him;
י   He is ever mindful of His covenant.
כ   ⁶ He revealed to His people His powerful works,
ל   in giving them the heritage of nations.
מ   ⁷ His handiwork is truth and justice;
נ   all His precepts are enduring,
ס   ⁸ well-founded for all eternity,
ע   wrought of truth and equity.
פ   ⁹ He sent redemption to His people;
צ   He ordained His covenant for all time;
ק   His name is holy and awesome.
ר   ¹⁰ The beginningᵇ of wisdom is the fear of the LORD;
ש   all who practice it gain sound understanding.
ת   Praise of Him is everlasting.

ᵇ⁻ᵇ *Or "after the manner of Melchizedek."*

ᵃ⁻ᵃ *Meaning of Heb. uncertain.*
ᵇ *Or "chief part."*

112 Hallelujah.

א Happy is the man who fears the LORD,
ב   who is ardently devoted to His commandments.
ג ² His descendants will be mighty in the land,
ד   a blessed generation of upright men.
ה ³ Wealth and riches are in his house,
ו   and his beneficence lasts forever.
ז ⁴ *ᵃ-A light shines*-ᵃ for the upright in the darkness;
ח   he is gracious, compassionate, and beneficent.
ט ⁵ All goes well with the man who lends generously,
י   who conducts his affairs with equity.
כ ⁶ He shall never be shaken;
ל   the beneficent man will be remembered forever.
מ ⁷ He is not afraid of evil tidings;
נ   his heart is firm, he trusts in the LORD.
ס ⁸ His heart is resolute, he is unafraid;
ע   in the end he will see the fall of his foes.
פ ⁹ He gives freely to the poor;
צ   his beneficence lasts forever;
ק   his horn is exalted in honor.
ר ¹⁰ The wicked man shall see it and be vexed;
ש   he shall gnash his teeth; his courage shall fail.
ת   The desire of the wicked shall come to nothing.

113 Hallelujah.

O servants of the LORD, give praise;
    praise the name of the LORD.
² Let the name of the LORD be blessed
    now and forever.
³ From east to west
    the name of the LORD is praised.

ᵃ⁻ᵃ *Or "He shines as a light."*

⁴ The Lord is exalted above all nations;
His glory is above the heavens.
⁵ Who is like the Lord our God,
who, enthroned on high,
⁶ sees what is below,
in heaven and on earth?
⁷ He raises the poor from the dust,
lifts up the needy from the refuse heap
⁸ to set them with the great,
with the great men of His people.
⁹ He sets the childless woman among her household
as a happy mother of children.
Hallelujah.

114 When Israel went forth from Egypt,
the house of Jacob from a people of strange speech,
² Judah became His *ᵃ-holy one,-ᵃ*
Israel, His dominion.
³ The sea saw them and fled,
Jordan ran backward,
⁴ mountains skipped like rams,
hills like sheep.
⁵ What alarmed you, O sea, that you fled,
Jordan, that you ran backward,
⁶ mountains, that you skipped like rams,
hills, like sheep?
⁷ Tremble, O earth, at the presence of the Lord,
at the presence of the God of Jacob,
⁸ who turned the rock into a pool of water,
the flinty rock into a fountain.

ᵃ⁻ᵃ *Or "sanctuary."*

115 Not to us, O Lord, not to us
but to Your name bring glory
for the sake of Your love and Your faithfulness.
² Let the nations not say,
"Where now is their God?"
³ when our God is in heaven
and all that He wills He accomplishes.
⁴ ªTheir idols are silver and gold,
the work of men's hands.
⁵ They have mouths, but cannot speak,
eyes, but cannot see;
⁶ they have ears, but cannot hear,
noses, but cannot smell;
⁷ they have hands, but cannot touch,
feet, but cannot walk;
they can make no sound in their throats.
⁸ Those who fashion them,
all who trust in them,
shall become like them.
⁹ O Israel, trust in the Lord!
He is their help and shield.
¹⁰ O house of Aaron, trust in the Lord!
He is their help and shield.
¹¹ O you who fear the Lord, trust in the Lord!
He is their help and shield.

¹² The Lord is mindful of us.
He will bless us;
He will bless the house of Israel;
He will bless the house of Aaron;
¹³ He will bless those who fear the Lord,
small and great alike.

ª *With vv. 4–11, cf. Ps. 135.15–20.*

14 May the LORD increase your numbers,
    yours and your children's also.
15 May you be blessed by the LORD,
    Maker of heaven and earth.
16 The heavens belong to the LORD,
    but the earth He gave over to man.
17 The dead cannot praise the LORD,
    nor any who go down into silence.
18 But we will bless the LORD
    now and forever.
    Hallelujah.

116 *a*-I love the LORD
        for He hears-*a* my voice, my pleas;
2   for He turns His ear to me
        whenever I call.
3 The bonds of death encompassed me;
    the torments of Sheol overtook me.
  I came upon trouble and sorrow
4   and I invoked the name of the LORD,
    "O LORD, save my life!"

5 The LORD is gracious and beneficent;
    our God is compassionate.
6 The LORD protects the simple;
    I was brought low and He saved me.
7 Be at rest, once again, O my soul,
    for the LORD has been good to you.
8 You*b* have delivered me from death,
    my eyes from tears,
    my feet from stumbling.
9 I shall walk before the LORD
    in the lands of the living.
10 *c*-I trust [in the LORD];

a-a *Heb. transposed for clarity. Others "I would love that the LORD hear," etc.*
b *I.e. God.*
c-c *Meaning of Heb. uncertain.*

out of great suffering I spoke-*c*

11 and said rashly,
"All men are false."

12 How can I repay the LORD
for all His bounties to me?
13 I raise the cup of deliverance
and invoke the name of the LORD.
14 I will pay my vows to the LORD
in the presence of all His people.
15 The death of His faithful ones
is grievous in the LORD's sight.

16 O LORD,
I am Your servant,
Your servant, the son of Your maidservant;
You have undone the cords that bound me.
17 I will sacrifice a thank offering to You
and invoke the name of the LORD.
18 I will pay my vows to the LORD
in the presence of all His people,
19 in the courts of the house of the LORD,
in the midst of*d* Jerusalem.
Hallelujah.

117 Praise the LORD, all you nations;
extol Him, all you peoples,
2 for great is His steadfast love toward us;
the faithfulness of the LORD endures forever.
Hallelujah.

---

d Others *"of you."*

118 Praise the LORD, for He is good,
His steadfast love is eternal.
2 Let Israel declare,
"His steadfast love is eternal."
3 Let the house of Aaron declare,
"His steadfast love is eternal."
4 Let those who fear the LORD declare,
"His steadfast love is eternal."

5 In distress I called on the LORD;
the Lord answered me and brought me relief.
6 The LORD is on my side,
I have no fear;
what can man do to me?
7 With the LORD on my side as my helper,
I will see the downfall of my foes.

8 It is better to take refuge in the LORD
than to trust in mortals;
9 it is better to take refuge in the LORD
than to trust in the great.

10 All nations have beset me;
by the name of the LORD I will surely *a*-cut them
down.*-a*
11 They beset me, they surround me;
by the name of the LORD I will surely cut them down.
12 They have beset me like bees;
they shall be extinguished like burning thorns;
by the name of the LORD I will surely cut them down.

13 You*b* pressed me hard,
I nearly fell;

---

a-a *Meaning of 'amilam in this and the following two verses uncertain.*
b *I.e. the enemy.*

but the LORD helped me.
14 The LORD is my strength and might;[c]
He has become my deliverance.

15 The tents of the victorious[d] resound with joyous shouts of
deliverance,
"The right hand of the LORD is triumphant!
16 The right hand of the LORD is exalted!
The right hand of the LORD is triumphant!"

17 I shall not die but live
and proclaim the works of the LORD.
18 The LORD punished me severely,
but did not hand me over to death.

19 Open the gates of victory[e] for me
that I may enter them and praise the LORD.
20 This is the gateway to the LORD—
the victorious[d] shall enter through it.

21 I praise You, for You have answered me,
and have become my deliverance.
22 The stone which the builders rejected
has become the chief cornerstone.
23 This is the LORD's doing;
it is marvelous in our sight.
24 This is the day that the LORD has made—
let us exult and rejoice on it.

25 O LORD, deliver us!
O LORD, let us prosper!

26 May he who enters be blessed in the name of the LORD;
we bless you from the House of the LORD.
27 The LORD is God;

[c] Others "song."
[d] Or "righteous."
[e] Or "righteousness."

He has given us light;
*ᶠbind the festal offering to the horns of the altar with
cords.ᶠ*

²⁸ You are my God and I will praise You;
You are my God and I will extol You.

²⁹ Praise the LORD for He is good,
His steadfast love is eternal.

119 א Happy are those whose way is blameless,
who follow the teaching of the LORD.

² Happy are those who observe His decrees,
who turn to Him wholeheartedly.

³ They have done no wrong,
but have followed His ways.

⁴ You have commanded that Your precepts
be kept diligently.

⁵ Would that my ways were firm
in keeping Your laws;

⁶ then I would not be ashamed
when I regard all Your commandments.

⁷ I will praise You with a sincere heart
as I learn Your just rules.

⁸ I will keep Your laws;
do not utterly forsake me.

ב ⁹ How can a young man keep his way pure?—
by holding to Your word.

¹⁰ I have turned to You with all my heart;
do not let me stray from Your commandments.

¹¹ In my heart I treasure Your promise;
therefore I do not sin against You.

¹² Blessed are You, O LORD;
train me in Your laws.

¹³ With my lips I rehearse

ᶠ⁻ᶠ *Meaning of Heb. uncertain.*

all the rules You proclaimed.
¹⁴ I rejoice over the way of Your decrees
    as over all riches.
¹⁵ I study Your precepts;
    I regard Your ways;
¹⁶ I take delight in Your laws;
    I will not neglect Your word.

ג ¹⁷ Deal kindly with Your servant,
    that I may live to keep Your word.
¹⁸ Open my eyes, that I may perceive
    the wonders of Your teaching.
¹⁹ I am only a sojourner in the land;
    do not hide Your commandments from me.
²⁰ My soul is consumed with longing
    for Your rules at all times.
²¹ You blast the accursed insolent ones
    who stray from Your commandments.
²² Take away from me taunt and abuse,
    because I observe Your decrees.
²³ Though princes meet and speak against me,
    Your servant studies Your laws.
²⁴ For Your decrees are my delight,
    my intimate companions.

ד ²⁵ My soul clings to the dust;
    revive me in accordance with Your word.
²⁶ I have declared my way, and You have answered me;
    train me in Your laws.
²⁷ Make me understand the way of Your precepts,
    that I may study Your wondrous acts.
²⁸ I am racked with grief;
    sustain me in accordance with Your word.
²⁹ Remove all false ways from me;
    favor me with Your teaching.

³⁰ I have chosen the way of faithfulness;
 I have set Your rules before me.
³¹ I cling to Your decrees;
 O LORD, do not put me to shame.
³² I eagerly pursue Your commandments,
 for You broaden my understanding.

ה ³³ Teach me, O LORD, the way of Your laws;
 I will observe them ᵃ‑to the utmost.‑ᵃ
³⁴ Give me understanding, that I may observe Your
 teaching
 and keep it wholeheartedly.
³⁵ Lead me in the path of Your commandments,
 for that is my concern.
³⁶ Turn my heart to Your decrees
 and not to love of gain.
³⁷ Avert my eyes from seeing falsehood;
 by Your ways preserve me.
³⁸ Fulfill Your promise to Your servant,
 which is for those who worship You.
³⁹ Remove the taunt that I dread,
 for Your rules are good.
⁴⁰ See, I have longed for Your precepts;
 by Your righteousness preserve me.

ו ⁴¹ May Your steadfast love reach me, O LORD,
 Your deliverance, as You have promised.
⁴² I shall have an answer for those who taunt me,
 for I have put my trust in Your word.
⁴³ Do not utterly take the truth away from my mouth,
 for I have put my hope in Your rules.
⁴⁴ I will always obey Your teaching,
 forever and ever.
⁴⁵ I will walk about at ease,
 for I have turned to Your precepts.

ᵃ‑ᵃ *Meaning of Heb. uncertain.*

⁴⁶ I will speak of Your decrees,
and not be ashamed in the presence of kings.
⁴⁷ I will delight in Your commandments,
which I love.
⁴⁸ I reach out for Your commandments, which I love;
I study Your laws.

ז ⁴⁹ Remember Your word to Your servant
through which You have given me hope.
⁵⁰ This is my comfort in my affliction,
that Your promise has preserved me.
⁵¹ Though the arrogant have cruelly mocked me,
I have not swerved from Your teaching.
⁵² I remember Your rules of old, O LORD,
and find comfort in them.
⁵³ I am seized with rage
because of the wicked who forsake Your teaching.
⁵⁴ Your laws are ᵇ⁻a source of strength to me⁻ᵇ
wherever I may dwell.
⁵⁵ I remember Your name at night, O LORD,
and obey Your teaching.
⁵⁶ This has been my lot,
for I have observed Your precepts.

ח ⁵⁷ The LORD is my portion;
I have resolved to keep Your words.
⁵⁸ I have implored You with all my heart;
have mercy on me, in accordance with Your promise.
⁵⁹ I have considered my ways,
and have turned back to Your decrees.
⁶⁰ I have hurried and not delayed
to keep Your commandments.
⁶¹ Though the bonds of the wicked are coiled round me,
I have not neglected Your teaching.
⁶² I arise at midnight to praise You
for Your just rules.

ᵇ⁻ᵇ *Or "songs for me."*

63 I am a companion to all who fear You,
  to those who keep Your precepts.
64 Your steadfast love, O LORD, fills the earth;
  teach me Your laws.

ט 65 You have treated Your servant well,
  according to Your word, O LORD.
66 Teach me good sense and knowledge,
  for I have put my trust in Your commandments.
67 Before I was humbled I went astray,
  but now I keep Your word.
68 You are good and beneficent;
  teach me Your laws.
69 Though the arrogant have accused me falsely,
  I observe Your precepts wholeheartedly.
70 Their minds are thick like fat;
  as for me, Your teaching is my delight.
71 It was good for me that I was humbled,
  so that I might learn Your laws.
72 I prefer the teaching You proclaimed
  to thousands of gold and silver pieces.

י 73 Your hands made me and fashioned me;
  give me understanding that I may learn Your command-
    ments.
74 Those who fear You will see me and rejoice,
  for I have put my hope in Your word.
75 I know, O LORD, that Your rulings are just;
  rightly have You humbled me.
76 May Your steadfast love comfort me
  in accordance with Your promise to Your servant.
77 May Your mercy reach me, that I might live,
  for Your teaching is my delight.
78 Let the insolent be dismayed, for they have
    wronged me without cause;
  I will study Your precepts.

79 May those who fear You,
    those who know Your decrees,
    turn again to me.
80 May I wholeheartedly follow Your laws
    so that I do not come to grief.

כ 81 I long for Your deliverance;
    I hope for Your word.
82 My eyes pine away for Your promise;
    I say, "When will You comfort me?"
83 Though I have become like a water-skin dried in smoke,
    I have not neglected Your laws.
84 How long has Your servant to live?
    when will You bring my persecutors to judgment?
85 The insolent have dug pits for me,
    flouting Your teaching.
86 All Your commandments are enduring;
    I am persecuted without cause; help me!
87 Though they almost wiped me off the earth,
    I did not abandon Your precepts.
88 As befits Your steadfast love, preserve me,
    so that I may keep the decree You proclaimed.

ל 89 The Lord exists forever;
    Your word stands firm in heaven.
90 Your faithfulness is for all generations;
    You have established the earth, and it stands.
91 They stand this day to [carry out] Your rulings,
    for all are Your servants.
92 Were not Your teaching my delight
    I would have perished in my affliction.
93 I will never neglect Your precepts,
    for You have preserved my life through them.
94 I am Yours; save me!
    For I have turned to Your precepts.

95 The wicked hope to destroy me,
   but I ponder Your decrees.
96 I have seen that all things have their limit,
   but Your commandment is broad beyond measure.

מ 97 O how I love Your teaching!
   It is my study all day long.
98 Your commandments make me wiser than my enemies;
   they always stand by me.
99 I have gained more insight than all my teachers,
   for Your decrees are my study.
100 I have gained more understanding than my elders,
   for I observe Your precepts.
101 I have avoided every evil way
   so that I may keep Your word.
102 I have not departed from Your rules,
   for You have instructed me.
103 How pleasing is Your word to my palate,
   sweeter than honey.
104 I ponder Your precepts;
   therefore I hate every false way.

נ 105 Your word is a lamp to my feet,
   a light for my path.
106 I have firmly sworn
   to keep Your just rules.
107 I am very much afflicted;
   O Lord, preserve me in accordance with Your word.
108 Accept, O Lord, my free-will offerings;
   teach me Your rules.
109 Though my life is always in danger,
   I do not neglect Your teaching.
110 Though the wicked have set a trap for me,
   I have not strayed from Your precepts.
111 Your decrees are my eternal heritage;

they are my heart's delight.
¹¹² I am resolved to follow Your laws
*-to the utmost-ᵃ forever.

ᴾ ¹¹³ I hate men of divided heart,
but I love Your teaching.
¹¹⁴ You are my protection and my shield;
I hope for Your word.
¹¹⁵ Keep away from me, you evildoers,
that I may observe the commandments of my God.
¹¹⁶ Support me as You promised, so that I may live;
do not thwart my expectation.
¹¹⁷ Sustain me that I may be saved,
and I will always muse upon Your laws.
¹¹⁸ You reject all who stray from Your laws,
for they are false and deceitful.
¹¹⁹ You do away with the wicked as if they were dross;
rightly do I love Your decrees.
¹²⁰ My flesh creeps from fear of You;
I am in awe of Your rulings.

ᵥ ¹²¹ I have done what is just and right;
do not abandon me to those who would wrong me.
¹²² Guarantee Your servant's well-being;
do not let the arrogant wrong me.
¹²³ My eyes pine away for Your deliverance,
for Your promise of victory.
¹²⁴ Deal with Your servant as befits Your steadfast love;
teach me Your laws.
¹²⁵ I am Your servant;
give me understanding,
that I might know Your decrees.
¹²⁶ It is a time to act for the LORD,
for they have violated Your teaching.
¹²⁷ Rightly do I love Your commandments

more than gold, even fine gold.
¹²⁸ Truly ^{c-}by all [Your] precepts I walk straight;^{-c}
I hate every false way.

 פ ¹²⁹ Your decrees are wondrous;
rightly do I observe them.
¹³⁰ ^{d-}The words You inscribed give^{-d} light,
and grant understanding to the simple.
¹³¹ I open my mouth wide, I pant,
longing for Your commandments.
¹³² Turn to me and be gracious to me,
as is Your rule with those who love Your name.
¹³³ Make my feet firm through Your promise;
do not let iniquity dominate me.
¹³⁴ Redeem me from being wronged by man,
that I may keep Your precepts.
¹³⁵ Show favor to Your servant,
and teach me Your laws.
¹³⁶ My eyes shed streams of water
because men do not obey Your teaching.

צ ¹³⁷ You are righteous, O LORD;
Your rulings are just.
¹³⁸ You have ordained righteous decrees;
they are firmly enduring.
¹³⁹ I am consumed with rage
over my foes' neglect of Your words.
¹⁴⁰ Your word is exceedingly pure,
and Your servant loves it.
¹⁴¹ Though I am belittled and despised,
I have not neglected Your precepts.
¹⁴² Your righteousness is eternal;
Your teaching is true.
¹⁴³ Though anguish and distress come upon me,
Your commandments are my delight.

^{c-c} Or "I declare all [Your] precepts to be just."
^{d-d} With Targum; or "The exposition of Your words gives"; meaning of Heb. uncertain.

144 Your righteous decrees are eternal;
    give me understanding, that I might live.

ק 145 I call with all my heart;
    answer me, O Lord,
    that I may observe Your laws.
146 I call upon You; save me,
    that I may keep Your decrees.
147 I rise before dawn and cry for help;
    I hope for Your word.
148 My eyes greet each watch of the night,
    as I meditate on Your promise.
149 Hear my voice as befits Your steadfast love;
    O Lord, preserve me, as is Your rule.
150 Those who pursue intrigue draw near;
    they are far from Your teaching.
151 You, O Lord, are near,
    and all Your commandments are true.
152 I know from Your decrees of old
    that You have established them forever.

ר 153 See my affliction and rescue me,
    for I have not neglected Your teaching.
154 Champion my cause and redeem me;
    preserve me according to Your promise.
155 Deliverance is far from the wicked,
    for they have not turned to Your laws.
156 Your mercies are great, O Lord;
    as is Your rule, preserve me.
157 Many are my persecutors and foes;
    I have not swerved from Your decrees.
158 I have seen traitors and loathed[e] them,
    because they did not keep Your word in mind.
159 See that I have loved Your precepts;
    O Lord, preserve me, as befits Your steadfast love.

e Or *"have contended with."*

160 Truth is the essence of Your word;
   Your just rules are eternal.

ע 161 Princes have persecuted me without reason;
   my heart thrills at Your word.
162 I rejoice over Your promise
   as one who obtains great spoil.
163 I hate and abhor falsehood;
   I love Your teaching.
164 I praise You seven times each day
   for Your just rules.
165 Those who love Your teaching enjoy well-being;
   they encounter no adversity.
166 I hope for Your deliverance, O LORD;
   I observe Your commandments.
167 I obey Your decrees
   and love them greatly.
168 I obey Your precepts and decrees;
   all my ways are before You.

ת 169 May my plea reach You, O LORD;
   grant me understanding according to Your word.
170 May my petition come before You;
   save me in accordance with Your promise.
171 My lips shall pour forth praise,
   for You teach me Your laws.
172 My tongue shall declare Your promise,
   for all Your commandments are just.
173 Lend Your hand to help me,
   for I have chosen Your precepts.
174 I have longed for Your deliverance, O LORD;
   Your teaching is my delight.
175 Let me live, that I may praise You;
   may Your rules be my help;
176   I have strayed like a lost sheep;

search for Your servant,
for I have not neglected Your commandments.

120 A song of ascents.[a]

In my distress I called to the Lord
and He answered me.
2 O Lord, save me from treacherous lips,
from a deceitful tongue!
3 What can you profit,
what can you gain,
O deceitful tongue?
4 A warrior's sharp arrows,
with hot coals of broom-wood.

5 Woe is me, that I live with Meshech,
that I dwell among the clans of Kedar.
6 Too long have I dwelt with those who hate peace.
7 I am all peace;
but when I speak,
they are for war.

121 A song for ascents.

I turn my eyes to the mountains;
from where will my help come?
2 My help comes from the Lord,
maker of heaven and earth.
3 He will not let your foot give way;
your guardian will not slumber.
4 See, the guardian of Israel
neither slumbers nor sleeps!
5 The Lord is your guardian,
the Lord is your protection

[a] *A term of uncertain meaning.*

at your right hand.
6 By day the sun will not strike you,
     nor the moon by night.
7 The LORD will guard you from all harm;
     He will guard your life.
8 The LORD will guard your going and coming
     now and forever.

122 A song of ascents. Of David.

1 rejoiced when they said to me,
     "We are going to the house of the LORD."
2 Our feet stood inside your gates, O Jerusalem,
3   Jerusalem built up, a city knit together,
4   to which tribes would make pilgrimage,
     the tribes of the LORD,
     —as was enjoined upon Israel—
     to praise the name of the LORD.
5 There the thrones of judgment stood,
     thrones of the house of David.
6 Pray for the well-being of Jerusalem:
     "May those who love you be at peace.
7 May there be well-being within your ramparts,
     peace in your citadels."
8 For the sake of my kin and friends,
     I pray for your well-being;
9   for the sake of the house of the LORD our God,
     I seek your good.

123 A song of ascents.

To You, enthroned in heaven,
     I turn my eyes.
2 As the eyes of slaves follow their master's hand,

as the eyes of a slave-girl follow the hand of her mistress,
so our eyes are toward the LORD our God,
awaiting His favor.

³ Show us favor, O LORD,
show us favor!
We have had more than enough of contempt.

⁴ Long enough have we endured
the scorn of the complacent,
the contempt of the haughty.

124 A song of ascents. Of David.

Were it not for the LORD, who was on our side,
let Israel now declare,
² were it not for the LORD, who was on our side
when men assailed us,
³ they would have swallowed us alive
in their burning rage against us;
⁴ the waters would have carried us off,
the torrent would have swept over us;
⁵ over us would have swept
the seething waters.
⁶ Blessed is the LORD, who did not let us
be ripped apart by their teeth.
⁷ We are like a bird escaped from the fowler's trap;
the trap broke and we escaped.
⁸ Our help is the name of the LORD,
maker of heaven and earth.

125 A song of ascents.

Those who trust in the LORD
are like Mount Zion

that cannot be moved,
enduring forever.
2 Jerusalem, hills enfold it,
and the LORD enfolds His people
now and forever.
3 a-The scepter of the wicked shall never rest
upon the land allotted to the righteous,
that the righteous not set their hand to wrongdoing.-a
4 Do good, O LORD, to the good,
to the upright in heart.
5 a-But those who in their crookedness act corruptly,-a
let the LORD make them go the way of evildoers.
May it be well with Israel!

126 A song of ascents.

When the LORD restores the fortunes of Zion
—a-we see it as in a dream-a—
2   our mouths shall be filled with laughter,
our tongues, with songs of joy.
Then shall they say among the nations,
"The LORD has done great things for them!"
3 The LORD will do great things for us
and we shall rejoice.

4 Restore our fortunes, O LORD,
like watercourses in the Negeb.
5 They who sow in tears
shall reap with songs of joy.
6 Though he goes along weeping,
carrying the seed-bag,
he shall come back with songs of joy,
carrying his sheaves.

a-a *Meaning of Heb. uncertain.*
a-a *Lit. "we are veritable dreamers."*

127 A song of ascents. Of Solomon.

Unless the LORD builds the house,
   its builders labor in vain on it;
   unless the LORD watches over the city,
   the watchman keeps vigil in vain.
² In vain do you rise early
   and stay up late,
   you who toil for the bread you eat;
   *a-*He provides as much for His loved ones while they
   sleep.*-a*

³ Sons are the provision*b* of the LORD;
   the fruit of the womb, His reward.
⁴ Like arrows in the hand of a warrior
   are sons born to a man in his youth.
⁵ Happy is the man who fills his quiver with them;
   they shall not be put to shame
   when they contend with the enemy in the gate.

128 A song of ascents.

Happy are all who fear the LORD,
   who follow His ways.
² You shall enjoy the fruit of your labors;
   you shall be happy and you shall prosper.
³ Your wife shall be like a fruitful vine within your house;
   your sons, like olive saplings around your table.
⁴ So shall the man who fears the LORD be blessed.

⁵ May the LORD bless you from Zion;
   may you share the prosperity of Jerusalem

---

a-a Meaning of Heb. uncertain.
b Lit. "heritage."

all the days of your life,
6   and live to see your children's children.
May all be well with Israel!

129 A song of ascents.

Since my youth they have often assailed me,
   let Israel now declare,
2   since my youth they have often assailed me,
   but they have never overcome me.
3 Plowmen plowed across my back;
   they made long furrows.
4 The LORD, the righteous one,
   has snapped the cords of the wicked.

5 Let all who hate Zion
   fall back in disgrace.
6 Let them be like grass on roofs
   that fades before it can be pulled up,
7   that affords no handful for the reaper,
   no armful for the gatherer of sheaves,
8   no exchange with passersby:
   "The blessing of the LORD be upon you."
"We bless you by the name of the LORD."

130 A song of ascents.

Out of the depths I call You, O LORD.
2 O Lord, listen to my cry;
   let Your ears be attentive
   to my plea for mercy.
3 If You keep account of sins, O LORD,
   Lord, who will survive?

⁴ Yours is the power to forgive
    so that You may be held in awe.

⁵ I look to the LORD;
    I look to Him;
    I await His word.
⁶ I am more eager for the Lord
    than watchmen for the morning,
    watchmen for the morning.

⁷ O Israel, wait for the LORD;
    for with the LORD is steadfast love
    and great power to redeem.
⁸ It is He who will redeem Israel from all their iniquities.

131   A song of ascents. Of David.

    O LORD, my heart is not proud
      nor my look haughty;
      I do not aspire to great things
      or to what is beyond me;
2   ᵃ⁻but I have taught myself to be contented
      like a weaned child with its mother;
      like a weaned child am I in my mind.⁻ᵃ
³ O Israel, wait for the LORD
    now and forever.

132   A song of ascents.

    O LORD, remember in David's favor
      his extreme self-denial,
2   how he swore to the LORD,
      vowed to the Mighty One of Jacob,

ᵃ⁻ᵃ *Meaning of Heb. uncertain.*

3 "I will not enter my house,
    nor will I mount my bed,
4 I will not give sleep to my eyes
    or slumber to my eyelids*a*
5 until I find a place for the LORD,
    an abode for the Mighty One of Jacob."

6 We heard it was in Ephrath;
    we came upon it in the region of Jaar.*b*
7 Let us enter His abode,
    bow at His footstool.
8 Advance, O LORD, to Your resting-place,
    You and Your mighty Ark!
9 Your priests are clothed in triumph;
    Your loyal ones sing for joy.
10 For the sake of Your servant David
    do not reject Your anointed one.

11 The LORD swore to David
    a firm oath that He will not renounce,
    "One of your own issue I will set upon your throne.
12 If your sons keep My covenant
    and My decrees that I teach them,
    then their sons also,
    to the end of time,
    shall sit upon your throne."
13 For the LORD has chosen Zion;
    He has desired it for His seat.
14 "This is my resting-place for all time;
    here I will dwell, for I desire it.
15 I will amply bless its store of food,
    give its needy their fill of bread.
16 I will clothe its priests in victory,
    its loyal ones shall sing for joy.
17 There I will make a horn sprout for David;

a Lit. "eyes."
b Cf. I Sam. 7.1–2; I Chron. 13.5–6.

I have prepared a lamp for My anointed one.
¹⁸ I will clothe his enemies in disgrace,
while on him his crown shall sparkle."

133 A song of ascents. Of David.

How good and how pleasant it is
that brothers dwell together.
² It is like fine oil on the head
running down onto the beard,
the beard of Aaron,
that comes down over the collar of his robe;
³ like the dew of Hermon
that falls upon the mountains of Zion.
There the LORD ordained blessing,
everlasting life.

134 A song of ascents.

Now bless the LORD,
all you servants of the LORD
who stand nightly
in the house of the LORD.
² Lift your hands toward the sanctuary
and bless the LORD.
³ May the LORD,
maker of heaven and earth,
bless you from Zion.

135 Hallelujah.

Praise the name of the LORD;
give praise, you servants of the LORD

2 who stand in the house of the Lord,
  in the courts of the house of our God.
3 Praise the Lord, for the Lord is good;
  sing hymns to His name, for it is pleasant.
4 For the Lord has chosen Jacob for Himself,
  Israel, as His treasured possession.

5 For I know that the Lord is great,
  that our Lord is greater than all gods.
6 Whatever the Lord desires He does
  in heaven and earth,
  in the seas and all the depths.
7 He makes clouds rise from the end of the earth;
  He makes lightning for the rain;
  He releases the wind from His vaults.
8 He struck down the firstborn of Egypt,
  man and beast alike;
9 He sent signs and portents against[a] Egypt,
  against Pharaoh and all his servants;
10 He struck down many nations
  and slew numerous kings—
11 Sihon king of the Amorites,
  Og king of Bashan,
  and all the royalty of Canaan—
12 and gave their lands as a heritage,
  as a heritage to His people Israel.

13 O Lord, Your name endures forever,
  Your fame, O Lord, through all generations;
14 for the Lord will champion His people,
  and obtain satisfaction for His servants.

15 [b]The idols of the nations are silver and gold,
  the work of men's hands.
16 They have mouths, but cannot speak;

a *Others "against you."*
b *With vv. 15–20, cf. Ps. 115.4–11.*

they have eyes, but cannot see;
17 they have ears, but cannot hear,
nor is there breath in their mouths.
18 Those who fashion them,
all who trust in them,
shall become like them.

19 O house of Israel, bless the LORD;
O house of Aaron, bless the LORD;
20 O house of Levi, bless the LORD;
you who fear the LORD, bless the LORD.
21 Blessed is the LORD from Zion,
He who dwells in Jerusalem.
Hallelujah.

136 Praise the LORD; for He is good,
His steadfast love is eternal.
2 Praise the God of gods,
His steadfast love is eternal.
3 Praise the Lord of lords,
His steadfast love is eternal;
4 Who alone works great marvels,
His steadfast love is eternal;
5 Who made the heavens with wisdom,
His steadfast love is eternal;
6 Who spread the earth over the water,
His steadfast love is eternal;
7 Who made the great lights,
His steadfast love is eternal;
8 the sun to dominate the day,
His steadfast love is eternal;
9 the moon and the stars to dominate the night,
His steadfast love is eternal;

¹⁰ Who struck Egypt through their firstborn,
　　His steadfast love is eternal:
¹¹ and brought Israel out of their midst,
　　His steadfast love is eternal;
¹² with a strong hand and outstretched arm,
　　His steadfast love is eternal;
¹³ Who split apart the Sea of Reeds,
　　His steadfast love is eternal;
¹⁴ and made Israel pass through it,
　　His steadfast love is eternal;
¹⁵ Who hurled Pharaoh and his army into the Sea of Reeds,
　　His steadfast love is eternal;
¹⁶ Who led His people through the wilderness,
　　His steadfast love is eternal;
¹⁷ Who struck down great kings,
　　His steadfast love is eternal;
¹⁸ and slew mighty kings,—
　　His steadfast love is eternal;
¹⁹ Sihon king of the Amorites,
　　His steadfast love is eternal;
²⁰ Og king of Bashan—
　　His steadfast love is eternal;
²¹ and gave their land as a heritage,
　　His steadfast love is eternal;
²² a heritage to His servant Israel,
　　His steadfast love is eternal;
²³ Who took note of us in our degradation,
　　His steadfast love is eternal;
²⁴ and rescued us from our enemies,
　　His steadfast love is eternal;
²⁵ Who gives food to all flesh,
　　His steadfast love is eternal.
²⁶ Praise the God of heaven,
　　His steadfast love is eternal.

137 By the rivers of Babylon,
    there we sat,
    sat and wept,
    as we thought of Zion.
2 There on the poplars
    we hung up our lyres,
3 for our captors asked us there for songs,
    our tormentors,*a* for amusement,
    "Sing us one of the songs of Zion."
4 How can we sing a song of the LORD
    on alien soil?
5 If I forget you, O Jerusalem,
    let my right hand wither;*b*
6 let my tongue stick to my palate
    if I cease to think of you,
    if I do not keep Jerusalem in memory
    even at my happiest hour.

7 Remember, O LORD, against the Edomites
    the day of Jerusalem's fall;
    how they cried, "Strip her, strip her
    to her very foundations!"
8 Fair Babylon, you predator,*c*
    a blessing on him who repays you in kind
    what you have inflicted on us;
9 a blessing on him who seizes your babies
    and dashes them against the rocks!

138 Of David.

I praise You with all my heart,
    sing a hymn to You before the divine beings;

---

a Meaning of Heb. uncertain.
b Others "forget its cunning."
c With Targum; others "who are to be destroyed."

2   I bow toward Your holy temple
    and praise Your name for Your steadfast love and
      faithfulness,
    because You have exalted *-Your name, Your word,
      above all.-*
3 When I called, You answered me,
    -You inspired me with courage.-
4 All the kings of the earth shall praise You, O LORD,
    for they have heard the words You spoke.
5 They shall sing of the ways of the LORD,
    "Great is the majesty of the LORD!"
6 High though the LORD is, He sees the lowly;
    lofty, He perceives from afar.
7 Though I walk among enemies,
    You preserve me in the face of my foes;
    You extend Your hand;
    with Your right hand You deliver me.
8 The LORD will settle accounts for me.
  O LORD, Your steadfast love is eternal;
    do not forsake the work of Your hands.

139   For the leader. Of David. A psalm.

    O LORD, You have examined me and know me.
2 When I sit down or stand up You know it;
    You discern my thoughts from afar.
3 *-You observe-* my walking and reclining,
    and are familiar with all my ways.
4 There is not a word on my tongue
    but that You, O LORD, know it well.
5 You hedge me before and behind;
    You lay Your hand upon me.
6 It is beyond my knowledge;
    it is a mystery; I cannot fathom it.

ᵃ⁻ᵃ *Meaning of Heb. uncertain.*

ᵃ⁻ᵃ *Meaning of Heb. uncertain.*

7 Where can I escape from Your spirit?
  Where can I flee from Your presence?
8 If I ascend to heaven, You are there;
  if I descend to Sheol, You are there too.
9 If I take wing with the dawn
  to come to rest on the western horizon,
10 even there Your hand will be guiding me,
  Your right hand will be holding me fast.
11 If I say, "Surely darkness *b*-will conceal me,
  night will provide me with cover,"-*b*
12 darkness is not dark for You;
  night is as light as day;
  darkness and light are the same.
13 It was You who created my conscience;*c*
  You fashioned me in my mother's womb.
14 I praise You,
  for I am awesomely, wondrously made;
  Your work is wonderful;
  I know it very well.
15 My frame was not concealed from You
  when I was shaped in a hidden place,
  knit together in the recesses of the earth.
16 Your eyes saw my unformed limbs;
  they were all recorded in Your book;
  in due time they were formed,
  a-to the very last one of them.-*a*
17 How weighty Your thoughts seem to me, O God,
  how great their number!
18 I count them—they exceed the grains of sand;
  I end—but am still with You.

19 O God, if You would only slay the wicked—
  you murderers, away from me!—
20 *a*-who invoke You for intrigue,
  Your enemies who swear by You falsely.-*a*
21 O LORD, You know I hate those who hate You,

b-b *Cf. Rashi, Ibn Ezra; meaning of Heb. uncertain.*
c *Lit. "kidneys."*

184

and loathe Your adversaries.
22 I feel a perfect hatred toward them;
   I count them my enemies.

23 Examine me, O God, and know my mind;
   probe me and know my thoughts.
24 See if I have vexatious ways,
   and guide me in ways everlasting.

140   For the leader. A psalm of David.

2 Rescue me, O LORD, from evil men;
   save me from the lawless,
3   whose minds are full of evil schemes,
   who plot war every day.
4 They sharpen their tongues like serpents;
   spiders' poison is on their lips.   *Selah.*

5 O LORD, keep me out of the clutches of the wicked;
   save me from lawless men
   who scheme to *a-*make me fall.*-a*
6 Arrogant men laid traps with ropes for me;
   they spread out a net along the way;
   they set snares for me.   *Selah.*

7 I said to the LORD: You are my God;
   give ear, O LORD, to my pleas for mercy.
8 O GOD, my Lord, the strength of my deliverance,
   You protected my head on the day of battle.*b*
9 O LORD, do not grant the desires of the wicked;
   do not let their plan succeed,
   *c-*else they be exalted.   *Selah.*

---

a-a *Lit. "push my feet."*
b *Lit. "arms."*
c-c *Meaning of Heb. uncertain.*

¹⁰ May the heads of those who beset me
   be covered with the mischief of their lips.⁻ᶜ
¹¹ May coals of fire drop down upon them,
   and they be cast into pits, never to rise again.
¹² Let slanderers have no place in the land;
   let the evil of the lawless man drive him into corrals.
¹³ I know that the LORD will champion
   the cause of the poor, the right of the needy.
¹⁴ Righteous men shall surely praise Your name;
   the upright shall dwell in Your presence.

141 A psalm of David.

I call You, O LORD, hasten to me;
   give ear to my cry when I call You.
² Take my prayer as an offering of incense,
   my upraised hands as an evening sacrifice.
³ O LORD, set a guard over my mouth,
   a watch at the door of my lips;
⁴   let my mind not turn to an evil thing,
   to practice deeds of wickedness
   with men who are evildoers;
   let me not feast on their dainties.
⁵ ᵃLet the righteous man strike me in loyalty,
   let him reprove me;
   let my head not refuse such choice oil.
My prayers are still against theirᵇ evil deeds.
⁶ May their judges slip on the rock,
   but let my words be heard, for they are sweet.
⁷ As when the earth is cleft and broken up
   our bones are scattered at the mouth of Sheol.
⁸ My eyes are fixed upon You, O GOD my Lord;
   I seek refuge in You, do not put me in jeopardy.
⁹ Keep me from the trap laid for me,

ᵃ *Meaning of vv. 5–7 uncertain.*
ᵇ *I.e. the evildoers of v. 4.*

and from the snares of evildoers.
¹⁰ Let the wicked fall into their nets
while I alone come through.

142 A *maskil* of David, while he was in the cave.^a A prayer.

² I cry aloud to the LORD;
I appeal to the LORD loudly for mercy.
³ I pour out my complaint before Him;
I lay my trouble before Him
⁴ when my spirit fails within me.
You know my course;
they have laid a trap in the path I walk.
⁵ Look at my right and see—
I have no friend;
there is nowhere I can flee,
no one cares about me.
⁶ So I cry to You, O LORD;
I say, "You are my refuge,
all I have in the land of the living."
⁷ Listen to my cry, for I have been brought very low;
save me from my pursuers,
for they are too strong for me.
⁸ Free me from prison,
that I may praise Your name.
The righteous ^{b-}shall glory in me^{-b}
for Your gracious dealings with me.

143 A psalm of David.

O LORD, hear my prayer;
give ear to my plea, as You are faithful;

―――――――――
^a *Cf. 1 Sam. 24.3–4.*
^{b-b} *Meaning of Heb. uncertain.*

answer me, as You are beneficent.
2 Do not enter into judgment with Your servant,
  for before You no creature is in the right.

3 My foe hounded me;
  he crushed me to the ground;
  he made me dwell in darkness
  like those long dead.
4 My spirit failed within me;
  my mind was numbed with horror.
5 Then I thought of the days of old;
  I rehearsed all Your deeds,
  recounted the work of Your hands.
6 I stretched out my hands to You,
  longing for You like thirsty earth.   Selah.

7 Answer me quickly, O LORD;
  my spirit can endure no more.
Do not hide Your face from me,
  or I shall become like those who descend into the Pit.
8 Let me learn of Your faithfulness by daybreak,
  for in You I trust;
  let me know the road I must take,
  for on You I have set my hope.
9 Save me from my foes, O LORD;
  a-to You I look for cover.-*a*
10 Teach me to do Your will,
  for You are my God.
Let Your gracious spirit lead me
  on level ground.
11 For the sake of Your name, O LORD, preserve me;
  as You are beneficent, free me from distress.
12 As You are faithful, put an end to my foes;
  destroy all my mortal enemies,
  for I am Your servant.

---

a-a *Meaning of Heb. uncertain.*

144 Of David.

Blessed is the LORD, my rock,
    who trains my hands for battle,
    my fingers for warfare;
2   my faithful one, my fortress,
    my haven and my deliverer,
    my shield, in whom I take shelter,
    who makes peoples^a subject to me.

3 O LORD, what is man that You should care about him,
    mortal man, that You should think of him?
4 Man is like a breath;
    his days are like a passing shadow.
5 O LORD, bend Your sky and come down;
    touch the mountains and they will smoke.
6 Make lightning flash and scatter them;
    shoot Your arrows and rout them.
7 Reach Your hand down from on high;
    rescue me, save me from the mighty waters,
    from the hands of foreigners,
8   whose mouths speak lies,
    and whose oaths^b are false.

9 O God, I will sing You a new song,
    sing a hymn to You with a ten-stringed harp,
10   to You who give victory to kings,
    who rescue His servant David from the deadly sword.
11 Rescue me, save me from the hands of foreigners,
    whose mouths speak lies,
    and whose oaths^b are false.

---

^a *So Targum, Saadia; others "my people."*
^b *With Rashi; lit. "right hand."*

12 ^cFor our sons are like saplings,
   well-tended in their youth;
   our daughters are like cornerstones
   trimmed to give shape to a palace.

13 Our storehouses are full,
   supplying produce of all kinds;
   our flocks number thousands,
   even myriads, in our fields;

14 our cattle are well cared for.
   There is no breaching and no sortie,
   and no wailing in our streets.

15 Happy the people who have it so;
   happy the people whose God is the LORD.

145 A song of praise. Of David.

א   I will extol You, my God and king,
    and bless Your name forever and ever.

ב ² Every day will I bless You
    and praise Your name forever and ever.

ג ³ Great is the LORD and much acclaimed;
    His greatness cannot be fathomed.

ד ⁴ One generation shall laud Your works to another
    and declare Your mighty acts.

ה ⁵ The glorious majesty of Your splendor
    ^{a-}and Your wondrous acts^{-a} will I recite.

ו ⁶ Men shall talk of the might of Your awesome deeds,
    and I will recount Your greatness.

ז ⁷ They shall celebrate Your abundant goodness,
    and sing joyously of Your beneficence.

ח ⁸ The LORD is gracious and compassionate,
    slow to anger and abounding in kindness.

---

^c *The meaning of several phrases in vv. 12–14 is uncertain.*

^{a-a} *A Qumran Pss. scroll reads: "they will speak of, and Your wonders."*

ס 9 The LORD is good to all,
    and His mercy is upon all His works.

י 10 All Your works shall praise You, O LORD,
    and Your faithful ones shall bless You.

כ 11 They shall talk of the majesty of Your kingship,
    and speak of Your might,

ל 12 to make His mighty acts known among men
    and the majestic glory of His kingship.

מ 13 Your kingship is an eternal kingship;
    Your dominion is for all generations.

ס 14 The LORD supports all who stumble,
    and makes all who are bent stand straight.

ע 15 The eyes of all look to You expectantly,
    and You give them their food when it is due.

פ 16 You give it openhandedly,
    feeding every creature to its heart's content.

צ 17 The LORD is beneficent in all His ways
    and faithful in all His works.

ק 18 The LORD is near to all who call Him,
    to all who call Him with sincerity.

ר 19 He fulfills the wishes of those who fear Him;
    He hears their cry and delivers them.

ש 20 The LORD watches over all who love Him,
    but all the wicked He will destroy.

ת 21 My mouth shall utter the praise of the LORD,
    and all creatures[b] shall bless His holy name forever and
    ever.

146 Hallelujah.
    Praise the LORD, O my soul!
  2 I will praise the LORD all my life,
    sing hymns to my God while I exist.

[b] Lit. "flesh."

³ Put not your trust in the great,
in mortal man who cannot save.
⁴ His breath departs;
he returns to the dust;
on that day his plans come to nothing.

⁵ Happy is he who has the God of Jacob for his help,
whose hope is in the LORD his God,
⁶   maker of heaven and earth,
the sea and all that is in them;
who keeps faith forever;
⁷   who secures justice for those who are wronged,
gives food to the hungry.
The LORD sets prisoners free;
⁸   The LORD restores sight to the blind;
the LORD makes those who are bent stand straight;
the LORD loves the righteous;
⁹   The LORD watches over the stranger;
He gives courage to the orphan and widow,
but makes the path of the wicked tortuous.

¹⁰ The LORD shall reign forever,
your God, O Zion, for all generations.
Hallelujah.

147 Hallelujah.
It is good to chant hymns to our God;
it is pleasant to sing glorious praise.

² The LORD rebuilds Jerusalem;
He gathers in the exiles of Israel.
³ He heals their broken hearts,
and binds up their wounds.

⁴ He reckoned the number of the stars;
 to each He gave its name.
⁵ Great is our LORD and full of power;
 His wisdom is beyond reckoning.
⁶ The LORD gives courage to the lowly,
 and brings the wicked down to the dust.

⁷ Sing to the LORD a song of praise,
 chant a hymn with a lyre to our God,
⁸ who covers the heavens with clouds,
 provides rain for the earth,
 makes mountains put forth grass;
⁹ who gives the beasts their food,
 to the raven's brood what they cry for.
¹⁰ He does not prize the strength of horses,
 nor value the fleetnessᵃ of men;
¹¹ but the LORD values those who fear Him,
 those who depend on His faithful care.

¹² O Jerusalem, glorify the LORD;
 praise your God, O Zion!
¹³ For He made the bars of your gates strong,
 and blessed your children within you.
¹⁴ He endows your realm with well-being,
 and satisfies you with choice wheat.

¹⁵ He sends forth His word to the earth;
 His command runs swiftly.
¹⁶ He lays down snow like fleece,
 scatters frost like ashes.
¹⁷ He tosses down hail like crumbs—
 who can endure His icy cold?
¹⁸ He issues a command—it melts them;
 He breathes—the waters flow.

ᵃ *Lit. "thighs."*

¹⁹ He issued His commands to Jacob,
His statutes and rules to Israel.
²⁰ He did not do so for any other nation;
of such rules they know nothing.
Hallelujah.

148 Hallelujah.
Praise the Lord from the heavens;
praise Him on high.
² Praise Him, all His angels,
praise Him, all His hosts.
³ Praise Him, sun and moon,
praise Him, all bright stars.
⁴ Praise Him, highest heavens,
and you waters that are above the heavens.
⁵ Let them praise the name of the Lord,
for it was He who commanded that they be created.
⁶ He made them endure forever,
establishing an order that shall never change.
⁷ Praise the Lord, O you who are on earth,
all sea monsters and ocean depths,
⁸ fire and hail, snow and smoke,
storm wind that executes His command,
⁹ all mountains and hills,
all fruit trees and cedars,
¹⁰ all wild and tamed beasts,
creeping things and winged birds,
¹¹ all kings and peoples of the earth,
all princes of the earth and its judges,
¹² youths and maidens alike,
old and young together.
¹³ Let them praise the name of the Lord,
for His name, His alone, is sublime;
His splendor covers heaven and earth.

¹⁴ He has exalted the horn of His people
    for the glory of all His faithful ones,
    Israel, the people close to Him.
    Hallelujah.

149 Hallelujah.
    Sing to the LORD a new song,
        His praises in the congregation of the faithful.
² Let Israel rejoice in its maker;
        let the children of Zion exult in their king.
³ Let them praise His name in dance;
        with timbrel and lyre let them chant His praises.
⁴ For the LORD delights in His people;
        He adorns the lowly with victory.
⁵ Let the faithful exult in glory;
        let them shout for joy upon their couches,
⁶   with paeans to God in their throats
        and two-edged swords in their hands,
⁷   to impose retribution upon the nations,
        punishment upon the peoples,
⁸   binding their kings with shackles,
        their nobles with chains of iron,
⁹   executing the doom decreed against them.
    This is the glory of all His faithful.
    Hallelujah.

150 Hallelujah.
    Praise God in His sanctuary;
        praise Him in the sky, His stronghold.
² Praise Him for His mighty acts;
        praise Him for*ᵃ* His exceeding greatness.
³ Praise Him with blasts of the horn;
        praise Him with harp and lyre.

ᵃ *Or "as befits."*

⁴ Praise Him with timbrel and dance;
  praise Him with lute and pipe.
⁵ Praise Him with resounding cymbals;
  praise Him with loud-clashing cymbals.
⁶ Let all that breathes praise the LORD.
  Hallelujah.

משלי

PROVERBS

משלי
PROVERBS

1 The proverbs of Solomon son of David, king of Israel:

² For learning wisdom and discipline;
For understanding words of discernment;
³ For acquiring the discipline for success,
Righteousness, justice, and equity;
⁴ For endowing the simple with shrewdness,
The young with knowledge and foresight.
⁵ —The wise man, hearing them, will gain more wisdom;
The discerning man will learn to be adroit;
⁶ For understanding proverb and epigram,
The words of the wise and their riddles.

⁷ The fear of the Lord is the beginning*a* of knowledge;
Fools despise wisdom and discipline.

⁸ My son, heed the discipline of your father,
And do not forsake the instruction of your mother;
⁹ For they are a graceful wreath upon your head,
A necklace about your throat.

¹⁰ My son, if sinners entice you, do not yield;
¹¹ If they say, "Come with us,
Let us set an ambush to shed blood,
Let us lie in wait for the innocent
(Without cause!)
¹² Like Sheol, let us swallow them alive;

ᵃ *Or "best part."*

Whole, like those who go down into the Pit.
¹³ We shall obtain every precious treasure;
We shall fill our homes with loot.
¹⁴ Throw in your lot with us;
We shall all have a common purse."
¹⁵ My son, do not set out with them;
Keep your feet from their path.
¹⁶ For their feet run to evil;
They hurry to shed blood.
¹⁷ In the eyes of every winged creature
The outspread net means nothing.
¹⁸ But they lie in ambush for their own blood;
They lie in wait for their own lives.
¹⁹ Such is the fate of all who pursue unjust gain;
It takes the life of its possessor.

²⁰ Wisdom[b] cries aloud in the streets,
Raises her voice in the squares.
²¹ At the head of the busy streets she calls;
At the entrance of the gates, in the city, she speaks out:
²² "How long will you simple ones love simplicity,
You scoffers be eager to scoff,
You dullards hate knowledge?
²³ You are indifferent to my rebuke;
I will now speak my mind to you,
And let you know my thoughts.
²⁴ Since you refused me when I called,
And paid no heed when I extended my hand,
²⁵ You spurned all my advice,
And would not hear my rebuke,
²⁶ I will laugh at your calamity,
And mock when terror comes upon you,
²⁷ When terror comes like a disaster,
And calamity arrives like a whirlwind,
When trouble and distress come upon you.

[b] *In Proverbs, wisdom is personified as a woman.*

28 Then they shall call me but I will not answer;
They shall seek me but not find me.
29 Because they hated knowledge,
And did not choose fear of the LORD;
30 They refused my advice,
And disdained all my rebukes,
31 They shall eat the fruit of their ways,
And have their fill of their own counsels.
32 The tranquillity of the simple will kill them,
And the complacency of dullards will destroy them.
33 But he who listens to me will dwell in safety,
Untroubled by the terror of misfortune."

2 My son, if you accept my words
And treasure up my commandments;
2 If you make your ear attentive to wisdom
And your mind open to discernment;
3 If you call to understanding
And cry aloud to discernment,
4 If you seek it as you do silver
And search for it as for treasures,
5 Then you will understand the fear of the LORD
And attain knowledge of God.
6 For the LORD grants wisdom;
Knowledge and discernment are by His decree.
7 He reserves ability for the upright
And is a shield for those who live blamelessly,
8 Guarding the paths of justice,
Protecting the way of those loyal to Him.
9 You will then understand what is right, just,
And equitable—every good course.
10 For wisdom will enter your mind
And knowledge will delight you.
11 Foresight will protect you,

And discernment will guard you.
[12] It will save you from the way of evil men,
From men who speak duplicity,
[13] Who leave the paths of rectitude
To follow the ways of darkness,
[14] Who rejoice in doing evil
And exult in the duplicity of evil men,
[15] Men whose paths are crooked
And who are devious in their course.
[16] It will save you from the forbidden[a] woman,
From the alien woman whose talk is smooth,
[17] Who forsakes the companion of her youth
And disregards the covenant of her God.
[18] Her house sinks down to Death,
And her course leads to the shades.
[19] All who go to her cannot return
And find again the paths of life.

[20] So follow the way of the good
And keep to the paths of the just.
[21] For the upright will inhabit the earth,
The blameless will remain in it.
[22] While the wicked will vanish from the land
And the treacherous will be rooted out of it.

3 My son, do not forget my teaching,
But let your mind retain my commandments;
[2] For they will bestow on you length of days,
Years of life and well-being.
[3] Let fidelity and steadfastness not leave you;
Bind them about your throat,
Write them on the tablet of your mind,
[4] And you will find favor and approbation
In the eyes of God and man.

---

[a] *Lit. "strange."*

5 Trust in the LORD with all your heart,
And do not rely on your own understanding.
6 In all your ways acknowledge Him,
And He will make your paths smooth.
7 Do not be wise in your own eyes;
Fear the LORD and shun evil.
8 It will be a cure for your body,[a]
A tonic for your bones.
9 Honor the LORD with your wealth,
With the best of all your income,
10 And your barns will be filled with grain,
Your vats will burst with new wine.
11 Do not reject the discipline of the LORD, my son;
Do not abhor His rebuke.
12 For whom the LORD loves, He rebukes,
As a father the son whom he favors.

13 Happy is the man who finds wisdom,
The man who attains understanding.
14 Her value in trade is better than silver,
Her yield, greater than gold.
15 She is more precious than rubies;
All of your goods cannot equal her.
16 In her right hand is length of days,
In her left, riches and honor.
17 Her ways are pleasant ways,
And all her paths, peaceful.
18 She is a tree of life to those who grasp her,
And whoever holds on to her is happy.

19 The LORD founded the earth by wisdom;
He established the heavens by understanding;
20 By His knowledge the depths burst apart,
And the skies distilled dew.
21 My son, do not lose sight of them;

---

[a] *Lit. "navel."*

Hold on to resourcefulness and foresight.
22 They will give life to your spirit
And grace to your throat.
23 Then you will go your way safely
And not injure your feet.
24 When you lie down you will be unafraid;
You will lie down and your sleep will be sweet.
25 You will not fear sudden terror
Or the disaster that comes upon the wicked,
26 For the LORD will be your trust;
He will keep your feet from being caught.

27 Do not withhold good from one who deserves it
When you have the power to do it [for him].
28 Do not say to your fellow, "Come back again;
I'll give it to you tomorrow," when you have it with you.
29 Do not devise harm against your fellow
Who lives trustfully with you.
30 Do not quarrel with a man for no cause,
When he has done you no harm.
31 Do not envy a lawless man,
Or choose any of his ways;
32 For the devious man is an abomination to the LORD,
But He is intimate with the straightforward.
33 The curse of the LORD is on the house of the wicked,
But He blesses the abode of the righteous.
34 At scoffers He scoffs,
But to the lowly He shows grace.
35 The wise shall obtain honor,
But dullards get disgrace as their portion.

4 Sons, heed the discipline of a father;
Listen and learn discernment,
2 For I give you good instruction;
Do not forsake my teaching.

³ Once I was a son to my father,
The tender darling of my mother.
⁴ He instructed me and said to me,
"Let your mind hold on to my words;
Keep my commandments and you will live.
⁵ Acquire wisdom, acquire discernment;
Do not forget and do not swerve from my words.
⁶ Do not forsake her and she will guard you;
Love her and she will protect you.
⁷ The beginning^a of wisdom is—acquire wisdom;
With all your acquisitions, acquire discernment.
⁸ Hug her to you and she will exalt you;
She will bring you honor if you embrace her.
⁹ She will adorn your head with a graceful wreath;
Crown you with a glorious diadem."

¹⁰ My son, heed and take in my words,
And you will have many years of life.
¹¹ I instruct you in the way of wisdom;
I guide you in straight courses.
¹² You will walk without breaking stride;
When you run, you will not stumble.
¹³ Hold fast to discipline; do not let go;
Keep it; it is your life.
¹⁴ Do not enter on the path of the wicked;
Do not walk on the way of evil men.
¹⁵ Avoid it; do not pass through it;
Turn away from it; pass it by.
¹⁶ For they cannot sleep unless they have done evil;
Unless they make someone fall they are robbed of
  sleep.
¹⁷ They eat the bread of wickedness
And drink the wine of lawlessness.
¹⁸ The path of the righteous is like radiant sunlight,
Ever brightening until noon.

^a Or "best part."

19 The way of the wicked is all darkness;
They do not know what will make them stumble.

20 My son, listen to my speech;
Incline your ear to my words.
21 Do not lose sight of them;
Keep them in your mind.
22 They are life to him who finds them,
Healing for his whole body.
23 More than all that you guard, guard your mind,
For it is the source of life.
24 Put crooked speech away from you;
Keep devious talk far from you.
25 Let your eyes look forward,
Your gaze be straight ahead.
26 Survey the course you take,
And all your ways will prosper.
27 Do not swerve to the right or the left;
Keep your feet from evil.

5 My son, listen to my wisdom;
Incline your ear to my insight,
2 That you may have foresight,
While your lips hold fast to knowledge.
3 For the lips of a forbidden*a* woman drip honey;
Her mouth is smoother than oil;
4 But in the end she is as bitter as wormwood,
Sharp as a two-edged sword.
5 Her feet go down to Death;
Her steps take hold of Sheol.
6 She does not chart a path of life;
Her course meanders for lack of knowledge.
7 So now, sons, pay heed to me,
And do not swerve from the words of my mouth.

a Lit. "strange."

8 Keep yourself far away from her;
Do not come near the doorway of her house
9 Lest you give up your vigor to others,
Your years to a ruthless one;
10 Lest strangers eat their fill of your strength,
And your toil be for the house of another;
11 And in the end you roar,
When your flesh and body are consumed,
12 And say,
"O how I hated discipline,
And heartily spurned rebuke.
13 I did not pay heed to my teachers,
Or incline my ear to my instructors.
14 Soon I was in dire trouble
Amidst the assembled congregation."
15 Drink water from your own cistern,
Running water from your own well.
16 Your springs will gush forth
In streams in the public squares.
17 They will be yours alone,
Others having no part with you.
18 Let your fountain be blessed;
Find joy in the wife of your youth—
19 A loving doe, a graceful mountain goat.
Let her breasts satisfy you at all times;
Be infatuated with love of her always.
20 Why be infatuated, my son, with a forbidden*a* woman?
Why clasp the bosom of an alien woman?
21 For a man's ways are before the eyes of God;
He surveys his entire course.
22 The wicked man will be trapped in his iniquities;
He will be caught up in the ropes of his sin.
23 He will die for lack of discipline,
Infatuated by his great folly.

6 My son, if you have stood surety for your fellow,
Given your hand for another,[a]
² You have been trapped by the words of your mouth,
Snared by the words of your mouth.
³ Do this, then, my son, to extricate yourself,
For you have come into the power of your fellow:
Go grovel—and badger your fellow;
⁴ Give your eyes no sleep,
Your pupils no slumber.
⁵ Save yourself like a deer out of the hand [of a hunter],
Like a bird out of the hand of a fowler.

⁶ Lazybones, go to the ant;
Study its ways and learn.
⁷ Without leaders, officers, or rulers,
⁸ It lays up its stores during the summer,
Gathers in its food at the harvest.
⁹ How long will you lie there, lazybones;
When will you wake from your sleep?
¹⁰ A bit more sleep, a bit more slumber,
A bit more hugging yourself in bed,
¹¹ And poverty will come [b-]calling upon you,[-b]
And want, like a man with a shield.

¹² A scoundrel, an evil man
Lives by crooked speech,
¹³ Winking his eyes,
Shuffling his feet,
Pointing his finger.
¹⁴ Duplicity is in his heart;
He plots evil all the time;
He incites quarrels.

---

[a] *Or "a stranger."*
[b-b] *Meaning of Heb. uncertain.*

15 Therefore calamity will come upon him without
   warning;
Suddenly he will be broken beyond repair.

16 Six things the LORD hates;
Seven are an abomination to Him:
17 A haughty bearing,
A lying tongue,
Hands that shed innocent blood,
18 A mind that hatches evil plots,
Feet quick to run to evil,
19 A false witness testifying lies,
And one who incites brothers to quarrel.

20 My son, keep your father's commandment;
Do not forsake your mother's teaching.
21 Tie them over your heart always;
Bind them around your throat.
22 When you walk it will lead you;
When you lie down it will watch over you;
And when you are awake it will talk with you.
23 For the commandment is a lamp,
The teaching is a light,
And the way to life is the rebuke that disciplines.
24 It will keep you from an evil woman,
From the smooth tongue of a forbidden*c* woman.
25 Do not lust for her beauty
Or let her captivate you with her eyes.
26 The last loaf of bread will go for a harlot;
A married woman will snare a person of honor.
27 Can a man rake embers into his bosom
Without burning his clothes?
28 Can a man walk on live coals
Without scorching his feet?

c Lit. "alien."

²⁹ It is the same with one who sleeps with his fellow's
wife;
None who touches her will go unpunished.
³⁰ A thief is not held in contempt
For stealing to appease his hunger;
³¹ Yet if caught he must pay sevenfold;
He must give up all he owns.
³² He who commits adultery is devoid of sense;
Only one who would destroy himself does such a thing.
³³ He will meet with disease and disgrace;
His reproach will never be expunged.
³⁴ The fury of the husband will be passionate;
He will show no pity on his day of vengeance.
³⁵ He will not have regard for any ransom;
He will refuse your bribe, however great.

7 My son, heed my words;
And store up my commandments with you.
² Keep my commandments and live,
My teaching, as the apple of your eye.
³ Bind them on your fingers;
Write them on the tablet of your mind.
⁴ Say to Wisdom, "You are my sister,"
And call Understanding a kinswoman.
⁵ She will guard you from a forbidden^a woman;
From an alien woman whose talk is smooth.

⁶ From the window of my house,
Through my lattice, I looked out
⁷ And saw among the simple,
Noticed among the youths,
A lad devoid of sense.
⁸ He was crossing the street near her corner,
Walking toward her house

^a Lit. "strange."

9 In the dusk of evening,
In the dark hours of night.
10 A woman comes toward him
b-Dressed like a harlot, with set purpose.-b
11 She is bustling and restive;
She is never at home.
12 Now in the street, now in the square,
She lurks at every corner.
13 She lays hold of him and kisses him;
Brazenly she says to him,
14 "I had to make a sacrifice of well-being;
Today I fulfilled my vows.
15 Therefore I have come out to you,
Seeking you, and have found you.
16 I have decked my couch with covers
Of dyed Egyptian linen;
17 I have sprinkled my bed
With myrrh, aloes, and cinnamon.
18 Let us drink our fill of love till morning;
Let us delight in amorous embrace.
19 For the man of the house is away;
He is off on a distant journey.
20 He took his bag of money with him
And will return only at mid-month."

21 She sways him with her eloquence,
Turns him aside with her smooth talk.
22 Thoughtlessly he follows her,
Like an ox going to the slaughter,
b-Like a fool to the stocks for punishment-b—
23 Until the arrow pierces his liver.
He is like a bird rushing into a trap,
Not knowing his life is at stake.
24 Now, sons, listen to me;
Pay attention to my words;

b-b *Meaning of Heb. uncertain.*

25 Let your mind not wander down her ways;
Do not stray onto her paths.
26 For many are those she has struck dead,
And numerous are her victims.
27 Her house is a highway to Sheol
Leading down to Death's inner chambers.

8   It is Wisdom calling,
Understanding raising her voice.
2 She takes her stand at the topmost heights,
By the wayside, at the crossroads,
3 Near the gates at the city entrance;
At the entryways, she shouts,
4 "O men, I call to you;
My cry is to all mankind.
5 O simple ones, learn shrewdness;
O dullards, instruct your minds.
6 Listen, for I speak noble things;
Uprightness comes from my lips;
7 My mouth utters truth;
Wickedness is abhorrent to my lips.
8 All my words are just,
None of them perverse or crooked;
9 All are straightforward to the intelligent man,
And right to those who have attained knowledge.
10 Accept my discipline rather than silver,
Knowledge rather than choice gold.
11 For wisdom is better than rubies;
No goods can equal her.

12 "I, Wisdom, live with Prudence;
I attain knowledge and foresight.
13 To fear the LORD is to hate evil;
I hate pride, arrogance, the evil way,

And duplicity in speech.
14 Mine are counsel and resourcefulness;
I am understanding; courage is mine.
15 Through me kings reign
And rulers decree just laws;
16 Through me princes rule,
Great men and all the *righteous judges.*
17 Those who love me I love,
And those who seek me will find me.
18 Riches and honor belong to me,
Enduring wealth and success.
19 My fruit is better than gold, fine gold,
And my produce better than choice silver.
20 I walk on the way of righteousness,
On the paths of justice.
21 I endow those who love me with substance;
I will fill their treasuries.

22 "The LORD created me at the beginning of His course
As the first of His works of old.
23 In the distant past I was fashioned,
At the beginning, at the origin of earth.
24 There was still no deep when I was brought forth,
No springs rich in water;
25 Before [the foundation of] the mountains were sunk,
Before the hills I was born.
26 He had not yet made earth and fields,
Or the world's first clumps of clay.
27 I was there when He set the heavens into place;
When He fixed the horizon upon the deep;
28 When He made the heavens above firm,
And the fountains of the deep gushed forth;
29 When He assigned the sea its limits,
So that its waters never transgress His command;
When He fixed the foundations of the earth,

a-a *According to some Heb. mss. and printed editions, "judges of the earth."*

³⁰ I was with Him as a confidant,
A source of delight every day,
Rejoicing before Him at all times,
³¹ Rejoicing in His inhabited world,
Finding delight with mankind.
³² Now, sons, listen to me;
Happy are they who keep my ways.
³³ Heed discipline and become wise;
Do not spurn it.
³⁴ Happy is the man who listens to me,
Coming early to my gates each day,
Waiting outside my doors.
³⁵ For he who finds me finds life
And obtains favor from the LORD.
³⁶ But he who misses me destroys himself;
All who hate me love death."

9 Wisdom has built her house,
She has hewn her seven pillars.
² She has prepared the feast,
Mixed the wine,
And also set the table.
³ She has sent out her maids to announce
On the heights of the town,
⁴ "Let the simple enter here";
To those devoid of sense she says,
⁵ "Come, eat my food
And drink the wine that I have mixed;
⁶ Give up simpleness and live,
Walk in the way of understanding."

⁷ To correct a scoffer,
^a-Or rebuke a wicked man for his blemish,
Is to call down abuse on oneself.^{-a}
⁸ Do not rebuke a scoffer, for he will hate you;

---

^{a-a} *Clauses transposed for clarity.*

Reprove a wise man, and he will love you.
9 Instruct a wise man, and he will grow wiser;
Teach a righteous man, and he will gain in learning.
10 The beginning of wisdom is fear of the LORD,
And knowledge of the Holy One is understanding.
11 For through me your days will increase,
And years be added to your life.
12 If you are wise, you are wise for yourself;
If you are a scoffer, you bear it alone.
13 The stupid woman bustles about;
She is simple and knows nothing.
14 She sits in the doorway of her house,
Or on a chair at the heights of the town,
15 Calling to all the wayfarers
Who go about their own affairs,
16 "Let the simple enter here";
And to those devoid of sense she says,
17 "Stolen waters are sweet,
And bread eaten furtively is tasty."
18 He does not know that the shades are there,
That her guests are in the depths of Sheol.

10

The proverbs of Solomon:

A wise son brings joy to his father;
A dull son is his mother's sorrow.
2 Ill-gotten wealth is of no avail,
But righteousness saves from death.
3 The LORD will not let the righteous go hungry,
But He denies the wicked what they crave.
4 Negligent hands cause poverty,
But diligent hands enrich.
5 He who lays in stores during the summer is a capable son,
But he who sleeps during the harvest is an incompetent.
6 Blessings light upon the head of the righteous,

But lawlessness covers the mouth of the wicked.

7 The name of the righteous is invoked in blessing,
But the fame of the wicked rots.

8 He whose heart is wise accepts commands,
But he whose speech is foolish comes to grief.

9 He who lives blamelessly lives safely,
But he who walks a crooked path will be found out.

10 He who winks his eye causes sorrow;
He whose speech is foolish comes to grief.

11 The mouth of the righteous is a fountain of life,
But lawlessness covers the mouth of the wicked.

12 Hatred stirs up strife,
But love covers up all faults.

13 Wisdom is to be found on the lips of the intelligent,
But a rod is ready for the back of the senseless.

14 The wise store up knowledge;
The mouth of the fool is an imminent ruin.

15 The wealth of a rich man is his fortress;
The poverty of the poor is his ruin.

16 The labor of the righteous man makes for life;
The produce of the wicked man makes for want.

17 He who follows discipline shows the way to life,
But he who ignores reproof leads astray.

18 He who conceals hatred has lying lips,
While he who speaks forth slander is a dullard.

19 Where there is much talking, there is no lack of trans-
gressing,
But he who curbs his tongue^a shows sense.

20 The tongue of a righteous man is choice silver,
But the mind of the wicked is of little worth.

21 The lips of the righteous sustain many,
But fools die for lack of sense.

22 It is the blessing of the LORD that enriches,
And no toil can increase it.

23 As mischief is sport for the dullard,

---

^{a} *Lit. "lips."*

So is wisdom for the man of understanding.
24 What the wicked man plots overtakes him;
What the righteous desire is granted.
25 When the storm passes the wicked man is gone,
But the righteous is an everlasting foundation.
26 Like vinegar to the teeth,
Like smoke to the eyes,
Is a lazy man to those who send him on a mission.
27 The fear of the LORD prolongs life,
While the years of the wicked will be shortened.
28 The righteous can look forward to joy,
But the hope of the wicked is doomed.
29 The way of the LORD is a stronghold for the blameless,
But a ruin for evildoers.
30 The righteous will never be shaken;
The wicked will not inhabit the earth.
31 The mouth of the righteous produces wisdom,
But the treacherous tongue shall be cut off.
32 The lips of the righteous know what is pleasing;
The mouth of the wicked [knows] duplicity.

11 False scales are an abomination to the LORD;
An honest*a* weight pleases Him.
2 When arrogance appears, disgrace follows,
But wisdom is with those who are unassuming.
3 The integrity of the upright guides them;
The deviousness of the treacherous leads them to ruin.
4 Wealth is of no avail on the day of wrath,
But righteousness saves from death.
5 The righteousness of the blameless man smooths his way,
But the wicked man is felled by his wickedness.
6 The righteousness of the upright saves them,
But the treacherous are trapped by their malice.
7 At death the hopes of a wicked man are doomed

---

a *Lit. "whole."*

And the ambition of evil men comes to nothing.
8 The righteous man is rescued from trouble
And the wicked man takes his place.
9 The impious man destroys his neighbor through speech,
But through their knowledge the righteous are rescued.
10 When the righteous prosper the city exults;
When the wicked perish there are shouts of joy.
11 A city is built up by the blessing of the upright,
But it is torn down by the speech of the wicked.
12 He who speaks contemptuously of his fellowman is devoid of sense;
A prudent man keeps his peace.
13 A base fellow gives away secrets,
But a trustworthy soul keeps a confidence.
14 For want of strategy an army falls,
But victory comes with much planning.
15 Harm awaits him who stands surety for another;*b*
He who spurns pledging shall be secure.
16 A graceful woman obtains honor;
Ruthless men obtain wealth.
17 A kindly man benefits himself;
A cruel man makes trouble for himself.
18 The wicked man earns illusory wages,
But he who sows righteousness has a true reward.
19 Righteousness is a prop of life,
But to pursue evil leads to death.
20 Men of crooked mind are an abomination to the LORD,
But those whose way is blameless please Him.
21 *c-*Assuredly,*-c* the evil man will not escape,
But the offspring of the righteous will be safe.
22 Like a gold ring in the snout of a pig
Is a beautiful woman bereft of sense.
23 What the righteous desire can only be good;
What the wicked hope for [stirs] wrath.
24 One man gives generously and ends with more;

b *Or "a stranger."*
c-c *Lit. "Hand to hand"; meaning of Heb. uncertain.*

Another stints on doing the right thing and incurs a loss.
25 A generous person enjoys prosperity;
He who satisfies others shall himself be sated.
26 He who withholds grain earns the curses of the people,
But blessings are on the head of the one who dispenses it.
27 He who earnestly seeks what is good pursues what is
   pleasing;
He who is bent on evil, upon him it shall come.
28 He who trusts in his wealth shall fall,
But the righteous shall flourish like foliage.
29 He who makes trouble for his household shall inherit
   the wind;
A fool is a slave to the wise-hearted.
30 The fruit of the righteous is a tree of life;
A wise man captivates people.
31 If the righteous on earth get their deserts,
How much more the wicked man and the sinner.

12 He who loves discipline loves knowledge;
He who spurns reproof is a brutish man.
2 A good man earns the favor of the LORD,
A man of intrigues, His condemnation.
3 A man cannot be established in wickedness,
But the root of the righteous will not be shaken loose.
4 A capable wife is a crown for her husband,
But an incompetent one is like rot in his bones.
5 The purposes of the righteous are justice,
The schemes of the wicked are deceit.
6 The words of the wicked are a deadly ambush,
But the speech of the upright saves them.
7 Overturn the wicked and they are gone,
But the house of the righteous will endure.
8 A man is commended according to his intelligence;

A twisted mind is held up to contempt.
⁹ Better to be lightly esteemed and have a servant
Than to put on airs and have no food.
¹⁰ A righteous man knows the needs of his beast,
But the compassion of the wicked is cruelty.
¹¹ He who tills his land shall have food in plenty,
But he who pursues vanities is devoid of sense.
¹² ᵃ⁻The wicked covet the catch of evil men;
The root of the righteous yields [fruit].⁻ᵃ
¹³ Sinful speech is a trap for the evil man,
But the righteous escapes from trouble.
¹⁴ A man gets his fill of good from the fruit of his speech;
One is repaid in kind for one's deeds.
¹⁵ The way of a fool is right in his own eyes;
But the wise man accepts advice.
¹⁶ A fool's vexation is known at once,
But a clever man conceals his humiliation.
¹⁷ He who testifies faithfully tells the truth,
But a false witness, deceit.
¹⁸ There is blunt talk like sword-thrusts,
But the speech of the wise is healing.
¹⁹ Truthful speech abides forever,
A lying tongue for but a moment.
²⁰ Deceit is in the minds of those who plot evil;
For those who plan good there is joy.
²¹ No harm befalls the righteous,
But the wicked have their fill of misfortune.
²² Lying speech is an abomination to the LORD,
But those who act faithfully please Him.
²³ A clever man conceals what he knows,
But the mind of a dullard cries out folly.
²⁴ The hand of the diligent wields authority;
The negligent are held in subjection.
²⁵ If there is anxiety in a man's mind let him quash it,
And turn it into joy with a good word.

ᵃ⁻ᵃ *Meaning of Heb. uncertain.*

26 A righteous man *a-*gives his friend direction,*-a*
But the way of the wicked leads astray.
27 A negligent man never has game to roast;
*a-*A diligent man has precious wealth.*-a*
28 The road of righteousness leads to life;
By way of its path there is no death.

13 A wise son—it is through the discipline of his father;
A scoffer—he never heard reproof.
2 A man enjoys good from the fruit of his speech;
But out of the throat of the treacherous comes lawlessness.
3 He who guards his tongue*a* preserves his life;
He who opens wide his lips, it is his ruin.
4 A lazy man craves, but has nothing;
The diligent shall feast on rich fare.
5 A righteous man hates lies;
The wicked man is vile and disgraceful.
6 Righteousness protects him whose way is blameless;
Wickedness subverts the sinner.
7 One man pretends to be rich and has nothing;
Another professes to be poor and has much wealth.
8 Riches are ransom for a man's life,
The poor never heard a reproof.
9 The light of the righteous is radiant;
The lamp of the wicked is extinguished.
10 *b-*Arrogance yields nothing but strife;*-b*
Wisdom belongs to those who seek advice.
11 Wealth may dwindle to less than nothing,
But he who gathers little by little increases it.
12 Hope deferred sickens the heart,
But desire realized is a tree of life.
13 He who disdains a precept will be injured thereby;
He who respects a command will be rewarded.
14 The instruction of a wise man is a fountain of life,

a Lit. *"mouth."*
b-b *Meaning of Heb. uncertain.*

Enabling one to avoid deadly snares.
[15] Good sense wins favor;
The way of treacherous men is unchanging.[c]
[16] Every clever man acts knowledgeably,
But a dullard exposes his stupidity.
[17] Harm befalls a wicked messenger;
A faithful courier brings healing.
[18] Poverty and humiliation are for him who spurns discipline;
But he who takes reproof to heart gets honor.
[19] Desire realized is sweet to the soul;
To turn away from evil is abhorrent to the stupid.
[20] He who keeps company with the wise becomes wise,
But he who consorts with dullards comes to grief.
[21] Misfortune pursues sinners,
But the righteous are well rewarded.
[22] A good man has what to bequeath to his grandchildren,
For the wealth of sinners is stored up for the righteous.
[23] The tillage of the poor yields much food;
But substance is swept away for lack of moderation.
[24] He who spares the rod hates his son,
But he who loves him disciplines him early.
[25] The righteous man eats to his heart's content,
But the belly of the wicked is empty.

14 The wisest of women builds her house,
But folly tears it down with its own hands.
[2] He who maintains his integrity fears the LORD;
A man of devious ways scorns Him.
[3] In the mouth of a fool is a rod of haughtiness,
But the lips of the wise protect them.
[4] If there are no oxen the crib is clean,
But a rich harvest comes through the strength of the ox.
[5] An honest witness will not lie;

---

[c] Or "harsh."

A false witness testifies lies.

⁶ A scoffer seeks wisdom in vain,
But knowledge comes easily to the intelligent man.

⁷ Keep your distance from a dullard,
For you will not learn wise speech.

⁸ It is the wisdom of a clever man to understand his course;
But the stupidity of the dullard is delusion.

⁹ Reparations mediate between fools,
Between the upright, good will.

¹⁰ The heart alone knows its bitterness,
And no outsider can share in its joy.

¹¹ The house of the wicked will be demolished,
But the tent of the upright will flourish.

¹² A road may seem right to a man,
But in the end it is a road to death.

¹³ The heart may ache even in laughter,
And joy may end in grief.

¹⁴ An unprincipled man reaps the fruits of his ways;
ᵃ⁻A good man, of his deeds.⁻ᵃ

¹⁵ A simple person believes anything;
A clever man ponders his course.

¹⁶ A wise man is diffident and shuns evil,
But a dullard rushes in confidently.

¹⁷ An impatient man commits folly;
A man of intrigues will be hated.

¹⁸ Folly is the lot of the simple,
But clever men ᵇ⁻glory in knowledge.⁻ᵇ

¹⁹ Evil men are brought low before the good,
So are the wicked at the gates of the righteous.

²⁰ A pauper is despised even by his peers,
But a rich man has many friends.

²¹ He who despises his fellow is wrong;
He who shows pity for the lowly is happy.

²² Surely those who plan evil go astray,
While those who plan good earn steadfast love.

ᵃ⁻ᵃ *Taking* 'al *as from* 'll; *cf. Hos. 12.3.*
ᵇ⁻ᵇ *Meaning of Heb. uncertain.*

23 From all toil there is some gain,
But idle chatter is pure loss.
24 The ornament of the wise is their wealth;
The stupidity of dullards is stupidity.
25 A truthful witness saves lives;
He who testifies lies [spreads] deceit.
26 Fear of the LORD is a stronghold,
A refuge for a man's children.
27 Fear of the LORD is a fountain of life,
Enabling one to avoid deadly snares.
28 A numerous people is the glory of a king;
Without a nation a ruler is ruined.
29 Patience results in much understanding;
Impatience gets folly as its portion.
30 A calm disposition gives bodily health;
Passion is rot to the bones.
31 He who withholds what is due to the poor affronts his
    Maker;
He who shows pity for the needy honors Him.
32 The wicked man is felled by his own evil;
The righteous man finds security in his death.
33 Wisdom rests quietly in the mind of a prudent man,
But among dullards it makes itself known.
34 Righteousness exalts a nation;
Sin is a reproach to any people.
35 The king favors a capable servant;
He rages at an incompetent one.

15 A gentle response allays wrath;
A harsh word provokes anger.
2 The tongue of the wise produces much knowledge,
But the mouth of dullards pours out folly.
3 The eyes of the LORD are everywhere,
Observing the bad and the good.

4 A healing tongue is a tree of life,
But a devious one makes for a broken spirit.
5 A fool spurns the discipline of his father,
But one who heeds reproof becomes clever.
6 In the house of the righteous there is much treasure,
But in the harvest of the wicked there is trouble.
7 The lips of the wise disseminate knowledge;
Not so the minds of dullards.
8 The sacrifice of the wicked is an abomination to the
  LORD,
But the prayer of the upright pleases Him.
9 The way of the wicked is an abomination to the LORD,
But He loves him who pursues righteousness.
10 Discipline seems bad to him who forsakes the way;
He who spurns reproof will die.
11 Sheol and Abaddon lie exposed to the LORD,
How much more the minds of men!
12 The scoffer dislikes being reproved;
He will not resort to the wise.
13 A joyful heart makes a cheerful face;
A sad heart makes a despondent mood.
14 The mind of a prudent man seeks knowledge;
The mouth of the dullard pursues folly.
15 All the days of a poor man are wretched,
But contentment is a feast without end.
16 Better a little with fear of the LORD
Than great wealth with confusion.
17 Better a meal of vegetables where there is love
Than a fattened ox where there is hate.
18 A hot-tempered man provokes a quarrel;
A patient man calms strife.
19 The way of a lazy man is like a hedge of thorns,
But the path of the upright is paved.
20 A wise son makes his father happy;
A fool of a man humiliates his mother.

²¹ Folly is joy to one devoid of sense;
A prudent man walks a straight path.
²² Plans are foiled for want of counsel,
But they succeed through many advisers.
²³ A ready response is a joy to a man,
And how good is a word rightly timed!
²⁴ For an intelligent man the path of life leads upward,
In order to avoid Sheol below.
²⁵ The Lord will tear down the house of the proud,
But He will establish the homestead of the widow.
²⁶ Evil thoughts are an abomination to the Lord,
But pleasant words are pure.
²⁷ He who pursues ill-gotten gain makes trouble for his
household;
He who spurns gifts will live long.
²⁸ The heart*a* of the righteous man rehearses his answer,
But the mouth of the wicked blurts out evil things.
²⁹ The Lord is far from the wicked,
But He hears the prayer of the righteous.
³⁰ What brightens the eye gladdens the heart;
Good news puts fat on the bones.
³¹ He whose ear heeds the discipline of life
Lodges among the wise.
³² He who spurns discipline hates himself;
He who heeds reproof gains understanding.
³³ The fear of the Lord is the discipline of wisdom;
Humility precedes honor.

16 A man may arrange his thoughts,
But what he says depends on the Lord.
² All the ways of a man seem right to him,
But the Lord probes motives.
³ Entrust your affairs to the Lord,
And your plans will succeed.

ᵃ *For* leb *as a source of speech, see note to Eccl. 5.1.*

⁴ The Lord made everything for a purpose,
Even the wicked for an evil day.
⁵ Every haughty person is an abomination to the Lord;
Assuredly,^a he will not go unpunished.
⁶ Iniquity is expiated by loyalty and faithfulness,
And evil is avoided through fear of the Lord.
⁷ When the Lord is pleased with a man's conduct,
He may turn even his enemies into allies.
⁸ Better a little with righteousness
Than a large income with injustice.
⁹ A man may plot out his course,
But it is the Lord who directs his steps.

¹⁰ There is magic on the lips of the king;
He cannot err in judgment.
¹¹ Honest scales and balances are the Lord's;
All the weights in the bag are His work.
¹² Wicked deeds are an abomination to kings,
For the throne is established by righteousness.
¹³ Truthful speech wins the favor of kings;
They love those who speak honestly.
¹⁴ The king's wrath is a messenger of death,
But a wise man can appease it.
¹⁵ The king's smile means life;
His favor is like a rain cloud in spring.

¹⁶ How much better to acquire wisdom than gold;
To acquire understanding is preferable to silver.
¹⁷ The highway of the upright avoids evil;
He who would preserve his life watches his way.
¹⁸ Pride goes before ruin,
Arrogance, before failure.
¹⁹ Better to be humble and among the lowly
Than to share spoils with the proud.
²⁰ He who is adept in a matter will attain success;

---

^a Lit. "Hand to hand"; meaning of Heb. uncertain.

Happy is he who trusts in the LORD.
21 The wise-hearted is called discerning;
One whose speech is pleasing gains wisdom.
22 Good sense is a fountain of life to those who have it,
And folly is the punishment of fools.
23 The mind of the wise man makes his speech effective
And increases the wisdom on his lips.
24 Pleasant words are like a honeycomb,
Sweet to the palate and a cure for the body.
25 A road may seem right to a man,
But in the end it is a road to death.
26 The appetite of a laborer labors for him,
Because his hunger[b] [c]forces him on.[c]

27 A scoundrel plots[c] evil;
What is on his lips is like a scorching fire.
28 A shifty man stirs up strife,
And a querulous one alienates his friend.
29 A lawless man misleads his friend,
Making him take the wrong way.
30 He closes his eyes while meditating deception;
He purses his lips while deciding upon evil.

31 Gray hair is a crown of glory;
It is attained by the way of righteousness.
32 Better to be forebearing than mighty,
To have self-control than to conquer a city.
33 Lots are cast into the lap;
The decision depends on the LORD.

17 Better a dry crust with peace
Than a house full of feasting with strife.
2 A capable servant will dominate an incompetent son
And share the inheritance with the brothers.

---

[b] *Lit. "mouth."*
[c-c] *Meaning of Heb. uncertain.*

3 For silver—the crucible;
For gold—the furnace,
And the LORD tests the mind.

4 An evildoer listens to mischievous talk;
A liar gives ear to malicious words.

5 He who mocks the poor affronts his Maker;
He who rejoices over another's misfortune will not go
   unpunished.

6 Grandchildren are the crown of their elders,
And the glory of children is their parents.

7 Lofty words are not fitting for a villain;
Much less lying words for a great man.

8 A bribe seems like a charm to him who uses it;
He succeeds at every turn.

9 He who seeks love overlooks faults,
But he who harps on a matter alienates his friend.

10 A rebuke works on an intelligent man
More than one hundred blows on a fool.

11 An evil man seeks only to rebel;
A ruthless messenger will be sent against him.

12 Sooner meet a bereaved she-bear
Than a fool with his nonsense.

13 Evil will never depart from the house
Of him who repays good with evil.

14 To start a quarrel is to open a sluice;
Before a dispute *-flares up,-*ᵃ drop it.

15 To acquit the guilty and convict the innocent—
Both are an abomination to the LORD.

16 What good is money in the hand of a fool
To purchase wisdom, when he has no mind?

17 A friend is devoted at all times;
A brother is born to share adversity.

18 Devoid of sense is he who gives his hand
To stand surety for his fellow.

19 He who loves transgression loves strife;

a-a *Meaning of Heb. uncertain.*

He who builds a high threshold invites broken bones.
20 Man of crooked mind comes to no good,
And he who speaks duplicity falls into trouble.
21 One begets a dullard to one's own grief;
The father of a villain has no joy.
22 A joyful heart makes for *b*-good health;-*b*
Despondency dries up the bones.
23 The wicked man draws a bribe out of his bosom
To pervert the course of justice.
24 Wisdom lies before the intelligent man;
The eyes of the dullard range to the ends of the earth.
25 A stupid son is vexation for his father
And a heartache for the woman who bore him.
26 To punish the innocent is surely not right,
Or to flog the great for their uprightness.
27 A knowledgeable man is sparing with his words;
A man of understanding is reticent.
28 Even a fool, if he keeps silent, is deemed wise;
Intelligent, if he seals his lips.

18 *a*-He who isolates himself pursues his desires;
He disdains all competence.-*a*
2 The fool does not desire understanding,
But only to air his thoughts.
3 Comes the wicked man comes derision,
And with the rogue, contempt.
4 The words a man speaks are deep waters,
A flowing stream, a fountain of wisdom.
5 It is not right to be partial to the guilty
And subvert the innocent in judgment.
6 The words of a fool lead to strife;
His speech invites blows.
7 The fool's speech is his ruin;
His words are a trap for him.
8 The words of a querulous man are bruising;*a*

b-b *Or "a cheerful face"; meaning of Heb. uncertain.*

a-a *Meaning of Heb. uncertain.*

They penetrate one's inmost parts.

9 One who is slack in his work
Is a brother to a vandal.

10 The name of the LORD is a tower of strength
To which the righteous man runs and is safe.

11 The wealth of a rich man is his fortress;
a-In his fancy-*a* it is a protective wall.

12 Before ruin a man's heart is proud;
Humility goes before honor.

13 To answer a man before hearing him out
Is foolish and disgraceful.

14 A man's spirit can sustain him through illness;
But low spirits—who can bear them?

15 The mind of an intelligent man acquires knowledge;
The ears of the wise seek out knowledge.

16 A man's gift eases his way
And gives him access to the great.

17 The first to plead his case seems right
Till the other party examines him.

18 The lot puts an end to strife
And separates those locked in dispute.

19 A brother offended is more formidable than a stronghold;
Such strife is like the bars of a fortress.

20 A man's belly is filled by the fruit of his mouth;
He will be filled by the produce of his lips.

21 Death and life are in the power of the tongue;
Those who love it will eat its fruit.

22 He who finds a wife has found happiness
And has won the favor of the LORD.

23 The poor man speaks beseechingly;
The rich man's answer is harsh.

24 There are companions to keep one company,
And there is a friend more devoted than a brother.

19 Better a poor man who lives blamelessly
Than one who speaks perversely and is a dullard.
² A person without knowledge is surely not good;
He who moves hurriedly blunders.
³ A man's folly subverts his way,
And his heart rages against the LORD.
⁴ Wealth makes many friends,
But a poor man loses his last friend.
⁵ A false witness will not go unpunished;
He who testifies lies will not escape.
⁶ Many court the favor of a great man,
And all are the friends of a dispenser of gifts.
⁷ All the brothers of a poor man despise him;
How much more is he shunned by his friends!
ᵃ⁻He who pursues words—they are of no avail.⁻ᵃ
⁸ He who acquires wisdom is his own best friend;
He preserves understanding and attains happiness.
⁹ A false witness will not go unpunished;
He who testifies falsely is doomed.
¹⁰ Luxury is not fitting for a dullard,
Much less that a servant rule over princes.
¹¹ A man shows intelligence by his forebearance;
It is his glory when he overlooks an offense.
¹² The rage of a king is like the roar of a lion;
His favor is like dew upon the grass.
¹³ A stupid son is a calamity to his father;
The nagging of a wife is like the endless dripping of water.
¹⁴ Property and riches are bequeathed by fathers,
But an efficient wife comes from the LORD.
¹⁵ Laziness induces sleep,
And a negligent person will go hungry.
¹⁶ He who has regard for his life pays regard to commandments;

ᵃ⁻ᵃ *Meaning of Heb. uncertain.*

He who is heedless of his ways will die.
¹⁷ He who is generous to the poor makes a loan to the
LORD;
He will repay him his due.
¹⁸ Discipline your son while there is still hope,
And^b do not ^{c-}set your heart on his destruction.^{-c}
¹⁹ A hot-tempered man incurs punishment;
^{a-}If you try to save him you will only make it worse.^{-a}
²⁰ Listen to advice and accept discipline
In order that you may be wise in the end.
²¹ Many designs are in a man's mind,
But it is the LORD's plan that is accomplished.
²² ^{a-}Greed is a reproach to a man;^{-a}
Better be poor than a liar.
²³ He who fears the LORD earns life;
^{a-}He shall abide in contentment,^{-a}
Free from misfortune.
²⁴ The lazy man buries his hand in the bowl;
He will not even bring it to his mouth.
²⁵ Beat the scoffer and the simple will become clever;
Reprove an intelligent man and he gains knowledge.
²⁶ A son who causes shame and disgrace
Plunders his father, puts his mother to flight.
²⁷ My son, cease to stray from words of knowledge
And receive discipline.
²⁸ A malicious witness scoffs at justice,
And the speech of the wicked conceals mischief.
²⁹ Punishments are in store for scoffers
And blows for the backs of dullards.

20 Wine is a scoffer, strong drink a roisterer;
He who is muddled by them will not grow wise.
² The terror of a king is like the roar of a lion;
He who provokes his anger risks his life.

^b or *"But."*
^{c-c} or *"pay attention to his moaning."*

³ It is honorable for a man to desist from strife,
But every fool *a*-becomes embroiled.-*a*
⁴ In winter the lazy man does not plow;
At harvesttime he seeks, and finds nothing.
⁵ The designs in a man's mind are deep waters,
But a man of understanding can draw them out.
⁶ He calls many a man his loyal friend,
But who can find a faithful man?
⁷ The righteous man lives blamelessly;
Happy are his children who come after him.
⁸ The king seated on the throne of judgment
Can winnow out all evil by his glance.
⁹ Who can say, "I have cleansed my heart,
I am purged of my sin"?
¹⁰ False weights and false measures,
Both are an abomination to the Lord.
¹¹ A child may be dissembling in his behavior
Even though his actions are blameless and proper.
¹² The ear that hears, the eye that sees—
The Lord made them both.
¹³ Do not love sleep lest you be impoverished;
Keep your eyes open and you will have plenty of food.
¹⁴ "Bad, bad," says the buyer,
But having moved off, he congratulates himself.
¹⁵ Gold is plentiful, jewels abundant,
But wise speech is a precious object.
¹⁶ Seize his garment, for he stood surety for another;*b*
Take it as a pledge, [for he stood surety] for an unfamiliar
  woman.
¹⁷ Bread gained by fraud may be tasty to a man,
But later his mouth will be filled with gravel.
¹⁸ Plans laid in council will succeed;
Wage war with stratagems.
¹⁹ He who gives away secrets is a base fellow;
Do not take up with a garrulous man.

a-a *Meaning of Heb. uncertain.*
b *Or "a stranger."*

20 One who reviles his father or mother,
Light will fail him when darkness comes.
21 An estate acquired in haste at the outset
Will not be blessed in the end.
22 Do not say, "I will requite evil";
Put your hope in the LORD and He will deliver you.
23 False weights are an abomination to the LORD;
Dishonest scales are not right.
24 A man's steps are decided by the LORD;
What does a man know about his own way?
25 It is a snare for a man *a*-to pledge a sacred gift rashly-*a*
And to give thought to his vows only after they have been
    made.
26 A wise king winnows out the wicked,
And turns the wheel upon them.
27 The lifebreath of man is the lamp of the LORD
Revealing all his inmost parts.
28 Faithfulness and loyalty protect the king;
He maintains his throne by faithfulness.
29 The glory of youths is their strength;
The majesty of old men is their gray hair.
30 Bruises and wounds are repayment*a* for evil,
Striking at one's inmost parts.

21 Like channeled water is the mind of the king in the LORD's
    hand;
He directs it to whatever He wishes.
2 All the ways of a man seem right to him,
But the LORD probes the mind.
3 To do what is right and just
Is more desired by the LORD than sacrifice.
4 Haughty looks, a proud heart—
The tillage of the wicked is sinful.
5 The plans of the diligent make only for gain;

All rash haste makes only for loss.

6 Treasures acquired by a lying tongue
-Are like driven vapor, heading for extinction.

7 The violence of the wicked sweeps them away,
For they refuse to act justly.

8 The way of a man may be tortuous and strange,
Though his actions are blameless and proper.

9 Dwelling in the corner of a roof is better
Than a contentious wife in a *-spacious house.*

10 The desire of the wicked is set upon evil;
His fellowman finds no favor in his eyes.

11 When a scoffer is punished, the simple man is edified;
When a wise man is taught, he gains insight.

12 The Righteous One observes the house of the wicked
man;
He subverts the wicked to their ruin.

13 Who stops his ears at the cry of the wretched,
He too will call and not be answered.

14 A gift in secret subdues anger,
A present in private, fierce rage.

15 Justice done is a joy to the righteous,
To evildoers, ruination.

16 A man who strays from the path of prudence
Will rest in the company of ghosts.

17 He who loves pleasure comes to want;
He who loves wine and oil does not grow rich.

18 The wicked are the ransom of the righteous;
The traitor comes in place of the upright.

19 It is better to live in the desert
Than with a contentious, vexatious wife.

20 Precious treasure and oil are in the house of the wise
man,
And a fool of a man will run through them.

21 He who strives to do good and kind deeds
Attains life, success, and honor.

22 One wise man prevailed over a city of warriors

a-a *Meaning of Heb. uncertain.*

And brought down its mighty stronghold.
23 He who guards his mouth and tongue
Guards himself from trouble.
24 The proud, insolent man, scoffer is his name,
Acts in a frenzy of insolence.
25 The craving of a lazy man kills him,
For his hands refuse to work.
26 All day long he is seized with craving
While the righteous man gives without stint.
27 The sacrifice of the wicked man is an abomination,
The more so as he offers it in depravity.
28 A false witness is doomed,
But one who really heard will testify with success.
29 The wicked man is brazen-faced;
The upright man discerns his course.
30 No wisdom, no prudence, and no counsel
Can prevail against the LORD.
31 The horse is readied for the day of battle,
But victory comes from the LORD.

22 Repute is preferable to great wealth,
Grace is better than silver and gold.
2 Rich man and poor man meet;
The LORD made them both.
3 The shrewd man saw trouble and took cover;
The simple kept going and paid the penalty.
4 The effect of humility is fear of the LORD,
Wealth, honor, and life.
5 Thorns and snares are in the path of the crooked;
He who values his life will keep far from them.
6 Train a lad in the way he ought to go;
He will not swerve from it even in old age.
7 The rich rule the poor,
And the borrower is a slave to the lender.
8 He who sows injustice shall reap misfortune;

His rod of wrath shall fail.

⁹ The generous man is blessed,
For he gives of his bread to the poor.

¹⁰ Expel the scoffer and contention departs,
Quarrel and contumely cease.

¹¹ A pure-hearted friend,
His speech is gracious;
He has the king for his companion.

¹² The eyes of the LORD watch the wise man;
He subverts the words of the treacherous.

¹³ The lazy man says, "There's a lion in the street;
I shall be killed *-if I step outside."-*

¹⁴ The mouth of a forbidden*ᵇ* woman is a deep pit;
He who is doomed by the LORD falls into it.

¹⁵ If folly settles in the heart of a lad,
The rod of discipline will remove it.

¹⁶ To profit by withholding what is due to the poor
Is like making gifts to the rich—pure loss.

¹⁷ Incline your ear and listen to the words of the sages;
Pay attention to my wisdom.

¹⁸ It is good that you store them inside you,
And that all of them be constantly on your lips,

¹⁹ That you may put your trust in the LORD.
I let you know today—yes, you—

²⁰ Indeed, I wrote down for you ᶜ-a threefold lore,-ᶜ
Wise counsel,

²¹ To let you know truly reliable words,
That you may give a faithful reply to him who sent you.

²² Do not rob the wretched because he is wretched;
Do not crush the poor man in the gate;

²³ For the LORD will take up their cause
And despoil those who despoil them of life.

²⁴ Do not associate with an irascible man,
Or go about with one who is hot-tempered,

²⁵ Lest you learn his ways

ᵃ⁻ᵃ *Lit. "in the square."*
ᵇ *Lit. "strange."*
ᶜ⁻ᶜ *Meaning of Heb. uncertain.*

And find yourself ensnared.
²⁶ Do not be one of those who give their hand,
Who stand surety for debts,
²⁷ Lest your bed be taken from under you
When you have no money to pay.
²⁸ Do not remove the ancient boundary stone
That your ancestors set up.
²⁹ See a man skilled at his work—
He shall attend upon kings;
He shall not attend upon ᶜobscure men.ᶜ

23 When you sit down to dine with a ruler,
Consider well who is before you.
² Thrust a knife into your gullet
If you have a large appetite.
³ Do not crave for his dainties,
For they are counterfeit food.

⁴ Do not toil to gain wealth;
Have the sense to desist.
⁵ You see it, then it is gone;
It grows wings and flies away,
Like an eagle, heavenward.

⁶ Do not eat of a stingy man's food;
Do not crave for his dainties;
⁷ He is like one keeping accounts;
"Eat and drink," he says to you,
But he does not really mean it.
⁸ The morsel you eat you will vomit;
You will waste your courteous words.

⁹ Do not speak to a dullard,
For he will disdain your sensible words.

¹⁰ Do not remove ancient boundary stones;
Do not encroach upon the field of orphans,
¹¹ For they have a mighty kinsman,
And He will surely take up their cause with you.

¹² Apply your mind to discipline
And your ears to wise sayings.
¹³ Do not withhold discipline from a child;
If you beat him with a rod he will not die.
¹⁴ Beat him with a rod
And you will save him from the grave.

¹⁵ My son, if your mind gets wisdom,
My mind, too, will be gladdened.
¹⁶ I shall rejoice with all my heart*a*
When your lips speak right things.
¹⁷ Do not envy sinners in your heart,
But only God-fearing men, at all times,
¹⁸ For then you will have a future,
And your hope will never fail.

¹⁹ Listen, my son, and get wisdom;
Lead your mind in a proper path.
²⁰ Do not be of those who guzzle wine,
Or glut themselves on meat;
²¹ For guzzlers and gluttons will be impoverished,
And drowsing will clothe you in tatters.

²² Listen to your father who begot you;
Do not disdain your mother when she is old.
²³ Buy truth and never sell it,
And wisdom, discipline, and understanding.
²⁴ The father of a righteous man will exult;
He who begets a wise son will rejoice in him.
²⁵ Your father and mother will rejoice;
She who bore you will exult.

ᵃ *Lit. "kidneys."*

²⁶ Give your mind to me, my son;
Let your eyes watch my ways.
²⁷ A harlot is a deep pit;
A forbidden[b] woman is a narrow well.
²⁸ She too lies in wait as if for prey,
And destroys the unfaithful among men.

²⁹ Who cries, "Woe!" who, "Alas!";
Who has quarrels, who complaints;
Who has wounds without cause;
Who has bleary eyes?
³⁰ Those whom wine keeps till the small hours,
Those who gather to drain the cups.
³¹ Do not ogle that red wine
As it lends its color to the cup,
As it flows on smoothly;
³² In the end, it bites like a snake;
It spits like a basilisk.
³³ Your eyes will see strange sights;
Your heart[c] will speak distorted things.
³⁴ You will be like one lying in bed on high seas,
Like one lying [d]on top of the rigging.[d]
³⁵ "They struck me, but I felt no hurt;
They beat me, but I was unaware;
As often as I wake,
I go after it again."

24 Do not envy evil men;
Do not desire to be with them;
² For their hearts[a] talk violence,
And their lips speak mischief.

³ A house is built by wisdom,
And is established by understanding;

---

[b] Lit. "alien."
[c] See note to 15.28.
[d-d] Meaning of Heb. uncertain.

[a] See note to 15.28.

4 By knowledge are its rooms filled
With all precious and beautiful things.

5 A wise man is strength;
A knowledgeable man exerts power;
6 For by stratagems you wage war,
And victory comes with much planning.

7 Wisdom is too lofty for a fool;
He does not open his mouth in the gate.
8 He who lays plans to do harm
Is called by men a schemer.
9 The schemes of folly are sin,
And a scoffer is an abomination to men.

10 If you showed yourself slack in time of trouble,
Wanting in power,
11 If you refrained from rescuing those taken off to death,
Those condemned to slaughter—
12 If you say, "We knew nothing of it,"
Surely He who fathoms hearts will discern [the truth],
He who watches over your life will know it,
And He will pay each man as he deserves.

13 My son, eat honey, for it is good;
Let its sweet drops be on your palate.
14 Know: such is wisdom for your soul;
If you attain it, there is a future;
Your hope will not be cut off.

15 Wicked man! Do not lurk by the home of the righteous
man;
Do no violence to his dwelling.
16 Seven times the righteous man falls and gets up,
While the wicked are tripped by one misfortune.

17 If your enemy falls, do not exult;
If he trips, let your heart not rejoice,
18 Lest the LORD see it and be displeased,
And avert His wrath from him.

19 Do not be vexed by evildoers;
Do not be incensed by the wicked;
20 For there is no future for the evil man;
The lamp of the wicked goes out.

21 Fear the LORD, my son, and the king,
And do not mix with dissenters,
22 For disaster comes from them suddenly;
The doom both decree who can foreknow?

23 These also are by the sages:

It is not right to be partial in judgment.
24 He who says to the guilty, "You are innocent,"
Shall be cursed by peoples,
Damned by nations;
25 But it shall go well with them who decide justly;
Blessings of good things will light upon them.

26 Giving a straightforward reply
Is like giving a kiss.
27 Put your external affairs in order,
Get ready what you have in the field,
Then build yourself a home.
28 Do not be a witness against your fellow without
good cause;
Would you mislead with your speech?

²⁹ Do not say, "I will do to him what he did to me;
I will pay the man what he deserves."

³⁰ I passed by the field of a lazy man,
By the vineyard of a man lacking sense.
³¹ It was all overgrown with thorns;
Its surface was covered with chickweed,
And its stone fence lay in ruins.
³² I observed and took it to heart;
I saw it and learned a lesson.
³³ A bit more sleep, a bit more slumber,
A bit more hugging yourself in bed,
³⁴ And poverty will come ᵇ-calling upon you,-ᵇ
And want, like a man with a shield.

25

These too are proverbs of Solomon, which the men of King Hezekiah of Judah copied:

² It is the glory of God to conceal a matter,
And the glory of a king to plumb a matter.
³ Like the heavens in their height, like the earth in its
depth,
Is the mind of kings—unfathomable.
⁴ The dross having been separated from the silver,
A vessel emerged for the smith.
⁵ Remove the wicked from the king's presence,
And his throne will be established in justice.
⁶ Do not exalt yourself in the king's presence;
Do not stand in the place of nobles.
⁷ For it is better to be told, "Step up here,"
Than to be degraded in the presence of the great.

Do not let what your eyes have seen
⁸ Be vented rashly in a quarrel;
Thinkᵃ of what it will effect in the end,

ᵇ⁻ᵇ *Meaning of Heb. uncertain.*

ᵃ *Lit. "Lest."*

When your fellow puts you to shame.
⁹ Defend your right against your fellow,
But do not give away the secrets of another,
¹⁰ Lest he who hears it reproach you,
And your bad repute never end.

¹¹ Like golden apples in silver showpieces*b*
Is a phrase well turned.
¹² Like a ring of gold, a golden ornament,
Is a wise man's reproof in a receptive ear.
¹³ Like the coldness of snow at harvesttime
Is a trusty messenger to those who send him;
He lifts his master's spirits.
¹⁴ Like clouds, wind—but no rain—
Is one who boasts of gifts not given.
¹⁵ Through forebearance a ruler may be won over;
A gentle tongue can break bones.
¹⁶ If you find honey, eat only what you need,
Lest, surfeiting yourself, you throw it up.
¹⁷ Visit your neighbor sparingly,
Lest he have his surfeit of you and loathe you.
¹⁸ Like a club, a sword, a sharpened arrow,
Is a man who testifies falsely against his fellow.
¹⁹ Like a loose tooth and an unsteady leg
Are a treacherous support in time of trouble.
²⁰ Disrobing on a chilly day,
Like vinegar on natron,
Is one who sings songs to a sorrowful soul.

²¹ If your enemy is hungry, give him bread to eat;
If he is thirsty, give him water to drink.
²² You will be heaping live coals on his head,
And the LORD will reward you.

²³ A north wind produces rain,
And whispered words, a glowering face.

b Meaning of Heb. uncertain.

²⁴ Dwelling in the corner of a roof is better
Than a contentious woman in *ᵇ*a spacious house.⁻ᵇ
²⁵ Like cold water to a parched throat
Is good news from a distant land.
²⁶ Like a muddied spring, a ruined fountain,
Is a righteous man fallen before a wicked one.
²⁷ It is not good to eat much honey,
*ᵇ*Nor is it honorable to search for honor.⁻ᵇ
²⁸ Like an open city without walls
Is a man whose temper is uncurbed.

26

Like snow in summer and rain at harvesttime,
So honor is not fitting for a dullard.
² As a sparrow must flit and a swallow fly,
So a gratuitous curse must backfire.*ᵃ*
³ A whip for a horse and a bridle for a donkey,
And a rod for the back of dullards.
⁴ Do not answer a dullard in accord with his folly,
Else you will become like him.
⁵ Answer a dullard in accord with his folly,
Else he will think himself wise.
⁶ He who sends a message by a dullard
Will wear out legs and *ᵇ*must put up with⁻ᵇ lawlessness.
⁷ As legs hang limp on a cripple,
So is a proverb in the mouth of dullards.
⁸ Like a pebble in a sling,
So is paying honor to a dullard.
⁹ As a thorn comes to the hand of a drunkard,
So a proverb to the mouth of a dullard.
¹⁰ *ᶜ*A master can produce anything,⁻ᶜ
But he who hires a dullard is as one who hires transients.*ᶜ*
¹¹ As a dog returns to his vomit,
So a dullard repeats his folly.
¹² If you see a man who thinks himself wise,
There is more hope for a dullard than for him.

ᵃ *Kethib, "fail."*
ᵇ⁻ᵇ *Lit. "drink."*
ᶜ⁻ᶜ *Meaning of Heb. uncertain.*

13 A lazy man says,
"There's a cub on the road, a lion in the squares."
14 The door turns on its hinge,
And the lazy man on his bed.
15 The lazy man buries his hand in the bowl;
He will not even bring it to his mouth.
16 The lazy man thinks himself wiser
Than seven men who give good advice.

17 A passerby who gets embroiled in someone else's
quarrel
Is like one who seizes a dog by its ears.
18 Like a madman^c scattering deadly firebrands, arrows,
19 Is one who cheats his fellow and says, "I was only
joking."

20 For lack of wood a fire goes out,
And without a querulous man contention is stilled.
21 Charcoal for embers and wood for a fire
And a contentious man for kindling strife.
22 The words of a querulous man are bruising;^c
They penetrate one's inmost parts.

23 Base silver laid over earthenware
Are ardent lips with an evil mind.
24 An enemy dissembles with his speech,
Inwardly he harbors deceit.
25 Though he be fair-spoken do not trust him,
For seven abominations are in his mind.
26 His hatred may be concealed by dissimulation,
But his evil will be exposed to public view.

27 He who digs a pit will fall in it,
And whoever rolls a stone, it will roll back on him.
28 A lying tongue hates ^cthose crushed by it;^{-c}
Smooth speech throws one down.

27 Do not boast of tomorrow,
For you do not know what the day will bring.
² Let the mouth of another praise you, not yours,
The lips of a stranger, not your own.
³ A stone has weight, sand is heavy,
But a fool's vexation outweighs them both.
⁴ There is the cruelty of fury, the overflowing of anger,
But who can withstand jealousy?
⁵ Open reproof is better than concealed love.
⁶ Wounds by a loved one are long lasting;
The kisses of an enemy are profuse.
⁷ A sated person disdains honey,
But to a hungry man anything bitter seems sweet.
⁸ Like a sparrow wandering from its nest
Is a man who wanders from his home.
⁹ Oil and incense gladden the heart,
And the sweetness of a friend is better than one's own
counsel.
¹⁰ Do not desert your friend and your father's friend;
Do not enter your brother's house in your time of
misfortune;
A close neighbor is better than a distant brother.
¹¹ Get wisdom, my son, and gladden my heart,
That I may have what to answer those who taunt me.
¹² The shrewd man saw trouble and took cover;
The simple kept going and paid the penalty.
¹³ Seize his garment, for he stood surety for another;ᵃ
Take it as a pledge, [for he stood surety] for an unfamiliar
woman.
¹⁴ He who greets his fellow loudly early in the morning
Shall have it reckoned to him as a curse.
¹⁵ An endless dripping on a rainy day
And a contentious wife are alike;
¹⁶ As soon repress her as repress the wind,

ᵃ Or "a stranger."

248

Or declare one's right hand to be oil.
¹⁷ As iron sharpens iron
So a man sharpens the wit*^b* of his friend.
¹⁸ He who tends a fig tree will enjoy its fruit,
And he who cares for his master will be honored.
¹⁹ As face answers to face in water,
So does one man's heart to another.
²⁰ Sheol and Abaddon cannot be satisfied,
Nor can the eyes of man be satisfied.
²¹ For silver—the crucible, for gold—the furnace,
And a man is tested by his praise.
²² Even if you pound the fool in a mortar
With a pestle along with grain,
His folly will not leave him.

²³ Mind well the looks of your flock;
Pay attention to your herds;
²⁴ For property does not last forever,
Or a crown for all generations.
²⁵ Grass vanishes, new grass appears,
And the herbage of the hills is gathered in.
²⁶ The lambs will provide you with clothing,
The he-goats, the price of a field.
²⁷ The goats' milk will suffice for your food,
The food of your household,
And the maintenance of your maids.

28 The wicked flee though no one gives chase,
But the righteous are as confident as a lion.
² When there is rebellion in the land, many are its rulers;
^a-But with a man who has understanding and knowledge,
stability will last.-*^a*
³ A poor man who withholds what is due to the wretched
Is like a destructive rain that leaves no food.
⁴ Those who forsake instruction praise the wicked,

^b *Lit. "face."*

^{a-a} *Meaning of Heb. uncertain.*

But those who heed instruction fight them.
⁵ Evil men cannot discern judgment,
But those who seek the LORD discern all things.
⁶ Better is a poor man who lives blamelessly
Than a rich man whose ways are crooked.
⁷ An intelligent son heeds instruction,
But he who keeps company with gluttons disgraces his
    father.
⁸ He who increases his wealth by loans at discount or
    interest
Amasses it for one who is generous to the poor.
⁹ He who turns a deaf ear to instruction—
His prayer is an abomination.
¹⁰ He who misleads the upright into an evil course
Will fall into his own pit,
But the blameless will prosper.
¹¹ A rich man is clever in his own eyes,
But a perceptive poor man can see through him.
¹² When the righteous exult there is great glory,
But when the wicked rise up men make themselves scarce.
¹³ He who covers up his faults will not succeed;
He who confesses and gives them up will find mercy.
¹⁴ Happy is the man who is anxious always,
But he who hardens his heart falls into misfortune.
¹⁵ A roaring lion and a prowling bear
Is a wicked man ruling a helpless people.
¹⁶ A prince who lacks understanding is very oppressive;
He who spurns ill-gotten gains will live long.
¹⁷ A man oppressed by bloodguilt will flee to a pit;
Let none give him support.
¹⁸ He who lives blamelessly will be delivered,
But he who is crooked in his ways will fall all at once.
¹⁹ He who tills his land will have food in plenty,
But he who pursues vanities will have poverty in plenty.
²⁰ A dependable man will receive many blessings,

But one in a hurry to get rich will not go unpunished.
²¹ To be partial is not right;
A man may do wrong for a piece of bread.
²² A miserly man runs after wealth;
He does not realize that loss will overtake it.
²³ He who reproves a man will in the end
Find more favor than he who flatters him.
²⁴ He who robs his father and mother and says,
"It is no offense,"
Is a companion to vandals.
²⁵ A greedy man provokes quarrels,
But he who trusts the Lord shall enjoy prosperity.
²⁶ He who trusts his own instinct is a dullard,
But he who lives by wisdom shall escape.
²⁷ He who gives to the poor will not be in want,
But he who shuts his eyes will be roundly cursed.
²⁸ When the wicked rise up, men go into hiding,
But when they perish the righteous increase.

29 One oft reproved may become stiff-necked,
But he will be suddenly broken beyond repair.
² When the righteous become great the people rejoice,
But when the wicked dominate the people groan.
³ A man who loves wisdom brings joy to his father,
But he who keeps company with harlots will lose
   his wealth.
⁴ By justice a king sustains the land,
But a fraudulent man tears it down.
⁵ A man who flatters his fellow
Spreads a net for his feet.
⁶ An evil man's offenses are a trap for himself,
But the righteous sing out joyously.
⁷ A righteous man is concerned with the cause of
   the wretched;

A wicked man cannot understand such concern.
⁸ Scoffers inflame a city,
But the wise allay anger.
⁹ When a wise man enters into litigation with a fool
There is ranting and ridicule, but no satisfaction.
¹⁰ Bloodthirsty men detest the blameless,
But the upright seek them out.
¹¹ A dullard vents all his rage,
But a wise man calms it down.
¹² A ruler who listens to lies,
All his ministers will be wicked.
¹³ A poor man and a fraudulent man meet;
The LORD gives luster to the eyes of both.
¹⁴ A king who judges the wretched honestly,
His throne will be established forever.
¹⁵ Rod and reproof produce wisdom,
But a lad out of control is a disgrace to his mother.
¹⁶ When the wicked increase, offenses increase,
But the righteous will see their downfall.
¹⁷ Discipline your son and he will give you peace;
He will gratify you with dainties.
¹⁸ For lack of vision a people lose restraint,
But happy is he who heeds instruction.
¹⁹ A slave cannot be disciplined by words;
Though he may comprehend, he does not respond.
²⁰ If you see a man hasty in speech,
There is more hope for a fool than for him.
²¹ A slave pampered from youth
ᵃ-Will come to a bad end.-ᵃ
²² An angry man provokes a quarrel;
A hot-tempered man commits many offenses
²³ A man's pride will humiliate him,
But a humble man will obtain honor.
²⁴ He who shares with a thief is his own enemy;
He hears the imprecation and does not tell.ᵇ
²⁵ A man's fears become a trap for him,

ᵃ⁻ᵃ *Meaning of Heb. uncertain.*
ᵇ *Cf. Lev. 5.1.*

But he who trusts in the LORD shall be safeguarded.
26 Many seek audience with a ruler,
But it is from the LORD that a man gets justice.
27 The unjust man is an abomination to the righteous,
And he whose way is straight is an abomination to the
wicked.

30 The words of Agur son of Jakeh, [man of] Massa;
The speech of the man to Ithiel, to Ithiel and Ucal:

2 I am brutish, less than a man;
I lack common sense.
3 I have not learned wisdom,
Nor do I possess knowledge of the Holy One.
4 Who has ascended heaven and come down?
Who has gathered up the wind in the hollow of his hand?
Who has wrapped the waters in his garment?
Who has established all the extremities of the earth?
What is his name or his son's name, if you know it?

5 Every word of God is pure,
A shield to those who take refuge in Him.
6 Do not add to His words,
Lest He indict you and you be proved a liar.

7 Two things I ask of you; do not deny them to me before
I die:
8 Keep lies and false words far from me;
Give me neither poverty nor riches,
But provide me with my daily bread,
9 Lest, being sated, I renounce, saying,
"Who is the LORD?"
Or, being impoverished, I take to theft
And profane*a* the name of my God.

---

a Meaning of Heb. uncertain.

¹⁰ Do not inform on a slave to his master,
Lest he curse you and you incur guilt.

¹¹ There is a breed of men that brings a curse on its fathers
And brings no blessing to its mothers,
¹² A breed that thinks itself pure,
Though it is not washed of its filth;
¹³ A breed so haughty of bearing, so supercilious;
¹⁴ A breed whose teeth are swords,
Whose jaws are knives,
Ready to devour the poor of the land,
The needy among men.

¹⁵ The leech has two daughters, "Give!" and "Give!"
Three things are insatiable;
Four never say, "Enough!":
¹⁶ Sheol, a barren womb,
Earth that cannot get enough water,
And fire which never says, "Enough!"

¹⁷ The eye that mocks a father
And disdains the homage due a mother—
The ravens of the brook will gouge it out,
Young eagles will devour it.

¹⁸ Three things are beyond me;
Four I cannot fathom:
¹⁹ How an eagle makes its way over the sky;
How a snake makes its way over a rock;
How a ship makes its way through the high seas;
How a man has his way with a maiden.
²⁰ Such is the way of an adulteress:
She eats, wipes her mouth,
And says, "I have done no wrong."

21 The earth shudders at three things,
At four which it cannot bear:
22 A slave who becomes king;
A scoundrel sated with food;
23 A loathsome woman who gets married;
A slave-girl who supplants her mistress.

24 Four are among the tiniest on earth,
Yet they are the wisest of the wise:
25 Ants are a folk without power,
Yet they prepare food for themselves in summer;
26 The badger is a folk without strength,
Yet it makes its home in the rock;
27 The locusts have no king,
Yet they all march forth in formation;
28 You can catch the lizard[b] in your hand,
Yet it is found in royal palaces.

29 There are three that are stately of stride,
Four that carry themselves well:
30 The lion is mightiest among the beasts,
And recoils before none;
31 [a]-The greyhound, the he-goat,
The king whom none dares resist.-[a]

32 If you have been scandalously arrogant,
If you have been a schemer,
Then clap your hand to your mouth.
33 As milk under pressure produces butter,
And a nose under pressure produces blood,
So patience under pressure produces strife.

b Or "spider."

31 The words of Lemuel, king of Massa, with which his mother admonished him:

> ² No, my son!
> No, O son of my womb!
> No, O son of my vows!
> ³ Do not give your strength to women,
> Your vigor,ᵃ ᵇ⁻to those who destroy kings.⁻ᵇ
> ⁴ Wine is not for kings, O Lemuel;
> Not for kings to drink,
> Nor any strong drink for princes,
> ⁵ Lest they drink and forget what has been ordained,
> And infringe on the rights of the poor.
> ⁶ Give strong drink to the hapless
> And wine to the embittered.
> ⁷ Let them drink and forget their poverty,
> And put their troubles out of mind.
> ⁸ Speak up for the dumb,
> For the rights of all the unfortunate.
> ⁹ Speak up, judge righteously,
> Champion the poor and the needy.

> א   ¹⁰ What a rare find is a capable wife!
> Her worth is far beyond that of rubies.
> ב   ¹¹ Her husband puts his confidence in her,
> And lacks no good thing.
> ג   ¹² She is good to him, never bad,
> All the days of her life.
> ד   ¹³ She looks for wool and flax,
> And sets her hand to them with a will.
> ה   ¹⁴ She is like a merchant fleet,
> Bringing her food from afar.
> ו   ¹⁵ She rises while it is still night,
> And supplies provisions for her household,

ᵃ *Lit. "ways."*
ᵇ⁻ᵇ *Meaning of Heb. uncertain.*

The daily fare of her maids.

ז 16 She sets her mind on an estate and acquires it;
She plants a vineyard by her own labors.

ח 17 She girds herself with strength,
c-And performs her tasks with vigor.*c*

ט 18 She sees*d* that her business thrives;
Her lamp never goes out at night.

י 19 She sets her hand to the distaff;
Her fingers work the spindle.

כ 20 She gives generously to the poor;
Her hands are stretched out to the needy.

ל 21 She is not worried for her household because of snow,
For her whole household is dressed in crimson.

מ 22 She makes covers for herself;
Her clothing is linen and purple.

נ 23 Her husband is prominent in the gates,
As he sits among the elders of the land.

ס 24 She makes cloth and sells it,
And offers a girdle to the merchant.

ע 25 She is clothed with strength and splendor;
She looks to the future cheerfully.

פ 26 Her mouth is full of wisdom,
Her tongue with kindly teaching.

צ 27 She oversees the activities of her household
And never eats the bread of idleness.

ק 28 Her children declare her happy;
Her husband praises her,

ר 29 "Many women have done well,
But you surpass them all."

ש 30 Grace is deceptive,
Beauty is illusory;
It is for her fear of the LORD
That a woman is to be praised.

ת 31 Extol her for the fruit of her hand,
And let her works praise her in the gates.

c-c Lit. "And exerts her arms."
d Lit. "tastes."

איוב

JOB

אִיוֹב
JOB

1 There was a man in the land of Uz named Job. That man was blameless and upright; he feared God and shunned evil. ² Seven sons and three daughters‧ were born to him; ³ his possessions were seven thousand sheep, three thousand camels, five hundred yoke of oxen and five hundred she-asses, and a very large household. That man was wealthier than anyone in the East.

⁴ It was the custom of his sons to hold feasts, each on his set day in his own home. They would invite their three sisters to eat and drink with them. ⁵ When a round of feast days was over, Job would send word to them to sanctify themselves, and, rising early in the morning, he would make burnt offerings, one for each of them; for Job thought, "Perhaps my children have sinned and blasphemed God in their thoughts." This is what Job always used to do.

⁶ One day the divine beings presented themselves before the LORD, ᵃ⁻and the Adversary⁻ᵃ came along with them. ⁷ The LORD said to the Adversary, "Where have you been?" The Adversary answered the LORD, "I have been roaming all over the earth." ⁸ The LORD said to the Adversary, "Have you noticed My servant Job? There is no one like him on earth, a blameless and upright man who fears God and shuns evil!" ⁹ The Adversary answered the LORD, "Does Job not have good reason to fear God? ¹⁰ Why, it is You who have fenced him round, him and his household and all that he has. You have blessed his efforts so that his possessions spread out in the land. ¹¹ But lay Your hand upon all that he has and he will surely blaspheme You to Your face." ¹² The LORD replied to the Adversary, "See, all that he has is in your power;

ᵃ⁻ᵃ *Heb.* ha-saṭan.

only do not lay a hand on him." The Adversary departed from the presence of the LORD.

¹³ One day, as his sons and daughters were eating and drinking wine in the house of their eldest brother, ¹⁴ a messenger came to Job and said, "The oxen were plowing and the she-asses were grazing alongside them ¹⁵ when Sabeans attacked them and carried them off, and put the boys to the sword; I alone have escaped to tell you." ¹⁶ This one was still speaking when another came and said, "God's fire fell from heaven, took hold of the sheep and the boys, and burned them up; I alone have escaped to tell you." ¹⁷ This one was still speaking when another came and said, "A Chaldean formation of three columns made a raid on the camels and carried them off and put the boys to the sword; I alone have escaped to tell you." ¹⁸ This one was still speaking when another came and said, "Your sons and daughters were eating and drinking wine in the house of their eldest brother ¹⁹ when suddenly a mighty wind came from the wilderness. It struck the four corners of the house so that it collapsed upon the young people and they died; I alone have escaped to tell you."

²⁰ Then Job arose, tore his robe, cut off his hair, and threw himself on the ground and worshiped. ²¹ He said, "Naked came I out of my mother's womb, and naked shall I return there; the LORD has given, and the LORD has taken away; blessed be the name of the LORD."

²² For all that, Job did not sin nor did he cast reproach on God.

2 One day the divine beings presented themselves before the LORD. The Adversary came along with them to present himself before the LORD. ² The LORD said to the Adversary, "Where have you been?" The Adversary answered the LORD, "I have been roaming all over the earth." ³ The LORD said to the Adversary, "Have you noticed My servant Job? There is no one like him on earth, a blameless and upright man who fears God and shuns evil. He still keeps his integrity; so you have incited Me against him

to destroy him for no good reason." ⁴ The Adversary answered the LORD, ᵃ-"Skin for skin-ᵃ—all that a man has he will give up for his life. ⁵ But lay a hand on his bones and his flesh, and he will surely blaspheme You to Your face." ⁶ So the LORD said to the Adversary, "See, he is in your power; only spare his life." ⁷ The Adversary departed from the presence of the LORD and inflicted a severe inflammation on Job from the sole of his foot to the crown of his head. ⁸ He took a potsherd to scratch himself as he sat in ashes. ⁹ His wife said to him, "You still keep your integrity! Blaspheme God and die!" ¹⁰ But he said to her, "You talk as any shameless woman might talk! Should we accept only good from God and not accept evil?" For all that, Job said nothing sinful.

¹¹ When Job's three friends heard about all these calamities that had befallen him, each came from his home—Eliphaz the Temanite, Bildad the Shuhite, and Zophar the Naamathite. They met together to go and console and comfort him. ¹² When they saw him from a distance, they could not recognize him, and they broke into loud weeping; each one tore his robe and threw dust into the air onto his head. ¹³ They sat with him on the ground seven days and seven nights. None spoke a word to him for they saw how very great was his suffering.

3 ᵃAfterward, Job began to speak and cursed the day of his birth. ² Job spoke up and said:

³ Perish the day on which I was born,
And the night it was announced,
"A male has been conceived!"
⁴ May that day be darkness;
May God above have no concern for it;
May light not shine on it;
⁵ May darkness and deep gloom reclaim it;
May a pall lie over it;
May ᵇ-what blackens-ᵇ the day terrify it.

ᵃ⁻ᵃ Apparently a proverb whose meaning is uncertain.

ᵃ There are many difficulties in the poetry of Job, making the interpretation of words, verses, and even chapters uncertain. The rubric "Meaning of Heb. uncertain" in this book indicates only some of the extreme instances.

ᵇ⁻ᵇ Meaning of Heb. uncertain.

⁶ May obscurity carry off that night;
May it not be counted among the days of the year;
May it not appear in any of its months;
⁷ May that night be desolate;
May no sound of joy be heard in it;
⁸ May those who cast spells upon the day^c damn it,
Those prepared to disable Leviathan;
⁹ May its twilight stars remain dark;
May it hope for light and have none;
May it not see the glimmerings of the dawn—
¹⁰ Because it did not block my mother's womb,
And hide trouble from my eyes.

¹¹ Why did I not die at birth,
Expire as I came forth from the womb?
¹² Why were there knees to receive me,
Or breasts for me to suck?
¹³ For now would I be lying in repose, asleep and at rest,
¹⁴ With the world's kings and counselors who rebuild ruins
for themselves,
¹⁵ Or with nobles who possess gold and who fill their
houses with silver.
¹⁶ Or why was I not like a buried stillbirth,
Like babies who never saw the light?
¹⁷ There the wicked cease from troubling;
There rest those whose strength is spent.
¹⁸ Prisoners are wholly at ease;
They do not hear the taskmaster's voice.
¹⁹ Small and great alike are there,
And the slave is free of his master.

²⁰ Why does He give light to the sufferer
And life to the bitter in spirit;
²¹ To those who wait for death but it does not come,
Who search for it more than for treasure,

---

^c Or "sea," taking Heb. yom as equivalent of yam; compare the combination of sea with
Leviathan in Ps. 74.13, 14 and with Dragon in Job 7.12; cf. also Isa. 27.1.

²² Who rejoice to exultation,
And are glad to reach the grave;
²³ To the man who has lost his way,
Whom God has hedged about?

²⁴ My groaning serves as my bread;
My roaring pours forth as water.
²⁵ For what I feared has overtaken me;
What I dreaded has come upon me.
²⁶ I had no repose, no quiet, no rest,
And trouble came.

4 Then Eliphaz the Temanite said in reply:

² If one ventures a word with you, will it be too much?
But who can hold back his words?
³ See, you have encouraged many;
You have strengthened failing hands.
⁴ Your words have kept him who stumbled from falling;
You have braced knees that gave way.
⁵ But now that it overtakes you, it is too much;
It reaches you, and you are unnerved.
⁶ Is not your piety your confidence,
Your integrity your hope?
⁷ Think now, what innocent man ever perished?
Where have the upright been destroyed?
⁸ As I have seen, those who plow evil
And sow mischief reap them.
⁹ They perish by a blast from God,
Are gone at the breath of His nostrils.
¹⁰ The lion may roar, the cub may howl,
But the teeth of the king of beasts ᵃ-are broken.-ᵃ
¹¹ The lion perishes for lack of prey,
And its whelps are scattered.

ᵃ-ᵃ *Meaning of Heb. uncertain.*

¹² A word came to me in stealth;
My ear caught a whisper of it.
¹³ In thought-filled visions of the night,
When deep sleep falls on men,
¹⁴ Fear and trembling came upon me,
Causing all my bones to quake with fright.
¹⁵ A wind passed by me,
Making the hair of my flesh bristle.
¹⁶ It halted; its appearance was strange to me;
A form loomed before my eyes;
I heard a murmur, a voice,
¹⁷ "Can mortals be acquitted by God?
Can man be cleared by his Maker?
¹⁸ If He cannot trust His own servants,
And casts reproach*ᵃ* on His angels,
¹⁹ How much less those who dwell in houses of clay,
Whose origin is dust,
Who are crushed like the moth,
²⁰ Shattered between daybreak and evening,
Perishing forever, unnoticed.
²¹ Their cord is pulled up
And they die, and not with wisdom."

5   Call now! Will anyone answer you?
To whom among the holy beings will you turn?
² Vexation kills the fool;
Passion slays the simpleton.
³ I myself saw a fool who had struck roots;
Impulsively, I cursed his home:
⁴ May his children be far from success;
May they be oppressed in the gate with none to deliver
     them;
⁵ May the hungry devour his harvest,
ᵃ-Carrying it off in baskets;

ᵃ⁻ᵃ *Meaning of Heb. uncertain.*

May the thirsty swallow their wealth.⁻ᵃ
⁶ Evil does not grow out of the soil,
Nor does mischief spring from the ground;
⁷ For man is born to [do] mischief,
Just as sparks fly upward.

⁸ But I would resort to God;
I would lay my case before God,
⁹ Who performs great deeds which cannot be fathomed,
Wondrous things without number;
¹⁰ Who gives rain to the earth,
And sends water over the fields;
¹¹ Who raises the lowly up high,
So that the dejected are secure in victory;
¹² Who thwarts the designs of the crafty,
So that their hands cannot gain success;
¹³ Who traps the clever in their own wiles;
The plans of the crafty go awry.
¹⁴ By day they encounter darkness,
At noon they grope as in the night.
¹⁵ But He saves the needy from the sword of their mouth,
From the clutches of the strong.
¹⁶ So there is hope for the wretched;
The mouth of wrongdoing is stopped.

¹⁷ See how happy is the man whom God reproves;
Do not reject the discipline of the Almighty.
¹⁸ He injures, but He binds up;
He wounds, but His hands heal.
¹⁹ He will deliver you from six troubles;
In seven no harm will reach you:
²⁰ In famine He will redeem you from death,
In war, from the sword.
²¹ You will be sheltered from the scourging tongue;
You will have no fear when violence comes.

²² You will laugh at violence and starvation,
And have no fear of wild beasts.
²³ For you will have a pact with the rocks in the field,
And the beasts of the field will be your allies.
²⁴ You will know that all is well in your tent;
When you visit your wife*ᵇ* you will never fail.
²⁵ You will see that your offspring are many,
Your descendants like the grass of the earth.
²⁶ You will come to the grave *ᵃ*-in ripe old age,-*ᵃ*
As shocks of grain are taken away in their season.
²⁷ See, we have inquired into this and it is so;
Hear it and accept it.

6 Then Job said in reply:

² If my anguish were weighed,
My full calamity laid on the scales,
³ It would be heavier than the sand of the sea;
That is why I spoke recklessly.*ᵃ*
⁴ For the arrows of the Almighty are in me;
My spirit absorbs their poison;
God's terrors are arrayed against me.
⁵ Does a wild ass bray when he has grass?
Does a bull bellow over his fodder?
⁶ Can what is tasteless be eaten without salt?
Does *ᵃ*-mallow juice-*ᵃ* have any flavor?
⁷ I refuse to touch them;
They are like food when I am sick.

⁸ Would that my request were granted,
That God gave me what I wished for;
⁹ Would that God consented to crush me,
Loosed His hand and cut me off.
¹⁰ Then this would be my consolation,

ᵇ *Lit. "home."*

ᵃ *Meaning of Heb. uncertain.*

a-As I writhed in unsparing-*a* pains:
That I did not *b*-suppress my words against the Holy One.-*b*
¹¹ What strength have I, that I should endure?
How long have I to live, that I should be patient?
¹² Is my strength the strength of rock?
Is my flesh bronze?
¹³ Truly, I cannot help myself;
I have been deprived of resourcefulness.

¹⁴ *a*-A friend owes loyalty to one who fails,
Though he forsakes the fear of the Almighty;-*a*
¹⁵ My comrades are fickle, like a wadi,
Like a bed on which streams once ran.
¹⁶ *a*-They are dark with ice;
Snow obscures them;-*a*
¹⁷ But when they thaw, they vanish;
In the heat, they disappear where they are.
¹⁸ Their course twists and turns;
They run into the desert and perish.
¹⁹ Caravans from Tema look to them;
Processions from Sheba count on them.
²⁰ They are disappointed in their hopes;
When they reach the place, they stand aghast.
²¹ So you are as nothing:*c*
At the sight of misfortune, you take fright.
²² Did I say to you, "I need your gift;
Pay a bribe for me out of your wealth;
²³ Deliver me from the clutches of my enemy;
Redeem me from violent men"?
²⁴ Teach me; I shall be silent;
Tell me where I am wrong.
²⁵ *a*-How trenchant honest words are;-*a*
But what sort of reproof comes from you?
²⁶ Do you devise words of reproof,
But count a hopeless man's words as wind?

b-b *Meaning of Heb. uncertain; others, "deny the words of the Holy One."*
c *Following* kethib, *with Targum; meaning of Heb. uncertain.*

²⁷ You would even cast lots over an orphan,
Or barter away your friend.
²⁸ Now be so good as to face me;
I will not lie to your face.
²⁹ Relent! Let there not be injustice;
Relent! I am still in the right.
³⁰ Is injustice on my tongue?
Can my palate not discern evil?

7 Truly man has a term of service on earth;
His days are like those of a hireling—
² Like a slave who longs for [evening's] shadows,
Like a hireling who waits for his wage.
³ So have I been allotted months of futility;
Nights of misery have been apportioned to me.
⁴ When I lie down, I think,
"When shall I rise?"
Night ᵃ-drags on,-ᵃ
And I am sated with tossings till morning twilight.
⁵ My flesh is covered with maggots and clods of earth;
My skin is broken and festering.
⁶ My days fly faster than a weaver's shuttle,
And come to their end ᵇ-without hope.-ᵇ
⁷ Consider that my life is but wind;
I shall never see happiness again.
⁸ The eye that gazes on me will not see me;
Your eye will seek me, but I shall be gone.
⁹ As a cloud fades away,
So whoever goes down to Sheol does not come up;
¹⁰ He returns no more to his home;
His place does not know him.

¹¹ On my part, I will not speak with restraint;
I will give voice to the anguish of my spirit;

ᵃ⁻ᵃ *Meaning of Heb. uncertain.*
ᵇ⁻ᵇ *Or "when the thread runs out."*

I will complain in the bitterness of my soul.
¹² Am I the sea or the Dragon,ᶜ
That You have set a watch over me?
¹³ When I think, "My bed will comfort me,
My couch will share my sorrow,"
¹⁴ You frighten me with dreams,
And terrify me with visions,
¹⁵ Till I prefer strangulation,
Death, to my wasted frame.
¹⁶ I am sick of it.
I shall not live forever;
Let me be, for my days are a breath.

¹⁷ What is man, that You make much of him,
That You fix Your attention upon him?
¹⁸ You inspect him every morning,
Examine him every minute.
¹⁹ Will You not look away from me for a while,
Let me be, till I swallow my spittle?
²⁰ If I have sinned, what have I done to You,
Watcher of men?
Why make of me Your target,
And a burden to myself?
²¹ Why do You not pardon my transgression
And forgive my iniquity?
For soon I shall lie down in the dust;
When You seek me, I shall be gone.

8 Bildad the Shuhite said in reply:

² How long will you speak such things?
Your utterances are a mighty wind!
³ Will God pervert the right?
Will the Almighty pervert justice?

ᶜ *See note at 3.8.*

⁴ If your sons sinned against Him,
He dispatched them for their transgression.
⁵ But if you seek God
And supplicate the Almighty,
⁶ If you are blameless and upright,
He will protect you,
And grant well-being to your righteous home.
⁷ Though your beginning be small,
In the end you will grow very great.

⁸ Ask the generation past,
Study what their fathers have searched out
⁹ —For we are of yesterday and know nothing;
Our days on earth are a shadow—
¹⁰ Surely they will teach you and tell you,
Speaking out of their understanding.
¹¹ Can papyrus thrive without marsh?
Can rushes grow without water?
¹² While still tender, not yet plucked,
They would wither before any other grass.
¹³ Such is the fate of all who forget God;
The hope of the impious man comes to naught—
¹⁴ Whose confidence is a ᵃthread of gossamer,⁻ᵃ
Whose trust is a spider's web.
¹⁵ He leans on his house—it will not stand;
He seizes hold of it, but it will not hold.
¹⁶ He stays fresh even in the sun;
His shoots spring up in his garden;
¹⁷ ᵃ⁻His roots are twined around a heap,
They take hold of a house of stones.⁻ᵃ
¹⁸ When he is uprooted from his place,
It denies him, [saying,]
"I never saw you."
¹⁹ Such is his happy lot;
And from the earth others will grow.

ᵃ⁻ᵃ *Meaning of Heb. uncertain.*

20 Surely God does not despise the blameless;
He gives no support to evildoers.
21 He will yet fill your mouth with laughter,
And your lips with shouts of joy.
22 Your enemies will be clothed in disgrace;
The tent of the wicked will vanish.

9 Job said in reply:

2 Indeed I know that it is so:
Man cannot win a suit against God.
3 If he insisted on a trial with Him,
He would not answer one charge in a thousand.
4 Wise of heart and mighty in power—
Who ever challenged Him and came out whole?—
5 Him who moves mountains without their knowing it,
Who overturns them in His anger;
6 Who shakes the earth from its place,
Till its pillars quake;
7 Who commands the sun not to shine;
Who seals up the stars;
8 Who by Himself spread out the heavens,
And trod on the back of the sea;
9 Who made the Bear*a* and Orion,
Pleiades, and the chambers of the south wind;
10 Who performs great deeds which cannot be fathomed,
And wondrous things without number.
11 He passes me by—I do not see Him;
He goes by me, but I do not perceive Him.
12 He snatches away—who can stop Him?
Who can say to Him, "What are You doing?"
13 God does not restrain His anger;
Under Him Rahab's*b* helpers sink down.
14 How then can I answer Him,

---

a *Meaning of Heb. uncertain.*
b *A primeval monster.*

Or choose my arguments against Him?
¹⁵ Though I were in the right, I could not speak out,
But I would plead for mercy with my judge.
¹⁶ If I summoned Him and He responded,
I do not believe He would lend me His ear.
¹⁷ For He crushes me ᶜfor a hair;⁻ᶜ
He wounds me much for no cause.
¹⁸ He does not let me catch my breath,
But sates me with bitterness.
¹⁹ If a trial of strength—He is the strong one;
If a trial in court—who will summon Him for me?
²⁰ Though I were innocent,
My mouth would condemn me;
Though I were blameless, He would prove me crooked.
²¹ I am blameless—I am distraught;
I am sick of life.
²² It is all one; therefore I say,
"He destroys the blameless and the guilty."
²³ When suddenly a scourge brings death,
He mocks as the innocent fail.
²⁴ The earth is handed over to the wicked one;
He covers the eyes of its judges.
If it is not He, then who?

²⁵ My days fly swifter than a runner;
They flee without seeing happiness;
²⁶ They pass like reed-boats,
Like an eagle swooping onto its prey.
²⁷ If I say, "I will forget my complaint;
Abandon my sorrowᵈ and be diverted,"
²⁸ I remain in dread of all my suffering;
I know that You will not acquit me.
²⁹ It will be I who am in the wrong;
Why then should I waste effort?
³⁰ If I washed with soap,

ᶜ⁻ᶜ *With Targum and Peshitta; or "with a storm."*
ᵈ *Lit. "face."*

274

Cleansed my hands with lye,
³¹ You would dip me in muck
Till my clothes would abhor me.
³² He is not a man, like me, that I can answer Him,
That we can go to law together.
³³ No arbiter is between us
To lay his hand on us both.
³⁴ If He would only take His rod away from me
And not let His terror frighten me,
³⁵ Then I would speak out without fear of Him;
For I know myself not to be so.

10 I am disgusted with life;
I will give rein to my complaint,
Speak in the bitterness of my soul.
² I say to God, "Do not condemn me;
Let me know what You charge me with.
³ Does it benefit You to defraud,
To despise the toil of Your hands,
While smiling on the counsel of the wicked?
⁴ Do You have the eyes of flesh?
Is Your vision that of mere men?
⁵ Are Your days the days of a mortal,
Are Your years the years of a man,
⁶ That You seek my iniquity
And search out my sin?
⁷ You know that I am not guilty,
And that there is none to deliver from Your hand.

⁸ "Your hands shaped and fashioned me,
Then destroyed every part of me.
⁹ Consider that You fashioned me like clay;
Will You then turn me back into dust?

¹⁰ You poured me out like milk,
Congealed me like cheese;
¹¹ You clothed me with skin and flesh
And wove me of bones and sinews;
¹² You bestowed on me life and care;
Your providence watched over my spirit.
¹³ Yet these things You hid in Your heart;
I know that You had this in mind:
¹⁴ To watch me when I sinned
And not clear me of my iniquity;
¹⁵ Should I be guilty—the worse for me!
And even when innocent, I cannot lift my head;
So sated am I with shame,
And drenched in my misery.
¹⁶ *ᵃ⁻*It is something to be proud of⁻ᵃ to hunt me like a lion,
To ᵇ⁻show Yourself wondrous through⁻ᵇ me time and
    again!
¹⁷ You keep sending fresh witnesses against me,
Letting Your vexation with me grow.
*ᵃ⁻*I serve my term and am my own replacement.⁻ᵃ

¹⁸ "Why did You let me come out of the womb?
Better had I expired before any eye saw me,
¹⁹ Had I been as though I never was,
Had I been carried from the womb to the grave.
²⁰ My days are few, so desist!
Leave me alone, let me be diverted awhile
²¹ Before I depart—never to return—
For the land of deepest gloom;
²² A land whose light is darkness,
All gloom and disarray,
Whose light is like darkness."

ᵃ⁻ᵃ *Meaning of Heb. uncertain.*
ᵇ⁻ᵇ *Or "make sport of"; cf. Pal. Aram. 'afli.*

11 Then Zophar the Naamathite said in reply:

² Is a multitude of words unanswerable?
Must a loquacious person be right?
³ Your prattle may silence men;
You may mock without being rebuked,
⁴ And say, "My doctrine is pure,
And I have been innocent in Your sight."
⁵ But would that God might speak,
And talk to you Himself.
⁶ He would tell you the secrets of wisdom,
*ᵃ*For there are many sides to sagacity;
And know that God has overlooked for you some of your
   iniquity.*⁻ᵃ*

⁷ Would you discover the mystery of God?
Would you discover the limit of the Almighty?
⁸ Higher than heaven—what can you do?
Deeper than Sheol—what can you know?
⁹ Its measure is longer than the earth
And broader than the sea.
¹⁰ *ᵃ*-Should He pass by, or confine,
Or call an assembly, who can stop Him?*⁻ᵃ*
¹¹ For He knows deceitful men;
When He sees iniquity, does He not discern it?
¹² *ᵃ*-A hollow man will get understanding,
When a wild ass is born a man.*⁻ᵃ*

¹³ But if you direct your mind,
And spread forth your hands toward Him—
¹⁴ If there is iniquity with you, remove it,
And do not let injustice reside in your tent—
¹⁵ Then, free of blemish, you will hold your head high,

ᵃ⁻ᵃ *Meaning of Heb. uncertain.*

And, *b*-when in straits,-*b* be unafraid.
16 You will then put your misery out of mind,
Consider it as water that has flowed past.
17 *a*-Life will be brighter than noon;-*a*
You will shine, you will be like the morning.
18 You will be secure, for there is hope,
a-And, entrenched,-*a* you will rest secure;
19 You will lie down undisturbed;
The great will court your favor.
20 But the eyes of the wicked pine away;
Escape is cut off from them;
They have only their last breath to look forward to.

12 Then Job said in reply:

2 Indeed, you are the [voice of] the people,
And wisdom will die with you.
3 But I, like you, have a mind,
And am not less than you.
Who does not know such things?
4 I have become a laughingstock to my friend—
"One who calls to God and is answered,
Blamelessly innocent"—a laughingstock.
5 *a*-In the thought of the complacent there is contempt for
    calamity;
It is ready for those whose foot slips.-*a*
6 Robbers live untroubled in their tents,
And those who provoke God are secure,
a-Those whom God's hands have produced.-*a*

7 But ask the beasts, and they will teach you;
The birds of the sky, they will tell you,
8 Or speak to the earth, it will teach you;
The fish of the sea, they will inform you.

---

b-b *Heb.* muṣaq; *other Heb. editions* muṣṣaq, *"you will be firm."*

a-a *Meaning of Heb. uncertain.*

⁹ Who among all these does not know
That the hand of the LORD has done this?
¹⁰ In His hand is every living soul
And the breath of all mankind.
¹¹ Truly, the ear tests arguments
As the palate tastes foods.
¹² Is wisdom in the aged
And understanding in the long-lived?
¹³ With Him are wisdom and courage;
His are counsel and understanding.
¹⁴ Whatever He tears down cannot be rebuilt;
Whomever He imprisons cannot be set free.
¹⁵ When He holds back the waters, they dry up;
When He lets them loose, they tear up the land.
¹⁶ With Him are strength and resourcefulness;
Erring and causing to err are from Him.
¹⁷ He makes counselors go about naked*b*
And causes judges to go mad.
¹⁸ He undoes the belts of kings,
And fastens loincloths on them.
¹⁹ He makes priests go about naked,*b*
And leads temple-servants*c* astray.
²⁰ He deprives trusty men of speech,
And takes away the reason of elders.
²¹ He pours disgrace upon great men,
And loosens the belt of the mighty.
²² He draws mysteries out of the darkness,
And brings obscurities to light.
²³ He exalts nations, then destroys them;
He expands nations, then leads them away.
²⁴ He deranges the leaders of the people,
And makes them wander in a trackless waste.
²⁵ They grope without light in the darkness;
He makes them wander as if drunk.

b A sign of madness.
c Cf. Ugaritic ytnm, *a class of temple servants; others "the mighty."*

13 My eye has seen all this;
My ear has heard and understood it.
² What you know, I know also;
I am not less than you.
³ Indeed, I would speak to the Almighty;
I insist on arguing with God.
⁴ But you invent lies;
All of you are quacks.
⁵ If you would only keep quiet
It would be considered wisdom on your part.
⁶ Hear now my arguments,
Listen to my pleading.
⁷ Will you speak unjustly on God's behalf?
Will you speak deceitfully for Him?
⁸ Will you be partial toward Him?
Will you plead God's cause?
⁹ Will it go well when He examines you?
Will you fool Him as one fools men?
¹⁰ He will surely reprove you
If in *-your heart-*ᵃ you are partial toward Him.
¹¹ His threat will terrify you,
And His fear will seize you.
¹² Your briefs are empty*ᵇ* platitudes;
Your responses are unsubstantial.*ᶜ*

¹³ Keep quiet; I will have my say,
Come what may upon me.
¹⁴ How long! I will take my flesh in my teeth;
I will take my life in my hands.
¹⁵ *ᵈ-*He may well slay me; I may have no hope;*-ᵈ*
Yet I will argue my case before Him.
¹⁶ In this too is my salvation:
That no impious man can come into His presence.

ᵃ⁻ᵃ *Lit. "secret."*
ᵇ *Lit. "ashen."*
ᶜ *Lit. "clayey."*
ᵈ⁻ᵈ *So with* kethib; *others with* qere *"Though He slay me, yet will I trust in Him."*

17 Listen closely to my words;
Give ear to my discourse.
18 See now, I have prepared a case;
I know that I will win it.
19 For who is it that would challenge me?
I should then keep silent and expire.
20 But two things do not do to me,
So that I need not hide from You:
21 Remove Your hand from me,
And let not Your terror frighten me.
22 Then summon me and I will respond,
Or I will speak and You reply to me.
23 How many are my iniquities and sins?
Advise me of my transgression and sin.
24 Why do You hide Your face,
And treat me like an enemy?
25 Will You harass a driven leaf,
Will You pursue dried-up straw,
26 That You decree for me bitter things
And make me *-answer for-*ᵉ the iniquities of my youth,
27 That You put my feet in the stocks
And watch all my ways,
*-Hemming in my footsteps?-*ᶠ
28 Man wastes away like a rotten thing,
Like a garment eaten by moths.

14 Man born of woman is short-lived and sated with trouble.
2 He blossoms like a flower and withers;
He vanishes like a shadow and does not endure.
3 Do You fix Your gaze on such a one?
Will You go to law with me?
4 *-Who can produce a clean thing out of an unclean one?
No one!-*ᵃ
5 His days are determined;

e-e Lit. "inherit."
f-f Meaning of Heb. uncertain.

a-a Meaning of Heb. uncertain.

You know the number of his months;
You have set him limits that he cannot pass.
6 Turn away from him, that he may be at ease
Until, like a hireling, he finishes out his day.

7 There is hope for a tree;
If it is cut down it will renew itself;
Its shoots will not cease.
8 If its roots are old in the earth,
And its stump dies in the ground,
9 At the scent of water it will bud
And produce branches like a sapling.
10 But mortals languish and die;
Man expires; where is he?
11 The waters of the sea fail,
And the river dries up and is parched.
12 So man lies down never to rise;
He will awake only when the heavens are no more,
Only then be aroused from his sleep.
13 O that You would hide me in Sheol,
Conceal me until Your anger passes,
Set me a fixed time to attend to me.
14 If a man dies, can he live again?
All the time of my service I wait
Until my replacement comes.
15 You would call and I would answer You;
You would set Your heart on Your handiwork.
16 Then You would not count my steps,
Or keep watch over my sin.
17 My transgression would be sealed up in a pouch;
You would coat over my iniquity.

18 Mountains collapse and crumble;
Rocks are dislodged from their place.
19 Water wears away stone;

Torrents wash away earth;
So you destroy man's hope,
²⁰ You overpower him for ever and he perishes;
You alter his visage and dispatch him.
²¹ His sons attain honor and he does not know it;
They are humbled and he is not aware of it.
²² He feels only the pain of his flesh,
And his spirit mourns in him.

15 Eliphaz the Temanite said in reply:

² Does a wise man answer with windy opinions,
And fill his belly with the east wind?
³ Should he argue with useless talk,
With words that are of no worth?
⁴ You subvert piety
And restrain prayer to God.
⁵ Your sinfulness dictates your speech,
So you choose crafty language.
⁶ Your own mouth condemns you—not I;
Your lips testify against you.

⁷ Were you the first man born?
Were you created before the hills?
⁸ Have you listened in on the council of God?
Have you sole possession of wisdom?
⁹ What do you know that we do not know,
Or understand that we do not?
¹⁰ Among us are gray-haired old men,
Older by far than your father.
¹¹ Are God's consolations not enough for you,
And His gentle words to you?
¹² How your heart has carried you away,
How your eyes ᵃ-have failed-ᵃ you,

ᵃ⁻ᵃ *Meaning of Heb. uncertain.*

13 That you could vent your anger on God,
And let such words out of your mouth!
14 What is man that he can be cleared of guilt,
One born of woman, that he be in the right?
15 He puts no trust in His holy ones;
The heavens are not guiltless in His sight;
16 What then of one loathsome and foul,
Man, who drinks wrongdoing like water!

17 I will hold forth; listen to me;
What I have seen, I will declare—
18 That which wise men have transmitted from their
  fathers,
And have not withheld,
19 To whom alone the land was given,
No stranger passing among them:
20 The wicked man writhes in torment all his days;
Few years are reserved for the ruthless.
21 Frightening sounds fill his ears;
When he is at ease a robber falls upon him.
22 He is never sure he will come back from the dark;
A sword stares him in the face.
23 He wanders about for bread—where is it?
He knows that the day of darkness has been readied
  for him.
24 Troubles terrify him, anxiety overpowers him,
Like a king *-expecting a siege.-*
25 For he has raised his arm against God
And played the hero against the Almighty.
26 He runs at Him defiantly*b*
a-With his thickly bossed shield.
27 His face is covered with fat
And his loins with blubber.-*a*
28 He dwells in cities doomed to ruin,
In houses that shall not be lived in,
That are destined to become heaps of rubble.

b Lit. "with neck."

284

²⁹ He will not be rich;
His wealth will not endure;
ᵃ-His produce shall not bend to the earth.⁻ᵃ
³⁰ He will never get away from the darkness;
Flames will sear his shoots;
ᵃ-He will pass away by the breath of His mouth.
³¹ He will not be trusted;
He will be misled by falsehood,
And falsehood will be his recompense.⁻ᵃ
³² He will wither before his time,
His boughs never having flourished.
³³ He will drop his unripe grapes like a vine;
He will shed his blossoms like an olive tree.
³⁴ For the company of the impious is desolate;
Fire consumes the tents of the briber;
³⁵ For they have conceived mischief, given birth to evil,
And their womb has produced deceit.

16 Job said in reply:

² I have often heard such things;
You are all mischievous comforters.
³ Have windy words no limit?
What afflicts you that you speak on?
⁴ I would also talk like you
If you were in my place;
I would barrage you with words,
I would wag my head over you.
⁵ I would encourage you with words,ᵃ
My moving lips would bring relief.
⁶ If I speak, my pain will not be relieved,
And if I do not—what have I lost?
⁷ Now He has truly worn me out;
You have destroyed my whole community.
⁸ You have shriveled me;

ᵃ *Lit. "my mouth."*

My gauntness serves as a witness,
And testifies against me.
9 In His anger He tears and persecutes me;
He gnashes His teeth at me;
My foe stabs me with his eyes.
10 They open wide their mouths at me;
Reviling me, they strike my cheeks;
They inflame themselves against me.
11 God hands me over to an evil man,
Thrusts me into the clutches of the wicked.
12 I had been untroubled, and He broke me in pieces;
He took me by the scruff and shattered me;
He set me up as His target;
13 His bowmen surrounded me;
He pierced my kidneys; He showed no mercy;
He spilled my bile onto the ground.
14 He breached me, breach after breach;
He rushed at me like a warrior.
15 I sewed sackcloth over my skin;
I *b*-buried my glory-*b* in the dust.
16 My face is red with weeping;
Darkness covers my eyes
17 *c*-For no injustice on my part
And for the purity of my prayer!-*c*

18 Earth, do not cover my blood;
Let there be no resting place for my outcry!
19 Surely now my witness is in heaven;
He who can testify for me is on high.
20 O my advocates, my fellows,
Before God my eyes shed tears;
21 Let Him arbitrate between a man and God
As between a man and his fellow.

b-b *Lit. "made my horn enter into."*
c-c *Or "Though I did no injustice,*
And my prayer was pure."

17

²² For a few more years will pass,
And I shall go the way of no return.
¹ My spirit is crushed, my days run out;
The graveyard waits for me.

² Surely mocking men keep me company,
And with their provocations I close my eyes.
³ Come now, stand surety for me!
Who will give his hand on my behalf?
⁴ You have hidden understanding from their minds;
Therefore You must not exalt [them].
⁵ He informs on his friends for a share [of their property],
And his children's eyes pine away.

⁶ He made me a byword among people;
I have become like Tophet*ᵃ* of old.
⁷ My eyes fail from vexation;
All shapes seem to me like shadows.
⁸ The upright are amazed at this;
The pure are aroused against the impious.
⁹ The righteous man holds to his way;
He whose hands are clean grows stronger.
¹⁰ But all of you, come back now;
I shall not find a wise man among you.
¹¹ My days are done, my tendons severed,
The strings of my heart.
¹² They say that night is day,
That light is here—in the face of darkness.
¹³ If I must look forward to Sheol as my home,
And make my bed in the dark place,
¹⁴ Say to the Pit, "You are my father,"
To the maggots, "Mother," "Sister"—
¹⁵ Where, then, is my hope?
Who can see hope for me?
¹⁶ Will it descend to Sheol?
Shall we go down together to the dust?

ᵃ *That consumed children; cf. Jer. 7.31.*

18 Then Bildad the Shuhite said in reply:

² How long? Put an end to talk!
Consider, and then we shall speak.
³ Why are we thought of as brutes,
Regarded by you as stupid?
⁴ You who tear yourself to pieces in anger—
Will *ᵃ*earth's order be disrupted*ᵃ* for your sake?
Will rocks be dislodged from their place?
⁵ Indeed, the light of the wicked fails;
The flame of his fire does not shine.
⁶ The light in his tent darkens;
His lamp fails him.
⁷ His iniquitous strides are hobbled;
His schemes overthrow him.
⁸ He is led by his feet into the net;
He walks onto the toils.
⁹ The trap seizes his heel;
The noose tightens on him.
¹⁰ The rope for him lies hidden on the ground;
His snare, on the path.
¹¹ Terrors assault him on all sides
And send his feet flying.
¹² His progeny hunger;
Disaster awaits his wife.*ᵇ*
¹³ The tendons under his skin are consumed;
Death's firstborn consumes his tendons.
¹⁴ He is torn from the safety of his tent;
Terror marches him to the king.*ᶜ*
¹⁵ It lodges in his desolate tent;
Sulfur is strewn upon his home.
¹⁶ His roots below dry up,
And above, his branches wither.

ᵃ⁻ᵃ *Lit. "the earth be abandoned."*
ᵇ *Lit. "rib" (cf. Gen. 2.22); or "stumbling."*
ᶜ *Viz. of the netherworld.*

17 All mention of him vanishes from the earth;
He has no name abroad.
18 He is thrust from light to darkness,
Driven from the world.
19 He has no seed or breed among his people,
No survivor where he once lived.
20 Generations to come will be appalled at his fate,
As the previous ones are seized with horror.
21 "These were the haunts of the wicked;
Here was the place of him who knew not God."

19 Job said in reply:

2 How long will you grieve my spirit,
And crush me with words?
3 *a*-Time and again-*a* you humiliate me,
And are not ashamed to abuse me.
4 If indeed I have erred,
My error remains with me.
5 Though you are overbearing toward me,
Reproaching me with my disgrace,
6 Yet know that God has wronged me;
He has thrown up siege works around me.
7 I cry, "Violence!" but am not answered;
I shout, but can get no justice.
8 He has barred my way; I cannot pass;
He has laid darkness upon my path.
9 He has stripped me of my glory,
Removed the crown from my head.
10 He tears down every part of me; I perish;
He uproots my hope like a tree.
11 He kindles His anger against me;
He regards me as one of His foes.
12 His troops advance together;

a-a *Lit. "Ten times."*

They build their road toward me
And encamp around my tent.
¹³ He alienated my kin from me;
My acquaintances disown me.
¹⁴ My relatives are gone;
My friends have forgotten me.
¹⁵ My dependents and maidservants regard me as a stranger;
I am an outsider to them.
¹⁶ I summon my servant but he does not respond;
I must myself entreat him.
¹⁷ My odor is repulsive to my wife;
I am loathsome to my children.
¹⁸ Even youngsters disdain me;
When I rise, they speak against me.
¹⁹ All my bosom friends detest me;
Those I love have turned against me.
²⁰ My bones stick to my skin and flesh;
I escape with the skin of my teeth.

²¹ Pity me, pity me! You are my friends;
For the hand of God has struck me!
²² Why do you pursue me like God,
ᵇ⁻Maligning me insatiably?⁻ᵇ
²³ O that my words were written down;
Would they were inscribed in a record,
²⁴ Incised on a rock forever
With iron stylus and lead!
²⁵ But I know that my Vindicator lives;
In the end He will testify on earth—
²⁶ This, after my skin will have been peeled off.
But I would behold God while still in my flesh,
²⁷ I myself, not another, would behold Him;
Would see with my own eyes:
My heartᶜ pines within me.

ᵇ⁻ᵇ Lit. "You are not satisfied with my flesh."
ᶜ Lit. "kidneys."

28 You say, "How do we persecute him?
The root of the matter is in him."d
29 Be in fear of the sword,
For [your] fury is iniquity worthy of the sword;
Know there is a judgment!

20 Zophar the Naamathite said in reply:

2 In truth, my thoughts urge me to answer
(It is because of my feelings
3 When I hear reproof that insults me);
A spirit out of my understanding makes me reply:
4 Do you not know this, that from time immemorial,
Since man was set on earth,
5 The joy of the wicked has been brief,
The happiness of the impious, fleeting?
6 Though he grows as high as the sky,
His head reaching the clouds,
7 He perishes forever, like his dung;
Those who saw him will say, "Where is he?"
8 He flies away like a dream and cannot be found;
He is banished like a night vision.
9 Eyes that glimpsed him do so no more;
They cannot see him in his place any longer.
10 His sons ingratiate themselves with the poor;
His own hands must give back his wealth.
11 His bones, still full of vigor,
Lie down in the dust with him.
12 Though evil is sweet to his taste,
And he conceals it under his tongue;
13 Though he saves it, does not let it go,
Holds it inside his mouth,
14 His food in his bowels turns
Into asps' venom within him.

d With many mss. and versions; printed editions, "me."

¹⁵ The riches he swallows he vomits;
God empties it out of his stomach.
¹⁶ He sucks the poison of asps;
The tongue of the viper kills him.
¹⁷ Let him not enjoy the streams,
The rivers of honey, the brooks of cream.
¹⁸ He will give back the goods unswallowed;
The value of the riches, undigested.
¹⁹ Because he crushed and tortured the poor,
He will not build up the house he took by force.
²⁰ He will not see his children tranquil;
He will not preserve one of his dear ones.^a
²¹ With no survivor to enjoy it,
His fortune will not prosper.
²² When he has all he wants, trouble will come;
Misfortunes of all kinds will batter him.
²³ Let that fill his belly;
Let Him loose His burning anger at him,
And rain down His weapons upon him.
²⁴ Fleeing from iron arrows,
He is shot through from a bow of bronze.
²⁵ Brandished and run through his body,
The blade, through his gall,
Strikes terror into him.
²⁶ Utter darkness waits for his treasured ones;
A fire fanned by no man will consume him;
Who survives in his tent will be crushed.
²⁷ Heaven will expose his iniquity;
Earth will rise up against him.
²⁸ His household will be cast forth by a flood,
Spilled out on the day of His wrath.
²⁹ This is the wicked man's portion from God,
The lot God has ordained for him.

---

^a *For this meaning of* beṭen *and* ḥamud, *cf. Hos. 9.16.*

21 Job said in reply:

2 Listen well to what I say,
And let that be your consolation.
3 Bear with me while I speak,
And after I have spoken, you may mock.
4 Is my complaint directed toward a man?
Why should I not lose my patience?
5 Look at me and be appalled,
And clap your hand to your mouth.
6 When I think of it I am terrified;
My body is seized with shuddering.

7 Why do the wicked live on,
Prosper and grow wealthy?
8 Their children are with them always,
And they see their children's children.
9 Their homes are secure, without fear;
They do not feel the rod of God.
10 Their bull breeds and does not fail;
Their cow calves and never miscarries;
11 They let their infants run loose like sheep,
And their children skip about.
12 They sing to the music of timbrel and lute,
And revel to the tune of the pipe;
13 They spend their days in happiness,
And go down to Sheol in peace.
14 They say to God, "Leave us alone,
We do not want to learn Your ways;
15 What is Shaddai that we should serve Him?
What will we gain by praying to Him?"
16 Their happiness is not their own doing.
(The thoughts of the wicked are beyond me!)

¹⁷ How seldom does the lamp of the wicked fail,
Does the calamity they deserve befall them,
Does He apportion [their] lot in anger!
¹⁸ Let them become like straw in the wind,
Like chaff carried off by a storm.
¹⁹ [You say,]"God is reserving his punishment for his
    sons";
Let it be paid back to him that he may feel it,
²⁰ Let his eyes see his ruin,
And let him drink the wrath of Shaddai!
²¹ For what does he care about the fate of his family,
When his number of months runs out?
²² Can God be instructed in knowledge,
He who judges from such heights?
²³ One man dies in robust health,
All tranquil and untroubled;
²⁴ His pails are full of milk;
The marrow of his bones is juicy.
²⁵ Another dies embittered,
Never having tasted happiness.
²⁶ They both lie in the dust
And are covered with worms.

²⁷ Oh, I know your thoughts,
And the tactics you will devise against me.
²⁸ You will say, "Where is the house of the great man—
And where the tent in which the wicked dwelled?"
²⁹ You must have consulted the wayfarers;
You cannot deny their evidence.
³⁰ For the evil man is spared on the day of calamity,
On the day when wrath is led forth.
³¹ Who will upbraid him to his face?
Who will requite him for what he has done?
³² He is brought to the grave,
While a watch is kept at his tomb.

³³ The clods of the wadi are sweet to him,
Everyone follows behind him,
Innumerable are those who precede him.
³⁴ Why then do you offer me empty consolation?
Of your replies only the perfidy remains.

22 Eliphaz the Temanite said in reply:

² Can a man be of use to God,
A wise man benefit Him?
³ Does Shaddai gain if you are righteous?
Does He profit if your conduct is blameless?
⁴ Is it because of your piety that He arraigns you,
And enters into judgment with you?
⁵ You know that your wickedness is great,
And that your iniquities have no limit.
⁶ You exact pledges from your fellows without reason,
And leave them naked, stripped of their clothes;
⁷ You do not give the thirsty water to drink;
You deny bread to the hungry.
⁸ The land belongs to the strong;
The privileged occupy it.
⁹ You have sent away widows empty-handed;
The strength of the fatherless is broken.
¹⁰ Therefore snares are all around you,
And sudden terrors frighten you,
¹¹ Or darkness, so you cannot see;
A flood of waters covers you.

¹² God is in the heavenly heights;
See the highest stars, how lofty!
¹³ You say, "What can God know?
Can He govern through the dense cloud?
¹⁴ The clouds screen Him so He cannot see

As He moves about the circuit of heaven."
15 Have you observed the immemorial path
That evil men have trodden;
16 How they were shriveled up before their time
And their foundation poured out like a river?
17 They said to God, "Leave us alone;
What can Shaddai do about it?"
18 But it was He who filled their houses with good things.
(The thoughts of the wicked are beyond me!)
19 The righteous, seeing it,ᵃ rejoiced;
The innocent laughed with scorn.
20 Surely their substance was destroyed,
And their remnant consumed by fire.

21 Be close to Him and wholehearted;
Good things will come to you thereby.
22 Accept instruction from His mouth;
Lay up His words in your heart.
23 If you return to Shaddai you will be restored,
If you banish iniquity from your tent;
24 If you regard treasure as dirt,
Ophir-gold as stones of the wadi,
25 And Shaddai be your treasure
And precious silver for you,
26 When you seek the favor of Shaddai,
And lift up your face to God,
27 You will pray to Him, and He will listen to you,
And you will pay your vows.
28 You will decree and it will be fulfilled,
And light will shine upon your affairs.
29 When others sink low, you will say it is pride;
For He saves the humble.
30 He will deliver the guilty;
He will be delivered through the cleanness of your hands.

ᵃ *Referring to v. 16.*

23 Job said in reply:

² Today again my complaint is bitter;
ᵃ-My strength is spent-*ᵃ* on account of my groaning.
³ Would that I knew how to reach Him,
How to get to His dwelling-place.
⁴ I would set out my case before Him
And fill my mouth with arguments.
⁵ I would learn what answers He had for me
And know how He would reply to me.
⁶ Would He contend with me overbearingly?
Surely He would not accuse me!
⁷ There the upright would be cleared by Him,
And I would escape forever from my judge.

⁸ But if I go East—He is not there;
West—I still do not perceive Him;
⁹ North—since He is concealed, I do not behold Him;
South—He is hidden, and I cannot see Him.
¹⁰ But He knows the way I take;
Would He assay me, I should emerge pure as gold.
¹¹ I have followed in His tracks,
Kept His way without swerving,
¹² I have not deviated from what His lips commanded;
I have treasured His words more than my daily bread.
¹³ He is one; who can dissuade Him?
Whatever He desires, He does.
¹⁴ For He will bring my term to an end,
But He has many more such at His disposal.
¹⁵ Therefore I am terrified at His presence;
When I consider, I dread Him.
¹⁶ God has made me fainthearted;
Shaddai has terrified me.

ᵃ⁻ᵃ *Lit. "My hand is heavy."*

¹⁷ Yet I am not cut off by the darkness;
He has concealed the thick gloom from me.

24 Why are times for judgment not reserved by Shaddai?
Even those close to Him cannot forsee His actions.^{*a*}
² People remove boundary-stones;
They carry off flocks and pasture them;
³ They lead away the donkeys of the fatherless,
And seize the widow's bull as a pledge;
⁴ They chase the needy off the roads;
All the poor of the land are forced into hiding.
⁵ Like the wild asses of the wilderness,
They go about their tasks, seeking food;
The wilderness provides each with food for his lads;
⁶ They harvest fodder in the field,
And glean the late grapes in the vineyards of the wicked.
⁷ They pass the night naked for lack of clothing,
They have no covering against the cold;
⁸ They are drenched by the mountain rains,
And huddle against the rock for lack of shelter.
⁹ ^{*b*}They snatch the fatherless infant from the breast,
And seize the child of the poor as a pledge.
¹⁰ They go about naked for lack of clothing,
And, hungry, carry sheaves;
¹¹ Between rows [of olive trees] they make oil,
And, thirsty, they tread the winepresses.
¹² Men groan in the city;
The souls of the dying cry out;
Yet God does not regard it as a reproach.

¹³ They are rebels against the light;
They are strangers to its ways,
And do not stay in its path.
¹⁴ The murderer arises ^{*c*}in the evening^{*c*}

^{*a*} *Lit. "days."*
^{*b*} *This verse belongs to the description of the wicked in vv. 2–4a.*
^{*c-c*} *Cf. Mishnaic Heb. 'or, Aramaic 'orta, "evening"; others "with the light."*

To kill the poor and needy,
And at night he acts the thief.
¹⁵ The eyes of the adulterer watch for twilight,
Thinking, "No one will glimpse me then."
He masks his face.
¹⁶ In the dark they break into houses;
By day they shut themselves in;
They do not know the light.
¹⁷ For all of them morning is darkness;
It is then that they discern the terror of darkness.
¹⁸ ^d May they be flotsam on the face of the water;
May their portion in the land be cursed;
May none turn aside by way of their vineyards.
¹⁹ May drought and heat snatch away their snow waters,
And Sheol, those who have sinned.
²⁰ May the womb forget him;
May he be sweet to the worms;
May he be no longer remembered;
May wrongdoers be broken like a tree.
²¹ May he consort with a barren woman who bears no
    child,
Leave his widow deprived of good.
²² Though he has the strength to seize bulls,
May he live with no assurance of survival.
²³ Yet [God] gives him the security on which he relies,
And keeps watch over his affairs.
²⁴ Exalted for a while, let them be gone;
Be brought low, and shrivel like mallows,
And wither like the heads of grain.

²⁵ Surely no one can confute me,
Or prove that I am wrong.

---

^d *From here to the end of the chapter the translation is largely conjectural.*

25 Bildad the Shuhite said in reply:

² Dominion and dread are His;
He imposes peace in His heights.
³ Can His troops be numbered?
On whom does His light not shine?
⁴ How can man be in the right before God?
How can one born of woman be cleared of guilt?
⁵ Even the moon is not bright,
And the stars are not pure in His sight.
⁶ How much less man, a worm,
The son-of-man, a maggot.

26 Then Job said in reply:

² You would help without having the strength;
You would deliver with arms that have no power.
³ Without having the wisdom, you offer advice
And freely give your counsel.
⁴ To whom have you addressed words?
Whose breath issued from you?

⁵ The shades tremble
Beneath the waters and their denizens.
⁶ Sheol is naked before Him;
Abaddon has no cover.
⁷ He it is who stretched out Zaphon*a* over chaos,
Who suspended earth over emptiness.
⁸ He wrapped up the waters in His clouds;
Yet no cloud burst under their weight.
⁹ *b-*He shuts off the view of His throne,
Spreading His cloud over it.*-b*

a *Used for heaven; cf. Isa. 14.13 and Ps. 48.3.*
b-b *Meaning of Heb. uncertain.*

10 He drew a boundary on the surface of the waters,
At the extreme where light and darkness meet.
11 The pillars of heaven tremble,
Astounded at His blast.
12 By His power He stilled the sea;
By His skill He struck down Rahab.
13 By His wind the heavens were calmed;
His hand pierced the ᶜElusive Serpent.ᶜ
14 These are but glimpses of His rule,
The mere whisper that we perceive of Him;
Who can absorb the thunder of His mighty deeds?

27 Job again took up his theme and said:

2 By God who has deprived me of justice!
By Shaddai who has embittered my life!
3 As long as there is life in me,
And God's breath is in my nostrils,
4 My lips will speak no wrong,
Nor my tongue utter deceit.
5 Far be it from me to say you are right;
Until I die I will maintain my integrity.
6 I persist in my righteousness and will not yield;
ᵃI shall be free of reproachᵃ as long as I live.

7 May my enemy be as the wicked;
My assailant, as the wrongdoer.
8 For what hope has the impious man when he is cut down,
When God takes away his life?
9 Will God hear his cry
When trouble comes upon him,
10 When he seeks the favor of Shaddai,
Calls upon God at all times?
11 I will teach you what is in God's power,

ᶜ⁻ᶜ *Cf. Isa. 27.1.*

ᵃ⁻ᵃ *Meaning of Heb. uncertain.*

And what is with Shaddai I will not conceal.
¹² All of you have seen it,
So why talk nonsense?
¹³ This is the evil man's portion from God,
The lot that the ruthless receive from Shaddai:
¹⁴ Should he have many sons—they are marked for the
    sword;
His descendants will never have their fill of bread;
¹⁵ Those who survive him will be buried in a plague,
And their widows will not weep;
¹⁶ Should he pile up silver like dust,
Lay up clothing like dirt—
¹⁷ He may lay it up, but the righteous will wear it,
And the innocent will share the silver.
¹⁸ The house he built is like a bird's nest,
Like the booth a watchman makes.
¹⁹ He lies down, a rich man, with [his wealth] intact;
When he opens his eyes it is gone.
²⁰ Terror overtakes him like a flood;
A storm wind makes off with him by night.
²¹ The east wind carries him far away, and he is gone;
It sweeps him from his place.
²² Then it hurls itself at him without mercy;
He tries to escape from its force.
²³ It claps its hands at him,
And whistles at him from its place.

28   There is a mine for silver,
And a place where gold is refined.
² Iron is taken out of the earth,
And copper smelted from rock.
³ He sets bounds for darkness;
To every limit man probes,
To rocks in deepest darkness.

4 *a*-They open up a shaft far from where men live,
[In places] forgotten by wayfarers,
Destitute of men, far removed.-*a*
5 Earth, out of which food grows,
Is changed below as if into fire.
6 Its rocks are a source of sapphires;
It contains gold dust too.
7 No bird of prey knows the path to it;
The falcon's eye has not gazed upon it.
8 The proud beasts have not reached it;
The lion has not crossed it.
9 Man sets his hand against the flinty rock
And overturns mountains by the roots.
10 He carves out channels through rock;
His eyes behold every precious thing.
11 He dams up the sources of the streams
So that hidden things may be brought to light.

12 But where can wisdom be found;
Where is the source of understanding?
13 No man can set a value on it;
It cannot be found in the land of the living.
14 The deep says, "It is not in me";
The sea says, "I do not have it."
15 It cannot be bartered for gold;
Silver cannot be paid out as its price.
16 The finest gold of Ophir cannot be weighed against it,
Nor precious onyx, nor sapphire.
17 Gold or glass cannot match its value,
Nor vessels of fine gold be exchanged for it.
18 Coral and crystal cannot be mentioned with it;
A pouch of wisdom is better than rubies.
19 Topaz from Nubia cannot match its value;
Pure gold cannot be weighed against it.

---

a-a *Meaning of Heb. uncertain.*

²⁰ But whence does wisdom come?
Where is the source of understanding?
²¹ It is hidden from the eyes of all living,
Concealed from the fowl of heaven.
²² Abaddon and Death say,
"We have only a report of it."
²³ God understands the way to it;
He knows its source;
²⁴ For He sees to the ends of the earth,
Observes all that is beneath the heavens.
²⁵ When He fixed the weight of the winds,
Set the measure of the waters;
²⁶ When He made a rule for the rain
And a course for the thunderstorms,
²⁷ Then He saw it and gauged it;
He measured it and probed it.
²⁸ He said to man,
"See! Fear of the Lord is wisdom;
To shun evil is understanding."

29 Job again took up his theme and said:

² O that I were as in months gone by,
In the days when God watched over me,
³ When His lamp shone over my head,
When I walked in the dark by its light,
⁴ When I was in my prime,
When God's company graced my tent,
⁵ When Shaddai was still with me,
When my lads surrounded me,
⁶ When my feet were bathed in cream,
And rocks poured out streams of oil for me.
⁷ When I passed through the city gates
To take my seat in the square,

⁸ Young men saw me and hid,
Elders rose and stood;
⁹ Nobles held back their words;
They clapped their hands to their mouths.
¹⁰ The voices of princes were hushed;
Their tongues stuck to their palates.
¹¹ The ear that heard me acclaimed me;
The eye that saw, commended me.
¹² For I saved the poor man who cried out,
The orphan who had none to help him.
¹³ I received the blessing of the lost;
I gladdened the heart of the widow.
¹⁴ I clothed myself in righteousness and it robed me;
Justice was my cloak and turban.
¹⁵ I was eyes to the blind
And feet to the lame.
¹⁶ I was a father to the needy,
And I looked into the case of the stranger.
¹⁷ I broke the jaws of the wrongdoer,
And I wrested prey from his teeth.
¹⁸ I thought I would end my days with my family,ᵃ
And ᵇ-be as long-lived as the phoenix,⁻ᵇ
¹⁹ My roots reaching water,
And dew lying on my branches;
²⁰ My vigor refreshed,
My bow ever new in my hand.
²¹ Men would listen to me expectantly,
And wait for my counsel.
²² After I spoke they had nothing to say;
My words were as drops [of dew] upon them.
²³ They waited for me as for rain,
For the late rain, their mouths open wide.
²⁴ When I smiled at them, they would not believe it;
They never expectedᶜ a sign of my favor.
²⁵ I decided their course and presided over them;

ᵃ *Lit. "nest."*
ᵇ⁻ᵇ *Others "multiply days like sand."*
ᶜ *Taking* yappilun *as from* pll; *cf. Gen. 48.11.*

I lived like a king among his troops,
Like one who consoles mourners.

30 But now those younger than I deride me,
[Men] whose fathers I would have disdained to put among
my sheep dogs.
² Of what use to me is the strength of their hands?
All their vigor*ᵃ* is gone.
³ Wasted from want and starvation,
They flee to a parched land,
To the gloom of desolate wasteland.
⁴ They pluck saltwort and wormwood;
The roots of broom are their food.
⁵ Driven out *ᵃ*-from society,-*ᵃ*
They are cried at like a thief.
⁶ They live in the gullies of wadis,
In holes in the ground, and in rocks,
⁷ Braying among the bushes,
Huddling among the nettles,
⁸ Scoundrels, nobodies,
Stricken from the earth.

⁹ Now I am the butt of their gibes;
I have become a byword to them.
¹⁰ They abhor me; they keep their distance from me;
They do not withhold spittle from my face.
¹¹ Because God*ᵇ* has disarmed*ᶜ* and humbled me,
They have thrown off restraint in my presence.
¹² Mere striplings assail me at my right hand:
They put me to flight;
They build their roads for my ruin.
¹³ They tear up my path;
They promote my fall,
Although it does them no good.

ᵃ⁻ᵃ Meaning of Heb. uncertain.
ᵇ Lit. "He."
ᶜ Lit. "loosened my [bow] string."

¹⁴ They come as through a wide breach;
They roll in ᵃ-like raging billows.⁻ᵃ
¹⁵ Terror tumbles upon me;
It sweeps away my honor like the wind;
My dignityᵈ vanishes like a cloud.
¹⁶ So now my life runs out;
Days of misery have taken hold of me.
¹⁷ By night my bones feel gnawed;
My sinews never rest.
¹⁸ ᵃ-With great effort I change clothing;
The neck of my tunic fits my waist.⁻ᵃ
¹⁹ He regarded me as clay,
I have become like dust and ashes.

²⁰ I cry out to You, but You do not answer me;
I wait, but You do [not] consider me.
²¹ You have become cruel to me;
With Your powerful hand You harass me.
²² You lift me up and mount me on the wind;
You make my courage melt.
²³ I know You will bring me to death,
The house assigned for all the living.
²⁴ ᵃ-Surely He would not strike at a ruin
If, in calamity, one cried out to Him.⁻ᵃ
²⁵ Did I not weep for the unfortunate?
Did I not grieve for the needy?
²⁶ I looked forward to good fortune, but evil came;
I hoped for light, but darkness came.
²⁷ My bowels are in turmoil without respite;
Days of misery confront me.
²⁸ I walk about in sunless gloom;
I rise in the assembly and cry out.
²⁹ I have become a brother to jackals,
A companion to ostriches.
³⁰ My skin, blackened, is peeling off me;

ᵈ *Heb.* yeshu'athi *taken as related to* shoa', *"noble."*

My bones are charred by the heat.
³¹ So my lyre is given over to mourning,
My pipe, to accompany weepers.

31 I have covenanted with my eyes
Not to gaze on a maiden.
² What fate is decreed by God above?
What lot, by Shaddai in the heights?
³ Calamity is surely for the iniquitous;
Misfortune, for the worker of mischief.
⁴ Surely He observes my ways,
Takes account of my every step.

⁵ Have I walked with worthless men,
Or my feet hurried to deceit?
⁶ Let Him weigh me on the scale of righteousness;
Let God ascertain my integrity.
⁷ If my feet have strayed from their course,
My heart followed after my eyes,
And a stain sullied my hands,
⁸ May I sow, but another reap,
May the growth of my field be uprooted!
⁹ If my heart was ravished by the wife of my neighbor,
And I lay in wait at his door,
¹⁰ May my wife grind for another,
May others kneel over her!
¹¹ For that would have been debauchery,
A criminal offense,
¹² A fire burning down to Abaddon,
Consuming the roots of all my increase.
¹³ Did I ever brush aside the case of my servants, man
or maid,
When they made a complaint against me?
¹⁴ What then should I do when God arises;

When He calls me to account, what should I answer Him?
¹⁵ Did not He who made me in my mother's belly make
    him?
Did not One form us both in the womb?
¹⁶ Did I deny the poor their needs,
Or let a^a widow pine away,
¹⁷ By eating my food alone,
The fatherless not eating of it also?
¹⁸ Why, from my youth he grew up with me as though I
    were his father;
Since I left my mother's womb I was her^b guide.
¹⁹ I never saw an unclad wretch,
A needy man without clothing,
²⁰ Whose loins did not bless me
As he warmed himself with the shearings of my sheep.
²¹ If I raised my hand against the fatherless,
Looking to my supporters in the gate,
²² May my arm drop off my shoulder;
My forearm break off ^cat the elbow.^c
²³ For I am in dread of God-sent calamity;
I cannot bear His threat.
²⁴ Did I put my reliance on gold,
Or regard fine gold as my bulwark?
²⁵ Did I rejoice in my great wealth,
In having attained plenty?
²⁶ If ever I saw the light shining,
The moon on its course in full glory,
²⁷ And I secretly succumbed,
And my hand touched my mouth in a kiss,
²⁸ That, too, would have been a criminal offense,
For I would have denied God above.
²⁹ Did I rejoice over my enemy's misfortune?
Did I thrill because evil befell him?
³⁰ I never let my mouth^d sin
By wishing his death in a curse.

^a Lit. "the eyes of a."
^b Viz. the widow's.
^{c-c} Lit. "from its shaft," i.e. the humerus.
^d Lit. "palate."

³¹ (Indeed, the men of my clan said,
"We would consume his flesh insatiably!")
³² No sojourner spent the night in the open;
I opened my doors to the road.
³³ Did I hide my transgressions like Adam,
Bury my wrongdoing in my bosom,
³⁴ That I should [now] fear the great multitude,
And am shattered by the contempt of families,
So that I keep silent and do not step outdoors?

³⁵ O that I had someone to give me a hearing;
O that Shaddai would reply to my writ,
Or my accuser draw up a true bill!
³⁶ I would carry it on my shoulder;
Tie it around me for a wreath.
³⁷ I would give him an account of my steps,
Offer it as to a commander.

³⁸ If my land cries out against me,
Its furrows weep together;
³⁹ If I have eaten its produce without payment,
And made its [rightful] owners despair,
⁴⁰ May nettles grow there instead of wheat;
Instead of barley, stinkweed!

The words of Job are at an end.

32 These three men ceased replying to Job, for he considered himself right. ² Then Elihu son of Barachel the Buzite, of the family of Ram, was angry—angry at Job because he thought himself right against God. ³ He was angry as well at his three friends, because they found no reply, but merely condemned Job. ⁴ Elihu waited out Job's speech, for they were all older than he. ⁵ But

when Elihu saw that the three men had nothing to reply, he was
angry.

6 Then Elihu son of Barachel the Buzite said in reply:

> I have but few years, while you are old;
> Therefore I was too awestruck and fearful
> To hold forth among you.
> 7 I thought, "Let age speak;
> Let advanced years declare wise things."
> 8 But truly it is the spirit in men,
> The breath of Shaddai, that gives them understanding.
> 9 It is not the aged who are wise,
> The elders, who understand how to judge.
> 10 Therefore I say, "Listen to me;
> I too would hold forth."
> 11 Here I have waited out your speeches,
> I have given ear to your insights,
> While you probed the issues;
> 12 But as I attended to you,
> I saw that none of you could argue with Job,
> Or offer replies to his statements.
> 13 I fear you will say, "We have found the wise course;
> God will defeat him, not man."
> 14 He did not set out his case against me,
> Nor shall I use your reasons to reply to him.
> 15 They have been broken and can no longer reply;
> Words fail them.
> 16 I have waited till they stopped speaking,
> Till they ended and no longer replied.
> 17 Now I also would have my say;
> I too would like to hold forth,
> 18 For I am full of words;
> The wind in my belly presses me.
> 19 My belly is like wine not yet opened,

Like jugs of new wine ready to burst.
²⁰ Let me speak, then, and get relief;
Let me open my lips and reply.
²¹ I would not show regard for any man,
Or temper my speech for anyone's sake;
²² For I do not know how to temper my speech—
My Maker would soon carry me off!

33 But now, Job, listen to my words,
Give ear to all that I say.
² Now I open my lips;
My tongue forms words in my mouth.
³ My words bespeak the uprightness of my heart;
My lips utter insight honestly.
⁴ The spirit of God formed me;
The breath of Shaddai sustains me.
⁵ If you can, answer me;
Argue against me, take your stand.
⁶ You and I are the same before God;
I too was nipped from clay.
⁷ You are not overwhelmed by fear of me;
My pressure does not weigh heavily on you.

⁸ Indeed, you have stated in my hearing,
I heard the words spoken,
⁹ "I am guiltless, free from transgression;
I am innocent, without iniquity.
¹⁰ But He finds reasons to oppose me,
Considers me His enemy.
¹¹ He puts my feet in stocks,
Watches all my ways."

¹² In this you are not right;
I will answer you: God is greater than any man.

¹³ Why do you complain against Him
That He does not reply to any of man's charges?
¹⁴ For God speaks ᵃtime and againᵃ
—Though man does not perceive it—
¹⁵ In a dream, a night vision,
When deep sleep falls on men,
While they slumber on their beds.
¹⁶ Then He opens men's understanding,
And by disciplining them leaves His signature
¹⁷ To turn man away from an action,
To suppress pride in man.
¹⁸ He spares him from the Pit,
His person, from perishing by the sword.
¹⁹ He is reproved by pains on his bed,
And the trembling in his bones is constant.
²⁰ He detests food;
Fine food [is repulsive] to him.
²¹ His flesh wastes away till it cannot be seen,
And his bones are rubbed away till they are invisible.
²² He comes close to the Pit,
His life [verges] on death.
²³ If he has a representative,
One advocate against a thousand
To declare the man's uprightness,
²⁴ Then He has mercy on him and decrees,
"Redeem him from descending to the Pit,
For I have obtained his ransom;
²⁵ Let his flesh be healthierᵇ than in his youth;
Let him return to his younger days."
²⁶ He prays to God and is accepted by Him;
He enters His presence with shouts of joy,
For He requites a man for his righteousness.
²⁷ Heᶜ declaresᵇ to men,
"I have sinned; I have perverted what was right;
But I was not paid back for it."

ᵃ⁻ᵃ *Lit. "once . . . twice."*
ᵇ *Meaning of Heb. uncertain.*
ᶜ *I.e. the contrite man.*

²⁸ He redeemed *d*-him from passing into the Pit;
He-*d* will enjoy the light.
²⁹ Truly, God does all these things
Two or three times to a man,
³⁰ To bring him back from the Pit,
That he may bask in the light of life.

³¹ Pay heed, Job, and hear me;
Be still, and I will speak;
³² If you have what to say, answer me;
Speak, for I am eager to vindicate you.
³³ But if not, you listen to me;
Be still, and I will teach you wisdom.

34 Elihu said in reply:

² Listen, O wise men, to my words;
You who have knowledge, give ear to me.
³ For the ear tests arguments
As the palate tastes food.
⁴ Let us decide for ourselves what is just;
Let us know among ourselves what is good.
⁵ For Job has said, "I am right;
God has deprived me of justice.
⁶ I declare the judgment against me false;
My arrow-wound is deadly, though I am free from trans-
    gression."
⁷ What man is like Job,
Who drinks mockery like water;
⁸ Who makes common cause with evildoers,
And goes with wicked men?
⁹ For he says, "Man gains nothing
When he is in God's favor."

ᵈ⁻ᵈ *Or, with* kethib, *"me . . . I."*

10 Therefore, men of understanding, listen to me;
Wickedness be far from God,
Wrongdoing, from Shaddai!
11 For He pays a man according to his actions,
And provides for him according to his conduct;
12 For God surely does not act wickedly;
Shaddai does not pervert justice.
13 Who placed the earth in His charge?
Who ordered the entire world?
14 If He but intends it,
He can call back His spirit and breath;
15 All flesh would at once expire,
And mankind return to dust.

16 If you would understand, listen to this;
Give ear to what I say.
17 Would one who hates justice govern?
Would you condemn the Just Mighty One?
18 Would you call a king a scoundrel,
Great men, wicked?
19 He is not partial to princes;
The noble are not preferred to the wretched;
For all of them are the work of His hands.
20 Some die suddenly in the middle of the night;
People are in turmoil and pass on;
Even great men are removed—not by human hands.
21 For His eyes are upon a man's ways;
He observes his every step.
22 Neither darkness nor gloom offer
A hiding-place for evildoers.
23 He has no set time for man
To appear before God in judgment.
24 He shatters mighty men without number
And sets others in their place.
25 Truly, He knows their deeds;

Night is over, and they are crushed.
26 He strikes them down with the wicked
Where people can see,
27 Because they have been disloyal to Him
And have not understood any of His ways;
28 Thus He lets the cry of the poor come before Him;
He listens to the cry of the needy.
29 When He is silent, who will condemn?
If He hides His face, who will see Him,
Be it nation or man?
30 The impious men rule no more,
Nor do those who ensnare the people.
31 Has he said to God,
"I will bear [my punishment] and offend no more.
32 What I cannot see You teach me.
If I have done iniquity, I shall not do so again"?
33 Should He requite as you see fit?
But you have despised [Him]!
You must decide, not I;
Speak what you know.
34 Men of understanding say to me,
Wise men who hear me,
35 "Job does not speak with knowledge;
His words lack understanding."
36 Would that Job were tried to the limit
For answers which befit sinful men.
37 He adds to his sin;
He increases his transgression among us;
He multiplies his statements against God.

35 Elihu said in reply:

2 Do you think it just
To say, "I am right against God"?

³ If you ask how it benefits you,
"What have I gained from not sinning?"
⁴ I shall give you a reply,
You, along with your friends.
⁵ Behold the heavens and see;
Look at the skies high above you.
⁶ If you sin, what do you do to Him?
If your transgressions are many,
How do you affect Him?
⁷ If you are righteous,
What do you give Him;
What does He receive from your hand?
⁸ Your wickedness affects men like yourself;
Your righteousness, mortals.

⁹ Because of contention the oppressed cry out;
They shout because of the power of the great.
¹⁰ But none says, "Where is my God, my Maker,
Who gives strength in the night;
¹¹ Who gives us more knowledge than the beasts of
    the earth,
Makes us wiser than the birds of the sky?"
¹² Then they cry out, but He does not respond
Because of the arrogance of evil men.
¹³ Surely it is false that God does not listen,
That Shaddai does not take note of it.
¹⁴ Though you say, "You do not take note of it,"
The case is before Him;
So wait for Him.
¹⁵ ᵃ⁻But since now it does not seem so,
He vents his anger;
He does not realize that it may be long drawn out.⁻ᵃ
¹⁶ Hence Job mouths empty words,
And piles up words without knowledge.

ᵃ⁻ᵃ *Meaning of Heb. uncertain.*

36 Then Elihu spoke once more.

2 Wait a little and let me hold forth;
There is still more to say for God.
3 I will make my opinions widely known;
I will justify my Maker.
4 In truth, my words are not false;
A man of sound opinions is before you.

5 See, God is mighty; He is not contemptuous;
He is mighty in strength and mind.
6 He does not let the wicked live;
He grants justice to the lowly.
7 He does not withdraw His eyes from the righteous;
With kings on thrones
He seats them forever, and they are exalted.
8 If they are bound in shackles
And caught in trammels of affliction,
9 He declares to them what they have done,
And that their transgressions are excessive;
10 He opens their understanding by discipline,
And orders them back from mischief.
11 If they will serve obediently,
They shall spend their days in happiness,
Their years in delight.
12 But if they are not obedient,
They shall perish by the sword,
Die for lack of understanding.
13 But the impious in heart become enraged;
They do not cry for help when He afflicts them.
14 They die in their youth;
[Expire] among the depraved.
15 He rescues the lowly from their affliction,

And opens their understanding through distress.
16 Indeed, He draws you away from the brink of distress
To a broad place where there is no constraint;
Your table is laid out with rich food.
17 You are obsessed with the case of the wicked man,
But the justice of the case will be upheld.
18 Let anger at his affluence not mislead you;
Let much bribery not turn you aside.
19 *a*-Will your limitless wealth avail you,-*a*
All your powerful efforts?
20 Do not long for the night
When peoples vanish where they are.
21 Beware! Do not turn to mischief;
Because of that you have been tried by affliction.
22 See, God is beyond reach in His power;
Who governs like Him?
23 Who ever reproached Him for His conduct?
Who ever said, "You have done wrong"?
24 Remember, then, to magnify His work,
Of which men have sung,
25 Which all men have beheld,
Men have seen, from a distance.
26 See, God is greater than we can know;
The number of His years cannot be counted.
27 He forms the droplets of water,
Which cluster into rain, from His mist.
28 The skies rain;
They pour down on all mankind.
29 Can one, indeed, contemplate the expanse of clouds,
The thunderings from His pavilion?
30 See, He spreads His lightning over it;
It fills the bed of the sea.
31 By these things He controls peoples;
He gives food in abundance.
32 Lightning fills His hands;

a-a *Meaning of Heb. uncertain.*

He orders it to hit the mark.
³³ Its noise tells of Him.
ᵃ⁻The kindling of anger against iniquity.⁻ᵃ

37 Because of this, too, my heart quakes,
And leaps from its place.
² Just listen to the noise of His rumbling,
To the sound that comes out of His mouth.
³ He lets it loose beneath the entire heavens—
His lightning, to the ends of the earth.
⁴ After it, He lets out a roar;
He thunders in His majestic voice.
No one can find a trace of it by the time His voice is heard.
⁵ God thunders marvelously with His voice;
He works wonders that we cannot understand.
⁶ He commands the snow, "Fall to the ground!"
And the downpour of rain, His mighty downpour of rain,
⁷ Is as a sign on every man's hand,
That all men may know His doings.
⁸ Then the beast enters its lair,
And remains in its den.
⁹ The storm wind comes from its chamber,
And the cold from the constellations.
¹⁰ By the breath of God ice is formed,
And the expanse of water becomes solid.
¹¹ He also loads the clouds with moisture
And scatters His lightning-clouds.
¹² ᵃ⁻He keeps turning events by His stratagems,⁻ᵃ
That they might accomplish all that He commands them
Throughout the inhabited earth,
¹³ Causing each of them to happen to His land,
Whether as a scourge or as a blessing.

¹⁴ Give ear to this, Job;
Stop to consider the marvels of God.

ᵃ⁻ᵃ *Meaning of Heb. uncertain.*

¹⁵ Do you know what charge God lays upon them
When His lightning-clouds shine?
¹⁶ Do you know the marvels worked upon the expanse of
  clouds
By Him whose understanding is perfect,
¹⁷ ᵃ⁻Why your clothes become hot⁻ᵃ
When the land is becalmed by the south wind?
¹⁸ Can you help him stretch out the heavens,
Firm as a mirror of cast metal?
¹⁹ Inform us, then, what we may say to Him;
We cannot argue because [we are in] darkness.
²⁰ Is anything conveyed to Him when I speak?
Can a man say anything when he is confused?
²¹ Now, then, one cannot see the sun,
Though it be bright in the heavens,
Until the wind comes and clears them [of clouds].
²² By the north wind the golden rays emerge;
The splendor about God is awesome.
²³ Shaddai—we cannot attain to Him;
He is great in power and justice
And abundant in righteousness; He does not torment.
²⁴ Therefore, men are in awe of Him
Whom none of the wise can perceive.

38

Then the LORD replied to Job out of the tempest and said:

² Who is this who darkens counsel,
Speaking without knowledge?
³ Gird your loins like a man;
I will ask and you will inform Me.

⁴ Where were you when I laid the earth's foundations?
Speak if you have understanding.
⁵ Do you know who fixed its dimensions
Or who measured it with a line?

⁶ Onto what were its bases sunk?
Who set its cornerstone
⁷ When the morning stars sang together
And all the divine beings shouted for joy?

⁸ Who closed the sea behind doors
When it gushed forth out of the womb,
⁹ When I clothed it in clouds,
Swaddled it in dense clouds,
¹⁰ When I made breakers My limit for it,
And set up its bar and doors,
¹¹ And said, "You may come so far and no farther;
Here your surging waves will stop"?

¹² Have you ever commanded the day to break,
Assigned the dawn its place,
¹³ So that it seizes the corners of the earth
And shakes the wicked out of it?
¹⁴ It changes like clay under the seal
Till [its hues] are fixed like those of a garment.
¹⁵ Their light is withheld from the wicked,
And the upraised arm is broken.

¹⁶ Have you penetrated to the sources of the sea,
Or walked in the recesses of the deep?
¹⁷ Have the gates of death been disclosed to you?
Have you seen the gates of deep darkness?
¹⁸ Have you surveyed the expanses of the earth?
If you know of these—tell Me.

¹⁹ Which path leads to where light dwells,
And where is the place of darkness,
²⁰ That you may take it to its domain
And know the way to its home?

21 Surely you know, for you were born then,
And the number of your years is many!

22 Have you penetrated the vaults of snow,
Seen the vaults of hail,
23 Which I have put aside for a time of adversity,
For a day of war and battle?
24 By what path is the west wind*a* dispersed,
The east wind scattered over the earth?
25 Who cut a channel for the torrents
And a path for the thunderstorms,
26 To rain down on uninhabited land,
On the wilderness where no man is,
27 To saturate the desolate wasteland,
And make the crop of grass sprout forth?
28 Does the rain have a father?
Who begot the dewdrops?
29 From whose belly came forth the ice?
Who gave birth to the frost of heaven?
30 Water congeals like stone,
And the surface of the deep compacts.

31 Can you tie cords to Pleiades
Or undo the reins of Orion?
32 Can you lead out Mazzaroth*b* in its season,
Conduct the Bear with her sons?
33 Do you know the laws of heaven
Or impose its authority on earth?

34 Can you send up an order to the clouds
For an abundance of water to cover you?
35 Can you dispatch the lightning on a mission
And have it answer you, "I am ready"?
36 Who put wisdom in the hidden parts?

a As Aramaic 'urya.
b Evidently a constellation.

Who gave understanding to the mind?[c]
[37] Who is wise enough to give an account of the heavens?
Who can tilt the bottles of the sky,
[38] Whereupon the earth melts into a mass,
And its clods stick together.

[39] Can you hunt prey for the lion,
And satisfy the appetite of the king of beasts?
[40] They crouch in their dens,
Lie in ambush in their lairs.
[41] Who provides food for the raven
When his young cry out to God
And wander about without food?

39 Do you know the season when the mountain goats give
birth?
Can you mark the time when the hinds calve?
[2] Can you count the months they must complete?
Do you know the season they give birth,
[3] When they couch to bring forth their offspring,
To deliver their young?
[4] Their young are healthy; they grow up in the open;
They leave and return no more.

[5] Who sets the wild ass free?
Who loosens the bonds of the onager,
[6] Whose home I have made the wilderness,
The salt land his dwelling-place?
[7] He scoffs at the tumult of the city,
Does not hear the shouts of the driver.
[8] He roams the hills for his pasture;
He searches for any green thing.

---

[c] *Or "rooster"; meaning of Heb. uncertain.*

⁹ Would the wild ox agree to serve you?
Would he spend the night at your crib?
¹⁰ Can you hold the wild ox by ropes to the furrow?
Would he plow up the valleys behind you?
¹¹ Would you rely on his great strength
And leave your toil to him?
¹² Would you trust him to bring in the seed
And gather it in from your threshing floor?

¹³ The wing of the ostrich beats joyously;
Are her pinions and plumage like the stork's?
¹⁴ She leaves her eggs on the ground,
Letting them warm in the dirt,
¹⁵ Forgetting they may be crushed underfoot,
Or trampled by a wild beast.
¹⁶ Her young are cruelly abandoned as if they were not
  hers;
Her labor is in vain for lack of concern.
¹⁷ For God deprived her of wisdom,
Gave her no share of understanding,
¹⁸ Else she would soar on high,
Scoffing at the horse and its rider.

¹⁹ Do you give the horse his strength?
Do you clothe his neck with a mane?
²⁰ Do you make him quiver like locusts,
His majestic snorting [spreading] terror?
²¹ He*a* paws with force, he runs with vigor,
Charging into battle.
²² He scoffs at fear; he cannot be frightened;
He does not recoil from the sword.
²³ A quiverful of arrows whizzes by him,
And the flashing spear and the javelin.
²⁴ Trembling with excitement, he swallows*b* the land;
He does not turn aside at the blast of the trumpet.

ᵃ *Lit. "They . . ."*
ᵇ *Or "digs up."*

25 As the trumpet sounds, he says, "Aha!"
From afar he smells the battle,
The roaring and shouting of the officers.

26 Is it by your wisdom that the hawk grows pinions,
Spreads his wings to the south?
27 Does the eagle soar at your command,
Building his nest high,
28 Dwelling in the rock,
Lodging upon the fastness of a jutting rock?
29 From there he spies out his food;
From afar his eyes see it.
30 His young gulp blood;
Where the slain are, there is he.

40 The LORD said in reply to Job.

2 a-Shall one who should be disciplined complain against
  Shaddai?-a
He who arraigns God must respond.

3 Job said in reply to the LORD:

4 See, I am of small worth; what can I answer You?
I clap my hand to my mouth.
5 I have spoken once, and will not reply;
Twice, and will do so no more.

6 Then the LORD replied to Job out of the tempest
  and said:

7 Gird your loins like a man;
I will ask, and you will inform Me.
8 Would you impugn My justice?

a-a Meaning of Heb. uncertain.

Would you condemn Me that you may be right?
9 Have you an arm like God's?
Can you thunder with a voice like His?
10 Deck yourself now with grandeur and eminence;
Clothe yourself in glory and majesty.
11 Scatter wide your raging anger;
See every proud man and bring him low.
12 See every proud man and humble him,
And bring them down where they stand.
13 Bury them all in the earth;
Hide their faces in obscurity.
14 Then even I would praise you
For the triumph your right hand won you.

15 Take now behemoth, whom I made as I did you;
He eats grass, like the cattle.
16 His strength is in his loins,
His might in the muscles of his belly.
17 a-He makes his tail stand up-a like a cedar;
The sinews of his thighs are knit together.
18 His bones are like tubes of bronze,
His limbs like iron rods.
19 He is the first of God's works;
Only his Maker can draw the sword against him.
20 The mountains yield him produce,
Where all the beasts of the field play.
21 He lies down beneath the lotuses,
In the cover of the swamp reeds.
22 The lotuses embower him with shade;
The willows of the brook surround him.
23 He can restrain the river from its rushing;
He is confident the stream*b* will gush at his command.
24 Can he be taken by his eyes?
Can his nose be pierced by hooks?
25 Can you draw out Leviathan by a fishhook?

b *Lit. "Jordan."*

Can you press down his tongue by a rope?
²⁶ Can you put a ring through his nose,
Or pierce his jaw with a barb?
²⁷ Will he plead with you at length?
Will he speak soft words to you?
²⁸ Will he make an agreement with you
To be taken as your lifelong slave?
²⁹ Will you play with him like a bird,
And tie him down for your girls?
³⁰ ^a-Shall traders traffic in him?-^a
Will he be divided up among merchants?
³¹ Can you fill his skin with darts
Or his head with fish-spears?
³² Lay a hand on him,
And you will never think of battle again.

41 See, any hope [of capturing] him must be disappointed;
One is prostrated by the very sight of him.
² There is no one so fierce as to rouse him;
Who then can stand up to Me?
³ Whoever confronts Me I will requite,
For everything under the heavens is Mine.
⁴ ^a-I will not be silent concerning him
Or the praise of his martial exploits.-^a
⁵ Who can uncover his outer garment?
Who can penetrate the folds of his jowls?
⁶ Who can pry open the doors of his face?
His bared teeth strike terror.
⁷ His protective scales are his pride,
Locked with a binding seal.
⁸ One scale touches the other;
Not even a breath can enter between them.
⁹ Each clings to each;
They are interlocked so they cannot be parted.

^{a-a} *Meaning of Heb. uncertain.*

¹⁰ His sneezings flash lightning,
And his eyes are like the glimmerings of dawn.
¹¹ Firebrands stream from his mouth;
Fiery sparks escape.
¹² Out of his nostrils comes smoke
As from a steaming, boiling cauldron.
¹³ His breath ignites coals;
Flames blaze from his mouth.
¹⁴ Strength resides in his neck;
Power leaps before him.
¹⁵ The layers of his flesh stick together;
He is as though cast hard; he does not totter.
¹⁶ His heart is cast hard as a stone,
Hard as the nether millstone.
¹⁷ Divine beings are in dread as he rears up;
As he crashes down, they cringe.
¹⁸ No sword that overtakes him can prevail,
Nor spear, nor missile, nor lance.
¹⁹ He regards iron as straw,
Bronze, as rotted wood.
²⁰ No arrow can put him to flight;
Slingstones turn into stubble for him.
²¹ Clubs*a* are regarded as stubble;
He scoffs at the quivering javelin.
²² His underpart is jagged shards;
It spreads a threshing-sledge on the mud.
²³ He makes the depths seethe like a cauldron;
He makes the sea [boil] like an ointment-pot.
²⁴ His wake is a luminous path;
He makes the deep seem white-haired.
²⁵ There is no one on land who can dominate him,
Made as he is without fear.
²⁶ He sees all that is haughty;
He is king over all proud beasts.

42 Job said in reply to the Lord:

² I know that You can do everything,
That nothing you propose is impossible for You.
³ Who is this who obscures counsel without knowledge?
Indeed, I spoke without understanding
Of things beyond me, which I did not know.
⁴ Hear now, and I will speak;
I will ask, and You will inform me.
⁵ I had heard You with my ears,
But now I see You with my eyes;
⁶ Therefore, I recant and relent,
Being but dust and ashes.

⁷ After the Lord had spoken these words to Job, the Lord said to Eliphaz the Temanite, "I am incensed at you and your two friends, for you have not spoken the truth about Me as did My servant Job. ⁸ Now take seven bulls and seven rams and go to My servant Job and sacrifice a burnt offering for yourselves. And let Job, My servant, pray for you; for to him I will show favor and not treat you vilely, since you have not spoken the truth about Me as did My servant Job." ⁹ Eliphaz the Temanite and Bildad the Shuhite and Zophar the Naamathite went and did as the Lord had told them, and the Lord showed favor to Job. ¹⁰ The Lord restored Job's fortunes when he prayed on behalf of his friends, and the Lord gave Job twice what he had before.

¹¹ All his brothers and sisters and all his former friends came to him and had a meal with him in his house. They consoled and comforted him for all the misfortune that the Lord had brought upon him. Each gave him one *kesitah*ᵃ and each one gold ring. ¹² Thus the Lord blessed the latter years of Job's life more than the former. He had fourteen thousand sheep, six thousand camels, one thousand yoke of oxen, and one thousand she-asses.

ᵃ *A unit of unknown value.*

[13] He also had seven sons and three daughters. [14] The first he named Jemimah, the second Keziah, and the third Keren-hap-puch. [15] Nowhere in the land were women as beautiful as Job's daughters to be found. Their father gave them estates together with their brothers. [16] Afterward, Job lived one hundred and forty years to see four generations of sons and grandsons. [17] So Job died old and contented.

שיר השירים

THE SONG OF SONGS

שיר השירים
THE SONG OF SONGS

1 The Song of Songs, by[a] Solomon.

² [b-]Oh, give me of the kisses of your mouth,[-b]
For your love is more delightful than wine.
³ Your ointments yield a sweet fragrance,
Your name is like finest[c] oil—
Therefore do maidens love you.
⁴ Draw me after you, let us run!
[d-]The king has brought me to his chambers.[-d]
Let us delight and rejoice in your love,
Savoring it more than wine—
[e-]Like new wine[-e] they love you!

⁵ I am dark, but comely,
O daughters of Jerusalem—
Like the tents of Kedar,
Like the pavilions of Solomon.
⁶ Don't stare at me because I am swarthy,
Because the sun has gazed upon me.
My mother's sons quarreled with me,
They made me guard the vineyards;
My own vineyard I did not guard.

⁷ Tell me, you whom I love so well;
Where do you pasture your sheep?
Where do you rest them at noon?

[a] *Or "concerning."*
[b-b] *Heb. "Let him give me of the kisses of his mouth!"*
[c] *Meaning of Heb. uncertain.*
[d-d] *Emendation yields "Bring me, O king, to your chambers."*
[e-e] *Understanding* mesharim *as related to* tirosh; *cf. Aramaic* merath.

Let me not be ^cas one who strays^c
Beside the flocks of your fellows.
⁸ If you do not know, O fairest of women,
Go follow the tracks of the sheep,
And graze your kids^f
By the tents of the shepherds.

⁹ I have likened you, my darling,
To a mare in Pharaoh's chariots:
¹⁰ Your cheeks are comely with plaited wreaths,
Your neck with strings of jewels.
¹¹ We will add wreaths of gold
To your spangles of silver.

¹² While the king was on his couch,
My nard gave forth its fragrance.
¹³ My beloved to me is a bag of myrrh
Lodged between my breasts.
¹⁴ My beloved to me is a spray of henna blooms
From the vineyards of En-gedi.

¹⁵ Ah, you are fair, my darling,
Ah, you are fair,
With your dove-like eyes!
¹⁶ And you, my beloved, are handsome,
Beautiful indeed!
Our couch is in a bower;
¹⁷ Cedars are the beams of our house,
Cypresses the rafters.

2 I am a rose^a of Sharon,
A lily of the valleys.

---

^f *As a pretext for coming.*
^a *Lit. "crocus."*

2 Like a lily among thorns,
So is my darling among the maidens.

3 Like an apple tree among trees of the forest,
So is my beloved among the youths.
I delight to sit in his shade,
And his fruit is sweet to my mouth.

4 He brought me to the banquet room
b-And his banner of love was over me.-*b*
5 "Sustain me with raisin cakes,
Refresh me with apples,
For I am faint with love."
6 His left hand was under my head,
His right arm embraced me.
7 I adjure you, O maidens of Jerusalem,
By gazelles or by hinds of the field:
Do not wake or rouse
Love until it please!

8 Hark! My beloved!
There he comes,
Leaping over mountains,
Bounding over hills.
9 My beloved is like a gazelle
Or like a young stag.
There he stands behind our wall,
Gazing through the window,
Peering through the lattice.
10 My beloved spoke thus to me,
"Arise, my darling;
My fair one, come away!
11 For now the winter is past,
The rains are over and gone.

---

b-b Meaning of Heb. uncertain.

¹² The blossoms have appeared in the land,
The time of pruning*c* has come;
The song of the turtledove
Is heard in our land.
¹³ The green figs form on the fig tree,
The vines in blossom give off fragrance.
Arise, my darling;
My fair one, come away!

¹⁴ "O my dove, in the cranny of the rocks,
Hidden by the cliff,
Let me see your face,
Let me hear your voice;
For your voice is sweet
And your face is comely."
¹⁵ Catch us the foxes,
The little foxes
That ruin the vineyards—
For our vineyard is in blossom.

¹⁶ My beloved is mine
And I am his
Who browses among the lilies.
¹⁷ When the day *d*-blows gently-*d*
And the shadows flee,*e*
Set out, my beloved,
Swift as a gazelle
Or a young stag,
For the hills of spices!*f*

3 Upon my couch at night*a*
I sought the one I love—
I sought, but found him not.

c Or "singing."
d-d Emendation yields "declines"; cf. Jer. 6.4.
e Septuagint reads "lengthen"; cf. Jer. 6.4.
f Heb. bather of uncertain meaning; 8.14 reads besamim, "spices."

a I.e. in a dream.

2 "I must rise and roam the town,
Through the streets and through the squares;
I must seek the one I love."
I sought but found him not.
3 *b*-I met the watchmen-*b*
Who patrol the town.
"Have you seen the one I love?"
4 Scarcely had I passed them
When I found the one I love.
I held him fast, I would not let him go
Till I brought him to my mother's house,
To the chamber of her who conceived me
5 I adjure you, O maidens of Jerusalem,
By gazelles or by hinds of the field:
Do not wake or rouse
Love until it please!

6 Who is she that comes up from the desert
Like columns of smoke,
In clouds of myrrh and frankincense,
Of all the powders of the merchant?
7 There is Solomon's couch,
Encircled by sixty warriors
Of the warriors of Israel,
8 All of them trained*c* in warfare,
Skilled in battle,
Each with sword on thigh
Because of terror by night.

9 King Solomon made him a palanquin
Of wood from Lebanon.
10 He made its posts of silver,
Its back*d* of gold,
Its seat of purple wool.

b-b *Lit. "The watchmen met me."*
c *Cf. Akkadian aḫāzu, "to learn."*
d *Meaning of Heb. uncertain.*

339

Within, it was decked with [e]love
By the maidens of Jerusalem.[-e]
[11] O maidens of Zion, go forth
And gaze upon King Solomon
Wearing the crown that his mother
Gave him on his wedding day,
On his day of bliss.

4   Ah, you are fair, my darling,
Ah, you are fair.
Your eyes are like doves
Behind your veil.
Your hair is like a flock of goats
Streaming down Mount Gilead.
[2] Your teeth are like a flock of ewes[a]
Climbing up from the washing pool;
All of them bear twins,
And not one loses her young.
[3] Your lips are like a crimson thread,
Your mouth is lovely.
Your brow behind your veil
[Gleams] like a pomegranate split open.
[4] Your neck is like the Tower of David,
Built [b]to hold weapons,[-b]
Hung with a thousand shields—
All the quivers of warriors.
[5] Your breasts are like two fawns,
Twins of a gazelle,
Browsing among the lilies.
[6] [c]When the day blows gently
And the shadows flee,
I will betake me to the mount of myrrh,
To the hill of frankincense.
[7] Every part of you is fair, my darling,

[e-e] *Emendation yields:*   "*ebony.*
                    O maidens of Jerusalem!"

[a] *Cf. 6.6; exact nuance of* qeṣuboth *uncertain, perhaps "shorn ones."*
[b-b] *Apparently a poetic figure for jewelry; meaning of Heb. uncertain.*
[c] *See notes at 2.17.*

There is no blemish in you
⁸ From Lebanon come with me;
From Lebanon, my bride, with me!
Trip down from Amana's peak,
From the peak of Senir*d* and Hermon,
From the dens of lions,
From the hills*e* of leopards.

⁹ You have captured my heart,
My own,*f* my bride,
You have captured my heart
With one [glance] of your eyes,
With one coil of your necklace.
¹⁰ How sweet is your love,
My own, my bride!
How much more delightful your love than wine,
Your ointments more fragrant
Than any spice!
¹¹ Sweetness drops
From your lips, O bride;
Honey and milk
Are under your tongue;
And the scent of your robes
Is like the scent of Lebanon.
¹² A garden locked
Is my own, my bride,
A fountain locked,
A sealed-up spring.
¹³ Your limbs are an orchard of pomegranates
And of all luscious fruits,
Of henna and of nard—
¹⁴ Nard and saffron,
Fragrant reed and cinnamon,
With all aromatic woods,
Myrrh and aloes—

d Cf. Deut. 3.9.
e Emendation yields "lairs"; cf. Nah. 2.13.
f Lit. "sister"; and so frequently below.

All the choice perfumes.
[15] *g*-[You are] a garden spring,
A well of fresh water,-*g*
A rill of Lebanon.

[16] Awake, O north wind,
Come, O south wind!
Blow upon my garden,
That its perfume may spread.
Let my beloved come to his garden
And enjoy its luscious fruits!

5 I have come to my garden,
My own, my bride;
I have plucked my myrrh and spice,
Eaten my honey and honeycomb,
Drunk my wine and my milk.

Eat, lovers, and drink:
Drink deep of love!

[2] *a*I was asleep,
But my heart was wakeful.
Hark, my beloved knocks!
"Let me in, my own,
My darling, my faultless dove!
For my head is drenched with dew,
My locks with the damp of night."
[3] I had taken off my robe—
Was I to don it again?
I had bathed my feet—
Was I to soil them again?
[4] My beloved *b*-took his hand off the latch,-*b*
And my heart was stirred *c*-for him.-*c*

---

g-g *Emendation yields:*
"The spring in my garden
Is a well of fresh water."

a *In vv. 2–8 the maiden relates a dream.*
b-b *Meaning of Heb. uncertain.*
c-c *Many manuscripts and editions read "within me" ('alai).*

⁵ I rose to let in my beloved;
My hands dripped myrrh—
My fingers, flowing myrrh—
Upon the handles of the bolt.
⁶ I opened the door for my beloved,
But my beloved had turned and gone.
I was faint *d*-because of what he said.-*d*
I sought, but found him not;
I called, but he did not answer.
⁷ I met the watchmen*e*
Who patrol the town;
They struck me, they bruised me.
The guards of the walls
Stripped me of my mantle.
⁸ I adjure you, O maidens of Jerusalem!
If you meet my beloved, tell him this:
That I am faint with love.

⁹ How is your beloved better than another,*f*
O fairest of women?
How is your beloved better than another*f*
That you adjure us so?

¹⁰ My beloved is clear-skinned and ruddy,
Preeminent among ten thousand.
¹¹ His head is finest gold,
His locks are curled
And black as a raven.
¹² His eyes are like doves
By watercourses,
Bathed in milk,
b-Set by a brimming pool.-*b*
¹³ His cheeks are like beds of spices,
g-Banks of-*g* perfume
His lips are like lilies;

---

d-d *Change of vocalization yields "because of him."*
e *See note at 3.3.*
f *Or "What sort of beloved is your beloved?"*
g-g *Septuagint vocalizes as participle, "producing."*

They drip flowing myrrh.
14 His hands are rods of gold,
Studded with beryl;
His belly a tablet of ivory,
Adorned with sapphires.
15 His legs are like marble pillars
Set in sockets of fine gold.
He is majestic as Lebanon,
Stately as the cedars.
16 His mouth is delicious
And all of him is delightful.
Such is my beloved,
Such is my darling,
O maidens of Jerusalem!

6 "Whither has your beloved gone,
O fairest of women?
Whither has your beloved turned?
Let us seek him with you."
2 My beloved has gone down to his garden,
To the beds of spices,
To browse in the gardens
And to pick lilies.
3 I am my beloved's
And my beloved is mine;
He browses among the lilies.

4 You are beautiful, my darling, as Tirzah,
Comely as Jerusalem,
a-Awesome as bannered hosts.-a
5 Turn your eyes away from me,
For they overwhelm me!
Your hair is like a flock of goats

a-a *Meaning of Heb. uncertain.*

Streaming down from Gilead.
6 Your teeth are like a flock of ewes
Climbing up from the washing pool;
All of them bear twins,
And not one loses her young.
7 Your brow behind your veil
[Gleams] like a pomegranate split open.
8 There are sixty queens,
And eighty concubines,
And damsels without number.
9 Only one is my dove,
My perfect one,
The only one of her mother,
The delight of her who bore her.
Maidens see and acclaim her;
Queens and concubines, and praise her.

10 Who is she that shines through like the dawn,
Beautiful as the moon,
Radiant as the sun
*a-*Awesome as bannered hosts?*-a*

11 I went down to the nut grove
To see the budding of the vale;
To see if the vines had blossomed,
If the pomegranates were in bloom.
12 *a-*Before I knew it,
My desire set me
Mid the chariots of Ammi-nadib.*-a*

7 Turn back, turn back,
O maid of Shulem!
Turn back, turn back,

That we may gaze upon you.
"Why will you gaze at the Shulammite
In*a* the Mahanaim dance?"

2 How lovely are your feet in sandals,
O daughter of nobles!
Your rounded thighs are like jewels,
The work of a master's hand.
3 Your navel is like a round goblet—
Let mixed wine not be lacking!—
Your belly like a heap of wheat
Hedged about with lilies.
4 Your breasts are like two fawns,
Twins of a gazelle.
5 Your neck is like a tower of ivory,
Your eyes like pools in Heshbon
By the gate of Bath-rabbim,
Your nose like the Lebanon tower
That faces toward Damascus.
6 The head upon you is like *b*crimson wool,*-b*
The locks of your head are like purple—
*c*A king is held captive in the tresses.*-c*
7 How fair you are, how beautiful!
O Love, with all its rapture!
8 Your stately form is like the palm,
Your breasts are like clusters.
9 I say: Let me climb the palm,
Let me take hold of its branches;
Let your breasts be like clusters of grapes,
Your breath like the fragrance of apples,
10 And your mouth like choicest wine.
"Let it flow to my beloved as new wine*d*
*c*Gliding over the lips of sleepers."*-c*

---

a *With many manuscripts and editions; others read "like." Meaning of entire line uncertain.*
b-b *So Ibn Janah and Ibn Ezra, taking karmel as a by-form of karmil: cf. II Chron. 2:6, 13; 3:14.*
c-c *Meaning of Heb. uncertain.*
d *See note at 1.4 end.*

¹¹ I am my beloved's,
And his desire is for me.
¹² Come, my beloved,
Let us go into the open;
Let us lodge ᵉ⁻among the henna shrubs.⁻ᵉ
¹³ Let us go early to the vineyards;
Let us see if the vine has flowered,
If its blossoms have opened,
If the pomegranates are in bloom.
There I will give my love to you.
¹⁴ The mandrakes yield their fragrance,
At our doors are all choice fruits;
Both freshly-picked and long-stored
Have I kept, my beloved, for you.

8   If only it could be as with a brother,
As if you had nursed at my mother's breast:
Then I could kiss you
When I met you in the street,
And no one would despise me.
² I would lead you, I would bring you
To the house of my mother,
Of her who taughtᵃ me—
I would let you drink of the spiced wine,
Of my pomegranate juice.

³ His left hand was under my head,
His right hand caressed me.
⁴ I adjure you, O maidens of Jerusalem:
Do not wake or rouse
Love until it please!

⁵ Who is she that comes up from the desert,
Leaning upon her beloved?

ᵉ⁻ᵉ *Or "in the villages."*

ᵃ *Emendation yields "bore"; cf. 6.9; 8.5.*

Under the apple tree I roused you;
It was there your mother conceived you,
There she who bore you conceived you.

6 Let me be a seal upon your heart,
Like the seal upon your hand.*b*
For love is fierce as death,
Passion is mighty as Sheol;
Its darts are darts of fire,
A blazing flame.
7 Vast floods cannot quench love,
Nor rivers drown it.
If a man offered all his wealth for love,
He would be laughed to scorn.

8 "We have a little sister,
Whose breasts are not yet formed.
What shall we do for our sister
When she is spoken for?
9 If she be a wall,
We will build upon it a silver battlement;
If she be a door,
We will panel it in cedar."
10 I am a wall,
My breasts are like towers.
So I became in his eyes
As one who finds favor.

11 Solomon had a vineyard
In Baal-hamon.
He had to post guards in the vineyard:
A man would give for its fruit
A thousand pieces of silver.
12 I have my very own vineyard:

b Lit. "arm."

348

You may have the thousand, O Solomon,
And the guards of the fruit two hundred!

[13] O you who linger in the garden,[c]
A lover[c] is listening;
Let me hear your voice.
[14] "Hurry, my beloved,
Swift as a gazelle or a young stag,
To the hills of spices!"

[c] *Heb. plural. Meaning of verse uncertain.*

רות

RUTH

רות
RUTH

1 In the days when the chieftains[a] ruled, there was a famine in the land; and a man of Bethlehem in Judah, with his wife and two sons, went to reside in the country of Moab. ² The man's name was Elimelech, his wife's name was Naomi, and his two sons were named Mahlon and Chilion—Ephrathites of Bethlehem in Judah. They came to the country of Moab and remained there.

³ Elimelech, Naomi's husband, died; and she was left with her two sons. ⁴ They married Moabite women, one named Orpah and the other Ruth, and they lived there about ten years. ⁵ Then those two—Mahlon and Chilion—also died; so the woman was left without her two sons and without her husband.

⁶ She started out with her daughters-in-law to return from the country of Moab; for in the country of Moab she had heard that the LORD had taken note of His people and given them food. ⁷ Accompanied by her two daughters-in-law, she left the place where she had been living; and they set out on the road back to the land of Judah.

⁸ But Naomi said to her two daughters-in-law, "Turn back, each of you to her mother's house. May the LORD deal kindly with you, as you have dealt with the dead and with me! ⁹ May the LORD grant that each of you find security in the house of a husband!" And she kissed them farewell. They broke into weeping ¹⁰ and said to her, "No, we will return with you to your people."

¹¹ But Naomi replied, "Turn back, my daughters! Why should you go with me? Have I any more sons in my body who might be husbands for you? ¹² Turn back, my daughters, for I am too old to be married. Even if I thought there was hope for me, even if

---

[a] *I.e. the leaders who arose in the period before the monarchy. Others "judges."*

I were married tonight and I also bore sons, [13] should you wait for them to grow up? Should you on their account debar yourselves from marriage? Oh no, my daughters! My lot is far more bitter than yours, for the hand of the LORD has struck out against me."

[14] They broke into weeping again, and Orpah kissed her mother-in-law farewell. But Ruth clung to her. [15] So she said, "See, your sister-in-law has returned to her people and her gods. Go follow your sister-in-law." [16] But Ruth replied, "Do not urge me to leave you, to turn back and not follow you. For wherever you go, I will go; wherever you lodge, I will lodge; your people shall be my people, and your God my God. [17] Where you die, I will die, and there I will be buried. *b*-Thus and more may the LORD do to me-*b* if anything but death parts me from you." [18] When [Naomi] saw how determined she was to go with her, she ceased to argue with her; [19] and the two went on until they reached Bethlehem.

When they arrived in Bethlehem, the whole city buzzed with excitement over them. The women said, "Can this be Naomi?" [20] "Do not call me Naomi,*c*" she replied. "Call me Mara,*d* for Shaddai*e* has made my lot very bitter. [21] I went away full, and the LORD has brought me back empty. How can you call me Naomi, when the LORD has *f*-dealt harshly with-*f* me, when Shaddai has brought misfortune upon me!"

[22] Thus Naomi returned from the country of Moab; she returned with her daughter-in-law Ruth the Moabite. They arrived in Bethlehem at the beginning of the barley harvest.

2 Now Naomi had a kinsman on her husband's side, a man of substance, of the family of Elimelech, whose name was Boaz. [2] Ruth the Moabite said to Naomi, "I would like to go to the fields and glean among the ears of grain, behind someone who may show me kindness." "Yes, daughter, go," she replied; [3] and off she went. She came and gleaned in a field, behind the reapers;

---

b-b *A formula of imprecation.*
c *I.e. "Pleasantness."*
d *I.e. "Bitterness."*
e *Usually rendered "the Almighty."*
f-f *Others "testified against."*

and, as luck would have it, it was the piece of land belonging to Boaz, who was of Elimelech's family.

⁴ Presently Boaz arrived from Bethlehem. He greeted the reapers, "The LORD be with you!" And they responded, "The LORD bless you!" ⁵ Boaz said to the servant who was in charge of the reapers, "Whose girl is that?" ⁶ The servant in charge of the reapers replied, "She is a Moabite girl who came back with Naomi from the country of Moab. ⁷ She said, 'Please let me glean and gather among the sheaves behind the reapers.' She has been on her feet ever since she came this morning. ᵃ-She has rested but little in the hut."-ᵃ

⁸ Boaz said to Ruth, ᵇ-"Listen to me, daughter.-ᵇ Don't go to glean in another field. Don't go elsewhere, but stay here close to my girls. ⁹ Keep your eyes on the field they are reaping, and follow them. I have ordered the men not to molest you. And when you are thirsty, go to the jars and drink some of [the water] that the men have drawn."

¹⁰ She prostrated herself with her face to the ground, and said to him, "Why are you so kind as to single me out, when I am a foreigner?"

¹¹ Boaz said in reply, "I have been told of all that you did for your mother-in-law after the death of your husband, how you left your father and mother and the land of your birth and came to a people you had not known before. ¹² May the LORD reward your deeds. May you have a full recompense from the LORD, the God of Israel, under whose wings you have sought refuge!"

¹³ She answered, "You are most kind, my lord, to comfort me and to speak gently to your maidservant—though I am not so much as one of your maidservants."

¹⁴ At mealtime, Boaz said to her, "Come over here and partake of the meal, and dip your morsel in the vinegar." So she sat down beside the reapers. He handed her roasted grain, and she ate her fill and had some left over.

¹⁵ When she got up again to glean, Boaz gave orders to his workers, "You are not only to let her glean among the sheaves,

ᵃ⁻ᵃ *Meaning of Heb. uncertain.*
ᵇ⁻ᵇ *Lit. "Have you not heard, daughter?"*

without interference, [16] but you must also pull some [stalks] out of the heaps and leave them for her to glean, and not scold her."

[17] She gleaned in the field until evening. Then she beat out what she had gleaned—it was about an *ephah* of barley—[18] and carried it back with her to the town. When her mother-in-law saw what she had gleaned, and when she also took out and gave her what she had left over after eating her fill, [19] her mother-in-law asked her, "Where did you glean today? Where did you work? Blessed be he who took such generous notice of you!" So she told her mother-in-law whom she had worked with, saying, "The name of the man with whom I worked today is Boaz."

[20] Naomi said to her daughter-in-law, "Blessed be he of the LORD, who has not failed in His kindness to the living or to the dead! For," Naomi explained to her daughter-in-law, "the man is related to us; he is one of our redeeming kinsmen.*c*" [21] Ruth the Moabite said, "He even told me, 'Stay close by my workers until all my harvest is finished.' " [22] And Naomi answered her daughter-in-law Ruth, "It is best, daughter, that you go out with his girls, and not be annoyed in some other field." [23] So she stayed close to the maidservants of Boaz, and gleaned until the barley harvest and the wheat harvest were finished. Then she stayed at home with her mother-in-law.

3 Naomi, her mother-in-law, said to her, "Daughter, I must seek a home for you, where you may be happy. [2] Now there is our kinsman Boaz, whose girls you were close to. He will be winnowing barley on the threshing floor tonight. [3] So bathe, anoint yourself, dress up, and go down to the threshing floor. But do not disclose yourself to the man until he has finished eating and drinking. [4] When he lies down, note the place where he lies down, and go over and uncover his feet and lie down. He will tell you what you are to do." [5] She replied, "I will do everything you tell me."

[6] She went down to the threshing floor and did just as her

---

c Cf. Lev. 25.25 and note; and Deut. 25.5–6. The fact that Boaz was a kinsman of Ruth's dead husband opened up the possibility of providing an heir for the latter.

mother-in-law had instructed her. [7] Boaz ate and drank, and in a cheerful mood went to lie down beside the grainpile. Then she went over stealthily and uncovered his feet and lay down. [8] In the middle of the night, the man gave a start and pulled back—there was a woman lying at his feet!

[9] "Who are you?" he asked. And she replied, "I am your handmaid Ruth. [a-]Spread your robe over your handmaid,[-a] for you are a redeeming kinsman."

[10] He exclaimed, "Be blessed of the LORD, daughter! Your latest deed of loyalty is greater than the first, in that you have not turned to younger men, whether poor or rich.[b] [11] And now, daughter, have no fear. I will do in your behalf whatever you ask, for all the [c-]elders of my town[-c] know what a fine woman you are. [12] But while it is true I am a redeeming kinsman, there is another redeemer closer than I. [13] Stay for the night. Then in the morning, if he will act as a redeemer, good! let him redeem. But if he does not want to act as redeemer for you, I will do so myself, as the LORD lives! Lie down until morning."

[14] So she lay at his feet until dawn. She rose before one person could distinguish another, for he thought, "Let it not be known that the woman came to the threshing floor." [15] And he said, "Hold out the shawl you are wearing." She held it while he measured out six measures of barley, and he put it on her back.

When she[d] got back to the town, [16] she came to her mother-in-law, who asked, "How is it with you, daughter?" She told her all that the man had done for her; [17] and she added, "He gave me these six measures of barley, saying to me, 'Do not go back to your mother-in-law empty-handed.'" [18] And Naomi said, "Stay here, daughter, till you learn how the matter turns out. For the man will not rest, but will settle the matter today."

4 Meanwhile, Boaz had gone to the gate and sat down there. And now the redeemer whom Boaz had mentioned passed by. He called, "Come over and sit down here, So-and-so!" And he came

---

[a-a] *A formal act of espousal; cf. Ezek. 16.8.*
[b] *I.e. she sought out a kinsman of her dead husband; see note at 2.20 above. Her first act of loyalty had been to return with Naomi.*
[c-c] *Lit. "gate of my people."*
[d] *So in many Heb. mss. Most mss. read "he."*

over and sat down. [2] Then [Boaz] took ten elders of the town and said, "Be seated here"; and they sat down.

[3] He said to the redeemer, "Naomi, now returned from the country of Moab, must sell the piece of land which belonged to our kinsman Elimelech. [4] I thought I should disclose the matter to you and say: Acquire it in the presence of those seated here and in the presence of the elders of my people. If you are willing to redeem it, redeem! But if you[a] will not redeem, tell me, that I may know. For there is no one to redeem but you, and I come after you." "I am willing to redeem it," he replied. [5] Boaz continued, "When you acquire the property from Naomi [b-]and from Ruth the Moabite, you must also acquire the wife of the deceased,[-b] so as to perpetuate the name of the deceased upon his estate." [6] The redeemer replied, "Then I cannot redeem it for myself, lest I impair my own estate.[c] You take over my right of redemption, for I am unable to exercise it."

[7] Now this was formerly done in Israel in cases of redemption or exchange: to validate any transaction, one man would take off his sandal and hand it to the other. Such was the practice[d] in Israel. [8] So when the redeemer said to Boaz, "Acquire for yourself," he drew off his sandal. [9] And Boaz said to the elders and to the rest of the people, "You are witnesses today that I am acquiring from Naomi all that belonged to Elimelech and all that belonged to Chilion and Mahlon. [10] I am also acquiring Ruth the Moabite, the wife of Mahlon, as my wife, so as to perpetuate the name of the deceased upon his estate, that the name of the deceased may not disappear from among his kinsmen and from the gate of his home town. You are witnesses today."

[11] All the people at the gate and the elders answered, "We are. May the LORD make the woman who is coming into your house like Rachel and Leah, both of whom built up the House of Israel! Prosper in Ephrathah[e] and perpetuate your name in Bethlehem!

[a] *So many Heb. mss., Septuagint, and Targum; most mss. read "he."*
[b-b] *Emendation yields "you must also acquire Ruth the Moabite, the wife of the deceased"; cf. v.10.*
[c] *I.e. by expending capital for property which will go to the son legally regarded as Mahlon's; see Deut. 25.5–6.*
[d] *Understanding Heb. te 'udah in the sense of the Arabic 'ādah and Syriac 'yādā. Cf. Ibn Ezra.*
[e] *Ephrathah is another name applied to Bethlehem; cf. 1.2; Gen. 35.16, 19; 48.7; Mic. 5.1.*

12 And may your house be like the house of Perez whom Tamar bore to Judah—through the offspring which the LORD will give you by this young woman."

13 So Boaz married Ruth; she became his wife, and he cohabited with her. The LORD let her conceive, and she bore a son. 14 And the women said to Naomi, "Blessed be the LORD, who has not withheld a redeemer from you today! May his name be perpetuated in Israel! 15 He will renew your life and sustain your old age; for he is born of your daughter-in-law, who loves you and is better to you than seven sons."

16 Naomi took the child and held it to her bosom. She became its foster mother, 17 and the women neighbors gave him a name, saying, "A son is born to Naomi!" They named him Obed; he was the father of Jesse, father of David.

18 This is the line of Perez: Perez begot Hezron, 19 Hezron begot Ram, Ram begot Amminadab, 20 Amminadab begot Nahshon, Nahshon begot Salmon,ᶠ 21 Salmon begot Boaz, Boaz begot Obed, 22 Obed begot Jesse, and Jesse begot David.

ᶠ *Heb. "Salmah."*

אֵיכָה

LAMENTATIONS

איכה
LAMENTATIONS

1 א *a*Alas!
Lonely sits the city
Once great with people!
She that was great among nations
Is become like a widow;
The princess among states
Is become a thrall.

ב ² Bitterly she weeps in the night,
Her cheek wet with tears.
There is none to comfort her
Of all her friends.
All her allies have betrayed her;
They have become her foes.

ג ³ Judah has gone into exile
Because of misery and harsh oppression;
When she settled among the nations,
She found no rest;
All her pursuers overtook her
*b*In the narrow places.*-b*

ד ⁴ Zion's roads are in mourning,
Empty of festival pilgrims;
All her gates are deserted.
Her priests sigh,
Her maidens are unhappy—
She is utterly disconsolate!

ה ⁵ Her enemies are now the masters,
Her foes are at ease,

---

a *Chapters 1–4 are alphabetical acrostics, i.e., the verses begin with the successive letters of the Heb. alphabet. Chapter 3 is a triple acrostic. In chapters 2–4 the letter pe precedes the 'ayin.*
b-b *Meaning of Heb. uncertain.*

Because the LORD has afflicted her
For her many transgressions;
Her infants have gone into captivity
Before the enemy.

ו ⁶ Gone from Fair Zion are all
That were her glory;
Her leaders were like stags
That found no pasture;
They could only walk feebly
Before the pursuer.

ז ⁷ All the precious things she had
In the days of old
Jerusalem recalled
In her days of woe and sorrow,
When her people fell by enemy hands
With none to help her;
When enemies looked on and gloated
Over her downfall.

ח ⁸ Jerusalem has greatly sinned,
Therefore she is become a mockery.
All who admired her despise her,
For they have seen her disgraced;
And she can only sigh
And shrink back.

ט ⁹ Her uncleanness clings to her skirts.
She gave no thought to her future;
She has sunk appallingly,
With none to comfort her.—
See, O LORD, my misery;
How the enemy jeers!

י ¹⁰ The foe has laid hands.
On everything dear to her.
She has seen her Sanctuary
Invaded by nations

Which You have denied admission
Into Your community.
כ ¹¹ All her inhabitants sigh
As they search for bread;
They have bartered their treasures for food,
To keep themselves alive.—
See, O Lord, and behold,
*c*How abject*c* I have become!

ל ¹² *b*May it never befall you,*b*
All who pass along the road!
Look about and see:
Is there any agony like mine,
Which was dealt out to me
When the Lord afflicted me
On His day of wrath?
מ ¹³ From above He sent a fire
Down into my bones.
He spread a net for my feet,
He hurled me backward;
He has left me forlorn,
In constant misery.
נ ¹⁴ *d*The yoke of my offenses is bound fast,
Lashed tight by His hand;
Imposed upon my neck,
It saps my strength;
The Lord has delivered me into the hands
Of those I cannot withstand.
ס ¹⁵ The Lord in my midst has rejected
All my heroes;
He has proclaimed a set time against me
To crush my young men.
As in a press the Lord has trodden
Fair Maiden Judah.
ע ¹⁶ For these things do I weep,

c-c *Or (ironically) "What a glutton"; cf. Prov. 23.20–21.*
d *Meaning of parts of vv. 14 and 15 uncertain.*

365

My eyes flow with tears:
Far from me is any comforter
Who might revive my spirit;
My children are forlorn,
For the foe has prevailed.

פ ¹⁷ Zion spreads out her hands,
She has no one to comfort her;
The LORD has summoned against Jacob
His enemies all about him;
Jerusalem has become among them
A thing unclean.

צ ¹⁸ The LORD is in the right,
For I have disobeyed Him.
Hear, all you peoples,
And behold my agony:
My maidens and my youths
Have gone into captivity!

ק ¹⁹ I cried out to my friends,
But they played me false.
My priests and my elders
Have perished in the city
As they searched for food
To keep themselves alive.

ר ²⁰ See, O LORD, the distress I am in!
My heart is in anguish,
ᵉ-I know how wrong I was-ᵉ
To disobey.
Outside the sword deals death;
Indoors, the plague.

שׁ ²¹ When they heard how I was sighing,
There was none to comfort me;
All my foes heard of my plight and exulted.
For it is Your doing:
ᶠ-You have brought on the day that You threatened.

ᵉ⁻ᵉ Lit. "My heart has turned over within me"; cf. Exod. 14.5; Hos. 11.8.
ᶠ⁻ᶠ Emendation yields: "Oh, bring on them what befell me,
    And let them become like me!"

Oh, let them become like me!*f*

ת 22 Let all their wrongdoing come before You,
And deal with them
As You have dealt with me
For all my transgressions.
For my sighs are many,
And my heart is sick.

2 א Alas!
The Lord in His wrath
Has shamed*a* Fair Zion,
Has cast down from heaven to earth
The majesty of Israel.
He did not remember His Footstool*b*
On His day of wrath.

ב 2 The Lord has laid waste without pity
All the habitations of Jacob;
He has razed in His anger
Fair Judah's strongholds.
He has brought low in dishonor
The kingdom and its leaders.

ג 3 In blazing anger He has cut down
All the might of Israel;
He has withdrawn His right hand
In the presence of the foe;
He has ravaged Jacob like flaming fire,
Consuming on all sides.

ד 4 He bent His bow like an enemy,
Poised His right hand like a foe;
He slew all who delighted the eye.
He poured out His wrath like fire
In the Tent of Fair Zion.

ה 5 The Lord has acted like a foe,
He has laid waste Israel,

---

a Meaning of Heb. uncertain.
b I.e. the Temple.

Laid waste all her citadels,
Destroyed her strongholds.
He has increased within Fair Judah
Mourning and moaning.

ו ⁶ He has stripped His Booth[b] like a garden,
He has destroyed His Tabernacle[c];
The LORD has ended in Zion
Festival and sabbath;
In His raging anger He has spurned
King and priest.

ז ⁷ The Lord has rejected His altar,
Disdained His Sanctuary.
He has handed over to the foe
The walls of its citadels;
They raised a shout in the House of the LORD
As on a festival day.

ח ⁸ The LORD resolved to destroy
The wall of Fair Zion;
[d-]He measured with a line,[-d] refrained not
From bringing destruction.
He has made wall and rampart to mourn,
Together they languish.

ט ⁹ Her gates have sunk into the ground,
He has smashed her bars to bits;
Her king and her leaders are [e-]in exile,[-e]
Instruction[f] is no more;
Her prophets, too, receive
No vision from the LORD.

י ¹⁰ Silent sit on the ground
The elders of Fair Zion;
They have strewn dust on their heads
And girded themselves with sackcloth;
The maidens of Jerusalem have bowed
Their heads to the ground.

כ ¹¹ My eyes are spent with tears,

[c] *Lit. "(Tent of) Meeting."*
[d-d] *I.e. He made His plans.*
[e-e] *Lit. "among the nations."*
[f] *Heb.* torah, *here priestly instruction; cf. Jer. 18.18; Hag. 2.11; Mal. 2.6.*

My heart is in tumult,
g-My being melts away-*g*
Over the ruin of *h*-my poor people,-*h*
As babes and sucklings languish
In the squares of the city.

ל 12 They keep asking their mothers,
"Where is bread and wine?"
As they languish like battle-wounded
In the squares of the town,
As their life runs out
In their mothers' bosoms.

מ 13 What can I *i*-take as witness-*i* or liken
To you, O Fair Jerusalem?
What can I match with you to console you,
O Fair Maiden Zion?
For your ruin is vast as the sea:
Who can heal you?

נ 14 Your seers prophesied to you
Delusion and folly.
They did not expose your iniquity
So as to restore your fortunes,
But prophesied to you oracles
Of delusion and deception.

ס 15 All who pass your way
Clap their hands at you;
They hiss and wag their head.
At Fair Jerusalem:*j*
"Is this the city that was called
Perfect in Beauty,
Joy of All the Earth?"

פ 16 All your enemies
Jeer at you;
They hiss and gnash their teeth,
And cry: "We've ruined her!

g-g Lit. "My liver spills on the ground."
h-h Lit. "the daughter of my people"; so elsewhere in poetry.
i-i Emendation yields "compare."
j These gestures were intended to ward off the calamity from the viewer; cf. e.g. Jer. 18.16 and note; Job 27.23.

Ah, this is the day we hoped for;
ᵏ⁻We have lived to see it!⁻ᵏ"

ע ¹⁷ The LORD has done what He purposed,
Has carried out the decree
That He ordained long ago;
He has torn down without pity.
He has let the foe rejoice over you,
Has exalted the might of your enemies.

צ ¹⁸ ˡ⁻Their heart cried out⁻ˡ to the Lord.
O wall of Fair Zion,
Shed tears like a torrent
Day and night!
Give yourself no respite,
Your eyes no rest.

ק ¹⁹ Arise, cry out in the night
At the beginning of the watches,
Pour out your heart like water
In the presence of the Lord!
Lift up your hands to Him
For the life of your infants,
Who faint for hunger
At every street corner,

ר ²⁰ See, O LORD, and behold,
To whom You have done this!
Alas, women eat their own fruit,
Their new-bornᵐ babes!
Alas, priest and prophet are slain
In the Sanctuary of the Lord!

ש ²¹ Prostrate in the streets lie
Both young and old.
My maidens and youths
Are fallen by the sword;
You slew them on Your day of wrath,

ᵏ⁻ᵏ *Lit. "We have attained, we have seen."*
ˡ⁻ˡ *Emendation yields "Cry aloud."*
ᵐ *The root has this meaning in Arabic. Others "dandled."*

You slaughtered without pity.

ת ²² You summoned, as on a festival,
My neighbors from round about.
On the day of the wrath of the LORD,
None survived or escaped;
Those whom I bore[m] and reared
My foe has consumed.

3 א I am the man [a-]who has known affliction
Under[-a] the rod of His wrath;
² Me He drove on and on
In unrelieved darkness;
³ On none but me He brings down His hand
Again and again, without cease.

ב ⁴ He has worn away my flesh and skin;
He has shattered my bones.
⁵ All around me He has built
Misery[b] and hardship;
⁶ He has made me dwell in darkness,
Like those long dead.

ג ⁷ He has walled me in and I cannot break out;
He has weighed me down with chains.
⁸ And when I cry and plead,
He shuts out my prayer;
⁹ He has walled in my ways with hewn blocks,
He has made my paths a maze.

ד ¹⁰ He is a lurking bear to me,
A lion in hiding;
¹¹ [c-]He has forced me off my way[-c] and mangled me,
He has left me numb.
¹² He has bent His bow and made me
The target of His arrows:

ה ¹³ He has shot into my vitals

[a-a] *Emendation yields "whom the Lord has shepherded with."*
[b] *Taking* rosh *as equivalent to* resh.
[c-c] *Meaning of Heb. uncertain.*

The shafts of His quiver.
14 I have become a laughingstock to all people,
The butt of their gibes all day long.
15 He has filled me with bitterness,
Sated me with wormwood.

ו 16 He has broken my teeth on gravel,
Has ground me into the dust.
17 My life was bereft of peace,
I forgot what happiness was.
18 I thought my strength and hope
Had perished before the LORD.
ז 19 To recall my distress and my misery
Was wormwood and poison;
20 Whenever I thought of them,
I was bowed low.

21 But this do I call to mind,
Therefore I have hope:
ח 22 The kindness of the LORD has not ended,
His mercies are not spent.
23 They are renewed every morning—
Ample is Your grace!
24 "The LORD is my portion," I say with full heart;
Therefore will I hope in Him.
ט 25 The LORD is good to those who trust in Him,
To the one who seeks Him;
26 It is good to wait patiently
Till rescue comes from the LORD.
27 It is good for a man, when young,
To bear a yoke;
י 28 Let him sit alone and be patient,
When He has laid it upon him.
29 Let him put his mouth to the dust—
There may yet be hope.

³⁰ Let him offer his cheek to the smiter;
Let him be surfeited with mockery.
כ ³¹ For the Lord does not
Reject forever,
³² But first afflicts, then pardons
In His abundant kindness.
³³ For He does not willfully bring grief
Or affliction to man,
ל ³⁴ Crushing under His feet
All the prisoners of the earth.
³⁵ To deny a man his rights
In the presence of the Most High,
³⁶ To wrong a man in his cause—
This the Lord does not choose.
מ ³⁷ Whose decree was ever fulfilled,
Unless the Lord willed it?
³⁸ Is it not at the word of the Most High,
That weal and woe befall?
³⁹ Of what shall a living man complain?
Each one of his own sins!

נ ⁴⁰ Let us search and examine our ways,
And turn back to the LORD;
⁴¹ Let us lift up our hearts with*ᵈ* our hands
To God in heaven:
⁴² We have transgressed and rebelled,
And You have not forgiven.
ס ⁴³ You have clothed Yourself in anger and pursued us,
You have slain without pity.
⁴⁴ You have screened Yourself off with a cloud,
That no prayer may pass through.
⁴⁵ You have made us filth and refuse
In the midst of the peoples.
פ ⁴⁶ All our enemies loudly
Rail against us.

ᵈ *Lit. "to"; emendation yields "rather than"; cf. Joel 2.13.*

⁴⁷ Panic and pitfall are out lot,
Death and destruction.
⁴⁸ My eyes shed streams of water
Over the ruin of my poor*ᵉ* people.

ע ⁴⁹ My eyes shall flow without cease,
Without respite,
⁵⁰ *ᶠ*Until the LORD looks down
And beholds from heaven.
⁵¹ My eyes have brought me grief*ᶠ*
Over all the maidens of my city.
צ ⁵² My foes have snared me like a bird,
Without any cause.
⁵³ They have ended my life in a pit
And cast stones at me.
⁵⁴ Waters flowed over my head;
I said: I am lost!

ק ⁵⁵ I have called on Your name, O LORD,
From the depths of the Pit.
⁵⁶ Hear my plea;
Do not shut Your ear
To my groan, to my cry!
⁵⁷ You have ever drawn nigh when I called You;
You have said, "Do not fear!"
ר ⁵⁸ You championed my cause, O Lord,
You have redeemed my life.
⁵⁹ You have seen, O LORD, the wrong done me;
Oh, vindicate my right!
⁶⁰ You have seen all their malice,
All their designs against me;
ש ⁶¹ You have heard, O LORD, their taunts,
All their designs against me,
⁶² The mouthings and pratings of my adversaries
Against me all day long.

ᵉ Lit. "the daughter of my"; so frequently in poetry.
ᶠ⁻ᶠ Emendation yields,
⁵⁰ *"Until the LORD looks down from heaven*
And beholds
⁵¹ *my affliction.*
The LORD has brought me grief."

⁶³ See how, at their ease or at work,
I am the butt of their gibes.

ת ⁶⁴ Give them, O LORD, their deserts
According to their deeds.
⁶⁵ Give them anguish*c* of heart;
Your curse be upon them!
⁶⁶ Oh, pursue them in wrath and destroy them
From under the heavens of the LORD!

4 א Alas!
The gold is dulled,*a*
Debased the finest gold!
The sacred*b* gems are spilled
At every street corner.

ב ² The precious children of Zion;
Once valued as gold—
Alas, they are accounted as earthen pots,
Work of a potter's hands!

ג ³ Even jackals offer the breast
And suckle their young;
But my poor people has turned cruel,
Like ostriches of the desert.

ד ⁴ The tongue of the suckling cleaves
To its palate for thirst.
Little children beg for bread;
None gives them a morsel.

ה ⁵ Those who feasted on dainties
Lie famished in the streets;
Those who were reared in purple
Have embraced refuse heaps.

ו ⁶ The guilt*c* of my poor*d* people
Exceeded the iniquity*c* of Sodom,
Which was overthrown in a moment,
Without a hand striking it.

---

a *Meaning of Heb. uncertain.*
b *Emendation yeilds "precious."*
c *I.e. punishment.*
d *See note at 3.48.*

א ⁷ Her elect were purer than snow,
Whiter than milk;
Their limbs were ruddier than coral,
Their bodies*ᵃ* were like sapphire.

ח ⁸ Now their faces are blacker than soot,
They are not recognized in the streets;
Their skin has shriveled on their bones,
It has become dry as wood.

ט ⁹ Better off were the slain of the sword
Than those slain by famine,
ᵃ-Who pined away, [as though] wounded,
For lack of-*ᵃ* the fruits of the field.

י ¹⁰ With their own hands, tenderhearted women
Have cooked their children;
Such became their fare,
In the disaster of my poor*ᵈ* people.

כ ¹¹ The Lord vented all His fury,
Poured out His blazing wrath;
He kindled a fire in Zion
Which consumed its foundations.

ל ¹² The kings of the earth did not believe,
Nor any of the inhabitants of the world,
That foe or adversary could enter
The gates of Jerusalem.

מ ¹³ It was for the sins of her prophets,
The iniquities of her priests,
Who had shed in her midst
The blood of the just.

נ ¹⁴ They wandered blindly through the streets,
Defiled with blood,
So that no one was able
To touch their garments.

ס ¹⁵ "Away! Unclean!" people shouted at them,
"Away! Away! Touch not!"
So they wandered and wandered again;

For the nations had resolved:
"They shall stay here no longer."

פ 16 ^eThe LORD's countenance has turned away from them,
He will look on them no more.
They showed no regard for priests,
No favor to elders.

ע 17 Even now our eyes pine away
In vain for deliverance.
As we waited, still we wait
For a nation that cannot help.

צ 18 Our steps were checked,
We could not walk ^fin our squares.^f
Our doom is near, our days are done—
Alas, our doom has come!

ק 19 Our pursuers were swifter
Than the eagles in the sky;
They chased us in the mountains,
Lay in wait for us in the wilderness.

ר 20 The breath of our life, the LORD's anointed,
Was captured in their traps—
He in whose shade we had thought
To live among the nations.

ש 21 Rejoice and exult, Fair Edom,
Who dwell in the land of Uz!
To you, too, the cup shall pass,
You shall get drunk and expose your nakedness.

ת 22 Your iniquity, Fair Zion, is expiated;
He will exile you no longer.
Your iniquity, Fair Edom, He will note;
He will uncover your sins.

5 Remember, O LORD, what has befallen us;
Behold, and see our disgrace!
2 Our heritage has passed to aliens,
Our homes to strangers.

---

^e *Meaning of line uncertain.*
^{f-f} *Or "With long strides."*

³ We have become orphans, fatherless;
Our mothers are like widows.
⁴ We must pay to drink our own water,
Obtain our own kindling at a price.
⁵ We are hotly*a* pursued;
Exhausted, we are given no rest.
⁶ We hold out a hand to Egypt;
To Assyria, for our fill of bread.
⁷ Our fathers sinned and are no more;
And we must bear their guilt.
⁸ Slaves are ruling over us,
With none to rescue us from them.
⁹ We get our bread at the peril of our lives,
Because of the *b-*sword of the wilderness.*-b*
¹⁰ Our skin glows like an oven,
With the fever of famine.
¹¹ They*c* have ravished women in Zion,
Maidens in the towns of Judah.
¹² Princes have been hanged by them;*c*
No respect has been shown to elders.
¹³ Young men must carry millstones,
And youths stagger under loads of wood.
¹⁴ The old men are gone from the gate,
The young men from their music.
¹⁵ Gone is the joy of our hearts;
Our dancing is turned into mourning.
¹⁶ The crown has fallen from our head;
Woe to us that we have sinned!

¹⁷ Because of this our hearts are sick,
Because of these our eyes are dimmed:
¹⁸ Because of Mount Zion, which lies desolate;
Jackals prowl over it.

ᵃ *Lit. "on our neck"; meaning of Heb. uncertain.*
ᵇ⁻ᵇ *Or "heat (cf. Deut. 28.22) of the wilderness"; meaning of Heb. uncertain.*
ᶜ *I.e. the slaves of v.8.*

¹⁹ But You, O Lord, are enthroned forever,
Your throne endures through the ages.
²⁰ Why have You forgotten us utterly,
Forsaken us for all time?
²¹ Take us back, O Lord, to Yourself,
And let us come back;
Renew our days as of old!
²² For truly, you have rejected us,
Bitterly raged against us.

> Take us back, O Lord, to Yourself,
> And let us come back;
> Renew our days as of old!

קהלת

ECCLESIASTES

קהלת
ECCLESIASTES

1 The words of Koheleth[a] son of David, king in Jerusalem.

2 Utter futility!—said Koheleth—
Utter futility! All is futile!
3 What real value is there for a man
In all the gains[b] he makes beneath the sun?

4 One generation goes, another comes,
But the earth remains the same forever.
5 The sun rises, and the sun sets—
And glides[c] back to where it rises.
6 Southward blowing,
Turning northward,
Ever turning blows the wind;
On its rounds the wind returns.
7 All streams flow into the sea,
Yet the sea is never full;
To the place [from] which they flow
The streams flow back again.[d]
8 All such things are wearisome:
No man can ever state them;
The eye never has enough of seeing,
Nor the ear enough of hearing.
9 Only that shall happen
Which has happened,
Only that occur
Which has occurred;

---

[a] *Probably "the Assembler," i.e. of hearers or of sayings; cf. 12. 9–11.*
[b] *So Rashbam. The Heb. 'amal usually has this sense in Ecclesiastes; cf. Ps. 105.44.*
[c] *So Targum; cf. Bereshith Rabbah on Gen. 1.17.*
[d] *According to popular belief, through tunnels; so Targum and Rashi.*

> There is nothing new
> Beneath the sun!

¹⁰ Sometimes there is a phenomenon of which they say, "Look, this one is new!"—it occurred long since, in ages that went by before us. ¹¹ The earlier ones are not remembered; so too those that will occur later ᵉ⁻will no more be remembered than⁻ᵉ those that will occur at the very end.

¹² I, Koheleth, was king in Jerusalem over Israel. ¹³ I set my mind to study and to probe with wisdom all that happens under the sun.—An unhappy business, that, which God gave men to be concerned with! ¹⁴ I observed all the happenings beneath the sun, and I found that all is futile and pursuitᶠ of wind:

> ¹⁵ A twisted thing that cannot be made straight,
> A lack that cannot be made good.

¹⁶ I said to myself: "Here I have grown richer and wiser than any that ruled before me over Jerusalem, and my mind has zealously absorbed wisdom and learning." ¹⁷ And so I set my mind to appraise wisdom and to appraise madness and folly. And I learned—that this too was pursuit of wind:

> ¹⁸ For as wisdom grows, vexation grows;
> To increase learning is to increase heartache.

2 I said to myself, "Come, I will treat you to merriment. Taste mirth!" That too, I found, was futile.

> ² Of revelry I said, "It's mad!"
> Of merriment, "What good is that?"

³ I ventured to tempt my flesh with wine, and to grasp folly, while letting my mind direct with wisdom, to the end that I might learn which of the two was better for men to practice in their few days of life under heaven. ⁴ I multiplied my possessions. I built myself houses and I planted vineyards. ⁵ I laid out gardens and

---

ᵉ⁻ᵉ *Lit. "will not be remembered like . . ." For* 'im *meaning "like," cf. 2.16; 7.11; Job 9.26.*
ᶠ *Lit. "tending," from root* ra'ah, *"to shepherd."*

groves, in which I planted every kind of fruit tree. [6] I constructed pools of water, enough to irrigate a forest shooting up with trees. [7] I bought male and female slaves, and I acquired stewards. I also acquired more cattle, both herds and flocks, than all who were before me in Jerusalem. [8] I further amassed silver and gold and treasures of kings and provinces; and I got myself male and female singers, as well as the luxuries of commoners—coffers[a] and coffers of them. [9] Thus, I gained more wealth than anyone before me in Jerusalem. In addition, my wisdom remained with me: [10] I withheld from my eyes nothing they asked for, and denied myself no enjoyment; rather, I got enjoyment out of[b] all my wealth. And that was all I got out of my wealth.

[11] Then my thoughts turned to all the fortune my hands had built up, to the wealth I had acquired and won—and oh, it was all futile and pursuit of wind; there was no real value under the sun! [12] [c]For what will the man be like who will succeed [d]the one who is ruling[d] over what was built up long ago?

My thoughts also turned to appraising wisdom and madness and folly. [13] I found that

Wisdom is superior to folly
As light is superior to darkness;
[14] A wise man has his eyes in his head,
Whereas a fool walks in darkness.

But I also realized that the same fate awaits them both. [15] So I reflected: "The fate of the fool is also destined for me; to what advantage, then, have I been wise?" And I came to the conclusion that that too was futile, [16] because the wise man, just like[e] the fool, is not remembered forever; for, as the succeeding days roll by, both are forgotten. Alas, the wise man dies, just like[e] the fool!

[17] And so I loathed life. For I was distressed by all that goes on under the sun, because everything is futile and pursuit of wind.

[18] So, too, I loathed all the wealth that I was gaining under the sun. For I shall leave it to the man who will succeed me—[19] and

---

[a] *The Heb.* shiddah *occurs only here in the Bible; in the Mishnah it designates a kind of chest.*
[b] *Septuagint and a few Heb. manuscripts have "(in exchange) for"; cf. 2.24; 3.13, 22; 5.17.*
[c] *The order of the two sentences in this verse is reversed in the translation for clarity.*
[d-d] *Change of vocalization yields "me, and who is to rule"; cf. vv. 18–19.*
[e] *See note on 1.11.*

who knows whether he will be wise or foolish?—and he will
control all the wealth that I gained by toil and wisdom under the
sun. That too is futile. 20 And so I came to view with despair all
the gains I had made under the sun. 21 For sometimes a person
whose fortune was made with wisdom, knowledge, and skill must
hand it on to be the portion of somebody who did not toil for it.
That too is futile, and a grave evil. 22 For what does a man get for
all the toiling and worrying he does under the sun? 23 All his days
his thoughts are grief and heartache, and even at night his mind
has no respite. That too is futile!

24 There is nothing worthwhile for a man but to eat and drink
and afford himself enjoyment with his means. And even that, I
noted, comes from God. 25 For who eats and who enjoys but
myself?/ 26 To the man, namely, who pleases Him He has given
g-the wisdom and shrewdness to enjoy himself;-g and to him who
displeases, He has given the urge to gather and amass—only for
handing on to one who is pleasing to God. That too is futile and
pursuit of wind.

3   A season is set for everything, a time for every experience
       under heaven:ᵃ
     2 A time for b-being born-b and a time for dying,
     A time for planting and a time for uprooting the planted;
     3 A time for c-slaying and a time for healing,-c
     A time for tearing down and a time for building up;
     4 A time for weeping and a time for laughing,
     A time for wailing and a time for dancing;
     5 A time for throwing stones and a time for gathering
       stones,
     A time for embracing and a time for shunning embraces;
     6 A time for seeking and a time for losing,
     A time for keeping and a time for discarding;
     7 A time for ripping and a time for sewing,
     A time for silence and a time for speaking;

---

f Some mss. and ancient versions read mimmennu, "by His doing."
g-g Lit. "wisdom and knowledge and enjoyment."

a I.e. all human experiences are preordained by God; see v. 11.
b-b Lit. "giving birth."
c-c Emendation yields "wrecking . . . repairing"; cf. I Kings 18.30.

⁸ A time for loving and a time for hating;
A time for war and a time for peace.

⁹ What value, then, can the man of affairs get from what he earns? ¹⁰ I have observed the business that God gave man to be concerned with: ¹¹ He brings everything to pass precisely at its time; He also puts eternity in their mind,*d* but without man ever guessing, from first to last, all the things that God brings to pass. ¹² Thus I realized that the only worthwhile thing there is for them is to enjoy themselves and do what is good*e* in their lifetime; ¹³ also, that whenever a man does eat and drink and get enjoyment out of all his wealth, it is a gift of God.

¹⁴ I realized, too, that whatever God has brought to pass will recur evermore:
Nothing can be added to it
And nothing taken from it—
and God has brought to pass that men revere Him.

¹⁵ ƒWhat is occurring occurred long since,
ˑAnd what is to occur occurred long since:
and God seeks the pursued. ¹⁶ And, indeed, I have observed under the sun:
Alongside justice there is wickedness,
Alongside righteousness there is wickedness.

¹⁷ I mused: "God will doom both righteous and wicked, for ᵍ-there isᵍ a time for every experience and for every happening." ¹⁸ ƒSo I decided, as regards men, to dissociate them [from] the divine beings and to face the fact that they are beasts.*h* ¹⁹ For in respect of the fate of man and the fate of beast, they have one and the same fate: as the one dies so dies the other, and both have the same lifebreath; man has no superiority over beast, since both amount to nothing. ²⁰ Both go to the same place; both came from dust and both return to dust. ²¹ Who knows if a man's lifebreath does rise upward and if a beast's breath does sink down into the earth?

²² I saw that there is nothing better for man than to enjoy his possessions, since that is his portion. For who can enable him to see what will happen afterward?

---

d *I.e. He preoccupies man with the attempt to discover the times of future events; cf. 8.17.*
e *I.e. what the author has already concluded (2.24) is good.*
f *Meaning of parts of verse uncertain.*
g-g *Shift of a diacritical point yields "He has set."*
h *Contrast Ps. 8.5–6.*

4 I further observed[a] all the oppression that goes on under the sun: the tears of the oppressed, with none to comfort them; and the power of their oppressors—with none to comfort them. [2] Then I accounted those who died long since more fortunate than those who are still living; [3] and happier than either are those who have not yet come into being and have never witnessed the miseries that go on under the sun.

[4] I have also noted that all labor and skillful enterprise come from men's envy of each other—another futility and pursuit of wind!

[5] [True,]
The fool folds his hands together[b]
And has to eat his own flesh.
[6] [But no less truly,]
Better is a handful of gratification
Than two fistfuls of labor which is pursuit of wind.

[7] And I have noted this further futility under the sun: [8] the case of the man who is alone, with no companion, who has neither son nor brother; yet he amasses wealth without limit, and his eye is never sated with riches. For whom, now, [c]is he amassing it while denying himself[c] enjoyment? That too is a futility and an unhappy business.

[9] [d]Two are better off than one, in that they have greater [e]benefit from[e] their earnings. [10] For should they fall, one can raise the other; but woe betide him who is alone and falls with no companion to raise him! [11] Further, when two lie together they are warm; but how can he who is alone get warm? [12] Also, if one attacks, two can stand up to him. A threefold cord is not readily broken!

---

[a] *Cf. 3.16.*
[b] *I.e. does not work; cf. Prov. 6.10; 24.33.*
[c-c] *Lit. "am I amassing . . . myself."*
[d] *4.9–5.8 consists of a series of observations of which each one is introduced by some slight association with what precedes. The theme of 4.4–8 is not resumed until 5.9.*
[e-e] *Emendation yields "hope for"; cf. 2.20.*

13 Better a poor but wise youth than an old but foolish king who no longer has the sense to heed warnings. 14 For the former can emerge from a dungeon to become king; while the latter, even if born to kingship, can become a pauper./ 15 [However,] I reflected about *g*-all the living who walk under the sun with-*g* that youthful successor who steps into his place. 16 Unnumbered are the multitudes of all those who preceded them;*h* and later generations will not acclaim him either.*i* For that*j* too is futile and pursuit of wind.

17 *k*-Be not overeager to go-*k* to the House of God: more acceptable is obedience than the offering of fools, for they know nothing [but] to do wrong.

5 Keep your mouth from being rash, and let not your throat*a* be quick to bring forth speech before God. For God is in heaven and you are on earth; that is why your words should be few. 2 Just as dreams come with much brooding, so does foolish utterance come with much speech. 3 When you make a vow to God, do not delay to fulfill it. For He has no pleasure in fools; what you vow, fulfill. 4 It is better not to vow at all than to vow and not fulfill. 5 Don't let your mouth bring you into disfavor, and don't plead before the messenger*b* that it was an error, *c*-but fear God;-*c* else God may be angered by your talk and destroy your possessions. 6 *d*For much dreaming leads to futility and to superfluous talk.

f *Taking* rash *as a verb; cf. Ps. 34.11.*
g-g *I.e. "the contemporaries of."*
h *And so never heard of the gifted youth.*
i *For despite his wisdom, he too will be forgotten; cf. 2.16.*
j *I.e. the advantage of wisdom over folly.*
k-k *Lit. "Guard your foot when it [or, you] would go."*

a *Heb.* leb, *lit. "heart," sometimes designates the organ of speech; cf. Isa. 33.18; 59.13; Ps. 19.15; 49.4; Job 8.10.*
b *Some ancient versions read "God."*
c-c *Moved up from v. 6 for clarity.*
d *Meaning of verse uncertain. Emendation yields: "Much brooding results in dreams; and much talk in futilities"; cf. v. 2.*

7 If you see in a province oppression of the poor and suppression of right and justice, don't wonder at the fact; for one high official is protected by a higher one, and both of them by still higher ones. 8 Thus the greatest advantage in all the land is his: he controls a field that is cultivated.*

9 A lover of money never has his fill of money, nor a lover of wealth his fill of income. That too is futile. 10 As his substance increases, so do those who consume it; what, then, does the success of its owner amount to but feasting his eyes? 11 A worker's*f* sleep is sweet, whether he has much or little to eat; but the rich man's abundance doesn't let him sleep.

12 Here is a grave evil I have observed under the sun: riches hoarded by their owner to his misfortune, 13 in that those riches are lost in some unlucky venture; and if he begets a son, he has nothing in hand.

14 *g-*Another grave evil is this: He must depart just as he came.*-g* As he came out of his mother's womb, so must he depart at last, naked as he came. He can take nothing of his wealth to carry with him. 15 So what is the good of his toiling for the wind? 16 Besides, all his days *h-*he eats in darkness,*-h* with much vexation and grief and anger.

17 Only this, I have found, is a real good: that one should eat and drink and get pleasure with all the gains he makes under the sun, during the numbered days of life that God has given him; for that is his portion. 18 Also, whenever a man is given riches and property by God, and is also permitted by Him to enjoy them and to take his portion and get pleasure for his gains—that is a gift of God. 19 For [such a man] will not brood much over the days of his life,*i* because God keeps him busy enjoying himself.

e *I.e. the high official profits from the labor of others; but meaning of verse uncertain.*
f *Some ancient versions have "slave's."*
g-g *Moved up from v. 15 for clarity.*
h-h *Septuagint reads "are [spent] in darkness and mourning."*
i *The thought of which is depressing; see v. 16.*

6 There is an evil I have observed under the sun, and a grave one it is for man: [2] that God sometimes grants a man riches, property, and wealth, so that he does not want for anything his appetite may crave, but God does not permit him to enjoy it; instead, a stranger will enjoy it. That is futility and a grievous ill. [3] Even if a man should beget a hundred children and live many years—no matter how many the days of his years may come to, if his gullet is not sated through his wealth, I say: The stillbirth, though it was not even accorded a burial,[a] is more fortunate than he. [4] Though it comes into futility and departs into darkness, and its very name is covered with darkness, [5] though it has never seen or experienced the sun, it is better off than he—[6] yes, even if the other lived a thousand years twice over but never had his fill of enjoyment! For are not both of them bound for the same place? [7] [b]All of man's earning is for the sake of his mouth, [c]yet his gullet is not sated. [8] What advantage then has the wise man over the fool, what advantage has the pauper who knows how to get on in life?[-c] [9] [d]Is the feasting of the eyes more important than the pursuit of desire? That, too, is futility and pursuit of wind.

[10] Whatever happens, it was designated long ago and it was known that it would happen; as for man, he cannot contend with what is stronger than he. [11] Often, much talk means much futility. How does it benefit a man? [12] Who can possibly know what is best for a man to do in life—the few days of his fleeting life? For[e] who can tell him what the future holds for him under the sun?

---

[a] *Stillbirths were cast into pits or hidden in the ground in no recognizable graves; cf. v. 4 end.*
[b] *Cf. Prov. 16.26.*
[c-c] *Meaning of Heb. uncertain; emendation yields "And if the gullet is not sated, [8]what advantage has the wise man over the fool, he who knows how to get on in life over the pauper?"*
[d] *Meaning of first half of verse uncertain.*
[e] *Lit. "according to the shadow that"; cf. Qumran Aramaic betel and Syriac meṭṭol; and see 8.13.*

7 *A good name is better than fragrant oil, and the day of death than the day of birth.*b

2 It is better to go to a house of mourning than to a house of feasting; for that is the end of every man, and a living one should take it to heart.

3 Vexation is better than revelry;*c for though the face be sad, the heart may be glad. 4 Wise men are drawn to a house of mourning, and fools to a house of merrymaking.

5 It is better to listen to a wise man's reproof than to listen to the praise of fools. 6 For the levity*d of the fool is like the crackling of nettles under a kettle.*e But that too is illusory; 7 for cheating*f may rob the wise man of reason and destroy the prudence of the cautious.*g

8 The end of a matter is better than the beginning
      of it.
   Better a patient spirit than a haughty spirit.

9 Don't let your spirit be quickly vexed, for vexation abides in the breasts of fools.

10 Don't say, "How has it happened that former times were better than these?" For it is not wise of you to ask that question.

11 Wisdom is as good as a patrimony, and even better, for those who behold the sun. 12 For to be in the shelter of wisdom is to be also in the shelter of money,*h and the advantage of intelligence is that wisdom preserves the life of him who possesses it.

13 *iConsider God's doing! Who can straighten what He has

---

a *The author now offers a number of practical maxims, which, however, he concludes (vv. 23–24) are of limited value.*

b *Until a man dies, there is always danger that he may forfeit his good name.*

c *For empty revelry precludes real happiness: cf. 2.2.*

d *Emendation yields "praise" (shbḥ).*

e *This section, to end of verse 7, is apparently a continuation of the thought in vv. 11–12 and 19.*

f *Emendation yields "riches."*

g *Lit. "caution"; cf. post-biblical mathun, "cautious."*

h *Emendation yields "For the possessor of wisdom becomes a possessor of money."*

i *Vv. 13–14 continue the thought of v. 10.*

twisted? [14] So in a time of good fortune enjoy the good fortune; and in a time of misfortune, reflect: The one no less than the other was God's doing; consequently, man may find no fault with Him.[j]

[15] In my own brief span of life, I have seen both these things: sometimes a good man perishes in spite of his goodness, and sometimes a wicked one endures in spite of his wickedness. [16] So don't overdo goodness and don't act the wise man to excess, or you may be dumfounded. [17] Don't overdo wickedness and don't be a fool, or you may die before your time. [18] It is best that you grasp the one without letting go of the other, for one who fears God will do his duty[k] by both.

[19] Wisdom is more of a stronghold to a wise man than [l]ten magnates[-l] that a city may contain.

[20] [m]For there is not one good man on earth who does what is best[n] and doesn't err.

[21] Finally, don't pay attention to everything that is said, so that you may not hear your slave reviling you; [22] for well you remember[o] the many times that you yourself have reviled others.

[23] All this I tested with wisdom. I thought I could fathom it,[n] but it eludes me. [24] [The secret of] what happens is elusive and deep, deep down; who can discover it? [25] I put my mind to studying, exploring, and seeking wisdom and the reason of things, and to studying wickedness, stupidity, madness, and folly. [26] Now, I find woman more bitter than death; she is all traps, her hands are fetters and her heart is snares. He who is pleasing to God escapes her, and he who is displeasing is caught by her. [27] See, this is what I found, said Koheleth, item by item in my search for the reason of things. [28] As for what I sought further but did not find, I found only one human being in a thousand, and the one I found among so many was never a woman. [29] But, see, this I did find: God made men plain, but they have engaged in too much reasoning.

---

[j] So Rashi; cf. the same thought in Job 1.22; 2.10.
[k] Cf. post-biblical yasa yede.
[l-l] Emendation yields "the riches of the magnates"; cf. Prov. 18.11.
[m] Apparently continuing the thought of v. 16.
[n] Refers back to 6.12.
[o] The same idiom occurs again in 8.5.

8 *a*-Who is like the wise man,-*a* and who knows the meaning of the adage:

"A man's wisdom lights up his face,
So that his deep discontent*b* is dissembled"?

2 I do! "Obey the king's orders—and *c*-don't rush-*c* into uttering an oath by God."*d* 3 *e*-Leave his presence; do not tarry-*e* in a dangerous situation, for he can do anything he pleases; 4 inasmuch as a king's command is authoritative, and none can say to him, "What are you doing?" 5 One who obeys orders will not suffer from the dangerous situation.

A wise man, however, will bear in mind*f* that there is a time of doom.*g* 6 For there is a time for every experience, including the doom; for a man's calamity*h* overwhelms him. 7 Indeed, he does not know what is to happen; even when it is on the point of happening, who can tell him? 8 No man has authority over the lifebreath—to hold back the lifebreath;*i* there is no authority over the day of death. There is no mustering out from that war; wickedness*j* is powerless to save its owner.

9 All these things I observed; I noted all that went on under the sun, while men still had authority over men to treat them unjustly. 10 And then I saw scoundrels *k*-coming from the Holy Site and being brought to burial,-*k* while such as had acted righteously were forgotten in the city.

---

a-a Some ancient versions read: "Who here is wise."
b Lit. "face"; cf. I Sam. 1.18; Job 9.27.
c-c Moved up from v. 3 for English word order.
d The answer to the inquiry about the implications of the proverb in v. 1 is given in the form of another proverb, of which only the first half is relevant and is enlarged upon.
e-e Or "Give ground before him; do not resist."
f The same idiom as in 7.22.
g Lit. "time and doom"; cf. the synonymous "time of misfortune," lit. "time and misfortune," 9.11.
h Still another term for death; cf. "the time of calamity" for "the hour of death," 9.12.
i From leaving the body when the time comes; see 12.7; cf. Ps. 104.29; 146.4.
j Emendation yields "riches."
k-k Meaning uncertain; emendation yields "approaching [to minister]. They would come and profane the Holy Site."

And here is another frustration: [11] the fact that the sentence imposed for evil deeds is not executed swiftly, which is why men are emboldened to do evil—[12] the fact that a sinner may do evil a hundred times and his [punishment] still be delayed. For although I am aware that "It will be well with those who revere God since they revere Him, [13] and it will not be well with the scoundrel, and he will not live long, because[l] he does not revere God"—[14] here is a frustration that occurs in the world: sometimes an upright man is requited according to the conduct of the scoundrel; and sometimes the scoundrel is requited according to the conduct of the upright. I say all that is frustration.

[15] I therefore praised enjoyment. For the only good a man can have under the sun is to eat and drink and enjoy himself. That much can accompany him, in exchange for his wealth, through the days of life that God has granted him under the sun.

[16] For I have set my mind to learn wisdom and to observe the business that goes on in the world—even to the extent of going without sleep day and night—[17] and I have observed all that God brings to pass. Indeed, man cannot guess the events that occur under the sun. For man tries strenuously, but fails to guess them; and even if a sage should think to discover them he would not be able to guess them.

9 For all this I noted, and I ascertained[a] all this: that the actions of even the righteous and the wise are determined by God. [b]Even love! Even hate! Man knows none of these in advance[2] —none![-b] For the same fate is in store for all: for the righteous, and for the wicked; for the good and pure,[c] and for the impure; for him who sacrifices, and for him who does not;[d] for him who is pleasing,[e]

[1] *See note on 6.12.*

[a] *Meaning of verb uncertain; construction as in Hos. 12.3; Ezra 3.12.*
[b-b] *Emendation yields: "Even love, even hate, no man can know in advance. All [2] are insignificant."*
[c] *I.e. those who observe the laws of ritual purity.*
[d] *Cf. 4.17.*
[e] *I.e. to God; cf. 2.26; 7.26.*

and for him who is displeasing; and for him who swears, and for him who shuns oaths.*f* 3 That is the sad thing about all that goes on under the sun: that the same fate is in store for all. (Not only that, but men's hearts are full of sadness, and their minds of madness, while they live; and then—to the dead!) 4 For he who is *g*reckoned among*g* the living has something to look forward to—even a live dog is better than a dead lion—5 since the living know they will die. But the dead know nothing; they have no more recompense,*h* for even the memory of them has died. 6 Their loves, their hates, their jealousies have long since perished; and they have no more share till the end of time in all that goes on under the sun.

7 Go, eat your bread in gladness, and drink your wine in joy; for your action was long ago approved by God.*i* 8 Let your clothes always be freshly washed, and your head never lack ointment. 9 Enjoy happiness with a woman you love all the fleeting days of life that have been granted to you under the sun—all your fleeting days. For that alone is what you can get out of life and out of the means you acquire under the sun. 10 Whatever it is in your power to do, do with all your might. For there is no action, no reasoning, no learning, no wisdom in Sheol, where you are going.

11 I have further observed under the sun that

The race is not won by the swift,

Nor the battle by the valiant;

Nor is bread won by the wise,

Nor wealth by the intelligent,

Nor favor by the learned.

For the time of mischance*j* comes to all.*k* 12 And a man cannot

---

f *Cf. 8.2.*
g-g *Lit. "joined to all."*
h *Emendation yields "hope."*
i *Cf. 2.24–25; 3.13; 5.18.*
j *Euphemism for death.*
k *I.e. the insignificant duration of life renders all successes illusory; cf. 4.15–16.*

even know his time. As fishes are enmeshed in a fatal net, and as birds are trapped in a snare, so men are caught at the time of calamity,^j when it comes upon them without warning.

13 This thing too I observed under the sun about wisdom, and it affected me profoundly. 14 There was a little city, with few men in it; and to it came a great king, who invested it and built mighty siege works against it. 15 Present in the city was a poor wise man ^l-who might have saved-^l it with his wisdom, but nobody thought of that poor man. 16 So I observed: Wisdom is better than valor; but

A poor man's wisdom is scorned,
And his words are not heeded.

17 ^mWords spoken softly by wise men are heeded ^n-sooner than those shouted by a lord in folly.-^n

18 Wisdom is more valuable than ^o-weapons of war,-^o but a single error destroys much of value.

10 Dead flies turn the perfumer's ointment fetid and putrid;^a so a little folly outweighs massive wisdom.

2 A wise man's mind tends toward the right hand, a fool's toward the left.^b 3 A fool's mind is also wanting when he travels, and he lets everybody know he is a fool.

4 If the wrath of a lord flares up against you, don't give up your post;^c for ^d-when wrath abates, grave offenses are pardoned.-^d

5 Here is an evil I have seen under the sun as great as an error

---

^l-l *Others "who saved."*
^m *9.17–10.19 is a group of loosely connected aphorisms.*
^n-n *Lit. "than the scream of a lord in [the manner of] the fools."*
^o-o *Emendation yields "everything precious."*

^a *Meaning of Heb. uncertain.*
^b *I.e. a wise man's mind brings him good luck; a fool's brings him bad luck.*
^c *Emendation yields "hope."*
^d-d *Lit. "abatement (II Chron. 36.16) remits grave offenses." For* hinniaḥ, *"to remit," cf. Abodah Zarah 13a; cf.* hanaḥah, *"remission of taxes," Esth. 2.18.*

committed by a ruler: [6] Folly was placed on lofty heights, while rich men sat in low estate. [7] I have seen slaves on horseback, and nobles walking on the ground like slaves.

[8] He who digs a pit will fall into it; he who breaches a stone fence will be bitten by a snake. [9] He who quarries stones will [e-]be hurt by them; he who splits wood will be harmed by[-e] it. [10] [f]If the ax has become dull and he has not whetted the edge, he must exert more strength. Thus the advantage of a skill [depends on the exercise of] prudence. [11] If the snake bites because no spell was uttered, no advantage is gained by the trained charmer.

[12] A wise man's talk brings him favor, but a fool's lips are his undoing. [13] His talk begins as silliness and ends as disastrous madness. [14] Yet the fool talks and talks!

[g]A man cannot know what will happen; who can tell him what the future holds?

[15] [h]A fool's exertions tire him out, for he doesn't know how to get to a town.

[16] Alas for you, O land whose king is a lackey and whose ministers dine in the morning! [17] Happy are you, O land whose king is a master and whose ministers dine at the proper time—with restraint, not with guzzling!

[18] Through slothfulness the ceiling sags,
Through lazy hands the house caves in.

[19] They[i] make a banquet for revelry; wine makes life merry, and money answers every need.

[20] Don't revile a king even among your intimates.[j]
Don't revile a rich man even in your bedchamber;
For a bird of the air may carry the utterance,
And a winged creature may report the word.

[e-e] *Emendation yields "profit . . . shall make use of."*
[f] *Meaning of verse uncertain.*
[g] *The thought of this sentence is resumed at v. 20.*
[h] *This verse continues the thought of v. 3.*
[i] *I.e. the ministers of v. 16.*
[j] *Others "thoughts"; meaning of Heb. uncertain.*

11 Send your bread forth upon the waters; for after many days you will find it. [2] Distribute portions to seven or even to eight, for you cannot know what misfortune may occur on earth.

[3] If the clouds are filled, they will pour down rain on the earth; and *a*-if a tree falls to the south or to the north, the tree will stay where it falls.*-a* [4] If one watches the wind, he will never sow; and if one observes the clouds, he will never reap. [5] Just as you do not know how the lifebreath passes into*b* the limbs within the womb of the pregnant woman, so you cannot foresee the actions of God, who causes all things to happen. [6] Sow your seed in the morning, and don't hold back your hand in the evening, since you don't know which is going to succeed, the one or the other, or if both are equally good.

[7] How sweet is the light, what a delight for the eyes to behold the sun! [8] Even if a man lives many years, let him enjoy himself in all of them, remembering how many the days of darkness are going to be. The only future is nothingness!

[9] O youth, enjoy yourself while you are young! Let your heart lead you to enjoyment in the days of your youth. Follow the desires of your heart and the glances of your eyes—but know well that God will call you to account for all such things—[10] and banish care from your mind, and pluck sorrow out of your flesh! For youth and black hair are fleeting.

12 So appreciate your vigor*a* in the days of your youth, before those days of sorrow come and those years arrive of which you will say, "I have no pleasure in them"; [2] before sun and light and moon and stars grow dark, and the clouds come back again after the rain:

a-a Emendation yields, "if a thunderbolt (lit. arrow, cf. e.g. II Sam. 22.15) falls . . . where the thunderbolt falls, only there will it strike."
b So many mss. and Targum; most mss. read "like."

a Cf. post-biblical bori; others "Remember thy Creator."

³ When the guards of the house*b* become shaky,
And the men of valor*c* are bent,
And the maids that grind,*d* grown few, are idle,
And the ladies that peer through the windows*e* grow dim,
⁴ And the doors to the street*f* are shut—
With the noise of the hand mill growing fainter,
And the song of the bird *g-*growing feebler,*-g*
And all the strains of music dying down;*h*
⁵ When one is afraid of heights
And there is terror on the road.—
For the almond tree may blossom,
*i-*The grasshopper be burdened,*-i*
And the caper bush may bud again;*j*
But man sets out for his eternal abode,
With mourners all around in the street.—
⁶ Before the silver cord snaps
And the golden bowl crashes,
The jar is shattered at the spring,
And the jug*k* is smashed at the cistern.*l*
⁷ And the dust returns to the ground
As it was,
And the lifebreath returns to God
Who bestowed it.
⁸ Utter futility—said Koheleth—
All is futile!

---

b *I.e. the arms.*
c *I.e. the legs.*
d *I.e. the teeth.*
e *I.e. the eyes.*
f *I.e. the ears.*
g-g *Exact meaning of Heb. uncertain.*
h *Cf. II Sam. 19.36.*
i-i *Emendation yields "The squill (post-biblical Heb. ḥaṣab) resume its burden," i.e. its blossom-stalk and its leaves.*
j *These plants, after seeming dead for part of the year, revive, unlike man. Cf. Job 14.7–10.*
k *So in Punic; others "wheel."*
l *Poetic figure for the end of life.*

⁹ A further word: Because Koheleth was a sage, he continued to instruct the people. He listened to and tested the soundness[m] of many maxims. ¹⁰ Koheleth sought to discover useful sayings and recorded[n] genuinely truthful sayings. ¹¹ The sayings of the wise are like goads, like nails fixed [o-]in prodding sticks.[-o] [p-]They were given by one Shepherd.[-p]

¹² A further word: [q-]Against them,[-q] my son, be warned!
The making of many books is without limit
And much study[r] is a wearying of the flesh.

¹³ The sum of the matter, when all is said and done: Revere God and observe His commandments! For this applies to all mankind: ¹⁴ that God will call every creature to account for [s-]everything unknown,[-s] be it good or bad.

The sum of the matter, when all is said and done: Revere God and observe His commandments! For this applies to all mankind.

---

[m] *A noun, like* dibber (Jer. 5.13), *which occurs in such post-biblical phrases as* shanim kethiq(qe)nan, *"normal years" (lit. "years according to their propriety").*

[n] Wekhathub *is equivalent to* wekhathob, *an infinitive employed as in Esth. 9.16 and elsewhere.*

[o-o] *Meaning of Heb. uncertain. Others "are those that are composed in collections."*

[p-p] *Meaning of Heb. uncertain. Emendation yields "They are accounted as a sharp ox goad" (post-biblical* mardea*).*

[q-q] *Emendation yields "Slow, there!" Cf. Arabic* mah *and* mah mah; *so also* mah (meh) *in Prov. 31.2.*

[r] *Meaning of Heb. uncertain.*

[s-s] *Emendation yields "all their conduct."*

אסתר
ESTHER

אסתר
ESTHER

1 It happened in the days of Ahasuerus—that Ahasuerus who reigned over a hundred and twenty-seven provinces from India to Nubia. ² In those days, when King Ahasuerus occupied the royal throne in the fortress*ᵃ* Shushan, ³ in the third year of his reign, he gave a banquet for all the officials and courtiers—the administration of Persia and Media, the nobles and the governors of the provinces in his service. ⁴ For no fewer than a hundred and eighty days he displayed the vast riches of his kingdom and the splendid glory of his majesty. ⁵ At the end of this period, the king gave a banquet for seven days in the court of the king's palace garden for all the people who lived in the fortress Shushan, high and low alike. ⁶ *ᵇ*[There were hangings of] white cotton and blue wool, caught up by cords of fine linen and purple wool to silver rods and alabaster columns; and there were couches of gold and silver on a pavement of marble, alabaster, mother-of-pearl, and mosaics. ⁷ Royal wine was served in abundance, as befits a king, in golden beakers, beakers of varied design. ⁸ And the rule for the drinking was, "No restrictions!" For the king had given orders to every palace steward to comply with each man's wishes. ⁹ In addition, Queen Vashti gave a banquet for women, in the royal palace of King Ahasuerus.

¹⁰ On the seventh day, when the king was merry with wine, he ordered Mehuman, Bizzetha, Harbona, Bigtha, Abagtha, Zethar, and Carcas, the seven eunuchs in attendance on King Ahasuerus, ¹¹ to bring Queen Vashti before the king wearing a royal diadem, to display her beauty to the peoples and the officials; for she was a beautiful woman. ¹² But Queen Vashti refused to come at the

---

ᵃ *I.e. the fortified city.*
ᵇ *Meaning of part of this verse uncertain.*

king's command conveyed by the eunuchs. The king was greatly incensed, and his fury burned within him.

13 Then the king consulted the sages learned in procedure.ᶜ (For it was the royal practice [to turn] to all who were versed in law and precedent. 14 His closest advisers were Carshena, She-thar, Admatha, Tarshish, Meres, Marsena, and Memucan, the seven ministers of Persia and Media who had access to the royal presence and occupied the first place in the kingdom.) 15 "What," [he asked,] "shall be done, according to law, to Queen Vashti for failing to obey the command of King Ahasuerus conveyed by the eunuchs?"

16 Thereupon Memucan declared in the presence of the king and the ministers: "Queen Vashti has committed an offense not only against Your Majesty but also against all the officials and against all the peoples in all the provinces of King Ahasuerus. 17 For the queen's behavior will make all wives despise their hus-bands, as they reflect that King Ahasuerus himself ordered Queen Vashti to be brought before him, but she would not come. 18 This very day the ladies of Persia and Media, who have heard of the queen's behavior, will cite it to all Your Majesty's officials, and there will be no end of scorn and provocation!

19 "If it please Your Majesty, let a royal edict be issued by you, and let it be written into the laws of Persia and Media, so that it cannot be abrogated, that Vashti shall never enter the presence of King Ahasuerus. And let Your Majesty bestow her royal state upon another who is more worthy than she. 20 Then will the judgment executed by Your Majesty resound throughout your realm, vast though it is; and all wives will treat their husbands with respect, high and low alike."

21 The proposal was approved by the king and the ministers, and the king did as Memucan proposed. 22 Dispatches were sent to all the provinces of the king, to every province in its own script and to every nation in its own language, that every man should wield authority in his home and speak the language of his own people.

ᶜ Lit. "the times."

2 Some time afterward, when the anger of King Ahasuerus subsided, he thought of Vashti and what she had done and what had been decreed against her. ² The king's servants who attended him said, "Let beautiful young virgins be sought out for Your Majesty. ³ Let Your Majesty appoint officers in every province of your realm to assemble all the beautiful young virgins at the fortress Shushan, in the harem under the supervision of Hege, the king's eunuch, guardian of the women. Let them be provided with their cosmetics. ⁴ And let the maiden who pleases Your Majesty be queen instead of Vashti." The proposal pleased the king, and he acted upon it.

⁵ In the fortress Shushan lived a Jew by the name of Mordecai, son of Jair son of Shimei son of Kish, a Benjaminite. ⁶ [Kish] had been exiled from Jerusalem in the group that was carried into exile along with King Jeconiah of Judah, which had been driven into exile by King Nebuchadnezzar of Babylon.—⁷ He was foster father to Hadassah—that is, Esther—his uncle's daughter, for she had neither father nor mother. The maiden was shapely and beautiful; and when her father and mother died, Mordecai adopted her as his own daughter.

⁸ When the king's order and edict was proclaimed, and when many girls were assembled in the fortress Shushan under the supervision of Hegai,ᵃ Esther too was taken into the king's palace under the supervision of Hegai, guardian of the women. ⁹ The girl pleased him and won his favor, and he hastened to furnish her with her cosmetics and her rations, as well as with the seven maids who were her due from the king's palace; and he treated her and her maids with special kindness in the harem. ¹⁰ Esther did not reveal her people or her kindred, for Mordecai had told her not to reveal it. ¹¹ Every single day Mordecai would walk about in front of the court of the harem, to learn how Esther was faring and what was happening to her.

¹² When each girl's turn came to go to King Ahasuerus at the

ᵃ Identical with Hege in v. 3.

end of the twelve months' treatment prescribed for women (for that was the period spent on beautifying them: six months with oil of myrrh and six months with perfumes and women's cosmetics, [13] and it was after that that the girl would go to the king), whatever she asked for would be given her to take with her from the harem to the king's palace. [14] She would go in the evening and leave in the morning for a second harem in charge of Shaashgaz, the king's eunuch, guardian of the concubines. She would not go again to the king unless the king wanted her, when she would be summoned by name. [15] When the turn came for Esther daughter of Abihail—the uncle of Mordecai, who had adopted her as his own daughter—to go to the king, she did not ask for anything but what Hegai, the king's eunuch, guardian of the women, advised. Yet Esther won the admiration of all who saw her.

[16] Esther was taken to King Ahasuerus, in his royal palace, in the tenth month, which is the month of Tebeth, in the seventh year of his reign. [17] The king loved Esther more than all the other women, and she won his grace and favor more than all the virgins. So he set a royal diadem on her head and made her queen instead of Vashti. [18] The king gave a great banquet for all his officials and courtiers, "the banquet of Esther." He proclaimed a remission of taxes[b] for the provinces and distributed gifts as befits a king.

[19] [c]When the virgins were assembled a second time, Mordecai sat in the palace gate. [20] But Esther still did not reveal her kindred or her people, as Mordecai had instructed her; for Esther obeyed Mordecai's bidding, as she had done when she was under his tutelage.

[21] At that time, when Mordecai was sitting in the palace gate, Bigthan and Teresh, two of the king's eunuchs who guarded the threshold, became angry, and plotted to do away with King Ahasuerus. [22] Mordecai learned of it and told it to Queen Esther, and Esther reported it to the king in Mordecai's name. [23] The matter was investigated and found to be so, and the two were impaled on stakes. This was recorded in the book of annals at the instance of the king.

[b] Or "an amnesty."
[c] Meaning of verse uncertain.

3 Some time afterward, King Ahasuerus promoted Haman son of Hammedatha the Agagite; he advanced him and seated him higher than any of his fellow officials. ² All the king's courtiers in the palace gate knelt and bowed low to Haman, for such was the king's order concerning him; but Mordecai would not kneel or bow low. ³ Then the king's courtiers who were in the palace gate said to Mordecai, "Why do you disobey the king's order?" ⁴ When they spoke to him day after day and he would not listen to them, they told Haman, in order to see whether Mordecai's resolve would prevail; for he had explained to them that he was a Jew.ᵃ ⁵ When Haman saw that Mordecai would not kneel or bow low to him, Haman was filled with rage. ⁶ But he disdained to lay hands on Mordecai alone; having been told who Mordecai's people were, Haman plotted to do away with all the Jews, Mordecai's people, throughout the kingdom of Ahasuerus.

⁷ In the first month, that is, the month of Nisan, in the twelfth year of King Ahasuerus, *pur*—which means "the lot"—was cast before Haman concerning every day and every month, [until it fell on] the twelfth month, that is, the month of Adar. ⁸ Haman then said to King Ahasuerus, "There is a certain people, scattered and dispersed among the other peoples in all the provinces of your realm, whose laws are different from those of any other people and who do not obey the king's laws; and it is not in Your Majesty's interest to tolerate them. ⁹ If it please Your Majesty, let an edict be drawn for their destruction, and I will pay ten thousand talents of silver to the stewards for deposit in the royal treasury." ¹⁰ Thereupon the king removed his signet ring from his hand and gave it to Haman son of Hammedatha the Agagite, the foe of the Jews. ¹¹ And the king said, "The money and the people are yours to do with as you see fit."

¹² On the thirteenth day of the first month, the king's scribes were summoned and a decree was issued, as Haman directed, to the king's satraps, to the governors of every province, and to the officials of every people, to every province in its own script and

---

ᵃ *I.e. that as a Jew he could not bow to a descendant of Agag, the Amalekite king: see I Sam. 15, and cf. Exod. 17.14–16; Deut. 25.17–19.*

to every people in its own language. The orders were issued in the name of King Ahasuerus and sealed with the king's signet. [13] Accordingly, written instructions were dispatched by couriers to all the king's provinces to destroy, massacre, and exterminate all the Jews, young and old, children and women, on a single day, on the thirteenth day of the twelfth month—that is, the month of Adar—and to plunder their possessions. [14] The text of the document was to the effect that a law should be proclaimed in every single province; it was to be publicly displayed to all the peoples, so that they might be ready for that day.

[15] The couriers went out posthaste on the royal mission, and the decree was proclaimed in the fortress Shushan. The king and Haman sat down to drink, but the city of Shushan was dumbfounded.

4 When Mordecai learned all that had happened, Mordecai tore his clothes and put on sackcloth and ashes. He went through the city, crying out loudly and bitterly, [2] until he came in front of the palace gate; for one could not enter the palace gate wearing sackcloth.—[3] Also, in every province that the king's command and decree reached, there was great mourning among the Jews, with fasting, weeping, and wailing, and everybody lay in sackcloth and ashes.—[4] When Esther's maidens and eunuchs came and informed her, the queen was greatly agitated. She sent clothing for Mordecai to wear, so that he might take off his sackcloth; but he refused.

[5] Thereupon Esther summoned Hathach, one of the eunuchs whom the king had appointed to serve her, and sent him to Mordecai to learn the why and wherefore of it all. [6] Hathach went out to Mordecai in the city square in front of the palace gate; [7] and Mordecai told him all that had happened to him, and all about the money that Haman had offered to pay into the royal treasury for the destruction of the Jews. [8] He also gave him the written text of the law that had been proclaimed in Shushan for

their destruction. [He bade him] show it to Esther and inform her, and charge her to go to the king and to appeal to him and to plead with him for her people. 9 When Hathach came and delivered Mordecai's message to Esther, 10 Esther told Hathach to take back to Mordecai the following reply: 11 "All the king's courtiers and the people of the king's provinces know that if any person, man or woman, enters the king's presence in the inner court without having been summoned, there is but one law for him—that he be put to death. Only if the king extends the golden scepter to him may he live. Now I have not been summoned to visit the king for the last thirty days."

12 When Mordecai was told what Esther had said, 13 Mordecai had this message delivered to Esther: "Do not imagine that you, of all the Jews, will escape with your life by being in the king's palace. 14 On the contrary, if you keep silent in this crisis, relief and deliverance will come to the Jews from another quarter, while you and your father's house will perish. And who knows, perhaps you have attained to royal position for just such a crisis." 15 Then Esther sent back this answer to Mordecai: 16 "Go, assemble all the Jews who live in Shushan, and fast in my behalf; do not eat or drink for three days, night or day. I and my maidens will observe the same fast. Then I shall go to the king, though it is contrary to the law; and if I am to perish, I shall perish!" 17 So Mordecai went about [the city] and did just as Esther had commanded him.

5 On the third day, Esther put on royal apparel and stood in the inner court of the king's palace, facing the king's palace, while the king was sitting on his royal throne in the throne room facing the entrance of the palace. 2 As soon as the king saw Queen Esther standing in the court, she won his favor. The king extended to Esther the golden scepter which he had in his hand, and Esther approached and touched the tip of the scepter. 3 "What troubles you, Queen Esther?" the king asked her. "And what is your request? Even to half the kingdom, it shall be

granted you." ⁴ "If it please Your Majesty," Esther replied, "let Your Majesty and Haman come today to the feast that I have prepared for him." ⁵ The king commanded, "Tell Haman to hurry and do Esther's bidding." So the king and Haman came to the feast that Esther had prepared.

⁶ At the wine feast, the king asked Esther, "What is your wish? It shall be granted you. And what is your request? Even to half the kingdom, it shall be fulfilled." ⁷ "My wish," replied Esther, "my request—⁸ if Your Majesty will do me the favor, if it please Your Majesty to grant my wish and accede to my request—let Your Majesty and Haman come to the feast which I will prepare for them; and tomorrow I will do Your Majesty's bidding."

⁹ That day Haman went out happy and lighthearted. But when Haman saw Mordecai in the palace gate, and Mordecai did not rise or even stir on his account, Haman was filled with rage at him. ¹⁰ Nevertheless, Haman controlled himself and went home. He sent for his friends and his wife Zeresh, ¹¹ and Haman told them about his great wealth and his many sons, and all about how the king had promoted him and advanced him above the officials and the king's courtiers. ¹² "What is more," said Haman, "Queen Esther gave a feast, and besides the king she did not have anyone but me. And tomorrow too I am invited by her along with the king. ¹³ Yet all this means nothing to me every time I see that Jew Mordecai sitting in the palace gate." ¹⁴ Then his wife Zeresh and all his friends said to him, "Let a stake be put up, fifty cubits high, and in the morning ask the king to have Mordecai impaled on it. Then you can go gaily with the king to the feast." The proposal pleased Haman, and he had the stake put up.

6 That night, sleep deserted the king, and he ordered the book of records, the annals, to be brought; and it was read to the king. ² There it was found written that Mordecai had denounced Bigthana and Teresh, two of the king's eunuchs who guarded the threshhold, who had plotted to do away with King Ahasuerus.

3 "What honor or advancement has been conferred on Mordecai for this?" the king inquired. "Nothing at all has been done for him," replied the king's servants who were in attendance on him. 4 "Who is in the court?" the king asked. For Haman had just entered the outer court of the royal palace, to speak to the king about having Mordecai impaled on the stake he had prepared for him. 5 "It is Haman standing in the court," the king's servants answered him. "Let him enter," said the king. 6 Haman entered, and the king asked him, "What should be done for a man whom the king desires to honor?" Haman said to himself, "Whom would the king desire to honor more than me?" 7 So Haman said to the king, "For the man whom the king desires to honor, 8 let royal garb which the king has worn be brought, and a horse on which the king has ridden and on whose head a royal diadem has been set; 9 and let the attire and the horse be put in the charge of one of the king's noble courtiers. And let the man whom the king desires to honor be attired and paraded on the horse through the city square, while they proclaim before him: This is what is done for the man whom the king desires to honor!" 10 "Quick, then!" said the king to Haman. "Get the garb and the horse, as you have said, and do this to Mordecai the Jew, who sits in the king's gate. Omit nothing of all you have proposed." 11 So Haman took the garb and the horse and arrayed Mordecai and paraded him through the city square; and he proclaimed before him: This is what is done for the man whom the king desires to honor!

12 Then Mordecai returned to the king's gate, while Haman hurried home, his head covered in mourning. 13 There Haman told his wife Zeresh and all his friends everything that had befallen him. His advisers and his wife Zeresh said to him, "If Mordecai, before whom you have begun to fall, is of Jewish stock, you will not overcome him; you will fall before him to your ruin."

14 While they were still speaking with him, the king's eunuchs arrived and hurriedly brought Haman to the banquet which Esther had prepared.

7 So the king and Haman came to feast with Queen Esther.
² On the second day, the king again asked Esther at the banquet,
"What is your wish, Queen Esther? It shall be granted you. And
what is your request? Even to half the kingdom, it shall be
fulfilled." ³ Queen Esther replied: "If Your Majesty will do me the
favor, and if it pleases Your Majesty, let my life be granted me
as my wish, and my people as my request. ⁴ For we have been
sold, my people and I, to be destroyed, massacred, and exter-
minated. Had we only been sold as bondmen and bondwomen,
I would have kept silent; for *ᵃ-the adversary-ᵃ* is not worthy of the
king's trouble."

⁵ Thereupon King Ahasuerus demanded of Queen Esther,
"Who is he and where is he who dared to do this?" ⁶ "The
adversary and enemy," replied Esther, "is this evil Haman!" And
Haman cringed in terror before the king and the queen. ⁷ The
king, in his fury, left the wine feast for the palace garden, while
Haman remained to plead with Queen Esther for his life; for he
saw that the king had resolved to destroy him. ⁸ When the king
returned from the palace garden to the banquet room, Haman
was lying prostrate on the couch on which Esther reclined. "Does
he mean," cried the king, "to ravish the queen in my own palace?" No sooner did these words leave the king's lips than
Haman's face *ᵇ-was covered.-ᵇ* ⁹ Then Harbonah, one of the eunuchs in attendance on the king, said, "What is more, a stake is
standing at Haman's house, fifty cubits high, which Haman made
for Mordecai—the man whose words saved the king." "Impale
him on it!" the king ordered. ¹⁰ So they impaled Haman on the
stake which he had put up for Mordecai, and the king's fury
abated.

ᵃ⁻ᵃ *Emendation yields "a trifle"* (hiṣṣar), *lit. "little finger."*
ᵇ⁻ᵇ *Meaning of Heb. uncertain. Emendation yields "blanched"; cf. Ps. 34.6.*

8 That very day King Ahasuerus gave the property of Haman, the enemy of the Jews, to Queen Esther. Mordecai presented himself to the king, for Esther had revealed how he was related to her. ² The king slipped off his ring, which he had taken back from Haman, and gave it to Mordecai; and Esther put Mordecai in charge of Haman's property.

³ Esther spoke to the king again, falling at his feet and weeping, and beseeching him to avert the evil plotted by Haman the Agagite against the Jews. ⁴ The king extended the golden scepter to Esther, and Esther arose and stood before the king. ⁵ "If it please Your Majesty," she said, "and if I have won your favor and the proposal seems right to Your Majesty, and if I am pleasing to you —let dispatches be written countermanding those which were written by Haman son of Hammedatha the Agagite, embodying his plot to annihilate the Jews throughout the king's provinces. ⁶ For how can I bear to see the disaster which will befall my people! And how can I bear to see the destruction of my kindred!"

⁷ Then King Ahasuerus said to Queen Esther and Mordecai the Jew, "I have given Haman's property to Esther, and he has been impaled on the stake for scheming against the Jews. ⁸ And you may further write with regard to the Jews as you see fit. [Write it] in the king's name and seal it with the king's signet, for an edict that has been written in the king's name and sealed with the king's signet may not be revoked."

⁹ So the king's scribes were summoned at that time, on the twenty-third day of the third month, that is, the month of Sivan; and letters were written, at Mordecai's dictation, to the Jews and to the satraps, the governors and the officials of the one hundred and twenty-seven provinces from India to Ethiopia: to every province in its own script and to every people in its own language, and to the Jews in their own script and language. ¹⁰ He had them written in the name of King Ahasuerus and sealed with the king's

signet. Letters were dispatched by mounted couriers, riding steeds *a*-used in the king's service, bred of the royal stud,-*a* 11 to this effect: The king has permitted the Jews of every city to assemble and fight for their lives; if any people or province attacks them, they may destroy, massacre, and exterminate its armed force together with women and children, and to plunder their possessions—12 on a single day in all the provinces of King Ahasuerus, namely, on the thirteenth day of the twelfth month, that is, the month of Adar. 13 The text of the document was to be issued as a law in every single province: it was to be publicly displayed to all the peoples, so that the Jews should be ready for that day to avenge themselves on their enemies. 14 The couriers, mounted on royal steeds, went out in urgent haste at the king's command; and the decree was proclaimed in the fortress Shushan.

15 Mordecai left the king's presence in royal robes of blue and white, with a magnificent crown of gold and a mantle of fine linen and purple wool. And the city of Shushan rang with joyous cries. 16 The Jews enjoyed light and gladness, happiness and honor. 17 And in every province and in every city, when the king's command and decree arrived, there was gladness and joy among the Jews, a feast and a holiday. And many of the people of the land professed to be Jews, for the fear of the Jews had fallen upon them.

9 And so, on the thirteenth day of the twelfth month—that is, the month of Adar—when the king's command and decree were to be executed, the very day on which the enemies of the Jews had expected to get them in their power, the opposite happened, and the Jews got their enemies in their power. 2 Throughout the provinces of King Ahasuerus, the Jews mustered in their cities to attack those who sought their hurt; and no one could withstand them, for the fear of them had fallen upon all the peoples. 3 Indeed, all the officials of the provinces—the satraps, the gover-

a-a *Meaning of Heb. uncertain.*

nors, and the king's stewards—showed deference to the Jews, because the fear of Mordecai had fallen upon them. ⁴ For Mordecai was now powerful in the royal palace, and his fame was spreading through all the provinces; the man Mordecai was growing ever more powerful. ⁵ So the Jews struck at their enemies with the sword, slaying and destroying; they wreaked their will upon their enemies.

⁶ In the fortress Shushan the Jews killed a total of five hundred men. ⁷ They also killedᵃ Parshandatha, Dalphon, Aspatha, ⁸ Poratha, Adalia, Aridatha, ⁹ Parmashta, Arisai, Aridai, and Vaizatha, ¹⁰ the ten sons of Haman son of Hammedatha, the foe of the Jews. But they did not lay hands on the spoil. ¹¹ When the number of those slain in the fortress Shushan was reported on that same day to the king, ¹² the king said to Queen Esther, "In the fortress Shushan alone the Jews have killed a total of five hundred men, as well as the ten sons of Haman. What then must they have done in the provinces of the realm! What is your wish now? It shall be granted you. And what else is your request? It shall be fulfilled." ¹³ "If it please Your Majesty," Esther replied, "let the Jews in Shushan be permitted to act tomorrow also as they did today; and let Haman's ten sons be impaled on the stake." ¹⁴ The king ordered that this should be done, and the decree was proclaimed in Shushan. Haman's ten sons were impaled: ¹⁵ and the Jews in Shushan mustered again on the fourteenth day of Adar and slew three hundred men in Shushan. But they did not lay hands on the spoil.

¹⁶ The rest of the Jews, those in the king's provinces, likewise mustered and fought for their lives. They disposed of their enemies, killing seventy-five thousand of their foes; but they did not lay hands on the spoil. ¹⁷ That was on the thirteenth day of the month of Adar; and they rested on the fourteenth day and made it a day of feasting and merrymaking. (¹⁸ But the Jews in Shushan mustered on both the thirteenth and fourteenth days, and so rested on the fifteenth, and made it a day of feasting and merrymaking.) ¹⁹ That is why village Jews, who live in unwalled

ᵃ *Moved up from v. 10 for greater clarity.*

towns, observe the fourteenth day of the month of Adar and make it a day of merrymaking and feasting, and as a holiday and an occasion for sending gifts to one another.

20 Mordecai recorded these events. And he sent dispatches to all the Jews throughout the provinces of King Ahasuerus, near and far, 21 charging them to observe the fourteenth and fifteenth days of Adar, every year—22 the same days on which the Jews enjoyed relief from their foes and the same month which had been transformed for them from one of grief and mourning to one of festive joy. They were to observe them as days of feasting and merrymaking, and as an occasion for sending gifts to one another and presents to the poor. 23 The Jews accordingly assumed as an obligation that which they had begun to practice and which Mordecai prescribed for them.

24 For Haman son of Hammedatha the Agagite, the foe of all the Jews, had plotted to destroy the Jews, and had cast *pur*—that is, the lot—with intent to crush and exterminate them. 25 But when [Esther] came before the king, he commanded: *b*-"With the promulgation of this decree,-*b* let the evil plot, which he devised against the Jews, recoil on his own head!" So they impaled him and his sons on the stake. 26 For that reason these days were named Purim, after *pur*.

In view, then, of all the instructions in the said letter and of what they had experienced in that matter and what had befallen them, 27 the Jews undertook and irrevocably obligated themselves and their descendants, and all who might join them, to observe these two days in the manner prescribed and at the proper time each year. 28 Consequently, these days are recalled and observed in every generation: by every family, every province, and every city. And these days of Purim shall never cease among the Jews, and the memory of them shall never perish among their descendants.

29 *c*Then Queen Esther daughter of Abihail wrote a second letter of Purim for the purpose of confirming with full authority the aforementioned one of Mordecai the Jew. 30 Dispatches were

b-b *Meaning of Heb. uncertain.*
c *Force of vv. 29–31 uncertain in part. V. 29 reads literally, "Then Queen Esther daughter of Abihail, and Mordecai the Jew, wrote with full authority to confirm this second letter of Purim."*

sent to all the Jews in the hundred and twenty-seven provinces of the realm of Ahasuerus with an ordinance of "equity and honesty*d*": 31 These days of Purim shall be observed at their proper time, as Mordecai the Jew—and now Queen Esther—has obligated them to do, and just as they have assumed for themselves and their descendants the obligation of the fasts with their lamentations.*e*

32 And Esther's ordinance validating these observances of Purim was recorded in a scroll.

10 King Ahasuerus imposed tribute on the mainland and the islands. 2 All his mighty and powerful acts, and a full account of the greatness to which the king advanced Mordecai, are recorded in the Annals of the Kings of Media and Persia. 3 For Mordecai the Jew ranked next to King Ahasuerus and was highly regarded by the Jews and popular with the multitude of his brethren; he sought the good of his people and interceded for the welfare of all his kindred.

---

d *I.e. of new holidays, the instituting of which is linked to love of equity and honesty in Zech. 8.19.*

e *The Jews had long been observing fast days in commemoration of national calamities; see Zech. 7.5; 8.19.*

דניאל

DANIEL

דניאל
DANIEL

1 In the third year of the reign of King Jehoiakim of Judah, King Nebuchadnezzar of Babylon came to Jerusalem and laid siege to it. ² The Lord delivered King Jehoiakim of Judah into his power, together with some of the vessels of the House of God, and he brought them to the land of Shinar to the house of his god; he deposited the vessels in the treasury of his god. ³ Then the king ordered Ashpenaz, his chief officer, to bring some Israelites of royal descent and of the nobility—⁴ youths without blemish, handsome, proficient in all wisdom, knowledgeable and intelligent, and capable of serving in the royal palace—and teach them the writings and the language of the Chaldeans. ⁵ The king allotted daily rations to them from the king's food and from the wine he drank. They were to be educated for three years, *a-*at the end of which they*-a* were to enter the king's service.

⁶ Among them were the Judahites Daniel, Hananiah, Mishael and Azariah. ⁷ The chief officer gave them new names; he named Daniel Belteshazzar, Hananiah Shadrach, Mishael Meshach, and Azariah Abed-nego. ⁸ Daniel resolved not to defile himself with the king's food or the wine he drank, so he sought permission of the chief officer not to defile himself, ⁹ and God disposed the chief officer to be kind and compassionate toward Daniel. ¹⁰ The chief officer said to Daniel, "I fear that my lord the king, who allotted food and drink to you, will notice that you look out of sorts, unlike the other youths of your age—and you will put my life*b* in jeopardy with the king." ¹¹ Daniel replied to the guard whom the chief officer had put in charge of Daniel, Hananiah, Mishael and Azariah, ¹² "Please test your servants for ten days,

---

a-a Or "and some of them."
b Lit. "head."

giving us legumes to eat and water to drink. [13] Then compare our appearance with that of the youths who eat of the king's food, and do with your servants as you see fit." [14] He agreed to this plan of theirs, and tested them for ten days. [15] When the ten days were over, they looked better and healthier than all the youths who were eating of the king's food. [16] So the guard kept on removing their food, and the wine they were supposed to drink, and gave them legumes. [17] God made all four of these young men intelligent and proficient in all writings and wisdom, and Daniel had understanding of visions and dreams of all kinds. [18] When the time the king had set for their presentation had come, the chief officer presented them to Nebuchadnezzar. [19] The king spoke with them, and of them all none was equal to Daniel, Hananiah, Mishael and Azariah; so these entered the king's service. [20] Whenever the king put a question to them requiring wisdom and understanding, he found them to be ten times better than all the magicians and exorcists throughout his realm. [21] Daniel was there until the first year of King Cyrus.

2 In the second year of the reign of Nebuchadnezzar, Nebuchadnezzar had a dream; his spirit was agitated, yet he [a]-was overcome by-[a] sleep. [2] The king ordered the magicians, exorcists, sorcerers, and Chaldeans to be summoned in order to tell the king what he had dreamed. They came and stood before the king, [3] and the king said to them, "I have had a dream and [b]-I am full of anxiety-[b] to know what I have dreamed." [4] The Chaldeans spoke to the king in Aramaic, "O king, live forever! Relate the dream to your servants, and we will tell its meaning." [5] The king said in reply to the Chaldeans, "I hereby decree: If you will not make the dream and its meaning known to me, you shall be torn limb from limb and your houses confiscated.[c] [6] But if you tell the dream and its meaning, you shall receive from me gifts, presents, and great honor; therefore, tell me the dream and its meaning." [7] Once again they answered, "Let the king relate the dream to his

---

[a]-[a] *Meaning of Heb. uncertain; others "could not."*
[b]-[b] *Lit. "My spirit is agitated."*
[c] *Meaning uncertain; or "turned into ruins."*

servants, and we will tell its meaning." [8] The king said in reply, "It is clear to me that you are playing for time, since you see that I have decreed [9] that if you do not make the dream known to me, there is but one verdict for you. You have conspired to tell me something false and fraudulent until circumstances change; so relate the dream to me, and I will then know that you can tell its meaning." [10] The Chaldeans said in reply to the king, "There is no one on earth who can [d-]satisfy the king's demand,[-d] for great king or ruler—none has ever asked such a thing of any magician, exorcist, or Chaldean. [11] The thing asked by the king is difficult; there is no one who can tell it to the king except the gods whose abode is not among mortals."[e] [12] Whereupon the king flew into a violent rage, and gave an order to do away with all the wise men of Babylon.

[13] The decree condemning the wise men to death was issued. Daniel and his companions were about to be put to death [14] when Daniel remonstrated with Arioch, the captain of the royal guard who had set out to put the wise men of Babylon to death. [15] He spoke up and said to Arioch, the royal officer, "Why is the decree of the king so urgent?" Thereupon Arioch informed Daniel of the matter. [16] So Daniel went to ask the king for time, that he might tell the meaning to the king. [17] Then Daniel went to his house and informed his companions, Hananiah, Mishael, and Azariah, of the matter, [18] that they might implore the God of Heaven for help regarding this mystery, so that Daniel and his colleagues would not be put to death together with the other wise men of Babylon.

[19] The mystery was revealed to Daniel in a night vision; then Daniel blessed the God of Heaven. [20] Daniel spoke up and said:

"Let the name of God be blessed forever and ever,
For wisdom and power are His.
[21] He changes times and seasons,
Removes kings and installs kings;
He gives the wise their wisdom
And knowledge to those who know.
[22] He reveals deep and hidden things,

[d-d] *Lit. "tell the king's matter."*
[e] *Lit. "flesh."*

Knows what is in the darkness,
And light dwells with Him.
23 I acknowledge and praise You,
O God of my fathers,
You who have given me wisdom and power,
For now You have let me know what we asked of You;
You have let us know what concerns the king."

24 Thereupon Daniel went to Arioch, whom the king had appointed to do away with the wise men of Babylon; he came and said to him as follows, "Do not do away with the wise men of Babylon; bring me to the king and I will tell the king the meaning!" 25 So Arioch rushed Daniel into the king's presence and said to him, "I have found among the exiles of Judah a man who can make the meaning known to the king!" 26 The king said in reply to Daniel (who was called Belteshazzar), "Can you really make known to me the dream that I saw and its meaning?" 27 Daniel answered the king and said, "The mystery about which the king has inquired—wise men, exorcists, magicians, and diviners cannot tell to the king. 28 But there is a God in heaven who reveals mysteries, and He has made known to King Nebuchadnezzar what is to be at the end of days. This is your dream and the vision that entered your mind in bed: 29 O king, the thoughts that came to your mind in your bed are about future events; He who reveals mysteries has let you know what is to happen. 30 Not because my wisdom is greater than that of other creatures has this mystery been revealed to me, but in order that the meaning should be made known to the king, and that you may know the thoughts of your mind.

31 "O king, as you looked on, there appeared a great statue. This statue, which was huge and its brightness surpassing, stood before you, and its appearance was awesome. 32 The head of that statue was of fine gold; its breast and arms were of silver; its belly and thighs, of bronze; 33 its legs were of iron, and its feet part iron and part clay. 34 As you looked on, a stone was hewn out, not by hands, and struck the statue on its feet of iron and clay and

crushed them. [35] All at once, the iron, clay, bronze, silver and
gold were crushed, and became like chaff of the threshing floors
of summer; a wind carried them off until no trace of them was left.
But the stone that struck the statue became a great mountain and
filled the whole earth.

[36] "Such was the dream, and we will now tell the king its meaning. [37] You, O king—king of kings, to whom the God of Heaven
has given kingdom, power, might, and glory; [38] into whose hands
He has given men, wild beasts, and the fowl of heaven, wherever
they may dwell; and to whom He has given dominion over them
all—you are the head of gold. [39] But another kingdom will arise
after you, inferior to yours; then yet a third kingdom, of bronze,
which will rule over the whole earth. [40] But the fourth kingdom
will be as strong as iron; just as iron crushes and shatters everything—and like iron that smashes—so will it crush and smash all
these. [41] You saw the feet and the toes, part potter's clay and part
iron; that means it will be a divided kingdom; it will have only
some of the stability of iron, inasmuch as you saw iron mixed with
common clay. [42] And the toes were part iron and part clay; that
[means] the kingdom will be in part strong and in part brittle.
[43] You saw iron mixed with common clay; that means: [f]they shall
intermingle with the offspring of men,[f] but shall not hold together, just as iron does not mix with clay. [44] And in the time of
those kings, the God of Heaven will establish a kingdom that shall
never be destroyed, a kingdom that shall not be transferred to
another people. It will crush and wipe out all these kingdoms, but
shall itself last forever—[45] just as you saw how a stone was hewn
from the mountain, not by hands, and crushed the iron, bronze,
clay, silver, and gold. The great God has made known to the king
what will happen in the future. The dream is sure and its interpretation reliable."

[46] Then King Nebuchadnezzar prostrated himself and paid
homage to Daniel and ordered that a meal offering and pleasing
offerings be made to him. [47] The king said in reply to Daniel,
"Truly your God must be the God of gods and Lord of kings and

[f-f] *Meaning uncertain.*

the revealer of mysteries to have enabled you to reveal this mystery." [48] The king then elevated Daniel and gave him very many gifts, and made him governor of the whole province of Babylon and chief prefect of all the wise men of Babylon. [49] At Daniel's request, the king appointed Shadrach, Meshach, and Abed-nego to administer the province of Babylon; while Daniel himself was at the king's court.

3 King Nebuchadnezzar made a statue of gold sixty cubits high and six cubits broad. He set it up in the plain of Dura in the province of Babylon. [2] King Nebuchadnezzar then sent word to gather the satraps, prefects, governors, counselors, treasurers, judges, officers, and all the provincial officials to attend the dedication of the statue that King Nebuchadnezzar had set up. [3] So the satraps, prefects, governors, counselors, treasurers, judges, officers, and all the provincial officials assembled for the dedication of the statue that King Nebuchadnezzar had set up, and stood before the statue that Nebuchadnezzar had set up. [4] The herald proclaimed in a loud voice, "You are commanded, O peoples and nations of every language, [5] when you hear the sound of the horn, pipe, zither, lyre, psaltery, bagpipe, and all other types of instruments, to fall down and worship the statue of gold that King Nebuchadnezzar has set up. [6] Whoever will not fall down and worship shall at once be thrown into a burning fiery furnace." [7] And so, as soon as all the peoples heard the sound of the horn, pipe, zither, lyre, psaltery, and all other types of instruments, all peoples and nations of every language fell down and worshiped the statue of gold that King Nebuchadnezzar had set up.

[8] Seizing the occasion, certain Chaldeans came forward to slander the Jews. [9] They spoke up and said to King Nebuchadnezzar, "O king, live forever! [10] You, O king, gave an order that everyone who hears the horn, pipe, zither, lyre, psaltery, bagpipe, and all types of instruments must fall down and worship the golden statue, [11] and whoever does not fall down and worship shall be

thrown into a burning fiery furnace. [12] There are certain Jews whom you appointed to administer the province of Babylon, Shadrach, Meshach, and Abed-nego; those men pay no heed to you, O king; they do not serve your god or worship the statue of gold that you have set up."

[13] Then Nebuchadnezzar, in raging fury, ordered Shadrach, Meshach, and Abed-nego to be brought; so those men were brought before the king. [14] Nebuchadnezzar spoke to them and said, "Is it true, Shadrach, Meshach, and Abed-nego, that you do not serve my god or worship the statue of gold that I have set up? [15] Now if you are ready to fall down and worship the statue that I have made when you hear the sound of the horn, pipe, zither, lyre, psaltery, and bagpipe, and all other types of instruments, [well and good]; but if you will not worship, you shall at once be thrown into a burning fiery furnace, and what god is there that can save you from my power?" [16] Shadrach, Meshach, and Abed-nego said in reply to the king, "O Nebuchadnezzar, we have no need to answer you in this matter, [17] for if so it must be, our God whom we serve is able to save us from the burning fiery furnace, and He will save us from your power, O king. [18] But even if He does not, be it known to you, O king, that we will not serve your god or worship the statue of gold that you have set up."

[19] Nebuchadnezzar was so filled with rage at Shadrach, Meshach, and Abed-nego that his visage was distorted, and he gave an order to heat up the furnace to seven times its usual heat. [20] He commanded some of the strongest men of his army to bind Shadrach, Meshach, and Abed-nego, and to throw them into the burning fiery furnace. [21] So these men, in their shirts, trousers, hats, and other garments, were bound and thrown into the burning fiery furnace. [22] Because the king's order was urgent, and the furnace was heated to excess, a tongue of flame killed the men who carried up Shadrach, Meshach, and Abed-nego. [23] But those three men, Shadrach, Meshach, and Abed-nego, dropped, bound, into the burning fiery furnace.

[24] Then King Nebuchadnezzar was astonished and, rising in haste, addressed his companions, saying, "Did we not throw

three men, bound, into the fire?" They spoke in reply, "Surely, O king." 25 He answered, "But I see four men walking about unbound and unharmed in the fire and the fourth looks like a divine being." 26 Nebuchadnezzar then approached the hatch of the burning fiery furnace and called, "Shadrach, Meshach, Abed-nego, servants of the Most High God, come out!" So Shadrach, Meshach, and Abed-nego came out of the fire. 27 The satraps, the prefects, the governors, and the royal companions gathered around to look at those men, on whose bodies the fire had had no effect, the hair of whose heads had not been singed, whose shirts looked no different, to whom not even the odor of fire clung. 28 Nebuchadnezzar spoke up and said, "Blessed be the God of Shadrach, Meshach, and Abed-nego, who sent His angel to save His servants who, trusting in Him, flouted the king's decree at the risk of their lives rather than serve or worship any god but their own God. 29 I hereby give an order that [anyone of] any people or nation of whatever language who blasphemes the God of Shadrach, Meshach, and Abed-nego shall be torn limb from limb, and his house confiscated, for there is no other God who is able to save in this way."

30 Thereupon the king promoted Shadrach, Meshach, and Abed-nego in the province of Babylon.

31 "King Nebuchadnezzar to all people and nations of every language that inhabit the whole earth: May your well-being abound! 32 The signs and wonders that the Most High God has worked for me I am pleased to relate. 33 How great are His signs; how mighty His wonders! His kingdom is an everlasting kingdom, and His dominion endures throughout the generations."

4 I, Nebuchadnezzar, was living serenely in my house, flourishing in my palace. 2 I had a dream that frightened me, and my thoughts in bed and the vision of my mind alarmed me. 3 I gave an order to bring all the wise men of Babylon before me to let

me know the meaning of the dream. ⁴ The magicians, exorcists, Chaldeans, and diviners came, and I related the dream to them, but they could not make its meaning known to me. ⁵ Finally, Daniel, called Belteshazzar after the name of my god, in whom the spirit of the holy gods was, came to me, and I related the dream to him, [saying], ⁶ "Belteshazzar, chief magician, in whom I know the spirit of the holy gods to be, and whom no mystery baffles, tell me the meaning of my dream vision that I have seen.
⁷ In the visions of my mind in bed

I saw a tree of great height in the midst of the earth;
⁸ The tree grew and became mighty;
Its top reached heaven,
⁹ And it was visible to the ends of the earth.
Its foliage was beautiful
And its fruit abundant;
There was food for all in it.
Beneath it the beasts of the field found shade,
And the birds of the sky dwelt on its branches;
All creatures fed on it.

¹⁰ In the vision of my mind in bed, I looked and saw a holy Watcher coming down from heaven. ¹¹ He called loudly and said:

'Hew down the tree, lop off its branches,
Strip off its foliage, scatter its fruit.
Let the beasts of the field flee from beneath it
And the birds from its branches,
¹² But leave the stump with its roots in the ground.
In fetters of iron and bronze
In the grass of the field,
Let him be drenched with the dew of heaven,
And share earth's verdure with the beasts.
¹³ Let his mind be altered from that of a man,
And let him be given the mind of a beast,
And let seven seasons pass over him.
¹⁴ This sentence is decreed by the Watchers;
This verdict is commanded by the Holy Ones

So that all creatures may know
That the Most High is sovereign over the realm of man,
And He gives it to whom He wishes
And He may set over it even the lowest of men.'

¹⁵ "I, King Nebuchadnezzar, had this dream; now you, Belteshazzar, tell me its meaning, since all the wise men of my kingdom are not able to make its meaning known to me, but you are able, for the spirit of the holy gods is in you."

¹⁶ Then Daniel, called Belteshazzar, was perplexed for awhile, and alarmed by his thoughts. The king addressed him, "Let the dream and its meaning not alarm you." Belteshazzar replied, "My lord, would that the dream were for your enemy and its meaning for your foe! ¹⁷ The tree that you saw grow and become mighty, whose top reached heaven, which was visible throughout the earth, ¹⁸ whose foliage was beautiful, whose fruit was so abundant that there was food for all in it, beneath which the beasts of the field dwelt, and in whose branches the birds of the sky lodged —¹⁹ it is you, O king, you who have grown and become mighty, whose greatness has grown to reach heaven, and whose dominion is to the end of the earth. ²⁰ The holy Watcher whom the king saw descend from heaven and say,

Hew down the tree and destroy it,
But leave the stump with its roots in the ground.
In fetters of iron and bronze
In the grass of the field,
Let him be drenched with the dew of heaven,
And share the lot of the beasts of the field
Until seven seasons pass over him—

²¹ this is its meaning, O king; it is the decree of the Most High which has overtaken my lord the king. ²² You will be driven away from men and have your habitation with the beasts of the field. You will be fed grass like cattle, and be drenched with the dew of heaven; seven seasons will pass over you until you come to know that the Most High is sovereign over the realm of man, and He gives it to whom He wishes. ²³ And the meaning of the command to leave the stump of the tree with its roots is that the

kingdom will remain yours from the time you come to know that Heaven is sovereign. ²⁴ Therefore, O king, may my advice be acceptable to you: Redeem your sins by beneficence and your iniquities by generosity to the poor; then your serenity may be extended."

²⁵ All this befell King Nebuchadnezzar. ²⁶ Twelve months later, as he was walking on the roof of the royal palace at Babylon, ²⁷ the king exclaimed, "There is great Babylon, which I have built by my vast power to be a royal residence for the glory of my majesty!" ²⁸ The words were still on the king's lips, when a voice fell from heaven, "It has been decreed for you, O King Nebuchadnezzar: The kingdom has passed out of your hands. ²⁹ You are being driven away from men, and your habitation is to be with the beasts of the field. You are to be fed grass like cattle, and seven seasons will pass over you until you come to know that the Most High is sovereign over the realm of man and He gives it to whom He wishes." ³⁰ There and then the sentence was carried out upon Nebuchadnezzar. He was driven away from men, he ate grass like cattle, and his body was drenched with the dew of heaven until his hair grew like eagle's [feathers] and his nails like [the talons of] birds.

³¹ "When the time had passed, I, Nebuchadnezzar, lifted my eyes to heaven, and my reason was restored to me. I blessed the Most High, and praised and glorified the Ever-Living One,

> Whose dominion is an everlasting dominion
> And whose kingdom endures throughout the generations.
> ³² All the inhabitants of the earth are of no account.
> He does as He wishes with the host of heaven,
> And with the inhabitants of the earth.
> There is none to stay His hand
> Or say to Him, 'What have You done?'

³³ There and then my reason was restored to me, and my majesty and splendor were restored to me for the glory of my kingdom. My companions and nobles sought me out, and I was reestablished over my kingdom, and added greatness was given me. ³⁴ So now I, Nebuchadnezzar, praise, exalt, and glorify the King

of Heaven, all of whose works are just and whose ways are right, and who is able to humble those who behave arrogantly."

5 King Belshazzar gave a great banquet for his thousand nobles, and in the presence of the thousand he drank wine. ² Under the influence of the wine, Belshazzar ordered the gold and silver vessels that his father Nebuchadnezzar had taken out of the temple at Jerusalem to be brought so that the king and his nobles, his consorts, and his concubines could drink from them. ³ The golden vessels that had been taken out of the sanctuary of the House of God in Jerusalem were then brought, and the king, his nobles, his consorts, and his concubines drank from them. ⁴ They drank wine and praised the gods of gold and silver, bronze, iron, wood, and stone. ⁵ Just then, the fingers of a human hand appeared and wrote on the plaster of the wall of the king's palace opposite the lampstand, so that the king could see the hand as it wrote. ⁶ The king's face darkened, and his thoughts alarmed him; the joints of his loins were loosened and his knees knocked together. ⁷ The king called loudly for the exorcists, Chaldeans, and diviners to be brought. The king addressed the wise men of Babylon, "Whoever can read this writing and tell me its meaning shall be clothed in purple and wear a golden chain on his neck, and shall rule as ᵃ-one of three-ᵃ in the kingdom."

⁸ Then all the king's wise men came, but they could not read the writing or make known its meaning to the king. ⁹ King Belshazzar grew exceedingly alarmed and his face darkened, and his nobles were dismayed. ¹⁰ Because of the state of the king and his nobles, the queen came to the banquet hall. The queen spoke up and said, "O king, live forever! Let your thoughts not alarm you or your face darken. ¹¹ There is a man in your kingdom who has the spirit of the holy gods in him; in your father's time, illumination, understanding, and wisdom like that of the gods were to be found in him, and your father, King Nebuchadnezzar, appointed him chief of the magicians, exorcists, Chaldeans, and diviners.

ᵃ-ᵃ *Cf. Dan. 6.3; or "third in rank."*

434

¹² Seeing that there is to be found in Daniel (whom the king called Belteshazzar) extraordinary spirit, knowledge, and understanding to interpret dreams, to explain riddles and solve problems, let Daniel now be called to tell the meaning [of the writing]."

¹³ Daniel was then brought before the king. The king addressed Daniel, "You are Daniel, one of the exiles of Judah whom my father, the king, brought from Judah. ¹⁴ I have heard about you that you have the spirit of the gods in you, and that illumination, knowledge, and extraordinary wisdom are to be found in you. ¹⁵ Now the wise men and exorcists have been brought before me to read this writing and to make known its meaning to me. But they could not tell what it meant. ¹⁶ I have heard about you, that you can give interpretations and solve problems. Now if you can read the writing and make known its meaning to me, you shall be clothed in purple and wear a golden chain on your neck and rule as one of three in the kingdom."

¹⁷ Then Daniel said in reply to the king, "You may keep your gifts for yourself, and give your presents to others. But I will read the writing for the king, and make its meaning known to him. ¹⁸ O king, the Most High God bestowed kingship, grandeur, glory, and majesty upon your father Nebuchadnezzar. ¹⁹ And because of the grandeur that He bestowed upon him, all the peoples and nations of every language trembled in fear of him. He put to death whom he wished, and whom he wished he let live; he raised high whom he wished and whom he wished he brought low. ²⁰ But when he grew haughty and willfully presumptuous, he was deposed from his royal throne and his glory was removed from him. ²¹ He was driven away from men, and his mind made like that of a beast, and his habitation was with wild asses. He was fed grass like cattle, and his body was drenched with the dew of heaven until he came to know that the Most High God is sovereign over the realm of man, and sets over it whom He wishes. ²² But you, Belshazzar his son, did not humble yourself although you knew all this. ²³ You exalted yourself against the Lord of Heaven, and had the vessels of His temple brought to you. You

and your nobles, your consorts, and your concubines drank wine from them and praised the gods of silver and gold, bronze and iron, wood and stone, which do not see, hear, or understand; but the God who controls your lifebreath and every move you make —Him you did not glorify! 24 He therefore made the hand appear, and caused the writing to be inscribed. 25 This is the writing that is inscribed: MENE MENE TEKEL UPHARSIN. 26 And this is its meaning: MENE—God has numbered*a* [the days of] your kingdom and brought it to an end; 27 TEKEL—*b-* you have been weighed*-b* in the balance and found wanting; 28 PERES—your kingdom *c-*has been divided*-c* and given to the Medes and the Persians." 29 Then, at Belshazzar's command, they clothed Daniel in purple, placed a golden chain on his neck, and proclaimed that he should rule as one of three in the kingdom.

30 That very night, Belshazzar, the Chaldean king, was killed, **6** 1 and Darius the Mede received the kingdom, being about sixty-two years old. 2 It pleased Darius to appoint over the kingdom one hundred and twenty satraps to be in charge of the whole kingdom; 3 over them were three ministers, one of them Daniel, to whom these satraps reported, in order that the king not be troubled. 4 This man Daniel surpassed the other ministers and satraps by virtue of his extraordinary spirit, and the king considered setting him over the whole kingdom. 5 The ministers and satraps looked for some fault in Daniel's conduct in matters of state, but they could find neither fault nor corruption, inasmuch as he was trustworthy, and no negligence or corruption was to be found in him. 6 Those men then said, "We are not going to find any fault with this Daniel, unless we find something against him in connection with the laws of his God." 7 Then these ministers and satraps came thronging in to the king and said to him, "O King Darius, live forever! 8 All the ministers of the kingdom, the prefects, satraps, companions, and governors are in agreement that a royal ban should be issued under sanction of an oath that whoever shall address a petition to any god or man, besides you, O king, during the next thirty days shall be thrown into a lions'

---

a *Aramaic* mena.
b-b *Aramaic* tekilta.
c-c *Aramaic* perisat.

den. ⁹ So issue the ban, O king, and put it in writing so that it be unalterable as a law of the Medes and Persians that may not be abrogated." ¹⁰ Thereupon King Darius put the ban in writing.

¹¹ When Daniel learned that it had been put in writing, he went to his house, in whose upper chamber he had had windows made facing Jerusalem, and three times a day he knelt down, prayed, and made confession to his God, as he had always done. ¹² Then those men came thronging in and found Daniel petitioning his God in supplication. ¹³ They then approached the king and reminded him of the royal ban: "Did you not put in writing a ban that whoever addresses a petition to any god or man besides you, O king, during the next thirty days, shall be thrown into a lions' den?" The king said in reply, "The order stands firm, as a law of the Medes and Persians that may not be abrogated." ¹⁴ Thereupon they said to the king, "Daniel, one of the exiles of Judah, pays no heed to you, O king, or to the ban that you put in writing; three times a day he offers his petitions [to his God]." ¹⁵ Upon hearing that, the king was very disturbed, and he set his heart upon saving Daniel, and until the sun set made every effort to rescue him. ¹⁶ Then those men came thronging in to the king and said to the king, "Know, O king, that it is a law of the Medes and Persians that any ban that the king issues under sanction of oath is unalterable." ¹⁷ By the king's order, Daniel was then brought and thrown into the lions' den. The king spoke to Daniel and said, "Your God, whom you serve so regularly, will deliver you." ¹⁸ A rock was brought and placed over the mouth of the den; the king sealed it with his signet and with the signet of his nobles, so that nothing might be altered concerning Daniel.

¹⁹ The king then went to his palace and spent the night fasting; no diversions were brought to him, and his sleep fled from him. ²⁰ Then, at the first light of dawn, the king arose and rushed to the lions' den. ²¹ As he approached the den, he cried to Daniel in a mournful voice; the king said to Daniel, "Daniel, servant of the living God, was the God whom you served so regularly able to deliver you from the lions?" ²² Daniel then talked with the king,

"O king, live forever! 23 My God sent His angel, who shut the mouths of the lions so that they did not injure me, inasmuch as I was found innocent by Him, nor have I, O king, done you any injury." 24 The king was very glad, and ordered Daniel to be brought up out of the den. Daniel was brought up out of the den, and no injury was found on him, for he had trusted in his God. 25 Then, by order of the king, those men who had slandered Daniel were brought and, together with their children and wives, were thrown into the lions' den. They had hardly reached the bottom of the den when the lions overpowered them and crushed all their bones.

26 Then King Darius wrote to all peoples and nations of every language that inhabit the earth, "May your well-being abound! 27 I have hereby given an order that throughout my royal domain men must tremble in fear before the God of Daniel, for He is the living God who endures forever; His kingdom is indestructible, and His dominion is to the end of time; 28 He delivers and saves, and performs signs and wonders in heaven and on earth, for He delivered Daniel from the power of the lions." 29 Thus Daniel prospered during the reign of Darius and during the reign of Cyrus the Persian.

7 In the first year of King Belshazzar of Babylon, Daniel saw a dream and a vision of his mind in bed; afterward he wrote down the dream. Beginning the account, 2 Daniel related the following:

"In my vision at night, I saw the four winds of heaven stirring up the great sea. 3 Four mighty beasts different from each other emerged from the sea. 4 The first was like a lion but had eagles' wings. As I looked on, its wings were plucked off, and it was lifted off the ground and set on its feet like a man and given the mind of a man. 5 Then I saw a second, different beast, which was like a bear but raised on one side, and with three fangs in its mouth among its teeth; it was told, 'Arise, eat much meat!'6 After that, as I looked on, there was another one, like a leopard, and it had on its back four wings like those of a bird; the beast had four heads, and dominion was given to it. [7] After that, as I looked on in the night vision, there was a fourth beast—fearsome, dreadful, and very powerful, with great iron teeth—that devoured and crushed, and stamped the remains with its feet. It was different from all the other beasts which had gone before it; and it had ten horns. [8] While I was gazing upon these horns, a new little horn sprouted up among them; three of the older horns were uprooted to make room for it. There were eyes in this horn like those of a man, and a mouth that spoke arrogantly. [9] As I looked on,

> Thrones were set in place,
> And the Ancient of Days took His seat.
> His garment was like white snow,
> And the hair of His head was like lamb's[a] wool.
> His throne was tongues of flame;
> Its wheels were blazing fire.
> [10] A river of fire streamed forth before Him;
> Thousands upon thousands served Him;
> Myriads upon myriads attended Him;
> The court sat and the books were opened.

[11] I looked on. Then, because of the arrogant words that the horn spoke, the beast was killed as I looked on; its body was destroyed and it was consigned to the flames. [12] The dominion of the other beasts was taken away, but an extension of life was given to them for a time and season. [13] As I looked on, in the night vision,

> One like a human being
> Came with the clouds of heaven;
> He reached the Ancient of Days
> And was presented to Him.
> [14] Dominion, glory, and kingship were given to him;
> All peoples and nations of every language must serve him.

[a] Or *"clean."*

His dominion is an everlasting dominion that shall not
   pass away,
And his kingship, one that shall not be destroyed.

[15] As for me, Daniel, my spirit was disturbed within me and the
vision of my mind alarmed me. [16] I approached one of the attendants and asked him the true meaning of all this. He gave me this
interpretation of the matter: [17] 'These great beasts, four in number [mean] four kingdoms[a] will arise out of the earth; [18] then holy
ones of the Most High will receive the kingdom, and will possess
the kingdom forever—forever and ever.' [19] Then I wanted to
ascertain the true meaning of the fourth beast, which was different from them all, very fearsome, with teeth of iron, claws of
bronze, that devoured and crushed, and stamped the remains;
[20] and of the ten horns on its head; and of the new one that
sprouted, to make room for which three fell—the horn that had
eyes, and a mouth that spoke arrogantly, and which was more
conspicuous than its fellows. [21] (I looked on as that horn made
war with the holy ones and overcame them, [22] until the Ancient
of Days came and judgment was rendered in favor of the holy
ones of the Most High, for the time had come, and the holy ones
took possession of the kingdom.) [23] This is what he said: 'The
fourth beast [means]—there will be a fourth kingdom upon the
earth which will be different from all the kingdoms; it will devour
the whole earth, tread it down, and crush it. [24] And the ten horns
[mean]—from that kingdom, ten kings will arise, and after them
another will arise. He will be different from the former ones, and
will bring low three kings. [25] He will speak words against the Most
High, and will harass the holy ones of the Most High. He will
think of changing times and laws, and they will be delivered into
his power for a [b]time, times, and half a time.[-b] [26] Then the court
will sit and his dominion will be taken away, to be destroyed and
abolished for all time. [27] The kingship and dominion and grandeur belonging to all the kingdoms under heaven will be given
to the people of the holy ones of the Most High. Their kingdom

---

[a] Lit. "kings."
[b-b] I.e. a year, two years, and half a year.

shall be an everlasting kingdom, and all dominions shall serve and obey them.' " [28] Here the account ends.

I, Daniel, was very alarmed by my thoughts, and my face darkened; and I could not put the matter out of my mind.

8 In the third year of the reign of King Belshazzar, a vision appeared to me, to me, Daniel, after the one that had appeared to me earlier. [2] I saw in the vision—at the time I saw it I was in the fortress of Shushan, in the province of Elam—I saw in the vision that I was beside the Ulai River. [3] I looked and saw a ram standing between me and the river; he had two horns; the horns were high, with one higher than the other, and the higher sprouting last. [4] I saw the ram butting westward, northward, and southward. No beast could withstand him, and there was none to deliver from his power. He did as he pleased and grew great. [5] As I looked on, a he-goat came from the west, passing over the entire earth without touching the ground. The goat had a conspicuous horn on its forehead. [6] He came up to the two-horned ram that I had seen standing between me and the river and charged at him with furious force. [7] I saw him reach the ram and rage at him; he struck the ram and broke its two horns, and the ram was powerless to withstand him. He threw him to the ground and trampled him, and there was none to deliver the ram from his power. [8] Then the he-goat grew very great, but at the peak of his power his big horn was broken. In its place, four conspicuous horns sprouted toward the four winds of heaven. [9] From one of them emerged a small horn, which extended itself greatly toward the south, toward the east, and toward the beautiful land. [10] It grew as high as the host of heaven and it hurled some stars of the [heavenly] host to the ground and trampled them. [11] It vaunted itself against the very chief of the host; on its account the regular offering was suspended, and His holy place was abandoned. [12] ^a-An army was arrayed iniquitously against the regular offer-

a-a Meaning of Heb. uncertain.

ing;-*a* it hurled truth to the ground and prospered in what it did.

¹³ Then I heard a holy being speaking, and another holy being said to whomever it was who was speaking, "How long will [what was seen in] the vision last—*a*the regular offering be forsaken because of transgression; the Sanctuary be surrendered and the [heavenly] host be trampled?"-*a* ¹⁴ He answered me,*b* "For twenty-three hundred evenings and mornings; then the sanctuary shall be cleansed." ¹⁵ While I, Daniel, was seeing the vision, and trying to understand it, there appeared before me one who looked like a man. ¹⁶ I heard a human voice from the middle of Ulai calling out, "Gabriel, make that man understand the vision." ¹⁷ He came near to where I was standing, and as he came I was terrified, and fell prostrate. He said to me, "Understand, O man, that the vision refers to the time of the end." ¹⁸ When he spoke with me, I was overcome by a deep sleep as I lay prostrate on the ground. Then he touched me and made me stand up, ¹⁹ and said, "I am going to inform you of what will happen when wrath is at an end, for [it refers] to the time appointed for the end.

²⁰ "The two-horned ram that you saw [signifies] the kings of Media and Persia; ²¹ and the buck, the he-goat—the king of Greece; and the large horn on his forehead, that is the first king. ²² One was broken and four came in its stead—that [means]: four kingdoms will arise out of a nation, but without its power. ²³ When their kingdoms are at an end, when the measure of transgression*c* has been filled, then a king will arise, impudent and versed in intrigue. ²⁴ He will have great strength, but not through his own strength. He will be extraordinarily destructive; he will prosper in what he does, and destroy the mighty and the people of holy ones. ²⁵ By his cunning, he will use deceit successfully. He will make great plans, will destroy many, taking them unawares, and will rise up against the chief of chiefs, but will be broken, not by [human] hands. ²⁶ What was said in the vision about evenings and mornings is true. Now you keep the vision a secret, for it pertains to far-off days." ²⁷ So I, Daniel, was stricken,*a* and languished many days. Then I arose and attended

b Several ancient versions "him."
c Lit. "transgressors."

to the king's business, but I was dismayed by the vision and no one could explain it.

9 In the first year of Darius son of Ahasuerus, of Median descent, who was made king over the kingdom of the Chaldeans— ² in the first year of his reign, I, Daniel, consulted the books concerning the number of years that, according to the word of the LORD that had come to Jeremiah the prophet, were to be the term of Jerusalem's desolation—seventy years. ³ I turned my face to the Lord God, devoting myself to prayer and supplication, in fasting, in sackcloth and ashes. ⁴ I prayed to the LORD my God, making confession thus: "O Lord, great and awesome God, who stays faithful to His covenant with those who love Him and keep His commandments! ⁵ We have sinned; we have gone astray; we have acted wickedly; we have been rebellious and have deviated from Your commandments and Your rules, ⁶ and have not obeyed Your servants the prophets who spoke in Your name to our kings, our officers, our fathers, and all the people of the land. ⁷ With you, O Lord, is the right, and the shame is on us to this very day, on the men of Judah and the inhabitants of Jerusalem, all Israel, near and far, in all the lands where You have banished them, for the trespass they committed against You. ⁸ The shame, O LORD, is on us, on our kings, our officers, and our fathers, because we have sinned against You. ⁹ To the Lord our God belong mercy and forgiveness, for we rebelled against Him, ¹⁰ and did not obey the LORD our God by following His teachings which He set before us through His servants the prophets. ¹¹ All Israel has violated Your teaching and gone astray, disobeying You; so the curse and the oath written in the Teaching of Moses, the servant of God, have been poured down upon us, for we have sinned against Him. ¹² He carried out the threat that He made against us, and against our rulers who ruled us, to bring upon us great misfortune; under the whole heaven there has never been done the like of what was done to Jerusalem. ¹³ All that calamity, just as is written in the Teaching of Moses, came upon us, yet we did not supplicate the LORD our God, did not repent of our iniquity or become wise through Your truth. 14 Hence the LORD was intent upon bringing calamity upon us, for the LORD our God is in the right in all that He has done, but we have not obeyed Him.

15 "Now, O Lord our God—You who brought Your people out of the land of Egypt with a mighty hand, winning fame for Yourself to this very day—we have sinned, we have acted wickedly. 16 O Lord, as befits Your abundant benevolence, let Your wrathful fury turn back from Your city Jerusalem, Your holy mountain; for because of our sins and the iniquities of our fathers, Jerusalem and Your people have become a mockery among all who are around us.

17 "O our God, hear now the prayer of Your servant and his plea, and show Your favor to Your desolate sanctuary, for the Lord's sake. 18 Incline Your ear, O my God, and hear; open Your eyes and see our desolation and the city to which Your name is attached. Not because of any merit of ours do we lay our plea before You but because of Your abundant mercies. 19 O Lord, hear! O Lord, forgive! O Lord, listen, and act without delay for Your own sake, O my God; for Your name is attached to Your city and Your people!"

20 While I was speaking, praying, and confessing my sin and the sin of my people Israel, and laying my supplication before the LORD my God on behalf of the holy mountain of my God— 21 while I was uttering my prayer, the man Gabriel, whom I had previously seen in the vision, was sent forth in flight and reached me about the time of the evening offering. 22 He made me understand by speaking to me and saying, "Daniel, I have just come forth to give you understanding. 23 A word went forth as you began your plea, and I have come to tell it, for you are precious; so mark the word and understand the vision.

²⁴ "Seventy weeks*ª* have been decreed for your people and your holy city until the measure of transgression is filled and that of sin complete, until iniquity is expiated, and eternal righteousness ushered in; and prophetic vision ratified,*ᵇ* and the holy of holies anointed. ²⁵ You must know and understand: From the issuance of the word to restore and rebuild Jerusalem until the [time of the] anointed leader is seven weeks; and for sixty-two weeks it will be rebuilt, square and moat, but in a time of distress. ²⁶ And after those sixty-two weeks, the anointed one will disappear and vanish.*ᶜ* The army of a leader who is to come will destroy the city and the sanctuary, but its end will come through a flood. Desolation is decreed until the end of war. ²⁷ During one week he will make a firm covenant with many. For half a week he will put a stop to the sacrifice and the meal offering. At the *ᶜ*corner [of the altar]*ᶜ* will be an appalling abomination until the decreed destruction will be poured down upon the appalling thing."

10 In the third year of King Cyrus of Persia, an oracle was revealed to Daniel, who was called Belteshazzar. That oracle was true, *ª*but it was a great task to understand the prophecy; understanding came to him through the vision.*ª*

² At that time, I, Daniel, kept three full weeks of mourning. ³ I ate no tasty food, nor did any meat or wine enter my mouth. I did not anoint myself until the three weeks were over. ⁴ It was on the twenty-fourth day of the first month, when I was on the bank of the great river—the Tigris—⁵ that I looked and saw a man dressed in linen, his loins girt in *ᵇ*fine gold.*ᵇ* ⁶ His body was like beryl, his face had the appearance of lightning, his eyes were like flaming torches, his arms and legs had the color of burnished bronze, and the sound of his speech was like the noise of a multitude.

⁷ I, Daniel, alone saw the vision; the men who were with me did not see the vision, yet they were seized with a great terror and fled

---

ª *Viz. of years.*
ᵇ *Lit. "sealed."*
ᶜ *Meaning of Heb. uncertain.*

ª⁻ª *Meaning of Heb. uncertain.*
ᵇ⁻ᵇ *Or "gold of Uphaz."*

445

into hiding. ⁸ So I was left alone to see this great vision. I was drained of strength, my vigor was destroyed, and I could not summon up strength. ⁹ I heard him speaking; and when I heard him speaking, overcome by a deep sleep, I lay prostrate on the ground. ¹⁰ Then a hand touched me, and shook me onto my hands and knees. ¹¹ He said to me, "O Daniel, precious man, mark what I say to you and stand up, for I have been sent to you." After he said this to me, I stood up, trembling. ¹² He then said to me, "Have no fear, Daniel, for from the first day that you set your mind to get understanding, practicing abstinence before your God, your prayer was heard, and I have come because of your prayer. ¹³ However, the prince of the Persian kingdom opposed me for twenty-one days; now Michael, a prince of the first rank, has come to my aid, after I was detained there with the kings of Persia. ¹⁴ So I have come to make you understand what is to befall your people in the days to come, for there is yet a vision for those days."

¹⁵ While he was saying these things to me, I looked down and kept silent. ¹⁶ Then one who looked like a man touched my lips, and I opened my mouth and spoke, saying to him who stood before me, "My lord, because of the vision, I have been seized with pangs and cannot summon strength. ¹⁷ How can this servant of my lord speak with my lord, seeing that my strength has failed and no spirit is left in me?" ¹⁸ He who looked like a man touched me again, and strengthened me. ¹⁹ He said, "Have no fear, precious man, all will be well with you; be strong, be strong!" As he spoke with me, I was strengthened, and said, "Speak on, my lord, for you have strengthened me!" ²⁰ Then he said, "Do you know why I have come to you? Now I must go back to fight the prince of Persia. When I go off, the prince of Greece will come in. ²¹ ᶜ‐No one is helping me against them except your prince, Michael. However, I will tell you what is recorded in the book of truth.‐ᶜ

ᶜ‐ᶜ *Order of clauses inverted for clarity.*

11 "In the first year of Darius the Mede, I took my stand to strengthen and fortify him. ² And now I will tell you the truth: Persia will have three more kings, and the fourth will be wealthier than them all; by the power he obtains through his wealth, he will stir everyone up against the kingdom of Greece. ³ Then a warrior king will appear who will have an extensive dominion and do as he pleases. ⁴ But after his appearance, his kingdom will be broken up and scattered to the four winds of heaven, but not for any of his posterity, nor with dominion like that which he had; for his kingdom will be uprooted and belong to others beside these.

⁵ "The king of the south will grow powerful; however, one of his officers will overpower him and rule, having an extensive dominion. ⁶ After some years, an alliance will be made, and the daughter of the king of the south will come to the king of the north to effect the agreement, but she will not maintain her strength, nor will his strength endure. She will be surrendered together with those who escorted her and the one who begot her and helped her during those times. ⁷ A shoot from her stock will appear in his place, will come against the army and enter the fortress of the king of the north; he will fight and overpower them. ⁸ He will also take their gods with their molten images and their precious vessels of silver and gold back to Egypt as booty. For some years he will leave the king of the north alone, ⁹ who will [later] invade the realm of the king of the south, but will go back to his land.

¹⁰ "His sons will wage war, collecting a multitude of great armies; he will advance and sweep through as a flood, and will again wage war as far as his stronghold. ¹¹ Then the king of the south, in a rage, will go out to do battle with him, with the king of the north. He will muster a great multitude, but the multitude will be delivered into his [foe's] power. ¹² But when the multitude is carried off, he will grow arrogant; he will cause myriads to perish, but will not prevail. ¹³ Then the king of the north will again

muster a multitude even greater than the first. After a time, a matter of years, he will advance with a great army and much baggage. [14] In those times, many will resist the king of the south, and the lawless sons of your people will assert themselves to confirm the vision, but they will fail. [15] The king of the north will advance and throw up siege ramps and capture a fortress city, and the forces of the south will not hold out; even the elite of his army will be powerless to resist. [16] His opponent will do as he pleases, for none will hold out against him; he will install himself in the beautiful land with destruction within his reach. [17] He will set his mind upon invading the strongholds throughout his [foe's] kingdom, but in order to destroy it he will effect an agreement with him and give him a daughter in marriage; he will not succeed at it and it will not come about. [18] He will turn to the coastlands and capture many; but a consul will put an end to his insults, nay pay him back for his insults. [19] He will head back to the strongholds of his own land, but will stumble, and fall, and vanish. [20] His place will be taken by one who will dispatch an officer to exact tribute for royal glory, but he will be broken in a few days, not by wrath or by war. [21] His place will be taken by a contemptible man, on whom royal majesty was not conferred; he will come in unawares and seize the kingdom through trickery. [22] The forces of the flood will be overwhelmed by him and will be broken, and so too the covenant leader. [23] And, from the time an alliance is made with him, he will practice deceit; and he will rise to power with a small band. [24] He will invade the richest of provinces unawares, and will do what his father and forefathers never did, lavishing on them[a] spoil, booty, and wealth; he will have designs upon strongholds, but only for a time.

[25] "He will muster his strength and courage against the king of the south with a great army. The king of the south will wage war with a very great and powerful army but will not stand fast, for they will devise plans against him. [26] Those who eat of his food will ruin him. His army will be overwhelmed, and many will fall slain. [27] The minds of both kings will be bent on evil; while sitting

---

[a] *I.e. his followers.*

at the table together, they will lie to each other, but to no avail, for there is yet an appointed term. ²⁸ He will return to his land with great wealth, his mind set against the holy covenant. Having done his pleasure, he will return to his land. ²⁹ At the appointed time, he will again invade the south, but the second time will not be like the first. ³⁰ Ships from Kittim will come against him. He will be checked, and will turn back, raging against the holy covenant. Having done his pleasure, he will then attend to those who forsake the holy covenant. ³¹ Forces will be levied by him; they will desecrate the temple, the fortress; they will abolish the regular offering and set up the appalling abomination. ³² He will flatter with smooth words those who act wickedly toward the covenant, but the people devoted to their God will stand firm. ³³ The knowledgeable among the people will make the many understand; and for a while they shall fall by sword and flame, suffer captivity and spoliation. ³⁴ In defeat, they will receive a little help, and many will join them insincerely. ³⁵ Some of the knowledgeable will fall, that they may be refined and purged and whitened until the time of the end, for an interval still remains until the appointed time.

³⁶ "The king will do as he pleases; he will exalt and magnify himself above every god, and he will speak awful things against the God of gods. He will prosper until wrath is spent, and what has been decreed is accomplished. ³⁷ He will not have regard for the god of his ancestors or for the one dear to women; he will not have regard for any god, but will magnify himself above all. ³⁸ He will honor the god of fortresses on his stand; he will honor with gold and silver, with precious stones and costly things, a god that his ancestors never knew. ³⁹ He will deal with fortified strongholds with the help of an alien god. He will heap honor on those who acknowledge him, and will make them master over many; he will distribute land for a price. ⁴⁰ At the time of the end, the king of the south will lock horns with him, but the king of the north will attack him with chariots and riders and many ships. He will invade lands, sweeping through them like a flood; ⁴¹ he will in-

vade the beautiful land, too, and many will fall, but these will escape his clutches: Edom, Moab, and the chief part of the Ammonites. 42 He will lay his hands on lands; not even the land of Egypt will escape. 43 He will gain control over treasures of gold and silver and over all the precious things of Egypt, and the Libyans and Cushites will follow at his heel. 44 But reports from east and north will alarm him, and he will march forth in a great fury to destroy and annihilate many. 45 He will pitch his royal pavilion between the sea and the beautiful holy mountain, and he will meet his doom with no one to help him.

12 "At that time, the great prince, Michael, who stands beside the sons of your people, will appear. It will be a time of trouble, the like of which has never been since the nation came into being. At that time, your people will be rescued, all who are found inscribed in the book. 2 Many of those that sleep in the dust of the earth will awake, some to eternal life, others to reproaches, to everlasting abhorrence. 3 And the knowledgeable will be radiant like the bright expanse of sky, and those who lead the many to righteousness will be like the stars forever and ever.

4 "But you, Daniel, keep the words secret, and seal the book until the time of the end. Many will range far and wide and knowledge will increase."

5 Then I, Daniel, looked and saw two others standing, one on one bank of the river, the other on the other bank of the river. 6 One said to the man clothed in linen, who was above the water of the river, "How long until the end of these awful things?" 7 Then I heard the man dressed in linen, who was above the water of the river, swear by the Ever-Living One as he lifted his right hand and his left hand to heaven: "For a *a*-time, times, and half a time;*-a* and when the breaking of the power of the holy people comes to an end, then shall all these things be fulfilled."

8 I heard and did not understand, so I said, "My lord, what will be the outcome of these things?" 9 He said, "Go, Daniel, for these words are secret and sealed to the time of the end. 10 Many will be purified and purged and refined; the wicked will act wickedly

a-a *See note at 7:25.*

and none of the wicked will understand; but the knowledgeable will understand. (¹¹ From the time the regular offering is abolished, and an appalling abomination is set up—it will be a thousand two hundred and ninety days. Happy the one who waits and reaches one thousand three hundred and thirty-five days.) ¹² But you, go on to the end; you shall rest, and arise to your destiny at the end of the days."

עזרא

EZRA

עזרא
EZRA

1 In the first year of King Cyrus of Persia, when the word of the LORD spoken by Jeremiah was fulfilled,[a] the LORD roused the spirit of King Cyrus of Persia to issue a proclamation throughout his realm by word of mouth and in writing as follows:

2 "Thus said King Cyrus of Persia: The LORD God of Heaven has given me all the kingdoms of the earth and has charged me with building Him a house in Jerusalem, which is in Judah. 3 Anyone of you of all His people—may his God be with him, and let him go up to Jerusalem that is in Judah and build the House of the LORD God of Israel, the God that is in Jerusalem; 4 and all who stay behind, wherever he may be living, let the people of his place assist him with silver, gold, goods, and livestock, beside the freewill offering to the House of God that is in Jerusalem."

5 So the chiefs of the clans of Judah and Benjamin, and the priests and Levites, all whose spirit had been roused by God, got ready to go up to build the House of the LORD that is in Jerusalem. 6 All their neighbors supported them with silver vessels, with gold, with goods, with livestock, and with precious objects, besides what had been given as a freewill offering. 7 King Cyrus of Persia released the vessels of the LORD's house which Nebuchadnezzar had taken away from Jerusalem and had put in the house of his god. 8 These King Cyrus of Persia released through the office of Mithredath the treasurer, who gave an inventory of them to Sheshbazzar the prince of Judah. 9 This is the inventory: 30 gold basins, 1000 silver basins, 29 knives, 10 30 gold bowls, 410 silver [b]double bowls,[-b] 1000 other vessels; 11 in all, 5400 gold

---

[a] Cf. Jer. 29.10.
[b-b] Meaning of Heb. uncertain.

and silver vessels. Sheshbazzar brought all these back when the exiles came back from Babylon to Jerusalem.

2 *These are the people of the province who came up from among the captive exiles whom King Nebuchadnezzar of Babylon had carried into exile to Babylon, who returned to Jerusalem and Judah, each to his own city, ² who came with Zerubbabel, Jeshua, Nehemiah, Seraiah, Reelaiah, Mordecai, Bilshan, Mispar, Bigvai, Rehum, Baanah:

The list of the men of the people of Israel: ³ the sons of Parosh —2172; ⁴ the sons of Shephatiah—372; ⁵ the sons of Arah—775; ⁶ the sons of Pahath-moab: the sons of Jeshua and Joab—2812; ⁷ the sons of Elam—1254; ⁸ the sons of Zattu—945; ⁹ the sons of Zaccai—760; ¹⁰ the sons of Bani—642; ¹¹ the sons of Bebai—623; ¹² the sons of Azgad—1222; ¹³ the sons of Adonikam—666; ¹⁴ the sons of Bigvai—2056; ¹⁵ the sons of Adin—454; ¹⁶ the sons of Ater: Hezekiah—98; ¹⁷ the sons of Bezai—323; ¹⁸ the sons of Jorah—112; ¹⁹ the sons of Hashum—223; ²⁰ the sons of Gibbar— 95; ²¹ the sons of Bethlehem—123; ²² the sons of Netophah—56; ²³ the sons of Anathoth—128; ²⁴ the sons of Azmaveth—42; ²⁵ the sons of Kiriath-arim: Chephirah and Beeroth—743; ²⁶ the sons of Ramah and Geba—621; ²⁷ the men of Michmas—122; ²⁸ the men of Beth-el and Ai—223; ²⁹ the men of Nebo—52; ³⁰ the sons of Magbish—156; ³¹ the sons of the other Elam—1254; ³² the sons of Harim—320; ³³ the sons of Lod, Hadid, and Ono—725; ³⁴ the sons of Jericho—345; ³⁵ the sons of Senaah—3630.

³⁶ The priests: the sons of Jedaiah: the house of Jeshua—973; ³⁷ the sons of Immer—1052; ³⁸ the sons of Pashhur—1247; ³⁹ the sons of Harim—1017.

⁴⁰ The Levites: the sons of Jeshua and Kadmiel: the sons of Hodaviah—74.

⁴¹ The singers: the sons of Asaph—128.

⁴² The gatekeepers: the sons of Shallum, the sons of Ater, the

---

ª *This chapter appears as Neh. 7.6–73 with variations in the names and numbers.*

sons of Talmon, the sons of Akkub, the sons of Hatita, the sons of Shobai, all told—139.

⁴³ The temple servants: the sons of Ziha, the sons of Hasupha, the sons of Tabbaoth, ⁴⁴ the sons of Keros, the sons of Siaha, the sons of Padon, ⁴⁵ the sons of Lebanah, the sons of Hagabah, the sons of Akkub, ⁴⁶ the sons of Hagab, the sons of Salmai, the sons of Hanan, ⁴⁷ the sons of Giddel, the sons of Gahar, the sons of Reaiah, ⁴⁸ the sons of Rezin, the sons of Nekoda, the sons of Gazzam, ⁴⁹ the sons of Uzza, the sons of Paseah, the sons of Besai, ⁵⁰ the sons of Asnah, the sons of Meunim, the sons of Nephusim, ⁵¹ the sons of Bakbuk, the sons of Hakupha, the sons of Harhur, ⁵² the sons of Bazluth, the sons of Mehida, the sons of Harsha, ⁵³ the sons of Barkos, the sons of Sisera, the sons of Temah, ⁵⁴ the sons of Neziah, the sons of Hatipha.

⁵⁵ The sons of Solomon's servants: the sons of Sotai, the sons of Hassophereth, the sons of Peruda, ⁵⁶ the sons of Jaalah, the sons of Darkon, the sons of Giddel, ⁵⁷ the sons of Shephatiah, the sons of Hattil, the sons of Pochereth-hazzebaim, the sons of Ami.

⁵⁸ The total of temple servants and the sons of Solomon's servants—392.

⁵⁹ The following were those who came up from Tel-melah, Tel-harsha, Cherub, Addan and Immer—they were unable to tell whether their father's house and descent were Israelite: ⁶⁰ the sons of Delaiah, the sons of Tobiah, the sons of Nekoda—652.

⁶¹ Of the sons of the priests, the sons of Habaiah, the sons of Hakkoz, the sons of Barzillai who had married a daughter of Barzillai and had taken his[b] name—⁶² these searched for their genealogical records, but they could not be found, so they were disqualified for the priesthood. ⁶³ The Tirshatha[c] ordered them not to eat of the most holy things until a priest with Urim and Thummim should appear.

⁶⁴ The sum of the entire community was 42,360, ⁶⁵ not counting their male and female servants, those being 7337; they also had 200 male and female singers. ⁶⁶ Their horses—736; their mules—245; ⁶⁷ their camels—435; their asses—6720.

b *Lit. "their."*
c *A Persian title.*

⁶⁸ Some of the chiefs of the clans, on arriving at the House of the LORD in Jerusalem, gave a freewill offering to erect the House of God on its site. ⁶⁹ In accord with their means, they donated to the treasury of the work: gold—6100 drachmas, silver—5000 minas, and priestly robes—100.

⁷⁰ The priests, the Levites and some of the people, and the singers, gatekeepers, and the temple servants took up residence in their towns and all Israel in their towns.

3 When the seventh month arrived—the Israelites being settled in their towns—the entire people assembled as one man in Jerusalem. ² Then Jeshua son of Jozadak and his brother priests, and Zerubbabel son of Shealtiel and his brothers set to and built the altar of the God of Israel to offer burnt offerings upon it as is written in the Teaching of Moses, the man of God. ³ They set up the altar on its site because they were in fear of the peoples of the land, and they offered burnt offerings on it to the LORD, burnt offerings each morning and evening. ⁴ Then they celebrated the festival of Tabernacles as is written, with its daily burnt offerings in the proper quantities, on each day as is prescribed for it, ⁵ followed by the regular burnt offering and the offerings for the new moons and for all the sacred fixed times of the LORD, and whatever freewill offerings were made to the LORD. ⁶ From the first day of the seventh month they began to make burnt offerings to the LORD, though the foundation of the Temple of the LORD had not been laid. ⁷ They paid the hewers and craftsmen with money, and the Sidonians and Tyrians with food, drink, and oil to bring cedarwood from Lebanon by sea to Joppa, in accord with the authorization granted them by King Cyrus of Persia.

⁸ In the second year after their arrival at the House of God, at Jerusalem, in the second month, Zerubbabel son of Shealtiel and Jeshua son of Jozadak, and the rest of their brother priests and Levites, and all who had come from the captivity to Jerusalem, as

their first step appointed Levites from the age of twenty and upward to supervise the work of the House of the LORD. ⁹ Jeshua, his sons and brothers, Kadmiel and his sons, *ᵃ*the sons of Judah,*⁻ᵃ* together were appointed in charge of those who did the work in the House of God; also the sons of Henadad, their sons and brother Levites.

¹⁰ When the builders had laid the foundation of the Temple of the LORD, priests in their vestments with trumpets, and Levites sons of Asaph with cymbals were stationed to give praise to the LORD, as King David of Israel had ordained. ¹¹ They sang songs extolling and praising the LORD, *ᵇ⁻*"For He is good, His steadfast love for Israel is eternal."*⁻ᵇ* All the people raised a great shout extolling the LORD because the foundation of the House of the LORD had been laid. ¹² Many of the priests and Levites and the chiefs of the clans, the old men who had seen the first house, wept loudly at the sight of the founding of this house. Many others shouted joyously at the top of their voices. ¹³ The people could not distinguish the shouts of joy from the people's weeping, for the people raised a great shout, the sound of which could be heard from afar.

4 When the adversaries of Judah and Benjamin heard that the returned exiles were building a temple to the LORD God of Israel, ² they approached Zerubbabel and the chiefs of the clans and said to them, "Let us build with you, since we too worship your God, having offered sacrifices to Him since the time of King Esarhaddon of Assyria, who brought us here." ³ Zerubbabel, Jeshua, and the rest of the chiefs of the clans of Israel answered them, "It is not for you and us to build a House to our God, but we alone will build it to the LORD God of Israel, in accord with the charge that the king, King Cyrus of Persia, laid upon us." ⁴ Thereupon the people of the land undermined the resolve of the people of Judah, and made them afraid to build. ⁵ They

---

ᵃ⁻ᵃ *I.e. Hodaviah of 2.40.*
ᵇ⁻ᵇ *Cf. Ps. 106.1; 136.*

bribed ministers in order to thwart their plans all the years of King Cyrus of Persia and until the reign of King Darius of Persia.

6 And in the reign of Ahasuerus, at the start of his reign, they drew up an accusation against the inhabitants of Judah and Jerusalem.

7 And in the time of Artaxerxes, Bishlam, Mithredath, Tabeel, and the rest of their colleagues wrote to King Artaxerxes of Persia, a letter written in Aramaic and translated.*

Aramaic:*b* 8 Rehum the commissioner and Shimshai the scribe wrote a letter concerning Jerusalem to King Artaxerxes as follows: (9 *c* Then Rehum the commissioner and Shimshai the scribe, and the rest of their colleagues, the judges, officials, officers, and overseers, the men of Erech, and of Babylon, and of Susa—that is the Elamites—10 and other peoples whom the great and glorious Osnappar deported and settled in the city of Samaria and the rest of the province of Beyond the River [wrote]—and now 11 this is the text of the letter which they sent to him:)—"To King Artaxerxes [from] your servants, men of the province of Beyond the River. And now 12 be it known to the king that the Jews who came up from you to us have reached Jerusalem and are rebuilding that rebellious and wicked city; they are completing the walls and repairing the foundation. 13 Now be it known to the king that if this city is rebuilt and the walls completed, they will not pay tribute, poll-tax, or land-tax, and in the end it will harm the kingdom. 14 Now since we eat the salt of the palace, and it is not right that we should see the king dishonored, we have written to advise the king [of this] 15 so that you may search the records of your fathers and find in the records and know that this city is a rebellious city, harmful to kings and states. Sedition has been rife in it from early times; on that account this city was destroyed. 16 We advise the king that if this city is rebuilt and its walls are completed, you will no longer have any portion in the province of Beyond the River."

---

a *Cf. below v. 18 and note d.*
b *A note indicating that what follows is in the Aramaic language.*
c *Vv. 9–11 amplify v. 8.*

17 The king sent back the following message: "To Rehum the commissioner and Shimshai the scribe, and the rest of their colleagues, who dwell in Samaria and in the rest of the province of Beyond the River, greetings. 18 Now the letter that you wrote me has been read to me in translation.*d* 19 At my order a search has been made, and it has been found that this city has from earliest times risen against kings, and that rebellion and sedition have been rife in it. 20 Powerful kings have ruled over Jerusalem and exercised authority over the whole province of Beyond the River, and tribute, poll-tax, and land-tax were paid to them. 21 Now issue an order to stop these men; this city is not to be rebuilt until I so order. 22 Take care not to be lax in this matter or there will be much damage and harm to the kingdom."

23 When the text of the letter of King Artaxerxes was read before Rehum and Shimshai the scribe and their colleagues, they hurried to Jerusalem, to the Jews, and stopped them by main force. 24 At that time, work on the House of God in Jerusalem stopped and remained in abeyance until the second year of the reign of King Darius of Persia.

5 Then the prophets, Haggai the prophet and Zechariah son of Iddo, prophesied to the Jews in Judah and Jerusalem, *a-*inspired by the God of Israel.*-a* 2 Thereupon Zerubbabel son of Shealtiel and Jeshua son of Jozadak began rebuilding the House of God in Jerusalem, with the full support of the prophets of God. 3 At once Tattenai, governor of the province of Beyond the River, Shethar-bozenai, and their colleagues descended upon them and said this to them, "Who issued orders to you to rebuild this house and complete its furnishing?" 4 Then we*b* said to them, "What are the names of the men who are engaged in the building?" 5 But God watched over the elders of the Jews and they were not stopped while a report went to Darius and a letter was sent back in reply to it.

d *I.e. from Aramaic to Persian.*

a-a *Lit. "with the name of the God of Israel upon them."*
b *The officials of v. 3; cf. v. 10. Greek and Syriac read "they."*

461

⁶ This is the text of the letter that Tattenai, governor of the province of Beyond the River, and Shethar-bozenai and his colleagues, the officials of Beyond the River, sent to King Darius. ⁷ They sent a message to him and this is what was written in it: "To King Darius, greetings, and so forth. ⁸ Be it known to the king, that we went to the province of Judah, to the house of the great God. It is being rebuilt of hewn stone, and wood is being laid in the walls. The work is being done with dispatch and is going well. ⁹ Thereupon we directed this question to these elders, 'Who issued orders to you to rebuild this house and to complete its furnishings?' ¹⁰ We also asked their names so that we could write down the names of their leaders for your information. ¹¹ This is what they answered us: 'We are the servants of the God of heaven and earth; we are rebuilding the house that was originally built many years ago; a great king of Israel built it and completed it. ¹² But because our fathers angered the God of Heaven, He handed them over to Nebuchadnezzar the Chaldean, king of Babylon, who demolished this house and exiled the people to Babylon. ¹³ But in the first year of King Cyrus of Babylon, King Cyrus issued an order to rebuild this House of God. ¹⁴ Also the silver and gold vessels of the House of God that Nebuchadnezzar had taken away from the temple in Jerusalem and brought to the temple in Babylon—King Cyrus released them from the temple in Babylon to be given to the one called Sheshbazzar whom he had appointed governor. ¹⁵ He said to him, "Take these vessels, go, deposit them in the temple in Jerusalem, and let the House of God be rebuilt on its original site." ¹⁶ That same Sheshbazzar then came and laid the foundations for the House of God in Jerusalem; and ever since then it has been under construction, but is not yet finished.' ¹⁷ And now, if it please the king, let the royal archives there in Babylon be searched to see whether indeed an order had been issued by King Cyrus to rebuild this House of God in Jerusalem. May the king convey to us his pleasure in this matter."

6 Thereupon, at the order of King Darius, they searched the archives where the treasures were stored in Babylon. ² But it was in the citadel of Ecbatana, in the province of Media, that a scroll was found in which the following was written: "Memorandum: ³ In the first year of King Cyrus, King Cyrus issued an order concerning the House of God in Jerusalem: 'Let the house be rebuilt, a place for offering sacrifices, with a base built up high. Let it be sixty cubits high and sixty cubits wide, ⁴ with a course of unused timber for each three courses of hewn stone. The expenses shall be paid by the palace. ⁵ And the gold and silver vessels of the House of God which Nebuchadnezzar had taken away from the temple in Jerusalem and transported to Babylon shall be returned, and let each go back to the temple in Jerusalem where it belongs; you shall deposit it in the House of God.'

⁶ "Now*ᵃ* you, Tattenai, governor of the province of Beyond the River, Shethar-bozenai and colleagues, the officials of the province of Beyond the River, stay away from that place. ⁷ Allow the work of this House of God to go on; let the governor of the Jews and the elders of the Jews rebuild this House of God on its site. ⁸ And I hereby issue an order concerning what you must do to help these elders of the Jews rebuild this House of God: the expenses are to be paid to these men with dispatch out of the resources of the king, derived from the taxes of the province of Beyond the River, so that the work not be stopped. ⁹ They are to be given daily, without fail, whatever they need of young bulls, rams, or lambs as burnt offerings for the God of Heaven, and wheat, salt, wine, and oil, at the order of the priests in Jerusalem, ¹⁰ so that they may offer pleasing sacrifices to the God of heaven and pray for the life of the king and his sons. ¹¹ I also issue an order that whoever alters this decree shall have a beam removed from his house, and he shall be impaled on it and his house confiscated.*ᵇ* ¹² And may the God who established His name there

---

ᵃ *This introduces the text of the reply of Darius that would have contained the preceding narrative (vv. 1–5) as a preliminary.*
ᵇ *Meaning uncertain; or "turned into ruins."*

cause the downfall of any king or nation that undertakes to alter or damage that House of God in Jerusalem. I, Darius, have issued the decree; let it be carried out with dispatch."

13 Then Tattenai, governor of the province of Beyond the River, Shethar-bozenai, and their colleagues carried out with dispatch what King Darius had written. 14 So the elders of the Jews progressed in the building, urged on by the prophesying of Haggai the prophet and Zechariah son of Iddo, and they brought the building to completion under the aegis of the God of Israel and by the order of Cyrus and Darius and King Arta-xerxes of Persia. 15 The house was finished on the third of the month of Adar in the sixth year of the reign of King Darius. 16 The Israelites, the priests, and the Levites, and all the other exiles celebrated the dedication of the House of God with joy. 17 And they sacrificed for the dedication of this House of God one hundred bulls, two hundred rams, four hundred lambs, and twelve goats as a purification offering for all of Israel, according to the number of the tribes of Israel. 18 They appointed the priests in their courses and the Levites in their divisions for the service of God in Jerusalem, according to the prescription in the Book of Moses.

19 c The returned exiles celebrated the Passover on the four-teenth day of the first month, 20 for the priests and Levites had purified themselves to a man; they were all pure. They slaugh-tered the passover offering for all the returned exiles, and for their brother priests and for themselves. 21 The children of Israel who had returned from the exile, together with all who joined them in separating themselves from the uncleanliness of the na-tions of the lands to worship the LORD God of Israel, ate of it. 22 They joyfully celebrated the Feast of Unleavened Bread for seven days, for the LORD had given them cause for joy by inclin-ing the heart of the Assyrian king toward them so as to give them support in the work of the House of God, the God of Israel.

c *Hebrew resumes here.*

7 After these events, during the reign of King Artaxerxes of Persia, Ezra son of Seraiah son of Azariah son of Hilkiah ² son of Shallum son of Zadok son of Ahitub ³ son of Amariah son of Azariah son of Meraioth ⁴ son of Zerahiah son of Uzzi son of Bukki ⁵ son of Abishua son of Phinehas son of Eleazar son of Aaron the chief priest—⁶ that Ezra came up from Babylon, a scribe expert in the Teaching of Moses which the LORD God of Israel had given, whose request the king had granted in its entirety, thanks to the benevolence of the LORD toward him.

(⁷ Some of the Israelites, the priests and Levites, the singers, the gatekeepers, and the temple servants set out for Jerusalem in the seventh year of King Artaxerxes, ⁸ arriving in Jerusalem in the fifth month in the seventh year of the king.) ⁹ On the first day of the first month the journey up from Babylon was started, and on the first day of the fifth month he arrived in Jerusalem, thanks to the benevolent care of his God for him. ¹⁰ For Ezra had dedicated himself to study the Teaching of the LORD so as to observe it, and to teach laws and rules to Israel.

¹¹ The following is the text of the letter which King Artaxerxes gave Ezra the priest-scribe, a scholar in matters concerning the commandments of the LORD and His laws to Israel:

¹² ᵃ "Artaxerxes king of kings, to Ezra the priest, scholar in the law of the God of heaven, ᵇ-and so forth.-ᵇ And now, ¹³ I hereby issue an order that anyone in my kingdom who is of the people of Israel and its priests and Levites who feels impelled to go to Jerusalem may go with you. ¹⁴ For you are commissioned by the king and his seven advisers to regulate Judah and Jerusalem according to the law of your God, which is in your care, ¹⁵ and to bring the freewill offering of silver and gold, which the king and his advisers made to the God of Israel, whose dwelling is in Jerusalem, ¹⁶ and whatever silver and gold that you find throughout the province of Babylon, together with the freewill offerings which the people and the priests will give for the House of their

ᵃ *Aramaic resumes here through v. 26.*
ᵇ⁻ᵇ *Meaning uncertain.*

God which is in Jerusalem. [17] You shall, therefore, with dispatch acquire with this money bulls, rams, and lambs, with their meal offerings and libations, and offer them on the altar of the House of your God in Jerusalem. [18] And whatever you wish to do with the leftover silver and gold, you and your kinsmen may do, in accord with the will of your God. [19] The vessels for the service of the House of your God which are given to you, deliver to God in Jerusalem, [20] and any other needs of the House of your God which it falls to you to supply, do so from the royal treasury. [21] I, King Artaxerxes, for my part, hereby issue an order to all the treasurers in the province of Beyond the River that whatever request Ezra the priest, scholar in the law of the God of Heaven, makes of you is to be fulfilled with dispatch [22] up to the sum of one hundred talents of silver, one hundred kor of wheat, one hundred bath of oil, and salt without limit. [23] Whatever is by order of the God of Heaven must be carried out diligently for the House of the God of Heaven, else wrath will come upon the king and his sons. [24] We further advise you that it is not permissible to impose tribute, poll tax, or land tax on any priest, Levite, singer, gatekeeper, temple servant, or other servant of this House of God. [25] And you, Ezra, by the divine wisdom you possess, appoint magistrates and judges to judge all the people in the province of Beyond the River who know the laws of your God, and to teach those who do not know them. [26] Let anyone who does not obey the law of your God and the law of the king be punished with dispatch, whether by death, corporal punishment, confiscation of possessions, or imprisonment."

[27] [c]Blessed is the LORD God of our fathers, who put it into the mind of the king to glorify the House of the LORD in Jerusalem, [28] and who inclined the king and his counselors and the king's military officers to be favorably disposed toward me. For my part, thanks to the care of the LORD for me, I summoned up courage and assembled leading men in Israel to go with me.

[c] *Hebrew resumes here.*

8 These are the chiefs of the clans and the register of the genealogy of those who came up with me from Babylon in the reign of King Artaxerxes: ² Of the sons of Phinehas, Gershom; of the sons of Ithamar, Daniel; of the sons of David, Hattush. ³ Of the sons of Shecaniah: of the sons of Parosh, Zechariah; through him the genealogy of 150 males was registered. ⁴ Eliehoenai son of Zerahiah, of the sons of Pahath-moab, and with him 200 males. ⁵ Of the sons of Shecaniah son of Jahaziel; and with him 300 males. ⁶ And of the sons of Adin, Ebed son of Jonathan; and with him 50 males. ⁷ And of the sons of Elam, Jeshaiah son of Athaliah; and with him 70 males. ⁸ And of the sons of Shephatiah, Zebadiah son of Michael; and with him 80 males. ⁹ Of the sons of Joab, Obadiah son of Jehiel; and with him 218 males. ¹⁰ And of the sons of Shelomith, the son of Josiphiah; and with him 160 males. ¹¹ And of the sons of Bebai, Zechariah son of Bebai; and with him 28 males. ¹² And of the sons of Azgad, Johanan son of Hakkatan; and with him 110 males. ¹³ And of the sons of Adonikam, who were the last; and these are their names: Eliphelet, Jeiel, and Shemaiah; and with them 60 males. ¹⁴ And of the sons of Bigvai, Uthai and Zaccur; and with them 70 males.

¹⁵ These I assembled by the river that enters Ahava, and we encamped there for three days. I reviewed the people and the priests, but I did not find any Levites there. ¹⁶ I sent for Eliezer, Ariel, Shemaiah, Elnathan, Jarib, Elnathan, Nathan, Zechariah, and Meshullam, the leading men, and also for Joiarib and Elnathan, the instructors, ¹⁷ and I gave them an order for Iddo, the leader at the place [called] Casiphia. I gave them a message to convey to Iddo [and] his brother temple servants at the place [called] Casiphia, that they should bring us attendants for the House of our God. ¹⁸ Thanks to the benevolent care of our God for us, they brought us a capable man of the family of Mahli son of Levi son of Israel, and Sherebiah and his sons and brothers,

eighteen in all, 19 and Hashabiah, and with him Jeshaiah of the family of Merari, his brothers and their sons, twenty in all; 20 and of the temple servants whom David and the officers had appointed for the service of the Levites—220 temple servants, all of them listed by name.

21 I proclaimed a fast there by the Ahava River to afflict ourselves before our God to beseech Him for a smooth journey for us and for our children and for all our possessions; 22 for I was ashamed to ask the king for soldiers and horsemen to protect us against any enemy on the way, since we had told the king, "The benevolent care of our God is for all who seek Him, while His fierce anger is against all who forsake Him." 23 So we fasted and besought our God for this, and He responded to our plea. 24 Then I selected twelve of the chiefs of the priests, namely Sherebiah and Hashabiah with ten of their brothers, 25 and I weighed out to them the silver, the gold, and the vessels, the contribution to the House of our God which the king, his counselors and officers, and all Israel who were present had made. 26 I entrusted to their safekeeping the weight of six hundred and fifty talents of silver, one hundred silver vessels of one talent each, one hundred talents of gold; 27 also, twenty gold bowls worth one thousand darics and two vessels of good, shining bronze, as precious as gold. 28 I said to them, "You are consecrated to the LORD, and the vessels are consecrated, and the silver and gold are a freewill offering to the LORD God of your fathers. 29 Guard them diligently until such time as you weigh them out in the presence of the officers of the priests and the Levites and the officers of the clans of Israel in Jerusalem in the chambers of the House of the LORD."

30 So the priests and the Levites received the cargo of silver and gold and vessels by weight, to bring them to Jerusalem to the House of our God. 31 We set out for Jerusalem from the Ahava River on the twelfth of the first month. We enjoyed the care of our God who saved us from enemy ambush on the journey.

³² We arrived in Jerusalem and stayed there three days. ³³ On the fourth day the silver, gold, and vessels were weighed out in the House of our God into the keeping of Meremoth son of Uriah the priest, with whom was Eleazar son of Phinehas. Jozabad son of Jeshua, and Noadiah son of Binnui, the Levites, were with them. ³⁴ Everything accorded as to number and weight, the entire cargo being recorded at that time.

³⁵ The returning exiles who arrived from captivity made burnt offerings to the God of Israel: twelve bulls for all Israel, ninety-six rams, seventy-seven lambs and twelve he-goats as a purification offering, all this a burnt offering to the LORD. ³⁶ They handed the royal orders to the king's satraps and the governors of the province of Beyond the River who gave support to the people and the House of God.

9 When this was over, the officers approached me, saying, "The people of Israel and the priests and Levites have not separated themselves from the peoples of the land whose abhorrent practices are like those of the Canaanites, the Hittites, the Perizzites, the Jebusites, the Ammonites, the Moabites, the Egyptians, and the Amorites. ² They have taken their daughters as wives for themselves and for their sons, so that the holy seed has become intermingled with the peoples of the land; and it is the officers and prefects who have taken the lead in this trespass."

³ When I heard this, I rent my garment and robe, I tore hair out of my head and beard, and I sat desolate. ⁴ Around me gathered all who were concerned over the words of the God of Israel because of the returning exiles' trespass, while I sat desolate until the evening offering. ⁵ At the time of the evening offering I ended my self-affliction; still in my torn garment and robe, I got down on my knees and spread out my hands to the LORD my God, ⁶ and said, "O my God, I am too ashamed and mortified to lift my face to You, O my God, for our iniquities *ᵃ-are overwhelming-ᵃ*

ᵃ⁻ᵃ *Lit. "are numerous above the head."*

and our guilt has grown high as heaven. 7 From the time of our fathers to this very day we have been deep in guilt. Because of our iniquities, we, our kings, and our priests have been handed over to foreign kings, to the sword, to captivity, to pillage, and to humiliation, as is now the case.

8 "But now, for a short while, there has been a reprieve from the LORD our God, who has granted us a surviving remnant and given us a stake in His holy place; our God has restored the luster to our eyes and furnished us with a little sustenance in our bondage. 9 For bondsmen we are, though even in our bondage God has not forsaken us, but has disposed the king of Persia favorably toward us, to furnish us with sustenance and to raise again the House of our God, repairing its ruins and giving us a hold*b* in Judah and Jerusalem.

10 "Now, what can we say in the face of this, O our God, for we have forsaken Your commandments, 11 which You gave us through Your servants the prophets when You said, 'The land which you are about to possess is a land unclean through the uncleanness of the peoples of the land, through their abhorrent practices with which they, in their impurity, have filled it from one end to the other. 12 Now then, do not give your daughters in marriage to their sons or let their daughters marry your sons; do nothing for their well-being or advantage, then you will be strong and enjoy the bounty of the land and bequeath it to your children forever.' 13 After all that has happened to us because of our evil deeds and our deep guilt—though You, our God, have been forebearing, [punishing us] less than our iniquity [deserves] in that You have granted us such a remnant as this—14 shall we once again violate Your commandments by intermarrying with these peoples who follow such abhorrent practices? Will You not rage against us till we are destroyed without remnant or survivor? 15 O LORD, God of Israel, You are benevolent,*c* for we have survived as a remnant, as is now the case. We stand before You in all our guilt, for we cannot face You on this account."

b *Lit. "fence."*
c *Or "in the right."*

10 While Ezra was praying and making confession, weeping and prostrating himself before the House of God, a very great crowd of Israelites gathered about him, men, women, and children; the people were weeping bitterly. ² Then Shecaniah son of Jehiel of the family of Elam spoke up and said to Ezra, "We have trespassed against our God by bringing into our homes foreign women from the peoples of the land; *ᵃ*-but there is still hope for Israel despite this.⁻ᵃ ³ Now then, let us make a covenant with our God to expel all these women and those who have been born to them, in accordance with the bidding of the LORD and of all who are concerned over the commandment of our God, and let the Teaching be obeyed. ⁴ Take action, for the responsibility is yours and we are with you. Act with resolve!"

⁵ So Ezra at once put the officers of the priests and the Levites and all Israel under oath to act accordingly, and they took the oath. ⁶ Then Ezra rose from his place in front of the House of God and went into the chamber of Jehohanan son of Eliashib; there, he ate no bread and drank no water, for he was in mourning over the trespass of those who had returned from exile. ⁷ Then a proclamation was issued in Judah and Jerusalem that all who had returned from the exile should assemble in Jerusalem, ⁸ and that anyone who did not come in three days would, by decision of the officers and elders, have his property confiscated and himself excluded from the congregation of the returning exiles.

⁹ All the men of Judah and Benjamin assembled in Jerusalem in three days; it was the ninth month, the twentieth of the month. All the people sat in the square of the House of God, trembling on account of the event and because of the rains. ¹⁰ Then Ezra the priest got up and said to them, "You have trespassed by bringing home foreign women, thus aggravating the guilt of Israel. ¹¹ So now, make confession to the LORD, God of your fathers, and do

ᵃ⁻ᵃ *Or "Is there . . . ?"*

His will, and separate yourselves from the peoples of the land and from the foreign women."

¹² The entire congregation responded in a loud voice, "We must surely do just as you say. ¹³ However, many people are involved, and it is the rainy season; it is not possible to remain out in the open, nor is this the work of a day or two, because we have transgressed extensively in this matter. ¹⁴ Let our officers remain on behalf of the entire congregation, and all our towns-people who have brought home foreign women shall appear before them at scheduled times, together with the elders and judges of each town, in order to avert the burning anger of our God from us on this account." ¹⁵ Only Jonathan son of Asahel and Jahzeiah son of Tikvah remained for this purpose, assisted by Meshullam and Shabbethai, the Levites. ¹⁶ The returning ex-iles did so. Ezra the priest and the men who were the chiefs of the ancestral clans—all listed by name—sequestered themselves on the first day of the tenth month to study the matter. ¹⁷ By the first day of the first month they were done with all the men who had brought home foreign women. ¹⁸ Among the priestly families who were found to have brought foreign women were Jeshua son of Jozadak and his brothers Maaseiah, Eliezer, Jarib, and Geda-liah. ¹⁹ They gave their word[b] to expel their wives and, acknowl-edging their guilt, offered a ram from the flock to expiate it. ²⁰ Of the sons of Immer: Hanani and Zebadiah; ²¹ of the sons of Harim: Maaseiah, Elijah, Shemaiah, Jehiel, and Uzziah; ²² of the sons of Pashhur: Elioenai, Maaseiah, Ishmael, Nethanel, Jozabad, and Elasah; ²³ of the Levites: Jozabad, Shimei, Kelaiah who is Kelita, Pethahiah, Judah and Eliezer. ²⁴ Of the singers: Eliashib. Of the gatekeepers: Shallum, Telem, and Uri. ²⁵ Of the Israelites: of the sons of Parosh: Ramiah, Izziah, Malchijah, Mijamin, Elea-zar, Malchijah and Benaiah; ²⁶ of the sons of Elam: Mattaniah, Zechariah, Jehiel, Abdi, Jeremoth, and Elijah; ²⁷ of the sons of Zattu: Elioenai, Eliashib, Mattaniah, Jeremoth, Zabad, and Aziza; ²⁸ of the sons of Bebai: Jehohanan, Hananiah, Zabbai, and Athlai; ²⁹ of the sons of Bani: Meshullam, Malluch, Adaiah, Jashub,

[b] Lit. "hand."

Sheal, and Ramoth; ³⁰ of the sons of Pahath-moab: Adna, Chelal, Benaiah, Maaseiah, Mattaniah, Bezalel, Binnui, and Manasseh; ³¹ of the sons of Harim: Eliezer, Isshijah, Malchijah, Shemaiah, and Shimeon; ³² also Benjamin, Malluch, and Shemariah; ³³ of the sons of Hashum: Mattenai, Mattattah, Zabad, Eliphelet, Jeremai, Manasseh and Shimei; ³⁴ of the sons of Bani: Maadai, Amram, and Uel; ³⁵ also Benaiah, Bedeiah, Cheluhu, ³⁶ Vaniah, Meremoth, Eliashib, ³⁷ Mattaniah, Mattenai, Jaasai, ³⁸ Bani, Binnui, Shimei, ³⁹ Shelemiah, Nathan, Adaiah, ⁴⁰ Machnadebai, Shashai, Sharai, ⁴¹ Azarel, Shelemiah, Shemariah, ⁴² Shallum, Amariah, and Joseph; ⁴³ of the sons of Nebo: Jeiel, Mattithiah, Zabad, Zebina, Jaddai, Joel, and Benaiah.

⁴⁴ All these had married foreign women, among whom were some women ^{c-}who had borne children.^{-c}

^{c-c} *Meaning of Heb. uncertain.*

נחמיה

NEHEMIAH

נחמיה
NEHEMIAH

1 The narrative of Nehemiah son of Hacaliah:

In the month of Kislev of the twentieth year,[a] when I was in the fortress of Shushan, ² Hanani, one of my brothers, together with some men of Judah, arrived, and I asked them about the Jews, the remnant who had survived the captivity, and about Jerusalem. ³ They replied, "The survivors who have survived the captivity there in the province are in dire trouble and disgrace; Jerusalem's wall is full of breaches, and its gates have been destroyed by fire."

⁴ When I heard that, I sat and wept, and was in mourning for days, fasting and praying to the God of heaven. ⁵ I said, "O LORD, God of heaven, great and awesome God, who stays faithful to His covenant with those who love Him and keep His commandments! ⁶ Let Your ear be attentive and Your eyes open to receive the prayer of Your servant that I am praying to You now, day and night, on behalf of the Israelites, Your servants, confessing the sins that we Israelites have committed against You, sins that I and my father's house have committed. ⁷ We have offended You by not keeping the commandments, the laws, and the rules that You gave to Your servant Moses. ⁸ Be mindful of the promise You gave to Your servant Moses: 'If you are unfaithful, I will scatter you among the peoples; ⁹ but if you turn back to Me, faithfully keep My commandments, even if your dispersed are at the ends of the earth,[b] I will gather them from there and bring them to the place where I have chosen to establish My name.' ¹⁰ For they are Your servants and Your people whom You redeemed by Your great power and Your mighty hand. ¹¹ O Lord! Let Your ear be attentive to the prayer of Your servant, and to the prayer of Your

---

[a] *I.e. of King Artaxerxes; cf. 2.1.*
[b] *Lit. "sky."*

servants who desire to hold Your name in awe. Grant Your servant success today, and dispose that man to be compassionate toward him!"

I was the king's cupbearer at the time.

2 In the month of Nisan, in the twentieth year of King Artaxerxes, wine was set before him; I took the wine and gave it to the king—I had never been out of sorts in his presence. ² The king said to me, "How is it that you look bad, though you are not ill? It must be bad thoughts." I was very frightened, ³ but I answered the king, "May the king live forever! How should I not look bad when the city of the graveyard of my ancestors lies in ruins, and its gates have been consumed by fire?" ⁴ The king said to me, "What is your request?" With a prayer to the God of heaven, ⁵ I answered the king, "If it please the king, and if your servant has found favor with you, send me to Judah, to the city of my ancestors' graves, to rebuild it." ⁶ With the consort seated at his side, the king said to me, "How long will you be gone and when will you return?" So it was agreeable to the king to send me, and I gave him a date. ⁷ Then I said to the king, "If it please the king, let me have letters to the governors of the province of Beyond the River, directing them to grant me passage until I reach Judah; ⁸ likewise, a letter to Asaph, the keeper of the King's Park, directing him to give me timber for roofing the gatehouses of the temple fortress and the city walls and for the house I shall occupy." The king gave me these, thanks to my God's benevolent care for me. ⁹ When I came to the governors of the province of Beyond the River I gave them the king's letters. The king also sent army officers and cavalry with me.

¹⁰ When Sanballat the Horonite and Tobiah the Ammonite servant heard, it displeased them greatly that someone had come, intent on improving the condition of the Israelites.

¹¹ I arrived in Jerusalem. After I was there three days ¹² I got up at night, I and a few men with me, and telling no one what my

God had put into my mind to do for Jerusalem, and taking no other beast than the one on which I was riding, ¹³ I went out by the Valley Gate, at night, toward the Jackals' Spring and the Dung Gate; and I surveyed the walls of Jerusalem that were breached, and its gates, consumed by fire. ¹⁴ I proceeded to the Fountain Gate and to the King's Pool, where there was no room for the beast under me to continue. ¹⁵ So I went up the wadi by night, surveying the wall, and, entering again by the Valley Gate, I returned. ¹⁶ The prefects knew nothing of where I had gone or what I had done, since I had not yet divulged it to the Jews—the priests, the nobles, the prefects, or the rest of the officials.

¹⁷ Then I said to them, "You see the bad state we are in— Jerusalem lying in ruins and its gates destroyed by fire. Come, let us rebuild the wall of Jerusalem and suffer no more disgrace." ¹⁸ I told them of my God's benevolent care for me, also of the things that the king had said to me, and they said, "Let us start building!" They were encouraged by [His] benevolence.

¹⁹ When Sanballat the Horonite and Tobiah the Ammonite servant and Geshem the Arab heard, they mocked us and held us in contempt and said, "What is this that you are doing? Are you rebelling against the king?" ²⁰ I said to them in reply, "The God of heaven will grant us success, and we, His servants, will start building. But you have no share or claim or stake^a in Jerusalem!"

3 Then Eliashib the high priest and his fellow priests set to and rebuilt the Sheep Gate; they consecrated it and set up its doors, consecrating it as far as the Hundred's Tower, as far as the Tower of Hananel. ² Next to him, the men of Jericho built. Next to them,^a Zaccur son of Imri. ³ The sons of Hassenaah rebuilt the Fish Gate; they roofed it and set up its doors, locks, and bars. ⁴ Next to them, Meremoth son of Uriah son of Hakkoz repaired; and next to him,^b Meshullam son of Berechiah son of Meshezabel. Next to him,^b Zadok son of Baana repaired. ⁵ Next to him,^b the Tekoites repaired, though their nobles would not take upon their shoul-

---

^a *Lit. "record."*

^a *Lit. "him."*
^b *Lit. "them."*

ders-*c* the work of their lord. ⁶ Joiada son of Paseah and Meshullam son of Besodeiah repaired the Jeshanah Gate; they roofed it and set up its doors, locks, and bars. *c-7* Next to them, Melatiah the Gibeonite and Jadon the Meronothite repaired, [with] the men of Gibeon and Mizpah, *d-*under the jurisdiction*-d* of the governor of the province of Beyond the River. ⁸ Next to them,*a* Uzziel son of Harhaiah, [of the] smiths, repaired. Next to him, Hananiah, of*e* the perfumers. They restored Jerusalem as far as the Broad Wall. ⁹ Next to them, Rephaiah son of Hur, chief of half the district of Jerusalem, repaired. ¹⁰ Next to him,*b* Jedaiah son of Harumaph repaired in front of his house. Next to him, Hattush son of Hashabneiah repaired. ¹¹ Malchijah son of Harim and Hasshub son of Pahath-moab repaired a second stretch, including the Tower of Ovens. ¹² Next to them,*a* Shallum son of Hallohesh,*f* chief of half the district of Jerusalem, repaired—he and his daughters. ¹³ Hanun and the inhabitants of Zanoah repaired the Valley Gate; they rebuilt it and set up its doors, locks, and bars. And [they also repaired] a thousand cubits of wall to the Dung Gate. ¹⁴ Malchijah son of Rechab, chief of the district of Beth-haccherem, repaired the Dung Gate; he rebuilt it and set up its doors, locks, and bars. ¹⁵ Shallun son of Col-hozeh, chief of the district of Mizpah, repaired the Fountain Gate; he rebuilt it and covered it, and set up its doors, locks, and bars, as well as the wall of the irrigation*g* pool of the King's Garden as far as the steps going down from the City of David. ¹⁶ After him, Nehemiah son of Azbuk, chief of half the district of Beth-zur, repaired, from in front of the graves of David as far as the artificial pool, and as far as the House of the Warriors. ¹⁷ After him, the Levites repaired: Rehum son of Bani. Next to him, Hashabiah, chief of half the district of Keilah, repaired for his district. ¹⁸ After him, their brothers repaired: Bavvai son of Henadad, chief of half the district of Keilah. ¹⁹ Next to him, Ezer son of Jeshua, the chief of Mizpah, repaired a second stretch, from in front of the ascent to the armory [at] the angle [of the wall]. ²⁰ After him, Baruch son of Zaccai zealously repaired a second stretch, from the angle to the entrance to the house of Eliashib, the high priest. ²¹ After him, Meremoth son of Uriah son

c-c Lit. "bring their neck into."
d-d Lit. "of the throne"; meaning of Heb. uncertain.
e Lit. "son of," i.e. member of the guild of.
f I.e. the charmer.
g Following Kimhi; cf. Mishnaic Heb. bet hashelahin, *irrigated field.*

of Hakkoz repaired a second stretch, from the entrance to Elia-shib's house to the end of Eliashib's house. [22] After him, the priests, inhabitants of the plain, repaired. [23] After them,[a] Benja-min and Hasshub repaired in front of their houses. After them,[a] Azariah son of Maaseiah son of Ananiah repaired beside his house. [24] After him, Binnui son of Henadad repaired a second stretch, from the house of Azariah to the angle, to the corner. [25] Palal son of Uzai—from in front of the angle and the tower that juts out of the house of the king, the upper [tower] of the prison compound. After him, Pedaiah son of Parosh. ([26] The temple servants were living on the Ophel, as far as a point in front of the Water Gate in the east, and the jutting tower.) [27] After him, the Tekoites repaired a second stretch, from in front of the great jutting tower to the wall of the Ophel. [28] Above the Horse Gate, the priests repaired, each in front of his house. [29] After them,[a] Zadok son of Immer repaired in front of his house. After him, Shemaiah son of Shechaniah, keeper of the East Gate, repaired. [30] After him, Hananiah son of Shelemiah and Hanun, the sixth son of Zalaph, repaired a second stretch. After them,[a] Meshullam son of Berechiah repaired in front of his chamber. [31] After him, Malchijah of the smiths repaired as far as the house of the temple servants and the merchants, [from] in front of the Muster Gate to the corner loft. [32] And between the corner loft to the Sheep Gate the smiths and the merchants repaired.

[33] When Sanballat heard that we were rebuilding the wall, it angered him, and he was extremely vexed. He mocked the Jews, [34] saying in the presence of his brothers and the Samarian force, "What are the miserable Jews doing? Will they restore, offer sacrifice, and finish one day? Can they revive those stones out of the dust heaps, burned as they are?" [35] Tobiah the Ammonite, alongside him, said, "That stone wall they are building—if a fox climbed it he would breach it!"

[36] Hear, our God, how we have become a mockery, and return their taunts upon their heads! Let them be taken as spoil to a land

of captivity! [37] Do not cover up their iniquity or let their sin be blotted out before You, for they hurled provocations at the builders.

[38] We rebuilt the wall till it was continuous all around to half its height; for the people's heart was in the work.

4 When Sanballat and Tobiah, and the Arabs, the Ammonites, and the Ashdodites heard that healing had come to the walls of Jerusalem, that the breached parts had begun to be filled, it angered them very much, [2] and they all conspired together to come and fight against Jerusalem and to throw it into confusion. [3] Because of them we prayed to our God, and set up a watch over them[a] day and night.

[4] Judah was saying,

"The strength of the basket-carrier has failed,
And there is so much rubble;
We are not able ourselves
To rebuild the wall."

[5] And our foes were saying, "Before they know or see it, we shall be in among them and kill them, and put a stop to the work." [6] When the Jews living near them[b] would arrive, they would tell us [c]time and again-[c] [d]" . . . from all the places where . . . you shall come back to us. . . ."-[d] [7] I stationed, on the lower levels of the place, behind the walls, on the bare rock—I stationed the people by families with their swords, their lances, and their bows. [8] Then I decided to exhort the nobles, the prefects, and the rest of the people, "Do not be afraid of them! Think of the great and awesome Lord, and fight for your brothers, your sons and daughters, your wives and homes!"

[9] When our enemies learned that it had become known to us, since God had thus frustrated their plan, we could all return to the wall, each to his work. [10] From that day on, half my servants did work and half held lances and shields, bows and armor. And the officers stood behind the whole house of Judah [11] who were

---

[a] *I.e. the workers on the walls.*
[b] *I.e. the foes.*
[c-c] *Lit. "ten times."*
[d-d] *Heb. seems to be abbreviated; a possible restoration of the sentence, with the missing elements enclosed in brackets, is: [of their evil plan; and we would say to them,] "From all the places where [you get such information] you shall come back to us [and convey it]."*

rebuilding the wall. The basket-carriers were burdened, doing work with one hand while the other held a weapon. ¹² As for the builders, each had his sword girded at his side as he was building. The trumpeter stood beside me. ¹³ I said to the nobles, the prefects, and the rest of the people, "There is much work and it is spread out; we are scattered over the wall, far from one another. ¹⁴ When you hear a trumpet call, gather yourselves to me at that place; our God will fight for us!" ¹⁵ And so we worked on, while half were holding lances, from the break of day until the stars appeared.

¹⁶ I further said to the people at that time, "Let every man with his servant lodge in Jerusalem, that we may use the night to stand guard and the day to work." ¹⁷ Nor did I, my brothers, my servants, or the guards following me ever take off our clothes,ᵉ[or] each his weapon, even at the water.⁻ᵉ

5 There was a great outcry by the common folk and their wives against their brother Jews. ² Some said, "Our sons and daughters are numerous; we must get grain to eat in order that we may live!" ³ Others said, "We must pawn our fields, our vineyards, and our homes to get grain to stave off hunger." ⁴ Yet others said, "We have borrowed money against our fields and vineyards to pay the king's tax. ⁵ Now ᵃ⁻we are as good as⁻ᵃ our brothers, and our children as good as theirs; yet here we are subjecting our sons and daughters to slavery—some of our daughters are already subjected—and we are powerless, while our fields and vineyards belong to others."

⁶ It angered me very much to hear their outcry and these complaints. ⁷ After pondering the matter carefully, I censured the nobles and the prefects, saying, "Are you pressing claims on loans made to your brothers?" Then I raised a large crowd against them ⁸ and said to them, "We have done our best to buy back our Jewish brothers who were sold to the nations; will you now sell your brothers so that they must be sold [back] to us?"

ᵉ⁻ᵉ *Meaning of Heb. uncertain.*

ᵃ⁻ᵃ *Lit. "our flesh is as good as the flesh of."*

They kept silent, for they found nothing to answer. [9] So I continued, "What you are doing is not right. You ought to act in a God-fearing way so as not to give our enemies, the nations, room to reproach us. [10] I, my brothers, and my servants also have claims of money and grain against them; let us now abandon those claims! [11] Give back at once their fields, their vineyards, their olive trees, and their homes, and [abandon] the claims for the hundred pieces of silver, the grain, the wine, and the oil that you have been pressing against them!" [12] They replied, "We shall give them back, and not demand anything of them; we shall do just as you say." Summoning the priests, I put them under oath to keep this promise. [13] I also shook out the bosom of my garment and said, "So may God shake free of his household and property any man who fails to keep this promise; may he be thus shaken out and stripped." All the assembled answered, "Amen," and praised the LORD.

The people kept this promise.

[14] Furthermore, from the day I was commissioned to be governor in the land of Judah—from the twentieth year of King Artaxerxes until his thirty-second year, twelve years in all—neither I nor my brothers ever ate of the governor's food allowance. [15] The former governors who preceded me laid heavy burdens on the people, and took from them for bread and wine more than[b] forty shekels of silver. Their servants also tyrannized over the people. But I, out of the fear of God, did not do so. [16] I also supported the work on this wall; we did not buy any land, and all my servants were gathered there at the work. [17] Although there were at my table, between Jews and prefects, one hundred and fifty men in all, beside those who came to us from surrounding nations; [18] and although what was prepared for each day came to one ox, six select sheep, and fowl, all prepared for me, and at ten-day intervals all sorts of wine in abundance—yet I did not resort to the governor's food allowance, for the [king's] service lay heavily on the people.

[b] Lit. "after"; meaning of Heb. uncertain.

19 O my God, remember to my credit all that I have done for this people!

6 When word reached Sanballat, Tobiah, Geshem the Arab, and the rest of our enemies that I had rebuilt the wall and not a breach remained in it—though at that time I had not yet set up doors in the gateways—2 Sanballat and Geshem sent a message to me, saying, "Come, let us get together in Kephirim in the Ono valley"; they planned to do me harm. 3 I sent them messengers, saying, "I am engaged in a great work and cannot come down, for the work will stop if I leave it in order to come down to you." 4 They sent me the same message four times, and I gave them the same answer. 5 Sanballat sent me the same message a fifth time by his servant, who had an open letter with him. 6 Its text was: "Word has reached the nations, and Geshem[a] too says that you and the Jews are planning to rebel—for which reason you are building the wall—and that you are to be their king. [b-]Such is the word.[-b] 7 You have also set up prophets in Jerusalem to proclaim about you, 'There is a king in Judah!' Word of these things will surely reach the king; so come, let us confer together."

8 I sent back a message to him, saying, "None of these things you mention has occurred; they are figments of your imagination"—9 for they all wished to intimidate us, thinking, "They will desist from the work, and it will not get done." Now strengthen my hands!

10 Then I visited Shemaiah son of Delaiah son of Mehetabel when he was housebound, and he said,

"Let us meet in the House of God, inside the sanctuary,
        And let us shut the doors of the sanctuary, for they are
            coming to kill you,
        By night they are coming to kill you."

11 I replied, "Will a man like me take flight? Besides, who such as I can go into the sanctuary and live? I will not go in." 12 Then I

---

[a] *Heb.* Gashmu.
[b-b] *Meaning of Heb. uncertain.*

realized that it was not God who sent him, but that he uttered that prophecy about me—Tobiah and Sanballat having hired him— ¹³ because he was a hireling, that I might be intimidated and act thus and commit a sin, and so provide them a scandal with which to reproach me.

¹⁴ "O my God, remember against Tobiah and Sanballat these deeds of theirs,ᶜ and against Noadiah the prophetess, and against the other prophets that they wished to intimidate me!"

¹⁵ The wall was finished on the twenty-fifth of Elul, after fifty-two days. ¹⁶ When all our enemies heard it, all the nations round about us were intimidated, and fell very low in their own estimation; they realized that this work had been accomplished by the help of our God.

¹⁷ Also in those days, the nobles of Judah kept up a brisk correspondence with Tobiah, and Tobiah with them. ¹⁸ Many in Judah were his confederates, for he was a son-in-law of Shecaniah son of Arah, and his son Jehohanan had married the daughter of Meshullam son of Berechiah. ¹⁹ They would also speak well of him to me, and would divulge my affairs to him. Tobiah sent letters to intimidate me.

7 When the wall was rebuilt and I had set up the doors, tasks were assigned to the gatekeepers, the singers, and the Levites. ² I put Hanani my brother and Hananiah, the captain of the fortress, in charge of Jerusalem, for he was a more trustworthy and God-fearing man than most. ³ I said to them, "The gates of Jerusalem are not to be opened until the heat of the day,ᵃ and ᵇbefore you leave your posts-ᵇ let the doors be closed and barred. And assign the inhabitants of Jerusalem to watches, each man to his watch, and each in front of his own house."

⁴ The city was broad and large, the people in it were few, and houses were not yet built. ⁵ My God put it into my mind to assemble the nobles, the prefects, and the people, in order to register them by families. I found the genealogical register of

ᶜ Lit. "his."

ᵃ Lit. "sun."
ᵇ⁻ᵇ Lit. "while they are still standing."

those who were the first to come up, and there I found written:
6 c These are the people of the province who came up from
among the captive exiles that Nebuchadnezzar, king of Babylon,
had deported, and who returned to Jerusalem and to Judah, each
to his own city, 7 who came with Zerubbabel, Jeshua, Nehemiah,
Azariah, Raamiah, Nahamani, Mordecai, Bilshan, Mispereth, Bigvai, Nehum, Baanah.

The number of the men of the people of Israel: 8 the sons of
Parosh—2172; 9 the sons of Shephatiah—372; 10 the sons of Arah
—652; 11 the sons of Pahath-moab: the sons of Jeshua and Joab
—2818; 12 the sons of Elam—1254; 13 the sons of Zattu—845;
14 the sons of Zaccai—760; 15 the sons of Binnui—648; 16 the sons
of Bebai—628; 17 the sons of Azgad—2322; 18 the sons of Adonikam—667; 19 the sons of Bigvai—2067; 20 the sons of Adin—655;
21 the sons of Ater: Hezekiah—98; 22 the sons of Hashum—328;
23 the sons of Bezai—324; 24 the sons of Hariph—112; 25 the sons
of Gibeon—95; 26 the men of Bethlehem and Netophah—188;
27 the men of Anathoth—128; 28 the men of Beth-azmaveth—
42;29 the men of Kiriath-jearim, Chephirah, and Beeroth—743;
30 the men of Ramah and Geba—621; 31 the men of Michmas—
122; 32 the men of Bethel and Ai—123; 33 the men of the other
Nebo—52; 34 the sons of the other Elam—1254; 35 the sons of
Harim—320; 36 the sons of Jericho—345; 37 the sons of Lod,
Hadid, and Ono—721; 38 the sons of Senaah—3930.

39 The priests: the sons of Jedaiah: the house of Jeshua—973;
40 the sons of Immer—1052; 41 the sons of Pashhur—1247; 42 the
sons of Harim—1017.

43 The Levites: the sons of Jeshua: Kadmiel, the sons of Ho-
deiah—74.

44 The singers: the sons of Asaph—148.

45 The gatekeepers: the sons of Shallum, the sons of Ater, the

c Vv. 6–43 appear as Ezra 2 with variations in the names and numbers.

sons of Talmon, the sons of Akkub, the sons of Hatita, the sons of Shobai—138.

46 The temple servants: the sons of Ziha, the sons of Hasupha, the sons of Tabbaoth, 47 the sons of Keros, the sons of Siah, the sons of Padon, 48 the sons of Lebanah, the sons of Hagabah, the sons of Shalmai, 49 the sons of Hanan, the sons of Giddel, the sons of Gahar, 50 the sons of Reaiah, the sons of Rezin, the sons of Nekoda, 51 the sons of Gazzam, the sons of Uzza, the sons of Paseah, 52 the sons of Besai, the sons of Meunim, the sons of Nephishesim, 53 the sons of Bakbuk, the sons of Hakupha, the sons of Harhur, 54 the sons of Bazlith, the sons of Mehida, the sons of Harsha, 55 the sons of Barkos, the sons of Sisera, the sons of Temah, 56 the sons of Neziah, the sons of Hatipha.

57 The sons of Solomon's servants: the sons of Sotai, the sons of Sophereth, the sons of Perida, 58 the sons of Jala, the sons of Darkon, the sons of Giddel, 59 the sons of Shephatiah, the sons of Hattil, the sons of Pochereth-hazzebaim, the sons of Amon.

60 The total of temple servants and the sons of Solomon's servants—392.

61 The following were those who came up from Tel-melah, Tel-harsha, Cherub, Addon, and Immer—they were unable to tell whether their father's house and descent were Israelite: 62 the sons of Delaiah, the sons of Tobiah, the sons of Nekoda—642.

63 Of the priests: the sons of Habaiah, the sons of Hakkoz, the sons of Barzillai who had married a daughter of Barzillai the Gileadite and had taken his*d* name—64 these searched for their genealogical records, but they could not be found, so they were disqualified for the priesthood. 65 The Tirshatha*e* ordered them not to eat of the most holy things until a priest with Urim and Thummim should appear.

66 The sum of the entire community was 42,360, 67 not counting their male and female servants, these being 7337; they also had 245 male and female singers. 68 *f*-[Their horses—736, their mules—245,]*f* camels—435, asses—6720.

---

d Lit. "their."
e A Persian title.
f-f These words are missing in some mss. and editions; but cf. Ezra 2.66.

⁶⁹ Some of the heads of the clans made donations for the work. The Tirshatha donated to the treasury: gold—1000 drachmas, basins—50, priestly robes—530.

⁷⁰ Some of the heads of the clans donated to the work treasury: gold—20,000 drachmas, and silver—2200 minas.

⁷¹ The rest of the people donated: gold—20,000 drachmas, silver—2000, and priestly robes—67.

⁷² The priests, the Levites, the gatekeepers, the singers, some of the people, the temple servants, and all Israel took up residence in their towns.

8 When the seventh month arrived—the Israelites being [settled] in their towns—¹ the entire people assembled as one man in the square before the Water Gate, and they asked Ezra the scribe to bring the scroll of the Teaching of Moses with which the Lord had charged Israel. ² On the first day of the seventh month, Ezra the priest brought the Teaching before the congregation, men and women and all who could listen with understanding. ³ He read from it, facing the square before the Water Gate, from the first light until midday, to the men and the women and those who could understand; the ears of all the people were given to the scroll of the Teaching.

⁴ Ezra the scribe stood upon a wooden tower made for the purpose, and beside him stood Mattithiah, Shema, Anaiah, Uriah, Hilkiah, and Maaseiah at his right, and at his left Pedaiah, Mishael, Malchijah, Hashum, Hashbaddanah, Zechariah, Meshullam. ⁵ Ezra opened the scroll in the sight of all the people, for he was above all the people; as he opened it, all the people stood up. ⁶ Ezra blessed the Lord, the great God, and all the people answered, "Amen, Amen," with hands upraised. Then they bowed their heads and prostrated themselves before the Lord with their faces to the ground. ⁷ Jeshua, Bani, Sherebiah, Jamin, Akkub, Shabbethai, Hodiah, Maaseiah, Kelita, Azariah, Jozabad, Hanan, Pelaiah, and the Levites explained the Teaching to the people,

while the people stood in their places. 8 They read from the scroll of the Teaching of God, translating it and giving the sense; so they understood the reading.

9 Nehemiah the Tirshatha, Ezra the priest and scribe, and the Levites who were explaining to the people said to all the people, "This day is holy to the LORD your God: you must not mourn or weep," for all the people were weeping as they listened to the words of the Teaching. 10 He further said to them, "Go, eat choice foods and drink sweet drinks and send portions to whoever has nothing prepared, for the day is holy to our Lord. Do not be sad, for your rejoicing in the LORD is the source of your strength." 11 The Levites were quieting the people, saying, "Hush, for the day is holy; do not be sad." 12 Then all the people went to eat and drink and send portions and make great merriment, for they understood the things they were told.

13 On the second day, the heads of the clans of all the people and the priests and Levites gathered to Ezra the scribe to study the words of the Teaching. 14 They found written in the Teaching that the LORD had commanded Moses that the Israelites must dwell in booths during the festival of the seventh month, 15 and that they must announce and proclaim throughout all their towns and Jerusalem as follows, "Go out to the mountains and bring leafy branches of olive trees, pine*a* trees, myrtles, palms and [other] leafy*a* trees to make booths, as it is written." 16 So the people went out and brought them, and made themselves booths on their roofs, in their courtyards, in the courtyards of the House of God, in the square of the Water Gate and in the square of the Ephraim Gate. 17 The whole community that returned from the captivity made booths and dwelt in the booths—the Israelites had not done so from the days of Joshua*b* son of Nun to that day— and there was very great rejoicing. 18 He read from the scroll of the Teaching of God each day, from the first to the last day. They celebrated the festival seven days, and there was a solemn gathering on the eighth, as prescribed.

a *Meaning of Heb. uncertain.*
b *Heb.* Jeshua.

9 On the twenty-fourth day of this month, the Israelites assembled, fasting, in sackcloth, and with earth upon them. [2] Those of the stock of Israel separated themselves from all foreigners, and stood and confessed their sins and the iniquities of their fathers. [3] Standing in their places, they read from the scroll of the Teaching of the LORD their God for one-fourth of the day, and for another fourth they confessed and prostrated themselves before the LORD their God. [4] On the raised platform of the Levites stood Jeshua and Bani, Kadmiel, Shebaniah, Bunni, Sherebiah, Bani, and Chenani, and cried in a loud voice to the LORD their God. [5] The Levites Jeshua, Kadmiel, Bani, Hashabniah, Sherebiah, Hodiah, and Pethahiah said, "Rise, bless the LORD your God who is from eternity to eternity: 'May Your glorious name be blessed, exalted though it is above every blessing and praise!'

[6] "You alone are the LORD. You made the heavens, the highest[a] heavens, and all their host, the earth and everything upon it, the seas and everything in them. You keep them all alive, and the host of heaven prostrate themselves before You. [7] You are the LORD God, who chose Abram, who brought him out of Ur of the Chaldeans and changed his name to Abraham. [8] Finding his heart true to You, You made a covenant with him to give the land of the Canaanite, the Hittite, the Amorite, the Perizzite, the Jebusite and the Girgashite—to give it to his descendants. And You kept Your word, for You are righteous. [9] You took note of our fathers' affliction in Egypt, and heard their cry at the Sea of Reeds. [10] You performed signs and wonders against Pharaoh, all his servants, and all the people of his land, for You knew that they acted presumptuously toward them. You made a name for Yourself that endures to this day. [11] You split the sea before them; they passed through the sea on dry land, but You threw their pursuers into the depths, like a stone into the raging waters.

[12] "You led them by day with a pillar of cloud, and by night with a pillar of fire, to give them light in the way they were to go.

[a] Lit. "the heavens of the."

¹³ You came down on Mount Sinai and spoke to them from heaven; You gave them right rules and true teachings, good laws and commandments. ¹⁴ You made known to them Your holy sabbath, and You ordained for them laws, commandments and Teaching, through Moses Your servant. ¹⁵ You gave them bread from heaven when they were hungry, and produced water from a rock when they were thirsty. You told them to go and possess the land that You swore to give them. ¹⁶ But they—our fathers— acted presumptuously; they stiffened their necks and did not obey Your commandments. ¹⁷ Refusing to obey, unmindful of Your wonders that You did for them, they stiffened their necks, and in their defiance resolved to return to their slavery. But You, being a forgiving God, gracious and compassionate, long-suffering and abounding in faithfulness, did not abandon them. ¹⁸ Even though they made themselves a molten calf and said, 'This is your God who brought you out of Egypt,' thus committing great impieties, ¹⁹ You, in Your abundant compassion, did not abandon them in the wilderness. The pillar of cloud did not depart from them to lead them on the way by day, nor the pillar of fire by night to give them light in the way they were to go. ²⁰ You endowed them with Your good spirit to instruct them. You did not withhold Your manna from their mouth; You gave them water when they were thirsty. ²¹ Forty years You sustained them in the wilderness so that they lacked nothing; their clothes did not wear out, and their feet did not swell.

²² "You gave them kingdoms and peoples, and ᵇ-allotted them territory.-ᵇ They took possession of the land of Sihon, the land of the king of Heshbon, and the land of Og, king of Bashan. ²³ You made their children as numerous as the stars of heaven, and brought them to the land which You told their fathers to go and possess. ²⁴ The sons came and took possession of the land; You subdued the Canaanite inhabitants of the land before them; You delivered them into their power, both their kings and the peoples of the land, to do with them as they pleased. ²⁵ They captured fortified cities and rich lands; they took possession of

ᵇ⁻ᵇ *Meaning of Heb. uncertain.*

houses filled with every good thing, of hewn cisterns, vineyards, olive trees, and fruit trees in abundance. They ate, they were filled, they grew fat; they luxuriated in Your great bounty. ²⁶ Then, defying You, they rebelled; they cast Your Teaching behind their back. They killed Your prophets who admonished them to turn them back to You; they committed great impieties.

²⁷ "You delivered them into the power of their adversaries who oppressed them. In their time of trouble they cried to You; You in heaven heard them, and in Your abundant compassion gave them saviors who saved them from the power of their adversaries. ²⁸ But when they had relief, they again did what was evil in Your sight, so You abandoned them to the power of their enemies, who subjugated them. Again they cried to You, and You in heaven heard and rescued them in Your compassion, time after time. ²⁹ You admonished them in order to turn them back to Your Teaching, but they acted presumptuously and disobeyed Your commandments, and sinned against Your rules, by following which a man shall live. They turned a defiant shoulder, stiffened their neck, and would not obey. ³⁰ You bore with them for many years, admonished them by Your spirit through Your prophets, but they would not give ear, so You delivered them into the power of the peoples of the lands. ³¹ Still, in Your great compassion You did not make an end of them or abandon them, for You are a gracious and compassionate God.

³² "And now, our God, great, mighty, and awesome God, who stays faithful to His covenant, do not treat lightly all the suffering that has overtaken us—our kings, our officers, our priests, our prophets, our fathers, and all Your people—from the time of the Assyrian kings to this day. ³³ Surely You are in the right with respect to all that has come upon us, for You have acted faithfully, and we have been wicked. ³⁴ Our kings, officers, priests, and fathers did not follow Your Teaching, and did not listen to Your commandments or to the warnings that You gave them. ³⁵ When they had their own kings and enjoyed the good that You lavished upon them, and the broad and rich land that You put at their

disposal, they would not serve You, and did not turn from their wicked deeds. ³⁶ Today we are slaves, and the land that You gave our fathers to enjoy its fruit and bounty—here we are slaves on it! ³⁷ On account of our sins it yields its abundant crops to kings whom You have set over us. They rule over our bodies and our beasts as they please, and we are in great distress.

10 "In view of all this, we make this pledge and put it in writing; and on the sealed copy [are subscribed] our officials, our Levites, and our priests.

² "On the sealed copy*ᵃ* [are subscribed]: Nehemiah the Tirshatha son of Hacaliah and Zedekiah, ³ Seraiah, Azariah, Jeremiah, ⁴ Pashhur, Amariah, Malchijah, ⁵ Hattush, Shebaniah, Malluch, ⁶ Harim, Meremoth, Obadiah, ⁷ Daniel, Ginnethon, Baruch, ⁸ Meshullam, Abijah, Mijamin, ⁹ Maaziah, Bilgai, Shemaiah; these are the priests.

¹⁰ "And the Levites: Jeshua son of Azaniah, Binnui of the sons of Henadad, and Kadmiel. ¹¹ And their brothers: Shebaniah, Hodiah, Kelita, Pelaiah, Hanan, ¹² Mica, Rehob, Hashabiah, ¹³ Zaccur, Sherebiah, Shebaniah, ¹⁴ Hodiah, Bani, and Beninu.

¹⁵ "The heads of the people: Parosh, Pahath-moab, Elam, Zattu, Bani, ¹⁶ Bunni, Azgad, Bebai, ¹⁷ Adonijah, Bigvai, Adin, ¹⁸ Ater, Hezekiah, Azzur, ¹⁹ Hodiah, Hashum, Bezai, ²⁰ Hariph, Anathoth, Nebai, ²¹ Magpiash, Meshullam, Hezir, ²² Meshezabel, Zadok, Jaddua, ²³ Pelatiah, Hanan, Anaiah, ²⁴ Hoshea, Hananiah, Hasshub, ²⁵ Hallohesh, Pilha, Shobek, ²⁶ Rehum, Hashabnah, Maaseiah, ²⁷ and Ahiah, Hanan, Anan, ²⁸ Malluch, Harim, Baanah.

²⁹ "And the rest of the people, the priests, the Levites, the gatekeepers, the singers, the temple servants, and all who separated themselves from the peoples of the lands to [follow] the Teaching of God, their wives, sons and daughters, all who know enough to understand, ³⁰ join with their noble brothers, and take

ᵃ *Heb. plural.*

494

an oath with sanctions to follow the Teaching of God, given through Moses the servant of God, and to observe carefully all the commandments of the LORD our Lord, His rules and laws.

³¹ "Namely: We will not give our daughters in marriage to the peoples of the land, or take their daughters for our sons.

³² "The peoples of the land who bring their wares and all sorts of foodstuff for sale on the sabbath day—we will not buy from them on the sabbath or a holy day.

"We will forgo [the produce of] the seventh year, and every outstanding debt.

³³ "We have laid upon ourselves obligations: To charge ourselves one-third of a shekel yearly for the service of the House of our God—³⁴ for the rows of bread, for the regular meal offering and for the regular burnt offering, [for those of the] sabbaths, new moons, festivals, for consecrations, for sin offerings to atone for Israel, and for all the work in the House of our God.

³⁵ "We have cast lots [among] the priests, the Levites, and the people, to bring the wood offering to the House of our God by clans annually at set times in order to provide fuel for the altar of the LORD our God, as is written in the Teaching.

³⁶ "And [we undertake] to bring to the House of the LORD annually the firstfruits of our soil, and of every fruit of every tree; ³⁷ also, the firstborn of our sons and our beasts, as is written in the Teaching; and to bring the firstlings of our cattle and flocks to the House of our God for the priests who minister in the House of our God.

³⁸ "We will bring to the storerooms of the House of our God the first part of our dough, and our gifts [of grain], and of the fruit of every tree, wine and oil for the priests, and the tithes of our land for the Levites—the Levites who collect the tithe in all our towns ᵇ⁻subject to royal service.⁻ᵇ ³⁹ An Aaronite priest must be with the Levites when they collect the tithe, and the Levites must bring up a tithe of the tithe to the House of our God, to the storerooms of the treasury. ⁴⁰ For it is to the storerooms that the Israelites and the Levites must bring the gifts of grain, wine, and

ᵇ⁻ᵇ *For this sense of* 'abodah, *"service," cf. 5.18.*

oil. The equipment of the sanctuary and of the ministering priests and the gatekeepers and the singers is also there.

"We will not neglect the House of our God."

11 The officers of the people settled in Jerusalem; the rest of the people cast lots for one out of ten to come and settle in the holy city of Jerusalem, and the other nine-tenths to stay in the towns. ² The people gave their blessing to all the men who willingly settled in Jerusalem.

³ These are the heads of the province who lived in Jerusalem —in the countryside*a* of Judah, the people lived in their towns, each on his own property, Israelites, priests, Levites, temple servants, and the sons of Solomon's servants, ⁴ while in Jerusalem some of the Judahites and some of the Benjaminites lived:

Of the Judahites: Athaiah son of Uzziah son of Zechariah son of Amariah son of Shephatiah son of Mahalalel, of the clan of Perez, ⁵ and Maaseiah son of Baruch son of Col-hozeh son of Hazaiah son of Adaiah son of Joiarib son of Zechariah son of the Shilonite. ⁶ All the clan of Perez who were living in Jerusalem— 468 valorous men.

⁷ These are the Benjaminites: Sallu son of Meshullam son of Joed son of Pedaiah son of Kolaiah son of Maaseiah son of Ithiel son of Jeshaiah. ⁸ After him, Gabbai and Sallai—928.

⁹ Joel son of Zichri was the official in charge of them, and Judah son of Hassenuah was the second-in-command of the city.

¹⁰ Of the priests: Jedaiah son of Joiarib, Jachin, ¹¹ Seraiah son of Hilkiah son of Meshullam son of Zadok son of Meraioth son of Ahitub, chief officer of the House of God, ¹² and their brothers, who did the work of the House—822; and Adaiah son of Jeroham son of Pelaliah son of Amzi son of Zechariah son of Pashhur son of Malchijah, ¹³ and his brothers, heads of clans—242; and Amashsai son of Azarel son of Ahzai son of Meshillemoth son of Immer, ¹⁴ and their brothers, valorous warriors—128. Zabdiel son of Haggedolim was the official in charge of them.

a Lit. "towns."

15 Of the Levites: Shemaiah son of Hasshub son of Azrikam son of Hashabiah son of Bunni, 16 and Shabbethai and Jozabad of the heads of the Levites were in charge of the external work of the House of God. 17 Mattaniah son of Micha son of Zabdi son of Asaph was the head; at prayer, he would lead off with praise; and Bakbukiah, one of his brothers, was his second-in-command; and Abda son of Shammua son of Galal son of Jeduthun. 18 All the Levites in the holy city—284.

19 And the gatekeepers: Akkub, Talmon, and their brothers, who stood watch at the gates—172.

20 And the rest of the Israelites, the priests, and the Levites in all the towns of Judah [lived] each on his estate.

21 The temple servants lived on the Ophel; Ziha and Gishpa were in charge of the temple servants.

22 The overseer of the Levites in Jerusalem was Uzzi son of Bani son of Hashabiah son of Mattaniah son of Micha, of the Asaphite singers, over the work of the House of God. 23 There was a royal order concerning them, a stipulation concerning the daily duties of the singers.

24 Petahiah son of Meshezabel, of the sons of Zerah son of Judah, advised the king concerning all the affairs of the people.

25 As concerns the villages with their fields: Some of the Judahites lived in Kiriath-arba and its outlying hamlets, in Dibon and its outlying hamlets, and in Jekabzeel and its villages; 26 in Jeshua, in Moladah, and in Beth-pelet; 27 in Hazar-shual, in Beer-sheba and its outlying hamlets; 28 and in Ziklag and in Meconah and its outlying hamlets; 29 in En-rimmon, in Zorah and in Jarmuth; 30 Zanoah, Adullam, and their villages; Lachish and its fields; Azekah and its outlying hamlets. They settled from Beer-sheba to the Valley of Hinnom.

31 The Benjaminites: from Geba, Michmash, Aija, and Bethel and its outlying hamlets; 32 Anathoth, Nob, Ananiah, 33 Hazor, Ramah, Gittaim, 34 Hadid, Zeboim, Neballat, 35 Lod, Ono, Geharashim. 36 Some of the Judahite divisions of Levites were [shifted] to Benjamin.

12 These are the priests and the Levites who came up with Zerubbabel son of Shealtiel and Jeshua:

Seraiah, Jeremiah, Ezra, ² Amariah, Malluch, Hattush, ³ Shecaniah, Rehum, Meramoth, ⁴ Iddo, Ginnethoi, Abijah, ⁵ Mijamin, Maadiah, Bilgah, ⁶ Shemaiah, Joiarib, Jedaiah, ⁷ Sallu, Amok, Hilkiah, Jedaiah. These were the heads of the priests and their brothers in the time of Jeshua.

⁸ The Levites: Jeshua, Binnui, Kadmiel, Sherebiah, Judah, and Mattaniah, in charge of thanksgiving songs,ᵃ he and his brothers; ⁹ and Bakbukiah and Unni [and] their brothers served opposite them by shifts.

¹⁰ Jeshua begot Joiakim; Joiakim begot Eliashib; Eliashib begot Joiada; ¹¹ Joiada begot Jonathan; Jonathan begot Jaddua.

¹² In the time of Joiakim, the heads of the priestly clans were: Meriaiah—of the Seraiah clan; Hananiah—of the Jeremiah clan; ¹³ Meshullam—of the Ezra clan; Jehohanan—of the Amariah clan; ¹⁴ Jonathan—of the Melicu clan; Joseph—of the Shebaniah clan; ¹⁵ Adna—of the Harim clan; Helkai—of the Meraioth clan; ¹⁶ Zechariah—of the Iddo clan; Meshullam—of the Ginnethon clan; ¹⁷ Zichri—of the Abijah clan . . . of the Miniamin clan; Piltai —of the Moadiah clan; ¹⁸ Shammua—of the Bilgah clan; Jehonathan—of the Shemaiah clan; ¹⁹ Mattenai—of the Joiarib clan; Uzzi —of the Jedaiah clan; ²⁰ Kallai—of the Sallai clan; Eber—of the Amok clan; ²¹ Hashabiah—of the Hilkiah clan; Nethanel—of the Jedaiah clan.

²² The Levites and the priests were listed by heads of clans in the days of Eliashib, Joiada, Johanan, and Jaddua, down to the reign of Darius the Persian. ²³ But the Levite heads of clans are listed in the book of the chronicles to the time of Johanan son of Eliashib.

²⁴ The heads of the Levites: Hashabiah, Sherebiah, Jeshua son of Kadmiel, and their brothers served opposite them, singing praise and thanksgiving hymns by the ordinance of David the

---

ᵃ *Meaning of Heb. uncertain.*

man of God—served opposite them in shifts; ²⁵ Mattaniah, Bakbukiah, Obadiah, Meshullam, Talmon, and Akkub, guarding as
gatekeepers by shifts at the vestibules of the gates.

²⁶ These were in the time of Joiakim son of Jeshua son of
Jozadak, and in the time of Nehemiah the governor, and of Ezra
the priest, the scribe.

²⁷ At the dedication of the wall of Jerusalem, the Levites, wher-
ever they lived, were sought out and brought to Jerusalem to
celebrate a joyful dedication with thanksgiving and with song,
accompanied by cymbals, harps, and lyres. ²⁸ The companies of
singers assembled from the [Jordan] plain, the environs of
Jerusalem, and from the Netophathite villages; ²⁹ from Beth-
hagilgal, from the countryside of Geba and Azmaveth, for the
singers built themselves villages in the environs of Jerusalem.

³⁰ The priests and Levites purified themselves; then they
purified the people, and the gates, and the wall.

³¹ I had the officers of Judah go up onto the wall, and I ap-
pointed two large thanksgiving [choirs] and processions. [One
marched] south on the wall, to the Dung Gate; ³² behind them
were Hoshaiah and half the officers of Judah, ³³ and Azariah,
Ezra, Meshullam, ³⁴ Judah, Benjamin, Shemaiah, and Jeremiah,
³⁵ and some of the young priests, with trumpets; Zechariah son
of Jonathan son of Shemaiah son of Mattaniah son of Micaiah son
of Zaccur son of Asaph, ³⁶ and his brothers Shemaiah, and Azarel,
Milalai, Gilalai, Maai, Nethanel, Judah, and Hanani, with the musical instruments of David, the man of God; and Ezra the scribe
went ahead of them. ³⁷ From there to the Fountain Gate, where
they ascended the steps of the City of David directly before them,
by the ascent on the wall, above the house of David, [and onward]
to the Water Gate on the east.

³⁸ The other thanksgiving [choir] marched on the wall in the
opposite direction, with me and half the people behind it, above
the Tower of Ovens to the Broad Wall; ³⁹ and above the Gate of
Ephraim, the Jeshanah Gate, the Fish Gate, the Tower of Hananel, the Tower of the Hundred, to the Sheep Gate; and they

halted at the Gate of the Prison Compound. ⁴⁰ Both thanksgiving choirs halted at the House of God, and I and half the prefects with me, ⁴¹ and the priests Eliakim, Maaseiah, Miniamin, Micaiah, Elioenai, Zechariah, Hananiah, with trumpets, ⁴² and Maaseiah and Shemaiah, Eleazar, Uzzi, Jehohanan, Malchijah, Elam, and Ezer. Then the singers sounded forth, with Jezrahiah in charge.

⁴³ On that day, they offered great sacrifices and rejoiced, for God made them rejoice greatly; the women and children also rejoiced, and the rejoicing in Jerusalem could be heard from afar.

⁴⁴ At that time men were appointed over the chambers that served as treasuries for the gifts, the firstfruits, and the tithes, into which the portions prescribed by the Teaching for the priests and Levites were gathered from the fields of the towns; for the people of Judah were grateful to the priests and Levites who were in attendance, ⁴⁵ who kept the charge of their God and the charge of purity, as well as to the singers and gatekeepers [serving] in accord with the ordinance of David and Solomon his son—⁴⁶ for the chiefs of the singers and songs of praise and thanksgiving to God already existed in the time of David and Asaph. ⁴⁷ And in the time of Zerubbabel, and in the time of Nehemiah, all Israel contributed the daily portions of the singers and the gatekeepers, and made sacred contributions for the Levites, and the Levites made sacred contributions for the Aaronites.

13 At that time they read to the people from the Book of Moses, and it was found written that no Ammonite or Moabite might ever enter the congregation of God, ² since they did not meet Israel with bread and water, and hired Balaam against them to curse them; but our God turned the curse into a blessing. ³ When they heard the Teaching, they separated all the alien admixture from Israel.

⁴ Earlier, the priest Eliashib, a relative of Tobiah, who had been appointed over the rooms in the House of our God, ⁵ had as-

signed to him*ᵃ* a large room where they used to store the meal offering, the frankincense, the equipment, the tithes of grain, wine, and oil, the dues of the Levites, singers and gatekeepers, and the gifts for the priests. ⁶ During all this time, I was not in Jerusalem, for in the thirty-second year of King Artaxerxes of Babylon, I went to the king, and only after a while did I ask leave of the king [to return]. ⁷ When I arrived in Jerusalem, I learned of the outrage perpetrated by Eliashib on behalf of Tobiah in assigning him a room in the courts of the House of God. ⁸ I was greatly displeased, and had all the household gear of Tobiah thrown out of the room; ⁹ I gave orders to purify the rooms, and had the equipment of the House of God and the meal offering and the frankincense put back.

¹⁰ I then discovered that the portions of the Levites had not been contributed, and that the Levites and the singers who performed the [temple] service had made off, each to his fields. ¹¹ I censured the prefects, saying, "How is it that the House of God has been neglected?" Then I recalled [the Levites] and installed them again in their posts; ¹² and all Judah brought the tithes of grain, wine, and oil into the treasuries. ¹³ I put the treasuries in the charge of the priest Shelemiah, the scribe Zadok, and Pedaiah of the Levites; and assisting them was Hanan son of Zaccur son of Mattaniah—for they were regarded as trustworthy persons, and it was their duty to distribute the portions to their brothers.

¹⁴ O my God, remember me favorably for this, and do not blot out the devotion I showed toward the House of my God and its attendants.

¹⁵ At that time I saw men in Judah treading winepresses on the sabbath, and others bringing heaps of grain and loading them onto asses, also wine, grapes, figs, and all sorts of goods, and bringing them into Jerusalem on the sabbath. I admonished them there and then for selling provisions. ¹⁶ Tyrians who lived there brought fish and all sorts of wares and sold them on the sabbath

ᵃ *I.e. Tobiah.*

to the Judahites in Jerusalem. ¹⁷ I censured the nobles of Judah, saying to them, "What evil thing is this that you are doing, profaning the sabbath day! ¹⁸ This is just what your ancestors did, and for it God brought all this misfortune on this city; and now you give cause for further wrath against Israel by profaning the sabbath!"

¹⁹ When shadows filled the gateways of Jerusalem at the approach of the sabbath, I gave orders that the doors be closed, and ordered them not to be opened until after the sabbath. I stationed some of my servants at the gates, so that no goods should enter on the sabbath. ²⁰ Once or twice the merchants and the vendors of all sorts of wares spent the night outside Jerusalem, ²¹ but I warned them, saying, "What do you mean by spending the night alongside the wall? If you do so again, I will lay hands upon you!" From then on they did not come on the sabbath. ²² I gave orders to the Levites to purify themselves and come and guard the gates, to preserve the sanctity of the sabbath.

This too, O my God, remember to my credit, and spare me in accord with your abundant faithfulness.

²³ Also at that time, I saw that Jews had married Ashdodite, Ammonite, and Moabite women; ²⁴ a good number of their children spoke the language of Ashdod and the language of those various peoples, and did not know how to speak Judean. ²⁵ I censured them, cursed them, flogged them, tore out their hair, and adjured them by God, saying, "You shall not give your daughters in marriage to their sons, or take any of their daughters for your sons or yourselves. ²⁶ It was just in such things that King Solomon of Israel sinned! Among the many nations there was not a king like him, and so well loved was he by his God that God made him king of all Israel, yet foreign wives caused even him to sin. ²⁷ How, then, can we acquiesce in your doing this great wrong, breaking faith with our God by marrying foreign women?" ²⁸ One of the sons of Joiada son of the high priest Eliashib was a son-in-law of Sanballat the Horonite; I drove him away from me.

[29] Remember to their discredit, O my God, how they polluted the priesthood, the covenant of the priests and Levites. [30] I purged them of every foreign element, and arranged for the priests and the Levites to work each at his task by shifts, [31] and for the wood offering [to be brought] at fixed times and for the firstfruits.

O my God, remember it to my credit!

דברי הימים א

I CHRONICLES

דברי הימים א
I CHRONICLES

1 Adam, Seth, Enosh; ² Kenan, Mahalalel, Jared; ³ Enoch, Me-
thuselah, Lamech; ⁴ Noah, Shem, Ham, and Japheth.

⁵ ᵃ The sons of Japheth: Gomer, Magog, Madai, Javan, Tubal,
Meshech, and Tiras. ⁶ The sons of Gomer: Ashkenaz, Diphath,
and Togarmah. ⁷ The sons of Javan: Elishah, Tarshish, Kittim,
and Rodanim.

⁸ The sons of Ham: Cush, Mizraim, Put, and Canaan. ⁹ The
sons of Cush: Seba, Havilah, Sabta, Raama, and Sabteca. The
sons of Raamah: Sheba and Dedan. ¹⁰ Cush begot Nimrod; he was
the first mighty one on earth.

¹¹ Mizraim begot the Ludim, the Anamim, the Lehabim, the
Naphtuhim, ¹² the Pathrusim, the Casluhim (whence the Philistines came forth), and the Caphtorim.

¹³ Canaan begot Sidon his firstborn, and Heth, ¹⁴ and the Jebusites, the Amorites, the Girgashites, ¹⁵ the Hivites, the Arkites, the
Sinites, ¹⁶ the Arvadites, the Zemarites, and the Hamathites.

¹⁷ The sons of Shem: Elam, Asshur, Arpachshad, Lud, Aram,
Uz, Hul, Gether, and Meshech. ¹⁸ Arpachshad begot Shelah; and
Shelah begot Eber. ¹⁹ Two sons were born to Eber: the name of
the one was Peleg (for in his days the earth was divided), and the
name of his brother Joktan. ²⁰ Joktan begot Almodad, Sheleph,
Hazarmaveth, Jerah, ²¹ Hadoram, Uzal, Diklah, ²² Ebal, Abimael,
Sheba, ²³ Ophir, Havilah, and Jobab; all these were the sons of
Joktan.

²⁴ Shem, Arpachshad, Shelah; ²⁵ Eber, Peleg, Reu; ²⁶ Serug,
Nahor, Terah; ²⁷ Abram, that is, Abraham.

²⁸ ᵇ The sons of Abraham: Isaac and Ishmael. ²⁹ This is their

ᵃ *With vv. 5–23, cf. Gen. 10. 1–30.*
ᵇ *With vv. 28–33, cf. Gen. 25. 1–16.*

line: The firstborn of Ishmael, Nebaioth; and Kedar, Abdeel, Mibsam, ³⁰ Mishma, Dumah, Massa, Hadad, Tema, ³¹ Jetur, Naphish, and Kedmah. These are the sons of Ishmael. ³² The sons of Keturah, Abraham's concubine: she bore Zimran, Jokshan, Medan, Midian, Ishbak, and Shuah. The sons of Jokshan: Sheba and Dedan. ³³ The sons of Midian: Ephah, Epher, Enoch, Abida, and Eldaah. All these were the descendants of Keturah.

³⁴ Abraham begot Isaac. The sons of Isaac: Esau and Israel. ³⁵ The sons of Esau: Eliphaz, Reuel, Jeush, Jalam, and Korah. ³⁶ The sons of Eliphaz: Teman, Omar, Zephi, Gatam, Kenaz, Timna, and Amalek. ³⁷ The sons of Reuel: Nahath, Zerah, Shammah, and Mizzah.

³⁸ The sons of Seir: Lotan, Shobal, Zibeon, Anah, Dishon, Ezer, and Dishan. ³⁹ The sons of Lotan: Hori and Homam; and Lotan's sister was Timna. ⁴⁰ The sons of Shobal: Alian, Manahath, Ebal, Shephi, and Onam. The sons of Zibeon: Aiah and Anah. ⁴¹ The sons of Anah: Dishon. The sons of Dishon: Hamran, Eshban, Ithran, and Cheran. ⁴² The sons of Ezer: Bilhan, Zaavan, and Jaakan. The sons of Dishan: Uz and Aran.

⁴³ ᶜ These are the kings who reigned in the land of Edom before any king reigned over the Israelites: Bela son of Beor, and the name of his city was Dinhabah. ⁴⁴ When Bela died, Jobab son of Zerah from Bozrah succeeded him as king. ⁴⁵ When Jobab died, Husham of the land of the Temanites succeeded him as king. ⁴⁶ When Husham died, Hadad son of Bedad, who defeated the Midianites in the country of Moab, succeeded him as king, and the name of his city was Avith. ⁴⁷ When Hadad died, Samlah of Masrekah succeeded him as king. ⁴⁸ When Samlah died, Saul of Rehoboth-on-the-River succeeded him as king. ⁴⁹ When Saul died, Baal-hanan son of Achbor succeeded him as king. ⁵⁰ When Baal-hanan died, Hadad succeeded him as king; and the name of his city was Pai, and his wife's name Mehetabel daughter of Matred daughter of Me-zahab. ⁵¹ And Hadad died.

The clans of Edom were the clans of Timna, Alvah, Jetheth,

ᶜ *With vv. 43–50, cf. Gen. 36. 31–43.*

⁵²Oholibamah, Elah, Pinon, ⁵³Kenaz, Teman, Mibzar, ⁵⁴Magdiel, and Iram; these are the clans of Edom.

2 These are the sons of Israel: Reuben, Simeon, Levi, Judah, Issachar, Zebulun, ²Dan, Joseph, Benjamin, Naphtali, Gad, and Asher. ³The sons of Judah: Er, Onan, and Shelah; these three, Bath-shua the Canaanite woman bore to him. But Er, Judah's firstborn, was displeasing to the LORD, and He took his life. ⁴His daughter-in-law Tamar also bore him Perez and Zerah. Judah's sons were five in all.

⁵The sons of Perez: Hezron and Hamul. ⁶The sons of Zerah: Zimri, Ethan, Heman, Calcol, and Dara, five in all. ⁷The sons of Carmi: Achar, the troubler of Israel, who committed a trespass against the proscribed thing; ⁸and Ethan's son was Azariah.

⁹The sons of Hezron, that were born to him: Jerahmeel, Ram, and Chelubai. ¹⁰Ram begot Amminadab, and Amminadab begot Nahshon, prince of the sons of Judah. ¹¹Nahshon was the father of Salma, Salma of Boaz, ¹²Boaz of Obed, Obed of Jesse. ¹³Jesse begot Eliab his firstborn, Abinadab the second, Shimea the third, ¹⁴Nethanel the fourth, Raddai the fifth, ¹⁵Ozem the sixth, David the seventh; ¹⁶their sisters were Zeruiah and Abigail. The sons of Zeruiah: Abishai, Joab, and Asahel, three. ¹⁷Abigail bore Amasa, and the father of Amasa was Jether the Ishmaelite.

¹⁸Caleb son of Hezron had children by his wife Azubah, and by Jerioth; these were her sons: Jesher, Shobab, and Ardon. ¹⁹When Azubah died, Caleb married Ephrath, who bore him Hur. ²⁰Hur begot Uri, and Uri begot Bezalel.

²¹Afterward Hezron had relations with the daughter of Machir father of Gilead—he had married her when he was sixty years old—and she bore him Segub; ²²and Segub begot Jair; he had twenty-three cities in the land of Gilead. ²³But Geshur and Aram took from them Havvoth-jair, Kenath and its dependencies, sixty towns. All these were the sons of Machir, the father of Gilead.

²⁴ After the death of Hezron, in Caleb-ephrathah, Abijah, wife of Hezron, bore Ashhur, the father of Tekoa.

²⁵ The sons of Jerahmeel the firstborn of Hezron: Ram his firstborn, Bunah, Oren, Ozem, and Ahijah. ²⁶ Jerahmeel had another wife, whose name was Atarah; she was the mother of Onam. ²⁷ The sons of Ram the firstborn of Jerahmeel: Maaz, Jamin, and Eker. ²⁸ The sons of Onam: Shammai and Jada. The sons of Shammai: Nadab and Abishur. ²⁹ The name of Abishur's wife was Abihail, and she bore him Ahban and Molid. ³⁰ The sons of Nadab: Seled and Appaim; Seled died childless. ³¹ The sons of Appaim: Ishi. The sons of Ishi: Sheshan. The sons of Sheshan: Ahlai. ³² The sons of Jada, Shammai's brother: Jether and Jonathan; Jether died childless. ³³ The sons of Jonathan: Peleth and Zaza. These were the descendants of Jerahmeel. ³⁴ Sheshan had no sons, only daughters; Sheshan had an Egyptian slave, whose name was Jarha. ³⁵ So Sheshan gave his daughter in marriage to Jarha his slave; and she bore him Attai. ³⁶ Attai begot Nathan and Nathan begot Zabad. ³⁷ Zabad begot Ephlal, and Ephlal begot Obed. ³⁸ Obed begot Jehu, and Jehu begot Azariah. ³⁹ Azariah begot Helez, and Helez begot Eleasah. ⁴⁰ Eleasah begot Sisamai, and Sisamai begot Shallum. ⁴¹ Shallum begot Jekamiah, and Jekamiah begot Elishama.

⁴² The sons of Caleb brother of Jerahmeel: Meshah his firstborn, who was the father of Ziph. The sons of Mareshah father of Hebron. ⁴³ The sons of Hebron: Korah, Tappuah, Rekem, and Shema. ⁴⁴ Shema begot Raham the father of Jorkeam, and Rekem begot Shammai. ⁴⁵ The son of Shammai: Maon, and Maon begot Bethzur. ⁴⁶ Ephah, Caleb's concubine, bore Haran, Moza, and Gazez; Haran begot Gazez. ⁴⁷ The sons of Jahdai: Regem, Jotham, Geshan, Pelet, Ephah, and Shaaph. ⁴⁸ Maacah, Caleb's concubine, bore Sheber and Tirhanah. ⁴⁹ She also bore Shaaph father of Madmannah, Sheva father of Machbenah and father of Gibea; the daughter of Caleb was Achsah. ⁵⁰ These were the descendants of Caleb.

The sons of Hur the firstborn of Ephrathah: Shobal father of

Kiriath-jearim, ⁵¹ Salma father of Bethlehem, Hareph father of Beth-gader. ⁵² Shobal father of Kiriath-jearim had sons: Haroeh, half of the Monuhoth. ⁵³ And the families of Kiriath-jearim: the Ithrites, the Puthites, the Shumathites, and the Mishraites; from these came the Zorathites and the Eshtaolites. ⁵⁴ The sons of Salma: Bethlehem, the Netophathites, Atroth-beth-joab, and half of the Manahathites, the Zorites. ⁵⁵ The families of the scribes that dwelt at Jabez: the Tirathites, the Shimeathites, the Sucathites; these are the Kenites who came from Hammath, father of the house of Rechab.

3 These are the sons of David who were born to him in Hebron: the firstborn Amnon, by Ahinoam the Jezreelite; the second Daniel, by Abigail the Carmelite; ² the third Absalom, son of Maacah daughter of King Talmai of Geshur; the fourth Adonijah, son of Haggith; ³ the fifth Shephatiah, by Abital; the sixth Ithream, by his wife Eglah; ⁴ six were born to him in Hebron. He reigned there seven years and six months, and in Jerusalem he reigned thirty-three years. ⁵ These were born to him in Jerusalem: Shimea, Shobab, Nathan, and Solomon, four by Bath-shua daughter of Ammiel; ⁶ then Ibhar, Elishama, Eliphelet, ⁷ Nogah, Nepheg, Japhia, ⁸ Elishama, Eliada, and Eliphelet—nine. ⁹ All were David's sons, besides the sons of the concubines; and Tamar was their sister.

¹⁰ The son of Solomon: Rehoboam; his son Abijah, his son Asa, his son Jehoshaphat, ¹¹ his son Joram, his son Ahaziah, his son Joash, ¹² his son Amaziah, his son Azariah, his son Jotham, ¹³ his son Ahaz, his son Hezekiah, his son Manasseh, ¹⁴ his son Amon, and his son Josiah. ¹⁵ The sons of Josiah: Johanan the firstborn, the second Jehoiakim, the third Zedekiah, the fourth Shallum. ¹⁶ The descendants of Jehoiakim: his son Jeconiah, his son Zedekiah; ¹⁷ and the sons of Jeconiah, the captive: Shealtiel his son, ¹⁸ Malchiram, Pedaiah, Shenazzar, Jekamiah, Hoshana, and Nedabiah; ¹⁹ the sons of Pedaiah: Zerubbabel and Shimei; the

sons of Zerubbabel: Meshullam and Hananiah, and Shelomith was their sister; 20 Hashubah, Ohel, Berechiah, Hasadiah, and Jushab-hesed—five. 21 And the sons of Hananiah: Pelatiah and Jeshaiah; the sons of [Jeshaiah]: Rephaiah; the sons of [Rephaiah]: Arnan; the sons of [Arnan]: Obadiah; the sons of [Obadiah]: Shecaniah. 22 And the sons of Shecaniah: Shemaiah; and the sons of Shemaiah: Hattush, and Igal, and Bariah, and Neariah, and Shaphat—six. 23 And the sons of Neariah: Elioenai, and Hizkiah, and Azrikam—three. 24 And the sons of Elioenai: Hodaviah, and Eliashib, and Pelaiah, and Akkub, and Johanan, and Delaiah, and Anani—seven.

4 The sons of Judah: Perez, Hezron, Carmi, Hur, and Shobal. 2 Reaiah son of Shobal begot Jahath, and Jahath begot Ahumai and Lahad. These were the families of the Zorathites. 3 These were [the sons of] the father of Etam: Jezreel, Ishma, and Idbash; and the name of their sister was Hazlelponi, 4 and Penuel was the father of Gedor, and Ezer the father of Hushah. These were the sons of Hur, the firstborn of Ephrathah, the father of Bethlehem. 5 Ashhur the father of Tekoa had two wives, Helah and Naarah; 6 Naarah bore him Ahuzam, Hepher, Temeni, and Ahashtari. These were the sons of Naarah. 7 The sons of Helah: Zereth, Zohar, and Ethnan. 8 Koz was the father of Anub, Zobebah, and the families of Aharhel son of Harum. 9 Jabez was more esteemed than his brothers; and his mother named him Jabez, "Because," she said, "I bore him in pain."[a] 10 Jabez invoked the God of Israel, saying, "Oh, bless me, enlarge my territory, stand by me, and make me not suffer pain from misfortune!" And God granted what he asked. 11 Chelub the brother of Shuhah begot Mehir, who was the father of Eshton. 12 Eshton begot Bethrapha, Paseah, and Tehinnah father of Ir-nahash. These were the men of Recah. 13 The sons of Kenaz: Othniel and Seraiah; and the sons of Othniel: 14 Hathath and Meonothai. He begot Ophrah. Seraiah begot Joab father of Ge-harashim,[b] so-called because they were crafts-

[a] Heb. 'oṣeb, connected with "Jabez."
[b] Lit. "the valley of the craftsmen."

men. [15] The sons of Caleb son of Jephunneh: Iru, Elah, and Naam; and the sons of Elah: Kenaz. [16] The sons of Jehallelel: Ziph, Ziphah, Tiria, and Asarel. [17] The sons of Ezrah: Jether, Mered, Epher, and Jalon. She[c] conceived and bore Miriam, Shammai, and Ishbah father of Eshtemoa. [18] And his Judahite wife bore Jered father of Gedor, Heber father of Soco, and Jekuthiel father of Zanoah. These were the sons of Bithiah daughter of Pharaoh, whom Mered married. [19] The sons of the wife of Hodiah sister of Naham were the fathers of Keilah the Garmite and Eshtemoa the Maacathite. [20] The sons of Shimon: Amnon, Rinnah, Ben-hanan, and Tilon. The sons of Ishi: Zoheth and Ben-zoheth. [21] The sons of Shelah son of Judah: Er father of Lecah, Laadah father of Mareshah, and the families of the linen factory at Beth-ashbea; [22] and Jokim, and the men of Cozeba and Joash, and Saraph, who married into Moab and Jahubi Lehem (the records are ancient). [23] These were the potters who dwelt at Netaim and Gederah; they dwelt there in the king's service.

[24] The sons of Simeon: Nemuel, Jamin, Jarib, Zerah, Shaul; [25] his son Shallum, his son Mibsam, his son Mishma. [26] The sons of Mishma: his son Hammuel, his son Zaccur, his son Shimei. [27] Shimei had sixteen sons and six daughters; but his brothers had not many children; in all, their families were not as prolific as the Judahites. [28] They dwelt in Beersheba, Moladah, Hazar-shual, [29] Bilhah, Ezem, Tolad, [30] Bethuel, Hormah, Ziklag, [31] Beth-marcaboth, Hazar-susim, Beth-biri, and Shaaraim. These were their towns until David became king, [32] together with their villages, Etam, Ain, Rimmon, Tochen, and Ashan—five towns, [33] along with all their villages that were around these towns as far as Baal; such were their settlements.

Registered in their genealogy were: [34] Meshobab, Jamlech, Joshash son of Amaziah, [35] Joel, Jehu son of Joshibiah son of Seraiah son of Asiel. [36] Elioenai, Jaakobah, Jeshohaiah, Asaiah, Adiel, Jesimiel, Benaiah, [37] Ziza son of Shiphi son of Allon son of Jedaiah son of Shimri son of Shemaiah—[38] these mentioned by name were chiefs in their families, and their clans increased

[c] *Apparently Bithiah; cf. v. 18.*

greatly. [39] They went to the approaches to Gedor, to the eastern side of the valley, in search of pasture for their flocks. [40] They found rich, good pasture, and the land was ample, quiet, and peaceful. The former inhabitants were of Ham; [41] those recorded by name came in the days of King Hezekiah of Judah, and attacked their encampments and the Meunim who were found there, and wiped them out forever, and settled in their place, because there was pasture there for their flocks. [42] And some of them, five hundred of the Simeonites, went to Mount Seir, with Pelatiah, Neariah, Rephaiah, and Uzziel, sons of Ishi, at their head, [43] and they destroyed the last surviving Amalekites, and they live there to this day.

5 The sons of Reuben the firstborn of Israel. (He was the firstborn; but when he defiled his father's bed, his birthright was given to the sons of Joseph son of Israel, so he is not reckoned as firstborn in the genealogy; [2] though Judah became more powerful than his brothers and a leader came from him, yet the birthright belonged to Joseph.) [3] The sons of Reuben, the firstborn of Israel: Enoch, Pallu, Hezron, and Carmi. [4] The sons of Joel: his son Shemaiah, his son Gog, his son Shimei, [5] his son Micah, his son Reaiah, his son Baal, [6] his son Beerah—whom King Tillegath-pilneser of Assyria exiled—was chieftain of the Reubenites. [7] And his kinsmen, by their families, according to their lines in the genealogy: the head, Jeiel, and Zechariah, [8] and Bela son of Azaz son of Shema son of Joel; he dwelt in Aroer as far as Nebo and Baal-meon. [9] He also dwelt to the east as far as the fringe of the wilderness this side of the Euphrates, because their cattle had increased in the land of Gilead. [10] And in the days of Saul they made war on the Hagrites, who fell by their hand; and they occupied their tents throughout all the region east of Gilead.

[11] The sons of Gad dwelt facing them in the land of Bashan as far as Salcah: [12] Joel the chief, Shapham the second, Janai, and

Shaphat in Bashan. [13] And by clans: Michael, Meshullam, Sheba, Jorai, Jacan, Zia, and Eber—seven. [14] These were the sons of Abihail son of Huri son of Jaroah son of Gilead son of Michael son of Jeshishai son of Jahdo son of Buz; [15] Ahi son of Abdiel son of Guni was chief of their clan, [16] and they dwelt in Gilead, in Bashan, and in its dependencies, and in all the pasturelands of Sharon, to their limits. [17] All of them were registered by genealogies in the days of King Jotham of Judah, and in the days of King Jeroboam of Israel.

[18] The Reubenites, the Gadites, and the half-tribe of Manasseh had warriors who carried shield and sword, drew the bow, and were experienced at war—44,760, ready for service. [19] They made war on the Hagrites—Jetur, Naphish, and Nodab. [20] They prevailed against them; the Hagrites and all who were with them were delivered into their hands, for they cried to God in the battle, and He responded to their entreaty because they trusted in Him. [21] They carried off their livestock: 50,000 of their camels, 250,000 sheep, 2,000 asses, and 100,000 people. [22] For many fell slain, because it was God's battle. And they dwelt in their place until the exile.

[23] The members of the half-tribe of Manasseh dwelt in the land; they were very numerous from Bashan to Baal-hermon, Senir, and Mount Hermon. [24] These were the chiefs of their clans: Epher, Ishi, Eliel, Azriel, Jeremiah, Hodaviah, and Jahdiel, men of substance, famous men, chiefs of their clans. [25] But they trespassed against the God of their fathers by going astray after the gods of the peoples of the land, whom God had destroyed before them. [26] So the God of Israel roused the spirit of King Pul of Assyria—the spirit of King Tillegath-pilneser of Assyria—and he carried them away, namely, the Reubenites, the Gadites, and the half-tribe of Manasseh, and brought them to Halah, Habor, Hara, and the river Gozan, to this day.

[27] [a] The sons of Levi: Gershom, Kohath, and Merari. [28] The sons of Kohath: Amram, Izhar, Hebron, and Uzziel. [29] The children of Amram: Aaron, Moses, and Miriam. The sons of Aaron: Nadab,

[a] *In some editions, ch. 6 begins here.*

Abihu, Eleazar, and Ithamar. [30] Eleazar begot Phinehas, Phinehas begot Abishua, [31] Abishua begot Bukki, Bukki begot Uzzi, [32] Uzzi begot Zerahiah, Zerahiah begot Meraioth, [33] Meraioth begot Amariah, Amariah begot Ahitub, [34] Ahitub begot Zadok, Zadok begot Ahimaaz, [35] Ahimaaz begot Azariah, Azariah begot Johanan, [36] and Johanan begot Azariah (it was he who served as priest in the House that Solomon built in Jerusalem). [37] Azariah begot Amariah, Amariah begot Ahitub, [38] Ahitub begot Zadok, Zadok begot Shallum, [39] Shallum begot Hilkiah, Hilkiah begot Azariah, [40] Azariah begot Seraiah, Seraiah begot Jehozadak; [41] and Jehozadak went into exile when the Lord exiled Judah and Jerusalem by the hand of Nebuchadnezzar.

6 The sons of Levi: Gershom, Kohath, and Merari. [2] And these are the names of the sons of Gershom: Libni and Shimei. [3] The sons of Kohath: Amram, Izhar, Hebron, and Uzziel. [4] The sons of Merari: Mahli and Mushi. These were the families of the Levites according to their clans. [5] Of Gershom: his son Libni, his son Jahath, his son Zimmah, [6] his son Joah, his son Iddo, his son Zerah, his son Jeatherai. [7] The sons of Kohath: his son Amminadab, his son Korah, his son Assir, [8] his son Elkanah, his son Ebiasaph, his son Assir, [9] his son Tahath, his son Uriel, his son Uzziah, and his son Shaul. [10] The sons of Elkanah: Amasai and Ahimoth, [11] his son Elkanah, his son Zophai, his son Nahath, [12] his son Eliab, his son Jeroham, his son Elkanah. [13] The sons of Samuel: his firstborn *a*-Vashni, and-*a* Abijah. [14] The sons of Merari: Mahli, his son Libni, his son Shimei, his son Uzzah, [15] his son Shimea, his son Haggiah, and his son Asaiah.

[16] These were appointed by David to be in charge of song in the House of the Lord, from the time the Ark came to rest. [17] They served at the Tabernacle of the Tent of Meeting with song until Solomon built the House of the Lord in Jerusalem; and they carried out their duties as prescribed for them. [18] Those were the appointed men; and their sons were: the Kohathites: Heman the singer, son of Joel son of Samuel [19] son of Elkanah

---

a-a Some ancient vv. read, "Joel, and the second"; cf. I Sam. 8.2.

son of Jeroham son of Eliel son of Toah [20] son of Zuph son of Elkanah son of Mahath son of Amasai [21] son of Elkanah son of Joel son of Azariah son of Zephaniah [22] son of Tahath son of Assir son of Ebiasaph son of Korah [23] son of Izhar son of Kohath son of Levi son of Israel; [24] and his kinsmen Asaph, who stood on his right, namely, Asaph son of Berechiah son of Shimea [25] son of Michael son of Baaseiah son of Malchijah [26] son of Ethni son of Zerah son of Adaiah [27] son of Ethan son of Zimmah son of Shimei [28] son of Jahath son of Gershom son of Levi. [29] On the left were their kinsmen: the sons of Merari: Ethan son of Kishi son of Abdi son of Malluch [30] son of Hashabiah son of Amaziah son of Hilkiah [31] son of Amzi son of Bani son of Shemer [32] son of Mahli son of Mushi son of Merari son of Levi; [33] and their kinsmen the Levites were appointed for all the service of the Tabernacle of the House of God.

[34] But Aaron and his sons made offerings upon the altar of burnt offering and upon the altar of incense, performing all the tasks of the most holy place, to make atonement for Israel, according to all that Moses the servant of God had commanded. [35] These are the sons of Aaron: his son Eleazar, his son Phinehas, his son Abishua, [36] his son Bukki, his son Uzzi, his son Zerahiah, [37] his son Meraioth, his son Amariah, his son Ahitub, [38] his son Zadok, his son Ahimaaz. [39] *b*These are their dwelling-places according to their settlements within their borders: to the sons of Aaron of the families of Kohathites, for theirs was the [first] lot; [40] they gave them Hebron in the land of Judah and its surrounding pasturelands, [41] but the fields of the city and its villages they gave to Caleb son of Jephunneh. [42] To the sons of Aaron they gave the cities*c* of refuge: Hebron and Libnah with its pasturelands, Jattir and Eshtemoa with its pasturelands, [43] Hilen with its pasturelands, Debir with its pasturelands, [44] Ashan with its pasturelands, and Beth-shemesh with its pasturelands. [45] From the tribe of Benjamin, Geba with its pasturelands, Alemeth with its pasturelands, and Anathoth with its pasturelands. All their cities throughout their families were thirteen.

[46] To the remaining Kohathites were given by lot out of the

---

b *With vv. 24–51, cf. Josh. 21.3–42.*
c *Josh. 21.13, "city."*

family of the tribe, out of the half-tribe, the half of Manasseh, ten cities. ⁴⁷ To the Gershomites according to their families were allotted thirteen cities out of the tribes of Issachar, Asher, Naphtali, and Manasseh in Bashan. ⁴⁸ To the Merarites according to their families were allotted twelve cities out of the tribes of Reuben, Gad, and Zebulun. ⁴⁹ So the people of Israel gave the Levites the cities with their pasturelands. ⁵⁰ They gave them by lot out of the tribe of the Judahites these cities which are mentioned by name, and out of the tribe of the Simeonites, and out of the tribe of the Benjaminites.

⁵¹ And some of the families of the sons of Kohath had cities of their territory out of the tribe of Ephraim. ⁵² They gave them the cities of refuge: Shechem with its pasturelands in the hill country of Ephraim, Gezer with its pasturelands, ⁵³ Jokmeam with its pasturelands, Beth-horon with its pasturelands, ⁵⁴ Aijalon with its pasturelands, Gath-rimmon with its pasturelands; ⁵⁵ and out of the half-tribe of Manasseh: Aner with its pasturelands, and Bileam with its pasturelands, for the rest of the families of the Kohathites.

⁵⁶ To the Gershomites; out of the half-tribe of Manasseh: Golan in Bashan with its pasturelands and Ashtaroth with its pasturelands; ⁵⁷ and out of the tribe of Issachar: Kedesh with its pasturelands, Dobrath with its pasturelands, ⁵⁸ Ramoth with its pasturelands, and Anem with its pasturelands; ⁵⁹ out of the tribe of Asher: Mashal with its pasturelands, Abdon with its pasturelands, ⁶⁰ Hukok with its pasturelands, and Rehob with its pasturelands; ⁶¹ and out of the tribe of Naphtali: Kedesh in Galilee with its pasturelands; Hammon with its pasturelands, and Kiriathaim with its pasturelands. ⁶² To the rest of the Merarites, out of the tribe of Zebulun: Rimmono with its pasturelands, Tabor with its pasturelands; ⁶³ and beyond the Jordan at Jericho, on the east side of the Jordan, out of the tribe of Reuben: Bezer in the wilderness with its pasturelands, Jahaz with its pasturelands, ⁶⁴ Kedemoth with its pasturelands, and Mephaath with its pasturelands; ⁶⁵ and out of the tribe of Gad: Ramoth in Gilead with

its pasturelands, Mahanaim with its pasturelands, ⁶⁶ Heshbon with its pasturelands, and Jazer with its pasturelands.

7 The sons of Issachar: Tola, Puah, Jashub, and Shimron— four. ² The sons of Tola: Uzzi, Rephaiah, Jeriel, Jahmai, Ibsam, Shemuel, chiefs of their clans, men of substance according to their lines; their number in the days of David was 22,600. ³ The sons of Uzzi: Izrahiah. And the sons of Izrahiah: Michael, Obadiah, Joel, and Isshiah—five. All of them were chiefs. ⁴ And together with them, by their lines, according to their clans, were units of the fighting force, 36,000, for they had many wives and sons. ⁵ Their kinsmen belonging to all the families of Issachar were in all 87,000 men of substance; they were all registered by genealogy.

⁶ [The sons of] Benjamin: Bela, Becher, and Jediael—three. ⁷ The sons of Bela: Ezbon, Uzzi, Uzziel, Jerimoth, and Iri—five, chiefs of clans, men of substance, registered by genealogy— 22,034 and thirty four. ⁸ The sons of Becher: Zemirah, Joash, Eliezer, Elioenai, Omri, Jeremoth, Abijah, Anathoth, and Alemeth. All these were the sons of Becher; ⁹ and they were registered by genealogy according to their lines, as chiefs of their clans, men of substance—20,200. ¹⁰ The sons of Jediael: Bilhan. And the sons of Bilhan: Jeush, Benjamin, Ehud, Chenaanah, Zethan, Tarshish, and Ahishahar. ¹¹ All these were the sons of Jediael, chiefs of the clans, men of substance—17,200, who made up the fighting force. ¹² And Shuppim and Huppim were the sons of Ir; Hushim the sons of Aher.

¹³ The sons of Naphtali: Jahziel, Guni, Jezer, and Shallum, the descendants of Bilhah.

¹⁴ The sons of Manasseh: Asriel, whom his Aramean concubine bore; she bore Machir the father of Gilead. ¹⁵ And Machir took wives for Huppim and for Shuppim. The name of his sister was Maacah. And the name of the second was Zelophehad; and Zelophehad had daughters. ¹⁶ And Maacah the wife of Machir bore a

son, and she named him Peresh; and the name of his brother was Sheresh; and his sons were Ulam and Rekem. ¹⁷ The sons of Ulam: Bedan. These were the sons of Gilead son of Machir son of Manasseh. ¹⁸ And his sister Hammolecheth bore Ishhod, Abiezer, and Mahlah. ¹⁹ The sons of Shemida were Ahian, Shechem, Likhi, and Aniam.

²⁰ The sons of Ephraim: Shuthelah, his son Bered, his son Tahath, his son Eleadah, his son Tahath, ²¹ his son Zabad, his son Shuthelah, also Ezer and Elead. The men of Gath, born in the land, killed them because they had gone down to take their cattle. ²² And Ephraim their father mourned many days, and his brothers came to comfort him. ²³ He cohabited with his wife, who conceived and bore a son; and she named him Beriah, because it occurred when there was misfortune*a* in his house. ²⁴ His daughter was Sheerah, who built both Lower and Upper Beth-horon, and Uzzen-sheerah. ²⁵ His son Rephah, his son Resheph, his son Telah, his son Tahan, ²⁶ his son Ladan, his son Ammihud, his son Elishama, ²⁷ his son Non, his son Joshua. ²⁸ Their possessions and settlements were Bethel and its dependencies, and on the east Naaran, and on the west Gezer and its dependencies, Shechem and its dependencies, and Aiah and its dependencies; ²⁹ also along the borders of the Manassites, Beth-shean and its dependencies, Taanach and its dependencies, Megiddo and its dependencies, Dor and its dependencies. In these dwelt the sons of Joseph son of Israel.

³⁰ The sons of Asher: Imnah, Ishvah, Ishvi, Beriah, and their sister Serah. ³¹ The sons of Beriah: Ḥeber and Malchiel, who was the father of Birzaith. ³² Heber begot Japhlet, Shomer, Hotham, and their sister Shua. ³³ The sons of Japhlet: Pasach, Bimhal, and Ashvath. These were the sons of Japhlet. ³⁴ The sons of Shemer: Ahi, Rohgah, Hubbah, and Aram. ³⁵ The sons of Helem his brother: Zophah, Imna, Shelesh, and Amal. ³⁶ The sons of Zophah: Suah, Harnepher, Shual, Beri, Imrah, ³⁷ Bezer, Hod, Shamma, Shilshah, Ithran, and Beera. ³⁸ The sons of Jether: Jephunneh, Pispa, and Ara. ³⁹ The sons of Ulla: Arah, Hanniel, and

---

a Heb bera‘ah.

Rizia. 40 All of these men of Asher, chiefs of the clans, select men, men of substance, heads of the chieftains. And they were registered by genealogy according to fighting force; the number of the men was 26,000 men.

8 Benjamin begot Bela his firstborn, Ashbel the second, Aharah the third, 2 Nohah the fourth, and Rapha the fifth. 3 And Bela had sons: Addar, Gera, Abihud, 4 Abishua, Naaman, Ahoah, 5 Gera, Shephuphan, and Huram. 6 These were the sons of Ehud —they were chiefs of clans of the inhabitants of Geba, and they were exiled to Manahath: 7 Naaman, Ahijah, and Gera—he exiled them and begot Uzza and Ahihud. 8 And Shaharaim had sons in the country of Moab after he had sent away Hushim and Baara his wives. 9 He had sons by Hodesh his wife: Jobab, Zibia, Mesha, Malcam, 10 Jeuz, Sachiah, and Mirmah. These were his sons, chiefs of clans. 11 He also begot by Hushim: Abitub and Elpaal. 12 The sons of Elpaal: Eber, Misham, and Shemed, who built Ono and Lod with its dependencies, 13 and Beriah and Shema—they were chiefs of clans of the inhabitants of Aijalon, who put to flight the inhabitants of Gath; 14 and Ahio, Shashak, and Jeremoth. 15 Zebadiah, Arad, Eder, 16 Michael, Ishpah, and Joha were sons of Beriah. 17 Zebadiah, Meshullam, Hizki, Heber, 18 Ishmerai, Izliah, and Jobab were the sons of Elpaal. 19 Jakim, Zichri, Zabdi, 20 Elienai, Zillethai, Eliel, 21 Adaiah, Beraiah, and Shimrath were the sons of Shimei. 22 Ishpan, Eber, Eliel, 23 Abdon, Zichri, Hanan, 24 Hananiah, Elam, Anthothiah, 25 Iphdeiah, and Penuel were the sons of Shashak. 26 Shamsherai, Shehariah, Athaliah, 27 Jaareshiah, Elijah, and Zichri were the sons of Jeroham. 28 These were the chiefs of the clans, according to their lines. These chiefs dwelt in Jerusalem.

29 The father of Gibeon dwelt in Gibeon, and the name of his wife was Maacah. 30 His firstborn son: Abdon; then Zur, Kish, Baal, Nadab, 31 Gedor, Ahio, Zecher. 32 Mikloth begot Shimeah. And they dwelt in Jerusalem opposite their kinsmen, with their

kinsmen. 33 Ner begot Kish, Kish begot Saul, Saul begot Jonathan, Malchi-shua, Abinadab, and Eshbaal; 34 and the son of Jonathan was Merib-baal; and Merib-baal begot Micah. 35 The sons of Micah: Pithon, Melech, Taarea, and Ahaz. 36 Ahaz begot Jehoaddah; and Jehoaddah begot Alemeth, Azmaveth, and Zimri; Zimri begot Moza. 37 Moza begot Binea; his son Eleasah, his son Azel. 38 Azel had six sons, and these are their names: Azrikam, Bocheru, Ishmael, Sheariah, Obadiah, and Hanan. All these were the sons of Azel. 39 The sons of Eshek his brother: Ulam his firstborn, Jeush the second, and Eliphelet the third. 40 The descendants of Ulam—men of substance, who drew the bow, had many children and grandchildren—one hundred and fifty; all these were Benjaminites.

9 All Israel was registered by genealogies; and these are in the book of the kings of Israel. And Judah was taken into exile in Babylon because of their trespass. 2 *a* The first to settle in their towns, on their property, were Israelites, priests, Levites, and temple servants, 3 while some of the Judahites and some of the Benjaminites and some of the Ephraimites and Manassehites settled in Jerusalem; 4 Uthai son of Ammihud son of Omri son of Imri son of Bani, from the sons of Perez son of Judah; 5 and of the Shilonites: Asaiah the firstborn and his sons. 6 Of the sons of Zerah: Jeuel and their kinsmen—690. 7 Of the Benjaminites: Sallu son of Meshullam son of Hodaviah son of Hassenuah, 8 Ibneiah son of Jeroham, Elah son of Uzzi son of Michri, and Meshullam son of Shephatiah son of Reuel son of Ibneiah; 9 and their kinsmen, according to their lines—956. All these were chiefs of their ancestral clans.

10 Of the priests: Jedaiah, Jehoiarib, Jachin, 11 and Azariah son of Hilkiah son of Meshullam son of Zadok son of Meraioth son of Ahitub, chief officer of the House of God; 12 and Adaiah son of Jeroham son of Pashhur son of Malchijah, and Maasai son of Adiel son of Jahzerah son of Meshullam son of Meshillemith son

a With vv. 2–17, cf. Neh. 11.3–19.

of Immer, [13] together with their kinsmen, chiefs of their clans—
1760, men of substance for the work of the service of the House
of God.

[14] Of the Levites: Shemaiah son of Hasshub son of Azrikam son
of Hashabiah, of the sons of Merari; [15] and Bakbakkar, Heresh,
Galal, and Mattaniah son of Mica son of Zichri son of Asaph;
[16] and Obadiah son of Shemaiah son of Galal son of Jeduthun,
and Berechiah son of Asa son of Elkanah, who dwelt in the villages of the Netophathites.

[17] The gatekeepers were: Shallum, Akkub, Talmon, Ahiman;
and their kinsman Shallum was the chief [18] hitherto in the King's
Gate on the east. They were the keepers belonging to the Levite
camp. [19] Shallum son of Kore son of Ebiasaph son of Korah, and
his kinsmen of his clan, the Korahites, were in charge of the work
of the service, guards of the threshold of the Tent; their fathers
had been guards of the entrance to the camp of the LORD. [20] And
Phinehas son of Eleazar was the chief officer over them in time
past; the LORD was with him. [21] Zechariah the son of Meshelemiah
was gatekeeper at the entrance of the Tent of Meeting. [22] All
these, who were selected as gatekeepers at the thresholds, were
212. They were selected by genealogies in their villages. David
and Samuel the seer established them in their office of trust.
[23] They and their descendants were in charge of the gates of the
House of the LORD, that is, the House of the Tent, as guards.
[24] The gatekeepers were on the four sides, east, west, north, and
south; [25] and their kinsmen in their villages were obliged to join
them every seven days, according to a fixed schedule. [26] The four
chief gatekeepers, who were Levites, were entrusted to be over
the chambers and the treasuries of the House of God. [27] They
spent the night near the House of God; for they had to do guard
duty, and they were in charge of opening it every morning.

[28] Some of them had charge of the service vessels, for they were
counted when they were brought back and taken out. [29] Some of
them were in charge of the vessels and all the holy vessels, and
of the flour, wine, oil, incense, and spices. [30] Some of the priests

blended the compound of spices. ³¹ Mattithiah, one of the Levites, the firstborn of Shallum the Korahite, was entrusted with making the flat cakes. ³² Also some of their Kohathite kinsmen had charge of the rows of bread, to prepare them for each sabbath.

³³ Now these are the singers, the chiefs of Levitical clans who remained in the chambers free of other service, for they were on duty day and night. ³⁴ These were chiefs of Levitical clans, according to their lines; these chiefs lived in Jerusalem.

³⁵ The father of Gibeon, Jeiel, lived in Gibeon, and the name of his wife was Maacah. ³⁶ His firstborn son, Abdon; then Zur, Kish, Baal, Ner, Nadab, ³⁷ Gedor, Ahio, Zechariah, and Mikloth; ³⁸ Mikloth begot Shimeam; and they lived in Jerusalem opposite their kinsmen, with their kinsmen. ³⁹ Ner begot Kish, Kish begot Saul, Saul begot Jonathan, Malchi-shua, Abinadab, and Eshbaal; ⁴⁰ and the son of Jonathan was Merib-baal; and Merib-baal begot Micah. ⁴¹ The sons of Micah: Pithon, Melech, Taharea; ⁴² Ahaz begot Jarah, and Jarah begot Alemeth, Azmaveth, and Zimri; Zimri begot Moza. ⁴³ Moza begot Binea; his son was Rephaiah, his son Eleasah, his son Azel. ⁴⁴ Azel had six sons and these were their names: Azrikam, Bocheru, Ishmael, Sheariah, Obadiah, and Hanan. These were the sons of Azel.

10 ᵃ The Philistines attacked Israel, and the men of Israel fled before the Philistines and [many] fell on Mount Gilboa. ² The Philistines pursued Saul and his sons, and the Philistines struck down Jonathan, Abinadab, and Malchi-shua, sons of Saul. ³ The battle raged around Saul, and the archers hit him, and he ᵇwas wounded⁻ᵇ by the archers. ⁴ Saul said to his arms-bearer, "Draw your sword and run me through, so that these uncircumcised may not come and make sport of me." But his arms-bearer, out of great awe, refused; whereupon Saul grasped the sword and fell upon it. ⁵ When the arms-bearer saw that Saul was dead, he too fell on his sword and died. ⁶ Thus Saul and his three sons and his

---

ᵃ With vv. 1–12, cf. I Sam. 31.1–13.
ᵇ⁻ᵇ Meaning of Heb. uncertain.

entire house died together. ⁷ And when all the men of Israel who
were in the valley saw that they^c had fled and that Saul and his
sons were dead, they abandoned their towns and fled; the Philistines then came and occupied them.

⁸ The next day the Philistines came to strip the slain, and they
found Saul and his sons lying on Mount Gilboa. ⁹ They stripped
him, and carried off his head and his armor, and sent them
throughout the land of the Philistines to spread the news to their
idols and among the people. ¹⁰ They placed his armor in the
temple of their god, and they impaled his head in the temple of
Dagan. ¹¹ When all Jabesh-gilead heard everything that the Philistines had done to Saul, ¹² all their stalwart men set out, removed
the bodies of Saul and his sons, and brought them to Jabesh.
They buried the bones under the oak tree in Jabesh, and they
fasted for seven days. ¹³ Saul died for the trespass which he had
committed against the LORD in not having fulfilled the command
of the LORD; moreover, he had consulted a ghost to seek advice,
¹⁴ and did not seek advice of the LORD; so He had him slain and
the kingdom transferred to David son of Jesse.

11 ^aAll Israel gathered to David at Hebron and said, "We are
your own flesh and blood. ² Long before now, even when Saul
was king, you were the leader of Israel; and the LORD your God
said to you: You shall shepherd My people Israel; you shall be
ruler of My people Israel." ³ All the elders of Israel came to the
king at Hebron, and David made a pact with them in Hebron
before the LORD. And they anointed David king over Israel, according to the word of the LORD through Samuel.

⁴ David and all Israel set out for Jerusalem, that is Jebus, where
the Jebusite inhabitants of the land lived. ⁵ David was told by the
inhabitants of Jebus, "You will never get in here!" But David
captured the stronghold of Zion; it is now the City of David.
⁶ David said, "Whoever attacks the Jebusites first will be the chief
officer"; Joab son of Zeruiah attacked first, and became the chief.

^c *I.e. Israel.*

^a *With vv. 1–9, cf. II Sam. 5.1–10, and with vv. 11–41, cf. II Sam. 23.8–39.*

⁷ David occupied the stronghold; therefore it was renamed the City of David. ⁸ David also fortified the surrounding area, from the Millo round about, and Joab rebuilt the rest of the city. ⁹ David kept growing stronger, for the LORD of Hosts was with him.

¹⁰ And these were David's chief warriors who strongly supported him in his kingdom, together with all Israel, to make him king, according to the word of the LORD concerning Israel.

¹¹ This is the list of David's warriors: Jashobeam son of Hachmoni, the chief officer; he wielded his spear against three hundred and slew them all on one occasion. ¹² Next to him was Eleazar son of Dodo, the Ahohite; he was one of the three warriors. ¹³ He was with David at Pas Dammim when the Philistines gathered there for battle. There was a plot of ground full of barley there; the troops had fled from the Philistines, ¹⁴ but they took their stand in the middle of the plot and defended it, and they routed the Philistines. Thus the LORD wrought a great victory.

¹⁵ Three of the thirty chiefs went down to the rock to David, at the cave of Adullam, while a force of Philistines was encamped in the Valley of Rephaim. ¹⁶ David was then in the stronghold, and a Philistine garrison was then at Bethlehem. ¹⁷ David felt a craving and said, "If only I could get a drink of water from the cistern which is by the gate of Bethlehem!" ¹⁸ So the three got through the Philistine camp, and drew water from the cistern which is by the gate of Bethlehem, and they carried it back to David. But David would not drink it, and he poured it out as a libation to the LORD. ¹⁹ For he said, "God forbid that I should do this! Can I drink the blood of these men who risked their lives?" —for they had brought it at the risk of their lives, and he would not drink it. Such were the exploits of the three warriors.

²⁰ Abshai, the brother of Joab, was head of another three. He once wielded his spear against three hundred and slew them. He won a name among the three; ²¹ among the three he was more

highly regarded than the other two, and so he became their commander. However, he did not attain to the other three.

²² Benaiah son of Jehoiada from Kabzeel was a brave soldier who performed great deeds. He killed the two [sons] of Ariel of Moab. Once, on a snowy day, he went down into a pit and killed a lion. ²³ He also killed an Egyptian, a giant of a man five cubits tall. The Egyptian had a spear in his hand, like a weaver's beam, yet [Benaiah] went down against him with a club, wrenched the spear out of the Egyptian's hand, and killed him with his own spear. ²⁴ Such were the exploits of Benaiah son of Jehoiada; and he won a name among the three warriors. ²⁵ He was highly regarded among the thirty, but he did not attain to the three. David put him in charge of his bodyguard.*b*

²⁶ The valiant warriors: Asahel brother of Joab, Elhanan son of Dodo from Bethlehem, ²⁷ Shammoth the Harorite, Helez the Pelonite, ²⁸ Ira son of Ikkesh from Tekoa, Abiezer of Anathoth, ²⁹ Sibbecai the Hushathite, Ilai the Ahohite, ³⁰ Mahrai the Netophathite, Heled son of Baanah the Netophathite, ³¹ Ittai son of Ribai from Gibeah of the Benjaminites, Benaiah of Pirathon, ³² Hurai of Nahale-gaash, Abiel the Arbathite, ³³ Azmaveth the Bahrumite, Eliahba of Shaalbon, ³⁴ the sons of Hashem the Gizonite, Jonathan son of Shageh the Hararite, ³⁵ Ahiam son of Sacar the Hararite, Eliphal son of Ur, ³⁶ Hepher the Mecherathite, Ahijah the Pelonite, ³⁷ Hezro the Carmelite, Naarai son of Ezbai, ³⁸ Joel brother of Nathan, Mibhar son of Hagri, ³⁹ Zelek the Ammonite, Naharai the Berothite—the arms-bearer of Joab son of Zeruiah—⁴⁰ Ira the Ithrite, Gareb the Ithrite, ⁴¹ Uriah the Hittite, Zabad son of Ahlai. ⁴² Adina son of Shiza the Reubenite, a chief of the Reubenites, and thirty with him; ⁴³ Hanan son of Maacah, and Joshaphat the Mithnite; ⁴⁴ Uzziah the Ashterathite, Shama and Jeiel sons of Hotham the Aroerite; ⁴⁵ Jedaiael son of Shimri, and Joha his brother, the Tizite; ⁴⁶ Eliel the Mahavite, and Jeribai and Joshaviah sons of Elnaam, and Ithmah the Moabite; ⁴⁷ Eliel, Obed, and Jaassiel the Mezobaite.

---

b Meaning of Heb. uncertain.

12 The following joined David at Ziklag while he was still in hiding from Saul son of Kish; these were the warriors who gave support in battle; [2] they were armed with the bow and could use both right hand and left hand to sling stones or shoot arrows with the bow; they were kinsmen of Saul from Benjamin. [3] At the head were Ahiezer and Joash, sons of Shemaah of Gibeah; and Jeziel and Pelet, sons of Azmaveth; and Beracah and Jehu of Anathoth; [4] Ishmaiah of Gibeon, a warrior among the thirty, leading the thirty; [5] Jeremiah, Jahaziel, Johanan, and Jozabad of Gederah; [6] Eluzai, Jerimoth, Bealiah, Shemariah, and Shephatiah the Hariphite; [7] Elkanah, Isshiah, Azarel, Joezer, and Jashobeam the Korahites; [8] Joelah and Zebadiah, sons of Jeroham of Gedor.[a] [9] Of the Gadites, there withdrew to follow David to the wilderness stronghold valiant men, fighters fit for battle, armed with shield and spear; they had the appearance of lions, and were as swift as gazelles upon the mountains: [10] Ezer the chief, Obadiah the second, Eliab the third, [11] Mashmannah the fourth, Jeremiah the fifth, [12] Attai the sixth, Eliel the seventh, [13] Johanan the eighth, Elzabad the ninth, [14] Jeremiah the tenth, Machbannai the eleventh. [15] Those were the Gadites, heads of the army. The least was equal to a hundred, the greatest to a thousand. [16] These were the ones who crossed the Jordan in the first month, when it was at its crest, and they put to flight all the lowlanders to the east and west. [17] Some of the Benjaminites and Judahites came to the stronghold to David, [18] and David went out to meet them, saying to them, "If you come on a peaceful errand, to support me, then I will make common cause with you, but if to betray me to my foes, for no injustice on my part, then let the God of our fathers take notice and give judgment." [19] Then the spirit seized Amasai, chief of the captains:

"We are yours, David,
On your side, son of Jesse;
At peace, at peace with you,

[a] *Or, "the troop," reading Heb.* gedud *with several mss.*

And at peace with him who supports you,
For your God supports you."
So David accepted them, and placed them at the head of his band.

20 Some Manassites went over to David's side when he came with the Philistines to make war against Saul, but they were of no help to them, because the lords of the Philistines in council dismissed him, saying, "He will go over to the side of his lord, Saul, and it will cost us our heads"; 21 when he went to Ziklag, these Manassites went over to his side—Adnah, Jozabad, Jediael, Michael, Jozabad, Elihu, and Zillethai, chiefs of the clans of Manasseh.

22 It was they who gave support to David against the band,*b* for all were valiant men; and they were officers of the force.

23 Day in day out, people came to David to give him support, until there was an army as vast as the army of God.

24 These are the numbers of the [men of the] armed bands who joined David at Hebron to transfer Saul's kingdom to him, in accordance with the word of the LORD:

25 Judahites, equipped with shield and spear—6800 armed men; 26 Simeonites, valiant men, fighting troops—7100; 27 of the Levites—4600; 28 Jehoiada, chief officer of the Aaronides; with him, 3700; 29 Zadok, a young valiant man, with his clan—22 officers; 30 of the Benjaminites, kinsmen of Saul, 3000 in their great numbers, hitherto protecting the interests of the house of Saul; 31 of the Ephraimites, 20,800 valiant men, famous in their clans; 32 of the half-tribe of Manasseh, 18,000, who were designated by name to come and make David king; 33 of the Issacharites, men who knew how to interpret the signs of the times, to determine how Israel should act; their chiefs were 200, and all their kinsmen followed them; 34 of Zebulun, those ready for service, able to man a battle line with all kinds of weapons, 50,000, giving support wholeheartedly; 35 of Naphtali, 1000 chieftains with their shields and lances—37,000; 36 Of the Danites, able to man the battle line —28,600; 37 of Asher, those ready for service to man the battle line—40,000; 38 from beyond the Jordan, of the Reubenites, the

b *I.e. the band of Amalekite raiders; cf. I Sam. 30.8,15.*

Gadites, and the half-tribe of Manasseh, together with all kinds of military weapons—120,000.

39 All these, fighting men, manning the battle line with whole heart, came to Hebron to make David king over all Israel. Likewise, all the rest of Israel was of one mind to make David king.

40 They were there with David three days, eating and drinking, for their kinsmen had provided for them.

41 And also, their relatives as far away as Issachar, Zebulun, and Naphtali brought food by ass, camel, mule, and ox—provisions of flour, cakes of figs, raisin-cakes, wine, oil, cattle, and sheep in abundance, for there was joy in Israel.

13 Then David consulted with the officers of the thousands and the hundreds, with every chief officer. 2 David said to the entire assembly of Israel, "If you approve, and if the LORD our God concurs,ᵃ let us send far and wide to our remaining kinsmen throughout the territories of Israel, including the priests and Levites in the towns where they have pasturelands, that they should gather together to us ³ in order to transfer the Ark of our God to us, for throughout the days of Saul we paid no regard to it." 4 The entire assembly agreed to do so, for the proposal pleased all the people. 5 David then assembled all Israel from Shihor of Egypt to Lebo-hamath, in order to bring the Ark of God from Kiriath-jearim. 6 ᵇDavid and all Israel went up to Baalah, Kiriath-jearim of Judah, to bring up from there the Ark of God, the LORD, Enthroned on the Cherubim, to which the Name was attached. 7 They transported the Ark of God on a new cart from the house of Abinadab; Uzza and Ahio guided the cart, 8 and David and all Israel danced before God with all their might—with songs, lyres, harps, timbrels, cymbals, and trumpets. 9 But when they came to the threshing floor of Chidon, Uzza put out his hand to hold the Ark of God because the oxen had stumbled.ᵃ
10 The LORD was incensed at Uzza, and struck him down, because he laid a hand on the Ark; and so he died there before God.

ᵃ Meaning of Heb. uncertain.
ᵇ With vv. 6–14, cf. II Sam. 6.2–11.

¹¹ David was distressed because the LORD ᶜ-had burst out-ᶜ against Uzza; and that place was named Perez-uzzah, as it is still called. ¹² David was afraid of God that day; he said, "How can I bring the Ark of God here?" ¹³ So David did not remove the Ark to his place in the City of David; instead, he diverted it to the house of Obed-edom the Gittite. ¹⁴ The Ark of God remained in the house of Obed-edom, in its own abode, three months, and the LORD blessed the house of Obed-edom and all he had.

14 ᵃKing Hiram of Tyre sent envoys to David with cedar logs, stonemasons, and carpenters to build a palace for him. ² Thus David knew that the LORD had established him as king over Israel, and that his kingship was highly exalted for the sake of His people Israel.

³ David took more wives in Jerusalem, and David begot more sons and daughters. ⁴ These are the names of the children born to him in Jerusalem:ᵇ Shammua, Shobab, Nathan, and Solomon; ⁵ Ibhar, Elishua, and Elpelet; ⁶ Nogah, Nepheg, and Japhia; ⁷ Elishama, Beeliada, and Eliphelet.

⁸ When the Philistines heard that David had been anointed king over all Israel, all the Philistines went up in search of David; but David heard of it, and he went out to them. ⁹ The Philistines came and raided the Valley of Rephaim. ¹⁰ David inquired of God, "Shall I go up against the Philistines? Will You deliver them into my hands?" And the LORD answered him, "Go up, and I will deliver them into your hands." ¹¹ Thereupon David ascended Baal-perazim, and David defeated them there. David said, "God ᶜ-burst out-ᶜ against my enemies by my hands as waters burst out." That is why that place was named Baal-perazim. ¹² They abandoned their gods there, and David ordered these to be burned.

¹³ Once again the Philistines raided the valley. ¹⁴ David inquired of God once more, and God answered, "Do not go up after them, but circle around them and confront them at the *baca*ᵈ

ᶜ⁻ᶜ *Heb.* paraṣ . . . pereṣ.

ᵃ *With vv. 1–16, cf. II Sam. 5.11–25.*
ᵇ *With the list in vv. 4–7, cf. also I Chron. 3.5–8.*
ᶜ⁻ᶜ *Heb.* paraṣ . . . pereṣ.
ᵈ *Meaning of Heb. uncertain.*

trees. [15] And when you hear the sound of marching in the tops of the *baca* trees, then go out to battle, for God will be going in front of you to attack the Philistine forces." [16] David did as God had commanded him; and they routed the Philistines from Gibeon all the way to Gezer. [17] David became famous throughout the lands, and the LORD put the fear of him in all the nations.

15 He had houses made for himself in the City of David, and he prepared a place for the Ark of God, and pitched a tent for it. [2] Then David gave orders that none but the Levites were to carry the Ark of God, for the LORD had chosen them to carry the Ark of the LORD and to minister to Him forever. [3] David assembled all Israel in Jerusalem to bring up the Ark of the LORD to its place, which he had prepared for it. [4] Then David gathered together the Aaronides and the Levites: [5] the sons of Kohath: Uriel the officer and his kinsmen—120; [6] the sons of Merari: Asaiah the officer and his kinsmen—220; [7] the sons of Gershom: Joel the officer and his kinsmen—130; [8] the sons of Elizaphan: Shemaiah the officer and his kinsmen—200; [9] the sons of Hebron: Eliel the officer and his kinsmen—80; [10] the sons of Uzziel: Amminadab the officer and his kinsmen—112.

[11] David sent for Zadok and Abiathar the priests, and for the Levites: Uriel, Asaiah, Joel, Shemaiah, Eliel, and Amminadab. [12] He said to them, "You are the heads of the clans of the Levites; sanctify yourselves, you and your kinsmen, and bring up the Ark of the LORD God of Israel to [the place] I have prepared for it. [13] *a-*Because you were not there the first time,*-a* the LORD our God burst out against us, for we did not show due regard for Him."

[14] The priests and Levites sanctified themselves in order to bring up the Ark of the LORD God of Israel. [15] The Levites carried the Ark of God by means of poles on their shoulders, as Moses had commanded in accordance with the word of the LORD. [16] David ordered the officers of the Levites to install their kins-

---

a-a *Meaning of Heb. uncertain.*

men, the singers, with musical instruments, harps, lyres, and cymbals, joyfully making their voices heard. [17] So the Levites installed Heman son of Joel and, of his kinsmen, Asaph son of Berachiah; and, of the sons of Merari their kinsmen, Ethan son of Kushaiah. [18] Together with them were their kinsmen of second rank, Zechariah, Ben, Jaaziel, Shemiramoth, Jehiel, Unni, Eliab, Benaiah, Maaseiah, Mattithiah, Eliphalehu, Mikneiah, Obed-edom and Jeiel the gatekeepers. [19] Also the singers Heman, Asaph, and Ethan to sound the bronze cymbals, [20] and Zechariah, Aziel, Shemiramoth, Jehiel, Unni, Eliab, Maaseiah, and Benaiah with harps *a*-on *alamoth;*-*a* [21] also Mattithiah, Eliphalehu, Mikneiah, Obed-edom, Jeiel, and Azaziah, with lyres to lead *a*-on the *sheminith;*-*a* [22] also Chenaniah, officer of the Levites in song;*a* he was in charge of the song*a* because he was a master. [23] Berechiah and Elkanah were gatekeepers for the Ark. [24] Shebaniah, Joshaphat, Nethanel, Amasai, Zechariah, Benaiah, and Eliezer the priests sounded the trumpets before the Ark of God, and Obed-edom and Jehiah were gatekeepers for the Ark. [25] *b* Then David and the elders of Israel and the officers of the thousands who were going to bring up the Ark of the Covenant of the LORD from the house of Obed-edom were joyful. [26] Since God helped the Levites who were carrying the Ark of the Covenant of the LORD, they sacrificed seven bulls and seven rams. [27] Now David and all the Levites who were carrying the Ark, and the singers and Chenaniah, officer of song of the singers, *a*-were wrapped-*a* in robes of fine linen, and David wore a linen ephod. [28] All Israel brought up the Ark of the Covenant of the LORD with shouts and with blasts of the horn, with trumpets and cymbals, playing on harps and lyres. [29] As the Ark of the Covenant of the LORD arrived at the City of David, Michal daughter of Saul looked out of the window and saw King David leaping and dancing, and she despised him for it.

[b] *Vv. 25–29 are found also in II Sam. 6.12–16.*

16 *a*They brought in the Ark of God and set it up inside the tent which David had pitched for it, and they sacrificed burnt offerings and offerings of well-being before God. ² When David finished sacrificing the burnt offerings and the offerings of well-being, he blessed the people in the name of the LORD. ³ And he distributed to every person in Israel—man and woman alike—to each a loaf of bread, *b*-a cake made in a pan, and a raisin cake.*-b* ⁴ He appointed Levites to minister before the Ark of the LORD, to invoke, to praise, and to extol the LORD God of Israel: ⁵ Asaph the chief, Zechariah second in rank, Jeiel, Shemiramoth, Jehiel, Mattithiah, Eliab, Benaiah, Obed-edom, and Jeiel, with harps and lyres, and Asaph sounding the cymbals, ⁶ and Benaiah and Jehaziel the priests, with trumpets, regularly before the Ark of the Covenant of God. ⁷ Then, on that day, David first commissioned Asaph and his kinsmen to give praise to the LORD:

⁸ "*c*Praise the LORD;
call on His name;
proclaim His deeds among the peoples.
⁹ Sing praises unto Him;
speak of all His wondrous acts.
¹⁰ Exult in His holy name;
let all who seek the LORD rejoice.
¹¹ Turn to the LORD, to His might;*d*
seek His presence constantly.
¹² Remember the wonders He has done;
His portents and the judgments He has pronounced,
¹³ O offspring of Israel, His servant,
O descendants of Jacob, His chosen ones.
¹⁴ He is the LORD our God;
His judgments are throughout the earth.
¹⁵ Be ever mindful of His covenant,
the promise He gave for a thousand generations,
¹⁶ that He made with Abraham,

ᵃ *With vv. 1–3, cf. II Sam. 6.17–19.*
ᵇ⁻ᵇ *Meaning of Heb. uncertain.*
ᶜ *With vv. 8–22, cf. Ps. 105.1–15.*
ᵈ *I.e. the Ark; cf. Ps. 78.61; 132.8.*

swore to Isaac,

17 and confirmed in a decree for Jacob,

for Israel, as an eternal covenant,

18 saying, 'To you I will give the land of Canaan

as your allotted heritage.'

19 You were then few in number,

a handful, merely sojourning there,

20 wandering from nation to nation,

from one kingdom to another.

21 He allowed no one to oppress them;

He reproved kings on their account,

22 'Do not touch My anointed ones;

do not harm My prophets.'

23 *e*"Sing to the LORD, all the earth.

proclaim His victory day after day.

24 Tell of His glory among the nations,

His wondrous deeds among all peoples.

25 For the LORD is great and much acclaimed,

He is held in awe by all divine beings.

26 All the gods of the peoples are mere idols,

but the LORD made the heavens.

27 Glory and majesty are before Him;

strength and joy are in His place.

28 "Ascribe to the LORD, O families of the peoples,

ascribe to the LORD glory and strength.

29 Ascribe to the LORD the glory of His name,

bring tribute and enter before Him,

bow down to the LORD majestic in holiness.

30 Tremble in His presence, all the earth!

The world stands firm; it cannot be shaken.

31 Let the heavens rejoice and the earth exult;

32 let the sea and all within it thunder,

the fields and everything in them exult;

e With vv. 23-33, cf. Ps. 96.1-13.

³³ then shall all the trees of the forest shout for joy
at the presence of the LORD,
for He is coming to rule the earth.
³⁴ Praise the LORD for He is good;
His steadfast love is eternal.
³⁵ ᶠ⁻Declare:
Deliver us, O God, our deliverer,
and gather us and save us from the nations,
to acclaim Your holy name,
to glory in Your praise.
³⁶ Blessed is the LORD, God of Israel, from eternity to eternity."
And all the people said, "Amen" and "Praise the LORD."ᶠ

³⁷ He left Asaph and his kinsmen there before the Ark of the
Covenant of the LORD to minister before the Ark regularly as
each day required, ³⁸ as well as Obed-edom with their kinsmen—
68; also Obed-edom son of Jedithun and Hosah as gatekeepers;
³⁹ also Zadok the priest and his fellow priests before the Tabernacle of the LORD at the shrine which was in Gibeon; ⁴⁰ to sacrifice
burnt offerings to the LORD on the altar of the burnt offering
regularly, morning and evening, in accordance with what was
prescribed in the Teaching of the LORD with which He charged
Israel. ⁴¹ With them were Heman and Jeduthun and the other
selected men designated by name to give praise to the LORD,
"For His steadfast love is eternal." ⁴² Heman and Jeduthun had
with them trumpets and cymbals to sound, and instruments for
the songs of God; and the sons of Jeduthun were to be at the gate.
⁴³ Then all the people went everyone to his home, and David
returned to greet his household.

17 ᵃWhen David settled in his palace, David said to the prophet
Nathan, "Here I am dwelling in a house of cedar, while the Ark
of the Covenant of the LORD is under tent-cloths." ² Nathan said
to David, "Do whatever you have in mind, for God is with you."
³ But that same night the word of God came to Nathan: ⁴ "Go

ᶠ⁻ᶠ *Cf. Ps. 106.47–48.*

ᵃ *With this chapter, cf. II Sam. 7.*

and say to My servant David: Thus said the LORD: You are not
the one to build a house for Me to dwell in. [5] From the day that
I brought out Israel to this day, I have not dwelt in a house, but
have [gone] from tent to tent and from one Tabernacle [to an-
other]. [6] As I moved about wherever Israel went, did I ever reproach any of the judges of Israel whom I appointed to care for
My people Israel: Why have you not built Me a house of cedar?

[7] "Further, say thus to My servant David: Thus said the LORD
of Hosts: I took you from the pasture, from following the flock,
to be ruler of My people Israel, [8] and I have been with you
wherever you went, and have cut down all your enemies before
you. Moreover, I will give you renown like that of the greatest
men on earth. [9] I will establish a home for My people Israel and
will plant them firm, so that they shall dwell secure and shall
tremble no more. Evil men shall not wear them down any more
as in the past, [10] ever since I appointed judges over My people
Israel. I will subdue all your enemies.

And I declare to you: The LORD will build a house[b] for you.
[11] When your days are done and you follow your fathers, I will
raise up your offspring after you, one of your own sons, and I will
establish his kingship. [12] He shall build a house for Me, and I will
establish his throne forever. [13] I will be a father to him, and he
shall be a son to Me, but I will never withdraw My favor from him
as I withdrew it from your predecessor. [14] I will install him in My
house and in My kingship forever, and his throne shall be established forever."

[15] Nathan spoke to David in accordance with all these words
and all this prophecy. [16] Then King David came and sat before the
LORD, and he said, "What am I, O LORD God, and what is my
family, that You have brought me thus far? [17] Yet even this, O
God, has seemed too little to You; for You have spoken of Your
servant's house for the future. [c]You regard me as a man of
distinction,[-c] O LORD God. [18] What more can David add regarding
the honoring of Your servant? You know Your servant. [19] O
LORD, [c]for Your servant's sake, and of Your own accord,[-c] You

[b] *I.e. a dynasty; play on "house" (i.e. Temple) in v. 4.*
[c-c] *Meaning of Heb. uncertain.*

have wrought this great thing, and made known all these great things. ²⁰ O LORD, there is none like You, and there is no other God but You, as we have always heard. ²¹ And who is like Your people Israel, a unique nation on earth, whom God went and redeemed as His people, winning renown for Yourself for great and marvelous deeds, driving out nations before Your people whom You redeemed from Egypt. ²² You have established Your people Israel as Your very own people forever; and You, O LORD, have become their God.

²³ "And now, O LORD, let Your promise concerning Your servant and his house be fulfilled forever; and do as You have promised. ²⁴ Let it be fulfilled that Your name be glorified forever, in that men will say, 'The LORD of Hosts, God of Israel, is Israel's God'; and may the house of Your servant David be established before You. ²⁵ Because You, my God, have revealed to Your servant that You will build a house for him, Your servant has ventured to pray to You. ²⁶ And now, O LORD, You are God and You have made this gracious promise to Your servant. ²⁷ Now, it has pleased You to bless Your servant's house, that it abide before You forever; for You, O LORD, have blessed and are blessed forever."

18 ᵃSome time afterward, David attacked the Philistines and subdued them; and David took Gath and its dependencies from the Philistines. ² He also defeated the Moabites; the Moabites became tributary vassals of David.

³ David defeated Hadadezer, king of Zobah-hamath, who was on his way to set up his monument at the Euphrates River. ⁴ David captured 1000 chariots and 7000 horsemen and 20,000 foot soldiers of his force; and David hamstrung all the chariot horses except for 100, which he retained. ⁵ And when the Arameans of Damascus came to the aid of King Hadadezer of Zobah-hamath, David struck down 22,000 of the Arameans. ⁶ David stationed [garrisons] in Aram of Damascus, and the Arameans became

ᵃ With this chapter, cf. II Sam. 8.

538

tributary vassals of David. The LORD gave David victory wherever he went. [7] David took the gold shields[b] carried by Hadadezer's retinue and brought them to Jerusalem; [8] and from Tibbath and Cun, towns of Hadadezer, David took a vast amount of copper, from which Solomon made the bronze tank, the columns, and the bronze vessels.

[9] When King Tou of Hamath heard that David had defeated the entire army of King Hadadezer of Zobah, [10] he sent his son Hadoram to King David to greet him and to congratulate him on his military victory over Hadadezer—for Hadadezer had been at war with Tou; [he brought with him] all manner of gold, silver, and copper objects. [11] King David dedicated these to the LORD, along with the other silver and gold that he had taken from all the nations: from Edom, Moab, and Ammon; from the Philistines and the Amalekites.

[12] Abshai son of Zeruiah struck down Edom in the Valley of Salt, 18,000 in all. [13] He stationed garrisons in Edom, and all the Edomites became vassals of David. The LORD gave David victory wherever he went.

[14] David reigned over all Israel, and David executed true justice among all his people. [15] Joab son of Zeruiah was commander of the army; Jehoshaphat son of Ahilud was recorder; [16] Zadok son of Ahitub and Abimelech son of Abiathar were priests; Shavsha was scribe; [17] Benaiah son of Jehoiada was commander of the Cherethites and the Pelethites; and David's sons were first ministers of the king.

19 [a]Some time afterward, Nahash the king of the Ammonites died, and his son succeeded him as king. [2] David said, "I will keep faith with Hanun son of Nahash, since his father kept faith with me." David sent messengers with condolences to him over his father. But when David's courtiers came to the land of Ammon to Hanun, with condolences, [3] the Ammonite officials said to Hanun, "Do you think David is really honoring your father just

[b] Or "quivers."

[a] With this chapter, cf. II Sam. 10.

because he sent you men with condolences? Why, it is to explore, to subvert, and to spy out the land that his courtiers have come to you." 4 So Hanun seized David's courtiers, shaved them, and cut away half of their garments up to the buttocks, and sent them off. 5 When David was told about the men, he dispatched others to meet them, for the men were greatly embarrassed. And the king gave orders, "Stay in Jericho until your beards grow back; then you can return."

6 The Ammonites realized that they had incurred the wrath of David; so Hanun and the Ammonites sent 1000 silver talents to hire chariots and horsemen from Aram-naharaim, Aram-maacah and Zobah. 7 They hired 32,000 chariots, the king of Maacah, and his army, who came and encamped before Medeba. The Ammonites were mobilized from their cities and came to do battle.

8 On learning this, David sent out Joab and the whole army, [including] the professional fighters. 9 The Ammonites marched out and took up their battle position at the entrance of the city, while the kings who came [took their stand] separately in the open. 10 Joab saw that there was a battle line against him both front and rear. So he made a selection from all the picked men of Israel and arrayed them against the Arameans, 11 and the rest of the troops he put under the command of his brother Abishai and arrayed them against the Ammonites. 12 Joab said, "If the Arameans prove too strong for me, you come to my aid; and if the Ammonites prove too strong for you, I will come to your aid. 13 Let us be strong and resolute for the sake of our people and the towns of our God; and the LORD will do what He deems right."

14 Joab and the troops with him marched into battle against the Arameans, who fled before him. 15 And when the Ammonites saw that the Arameans had fled, they too fled before his brother Abishai, and withdrew into the city. So Joab went to Jerusalem.

16 When the Arameans saw that they had been routed by Israel, they sent messengers to bring out the Arameans from across the Euphrates; Shophach, Hadadezer's army commander, led them.

¹⁷ David was informed of it; he assembled all Israel, crossed the Jordan, and came and took up positions against them. David drew up his forces against Aram; and they fought with him. ¹⁸ But the Arameans were put to flight by Israel. David killed 7000 Aramean charioteers and 40,000 footmen; he also killed Shophach, the army commander. ¹⁹ And when all the vassals of Hadadezer saw that they had been routed by Israel, they submitted to David and became his vassals. And the Arameans would not help the Ammonites anymore.

20 ᵃAt the turn of the year, the season when kings go out [to battle], Joab led out the army force and devastated the land of Ammon, and then besieged Rabbah, while David remained in Jerusalem; Joab reduced Rabbah and left it in ruins. ² David took the crown from the head of their king; he found that it weighed a talent of gold, and in it were precious stones. It was placed on David's head. He also carried off a vast amount of booty from the city. ³ He led out the people who lived there and ᵇ-he hacked them-ᵇ with saws and iron threshing boards and axes;ᶜ David did thus to all the towns of Ammon. Then David and all the troops returned to Jerusalem. ⁴ After this, fighting broke out with the Philistines at Gezer; that was when Sibbecai the Hushathite killed Sippai, a descendant of the Rephaim, and they were humbled.

⁵ Again there was fighting with the Philistines, and Elhanan son of Jair killed Lahmi, the brother of Goliath the Gittite; his spear had a shaft like a weaver's beam. ⁶ Once again there was fighting at Gath. There was a giant of a man who had twenty-four fingers [and toes], six [on each hand] and six [on each foot]; he too was descended from the Raphah. ⁷ When he taunted Israel, Jonathan son of David's brother Shimea killed him. ⁸ These were descended from the Raphah in Gath, and they fell by the hands of David and his men.

ᵃ *With vv. 1–3, cf. II Sam. 11.1; 12.30–31.*
ᵇ⁻ᵇ *Meaning of Heb. uncertain. II Sam. 12.31 has "set them to work."*
ᶜ *Heb.* megeroth; *cf. II Sam. 12.31* magzeroth, *"axes."*

21 ᵃSatan arose against Israel and incited David to number Israel. ² David said to Joab and to the commanders of the army, "Go and count Israel from Beer-sheba to Dan and bring me information as to their number." ³ Joab answered, "May the LORD increase His people a hundredfold; my lord king, are they not all subjects of my lord? Why should my lord require this? Why should it be a cause of guilt for Israel?"

⁴ However, the king's command to Joab remained firm, so Joab set out and traversed all Israel; he then came to Jerusalem. ⁵ Joab reported to David the number of the people that had been recorded. All Israel comprised 1,100,000 ready to draw the sword, while in Judah there were 470,000 men ready to draw the sword. ⁶ He did not record among them Levi and Benjamin, because the king's command had become repugnant to Joab. ⁷ God was displeased about this matter and He struck Israel.

⁸ David said to God, "I have sinned grievously in having done this thing; please remit the guilt of Your servant, for I have acted foolishly." ⁹ The LORD ordered Gad, David's seer: ¹⁰ "Go and tell David: Thus said the LORD: I offer you three things; choose one of them and I will bring it upon you." ¹¹ Gad came to David and told him, "Thus said the LORD: Select for yourself ¹² a three-year famine; or that you be swept away three months before your adversaries with the sword of your enemies overtaking you; or three days of the sword of the LORD, pestilence in the land, the angel of the LORD wreaking destruction throughout the territory of Israel. Now consider what reply I shall take back to Him who sent me." ¹³ David said to Gad, "I am in great distress. Let me fall into the hands of the LORD, for His compassion is very great; and let me not fall into the hands of men."

¹⁴ The LORD sent a pestilence upon Israel, and 70,000 men fell in Israel. ¹⁵ God sent an angel to Jerusalem to destroy it, but as he was about to wreak destruction, the LORD saw and renounced further punishment and said to the destroying angel, "Enough!

ᵃ With vv. 1–26, cf. II Sam. 24.

Stay your hand!" The angel of the LORD was then standing by the threshing floor of Ornan the Jebusite. ¹⁶ David looked up and saw the angel of the LORD standing between heaven and earth, with a drawn sword in his hand directed against Jerusalem. David and the elders, covered in sackcloth, threw themselves on their faces. ¹⁷ David said to God, "Was it not I alone who ordered the numbering of the people? I alone am guilty, and have caused severe harm; but these sheep, what have they done? O LORD my God, let Your hand fall upon me and my father's house, and let not Your people be plagued!" ¹⁸ The angel of the LORD told Gad to inform David that David should go and set up an altar to the LORD on the threshing floor of Ornan the Jebusite. ¹⁹ David went up, following Gad's instructions which he had delivered in the name of the LORD. ²⁰ Ornan too saw the angel; his four sons who were with him hid themselves while Ornan kept on threshing wheat. ²¹ David came to Ornan; when Ornan looked up, he saw David and came off the threshing floor and bowed low to David, with his face to the ground. ²² David said to Ornan, "Sell me the site of the threshing floor, that I may build on it an altar to the LORD. Sell it to me at the full price, that the plague against the people will be checked." ²³ Ornan said to David, "Take it and let my lord the king do whatever he sees fit. See, I donate oxen for burnt offerings, and the threshing boards for wood, as well as wheat for a meal offering—I donate all of it." ²⁴ But King David replied to Ornan, "No, I will buy them at the full price. I cannot make a present to the LORD of what belongs to you, or sacrifice a burnt offering that has cost me nothing." ²⁵ So David paid Ornan for the site 600 shekels' worth of gold. ²⁶ And David built there an altar to the LORD and sacrificed burnt offerings and offerings of well-being. He invoked the LORD, who answered him with fire from heaven on the altar of burnt offerings. ²⁷ The LORD ordered the angel to return his sword to its sheath. ²⁸ At that time, when David saw that the LORD answered him at the threshing floor of Ornan the Jebusite, then he sacrificed there—²⁹ for the Tabernacle of the LORD, which Moses had made in the wilderness, and the altar of burnt offerings, were at that time in the shrine at Gibeon, [30] and David was unable to go to it to worship the LORD because he was terrified by the sword of the angel of the LORD.[1] David said, "Here will be the House of the LORD and here the altar of

22 burnt offerings for Israel."

[2] David gave orders to assemble the aliens living in the land of Israel, and assigned them to be hewers, to quarry and dress stones for building the House of God. [3] Much iron for nails for the doors of the gates and for clasps did David lay aside, and so much copper it could not be weighed, [4] and cedar logs without number—for the Sidonians and the Tyrians brought many cedar logs to David.

[5] For David thought, "My son Solomon is an untried youth, and the House to be built for the LORD is to be made exceedingly great to win fame and glory throughout all the lands; let me then lay aside material for him." So David laid aside much material before he died. [6] Then he summoned his son Solomon and charged him with building the House for the LORD God of Israel.

[7] David said to Solomon, "My son, I wanted to build a House for the name of the LORD my God. [8] But the word of the LORD came to me, saying, 'You have shed much blood and fought great battles; you shall not build a House for My name for you have shed much blood on the earth in My sight. [9] But you will have a son who will be a man at rest, for I will give him rest from all his enemies on all sides; Solomon[a] will be his name and I shall confer peace[b] and quiet on Israel in his time. [10] He will build a House for My name; he shall be a son to Me and I to him a father, and I will establish his throne of kingship over Israel forever.' [11] Now, my son, may the LORD be with you, and may you succeed in building the House of the LORD your God as He promised you would. [12] Only let God give you sense and understanding and put you in charge of Israel and the observance of the Teaching of the LORD your God. [13] Then you shall succeed, if you observantly carry out the laws and the rules which the LORD charged Moses to lay upon Israel. Be strong and of good courage; do not be

[a] *Heb.* Shelomoh.
[b] *Heb.* shalom.

afraid or dismayed. [14] See, *by denying myself,* I have laid aside for the House of the LORD one hundred thousand talents of gold and one thousand talents of silver, and so much copper and iron it cannot be weighed; I have also laid aside wood and stone, and you shall add to them. [15] An abundance of workmen is at your disposal—hewers, workers in stone and wood, and every kind of craftsman in every kind of material—[16] gold, silver, copper, and iron without limit. Go and do it, and may the LORD be with you."

[17] David charged all the officers of Israel to support his son Solomon, [18] "See, the LORD your God is with you, and He will give you rest on every side, for He delivered the inhabitants of the land into my hand so that the land lies conquered before the LORD and before His people. [19] Now, set your minds and hearts on worshiping the LORD your God, and go build the Sanctuary of the LORD your God so that you may bring the Ark of the Covenant of the LORD and the holy vessels of God to the house that is built for the name of the LORD."

23 When David reached a ripe old age, he made his son Solomon king over Israel. [2] Then David assembled all the officers of Israel and the priests and the Levites. [3] The Levites, from the age of thirty and upward, were counted; the head-count of their males was 38,000: [4] of these there were 24,000 in charge of the work of the House of the LORD, 6000 officers and magistrates, [5] 4000 gatekeepers, and 4000 for praising the LORD "with instruments I devised for singing praises." [6] David formed them into divisions:

The sons of Levi: Gershon, Kohath, and Merari. [7] The Gershonites: Ladan and Shimei. [8] The sons of Ladan: Jehiel the chief, Zetham, and Joel—3. [9] The sons of Shimei: Shelomith, Haziel, and Haran—3. These were the chiefs of the clans of the Ladanites. [10] And the sons of Shimei: Jahath, Zina, Jeush, and Beriah; these were the sons of Shimei—4. [11] Jahath was the chief and Zizah the second, but Jeush and Beriah did not have many chil-

---

c-c With Targum; or "in my poverty."

dren, so they were enrolled together as a single clan. [12] The sons of Kohath: Amram, Izhar, Hebron, and Uzziel—4. [13] The sons of Amram: Aaron and Moses. Aaron was set apart, he and his sons, forever, to be consecrated as most holy, to make burnt offerings to the LORD and serve Him and pronounce blessings in His name forever. [14] As for Moses, the man of God, his sons were named after the tribe of Levi. [15] The sons of Moses: Gershom and Eliezer. [16] The sons of Gershom: Shebuel the chief. [17] And the sons of Eliezer were: Rehabiah the chief. Eliezer had no other sons, but the sons of Rehabiah were very numerous. [18] The sons of Izhar: Shelomith the chief. [19] The sons of Hebron: Jeriah the chief, Amariah the second, Jahaziel the third, and Jekameam the fourth. [20] The sons of Uzziel: Micah the chief and Isshiah the second. [21] The sons of Merari: Mahli and Mushi. The sons of Mahli: Eleazar and Kish. [22] Eleazar died having no sons but only daughters; the sons of Kish, their kinsmen, married them. [23] The sons of Mushi: Mahli, Eder, and Jeremoth—3.

[24] These are the sons of Levi by clans, with their clan-chiefs as they were enrolled, with a list of their names by heads, who did the work of the service of the House of the LORD from the age of twenty and upward. [25] For David said, "The LORD God of Israel has given rest to His people and made His dwelling in Jerusalem forever. [26] Therefore the Levites need not carry the Tabernacle and all its various service vessels." [27] Among the last acts of David was the counting of the Levites from the age of twenty and upward. [28] For their appointment was alongside the Aaronites for the service of the House of the LORD, to look after the courts and the chambers, and the purity of all the holy things, and the performance of the service of the House of God, [29] and the rows of bread, and the fine flour for the meal offering, and the unleavened wafers, and the cakes made on the griddle and soaked, and every measure of capacity and length; [30] and to be present every morning to praise and extol the LORD, and at evening too, [31] and whenever offerings were made to the LORD, according to the quantities prescribed for them, on sabbaths, new moons and

holidays, regularly, before the LORD; [32] and so to keep watch over the Tent of Meeting, over the holy things, and over the Aaronites their kinsmen, for the service of the House of the LORD.

24

The divisions of the Aaronites were:

The sons of Aaron: Nadab and Abihu, Eleazar and Itha-mar. [2] Nadab and Abihu died in the lifetime of their father, and they had no children, so Eleazar and Ithamar served as priests.

[3] David, Zadok of the sons of Eleazar, and Ahimelech of the sons of Ithamar divided them into offices by their tasks. [4] The sons of Eleazar turned out to be more numerous by male heads than the sons of Ithamar, so they divided the sons of Eleazar into sixteen chiefs of clans and the sons of Ithamar into eight clans. [5] They divided them by lot, both on an equal footing, since they were all Sanctuary officers and officers of God—the sons of Eleazar and the sons of Ithamar. [6] Shemaiah son of Nathanel, the scribe, who was of the Levites, registered them under the eye of the king, the officers, and Zadok the priest, and Ahimelech son of Abiathar, and the chiefs of clans of the priests and Levites— *a*-one clan more taken for Eleazar for each one taken of Ithamar.-*a*

[7] The first lot fell on Jehoiarib; the second on Jedaiah; [8] the third on Harim; the fourth on Seorim; [9] the fifth on Malchijah; the sixth on Mijamin; [10] the seventh on Hakkoz; the eighth on Abijah; [11] the ninth on Jeshua; the tenth on Shecaniah; [12] the eleventh on Eliashib; the twelfth on Jakim; [13] the thirteenth on Huppah; the fourteenth on Jeshebeab; [14] the fifteenth on Bilgah; the sixteenth on Immer; [15] the seventeenth on Hezir; the eighteenth on Happizzez; [16] the nineteenth on Pethahiah; the twentieth on Jehezkel; [17] the twenty-first on Jachin; the twenty-second on Gamul [18] the twenty-third on Delaiah; the twenty-fourth on Maaziah.

[19] According to this allocation of offices by tasks, they were to enter the House of the LORD as was laid down for them by Aaron their father, as the LORD God of Israel had commanded him.

[20] The remaining Levites: the sons of Amram: Shubael; the

a-a *Meaning of Heb. uncertain.*

sons of Shubael: Jehdeiah; ²¹ Rehabiah. The sons of Rehabiah:
Isshiah, the chief. ²² Izharites: Shelomoth. The sons of Shelomoth: Jahath ²³ and Benai, Jeriah; the second, Amariah; the third,
Jahaziel; the fourth, Jekamean. ²⁴ The sons of Uzziel: Micah. The
sons of Micah: Shamir. ²⁵ The brother of Micah: Isshiah. The sons
of Isshiah: Zechariah. ²⁶ The sons of Merari: Mahli and Mushi.
The sons of Jaazaiah, his son ²⁷ —the sons of Merari by Jaazaiah
his son: Shoham, Zakkur, and Ibri. ²⁸ Mahli: Eleazar; he had no
sons. ²⁹ Kish: the sons of Kish: Jerahmeel. ³⁰ The sons of Mushi:
Mahli, Eder, and Jerimoth. These were the sons of the Levites by
their clans.

³¹ These too cast lots corresponding to their kinsmen, the sons
of Aaron, under the eye of King David and Zadok and Ahimelech
and the chiefs of the clans of the priests and Levites, on the
principle of "chief and youngest brother alike."

25

David and the officers of the army set apart for service the
sons of Asaph, of Heman, and of Jeduthun, who prophesied to
the accompaniment of lyres, harps, and cymbals. The list of men
who performed this work, according to their service, was:

² Sons of Asaph: Zaccur, Joseph, Nethaniah, and Asarelah—
sons of Asaph under the charge of Asaph, who prophesied by
order of the king. ³ Jeduthun—the sons of Jeduthun: Gedaliah,
Zeri, Jeshaiah, Hashabiah, Mattithiah—6, under the charge of
their father Jeduthun, who, accompanied on the harp, prophesied, praising and extolling the LORD. ⁴ Heman—the sons of
Heman: Bukkiah, Mattaniah, Uzziel, Shebuel, Jerimoth, Hananiah, Hanani, Eliathah, Giddalti, Romamti-ezer, Joshbekashah,
Mallothi, Hothir, and Mahazioth; ⁵ all these were sons of Heman,
the seer of the king, [who uttered] prophecies of God for His
greater glory. God gave Heman fourteen sons and three daughters; ⁶ all these were under the charge of their father for the
singing in the House of the LORD, to the accompaniment of
cymbals, harps, and lyres, for the service of the House of God by

order of the king. Asaph, Jeduthun, and Heman—7 their total number with their kinsmen, trained singers of the LORD—all the masters, 288.

8 They cast lots for shifts on the principle of "small and great alike, like master like apprentice."

9 The first lot fell to Asaph—to Joseph; the second, to Gedaliah, he and his brothers and his sons—12; 10 the third, to Zaccur: his sons and his brothers—12; 11 the fourth, to Izri: his sons and his brothers—12; 12 the fifth, to Nethaniah: his sons and his brothers—12; 13 the sixth, to Bukkiah: his sons and his brothers —12; 14 the seventh, to Jesarelah: his sons and his brothers—12; 15 the eighth, to Jeshaiah: his sons and his brothers—12; 16 the ninth, to Mattaniah: his sons and his brothers—12; 17 the tenth, to Shimei: his sons and his brothers—12; 18 the eleventh to Azarel; his sons and his brothers—12; 19 the twelfth, to Hashabiah: his sons and his brothers—12; 20 the thirteenth, to Shubael: his sons and his brothers—12; 21 the fourteenth, to Mattithiah: his sons and his brothers—12; 22 the fifteenth, to Jeremoth: his sons and his brothers—12; 23 the sixteenth, to Hananiah: his sons and his brothers—12; 24 the seventeenth, to Joshbekashah: his sons and his brothers—12; 25 the eighteenth, to Hanani: his sons and his brothers—12; 26 the nineteenth, to Mallothi: his sons and his brothers—12; 27 the twentieth, to Eliathah; his sons and his brothers—12; 28 the twenty-first, to Hothir: his sons and his brothers—12; 29 the twenty-second, to Giddalti: his sons and his brothers—12; 30 the twenty-third, to Mahazioth: his sons and his brothers—12; 31 the twenty-fourth, to Romamtiezer: his sons and his brothers—12.

26 The divisions of the gatekeepers: Korahites: Meshelemiah son of Kore, of the sons of Asaph. 2 Sons of Meshelemiah: Zechariah the firstborn, Jediael the second, Zebediah the third, Jathniel the fourth, 3 Elam the fifth, Jehohanan the sixth, Eliehoenai the seventh. 4 Sons of Obed-edom: Shemaiah the firstborn,

Jehozabad the second, Joah the third, Sacar the fourth, Nethanel the fifth, 5 Ammiel the sixth, Issachar the seventh, Peullethai the eighth—for God had blessed him. 6 To his son Shemaiah were born sons who exercised authority in their clans because they were men of substance. 7 The sons of Shemaiah: Othni, Rephael, Obed, Elzabad—his brothers, men of ability, were Elihu and Semachiah. 8 All these, sons of Obed-edom; they and their sons and brothers, strong and able men for the service—62 of Obed-edom. 9 Meshelemiah had sons and brothers, able men—18. 10 Hosah of the Merarites had sons: Shimri the chief (he was not the firstborn, but his father designated him chief), 11 Hilkiah the second, Tebaliah the third, Zechariah the fourth. All the sons and brothers of Hosah—13.

12 These are the divisions of the gatekeepers, by their chief men, [who worked in] shifts corresponding to their kinsmen, ministering in the House of the LORD. 13 They cast lots, small and great alike, by clans, for each gate.

14 The lot for the east [gate] fell to Shelemiah. Then they cast lots [for] Zechariah his son, a prudent counselor, and his lot came out to be the north [gate]. 15 For Obed-edom, the south [gate], and for his sons, the vestibule. 16 For Shuppim and for Hosah, the west [gate], with the Shallecheth gate on the ascending highway. Watch corresponded to watch: 17 At the east—six Levites; at the north—four daily; at the south—four daily; at the vestibule—two by two; 18 at the colonnade on the west—four at the causeway and two at the colonnade. 19 These were the divisions of the gatekeepers of the sons of Korah and the sons of Merari.

20 And the Levites: Ahijah over the treasuries of the House of God and the treasuries of the dedicated things. 21 The sons of Ladan: the sons of the Gershonites belonging to Ladan; the chiefs of the clans of Ladan, the Gershonite—Jehieli. 22 The sons of Jehieli: Zetham and Joel; his brother was over the treasuries of the House of the LORD.

23 Of the Amramites, the Izharites, the Hebronites, the Uzzielites: 24 Shebuel son of Gershom son of Moses was the chief officer

over the treasuries. ²⁵ And his brothers: Eliezer, his son Rehabiah, his son Jeshaiah, his son Joram, his son Zichri, his son
Shelomith—²⁶ that Shelomith and his brothers were over all the
treasuries of dedicated things that were dedicated by King David
and the chiefs of the clans, and the officers of thousands and
hundreds and the other army officers; ²⁷ they dedicated some of
the booty of the wars to maintain the House of the Lord. ²⁸ All
that Samuel the seer had dedicated, and Saul son of Kish, and
Abner son of Ner, and Joab son of Zeruiah—or [what] any other
man had dedicated, was under the charge of Shelomith and his
brothers.

²⁹ The Izharites: Chenaniah and his sons were over Israel as
clerks and magistrates for affairs outside [the Sanctuary]. ³⁰ The
Hebronites: Hashabiah and his brothers, capable men, 1700,
supervising Israel on the west side of the Jordan in all matters of
the Lord and the service of the king. ³¹ The Hebronites: Jeriah,
the chief of the Hebronites—they were investigated in the forti-
eth year of David's reign by clans of all their lines, and men of
substance were found among them in Jazer-gilead. ³² His brothers, able men, 2700, chiefs of clans—David put them in charge
of the Reubenites, the Gadites and the half-tribe of Manasseh in
all matters of God and matters of the king.

27 The number of Israelites—chiefs of clans, officers of thousands and hundreds and their clerks, who served the king in all
matters of the divisions, who worked in monthly shifts during all
the months of the year—each division, 24,000. ² Over the first
division for the first month—Jashobeam son of Zabdiel; his division had 24,000. ³ Of the sons of Perez, he, the chief of all the
officers of the army, [served] for the first month. ⁴ Over the division of the second month—Dodai the Ahohite; Mikloth was chief
officer of his division; his division had 24,000. ⁵ The third army
officer for the third month—Benaiah son of Jehoiada, the chief
priest; his division had 24,000. ⁶ That was Benaiah, one of the

warriors of the thirty and over the thirty; and [over] his division was Ammizabad his son. 7 The fourth, for the fourth month, Asahel brother of Joab, and his son Zebadiah after him; his division had 24,000. 8 The fifth, for the fifth month, the officer Shamhut the Izrahite; his division had 24,000. 9 The sixth, for the sixth month, Ira son of Ikkesh the Tekoite; his division had 24,000. 10 The seventh, for the seventh month, Helez the Pelonite, of the Ephraimites; his division had 24,000. 11 The eighth, for the eighth month, Sibbecai the Hushathite, of Zerah; his division had 24,000. 12 The ninth, for the ninth month, Abiezer the Anathothite, of Benjamin; his division had 24,000. 13 The tenth, for the tenth month, Mahrai the Netophathite, of Zerah; his division had 24,000. 14 The eleventh, for the eleventh month, Menaiah the Pirathonite, of the Ephraimites; his division had 24,000. 15 The twelfth, for the twelfth month, Heldai the Netophathite, of Othniel; his division had 24,000.

16 Over the tribes of Israel: Reuben: the chief officer, Eliezer son of Zichri. Simeon: Shephatiah son of Maaca. 17 Levi: Hashabiah son of Kemuel. Aaron: Zadok. 18 Judah: Elijah, of the brothers of David. Issachar: Omri son of Michael. 19 Zebulun: Ishmaiah son of Obadiah. Naphtali: Jerimoth son of Azriel. 20 Ephraimites: Hoshea son of Azaziah. The half-tribe of Manasseh: Joel son of Pedaiah. 21 Half Manasseh in Gilead: Iddo son of Zechariah. Benjamin: Jaasiel son of Abner. 22 Dan: Azarel son of Jeroham. These were the officers of the tribes of Israel.

23 David did not take a census of those under twenty years of age, for the LORD had promised to make Israel as numerous as the stars of heaven. 24 Joab son of Zeruiah did begin to count them, but he did not finish; wrath struck Israel on account of this, and the census was not entered into the account of the chronicles of King David.

25 Over the royal treasuries: Azmaveth son of Adiel. Over the treasuries in the country—in the towns, the hamlets, and the citadels: Jonathan son of Uzziah. 26 Over the field laborers in agricultural work: Ezri son of Chelub. 27 Over the vineyards: Shi-

mei the Ramathite. And over the produce in the vineyards for wine-cellars: Zabdi the Shiphmite. ²⁸ Over the olive trees and the sycamores in the Shephelah: Baal-hanan the Gederite. Over the oil-stores: Joash. ²⁹ Over the cattle pasturing in Sharon: Shirtai the Sharonite. And over the cattle in the valleys: Shaphat son of Adlai. ³⁰ Over the camels: Obil the Ishmaelite. And over the she-asses: Jehdeiah the Meronothite. ³¹ Over the flocks: Jaziz the Hagrite. All these were stewards of the property of King David. ³² Jonathan, David's uncle, was a counselor, a master, and a scribe: Jehiel son of Hachmoni was with the king's sons. ³³ Ahitophel was a counselor to the king. Hushai the Archite was the king's friend. ³⁴ After Ahitophel were Jehoiada son of Benaiah and Abiathar. The commander of the king's army was Joab.

28 David assembled all the officers of Israel—the tribal officers, the divisional officers who served the king, the captains of thousands and the captains of hundreds, and the stewards of all the property and cattle of the king and his sons, with the eunuchs and the warriors, all the men of substance—to Jerusalem. ² King David rose to his feet and said, "Hear me, my brothers, my people! I wanted to build a resting-place for the Ark of the Covenant of the LORD, for the footstool of our God, and I laid aside material for building. ³ But God said to me, 'You will not build a house for My name, for you are a man of battles and have shed blood.' ⁴ The LORD God of Israel chose me of all my father's house to be king over Israel forever. For He chose Judah to be ruler, and of the family of Judah, my father's house; and of my father's sons, He preferred to make me king over all Israel; ⁵ and of all my sons—for many are the sons the LORD gave me— He chose my son Solomon to sit on the throne of the kingdom of the LORD over Israel. ⁶ He said to me, 'It will be your son Solomon who will build My House and My courts, for I have chosen him to be a son to Me, and I will be a father to him. ⁷ I will establish his kingdom forever, if he keeps firmly to the observance of My commandments and rules as he does now.' [8] And now, in the sight of all Israel, the congregation of the LORD, and in the hearing of our God, [I say:] Observe and apply yourselves to all the commandments of the LORD your God in order that you may possess this good land and bequeath it to your children after you forever.

[9] "And you, my son Solomon, know the God of your father, and serve Him with single mind and fervent heart, for the LORD searches all minds and discerns the design of every thought; if you seek Him He will be available to you, but if you forsake Him He will abandon you forever. [10] See then, the LORD chose you to build a House as the Sanctuary; be strong and do it."

[11] David gave his son Solomon the plan of the porch and its houses, its storerooms and its upper chambers and inner chambers; and of the place of the Ark-cover; [12] and the plan of all that he had by the spirit: of the courts of the House of the LORD and all its surrounding chambers, and of the treasuries of the House of God and of the treasuries of the holy things; [13] the divisions of priests and Levites for all the work of the service of the House of the LORD and all the vessels of the service of the House of the LORD; [14] and gold, the weight of gold for vessels of every sort of use; silver for all the vessels of silver by weight, for all the vessels of every kind of service; [15] the weight of the gold lampstands and their gold lamps, and the weight of the silver lampstands, each lampstand and its silver lamps, according to the use of every lampstand; [16] and the weight of gold for the tables of the rows of bread, for each table, and of silver for the silver tables; [17] and of the pure gold for the forks and the basins and the jars; and the weight of the gold bowls, every bowl; and the weight of the silver bowls, each and every bowl; [18] the weight of refined gold for the incense altar and the gold for the figure of the chariot—the cherubs—those with outspread wings screening the Ark of the Covenant of the LORD. [19] "All this that the LORD made me understand by His hand on me, I give you in writing—the plan of all the works."

²⁰ David said to his son Solomon, "Be strong and of good courage and do it; do not be afraid or dismayed, for the LORD God my God is with you; He will not fail you or forsake you till all the work on the House of the LORD is done. ²¹ Here are the divisions of the priests and Levites for all kinds of service of the House of God, and with you in all the work are willing men, skilled in all sorts of tasks; also the officers and all the people are at your command."

29 King David said to the entire assemblage, "God has chosen my son Solomon alone, an untried lad, although the work to be done is vast—for the temple^a is not for a man but for the LORD God. ² I have spared no effort to lay up for the House of my God gold for golden objects, silver for silver, copper for copper, iron for iron, wood for wooden, onyx-stone and inlay-stone, stone of antimony and variegated colors—every kind of precious stone and much marble. ³ Besides, out of my solicitude for the House of my God, I gave over my private hoard of gold and silver to the House of my God—in addition to all that I laid aside for the holy House: ⁴ 3000 gold talents of Ophir gold, and 7000 talents of refined silver for covering the walls of the houses ⁵ (gold for golden objects, silver for silver for all the work)—into the hands of craftsmen. Now who is going to make a freewill offering and devote himself today to the LORD?"

⁶ The officers of the clans and the officers of the tribes of Israel and the captains of thousands and hundreds and the supervisors of the king's work made freewill offerings, ⁷ giving for the work of the House of God: 5000 talents of gold, 10,000 darics, 10,000 talents of silver, 18,000 talents of copper, 100,000 talents of iron. ⁸ Whoever had stones in his possession gave them to the treasury of the House of the LORD in the charge of Jehiel the Gershonite. ⁹ The people rejoiced over the freewill offerings they made, for with a whole heart they made freewill offerings to the LORD; King David also rejoiced very much.

^a *Lit. "fortress."*

¹⁰ David blessed the LORD in front of all the assemblage; David said, "Blessed are You, LORD, God of Israel our father, from eternity to eternity. ¹¹ Yours, LORD, are greatness, might, splendor, triumph, and majesty—yes, all that is in heaven and on earth; to You, LORD, belong kingship and preeminence above all. ¹² Riches and honor are Yours to dispense; You have dominion over all; with You are strength and might, and it is in Your power to make anyone great and strong. ¹³ Now, God, we praise You and extol Your glorious name. ¹⁴ Who am I and who are my people, that we should have the means to make such a freewill offering; but all is from You, and it is Your gift that we have given to You. ¹⁵ For we are sojourners with You, mere transients like our fathers; our days on earth are like a shadow, with nothing in prospect. ¹⁶ O LORD our God, all this great mass that we have laid aside to build You a House for Your holy name is from You, and it is all Yours. ¹⁷ I know, God, that You search the heart and desire uprightness; I, with upright heart, freely offered all these things; now Your people, who are present here—I saw them joyously making freewill offerings. ¹⁸ O LORD God of Abraham, Isaac, and Israel, our fathers, remember this to the eternal credit of the thoughts of Your people's hearts, and make their hearts constant toward You. ¹⁹ As to my son Solomon, give him a whole heart to observe Your commandments, Your admonitions, and Your laws, and to fulfill them all, and to build this temple*a* for which I have made provision."

²⁰ David said to the whole assemblage, "Now bless the LORD your God." All the assemblage blessed the LORD God of their fathers, and bowed their heads low to the LORD and the king. ²¹ They offered sacrifices to the LORD and made burnt offerings to the LORD on the morrow of that day: 1000 bulls, 1000 rams, 1000 lambs, with their libations; [they made] sacrifices in great number for all Israel, ²² and they ate and drank in the presence of the LORD on that day with great joy. They again proclaimed Solomon son of David king, and they anointed him as ruler before the LORD, and Zadok as high priest. ²³ Solomon successfully

---

ª *Lit. "fortress."*

took over the throne of the LORD as king instead of his father David, and all went well with him. All Israel accepted him; 24 all the officials and the warriors, and the sons of King David as well, gave their hand in support of King Solomon. 25 The LORD made Solomon exceedingly great in the eyes of all Israel, and endowed him with a regal majesty that no king of Israel before him ever had.

26 Thus David son of Jesse reigned over all Israel; 27 the length of his reign over Israel was 40 years: he reigned 7 years in Hebron and 33 years in Jerusalem. 28 He died at a ripe old age, having enjoyed long life, riches and honor, and his son Solomon reigned in his stead. 29 The acts of King David, early and late, are recorded in the history of Samuel the seer, the history of Nathan the prophet, and the history of Gad the seer, 30 together with all the mighty deeds of his kingship and the events that befell him and Israel and all the kingdoms of the earth.

דברי הימים ב

II CHRONICLES

דברי הימים ב
II CHRONICLES

1 [a]Solomon son of David took firm hold of his kingdom, for the LORD his God was with him and made him exceedingly great. [2] Solomon summoned all Israel—the officers of thousands and of hundreds, and the judges, and all the chiefs of all Israel, the heads of the clans. [3] Then Solomon, and all the assemblage with him, went to the shrine at Gibeon, for the Tent of Meeting, which Moses the servant of the LORD had made in the wilderness, was there. ([4] But the Ark of God David had brought up from Kiriath-jearim to the place which David had prepared for it; for he had pitched a tent for it in Jerusalem.) [5] The bronze altar, which Bezalel son of Uri son of Hur had made, was also there before the Tabernacle of the LORD, and Solomon and the assemblage resorted to it. [6] There Solomon ascended the bronze altar before the LORD, which was at the Tent of Meeting, and on it sacrificed a thousand burnt offerings.

[7] That night, the LORD appeared to Solomon and said to him, "Ask, what shall I grant you?" [8] Solomon said to God, "You dealt most graciously with my father David, and now You have made me king in his stead. [9] Now, O LORD God, let Your promise to my father David be fulfilled; for You have made me king over a people as numerous as the dust of the earth. [10] Grant me then the wisdom and the knowledge [b]-to lead this people,-[b] for who can govern Your great people?" [11] God said to Solomon, "Because you want this, and have not asked for wealth, property, and glory, nor have you asked for the life of your enemy, or long life for yourself, but you have asked for the wisdom and the knowledge to be able to govern My people over whom I have made you king,

---

[a] *With vv. 3–13, cf. I Kings 3.4–15; with vv. 14–17, cf. I Kings 10.26–29.*
[b-b] *Lit. "that I may go out before this people and come in."*

[12] wisdom and knowledge are granted to you, and I grant you also wealth, property, and glory, the like of which no king before you has had, nor shall any after you have." [13] From the shrine at Gibeon, from the Tent of Meeting, Solomon went to Jerusalem and reigned over Israel.

[14] Solomon assembled chariots and horsemen; he had 1400 chariots and 12,000 horses that he stationed in the chariot towns and with the king in Jerusalem. [15] The king made silver and gold as plentiful in Jerusalem as stones, and cedars as plentiful as the sycamores in the Shephelah. [16] Solomon's horses were imported from Egypt and from Que; the king's traders would buy them from Que at the market price. [17] A chariot imported from Egypt cost 600 shekels of silver, and a horse 150. These in turn were exported by them[c] to all the kings of the Hittites and the kings of the Arameans.

[18] Then Solomon resolved to build a House for the name of the
2 Lord and a royal palace for himself.

[a]Solomon mustered 70,000 basket carriers and 80,000 quarriers in the hills, with 3600 men supervising them. [2] Solomon sent this message to King Huram of Tyre, "In view of what you did for my father David in sending him cedars to build a palace for his residence—[3] see, I intend to build a House for the name of the Lord my God; I will dedicate it to Him for making incense offering of sweet spices in His honor, for the regular rows of bread, and for the morning and evening burnt offerings on sabbaths, new moons, and festivals, as is Israel's eternal duty. [4] The House that I intend to build will be great, inasmuch as our God is greater than all gods. [5] Who indeed is capable of building a House for Him! Even the heavens to their uttermost reaches cannot contain Him, and who am I that I should build Him a House—except as a place for making burnt offerings to Him? [6] Now send me a craftsman to work in gold, silver, bronze, and iron, and in purple, crimson, and blue yarn, and who knows how to engrave, alongside the craftsmen I have here in Judah and in

[c] *That is, Solomon's dealers.*

[a] *Cf. I Kings 5.*

Jerusalem, whom my father David provided. [7] Send me cedars, cypress, and algum wood from the Lebanon, for I know that your servants are skilled at cutting the trees of Lebanon. My servants will work with yours [8] to provide me with a great stock of timber; for the House which I intend to build will be singularly great. [9] I have allocated for your servants, the wood-cutters who fell the trees, 20,000 kor of crushed wheat and 20,000 kor of barley, 20,000 bath of wine and 20,000 bath of oil."

[10] Huram, king of Tyre, sent Solomon this written message in reply, "Because the LORD loved His people, He made you king over them."

[11] Huram continued, "Blessed is the LORD, God of Israel, who made the heavens and the earth, who gave King David a wise son, endowed with intelligence and understanding, to build a House for the LORD and a royal palace for himself. [12] Now I am sending you a skillful and intelligent man, my master[b] Huram,[13] the son of a Danite woman, his father a Tyrian. He is skilled at working in gold, bronze, iron, precious stones, and wood; in purple, blue, and crimson yarn and in fine linen; and at engraving and designing whatever will be required of him, alongside your craftsmen and the craftsmen of my lord, your father David. [14] As to the wheat, barley, oil, and wine which my lord mentioned, let him send them to his servants. [15] We undertake to cut down as many trees of Lebanon as you need, and deliver them to you as rafts by sea to Jaffa; you will transport them to Jerusalem."

[16] Solomon took a census of all the aliens who were in the land of Israel, besides the census taken by his father David, and they were found to be 153,600. [17] He made 70,000 of them basket carriers, and 80,000 of them quarriers, with 3600 supervisors to see that the people worked.

3 [a]Then Solomon began to build the House of the LORD in Jerusalem on Mount Moriah, where [the LORD] had appeared to his father David, at the place which David had designated, at the

[b] Lit. "my father."

[a] With vv. 2–17, cf. I Kings 6, 7.1–22.

threshing floor of Ornan the Jebusite. ² He began to build on the second day of the second month of the fourth year of his reign. ³ These were the dimensions Solomon established for building the House of God: its length in cubits, by the former measure, was 60, and its breadth was 20. ⁴ The length of the porch in front [was equal] to the breadth of the House—20 cubits, and its height was 120. Inside he overlaid it with pure gold. ⁵ The House itself he paneled with cypress wood. He overlaid it with fine gold and embossed on it palms and chains. ⁶ He studded the House with precious stones for decoration; the gold was from Parvaim. ⁷ He overlaid the House with gold—the beams, the thresholds, its walls and doors; he carved cherubim on the walls. ⁸ He made the Holy of Holies: its length was [equal to] the breadth of the house —20 cubits, and its breadth was 20 cubits. He overlaid it with 600 talents of fine gold. ⁹ The weight of the nails was 50 shekels of gold; the upper chambers he overlaid with gold. ¹⁰ He made two sculptured cherubim in the Holy of Holies, and they were overlaid with gold. ¹¹ The outspread wings of the cherubim were 20 cubits across: one wing five cubits long touching one wall of the House, and the other wing five cubits long touching the wing of the other cherub; ¹² one wing of the other [cherub] five cubits long extending to the other wall of the House, and its other wing five cubits long touching the wing of the first cherub. ¹³ The wingspread of these cherubim was thus 20 cubits across, and they were standing up facing the House. ¹⁴ He made the curtain of blue, purple, and crimson yarn and fine linen, and he worked cherubim into it. ¹⁵ At the front of the House he made two columns 35 cubits high; the capitals*^b* on top of them were five cubits high. ¹⁶ He made chainwork in the inner Sanctuary and set it on the top of the columns; he made a hundred pomegranates and set them into the chainwork. ¹⁷ He erected the columns in front of the Great Hall, one to its right and one to its left; the one to the right was called Jachin, and the one to the left, Boaz.

^b *Meaning of Heb. uncertain.*

4 [a]He made an altar of bronze 20 cubits long, 20 cubits wide, and 20 cubits high.

2 He made the sea[b] of cast metal ten cubits across from brim to brim, perfectly round; it was five cubits high, and its circumference was 30 cubits. 3 Beneath were figures of oxen set all around it, of ten cubits, encircling the sea; the oxen were in two rows, cast in one piece with it. 4 It stood upon 12 oxen: three faced north, three faced west, three faced south, and three faced east, with the sea resting upon them; their haunches were all turned inward. 5 It was a handbreadth thick, and its brim was made like that of a cup, like the petals of a lily. It held 3,000 bath.

6 He made ten bronze lavers for washing; he set five on the right and five on the left; they would rinse off in them the parts of the burnt offering; but the sea served the priests for washing. 7 He made ten lampstands of gold as prescribed, and placed them in the Great Hall, five on the right and five on the left. 8 He made ten tables and placed them in the Great Hall, five on the right and five on the left. He made one hundred gold basins. 9 He built the court of the priests and the great court, and doors for the great court; he overlaid the doors with bronze. 10 He set the sea on the right side, at the southeast corner.

11 Huram made the pails, the shovels, and the basins. With that Huram completed the work he had undertaken for King Solomon in the House of God: 12 the two columns, the globes, and the two capitals on top of the columns; and the two pieces of network to cover the two globes of the capitals on top of the columns; 13 the 400 pomegranates for the two pieces of network, two rows of pomegranates for each network, to cover the two globes of the capitals on top of the columns; 14 he made the stands and the lavers upon the stands; 15 one sea with the twelve oxen beneath it; 16 the pails, the shovels, and the bowls.[c] And all the vessels made for King Solomon for the House of the LORD by Huram his master were of burnished bronze. 17 The king had them cast in

[a] Cf. I Kings 7.23–50.
[b] I.e. a large basin.
[c] Or "forks."

molds dug out of the earth, in the plain of the Jordan between Succoth and Zeredah. 18 Solomon made a very large number of vessels; the weight of the bronze used could not be reckoned. 19 And Solomon made all the furnishings that were in the House of God: the altar of gold; the tables for the bread of display; 20 the lampstands and their lamps, to burn as prescribed in front of the inner Sanctuary, of solid gold; 21 and the petals, lamps, and tongs, of purest gold; 22 the snuffers, basins, ladles, and fire pans, of solid gold; and the entrance to the House: the doors of the innermost part of the House, the Holy of Holies, and the doors of the Great Hall of the House, of gold.

5 *a*When all the work that King Solomon undertook for the House of the LORD was completed, Solomon brought the things that his father David had consecrated—the silver, the gold, and the utensils—and deposited them in the treasury of the House of God.

2 Then Solomon convoked the elders of Israel—all the heads of the tribes and the ancestral chiefs of the Israelites—in Jerusalem, to bring up the Ark of the Covenant of the LORD from the City of David, that is, Zion.

3 All the men of Israel assembled before the king at the Feast,*b* in the seventh month. 4 When all the elders of Israel had come, the Levites carried the Ark. 5 They brought up the Ark and the Tent of Meeting and all the holy vessels that were in the Tent— the Levite priests brought them up. 6 Meanwhile, King Solomon and the whole community of Israel, who had gathered to him before the Ark, were sacrificing sheep and oxen in such abundance that they could not be numbered or counted.

7 The priests brought the Ark of the LORD's Covenant to its place in the inner Sanctuary of the House, in the Holy of Holies, beneath the wings of the cherubim; 8 for the cherubim had their wings spread out over the place of the Ark so that the cherubim covered the Ark and its poles from above. 9 The poles projected

---

a Cf. I Kings 7.51–8.11.
b I.e. of Tabernacles.

beyond the Ark and the ends of the poles were visible from the front of the inner Sanctuary, but they could not be seen from the outside; and there they remain to this day. ¹⁰ There was nothing inside the Ark but the two tablets which Moses placed [there] at Horeb, when the LORD made [a Covenant] with the Israelites after their departure from Egypt. ¹¹ When the priests came out of the Sanctuary—all the priests present had sanctified themselves, without keeping to the set divisions—¹² all the Levite singers, Asaph, Heman, Jeduthun, their sons and their brothers, dressed in fine linen, holding cymbals, harps, and lyres, were standing to the east of the altar, and with them were 120 priests who blew trumpets. ¹³ The trumpeters and the singers joined in unison to praise and extol the LORD; and as the sound of the trumpets, cymbals, and other musical instruments, and the praise of the LORD, "For He is good, for His steadfast love is eternal," grew louder, the House, the House of the LORD, was filled with a cloud. ¹⁴ The priests could not stay and perform the service because of the cloud, for the glory of the LORD filled the House of God.

6 ^aThen Solomon declared:
>"The LORD has chosen
>To abide in a thick cloud;
>² I have built for You
>A stately House,
>And a place where You
>May dwell forever."

³ Then, as the whole congregation of Israel stood, the king turned and blessed the whole congregation of Israel. ⁴ He said, "Blessed is the LORD God of Israel, ^bwho made a promise to my father David and fulfilled it.^{-b} For He said, ⁵ 'From the time I brought My people out of the land of Egypt, I never chose a city from among all the tribes of Israel to build a House where My name might abide; nor did I choose anyone to be the leader of

---

^a Cf. I. Kings 8.12–53.
^{b-b} Lit. "who spoke with His own mouth a promise to my father David and has fulfilled with His own hands."

my people Israel. [6] But then I chose Jerusalem for My name to abide there, and I chose David to rule My people Israel.'

[7] "Now my father David had wanted to build a House for the name of the Lord God of Israel. [8] But the Lord said to my father David, 'As for your wanting to build a House for My name, you do well to want that. [9] However, you shall not build the House; your son, the issue of your loins, he shall build the House for My name.' [10] Now the Lord has fulfilled the promise that He made. I have succeeded[c] my father David and have ascended the throne of Israel, as the Lord promised. I have built the House for the name of the Lord God of Israel, [11] and there I have set the Ark containing the Covenant which the Lord made with the Israelites."

[12] Then, standing before the altar of the Lord in front of the whole congregation of Israel, he spread forth his hands. [13] Solomon had made a bronze platform[d] and placed it in the midst of the Great Court; it was five cubits long and five cubits wide and three cubits high. He stood on it; then, kneeling in front of the whole congregation of Israel, he spread forth his hands to heaven [14] and said, "O Lord God of Israel, there is no god like You in the heavens and on the earth, You who steadfastly maintain the Covenant with Your servants who walk before You with all their heart; [15] You who have kept the promises You made to Your servant, my father David; You made a promise and have fulfilled it—as is now the case. [16] And now, O Lord God of Israel, keep that promise that You made to Your servant, my father David, 'You shall never lack a descendant in My sight sitting on the throne of Israel if only your children will look to their way and walk in the [path] of My teachings as you have walked before Me.' [17] Now, therefore, O God of Israel, let the promise that You made to Your servant, my father David, be confirmed.

[18] "Does God really dwell with man on earth? Even the heavens to their uttermost reaches cannot contain You, how much less this House that I have built! [19] Yet turn, O Lord my God, to the prayer and supplication of Your servant, and hear the cry and the

[c] *Lit. "risen in place of."*
[d] *Meaning of Heb. uncertain.*

prayer which Your servant offers to You. ²⁰ May Your eyes be open day and night toward this House, toward the place where You have resolved to make Your name abide; may You heed the prayers which Your servant offers toward this place. ²¹ And when You hear the supplications which Your servant and Your people Israel offer toward this place, give heed in Your heavenly abode—give heed and pardon.

²² "If a man commits an offense against his fellow, and an oath is exacted from him, causing him to utter an imprecation against himself, and he comes with his imprecation before Your altar in this House, ²³ may You hear in heaven and take action to judge Your servants, requiting him who is in the wrong by bringing down the punishment of his conduct on his head, vindicating him who is in the right by rewarding him according to his righteousness.

²⁴ "Should Your people Israel be defeated by an enemy because they have sinned against You, and then once again acknowledge Your name and offer prayer and supplication to You in this House, ²⁵ may You hear in heaven and pardon the sin of Your people Israel, and restore them to the land that You gave to them and to their fathers.

²⁶ "Should the heavens be shut up and there be no rain because they have sinned against You, and then they pray toward this place and acknowledge Your name and repent of their sins, because You humbled them, ²⁷ may You hear in heaven and pardon the sin of Your servants, Your people Israel, when You have shown them the proper way in which they are to walk, and send down rain upon the land which You gave to Your people as their heritage. ²⁸ So, too, if there is a famine in the land, if there is pestilence, blight, mildew, locusts, or caterpillars, or if an enemy oppresses them in any of the settlements of their land.

"In any plague and in any disease, ²⁹ any prayer or supplication offered by any person among all Your people Israel—each of whom knows his affliction and his pain—when he spreads forth his hands toward this House, ³⁰ may You hear in Your heavenly abode, and pardon. Deal with each man according to his ways as You know his heart to be—for You alone know the hearts of all men—[31] so that they may revere You all the days that they live on the land that You gave to our fathers.

[32] "Or if a foreigner who is not of Your people Israel comes from a distant land for the sake of Your great name, Your mighty hand, and Your outstretched arm, if he comes to pray toward this House, [33] may You hear in Your heavenly abode and grant whatever the foreigner appeals to You for. Thus all the peoples of the earth will know Your name and revere You, as does Your people Israel; and they will recognize that Your name is attached to this House that I have built.

[34] "When Your people take the field against their enemies in a campaign on which You send them, and they pray to You in the direction of the city which You have chosen and the House which I have built to Your name, [35] may You hear in heaven their prayer and supplication and uphold their cause.

[36] "When they sin against You—for there is no person who does not sin—and You are angry with them and deliver them to the enemy, and their captors carry them off to an enemy land, near or far; [37] and they take it to heart in the land to which they have been carried off, and repent and make supplication to You in the land of their captivity, saying, 'We have sinned, we have acted perversely, we have acted wickedly,' [38] and they turn back to You with all their heart and soul, in the land of their captivity where they were carried off, and pray in the direction of their land which You gave to their fathers and the city which You have chosen, and toward the House which I have built for Your name— [39] may You hear their prayer and supplication in Your heavenly abode, uphold their cause, and pardon Your people who have sinned against You. [40] Now My God, may Your eyes be open and Your ears attentive to prayer from this place, and now,

[41] Advance, O Lord God, to your resting-place,
You and Your mighty Ark.
Your priests, O Lord God, are clothed in triumph;

Your loyal ones will rejoice in [Your] goodness.
42 O LORD God,
do not reject Your anointed one;
remember the loyalty of Your servant David."

7 *a*When Solomon finished praying, fire descended from heaven and consumed the burnt offering and the sacrifices, and the glory of the LORD filled the House. 2 The priests could not enter the House of the LORD, for the glory of the LORD filled the House of the LORD. 3 All the Israelites witnessed the descent of the fire and the glory of the LORD on the House; they knelt with their faces to the ground and prostrated themselves, praising the LORD, "For He is good, for His steadfast love is eternal."

4 Then the king and all the people offered sacrifices before the LORD. 5 King Solomon offered as sacrifices 22,000 oxen and 120,000 sheep; thus the king and all the people dedicated the House of God. 6 The priests stood at their watches; the Levites with the instruments for the LORD's music which King David had made to praise the LORD, "For His steadfast love is eternal," by means of the psalms of David that they knew. The priests opposite them blew trumpets while all Israel were standing.

7 Solomon consecrated the center of the court in front of the House of the LORD, because he presented there the burnt offerings and the fat parts of the offerings of well-being, since the bronze altar that Solomon had made was not able to hold the burnt offerings, the meal offerings, and the fat parts. 8 At that time Solomon kept the Feast for seven days—all Israel with him —a great assemblage from Lebo-hamath to the Wadi of Egypt.

9 On the eighth day they held a solemn gathering; they observed the dedication of the altar seven days, and the Feast seven days. 10 On the twenty-third day of the seventh month he dismissed the people to their homes, rejoicing and in good spirits over the goodness that the LORD had shown to David and Solomon and His people Israel.

a Cf. I Kings 8.54–9.9.

¹¹ Thus Solomon finished building the House of the LORD and the royal palace; Solomon succeeded in everything he had set his heart on accomplishing with regard to the House of the LORD and his palace. ¹² The LORD appeared to Solomon at night and said to him, "I have heard your prayer and have chosen this site as My House of sacrifice. ¹³ If I shut up the heavens and there is no rain; if I command the locusts to ravage the land; or if I let loose pestilence against My people, ¹⁴ when My people, who bear My name, humble themselves, pray, and seek My favor and turn from their evil ways, I will hear in My heavenly abode and forgive their sins and heal their land. ¹⁵ Now My eyes will be open and My ears attentive to the prayers from this place. ¹⁶ And now I have chosen and consecrated this House that My name be there forever. My eyes and My heart shall always be there. ¹⁷ As for you, if you walk before Me as your father David walked before Me, doing all that I have commanded you, keeping My laws and rules, ¹⁸ then I will establish your royal throne over Israel forever, in accordance with the Covenant I made with your father David, saying, 'You shall never lack a descendant ruling over Israel.' ¹⁹ But if you turn away from Me and forsake My laws and commandments which I set before you, and go and serve other gods and worship them, ²⁰ then I will uproot them*b* from My land which I gave them, and this House which I consecrated to My name I shall cast out of my sight, and make it a proverb and a byword among all peoples. ²¹ And as for this House, once so exalted, everyone passing by it shall be appalled and say, 'Why did the LORD do thus to this land and to this House?' ²² And the reply will be, 'It is because they forsook the LORD God of their fathers who freed them from the land of Egypt, and adopted other gods and worshiped them and served them; therefore He brought all this calamity upon them.' "

ᵇ *I.e. Israel; cf. I Kings 9.7.*

8 *a*At the end of twenty years, during which Solomon con-structed the House of the LORD and his palace—*2* Solomon also rebuilt the cities that Huram had given to him,*b* and settled Israel-ites in them—*3* Solomon marched against Hamath-zobah and overpowered it. *4* He built Tadmor in the desert and all the garri-son towns which he built in Hamath. *5* He built Upper Beth-horon and Lower Beth-horon as fortified cities with walls, gates, and bars, *6* as well as Baalath and all of Solomon's garrison towns, chariot towns, and cavalry towns—everything that Solomon desired to build in Jerusalem and in the Lebanon, and through-out the territory that he ruled. *7* All the people that were left of the Hittites, Amorites, Perizzites, Hivites, and Jebusites, none of whom were of Israelite stock—*8* those of their descendants who were left after them in the land, whom the Israelites had not annihilated—these Solomon subjected to forced labor, as is still the case. *9* But the Israelites, none of whom Solomon enslaved for his works, served as soldiers and as his chief officers, and as commanders of his chariotry and cavalry. *10* These were King Solomon's prefects—250 foremen over the people. *11* Solomon brought up Pharaoh's daughter from the City of David to the palace which he had built for her, for he said, "No wife of mine shall dwell in a palace of King David of Israel, for [the area] is sacred since the Ark of the LORD has entered it."

12 At that time, Solomon offered burnt offerings on the altar which he had built in front of the porch. *13* What was due for each day he sacrificed according to the commandment of Moses for the sabbaths, the new moons, and the thrice-yearly festivals—the Feast of Unleavened Bread, the Feast of Weeks, and the Feast of Booths. *14* Following the prescription of his father David, he set up the divisions of the priests for their duties, and the Levites for their watches, to praise and to serve alongside the priests, accord-ing to each day's requirement, and the gatekeepers in their watches, gate by gate, for such was the commandment of David,

a Cf. I Kings 9.10–28.
b Lit. "Solomon."

the man of God. [15] They did not depart from the commandment of the king relating to the priests and the Levites in all these matters and also relating to the treasuries. [16] And all of Solomon's work was well executed from the day the House of the LORD was founded until the House of the LORD was completed to perfection.

[17] At that time Solomon went to Ezion-geber and to Eloth on the seacoast of the land of Edom. [18] Huram sent him, under the charge of servants, a fleet with a crew of expert seamen; they went with Solomon's men to Ophir, and obtained gold there in the amount of 450 talents, which they brought to King Solomon.

9 [a]The queen of Sheba heard of Solomon's fame, and came to Jerusalem to test Solomon with hard questions, accompanied by a very large retinue, including camels bearing spices, a great quantity of gold, and precious stones. When she came to Solomon, she spoke to him of all that she had on her mind. [2] Solomon had answers for all her questions; there was nothing that Solomon did not know, nothing to which he could not give her an answer.

[3] When the queen of Sheba saw how wise Solomon was and the palace he had built, [4] the fare of his table, the seating of his courtiers, the service and attire of his attendants, his butlers and their attire, and the procession with which he went up to the House of the LORD, it took her breath away. [5] She said to the king, "What I heard in my own land about you and your wisdom was true. [6] I did not believe what they said until I came and saw with my own eyes that not even the half of your great wisdom had been described to me; you surpass the report that I heard. [7] How fortunate are your men and how fortunate are these courtiers of yours who are always in attendance on you and can hear your wisdom! [8] Blessed is the LORD your God, who favored you and set you on His throne as a king before the LORD. It is because of your God's love for Israel and in order to establish them forever

[a] *Cf. I. Kings 10, 11.41–43.*

that He made you king over them to execute righteous justice."

⁹ She presented the king with 120 talents of gold, and a vast quantity of spices and precious stones. There were no such spices as those which the queen of Sheba gave to King Solomon— ¹⁰ also, the servants of Huram and Solomon who brought gold from Ophir brought algum-wood and precious stones. ¹¹ The king made of the algum-wood ramps for the House of the LORD and for the royal palace, and lyres and harps for the musicians, whose like had never before been seen in the land of Judah— ¹² King Solomon, in turn, gave the queen of Sheba everything she expressed a desire for, exceeding a return for what she had brought to the king. Then she and her courtiers left and returned to her own land.

¹³ The gold which Solomon received every year weighed 666 gold talents, ¹⁴ besides what traders and merchants brought, and the gold and silver that all the kings of Arabia and governors of the regions brought to Solomon. ¹⁵ King Solomon made 200 shields of beaten gold—600 shekels of beaten gold for each shield, ¹⁶ and 300 bucklers of beaten gold—300 [shekels] of gold for each buckler. The king placed them in the Lebanon Forest House. ¹⁷ The king also made a large throne of ivory, overlaid with pure gold. ¹⁸ Six steps led up to the throne; and the throne had a golden footstool attached to it, and arms on either side of the seat. Two lions stood beside the arms, ¹⁹ and twelve lions stood on the six steps, six on either side. None such was ever made for any other kingdom. ²⁰ All of King Solomon's drinking vessels were of gold, and all the utensils of the Lebanon Forest House were of pure gold; silver counted for nothing in Solomon's days. ²¹ The king's fleet traveled to Tarshish with Huram's servants. Once every three years, the Tarshish fleet came in, bearing gold and silver, ivory, apes, and peacocks.

²² King Solomon surpassed all the kings of the earth in wealth and wisdom. ²³ All the kings of the earth came to pay homage to Solomon and to listen to the wisdom with which God had endowed him. ²⁴ Each brought his tribute—silver and gold objects,

robes, weapons, and spices, horses and mules—in the amount due each year. ²⁵ Solomon had 4000 stalls for horses and chariots, and 12,000 horsemen, which he stationed in the chariot towns and with the king in Jerusalem. ²⁶ He ruled over all the kings from the Euphrates to the land of the Philistines and to the border of Egypt. ²⁷ The king made silver as plentiful in Jerusalem as stones, and cedars as plentiful as sycamores in the Shephelah. ²⁸ Horses were brought for Solomon from Egypt and all the lands. ²⁹ The other events of Solomon's reign, early and late, are recorded in the chronicle of the prophet Nathan and in the prophecies of Ahijah the Shilonite and in the visions of Jedo the seer concerning Jeroboam son of Nebat. ³⁰ Solomon reigned forty years over all Israel in Jerusalem. ³¹ Solomon slept with his fathers and was buried in the city of his father David; his son Rehoboam succeeded him as king.

10 ᵃRehoboam went to Shechem, for all Israel had come to Shechem to acclaim him king. ² Jeroboam son of Nebat learned of it while he was in Egypt where he had fled from King Solomon, and Jeroboam returned from Egypt. ³ They sent for him; and Jeroboam and all Israel came and spoke to Rehoboam as follows: ⁴ "Your father made our yoke heavy. Now lighten the harsh labor and the heavy yoke which your father laid on us, and we will serve you." ⁵ He answered them, "Come back to me in three days." So the people went away.

⁶ King Rehoboam took counsel with the elders who had served during the lifetime of his father Solomon. He said, "What answer do you counsel to give these people?" ⁷ They answered him, "If you will be good to these people and appease them and speak to them with kind words, they will be your servants always." ⁸ But he ignored the counsel that the elders gave him, and took counsel with the young men who had grown up with him and were serving him. ⁹ "What," he asked, "do you counsel that we reply to these people who said to me, 'Lighten the yoke that your father laid on us'?" ¹⁰ And the young men who had grown up with him an-

ᵃ *Cf. I Kings 12.1–19.*

swered, "Speak thus to the people who said to you, 'Your father made our yoke heavy, now you make it lighter for us.' Say to them, 'My little finger is thicker than my father's loins. ¹¹ My father imposed a heavy yoke on you, and I will add to your yoke; my father flogged you with whips, but I [will do so] with scorpions.' "

¹² Jeroboam and all the people came to Rehoboam on the third day, since the king had told them, "Come back on the third day." ¹³ The king answered them harshly; thus King Rehoboam ignored the elders' counsel. ¹⁴ He spoke to them in accordance with the counsel of the young men, and said, ᵇ-"I will make-ᵇ your yoke heavy, and I will add to it; my father flogged you with whips, but I [will do so] with scorpions." ¹⁵ The king did not listen to the people, for God had brought it about in order that the LORD might fulfill the promise which He had made through Ahijah the Shilonite to Jeroboam son of Nebat. ¹⁶ When all Israel [saw] that the king had not listened to them, the people answered the king:

> "We have no portion in David,
> No share in Jesse's son!
> To your tents, O Israel!
> Now look to your own house, O David."

So all Israel returned to their homes.ᶜ ¹⁷ But Rehoboam continued to reign over the Israelites who lived in the towns of Judah. ¹⁸ King Rehoboam sent out Hadoram, who was in charge of the forced labor, but the Israelites pelted him to death with stones. Thereupon, King Rehoboam hurriedly mounted his chariot and fled to Jerusalem. ¹⁹ Israel has been in revolt against the house of David to this day.

11 ᵃWhen Rehoboam arrived in Jerusalem, he mustered the house of Judah and Benjamin, 180,000 picked fighting men, to make war with Israel in order to restore the kingdom to Rehoboam. ² But the word of the LORD came to Shemaiah, the man of God, ³ "Say to Rehoboam son of Solomon king of Judah, and to all Israel in Judah and Benjamin: ⁴ Thus said the LORD: You shall

---

ᵇ⁻ᵇ *Some mss. and printed editions read "my father made"; cf. I Kings 12.14.*
ᶜ *Lit. "tents."*

ᵃ *With 11.1–4, cf. I Kings 12.21–24.*

not set out to make war on your kinsmen. Let every man return to his home, for this thing has been brought about by Me." They heeded the words of the LORD and refrained from marching against Jeroboam. [5] Rehoboam dwelt in Jerusalem and built fortified towns in Judah. [6] He built up Bethlehem, and Etam, and Tekoa, [7] and Beth-zur, and Soco, and Adullam, [8] and Gath, and Mareshah, and Ziph, [9] and Adoraim, and Lachish, and Azekah, [10] and Zorah, and Aijalon, and Hebron, which are in Judah and in Benjamin, as fortified towns. [11] He strengthened the fortified towns and put commanders in them, along with stores of food, oil, and wine, [12] and shields and spears in every town. He strengthened them exceedingly; thus Judah and Benjamin were his.

[13] The priests and the Levites, from all their territories throughout Israel, presented themselves to him. [14] The Levites had left their pasturelands and their holdings and had set out for Judah and Jerusalem, for Jeroboam and his sons had prevented them from serving the LORD, [15] having appointed his own priests for the shrines, goat-demons, and calves which he had made. [16] From all the tribes of Israel, those intent on seeking the LORD God of Israel followed them to Jerusalem, to sacrifice to the LORD God of their fathers. [17] They strengthened the kingdom of Judah, and supported Rehoboam son of Solomon for three years, for they followed the ways of David and Solomon for three years.

[18] Rehoboam married Mahalath daughter of Jerimoth son of David, and Abihail daughter of Eliab son of Jesse. [19] She bore him sons: Jeush, Shemariah, and Zaham. [20] He then took Maacah daughter of Absalom; she bore him Abijah, Attai, Ziza, and Shelomith. [21] Rehoboam loved Maacah daughter of Absalom more than his other wives and concubines—for he took eighteen wives and sixty concubines; he begot twenty-eight sons and sixty daughters. [22] Rehoboam designated Abijah son of Maacah as chief and leader among his brothers, for he intended him to be his successor. [23] He prudently distributed all his sons throughout the regions of Judah and Benjamin and throughout the fortified

towns; he provided them with abundant food, and he sought many wives for them.

12 When the kingship of Rehoboam was firmly established, and he grew strong, he abandoned the Teaching of the LORD, he and all Israel with him.

2 In the fifth year of King Rehoboam, King Shishak of Egypt marched against Jerusalem—for they had trespassed against the LORD—3 with 1200 chariots, 60,000 horsemen and innumerable troops who came with him from Egypt: Lybians, Sukkites and Kushites. 4 He took the fortified towns of Judah and advanced on Jerusalem. 5 The prophet Shemaiah came to Rehoboam and the officers of Judah, who had assembled in Jerusalem because of Shishak, and said to them, "Thus said the LORD: You have abandoned Me, so I am abandoning you to Shishak." 6 Then the officers of Israel and the king humbled themselves and declared, "The LORD is in the right." 7 When the LORD saw that they had submitted, the word of the LORD came to Shemaiah, saying, "Since they have humbled themselves, I will not destroy them but will grant them some measure of deliverance, and My wrath will not be poured out on Jerusalem through Shishak. 8 They will be subject to him, and they will know the difference between serving Me and serving the kingdoms of the earth." King Shishak of Egypt marched against Jerusalem. 9 *a*He took away the treasures of the House of the LORD and the treasures of the royal palace; he took away everything; he took away the golden shields that Solomon had made. 10 King Rehoboam had bronze shields made in their place, and entrusted them to the officers of the guard*b* who guarded the entrance to the royal palace. 11 Whenever the king entered the House of the LORD, the guards would carry them and then bring them back to the armory of the guards. 12 After he had humbled himself, the anger of the LORD was averted and He did not destroy him entirely; in Judah, too, good things were found.

^a *With vv. 9–16, cf. I Kings 14.26–31.*
^b *Lit. "runners."*

¹³ King Rehoboam grew strong in Jerusalem and exercised kingship. Rehoboam was forty-one years old when he became king, and he reigned seventeen years in Jerusalem—the city the LORD had chosen out of all the tribes of Israel to establish His name there. His mother's name was Naamah the Ammonitess. ¹⁴ He did what was wrong, for he had not set his heart to seek the LORD. ¹⁵ The deeds of Rehoboam, early and late, are recorded in the chronicles of the prophet Shemaiah and Iddo the seer, in the manner of genealogy. There was continuous war between Rehoboam and Jeroboam. ¹⁶ Rehoboam slept with his fathers and was buried in the City of David. His son Abijah succeeded him as king.

13 In the eighteenth year of King Jeroboam, Abijah became king over Judah. ² He reigned three years in Jerusalem; his mother's name was Micaiah daughter of Uriel of Gibeah. There was war between Abijah and Jeroboam. ³ Abijah joined battle with a force of warriors, 400,000 picked men. Jeroboam arrayed for battle against him 800,000 picked men, warriors. ⁴ Abijah stood on top of Mount Zemaraim in the hill country of Ephraim and said, "Listen to me, Jeroboam and all Israel. ⁵ Surely you know that the LORD God of Israel gave David kingship over Israel forever—to him and his sons—by a covenant of salt. ⁶ Jeroboam son of Nebat had been in the service of Solomon son of David, but he rose up and rebelled against his master. ⁷ Riffraff and scoundrels gathered around him and pressed hard upon Rehoboam son of Solomon. Rehoboam was inexperienced and faint-hearted and could not stand up to them. ⁸ Now you are bent on opposing the kingdom of the LORD, which is in the charge of the sons of David, because you are a great multitude and possess the golden calves which Jeroboam made for you as gods. ⁹ Did you not banish the priests of the LORD, the sons of Aaron and the Levites, and, like the peoples of the land, appoint your own priests? Anyone who offered himself for ordination with a young

bull of the herd and seven rams became a priest of no-gods!
[10] As for us, the LORD is our God, and we have not forsaken Him.
The priests who minister to the LORD are the sons of Aaron, and
the Levites are at their tasks. [11] They offer burnt offerings in
smoke each morning and each evening, and the aromatic incense,
the rows of bread on the pure table; they kindle the golden
lampstand with its lamps burning each evening, for we keep the
charge of the LORD our God, while you have forsaken it. [12] See,
God is with us as our chief, and His priests have the trumpets for
sounding blasts against you. O children of Israel, do not fight the
LORD God of your fathers, because you will not succeed."
[13] Jeroboam, however, had directed the ambush to go around and
come from the rear, thus *a-the main body was-a* in front of Judah,
while the ambush was behind them. [14] When Judah turned
around and saw that the fighting was before and behind them,
they cried out to the LORD, and the priests blew the trumpets.
[15] The men of Judah raised a shout; and when the men of Judah
raised a shout, God routed Jeroboam and all Israel before Abijah
and Judah. [16] The Israelites fled before Judah, and God delivered
them into their hands. [17] Abijah and his army inflicted a severe
defeat on them; 500,000 men of Israel fell slain. [18] The Israelites
were crushed at that time, while the people of Judah triumphed
because they relied on the LORD God of their fathers. [19] Abijah
pursued Jeroboam and captured some of his cities—Bethel with
its dependencies, Jeshanah with its dependencies and Ephrain
with its dependencies. [20] Jeroboam could not muster strength
again during the days of Abijah. The LORD struck him down and
he died. [21] But Abijah grew powerful; he married fourteen wives
and begat twenty-two sons and sixteen daughters.

[22] The other events of Abijah's reign, his conduct and his acts,
are recorded in the story of the prophet Iddo. [23] Abijah slept with
his fathers and was buried in the city of David; his son Asa succeeded him as king. The land was untroubled for ten years.

---

a-a *Lit. "they were."*

14 Asa did what was good and pleasing to the LORD his God. [2] He abolished the alien altars and shrines; he smashed the pillars and cut down the sacred posts. [3] He ordered Judah to turn to the LORD God of their fathers and to observe the Teaching and the Commandment. [4] He abolished the shrines and the incense stands throughout the cities of Judah, and the kingdom was untroubled under him. [5] He built fortified towns in Judah, since the land was untroubled and he was not engaged in warfare during those years, for the LORD had granted him respite. [6] He said to Judah, "Let us build up these cities and surround them with walls and towers, gates and bars, while the land is at our disposal because we turned to the LORD our God—we turned [to Him] and He gave us respite on all sides." They were successful in their building.

[7] Asa had an army of 300,000 men from Judah bearing shields and spears, and 280,000 from Benjamin bearing bucklers and drawing the bow; all these were valiant men. [8] Zerah the Cushite marched out against them with an army of a thousand thousand and 300 chariots. When he reached Mareshah [9] Asa confronted him, and the battle lines were drawn in the valley of Zephat by Mareshah. [10] Asa called to the LORD his God, and said, "O LORD, it is all the same to You to help the numerous and the powerless. Help us, O LORD our God, for we rely on You, and in Your name we have come against this great multitude. You are the LORD our God. Let no mortal hinder You." [11] So the LORD routed the Cushites before Asa and Judah, and the Cushites fled. [12] Asa and the army with him pursued them as far as Gerar. Many of the Cushites fell wounded beyond recovery, for they broke before the LORD and His camp. Very much spoil was taken. [13] All the cities in the vicinity of Gerar were ravaged, for a terror of the LORD seized them. All the cities were plundered, and they yielded much booty. [14] They also ravaged the encampment of herdsmen, capturing much sheep and camels. Then they returned to Jerusalem.

15 The spirit of God came upon Azariah son of Oded. [2] He came to Asa and said to him, "Listen to me, Asa and all Judah and Benjamin; the LORD is with you as long as you are with Him. If you turn to Him, He will respond to you, but if you forsake Him, He will forsake you. [3] Israel has gone many days without the true God, without a priest to give instruction and without Teaching. [4] But in distress it returned to the LORD God of Israel, and sought Him, and He responded to them. [5] At those times, *a-no wayfarer-a* was safe, for there was much tumult among all the inhabitants of the lands. [6] Nation was crushed by nation and city by city, for God threw them into panic with every kind of trouble. [7] As for you, be strong, do not be disheartened, for there is reward for your labor."

[8] When Asa heard these words, the prophecy of Oded the prophet, he took courage and removed the abominations from the entire land of Judah and Benjamin and from the cities which he had captured in the hill country of Ephraim. He restored the altar of the LORD in front of the porch of the LORD. [9] He assembled all the people of Judah and Benjamin and those people of Ephraim, Manasseh, and Simeon who sojourned among them, for many in Israel had thrown in their lot with him when they saw that the LORD his God was with him. [10] They were assembled in Jerusalem in the third month of the fifteenth year of the reign of Asa. [11] They brought sacrifices to the LORD on that day; they brought 700 oxen and 7000 sheep of the spoil. [12] They entered into a covenant to worship the LORD God of their fathers with all their heart and with all their soul. [13] Whoever would not worship the LORD God of Israel would be put to death, whether small or great, whether man or woman. [14] So they took an oath to the LORD in a loud voice and with shouts, with trumpeting and blasts of the horn. [15] All Judah rejoiced over the oath, for they swore with all their heart and sought Him with all their will. He responded to them and gave them respite on every side.

[16] *b*He*c* also deposed Maacah mother of King Asa from the rank

---

a-a *Lit. "one who goes out and one who comes in."*
b *With vv. 16–19, cf. I Kings 15.13–16.*
c *I.e. Asa.*

of queen mother, because she had made an abominable thing for [the goddess] Asherah. Asa cut down her abominable thing, reduced it to dust, and burned it in the Wadi Kidron. [17] The shrines, indeed, were not abolished in Israel; however, Asa was wholehearted [with the LORD] all his life. [18] He brought into the House of God the things that he and his father had consecrated—silver, gold, and utensils. [19] There was no war until the thirty-fifth year of the reign of Asa.

16

[a]In the thirty-sixth year of the reign of Asa, King Baasha of Israel marched against Judah and built up Ramah to block [b-]all movement[-b] of King Asa of Judah. [2] Asa took all the silver and gold from the treasuries of the House of the LORD and the royal palace, and sent them to King Ben-hadad of Aram, who resided in Damascus, with this message: [3] "There is a pact between me and you, as there was between my father and your father. I herewith send you silver and gold; go and break your pact with King Baasha of Israel so that he may withdraw from me." [4] Ben-hadad acceded to King Asa's request; he sent his army commanders against the towns of Israel and ravaged Ijon, Dan, Abel-maim, and all the garrison towns of Naphtali. [5] When Baasha heard about it, he stopped building up Ramah and put an end to the work on it. [6] Then King Asa mustered all Judah, and they carried away the stones and timber with which Baasha had built up Ramah; with these King Asa built up Geba and Mizpah.

[7] At that time, Hanani the seer came to King Asa of Judah and said to him, "Because you relied on the king of Aram and did not rely on the LORD your God, therefore the army of the king of Aram has slipped out of your hands. [8] The Cushites and Lybians were a mighty army with chariots and horsemen in very great numbers, yet because you relied on the LORD He delivered them into your hands. [9] For the eyes of the LORD range over the entire earth, to give support to those who are wholeheartedly with Him.

[a] Cf. I Kings 15.17–24.
[b-b] Lit. "one who goes out and one who comes in."

You have acted foolishly in this matter, and henceforth you will be beset by wars." [10] Asa was vexed at the seer and put him into the stocks,[c] for he was furious with him because of that. Asa inflicted cruelties on some of the people at that time.

[11] The acts of Asa, early and late, are recorded in the annals of the kings of Judah and Israel. [12] In the thirty-ninth year of his reign, Asa suffered from an acute foot ailment; but ill as he was, he still did not turn to the LORD but to physicians. [13] Asa slept with his fathers. He died in the forty-first year of his reign [14] and was buried in the grave that he had made for himself in the City of David. He was laid in his resting-place, which was filled with spices of all kinds, expertly blended; a very great fire was made in his honor.

17 His son Jehoshaphat succeeded him as king, and took firm hold of Israel. [2] He stationed troops in all the fortified towns of Judah, and stationed garrisons throughout the land of Judah and the cities of Ephraim which his father Asa had captured. [3] The LORD was with Jehoshaphat because he followed the earlier ways of his father David, and did not worship the Baalim, [4] but worshiped the God of his father and followed His commandments—unlike the behavior of Israel. [5] So the LORD established the kingdom in his hands, and all Judah gave presents to Jehoshaphat. He had wealth and glory in abundance. [6] His mind was elevated in the ways of the LORD. Moreover, he abolished the shrines and the sacred posts from Judah.

[7] In the third year of his reign he sent his officers Ben-hail, Obadiah, Zechariah, Nethanel, and Micaiah throughout the cities of Judah to offer instruction. [8] With them were the Levites, Shemaiah, Nethaniah, Zebadiah, Asahel, Shemiramoth, Jehonathan, Adonijah, Tobijah and Tob-adonijah the Levites; with them were Elishama and Jehoram the priests. [9] They offered instruction throughout Judah, having with them the Book of the Teaching of

[c] *Meaning of Heb. uncertain.*

the LORD. They made the rounds of all the cities of the LORD and instructed the people. 10 A terror of the LORD seized all the kingdoms of the lands around Judah, and they did not go to war with Jehoshaphat. 11 From Philistia a load of silver was brought to Jehoshaphat as tribute. The Arabs, too, brought him flocks: 7700 rams and 7700 he-goats. 12 Jehoshaphat grew greater and greater, and he built up fortresses and garrison towns in Judah. 13 He carried out extensive works in the towns of Judah, and had soldiers, valiant men, in Jerusalem. 14 They were enrolled according to their clans. Judah: chiefs of thousands, Adnah the chief, who had 300,000 valiant men; 15 next to him was Jehohanan the captain, who had 280,000; 16 next to him was Amasiah son of Zichri, who made a freewill offering to the LORD. He had 200,000 valiant men. 17 Benjamin: Eliada, a valiant man, who had 200,000 men armed with bow and buckler; 18 next to him was Jehozabad, who had 180,000 armed men. 19 These served the king, besides those whom the king assigned to the fortified towns throughout Judah.

18 *a*So Jehoshaphat had wealth and honor in abundance, and he allied himself by marriage to Ahab. 2 After some years had passed, he came to visit Ahab at Samaria. Ahab slaughtered sheep and oxen in abundance for him and for the people with him, and persuaded him to march against Ramoth-gilead. 3 King Ahab of Israel said to King Jehoshaphat of Judah, "Will you accompany me to Ramoth-gilead?" He answered him, "I will do what you do; my troops shall be your troops and shall accompany you in battle." 4 Jehoshaphat then said to the king of Israel, "But first inquire of the LORD."

5 So the king of Israel gathered the prophets, four hundred men, and asked them, "Shall I march upon Ramoth-gilead for battle, or shall I not?" "March," they said, "and God will deliver it into the king's hands." 6 Then Jehoshaphat asked, "Is there not another prophet of the LORD here through whom we can in-

---

a *Cf. I Kings 22.*

quire?" ⁷ And the king of Israel answered Jehoshaphat, "There is one more man through whom we can inquire of the Lord; but I hate him, because he never prophesies anything good for me but always misfortune. He is Micaiah son of Imlah." Jehoshaphat replied, "Let the king not say such a thing." ⁸ So the king of Israel summoned an officer and said, "Bring Micaiah son of Imlah at once."

⁹ The king of Israel and King Jehoshaphat of Judah, wearing their robes, were seated on their thrones situated in the threshing floor at the entrance of the gate of Samaria; and all the prophets were prophesying before them. ¹⁰ Zedekiah son of Chenaanah had provided himself with iron horns; and he said, "Thus said the Lord: With these you shall gore the Arameans till you make an end of them." ¹¹ All the other prophets were prophesying similarly, "March against Ramoth-gilead and be victorious! The Lord will deliver it into Your Majesty's hands."

¹² The messenger who had gone to summon Micaiah said to him, "Look, the words of the prophets are unanimously favorable to the king. Let your word be like that of the rest of them; speak a favorable word." ¹³ "By the life of the Lord," Micaiah answered, "I will speak only what my God tells me." ¹⁴ When he came before the king, the king said to him, "Micah,ᵇ shall we march against Ramoth-gilead for battle or shall we not?" He answered him, "March and be victorious! They will be delivered into your hands." ¹⁵ The king said to him, "How many times must I adjure you to tell me nothing but the truth in the name of the Lord?" ¹⁶ Then he said, "I saw all Israel scattered over the hills like sheep without a shepherd; and the Lord said, 'These have no master; let everyone return to his home in safety.'" ¹⁷ The king of Israel said to Jehoshaphat, "Did I not tell you that he would not prophesy good fortune for me, but only misfortune?"

¹⁸ Then [Micaiah] said, "Indeed, hear now the word of the Lord! I saw the Lord seated upon His throne, with all the host of heaven standing in attendance to the right and to the left of

ᵇ *A shortened form of Micaiah.*

Him. ¹⁹ The LORD asked, 'Who will entice King Ahab of Israel so that he will march and fall at Ramoth-gilead?' Then one said this and another said that, ²⁰ until a certain spirit came forward and stood before the LORD and said, 'I will entice him.' 'How?' said the LORD to him. ²¹ And he replied, 'I will go forth and become a lying spirit in the mouth of all his prophets.' Then He said, 'You will entice with success. Go forth and do it.' ²² Thus the LORD has put a lying spirit in the mouth of all these prophets of yours; for the LORD has decreed misfortune for you."

²³ Thereupon Zedekiah son of Chenaanah came up and struck Micaiah on the cheek, and exclaimed, "However did the spirit of the LORD pass from me to speak with you!" ²⁴ Micaiah replied, "You will see on the day when you try to hide in the innermost room." ²⁵ Then the king of Israel said, "Take Micaiah and turn him over to Amon, the governor of the city, and to Prince Joash, ²⁶ and say, 'The king's orders are: Put this fellow in prison, and let his fare be scant bread and scant water until I come home safe.' " ²⁷ To which Micaiah retorted, "If you ever come home safe, the LORD has not spoken through me." He said further, ᶜ-"Listen, all you peoples!"-ᶜ

²⁸ The king of Israel and King Jehoshaphat of Judah marched against Ramoth-gilead. ²⁹ The king of Israel said to Jehoshaphat, ᵈ-"I will disguise myself and go-ᵈ into the battle, but you, wear your robes." So the king of Israel disguised himself, and they went into the battle. ³⁰ The king of Aram had given these instructions to his chariot officers: "Do not attack anyone, small or great, except the king of Israel." ³¹ When the chariot officers saw Jehoshaphat, whom they took for the king of Israel, they wheeled around to attack him, and Jehoshaphat cried out and the LORD helped him, and God diverted them from him. ³² And when the chariot officers realized that he was not the king of Israel, they gave up the pursuit. ³³ Then a man drew his bow at random and hit the king of Israel between the ᵉ-plates of the-ᵉ armor and he said to his charioteer, "Turn around and get me behind the lines; I am wounded." ³⁴ The battle ᵉ-raged all day long,-ᵉ and the king

---

ᶜ⁻ᶜ *Cf. Mic. 1.2.*
ᵈ⁻ᵈ *Infinitives used for finite verb; cf. note at I Kings 22.30.*
ᵉ⁻ᵉ *Meaning of Heb. uncertain*

remained propped up in the chariot facing Aram until dusk; he died as the sun was setting.

19 King Jehoshaphat of Judah returned safely to his palace, to Jerusalem. ² Jehu son of Hanani the seer went out to meet King Jehoshaphat and said to him, "Should one give aid to the wicked and befriend those who hate the LORD? For this, wrath is upon you from the LORD. ³ However, there is some good in you, for you have purged the land of the sacred posts and have dedicated yourself to worship the LORD."

⁴ Jehoshaphat remained in Jerusalem awhile and then went out among the people from Beer-sheba to the hill country of Ephraim; he brought them back to the LORD God of their fathers. ⁵ He appointed judges in the land in all the fortified towns of Judah, in each and every town. ⁶ He charged the judges: "Consider what you are doing, for you judge not on behalf of man, but on behalf of the LORD, and He is with you when you pass judgment. ⁷ Now let the dread of the LORD be upon you; act with care, for there is no injustice or favoritism or bribe-taking with the LORD our God." ⁸ Jehoshaphat also appointed in Jerusalem some Levites and priests and heads of the clans of Israelites for rendering judgment in matters of the LORD, and for disputes. Then they returned to Jerusalem. ⁹ He charged them, "This is how you shall act: in fear of the LORD, with fidelity, and with whole heart. ¹⁰ When a dispute comes before you from your brothers living in their towns, whether about homicide, or about ritual, or laws or rules, you must instruct them so that they do not incur guilt before the LORD and wrath be upon you and your brothers. Act so and you will not incur guilt. ¹¹ See, Amariah the chief priest is over you in all cases concerning the LORD, and Zebadiah son of Ishmael is the commander of the house of Judah in all cases concerning the king; the Levitical officials are at your disposal; act with resolve and the LORD be with the good."

20 After that, Moabites, Ammonites, together with some Ammonim,[a] came against Jehoshaphat to wage war. 2 The report was brought to Jehoshaphat: "A great multitude is coming against you from beyond the sea, from Aram, and is now in Hazazontamar"—that is, Ein-gedi. 3 Jehoshaphat was afraid; he decided to resort to the LORD and proclaimed a fast for all Judah. 4 Judah assembled to beseech the LORD. They also came from all the towns of Judah to seek the LORD.

5 Jehoshaphat stood in the congregation of Judah and Jerusalem in the House of the LORD at the front of the new court. 6 He said, "LORD God of our fathers, truly You are the God in heaven and You rule over the kingdoms of the nations; power and strength are Yours; none can oppose You. 7 O our God, you dispossessed the inhabitants of this land before Your people Israel, and You gave it to the descendants of Your friend Abraham for ever. 8 They settled in it and in it built for You a House for Your name. They said, 9 'Should misfortune befall us —the punishing sword, pestilence, or famine, we shall stand before this House and before You—for Your name is in this House —and we shall cry out to You in our distress, and You will listen and deliver us.' 10 Now the people of Ammon, Moab, and the hill country of Seir, into whose [land] You did not let Israel come when they came from Egypt, but they turned aside from them and did not wipe them out, 11 these now repay us by coming to expel us from Your possession which You gave us as ours. 12 O our God, surely You will punish them, for we are powerless before this great multitude that has come against us, and do not know what to do, but our eyes are on You." 13 All Judah stood before the LORD with their little ones, their womenfolk, and their children.

14 Then in the midst of the congregation the spirit of the LORD came upon Jahaziel son of Zechariah son of Benaiah son of Jeiel son of Mattaniah the Levite, of the sons of Asaph, 15 and he said,

---

[a] *Probably for* m'nym *"Meunites" (I Chron. 4.41); cf. Kimhi.*

"Give heed, all Judah and the inhabitants of Jerusalem and King Jehoshaphat; thus said the LORD to you, 'Do not fear or be dismayed by this great multitude, for the battle is God's, not yours. ¹⁶ March down against them tomorrow as they come up by the Ascent of Ziz; you will find them at the end of the wadi in the direction of the wilderness of Jeruel. ¹⁷ It is not for you to fight this battle; stand by, wait, and witness your deliverance by the LORD, O Judah and Jerusalem; do not fear or be dismayed; go forth to meet them tomorrow and the LORD will be with you.'" ¹⁸ Jehoshaphat bowed low with his face to the ground, and all Judah and the inhabitants of Jerusalem threw themselves down before the LORD to worship the LORD. ¹⁹ Levites of the sons of Kohath and of the sons of Korah got up to extol the LORD God of Israel at the top of their voices.

²⁰ Early the next morning they arose and went forth to the wilderness of Tekoa. As they went forth, Jehoshaphat stood and said, "Listen to me, O Judah and inhabitants of Jerusalem: Trust firmly in the LORD your God and you will stand firm; trust firmly in His prophets and you will succeed." ²¹ After taking counsel with the people, he stationed singers to the LORD extolling the One majestic in holiness as they went forth ahead of the vanguard, saying, "Praise the LORD, for His steadfast love is eternal." ²² As they began their joyous shouts and hymns, the LORD set ambushes for the men of Amon, Moab, and the hill country of Seir, who were marching against Judah, and they were routed. ²³ The Ammonites and Moabites turned against the men of the hill country of Seir to exterminate and annihilate them. When they had made an end of the men of Seir, each helped to destroy his fellow.

²⁴ When Judah reached the lookout in the wilderness and looked for the multitude, they saw them lying on the ground as corpses; not one had survived. ²⁵ Jehoshaphat and his army came to take the booty, and found an abundance of goods, corpses, and precious objects, which they pillaged, more than they could carry off. For three days they were taking booty, there was so much of

it. ²⁶ On the fourth day they assembled in the Valley of Blessing —for there they blessed the LORD; that is why that place is called the Valley of Blessing to this day. ²⁷ All the men of Judah and Jerusalem with Jehoshaphat at their head returned joyfully to Jerusalem, for the LORD had given them cause for rejoicing over their enemies. ²⁸ They came to Jerusalem to the House of the LORD, to the accompaniment of harps, lyres, and trumpets. ²⁹ The terror of God seized all the kingdoms of the lands when they heard that the LORD had fought the enemies of Israel. ³⁰ The kingdom of Jehoshaphat was untroubled, and his God granted him respite on all sides.

³¹ ^bJehoshaphat reigned over Judah. He was thirty-five years old when he became king, and he reigned in Jerusalem for twenty-five years. His mother's name was Azubah daughter of Shilhi. ³² He followed the course of his father Asa and did not deviate from it, doing what was pleasing to the LORD. ³³ However, the shrines did not cease; the people still did not direct their heart toward the God of their fathers. ³⁴ As for the other events of Jehoshaphat's reign, early and late, they are recorded in the annals of Jehu son of Hanani, which were included in the Book of the Kings of Israel.

³⁵ Afterward, King Jehoshaphat of Judah entered into a partnership with King Ahaziah of Israel, thereby acting wickedly. ³⁶ He joined with him in constructing ships to go to Tarshish; the ships were constructed in Ezion-geber. ³⁷ Eliezer son of Dodavahu of Mareshah prophesied against Jehoshaphat, "As you have made a partnership with Ahaziah, the LORD will break up your work." The ships were wrecked and were unable to go to Tarshish.

21 ^aJehoshaphat slept with his fathers and was buried with his fathers in the City of David; his son Jehoram succeeded him as king. ² He had brothers, sons of Jehoshaphat: Azariah, Jehiel,

^b *With vv. 31–37, cf. I Kings 22.41–49.*

^a *Cf. II Kings 8.17–24.*

Zechariah, Azariahu, Michael and Shephatiah; all these were sons of King Jehoshaphat of Israel. ³ Their father gave them many gifts of silver, gold, and [other] presents, as well as fortified towns in Judah, but he gave the kingdom to Jehoram because he was the firstborn.

⁴ Jehoram proceeded to take firm hold of his father's kingdom and put to the sword all his brothers, as well as some of the officers of Israel. ⁵ Jehoram was thirty-two years old when he became king, and he reigned in Jerusalem eight years. ⁶ He followed the practices of the kings of Israel doing what the House of Ahab had done, for he married a daughter of Ahab; he did what was displeasing to the LORD. ⁷ However, the LORD refrained from destroying the House of David for the sake of the covenant he had made with David, and in accordance with his promise to maintain a lamp for him and his descendants for all time. ⁸ During his reign, the Edomites rebelled against Judah's rule and set up a king of their own. ⁹ Jehoram advanced [against them] with his officers and all his chariotry. He arose by night and attacked the Edomites, who surrounded him and the chariot commanders. ¹⁰ Edom has been in rebellion against Judah, to this day; Libnah also rebelled against him at that time, because he had forsaken the LORD God of his fathers. ¹¹ Moreover, he built shrines in the hill country of Judah; he led astray the inhabitants of Jerusalem and made Judah wayward.

¹² A letter from Elijah the prophet came to him which read, "Thus says the LORD God of your father David: Since you have not followed the practices of your father Jehoshaphat and the practices of King Asa of Judah, ¹³ but have followed the practices of the kings of Israel, leading astray Judah and the inhabitants of Jerusalem as the House of Ahab led them astray, and have also killed your brothers of your father's house, who were better than you, ¹⁴ therefore, the LORD will inflict a great blow upon your people, your sons, and your wives and all your possessions. ¹⁵ As for you, you will be severely stricken with a disorder of the bowels year after year until your bowels drop out."

¹⁶ The LORD stirred up the spirit of the Philistines and the Arabs who were neighbors of the Cushites against Jehoram. ¹⁷ They marched against Judah, breached its defenses, and carried off all the property that was found in the king's palace, as well as his sons and his wives. The only son who remained was Jehoahaz, his youngest. ¹⁸ After this, the LORD afflicted him with an incurable disease of the bowels. ¹⁹ Some years later, when a period of two years had elapsed, his bowels dropped out because of his disease, and he died a gruesome death. His people did not make a fire for him like the fire for his fathers. ²⁰ He was thirty-two years old when he became king, and he reigned in Jerusalem eight years. He departed unpraised,^b and was buried in the City of David, but not in the tombs of the kings.

22 ^aThe inhabitants of Jerusalem made Ahaziah, his youngest son, king in his stead, because all the older ones had been killed by the troops that penetrated the camp with the Arabs. Ahaziah son of Jehoram reigned as king of Judah. ² Ahaziah was forty-two years old when he became king, and he reigned in Jerusalem one year; his mother's name was Athaliah daughter of Omri. ³ He too followed the practices of the house of Ahab, for his mother counseled him to do evil. ⁴ He did what was displeasing to the LORD, like the house of Ahab, for they became his counselors after his father's death, to his ruination. ⁵ Moreover, he followed their counsel and marched with Jehoram son of King Ahab of Israel to battle against King Hazael of Aram at Ramoth-gilead, where the Arameans wounded Joram. ⁶ He returned to Jezreel to recover from the wounds inflicted on him at Ramah when he fought against King Hazael of Aram. King Azariah son of Jehoram of Judah went down to Jezreel to visit Jehoram son of Ahab while he was ill. ⁷ The LORD caused the downfall of Ahaziah because he visited Joram. During his visit he went out with Jehoram to Jehu son of Nimshi, whom the LORD had anointed to cut off the house of Ahab. ⁸ In the course of bringing the house of Ahab to judg-

---

^b *Following Septuagint; cf. Arabic* ḥamada, *"praise."*

^a *With vv. 1–6, cf. II Kings 8.25–29; with vv. 8–9, cf. II Kings 9.27–28; with vv. 10–12, cf. II Kings 11.1–3.*

ment, Jehu came upon the officers of Judah and the nephews of Ahaziah, ministers of Ahaziah, and killed them. ⁹ He sent in search of Ahaziah, who was caught hiding in Samaria, was brought to Jehu, and put to death. He was given a burial, because it was said, "He is the son of Jehoshaphat who worshiped the LORD wholeheartedly." So the house of Ahaziah could not muster the strength to rule.

¹⁰ When Athaliah, Ahaziah's mother, learned that her son was dead, she promptly did away with all who were of the royal stock of the house of Judah. ¹¹ But Jehoshabeath, daughter of the king, spirited away Ahaziah's son Joash from among the princes who were being slain, and put him and his nurse in a bedroom. Jehoshabeath, daughter of King Jehoram, wife of the priest Jehoiada —she was the sister of Ahaziah—kept him hidden from Athaliah so that he was not put to death. ¹² He stayed with them for six years, hidden in the House of God, while Athaliah reigned over the land.

23 ᵃIn the seventh year, Jehoiada took courage and brought the chiefs of the hundreds, Azariah son of Jehoram, Ishmael son of Jehohanan, Azariah son of Obed, Maaseiah son of Adaiah, and Elishaphat son of Zichri, into a compact with him. ² They went through Judah and assembled the Levites from all the towns of Judah, and the chiefs of the clans of Israel. They came to Jerusalem ³ and the entire assembly made a covenant with the king in the House of God. Heᵇ said to them, "The son of the king shall be king according to the promise the LORD made concerning the sons of David. ⁴ This is what you must do: One third of you, priests and Levites, who are on duty for the week, shall be gatekeepers at the thresholds; ⁵ another third shall be stationed in the royal palace, and the other third at the Foundation Gate. All the people shall be in the courts of the House of the LORD. ⁶ Let no one enter the House of the LORD except the priests and the ministering Levites. They may enter because they are sanctified,

ᵃ *Cf. II Kings 11. 4–20.*
ᵇ *I.e. Jehoiada.*

but all the people shall obey the proscription of the LORD. 7 The Levites shall surround the king on every side, every man with his weapons at the ready; and whoever enters the House shall be killed. Stay close to the king in his comings and goings." 8 The Levites and all Judah did just as Jehoiada the priest ordered: each took his men—those who were on duty that week and those who were off duty that week, for Jehoiada the priest had not dismissed the divisions. 9 Jehoiada the priest gave the chiefs of the hundreds King David's spears and shields and quivers that were kept in the House of God. 10 He stationed the entire force, each man with his weapons at the ready, from the south end of the House to the north end of the House, at the altar and the House, to guard the king on every side. 11 Then they brought out the king's son, and placed upon him the crown and the insignia. They proclaimed him king, and Jehoiada and his sons anointed him and shouted, "Long live the king!"

12 When Athaliah heard the shouting of the people and the guards and the acclamation of the king, she came out to the people, to the House of the LORD. 13 She looked about and saw the king standing by his pillar at the entrance, the chiefs with their trumpets beside the king, and all the people of the land rejoicing and blowing trumpets, and the singers with musical instruments leading the hymns. Athaliah rent her garments and cried out, "Treason, treason!" 14 Then the priest Jehoiada ordered out the army officers, the chiefs of hundreds, and said to them, "Take her out between the ranks, and if anyone follows her, put him to the sword." For the priest thought, "Let her not be put to death in the House of the LORD." 15 They cleared a passage for her and she came to the entrance of the Horse Gate to the royal palace; there she was put to death.

16 Then Jehoiada solemnized a covenant between himself and the people and the king that they should be the people of the LORD. 17 All the people then went to the temple of Baal; they tore it down and smashed its altars and images to bits, and they slew Mattan, the priest of Baal, in front of the altars. 18 Jehoiada put

596

the officers of the House of the LORD in the charge of Levite priests whom David had assigned over the House of the LORD to offer up burnt offerings, as is prescribed in the Teaching of Moses, accompanied by joyful song as ordained by David. 19 He stationed the gatekeepers at the gates of the House of the LORD to prevent the entry of anyone unclean for any reason. 20 He took the chiefs of hundreds, the nobles, and the rulers of the people and all the people of the land, and they escorted the king down from the House of the LORD into the royal palace by the upper gate, and seated the king on the royal throne. 21 All the people of the land rejoiced, and the city was quiet. As for Athaliah, she had been put to the sword.

24 *a*Jehoash was seven years old when he became king, and he reigned in Jerusalem forty years. His mother's name was Zibiah of Beer-sheba. 2 All the days of the priest Jehoiada, Jehoash did what was pleasing to the LORD. 3 Jehoiada took two wives for him, by whom he had sons and daughters.

4 Afterward, Joash decided to renovate the House of the LORD. 5 He assembled the priests and the Levites and charged them as follows: "Go out to the towns of Judah and collect money from all Israel for the annual repair of the House of your God. Do it quickly." But the Levites did not act quickly. 6 The king summoned Jehoiada the chief and said to him, "Why have you not seen to it that the Levites brought the tax imposed by Moses, the servant of the LORD, and the congregation of Israel from Judah and Jerusalem to the Tent of the Pact?" 7 For the children of the wicked Athaliah had violated the House of God and had even used the sacred things of the House of the LORD for the Baals. 8 The king ordered that a chest be made and placed on the outside of the gate of the House of the LORD. 9 A proclamation was issued in Judah and Jerusalem to bring the tax imposed on Israel in the wilderness by Moses, the servant of God. 10 All the officers

a Cf. II Kings 12.1–22.

and all the people gladly brought it and threw it into the chest till it was full. [11] Whenever the chest was brought to the royal officers by the Levites, and they saw that it contained much money, the royal scribe and the agent of the chief priest came and emptied out the chest and carried it back to its place. They did this day by day, and much money was collected. [12] The king and Jehoiada delivered the money to those who oversaw the tasks connected with the work of the House of the LORD. They hired masons and carpenters to renovate the House of the LORD, as well as craftsmen in iron and bronze to repair the House of the LORD. [13] The overseers did their work; under them the work went well and they restored the House of God to its original form and repaired it. [14] When they had finished, they brought the money that was left over to the king and Jehoiada; it was made into utensils for the House of the LORD: buckets and ladles, golden and silver vessels. Burnt offerings were offered up regularly in the House of the LORD all the days of Jehoiada. [15] Jehoiada reached a ripe old age and died; he was one hundred and thirty years old at his death. [16] They buried him in the City of David together with the kings, because he had done good in Israel, and on behalf of God and His House.

[17] But after the death of Jehoiada, the officers of Judah came, bowing low to the king; and the king listened to them. [18] They forsook the House of the LORD God of their fathers to serve the sacred posts and idols; and there was wrath upon Judah and Jerusalem because of this guilt of theirs. [19] The LORD sent prophets among them to bring them back to Him; they admonished them but they would not pay heed. [20] Then the spirit of God enveloped Zechariah son of Jehoiada the priest; he stood above the people and said to them, "Thus God said: Why do you transgress the commandments of the LORD when you cannot succeed? Since you have forsaken the LORD, He has forsaken you." [21] They conspired against him and pelted him with stones in the court of the House of the LORD, by order of the king. [22] King Joash disregarded the loyalty that his father Johoiada had shown to him, and

killed his son. As he was dying, he said, "May the LORD see and requite it."

23 At the turn of the year, the army of Aram marched against him; they invaded Judah and Jerusalem, and wiped out all the officers of the people from among the people, and sent all the booty they took to the king of Damascus. 24 The invading army of Aram had come with but a few men, but the LORD delivered a very large army into their hands, because they had forsaken the LORD God of their fathers. They inflicted punishments on Joash. 25 When they withdrew, having left him with many wounds, his courtiers plotted against him because of the murder*b* of the sons of Jehoiada the priest, and they killed him in bed. He died and was buried in the City of David; he was not buried in the tombs of the kings. 26 These were the men who conspired against him: Zabad son of Shimeath the Ammonitess, and Jehozabad son of Shimrith the Moabitess. 27 As to his sons, and the many pronouncements against him, and his rebuilding of the House of God, they are recorded in the story in the book of the kings. His son Amaziah succeeded him as king.

25 *a*Amaziah was twenty-five years old when he became king, and he reigned twenty-nine years in Jerusalem; his mother's name was Jehoaddan of Jerusalem. 2 He did what was pleasing to the LORD, but not with a whole heart. 3 Once he had the kingdom firmly under control, he executed the courtiers who had assassinated his father the king. 4 But he did not put their children to death for [he acted] in accordance with what is written in the Teaching, in the Book of Moses, where the LORD commanded, *b*-"Parents shall not die for children, nor shall children die for parents, but every person shall die only for his own crime."-*b*

5 Amaziah assembled the men of Judah, and he put all the men of Judah and Benjamin under officers of thousands and officers of hundreds, by clans. He mustered them from the age of twenty upward, and found them to be 300,000 picked men fit for service,

b *Lit. "blood."*

a *Cf. II Kings 14.*
b-b *Cf. Deut. 24.16.*

able to bear spear and shield. ⁶ He hired 100,000 warriors from Israel for 100 talents of silver. ⁷ Then a man of God came to him and said, "O king! Do not let the army of Israel go with you, for the LORD is not with Israel—all these Ephraimites. ⁸ But go by yourself and do it; take courage for battle, [else] God will make you fall before the enemy. For in God there is power to help one or make one fall!" ⁹ Amaziah said to the man of God, "And what am I to do about the 100 talents I gave for the Israelite force?" The man of God replied, "The LORD has the means to give you much more than that." ¹⁰ So Amaziah detached the force that came to him from Ephraim, [ordering them] to go back to their place. They were greatly enraged against Judah and returned to their place in a rage.

¹¹ Amaziah took courage and, leading his army, he marched to the Valley of Salt. He slew 10,000 men of Seir; ¹² another 10,000 the men of Judah captured alive and brought to the top of Sela. They threw them down from the top of Sela and every one of them was burst open. ¹³ The men of the force that Amaziah had sent back so they would not go with him into battle made forays against the towns of Judah from Samaria to Beth-horon. They slew 3000 of them, and took much booty.

¹⁴ After Amaziah returned from defeating the Edomites, he had the gods of the men of Seir brought, and installed them as his gods; he prostrated himself before them, and to them he made sacrifice. ¹⁵ The LORD was enraged at Amaziah, and sent a prophet to him who said to him, "Why are you worshiping the gods of a people who could not save their people from you?" ¹⁶ As he spoke to him, [Amaziah] said to him, "Have we appointed you a counselor to the king? Stop, else you will be killed!" The prophet stopped, saying, "I see God has counseled that you be destroyed, since you act this way and disregard my counsel."

¹⁷ Then King Amaziah of Judah took counsel and sent this message to Joash son of Jehoahaz son of Jehu, king of Israel, "Come, let us confront each other!" ¹⁸ King Joash of Israel sent

back this message to King Amaziah of Judah, "The thistle in Lebanon sent this message to the cedar in Lebanon, 'Give your daughter to my son in marriage.' But a wild beast in Lebanon passed by and trampled the thistle. [19] You boast that you have defeated the Edomites and you are ambitious to get more glory. Now stay at home, lest, provoking disaster you fall, dragging Judah down with you." [20] But Amaziah paid no heed—it was God's doing, in order to deliver them up because they worshiped the gods of Edom. [21] King Joash of Israel marched up, and he and King Amaziah of Judah confronted each other at Beth-shemesh in Judah. [22] The men of Judah were routed by Israel, and they all fled to their homes. [23] King Joash of Israel captured Amaziah son of Joash son of Jehoahaz, king of Judah, in Beth-shemesh. He brought him to Jerusalem and made a breach of 400 cubits in the wall of Jerusalem, from the Ephraim Gate to the Corner Gate. [24] Then, with all the gold and silver and all the utensils that were to be found in the House of God in the custody of Obed-edom, and with the treasuries of the royal palace, and with the hostages, he returned to Samaria.

[25] King Amaziah son of Joash of Judah lived fifteen years after the death of King Joash son of Jehoahaz of Israel. [26] The other events of Amaziah's reign, early and late, are recorded in the book of the kings of Judah and Israel. [27] From the time that Amaziah turned from following the LORD, a conspiracy was formed against him in Jerusalem, and he fled to Lachish; but they sent men after him to Lachish and they put him to death there. [28] They brought his body back on horses and buried him with his fathers in the city of Judah.

26

Then all the people of Judah took Uzziah, who was sixteen years old, and proclaimed him king to succeed his father Amaziah. [2] It was he who rebuilt Eloth and restored it to Judah after King [Amaziah] slept with his fathers.

[3] Uzziah was sixteen years old when he became king, and he

reigned fifty-two years in Jerusalem; his mother's name was Jeco-liah of Jerusalem. [4] He did what was pleasing to the LORD just as his father Amaziah had done. [5] He applied himself to the worship of God during the time of Zechariah, instructor in the visions[a] of God; during the time he worshiped the LORD, God made him prosper. [6] He went forth to fight the Philistines, and breached the wall of Gath and the wall of Jabneh and the wall of Ashdod; he built towns in [the region of] Ashdod and among the Philistines. [7] God helped him against the Philistines, against the Arabs who lived in Gur-baal, and the Meunites. [8] The Ammonites paid trib-ute to Uzziah, and his fame spread to the approaches of Egypt, for he grew exceedingly strong. [9] Uzziah built towers in Jerusa-lem on the Corner Gate and the Valley Gate and on the Angle, and fortified them. [10] He built towers in the wilderness and hewed out many cisterns, for he had much cattle, and farmers in the foothills and on the plain, and vinedressers in the mountains and on the fertile lands, for he loved the soil.

[11] Uzziah had an army of warriors, a battle-ready force who were mustered by Jeiel the scribe and Maasseiah the adjutant under Hananiah, one of the king's officers. [12] The clan chiefs, valiants, totaled 2600; [13] under them was the trained army of 307,500, who made war with might and power to aid the king against the enemy. [14] Uzziah provided them—the whole army—with shields and spears, and helmets and mail, and bows and slingstones. [15] He made clever devices in Jerusalem, set on the towers and the corners, for shooting arrows and large stones. His fame spread far, for he was helped wonderfully, and he became strong.

[16] When he was strong, he grew so arrogant he acted corruptly: he trespassed against his God by entering the Temple of the LORD to offer incense on the incense altar. [17] The priest Azariah, with eighty other brave priests of the LORD, followed him in [18] and, confronting King Uzziah, said to him, "It is not for you, Uzziah, to offer incense to the LORD, but for the Aaronite priests, who have been consecrated, to offer incense. Get out of the

[a] *Some Heb. mss. read* byr't; *compare ancient versions, "fear."*

Sanctuary, for you have trespassed; there will be no glory in it for you from the LORD God." ¹⁹ Uzziah, holding the censer and ready to burn incense, got angry; but as he got angry with the priests, leprosy broke out on his forehead in front of the priests in the House of the LORD beside the incense altar. ²⁰ When the chief priest Azariah and all the other priests looked at him, his forehead was leprous, so they rushed him out of there; he too made haste to get out, for the LORD had struck him with a plague. ²¹ King Uzziah was a leper until the day of his death. He lived in *ᵇ⁻ isolated quarters⁻ᵇ* as a leper, for he was cut off from the House of the LORD—while Jotham his son was in charge of the king's house and governed the people of the land.

²² The other events of Uzziah's reign, early and late, were recorded by the prophet Isaiah son of Amoz. ²³ Uzziah slept with his fathers in the burial field of the kings, because, they said, he was a leper; his son Jotham succeeded him as king.

27 Jotham was twenty-five years old when he became king, and he reigned sixteen years in Jerusalem; his mother's name was Jerushah daughter of Zadok. ² He did what was pleasing to the LORD just as his father Uzziah had done, but he did not enter the Temple of the LORD; however, the people still acted corruptly. ³ It was he who built the Upper Gate of the House of the LORD; he also built extensively on the wall of Ophel. ⁴ He built towns in the hill-country of Judah, and in the woods he built fortresses and towers. ⁵ Moreover, he fought with the king of the Ammonites and overcame them; the Ammonites gave him that year 100 talents of silver and 10,000 kor of wheat and another 10,000 of barley; that is what the Ammonites paid him, and [likewise] in the second and third years. ⁶ Jotham was strong because he maintained a faithful course before the LORD his God.

⁷ The other events of Jotham's reign, and all his battles and his conduct are recorded in the book of the kings of Israel and Judah. ⁸ He was twenty-five years old when he became king, and he

ᵇ⁻ᵇ *Meaning of Heb. uncertain.*

reigned sixteen years in Jerusalem. ⁹ Jotham slept with his fathers, and was buried in the City of David; his son Ahaz succeeded him as king.

28 Ahaz was twenty years old when he became king, and he reigned sixteen years in Jerusalem. He did not do what was pleasing to the LORD as his father David had done, ² but followed the ways of the kings of Israel; he even made molten images for the Baals. ³ He made offerings in the Valley of Ben-hinnom and burned his sons in fire, in the abhorrent fashion of the nations which the LORD had dispossessed before the Israelites. ⁴ He sacrificed and made offerings at the shrines, on the hills, and under every leafy tree. ⁵ The LORD his God delivered him over to the king of Aram, who defeated him and took many of his men captive, and brought them to Damascus. He was also delivered over to the king of Israel, who inflicted a great defeat on him. ⁶ Pekah son of Remaliah killed 120,000 in Judah—all brave men —in one day, because they had forsaken the LORD God of their fathers. ⁷ Zichri, the champion of Ephraim, killed Maaseiah the king's son, and Azrikam chief of the palace, and Elkanah, the second to the king. ⁸ The Israelites captured 200,000 of their kinsmen, women, boys, and girls; they also took a large amount of booty from them and brought the booty to Samaria.

⁹ A prophet of the LORD by the name of Oded was there, who went out to meet the army on its return to Samaria. He said to them, "Because of the fury of the LORD God of your fathers against Judah, He delivered them over to you, and you killed them in a rage that reached heaven. ¹⁰ Do you now intend to subjugate the men and women of Judah and Jerusalem to be your slaves? As it is, you have nothing but offenses against the LORD your God. ¹¹ Now then, listen to me, and send back the captives you have taken from your kinsmen, for the wrath of the LORD is upon you!" ¹² Some of the chief men of the Ephraimites—Azariah son of Jehohanan, Berechiah son of Meshillemoth, Jehizkiah son of Shallum, and Amasa son of Hadlai—confronted those return-

ing from the campaign ¹³ and said to them, "Do not bring these captives here, for it would mean our offending the LORD, adding to our sins and our offenses; for our offense is grave enough, and there is already wrath upon Israel." ¹⁴ So the soldiers released the captives and the booty in the presence of the officers and all the congregation. ¹⁵ Then the men named above proceeded to take the captives in hand, and with the booty they clothed all the naked among them—they clothed them and shod them and gave them to eat and drink and anointed them and provided donkeys for all who were failing and brought them to Jericho, the city of palms, back to their kinsmen. Then they returned to Samaria.

¹⁶ At that time, King Ahaz sent to the king of Assyria for help. ¹⁷ Again the Edomites came and inflicted a defeat on Judah and took captives. ¹⁸ And the Philistines made forays against the cities of the Shephelah and the Negeb of Judah; they seized Beth-shemesh and Aijalon and Gederoth, and Soco with its villages, and Timnah with its villages, and Gimzo with its villages; and they settled there. ¹⁹ Thus the LORD brought Judah low on account of King Ahaz of Israel,ᵃ for he threw off restraint in Judah and trespassed against the LORD. ²⁰ Tillegath-pilneser, king of Assyria, marched against him and gave him trouble, instead of supporting him. ²¹ For Ahaz plundered the House of the LORD and the house of the king and the officers, and made a gift to the king of Assyria—to no avail.

²² In his time of trouble, this King Ahaz trespassed even more against the LORD, ²³ sacrificing to the gods of Damascus which had defeated him, for he thought, "The gods of the kings of Aram help them; I shall sacrifice to them and they will help me"; but they were his ruin and that of all Israel. ²⁴ Ahaz collected the utensils of the House of God, and cut the utensils of the House of God to pieces. He shut the doors of the House of the LORD and made himself altars in every corner of Jerusalem. ²⁵ In every town in Judah he set up shrines to make offerings to other gods, vexing the LORD God of his fathers.

ᵃ *Some mss. and ancient versions read "Judah."*

26 The other events of his reign and all his conduct, early and late, are recorded in the book of the kings of Judah and Israel. 27 Ahaz slept with his fathers and was buried in the city, in Jerusalem; his body was not brought to the tombs of the kings of Israel. His son Hezekiah succeeded him as king.

29 Hezekiah became king at the age of twenty-five, and he reigned twenty-nine years in Jerusalem; his mother's name was Abijah daughter of Zechariah. 2 He did what was pleasing to the LORD, just as his father David had done.

3 He, in the first month of the first year of his reign, opened the doors of the House of the LORD and repaired them. 4 He summoned the priests and the Levites and assembled them in the east square. 5 He said to them, "Listen to me, Levites! Sanctify yourselves and sanctify the House of the LORD God of your fathers, and take the abhorrent things out of the holy place. 6 For our fathers trespassed and did what displeased the LORD our God; they forsook Him and turned their faces away from the dwelling-place of the LORD, turning their backs on it. 7 They also shut the doors of the porch and put out the lights; they did not offer incense and did not make burnt offerings in the holy place to the God of Israel. 8 The wrath of the LORD was upon Judah and Jerusalem; He made them an object of horror, amazement, and hissing a as you see with your own eyes. 9 Our fathers died by the sword, and our sons and daughters and wives are in captivity on account of this. 10 Now I wish to make a covenant with the LORD God of Israel, so that His rage may be withdrawn from us. 11 Now, my sons, do not be slack, for the LORD chose you to attend upon Him, to serve Him, to be His ministers and to make offerings to Him."

12 So the Levites set to—Mahath son of Amasai and Joel son of Azariah of the sons of Kohath; and of the sons of Merari, Kish son of Abdi and Azariah son of Jehallelel; and of the Gershonites, Joah son of Zimmah and Eden son of Joah; 13 and of the sons of

a See note at Jer. 18.16.

Elizaphan, Shimri and Jeiel; and of the sons of Asaph, Zechariah and Mattaniah; ¹⁴ and of the sons of Heman, Jehiel and Shimei; and of the sons of Jeduthun, Shemaiah and Uzziel—¹⁵ and, gathering their brothers, they sanctified themselves and came, by a command of the king concerning the LORD's ordinances, to purify the House of the LORD. ¹⁶ The priests went into the House of the LORD to purify it, and brought all the unclean things they found in the temple of the LORD out into the court of the House of the LORD; [there] the Levites received them, to take them outside to Wadi Kidron. ¹⁷ They began the sanctification on the first day of the first month; on the eighth day of the month they reached the porch of the LORD. They sanctified the House of the LORD for eight days, and on the sixteenth day of the first month they finished. ¹⁸ Then they went into the palace of King Hezekiah and said, "We have purified the whole House of the LORD and the altar of burnt offering and all its utensils, and the table of the bread of display and all its utensils; ¹⁹ and all the utensils which King Ahaz had befouled during his reign, when he trespassed, we have made ready and sanctified. They are standing in front of the altar of the LORD."

²⁰ King Hezekiah rose early, gathered the officers of the city, and went up to the House of the LORD. ²¹ They brought seven bulls and seven rams and seven lambs and seven he-goats as a sin offering for the kingdom and for the Sanctuary and for Judah. He ordered the Aaronite priests to offer them on the altar of the LORD. ²² The cattle were slaughtered, and the priests received the blood and dashed it against the altar; the rams were slaughtered and the blood was dashed against the altar; the lambs were slaughtered and the blood was dashed against the altar. ²³ The he-goats for the sin offering were presented to the king and the congregation, who laid their hands upon them. ²⁴ The priests slaughtered them and performed the purgation-rite with the blood against the altar, to expiate for all Israel, for the king had designated the burnt offering and the sin offering to be for all Israel. ²⁵ He stationed the Levites in the House of the LORD with

cymbals and harps and lyres, as David and Gad the king's seer and Nathan the prophet had ordained, for the ordinance was by the LORD through His prophets.

26 When the Levites were in place with the instruments of David, and the priests with their trumpets, 27 Hezekiah gave the order to offer the burnt offering on the altar. When the burnt offering began, the song of the LORD and the trumpets began also, together with the instruments of King David of Israel. 28 All the congregation prostrated themselves, the song was sung and the trumpets were blown—all this until the end of the burnt offering. 29 When the offering was finished, the king and all who were there with him knelt and prostrated themselves. 30 King Hezekiah and the officers ordered the Levites to praise the LORD in the words of David and Asaph the seer; so they praised rapturously, and they bowed and prostrated themselves.

31 Then Hezekiah said, "Now you have consecrated yourselves to the LORD; come, bring sacrifices of well-being and thanksgiving to the House of the LORD." The congregation brought sacrifices of well-being and thanksgiving, and all who felt so moved brought burnt offerings. 32 The number of burnt offerings that the congregation brought was 70 cattle, 100 rams, 200 lambs—all these for burnt offerings to the LORD. 33 The sacred offerings were 600 large cattle and 3000 small cattle. 34 The priests were too few to be able to flay all the burnt offerings, so their kinsmen, the Levites, reinforced them till the end of the work, and till the [rest of the] priests sanctified themselves. (The Levites were more conscientious about sanctifying themselves than the priests.) 35 For beside the large number of burnt offerings, there were the fat parts of the sacrifices of well-being and the libations for the burnt offerings; so the service of the House of the LORD was properly accomplished. 36 Hezekiah and all the people rejoiced over what God had enabled the people to accomplish, because it had happened so suddenly.

30 Hezekiah sent word to all Israel and Judah; he also wrote letters to Ephraim and Manasseh to come to the House of the LORD in Jerusalem to keep the Passover for the LORD God of Israel. [2] The king and his officers and the congregation in Jerusalem had agreed to keep the Passover in the second month, [3] for at the time, they were unable to keep it,[a] for not enough priests had sanctified themselves, nor had the people assembled in Jerusalem. [4] The king and the whole congregation thought it proper [5] to issue a decree and proclaim throughout all Israel from Beer-sheba to Dan that they come and keep the Passover for the LORD God of Israel in Jerusalem—not often did they act in accord with what was written. [6] The couriers went out with the letters from the king and his officers through all Israel and Judah, by order of the king, proclaiming, "O you Israelites! Return to the LORD God of your fathers, Abraham, Isaac, and Israel, and He will return to the remnant of you who escaped from the hand of the kings of Assyria. [7] Do not be like your fathers and brothers who trespassed against the LORD God of their fathers and He turned them into a horror, as you see. [8] Now do not be stiff-necked like your fathers; submit yourselves to the LORD and come to His Sanctuary, which He consecrated forever, and serve the LORD your God so that His anger may turn back from you. [9] If you return to the LORD, your brothers and children will be regarded with compassion by their captors, and will return to this land; for the LORD your God is gracious and merciful; He will not turn His face from you if you return to Him."

[10] As the couriers passed from town to town in the land of Ephraim and Manasseh till they reached Zebulun, they were laughed at and mocked. [11] Some of the people of Asher and Manasseh and Zebulun, however, were contrite, and came to Jerusalem. [12] The hand of God was on Judah, too, making them of a single mind to carry out the command of the king and officers concerning the ordinance of the LORD. [13] A great crowd assem-

---

[a] *I.e. on its proper date; cf. Num. 9.1–14.*

bled at Jerusalem to keep the Feast of Unleavened Bread in the second month, a very great congregation. [14] They set to and removed the altars that were in Jerusalem, and they removed all the incense stands and threw them into Wadi Kidron. [15] They slaughtered the paschal sacrifice on the fourteenth of the second month. The priests and Levites were ashamed, and they sanctified themselves and brought burnt offerings to the House of the LORD. [16] They took their stations, as was their rule according to the Teaching of Moses, man of God. The priests dashed the blood [which they received] from the Levites. [17] Since many in the congregation had not sanctified themselves, the Levites were in charge of slaughtering the paschal sacrifice for everyone who was not clean, so as to consecrate them to the LORD. [18] For most of the people—many from Ephraim and Manasseh, Issachar and Zebulun—had not purified themselves, yet they ate the paschal sacrifice in violation of what was written. Hezekiah prayed for them, saying, "The good LORD will provide atonement for [19] everyone who set his mind on worshiping God, the LORD God of his fathers, even if he is not purified for the sanctuary." [20] The LORD heard Hezekiah and healed the people.

[21] The Israelites who were in Jerusalem kept the Feast of Unleavened Bread seven days, with great rejoicing, the Levites and the priests praising the LORD daily with powerful instruments for the LORD. [22] Hezekiah persuaded all the Levites who performed skillfully for the LORD to spend the seven days of the festival making offerings of well-being, and confessing to the LORD God of their fathers. [23] All the congregation resolved to keep seven more days, so they kept seven more days of rejoicing. [24] King Hezekiah of Judah contributed to the congregation 1000 bulls and 7000 sheep. And the officers contributed to the congregation 1000 bulls and 10,000 sheep. And the priests sanctified themselves in large numbers. [25] All the congregation of Jerusalem and the priests and the Levites and all the congregation that came from Israel, and the resident aliens who came from the land of Israel and who lived in Judah rejoiced. [26] There was great rejoic-

ing in Jerusalem, for since the time of King Solomon son of David of Israel nothing like it had happened in Jerusalem. ²⁷ The Levite priests rose and blessed the people, and their voice was heard, and their prayer went up to His holy abode, to heaven.

31 When all this was finished, all Israel who were present went out into the towns of Judah and smashed the pillars, cut down the sacred posts, demolished the shrines and altars throughout Judah and Benjamin, and throughout Ephraim and Manasseh, to the very last one. Then all the Israelites returned to their towns, each to his possession.

² Hezekiah reconstituted the divisions of the priests and Levites, each man of the priests and Levites according to his office, for the burnt offerings, the offerings of well-being, to minister, and to sing hymns and praises in the gates of the courts of the LORD; ³ also the king's portion, from his property, for the burnt offerings—the morning and evening burnt offering, and the burnt offerings for sabbaths, and new moons, and festivals, as prescribed in the Teaching of the LORD.

⁴ He ordered the people, the inhabitants of Jerusalem, to deliver the portions of the priests and the Levites, so that they might devote themselves to the Teaching of the LORD. ⁵ When the word spread, the Israelites brought large quantities of grain, wine, oil, honey, and all kinds of agricultural produce, and tithes of all, in large amounts. ⁶ The men of Israel and Judah living in the towns of Judah—they too brought tithes of cattle and sheep and tithes of sacred things consecrated to the LORD their God, piling them in heaps. ⁷ In the third month the heaps began to accumulate, and were finished in the seventh month. ⁸ When Hezekiah and the officers came and saw the heaps, they blessed the LORD and his people Israel. ⁹ Hezekiah asked the priests and Levites about the heaps. ¹⁰ The chief priest Azariah, of the house of Zadok, replied to him, saying, "Ever since the gifts began to be brought to the House of the LORD, people have been eating to satiety and leav-

ing over in great amounts, for the Lord has blessed His people; this huge amount is left over!" ¹¹ Hezekiah then gave orders to prepare store-chambers in the House of the Lord; and they were prepared. ¹² They brought in the gifts and the tithes and the sacred things faithfully. Their supervisor was Conaniah the Levite, and Shimei his brother was second in rank. ¹³ Jehiel and Azaziah and Nahath and Asahel and Jerimoth and Jozabad and Eliel and Ismachiah and Mahath and Benaiah were commissioners under Conaniah and Shimei his brother by appointment of King Hezekiah; Azariah was supervisor of the House of God. ¹⁴ Kore son of Imnah the Levite, the keeper of the East Gate, was in charge of the freewill offerings to God, of the allocation of gifts to the Lord, and the most sacred things. ¹⁵ Under him were Eden, Miniamin, Jeshua, Shemaiah, Amariah, and Shecaniah, in offices of trust in the priestly towns, making allocation to their brothers by divisions, to great and small alike; ¹⁶ besides allocating their daily rations to those males registered by families from three years old and up, all who entered the House of the Lord according to their service and their shift by division; ¹⁷ and in charge of the registry of priests by clans, and of the Levites, from twenty years old and up, by shifts, in their divisions; ¹⁸ and the registry of the dependents of their whole company—wives, sons, and daughters—for, relying upon them, they sanctified themselves in holiness. ¹⁹ And for the Aaronite priests, in each and every one of their towns with adjoining fields, the above-named men were to allocate portions to every male of the priests and to every registered Levite. ²⁰ Hezekiah did this throughout Judah. He acted in a way that was good, upright, and faithful before the Lord his God. ²¹ Every work he undertook in the service of the House of God or in the Teaching and the Commandment, to worship his God, he did with all his heart; and he prospered.

32 ^aAfter these faithful deeds, King Sennacherib of Assyria invaded Judah and encamped against its fortified towns with the aim of taking them over. ² When Hezekiah saw that Sennacherib had come, intent on making war against Jerusalem, ³ he consulted with his officers and warriors about stopping the flow of the springs outside the city, and they supported him. ⁴ A large force was assembled to stop up all the springs and the wadi that flowed through the land, for otherwise, they thought, the king of Assyria would come and find water in abundance. ⁵ He acted with vigor, rebuilding the whole breached wall, raising towers on it, and building another wall outside it. He fortified the Millo of the City of David, and made a great quantity of arms and shields. ⁶ He appointed battle officers over the people; then, gathering them to him in the square of the city gate, he rallied them, saying, ⁷ "Be strong and of good courage; do not be frightened or dismayed by the king of Assyria or by the horde that is with him, for we have more with us than he has with him. ⁸ With him is an arm of flesh, but with us is the LORD our God, to help us and to fight our battles." The people were encouraged by the speech of King Hezekiah of Judah.

⁹ Afterward, King Sennacherib of Assyria sent his officers to Jerusalem—he and all his staff being at Lachish—with this message to King Hezekiah of Judah and to all the people of Judah who were in Jerusalem: ¹⁰ "Thus said King Sennacherib of Assyria: On what do you trust to enable you to endure a siege in Jerusalem? ¹¹ Hezekiah is seducing you to a death of hunger and thirst, saying, 'The LORD our God will save us from the king of Assyria.' ¹² But is not Hezekiah the one who removed His shrines and His altars and commanded the people of Judah and Jerusalem saying, 'Before this one altar you shall prostrate yourselves, and upon it make your burnt offerings'? ¹³ Surely you know what I and my fathers have done to the peoples of the lands? Were the gods of the nations of the lands able to save their lands from me?

^a *Cf. II Kings 18–20; Isa. 36–39.*

¹⁴ Which of all the gods of any of those nations whom my fathers destroyed was able to save his people from me, that your God should be able to save you from me? ¹⁵ Now then, do not let Hezekiah delude you; do not let him seduce you in this way; do not believe him. For no god of any nation or kingdom has been able to save his people from me or from my fathers—much less your God, to save you from me!" ¹⁶ His officers said still more things against the LORD God and against His servant Hezekiah. ¹⁷ He also wrote letters reviling the LORD God of Israel, saying of Him, "Just as the gods of the other nations of the earth did not save their people from me, so the God of Hezekiah will not save his people from me." ¹⁸ They called loudly in the language of Judah to the people of Jerusalem who were on the wall, to frighten them into panic, so as to capture the city. ¹⁹ They spoke of the God of Jerusalem as though He were like the gods of the other peoples of the earth, made by human hands. ²⁰ Then King Hezekiah and the prophet Isaiah son of Amoz prayed about this, and cried out to heaven.

²¹ The LORD sent an angel who annihilated every mighty warrior, commander, and officer in the army of the king of Assyria, and he returned in disgrace to his land. He entered the house of his god, and there some of his own offspring struck him down by the sword. ²² Thus the LORD delivered Hezekiah and the inhabitants of Jerusalem from King Sennacherib of Assyria, and from everyone; He provided for them on all sides. ²³ Many brought tribute to the LORD to Jerusalem, and gifts to King Hezekiah of Judah; thereafter he was exalted in the eyes of all the nations.

²⁴ At that time, Hezekiah fell deathly sick. He prayed to the LORD, who responded to him and gave him a sign. ²⁵ Hezekiah made no return for what had been bestowed upon him, for he grew arrogant; so wrath was decreed for him and for Judah and Jerusalem. ²⁶ Then Hezekiah humbled himself where he had been arrogant, he and the inhabitants of Jerusalem, and no wrath of the LORD came on them during the reign of Hezekiah. ²⁷ Hezekiah enjoyed riches and glory in abundance; he filled

treasuries with silver and gold, precious stones, spices, shields, and all lovely objects; [28] and store-cities with the produce of grain, wine, and oil, and stalls for all kinds of beasts, and flocks for sheepfolds. [29] And he acquired towns, and flocks of small and large cattle in great number, for God endowed him with very many possessions. [30] It was Hezekiah who stopped up the spring of water of Upper Gihon, leading it downward west of the City of David; Hezekiah prospered in all that he did. [31] So too in the matter of the ambassadors of the princes of Babylon, who were sent to him to inquire about the sign that was in the land, when God forsook him in order to test him, to learn all that was in his mind.

[32] The other events of Hezekiah's reign, and his faithful acts, are recorded in the visions of the prophet Isaiah son of Amoz and in the book of the kings of Judah and Israel. [33] Hezekiah slept with his fathers, and was buried on the upper part of the tombs of the sons of David. When he died, all the people of Judah and the inhabitants of Jerusalem accorded him much honor. Manasseh, his son, succeeded him.

33 [a]Manasseh was twelve years old when he became king, and he reigned fifty-five years in Jerusalem. [2] He did what was displeasing to the LORD, following the abhorrent practices of the nations which the LORD had dispossessed before the Israelites. [3] He rebuilt the shrines that his father Hezekiah had demolished; he erected altars for the Baals and made sacred posts. He bowed down to all the host of heaven and worshiped them, [4] and he built altars [to them] in the House of the LORD, of which the LORD had said, "My name will be in Jerusalem forever." [5] He built altars for all the host of heaven in the two courts of the House of the LORD. [6] He consigned his sons to the fire in the Valley of Ben-hinnom, and he practiced soothsaying, divination, and sorcery, and consulted ghosts and familiar spirits; he did much that was displeasing to the LORD in order to vex Him. [7] He placed a sculptured

---

[a] *Cf. II Kings 21.*

image that he made in the House of God, of which God had said to David and to his son Solomon, "In this House and in Jerusalem, which I chose out of all the tribes of Israel, I will establish My name forever. 8 And I will never again remove the feet of Israel from the land that I assigned to their fathers, if only they observe faithfully all that I have commanded them—all the teaching and the laws and the rules given by Moses." 9 Manasseh led Judah and the inhabitants of Jerusalem astray into evil greater than that done by the nations that the LORD had destroyed before the Israelites.

10 The LORD spoke to Manasseh and his people, but they would not pay heed, 11 so the LORD brought against them the officers of the army of the king of Assyria, who took Manasseh captive in manacles, bound him in fetters, and led him off to Babylon. 12 In his distress, he entreated the LORD his God and humbled himself greatly before the God of his fathers. 13 He prayed to Him, and He granted his prayer, heard his plea, and returned him to Jerusalem to his kingdom. Then Manasseh knew that the LORD alone was God. 14 Afterward he built the outer wall of the City of David west of Gihon in the wadi on the way to the Fish Gate, and it encircled Ophel; he raised it very high. He also placed army officers in all the fortified towns of Judah. 15 He removed the foreign gods and the image from the House of the LORD, as well as all the altars that he had built on the Mount of the House of the LORD and in Jerusalem, and dumped them outside the city. 16 He rebuilt the altar of the LORD and offered on it sacrifices of well-being and thanksgiving, and commanded the people of Judah to worship the LORD God of Israel. 17 To be sure, the people continued sacrificing at the shrines, but only to the LORD their God.

18 The other events of Manasseh's reign, and his prayer to his God, and the words of the seers who spoke to him in the name of the LORD God of Israel are found in the chronicles of the kings of Israel. 19 His prayer and how it was granted to him, the whole account of his sin and trespass, and the places in which he built

shrines and installed sacred posts and images before he humbled himself are recorded in the words of Hozai.[b] [20] Manasseh slept with his fathers and was buried on his palace grounds; his son Amon succeeded him as king.

[21] Amon was twenty-two years old when he became king, and he reigned two years in Jerusalem. [22] He did what was displeasing to the LORD, as his father Manasseh had done. Amon sacrificed to all the idols that his father Manasseh had made and worshiped them. [23] He did not humble himself before the LORD, as his father Manasseh had humbled himself; instead, Amon incurred much guilt. [24] His courtiers conspired against him and killed him in his palace. [25] But the people of the land struck down all who had conspired against King Amon; and the people of the land made his son Josiah king in his stead.

34 [a]Josiah was eight years old when he became king, and he reigned thirty-one years in Jerusalem. [2] He did what was pleasing to the LORD, following the ways of his father David without deviating to the right or to the left. [3] In the eighth year of his reign, while he was still young, he began to seek the God of his father David, and in the twelfth year he began to purge Judah and Jerusalem of the shrines, the sacred posts, the idols, and the molten images. [4] At his bidding, they demolished the altars of the Baals, and he had the incense stands above them cut down; he smashed the sacred posts, the idols, and the images, ground them into dust, and strewed it onto the graves of those who had sacrificed to them. [5] He burned the bones of priests on their altars and purged Judah and Jerusalem. [6] In the towns of Manasseh and Ephraim and Simeon, as far as Naphtali, [lying] in ruins on every side, [7] he demolished the altars and the sacred posts and smashed the idols and ground them into dust; and he hewed down all the incense stands throughout the land of Israel. Then he returned to Jerusalem.

[8] In the eighteenth year of his reign, after purging the land and

[b] *Or "seers."*

[a] *Cf. II Kings 22, 23.1–20.*

the House, he commissioned Shaphan son of Azaliah, Maaseiah the governor of the city, and Joah son of Joahaz the recorder to repair the House of the Lord his God. ⁹ They came to the high priest Hilkiah and delivered to him the silver brought to the House of God, which the Levites, the guards of the threshold, had collected from Manasseh and Ephraim and from all the remnant of Israel and from all Judah and Benjamin and ᵇ-the inhabitants of Jerusalem.-ᵇ ¹⁰ They delivered it into the custody of the overseers who were in charge at the House of the Lord, and the overseers who worked in the House of the Lord spent it on examining and repairing the House. ¹¹ They paid it out to the artisans and the masons to buy quarried stone and wood for the couplings and for making roof-beams for the buildings that the kings of Judah had allowed to fall into ruin. ¹² The men did the work honestly; over them were appointed the Levites Jahath and Obadiah, of the sons of Merari, and Zechariah and Meshullam, of the sons of Kohath, to supervise; while other Levites, all the master musicians, ¹³ were over the porters, supervising all who worked at each and every task; some of the Levites were scribes and officials and gatekeepers.

¹⁴ As they took out the silver that had been brought to the House of the Lord, the priest Hilkiah found a scroll of the Lord's Teaching given by Moses. ¹⁵ Hilkiah spoke up and said to the scribe Shaphan, "I have found a scroll of the Teaching in the House of the Lord"; and Hilkiah gave the scroll to Shaphan. ¹⁶ Shaphan brought the scroll to the king and also reported to the king, "All that was entrusted to your servants is being done; ¹⁷ they have melted down the silver that was found in the House of the Lord and delivered it to those who were in charge, to the overseers." ¹⁸ The scribe Shaphan also told the king, "The priest Hilkiah has given me a scroll"; and Shaphan read from it to the king. ¹⁹ When the king heard the words of the Teaching, he tore his clothes. ²⁰ The king gave orders to Hilkiah, and Ahikam son of Shaphan, and Abdon son of Micah, and the scribe Shaphan, and Asaiah the king's minister, saying, ²¹ "Go, inquire of the

ᵇ⁻ᵇ *With* kethib *and ancient versions;* qere *"they returned to Jerusalem."*

LORD on my behalf and on behalf of those who remain in Israel and Judah concerning the words of the scroll that has been found, for great indeed must be the wrath of the LORD that has been poured down upon us because our fathers did not obey the word of the LORD and do all that is written in this scroll."

²² Hilkiah and those whom the king [had ordered] went to the prophetess Huldah, wife of Shallum son of Tokhath son of Hasrah, keeper of the wardrobe, who was living in Jerusalem in the Mishneh,^c and spoke to her accordingly. ²³ She responded to them: "Thus said the LORD God of Israel: Say to the man who sent you to Me, '²⁴ Thus said the LORD: I am going to bring disaster upon this place and its inhabitants—all the curses that are written in the scroll that was read to the king of Judah— ²⁵ because they forsook Me and made offerings to other gods in order to vex Me with all the works of their hands; My wrath shall be poured out against this place and not be quenched.' ²⁶ But say this to the king of Judah who sent you to inquire of the LORD: 'Thus said the LORD God of Israel: As for the words which you have heard, ²⁷ since your heart was softened and you humbled yourself before God when you heard His words concerning this place and its inhabitants, and you humbled yourself before Me and tore your clothes and wept before Me, I for My part have listened, declares the LORD. ²⁸ Assuredly, I will gather you to your fathers, and you will be laid in your grave in peace; your eyes shall see nothing of the disaster which I will bring upon this place and its inhabitants.' " They reported this back to the king.

²⁹ Then the king sent word and assembled all the elders of Judah and Jerusalem. ³⁰ The king went up to the House of the LORD with all the men of Judah and the inhabitants of Jerusalem and the priests and the Levites—all the people, young and old— and he read to them the entire text of the covenant scroll that was found in the House of the LORD. ³¹ The king stood in his place and solemnized the covenant before the LORD: to follow the LORD and observe His commandments, His injunctions, and His laws with all his heart and soul, to fulfill all the terms of the

^c *A quarter in Jerusalem; cf. Zeph. 1.10.*

covenant written in this scroll. ³² He obligated all the men of Jerusalem and Benjamin who were present; and the inhabitants of Jerusalem acted in accord with the Covenant of God, God of their fathers. ³³ Josiah removed all the abominations from the whole territory of the Israelites and obliged all who were in Israel to worship the LORD their God. Throughout his reign they did not deviate from following the LORD God of their fathers.

35 ^aJosiah kept the Passover for the LORD in Jerusalem; the passover sacrifice was slaughtered on the fourteenth day of the first month. ² He reinstated the priests in their shifts and rallied them to the service of the House of the LORD. ³ He said to the Levites, consecrated to the LORD, who taught all Israel, "Put the Holy Ark in the House that Solomon son of David, king of Israel, built; as you no longer carry it on your shoulders, see now to the service of the LORD your God and His people Israel, ⁴ and dispose yourselves by clans according to your divisions, as prescribed in the writing of King David of Israel and in the document of his son Solomon, ⁵ and attend in the Sanctuary, by clan divisions, on your kinsmen, the people—by clan divisions of the Levites. ⁶ Having sanctified yourselves, slaughter the passover sacrifice and prepare it for your kinsmen, according to the word of God given by Moses." ⁷ Josiah donated to the people small cattle— lambs and goats, all for passover sacrifices for all present—to the sum of 30,000, and large cattle, 3000—these from the property of the king. ⁸ His officers, priests, and Levites gave a freewill offering to the people, to the priests and to the Levites. Hilkiah and Zechariah and Jehiel, the chiefs of the House of God, donated to the priests for passover sacrifices 2600 [small cattle] and 300 large cattle. ⁹ Conaniah, Shemaiah, and Nethanel, his brothers, and Hashabiah and Jeiel and Jozabad, officers of the Levites, donated 5000 [small cattle] and 500 large cattle to the Levites for passover sacrifices.

¹⁰ The service was arranged well: the priests stood at their posts

---

^a *Cf. II Kings 23.21–30.*

and the Levites in their divisions, by the king's command. [11] They slaughtered the passover sacrifice and the priests [received its blood] from them and dashed it, while the Levites flayed the animals. [12] They removed the parts to be burnt, distributing them to divisions of the people by clans, and making the sacrifices to the LORD, as prescribed in the scroll of Moses; they did the same for the cattle. [13] They roasted the passover sacrifice in fire, as prescribed, while the sacred offerings they cooked in pots, cauldrons, and pans, and conveyed them with dispatch to all the people. [14] Afterward they provided for themselves and the priests, for the Aaronite priests were busy offering the burnt offerings and the fatty parts until nightfall, so the Levites provided both for themselves and for the Aaronite priests. [15] The Asaphite singers were at their stations, by command of David and Asaph and Heman and Jeduthun, the seer of the king; and the gatekeepers were at each and every gate. They did not have to leave their tasks, because their Levite brothers provided for them. [16] The entire service of the LORD was arranged well that day, to keep the Passover and to make the burnt offerings on the altar of the LORD, according to the command of King Josiah. [17] All the Israelites present kept the Passover at that time, and the Feast of Unleavened Bread for seven days. [18] Since the time of the prophet Samuel, no Passover like that one had ever been kept in Israel; none of the kings of Israel had kept a Passover like the one kept by Josiah and the priests and the Levites and all Judah and Israel there present and the inhabitants of Jerusalem. [19] That Passover was kept in the eighteenth year of the reign of Josiah.

[20] After all this furbishing of the Temple by Josiah, King Necho of Egypt came up to fight at Carchemish on the Euphrates, and Josiah went out against him. [21] [Necho] sent messengers to him, saying, "What have I to do with you, king of Judah? I do not march against you this day but against the kingdom that wars with me, and it is God's will that I hurry. Refrain, then, from interfering with God who is with me, that He not destroy you." [22] But Josiah would not let him alone; instead, *b*he donned [his armor]*-b*

b-b *With Targ.*

to fight him, heedless of Necho's words from the mouth of God; and he came to fight in the plain of Megiddo. [23] Archers shot King Josiah, and the king said to his servants, "Get me away from here, for I am badly wounded." [24] His servants carried him out of his chariot and put him in the wagon of his second-in-command, and conveyed him to Jerusalem. There he died, and was buried in the grave of his fathers, and all Judah and Jerusalem went into mourning over Josiah. [25] Jeremiah composed laments for Josiah which all the singers, male and female, recited in their laments for Josiah, as is done to this day; they became customary in Israel and were incorporated into the laments. [26] The other events of Josiah's reign and his faithful deeds, in accord with the Teaching of the LORD, [27] and his acts, early and late, are recorded in the book of the kings of Israel and Judah.

36 [a]The people of the land took Jehoahaz son of Josiah and made him king instead of his father in Jerusalem. [2] Jehoahaz was twenty-three years old when he became king and he reigned three months in Jerusalem. [3] The king of Egypt deposed him in Jerusalem and laid a fine on the land of 100 silver talents and one gold talent. [4] The king of Egypt made his brother Eliakim king over Judah and Jerusalem, and changed his name to Jehoiakim; Necho took his brother Joahaz and brought him to Egypt.

[5] Jehoiakim was twenty-five years old when he became king, and he reigned eleven years in Jerusalem; he did what was displeasing to the LORD his God. [6] King Nebuchadnezzar of Babylon marched against him; he bound him in fetters to convey him to Babylon. [7] Nebuchadnezzar also brought some vessels of the House of the LORD to Babylon, and set them in his palace in Babylon. [8] The other events of Jehoiakim's reign, and the abominable things he did, and what was found against him, are recorded in the book of the kings of Israel and Judah. His son Jehoiachin succeeded him as king.

[9] Jehoiachin was eight years old when he became king, and he

[a] With vv. 1–13, cf. II Kings 23.28–37, II Kings 24.1–20.

reigned three months and ten days in Jerusalem; he did what was displeasing to the LORD. [10] At the turn of the year, King Nebuchadnezzar sent to have him brought to Babylon with the precious vessels of the House of the LORD, and he made his kinsman Zedekiah king over Judah and Jerusalem.

[11] Zedekiah was twenty-one years old when he became king, and he reigned eleven years in Jerusalem. [12] He did what was displeasing to the LORD his God; he did not humble himself before the prophet Jeremiah, who spoke for the LORD. [13] He also rebelled against Nebuchadnezzar, who made him take an oath[b] by God; he stiffened his neck and hardened his heart so as not to turn to the LORD God of Israel. [14] All the officers of the priests and the people committed many trespasses, following all the abominable practices of the nations. They polluted the House of the LORD which He had consecrated in Jerusalem. [15] The LORD God of their fathers had sent word to them through His messengers daily without fail, for He had pity on His people and His dwelling-place. [16] But they mocked the messengers of God and disdained His words and taunted His prophets until the wrath of the LORD against His people grew beyond remedy. [17] He therefore brought the king of the Chaldeans upon them, who killed their youths by the sword in their Sanctuary; He did not spare youth, maiden, elder, or graybeard, but delivered all into his hands. [18] All the vessels of the House of God, large and small, and the treasures of the House of the LORD and the treasures of the king and his officers were all brought to Babylon. [19] They burned the House of God and tore down the wall of Jerusalem, burned down all its mansions, and consigned all its precious objects to destruction. [20] Those who survived the sword he exiled to Babylon, and they became his and his sons' servants till the rise of the Persian kingdom, [21] in fulfillment of the word of the LORD spoken by Jeremiah, until the land paid back its sabbaths; as long as it lay desolate it kept sabbath, till seventy years were completed.

[22] And in the first year of King Cyrus of Persia, when the word of the LORD spoken by Jeremiah was fulfilled, the LORD roused

[b] Viz. a vassal oath.

the spirit of King Cyrus of Persia to issue a proclamation throughout his realm by word of mouth and in writing, as follows: 23 "Thus said King Cyrus of Persia: The LORD God of Heaven has given me all the kingdoms of the earth, and has charged me with building Him a House in Jerusalem, which is in Judah. Anyone of you of all His people, the LORD His God be with him and let him go up."

Inhaltsübersicht

Luther, Zwingli, Calvin in ihren Liedern

Alle drei Haupt-Reformatoren haben geistliche Lieder verfaßt. Unter verschiedenen Bedingungen zwar, in unterschiedlicher Zahl, mit ungleichem Können, in nicht völlig einheitlicher Absicht, aber immerhin in allen drei Fällen geistliche Lieder in der Volkssprache. Luther hochdeutsch, Zwingli alemannisch, Calvin französisch. Und alle drei haben in erster Linie nach dem biblischen Psalter gegriffen, alle drei kennen aber auch andere Liedstoffe. Keiner von den dreien hat nur einmal nebenbei ein Liedlein geschrieben, sondern alle drei haben sich mehrfach mit diesen Schöpfungen befaßt und also dem Lied keine ganz nebensächliche Rolle zugeschrieben. Und für alle drei war ein Lied eine Einheit aus Text und Musik. Zwingli hat alle seine Lieder selbst vertont, Luther einen Teil, während er in anderen Fällen auf vorhandene Melodien dichtete, und Calvin hat teils auf vorhandene Melodien gedichtet, teils seine Texte nachher von andern mit Melodien versehen lassen. Auch wenn er nicht selbst musikschöpferisch tätig war, so war ihm diese Seite des Liedes doch keineswegs gleichgültig, wie seine Gesangbuch-Vorrede zeigt. Alle drei haben also persönlich für die Singbarkeit ihrer Dichtungen gesorgt.

Wenn diese recht erstaunliche Tatsache auch reformationsgeschichtlich sonst gut informierten Leuten nicht ohne weiteres oder doch nicht in ihrem ganzen Umfang bewußt ist, dann liegt das vor allem daran, daß die Liedschöpfungen der drei Reformatoren vollständig und als textlich-musikalische Einheit bisher nur den Spezialisten zugänglich waren. Der Großteil von Luthers Liedern steht zwar heute in jedem evangelischen Gesangbuch; aber die deutschen Luther-Ausgaben (mit Ausnahme der nur dem Wissenschafter zugänglichen und nur für ihn brauchbaren Weimarer Ausgabe) bringen stets nur die Texte. Von Zwinglis Liedern ist bisher sogar in der maßgebenden wissenschaftlichen Gesamt-Ausgabe nur ein einziges und dieses erst noch nur dem Text nach zugänglich. Die andern muß man in der Spezial-Literatur suchen, und noch schlimmer steht es bei Calvin: Seine Lied-Texte stehen zwar in der wissenschaftlichen Gesamtausgabe seiner Werke. Aber mit den zugehörigen Melodien zusammen findet man sie weder in einer französischen, noch in einer deutschen Publikation; man muß dafür zu einer englischen greifen.

Was lag deshalb näher, als jetzt, da sich die nur wenige Wochen auseinander liegenden Geburtstage Luthers und Zwinglis zum 500. Mal jähren, die Lieder der genannten drei Reformatoren einmal im vol-

len Umfang und in ihrer textlich-musikalischen Einheit allgemein zugänglich zu machen. Der Spezialist wird für den dabei sich ergebenden Überblick ebenso dankbar sein wie der musik-, literatur- und kirchengeschichtlich interessierte Laie, an den bei der vorliegenden Ausgabe in erster Linie gedacht wird. Wir verzichten gerade deshalb hier auf jeglichen gelehrten Apparat. Wir bieten die Texte in einer dem Original gegenüber verantwortbaren, aber für den heutigen Menschen soweit als möglich verständlichen Fassung und die Melodien in heutiger Notation. Auf die Mitteilung von Varianten zu den Texten und Melodien wird verzichtet. Die Beigaben zu jedem Lied beschränken wir auf ein Mindestmaß. In Anmerkungen werden die Stellen erläutert, die vom sprachgeschichtlich ungeschulten Leser falsch oder überhaupt nicht verstanden werden und die man doch nicht ändern konnte, weil sonst der Reim oder das Metrum gestört worden wären. Die Erläuterungen, die den einzelnen Stücken beigegeben sind, sollen Aufschluß geben über Hintergrund, Entstehung, Überlieferung und Besonderheiten des Textes und der musikalischen Gestalt. Die wissenschaftlichen Belege für das dort wie in der allgemeinen Einleitung zu jeder der drei Liedergruppen Gesagte müssen in der am Schluß angeführten Fachliteratur gesucht werden. Mit Einzelhinweisen darauf wollten wir jedoch den Leser nicht langweilen. Die hymnologischen Fachausdrücke, deren Verwendung sich nicht umgehen ließ, sind auf S. 283–290 kurz erläutert.

Die Lieder sollen im übrigen für sich sprechen. Und sie sollen nicht nur sprechen, sondern auch klingen. Mancher Text erschließt sich einem erst dann richtig, wenn man singend ihn sich aneignet. Vielleicht können diese alten Lieder auch heute noch da und dort etwas von dem bewirken, wozu sie geschrieben worden sind: Glauben wecken, stärken, vertiefen, aussprechen.

MARTIN LUTHER

Luthers Weg zum Kirchenlied

Luther ging voran. Er kannte das deutsche geistliche Lied aus seiner Jugendzeit ebenso gut wie den lateinischen liturgischen Gesang. Als Schüler ist er mit seinen Kameraden in den Festzeiten von Haus zu Haus gezogen, um lateinische und deutsche volkstümliche Weihnachts- und Osterlieder zu singen. Manche unter ihnen hat er zeitlebens als köstlichen Schatz bewahrt und ihre Pflege auch in der erneuerten Kirche empfohlen, so den Kommunionsgesang Gott sei gelobet und gebenedeiet, *den er nur an einer Stelle gebessert wissen wollte, das Weihnachtslied* Ein Kindelein so löbelich, *das er in Predigten häufig zitiert, oder die Oster-Leise* Christ ist erstanden, *von der er über Tisch einmal sagte:* Aller Lieder singt man sich mit der Zeit müde, aber das ‹Christ ist erstanden› muß jedes Jahr wieder hervorgenommen werden!

Doch zum Liedermacher wurde Luther erst, als die Reformation bereits Tatsache war. Er hatte 1522 von der Wartburg aus «seinen lieben Deutschen» das Neue Testament in ihrer Sprache geschenkt und dann in Wittenberg die von andern allzu ungestüm angebahnte Neuordnung des Gottesdienstes in geordnetere Bahnen zu lenken gesucht. Dabei mögen ihn schon die Gedanken bewegt haben, die er dann gegen Ende des Jahres 1523 in seiner lateinischen Schrift über die rechte Art, Messe und Kommunion zu halten, aussprach: Ich möchte, daß wir möglichst viele Lieder hätten, die das Volk während der Messe singen könnte, zum Graduale, zum Sanctus, zum Agnus Dei. Aber, *so fährt er kurz danach weiter,* es fehlen uns die Dichter oder sind noch nicht bekannt, die uns fromme und geistliche Lieder (wie Paulus sie nennt) sängen, die dann geeignet wären, in der Versammlung Gottes immer wieder gebraucht zu werden. *Die obgenannten deutschen Lieder werden dann als vorläufiger Ersatz empfohlen, und der Abschnitt schließt mit einem förmlichen Aufruf an die deutschen Dichter, sie sollten Glaubenslieder drucken lassen. Offensichtlich denkt Luther noch kaum daran, daß gerade er berufen sein könnte, hier den entscheidenden Anfang zu machen.*

Der Anstoß dazu kam nicht von der Seite des praktischen Bedürfnisses her – und das erklärt auch später manches –, sondern aus einer persönlichen Erschütterung und dem Willen, das Ereignis, welches sie bewirkte, reformationspropagandistisch auszunutzen: Am 1. Juli 1523 waren auf dem Marktplatz zu Brüssel zwei junge Ordensbrüder Luthers aus dem Antwerpener Augustiner-Kloster als Ketzer ver-

brannt worden, weil sie sich zu Luthers Lehre bekannt hatten. Luther weiß, wie ernst es der Gegenpartei nun ist. Er sendet den bedrängten Glaubensgenossen in den Niederlanden ein bewegendes Trostschreiben. Aber vielleicht noch vorher wird er zum Dichter. Seit der Erfindung der Buchdruckerkunst war es Brauch, Helden- und Schlachtenlieder, aber auch Lebensbeschreibungen von Heiligen und Märtyrern in Liedform als kleine Flugschriften zu verbreiten. Diese Form schien Luther das richtige Mittel zu sein, um dem Ereignis vom 1. Juli die erwünschte Breitenwirkung zu geben. Im Stil dieser sogenannten historischen Volkslieder beginnt er: Ein neues Lied wir heben an – das walt Gott, unser Herre (23). Es ist zwar keiner der frühen Drucke mit diesem Lied erhalten, aber es kann kein Zweifel daran bestehen, daß es – wie übrigens der größere Teil von Luthers Liedern – zuerst in dieser Form verbreitet wurde. Und es ist auch kaum zu bezweifeln, daß Luther selbst es war, der diesem bewegenden Hochgesang von der Kraft des Evangeliums seine hochgemute Melodie gab, wenngleich äußere Zeugnisse dafür fehlen.

Wohl nicht lange danach gelang Luther mit Nun freut euch, lieben Christen gmein (18) ein zweites, ähnliches Lied. Es schildert die Heilsgeschichte in überaus kühner Weise in der Form einer autobiographischen Erzählung: Luther besingt die Erlösungstat Gottes in Jesus Christus so, als wäre sie eigens für ihn ins Werk gesetzt worden. Sein innerer Weg zur reformatorischen Erkenntnis wird in diesen Strophen in einer Weise geschildert, wie keine Biographie das so aufrüttelnd zu tun vermöchte.

Auch hier hat der Reformator dem Liede sein Klang-Kleid auf den Leib geschnitten, wenn auch wahrscheinlich erst in einem zweiten Anlauf, denn entstanden ist das Lied offensichtlich als Kontrafaktur auf das Osterprozessionslied Freut euch, alle Christenheit, / daß Christ ist auferstanden, in anderer Fassung: Nun freut euch, Frauen unde Mann, / daß Christ ist auferstanden. Textanfang, Strophenmaß, Melodie und die österliche Grundstimmung sind von hier übernommen.

Und nun war der Born geöffnet. Wir haben Grund zur Annahme, daß noch im selben Jahr 1523 mindestens 9 weitere geistliche Lieder aus Luthers Feder flossen. Ehe wir aber auf diese weiteren Lieder eingehen, sei festgehalten, daß demnach das evangelische Kirchenlied, soweit der entscheidende Impuls dafür von Wittenberg ausgegangen ist, nicht im liturgischen oder katechetischen Bedürfnis, sondern allein in dem ganz persönlichen Drang nach künstlerischer Gestaltung wurzelt, wie er sich bei Luther unter dem Druck der Anfechtung und

als Weg zu ihrer Bewältigung in dieser Stunde seines Lebens – kurz vor Vollendung seines 40.Lebensjahres – einstellte. So sind auch diese beiden ersten Lieder erst nachträglich zu Gemeindeliedern geworden. Ihr ursprünglicher «Sitz im Leben» ist weder die Katechese noch die Liturgie, sondern die Evangeliumsverkündigung in einem denkbar weiten Sinne durch das Medium des Liedes. Dabei wird es uns wohl immer verborgen bleiben, ob der entscheidende Anstoß zum poetischen Schaffen mehr von innen oder stärker von außen kam. Vielleicht kommt man der Wahrheit am nächsten, wenn man annimmt, daß der äußere Anstoß bei Luther auf eine innere Prädisposition stieß. In gleicher Weise werden das persönliche Verarbeiten der inneren Berufung und die Absicht nach reformatorischer «Propaganda» zueinander in Spannung gestanden und einander beeinflußt haben.

Luthers Erfindung: Psalmen in Liedform

Man nimmt gewöhnlich an, daß die ersten unter Luthers weiteren Liedern die Psalmlieder waren. Meist wird angenommen, seine Liedbearbeitung des 67.Psalms (27) sei sein erstes Psalmlied, weil es schon um die Wende 1523/24 im Anhang zur deutschen Übersetzung der vorhin erwähnten Schrift Luthers über Messe und Kommunion überliefert ist. Aber das besagt wenig. Denn um weniges früher ist das Vorhandensein der Bearbeitung des 130.Psalms (30), bezeugt durch einen Brief, mit dem Luther um die Jahreswende mehrere Freunde um die Bereimung von bestimmten Psalmen bat und dem er als Muster sein Lied zu Psalm 130 beilegte. Dieses aber gehört zu einer Gruppe von vier Psalmliedern, die alle die gleiche Grundstimmung aufweisen und alle im selben Metrum geschrieben sind, dem jenes Oster-Prozessionsliedes, zu welchem Nun freut euch, lieben Christen gmein (18) im Kontrafaktur-Verhältnis steht. Diese vier Lieder über die Psalmen 12 (24), 14 (25), 124 (28) und 130 (30) lassen sich alle ohne Mühe in die Stimmung des Märtyrerliedes einfügen. Mithin dürften sie in zeitlicher Nähe zu den ersten beiden Liedern Luthers entstanden sein; denn mit dem einen sind sie inhaltlich, mit dem andern formal verbunden. Ja, es ist nicht einmal ganz ausgeschlossen, daß Luther, der vom klösterlichen Stundengebet und vom Brevierbeten her mit der Psalmenfrömmigkeit tief vertraut war, zunächst zu diesem Stoff griff, um seiner Stimmung Form zu geben, und erst danach zu den beiden stärker eigenständigen Liedern (18, 23) vorstieß. Das Verständnis des Psalters ist Luther erst in der An-

Abb. 1. Zwei Seiten aus einem Tenor-Stimmbuch, das Luthers musikalischer Berater, der Torgauer Kantor Johann Walter, um 1540 für seine Kantorei eigenhändig niedergeschrieben hat. Der Melodie des Liedes Nr. 26 sind die erste und dritte Strophe

fechtung aufgegangen. In diesem Falle würde nicht nur Luthers Liedschaffen im allgemeinen, sondern auch die Psalmlieddichtung zunächst nicht in der Absicht nach liturgischer Dichtung wurzeln, sondern in jenem Freiraum unmittelbaren künstlerischen Ausdrucks für religiöse Gefühle, in welchem schon die alttestamentlichen Psalmen selbst sehr wahrscheinlich größerenteils entstanden sind.

Sei dem, wie ihm wolle, eines ist gewiß: Luther hat als Erfinder des Psalmliedes zu gelten, einer Liedgattung, die es vorher nicht gab, auch nicht in Ansätzen oder Vorstufen, die aber sofort eine gewaltige Breitenwirkung hatte. Außer den schon genannten fünf Psalmliedern hat er selbst dann 1524 noch den Hauspsalm 128 gereimt (29) und 1528 schließlich jene ganz andersartige Psalmbearbeitung geschaffen, die sein berühmtestes Lied wurde: Ein feste Burg ist unser Gott (26).

Wenn man feststellt, daß Psalm 124 sich als Eingangslied des Gottesdienstes eignet und Psalm 67 zum Schluß, könnte man sich fragen, ob Luther hier nicht doch ganz deutlich an die liturgischen Bedürfnisse dachte. Das ist möglich, aber nicht zwingend, und es blieben

18

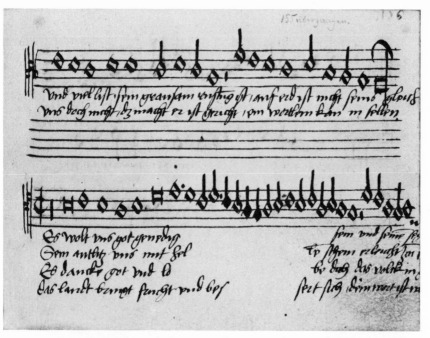

untergelegt; die zweite und vierte sang die Gemeinde. Anschließend der Anfang von Nr. 27, in der gleichen Weise textiert. Nürnberg, Germanisches Nationalmuseum.

immer noch die drei Psalmen *12*, *14* und *130*, die jene frühe «vorliturgische» Psalmlied-Gruppe bilden könnten. Als Luther den Brief an Spalatin und die andern Freunde schrieb, Ende *1523*, hatte er allerdings bereits die gottesdienstliche Verwendung im Auge. Die Geburtsstunde des deutschen evangelischen Gemeindeliedes muß also kurz zuvor geschlagen haben.

Hymnenübertragungen

Ein äußerer Anlaß dafür wird erkennbar, wenn wir eine weitere Gattung von Bearbeitungen fremder Vorlagen durch Luther näher betrachten: seine Übertragungen mittelalterlicher Hymnen. Luther dürfte dazu angeregt worden sein durch den Versuch des Spiritualisten und begabten Außenseiters Thomas Müntzer, der in seiner Verdeutschung von Messe und Stundengebet die gregorianischen Weisen unverändert beibehielt und ihnen lediglich einen silbengleichen deutschen Text unterlegte. In seiner 1525 erschienenen Schrift Wi-

19

der die himmlischen Propheten *sagt Luther nämlich:* Daß man den lateinischen Text übersetzt und die lateinische Melodie, beziehungsweise Noten beibehält, mag man hinnehmen, aber es klingt nicht richtig und wie es soll. Es muß beides, Text und Noten, Betonung,

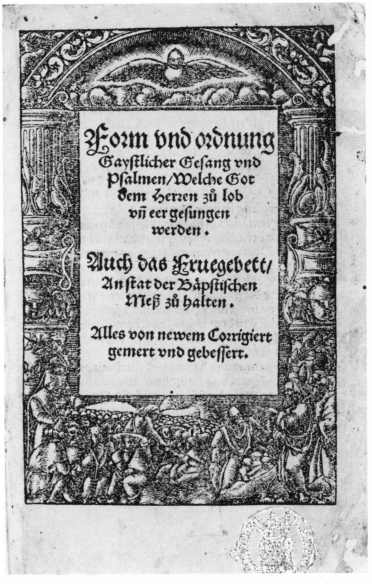

Abb. 2. Der älteste erhaltene Druck von Luthers berühmtestem Lied Nr. 26, ein

Tonfall und Sprachgebärde aus der echten Muttersprache und ihrem Klang kommen, sonst ist es alles ein Nachahmen, wie die Affen tun. *Dementsprechend verfährt nun Luther in seinen Hymnen-Übertragungen: Er übersetzt den Text (wobei er sich oft geradezu sklavisch*

werd ich dancken schiere/ vmb das hail seines angesicht/ erlösung hatt er zügericht/ durch Jesum Christum Amen.

⁋ Der. 46. Ain trost psalm.

In seiner aygnen weyß.

Ain feste burg ist vnnser Gott/ ain güte wör vnd waffen/ Er hilfft vns frey auß aller nott/ die vns yetz hatt betroffen/ der alt böse feyndt/ mitt ernst ers yetz meint/ groß macht vnd vil list/ sein grawsam rüstung ist/ auff erd ist nicht seins gleichen.

⁋ Mit vnnser macht ist nichts gethan/ wir seind gar bald verloren/ Es streyt für vns der rechte man/ den Got hat selbs erkorn/ Fragst du wer der ist/ er hayst Jesu Christ/ der Herr Zebaoth/ vnnd ist kain ander Gott/ das feld müß er behalten.

⁋ Vnd wen̄ die welt vol teüfel wer/ vnd wolt vns gar verschlingen/ So fürchten wir vnns nicht zü ser/ es sol vns doch gelinge̅/ Der Fürst diser wellt/ wie saur er sich stellt/ thůt er vns doch nicht/ das macht er ist gericht/ ain wörtlin kan jn fellen.

⁋ Das wort sy sollen lassen stan/ vnnd kain danck darzů haben/ Er ist bey vnns wol auff dem plan/ mit seinem gayst vnd gabe̅/ nemen

Augsburger Gesangbuch von 1529. Stuttgart, Württembergische Landesbibliothek.

an die Vorlage hält) und arbeitet dann die ursprüngliche melismenreiche Melodie zu einer dem Text besser entsprechenden metrischen und syllabischen Liedweise um. In dieser Weise werden – nimmt man an – auf die Weihnachtszeit 1523 hin der klassische ambrosianische Adventshymnus Veni redemptor gentium (1) und der ebenfalls aus der Frühzeit der Hymnendichtung stammende Weihnachtshymnus A solis ortus cardine von Caelius Sedulius (2) bearbeitet. Auf Pfingsten 1524 kommt dann der ebenso berühmte Heilig-Geist-Hymnus des Hrabanus Maurus Veni Creator Spiritus hinzu, der in der gleichen Weise textlich und musikalisch bearbeitet wird (10). 1541 hat Luther schließlich noch eine weitere Hymnen-Übertragung geschaffen mit dem Epiphanias-Lied Was fürchtst du, Feind Herodes, sehr (6) mit einem weiteren Teil jenes Leben-Jesu-Liedes von Caelius Sedulius, dessen erste sieben Strophen er bereits 20 Jahre früher übertragen hatte. Und auch der letzte Lied-Text, den wir von seiner Hand besitzen, ist eine Hymnen-Übertragung: Das erst 1543 erscheinende Abendlied Der du bist drei in Einigkeit (37).

Die Melodie des Advents-Hymnus Veni redemptor gentium hat Luther später noch zweimal beschäftigt: Er zog sie 1529 heran für seine Lied-Übertragung der Antiphon Da pacem Domine, die er mit der Strophe Verleih uns Frieden gnädiglich (32) wiedergab, und nochmals 1541/42, als er in der erneuten Bedrohung durch die Türken das Kinderlied Erhalt uns, Herr, bei deinem Wort (36) schuf.

Luthers wörtliche Übertragungen vorgegebener Texte (seien es Psalmen oder Hymnen) erscheinen uns oft etwas ungelenk, hölzern und schwerverständlich. Wem soll beispielsweise die Zeile Und blühet ein Frucht Weibs Fleisch (1, 2) mit den drei aneinandergereihten Substantiven etwas sagen? Man versteht sie nur, wenn man den lateinischen Urtext kennt: «ventrisque fructus floruit» (und die Frucht des Mutterleibes blühte auf). Es mag tatsächlich vor allem die Bindung an die Vorlage sein, die den Dichter hier in der Entfaltung seiner Begabung behindert.

Leisen

In die Zeit vor Weihnachten 1523 setzt man auch die Entstehung des Weihnachtsliedes Gelobet seist du, Jesu Christ (3) an. Luther geht zwar auch hier von der Tradition aus, aber auf eine andere Weise, die ihm viel mehr Spielraum läßt: Was ihm da vorgegeben war, ist die erste Strophe mit der Melodie, eine nach dem abschließenden Ruf so

genannte Leise. *Diese eine Strophe, die im Zusammenhang mit der* Weihnachtssequenz Grates nunc omnes reddamus, *aber auch sonst in der Weihnachtszeit vom Volk gesungen wurde, hat Luther zum sie-benstrophigen Gemeindelied erweitert. Für seine sechs Zusatzstro-phen war er an keine Vorlage gebunden. Und damit ist dieses Lied das erste frei gedichtete deutsche evangelische Kirchenlied geworden – Kirchenlied im engeren Sinn als primär für den Gottesdienst be-stimmtes Gemeindelied verstanden.*

Luther hat auch hier weitergearbeitet: Noch im Laufe desselben Kirchenjahres hat er die Pfingst-Leise Nun bitten wir den Heiligen Geist *(12) und die Fronleichnams-Leise* Gott sei gelobet und gebene-deiet *(22) in der gleichen Weise zu Liedern erweitert. In den Quellen des Jahres 1524 finden wir auch ein Osterlied, das seiner Form nach eine Leise ist und in der Überschrift dieselbe Bezeichnung «Lobge-sang» trägt, wie sie sonst – von einer Ausnahme (7) abgesehen – nur die Leisen tragen:* Jesus Christus, unser Heiland, der den Tod über-wand *(9). Eine mittelalterliche Leise läßt sich hier als Vorlage nicht nachweisen, und so ist mit der Möglichkeit zu rechnen, daß Luther hier einem neuen Lied diese Form gab. Wenn er die Osterleise* Christ ist erstanden *(38) nicht in gleicher Weise bearbeitete, dann offenbar, weil er das, was er hier sagen wollte, in den knappen Leisen-Stro-phen nicht unterbringen konnte. Als erneuertes* Christ ist erstanden *finden wir in den Quellen des Jahres 1524 das große Osterlied* Christ lag in Todesbanden *(8) in sieben Strophen zu sieben Zeilen. Daß Luther mit diesem* Christ ist erstanden, *gebessert die von ihm so hochgeschätzte Osterleise nicht verdrängen wollte, wird daran deut-lich, daß er 1529 die alte Leise in nur leichter Überarbeitung neben diesem neuen Osterlied in sein Gesangbuch aufgenommen hat (38). Im übrigen hat er für sein Osterlied nicht nur die Leise, sondern auch die Ostersequenz* Victimae paschali laudes, *mit der die Leise in der Liturgie verbunden war, herangezogen. Das Lied ist somit die Wei-terführung des mit* Gelobet seist du, Jesu Christ *(3) gegebenen An-satzes. Das auch formal frei gedichtete Festlied ist geschaffen.*

Genau dieselbe Entwicklungslinie ist auch an den Melodien ables-bar: Bisher hatte Luther – von der Märtyrer-Ballade abgesehen – auf vorliegende Melodien gedichtet oder die durch die Tradition gege-benen Melodien überarbeitet. Nun schafft er für dieses Osterlied eine neue Weise, für welche er sich allerdings in den beiden ersten Zeilen noch an die Melodie der Leise anlehnt, so wie es ja auch der Text tut.

Möglicherweise hat Luther gegen Ende seines Lebens auch die Passions-Leise O du armer Judas *noch bearbeitet. Es ist nicht ausgeschlossen, daß der Text* Unsre große Sünde und schwere Missetat *(44) in Rhaus' Schulgesangbuch von 1544 auf Luther zurückgeht. Damit wäre dann der Kranz von Liedern zu den Hauptfesten des Kirchenjahres, die wir von Luthers Hand haben, beinahe geschlossen; nur ein Himmelfahrtslied würde dann noch fehlen.*

Eine weitere Leise, die Luther schon 1524 bearbeitet hat, ist ihrer Form, ihrem Inhalt und ihrer Entstehungsgeschichte nach ein Sonderfall: Mitten wir im Leben sind *(16). Es handelt sich hier nicht um eine Strophe, welche als Einschub in eine Fest-Sequenz entstand, sondern um die spätmittelalterliche deutsche Übertragung der Antiphon* Media vita in morte sumus. *Da sie mit «Kyrieleis» schließt, rechnet man sie unter die Leisen, was auch Luther mit der Bezeichnung «Lobgesang» tut. Dies ist also deutlich eine Gattungsbezeichnung, denn dieses Lied ist ja eher ein Bitt-, Anbetungs- und Bekenntnis- als ein Lob-Gesang. Die Forschung hält es für erwiesen, daß Luther hier nochmals nicht durch ein liturgisches Bedürfnis, sondern durch persönliches Erleben zum Liedschöpfer wurde. Die Technik, die er anwandte – Überarbeitung und Erweiterung einer bisher schon gesungenen Strophe unter Übernahme der bekannten Melodie –, hatte er inzwischen an Liedern erprobt, die für den liturgischen Gebrauch geschaffen waren.*

Hier ist schließlich auch das Pfingstlied Komm, Heiliger Geist, Herre Gott *(11) zu nennen, weil es wie* Mitten wir im Leben sind *eine spätmittelalterliche deutsche Strophe aufnimmt, die ihrerseits auf einen lateinischen liturgischen Text zurückgeht; daran sind auch hier zwei weitere, gleichgebaute Strophen angefügt. Eine Leise ist das allerdings nicht, weil die Strophe nicht mit «Kyrieleis», sondern mit «Halleluja» schließt. Luther setzt daher auch nicht die (hier dem Wortsinn nach viel eher berechtigte) Überschrift «Lobgesang».*

Und noch eins muß dem angefügt werden, weil es ebenfalls die Bearbeitung einer spätmittelalterlichen Vorlage ist: Gott, der Vater wohn uns bei *(13). Aus einem Lied zur Heiligen-Anrufung (möglicherweise eine Lied-Bearbeitung der Allerheiligen-Litanei) macht Luther ein trinitarisches Bittlied. Man rechnet mit der Entstehung um Trinitatis 1524. Auch hier wird die alte Melodie mitübernommen.*

Katechismus-Lieder

Mit den bisher aufgezählten sind aber weder die Liedtypen noch die Lieder, mit denen Luther im ersten Jahr seiner lied-schöpferischen Tätigkeit hervortritt, schon erschöpft. Es ist in erster Linie nun die Gruppe der Katechismus-Lieder zu nennen, mit denen Luther der Jugend die Grundlagen und Hauptzeugnisse des Glaubens ins Herz singen möchte. Da ist einmal das Lied über das Gesetz Dies sind die heilgen Zehn Gebot *(14). Man könnte es in die Gruppe der Leisen einordnen, denn Luther schreibt es im Ton einer Leise, des Jerusalem-Pilger-Liedes* In Gottes Namen fahren wir. *Er will damit sagen, die wahre Pilgerschaft des Christen sei ein Leben im Gehorsam gegenüber Gottes Geboten. Jedes Gebot bekommt eine Strophe. Noch im gleichen Jahr, nur etwas später, hat Luther dann denselben Stoff nochmals in gedrängterer Form (5 Strophen) behandelt:* Mensch, willst du leben seliglich *(15). Man denkt beim Nebeneinander dieser beiden Lieder unwillkürlich an das Nebeneinander von Großem und Kleinem Katechismus fünf Jahre später, dort allerdings in umgekehrter Abfolge.*

Die Liedbearbeitung des Glaubensbekenntnisses (17) könnte man insofern noch der vorangehenden Gruppe zuzählen, als auch hier nachweislich ein älteres Credo-Lied überarbeitet wird, allerdings diesmal recht eingreifend, sowohl was den Text als auch was die Melodie angeht. Auch mag Luther hier ebensosehr wie an die Glaubensunterweisung auch an den Gottesdienst gedacht haben. Das erhellt schon aus dem Titel, noch mehr aber daraus, daß er dem Lied nicht das damals im Unterricht verwendete Apostolicum, sondern das Meß-Symbol, das Nizaenokonstantinopolitanum, zugrunde legt.

Daß Luther aber doch einen gereimten Katechismus im Auge hatte, wird daraus ersichtlich, daß er schon fünf Jahre später in seinem Gesangbuch eine eigene Abteilung mit Katechismus-Liedern schuf und diese danach mit Liedern zum Vaterunser (19) und zur Taufe (20) vervollständigte, schließlich 1543 auch mit einer besonderen Einleitung versah (S. 71).

Kinderlieder

Luther war von seinem Amt her – er war Theologieprofessor und nicht Pfarrer – nicht unmittelbar mit der Aufgabe der Unterweisung der Kinder konfrontiert. Als Vater von sechs Kindern war ihm den-

noch das Denken und Reden des Kindes nicht fern, und so besitzen wir von ihm außer den Katechismus-Liedern zwei von ihm selbst so bezeichnete Kinderlieder. Das Weihnachtslied Vom Himmel hoch, da komm ich her *(4)* ist besonders in seinen Strophen der kindlichen Krippenanbetung ein eindrückliches Zeugnis für Luthers Einfühlungsgabe in das kindliche Wesen. Das Bittlied in der Türkennot von *1543 (36)* mag man von einem heutigen Standpunkt aus als wenig kindgemäß ansehen. In seiner unkomplizierten Redeweise ist es jedoch im Munde von Kindern durchaus denkbar. Auch bei seinem späteren Weihnachtslied *(5)* hat Luther an den Kindergesang gedacht, denn er gibt auf der Druckvorlage dafür eine besondere Melodie an *(5 B)*.

Hofweisen

Eine formale Liedgattung eigener Art, die bei Luther zwar nicht sehr stark, aber doch eindeutig vertreten ist, ist die des bürgerlichen Gesellschaftsliedes: die sogenannte Hofweise. Es handelt sich dabei um Sololieder mit Begleitung eines Streicher- oder Bläser-Ensembles; bisweilen sang man sie wohl auch zur Laute oder – wie man damals sagte – in ein Orgelwerk (Positiv, Portativ, Regal). Ihre Texte sind in der Regel weltlich, ihre Melodien stark formelhaft, melismatisch und oft rhythmisch kompliziert. Luther wendet nun diesen Formtyp auf das geistliche Lied an. Da ist im Jahre 1524 zuerst die Liedbearbeitung des Canticum Simeonis Mit Fried und Freud ich fahr dahin (7). Die Melodie, die mit dem völlig neuen Versmaß zusammen erfunden worden sein muß, wird man Luther zuschreiben müssen; Johann Walter könnte sie höchstens überarbeitet haben. Sie ist solistisch und nicht für die Gemeinde gedacht, auch wenn sie bis heute in den Gemeindegesangbüchern überliefert wird.

Daß Luther von den drei neutestamentlichen Cantica nur dies eine übertragen hat, vor allem, daß er das von ihm so hoch geschätzte Magnificat nicht bearbeitet hat, mag Erstaunen wecken. Aber es ist so. Immerhin kommt sein anderes Lied im Hofweisen-Stil; das Lied von der Kirche Sie ist mir lieb, die werte Magd (35), das erst 1535 im Wittenberger Gesangbuch auftaucht (die Melodie sogar erst 10 Jahre später) ihm insofern inhaltlich nahe, als Luther hier jenes Bild aus Offenbarung 12 heraufbeschwört, das stets als Quelle für die Mariendarstellung diente. Maria als Mutter der Kirche – diese Vorstellung ist auch im Magnificat lebendig, im Lobgesang, den die Kirche mit den Worten der Mutter Jesu singt.

Den Hofweisen-Stil vertritt im Grunde auch Ein feste Burg ist unser Gott *(26). Die Melodie dieses Liedes – mit Sicherheit ein Werk Luthers – lebt ja auch kaum in ihrer rhythmisch anspruchsvollen Urgestalt im Gemeindegesang.*

Kontrafaktur

Einer weiteren Gepflogenheit seiner Zeit zollt Luther Tribut mit der Anwendung des Kontrafaktur-Verfahrens, d. h. der bewußten Anknüpfung bei einem allgemein bekannten weltlichen oder geistlichen Lied, dessen Melodie übernommen wird und dessen Text in irgendeiner Weise den Hintergrund für den neuen Text abgibt. Ein klassisches Beispiel dafür hat er mit seinem Kinderlied auf Weihnachten Vom Himmel hoch, da komm ich her *(4) geliefert. Hierher gehört aber auch* Nun freut euch, lieben Christen gmein *(18, als geistliche Parallel-Kontrafaktur) und (im gleichen Sinne) wohl auch das längere Zehn-Gebote-Lied (14). Auch die Kontrafaktur von geistlich zu weltlich liegt übrigens bei Luther vor, und zwar mit einem Schmählied auf Herzog Heinrich von Braunschweig-Wolfenbüttel, der den Evangelischen übel gesonnen war, nach dem Passionslied* Ach du armer Judas, was hast du getan: Ach du arger Heinze, was hast du getan.

Freie Lieder

Bleiben wir zunächst noch im Bereiche der Liedform im engeren Sinn, so stellt sich die Frage, ob denn Luther keine freien Lieder – unabhängig von jeder Vorlage – geschaffen habe. Wenn man unter einem vorlagefreien Lied eins verstehen will, bei dem weder der Text von einem Bibeltext oder einem älteren liturgischen Gesang abhängig ist, noch die Melodie von einer fremden Vorlage hergeleitet werden kann, dann ist hier nur Ein neues Lied wir heben an *(23) zu nennen, allenfalls noch das Kinderlied* Erhalt uns, Herr, bei deinem Wort *(36), wenn man davon absieht, daß die Melodie in den beiden ersten Zeilen sich sehr stark (und wohl nicht zufällig) an die von* Veni redemptor gentium *anlehnt, und das Tauflied (20), wenn man davon absieht, daß es auf eine schon vorhandene Melodie gedichtet ist.*

Man würde allerdings Luther verkennen, wollte man ihn vorwiegend als einen – zwar originellen, ja teilweise genialen – Bearbeiter fremder Vorlagen verstehen. Nur 17 seiner Lieder und gereimten

Gesänge sind reine Übersetzungen oder Übertragungen biblischer oder liturgischer Texte (1, 2, 4 [Str. 1–5], 6, 7, 10, 15, 24, 25, 27–33, 37). Daneben stehen 6 freiere Paraphrasen, bzw. stärker eingreifende Bearbeitungen von Vorlagen (5, 13, 14, 17, 19, 21) und zwei Texte, in denen Luther sich an seine Vorlagen nur lose anlehnt (8, 26) und die nun schon nahezu unter die freien Dichtungen gezählt werden dürfen, was vollends von jenen Liedern gelten muß, in denen Luther zwar von einer vorgegebenen Strophe ausgeht, dann aber frei weiterdichtet (3, 4 [Str. 6–15], 11, 12, 16, 22). (Ungewiß muß der Fall von 9 bleiben.) Ähnlich verhält es sich mit den Melodien; doch davon später.

Gesänge in offener Form für den Gottesdienst

Nun hat Luther aber auch einige nicht-liedmäßige liturgische Gesänge geschaffen. Zunächst sind zwei zu nennen, die, wenn auch nicht liedförmig, so doch gereimt sind und darum meist unter die Lieder gerechnet werden (und in diesem Sinne auch eben mitgezählt wurden): Ende 1525 schuf Luther für seine deutsche evangelische Bearbeitung des Meßformulars ein deutsches Sanctus, und zwar nicht als Liedfassung des liturgischen Textes, wie Nikolaus Decius das 1523 versucht hatte, sondern als Nacherzählung von Jesaja 6, 1–4 in 16 fünfhebigen, paarig gereimten Versen, zu singen auf eine neue Melodie, die sich an eine Sanctus-Weise aus dem Mittelalter leicht anlehnt (31).

Während wir andere musikalische Teile dieses Gottesdienst-Formulars, weil für den Gesang des Liturgen am Altar bestimmt, beiseite lassen, ist die Melodie zum Kyrie (43) zu nennen. Ein Gloria fehlt in diesem Formular, und das Agnus Dei wird nur erwähnt. In der von Wittenberger Stadtpfarrer Johannes Bugenhagen bearbeiteten und 1528 in Wittenberg gedruckten Gottesdienstordnung für Braunschweig findet sich dann ein Agnus Dei, das nach den gleichen Prinzipien wie das eben genannte Kyrie angelegt ist und von dem man allgemein annimmt, es stamme ebenfalls von Luther (44). Er hat es allerdings, im Gegensatz zum Sanctus aus der deutschen Messe von 1526, nie in sein Gesangbuch übernommen. Eine Gloria-Bearbeitung gibt es von Luther nicht. Die Vers-Übertragung All Ehr und Lob soll Gottes sein, für die später von einigen wenigen Quellen sein Name überliefert wird, stammt mit Sicherheit nicht von ihm.

Hingegen hat Luther 1529 den ebenso berühmten und ebenso alten Lobgesang, das Te Deum, bearbeitet, allerdings nicht in Lied-

form, sondern wiederum in lauter gereimten achtsilbigen Versen, welche auf zwei Chöre verteilt sind – eine sehr originelle Umformung dieses altkirchlichen Kunstwerkes, die von Luthers liturgiegerechter Form-Phantasie zeugt *(33)*. Luther hat das Stück *1529* unter seine Lieder aufgenommen.

An letzter Stelle unter Luthers eigenen Kirchengesängen steht im Wittenberger Gesangbuch von *1529* die deutsche Litanei *(34)*, der Luther dann in einer zweiten Auflage auch noch eine lateinische Fassung an die Seite gestellt hat. Auch dieses Stück ist (in beiden Formen) zweichörig angelegt.

Fünf weitere nicht-liedmäßige liturgische Gemeindegesänge müssen Luther zugeschrieben werden: Davon stehen drei Versuche in deutscher Gemeinde-Psalmodie im Wittenberger Gemeindegesangbuch: Die Psalmen *117* (für den Predigt-Gottesdienst) und *111* (für den Abendmahlsgottesdienst) und das Benedictus *(40, 39, 41)*. Diese Texte entnahm Luther seiner Bibelübersetzung; die musikalische Bearbeitung aber stellt einen eigenständigen neuen Versuch von seiner Hand dar.

Melodien

Für Luther war ein Kirchengesang eine Einheit aus Wort und Ton. Er hat seine Lieder gesungen. Wenn auch Texte wie Nun freut euch, lieben Christen gmein *(18)* oder Ein feste Burg ist unser Gott *(26)* schon als Gedichte Schöpfungen von imponierender Kraft sind und darum keine Anthologie deutscher Lyrik, die das *16.* Jahrhundert miteinbezieht, an Luther völlig vorbeigehen wird, so schließen sich doch manche der Liedschöpfungen Luthers erst dem ganz auf, der sie sich singend aneignet. Das gilt erst recht natürlich von den übrigen liturgischen Gesängen. Sei es, daß Luther auf eine bereits vorhandene Melodie dichtet, sei es, daß er eine überlieferte Melodie bearbeitet, sei es, daß er eine ganz neue Singweise anbietet, immer ist das, was entsteht, eine Einheit aus Wort und Ton. Ja selbst dann, wenn ein anderer es war, der nachträglich zu Luthers Wort die Töne fügte, sind es erst sie, die das Wort zum richtigen Leben rufen.

Wir geben deshalb alle Texte Luthers hier mit den Melodien wieder, die ihnen in den Quellen bis zu Luthers Tod beigegeben sind. Das sind nicht selten mehrere. Schon Luther selbst hat in einigen Fällen eine bereits vorhandene fremde Melodie später durch eine eigene neue ersetzt, so bei den Kontrafakturen *(18 und 4)*, wahrscheinlich auch bei einigen der Psalmlieder im Metrum der «Lutherstro-

phe» (24, 25, 18, 30). In drei Fällen hat er sogar eigene Melodien später durch andere ersetzt (18, 19, 24).

Durch ein Zeugnis von Luthers musikalischem Mitarbeiter Johann Walter wissen wir, daß Luther die Melodie zu seinem deutschen Sanctus (31) selbst geschaffen hat. Vom Vaterunser-Lied (19) liegt die Urschrift Luthers vor. Darauf steht von seiner Hand der Entwurf einer Melodie, die in den gedruckten Quellen dann allerdings durch eine andere ersetzt ist; auch sie – die Bearbeitung einer fremden Weise – muß von Luthers Hand stammen. Mit sehr großer Wahrscheinlichkeit lassen sich außer den beiden genannten (31 und 19A) noch elf Liedmelodien Luther zuweisen (4B, 8, 18B und C, 23, 24B und G, 26, 27B = 20, 30B, 35A oder B), mit einiger Wahrscheinlichkeit auch zwei weitere (7 und 29C). Mehr oder weniger eingreifende Bearbeitungen älterer Melodien von Luthers Hand liegen sehr wahrscheinlich bei acht Liedern vor (1, 2, 10, 17A oder B, 33, 36), während in zwölf anderen Fällen (3, 11, 12, 13, 14, 16, 22, 32, 37, 38, 44, 45) Luther die Melodie nur leicht oder gar nicht bearbeitet hat. Vier Texte sind auf vorhandene Melodien gedichtet und haben bei Luther keine eigene erhalten (5, 6, 15, 20). In acht Fällen schließlich glaubt man auf Grund der Quellenlage annehmen zu dürfen, daß wir die Erstvertonung Johann Walter zu verdanken haben (4C, 9B, 15B, 29C, 25B, 28A und D, 29B); als Bearbeiter kommt er bei 8, 16 und vielleicht 7 in Frage. Für die musikalische Gestalt der nicht-liedmäßigen Stücke 39–43 müssen wir Luther in Anspruch nehmen.

Vom Flugblatt zum Chorgesangbuch

Luthers Lieder verbreiteten sich – wie alle seine Schriften – mit Windeseile. Am aktivsten nahm man sie in Straßburg auf. Sei es, weil man die in den ersten Drucken stehenden Wittenberger Melodien für ungeeignet hielt, sei es, weil dort mehrere Texte auf dieselbe Weise verwiesen wurden, sei es, weil diese Drucke überhaupt keine Melodien enthielten, jedenfalls entstanden in Straßburg sofort neue Melodien zu Luthers Psalmliedern. Die zu Aus tiefer Not (30C) findet man schon im Jahr 1524 in einem Straßburger liturgischen Druck, andere folgen bald danach (14B und C, 24E, 30E). Die Straßburger musikalische Fassung der Lutherlieder wurde über das Konstanzer Gesangbuch dann bestimmend für die reformierte Tradition.

Luther hatte schon vor der Entstehung seiner ersten Lieder eine eindeutige Vorstellung von dem, was evangelischer Gemeindege-

30

sang sein sollte. Aber das, was er selbst dafür zu leisten hatte, wuchs erst nach und nach zu dem heran, was es schließlich wurde. Es gilt heute als erwiesen, daß der größte Teil von Luthers Liedern zunächst in der Form von Flugblättern erschien. Daß keiner dieser Ur-Drucke erhalten geblieben ist, darf uns nicht wundernehmen. Wie viele von den hektographierten Liedblättern, auf denen manche Lieder unserer Zeitgenossen, für einen bestimmten Gottesdienst geschrieben und zunächst für den Eigenbedarf mehr oder weniger behelfsmäßig vervielfältigt, wird man im Jahre 2400 noch nachweisen können? Immerhin ist eine ganze Reihe von frühen Nachdrucken solcher Liedblätter erhalten geblieben und in einem Fall sogar Luthers Manuskript, das für den Druck eines solchen verwendet wurde (5).

Schon wenige Monate nach dem Erscheinen der ersten Liedblätter haben tüchtige Buchdrucker sich dieses offenbar begehrten Produktes angenommen. In Nürnberg erscheint 1524 eine Zusammenfassung mehrerer derartiger Liedblätter in drei Auflagen; in Augsburg wird diese kleine Sammlung von acht Liedern (vier davon von Luther) sofort nachgedruckt. Zwei Erfurter Drucker gehen noch weiter: Sie drucken – ebenfalls schon 1524 – ein kleines Handbüchlein mit den ihnen erreichbaren Liedern; unter den 26 Stücken sind 18 der frühen Lutherlieder. Nun erst denkt Luther selbst an die Zusammenfassung des bis dahin Geleisteten in einem Buch. Er übergibt – so nimmt man heute an – das bisher erschienene Liedmaterial dem Hofkomponisten des sächsischen Kurfürsten, dem damals 30 Jahre alten Johann Walter, und bittet ihn, diese Lieder für den Gebrauch in Schule und Gottesdienst mehrstimmig zu vertonen. Was dabei entsteht, ist das erste große Werk der evangelischen Kirchenmusik, das Wittenberger Chorgesangbuch, eine Sammlung von 38 deutschen Liedern (darunter 24 von Luther) und 5 lateinischen Motetten. Luther schreibt dazu ein programmatisches Vorwort (S. 39f.). Aus dieser Tatsache hat man schon die unterschiedlichsten Schlüsse gezogen. Am ehesten dürften die Dinge so liegen – und Einzelbeobachtungen bestätigen das –, daß Luther Johann Walter einen Auftrag gab und ihm das Liedmaterial nannte oder zur Verfügung stellte, dem Komponisten aber sonst freie Hand ließ. Mit seiner Vorrede gab er dem Unternehmen seine Legitimation. Eine redaktionelle Mitarbeit Luthers im einzelnen darf man nicht voraussetzen. Die Lieder sind in einem ziemlich willkürlichen Durcheinander angeordnet. Vermutlich wurden die Noten vorweg geschnitten und die Texte vorweg gesetzt, wie der Komponist sie ablieferte.

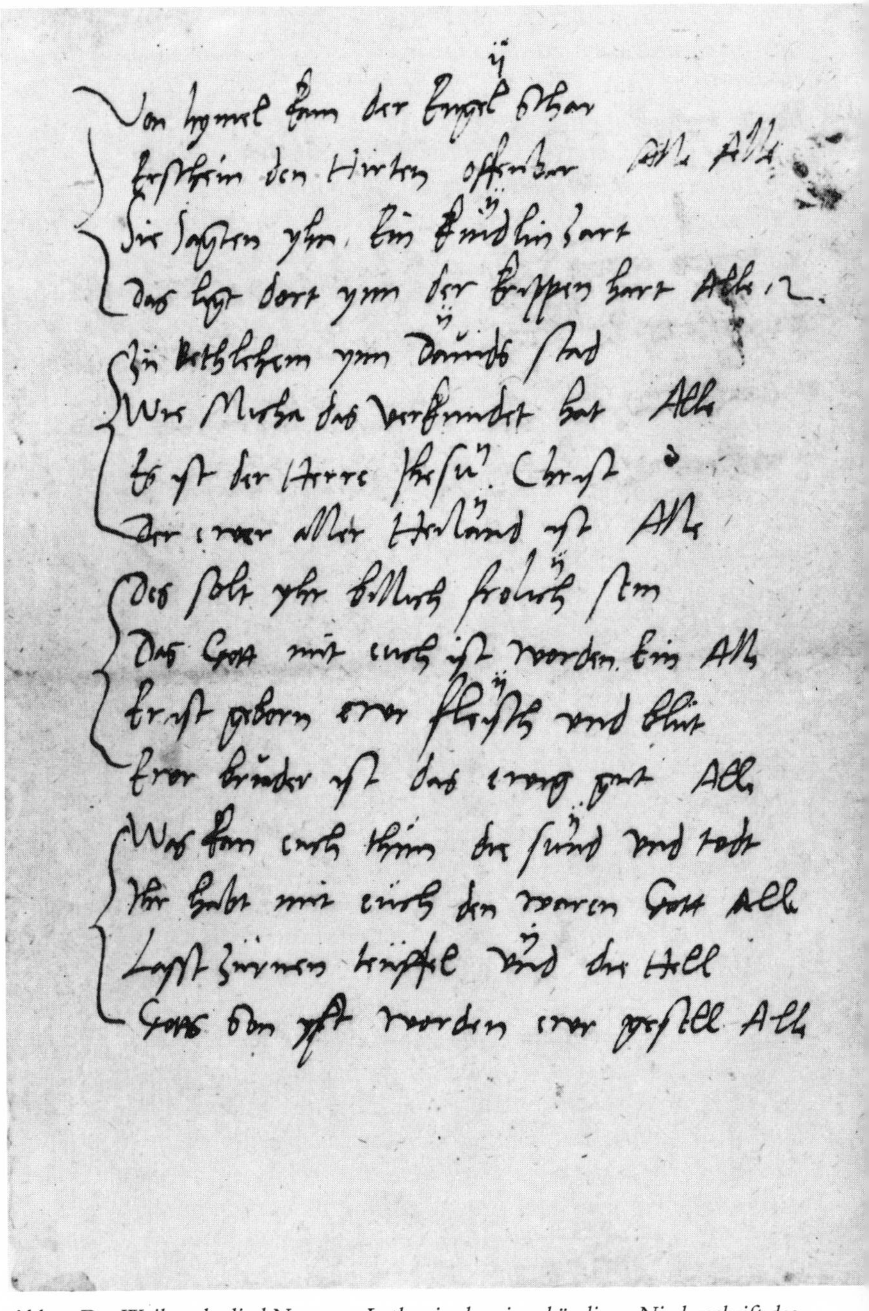

Von hymel kom der Engel schar
Erschein den Hirten offenbar
Sie sagten yhn, ein kindlin zart
das legt dort ynn der krippen hart   All. 2.

Zu Bethlehem ynn Dauids stad
Wie Micha das verkündet hat   All
Es ist der Herre Jhesu Christ
der ewer Aller Heiland ist   All

Des solt yhr billich frolich sein
Das Gott mit euch ist worden ein   All
Er ist geborn ewer fleisch vnd blut
Ewer bruder ist das ewig gut   All

Was kan euch thun die sünd vnd todt
Ihr habt mit euch den waren Gott   All
Last zurnen teuffel vnd die Hell
Gotts son ist worden ewer gesell   All

Abb. 3. Das Weihnachtslied Nr. 5 von Luther in der eigenhändigen Niederschrift des
Dichters. Es handelt sich offensichtlich um die Vorlage für die Drucklegung als klei-

32

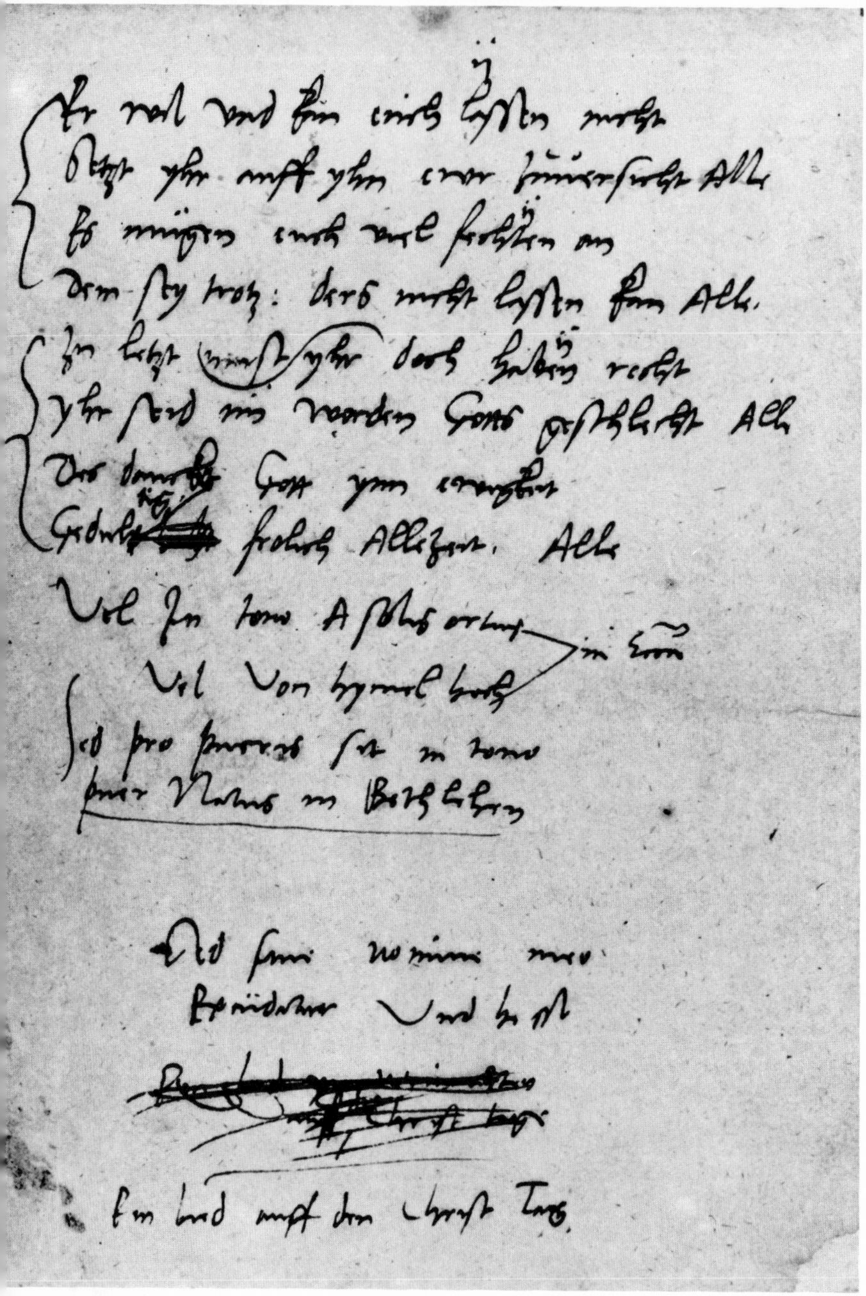

nes Liedblatt, das nach Luthers Willen anonym erscheinen sollte. Wien, Österreichische Nationalbibliothek.

Gott gebe vns allen ein
Glückſäliges neüwes Jar.

VOn Hemmel kam der Engel ſchar/
Erſchein den Hirten offenbar/
Sie ſagten jhn/Ein kindlein zart/
Das ligt dort in der kripffen hart.

Zů Bethlehem in Dauids ſtat/
Wie Micha das verkündet hat/
Es iſt der Herre Jeſu Chriſt/
Der ewer aller Heyland iſt.

Des ſolt jr billich frölich ſein/
Das Gott mit eüch iſt worden ein/
Er iſt geboren ewer fleiſch vnd blůt/
Ewr Brůder iſt das ewig gůt.

Was kan eüch thůn die ſünd vñ tod/
Ir habt mit eüch den waren Gott/
Laßt zürnen Teüffel vnd die Hell/
Gotts Son iſt worden ewer gſell.

Er will vnd kan eüch laſſen nicht/
Setzt jr auff ſn ewr zůuerſicht/
Es mögen eüch vil fechten an/
Dem ſey trotz ders nit laſſen kan.

Zů letſt můſſe jr doch haben recht/
Ir ſeidt nun worden Gottes geſchlecht/
Des dancket Gott in ewigkeyt/
Gedultig/frölich alle zeit. AMEN.

Dieses Gesangbuch war für den Schülerchor bestimmt. Es diente dem Musikunterricht in der Schule. Die Kantorei repräsentierte im Gottesdienst anfänglich die singende Gemeinde.

Zu diesem noch *1524*, aber vermutlich erst gegen Ende des Jahres erschienenen Chorwerk wurde *1525* eine Ausgabe «für die Laien», d. h. für die Hand der Gemeinde veranstaltet. Darin waren nur die Texte und Melodien der Lieder, jedoch in derselben Anordnung und begleitet von derselben Vorrede, enthalten. *1526* erschien eine im wesentlichen unveränderte Neuausgabe davon.

Luthers Gesangbuch

Im Frühling *1529* erscheint in Wittenberg – nun unabhängig vom Chorgesangbuch – eine Sammlung geistlicher Lieder für die Gemeinde, die erst das darstellt, was wir heute unter einem Kirchengesangbuch verstehen: ein inhaltlich einigermaßen umfassendes und nach einem bestimmten Plan geordnetes Sammelwerk. Luthers Name und Wappen auf dem Titelblatt, sein Name über jedem seiner Lieder, das Vorwort aus dem Chorgesangbuch und dazu eine neue Vorrede von seiner Hand samt kurzen Einleitungen zu dreien der fünf Abteilungen, in welchen der Stoff untergebracht ist, zeigen, daß hier Luther persönlich am Werk ist. Seine eigenen Lieder stehen geschlossen voran, zuerst die zu den Festen des Kirchenjahres (*1–3, 6, 8–13*), dann die zum Katechismus (*14–18, 21–23*), wobei Mitten wir im Leben sind (*16*) den Zehn Geboten und Nun freut euch, lieben Christen gmein (*18*) dem Credolied als Antwort und vertiefende Deutung beigegeben sind, während das Märtyrerlied (*23*) diesen Zyklus zusammenfassend abschließt; als Lied vom Bekennen und von der Feuertaufe vertritt es vorläufig vielleicht die Stelle eines Taufliedes. Es folgen die sechs Psalmbereimungen von *1524*, vermehrt um das inzwischen entstandene Lied zu Psalm 46 (*24–30*), und schließlich die übrigen liturgischen Gesänge (*31–34*), die alle inzwischen entstanden sind. Die zweite Abteilung bringt 8 Lieder von weiteren Wittenberger Autoren, deren Namen ebenfalls bei jedem Lied ge-

Abb. 4 (nebenstehend). Einblattdruck mit Luthers Weihnachtslied Nr. 5, um 1550, möglicherweise aus einer Straßburger Presse. Es dürfte sich um einen frühen Nachdruck des anonymen Urdruckes (vgl. Abb. 3) handeln, weshalb auch hier Luthers Name fehlt. Das Blatt ist verschollen; Rückvergrößerung der Abbildung auf Tafel II in: Catalogue No. 1: Original Engravings and Woodcuts by the Old Masters. H. Gilhofer & H. Ranschburg Ltd., Luzern o. J.

nannt sind. Die dritte Abteilung mit 6 Liedern aus der Tradition erhält eine eigene kurze Einleitung (S. 148). Von diesen Liedern nahmen wir Christ ist erstanden (38) in diese Sammlung auf, weil wir der Ansicht sind, die hier überlieferte Text- und die Melodiefassung, die vorher nicht anzutreffen sind, stammten von Luther. Es folgen, wieder mit einer kurzen, ganz offensichtlich von Luther selbst formulierten Einleitung (S. 150), eine vierte Abteilung mit einer kleinen Auswahl aus dem übrigen zeitgenössischen evangelischen Liedgut und als fünfte und letzte Abteilung 11 Cantica aus dem Alten Testament und die vier aus dem Neuen Testament; auch dieser Teil ist mit einer Einleitung versehen, die offensichtlich von Luthers Hand stammt (S. 150). Das Büchlein ist mit 12 ganzseitigen Holzschnittbildern geschmückt.

Ende 1529 muß eine Neuauflage erschienen sein, die wenige Erweiterungen brachte. 1533 erscheint die erste uns erhaltene Ausgabe. Hier werden im ersten Teil der Lutherlieder 8 kurze Gebete zwischen die Lieder eingestreut und in der fünften Abteilung 10 vierstimmige Psalmodie-Modelle Johann Walters aufgenommen. In weiteren Auflagen (erhalten sind solche von 1535, 1544 und 1545, nachgewiesen auch eine von 1543) kommen nach und nach die späteren Lieder Luthers (4, 5, 7, 19, 20, 35−37) hinzu, und es werden in der Anordnung gewisse Umstellungen vorgenommen.

Für die vorliegende Ausgabe wählen wir jedoch die originelle und ursprüngliche Reihenfolge der Lieder von 1529 und fügen nur an der jeweils passenden Stelle die später erschienenen Gesänge ein.

Dieses Gesangbuch Luthers – als Werk des Reformators bisher weder erkannt noch gewürdigt – war von nicht geringerer Auswirkung als seine Bibelübersetzung. Kaum ein evangelisches Gesangbuch der Folgezeit, das nicht Luthers Lieder übernahm, kaum eins, das sich nicht – wenigstens teilweise – an dessen Anordnung orientierte. Selbst katholische Gesangbücher zeigen sich als unmittelbar von demjenigen Luthers beeinflußt. Luther hat der Christenheit deutscher Zunge nicht nur die Bibel, sondern auch das Gesangbuch geschenkt.

Es darf hierbei nicht übersehen werden, daß die erste Ausgabe dieses Gesangbuches sozusagen gleichzeitig mit dem Kleinen und Großen Katechismus erschien und im gleichen Jahr auch eine Neuausgabe von Luthers Betbüchlein auf den Markt kam, welches das gleiche Format und die gleichen Illustrationen aufweist wie das Gesangbuch. Luther legte mit diesen drei Veröffentlichungen den Grund

zum Aufbau einer evangelischen Frömmigkeit. Dabei war das Gesangbuch nicht nur ein liturgisches Buch, sondern auch ein Schul- und Hausbuch.

Das Begräbnisgesangbuch

Für eine besondere Gelegenheit, für das Begräbnis, schuf Luther dann 1542 noch ein eigenes Gesangbuch. Die dafür geschriebene Vorrede geht über diesen unmittelbaren Zweck hinaus und gibt eine Reihe praktischer Anregungen für ein evangeliumgemäßes Begräbniswesen. Die in diesem Büchlein stehenden deutschen Lieder sind bis auf eines dem Gesangbuch entnommen. Dieses eine, Nun laßt uns den Leib begraben (45), ist die leichte Bearbeitung und Erweiterung eines Begräbnisliedes von Michael Weiße durch Luther. Das Besondere an diesem Büchlein, Luthers lateinische Neutextierung einiger gregorianischer Begräbnisgesänge, muß hier unberücksichtigt bleiben.

1545 – ein Jahr vor Luthers Tod – erschien in Leipzig eine Prachtausgabe des Wittenberger Gesangbuches. Das Format ist größer. Jede Seite ist mit Zierleisten eingefaßt. Die Illustrationen sind in größerem Format neu gestaltet und die Noten in sehr schöner Weise neu geschnitten. Das Begräbnisbüchlein ist ins Gesangbuch eingefügt, selbstverständlich nun unter Weglassung der im Gesangbuch selbst schon stehenden Lieder. Luther wurde vom Drucker gebeten, zu diesem Gesangbuch eine neue Vorrede zu schreiben, und er hat dieser Bitte entsprochen mit einer sehr kühnen, aber zu Herzen gehenden Auslegung von Psalm 96,1 (S. 170f.).

Das Ganze

Luther war nicht ohne schriftstellerisches Selbstbewußtsein. Aber von seinen poetischen Fähigkeiten war er nicht sonderlich überzeugt, wie mehrere Äußerungen zeigen. Damit mag es zusammenhängen, daß er auf keinem Gebiet seines Liedschaffens Vollständigkeit anstrebte. Eine vollständige Bereimung des Psalters – ein Gedanke, der doch sehr nahe gelegen hätte, wie sich bei Calvin zeigen wird – hat er offenbar nie ins Auge gefaßt. Besonders auffällig ist, daß Luther von den Cantica nur das Nunc dimittis liedmäßig bearbeitet hat, nicht aber das Benedictus und – vor allem – nicht das von ihm so hoch geschätzte Magnificat. Der Zyklus von Festliedern bleibt unvollständig, auch wenn wir die Passions-Leise aus dem Rhaw'schen

Schulgesangbuch von *1544 (44)* als Werk Luthers anerkennen sollten. Denn ein Himmelfahrtslied findet sich in seinem Gesangbuch
nur im dritten Teil unter den Liedern «der Alten» (Christ fuhr gen
Himmel). Auch ein Zyklus von Ordinariums-Liedern liegt nicht vor.
Ein Gloria-Lied fehlt, und zwar gewiß nicht deswegen, weil Luther
das Gloria-Lied des Nicolaus Decius von *1523* (Allein Gott in der
Höh sei Ehr) für genügend gehalten hätte. Es ist zweifelhaft, ob er es
gekannt hat, denn es erscheint in seinem Gesangbuch nicht. Aber
auch die Auswahl von Hymnen, die Luther bearbeitet hat *(1, 2, 6, 10,
37)*, erscheint reichlich zufällig; neben dem Abendlied *(36)* würde
man zumindest ein Morgenlied erwarten.

Luthers Kirchenlied-Opus wirkt trotz alledem nicht torsohaft.
Und wenn es auch von Späteren mannigfach ergänzt wurde und
heute zum Teil durch andere Lieder ersetzt werden muß, so macht es
doch, wenn man es einmal so geschlossen vor sich hat, einen so voll-
kommenen Eindruck wie kaum eines Späteren hymnodische Hinter-
lassenschft. Luther ist und bleibt – wenn auch Decius ihm zeitlich
voranging – der Vater des deutschen evangelischen Kirchenliedes
und – wenn auch die böhmischen Brüder schon vor ihm ein volks-
sprachliches Gesangbuch besaßen – der Schöpfer des deutschen evangelischen Gesangbuches.

Die Vorrede zum Wittenberger Chorgesangbuch
1524

Daß geistliche Lieder zu singen gut und Gott wohlgefällig ist, denke ich, sei keinem Christen verborgen, da doch jedem nicht nur das Beispiel der Propheten und Könige im Alten Testament (die mit Singen und Klingen, mit Dichten und allerlei Saitenspiel Gott gelobt haben) vertraut ist, sondern auch dieser Brauch selbst, besonders im Psalmengesang, der ganzen Christenheit von Anfang an bekannt ist. Auch hat ja St.Paulus dies in 1.Korinther 14,15–26 angeordnet und gebietet den Kolossern (3,16), von Herzen dem Herrn geistliche Lieder und Psalmen zu singen, damit dadurch Gottes Wort und die christliche Lehre auf allerlei Weise getrieben und geübt werden.

Deshalb habe auch ich – mit einigen andern zusammen –, um einen guten Anfang zu machen und um denen Anlaß zu geben, die es besser vermögen, etliche geistliche Lieder gesammelt, um das heilige Evangelium, das jetzt durch Gottes Gnade wieder hervorgekommen ist, zu treiben und in Schwang zu bringen, damit auch wir uns rühmen möchten, wie Mose in seinem Gesang es tut (Exodus 15), so daß Christus unser Lob und Gesang sei und wir nichts wissen sollen zu singen noch zu sagen, als Jesus Christus, unsern Heiland, wie Paulus sagt in 1.Korinther 2,2.

Und diese Lieder sind dazu auch in vier Stimmen gesetzt, aus keinem anderen Grunde, als daß ich gerne möchte, daß die Jugend, die ohnehin soll und muß in der Musik und anderen rechten Künsten erzogen werden, etwas hätte, damit sie die Buhllieder und fleischlichen Gesänge los würde und statt derselben etwas Heilsames lernte und so das Gute mit Lust, wie es den Jungen gebührt, einginge. Ich bin auch nicht der Meinung, daß durchs Evangelium sollten alle Künste zu Boden geschlagen werden und vergehen, wie etliche falsche Eiferer vorgeben, sondern ich möchte alle Künste, besonders die Musik, gerne sehen im Dienste dessen, der sie gegeben und geschaffen hat. Ich bitte deshalb, daß ein jeder fromme Christ sich das gefallen lassen wolle und er da, wo ihm Gott mehr oder dasselbe verliehen hat, dies fördern helfe. Es ist ohnehin leider alle Welt viel zu nachlässig und zu gedankenlos, die arme Jugend zu erziehen und zu lehren, als daß man allen voran auch noch Anlaß dazu geben dürfte. Gott gebe uns seine Gnade. Amen.

Das in vier Stimmbüchern 1524 in Wittenberg erschienene Chorgesangbuch enthält Luthers erste zusammenhängende Äußerung zum

gottesdienstlichen Liedgesang. Es liegt Luther offenbar viel daran, daß allen voran die Jugend die neuen Lieder lerne und Freude daran bekomme. Als Autor der meist vierstimmigen Sätze gibt sich am Schluß des Alt-Stimmbuches der Torgauer Kantor Johann Walter (1496–1570) zu erkennen. (Das Alt-Stimmbuch der Erstauflage von 1524 ist verloren, aber ein sehr getreuer Wormser Nachdruck vom Jahr 1525 ist vollständig erhalten geblieben.) Welches Luthers Anteil an dem Werk ist, bleibt immer noch umstritten. Ohne Zweifel stammt nicht nur die Anregung von Luther, sondern auch das Melodie- und Textmaterial muß weitgehend der Reformator selbst Walter zur Verfügung gestellt haben. Hingegen darf man mit Fug und Recht bezweifeln, ob Luther an der Redaktion im Einzelnen mitgewirkt hat.

Eine Ausgabe für die Hand der Gemeinde (mit denselben Liedern in derselben Anordnung und mit derselben Vorrede Luthers) erschien erst im Jahr darauf. Erhalten ist ein geringfügig erweiterter Nachdruck vom Jahre 1526.

Die neue Vorrede zum Wittenberger Gemeindegesangbuch
1529

Nun haben sich etliche als tüchtig erwiesen und die Lieder vermehrt, so daß sie mich bei weitem übertreffen und hierin gewiß meine Meister sind. Aber daneben haben die andern wenig Gutes dazu getan. Und weil ich sehe, daß das tägliche Hinzutun ohne jede Unterscheidung, wie es jedem gerade gut dünkt, ins Uferlose wächst und außerdem auch die ersten unter unseren Liedern je länger desto fehlerhafter gedruckt werden,[1] habe ich Sorge, es werde diesem Büchlein auf die Länge gehen, wie es allezeit guten Büchern ergangen ist: daß sie durch Zutaten unberufener Köpfe so sehr überdeckt und verunstaltet worden sind, daß man das Gute darunter verloren und allein das Unnütze im Gebrauch behalten hat, wie wir sehen aus St. Lukas im ersten Kapitel (1, 1–4), daß im Anfang jedermann Evangelien hat schreiben wollen, bis man beinahe das rechte Evangelium verloren hatte unter so vielen Evangelien. So ist's auch des St. Hieronymus und Augustinus und vieler Anderer Büchern ergangen. Summa: Es muß stets der Mäuse Mist unter dem Pfeffer sein.

Damit nun dies, soweit wir können, verhindert werde, habe ich dies Büchlein wiederum aufs neue durchgesehen und die Lieder der

---

[1] *Hier übertreibt Luther. Die Abdrucke seiner Lieder in rund 60 Quellen zwischen 1524 und 1529 lassen eine solche Tendenz nicht erkennen.*

Unseren zusammen nacheinander mit Angabe der Verfassernamen[2] eingereiht – was ich zuvor der Ehrsucht wegen vermieden hatte, nun aber zu tun gezwungen bin, damit nicht unter unserem Namen fremde, untaugliche Gesänge verkauft werden. Danach habe ich die andern, die wir als die besten ansehen und für brauchbar halten, hinten angefügt.[3] Ich bitte und ermahne alle, die das reine Wort liebhaben, sie möchten dieses unser Büchlein hinfort ohne unser Wissen und Wollen nicht mehr verbessern oder erweitern. Wo es aber ohne unser Wissen gebessert würde, soll es so geschehen, daß man erkenne, inwiefern es nicht unser zu Wittenberg herausgegebenes Büchlein ist. Es kann ja jeder selbst sein eigenes Büchlein mit Liedern zusammenstellen und das unsrige unangetastet lassen, wie wir bitten, begehren und hiemit bezeugt haben wollen. Denn wir möchten ja auch gerne unsere Münze in unserer Währung behalten, wobei es niemandem verwehrt ist, für sich eine bessere zu machen. Auf daß Gottes Name allein gepriesen und unser Name nicht gesucht werde. Amen.

Das erste evangelische Gemeindegesangbuch, das diesen Namen verdient, ist dasjenige, das Luther in Wittenberg 1529 bei Joseph Klug drucken ließ. Es stellt eine höchst beachtliche Leistung Luthers dar, und wir haben allen Grund zur Annahme, daß er dieses Werk persönlich redigiert hat. Zu zahlreich sind die Maßnahmen daran, die nur auf ihn zurückgehen können – Anordnung und Auswahl der Lieder, Einleitungen zu einzelnen Teilen, neue Melodien zu eigenen Texten, Neubearbeitung von Melodien, Einführung der Verfassernamen – und deren letzte er in dem neuen Vorwort ausführlich begründet.

Daß dieses Vorwort schon in einem Gesangbuch von 1528 gestanden habe, wie man längere Zeit annahm, ist heute als irrig erwiesen. Die Erstausgabe dieses epochemachenden Wittenberger Gemeindegesangbuches fällt ins Jahr 1529. Ein Exemplar war noch Anfang des 19. Jahrhunderts vorhanden, ist aber seither verschollen, doch läßt sich der Inhalt des Buches auf Grund zweier Beschreibungen, eines Erfurter Nachdrucks von 1531 und der ältesten erhaltenen Auflage von 1533 zweifelsfrei rekonstruieren.

---

[2] *Weder das Wittenberger Chorgesangbuch von 1524 noch das Gemeindegesangbuch von (1525) 1526 enthalten Autorennamen; diese tauchen tatsächlich erst 1529 auf.* [3] *Vgl. Luthers Einleitung zu diesem Teil des Gesangbuches, hier S. 150.*

I

Der Hymnus ‹Veni redemptor gentium›, verdeutscht

1 Nun komm, der Hei-den Hei-land, der Jung-frau-en Kind er-kannt.[1]

Daß sich wundre al - le Welt, Gott solch Ge-burt ihm be-stellt.[2]

2 Nicht von Manns Blut noch vom Fleisch,
allein von dem Heilgen Geist
ist Gotts Wort worden ein Mensch
und blühet ein Frucht Weibs Fleisch.[3]

3 Der Jungfrau Leib schwanger ward,
doch blieb Keuschheit rein bewahrt.
Leucht' hervor manch Tugend schön.
Gott war da in seinem Thron.

4 Er ging aus der Kammer sein,
dem könglichen Saal so rein.
Gott von Art und Mensch, ein Held[4]
sein' Weg er zu laufen eilt.

5 Sein Lauf kam vom Vater her
und kehrt wieder zum Vater,
fuhr hinunter zu der Höll
und wieder zu Gottes Stuhl.

6 Der du bist dem Vater gleich,
führ hinaus den Sieg im Fleisch,
daß dein ewig Gottsgewalt
in uns das krank Fleisch erhalt.[5]

7 Dein Krippe glänzt hell und klar,
die Nacht gibt ein neu Licht dar;
Dunkel darf nicht kommen drein;
der Glaub bleibt immer im Schein.[6]

8 Lob sei Gott dem Vater tan,
Lob sei Gott, seim eingen Sohn,
Lob sei Gott dem Heiligen Geist
immer und in Ewigkeit.

---

[1] *als Kind der Jungfrau bekannt (anerkannt).* [2] *damit alle Welt staune, hat Gott ihm (seinem Sohn) eine solche Geburt (nämlich von der Jungfrau) bereitet (oder:*

richtet Gott sich eine solche Geburt zu). ³ *und es blüht auf eine Frucht aus dem Fleisch des Weibes.* ⁴ *seinem Wesen nach (zugleich) Gott und Mensch, eilt er, seinen Weg wie ein Held zu durchlaufen.* ⁵ krank = *schwach.* ⁶ im Schein = *im Licht, offenbar.*

Wohl kurz vor der Weihnachtszeit 1523 hat Luther die drei ersten der hier abgedruckten Lieder verfaßt und wahrscheinlich als Einzeldruck veröffentlicht. Jedenfalls stehen sie 1524 in den Erfurter Enchiridien und im Walter'schen Chorgesangbuch, die sonst untereinander nicht zusammenhängen, in einer auch in Einzelheiten so weitgehend übereinstimmenden Fassung, daß man eine gemeinsame Vorlage annehmen muß.

Das vorliegende Lied ist eine sehr wörtliche Übersetzung des klassischen Advents-Hymnus des Mailänder Bischofs Ambrosius, des Vaters des abendländischen Hymnengesangs (entstanden wahrscheinlich im Jahre 386). Luther hat die überlieferte Melodie in genialer Weise aus der melismenreichen, rhythmisch unbestimmten in eine metrische Fassung umgearbeitet. Dabei hat er das Strophen-Metrum von 4 × 8 auf 4 × 7 Silben verkürzt. Der Text ist ohne Kenntnis der lateinischen Vorlage stellenweise fast unverständlich; ob das poetisches Unvermögen Luthers ist oder damit zusammenhängt, daß ihm in diesem Fall die volkstümliche Verständlichkeit weniger wichtig war als die richtige Wiedergabe dieses dogmatisch befrachteten Textes, ist schwer zu entscheiden.

2

Der Hymnus ‹A solis ortus cardine›

A

1 Chri - stus wir sol - len lo - ben schon,¹ der rei - nen Magd Ma - ri - a Sohn, so weit die lie - be Son - ne leucht' und an al - ler Welt En - de reicht.

B

1 Chri-stus wir sol - len lo - - - ben __ schon,[1]
der rei - nen Magd Ma - ri - a __ Sohn,
so weit die lie - be __ Son - ne leucht' __
und an al - ler Welt __ En - de __ reicht. __

2 Der selig Schöpfer aller Ding
   zog an eins Knechtes Leib gering,
   daß er das Fleisch durch Fleisch erwürb[2]
   und sein Geschöpf nicht ganz verdürb.

3 Die göttlich Gnad vom Himmel groß
   sich in die keusche Mutter goß.
   Ein Maidlein trug ein heimlich Pfand,[3]
   das der Natur war unbekannt.

4 Das züchtig Haus des Herzens zart
   gar bald ein Tempel Gottes ward;
   die kein Mann 'rühret noch erkannt,[4]
   von Gotts Wort sie man schwanger fand.

5 Die edle Mutter hat geborn,
   den Gabriel verhieß zuvorn,[5]
   den Sankt Johann mit Springen zeigt,
   da er noch lag im Mutterleib.[6]

6 Er lag im Heu mit Armut groß,
   die Krippe hart ihn nicht verdroß.
   Es ward ein wenig Milch sein Speis,
   der nie kein Vöglein hungern ließ.

7 Des Himmels Chör sich freuen drob,
   und die Engel singen Gott Lob;
   den armen Hirten wird vermeldt
   der Hirt und Schöpfer aller Welt.

8 Lob, Ehr und Dank sei dir gesagt,
  Christ, geborn von der reinen Magd,
  mit Vater und dem Heilgen Geist,
  von nun an bis in Ewigkeit.

[1] schon = *schön, auf angemessene Weise.*   [2] *Hebräer 2,14–18; erwerben = erkaufen, erlösen.*   [3] *heimlich = geheimnisvoll; Pfand = Kind (oder: anvertraute Gabe).*   [4] *Matthäus 1,25.*   [5] *Lukas 1,31.*   [6] *Lukas 1,41.*

Luther hat vier Weihnachtslieder geschrieben. Dieses ist wie Nr. 1 die getreue Übertragung eines Hymnus aus der kirchlichen Tradition. Der Spanier Caelius Sedulius schrieb um die Mitte des 5. Jahrhunderts ein Gedicht über das Leben Jesu, in welchem jede Strophe der Reihe nach mit einem Buchstaben des lateinischen Alphabets beginnt: A solis ortus cardine ... Beatus auctor saeculi ..., Castae Parentis viscera ... usw. Die ersten sieben Strophen davon (zusammen mit einer Doxologie-Strophe) erhielten sich im kirchlichen Gebrauch als Weihnachtslied. Daher ist der Charakter dieses Liedes völlig anders als der des vorangehenden: Jenes ist ein lobpreisendes Lehrlied, dies ein betrachtendes Erzähllied. Auch hier hat Luther die überlieferte melismatische Melodie in genialer Weise bearbeitet (A). Leider hat er diese erste Bearbeitung 1529 durch eine weniger gut gelungene zweite ersetzt. Vielleicht ist das der Grund, weshalb dieses Weihnachtslied später nicht die Verbreitung gehabt hat, die das Adventslied erfahren hat. Dem Text nach wäre es leichter zugänglich als jenes. Zur Entstehung und ersten Verbreitung ist dasselbe zu sagen wie zu Nr. 1. Die zugrundeliegende Choralweise (B) wurde seit 1545 von den Straßburger Gesangbüchern verbreitet.

3
Ein Lobgesang von der Geburt Christi

1 Ge-lo-bet seist du, Je-su Christ, daß du Mensch ge-
bo-ren bist[1] von ei-ner Jung-frau, das ist wahr;
des[2] freu-et sich der En-gel Schar. Ky-ri-e-leis.

2 Des ewgen Vaters einig Kind
jetzt man in der Krippe findt.
In unser armes Fleisch und Blut
verkleidet sich das ewig Gut.
Kyrieleis.

3 Den aller Welt Kreis nie beschloß,[3]
der liegt in Marien Schoß.
Er ist ein Kindlein worden klein,
der alle Ding erhält allein.
Kyrieleis.

4 Das ewig Licht geht da herein,
gibt der Welt ein' neuen Schein.
Es leucht' wohl mitten in der Nacht
und uns des Lichtes Kinder macht.[4]
Kyrieleis.

5 Der Sohn des Vaters, Gott von Art,
ein Gast in der Welte ward[5]
und führt uns aus dem Jammertal;
er macht uns Erben in seim Saal.[6]
Kyrieleis.

6 Er ist auf Erden kommen arm,
daß er unser sich erbarm
und in dem Himmel machet' reich[7]
und seinen lieben Engeln gleich.
Kyrieleis.

7 Das hat er alles uns getan,
sein groß Lieb zu zeigen an.
Des freu sich alle Christenheit[8]
und dank ihm des in Ewigkeit.
Kyrieleis.

[1] *als Mensch geboren, in deiner Geburt Mensch geworden.* [2] *des = dessen, darüber.* [3] *beschloß = umschloß, fassen konnte.* [4] *und uns zu Kindern des Lichtes macht.* [5] *Welte: Luther schreibt «Welt» zweisilbig: Werlet. Die Einfügung «Welt hie» ist eine erst in späteren Gesangbüchern auftauchende Variante.* [6] *er macht uns zu Erben (Römer 8,17).* [7] *erbarme und uns reich mache (2. Korinther 8,9).* [8] *darüber freue sich die ganze Christenheit.*

Die zugrundeliegende Leise ist in mehreren vorreformatorischen Quellen überliefert, von denen zwei in das Zisterzienserinnenkloster Medingen in der Lüneburger Heide gehören. Das ist der Kulturkreis, mit dem Luther in seiner Magdeburger Schulzeit sehr wahrscheinlich in Berührung kam. Eine lesbare Aufzeichnung der Melodie aus dem

Mittelalter gibt es nicht. Es ist aber anzunehmen, daß Luther nebst der ersten Strophe auch die Melodie im wesentlichen unverändert übernommen hat. Auffallend ist, daß die zweite Zeile nur 7 Silben hat und volltaktig beginnt. Die Strophen 2 bis 7 hat Luther ohne jede Vorlage frei gedichtet. Sie sind dadurch aufs engste mit der ersten verknüpft, daß inhaltlich eine strenge Symmetrie besteht: Die Strophen 1 und 7, 2 und 6, 3 und 5 entsprechen sich, und in der Mittelstrophe 4 wird die zentrale Aussage gemacht. Das Ganze ist eines der kostbarsten deutschen Weihnachtslieder. Für die Entstehung und erste Verbreitung gilt dasselbe wie für Nr. 1.

4
Ein Kinderlied auf die Weihnacht Christi

C

1 «Vom Himmel hoch, da komm ich her; ich bring euch gute
neu - e Mär.[1] Der gu - ten Mär bring ich so viel, da-von ich
singen und sa - gen will, da-von ich singen und sa - gen will:

2 Euch ist ein Kindlein heut geborn
   von einer Jungfrau auserkorn,
   ein Kindelein so zart und fein,
   das soll eur Freud und Wonne sein.

3 Es ist der Herr Christ, unser Gott;
   der will euch führn aus aller Not.
   Er will eur Heiland selber sein,
   von allen Sünden machen rein.

4 Er bringt euch alle Seligkeit,
   die Gott der Vater hat bereit',
   daß ihr mit uns im Himmelreich
   sollt leben nun und ewiglich.

5 So merket nun das Zeichen recht:[2]
   die Krippe, Windelein so schlecht;[3]
   da findet ihr das Kind gelegt,
   das alle Welt erhält und trägt.»

6 Des laßt uns alle fröhlich sein[4]
   und mit den Hirten gehn hinein,
   zu sehn, was Gott uns hat beschert
   mit seinem lieben Sohn verehrt.[5]

7 Merk auf, mein Herz, und sieh dorthin:
   Was liegt doch in dem Krippelin?
   Wes ist das schöne Kindelin?
   Es ist das liebe Jesulin.

8 Sei willekomm, du edler Gast.[6]
   Den Sünder nicht verschmähet hast
   und kommst ins Elend her zu mir.[7]
   Wie soll ich immer danken dir?

9 Ach Herr, du Schöpfer aller Ding,
   wie bist du worden so gering,
   daß du da liegst auf dürrem Gras,
   davon ein Rind und Esel aß.

10 Und wär die Welt vielmal so weit
   von Edelstein und Gold bereit',[8]
   so wär sie doch dir viel zu klein
   zu sein ein enges Wiegelein.

11 Der Sammet und die Seide dein,
   das ist grob Heu und Windelein.
   Darauf du Kön'g so groß und reich
   herprangst, als wär's dein Himmelreich.[9]

12 Das hat also gefallen dir,
   die Wahrheit anzuzeigen mir,
   wie aller Welt Macht, Ehr und Gut
   vor dir nichts gilt, nichts hilft noch tut.[10]

13 Ach mein herzliebes Jesulin,
   mach dir ein rein, sanft Bettelin,
   zu ruhen in meins Herzens Schrein,
   daß ich nimmer vergesse dein.

14 Davon ich allzeit fröhlich sei,
   zu springen, singen immer frei[11]
   das rechte Susaninne schon,[12]
   mit Herzenslust den süßen Ton.[13]

15 Lob, Ehr sei Gott im höchsten Thron,
   der uns schenkt seinen eingen Sohn.
   Des freuen sich der Engel Schar'[14]
   und singen uns solch neues Jahr.[15]

---

[1] Mär = *Kunde, Nachricht.*   [2] *gebt sorgsam Acht auf das Zeichen (Lukas 2,12a).*
[3] schlecht = *schlicht, einfach.*   [4] des = *dessen, darüber.*   [5] verehrt = *geschenkt.*
[6] sei willekomm = *sei willkommen.*   [7] ins Elend = *in die Fremde.*   [8] bereit = *zubereitet.*   [9] herprangst = *mit Pracht daherkommst.*   [10] tut = *ausrichtet.*
[11] springen = *tanzen; frei = ungehindert, ausgelassen, frisch.*   [12] Susaninne: Kosewort der Mutter an der Wiege.*   [13] Ton = *Melodie.*   [14] Schar' = *Scharen.*   [15] In Sachsen schrieb man damals die neue Jahreszahl schon von Weihnachten an (sog. Natalstil der Datierung).*

Dieses dritte und bekannteste Weihnachtslied Luthers begegnet uns zum ersten Mal in der zweiten erhaltenen Ausgabe des Klug'schen Wittenberger Gesangbuchs von 1535. Man nimmt an, daß Luther es auf Weihnachten 1534 geschaffen hat. Eindeutig klar ist, daß es sich um das klassische Beispiel einer Kontrafaktur von weltlich zu geist-

*lich handelt: Noch zu Luthers Lebenszeit ist ein wohl auf das
15.Jahrhundert zurückgehendes Spiellied überliefert, ein* Ringeltanz,
wie man um den Kranz singet. *Der von Luther hochgeschätzte Komponist Ludwig Senfl hat dazu einen großartigen sechsstimmigen Satz
in drei Strophen geschrieben. Der Text läßt den Spielablauf vermuten: Ein Einzelsänger beginnt, indem er in den Kreis der Singenden
und Tanzenden tritt:*

> Mit Lust tritt ich an diesen Tanz.
> Ich hoff, mir werd ein schöner Kranz
> von einem schönen Jungfräulein;
> darum will ich ihr eigen sein.

*Es geht demnach bei diesem Spiel offenbar um eine Art Wettbewerb
unter Jugendlichen, in welchem ein Mädchen dann in Form eines
Kranzes dem Sieger die Auszeichnung übergibt. Worum es dabei
ging, das zeigt eine weitere Strophe, mit der bisweilen auch das
ganze Lied zitiert wird:*

> Ich komm aus fremden Landen her
> (oder: Aus fremden Landen komm ich her)
> und bring euch viel der neuen Mär.
> Der neuen Mär bring ich so viel,
> mehr dann ich euch hie sagen will.

*Mit dieser Strophe beginnt ein Einzelner in der Rolle des Nachrichtensängers. Vermutlich schloß er an diese erste Strophe irgendeinen
Bericht an, der sich dann mit den (wohl meist fingierten) Berichten
anderer messen mußte. So wie dieser «Bänkelsänger» (wie man seit
dem 17.Jahrhundert sagen würde) beim Abendtanz unter der Dorflinde in den Kreis tritt, so kommt der Engel in der Christnacht zu
den Hirten. Auch er hat eine «Mär», eine Nachricht, aber nicht einfach irgendeine Mär, sondern* die gute Mär, *das Eu-Angelion (Lukas
2,9–13). Wie ließe sich dieses Luther so liebe Wort besser veranschaulichen als gerade mit dieser Strophe in dieser Situation? Durch
diese Anknüpfung bei jenem Spiellied erhielt das neue Lied für alle,
die das alte kannten, eine Prägnanz, die wir so unmittelbar nicht
mehr nachempfinden können, weshalb schon Valentin Triller in seinem «Schlesisch Singebüchlein» von 1555 dem Lied eine die Situation klärende Einleitungsstrophe glaubte vorausschicken zu müssen:*

> Es kam ein Engel hell und klar
> von Gott aufs Feld zun Hirten dar;
> der war gar sehr von Herzen froh
> und sprach fröhlich zu ihn' also:

Luther hat sein Lied als «Kinderlied» bezeichnet und es auch – so weit man das von einem Autor des 16. Jahrhunderts erwarten kann – kindlichem Verständnis gemäß gestaltet. Ob er es von Kindern «aufgeführt» wissen wollte, wie manche Autoren meinen, ist ungewiß, aber meines Erachtens doch denkbar. Luthers ältestes Kind Hans (geboren 7. Juni 1526) wäre zu Weihnachten 1534 8 jährig gewesen und hätte die Rolle des Engels singen können. Magdalena (geboren 4. Mai 1529), Martin (geboren 7. November 1531) und Paul (geboren 28. Januar 1533), zusammen vielleicht mit Kindern von Freunden und Gästen, hätten dann die Hirten gespielt. Und wenn diese sich nach der 5. Strophe des Engels auf den Weg zur Wiege des eben am 17. Dezember geborenen jüngsten Geschwisterchens Margareta als Christkind aufgemacht hätten, würden sich die Eltern dann mit der 6. Strophe (entsprechend Lukas 2, 15) dem Zuge angeschlossen haben. An der Wiege des Christkindes hätte dann Magdalena als erster Hirte die 7. Strophe gesungen, während man eine Strophe wie die 12. sich etwa im Munde des Vaters vorstellen könnte. Mit der 14. Strophe würde das kleinste der die Hirten darstellenden Kinder den Reigen beschlossen haben, worauf der von allen gesungene «Chorschluß» der 15. Strophe folgte.

Auf jeden Fall hat Luther das Lied nicht als feierlichen Weihnachts-«Choral» geschrieben. Es dürfte als Liedblatt hinausgegangen sein, versehen mit jener Volksweise (A). So kam es dann ins Wittenberger Gesangbuch von 1535. Es scheint sich daraufhin entgegen Luthers ursprünglicher Absicht als Gemeindelied durchgesetzt zu haben, was Luther veranlaßt haben muß, auch diesem Lied eine eigene Weise zu geben. Sie dürfte zuerst in einer verlorenen Ausgabe des Wittenberger Gesangbuches aus den Jahren 1536 bis 1538 gestanden haben und wird uns in einem Leipziger Gesangbuch von 1539 greifbar (B). 1544 schon wird in Wittenberg ein fünfstimmiger Tonsatz Georg Forsters veröffentlicht, der beide Melodien in kunstvoller Weise als Doppel-cantus firmus kombiniert. Eine dritte Melodie (C) verdanken wir Johann Walter. Sie steht als Unterstimme eines dreistimmigen Satzes «auf Bergreihenweise», d. h. mit langen Melismen am Ende der Zeilen 2 und 4 in den Begleitstimmen, in einer Nürnberger Tricinien-Sammlung von 1541. Sie ist seit 1927 verbreitet als Singweise zu Johannes Zwicks All Morgen ist ganz frisch und neu. Die Dehnungen in der 3. Zeile kommen jedoch erst mit Luthers Text Der guten Mär bring ich so viel zu voller Geltung.

Die weitverbreitete Abweichung in der letzten Zeile der Haupt-

51

melodie *(5. Ton a statt g) ist eine spätere Angleichung an den Melodieverlauf in der Schlußzeile von* Ein feste Burg *(26).*

5
Ein ander Christlied, im vorigen Ton

2 zu Bethlehem, in Davids Stadt,
wie Micha das verkündet hat.[2]
Es ist der Herre Jesus Christ,
der euer aller Heiland ist.

3 Des sollt ihr billig fröhlich sein,[3]
daß Gott mit euch ist worden eins.
Er ist geborn eur Fleisch und Blut.[4]
Eur Bruder ist das ewig Gut.[5]

4 Was kann euch tun die Sünd und Tod?[6]
Ihr habt mit euch den wahren Gott.
Laßt zürnen Teufel und die Höll:
Gotts Sohn ist worden eur Gesell.[7]

5 Er will und kann euch lassen nicht,
setzt ihr auf ihn eur Zuversicht.
Es mögen euch viel' fechten an:
Dem sei Trotz, der's nicht lassen kann.[8]

6 Zuletzt müßt ihr doch haben recht.
Ihr seid nun worden Gotts Geschlecht.
Des danket Gott in Ewigkeit,
geduldig, fröhlich allezeit.»

Ein Lied auf den Christtag

1 Vom Him-mel kam der En - gel Schar, der En - - - - gel
Schar; ____ er-schien den Hir - ten of - fen - bar.[1]
Hal - le - lu - ja. Hal - le - - - - lu - ja.

2 Sie sagten ihn': «Ein |: Kindlein zart, :|
das liegt dort in der Krippe hart,
Halleluja, Halleluja.

3 zu Bethlehem in |: Davids Stadt, :|
wie Micha das verkündet hat.[2]
Halleluja, Halleluja.

4 Es ist der Herre |: Jesus Christ, :|
der euer aller Heiland ist.
Halleluja, Halleluja.

5 Des sollt ihr billig |: fröhlich sein, :|[3]
daß Gott mit euch ist worden eins.
Halleluja, Halleluja.

6 Er ist geborn eur |: Fleisch und Blut. :|[4]
Eur Bruder ist das ewig Gut.[5]
Halleluja, Halleluja.

7 Was kann euch tun die |: Sünd und Tod? :|[6]
Ihr habt mit euch den wahren Gott.
Halleluja, Halleluja.

8 Laßt zürnen Teufel |: und die Höll: :|
Gotts Sohn ist worden eur Gesell.[7]
Halleluja, Halleluja.

9 Er will und kann euch |: lassen nicht, :|
setzt ihr auf ihn eur Zuversicht.
Halleluja, Halleluja.

10 Es mögen euch viel' |: fechten an: :|
Dem sei Trotz, der's nicht lassen kann.[8]
Halleluja, Halleluja.

11 Zuletzt müßt ihr doch |: haben recht. :|
Ihr seid nun worden Gotts Geschlecht.
Halleluja, Halleluja.

12 Des danket Gott in |: Ewigkeit, :|
geduldig, fröhlich allezeit.»
Halleluja, Halleluja.

[1] *offenbar = sichtbar.* [2] *Micha 5,1; Matthäus 2,5.* [3] *darüber dürft ihr mit Recht fröhlich sein.* [4] *als euer Fleisch und Blut.* [5] *Hebräer 12,11.* [6] *Römer 8,38f.* [7] *Gesell = Gefährte.* [8] *dem widersteht, der es nicht bleiben lassen kann, euch anzufechten.*

Wenn man annehmen dürfte, daß das Weihnachtslied Nr. 4 von Luther für die Weihnachtsfeier in seinem Hause geschrieben und dann gewiß auch seither immer wieder so gebraucht wurde, dann würde man verstehen, warum wir im Wittenberger Gesangbuch von 1543 unerwartet eine neuerliche Bearbeitung der Engelsbotschaft von Lukas 2,9–13 finden, und zwar so deutlich als Trostlied gefaßt: Das Lied dürfte auf Weihnachten 1542 hin entstanden sein. Am 20. September jenes Jahres war Luthers zweites Kind, das früher bei der Krippe das Susaninne gesungen hatte, nach mehrwöchiger Krankheit gestorben. An dem darauffolgenden Weihnachtsfest wollte Luther wohl sich und die Seinen mit einer Deutung der Engelsworte trösten lassen, die dieser Situation angepaßt war. Die zwölf Strophen dieses Liedes könnten sehr wohl die fünf ersten von Nr. 4 ersetzen.

Von diesem (abgesehen von Nr. 37 und 44) letzten Lied Luthers hat sich die handschriftliche Vorlage des Autors für den Erstdruck

(wohl als Liedblatt) erhalten. Darauf steht die ausdrückliche Anweisung, das Lied solle ohne seinen Namen gedruckt werden. Im übrigen ist diese Erstfassung – wir drucken sie unter C gesondert ab – bis heute kaum beachtet worden. Luther hat dem Liede keine eigene Melodie gegeben, sondern es auf die Melodie der Weihnachts-Cantio Puer natus in Bethlehem, die im dritten Teil seines Gesangbuches stand, geschrieben. Deshalb hat er den Text in zweizeiligen Strophen mit angehängtem doppeltem Halleluja und mit Wiederholung der drei letzten Silben der jeweils ersten Zeile konzipiert. Für den Gesang der Gemeinde sieht Luther allerdings schon auf der Handschrift die Melodie von Nr. 4 vor, auf welche denn auch im Gesangbuch verwiesen wird (A). Als weitere Möglichkeit nennt Luther auf seiner ersten Niederschrift die Hymnenweise von Nr. 6 (B). Im Blick auf diese beiden Melodien hat er dann durch Klammern am linken Rand die Möglichkeit angedeutet, je zwei Strophen zu einer zusammenzufassen.

Erst später hat man diesen Text mit der ersten, nun herrenlos gewordenen Melodie von Nr. 4 verbunden.

6

Der Hymnus ‹Hostis Herodes impie›,
im Ton ‹A solis ortus cardine›

1 Was fürchtst du, Feind He - ro - des, sehr,   daß uns geboren kommt Christ, der Herr?[1]   Er sucht kein sterb - lich Kö - nig - reich,   der zu uns bringt sein Him - mel - reich.

1 Was fürchtst du, Feind He - ro - des, sehr, daß uns ge - born

kommt Christ, der Herr?[1] Er sucht kein sterb - lich Kö -

nig - reich, der zu uns bringt sein Him - mel - reich.

2 Dem Stern die Weisen folgen nach.
Solch Licht zum rechten Licht sie bracht.
Sie zeigen mit den Gaben drei,
dies Kind Gott, Mensch und König sei.

3 Die Tauf im Jordan an sich nahm[2]
das himmlische Gotteslamm,
dadurch der nie kein Sünde tat
von Sünden uns gewaschen hat.

4 Ein Wunderwerk da neu geschah:[3]
Sechs steinern' Krüge man da sah
voll Wassers, das verlor sein Art;[4]
roter Wein durch sein Wort draus ward.

5 Lob, Ehr und Dank sei dir gesagt,
Christ, geborn von der reinen Magd,
mit Vater und dem Heilgen Geist,
von nun an bis in Ewigkeit.
Amen.

[1] *Matthäus 2,3; daß in seiner Geburt zu uns kommt Christ, der Herr.* [2] *Matthäus 3,13–17; Johannes 1,29–34.* [3] *Johannes 2,1–11.* [4] Art = *Eigenschaft.*

Zu diesem Lied ist das Entstehungsdatum zuverlässig überliefert: 12. Dezember 1541. Wir gehen also nicht fehl, wenn wir auch bei anderen Festliedern Luthers eine Entstehung kurz vor der betreffenden Festzeit annehmen. Anlaß war in diesem Fall wohl doch der Wunsch Luthers, auch für Epiphanias (6. Januar), das Fest, welches die Weihnachtszeit im engeren Sinne beschließt, ein eigenes Lied zu haben. Es handelt sich um die Übertragung von vier weiteren Strophen aus jenem alphabetischen Hymnus des Caelius Sedulius, dessen erste Strophen er in Nr. 2 schon früher bearbeitet hatte. Mit jenem Lied teilt dieses auch die Melodie (A). In ihrer ursprünglichen Gestalt gab man die Hymnenweise dem Lied seit 1545 in Straßburg bei (B).

7

Der Lobgesang Simeonis: ‹Nunc dimittis›

1 Mit Fried und Freud ich fahr da - hin in_____ Gotts_____ Wil - le.[1] Ge-trost ist mir mein Herz_ und Sinn, sanft und stil - le, wie _____ Gott mir ver-hei - ßen _ hat. Der Tod ist mein Schlaf wor - den.

2 Das macht Christus, wahr' Gottes Sohn,
   der treu Heiland,
   den du mich, Herr, hast sehen lon[2]
   und 'macht bekannt,[3]
   daß er sei das Leben mein[4]
   und Heil in Not und Sterben.

3 Den hast du allen vorgestellt
   mit groß Gnaden,
   zu seinem Reich die ganze Welt
   heißen laden
   durch dein teuer heilsams Wort
   an allem Ort erschollen.

4 Er ist das hell und selig Licht
   für die Heiden,
   zu 'rleuchten, die dich kennen nicht,
   und zu weiden.
   Er ist deins Volks Israel
   der Preis, Ehr, Freud und Wonne.

[1] *nach Gottes Willen.*   [2] *lon = lassen.*   [3] *und bekanntgemacht hast, von dem du verkündet hast.*   [4] *Das Wort «mein» fehlt im Urtext; das Metrum erfordert jedoch hier noch eine Silbe.*

Dies ist von den drei neutestamentlichen Cantica das einzige, wel-ches Luther in einem Lied bearbeitet hat; in psalmodischer Form hat

57

er alle drei in sein Gesangbuch aufgenommen (vgl. zu Nr. 41).
Warum Luther gerade den Lobgesang Simeons (Lukas 2,29–32)
liedmäßig bearbeitet hat, ist schwer zu sagen. Ein liturgisches Anliegen (wie bei Calvin, Nr. 7) kann kaum dahinterstehen, denn diese
Bearbeitung ist ein ausgesprochenes Sololied. Luther könnte immerhin an eine liturgische Verwendung am Fest Mariae Reinigung (2. Februar) gedacht haben; jedenfalls ordnet er das Lied 1529 so ein.

Die Beziehung zur Bestattung, die dann bei der Übernahme dieses
Liedes in die Begräbnisgesänge von 1542 (s. zu Nr. 44) deutlich wird,
mag immerhin auch bei der Entstehung Luther vor Augen gestanden
haben. Daß das Lied um den 2. Februar 1524 herum entstanden sein
sollte, ist einigermaßen unwahrscheinlich, denn es steht erst in dem
wohl gegen Ende des Jahres 1524 erschienenen Walterschen Chorgesangbuch. Von allen anderen Liedern dieses Jahres unterscheidet es
sich im übrigen durch seinen überaus kunstvollen Strophenbau und
eine diesem entsprechende Melodiegestalt. Ähnliches hat Luther später nur noch in Ein feste Burg (26) und Sie ist mir lieb (35) geleistet.
Die Melodie muß wohl von Luther stammen, denn er hätte diesen
Text kaum ohne eine solche gedichtet. Denkbar wäre höchstens, daß
Johann Walter sie verbessert hätte; doch gibt es auch dafür (im Gegensatz zu Nr. 8) keine Anhaltspunkte.

8
Christ ist erstanden, gebessert

b

1 Christ lag in To-des-ban - den, für uns-re Sünd ge-ge-ben.
Der ist wie-der er - stan - den und hat uns bracht das Leben.

Des wir sol-len fröhlich sein, Gott lo-ben und __ dank-bar sein

und sin-gen: Hal - le - lu - ja, Hal - le - lu - ja.

2 Den Tod niemand zwingen konnt
   bei allen Menschenkinden.
   Das macht alles unser Sünd;
   kein Unschuld war zu finden.
      Davon kam der Tod so bald
      und nahm über uns Gewalt,
      hielt uns in seim Reich gefangen.
      Halleluja.

3 Jesus Christus, Gottes Sohn,
   an unsrer Statt ist kommen
   und hat die Sünd abgetan,
   damit dem Tod genommen
      all sein Recht und sein Gewalt;[1]
      da bleibt nichts, denn Tods Gestalt;[2]
      den Stachel hat er verloren.[3]
      Halleluja.

4 Es war ein wunderlich Krieg,
   da Tod und Leben rungen.[4]
   Das Leben behielt den Sieg;
   es hat den Tod verschlungen.
      Die Schrift hat verkündet das,[5]
      wie ein Tod den andern fraß;
      ein Spott aus dem Tod ist worden.[6]
      Halleluja.

5 Hier ist das recht Osterlamm,[7]
   davon Gott hat geboten.
   Das ist an des Kreuzes Stamm
   in heißer Lieb gebraten.

59

Das Blut zeichnet unsre Tür;
das hält der Glaub dem Tod für.[8]
Der Würger kann uns nicht rühren.[9]
Halleluja.

6 So feiern wir dies hoch Fest[10]
mit Herzensfreud und Wonne,
das uns der Herr scheinen läßt;
er ist selber die Sonne,
der durch seiner Gnaden Glanz
erleucht unsre Herzen ganz;
der Sünden Nacht ist vergangen.
Halleluja.

7 Wir essen und leben wohl[11]
in rechten Osterfladen.
Der alte Saurteig nicht soll
sein bei dem Wort der Gnaden.
Christus will die Koste sein[12]
und speisen die Seel allein;
der Glaub will keins andern leben.[13]
Halleluja.

[1] Gewalt = *Kraft.* [2] *es bleibt nur die äußere Gestalt des Todes (aber Kraft hat er nicht mehr); 1. Korinther 15,55.* [3] *Hosea 13,14; 1. Korinther 15,54.55.* [4] *In der Oster-Sequenz heißt es: Tod und Leben waren in einen wunderlichen Zwiekampf verstrickt.* [5] *Gemeint ist Hosea 13,14.* [6] *Der Tod ist zum Spotte (zu Schanden) geworden.* [7] *1. Korinther 5,7; 2. Mose 12 (zur ganzen Strophe).* [8] *für = vor.* [9] *rühren = berühren, uns nichts antun.* [10] *hoch = hohe.* [11] *Johannes 6,35; 1. Korinther 5,7.8; 2. Mose 12,8.15–20.* [12] *Koste = Nahrung.* [13] *der Glaube will von nichts anderem leben.*

Wie die Überschrift gemeint ist, wird deutlich, sobald man die Melodie mit dem Text des zweiten Stollens ansieht: Luther geht aus von der Oster-Leise Christ ist erstanden *(38). Mit dem «gebessert» will Luther nicht sagen, er hielte die (von ihm ja so hoch geschätzte) Leise für schlecht oder doch verbesserungsbedürftig. Das Wort meint einfach: bearbeitet, erweitert. Luther konnte sich in diesem Fall nicht auf den engen Raum der Leisenstrophe beschränken, sondern wollte mehr Raum haben. So schuf er eine siebenzeilige Strophe, deren erste sechs Zeilen auch sieben Silben haben. Der Inhalt der ersten Leisenstrophe ist in der ersten Liedstrophe enthalten. Daran schließen sich (wie beim Weihnachtslied Nr. 3) sechs weitere Strophen an, wobei wiederum die Mittelstrophe die Hauptaussage enthält. In ihr wird übrigens die Ostersequenz des Wipo von Burgund* Victimae paschali

laudes, *von welcher die Leise ihrer Entstehung und ihrer liturgischen Funktion nach abhängt, zitiert. Der Melodie, wie sie in den frühen Quellen des Jahres 1524 steht (a), fügt Johann Walter in seinem Chorgesangbuch eine zweite, im Abgesang geschmeidigere Fassung bei, die sich später auch durchgesetzt hat (b). Wahrscheinlich hat der Berufsmusiker Walter hier das Werk des begabten Dilettanten Luther überarbeitet.*

9

Ein Lobgesang auf das Osterfest

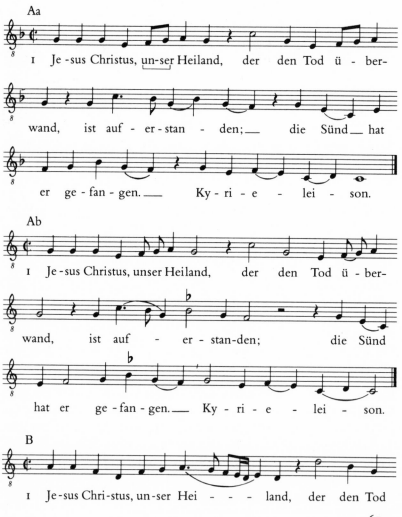

Aa

1 Je -sus Christus, un-ser Heiland, der den Tod ü - ber-
wand, ist auf - er-stan - den;___ die Sünd___ hat
er ge - fan - gen. ___ Ky - ri - e - lei - son.

Ab

1 Je -sus Christus, unser Heiland, der den Tod ü - ber-
wand, ist auf - er - stan-den; die Sünd
hat er ge - fan - gen.___ Ky - ri - e - lei - son.

B

1 Je -sus Chri-stus, un-ser Hei - - - land, der den Tod

61

ü - ber - - - wand, ist auf-er-stan - den; die

Sünd hat er ___ ge - fan-gen. Ky -ri - e - lei - son.

C

1 Je - sus Chri-stus, un - ser Hei - land, der den Tod

ü - ber - wand, ist auf - er - stan - den; die Sünd hat

er ge - fan - gen. Ky - ri - e - lei - son.

2 Der ohn Sünden war geborn,[1]
  trug für uns Gottes Zorn,
  hat uns versöhnet,
  daß Gott uns sein Huld gönnet.
  Kyrieleison.

3 Tod, Sünd, Leben und auch Gnad,
  alls in Händen er hat.
  Er kann erretten
  alle, die zu ihm treten.
  Kyrieleison.

---

[1] *Auch hier (wie in Nr. 8) wird auf die Oster-Sequenz angespielt: Christus, der Unschuldige, versöhnte die Sünder mit dem Vater.*

Die Überschrift und die Strophenform weisen dieses Osterlied als Leise aus. Ob es eine altüberlieferte Leise ist oder ob Luther für ein neugeschaffenes Lied diese Form gewählt hat, ist nicht auszumachen, da hier keine mittelalterliche Bezeugung vorliegt. Mit der Melodie Aa ist das Lied nicht nur in den Erfurter Enchiridien, sondern auch auf einem kürzlich aufgefundenen Augsburger Einblattdruck, der auf dem Wittenberger Urdruck beruhen dürfte, überliefert. Johann Wal-

ter hat in seinem Chorgesangbuch von *1524* zu dieser Weise (in etwas abweichender Form: Ab) einen Satz geschrieben, daneben dem
Text aber noch eine eigene Melodie gegeben (B). Eine dritte Weise
(C) taucht im Wittenberger Gemeindegesangbuch von *1529* auf. Sie
läßt sich als dorische Variante der mixolydischen Melodie A auffas-
sen und zeigt das in diesem Gesangbuch an mehreren Stellen deutlich werdende Bestreben nach gemeindegemäßer Einfachheit. Mindestens diese Bearbeitung könnte dann von Luther stammen. Am
Anfang der *1.* und *3.* Zeile steht in der Vorlage eine Note von doppel-
ter Länge.

Wahrscheinlich hat Luther dieses ganz knappe Osterzeugnis bewußt der sehr weit ausgreifenden Dichtung Nr. *8* an die Seite gestellt. Als drittes Osterlied kommt dann *1529* in der Abteilung der
«Lieder der Alten» noch das klassische Christ ist erstanden *(38)* hinzu.

10
Der Hymnus ‹Veni creator spiritus›

1 Komm, Gott Schöp-fer, Hei-li-ger Geist, be-
such das Herz der Men-schen dein. Mit Gna-den
sie füll, wie du weißt, daß dein Geschöpf vor-hin sein.[1]

   2 Denn du bist der Tröster genannt,
     des Allerhöchsten Gabe teur,
     ein geistlich Salb an uns gewandt,[2]
     ein lebend Brunn, Lieb und Feur.

   3 Zünd uns ein Licht an im Verstand,
     gib uns ins Herz der Liebe Brunst.[3]
     Das schwach Fleisch in uns, dir bekannt,[4]
     erhalt fest dein Kraft und Gunst.

   4 Du bist mit Gaben siebenfalt
     der Finger an Gotts rechter Hand.

63

Des Vaters Wort gibst du gar bald
mit Zungen in alle Land.

5 Des Feindes List treib von uns fern,
den Fried schaff bei uns deine Gnad,
daß wir dei'm Leiten folgen gern[5]
und meiden der Seele Schad'.

6 Lehr uns den Vater kennen wohl,
dazu Jesus Christ, seinen Sohn,
daß wir des Glaubens werden voll,
dich, beider Geist, zu verstahn.[6]

7 Gott Vater sei Lob und dem Sohn,
der von den Toten auferstund;
dem Tröster sei dasselb getan
in Ewigkeit alle Stund.

[1] *wie Du ja weißt, daß sie von Anfang an deine Geschöpfe sind.*   [2] Salb = *Salbung.*   [3] Brunst = *Brand.*   [4] das schwach Fleisch: *Akkusativobjekt.*   [5] dei'm = *deinem.*   [6] verstahn *(eigentlich: verstohn)* = *verstehen.*

Auch der Gruppe der Pfingstlieder schickt Luther (wie derjenigen der Weihnachtslieder) ein klassisches lateinisches Lehrlied in deutscher Übertragung voraus. Dem Text wie der Melodie dieses Liedes liegt der Hymnus Veni creator Spiritus *des Hrabanus Maurus von 809 zu Grunde, sehr wahrscheinlich geschrieben für die Synode von Aachen, die den Einschub «filioque» (und vom Sohne) in den dritten Artikel des Nizänischen Glaubensbekenntnisses beschließen sollte. Der Hymnus wurde dann das Lehrlied vom Heiligen Geist und der Eröffnungsgesang für kirchliche Versammlungen. Der lateinische Text zitiert in der einleitenden Anrufung wie in einem weiteren Vers wörtlich den ambrosianischen Hymnus* Veni redemptor gentium, *und man nimmt an, daß sich in seiner Melodie auch die ambrosianische Melodie jenes Adventshymnus erhalten hat.*

Luther hat auch hier in die Form eingegriffen, indem er die letzte Zeile der Strophe um eine Silbe kürzte. Bei der Umgestaltung der melismatischen Choralweise zu einer syllabischen Mensuralweise ergab das eine Synkope auf dem vorletzten Ton. Außerdem hat Luther die Strophen 3 und 4 der Vorlage in der Reihenfolge umgestellt. Ob dieser Eingriff bewußt erfolgte oder ob Luther schon den lateinischen Text nur in dieser Form kannte, ist nicht mit Sicherheit festzustellen.

Wie bei Nr. 2 hat Luther auch hier die erste Bearbeitung der Melodie von 1524 im Wittenberger Gemeindegesangbuch von 1529

durch eine neue ersetzt, die jedoch in diesem Fall besser gelungen ist als die erste und sich zu Recht später durchgesetzt hat.

11

‹Veni sancte spiritus›, gebessert

a

1 Komm, Hei - li - ger__ Geist, Her - re Gott, erfüll mit dei - ner

Gna - de Gut dei -ner Gläub-gen Herz, Mut und Sinn; dein

bren-nend Lieb ent-zünd in ihn'. O Herr, durch dei - nes

Lich - tes Glast[1] zu dem Glau-ben ver - sam-melt hast das

Volk aus al - ler Welt Zun-gen; das sei dir, Herr, zu

Lob ge - sun - gen. Hal-le - lu - ja. Hal - le - lu - ja.

b

1 Komm, Hei - li -ger Geist, Her - - re Gott, er -

füll mit __ dei - ner __ Gna - de __ Gut dei-

65

ner — Gläu - bi- gen Herz, Mut — und — Sinn; dein bren-nend

Lieb — ent-zünd — in ihn'. O Herr, durch dei - nes

Lich - tes Glast[1] zu dem Glau - ben — ver - sam -

melt — hast das Volk — aus al - ler Welt Zun -

gen; das sei dir, Herr, — zu Lob ge - sun -gen.

Hal - le - lu - - ja. Hal - le - lu - ja.

2 Du heiliges Licht, edler Hort,[2]
laß uns leuchten des Lebens Wort;
und lehr uns Gott recht erkennen,
von Herzen Vater ihn nennen.
O Herr, behüt vor fremder Lehr,
daß wir nicht Meister suchen mehr,
denn Jesus mit rechtem Glauben,
und ihm aus ganzer Macht vertrauen.[3]
Halleluja, Halleluja.

3 Du heilige Glut, süßer Trost,
nun hilf uns fröhlich und getrost
in deim Dienst beständig bleiben,
die Trübsal uns nicht wegtreiben.
O Herr, durch dein Kraft uns bereit'
und stärk des Fleisches Blödigkeit,[4]
daß wir hier ritterlich ringen,
durch Tod und Leben zu dir dringen.
Halleluja. Halleluja.

[1] Glast = *Glanz*. [2] Hort = *Trost, Schatz (vgl. Nr. 30 b: 3,6)*. [3] Macht = *Kraft,*
Vermögen. [4] Blödigkeit = *Schwachheit, Verzagtheit (Matthäus 26,41)*.

Auch mit seinem zweiten Pfingstlied knüpft Luther bei der Tradition an. Zugrunde liegt die Pfingst-Antiphon Veni sancte Spiritus: «Komm, Heiliger Geist, erfülle die Herzen deiner Gläubigen, und entzünde in ihnen das Feuer deiner Liebe, der du aus der Verschiedenheit der Sprachen die Völker zur Einheit des Glaubens versammelt hast. Halleluja. Halleluja.» Sie ist schon im 14. Jahrhundert als deutsche Strophe gesungen worden. Die Melodie gehört von Anfang an zu diesem deutschen Text. Luther hat gelegentlich seiner Begeisterung für diese Strophe mit der Behauptung Ausdruck gegeben, der Heilige Geist selber habe diesen Text und diese Melodie gemacht. Diese deutsche Strophe hat Luther leicht überarbeitet (die nochmalige Anrede «O Herr» in der Mitte der Strophe scheint auf ihn zurückzugehen) und um zwei eigene, gleichgebaute Strophen erweitert, wobei er vor allem in der Mittelstrophe sehr deutlich sein evangelisches Bekenntnis des Glaubens an Christus allein und gegen andere Quellen und Beziehungspersonen des Glaubens ausspricht.

Da das Lied um Pfingsten 1524 entstanden sein muß, in einer Zeit, in welcher Luther sich intensiv mit der Heiligenverehrung befaßte, ist diese Zuspitzung in Strophe 2 verständlich.

Das Lied steht in den Erfurter Enchiridien, die – falls das Lied wirklich um Pfingsten 1524 geschrieben ist – erst im Sommer des Jahres erschienen sein können. Die im Gegensatz zu den mittelalterlichen Melodiefassungen weitgehend syllabisierte und isometrisierte Fassung der Melodie, die wir dort finden und die sich seit 1545 durchgesetzt hat (a), dürfte auf Luther zurückgehen. Aber auch die mittelalterliche Melodieform lebte mit Luthers Text weiter. Wir finden sie seit 1533 im Wittenberger Gesangbuch und bald auch anderwärts (b).

I 2
Der Lobgesang ‹Nun bitten wir den Heiligen Geist›

a

1 Nun bit-ten wir den Hei - li - gen Geist   um den

rech -ten Glau-ben al - ler - meist,   daß er uns be-

hü - te an un-serm En - de, wenn wir heim-fahrn aus

die-sem E - len - de.[1] Ky - ri - e - - leis.

b

1 Nun bit-ten wir den Heil-gen Geist um den

rech-ten Glau-ben al - ler-meist, daß er uns be-

hü - te an un-serm En - de, wenn wir heim-fahrn aus

die-sem E - len - de.[1]____ Ky - ri - e - lei - son.

2 Du wertes Licht, gib uns deinen Schein,[2]
lehr uns Jesus Christ kennen allein,
daß wir an ihm bleiben, dem treuen Heiland,
der uns 'bracht hat zum rechten Vaterland.
Kyrieleis.

3 Du süße Lieb, schenk uns deine Gunst;
laß uns empfinden der Liebe Brunst,[3]
daß wir uns von Herzen einander lieben
und im Frieden auf einem Sinn bleiben.
Kyrieleis.

4 Du höchster Tröster in aller Not,
hilf, daß wir nicht fürchten Schand noch Tod,
daß in uns die Sinne nicht verzagen,[4]
wenn der Feind wird das Leben verklagen.[5]
Kyrieleis.

[1] Elende = *Fremde (weil der Himmel unsere wahre Heimat ist, s. 2,4).* [2] Schein
= *Glanz.* [3] Brunst = *Brand, Brennen.* [4] *daß wir nicht verzagen (möglicherweise hieß der Vers jedoch ursprünglich: daß uns unsere Sünde nicht mach verza-*

gen). [5] *wenn der Teufel unser Leben einklagen, uns auf Verlust des Lebens, also mit Antrag auf Tod, verklagen wird.*

Nachdem Luther die klassischen Leisen zu Weihnachten *(3)* und Ostern *(8)* bearbeitet hat, ist es nahezu selbstverständlich, daß er auch die weitverbreitete Pfingstleise in gleicher Weise für den neuen Gemeindegesang aufwertet. Die deutsche Einschaltstrophe in die Pfingstsequenz Veni sancte Spiritus *(nicht zu verwechseln mit der Antiphon gleichen Anfangs)* dürfte wie die Osterleise *(38)* ins *12.* Jahrhundert zurückreichen. Jedenfalls wird sie schon im *13.* Jahrhundert von Berthold von Regensburg *(gestorben 1273)* in einer Predigt zitiert: «Es war ein weiser Mann, der dieses Lied erfand.» Auch Luther hat die Strophe schon um *1509/10* in einer Erfurter Predigt zitiert und *1523* für den evangelischen Gottesdienst empfohlen. Ob seine Erweiterung wie Nr. *11* schon um Pfingsten *1524* entstanden ist, kann man deshalb bezweifeln, weil dieses Lied im Gegensatz zu Nr. *11* nicht in den Erfurter Enchiridien steht, sondern erst gegen Ende des Jahres in Straßburg und bei Johann Walter erscheint. Daß die Gesangbücher es als Pfingstlied einreihen, daran ist Luther selbst schuld, der es *1529* so eingeordnet hat. Er hat es aber vorher in seiner Deutschen Messe von *1526* als Graduallied empfohlen und *1542* in seine Sammlung von Begräbnisgesängen aufgenommen. Das Straßburger Kirchenamt will es im Predigtgottesdienst als Wort-Epiklese verwendet wissen.

Die schon vor der Reformation mehrfach überlieferte Weise findet sich bei Johann Walter in der Fassung a. Sie wurde in nur wenig abweichender Gestalt so auch ins Gemeindegesangbuch Luthers von *1529* übernommen, obwohl es sich eindeutig um eine Chor-Fassung handelt, in welcher die beiden ersten Liedzeilen in gegenüber der zweiten Melodiehälfte verdoppelten Notenwerten gesungen werden. Straßburg hingegen überliefert schon seit *1524* die gemeindegemäßere und ohne Zweifel der mittelalterlichen volkstümlichen Singpraxis entsprechende Fassung b.

13
Gott der Vater wohn uns bei

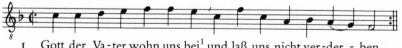

1 Gott der Va-ter wohn uns bei[1] und laß uns nicht ver-der - ben,
mach uns al-ler Sün-den frei und helf uns se-lig ster - ben.

Vor dem Teu-fel uns be-wahr, halt uns bei fe-stem Glau-

ben, und auf dich laß uns bau – – en, aus Herzens-

grund ver-trau – en, dir uns la-ßen ganz und gar,[2]

mit al-len rech-ten Chri-sten ent-flie-hen Teu-fels

Li – sten, mit Waf-fen Gotts uns fri – sten.[3] A-men.

A-men, das sei wahr, so sin-gen wir Hal-le-lu-ja.

2 Jesus Christus wohn uns bei[1]
  und laß uns nicht . . .

3 Heilig Geist, der wohn uns bei[1]
  und laß uns nicht . . .

[1] wohn uns bei: *Der Sinn dieser Ausdrucksweise erschöpft sich nicht in der Übersetzung «steh uns bei». Es geht nicht bloß um irgend einen Beistand Gottes, sondern
um sein persönliches Dabeisein (vgl. 19: 3,3).*   [2] *dir uns überlassen, auf dich uns
verlassen, dir uns anvertrauen.*   [3] *mit Gottes Waffen uns begnügen.*

Den Kranz von Liedern zu den Festen des Kirchenjahres schließt Luther in seinem Gesangbuch von 1529 mit diesem trinitarischen Bittlied ab. So wenig wie die drei vorangehenden Lieder typische
Pfingstlieder sind, ist dies ein eigentliches Trinitatis-Lied. Das wird
deutlich, wenn wir seine Herkunft beachten: Im Erfurter Gesangbuch von 1525 trägt das Lied den möglicherweise von Luther stammenden Titel: Der Lobgesang «Gott der Vater wohn uns bei», gebessert und christlich korrigiert. Auch hier hat also Luther ein überliefertes Lied überarbeitet. Die von Luther verwendete Melodie ist kürzlich in einem um 1500 geschriebenen Chorbuch aus Halberstadt

(heute in Berlin) entdeckt worden. Ob das Lied im Mittelalter auch trinitarisch begonnen hat, ist nicht ganz sicher, aber wahrscheinlich; überliefert sind nur Strophen, die sich an Maria, an Petrus, den Erzengel Michael, an Christophorus und an Nikolaus wenden. Es scheint sich somit um ein Allerheiligen-Litanei-Lied zu handeln. Und diese Litanei beginnt mit der Anrufung der Dreieinigkeit. Luther hat hier auf jeden Fall den Text der Strophe nicht unverändert übernommen. Was er daran geändert hat, ist schwer zu sagen, weil wir trotz des Berliner Fundes die Fassung, welche Luther vorlag, nicht kennen. Aus der angeführten Überschrift geht jedoch hervor, daß er hier einiges in evangelischem Sinne geändert hat. Merkwürdigerweise gehört dazu auch, daß er dieser Leise ihr Haupt-Erkennungsmerkmal, das «Kyrieleison, Christe eleison», das ursprünglich in der vorletzten Zeile stand, weggenommen hat. Luthers Text steht im Jahre 1524 nur im Walterschen Chorgesangbuch; er dürfte also später entstanden sein als jene, die in die Erfurter Gesangbücher Aufnahme fanden.

Nun folgen geistliche Gesänge, in denen der Katechismus zusammengefaßt ist, weil wir doch gerne möchten, daß die christliche Lehre auf allerlei Weise, durch Predigen, Lesen, Singen usw., betätigt und stets den jungen und unwissenden Leuten eingeprägt und auf diese Weise immerfort rein erhalten und unseren Nachkommen weitergegeben werde. Dazu verleihe uns Gott seine Gnade und seinen Segen durch Jesus Christus. Amen.

14
Die Zehn Gebote Gottes, lang

1 Dies sind die heil-gen Zehn Ge-bot, die uns gab un-ser Her-re Gott durch Mo-se, sei-nen Die-ner treu, hoch auf dem Berg Si-na-i. Kyri-e-leis.

2 Ich bin allein dein Gott, der Herr,
  kein' Götter sollst du haben mehr.[1]
  Du sollst mir ganz vertrauen dich,[2]
  von Herzensgrund lieben mich.
  Kyrieleis.

3 Du sollst nicht brauchen zu Unehrn
  den Namen Gottes, deines Herrn;
  du sollst nichts preisen recht noch gut,
  als was Gott selbst redt und tut.
  Kyrieleis.

4 Du sollst heilgen den siebent' Tag,
  daß du und dein Haus ruhen mag;

du sollst von deim Tun lassen ab,
daß Gott sein Werk in dir hab.
Kyrieleis.

5 Du sollst ehrn und gehorsam sein
dem Vater und der Mutter dein,
und wo dein Hand ihn' dienen kann;
so wirst du langs Leben han.[3]
Kyrieleis.

6 Du sollst nicht töten zorniglich,
nicht hassen noch selbst rächen dich,
Geduld haben und sanften Mut
und auch dem Feind tun das Gut'.
Kyrieleis.

7 Dein Eh sollst du bewahren rein,
daß auch dein Herz kein ander' mein,[4]
und halten keusch das Leben dein
mit Zucht und Mäßigkeit fein.
Kyrieleis.

8 Du sollst nicht stehlen Geld noch Gut,
nicht wuchern jemands Schweiß und Blut;[5]
du sollst auftun dein milde Hand
den Armen in deinem Land.
Kyrieleis.

9 Du sollst kein falscher Zeuge sein,
nicht lügen auf den Nächsten dein.
Sein Unschuld sollst auch retten du
und seine Schand decken zu.
Kyrieleis.

10 Du sollst deins Nächsten Weib und Haus
begehren nicht, noch etwas draus;
du sollst ihm wünschen alles Gut',
wie dir dein Herz selber tut.
Kyrieleis.

11 Die Gebot all uns geben sind,
daß du dein Sünd, o Menschenkind,
erkennen sollst und lernen wohl,
wie man vor Gott leben soll.
Kyrieleis.

12 Das helf uns der Herr Jesus Christ,
der unser Mittler worden ist.
Es ist mit unserm Tun verlorn,[6]
verdienen doch eitel Zorn.
Kyrieleis.

[1] *keine weiteren (anderen) Götter sollst du haben.* [2] *du sollst dich mir ganz anvertrauen.* [3] han = *haben.* [4] mein = *meine = im Auge habe, erstrebe.* [5] wuchern = *ausbeuten.* [6] verlorn = *umsonst (vgl. Nr. 30 b: 2,3).*

Dieses Lied zum – nach Luthers Ordnung – ersten Katechismus-Stück eröffnet die Erfurter Sammlungen des Jahres 1524. Nach der Wittenberger Kirchenordnung von 1533 wurde es zum Anfang der Katechismus-Predigt am Sonntagnachmittag gesungen. Den Beschluß machte jeweils Nr. 15. Zu beachten ist, daß gemäß mittelalterlicher Überlieferung das Bilderverbot weggelassen ist. Sonst hat jedes Gebot eine Strophe, das 9. und 10. nach mittelalterlicher Zählung sind jedoch in eine Strophe zusammengefaßt. So ergibt sich durch Zufügung einer Einleitungs- und zweier Schluß-Strophen das 12strophige Lied. Als Melodie wählte Luther die Jerusalem-Pilger-Leise In Gottes Namen fahren wir *(A). Es ist kaum anzunehmen, daß er damit einer mittelalterlichen Tradition folgte. Vielmehr wird er – in der Art der Kontrafaktur – damit das Leben nach Gottes Geboten als die wahre Pilgerschaft des Christen haben bezeichnen wollen.*

In Straßburg hat man diese Melodie nicht übernommen; Wolfgang Dachstein hat eine neue geschaffen (1525 erstmals gedruckt), die dann auch von Calvin für sein Zehn-Gebote-Lied benützt wurde (B). Eine dritte Melodie taucht dann in Straßburg 1545 auf (C). Was zu ihrer Entstehung Anlaß gab, ist unklar.

15

Die Zehn Gebote, kurz

A

B

1 Mensch, willst du le - ben se - lig-lich und bei Gott blei-ben

e - - - wig-lich, sollst du hal-ten die Zehn Ge-

bot, die uns ge - beut un - ser Gott.[1] Ky - ri - e - leis.

C

1 Mensch, willst du le - ben se - lig - lich und bei Gott

blei - ben e - wig - lich, sollst du halten die Zehn Gebot,

die uns ge-beut un - ser Gott.[1] Ky - ri - e - le - i - son.

2 Dein Gott allein und Herr bin ich;
  kein andrer Gott soll irren dich.[2]
  Trauen soll mir das Herze dein;
  mein eigen Reich sollst du sein.
  Kyrieleis.

3 Du sollst mein' Namen ehren schon[3]
  und in der Not mich rufen an.
  Du sollst heilgen den Sabbattag,
  daß ich in dir wirken mag.[4]
  Kyrieleis.

4 Dem Vater und der Mutter dein
  sollst du nach mir gehorsam sein,[5]
  niemand töten noch zornig sein
  und deine Eh' halten rein.
  Kyrieleis.

5 Du sollst ei'm andern stehlen nicht,
  auf niemand Falsches zeugen icht,[6]

deines Nächsten Weib nicht begehrn
und all sein Gut gern entbehrn.
Kyrieleis.

[1] gebeut = *gebietet.*   [2] irren = *beirren, irreführen.*   [3] schon = *schön, richtig.*
[4] mag = *kann.*   [5] nach mir = *nebst mir.*   [6] icht = *etwas (auf niemand etwas
Falsches zeugen).*

*Das kürzere Zehn-Gebote-Lied ist ein kleines Meisterwerk. Ohne
den Worten Gewalt anzutun, bringt Luther nach der Einleitungs-
Strophe in regelmäßig steigender Zahl zuerst 1, dann 2, dann 3 und
zuletzt 4 Gebote in je einer Strophe unter, was für die beiden Tafeln
je zwei Strophen ergibt. Als Melodie hat er zunächst die von Nr. 14
vorgesehen (A). Johann Walter, in dessen Chorgesangbuch von 1524
der Text zum ersten Mal überliefert ist, hat – im Bestreben, jedem
Text sein eigenes Tongewand zu geben – für diesen Text eine eigene
Weise geschaffen (B), die sich dann auch im Gemeindegesang durchsetzte. Die Straßburger Gesangbücher behielten ihre Melodie von
Nr. 14 auch für dieses Lied bei (C).*

16

Der Lobgesang ‹Mitten wir im Leben sind›

Her - re Gott, hei - li - ger star - ker Gott,
hei - li - ger barm - her - zi - ger Hei - land, du e -
wi - ger Gott, laß uns nicht ver - sin - ken
in des bit - tern To - des Not. Ky - ri - e - lei - son.

2 Mitten in dem Tod anficht
uns der Hölle Rachen.
Wer will uns aus solcher Not
frei und ledig machen?
  Das tust du, Herr, alleine.
  Es jammert dein Barmherzigkeit
  unser Klag und großes Leid.
  Heiliger Herre Gott,
  heiliger starker Gott,
  heiliger barmherziger Heiland,
  du ewiger Gott,
  laß uns nicht verzagen
  vor der tiefen Hölle Glut.
  Kyrieleison.

3 Mitten in der Höllen Angst
unsre Sünd' uns treiben.
Wo solln wir denn fliehen hin,
da wir können bleiben?
  Zu dir, Herr Christ, alleine.
  Vergossen ist dein teures Blut,
  das gnug für die Sünden tut.
  Heiliger Herre Gott,
  heiliger starker Gott,
  heiliger barmherziger Heiland,
  du ewiger Gott,
  laß uns nicht abfallen
  von des rechten Glaubens Trost.
  Kyrieleison.

Luther überschreibt dieses Lied mit «Lobgesang»; wir würden es eher als Bittlied bezeichnen. Es wird in heutigen Gesangbüchern im Abschnitt «Buße» oder «Tod und Ewigkeit» geführt. Für Luther ist es jedoch geprägt durch das abschließende «Kyrie eleison»; und die Leisen nennt er «Lobgesänge». Inhaltlich ist es ein sehr umfassendes Lied. Luther hat es 1542 unter die Begräbnisgesänge aufgenommen. Daß er aber darin mehr gesehen hat als ein Sterbelied, zeigt die Einordnung im Wittenberger Gesangbuch von 1529, die sich gerade durch Maßnahmen wie diese als Luthers ureigenstes Werk erweist: Er ordnet diese Leise den beiden Liedern zum ersten Katechismusstück als «Deutelied» zu. Die Wahl einer Leisen-Melodie für jene beiden Lieder bekommt dadurch vermehrtes Gewicht, daß die christliche Antwort auf das alttestamentliche Gebot ebenfalls von der Christus-Anrufung «Kyrie eleison» getragen ist.

Luther benützt auch hier eine allgemein bekannte Liedstrophe aus der Tradition als Ausgangspunkt. Sie ist erstmals 1456 in Salzburg überliefert, und zwar mit der vorliegenden Melodie. Der Text geht zurück auf einen lateinischen Kirchengesang. Aber die bis in unsere Tage kolportierte Nachricht, es handle sich dabei um eine Sequenz, die Notker beim Anblick lebensgefährlicher Bauarbeiten an einer Brücke über das Martinstobel bei St. Gallen gefunden habe, entbehrt jeglichen historischen Rückhalts. Es handelt sich nicht um eine Sequenz, sondern um eine Antiphon, und diese stammt nicht aus St. Gallen, sondern wahrscheinlich aus der gallikanischen Tradition und ist älter als Notker; das Stück ist in England bereits früher überliefert als in St. Gallen.

Eine andere biographische Verankerung des Liedes jedoch hat einiges für sich, die begründete Vermutung nämlich, Luther habe seine meisterhafte Fortdichtung dieser Strophe geschaffen, nachdem am 5. Juli 1524 ein Freund Melanchtons und Jonas', der Humanist Wilhelm Neesen, bei einem Schiffsunglück auf der Elbe bei Wittenberg vor den Augen seiner Freunde ertrank. Luther war bei dem Unglück vielleicht nicht zugegen, aber es hat ihn tief getroffen, wie seine Briefe aus dieser Zeit zeigen. Der Text steht erstmals in den Erfurter Enchiridien von 1524, die, wenn diese Annahme richtig ist, erst im Frühherbst des Jahres erschienen sein können. Die Melodie wird dort als bekannt vorausgesetzt. Die Fassung, in welcher sie dann seit Walters Chorgesangbuch von 1524 in den Gesangbüchern verbreitet ist, dürfte Johann Walter ihr gegeben haben.

Sowohl in der Tiefe und schlichten Klarheit der Text-Aussagen als

auch hinsichtlich des vollkommen identischen Aufbaus der drei Strophen (vgl. z. B. an derselben Stelle in Strophe *1*: Leben–Tod, in Strophe *2*: Tod–Hölle, in Strophe *3*: Hölle–Sünde) und bezüglich des Wort–Ton-Verhältnisses (die betonte Silbe des wichtigsten Wortes bekommt in allen drei Strophen jeweils den höchsten Ton in der Zeile) ist dies wohl die großartigste Liedschöpfung Luthers.

17

Das deutsche Credo

1 Wir glau - ben all an ei - nen Gott, Schöp - fer Him - mels und der Er - den, der sich zum Va - ter ge - ben hat,[1] daß wir sei - ne Kin - der wer - den. Er will uns all-zeit er - näh - ren, Leib und Seel auch wohl be- wah - ren. Al - lem Un - fall will er weh - ren; kein Leid soll uns wi - der - fah - ren. Er sor - get für uns, hüt' und wacht; es steht al - les in sei - ner Macht.

b

1 Wir glau-ben all an ei-nen Gott, Schöpfer Himmels und der
der sich zum Va-ter ge-ben hat,[1] daß wir sei-ne Kin-der

Er - den,
wer-den. Er will uns all-zeit er-näh-ren, Leib und Seel auch

wohl be-wah - ren. Al-lem Un-fall will er weh - ren;

kein Leid soll uns wi-der-fah-ren. Er sor-get für uns,

hüt' und wacht; es steht al-les in sei-ner Macht.

2 Wir glauben auch an Jesus Christ,
seinen Sohn und unsern Herren,
der ewig bei dem Vater ist,
gleicher Gott von Macht und Ehren.
Von Maria, der Jungfrauen,
ist ein wahrer Mensch geboren[2]
durch den Heilgen Geist im Glauben,
für uns, die wir warn verloren,
am Kreuz gestorben und vom Tod
wieder auferstanden durch Gott.

3 Wir glauben an den Heilgen Geist,
Gott mit Vater und dem Sohne,
der aller Schwachen Tröster heißt
und mit Gaben zieret schöne.
Die ganz Christenheit auf Erden
hält in einem Sinn gar eben.[3]
Hier all Sünd vergeben werden,
das Fleisch soll auch wieder leben.
Nach diesem Elend ist bereit'[4]
uns ein Leben in Ewigkeit.

80

¹ geben = *hingegeben*.   ² *ist er als ein wahrer Mensch geboren*.   3 *(und der)*
die ganze Christenheit auf Erden in einerlei Gesinnung ganz gleichmäßig erhält (zu-
sammenhält).   ⁴ Elend = *Fremde.*

Luthers Lied zum zweiten Katechismus-Hauptstück, dem Glaubens-
bekenntnis, ist eine Paraphrase des Nizänokonstantinopolitanums in
drei zehnzeiligen Strophen, für jeden Artikel eine. Luther lehnt sich
dabei wieder an eine spätmittelalterliche Vorlage an. Es gab ein ähnli-
ches lateinisches Credo-Lied und eine deutsche Übersetzung davon
schon im 15. Jahrhundert. Luthers Anteil an der vorliegenden Text-
und Melodiegestalt ist einstweilen nicht genau zu eruieren, weil es
nicht sicher ist, ob er das mittelalterliche Lied in der Gestalt gekannt
hat, in der es uns überliefert ist. Auch gibt es zwei recht unterschied-
liche reformatorische Melodiefassungen, von denen wir nicht mit
Sicherheit sagen können, welche diejenige Luthers ist. Die eine (a)
steht bei Johann Walter und verbreitete sich allgemein, die andere
(b) findet sich im Zwickauer Gesangbuch von 1525.

Auch über Luthers Absicht bei der Schaffung des Liedes herrscht
unter den Forschern keine Einigkeit. Daß Luther es zunächst für das
Trinitatis-Fest bestimmt hat, wie man heute meist noch liest, ist un-
wahrscheinlich. Die Reihenfolge der Lieder in der ältesten Quelle
dieses Stücks, dem Walterschen Chorgesangbuch von 1524, sagt über
die liturgische Verwendung der Lieder nichts aus. Zwar hat Luther
das Lied 1526 in seiner Deutschen Messe als Credo-Lied der Ge-
meinde empfohlen. Aber wahrscheinlicher scheint mir, daß Luther
hier, wie bei den Zehn Geboten, in erster Linie an die katechetische
Verwendung dachte.

18
Ein fein geistlich Lied, wie der Sünder zur Gnade kommt

A

1 Nun freut euch, lie - ben Chri - sten gmein,¹ und
  daß wir ge - trost und all in ein³ mit

laßt uns fröh - lich sprin - gen,²
Lust und Lie - be sin - gen,   was Gott an

81

uns ge - wen - det hat und sei - ne sü - ße

Wun - der - tat. Gar - teur hat er's er - wor - ben.[4]

B

1 Nun freut euch, lie - ben Chri - sten - gmein,[1] und
daß wir ge - trost und all in ein[3] mit

laßt uns fröh - lich sprin - gen,[2]
Lust und Lie - be sin - gen,   was Gott an

uns ge - wen - det hat und sei - ne sü - ße

Wun - der - tat. Gar - teur hat er's er - wor - ben.[4]

C

1 Nun freut euch, lie - ben Chri - sten gmein,[1] und
daß wir ge - trost und all in ein[3] mit

laßt uns fröh - lich sprin - gen,[2]
Lust und Lie - be sin - gen,   was Gott an

uns ge - wen - det hat und sei - ne sü - ße

Wun - der - tat. Gar - teur hat er's er - wor - ben.[4]

82

D

1 Nun freut euch, lieben Christen gmein,[1] und laßt uns
daß wir getrost und all in ein[3] mit Lust und

fröhlich springen,[2]
Liebe singen,
was Gott an uns ge-

wendet hat und sei - ne sü - ße Wunder-

tat. Gar - teur hat er's er - wor - ben.[4]

2 Dem Teufel ich gefangen lag,
im Tod war ich verloren.
Mein Sünd mich quälte Nacht und Tag,
darin ich war geboren.
Ich fiel auch immer tiefer drein.
Es war kein Guts am Leben mein.
Die Sünd hatt' mich besessen.

3 Mein guten Werk', die galten nicht;
es war mit ihn' verdorben.
Der frei Will haßte Gotts Gericht;
er war zum Gut'n gestorben.
Die Angst mich zu verzweifeln trieb,
daß nichts denn Sterben bei mir blieb.
Zur Hölle mußt ich sinken.

4 Da jammert Gott in Ewigkeit
mein Elend übermaßen.
Er dacht an sein Barmherzigkeit,
er wollt mir helfen lassen.
Er wandt zu mir das Vaterherz.
Es war bei ihm fürwahr kein Scherz.
Er ließ's sein Bestes kosten.[5]

5 Er sprach zu seinem lieben Sohn:
«Die Zeit ist hie zu 'rbarmen.[6]
Fahr hin, meins Herzens werte Kron,
und sei das Heil dem Armen,

und hilf ihm aus der Sünden Not.
Erwürg für ihn den bittern Tod,
und laß ihn mit dir leben.»

6 Der Sohn dem Vater g'horsam ward:
Er kam zu mir auf Erden
von einer Jungfrau rein und zart.
Er sollt mein Bruder werden.
Gar heimlich führt' er sein Gewalt:[7]
Er ging in meiner armen Gstalt.
Den Teufel wollt er fangen.

7 Er sprach zu mir: «Halt dich an mich,
es soll dir jetzt gelingen.
Ich geb mich selber ganz für dich;
da will ich für dich ringen.
Denn ich bin dein, und du bist mein;
und wo ich bleib, da sollst du sein.
Uns soll der Feind nicht scheiden.

8 Vergießen wird er mir mein Blut,[8]
dazu mein Leben rauben.
Das leid ich alles dir zugut;
das halt mit festem Glauben.
Den Tod verschlingt das Leben mein;
mein Unschuld trägt die Sünde dein.
Da bist du selig worden.

9 Gen Himmel zu dem Vater mein
fahr ich von diesem Leben.
Da will ich sein der Meister dein.
Den Geist will ich dir geben,
der dich in Trübnis trösten soll[9]
und lernen mich erkennen wohl
und in der Wahrheit leiten.

10 Was ich getan hab und gelehrt,
das sollst du tun und lehren,
damit das Reich Gotts werd gemehrt
zu Lob und seinen Ehren.
Und hüt dich vor der Menschen Gsatz,[10]
davon verdirbt der edle Schatz.[11]
Das laß ich dir zur Letze.»[12]

---

[1] gmein = *insgemein, miteinander.*   [2] springen = *tanzen.*   [3] all in ein = *alle einmütig.*   [4] *1. Petrus 1,18.*   [5] *er ließ es sich.*   [6] *es ist Zeit geworden, daß ich mich erbarme (Galater 4,4).*   [7] *in Verborgenheit übte er seine Macht aus.*   [8] er = *der Feind (der Teufel).*   [9] Trübnis = *Trübsal.*   [10] Gsatz = *Gesetz.*   [11] der

edle Schatz = *das Evangelium, überhaupt die ganze Befreiung durch die hier ge-*
schilderte Erlösungstat Christi. [12] *zur Letze: Bedeutung umstritten, am ehesten*
wohl = zum Abschiedstrost. Die Bedeutung «Lektion», die an sich möglich wäre,
liegt in diesem Zusammenhang (Gegensatz zu «der Menschen Gsatz»!) nicht nahe.

Dies ist ohne Zweifel die originellste aller Liedschöpfungen Luthers.
Zwar geht Luther mit dieser Kontrafaktur offensichtlich (Strophen-
schema, Melodie A, Textanfang, Grundstimmung) von dem seit
Ende des 14. Jahrhunderts überlieferten Oster-Prozessionslied (Nun)
freut euch, alle Christenheit *(auch* Nun freut euch, Frauen unde
Mann) *aus. Was dabei entstanden ist, läßt jedoch die Vorlage restlos*
vergessen. Luther verknüpft eine Schilderung seines persönlichen
Weges zum reformatorischen Glauben mit einer persönlichen Appli-
kation der Heilsgeschichte. Dabei ist zu bedenken, daß das Ich dieses
Liedes (gleich dem Ich der Psalmen) in der Absicht des Dichters sich
nicht ausschließlich auf seine eigene Person bezieht, sondern zum Ich
eines jeden, der dieses Lied singt, werden kann und soll.

So stellt Luther dieses Glaubenszeugnis in seinem Gesangbuch
von 1529 als «Deutelied» neben das Credo-Lied Nr. 17, gibt ihm in-
nerhalb der Katechismus-Lieder also eine ähnliche Funktion, wie sie
das andere zentrale Glaubenslied Nr. 15 erhielt.

Da auch das Glaubenslied des Paulus Speratus Es ist das Heil uns
kommen her *auf jene Ostermelodie gedichtet war, hat Luther für*
diesen Text, der ihm offenbar sehr wichtig war, eine eigene Melodie
(C) geschaffen, die wie der Text stark solistischen Charakter trägt,
sich dann aber als Hauptmelodie dieses Liedes durchsetzte. In dieser
Form erschien das Lied schon 1523 als Einblattdruck; ein Nachdruck
davon aus dem Jahre 1524 ist erhalten geblieben. Daß diese Melodie
sich durchsetzen würde, konnte Luther 1529, als er sein Gesangbuch
schuf, nicht ahnen. Er hat darum dem Lied damals eine gemeindege-
mäßere neue Weise (D) gegeben, für welche man ihn als Autor eben-
falls in Anspruch nehmen muß; die frühere Melodie wird als Zweit-
melodie immerhin mit abgedruckt. Auch diese neue Melodie hat mit
Luthers Text eine weite Verbreitung gefunden, wird aber heute zu-
meist zu anderen Texten gesungen (Es ist gewißlich an der Zeit; Ich
steh an deiner Krippe hier; Gott, Deine Güte reicht so weit). *Als Jo-*
hann Walter im Auftrage Luthers 1524 sein Chorgesangbuch schuf,
dürfte ihm das Lied mit der Ostermelodie (oder einem Verweis dar-
auf) vorgelegen haben. Diese stand aber auch beim Bekenntnis-Lied
des Speratus. Weil Walter jedem Lied seine eigene Weise geben
wollte und ihm offenbar die erste Originalweise Luthers noch nicht

bekannt war, schuf er eine eigene im fröhlich-springenden Dreiertakt. Weil er im Tenor-Stimmbuch konsequent auf der linken von zwei aufgeschlagenen Seiten die Noten und auf der rechten die Textstrophen gedruckt wissen wollte, der lange Text dieses Liedes aber auf einer Seite nicht Platz fand, entstand bei dieser Nummer eine Leerseite. Dort hat er dann – vielleicht erst kurz vor dem Druck – einen zweiten Satz zu diesem Lied untergebracht, der nun in freier Weise die erste Original-Weise Luthers (B) verarbeitet.

19
Das Vaterunser, kurz ausgelegt und in ein Lied gebracht

A

1 Va - ter un - ser im Him - mel - reich, der du uns

al - le hei - ßest gleich[1] Brü - der sein und dich ru - fen an

und willst das Be - ten von uns han, gib, daß nicht

bet al - lein der Mund; hilf, daß es geh von Her - zens - grund

B

1 Va - ter un - ser im Him - mel - reich, der du uns al - le

hei - ßest gleich[1] Brü - der sein und dich ru - fen an

und willst das Be - ten von uns han, gib, daß nicht

bet al-lein der Mund; hilf, daß es geh von Her-zens-grund

C

1 Va - ter un - ser im Him - mel - reich, der

du uns al - le hei - ßest gleich[1] Brü - der sein

und dich ru - fen an und willst das Be - ten

von uns han, gib, daß nicht bet al - lein der

Mund; hilf, daß es geh von Her - zens - grund

2 Geheiligt werd der Name dein.
Dein Wort bei uns hilf halten rein,
daß wir auch leben heiliglich
nach deinem Namen würdiglich.
Behüt uns, Herr, vor falscher Lehr.
Das arm, verführet Volk bekehr.

3 Es komm dein Reich zu dieser Zeit
und dort hernach in Ewigkeit.
Der Heilig Geist uns wohne bei[2]
mit seinen Gaben mancherlei.
Des Satans Zorn und groß Gewalt
zerbrich; vor ihm dein Kirch erhalt.

4 Dein Will gescheh, Herr Gott, zugleich
auf Erden wie im Himmelreich.
Gib uns Geduld in Leidenszeit,
gehorsam sein in Lieb und Leid.
Wehr und steur allem Fleisch und Blut,
das wider deinen Willen tut.

5 Gib uns heut unser täglich Brot
und was man braucht zur Leibesnot.
B'hüt uns, Herr, vor Unfried und Streit,[3]
vor Seuchen und vor teurer Zeit,
daß wir in gutem Frieden stehn,
der Sorg und Geizens müßiggehn.

6 All unser' Schuld' vergib uns, Herr,
daß sie uns nicht betrüben mehr,
wie wir auch unsern Schuldigern
ihr' Schuld und Fehl vergeben gern.[4]
Zu dienen mach uns all bereit
in rechter Lieb und Einigkeit.

7 Führ uns, Herr, in Versuchung nicht,
wenn uns der böse Geist anficht
zur linken und zur rechten Hand;
hilf uns tun starken Widerstand,
im Glauben fest und wohlgerüst'
und durch des Heilgen Geistes Trost.

8 Von allem Übel uns erlös.
Es sind die Zeit' und Tage bös.
Erlös uns von dem ewgen Tod[5]
und tröst uns in der letzten Not.
Bescher uns auch ein selges End;
nimm unsre Seel in deine Händ.

9 Amen, das ist: Es werde wahr.
Stärk unsern Glauben immerdar,
auf daß wir ja nicht zweifeln dran,[6]
was wir hiemit gebetet han
auf dein Wort in dem Namen dein.
So sprechen wir das Amen fein.

---

[1] gleich = *miteinander.*   [2] uns wohne bei = *sei und bleibe bei uns (vgl. zu 13: 1,1).*   [3] *so nach der Handschrift Luthers (die Drucke haben «Behüt» und somit eine Silbe zuviel).*   [4] Fehl = *Mangel, Versäumnis.*   [5] *so nach der Handschrift (die Drucke haben: erlös uns vom ewigen Tod).*   [6] *nicht zweifeln an dem, was wir hiermit gebetet (erbeten) haben.*

1529 war der Zyklus der Katechismus-Lieder noch unvollständig. Diese Lied-Paraphrase zum Gebet des Herrn kommt erst zwischen 1535 und 1539 hinzu. Als Erstdruck muß man einen Einzeldruck vermuten. Erhalten ist uns aber erst der Abdruck in einem Leipziger Gesangbuch von 1539. In Luthers Gesangbuch wurde das Lied spätestens 1543 aufgenommen. Es steht dort im Abschnitt der Katechis-

mus-Lieder, der nun auch eine besondere Einleitung erhalten hat
(S. 71).

In diesem Fall ist sogar Luthers handschriftlicher Entwurf erhalten
geblieben. (Wo sich das Blatt befindet, ist nicht bekannt, aber es gibt
eine zuverlässige Ablichtung davon, die in verschiedenen Werken re-
produziert ist.) Man kann auf diesem Entwurf erkennen, wie Luther
am Text gefeilt hat. Und am Schluß hat er auch einen Melodie-Ent-
wurf notiert. Diese Melodie (A) trägt ähnliche Züge wie andere Lu-
ther-Melodien, wurde jedoch von Luther verworfen; sie erscheint
im Druck nirgends. Luther verwendet diesen Typus von ionischen
Melodien im Oktavraum vorwiegend für verkündigende Texte. Als
er sie schrieb, mag er stärker an die katechetische Verwendung des
Liedes gedacht haben. Dann aber kehrte er zu der meditativeren böhmischen Vaterunser-Melodie zurück, die er, wie das gewählte Metrum zeigt, offenbar von Anfang an im Sinn hatte. Das Lied wird im
Druck von Anfang an mit dieser Melodie (B) verbreitet, die einer
schon 1519 im Gesangbuch der böhmischen Brüder überlieferten
Vaterunser-Melodie nachgebildet ist.

Eine weitere Melodie (C) erhielt das Lied 1544 im Schulgesangbuch Georg Rhaus. Sie ist dort einem Zyklus von sechs Vertonungen
durch Sixt Dietrich als Cantus firmus zu Grunde gelegt. Es ist daher
die Möglichkeit nicht auszuschließen, daß dieser Konstanzer Musiker ihr Autor ist.

20

Ein geistlich Lied von unserer heiligen Taufe,
darin fein kurz zusammengefaßt, was sie sei,
wer sie gestiftet habe, was sie nütze

1 Christ,   un - ser Herr, zum Jor - dan kam   nach sei - nes
  von   Sankt Jo - hann die Tau - fe nahm,   sein Werk und

Va - ters   Wil - len,
Amt   zu   'rfül - len.   Da wollt er   stif - ten

uns ein Bad,   zu wa-schen uns von Sün - den,   er -

säu - fen auch den bit - tern Tod durch sein selbst

Blut und Wun - den.[1] Es galt ein neu-es Le - ben.

2 So hört und merket alle wohl,
   was Gott heißt selbst die Taufe[2]
   und was ein Christ da glauben soll,
   zu meiden Ketzerhaufen:[3]
       Gott spricht und will, daß Wasser sei,
       doch nicht allein schlicht Wasser;
       sein heiligs Wort ist auch dabei
       mit reichem Geist ohn Maßen.
       Der ist allhie der Täufer.

3 Solchs hat er uns bewiesen klar
   mit Bildern und mit Worten.
   Des Vaters Stimm man offenbar[4]
   daselbst am Jordan hörte.
       Er sprach: «Das ist mein lieber Sohn,
       an dem ich hab Gefallen.
       Den will ich euch befohlen han,[5]
       daß ihr ihn höret alle
       und folget seinem Lehren.»

4 Auch Gottes Sohn hier selber steht
   in seiner zarten Menschheit.[6]
   Der Heilig Geist herniederfährt
   in Taubenbild verkleidet,
       daß wir nicht sollen zweifeln dran,
       wenn wir getaufet werden,
       all drei Person' getaufet han,
       damit bei uns auf Erden
       zu wohnen sich ergeben.[7]

5 Sein' Jünger heißt der Herre Christ:
   «Geht hin, all Welt zu lehren,
   daß sie verlorn in Sünden ist,
   sich soll zur Buße kehren.
       Wer glaubet und sich taufen läßt,
       soll dadurch selig werden.
       Ein neugeborner Mensch er heißt,
       der nicht mehr könne sterben,
       das Himmelreich soll erben.»[8]

6 Wer nicht glaubt dieser großen Gnad,
der bleibt in seinen Sünden
und ist verdammt zum ewgen Tod
tief in der Hölle Gründen.
Nichts hilft sein eigen Heiligkeit;
all sein Tun ist verloren.[9]
Die Erbsünd macht's zur Nichtigkeit,
darin er ist geboren;[10]
er kann sich selbst nicht helfen.

7 Das Aug allein das Wasser sieht,
wie Menschen Wasser gießen.
Der Glaub im Geist die Kraft versteht
des Blutes Jesu Christi,
und ist vor ihm ein rote Flut,[11]
von Christi Blut gefärbet,
die allen Schaden heilen tut,
von Adam her geerbet,
auch von uns selbst begangen.

[1] *durch sein eigenes Blut und seine eigenen Wunden.*   [2] *was Gott selbst unter der Taufe versteht.*   [3] *um sich von der Schar der Ketzer fernzuhalten (hier dürften in erster Linie die Wiedertäufer gemeint sein).*   [4] *offenbar = öffentlich.*   [5] *han = haben.*   [6] *zart = edel.*   [7] *womit sie (die drei Personen der göttlichen Trinität) sich bei uns auf Erden zu wohnen hingegeben haben.*   [8] *der nicht mehr sterben kann und das Himmelreich erben soll.*   [9] *verloren = umsonst.*   [10] *darin er ist geboren bezieht sich auf «Erbsünde».*   [11] *und es (das Wasser) ist vor ihm (dem Glauben, d.h. vor den Augen des Glaubens) eine rote Flut.*

Während das Lied zum Gebet des Herrn (19) jede der sieben Bitten durch eine Gebets-Paraphrase indirekt erläutert, haben wir hier ein reines Lehr-Lied vor uns, wie wir sonst von Luther höchstens in dem Osterlied Nr. 8 etwas Vergleichbares besitzen. Es kam zu den Katechismus-Liedern als letztes hinzu. Da sich in zwei Taufpredigten Luthers von 1540 auffallende Parallelen zu diesem Lied finden und seit 1541 eine ganze Reihe von Einzeldrucken und Liederblättern mit diesem Lied auftauchen, nimmt man 1540/41 als Entstehungszeit und 1541 als Jahr des Erstdrucks an. 1543 steht das Lied unter den Katechismus-Liedern im Wittenberger Gesangbuch, gleichzeitig auch in einem Leipziger Gesangbuch.

Eine merkwürdige Tatsache ergibt sich hinsichtlich der Melodie: Luther wählt das nicht ganz gewöhnliche Metrum seines 67. Psalms (27). Dort hatte sich die Überlieferung ja schon früh gegen die Melodie Luthers (27 A) und für die Greiters (27 B) entschieden. Jene somit

herrenlos gewordene (großartige!) Luther-Weise taucht nun bei diesem Tauflied wieder auf. Soll man sich vorstellen, daß Luther von dem Umstand wußte, daß jene Weise «frei» war, und sie deshalb für dieses Lied zu Ehren zog? Schon 1544 finden wir in dem Rhauschen Wittenberger Schulgesangbuch einen Satz von Wolff Heintz dazu.

21
St. Johannes Hus Lied, gebessert

A

1 Je - sus Chri - stus, un - ser Hei - - - land, der von uns den Got - tes - zorn wandt,[1] durch das bitt - re Lei - den sein half er uns aus der Höl - le Pein.

B

1 Je - sus Chri - stus, un - ser Hei - land, der von uns den Got - tes - zorn wandt,[1] durch das bitt - re Lei - den sein half er uns aus der Höl - le Pein.

2 Daß wir nimmer des vergessen,
gab er uns sein' Leib zu essen,
verborgen im Brot so klein,
und zu trinken sein Blut im Wein.

3 Wer sich will zu dem Tisch machen,[2]
der hab wohl acht auf sein' Sachen.
Wer unwürdig hinzugeht,
statt des Lebens den Tod empfäht.[3]

4 Du sollst Gott, den Vater, preisen,
daß er dich so wohl wollt speisen
und für deine Missetat
in den Tod sein' Sohn geben hat.

5 Du sollst glauben und nicht wanken,
daß ein' Speise sei den Kranken,
den' ihr Herz von Sünden schwer
und vor Angst ist betrübet sehr.

6 Solch groß Gnad und Barmherzigkeit
sucht ein Herz in großer Arbeit;[4]
ist dir wohl, so bleib davon,
daß du nicht kriegest bösen Lohn.[5]

7 Er spricht selber: «Kommt, ihr Armen,[6]
laßt mich über euch erbarmen;
kein Arzt ist dem Starken not,[7]
sein Kunst wird an ihm gar ein Spott.

8 Hättst du dir was kunnt erwerben,
was braucht' denn ich für dich sterben?[8]
Dieser Tisch auch dir nicht gilt,
so du selber dir helfen willt.

9 Glaubst du das von Herzensgrunde
und bekennest mit dem Munde,
so bist du recht wohl geschickt,[9]
und die Speise dein Seel erquickt.

10 Die Frucht darf auch nicht ausbleiben:
Deinen Nächsten sollst du lieben,
daß er dein genießen kann,[10]
wie dein Gott hat an dir getan.»

---

[1] wandt = *abwandte.*   [2] *wer sich dem Tisch nahen will (1. Korinther 11,27–29).*
[3] empfäht = *empfängt.*   [4] Arbeit = *Mühe.*   [5] *ist es dir jedoch wohl (in deinem Sündersein), dann bleib (dem Tische des Herrn) fern, damit du nicht bösen Lohn empfängst.*   [6] *Das hier zitierte Jesus-Wort Matthäus 11,28 war auch ein Lieblingswort Zwinglis.*   [7] *der Gesunde bedarf keines Arztes; dessen Kunst wird an ihm*

völlig zuschanden (Matthäus 12,20). [8] *Luther läßt weiterhin Christus in direkter Rede sprechen, obwohl hier kein Zitat aus dem Evangelium mehr vorliegt: Wenn du dir (für deine Seligkeit) selber etwas hättest erwerben können, wozu hätte ich dann für dich zu sterben brauchen?* [9] geschickt = *geeignet, vorbereitet (für den Genuß des Abendmahls).* [10] *daß er von dir Nutzen haben, deiner froh werden kann.*

Zum letzten Hauptstück des Katechismus – Vom Abendmahl – gibt es kein dem Tauflied verwandtes, umfassendes Lehrlied Luthers, sondern lediglich zwei Lieder, die zum Vollzug des Abendmahls gehören – dieses davor, das nächste danach zu singen –, die aber seit 1529 gleichwohl bei den Katechismus-Liedern eingeordnet sind. Das allein zeigt schon, welch hohe Bedeutung Luther der katechetischen Zielsetzung bei seiner Gesangbucharbeit beimaß.

Das erste dieser beiden Lieder, das man eher noch als Lehrlied ansprechen könnte, ist in loser Anlehnung an eine lateinische Cantio (Jesus Christus nostra salus) gedichtet. Dieses stammt allerdings nicht von Johannes Hus, wie man zu Luthers Zeit aufgrund des Akrostichons «Johannes» allgemein annahm, sondern wahrscheinlich von dem Prager Bischof Johannes von Jenstein (1348–1400).

Man nimmt an, das Lied sei kurz vor Ostern 1524 entstanden, denn in Luthers Predigten vom Palmsonntag und vom Gründonnerstag dieses Jahres finden sich auffallende inhaltliche Parallelen dazu. Wenn Luther das Lied für jene Gottesdienste geschrieben und dort vom Chor hätte singen lassen, dann wäre dies nicht der einzige derartige Fall in der Kirchenlied-Geschichte.

Die erste Melodie (A) stammt wahrscheinlich aus dem Mittelalter. Einen Beleg für diese Vermutung hat man allerdings noch nicht gefunden. Die älteste Überlieferung für dieses Lied Luthers ist ein Augsburger Flugblatt, ohne Zweifel ein Nachdruck des Wittenberger Urdrucks. Die Melodie steht darauf (und gewiß auch auf der Wittenberger Vorlage) in einem zweistimmigen Satz: Zur Liedweise ist eine Diskantstimme hinzugefügt. Wenn diese Stimme nicht von Luther stammt, dann gehört sie zur mittelalterlichen Überlieferung der Melodie. 1529 stellte Luther dieser für den Chorgesang bestimmten Melodie eine gemeindegemäße voran, die nun auf jeden Fall von seiner Hand stammen dürfte.

22

Der Gesang Gott sei gelobet

1 Gott sei ge - lo - bet und ge-be - ne - dei - et,
mit sei -nem Flei - sche und mit sei-nem Blu - te;
der uns sel - ber hat ge - spei - set
das gib uns, Herr Gott, zu gu - te.[1]
Ky - ri - e - lei - - son. Herr, durch dei - nen
hei - li - gen Leich-nam, der von dei - ner Mut - ter Ma-
ri - a kam, und das hei - li - ge Blut hilf uns,
Herr, aus al - ler Not. Ky - ri - e - lei - - son.

2 Der heilig Leichnam ist für uns gegeben[2]
zum Tod, daß wir dadurch leben.
Nicht größre Güte konnte er uns schenken;
dabei solln wir sein gedenken.
Kyrieleison.
    Herr, dein Lieb so groß dich zwungen hat,
daß dein Blut an uns groß Wunder tat
und bezahlt unsre Schuld,
daß uns Gott ist worden hold.
Kyrieleison.

3 Gott geb uns allen seiner Gnade Segen,
daß wir gehn auf seinen Wegen
in rechter Lieb und brüderlicher Treue,
daß uns die Speis nicht gereue.[3]
Kyrieleison.

Herr, dein Heilger Geist uns nicht verlaß,
der uns geb zu halten rechte Maß,[4]
daß dein arm Christenheit
leb in Fried und Einigkeit.
Kyrieleison.

[1] *das laß uns zum Guten gedeihen.*   [2] Leichnam = *Leib.*   [3] *daß uns der Empfang des Abendmahls nicht zum Schaden gereiche (vgl. 21:16,4 und 1.Korinther 11,27–29).*   [4] *in der rechten Weise zu leben (nicht etwa: Maß zu halten!).*

Wie die anderen mit «Kyrieleis» endenden Lieder Luthers ist auch dieses die Erweiterung einer Leise, nur daß es sich in diesem Fall um eine Art «Doppel-Leise» handelt, eine Strophe von 2 × 4 Zeilen mit «Kyrieleis» in der Mitte und am Schluß. Und auch diese Leise gehört zu einer Festtags-Sequenz, nämlich zu derjenigen, die Thomas von Aquino 1264 für das damals in Rom aufkommende Fronleichnamsfest geschrieben haben soll: Lauda Sion salvatorem. Nur, daß dieses Fest in Wittenberg seit 1523 abgeschafft ist, womit das Lied seinen Festtags-Bezug verliert und als allgemeines Danklied nach der Kommunion einen neuen Sitz im Leben erhält, der durch die beiden Zusatzstrophen Luthers noch verdeutlicht wird.

Die Leise ist – in ihrem ursprünglichen Zusammenhang mit der Sequenz – erstmals in jenem Prozessionale aus dem Ende des 14. Jahrhunderts überliefert, das auch die älteste Überlieferung jenes Osterliedes bringt, das Luther für seine frühesten Psalmlieder (24, 25, 28, 30) und für sein erstes freigedichtetes Lied (18) zum Ausgangspunkt wählte. Sie scheint sich im Laufe des 15. Jahrhunderts dann stark verbreitet zu haben, so daß Luther sie in seiner liturgischen Schrift von 1523 (Formula missae) und in der Deutschen Messe von 1526 als allgemein bekannt voraussetzen konnte. Das gilt für die Melodie auch in den Erfurter Enchiridien, die nur den Text abdrucken. Die beiden Zusatzstrophen müssen also in der ersten Hälfte des Jahres 1524 entstanden sein. In seinem trinitarischen, sehr einfachen und konsequenten Aufbau steht dieses dreistrophige Lied dem Mitten wir im Leben sind (16) sehr nahe.

23

Ein Lied von den zwei Märtyrern Christi, zu Brüssel von den Sophisten von Löwen verbrannt, geschehen im Jahr 1523

1 Ein neu - es Lied wir he - ben an[1] — das walt Gott,
zu sin - gen, was Gott hat ge - tan zu sei - nem

un - ser Her - re —,
Lob und Eh - re.
Zu Brüs - sel in dem Nie - der -

land wohl durch zwei jun - ge Kna - - - ben[2] hat

er sein Wun - der macht be - kannt, die er mit

(a)

sei - nen Ga - - - ben[3] so reichlich hat ge - zie - ret.

(b)

Schluß

so reichlich hat ge - zie - ret.

2 Der erst mit Recht Johannes heißt,
   so reich an Gottes Hulden,[4]
   sein Bruder Heinrich nach dem Geist,[5]
   ein rechter Christ ohn Schulden,
      von dieser Welt geschieden sind.
   Sie han die Kron erworben,[6]
   recht wie die frommen Gotteskind
   für sein Wort sind gestorben;
      sein Märtrer sind sie worden.

97

3 Der alte Feind sie fangen ließ,
  erschreckt sie lang mit Dräuen.[7]
Das Wort Gotts er sie leugnen hieß,
  mit List auch wollt sie 'täuben.[8]
    Von Löwen der Sophisten viel[9]
    mit ihrer Kunst verloren[10]
    versammelt er zu diesem Spiel.
    Der Geist sie macht zu Toren;
    sie konnten nichts gewinnen.

4 Sie sangen süß, sie sangen saur,[11]
  versuchten manche Listen.
Die Knaben standen wie ein' Maur,
  veracht'en die Sophisten.
    Den alten Feind das sehr verdroß,
    daß er war überwunden
    von solchen Jungen, er so groß.
    Er ward voll Zorn; von Stund an
    gedacht sie zu verbrennen.

5 Sie raubten ihn' das Klosterkleid,
  die Weih sie ihn' auch nahmen.[12]
Die Knaben waren des bereit;[13]
  sie sprachen fröhlich Amen.
    Sie dankten ihrem Vater Gott,
    daß sie los sollten werden
    des Teufels Larvenspiel und Spott,[14]
    darin durch falsche 'Bärden[15]
    die Welt er gar betrüget.

6 Das schickt Gott durch sein Gnad also,
  daß sie recht Priester worden,[16]
sich selbst ihm mußten opfern do
  und gehn im Christenorden,[17]
    der Welt ganz abgestorben sein,
    die Heuchelei ablegen,
    zum Himmel kommen frei und rein,
    die Möncherei ausfegen
    und Menschentand hier lassen.

7 Man schrieb ihn' vor ein Brieflein klein,[18]
  das hieß man sie selbst lesen.[19]
Die Stück sie zeich'ten alle drein,[20]
  was ihr Glaub war gewesen.
    Der höchste Irrtum dieser war:
    Man muß allein Gott glauben;

der Mensch lügt und trügt immerdar,
dem soll man nichts vertrauen.
Drum mußten sie verbrennen.

8 Zwei große Feur sie zündten an;
die Knaben sie herbrachten.
Es nahm groß wunder jedermann,
daß sie solch Pein veracht'en.
Mit Freuden sie sich gaben drein,
mit Gottes Lob und Singen.
Der Mut ward den Sophisten klein
vor diesen neuen Dingen,
daß sich Gott ließ so merken.

(der jüngere Liedschluß:)

9 Der Schimpf sie nun gereuet hat,[21]
sie wollten's gern schön machen.[22]
Sie thurn nicht rühmen sich der Tat;[23]
sie 'bergen fast die Sachen.[24]
Die Schand im Herzen beißet sie
und klagen's ihrn Genossen.
Doch kann der Geist nicht schweigen hie:
Des Abels Blut vergossen,
es muß den Kaïn melden.[25]

10 Die Asche will nicht lassen ab,
sie stäubt in allen Landen.
Hie hilft kein Bach, Loch, Grub noch Grab;
sie macht den Feind zuschanden.
Die er im Leben durch den Mord
zu schweigen hat gezwungen,
die muß er tot an allem Ort
mit aller Stimm und Zungen
gar fröhlich lassen singen.

(der ältere Liedschluß:)

11 Noch lassen sie ihr Lügen nicht,[26]
den großen Mord zu schmücken:[27]
Sie geben vor ein falsch Gedicht;[28]
ihr Gwissen tut sie drücken.
Die Heilgen Gotts auch nach dem Tod
von ihn' gelästert werden.
Sie sagen, in der letzten Not
die Knaben noch auf Erden
sich sollen han umkehret.[29]

12 Die laß man lügen immerhin;[30]
sie haben's kleinen Frommen.[31]
Wir sollen danken Gott darin;[32]
sein Wort ist wiederkommen.
Der Sommer ist hart vor der Tür,[33]
der Winter ist vergangen,
die zarten Blumen gehn herfür.[34]
Der das hat angefangen,
der wird es wohl vollenden.[35]

[1] anheben = anfangen.   [2] Knaben = Jünglinge   [3] bezieht sich auf «Knaben», nicht auf «Wundermacht».   [4] Johann van der Eschen. Die Etymologie des Namens Johannes (hebräisch Jochanan) ist tatsächlich: Gott ist gnädig.   [5] Heinrich Voes. Hier scheint keine Anspielung auf den Namen vorzuliegen. Gemeint ist: Heinrich, sein Bruder nach dem Geist.   [6] han = haben.   [7] Dräuen = Drohen.   [8] 'täuben = betäuben, zum Schweigen bringen.   [9] Die Universität Löwen war neben Köln eines der frühesten und wichtigsten Zentren des Widerstandes gegen Luther. Als «Sophisten» bezeichnet Luther die altgläubigen Theologen stets.   [10] mit ihrem nutzlosen Wissen.   [11] sie lockten, sie drohten.   [12] Das war das übliche Vorgehen bei einer Ketzer-Verbrennung.   [13] des = dazu.   [14] Larvenspiel = Schwindel, vielleicht aber auch wörtlich das Sich-Verstecken hinter allerlei Masken; Spott = Lästerung (Gottes).   [15] falsche 'Bärden = trügerisches Gebaren.   [16] Die Kirche hat sie ihrer Priesterwürde beraubt (5, 2); nun sind sie wahre Priester.   [17] Die Kirche hat sie aus ihrem Orden ausgestoßen (5, 1); aber nun sind sie Glieder des wahren Ordens.   [18] man setzte ihnen ein kurzes Schriftstück auf.   [19] lesen = vorlesen.   [20] darin verzeichneten sie alle Punkte.   [21] Schimpf = Scherz, Spiel.   [22] schön machen = richtigstellen, ungeschehen machen.   [23] sie getrauen sich nicht, sich dieser Tat zu rühmen.   [24] sie verbergen die Angelegenheit sorgfältig (während es Luther wichtig ist, sie durch sein Lied möglichst weit bekanntzumachen).   [25] Kaïn: der Name ist hier zweisilbig zu lesen; melden = verraten, verklagen.   [26] noch = dennoch.   [27] schmücken = beschönigen.   [28] sie bringen eine erlogene Fabel vor.   [29] seien (auf ihrem falschen Weg) umgekehrt (hätten widerrufen).   [30] immerhin = immerzu.   [31] sie haben geringen Nutzen davon.   [32] darin = in, mit und wegen dieser an sich traurigen Geschichte.   [33] hart = dicht.   [34] gehn herfür = kommen hervor.   [35] wohl = gut, herrlich, glücklich.

Im allgemeinen nimmt man an, dies sei Luthers allererstes poetisches Werk. Der ihn aufs tiefste erschütternde Märtyrertod der beiden Antwerpener Ordensbrüder in Brüssel, die seiner Lehre anhingen und deshalb von der Kirche zur Rechenschaft gezogen wurden, hätten bei ihm den poetischen Born zum Fließen gebracht. Beweisbar ist diese Abfolge (23, 18, 27, 30 usw.) allerdings nicht. Es ist nur so viel sicher, daß diese Ballade bald nach dem Bekanntwerden des Ereignisses vom 1. Juli 1523, etwa Anfang August 1523, entstanden sein muß. Luther folgt hier einem Brauch der Zeit, welche es liebte, bedeutsame Ereignisse in der Form des später so genannten historischen

Volksliedes bekanntzumachen. Ein solches, das die Hinrichtung des Augsburger Bürgermeisters Hans Vitel (1477) erzählt, beginnt Nun wollen wir es heben an, ein neues Lied zu singen. Während sich aber andere Autoren dabei jeweils irgendeines bekannten «Tons» bedienten, hat Luther hier als musikalische Form mit dem Text zusammen eine neue Weise geschaffen, welche dem Stil der Hofweisen nahesteht.

In den ältesten erhaltenen Quellen, die sehr wahrscheinlich auf einem verlorenen Flugblatt beruhen, fehlen die Strophen 9 und 10. Strophe 11 schließt denn auch nahtlos an Strophe 8 an, was man von dem Übergang von der 10. zur 11. Strophe nicht behaupten kann. Die Strophen 9 und 10 finden sich erstmals in Johann Walters Chorgesangbuch. Man muß annehmen, Luther habe sie dem Komponisten als Ersatz für die Strophen 11 und 12, also als neuen Liedschluß, übersandt. Strophe 10 bringt ja einen ebenso zwingenden und fröhlichen Abschluß wie Strophe 12. Entweder Walter oder der Setzer haben das dann mißverstanden und fügten an den neuen Liedschluß den älteren noch an.

Ähnlich muß es mit der Melodie gegangen sein. In den ältesten Quellen finden wir den Schluß a auf dem Grundton. Bei Walter taucht dann der Dominant-Schluß b auf, von dem man vermutet, er sei für die Strophen 1–9 bestimmt gewesen, während die letzte Strophe dann auf der Tonika geschlossen hätte. Walter ist in seinen späteren Ausgaben (seit 1534) zum ursprünglichen Melodie-Schluß zurückgekehrt, während die Gesangbücher mit wenigen Ausnahmen den Schluß b beibehielten.

Das Lied beschließt im Gesangbuch Luthers von 1529 die Gruppe der Katechismuslieder. Es bringt die aktuelle Konkretisierung dessen, was Glauben und Leben aus dem Glauben heißt. Es vertritt als Bericht über eine Bluttaufe den noch nicht mit einem Lied versehenen Artikel von der Taufe und mit seinem fröhlichen Bekenntnis zum Sieg der Reformation den Artikel von der Kirche.

Nun folgen etliche Psalmen, durch D. Martin Luther
zu geistlichen Liedern gemacht, und zuerst

24

der 12.: ‹Salvum me fac, Domine›

A

1 Ach Gott, vom Him - mel sieh dar - ein   und laß dich
wie we - nig sind der Heil-gen dein;   ver-las - sen

das er - bar - men,   Dein Wort man läßt nicht haben wahr;[1] der
sind wir Ar - men.

Glaub ist auch er - lo-schen gar[2]   bei al - len Menschenkin - dern.

B

1 Ach Gott, vom Himmel sieh dar-ein   und laß dich das er -
wie we - nig sind der Heil-gen dein;   ver- las-sen sind wir

bar - men,
Ar -   men. Dein Wort man läßt nicht ha-ben wahr;[1] der

Glaub ist auch er - lo-schen gar[2]   bei al - len Menschenkin - dern.

C

1 Ach Gott, vom Himmel sieh dar-ein   und laß dich das   er -
wie we - nig sind der Heil-gen dein; ver-las-sen sind wir

bar - men,

Ar - men. Dein Wort man läßt nicht ha - ben wahr;[1] der

Glaub ist auch er - lo-schen gar[2] bei al - len Menschenkin - dern.

D

1 Ach Gott, vom Himmel sieh darein und laß dich das er-bar-men,
wie we-nig sind der Heilgen dein; ver-las-sen sind wir Ar-men.

Dein Wort man läßt nicht ha - ben wahr;[1] der Glaub ist auch er –

lo-schen gar[2] bei al - len Men-schen-kin - dern.

E

1 Ach Gott, vom Himmel sieh dar-ein und laß dich das
wie we - nig sind der Heil-gen dein; ver - las - sen sind

er - bar - men,
wir ___ Ar - men.

Dein Wort man läßt nicht ha -ben

wahr;[1] der Glaub ist auch er - lo-schen gar[2]

bei al - len Men-schen-kin - - - - - - - dern.

103

2 Sie lehren eitel falsche List,[3]
was eigen Witz erfindet.[4]
Ihr Herz nicht *eines* Sinnes ist
in Gottes Wort gegründet.
Der wählet dies, der andre das;
sie trennen uns ohn alle Maß
und gleißen schön von außen.

3 Gott woll ausrotten alle Lahr',[5]
die falschen Schein uns lehren.
Dazu ihr Zung stolz offenbar[6]
spricht: «Trotz, wer wills uns wehren?
Wir haben Recht und Macht allein;
was wir setzen, das gilt gemein.[7]
Wer ist, der uns soll meistern?»[8]

4 Darum spricht Gott: «Ich muß auf sein;[9]
die Armen sind verstöret.
Ihr Seufzen dringt zu mir herein;
ich hab ihr Klag erhöret.
Mein heilsam Wort soll auf den Plan,[10]
getrost und frisch sie greifen an[11]
und sein die Kraft der Armen.»

5 Das Silber, durchs Feur siebenmal
bewährt, wird lauter 'funden.[12]
Am Gotteswort man warten soll
desgleichen alle Stunden.[13]
Es will durchs Kreuz bewähret sein;
da wird sein Kraft erkannt und Schein[14]
und leucht' stark in die Lande.

6 Das wollst du, Gott, bewahren rein[15]
vor diesem argen Gschlechte,
und laß uns dir befohlen sein,
das sich's in uns nicht flechte.[16]
Der gottlos Hauf sich umher findt,
wo diese losen Leute sind
in deinem Volk erhaben.[17]

---

[1] *dein Wort läßt man nicht gelten (wahr sein, Recht haben).* [2] gar = ganz. [3] *sie (die Irrlehrer, vor allem die Schwärmer) lehren lauter trügerisches Wissen.* [4] Witz = *Verstand.* [5] Lahr' = *Lehrer (aus der Grammatik des Satzes und aus dem ganzen Zusammenhang kann sich nicht der Sinn «Lehre», sondern nur «Lehrer» ergeben; vgl. «gelahrt»).* [6] *ihre stolze Zunge spricht öffentlich.* [7] *was wir festsetzen (als gültig erklären), das soll allgemein gelten.* [8] *Wer sollte uns zurecht weisen können?* [9] *ich muß mich aufmachen.* [10] *mein heilbringendes Wort soll zur Stelle sein.* [11] *angreifen: nicht in feindlichem Sinne, sondern im Sinne von «un-*

ter die Arme greifen». ¹² bewährt = geläutert, geprüft. ¹³ dasselbe soll man bei Gottes Wort jederzeit erwarten. ¹⁴ entweder: da wird seine (des Gotteswortes) Kraft und sein Glanz erkannt; oder: da wird seine Kraft erkannt und offenbar. ¹⁵ das = das Wort. ¹⁶ daß es (das arge Geschlecht = die von den Irrlehrern Verführten) sich nicht unter uns mische, sich nicht mit uns verflechte. ¹⁷ die Gottlosen scharen sich zusammen, wo diese nichtsnutzigen Leute sich in deinem Volk groß aufspielen.

Der älteste erhaltene Druck dieses Liedes ist eine Zusammenfassung mehrerer früherer reformatorischer Liedflugblätter durch den Nürnberger Drucker Jobst Gutknecht von 1524, das nach der Anzahl der darin enthaltenen Lieder sogenannte Achtliederbuch. Es enthält nach Luthers Nr. 18 und zwei Liedern von Paulus Speratus die drei Psalmlieder Luthers Nr. 24, 25 und 30, die alle dasselbe Metrum haben und auf eine und dieselbe Melodie, die jenes Oster-Prozessionsliedes, verwiesen werden, das auch für Nr. 18 den formalen Ausgangspunkt bildete (A). Man darf annehmen, daß dem Drucker ein Wittenberger Dreiliederblatt mit diesen drei Psalmen und ihrer gemeinsamen Melodie vorlag.

Die Wahl dieses Psalms durch Luther dürfte durch seine Auseinandersetzung mit den Schwärmern veranlaßt sein. Der ziemlich unverblümte Bezug auf diesen «inneren Feind» der Reformation läßt Luther hier den Psalm in zwar treuer, aber breiterer Weise paraphrasieren als in anderen Fällen.

In den Erfurter Enchiridien taucht dann für die beiden ersten Psalmlieder dieser Gruppe eine Eigenweise von hoher Qualität auf, die man Luther zuschreiben muß (B). Mit ihrem a-hypophrygisch trifft sie den Ton dieser Klagepsalmen ausgezeichnet. Auch Walter hat das Lied offenbar nur mit der fremden Weise kennengelernt, weshalb er seinerseits eine neue Melodie dafür aufsetzt (C). In der Folge hielt Luther seine Weise als für den Gemeindegesang zu schwierig und schuf (wie bei Nr. 18) eine zweite, gemeindegemäßere Weise (D), fügte aber diejenige von 1524 als Zweitmelodie noch bei. Sie hat sich auf die Länge durchgesetzt. Auch in Straßburg war man mit der ersten Lösung nicht zufrieden. Matthäus Greiter schuf schon 1524 eine neue Weise (E), die sich jedoch leider nicht durchsetzte. Sie ist der Lutherschen von 1529 deutlich überlegen.

Luther zitiert in den Überschriften seiner Psalmlieder (24–30) stets den lateinischen Psalmanfang, wie er ihm aus dem klösterlichen Stundengebet und vom Brevier des Priesters her vertraut war.

Der 14. Psalm: ‹Dixit insipiens in corde suo›

A

1 Es spricht der Un-wei-sen Mund wohl: «Den rech ten Gott wir
  Doch ist ihr Herz Un-glau-bens voll; mit Tat sie ihn ver -

mei - nen.»
nei - nen.[1]   Ihr We - sen ist ver - der - bet zwar;   vor

Gott ist es ein Greu-el gar.[2]   Es tut ihr' kei-ner kein __ gut.[3]

B

1 Es spricht der Un - wei - sen Mund wohl: «Den
  Doch ist ihr Herz Un - glau- bens - voll;   mit

|1. |2.

rech-ten Gott wir mei - nen.»
Tat sie ihn ver - nei -   nen.[1]   Ihr We - sen

ist ver - der - bet zwar;   vor Gott ist es ein

Greu - el gar.[2]   Es tut ihr' kei - ner kein __ gut.[3]

C

1 Es spricht der Un - wei - sen Mund wohl: «Den
  Doch ist ihr Herz Un - glau - bens - voll;   mit

rech - ten Gott wir mei - nen.»
Tat sie ihn ver - nei - nen.[1] Ihr We - sen

ist ver - der - bet zwar; vor Gott ist es ein

Greu - el gar.[2] Es tut ihr' kei - ner kein_____ gut.[3]

2 Gott selbst vom Himmel sah herab
auf aller Menschen Kinder.
Zu schauen sie er sich begab,
ob er jemand würd finden,
    der sein' Verstand gerichtet hätt,[4]
    mit Ernst nach Gottes Worten tät
    und fragt' nach seinem Willen.

3 Da war niemand auf rechter Bahn,
sie waren all ausgschritten.[5]
Ein jeder ging nach seinem Wahn
und hielt verlorne Sitten.[6]
    Es tat ihr' keiner doch kein gut,[7]
    wiewohl gar viel' betrog der Mut,[8]
    ihr Tun müßt Gott gefallen.

4 Wie lang wollen unwissend sein,
die solche Müh aufladen
und fressen dafür das Volk mein
und nährn sich mit sei'm Schaden?
    Es steht ihr Trauen nicht auf Gott,
    sie rufen ihn nicht in der Not,
    sie wolln sich selbst versorgen.

5 Darum ist ihr Herz nimmer still
und steht allzeit in Forchten.[9]
Gott bei den Frommen bleiben will,
dem sie mit Glauben horchen.[10]
    Ihr aber schmäht des Armen Rat
    und höhnet alles, was er sagt,[11]
    daß Gott sein Trost ist worden.

6 Wer soll Israel, dem armen,
   zu Zion Heil erlangen?
   Gott wird sich seins Volks erbarmen
   und lösen, die gefangen.
   Das wird er tun durch seinen Sohn,
   davon wird Jakob Wonne han
   und Israel sich freuen.

[1] mit Tat = *mit ihrem Tun.* [2] gar = *ganz.* [3] *es tut keiner von ihnen das, was gut (recht) ist.* [4] *der sein Verstehen ausgerichtet hätte (auf Gottes Wort).* [5] *ausgschritten = (vom rechten Weg) abgewichen.* [6] *hielt sich an nutzlose, sinnlose Bräuche.* [7] *wie Anmerkung 3* [8] *?* [9] Forchten = *Furcht.* [10] horchen = *gehorchen.* [11] höhnet = *verhöhnet.*

Dieses Lied über Psalm 14 teilt mit dem vorangehenden den Anlaß und die Zeit der Entstehung, das Metrum, die Melodie (in den beiden ältesten Quellen) und die Art der getreuen, aber recht breiten Paraphrasierung des Psalms. In beiden Fällen hebt der Dichter ganz kurz den Vorhang und läßt sein christliches Bekenntnis erkennen, dort in der Erwähnung des Kreuzes, hier durch die Nennung des Sohnes Gottes.

Auch im Chorgesangbuch Walters tritt dieses Lied als Paar mit dem vorangehenden zusammen auf, aber nun mit einer Eigenweise (B), die von Walter stammen muß. Sie ist dann seit 1529 auch ins Gemeindegesangbuch übernommen worden.

Das Lied ist eine der schwächeren Dichtungen Luthers, wenn nicht die schwächste.

26

Der 46. Psalm: ‹Deus noster refugium et virtus›

1 Ein fe - ste Burg ist un - ser Gott, ein gu - te
   Er hilft uns frei aus al - ler Not,[2] die uns jetzt

Wehr und Waf - fen.[1] Der alt____ bö - se
hat ge - trof - fen.

108

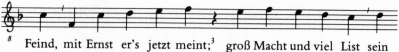

8 Feind, mit Ernst er's jetzt meint;[3] groß Macht und viel List sein

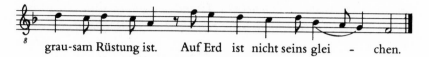

8 grau-sam Rüstung ist. Auf Erd ist nicht seins glei - chen.

2 Mit unsrer Macht ist nichts getan,[4]
wir sind gar bald verloren.
Es streit' für uns der rechte Mann,
den Gott hat selbst erkoren.
   Fragst du, wer der ist?
   Er heißt Jesus Christ,
   der Herr Zebaoth,
   und ist kein andrer Gott.
   Das Feld muß er behalten.[5]

3 Und wenn die Welt voll Teufel wär
und wollt' uns gar verschlingen,[6]
so fürchten wir uns nicht zu sehr.
Es soll uns doch gelingen.[7]
   Der Fürst dieser Welt,
   wie saur er sich stellt,
   tut er uns doch nicht;[8]
   das macht: Er ist gericht'.[9]
   Ein Wörtlein kann ihn fällen.

4 Das Wort sie sollen lassen stan[10]
und kein' Dank dazu haben.[11]
Er ist bei uns wohl auf dem Plan[12]
mit seinem Geist und Gaben.
   Nehmen sie den Leib,
   Gut, Ehr, Kind und Weib,
   laß fahren dahin;
   sie haben's kein' Gewinn.[13]
   Das Reich muß uns doch bleiben.

[1] *Einzahl.* [2] *er hilft uns aus aller Not hinaus; oder: er hilft uns ohne Entgelt, ko-stenlos, aus aller Not.* [3] *er geht jetzt mit Eifer ans Werk, es ist ihm ernst bei dem, was er unternimmt.* [4] *mit unserem Können läßt sich nichts ausrichten.* [5] *Feld = Schlachtfeld (er wird siegreich sein).* [6] *gar = ganz.* [7] *es = daß wir siegen gegen die satanische Anfechtung; doch = dennoch.* [8] *wie grimmig auch der Fürst dieser Welt (der Teufel) auftritt, so wird er uns doch nichts antun können; sauer = bitter, bitterböse, erbittert.* [9] *das bedeutet, daß er gerichtet, verurteilt, er-ledigt ist (Matthäus 4, 1–11).* [10] *sie: unvermittelt und ohne nähere Kennzeich-*

nung werden hier die Feinde der Reformation eingeführt; sollen = müssen. [11] ob sie wollen oder nicht. [12] Plan = Platz, Stelle. [13] sie haben nichts davon.

Das wohl berühmteste Lied Luthers hat auch der Forschung von allen am meisten Mühe gemacht. Die Literatur darüber füllt ein ganzes Büchergestell. Doch scheinen die Fragen heute weitgehend geklärt zu sein.

Der Abstand zu den anderen sechs Psalmliedern ist groß. Psalm 46 wird hier in sehr freier, aber sachlich durchaus angemessener Weise bearbeitet, und man hätte nie daran zweifeln sollen, ob die Nennung des 46. Psalms hier zu Recht geschieht. In den drei ersten Strophen lassen sich sogar ohne große Mühe die drei Strophen des Psalmtextes wieder erkennen.

Das Lied erscheint erstmals 1529 in Luthers Gemeindegesangbuch. Es kann kurz zuvor noch als Einzeldruck erschienen sein. Ein solcher muß nach Augsburg gelangt sein, wo der Text ohne Melodie noch im gleichen Jahr unter dem Titel «Ein Trostlied» erscheint.

Dieser Titel ist richtig: Das Lied ist nicht das Trutz- oder Kampflied, als welches man es bei Reformationsfeiern und in der Armee lange Zeit mißbrauchte. Luther suchte und fand im 46. Psalm Trost in schwerer Anfechtung. Luther wurde von körperlichen Beschwerden geplagt, die mit inneren Anfechtungen Hand in Hand gingen. Dann brach in Wittenberg die Pest aus, und es kam die Nachricht, daß in Scherding wieder ein Bekenner des evangelischen Glaubens, Leonhard Kaiser, zum Blutzeugen geworden ist. Der 10. Jahrestag des Reformationsbeginns mit der Veröffentlichung der 95 Thesen nahte. Gleichzeitig sah Luthers Frau ihrer zweiten Entbindung entgegen. In solcher Not, wie sie den größeren Teil des Jahres 1527 ausfüllte, schrieb Luther wahrscheinlich dieses Trostlied.

Es ist nicht verwunderlich, daß es ein sehr persönliches Lied ist. Das prägt auch seine Form. Text und Weise sind eindeutig im Hofweisen-Stil gehalten. Beides ist meisterlich gelungen, wenn auch ein Bruch zwischen den Strophen 3 und 4 zu bemerken ist und die 4. Strophe inhaltlich und in der Art zu reden in etwas anderer Richtung geht.

Auch hier hat das Solo-Lied schon früh eine Umdeutung zum Gemeinde-Lied erfahren. Aber Luther hat es nie für nötig gehalten, seine nicht ganz einfache Melodie durch eine gemeindegemäßere zu ersetzen.

27
Der 67. Psalm

A

1 Es woll uns Gott ge - nä - dig sein _____
Sein Ant - litz uns mit hel - lem Schein _____

und sei - nen Se - gen ge - - - - ben.
er - leucht zum ew - gen Le - - - - ben.

Daß wir er - ken - nen sei - ne Werk und was ihm 'liebt auf Er -

den,[1] und Je - su Chri - sti Heil und Stärk[2] be - kannt den

Hei - den wer - den und sie zu Gott be - keh - ren.

B

1 Es woll uns Gott ge - nä - dig sein und sei - nen
Sein Ant - litz uns mit hel - lem Schein er - leucht zum

1. 2.

Se - gen ge - ben.
e - wgen Le - ben. Daß wir er - ken - nen

sei - ne Werk und was ihm 'liebt auf Er - - - den,[1]

und Je - su Chri - sti Heil und Stärk[2] be - kannt den

III

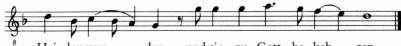

8 Hei-den wer - den und sie zu Gott be-keh - ren.

2 So danken, Gott, und loben dich
die Heiden überalle,
und alle Welt, die freue sich
und sing mit großem Schalle,
daß du auf Erden Richter bist
und läß't die Sünd nicht walten;[3]
dein Wort die Hut und Weide ist,[4]
die alles Volk erhalten,
in rechter Bahn zu wallen.[5]

3 Es danke, Gott, und lobe dich
das Volk in guten Taten.
Das Land bringt Frucht und bessert sich,
dein Wort ist wohl geraten.
Uns segne Vater und der Sohn,
uns segne Gott, der Heilig Geist,
dem alle Welt die Ehre tun,[6]
vor ihm sich fürcht allermeist.
Nun sprecht von Herzen: Amen.

[1] liebt = *beliebt* = *wohlgefällig ist.*   [2] *und daß ...*   [3] walten = *herrschen.*
[4] Hut und Weide = *Schutz und Nahrung.*   [5] *auf rechtem Weg zu gehen.*   [6] alle
Welt = *alle Menschen (daher die Mehrzahl* tun = *erweisen).*

*Während die beiden Psalmlieder Nr. 24 und 25 stark den Charakter
reformatorischer Polemik tragen, liegt hier ein Lied vor, das deutli-
cher auf den liturgischen Gebrauch ausgerichtet ist. Es erscheint
darum auch, sozusagen als Musterbeispiel, zuerst im Anhang zur
Übersetzung von Luthers Schrift über Meß-Kanon und Kommunion
durch Justus Jonas Anfang 1524 (neben Johannes Agricolas Lied
über Psalm 117) – der älteste Druck eines Lutherliedes, den wir
heute noch besitzen. Daß dieses deshalb auch das älteste Psalmlied
Luthers sei, das zu behaupten, ist ein Kurzschluß. Denn kurz zuvor
erwähnt Luther in einem Brief seine Bearbeitung des 130. Psalms
(30), und zwar ebenfalls unter dem Gesichtspunkt des Beitrags zum
liturgischen Gemeindegesang.*

*Ob es ein Zufall ist, daß Luther hier das (wahrscheinlich von ihm
erstmals verwendete) Metrum seiner Märtyrer-Ballade (23) wählt?
Sollte er zunächst gar jene Melodie auch für dieses Lied im Auge gehabt haben?*

112

Die Melodie-Frage ist bei diesem Liede allerdings auch ohne diese Überlegung schon problembeladen genug. Im genannten Erstdruck fehlt die Melodie und ist keine angegeben. In Straßburg wird das Lied schon *1524* mit einer Weise gedruckt, die alle Merkmale des Greiterschen Melodie-Stils trägt (A). Da auch die anderen frühen Luther-Psalmen in Straßburg sofort eigene Melodien erhalten, ist es wahrscheinlich, daß auch dies eine Straßburger Weise ist. Nun hat sich aber ein ebenfalls *1524* datiertes Liederblatt mit dieser Straßburger Melodie erhalten, das im fernen Magdeburg gedruckt ist. Und zudem läßt sich die Magdeburger mensurale Notierung wohl als Übertragung der choralen aus Straßburg erklären, während die Magdeburger Notierung, in Choralnoten übertragen, nicht das vorhandene Notenbild ergäbe. Wir sind also zur Annahme gezwungen, daß – auf welchem Wege auch immer – die Straßburger Weise nach Magdeburg und von da in andere Liedzentren der lutherischen Stammlande gelangt ist und so zur Hauptmelodie dieses Liedes wurde.

Inzwischen hat aber offenbar Luther selbst (oder Johann Walter?) dem Lied auch eine Weise gegeben, die uns erstmals in Walters Chorgesangbuch von *1524* begegnet (B). Sie hat sich jedoch nicht verbreitet, und schon das Wittenberger Gesangbuch von *1526*, das sonst ganz auf dem Chorgesangbuch fußt, hat die Straßburger Weise. Die Melodie aus dem Chorgesangbuch kommt erst zu ihrem Recht, seit Luther *1541* sein Tauflied (20) darauf singen läßt.

28
Der 124. Psalm

A

1 Wär Gott nicht mit uns die - se Zeit, so soll Is-
wär Gott nicht mit uns die se Zeit, wir hät ten

[1.
ra - el sa - - gen,
'mußt ver - za -

[2.
gen,[1] die so ein

klei - nes Häuf - lein sind, ver-acht' von so viel

Men-schen-kind', die uns zu-set-zen al - le.[2]

B

1 Wär Gott nicht mit uns die-se Zeit, so soll Is-ra-el
wär Gott nicht mit uns die-se Zeit, wir hätten 'mußt ver-

sa - gen,
za - gen,[1] die so ein klei-nes Häuf-lein sind, ver-
acht' von so viel Menschenkind', die uns zu-set-zen al - le.[2]

C

1 Wär Gott nicht mit uns die - se Zeit,
wär Gott nicht mit uns die - se Zeit,

so soll Is - ra - el sa - gen,
wir hät - ten 'mußt ver - za - gen,[1] die so ein

ar - mes Häuf - lein sind, ver-acht' von so viel

Men-schen kind', die uns zu - set - zen al - le.[2]

114

D

1 Wär Gott nicht mit uns die - se Zeit, so soll Is -
  wär Gott nicht mit uns die - se Zeit, wir hät - ten

ra - el sa - gen,
'mußt ver - za - gen,[1] die so ein

ar - mes Häuf - lein sind, ver - acht' von so viel Menschen

kind', die uns zu - set - zen al - le.[2]

E

1 Wär Gott nicht mit uns die - se Zeit, so soll Is -
  wär Gott nicht mit uns die - se Zeit, wir hät - ten

ra - el sa - gen,
'mußt ver - za - gen,[1] die so ein ar - mes

Häuf - lein sind, ver - acht' von so viel Menschenkind',

die uns zu - set - zen al - - - - - le.[2]

2 Auf uns so zornig ist ihr Sinn.
  Wo Gott hätt das zugeben,[3]
  verschlungen hätten sie uns hin
  mit ganzem Leib und Leben.

Wir wärn als die ein Flut ersäuft[4]
und über die groß Wasser läuft
und mit Gewalt verschwemmet.[5]

3 Gott Lob und Dank, der nicht zugab,
daß ihr Schlund uns möcht fangen.
Wie ein Vogel des Stricks kommt ab,[6]
ist unser Seel entgangen.
Strick ist entzwei und wir sind frei;[7]
des Herren Name steht uns bei,
des Gotts Himmels und Erden.

[1] *wir hätten verzagen müssen.* [2] *die uns alle zusetzen, uns angreifen.* [3] *wenn Gott es zugelassen hätte.* [4] *wir wären wie die, welche eine Flut ersäuft.* [5] *und mit Macht überschwemmte.* [6] *vom Strick (des Vogelfängers) loskommt.* [7] *Dieser Binnenreim hat eine starke Schlußwirkung.*

Auch hier hat Luther jenes Metrum gewählt, das wir bei Nr. 24 und 25 antreffen. Und mehr als das: Seinem Inhalt nach erscheint dieses Psalmlied als die getroste Antwort auf die Klagen jener beiden andern. In den Feinden, von denen der Psalmsänger spricht, sieht der Reformator die äußeren und inneren Feinde der Reformation, in diesem Fall offensichtlich die römische Partei. Es könnte also durchaus mit jenen frühen Psalmliedern zusammen entstanden sein. Wenn es in den Erfurter Enchiridien von 1524 nicht steht, dann vielleicht nur darum, weil dort eine längere Bearbeitung dieses Psalms von Justus Jonas (Wo Gott, der Herr, nicht bei uns hält) aufgenommen wurde. Im Walterschen Chorgesangbuch von 1524, wo wir diese Psalmbereimung zum ersten Mal finden, steht sie ebenfalls mit den anderen in einer Gruppe beisammen. Das Lied ist wohl als Gottesdienst-Eingangslied brauchbar und somit ein Gegenstück zu dem Segenslied Nr. 27, aber ob es als solches von Anfang an gemeint war, ist nach dem eben Gesagten zu bezweifeln. Wie bei anderen Psalmliedern gibt es auch hier eine reiche Melodie-Überlieferung schon zu Lebzeiten Luthers: Die Melodie A, mit der das Lied bei Walter steht, dürfte von diesem Tonsetzer stammen, der jedem Lied seine eigene Weise geben wollte, während Luther wohl auch dieses Lied ursprünglich auf die gleiche Weise sang wie Nr. 24, 25 und 30. In Straßburg wird es seit 1525 mit Melodie A überliefert, während man in Konstanz dem Texte Luthers die beim 1. Psalm von Ludwig Oeler (Wohl dem Menschen, der wandlet nit) stehende Straßburger Melodie von Nr. 24 beigab (E). Im Zwickauer Enchiridion von 1528 steht dann die Melodie der Jonasschen Bearbeitung dieses Psalms bei der-

jenigen Luthers (C), und schließlich hat Walter in seinem Chorgesangbuch seit 1534 die Melodie A durch eine neue, in der letzten
Zeile jedoch gleich lautende (D) ersetzt. Auf die Melodie B verweist
ein Erfurter Enchiridion von 1525 den Text.

29

Der 128. Psalm

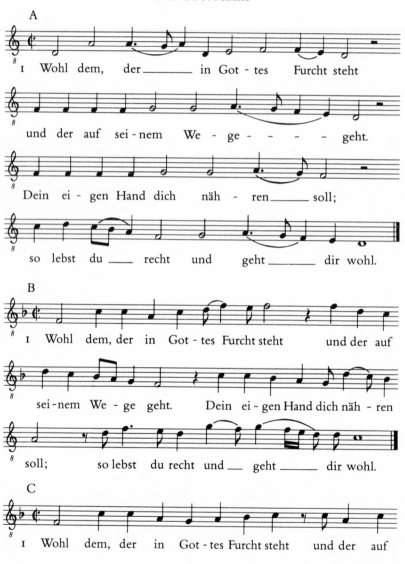

sei - nem We - ge geht.   Dein ei - gen Hand dich näh - ren

soll;   so lebst du recht und geht dir wohl.

D

1 Wohl dem, der in Got - tes Furcht steht   und der auf
seim We - - - ge geht.   Dein ei - gen Hand dich
näh - ren soll;   so lebst du recht und geht dir wohl.

E

1 Wohl dem,   der in Got-tes Furcht steht   und
der   auf sei-nem We-ge geht.   Dein ei-gen
Hand dich näh-ren soll;   so lebst du recht und geht dir wohl.

2 Dein Weib wird in deim Hause sein
   wie ein Reben voll Trauben fein[1]
   und dein Kinder um deinen Tisch
   wie Ölpflanzen gesund und frisch.[2]

3 Sieh, so reich Segen hangt dem an,[3]
   wo in Gottes Furcht lebt ein Mann.
   Von ihm läßt der alt Fluch und Zorn,
   den Menschenkindern angeborn.

4 Aus Zion wird Gott segnen dich,
   daß du wirst schauen stetiglich

das Glück der Stadt Jerusalem,
vor Gott in Gnaden angenehm.

5 Fristen wird er das Leben dein⁴
und mit Güte stets bei dir sein,
daß du sehen wirst Kindeskind
und daß Israel Friede find.

¹ der Reben = *der Weinstock.*   ² Ölpflanzen = *Ölbäumchen.*   ³ hangt dem an
= *ist damit verbunden.*   ⁴ fristen = *erhalten, vor Schaden bewahren.*

*Am 13. Juni 1525 schloß Luther die Ehe mit Katharina von Bora.
Dieser Ehepsalm aber steht schon 1524 in den Erfurter Enchiridien,
und so kann er mit diesem Ereignis in Luthers Leben nicht in Zusammenhang
gebracht werden. Auch daß Luther ihn für den zweiten
Sonntag der Epiphanias-Zeit 1524 (17. Januar), als er über die Hochzeit
zu Kana (Johannes 2, 1–11) predigte, geschaffen habe, ist wohl
allzuweit hergeholt. Ob das Lied noch 1523 entstanden ist, als Luther
begann, sich mit der Psalmbereimung zu befassen, oder erst Anfang
1524, wissen wir nicht.*

*Die Erfurter Enchiridien schreiben die Melodie des Abendmahlliedes
Nr. 21 vor (A). Ob das die Melodie ist, auf die Luther gedichtet
hat? In der uns vorliegenden Form geht sie schlecht auf diesen Text.
Johann Walter hat dann eine recht anspruchsvolle Melodie im Stil
der solistischen Hofweise geschaffen (B). Erst mit einer dritten
Weise, die im Wittenberger Gesangbuch Luthers von 1529 auftaucht
und die vom Textdichter selbst stammen muß (C), wird das Lied
zum Gemeindelied. Auch Johann Walter hat dann noch eine Melodie
beigesteuert (D). Wahrscheinlich ist die einschneidende Neubearbeitung
seines Chorgesangbuches, die wir nur in einem Straßburger
Nachdruck von 1534 kennen, in Wittenberg schon vor 1529 erschienen,
und so stand Luthers gemeindegemäße Melodie Walter
noch nicht zur Verfügung.*

30a
Der 130. Psalm

A

1 Aus tie - fer Not schrei ich zu dir: Herr Gott,
Dein gnä - dig Oh - ren kehr zu mir¹ und mei-

er - hör mein Ru - fen.
ner Bitt sie öf - fen.[2]

Denn so du

willst das se - hen an, wie man - che Sünd ich

hab ge - tan: Wer kann, Herr, vor dir blei - ben?

B

1 Aus tie - fer Not schrei ich zu dir: Herr Gott, er -
Dein gnä - dig Oh - ren kehr zu mir[1] und mei - ner

1. 2.

hör mein Ru - fen.
Bitt sie öf - fen.[2] Denn so du

willst das se - hen an, wie man - che Sünd ich

hab ge - tan: Wer kann, Herr, vor dir blei - ben?

C

1 Aus tie - fer Not schrei ich zu dir: Herr Gott, er -
Dein gnä - dig Oh - ren kehr zu mir[1] und mei - ner

1. 2.

hör mein Ru - fen.
Bitt sie öf - fen.[2] Denn so du

willst das se - hen an, wie man - che Sünd ich

hab ge - tan: Wer kann, Herr, vor dir blei - ben?

D

1 Aus tie-fer Not schrei ich zu dir: Herr Gott, er-hör
Dein gnä-dig Oh - ren kehr zu mir[1] und mei-ner Bitt

mein __ Ru - fen.
sie __ öf - fen.[2] Denn so du willst das

se - hen an, wie man-che Sünd ich hab ge -

tan: Wer kann, Herr, vor dir blei - ben?

2 Es steht bei deiner Macht allein,
die Sünden zu vergeben,
daß dich fürcht' beide, groß und klein,[3]
auch in dem besten Leben.
   Darum auf Gott will hoffen ich;
   mein Herz auf ihn soll lassen sich.
   Ich will seins Worts erharren.[4]

3 Und ob es währt bis in die Nacht
und wieder an den Morgen,
doch soll mein Herz an Gottes Macht
verzweifeln nicht noch sorgen.
   So tu Israel rechter Art,[5]
   der aus dem Geist erzeuget ward,
   und seines Gotts erharre.[6]

4 Ob bei uns ist der Sünden viel,
bei Gott ist viel mehr Gnaden.[7]

121

Sein Hand zu helfen hat kein Ziel,[8]
wie groß auch sei der Schaden.
Er ist allein der gute Hirt,
der Israel erlösen wird[9]
aus seinen Sünden allen.

[1] kehr zu mir = *wende mir zu.*   [2] öffen = *öffne. Wenn man annehmen dürfte,
daß Luther hier zunächst niedersächsisch hörte, ergäbe sich der reine Reim: Röpen/
öpen.*   [3] *daß Große und Kleine dich fürchten.*   [4] *ich will an seinem Wort festhalten, mit meinem Vertrauen auf Gottes Zusage durchhalten.*   [5] *Israel (Jakob,
der Gottesstreiter, s. 1. Mose 32, 29) ist hier noch stärker als Person gesehen = der
Gläubige, in der nächsten Strophe dann stärker als Kollektiv = die Kirche, also
hier: so verhalte sich ein rechter Gottesstreiter.*   [6] *und an seinem Gott halte er fest.*
[7] *dem Plural Sünden entspricht hier der Plural Gnaden.*   [8] *dem Helfen seiner
Hand ist keine Grenze gesetzt.*   [9] *Israel = das Gottesvolk, die Kirche.*

30 b
Der 130. Psalm

1 Aus tie-fer Not schrei ich zu dir: Herr Gott, er-
Dein gnä-dig Oh-ren kehr zu mir[1] und mei-ner

hör mein Ru - - fen.
Bitt sie öf - fen.[2] Denn so du

willst das se - hen an, was Sünd und Un-recht

ist__ ge-tan, wer kann, Herr, vor dir blei - ben?

2 Bei dir gilt nichts denn Gnad und Gunst,
die Sünden zu vergeben.
Es ist doch unser Tun umsonst,
auch in dem besten Leben.
Vor dir niemand sich rühmen kann;
des muß dich fürchten jedermann[3]
und deiner Gnade leben.

3 Darum auf Gott will hoffen ich,
auf mein Verdienst nicht bauen.
Auf ihn mein Herz soll lassen sich[4]
und seiner Güte trauen,
die mir zusagt sein wertes Wort;
das ist mein Trost und treuer Hort.
Des will ich allzeit harren.[5]

4 Und ob es währt bis in die Nacht
und wieder an den Morgen,
doch soll mein Herz an Gottes Macht[6]
verzweifeln nicht noch sorgen.
So tu Israel rechter Art,[7]
der aus dem Geist erzeuget ward,
und seines Gotts erharre.[8]

5 Ob bei uns ist der Sünden viel,
bei Gott ist viel mehr Gnaden.[9]
Sein Hand zu helfen hat kein Ziel,[10]
wie groß auch sei der Schaden.
Er ist allein der gute Hirt,
der Israel erlösen wird
aus seinen Sünden allen.

[1] kehr zu mir = *wende mir zu.* [2] öffen = *öffne. Wenn man annehmen dürfte, daß Luther hier zunächst niedersächsisch hörte, ergäbe sich der reine Reim: Röpen/öpen.* [3] des = *dessen, deshalb.* [4] sich lassen = *sich verlassen.* [5] *daran will ich stets festhalten.* [6] doch = *dennoch.* [7] *s. 30 a, Anmerkung 5.* [8] *an seinem Gott halte er fest.* [9] *Dem Plural* Sünden *entspricht der Plural* Gnaden. [10] *dem Helfen seiner Hand ist keine Grenze gesetzt.*

Diese nach Nr. 26 zweitberühmteste Psalmbereimung Luthers ist nachweislich Ende 1523 schon vorhanden gewesen. Als Luther um jene Zeit eine Reihe von Freunden um die Bearbeitung der Bußpsalmen bat, stellte er den Psalm 130 beiseite und schrieb: De profundis a me versus est *(«Aus der Tiefe» ist von mir schon übertragen.) In den Erfurter Enchiridien steht denn auch Luthers Lied über diesen Psalm, und auch in Straßburg findet es sich schon in einem Druck von 1524. Die genannten Quellen enthalten die 4 strophige Fassung (a), die sich sehr genau an den Psalmtext hält, wie Luther das in jenem Brief forderte: …wie ich es im beiliegenden Beispiel getan habe: … so nahe wie möglich am Psalmtext. Im Walterschen Chorgesangbuch steht dann eine 5 strophige Fassung (b), in welcher außer einer Variante in der ersten Strophe der Inhalt der 2. Strophe auf zwei Strophen verteilt ist. Damit erhält der Psalmvers «Denn bei dir ist Vergebung, daß man*

dich fürchte» (V.4), in welchem Luther die reformatorische Zentrallehre von der Rechtfertigung des Sünders aus Gnaden allein erkannte, ein starkes Übergewicht.

Während man eine Zeitlang annahm, die 4 strophige Fassung sei durch mangelhafte Überlieferung entstanden, ist man heute zur früheren Auffassung zurückgekehrt, wonach die knappere und Psalmnähere Fassung Luthers Erstfassung von 1523 ist. Er selbst hat dann 1524 das Psalmlied durch die eindrucksvolle Erweiterung um eine Strophe zum reformatorischen Glaubenslied umgeformt.

Auch dieses Lied hat der Reformator im Metrum der sogenannten «Lutherstrophe» gedichtet: Im «Achtliederbuch» wird es auf die Melodie des Oster-Prozessions-Liedes verwiesen (A). Schon in den Erfurter Enchiridien erhält es jedoch eine offenbar von Luther selbst stammende eindrückliche phrygische Eigenweise mit dem «rufenden» Einsatz auf der Dominante (B). Straßburg bringt auch hier eine neue Melodie (C), offenbar von Wolfgang Dachstein. Wer sie für zu oberflächlich und für dieses Bußlied allzu fröhlich hält, übersieht die Besonderheit gerade dieses Liedes, das von der Buße in die getroste, ja fröhliche Vergebungsgewißheit hinüberführt. Luthers Weise interpretiert den Text von seiner 1. Strophe her, die Dachsteinsche von der letzten her. Da die Straßburger zunächst nur den 4 strophigen Text kannten, ist die Straßburger Melodie in der reformierten Tradition, die teilweise beide Texte nebeneinander überlieferte, ausschließlich mit dem 4 strophigen Text verbunden geblieben. Wir geben diesen daher mit allen drei Melodien wieder, den 5 strophigen jedoch nur mit der Melodie Luthers (B).

31
Das deutsche Sanctus

Je - sa - ja, dem Pro - phe - ten, das ge - schah,

daß er im Geist den Her - ren sit - zen sah

auf ei - nem ho - hen Thron in hel - lem Glanz;

sei - nes Klei - des Saum den Chor fül - let ganz.[1]

Es stan - den zwei Se - raph' bei ihm da - ran.

Sechs Flü - gel sah er ei - nen je - den han;[2]

mit zwein ver - bar - gen sie ihr Ant - litz klar,

mit zwein be - deck - ten sie die Fü - ße gar,

und mit den an - dern zwein sie flo - gen frei,[3]

gen 'an - der rie - fen sie mit gro - ßem Gschrei:[4]

«Hei - lig ist Gott, der Her - re Ze - ba - oth.

Hei - lig ist Gott, der Her - re Ze - ba - oth.

Hei - lig ist Gott, der Her - re Ze - ba - oth.

Sein Ehr die gan - ze Welt er - fül - let hat.»

8 Von dem Gschrei zit - tert Schwell und Bal - ken gar;

8 das Haus auch ganz voll Rauch und Ne - bel war.

[1] Chor: *Luther stellt sich den Tempel nach der Art einer gotischen Kirche vor und setzt das Allerheiligste mit dem Chor gleich.* [2] han = haben. [3] frei = unbehindert (?). [4] gen' ander = gegeneinander (im Wechselgesang).

Entgegen der Überschrift ist dieser Gesang kein eigentliches Sanctus. Zum Wesen dieses liturgischen Stücks gehört es, daß die Singenden damit in die Präfation des Liturgen einfallen. Luther aber hat in seiner Deutschen Messe von 1525 (gedruckt um Weihnachten und daher 1526 datiert) mitsamt dem Meß-Kanon auch die Präfation gestrichen. Das Sanctus und das Agnus Dei (43) läßt er vom Chor während der Kommunion singen und kann daher den Ruf aus Jesaja 6,3 einbetten in den ursprünglichen biblischen Zusammenhang: Er bringt Jesaja 6,1–4 in Verse. Johann Walter bezeugt in einer Nachricht, die von Michael Praetorius 1615 überliefert wird, daß Luther auch die Melodie zu diesem liturgischen Gesang geschaffen habe. Sie lehnt sich an das gregorianische Sanctus der Adventszeit an. Denn Luther hat dieses sein erstes und einziges liturgisches Formular wahrscheinlich in dieser Kirchen-Jahreszeit zum ersten Mal verwendet.

32
‹Da pacem Domine› deutsch

a

8 Ver-leih uns Frie-den gnä-dig-lich, Herr Gott, zu un-sern

8 Zei-ten.[1] Es ist doch ja kein and - rer ____ nicht, der

8 für uns könn - te strei - ten, denn du, un-ser Gott, al-lei-ne.

Bestellkarte

Huldreich Zwinglis sämtliche Werke

Ex. Bd. 1	Fr. 170.–/DM 200.–	
Ex. Bd. 2	Fr. 210.–/DM 250.–	
Ex. Bd. 3	Fr. 240.–/DM 290.–	
Ex. Bd. 4	Fr. 240.–/DM 290.–	
Ex. Bd. 5	Fr. 240.–/DM 290.–	
Ex. Bd. 6/1	Fr. 240.–/DM 290.–	
Ex. Bd. 6/2	Fr. 270.–/DM 320.–	
Ex. Bd. 6/3	Fr. 270.–/DM 320.–	

Ex. Bd. 7	Fr. 180.–/DM 210.–	
Ex. Bd. 8	Fr. 210.–/DM 250.–	
Ex. Bd. 9	Fr. 180.–/DM 210.–	
Ex. Bd. 10	Fr. 180.–/DM 210.–	
Ex. Bd. 11	Fr. 180.–/DM 210.–	
Ex. Bd. 12/1	Fr. 140.–/DM 170.–	
Ex. Bd. 13	Fr. 270.–/DM 320.–	
Ex. Bd. 14	Fr. 270.–/DM 320.–	

Heinrich Bullinger-Werke

Ex. Bibliographie Bd. 1	Fr. 48.–/DM 58.–
Ex. Bibliographie Bd. 2	Fr. 58.–/DM 68.–
Ex. Briefe Bd. 1	Fr. 53.–/DM 63.–
Ex. Briefe Bd. 2	Fr. 93.–/DM 107.–
Ex. Briefe Bd. 3	Fr. 110.–/DM 125.–
Ex. Theol. Schriften Bd. 1	Fr. 80.–/DM 92.–
Ex. Zürcher Bibel 1531 (ab 1.1.1984 Fr. 115.–/DM 130.–)	Fr. 95.–/DM 115.–

Heidelberger-Katechismus 1563

Ex. Luxusausgabe	Fr. 180.–/DM 196.–
Ex. Leinenausgabe	Fr. 24.–/DM 26.–
Ex. Henss, Heidelberger...	Fr. 12.–/DM 14.–
Ex. Jenny, Luther, Zwingli, Calvin	Fr. 56.–/DM 62.–

Datum/Unterschrift

Absender auf Vorderseite nicht vergessen! Preisänderungen jederzeit vorbehalten.

Richten Sie Ihre Bestellung an Ihre Buch-
handlung oder an:

Theologischer Verlag
Postfach
8026 Zürich

Chr. Kaiser-Verlag
Postfach 509
8000 München 40

Name

Vorname

Strasse/Hausnummer

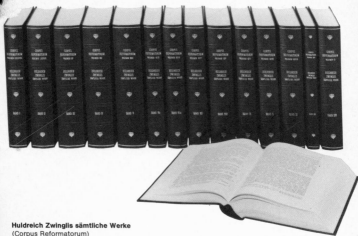

Huldreich Zwinglis sämtliche Werke

(Corpus Reformatorum)

Das Werk kann vollständig subskribiert werden oder ab Band 6/3 (erscheint August 1983) zur Fortsetzung bestellt werden. Subs.-Preis ca. 10 % günstiger als Einzelpreise.

Die Zürcher Bibel 1531
Auf 17×25 cm verkleinerte faksi-
milierte Ausgabe der Zürcher
Bibel, gedruckt 1531 bei
Froschour, Zürich.

1376 S., Ln., Einführungspreis
Fr. 95.–/DM 115.–, ab 1.1.1984
Fr. 115.–/DM 130.–

Walter Henss
**Der Heidelberger Katechismus
im konfessionspolitischen
Kräftespiel seiner Frühzeit**
Historisch-bibliographische Einführung zur ersten vollständigen
deutschen Fassung von 1563
und der dazugehörigen lateinischen Fassung.

78 S., br., Fr. 12.–/DM 14.–

**Der Heidelberger Katechismus
von 1563**
Reprint der ersten vollständigen
Ausgabe von 1563 der deutschen
und lateinischen Ausgabe.

Luxusausgabe, Einbandfaksimile
des «Reformatoreneinbandes»,
Leder mit Schliessen, Fr. 180.–/
DM 196.–

Sonderausgabe in Leinen,
Fr. 24.–/DM 26.–

Markus Jenny
**Luther-Zwingli-Calvin in ihren
Liedern**
Erstmals erscheinen alle Lieder
der drei grossen Reformatoren
mit vollem Text und Notensatz
der Melodien.

288 S., Ln., Fr. 56.–/DM 62.–

Heinrich-Bullinger-Werke
Bibliographie
Bd. 1: Werke von Bullinger
Bd. 2: Werke über Bullinger

Briefwechsel
Bd. 1: Briefe 1524–1531
Bd. 2: Briefe 1532
Bd. 3: Briefe 1533

Theologische Schriften
Bd. 1: Exegetische Schriften aus
den Jahren 1525–1527

b

Ver - leih uns Frie-den gnä-dig-lich, Herr Gott, zu un - sern

Zei - ten.[1] Es ist doch ja kein and - rer nicht, der

für uns könnte strei - ten, denn du, un - ser Gott, al - lei - ne.

[1] *Plural wie im lateinischen Text (in diebus nostris); vgl. unseren Ausdruck «diese Zeitläufte».*

Der älteste erhaltene Druck dieses Liedes ist ein Nürnberger Druck der Litanei (34) von 1529, in welchem diese Strophe jenen liturgischen Gesang abschließt. Sie stand auch im Wittenberger Gesangbuch von 1529 und ist dort in der späteren Auflage von 1533 erhalten. Diese Bitte um Frieden muß Luther wichtig geworden sein im Zusammenhang mit der Bedrohung durch die Türken, die auch für die Schaffung der Litanei (34) der Anlaß war. Textlich ist sie die fast wörtliche Übersetzung einer Antiphon (Da pacem Domine) aus dem 9. Jahrhundert. Musikalisch hat sie damit gar nichts zu tun. Luther hat nämlich einfach die Melodie jenes Advents-Hymnus Veni redemptor gentium genommen, die er in Nr. 1 mensural bearbeitet hatte, und zwar nahezu (oder ganz?) in ihrer ursprünglichen Gestalt. An sie hängt er – eine kühne, aber bestgelungene und wirkungsvolle Maßnahme – eine fünfte Zeile an, die dadurch ein sehr starkes Gewicht bekommt. Das reformatorische «Allein» (Gott allein die Ehre, allein durch den Glauben, allein durch Gnade, allein die Schrift) wird hier in unüberhörbarer Deutlichkeit ausgesprochen: (... kein andrer nicht), denn Du, unser Gott, alleine.

Die Melodie wird schon 1529 in zwei Varianten, einer mehr choralen (a) und einer mehr mensuralen und rein syllabischen (b), überliefert. Wahrscheinlich hat Luther das Stück zunächst mit der ersten Fassung in Einzeldrucken veröffentlicht und aufgrund von Erfahrungen bald danach für das Wittenberger Gesangbuch von 1529 die gemeindegemäßere syllabische Fassung erstellt.

Die Wahl der Melodie dürfte von Bedeutung sein: Gott wird in der Bedrohung durch die Heiden angerufen als der Erlöser der Völker.

127

33

‹Te Deum laudamus› verdeutscht

Der erste Chor

Herr Gott, dich lo - ben wir.

Dich, Va - ter in E - wig - keit

All En - gel und Him - mels Heer

auch Che - ru - bim und Se - ra - phim

«Hei - lig - ist un - ser Gott,

hei - lig ist un - ser Gott, der Her - re Ze - ba - oth.»

Dein gött - lich Macht und Herr - lich - keit

Der hei - li - gen zwölf Bo - ten Zahl

die teu - ren Märt'- rer all - zu - mal

Die gan - ze wer - te Chri - sten - heit

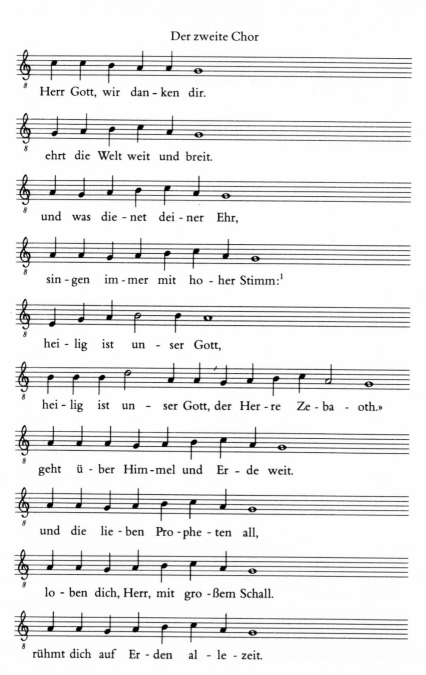

Der zweite Chor

Herr Gott, wir dan - ken dir.

ehrt die Welt weit und breit.

und was die - net dei - ner Ehr,

sin - gen im - mer mit ho - her Stimm:[1]

hei - lig ist un - ser Gott,

hei - lig ist un - ser Gott, der Her - re Ze - ba - oth.»

geht ü - ber Him - mel und Er - de weit.

und die lie - ben Pro - phe - ten all,

lo - ben dich, Herr, mit gro - ßem Schall.

rühmt dich auf Er - den al - le - zeit.

Der erste Chor

Dich, Gott Va - ter im höch-sten Thron,

den Hei-li-gen Geist und Trö - ster wert

Du Kö-nig der Eh - ren, Je - sus Christ,

Der Jung-frau Leib nicht hast ver-schmächt,[2]

Du hast dem Tod zer-stört sein Macht

Du sitzt zur Rech-ten Got - tes gleich[3]

Ein Rich -ter du zu -künf -tig bist

Nun hilf uns, Herr, den Die - nern dein,

Laß uns im Him-mel ha - ben teil

Hilf dei-nem Volk, Herr Je - sus Christ,

Wart' und pfleg es zu al - ler Zeit

Der zweite Chor

dei - nen rech - ten und ei - ni-gen Sohn,

mit rech - tem Dienst sie lobt und ehrt.

Gott Va - ters e - wi-ger Sohn du bist.

zu 'r lö - sen das menschlich Ge-schlecht.

und all' Chri-sten zum Him-mel 'bracht.

mit al - ler Ehr in's Va - ters Reich.

al - lem, was tot und le - bend ist.[4]

die mit dei'm teurn Blut er - lö - set sein.[5]

mit den Hei - li-gen am e - wi-gen Heil.

und seg - ne, was dein Erb - teil ist.

und heb es hoch in E - wig - keit.

131

Der erste Chor

Täg-lich, Herr Gott, wir lo - ben dich

Be - hüt uns heut, o treu - er Gott,

Sei uns gnä-dig, o Her - re Gott,

Zeig uns dei - ne Barm-her-zig-keit,

Auf dich hof - fen wir, lie - ber Herr,

A – – – – men.

Der zweite Chor

und ehrn dein' Na - men ste - tig - lich.

vor al - ler Sünd und Mis - se - tat.

sei uns gnä - dig in al - ler Not.

wie uns - re Hoff-nung zu dir steht.[6]

in Schan - den laß uns nim - mer - mehr.

A - - - - - men.

[1] mit hoher Stimm = *mit lauter Stimme.* [2] verschmächt = *verschmäht.*
[3] gleich = *ihm gleichgestellt.* [4] *du bist im Kommen, du wirst kommen als Richter über alles.* [5] sein = *sind.* [6] *wie = so, wie.*

Was Luther 1523 und 1524 für den evangelischen Gemeindegesang schuf, sind ausnahmslos Lieder. 1525 kam die Bearbeitung von Jesaja 6, 1–4 (31) hinzu, die zwar der Liedform noch nahesteht, ihr aber im strengen Sinne nicht mehr zugehört. Seit 1529 kommen weitere liturgische Gesänge hinzu, die sich nun ganz von der Liedform abwenden. Der wichtigste unter ihnen ist diese deutsche Bearbeitung des Te Deum. Luther hat den aus dem 4. Jahrhundert stammenden, psalmähnlichen Text in gereimte Zeilenpaare von 6–9 Silben übertragen und auf zwei Chöre verteilt – eine von der mittelalterlichen Gesangspraxis her in diesem Fall nicht gegebene, originelle Maßnahme. Die Choralweise hat er meisterhaft in eine syllabische Form zu überführen gewußt. Nach der Wittenberger Kirchenordnung von 1533 sollte eine Gruppe von Schülern als erster Chor singen und die Gemeinde als zweiter Chor antworten.

34
Die deutsche Litanei

Der erste Chor

Ky - ri - e

Chri - ste

Ky - ri - e

Chri - ste,

Herr, Gott Va - ter im Him - mel,
Herr, Gott Sohn, der Welt Hei - land,
Herr, Gott Hei - li - ger   Geist,

Sei uns gnä - dig,
Sei uns gnä - dig,

Vor al - len Sün - den
Vor al - lem Irr - tum
Vor al - lem Ü - bel

Vor des Teu - fels Trug und List
Vor bö - sem, schnel - lem Tod[1]
Vor Pe - sti - lenz und teu - rer Zeit
Vor Krieg und Blut
Vor Auf - ruhr und Zwie - tracht

Der zweite Chor

e - le - i - son.

e - le - i - son.

e - le - i - son.

er - hö - re   uns.

er - barm dich   ü - ber   uns.
er - barm dich   ü - ber   uns.
er - barm dich   ü - ber   uns.

ver-schon uns,   lie - ber   Her - re   Gott.
hilf   uns,   lie - ber   Her - re   Gott.

be - hüt   uns,   lie - ber   Her - re   Gott.
be - hüt   uns,   lie - ber   Her - re   Gott.
be - hüt   uns,   lie - ber   Her - re   Gott.

be - hüt   uns,   lie - ber   Her - re   Gott.
be - hüt   uns,   lie - ber   Her - re   Gott.
be - hüt   uns,   lie - ber   Her - re   Gott.
be - hüt   uns,   lie - ber   Her - re   Gott.
be - hüt   uns,   lie - ber   Her - re   Gott.

Vor Ha - gel und Un - ge - wit - ter
Vor dem e - wi - gen Tod

Durch dei - ne hei - li - ge   Ge - burt
Durch dei - nen Todeskampf und blu - ti - gen Schweiß
                        Durch dein Kreuz und Tod

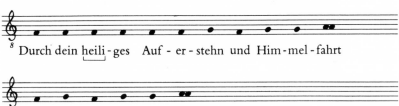

Durch dein heili - ges Auf - er - stehn und Him - mel - fahrt

In uns - rer letz - ten Not

Im jüng - sten Ge - richt

Wir ar - men Sün - der bit - ten,

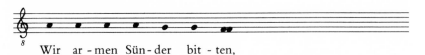

und dei - ne hei - li - ge christ - li - che
                Kir - che re - gie - ren und füh - ren,
al - le Bi - schöfe, Pfar - rer und Kir - chen -
die - ner im heil - sa - men Wort und hei -
                li - gen Le - ben be - hal - ten,
        al - len Rot - ten und Är - ger - nis - sen weh - ren,[2]
al - le Ir - ren - den und Ver - führ - ten
                wie - der - brin - gen,
    den Sa - tan un - ter un - sre Fü - ße tre - ten,
treu - e Ar - bei - ter in dei - ne Ern - te sen - den,
        dei - nen Geist und Kraft zum Wort ge - ben,

be - hüt uns, lie - ber Her - re Gott.
be - hüt uns, lie - ber Her - re Gott.

hilf uns, lie - ber Her - re Gott.
hilf uns, lie - ber Her - re Gott.
hilf uns, lie - ber Her - re Gott.

hilf uns, lie - ber Her - re Gott.

hilf uns, lie - ber Her - re Gott.

hilf uns, lie - ber Her - re Gott.

du wollst uns hö - ren, lie - ber Her - re Gott,

– er - hör uns, lie - ber Her - re Gott! –

– er - hör uns, lie - ber Her - re Gott! –
– er - hör uns, lie - ber Her - re Gott! –

– er - hör uns, lie - ber Her - re Gott! –
– er - hör uns, lie - ber Her - re Gott! –
– er - hör uns, lie - ber Her - re Gott! –
– er - hör uns, lie - ber Her - re Gott! –

Der erste Chor

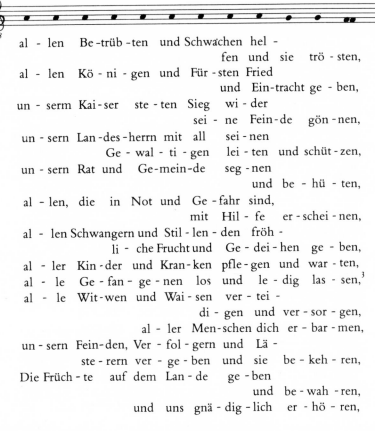

al - len   Be -trüb -ten   und Schwa'chen hel -
                                    fen und sie   trö - sten,
al - len   Kö - ni - gen und Für -sten Fried
                                    und   Ein-tracht ge - ben,
un - serm Kai-ser   ste - ten Sieg   wi - der
                                    sei - ne Fein-de   gön -nen,
un - sern Lan-des-herrn mit all   sei - nen
                          Ge - wal - ti - gen   lei - ten und schüt-zen,
un - sern Rat und   Ge-mein-de   seg -nen
                                    und be - hü - ten,
al - len, die in Not und Ge -fahr sind,
                          mit Hil - fe   er -schei -nen,
al - len Schwangern und Stil - len - den   fröh -
                          li - che Frucht und   Ge - dei - hen ge - ben,
al - ler Kin -der und Kran-ken pfle-gen und war -ten,
al - le   Ge - fan - ge - nen los und le - dig las - sen,[3]
al - le   Wit-wen und Wai - sen   ver - tei -
                          di - gen und ver - sor - gen,
                          al - ler Men-schen dich er - bar - men,
un - sern Fein-den, Ver - fol - gern und Lä -
                          ste - rern ver - ge - ben und sie   be - keh - ren,
Die Früch - te   auf dem Lan - de   ge -ben
                                    und be - wah -ren,
                          und uns gnä - dig - lich   er - hö - ren,

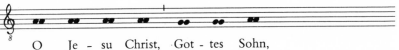

O   Je - su Christ, Got - tes   Sohn,

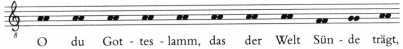

O   du   Got - tes - lamm, das   der   Welt Sün - de   trägt,
O   du   Got - tes - lamm, das   der   Welt Sün - de   trägt,
O   du   Got - tes - lamm, das   der   Welt Sün - de   trägt,

Chri - ste,

Der zweite Chor

– er - hör uns, lie - ber Her - re Gott! –

– er - hör uns, lie - ber Her - re Gott! –

– er - hör uns, lie - ber Her - re Gott! –

– er - hör uns, lie - ber Her - re Gott! –

– er - hör uns, lie - ber Her - re Gott! –

– er - hör uns, lie - ber Her - re Gott! –

– er - hör uns, lie - ber Her - re Gott! –
– er - hör uns, lie - ber Her - re Gott! –
– er - hör uns, lie - ber Her - re Gott! –

– er - hör uns, lie - ber Her - re Gott! –
– er - hör uns, lie - ber Her - re Gott! –

– er - hör uns, lie - ber Her - re Gott! –

– er - hör uns, lie - ber Her - re Gott! –
– er - hör uns, lie - ber Her - re Gott! –

er - hör uns, lie - ber Her - re Gott.

er - barm dich ü - ber uns.
er - barm dich ü - ber uns.
ver - leih uns ste - ten Fried.

er - hö - re uns.

139

Der erste Chor

Ky - ri - e

Chri - ste

Beide Chöre zusammen

Ky - ri - e - e - le - i - son. A - men.

[1] *vor plötzlichem Sterben.*   [2] *allen Sekten und allen Hindernissen (für den Glauben) wehren.*   [3] *freilassen.*

An letzter Stelle unter den Liedern Luthers steht im Wittenberger Gesangbuch von 1529 die Litanei. Sie ist, gleich vielen Liedern Luthers, zunächst als Einzeldruck veröffentlicht worden. Aus brieflichen Äußerungen wissen wir, daß Luther sich Anfang 1529 mit der Wiedereinführung des Litaneisingens in Wittenberg befaßte und selbst an der Bereitstellung dieses liturgischen Stücks arbeitete; am 13. März lag die deutsche Litanei gedruckt vor. 1520/21 war das Litaneisingen in Wittenberg, wahrscheinlich durch Andreas Karlstadt, im Rahmen einer recht überstürzten Liturgiereform abgeschafft worden. Für Luther lag der Anlaß zur Wiedereinführung in den Zeitereignissen: Seit der türkische Sultan Suleiman II. 1526 in der Schlacht bei Mohács gesiegt hatte und die Städte Buda und Pest ihm ihre Tore hatten öffnen müssen, waren die Türken in unaufhaltsamem Vormarsch nach Mitteleuropa begriffen. Die Belagerung Wiens stand bevor. Und wenn Wien fallen sollte, dann wäre es um das christliche Europa bald einmal geschehen. Nun konnte nur noch das Gebet der Christen helfen.

Luthers deutsche Litanei hatte in den Einzeldrucken noch eine etwas abweichende Gestalt (der zweite Chor setzt stets auf f ein); für das Gesangbuch hat der Autor sie dann nochmals überarbeitet, so daß der zweite Chor nun stets mit dem Ton beginnt, mit welchem der erste geschlossen hat – ohne Zweifel eine Erleichterung für die Gemeinde, wie das Gesangbuch Luthers von 1529 deren ja viele enthält. Wir geben nur diese letztgenannte Fassung wieder. Gleichzeitig

140

Der zweite Chor

e - le - i - son.

e - le - i - son.

Beide Chöre zusammen

Ky - ri - e   e - le - i - son.   A - men.

mit der deutschen überarbeitete Luther auch eine lateinische Fassung der Litanei, die dann in der zweiten, ebenfalls verschollenen Ausgabe des Wittenberger Gemeindegesangbuches, die Ende *1529* erschien, nach der deutschen abgedruckt ist.

Die Melodie der deutschen Fassung ist der mittelalterlichen Vorlage in freier Weise nachgestaltet.

Es folgen nun (*35–37*) drei weitere Lieder Luthers aus den *40*er Jahren.

35
Ein Lied von der heiligen christlichen Kirche
aus dem 12. Kapitel der Offenbarung

1 Sie ist mir lieb, die wer - - - - - - te Magd, und kann ihr' nicht ver - ges - - - - - - - - - - sen.

Lob, Ehr und Zucht von ihr_____ man sagt; sie hat mein Herz be - ses - - - - - - - - -

sen.[1] Ich bin ihr hold, und wenn ich sollt groß Un - glück han,[2] da liegt nichts dran; sie wird_____ mich des er - get - - - - - zen[3] mit ih - rer Lieb und Treu an mir, die sie zu mir will set - - - - - zen, und tun all_____ mein Be - gier.[4]

B

1 Sie ist mir lieb, die wer - te Magd, und kann ihr'
Lob, Ehr und Zucht von ihr — man sagt; sie hat mein
nicht ver - ges - sen.
Herz be - ses - sen.[1]
Ich bin ihr hold,
und wenn — ich sollt groß Un - glück han,[2] da liegt nichts
dran; sie wird mich des — er - get - zen[3] mit
ih - rer Lieb und Treu an mir, die sie zu
mir will set - zen, und tun all mein — Be - gier.[4]

2 Sie trägt von Gold so rein ein' Kron,
da leuchten drin zwölf Sterne.
Ihr Kleid ist wie die Sonne schön;
das glänzet hell und ferne.[5]
Und auf dem Mon[6]
ihr' Füße stohn.[7]
Sie ist die Braut,
dem Herrn vertraut.[8]
Ihr ist weh und muß gebären
ein schönes Kind, den edlen Sohn
und aller Welt ein' Herren.
Dem ist sie unterton.[9]

3 Das tut dem alten Drachen Zorn;[10]
er will das Kind verschlingen.
Sein Toben ist doch ganz verlorn;[11]
es kann ihm nicht gelingen.

Das Kind ist doch
gen Himmel hoch
genommen hin
und lässet ihn
auf Erden gar sehr wüten.
Die Mutter muß gar sein allein;
doch will sie Gott behüten
und der recht Vater sein.

[1] besessen = *in Besitz genommen.*   [2] han = *haben.*   [3] *sie wird mich dafür entschädigen.*   [4] *mit ihrer Liebe und Treue mir gegenüber, die sie mir erzeigen will, und (sie wird) all mein Wünschen stillen.*   [5] ferne = *in die Ferne, weithin.*   [6] Mon = *Mond.*   [7] stohn = *stehen.*   [8] *dem Herrn angetraut.*   [9] unterton = *untertan.*   [10] tut = *verursacht.*   [11] *sein Toben ist jedoch völlig vergeblich.*

Auf seine Weise ist dies das originellste Lied Luthers, aber wir wissen nicht, wie er auf den Gedanken kam, so etwas zu schreiben. Als Lied für den Gottesdienst ist es bestimmt nicht gedacht. Die Form ist die der Hofweise, in diesem Fall auch in bezug auf den (jedenfalls in der ersten Strophe) kühl-formelhaften Text, der die weitere Absicht des Liedes zwar nicht verleugnet, aber vollkommen verhüllt. Die erste Strophe könnte einem Liebeslied angehören, doch ist weder dieser Text noch auch nur dieses Metrum sonst überliefert, so daß man den Gedanken an eine Kontrafaktur wohl fallenlassen und eine Luthersche Schöpfung vermuten muß. Offenbar wollte Luther seinem Verhältnis zur Kirche für einmal diese zunächst in die Form des Liebesliedes verschlüsselte und auch in den beiden folgenden Strophen durch die Verwendung des Bildes aus Offenbarung 12 verhüllende Form geben. Ob Luther mit diesem Lied auch einen Beitrag zu einer evangelischen Mariologie leisten wollte, muß eine offene Frage bleiben. Auf jeden Fall ist dieser Schriftabschnitt im Mittelalter vorwiegend auf Maria, von Luther aber stets auf die Kirche bezogen worden. Seiner Absicht nach steht das Lied den frühen Trostpsalmen für die angefochtene Kirche (24, 25, 28, 30) und dem Trostlied über Psalm 46 (26) von 1528 nahe. Was auch die Offenbarung will, das tut Luther mit diesem Lied: die angefochtene Kirche trösten.

Der Text wird für uns erstmals greifbar im Wittenberger Gesangbuch von 1535. Er hat dort weder eine Melodie noch eine Tonangabe. Erst das Leipziger Gesangbuch von 1545, das sich auch sonst in der Liedtradition selbständig und – auch musikalisch – gut informiert zeigt, weiß eine Singweise beizubringen (A). Eine zweite (B), die ebenfalls schon zu Luthers Lebzeiten geschaffen worden sein

muß, steht in einem Frankfurter Gesangbuch von 1565, dessen ver-
schollene erste Ausgabe schon 1544 erschienen ist. Daß nur eine der
beiden die Originalweise Luthers sein kann, ist klar. Aber welche?
Die größere Wahrscheinlichkeit liegt bei A.

36
Ein Kinderlied, zu singen wider die beiden Erzfeinde Christi
und seiner heiligen Kirche, den Papst und die Türken

2 Beweis dein Macht, Herr Jesus Christ,
 der du Herr aller Herren bist.
 Beschirm dein arme Christenheit,
 daß sie dich lob in Ewigkeit.

3 Gott Heilger Geist, du Tröster wert,
 gib dei'm Volk einrlei Sinn auf Erd.[3]
 Steh bei uns in der letzten Not.
 G'leit uns ins Leben aus dem Tod.

¹ steur' = wehre, gebiete Einhalt. ² Luther schreibt «wollten» und nicht «wollen»; das ist Optativ, nicht Indikativ, daher heute mit «möchten» wiederzugeben. Luther weiß: Sie möchten es, aber sie können es nicht. ³ einrlei Sinn = einerlei Gesinnung.

Wieder, wie 1529 (s. zu 34), rücken die Türken durch Ungarn vor. Suleiman II. besiegt im August 1541 bei Ofen Ferdinands Heer. Auf Veranlassung seines Kurfürsten läßt Luther am 11. Oktober die Vermahnung zum Gebet wider die Türken erscheinen. Im November vernimmt man, daß die Flotte Kaiser Karls V. bei Algier vernichtet wurde. Im Sommer 1542 schließt der König von Frankreich ein Bündnis mit dem türkischen Sultan gegen den deutschen Kaiser, und das Gerücht geht um, auch der Papst sei diesem Bündnis beigetreten. Wenn jemand den Türken etwas tun soll, so werden's die einfältigen Kinderchen tun, die das Vaterunser beten. Unser Wall und Büchsen und alle Fürsten, die werden den Türken wohl ungeschoren lassen. Das ist Luthers Überzeugung. Und so schreibt er dieses Kinderlied, zu singen wider die beiden Erzfeinde Christi und seiner heiligen Kirche, den Papst und die Türken. Wann das geschah, ist ungewiß. Ein heute nicht mehr nachweisbarer Einzeldruck aus dem Jahre 1542 wird 1735 beschrieben. 1543 steht das Lied dann im Wittenberger Gemeindegesangbuch. In sein Chorgesangbuch hat Walter es nie aufgenommen. Erst 1566 hat er als Siebzigjähriger mit einem großangelegten sechsteiligen Liedzyklus diesem Liede die nötige Nachachtung verschafft. Die Melodie kann nur von Luther selbst stammen. Nochmals greift er die Hymnus-Melodie Veni redemptor gentium (vgl. 1 und 30) auf. Die erste Zeile verläuft gleich wie bei dem Friedensgebet von 1529; sie wird aber durch das Herausheben der Betonung «Erhált» intensiver. Dasselbe gilt von der zweiten Zeile mit der Vorverlegung des Hochtons auf «deíner». Dann aber verläßt der Melodieschöpfer die Vorlage und weitet auf die entscheidenden Worte «Jesus Christus» den Umfang der Melodie nach oben aus bis zur Oktav des Grundtons.

Auch hier liegen – wie bei Nr. 30 – von Anfang an zwei Melodiefassungen vor. Im Wittenberger Gesangbuch steht die uns vertraute, jedoch in Choralnoten und ohne Dehnung der Zeilen-Anfangs- und -Schlußtöne (a), im Leipziger Gesangbuch von 1545 jedoch eine mensurierte mit einem in den mittleren beiden Zeilen abweichenden rhythmischen und melodischen Verlauf (b). Die Wittenberger Fassung dürfte die ursprüngliche sein.

37
Der Hymnus ‹O lux beata trinitas› verdeutscht

1 Der du bist___ drei ___ in Ei - nig - keit,[1]___
   ein wah - rer___ Gott___ von E - wig - keit: ___

Die Sonn mit dem___ Tag___ von uns ___ weicht;

laß leuch - - - ten uns dein gött - lich Licht.

1 Der du___ bist drei in Ei - nig -keit,[1]   Die Sonn mit dem Tag
   ein wah - rer Gott von E - wig -keit:

von uns weicht; laß leuch - ten uns dein gött - lich Licht.

2 Des morgens, Gott, dich loben wir,
   des abends auch beten vor dir.
      Unser armes Lied rühmet dich
      jetzund, immer und ewiglich.

3 Gott Vater, dem sei ewig Ehr,
   Gott Sohn, der ist der einig Herr,[2]
      und dem Tröster Heiligen Geist
      von nun an bis in Ewigkeit.
      Amen.

[1] Einigkeit = *Einheit (unitas).*   [2] einig = *alleinige (unicus).*

*Daraus, daß dieses Lied in der ältesten Quelle, dem Wittenberger
Gesangbuch von 1543, nicht unter den Liedern Luthers steht, son-*
dern unter den Geistlichen Liedern, von Christen gemacht, die vor
unserer Zeit gewesen sind, *schließt man, es sei kurz vor oder sogar*

während der Drucklegung dieser Auflage von Luthers Gesangbuch entstanden und ihm nachträglich noch angefügt worden. Das ist möglich, aber nicht zwingend. Wäre diese Annahme richtig, so wäre dies das letzte der unter Luthers Namen überlieferten Lieder.

Es handelt sich um die (mit Ausnahme der 2. Zeile) wörtliche Übersetzung des Vesper-Hymnus O lux beata Trinitas aus dem 5. Jahrhundert. Es trifft sich gut, daß der Reigen der eigentlichen Liedschöpfungen Luthers sich mit diesem Abendlied und der Bearbeitung eines Bestattungsliedes (45) schließt. Das demütige Bekenntnis Unser armes Lied rühmet dich mag wie eine Schlußschrift unter Luthers Liedschaffen erscheinen und kommt so auf besondere Weise zum Leuchten. Nur dürfen solche Beobachtungen nicht als historische Auskünfte über Anlaß, Absicht und Ziel der Entstehung dieses vielleicht spätesten Lutherliedes genommen werden. Darüber wissen wir nichts, ebensowenig wie über die Gründe für das Fehlen einer Melodie. Zwanzig Jahre früher hätte Luther doch wohl der Übersetzung eines lateinischen Hymnus auch die gemeindegemäße Übertragung seiner Melodie beigegeben. Hier setzt er offenbar voraus, daß man den deutschen Text auf die überlieferte Choralweise singt. In Leipzig (a) wie in Straßburg (b) hat man denn auch 1545 dem Text diese alte Weise beigedruckt, je in etwas verschiedener Bearbeitung.

Soweit die mit Luthers Namen gezeichneten Beiträge zu seinem Gesangbuch! In zwei Fällen schon 1529, in zwei weiteren seit 1533 finden wir darin jedoch noch weitere Gesänge, denen er die vorliegende textliche und musikalische Gestalt gegeben haben muß. Zudem werden drei der vier weiteren Abteilungen des Gesangbuchs mit Einleitungen eröffnet, die offensichtlich von Luther verfaßt sind und die – gewissermaßen als Fortsetzung der Vorrede – seine Absichten bei der Gestaltung dieses Werkes deutlich hervortreten lassen.

Auf die erste Abteilung mit seinen eigenen Liedern läßt er unter dem Titel Andere der Unsern Lieder in der Erstausgabe von 1529 acht Lieder von Autoren aus seinem Freundeskreis folgen: Wo Gott, der Herr, nicht bei uns hält (Justus Jonas), Fröhlich wollen wir Halleluja singen (Johannes Agricola), Erbarm dich mein, o Herre Gott (Erhard Hegenwald), Es ist das Heil uns kommen her (Paulus Speratus), Durch Adams Fall ist ganz verderbt (Lazarus Spengler), Herr Christ, der einig Gotts Sohn (Elisabeth Cruciger), Hilf, Gott, wie ist des Menschen Not und In Gott gelaub ich, daß er hat (Paulus Speratus).

Daran schließt sich eine dritte Abteilung an, aus der wir Nr. 38 wie-
dergeben. Dieser Teil wird von Luther folgendermaßen eingeleitet:

Die alten Lieder, die hier folgen, haben wir mit aufgenommen als
das Zeugnis einiger frommer Christen, die vor uns gelebt haben in
der großen Finsternis der falschen Lehre, damit man deutlich erkennen möge, wie dennoch zu allen Zeiten Leute gewesen sind, die
Christus recht erkannt haben und trotz allem wunderbarerweise in
dieser Erkenntnis durch Gottes Gnade erhalten wurden.

Es handelt sich um die Weihnachts-Cantio Dies est laetitiae, *ihre*
deutsche Fassung Der Tag, der ist so freudenreich *(mit der von Lu-*
ther besonders hochgeschätzten Strophe Ein Kindelein so löbelich),
die lateinisch-deutsche Weihnachts-Cantio In dulci jubilo, *eine Neu-*
fassung der Oster-Leise Christ ist erstanden *(hier Nr. 38), das Abend-*
lied Christe, der du bist Tag und Licht *(Übersetzung des Vesperhym-*
nus Christe qui lux es et dies) *und schließlich Adam von Fuldas* Ach
hilf mich Leid und sehnlich Klag *in einer evangelischen Umarbei-*
tung.

38
Christ ist erstanden

1 Christ ist er - stan - den[1] von der Mar - ter al - le; des
sol-len wir al - le froh __ sein.[2] Christ will un - ser
Trost sein.[3] Ky - ri - e - leis. Wär er nicht er - stan - den,[1] die
Welt, die wär ver - gan - gen; seit daß er er - stan-den ist, so
lobn wir den Va - ter Je - su Christ. Ky - ri - e - leis.

Hal - le - lu - ja, Hal - le - lu - ja,

Hal - le - lu - ja. Des sol-len wir al - le froh__sein.

Christ will un - ser Trost[3]__ sein. Ky - ri - e - leis.

[1] erstanden = auferstanden.   [2] des = darüber.   [3] Trost = Helfer.

Von allen mittelalterlichen Leisen ist dies die am weitesten verbreitete und wohl auch eine der ältesten. Sie ist seit dem 12. Jahrhundert belegt, und Luther hat sie schon 1523 in seiner Osterpredigt erwähnt. Seit 1531 kommt sie dann in den Nachschriften Lutherscher Predigten häufiger vor. Offenbar hat Luther eingesehen, daß sein Osterlied (8) die Leise an volkstümlicher Prägnanz nicht erreicht und sie deshalb nicht ersetzen kann. Er hat sie deshalb in den evangelischen Kirchengesang eingeführt, und zwar – im Gegensatz zu den anderen von ihm übernommenen Leisen – ohne ihr weitere Strophen anzufügen. Dreistrophig war sie ja schon seit dem 15. Jahrhundert, und was er zu Ostern zu sagen hatte, war in dem Osterlied von 1524 bereits gesagt.

Die hier vorliegende Fassung von Text und Melodie kommt in der reichen mittelalterlichen Überlieferung dieser Leise ebenso wenig vor wie bei Johann Walter, der die Osterleise fünfmal vertont hat, weshalb wir allen Grund haben, sie Luther zuzuschreiben.

In der vierten Abteilung seines Gesangbuches bringt Luther die Lieder O Gott Vater, du hast Gewalt *(Hans Sachs),* Capitan, Herr Gott, Vater mein *und* Genad mir, Herr, ewiger Gott *(Herzog Albrecht von Preußen),* O Herre Gott, dein göttlich Wort *(Anarg, Herr zu Wildenfels),* Hilf Gott, wie geht es immer zu *(Andreas Knöppgen),* Wo Gott zum Haus nicht gibt sein Gunst *(Johannes Kolroß?),* Ich ruf zu dir, Herr Jesu Christ *(Johannes Agricola) und* Mag ich Unglück nicht widerstahn *(Herzog Albrecht von Preußen). Luther leitet diese Abteilung unter Hinweis auf seine neue Vorrede (s. S. 40 f.) folgendermaßen ein:*

Es sind auch von anderen Zeitgenossen geistliche Lieder gemacht worden. Weil sie aber sehr zahlreich sind und der größere Teil davon nicht besonders viel taugt, habe ich sie nicht alle in unser Gesangbüchlein übernehmen wollen, sondern habe die besten darunter herausgesucht und füge sie hier an. Was mich aber dazu veranlaßt hat, darüber wird dich die neue Vorrede belehren.

Der fünfte und letzte Teil des Gesangbuches bringt die Cantica. Daraus muß hier das Benedictus (41) mitgeteilt werden. Noch vorher aber geben wir zwei psalmodische Stücke wieder, die Luther in die Neuausgabe seines Gesangbuches von 1533 eingefügt hat (39, 40). Deren zweites steht dort ebenfalls im Cantica-Teil, dessen Einleitung Luther so formuliert hat:

Wir haben auch – als gute Vorbilder – in dieses Büchlein aufgenommen die heiligen Lieder aus der Heiligen Schrift, welche die lieben Patriarchen und Propheten gemacht und gesungen haben, damit wir nicht nur als neue Meister betrachtet werden in dieser Arbeit, sondern auch vor uns das Beispiel aller Heiligen vorweisen können. So wird jeder Christ ohne Mühe erkennen, wie sie – gleich wie wir es tun – auch allein Gottes Gnade und nicht Menschenwerk preisen. Sie aber wird man nicht dermaßen zu verdammen sich getrauen wie uns, wenn man sie auch ebensosehr verachtet wie uns.

Vor allem aber deshalb, weil wir diese Lieder oder Psalmen mit Ernst und Andacht, mit Herz und Verständnis gesungen haben möchten, nicht wie man sie in den Stiften und Klöstern in großem Mißbrauch und großer Abgötterei noch heutigen Tages blökt und heult und dabei nichts versteht noch zu verstehen willig oder bemüht ist, geschweige daß man mit Andacht oder Gewinn sänge, weshalb denn auch Gott damit mehr erzürnt als versöhnt wird.

39
Der 111. Psalm
zu singen, wenn man das Sakrament empfängt

Ich danke dem Herrn von ganzem Herzen   im Rat der From-men

151

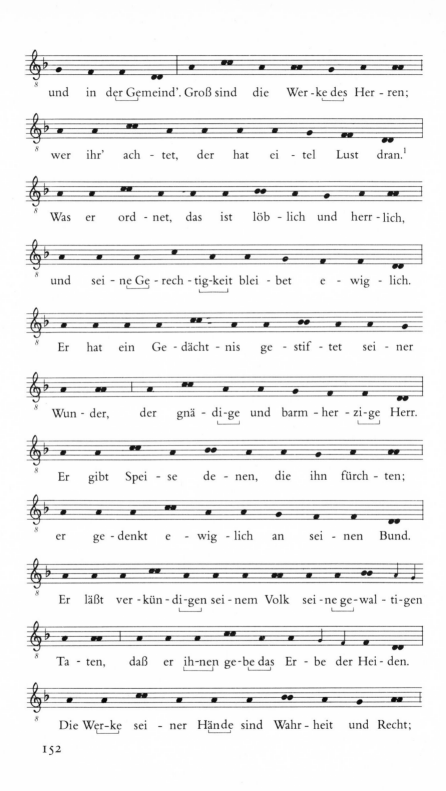

und in der Gemeind'. Groß sind die Wer-ke des Her-ren;

wer ihr' ach-tet, der hat ei-tel Lust dran.[1]

Was er ord-net, das ist löb-lich und herr-lich,

und sei-ne Ge-rech-tig-keit blei-bet e-wig-lich.

Er hat ein Ge-dächt-nis ge-stif-tet sei-ner

Wun-der, der gnä-di-ge und barm-her-zi-ge Herr.

Er gibt Spei-se de-nen, die ihn fürch-ten;

er ge-denkt e-wig-lich an sei-nen Bund.

Er läßt ver-kün-di-gen sei-nem Volk sei-ne ge-wal-ti-gen

Ta-ten, daß er ih-nen ge-be das Er-be der Hei-den.

Die Wer-ke sei-ner Hän-de sind Wahr-heit und Recht;

152

al – le sei – ne Ge – bo – te sind recht – schaf – fen.

Sie wer – den er – hal – ten im – mer und e – wig – lich

und ge – sche – hen treu – lich und red – lich.

Er sen – det Er – lö – sung sei – nem Volk;

er ver – heißt, daß sein Bund e – wig – lich blei – ben soll.

Sein Na – me ist hei – lig und hehr. Die Furcht

des Her – ren ist der Weis – heit An – fang.

Das ist ei – ne fei – ne Klug – heit; wer dar-

nach tut, des Lob blei – bet e – wig – lich.

Lob und Preis sei Gott dem Va – ter

und dem Sohn und dem Hei – li – gen Geist,

wie es war von An - fang, jetzt und im - mer - dar

und von E - wig - keit zu E - wig - keit.

A - - - - - - men.

[1] *wer sie in Ehren hält.*

In der Einleitung zu seiner Auslegung dieses Psalms vom Jahre 1530 sagt Luther, er habe ein Abendmahlslied schreiben wollen. Aber es sei ihm nicht gelungen und da habe er sich gesagt, es sei ja auch nicht nötig, denn der Heilige Geist habe doch bereits viel bessere Lieder gemacht: die Psalmen. Und so legt er diesen Psalm aus. In der nächsten erhaltenen Ausgabe seines Gesangbuches – es ist die von 1533 – erscheint denn auch im Anschluß an die Abendmahlslieder im Katechismus-Teil dieser Psalm nicht als Lied, sondern als Gemeindepsalmodie zur Kommunion. Der Text ist derjenige der Psalmenübersetzung von 1533. Und in Anlehnung an die lateinische mittelalterliche Psalmodie-Tradition schafft Luther hier ein rein syllabisches Psalmodie-Modell, das er jedoch zwecks leichterer Ausführbarkeit durch die Gemeinde wie eine komponierte Melodie ausschreibt. So war Luther nicht gezwungen, die allereinfachste Möglichkeit zu wählen, sondern er konnte den ersten Halbvers zweiakzentig gestalten. Als Psalmton wählte er den ersten, den auch für das Kyrie (43) und das Agnus Dei (44) verwendeten. Auf eine Antiphon hat Luther verzichtet. Hingegen hat er das «Amen» entgegen sonstigem Brauch nicht als Bestandteil des letzten Verses aufgefaßt, sondern dafür einen eigenen Melodieteil geschaffen.

40

Der 117. Psalm
zu singen, um Gott zu danken für das Evangelium und Reich Christi

Lo - bet den Her - ren, al - le Hei - den. Prei - set ihn,

al - le Völ - ker. Denn sei - ne Gnad und Wahr - heit

wal - tet ü - ber uns in E - wig - keit. Lob und Preis sei

Gott dem Va - ter und dem Sohn und dem Hei - li - gen Geist,

wie es war von An - fang, jetzt und im - mer - dar und von

E - wig - keit zu E - wig - keit. A - men. Lo - bet den

Her - ren, al - le Hei - den. Prei - set ihn, al - le Völ - ker.

Denn sei - ne Gnad und Wahr - heit wal - tet

ü - ber uns in E - wig - keit. Hal - le - lu - ja.

Diese psalmodische Vertonung des 117. Psalms ist gleichzeitig mit Nr. 39 in Luthers Gesangbuch aufgenommen worden. Ist jene für

den Sakraments-Gottesdienst bestimmt, so diese für den Wortgottes-
dienst. Eingereiht wurde sie etwas unglücklich im fünften Teil des
Gesangbuchs zwischen den alt- und den neutestamentlichen Cantica.
Luther wählt in diesem Fall eine Variante des dritten Psalmtons. Das
Amen ist in den zweiten Vers des Gloria patri einbezogen. Eine Antiphon gibt Luther auch hier dem Psalm nicht bei, hingegen folgt auf
das Gloria patri nochmals der Psalm in einer freien Vertonung, abge-
schlossen mit «Halleluja». Im letzten Halbvers verwendet Luther zur
Heraushebung der vier wichtigsten Textsilben die Tristropha, eine
seltene chorale Notenform, die eine gegenüber dem Grundwert etwa
dreifache Dauer des betreffenden Tons anzeigt. Der Text hat auch
hier die Fassung des Psalters von 1533.

41
Der Lobgesang des Zacharias,
des Vaters Johannes des Täufers, daraus lerne, nach seinem
Vorbild Gott dankbar zu sein
für sein heiliges wertes Evangelium etc.

und hat aufgerichtet ein Horn des Heils
    im Haus seines Dieners David,
wie er vorzeiten geredet hat
    durch den Mund seiner heiligen Propheten.
Daß er uns errettete von unsern Feinden
    und von der Hand aller, die uns hassen,
und die Barmherzigkeit erzeigte unsern Vätern
    und gedächte an seinen heiligen Bund
und an den Eid, den er geschworen hat unserm Vater Abraham,
    uns zu geben,
daß wir, erlöst aus der Hand unsrer Feinde,
    ihm dienten ohne Furcht unser Leben lang
in Heiligkeit und Gerechtigkeit,
    die ihm gefällig ist.

Und du, Kindlein, wirst ein Prophet des Höchsten heißen;
du wirst vor deinem Herrn hergehen, daß du seinen Weg bereitest
und Erkenntnis des Heils gebest seinem Volk,
die da ist in der Vergebung ihrer Sünden,
durch die herzliche Barmherzigkeit unseres Gottes,
durch welche uns besucht hat der Aufgang aus der Höhe,
auf daß er erscheine denen, die da sitzen in Finsternis und Schatten des Todes,
und richte unsere Füße auf den Weg des Friedens.
Lob und Ehr sei Gott, dem Vater, und dem Sohn
und dem Heiligen Geist,
wie es war von Anfang, jetzt und immerdar
und von Ewigkeit zu Ewigkeit. Amen.

Ge - lo - bet sei der Herr, der Gott Is - ra - els,

denn er hat be - sucht und er - lö - set sein Volk.

In seiner ursprünglichen Gestalt von 1529 enthielt Luthers Gesangbuch elf alttestamentliche und die vier neutestamentlichen Cantica. 1533 sind diese Cantica mit 9 vierstimmigen Psalmodie-Modellen Johann Walters versehen, die 1529 noch fehlten. So fielen beim Magnificat und beim Nunc dimittis die Psalmodie-Modelle, die Luther wahrscheinlich dafür geschaffen hatte, dahin. Einzig der für die Mette bestimmte Lobgesang des Zacharias (Lukas 1,68–79) erhielt kein vierstimmiges Psalmodie-Modell, und so blieb hier das ohne Zweifel von Luther bearbeitete einstimmige Modell im 7. Psalmton stehen.

Auch hier verzichtet Luther auf eine Antiphon, beschließt aber das Ganze nach dem Gloria patri mit einer Wiederholung des ersten Verses mit einer neuen, frei komponierten Melodie.

Vorrede auf alle guten Gesangbücher
1538

Frau Musica *[spricht]:*

Vor allen Freuden auf Erden
kann niemandem eine schönere werden,
denn die ich geb mit mei'm Singen
und mit manchem süßen Klingen.
Hier kann nicht sein ein böser Mut,[1]
wo da singen Gesellen gut.[2]
Hier bleibt kein Zorn, Zank, Haß noch Neid;
weichen muß alles Herzeleid.
Geiz, Sorg und was sonst hart anleit[3]
fährt hin mit aller Traurigkeit.[4]
Auch ist ein jeder des wohl frei,[5]
daß solche Freud kein Sünde sei,
sondern auch Gott viel besser gefällt
denn alle Freud der ganzen Welt.
Dem Teufel sie sein Werk zerstört
und verhindert viel böser Mörd.
Das bezeugt Davids, des Königs, Tat,
der dem Saul oft gewehret hat
mit gutem, süßem Harfenspiel,
daß er in großen Mord nicht fiel.
Zum göttlichen Wort und Wahrheit
macht sie das Herz still und bereit.
Solchs hat Elisäus bekannt,[6]
da er den Geist durchs Harfen fand.[7]
Die beste Zeit im Jahr ist mein;[8]
da singen alle Vögelein.
Himmel und Erde ist der voll;[9]
viel gut Gesang da lautet wohl.
Voran die liebe Nachtigall
macht alles fröhlich überall
mit ihrem lieblichen Gesang.
Des muß sie haben immer Dank.[10]
Viel mehr der liebe Herre Gott,
der sie also geschaffen hat,
zu sein die rechte Sängerin,
der Musica ein' Meisterin.

Dem singt und springt sie Tag und Nacht;
seins Lobes sie nichts müde macht.
Den ehrt und lobt auch mein Gesang
und sagt ihm einen ewigen Dank.

[1] *Mut = Gemüt, Sinn.* [2] *Gesellen = Kameraden.* [3] *anleit = anliegt, bedrängt.*
[4] *fährt hin = verschwindet.* [5] *des wohl frei = darin ganz unbehindert, also:*
völlig im Recht, zu behaupten, daß. [6] *Elisäus = Elisa (2. Könige 3, 15).* [7] *durchs*
Harfen = durchs Harfenspiel. [8] *ist mein = gehört mir, der Frau Musica (und*
nicht etwa = ist Mai'n = Maien, wie man gelegentlich in Liederbüchern liest).
[9] *der = deren = davon.* [10] *des = dafür.*

Dieses Gedicht Luthers wird für uns erstmals 1538 greifbar als Vor-
wort zu einer Schrift ähnlicher Form und ähnlichen Inhalts von Jo-
hann Walter, betitelt: Lob und Preis der löblichen Kunst Musica. *Es*
ist unwahrscheinlich, daß Luther diese Verse für diese Schrift Walters
verfaßte, sonst würden Walter oder sein Drucker mit Stolz auf dem
Titelblatt diese Tatsache vermerkt haben. Viel eher wird man anneh-
men dürfen, daß dieses Gedicht schon vor 1543, wo wir es dann im
Klugschen Wittenberger Gesangbuch ganz am Schluß, vor dem Re-
gister, finden, schon in einer verschollenen Ausgabe dieses Gesang-
buches stand, die zwischen 1535 und 1538 erschienen sein muß.

Christliche Gesänge, lateinisch und deutsch, zum Begräbnis
1542

Dem christlichen Leser
D. Martin Luther

St. Paulus schreibt denen zu Thessalonich (1. Thess. 4, 13), daß sie über die Toten nicht betrübt sein sollen wie die andern, die keine Hoffnung haben, sondern sich trösten sollen durch Gottes Wort, als solche, die sichere Hoffnung haben auf das Leben und die Auferstehung der Toten.

Denn daß die betrübt sind, die keine Hoffnung haben, ist nicht verwunderlich, ist ihnen auch nicht zu verdenken, da sie doch dem Glauben an Christus fernstehen und entweder allein dieses zeitliche Leben schätzen und lieb haben müssen und es ungern verlieren oder nach diesem Leben den ewigen Tod und den Zorn Gottes in der Hölle erwarten müssen und ungern darauf zugehen.

Wir Christen aber, die wir von dem allem durch das kostbare Blut des Sohnes Gottes erlöst sind, sollen uns üben und gewöhnen im Glauben, den Tod zu verachten und als einen tiefen, starken, süßen Schlaf anzusehen, den Sarg nicht anders denn als unseres Herrn Christi Schoß oder Paradies, das Grab für nichts anderes als einen weichen Pfuhl oder Ruhebett zu halten. So ist es ja vor Gott in Wahrheit, wie er spricht (Joh. 11, 11): «Lazarus, unser Freund, schläft.» Und Matthäus 9, 24: «Das Mädchen ist nicht tot, sondern es schläft.»

So hält es auch St. Paulus im 1. Korinther 15: Er rückt aus unseren Augen alle häßlichen Gestalten des Todes in unserem sterblichen Leibe und zeigt uns lauter holdselige und tröstliche Gestalten des Lebens, wenn er spricht (1. Kor. 15, 42–44): «Es wird gesät verweslich und wird auferstehen unverweslich. Es wird gesät in Unehre (das heißt: in häßlicher, schandbarer Gestalt) und wird auferstehen in Herrlichkeit. Es wird gesät in Schwachheit und wird auferstehen in Kraft. Es wird gesät ein natürlicher Leib und wird auferstehen ein geistlicher Leib.»

Darum haben wir in unseren Kirchen die päpstlichen Greuel wie Vigilien, Seelenmessen, Jahrtage, Fegefeuer und alles andere Gaukelwerk, das für die Toten getrieben wird, abgeschafft und gänzlich ausgeräumt und wollen unsere Kirchen nicht mehr Klagehäuser und Leidstätten sein lassen, sondern, wie auch die alten Kirchenväter sie genannt hatten: Koemiteria, das heißt: für Schlafhäuser und Ruhestätten halten.

Wir singen auch weder Trauerlieder noch Klagegesänge bei unseren Toten, sondern tröstliche Lieder von Vergebung der Sünden, von Ruhe, Schlaf, Leben, Auferstehung der verstorbenen Christen, womit unser Glaube gestärkt und die Leute zu rechter Andacht ermuntert werden.

Denn es ist auch billig und recht, daß man das Begräbnis würdig begehe und durchführe, zu Lob und Ehren dem tröstlichen Artikel unseres Glaubensbekenntnisses, nämlich von der Auferstehung der Toten, und zum Trotz dem schrecklichen Feinde, dem Tode, der uns so schändlich dahinfrißt ohne Unterlaß in allerlei scheußlicher Gestalt und Weise.

So haben (wie wir lesen) die heiligen Patriarchen, Abraham, Isaak, Jakob, Joseph usw., ihr Begräbnis herrlich begangen und mit großem Eifer angeordnet. Hernach haben die Könige von Juda großes Gepränge getrieben über den Leichen mit köstlichem Räucherwerk von allerlei gutem, edlem Gewürz, alles, um den stinkenden, schändlichen Tod zu dämpfen und die Auferstehung der Toten zu preisen und zu bekennen, um damit die Schwachgläubigen und Traurigen zu trösten.

Dazu gehört auch, was die Christen bisher getan haben und heute noch tun an den Leichen und Gräbern: daß man sie herrlich trägt, schmückt, besingt und mit Grabzeichen ziert. Es geht alles um den einen Artikel von der Auferstehung, daß er fest in uns gegründet werde, denn er ist unser dauernder, seliger, ewiger Trost und unsere Freude wider Tod, Hölle, Teufel und alle Traurigkeit.

Zudem haben wir auch, als gute Beispiele, die schönen Musikstücke oder Gesänge, die im Papsttum in Vigilien, in Seelenmessen und beim Begräbnis gebraucht werden, genommen, davon einige in dies Büchlein drucken lassen und wollen mit der Zeit davon weitere übernehmen (oder wer es besser kann als wir). Doch haben wir andere Texte daruntergesetzt, um damit unseren Artikel von der Auferstehung zu schmücken, nicht das Fegefeuer mit seiner Strafe und Genugtuung, deretwegen ihre Verstorbenen nicht schlafen und ruhen können. Der Gesang und die Noten sind köstlich; schade wäre es, wenn sie untergehen sollten. Aber unchristlich und ungereimt sind die Texte oder Worte; die sollten untergehen.

Gleichwie auch in allen anderen Stücken sind sie uns hier weit voraus, haben die schönsten Gottesdienste, schöne, herrliche Stifte und Klöster. Aber das Predigen und Lehren, das sie darin treiben, dient zum größeren Teil dem Teufel und lästert Gott. Denn er [der

Teufel] ist der Welt Fürst und Gott; darum muß er auch das Edelste, Beste und Schönste haben.

Auch haben sie köstliche goldene und silberne Monstranzen und Bilder, geziert mit Kleinoden und Edelsteinen. Aber darin sind Totengebeine vom Schindanger und anderswoher. Weiter haben sie köstliche Kirchenkleider, Kaseln, Mäntel, Röcke, Hüte, Infuln. Aber wer ist darunter oder damit bekleidet? Faule Bäuche, böse Wölfe, gottlose Säue, die Gottes Wort verfolgen und lästern.

So haben sie auch wahrlich viel treffliche, schöne Musik oder Gesänge, besonders in den Stiften und Pfarren, aber viele unsaubere, abgöttische Texte damit geziert. Darum haben wir solche abgöttischen, toten und tollen Texte entkleidet, ihnen die schöne Musik abgestreift und sie dem lebendigen, heiligen Gotteswort angezogen, es damit zu singen, zu loben und zu ehren, damit so dieser schöne Schmuck der Musik in rechtem Gebrauch ihrem lieben Schöpfer und seinen Christen diene, so daß er gelobt und geehrt, wir aber durch sein heiliges Wort, welches mit süßem Gesang ins Herz dringt, gebessert und im Glauben gestärkt werden. Das helfe uns Gott der Vater mit dem Sohn und dem Heiligen Geist. Amen.

Doch ist nicht dies unsere Meinung, daß diese Noten genau so in allen Kirchen gesungen werden müßten. Eine jede Kirche behalte ihre Noten nach ihrem Buch und Brauch. Denn ich selbst höre es auch nicht gerne, wenn in einem Responsorium oder einem anderen Gesang die Noten geändert sind und sie anders gesungen werden bei uns als ich es aus meiner Jugend gewöhnt bin. Es geht um die Veränderung des Textes und nicht der Noten.

Wenn man ferner auch die Gräber ehren möchte, wäre es schön, an die Wände über den Gräbern gute Epitaphe oder Sprüche aus der Schrift zu malen oder zu schreiben, damit sie denen vor Augen sind, die zur Bestattung oder auf den Kirchhof gehen.[1] Solche Sprüche und Grabschriften würden die Kirchhöfe besser zieren als andere, weltliche Zeichen wie Wappen, Helme usw.[2] Wo aber jemand begabt und

[1] *Luther führt hier die folgenden 23 Bibelstellen im Wortlaut an: 1.Mose 25,8 (und öfter); Hiob 19,25–27; Psalm 3,6; Psalm 4,9; Psalm 17,15; Psalm 49,16; Psalm 116,15; Jesaja 25,7.8; Jesaja 26,19; Jesaja 26,20; Jesaja 57,1.2; Ezechiel 37,12.13; Daniel 12,2; Hosea 13,14; Matthäus 22,32; Johannes 6,39; Johannes 11,25.26; Römer 14,7–9; 1.Korinther 15,19; 1.Korinther 15,22; 1.Korinther 15,55–57; Philipper 1,21; 1.Thessalonicher 4,14.* [2] *Wahrscheinlich nur aus drucktechnischen Gründen sind schon an dieser Stelle die Gesänge eingeschoben, nämlich 7 lateinische Prosagesänge mit Choralnoten, das lateinische Bestattungslied* Iam maesta quiesce querela *des Prudentius mit einer möglicherweise von Luther geschaffenen*

bereit wäre, solche Sprüche in gute, schöne Verse zu bringen, so würde das dazu dienen, daß sie um so leichter behalten und um so lieber gelesen würden. Denn Reime oder Verse ergeben gute Merk- oder Sprichwörter, die man lieber gebraucht als die schlichte Rede-weise.[3]

Lukas 2,29–32

Im Fried' bin ich dahingefahrn,
denn mein' Augen gesehen han
dein' Heiland, Herr, von dir bereit'
zum Licht der ganzen Christenheit.
Indes ruh ich in dieser Gruft
bis auf meins Herren Wiederkunft.

Lukas 2,29–32

Mit Fried und Freud in guter Ruh
getrost tat ich mein' Augen zu
und legt mich schlafen in mein Grab,
weil ich dein' Heiland gsehen hab,
den du für uns all hast bereit'
zu Heil der ganzen Christenheit,
daß er das ewig Licht sollt sein
den Heiden zum seligen Schein
und daß auch Israel darob
hab Herrlichkeit und ewigs Lob.

Johannes 11,25.26

Christ ist die Wahrheit und das Leben;
die Auferstehung will er geben.
Wer an ihn glaubt, das Leb'n erwirbt,
ob er gleich hie auch leiblich stirbt.
Wer lebt und glaubt, gibt ihm die Ehr,
wird gwißlich sterben nimmermehr.

Hiob 19,25–27

In mei'm Elend war dies mein Trost:
Ich sprach: Es lebt, der mich erlöst.
Auf den ich in der Not vertraut,
wird mich wieder mit meiner Haut

Melodie, die Nrn. 30, 16, 17, 7, 42 und 12 der vorliegenden Ausgabe (mit Noten)
und schließlich nochmals vier lateinische Prosagesänge mit Choralnoten, darunter
das Media vita *(vgl. Nr. 16).* [3] *Was folgt, sind Beispiele von Luthers Hand.*

umgeben, daß ich aus der Erd
vom Tod wieder erwecket werd.
In meinem Fleisch werd ich Gott sehen.
Ist gwißlich wahr, und wird geschehen.

Die deutschen Gesänge «Mit Fried und Freud ich fahr dahin», «Wir glauben all an einen Gott», «Nun bitten wir den Heiligen Geist», «Nun laßt uns den Leib begraben» usw. kann man einen nach dem andern singen, wenn man vom Begräbnis heimgeht. So mag man es auch mit den lateinischen Gesängen halten: «Iam maesta quiesce querela», «Si enim credimus», «Corpora sanctorum», «In pace sumus» usw.

Eines der letzten Werke Luthers zur kirchlichen Praxis sind seine lateinischen und deutschen Begräbnisgesänge von 1542. Das Ganze ist nicht nur ein Gesangbuch zur Bestattung, denn diese Einleitung dazu ist ein bemerkenswerter Beitrag zu einem evangelischen Bestattungswesen überhaupt. Das Interessanteste an dem Werk und eine Arbeit Luthers, der bisher überhaupt keine Beachtung geschenkt wurde, sind die voranstehenden sieben Bearbeitungen lateinischer Bestattungs-Responsorien. Doch können uns diese hier nicht beschäftigen. Und die fünf aus dem Gesangbuch bekannten Lieder Luthers (30, 16, 17, 7, 12), die hier mit Text und Melodie abgedruckt sind, bringen nichts Neues. Das Werk ist jedoch, abgesehen von seiner Vorrede, die mit unter Luthers Gesangbuch-Vorreden zählt, hier auch zu nennen als Quelle für das Lied Nr. 42, das (abgesehen von einem lateinischen) einzige eigentliche Bestattungslied in diesem Singheft.

42
Nun laßt uns den Leib begraben
Ein geistlich Lied zum Begräbnis der Verstorbenen

A

1 Nun laßt uns den Leib be - gra - ben, da - ran gar
kein Zwei - fel ha - ben, er werd am jüng - sten

Tag auf-stehn und un - ver - wes -lich her - vor -gehn.

B

1 Nun laßt uns den Leib be - gra - ben, da - ran gar

kein Zwei-fel ha - ben, er werd am jüng - sten Tag

auf - stehn und un - ver - wes - lich her - vor - gehn.

2 Erd ist er und von der Erden,
wird auch zu Erd wieder werden
und von der Erd wieder aufstehn,
wenn Gottes Posaun wird angehn.

3 Seine Seel lebt ewig in Gott,
der sie allhier aus lauter Gnad
von aller Sünd und Missetat
durch seinen Sohn erlöset hat.

4 Sein Arbeit, Trübsal und Elend[1]
ist kommen zu ei'm selgen End.
Er hat getragen Christi Joch,
ist gstorben und lebet doch noch.

5 Die Seele lebt ohn alle Klag,
der Leib schläft bis an Jüngsten Tag,
an welchem Gott ihn verklären
und ewger Freud wird gewähren.

6 Hier ist er in Angst gewesen,
dort aber wird er genesen,
in herrlicher Freud und Wonne
leuchten wie die helle Sonne.

7 Nun lassen wir ihn hier schlafen
und gehn allsamt unsre Straßen,
schicken uns auch mit allem Fleiß,[2]
denn der Tod kommt uns gleicherweis.

8 Das helf uns Christus, unser Trost,
der uns durch sein Blut hat erlöst
von's Teufels Gwalt und ewger Pein.
Ihm sei Lob, Preis und Ehr allein.

Amen.

[1] *Elend = Fremde, Fremdlingschaft.* [2] *schicken = sich bereitmachen.*

Dieses Begräbnislied wird in seiner authentischen Text- und Melodiequelle, Luthers Begräbnisgesängen von 1542, ausdrücklich als Werk Luthers bezeichnet. Dasselbe gilt vom Leipziger Gesangbuch Valentin Bapsts von 1545, welches die Begräbnisgesänge samt der Einleitung (nur unter Weglassung der bereits im Gesangbuch stehenden Lieder) in vollem Umfang integriert hat. Nun hat aber Luther gerade am Schluß der Vorrede zum genannten Leipziger Gesangbuch seine Autorschaft an diesem Lied unter Hinweis auf den eigentlichen Autor bestritten (s. S. 171). Und er hat damit insofern Recht, als dem Liede tatsächlich ein Bestattungslied von Michael Weiße aus dem ersten deutschen Gesangbuch der Böhmischen Brüder von 1531 zugrunde liegt. Der Text Weißes ist leicht überarbeitet und um eine neue Schluß-Strophe erweitert. Luther war insofern also berechtigt, seinen Namen dazuzusetzen, aber er ist offenbar des Plagiats bezichtigt worden und hat wohl aus diesem Grunde darum gebeten, seinen Namen bei dem Lied zu streichen. Wenn wir diesen Sachverhalt kennen, werden wir das Lied als Bearbeitung durch Luther unter den Werken des Reformators ohne weiteres aufführen dürfen. Im Wittenberger Gesangbuch ist es 1543, als Nachtrag, an letzter Stelle hinter den Cantica abgedruckt worden.

Die erst in der Schlußzeile als mixolydisch erkennbare Melodie A dürfte von Luther stammen, während die melodisch wie rhythmisch merkwürdig unsangliche Weise B aus dem Leipziger Gesangbuch von 1542 zwar gleichzeitig mit der Melodie A auftaucht und 1545 dann auch in das Bapstsche Gesangbuch übernommen wurde, aber nicht den Eindruck macht, als hätte man das Lied je so gesungen. Wahrscheinlich verdankt diese Melodie ihr Dasein in dieser Form irgendeinem Versehen.

Die folgenden drei Stücke sind in keiner Ausgabe des Wittenberger Gesangbuches anzutreffen. Daß sie dennoch von Luther stammen, ist im ersten Fall so gut wie sicher, im zweiten wahrscheinlich und im dritten möglich.

43
Kyrie eleison

In der Deutschen Messe Luthers von 1526 steht außer dem Sanctus (31) auch ein Kyrie, das ebenfalls von Luther für die singende Gemeinde eingerichtet wurde. Er hat den Text in seiner griechischen Form belassen und die aus nur vier Tönen bestehende, in ihrer Schlichtheit überzeugende Melodie aus dem ersten Psalmton der Meß-Psalmodie entwickelt.

44
Christe, du Lamm Gottes

Das Agnus Dei hat Luther in der Deutschen Messe wohl erwähnt, aber – im Gegensatz zum Sanctus (31) – nicht mitgeteilt. Hingegen finden wir ein gemeindegemäßes deutsches Agnus Dei in der vom Wittenberger Stadtpfarrer Johannes Bugenhagen bearbeiteten und 1528 bei Joseph Klug in Wittenberg gedruckten Kirchenordnung der Stadt Braunschweig. Das Stück ist melodisch, wie das Kyrie, auf dem 1.Psalmton aufgebaut, nur daß hier der ganze Sechstonraum ausgenützt wird. Das gibt der Vermutung starkes Gewicht, daß auch hier Luther der Schöpfer ist. Textlich ist die Anrede an das Lamm im lateinischen Text durch die Anrede an Christus ersetzt, eine Freiheit im Umgang mit der Tradition, die man Luther ohne weiteres zutraut.

45
O du armer Judas

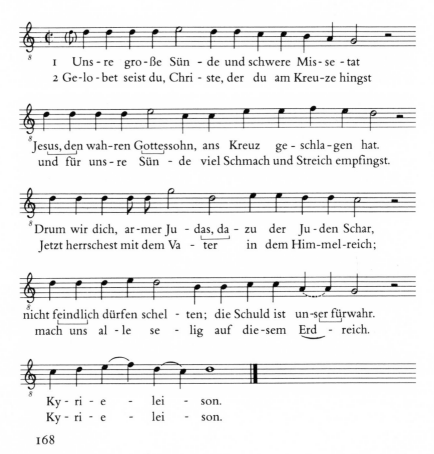

1 Uns-re gro-ße Sün - de und schwere Mis-se-tat
2 Ge-lo-bet seist du, Chri - ste, der du am Kreu-ze hingst

Jesus, den wah-ren Gottessohn, ans Kreuz ge - schla-gen hat.
und für uns-re Sün - de viel Schmach und Streich empfingst.

Drum wir dich, ar-mer Ju - das, da - zu der Ju-den Schar,
Jetzt herrschest mit dem Va - ter in dem Him-mel-reich;

nicht feindlich dürfen schel - ten; die Schuld ist un-ser fürwahr.
mach uns al - le se - lig auf die-sem Erd - reich.

Ky - ri - e - lei - son.
Ky - ri - e - lei - son.

168

Im Jahre *1544* hat der Wittenberger Musiksammler, Musiker, Drukker und Verleger Georg Rhau *(1488–1548)* im Rahmen eines umfassenden Musikwerkes, das den gesamten Bedarf der damaligen lutherischen Liturgie der Haupt- und Nebengottesdienste an mehrstimmiger Vokalmusik decken sollte, eine Sammlung von deutschen Kirchenliedsätzen seiner Zeit herausgebracht, das erste derartige Werk nach Walters Chorgesangbuch. Es enthält Sätze zu fast allen Liedern Luthers, aber auch zu den Liedern anderer Dichter jenes Umkreises. In diesem Werk finden sich zwei Sätze zu der Passions-Leise O Du armer Judas, was hast du getan, einer von Thomas Stoltzer und einer von Ludwig Senfl. Keiner dieser beiden Sätze hat jedoch den – ziemlich unerbaulichen! – Text dieser Leise, sondern es sind zwei offensichtlich zusammengehörige Strophen untergelegt, die man vorher nirgends findet. Die erste steht zum alten Text deutlich im Kontrafaktur-Verhältnis: Statt den «armen Judas» anzuklagen, klagt der Christenmensch sich selber an. Und dann wird, wie in der alten Leise, Judas angeredet, aber es wird ihm gesagt, wie unrecht der alte Text hat. Die 2. Strophe ist dann eine Übersetzung der lateinischen Strophe Laus tibi Christe qui pateris aus dem *14.* Jahrhundert, die bereits mit dieser Leisen-Melodie verbunden war. Luther kannte, wie man aus seinen Tischreden weiß, diese Judas-Leise, und so wurde verschiedentlich die Vermutung ausgesprochen, diese Bearbeitung könnte von ihm stammen. Sie würde eine Lücke in Luthers Liedern zum Kirchenjahr schließen, und es wäre dann müßig, sich weiter darüber Gedanken zu machen, warum Luther kein Passionslied geschrieben hat.

Die hier abgedruckte Melodiefassung ist die Grundform, die sich aus den melodietragenden Stimmen der beiden genannten Figuralsätze ergibt.

Die Vorrede zum Leipziger Gesangbuch des Valentin Babst
1545

Der 96. Psalm spricht: «Singet dem Herrn ein neues Lied. Singet dem Herrn, alle Welt.» Es war im Alten Testament unter dem Gesetz Moses der Gottesdienst sehr beschwerlich und mühevoll, da sie so viele und mancherlei Opfer bringen mußten von allem, was sie in Haus und Feld hatten. Das tat das Volk, das faul und geizig war oder alles nur um des zeitlichen Genießens willen tat, gar ungerne, wie der Prophet Maleachi (1, 10) sagt: «Wer ist unter euch, der umsonst eine Tür zuschlösse oder ein Licht auf meinem Altar anzündete?» Wo aber ein solch faules, unwilliges Herz ist, da kann gar nichts oder nichts Gutes gesungen werden. Fröhlich und voller Lust müssen Herz und Gemüt sein, wo man singen soll. Darum hat Gott solchen faulen und unwilligen Gottesdienst verworfen, wie er daselbst (Mal. 1, 10f.) weiter spricht: «Ich habe keine Lust zu euch, spricht der Herr Zebaoth, und eure Speisopfer gefallen mir nicht von euren Händen. Denn vom Aufgang der Sonne bis zu ihrem Niedergang ist mein Name herrlich unter den Heiden, und an allen Orten wird meinem Namen Räucherwerk geopfert und ein reines Speisopfer. Denn groß ist mein Name unter den Heiden, spricht der Herr Zebaoth.»

So ist nun im Neuen Testament ein besserer Gottesdienst, wovon hier der Psalm sagt: «Singet dem Herrn ein neues Lied. Singet dem Herrn, alle Welt.» Denn Gott hat unser Herz und Gemüt fröhlich gemacht durch seinen lieben Sohn, welchen er für uns hingegeben hat zur Erlösung von Sünden, Tod und Teufel. Wer dies mit Ernst glaubt, der kann's nicht lassen: Er muß fröhlich und mit Lust davon singen und sagen, damit es andere auch hören und herzukommen. Wer aber nicht davon singen und sagen will, das ist ein Zeichen dafür, daß er's nicht glaubt und nicht ins neue, fröhliche Testament, sondern unter das alte, faule, unlustige Testament gehört.

Darum tun die Drucker sehr wohl daran, daß sie gute Lieder fleißig drucken und mit allerlei Zierde den Leuten angenehm machen, damit sie zu solcher Freude des Glaubens gereizt werden und gerne singen. Wie denn dieser Druck Valentin Babsts sehr anmutig ausgeschmückt ist.[1] Gott gebe, daß damit dem Römischen Papst, der nichts als Heulen, Trauern und Leid in aller Welt angerichtet hat durch

---

[1] *Das Bapst'sche Gesangbuch ist das am reichsten und schönsten ausgestattete der Reformationszeit. Das Format und die Illustrationen sind größer als beim Wittenberger Gesangbuch; zudem ist jede Seite mit Zierleisten eingefaßt.*

170

seine verdammten, unerträglichen und leidbringenden Gesetze, großer Abbruch und Schaden geschehe. Amen.[2]

Ich muß aber noch darauf aufmerksam machen: Das Lied, welches man zum Begräbnis singt: «Nun laßt uns den Leib begraben», trägt meinen Namen; aber es stammt nicht von mir, und mein Name soll hier entfernt werden. Nicht, daß ich dieses Lied verwerfe, denn es gefällt mir sehr gut, und es hat's ein guter Dichter geschrieben mit Namen Johannes Weiß[3] (nur daß er etwas verstiegene Ansichten über das Sakrament hatte). Aber ich will nicht eines andern Arbeit mir aneignen.[4]

Und im «De profundis»[5] muß es so heißen: «Des muß dich fürchten jedermann.» Es ist entweder ein Versehen oder Besserwisserei, wenn in manchen Büchern steht: «Des muß sich fürchten jedermann.» Ut timearis[6]. Denn es ist eine hebräische Ausdrucksweise, wie Matthäus 15,9: «Vergeblich fürchten sie mich mit Menschenlehre» und Psalm 14 und 53: «Sie rufen den Herrn nicht an. Sie fürchten da, wo nichts zu fürchten ist.»[7] Das bedeutet: Sie üben viel Demut, sich Bücken und Dücken in ihrem Gottesdienst, da wo ich gar keinen Gottesdienst haben will. So ist es auch hier gemeint: Weil sonst nirgends Vergebung der Sünden zu finden ist als bei dir, müssen sie wirklich alle Abgötterei bleiben lassen, und sie tun es gern, daß sie sich vor dir bücken, dücken und zu Kreuz kriechen und dich allein in Ehren halten, bei dir Zuflucht suchen und dir dienen als solche, die von deiner Gnade leben und nicht von ihrer eigenen Gerechtigkeit usw.

[2] *Luther hat diese Vorrede geschrieben, als mindestens der erste Teil des Gesangbuches schon gedruckt war. Der Titelbogen mit dieser Vorrede wurde offensichtlich nachträglich gedruckt. Die Vorrede füllte den Raum bis zum Register, das die letzten sieben Seiten des Bogens füllt, nicht ganz aus, und so nützte Luther den Platz für die beiden nachfolgenden Hinweise aus.* [3] *Der Dichter heißt in Wirklichkeit Michael Weiße (s. zu Nr. 42).* [4] *Darüber, daß diese Ausführungen Luthers Autorschaft für die Bearbeitung des Liedes nicht ausschließen, s. zu Nr. 42.* [5] *Gemeint ist mit dem lateinischen Anfang von Psalm 130 Luthers Lied Nr. 30b.* [6] *Mit der lateinischen Übersetzung verdeutlicht Luther den Fehler.* [7] *Psalm 53,5 f.; die erste Stellenangabe meint den gleichlautenden Psalm 14, in welchem Luther diesen Vers (4 f.) jedoch anders übersetzt hat.*

HULDRYCH ZWINGLI

Gegner des Kirchengesanges?

Der Schweizer Huldrych Zwingli – keine drei Monate jünger als Lu-
ther – ist weithin nur bekannt als der Vater des kirchengesanglosen
Gottesdienstes der Zürcher Kirche im Reformationszeitalter. In die-
ser Eigenschaft könnte er im vorliegenden Zusammenhang höch-
stens als negatives Gegenbild zu Luther genannt werden. Nun
stimmt es zwar, daß Zwingli in Zürich den mittelalterlichen liturgi-
schen Gesang bekämpft und abgeschafft und den evangelischen Kir-
chengesang nicht eingeführt hat. Daß er den Gemeindegesang im er-
neuerten Gottesdienst abgelehnt hätte, das hingegen läßt sich aus den
Quellen nicht belegen. Spätestens seit dem 23. November 1524, als
die Straßburger Reformatoren ihm brieflich ihren nach der Schrift
erneuerten Gottesdienst schilderten, wußte er, daß die Gemeinde
dort Liedpsalmen und andere Kirchenlieder sang, und er hat sich in
seiner Antwort, auch im Namen seiner Zürcher Amtsbrüder, am
16. Dezember 1524 ausdrücklich positiv geäußert: Was ihr von deutschen Liedern und Psalmen schreibt, findet hier bei allen Brüdern
Zustimmung. *Und im Jahr darauf äußerte der Zürcher Reformator*
sich auch öffentlich – einmal im Vorwort zu seinem neuen Abend-
mahls-Formular und einmal in einer Predigt über Psalm 92, 1 – im
gleichen Sinne. Warum er den Kirchengesang dennoch nicht einge-
führt hat, ist ein Rätsel, für dessen Lösung allerhand Vorschläge vor-
liegen. Völlig einleuchtend wird Zwinglis Haltung dadurch nicht.
Aber es ist hier nicht der Ort, dieser Frage nachzugehen. Es bleibt bei
der Tatsache, daß der mittlere der drei großen Reformatoren für den
Kirchengesang nichts getan hat. Erst zwei Jahre nach seinem frühen
Tode wurde in Zürich das erste Schweizer Gesangbuch gedruckt, das
sanktgallische des Dominik Zyli, und wenig später wohl auch das der
Konstanzer Reformatoren, das dann etwa von der Jahrhundertmitte
an für den Kirchengesang in der reformierten Schweiz im Reforma-
tions-Jahrhundert maßgebend werden sollte. Es darf als das Gesang-
buch des Zwinglianismus bezeichnet werden. Das erste Zürcher Ge-
sangbuch von 1598 fußt denn auch ganz darauf.

Musiker – Dichter – Komponist

In diesem Gesangbuch, das von Anfang an nach dem Vorbild Luthers
zu jedem Lied den Namen des Autors nennt, stehen nun nicht weni-
ger als drei geistliche Lieder, die den Namen Zwinglis tragen, eines

schon in der Ausgabe von etwa 1537, zwei weitere dann in der über-nächsten. Das mag überraschen. Aber die Autorschaft Zwinglis ist so gut bezeugt, daß keine Zweifel möglich sind: Zwingli ist unter die Liedschöpfer der Reformationszeit einzureihen. Und zwar ist er als Schöpfer sowohl der poetisch sehr hoch stehenden Texte wie auch der überaus stark eigengeprägten Melodien klar und eindeutig nach-gewiesen.

Zwinglis Musikbegabung trat schon in seiner Jugendzeit zutage: Als er zur Vervollkommnung seiner Mittelschulbildung in Bern bei den Dominikanern weilte, wollten diese ihn seiner schönen Stimme wegen zum Novizen machen. Es bedurfte eines Eingriffs von väterli-cher Seite, um dieses Vorhaben zu vereiteln. Nach dem verläßlichen Zeugnis von Zeitgenossen spielte Zwingli mindestens ein halbes Dutzend von Instrumenten; er selbst bekennt sich ausdrücklich und in positivem Sinne zu seinem Lauten- und Geigenspiel. Das erste dieser beiden Instrumente beherrschte er nach dem Urteil von Zeit-genossen in hervorragender Weise.

Auch das Kunstmittel der Poesie war Zwingli schon früh zur Hand. Zwei größere Werke lassen seine starke Begabung auf diesem Ge-biete erkennen: Das Fabelgedicht vom Ochsen, sein in einer lateini-schen Fassung von 99 Hexametern und in einer alemannischen von 184 paarweise gereimten Versen überliefertes ältestes erhaltenes Werk, entstanden im Herbst 1510, und das Gedicht Der Labyrinth in 242 alemannischen Versen, wohl vom Herbst 1516, beides leidenschaft-liche, aber kluge Stellungnahmen im Kampf um die Reisläuferei.

So sind wir nicht erstaunt, aus der Korrespondenz des Zürcher Re-formators zu erfahren, daß er Lauten-Lieder schreibt. Am 27. Septem-ber 1530 bittet aus Straßburg Wolfgang Capito: Schick uns Lieder, aber auch solche zur Laute, wenn Du kannst, wo Du so mit Arbeit überladen bist. *Ein Vierteljahr später (22. Januar 1531) wird die Bitte wiederholt:* Ich möchte unbedingt von Dir komponierte Lieder ha-ben, denn meine Familie wünscht solche dringend. Ich bringe sie dann zu Bernhard Friedrich, wo alles, was von Zwingli kommt, hochgeschätzt wird. *Im Hause des Ratsherrn Bernhard Ott Friedrich wurden nachweislich Kompositionen Zwinglis musiziert. Und eines der erhaltenen Lieder Zwinglis, das Kappeler Lied, wurde spätestens 1537 gleichzeitig in Straßburg und in Zürich gedruckt, wobei die Straßburger Melodiefassung an einer Stelle von der Zürcher ab-weicht. Damit ist erwiesen, daß es in Straßburg eine eigenständige Zwingli-Tradition gab.*

176

Und noch eine Kunde haben wir von Zwinglis kompositorischer Tätigkeit: Am Neujahrstag *1531* wurde am Zürcher Carolinum, dem Vorläufer der heutigen Universität, die Komödie «Plutos» von Aristophanes durch Lehrer und Schüler in griechischer Sprache aufgeführt. Die Bühnenmusik dazu (worum es sich im einzelnen handelte, wissen wir nicht) schrieb Zwingli. Und ein Zeitgenosse weiß zu berichten, daß er bei dieser «Premiere» vor Rührung weinte.

Instrumentalmusik, Dichtung, Gesang, Musiktheater: Da schlug offenbar Zwinglis Herz höher. Er hat keine theologischen Aussagen über die Musik gemacht, wie wir sie von Luther kennen. Aber er hat die Musik geliebt – so sehr, daß ihm das von römischer Seite wie von Extremisten auf evangelischer Seite zum Vorwurf gemacht wurde.

Der Liedschöpfer

Es müßte im höchsten Grad verwunderlich erscheinen, wenn von Zwinglis poetisch-musikalischem Schaffen keine Silbe und keine Note erhalten geblieben wäre. Beiträge zu einer gesungenen Liturgie müssen wir von ihm freilich nicht erwarten. (Daß er immerhin auch davon einiges verstand, zeigen seine Anweisungen an die im säkularisierten Kloster Rüti verbliebenen, evangelisch gewordenen Mönche von 1525.) Kirchenlieder, wie Luther sie aus der Tradition sammelte und bearbeitete oder neu schuf, dürfen wir beim Zürcher nicht suchen. Wenn es hier etwas geben könnte, dann wären es Stücke, die auf der Linie von Luthers frühesten Liedern lägen: persönlicher poetischer Ausdruck für den Kampf und den Sieg des Reformators, sei es anhand von Psalmstoffen, sei es in freier Gestaltung, Parallelen also zu Luthers ersten Psalmliedern, zum Märtyrerlied, zu Nun freut euch, lieben Christen gmein. *Und tatsächlich: Genau das liegt vor.*

Daß einige wenige derartige Schöpfungen von Zwinglis Hand erhalten geblieben sind, dafür haben in einem Fall die Straßburger und die Konstanzer Gesangbuchredaktoren gesorgt. In den beiden anderen waren es Basler Musikfreunde, die solche Dinge in ihren Musik-Handschriften festhielten, ferner der Konstanzer Buchhändler und spätere Mitarbeiter des Zürcher Druckers Christoffel Froschauer, Gregor Mangolt, als der Betreuer des Konstanzer Gesangbuches seit 1548, sowie Zwinglis Freund und Nachfolger Heinrich Bullinger, der in seiner Reformationsgeschichte der Nachwelt ins einzelne gehende Kunde gibt von der Entstehung zweier Lieder Zwinglis.

Formwahl

Zwingli galt manchen seiner Zeitgenossen als «Lutheraner». Es läßt sich viel sagen über seinen selbständigen Weg zum Reformator. Aber die von Luther ausgehende Bewegung hat ihre gewaltige Wirkung auch auf Zwingli gehabt. Nicht umsonst hat er geweint, als es im Oktober 1529 in Marburg nicht zur Einigung mit dem großen Wittenberger kommen wollte. Was im großen gilt, behält auch im kleinen seine Richtigkeit: Luther war der erste, der auf den Gedanken kam, einen Psalm in die Liedform umzugießen. Zwingli nahm den Anstoß auf. Wie Luther wählte er dafür einen Klagepsalm. Es war der neunundsechzigste. Aber dann ging er einen anderen Weg. Während Luther seine Klage und seinen Trost, die er im Psalter vorgezeichnet fand, jener Osterprozessions-Weise unterlegte, suchte Zwingli sich eine eigenständige Form. Er schuf ein recht kompliziertes neues Strophengebilde und eine Melodie im Stile der Hofweise. In sieben langen Strophen brachte er mit großer Sorgfalt die 42 Verse des Psalms in Reime, lediglich am Schluß ein wenig raffend (1). Es ist von Bedeutung, den Leser dieser Verse darauf hinzuweisen, daß Zwingli eine Eigenheit des Hofweisenstils hervorragend beherrscht: das, was man die «Jambenglätte» genannt hat, d. h. das Zusammenfallen von Wortbetonung und Versakzent. Was wir etwa bei Hans Sachs, aber auch in einzelnen Liedern Luthers als Geholper empfinden (Vatér unsér im Himmelreich... Brüdér sein únd Dich rufen an..., oder ...möchtén stürzén von deinem Thron), das gibt es in Zwinglis Liedern nur an acht Stellen. Gerade hierin unterscheidet sich der Hofweisenstil von der Meistersingerei, mit der er sonst manches gemeinsam hat. In musikalischer Hinsicht ist der wiederholte Gebrauch von bestimmten Melodieformeln und die sehr differenzierte rhythmische Gestalt (u. a. Synkopen) typisch. Vergleicht man Zwinglis Hofweisen mit denen Luthers, so fragt man sich, ob Zwingli nicht diesen Stil souveräner beherrschte als Luther.

Datierung und Deutung

Bullinger hat Zwinglis bedeutendste Liedschöpfung, das Pestlied (2), auf die Wende 1519/20 datiert, in die Zeit, da Zwingli wunderbarerweise von einer Pesterkrankung genas. Die jüngere Zwingliforschung hält diese Datierung für falsch. Die reformatorische Erkenntnis, die sich in diesem Liede ausspricht, ist Zwingli nachweislich erst

CCLXXXII Geiſtliche
In mitten der kranckheit.

Tröſt Herr Gott tröſt/ die kranckheit wachßt/
Wee vnd angſt faßt min ſeel vnd lyb/ Darumb dich
ſchub/ gen mir einiger troſt mit gnad:/: Die gwüß
erlöſt ein yeden der/ſin hertzlich bgär/vnd hoffnung
ſetzt in dich verſchetzt / Darzu diß int all nutz vnnd
ſchad. Nun iſt es vmb/min zung iſt ſtumm/ mag
ſprechen nit ein wort/min ſinn ſtad all verdort. Darumb iſt int/ das du min ſinnt/ fürſt fürhin/ ſo ich
nit bin/ſo ſtarck das ich/ mög dapfferlich/ thün wi-
derſtand des Tüffels facht/vnd fräffner hand/doch
wirt min gmüt/ſtät blyben dir wie er ioch wüt.

In der Beſſerung.
Gſund Herr Gott gſund/ich mein ich ker/ ſchon
widrumb här/ja wenn dich dunckt/der ſünd ſunck/
werd nit mer bherrſchen mich vff erd:/: So müß
min mund din lob vnnd leer/ vßſprechen mer/ dann
vormals ye/ wie es ioch gee/ einfaltigklich en alle
gferd/ Wiewol ich müſſ/ des todes bäſz erleyden
zwar ein mal/vilicht mit gröſſerm qual/ daß ietzüd
wer/geſchähen her/ſo ich ſunſt bin/ nach gfaren hin/
ſo wil ich doch/den trutz vnd boch/ in diſer wält/ tra
gen frölich vmb widergelt/mit hülffe din/on den nüt
mag volkommen ſin.

Abb. 5. Der älteste erhaltene Druck von Zwinglis Pestlied (Nr. 2) in der um 1552 bei Froschauer in Zürich erschienenen Ausgabe des einstigen Konstanzer Gesangbuchs. Zentralbibliothek Zürich.

179

Abb. 6. Zwinglis Lied über den 69. Psalm (Nr. 1) aus dem ersten offiziellen Zürcher Gesangbuch von 1598. Die Noten sind nicht mehr in Holz geschnitten, wie z. B. in

um die Mitte des Jahres 1520 aufgegangen. Und sie steht mit Sicherheit in keinem ursächlichen Zusammenhang mit der Pesterkrankung. So kann das Lied frühestens Mitte 1520 entstanden sein. Aber nichts hindert uns, es noch später anzusetzen. Luthers Nun freut euch, lieben Christen gmein, dem Liede Zwinglis in manchem verwandt, wird ja auch nicht in die Zeit unmittelbar nach den Erfurter Klostererlebnissen datiert, die in den Strophen 2–4 sehr deutlich heraufbeschworen werden.

Abb. 5, sondern mit beweglichen Metalltypen gesetzt. Bibliothek des Verfassers.

Sichere Anhaltspunkte für eine Datierung von Zwinglis Pestlied lassen sich nicht finden. Es erscheint aber als wahrscheinlich, daß Zwingli dieses, verglichen mit dem Psalmlied, noch vollendetere Lied nach jenem geschaffen hat. Nach Form und Inhalt stehen beide Lieder sich sehr nahe, nur daß im Pestlied das eigene Krankheitserlebnis an die Stelle dessen tritt, was im Psalm ein fremdes, künstlerisch bereits von einem anderen durchgeformtes Erleben hergab. Wenn man annehmen will, daß auch bei Luther jene Klagepsalmen

der freien Dichtung Nun freut euch, lieben Christen gmein *voran-gingen, hätten wir bei beiden Reformatoren den gleichen Vorgang vor uns: Die poetische Bewältigung der Einsicht, zum leidvollen Weg des reformatorischen Kampfes berufen zu sein, hält sich zuerst an das Vorbild des Klagepsalms und erhebt sich dann zu eigenwüchsiger Gestaltung.*

Ob diese Chronologie richtig ist oder nicht, so hilft uns jedenfalls die Parallele zu Luthers autobiographischem Lied dasjenige Zwinglis besser verstehen. Nicht das Biographische ist der eigentliche Gegenstand des Liedes; es ist nur Metapher. Gegenstand ist die Darstellung des Durchbruchs zum restlosen Vertrauen auf Gottes freimachende Zuwendung in Christus, das Urerlebnis des echten Glaubens.

Zwinglis drittes Lied wird wie das Pestlied einer bestimmten historischen Stunde im Leben des Reformators zugeordnet. Das hat dem Lied auch seinen Namen eingebracht: Kappeler Lied. Es soll im Juni 1529, als sich die Zürcher und die Innerschweizer Truppen bei Kappel gegenüberlagen, dort im Felde gedichtet, vertont und gesungen worden sein. Auch das ist in dieser Form unmöglich. Nur wenn das Lied wesentlich früher entstanden ist, läßt sich die Tatsache erklären, daß es in einer Basler Handschrift mit zwei Melodien überliefert ist, einer im Hofweisen-Stil (dem auch der Text trotz seiner Knappheit angehört) und einer zweiten von mehr volksliedhaftem Charakter. Diese zweite Melodie könnte vielleicht im Felde bei Kappel entstanden sein. Schwerer noch wiegt, daß das Kappeler Lied inhaltlich den beiden andern Liedern Zwinglis sehr nahe steht. Man vergleiche nur das Akrostichon des Kappeler Liedes Herr Gott hilf *mit den Anfängen der beiden anderen:* Hilf, Gott, das Wasser geht mir bis an d'Seel *und* Hilf, Herr Gott, hilf in dieser Not. *Es muß die anfechtungsreiche Zeit um 1525/26 gewesen sein, die Zwingli diesen Seufzer abrang. In jener Zeit hat er über die Psalmen gepredigt, und zwischen seiner Erklärung des 69. Psalms und dem Lied über diesen Psalm besteht eine so nahe Verwandtschaft, daß man beides gerne in die gleiche Zeit setzen möchte. In jenen Tagen, da sich in Zürich selbst der Widerstand gegen Zwingli zu regen begann, war die Bitte, Gott möge den Fortgang der Dinge selbst in die Hand nehmen, weil sonst ein unglücklicher Ausgang zu befürchten sei, am Platz; 1529 bei Kappel nicht; dort wußte Zwingli, was er wollte und was zu dem von ihm erstrebten glücklichen Fortgang der Reformation führen würde. Aber daß das Lied dort, wenngleich in anderer Interpretation, gesungen wurde, läßt sich ernsthaft nicht bezweifeln.*

Abb. 7. Zwinglis Kappeler Lied (Nr. 3) mit der endgültigen Melodie, von unbekann-
ter Hand um 1530 in eine Sammelhandschrift mit vierstimmigen Sätzen eingetra-
gen, von der leider nur das Tenor-Stimmbuch erhalten geblieben ist. Universitäts-
bibliothek Basel.

Inhaltlich kann man das Kappeler Lied sehr wohl mit Luthers Erhalt uns, Herr, bei deinem Wort vergleichen. Es ist zwar nicht so eindeutig trinitarisch wie jenes, läßt sich aber zum mindesten ohne Mühe so deuten. Die drei kurzen Strophen lassen die Verwandtschaft besonders stark ins Auge fallen. In beiden Fällen ruft der Sänger Gott in der Stunde der Bedrohung durch den Feind, der die Gemeinde vernichten will, um Hilfe an. Beide Lieder enden mit der Bitte um die Einheit der Kirche – in der Situation des Kampfes um die Identität der neu entstandenen Gemeinde durchaus keine Selbstverständlichkeit. Und für beide Reformatoren ist das Lob Gottes das Ziel – bei Luther am Ende der zweiten, bei Zwingli am Ende der dritten Strophe.

Es ist erstaunlich: Für alle drei Lieder Zwinglis finden sich mithin recht genaue Parallelen in Luthers Liedschaffen. Dabei dürften die beiden Dichter-Komponisten kaum um diese Einmütigkeit gewußt haben, schon gar nicht in diesem letzten, deutlichsten Fall, wo nahezu 20 Jahre zwischen der Entstehung der beiden Lieder liegen.

Die mehrstimmigen Liedsätze

Zu den beiden zuletzt genannten Liedern Zwinglis weiß Bullinger, daß der Zürcher Reformator selbst sie vierstimmig vertont habe. Die Hofweisen-Tenöre, wie Zwingli sie schreibt, sind tatsächlich in der Regel Bestandteil eines oft recht komplizierten vierstimmigen Satzes. Die genannte zeitgenössische Basler Handschrift, die weiter vorne auch das Pestlied Zwinglis enthält, ist denn auch das Tenor-Stimmbuch aus einem Satz von ursprünglich vier Stimmbüchern; die andern drei sind verloren. Jene Zeit kannte die Partitur-Notierung von Sätzen für mehrere Singstimmen oder Instrumente noch nicht, was manchen schmerzlichen Verlust mit sich bringt. So auch hier: Wir wissen nur, daß es diese Sätze gab; aber sie sind verloren.

Auch der 69. Psalm ist in einer Basler Handschrift bezeugt. Ein Student hat um 1574 einige Sätze aus der Sammlung seines Onkels, des Humanisten Bonifacius Amerbach, kopiert. Von den vier zierlichen Stimmheftchen sind zwei verloren. Immerhin besitzen wir hier außer dem Tenor nun auch den Contratenor oder Alt, der uns erlaubt, den Satz annäherungsweise zu rekonstruieren. Vier zeitgenössische Instrumentalsätze zum Kappeler Lied, die man bisweilen Zwingli zuzuschreiben versuchte, stammen wohl nicht von ihm, zeigen aber immerhin, wie beliebt weit herum Zwinglis Lieder waren,

obwohl keinerlei liturgischer Gebrauch diese Verbreitung begünstigte. Bullinger dürfte also recht haben, wenn er zu berichten weiß, daß Zwinglis Sätze weit und breit an Fürstenhöfen gesungen und geblasen wurden.

Weitere Melodien Zwinglis?

Im Konstanzer Gesangbuch finden wir zwei Psalmlieder von Zwinglis Freund und Amtsbruder an St. Peter, Leo Jud, mit Melodien, die einen von dem der Straßburger, Wittenberger und Konstanzer Melodien auffallend abweichenden, dem der Zwingli-Lieder aber sehr nahestehenden Stil aufweisen. Da von einer musikschöpferischen Tätigkeit Leo Juds nichts bekannt ist, kommt die Vermutung auf, Zwingli könnte diese Melodien geschaffen haben. Das müßte dann auch für die am selben Ort überlieferte Weise zu einem Psalmlied des 1529 in Konstanz hingerichteten Spiritualisten Ludwig Hätzer gelten. Wir geben diese Melodien hier wieder.

Nachhall

Da der 69. Psalm und das Pestlied Zwinglis für den Gemeindegesang zu schwierig waren, erlebten sie keine weite Verbreitung. Noch während des 17. Jahrhunderts verschwinden sie aus den Gesangbüchern. Das Pestlied taucht in einer Neubearbeitung, welche jedoch das Strophenschema nicht wahrt, 1891 im Gesangbuch wieder auf. Das Kappeler Lied hielt sich im Zürcher Gesangbuch länger und erfuhr durch Friedrich Spitta schon 1898 eine meisterliche hochdeutsche Neufassung, die ihm den Weg in zahlreiche Lieder- und Gesangbücher bis zum heutigen Tag bahnte.

So bleibt Zwingli auch unserer Zeit als Dichter und Sänger im Bewußtsein. War seine Liebe zu Musik und Gesang eine so andersartige als die Luthers? Aus dem Abstand der Zeit betrachtet, rücken beide zusammen als Vorsänger einer im Liede Gott lobenden Christenheit:

... daß sie dich lob in Ewigkeit.
... daß wir ewig lobsingen dir.

Der 69. Psalm

1 Hilf, Gott, das Was - ser gaht mir bis an d'Seel.
Ich bin im tie - fen Meer, das Gwill zer - schlächt

Im Kat steck ich und find keins Bo - dens Grund.
mich sehr; vom Gschrei ist wor - den müed min Mund.

Ich heis - ren fast; der Au - gen Glast

nimmt ab, _____ so ich stets uf _____ dich sich

und hoff, min Gott; der Haß - - ren Rott,

die mich ohn Ur - sach föcht, wohl ü - ber - tref - - fen

möcht die Haar mins Kopfs; die fal - schen Find

mir viel ze - stark wor - - - den sind. Das ich nit ge-

nom-men hab, mueß ich al - les tra - - - gen ab.

1 *Hilf, Gott, das Wasser geht*
mir bis an die Seele. Im Dreck
stecke ich und finde keinen festen Boden (keines Bodens Grund).
Ich bin im tiefen Meer
das Gewoge zerschlägt mich völlig;
vom Schreien ist mein Mund müde geworden.
  Ich bin ganz heiser;
  das Licht der Augen
  nimmt ab, dieweil ich
  stets auf dich schaue
  und hoffe, mein Gott;
  die Bande der Hasser,
  die mich ohne Ursache bekämpft (anficht),
  mag wohl bald die Haare meines Kopfes
  [an Zahl] übertreffen; diese lügnerischen Feinde
  sind mir viel zu stark geworden.
  Was ich nicht genommen habe,
  muß ich alles zurückzahlen.

2 Min Torheit ist, o Gott,
dir bkannt und Missetat.
Nit laß zue Schwachheit kommen, die
in dich vertruend, Herr,
noch den gschändt werden, der
dich suecht, drum daß ich gsündt hab hie.
Dann ich trag noch
nit kleine Schmoch
um dich, o Gott,
bin ganz schamrot.
Min Brüeder sind,
sam sie nit Kind
sigend der Mueter min,
frömd worden mir. Der Grin
und Yfer dines Hus' mich fraß;
drum din Schmäher uf mich saß.
Was min Seel weint, fastet, btracht,
ward mir alls zue Gspött gemacht.

3 Sobald ich härin Gwand
anlegt, ein Sprüchwort fand
min Widerpart. Sie redtend fry
bin Porten wider mich.
Und wo sie samlend sich
bim Wyn und Praß, da singend sie
ein Lied von mir.
Ach Herr, zue dir
ich ernstlich bitt
– abschlach mir's nit – :
Durch all din Güet
mir hilf und bhüet.
Erlös mich us dem Lätt,
das mich schier versenkt hätt,
daß ich von mynem Fynd und Waag
's tieffen Wassers mich entsag,
dem Gwill und Grueb so entflüch.
Das nit ob mir zämenzüch.

4 Herr, der barmherzig bist
und güetig z'aller Frist,
wend dich gen mir durch all din Gnad.
Verbirg din Angsicht nit
vor dym Knecht, den Angst schütt.
Yl, daß du mich verhörist grad.

2 Meine Torheit und Missetat
ist dir, o Gott, bekannt.
Laß die nicht schwach werden, die
auf dich vertrauen, Herr,
noch den in Schande fallen, der
dich sucht, weil ich hienieden gesündigt habe.
    Denn ich trage noch immer
    keine geringe Schmach
    um deinetwillen, o Gott;
    ich bin völlig rot vor Scham.
    Meine Brüder sind
    – als ob sie nicht Kinder
    meiner Mutter wären –
    mir fremd geworden. Der Grimm
    und Eifer um dein Haus hat mich gefressen;
    darum saß dein Schmäher mir auf.
    Was [auch immer] meine Seele weinte, fastete, nachdachte,
    [das] wurde alles Anlaß zum Spott über mich.

3 Sobald ich ein härenes Kleid [zum Zeichen der Buße]
anzog, erfand die Partei meiner Gegner
ein Sprüchlein [über mich]. Sie redeten ungehemmt
im Tor über mich.
Und wo sie sich beim Wein und zum Prassen
versammeln, da singen sie
    ein Lied über mich.
    Ach Herr, zu dir
    bitte ich ernstlich
    – schlag mir's nicht ab – :
    Durch all deine Güte
    hilf mir und behüte mich.
    Erlöse mich aus dem Schlamm,
    der mich beinahe hätte untergehen lassen,
    damit ich mich meines Feindes und der Woge(n)
    des tiefen Wassers entschlage
    [und] den Wellen und dem Grab so entfliehe.
    Laß das nicht über mir zusammenschlagen
    (zieh das nicht über mir zusammen).

4 Herr, der du barmherzig bist
und gütig zu jeder Zeit,
    wende dich mir zu mit all deiner Gnade.
    Verbirg dein Antlitz nicht
    vor deinem Knecht, den [die] Angst schüttelt.
    Eile, mich gleich zu erhören.

Näch myner Seel,
o Gott, du wel-
list lösen sy,
daß nit die Kry
myns Fygends bstand.
Du weißt, was Schand
und Schmach ich lyd; vor dir
sind bkannt, die Leids tuend mir.
Ihr Unbill schwächt und bricht min Herz;
niemand btrachtet minen Schmerz.
Ich umsach, ob neißwar mit-
lidt, fand einen Tröster nit.

5 Sie hond mit Gallen mich
gspyst und tränkt mit essich.
Den Tisch, o Herr, jn widergilt
mit schwerem Fall und Strick.
Blend sie, daß sie kein Stick
sähend, zerknütsch on alle Mild
ihr stark Ruckbein.
Bgüß sie all gmein
mit dinr Ungnad;
dins Zornes Schad
streng uf sie schlach.
Ihr' Wohnung mach
einöd, ihr' Hüser lär.
Dann den du gschlagen schwär,
zerschlahends gar; wo du mich eh
gwundt hast, da verwundends meh.
Spar's jn alles zämen, Herr,
und begnad sie nimmermehr.

6 Vertilg sie us dem Buech
der Läbenden; nit suech
sie zue den Frommen z'schryben, Herr.
Mich Armen aber, Gott,
und Kranken arzen sott,
din Hilf mir nimmer machen feer.
Wil ich mit Gsang
und großem Dank
din Lob und Ehr
stäts prysen mehr,
welchs dir viel bas
gefällt, dann daß

Nahe dich meiner Seele,
o Gott; du wollest
sie erlösen,
damit nicht das Schlachtgeschrei
meines Feindes Bestand habe.
Du weißt, welche Schande
und Schmach ich leide; vor dir
sind bekannt, die mir Leid antun.
Ihre [mir zugefügte] Unbill schwächt und bricht mein Herz;
[aber] niemand beachtet meinen Schmerz.
Ich schaute aus (sah mich um), ob jemand mit mir Mitleid habe,
[aber] ich fand keinen Tröster.

5 Sie haben mit Galle mich
gespeist und getränkt mit Essig.
Diese Bewirtung, o Herr, vergilt ihnen
mit schwerem Fall und Strick.
Blende sie, daß sie kein Stück [weit]
[mehr] sehen, zermalme ohne alle Milde
    ihr starkes Rückgrat.
Begieße sie alle zusammen
mit deiner Ungnade;
die Schädigung durch deinen Zorn
schlage unerbittlich auf sie.
Ihre Wohnung mach
zur Einöde, ihre Häuser leer.
Denn [der], welchen du [schon] schwer geschlagen hast,
[den] zerschlagen sie [noch] vollends; wo du mich schon
verwundet hast, da verwunden sie noch mehr.
Hebe es ihnen alles auf, Herr,
und begnadige sie nie mehr.

6 Vertilge sie aus dem Buch
der Lebenden; trachte nicht,
sie zu den Frommen zu zählen, Herr.
Mich Armen aber, Gott,
und Kranken wollest du heilen (als Arzt behandeln),
mit deiner Hilfe mir nicht fernbleiben.
    Dieweil werde ich mit Gesang
    und großem Dank
    dein Lob und Ehr
    stets mehr preisen,
    was dir viel besser
    gefällt, denn daß

man dir die Ochsen schlach
und Stier, die alls Gemach
mit Horn und Klauen habend schon,
ufgricht' sind und wohlgeton.
Das gfallt dir für alle vych,
wenn der Mensch ufopfert sich.

7 Das sähend an, ihr, die
verkümmert werdend hie;
erfreuend üch und suechend Gott.
Der wird üch üer Herz
erquicken, wenden Schmerz;
er merkt uf aller Menschen Not,
die Kummer drängt
ald Gfängnus ängt.
Er schupft sie nit.
Das lobind hüt
ihn, Himmel, Erd
und alles werd,
das sich im Meer bewegt.
Gott ist, der Zion trägt
und Juda Städt erbut und halt,
daß da wohnind jung und alt
und sie bsitzind ewiglich.
Das ists heilig Himmelrych.

man dir die Ochsen schlachte
und Stiere, die alle Glieder
mit Horn und Klauen in Ordnung (schön) haben,
gesund und wohlgestaltet sind.
Das gefällt dir mehr als alle [Opfer-]Tiere,
wenn der Mensch sich aufopfert.

7 Das schaut an, ihr, die
[ihr] hier mit Kummer beladen werdet;
freut euch und suchet Gott.
Er wird euch euer Herz
erquicken, den Schmerz [in Freude] kehren;
er achtet auf aller Menschen Not,
   die Kummer bedrängt
   oder Gefangenschaft beengt.
Er verstößt sie nicht.
Deshalb loben ihn (Gott) heute
Himmel, Erde
und fröhlich alles,
was sich im Meer bewegt.
Gott ist [es], der Zion trägt
und Judas Städte erbaut und erhält,
daß Jung und Alt da wohnen [können]
und sie ewiglich besitzen.
Das ist das heilige Himmelreich.

Wir lassen hier einen vierstimmigen Satz zum vorangehenden Lied folgen, der nur fragmentarisch (die oberste und die unterste der drei Begleitstimmen sind ergänzt) und nur in einer um ein halbes Jahrhundert jüngeren Quelle überliefert ist, aber dennoch sehr wahrscheinlich von Zwingli selbst stammt. Er ist hier so notiert, daß die Begleitung auf einem Tasteninstrument ausgeführt werden kann. Wird die Melodie von einer Frauenstimme gesungen, so ist der Satz eine Oktave höher zu spielen.

1 Hilf, Gott, _____ das Was - ser _____
Ich bin _____ im tie - fen _____

gaht _____ mir bis an _____ d'Seel.
Meer, _____ das Gwill zer - schlächt

Im Kat _____ steck _____ ich _____ und
mich sehr; _____ vom _____ Gschrei _____ ist

find _____ keins _____ Bo - dens _____ Grund.
wor - den _____ müed _____ min _____ Mund. Ich

mich ohn Ur - sach föcht, wohl ü - ber tref - - -

fen möcht___ die Haar mins___ Kopfs; die

fal - schen___ Find___ mir viel ze-

stark wor - - - den sind.___

Das ich nit ge - nom - men hab, ____ mueß ich____ al - les tra - - - - - gen ab.

Wie Luther in seinen frühesten Psalmliedern, so wählt auch Zwingli einen individuellen Klagepsalm als Grundlage dieses Liedes. Er macht nicht den Versuch, es in eine andere Gattung zu überführen, sondern greift zur solistischen Form des Hofliedes. Den Psalminhalt deutet er nicht (jedenfalls nicht explizit) christologisch, wie das schon seit urchristlicher Zeit geschehen war, sondern auf sich selbst in dem Kampf um das unverfälschte Evangelium und die Erneuerung der Kirche. Im Gegensatz zu den beiden folgenden Liedern verfügen wir für die Autorschaft Zwinglis an diesem Psalmlied über keine literarischen Zeugnisse. Das hat dazu geführt, daß man da und dort an der Autorschaft Zwinglis für das Psalmlied zweifelte. Sollten diese Zweifel jedoch zu Recht bestehen, so müßte man sie für Dutzende von Kirchenliedern, darunter auch solche Luthers, anmelden. Das älteste Zeugnis für dieses Lied, ein um 1552 in Zürich gedrucktes Gesangbuch, nennt Zwingli als Autor. Als Bearbeiter dieser zweiten für die Schweiz gedruckten Ausgabe des Konstanzer Gesangbuches hat man den Buchhändler und Mitarbeiter des Druckers Christoffel Froschauer, einen persönlichen Freund Zwinglis und Bullingers, Gregor Mangolt, eruieren können, der damals in Zürich lebte und somit ein ebenso verläßlicher Zeuge ist wie Heinrich Bullinger. Und als der Zürcher Pfarrer Raphael Egli 1598 das erste Zürcher Gesangbuch bearbeitete, druckte er das Psalmlied unter Zwinglis Namen ab, jedoch in einer Fassung, die an drei Stellen besser ist als die Mangolts. Er scheint also noch über andere Quellen verfügt zu haben, und so ist sein Zeugnis für die Autorschaft Zwinglis von selbständigem Wert.

Eine weitere selbständige Überlieferung dieses Liedes stellen zwei Stimmheftchen dar, die der Basler Student Ludwig Iselin um 1574 niedergeschrieben hat. Darin steht unter Stücken, die er nachweislich aus Musikhandschriften und Drucken aus dem Besitz seines Onkels Bonifacius Amerbach kopiert hat, auch unser Lied. Da es in der Musikaliensammlung Amerbachs eine Handschrift mit Zwinglis Pestlied und den beiden Melodien und dem gesamten Text des Kappeler Liedes gibt, liegt die Vermutung nahe, es habe in einer anderen, heute verschwundenen Handschrift aus dem Kreise um Amerbach auch dieses Lied Zwinglis gestanden. Daß es sich bei dem (ohne Zweifel einst vierstimmigen) Satz, in welchem die Melodie hier überliefert ist, um den Originalsatz Zwinglis handelt, ist so gut wie sicher. Die beiden verlorenen Stimmen lassen sich nach Maßgabe der erhaltenen Altus- (bzw. Contratenor-)Stimme ergänzen. Der hier vorliegende Ergänzungsversuch stammt von Marguerite Jenny-Loeliger.

Eine metrische und gereimte Übertragung des Textes ins Hoch-
deutsche wäre ein nutzloses Unterfangen; es käme auf weite Strek-
ken einer Neudichtung in Zwinglis Versmaß gleich. Um die allzu
zahlreichen Fußnoten zu vermeiden, die hier zur Erklärung des Tex-
tes nötig wären, geben wir dem Texte Zwinglis eine nicht singbare
Prosa-Übersetzung bei.

Zum Vortrag des Originaltextes beachte man die Bemerkung am
Schluß der Erläuterungen zum Pestlied (2). Ferner muß beachtet wer-
den, daß Zwingli hier in der drittletzten Zeile ein Mißgeschick pas-
siert ist: Das Metrum verlangt an dieser Stelle x́ x x́ x x́ x x́. Gerade
die erste Strophe verstößt jedoch dagegen: mir víl ze stárk (wórden
sínd). Da die Melodie sich auf die erste Strophe bezieht, werden an
dieser Stelle nun aber die anderen sechs Strophen ins Unrecht ver-
setzt.

Das Pestlied

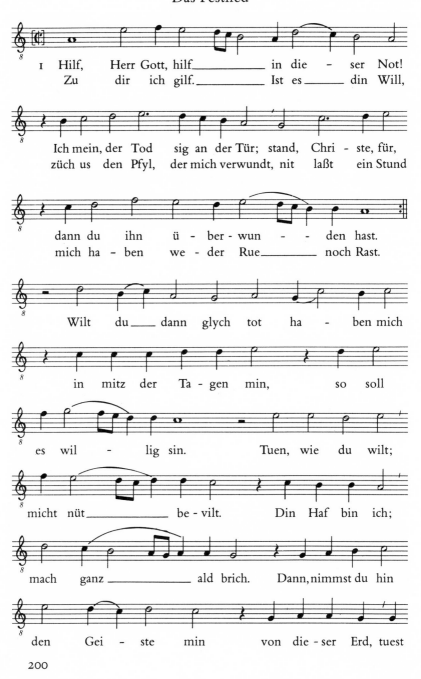

1 Hilf, Herr Gott, hilf_____ in die - ser Not!
Zu dir ich gilf._____ Ist es_____ din Will,

Ich mein, der Tod sig an der Tür; stand, Chri - ste, für,
züch us den Pfyl, der mich verwundt, nit laßt ein Stund

dann du ihn ü - ber - wun - - den hast.
mich ha - ben we - der Rue_____ noch Rast.

Wilt du_____ dann glych tot ha - ben mich

in mitz der Ta - gen min, so soll

es wil - lig sin. Tuen, wie du wilt;

micht nüt_____ be - vilt. Din Haf bin ich;

mach ganz _____ ald brich. Dann, nimmst du hin

den Gei - ste min von die - ser Erd, tuest

1 *Hilf, Herr Gott, hilf*
   in dieser Not!
   Mir ist, der Tod
   sei an der Tür;
   Christus, stelle dich vor mich,
   denn du hast ihn überwunden.
   Zu dir schreie ich.
   Ist es dein Wille, [so] zieh aus den Pfeil,
   der mich verwundet,
   nicht eine Stunde
   mir weder Ruhe noch Rast läßt.
     Willst du [aber] dennoch
     mich tot haben,
     inmitten meiner Tage,[1]
     so soll es eben sein.
   Tu, wie du willst;
   nichts ist mir zuviel (nichts verdrießt mich).
   Dein Gefäß bin ich;
   stelle [es] wieder her oder zerbrich [es].
   Denn, wenn du
   meinen Geist hinnimmst
   von dieser Erde,
   [dann] tust du es, damit er nicht schlimmer werde
   oder anderen nicht
   ihre Frömmigkeit und Lebensführung beflecke.

---

[1] *Zwingli war zur Zeit der Pesterkrankung 3 5 ¾ Jahre alt, zur Zeit der Abfassung dieses Liedes etwa 40. Das ist nach Psalm 90, 10 genau die Mitte des Lebens.*

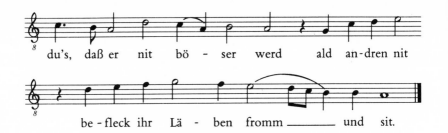

du's, daß er nit bö - ser werd ald an-dren nit

be - fleck ihr Lä - ben fromm _____ und sit.

2 Tröst, Herr Gott, tröst!
Die Krankheit wachst;
Weh und Angst faßt
min Seel und Lyb.
Darum dich schieb
gen mir, einiger Trost, mit Gnad,
die gwüß erlöst
ein jeden, der
sin herzlich Bgehr
und Hoffnung setzt
in dich, verschätzt
darzue dies Zyts all Nutz und Schad.
 Nun ist es um;
 min Zung ist stumm,
 mag sprechen nit ein Wort;
 min Sinn sind all verdorrt.
 Darum ist Zyt,
 daß du min Stryt
 füerist fürhin,
 so ich nit bin
 so stark, daß ich
 mög dapferlich
 tuen Widerstand
 des Tüfels Facht und frevner Hand.
 Doch wird min Gmüet
 stet blyben dir, wie er joch wüet.

3 Gsund, Herr Gott, gsund!
Ich mein, ich kehr
schon widrum her.
Ja, wenn dich dunk,
der Sünden Funk
werd nit mehr bherrschen mich uf Erd,
so mueß min Mund
din Lob und Lehr
ussprechen mehr

2 *Tröst, Herr Gott, tröst!*
Die Krankheit wächst.
Weh und Angst faßt
meine Seele und [meinen] Leib.
Darum nahe dich mir,
alleinziger Trost, mit [der] Gnade,
die gewißlich einen jeden
erlöst, der
sein herzliches Begehren
und seine Hoffnung
auf dich setzt und dazu gering achtet
zeitlichen Nutzen oder Schaden.
 Nun ist es vorüber;
 meine Zunge ist stumm,
 mag kein Wort [mehr] sprechen.
Meine Sinne sind alle verdorrt.
Darum ist es an der Zeit,
daß du meinen Streit
fortan führest,
denn ich bin nicht [mehr]
stark genug, daß ich
könnte tapfer
Widerstand leisten
der Anfechtung und frevelhaften Hand des Teufels.
Doch wird mein Gemüt
dir treu bleiben, wie er auch wüte.

3 *Gesund, Herr Gott, gesund!*
Mir ist, ich kehre
unversehrt wieder zurück.
Ja, wenn es dich dünkt,
der Brand der Sünde
werde mich auf Erden nicht mehr beherrschen,
so muß mein Mund
dein Lob und deine Lehre
mehr denn je zuvor

dann vormals je,
wie es joch geh,
einfaltiglich ohn alle Gferd.
Wiewohl ich mueß
des Todes Bueß
erlyden zwar einmal,
vilicht mit größerm Qual,
dann jetzund wär
geschehen, Herr,
so ich sust bin
nach gfahren hin,
so will ich doch
den Trutz und Boch
in dieser Welt
tragen fröhlich um Widergelt
mit Hilfe din,
ohn den nüt mag vollkommen sin.

aussprechen,
wie es auch gehe,
in Einfalt und aus lauterem Herzen.
  Wiewohl ich
  die Strafe des Todes
  einmal werde erleiden müssen
  – vielleicht mit größerer Qual,
  als es jetzt
  geschehen wäre, Herr,
  da ich beinahe (nach) ohne solche (sust)
  hingegangen wäre –,
  so will ich doch
  Widerstand und Gewalt
  in dieser Welt
  fröhlich ertragen [in der Hoffnung] auf den [himmlischen] Lohn, [2]
  mit deiner Hilfe,
  [du,] ohne den nichts vollkommen sein kann. [3]

[2] *Römer 8, 18.*   [3] *Johannes 15, 5; Philipper 2, 13.*

Zwinglis Pestlied ist eine der hervorragendsten und eigengeprägtesten poetischen Schöpfungen der Reformationszeit. Es gibt keinerlei Vorlage, die dem Dichter als Anregung hätte dienen können, wenn man von den Psalmen absieht, in welchen auf ähnliche Weise persönliches Erleben und Erleiden ins allgemein Gültige erhoben wird. Man hat lange geglaubt, Zwingli habe hier einfach seine Gefühle und Gedanken während der Pesterkrankung dargestellt. Heinrich Bullingers Nachricht in seiner 1567 niedergeschriebenen Reformationsgeschichte, Zwingli habe dieses Lied unmittelbar nach seiner Genesung von der Pest um die Wende 1519/20 verfaßt, und die in gleicher Richtung gehende Überschrift Gregor Mangolts in der um 1552 erschienenen Ausgabe des einstigen Konstanzer Gesangbuches mußten einen in dieser Auffassung bestärken. Es ist jedoch völlig undenkbar, daß ein von der Pest Genesender ein so anspruchsvolles Lied wie das vorliegende dichtet. Zwinglis Briefe aus den ersten Monaten des Jahres 1520 zeigen denn auch, wie langsam die Genesung fortschritt und wie große Mühe sie ihm bereitete.

Was aber noch mehr ins Gewicht fällt, ist, daß sich auffallende Parallelen zu den wesentlichen Aussagen dieses Liedes in den schriftlichen Äußerungen Zwinglis erst seit Mitte 1520 finden, dann aber bis zum Ende seines Lebens. Am 24. Juli 1520 schreibt Zwingli an Oswald Myconius in Basel: Ich bitte Christus nur um das eine, daß er

mir verleihe, alles mit einem mannhaften Herzen zu tragen, und daß
er mich, sein Geschirr, zerbreche oder festmache, wie es ihm gefällt.
Man vergleiche dazu den Abgesang der 1. Strophe. Und dieser Ge-
danke findet sich von nun an bei Zwingli immer wieder, bis hin zu
jenem Gedicht für einen Kalender, das er wenige Tage vor seinem
Tode zu seinem Drucker brachte und in dem es heißt:

> So er *(Gott)* nun euch zue sinem Gschir
> für andre gkiest *(vor andern erkoren)*, so glaubet mir:
> Er will etwas damit schaffen.

Der Mensch als Gottes Geschöpf ist sein Geschirr – was nach alemanni-
schem Sprachgebrauch sowohl Werkzeug als auch Gefäß bedeutet –:
In diesem durchaus nicht fatalistisch verstandenen Abhängigkeitsge-
fühl hat man eines der Leitmotive zwinglischer Theologie und Spiritu-
alität erkannt. Das Pestlied nimmt also im Werk Zwinglis eine genauso
zentrale Stelle ein wie Luthers Lieder im Werk des Wittenberger Refor-
mators.

Die Mitteilung Bullingers, Zwingli habe nicht nur den Text dieses
Liedes, sondern auch die Melodie und den vierstimmigen Satz geschaf-
fen, ist durchaus glaubwürdig. Bei den Liedern dieses Formtyps, den
Hofliedern, ist die Einheit von Textdichter, Melodieerfinder und Satz-
schöpfer durchaus normal und durch viele Beispiele belegbar. Zudem
existiert in diesem Fall eine Niederschrift der Melodie (die zugehörige
Textniederschrift ist fragmentarisch) im Tenor-Stimmbuch einer Bas-
ler Handschrift, die einst vier Stimmbücher umfaßt haben muß. Dieser
Eintrag in die Handschrift ist auf etwa 1529 zu datieren, reicht also in
Zwinglis Lebenszeit zurück. Eine selbständige Textüberlieferung liegt
der Wiedergabe des Gedichtes in Bullingers Reformationsgeschichte
zugrunde. Schon vorher hat Gregor Mangolt Text und Melodie in die
zweite Ausgabe seiner Neubearbeitung des Konstanzer Gesangbuches
(um 1552) aufgenommen. Er hat den Text wahrscheinlich bereits nicht
mehr in seinem ursprünglichen Sinne verstanden, sondern als Trostlied
für Kranke gedeutet und darum die drei Strophen mit «Im Anfang der
Krankheit», «Inmitten der Krankheit» und «In der Besserung» über-
schrieben. Daß die letzten zehn Zeilen der 2. Strophe dann ihren Sinn
verlieren, hat er nicht bemerkt. Aber seine Wiedergabe ist der älteste
erhaltene Druck des Liedes.

Eine Wiedergabe dieses Gedichtes in hochdeutscher Fassung wäre
mit derart starken Eingriffen in Zwinglis Text verbunden, daß wir, nach
mehrfachen Versuchen, darauf verzichtet haben. Der Leser und der Sän-

ger, welcher das Alemannische nicht beherrscht, muß sich mit dem Sinn des Textes anhand der beigegebenen Prosa-Übersetzung vertraut machen und dann den Text Zwinglis zu sprechen oder zu singen versuchen. Dabei ist zu beachten, daß ie und ue (damals ů geschrieben) als Diphtonge mit einem gegen ä hin gefärbten, fast tonlosen e zu sprechen sind («die» also z. B. nicht wie hochdeutsch «die», sondern etwa «diä»). Das st ist auch im Auslaut als scht zu sprechen (z. B. «hast» = «hascht»). Das ch ist stets (auch nach e, i usw.) zu sprechen wie in «Nacht».

3

Das Kappeler Lied

207

1 *Herr,* nun heb den Wagen selb.
Schelb wird sust all unser Fahrt;
das brächt Lust der Widerpart,
die dich
veracht so frävenlich.

2 *Gott,* erhöch den Namen din
in der Straf der bösen Böck.
Dine Schaf widrum erweck,
die dich
liebhabend inniglich.

3 *Hilf,* daß alle Bitterkeit
scheid in d'Feer, und alte Trü
widerkehr und werde nü,
daß wir
ewig lobsingind dir.

1 Herr, *nun selbst den Wagen halt,*
bald abseit geht sonst die Fahrt;
das brächt Freud dem Widerpart,
der dich
veracht' so freventlich.

2 Gott, *erhöh deins Namens Ehr:*
Wehr und straf der Bösen Grimm.
Weck die Schaf mit deiner Stimm,
die dich
liebhaben inniglich.

3 Hilf, *daß alle Bitterkeit*
scheid, o Herr, und alte Treu
wiederkehr und werde neu,
daß wir
ewig lobsingen dir.

Das Kappeler Lied ist Zwinglis kunstvollste Liedschöpfung. Außer dem Endreim kennt es auch den Schlagreim und den Binnenreim. Ferner sind die Strophen, wie das bei den Hofweisen nicht selten der Fall ist, durch ein Akrostichon zusammengehalten: Die Anfangsworte aller drei Strophen ergeben hintereinander gelesen die Bitte: «Herr Gott hilf.» Dieses Akrostichon schlägt die Brücke hinüber zu den beiden anderen Liedern Zwinglis, die mit diesem Ruf beginnen.

Die Basler Handschrift, die (in einem früher niedergeschriebenen Teil) das Pestlied Zwinglis enthält, überliefert um 1535 auch das Kappeler Lied, und zwar signiert und datiert: V.Z. 1529. Man hat Grund zur Annahme, daß diese Niederschrift unmittelbar auf eine Urschrift Zwinglis zurückgeht. Einzig in dieser Handschrift ist das Lied mit zwei Melodien überliefert. Die Melodie A trägt die Merkmale des Hofweisen-Stils und steht den Melodien der beiden anderen Zwingli-Lieder stilistisch sehr nahe. Es muß sich um die ursprüngliche Singweise handeln. Melodie B hat viel stärker volkstümlichen Charakter. In Heinrich Isaacs († 1517) «Missa carminum» (Messe über Volksliedmelodien) hat man eine verwandte Melodie gefunden. Und auch das von Caspar Othmayr 1549 mit einem Satz versehene Lied Ich weiß mir ein Maidlein hübsch und fein zeigt ähnliche Züge. Doch ist unter diesen drei Melodien in keiner Richtung eine eindeutige Abhängigkeit zu beweisen, von einem Kontrafaktur-Verhältnis gar nicht zu reden. Zwinglis Weise ist eine originale und originelle Schöpfung.

Bullinger berichtet in einem Nachtrag zu seiner Reformationsgeschichte von 1567 aufgrund der Stumpfschen Chronik, Zwingli habe

dieses Lied während des ersten Kappeler Krieges im Juni 1529 im Feldlager bei Kappel gedichtet und vertont und dann von den Soldaten singen lassen. Diese Nachricht dürfte aber ebensowenig zutreffen wie diejenige über die Entstehung des Pestliedes während oder unmittelbar nach der Pesterkrankung, die übrigens ebenfalls auf Johannes Stumpf zurückgeht. Die stilistische und inhaltliche Verwandtschaft des Kappeler Liedes mit den beiden andern Liedern Zwinglis läßt uns vermuten, daß der Reformator auch dieses sein drittes Lied damals um 1525 geschaffen hat, wobei es zuerst die Melodie A erhielt. 1529, möglicherweise nun vor Kappel, gab Zwingli ihm dann die zweite Melodie, die das Lied erst für den Gesang der Soldaten geeignet machte. Das wäre ein Vorgang, wie wir ihn bei Luther mehrfach beobachten konnten. Allerdings hat hier auch der Text eine Veränderung erfahren, nicht dem Wortlaut nach, wohl aber, was seinen inhaltlichen Bezug betrifft. Die «alte Treue», um deren Wiederkehren die 3. Strophe bittet, war ursprünglich die zwischen der Reformationspartei und dem radikalen Flügel, den Täufern, die damals von Zwingli abzurücken begannen. Jetzt ist es die alte Einheit der Eidgenossen, die im Begriffe ist, endgültig zu zerbrechen.

Das Kappeler Lied tritt schon vor den beiden anderen Liedern auch in den Gesangbüchern auf. Es ist das einzige Lied Zwinglis, das sich über die Schweiz hinaus verbreitet hat. Über Straßburg ist es bis in das Heidelberger und in das Bonner Gesangbuch, ja sogar bis in ein Königsberger Gesangbuch gelangt. Die ungefähr gleichzeitige Überlieferung im Konstanzer Gesangbuch wurde für die Schweiz maßgebend, wo man das Lied im Zürcher Gesangbuch noch Anfang des 19. Jahrhunderts findet.

Die weit verbreitete Textunterlegung, welche die 4. und 5. Textzeile zusammenhängt, als wäre es eine einzige, und auf der drittletzten Silbe dann ein Melisma von vier Tönen erhält, ist durch die unsorgfältige Textunterlegung in der ältesten Straßburger Quelle (um 1537) entstanden. Es kann aber kein Zweifel bestehen, daß allein jene Unterlegung die Meinung Zwinglis trifft, die auch in der Melodie deutlich werden läßt, daß das Lied fünf Zeilen hat und das Wort «freventlich» unter die drei letzten Töne bringt, so daß die im Ostschweizer Dialekt Zwinglis kurze erste Silbe dieses Wortes auch den kurzen Ton erhält wie vorher bei «Wagen» bzw. «Namen». Die sorgfältige Darstellung der Noten, wie sie für die um 1549 erschienene erste Schweizer Ausgabe des Konstanzer Gesangbuches in Holz geschnitten und dann bis 1608 weiter verwendet wurde, beweist das eindeutig.

Wir geben in diesem Fall die Übertragung Friedrich Spittas von *1898 ins Hochdeutsche bei, weil sie (von der eben genannten Feinheit in der Wort-Ton-Beziehung abgesehen) auf keines der von Zwingli angewandten Kunstmittel verzichtet und dennoch ebenso natürlich-volksnah daherkommt wie der Urtext. Und in dieser Form steht das Lied jedem Kirchengesangbuch wohl an. Man wird es allerdings nicht, wie das seit 1537 wegen der Verbindung mit Kappel geschah, unter den Titel «Um Hilfe und Beistand Gottes in Kriegsgefahr» in die Abteilung «Lieder für Volk und Vaterland» oder gar unter die Soldatenlieder ein-reihen dürfen. Es gehört vielmehr mit dem ihm nahe verwandten Lied Luthers* Erhalt uns, Herr, bei deinem Wort *zusammen unter die Lieder von der Kirche. Obwohl die Reformatoren das ökumenische Anliegen in der uns geläufigen Ausprägung noch nicht kannten – nicht kennen konnten –, sind diese beiden Lieder recht eigentlich ökumenische Bitt-lieder:* Gib deim Volk einrlei Sinn auf Erd – Hilf, daß alle Bitterkeit scheid, o Herr, und alte Treu wiederkehr und werde neu, daß wir ewig lobsingen dir.

4

Der 9. Psalm

Confitebor tibi domine in toto corde meo etc.

Leo Jud

Dir, o Herr, will ich sin - gen us gan - zem Her-
in Freuden mich er - sprin - gen zue Lob — dem Na-

zen mein, dein Wun - der - ta - ten _____ al - le
men sein;

will ich mit Freud und Schal - le, din' Na - men

frei, wie hoch _____ der sei,

prei - sen von jetzt in E - - - - wig - keit.

(weitere 7 Strophen)

Zwinglis Nachfolger als Leutpriester in Einsiedeln und seit Ende 1522 sein Amtsbruder an St.Peter in Zürich war der Elsässer Leo Jud (1482–1542). Schon in seiner Einsiedler Zeit verband ihn eine innige Freundschaft mit Zwingli. Sein Sohn Johannes berichtet von seinem Vater: Er war auch gern bei der Musik und beim Saitenspiel, denn er war ein herrlicher und guter Musicus, hatte eine herrliche Stimme zum Discant *(oberste Stimme des vierstimmigen Satzes, sonst meist von Knaben gesungen),* den er so hell sang, daß ihn keiner übertraf. Es kamen oft zu ihm Herr Dietrich Wanner, Pfarrer zu Horgen *(seit 1525),* und Herr Jakob Leu, Kilchherr zu Thalwil *(seit 1541),* und andere Musici, aßen jeweils mit ihm, und danach sangen sie miteinander. Er hat auch etliche Psalmen gedichtet, die man noch jetzt im Psalmenbüchlein findet, wie «Dem König und Regenten dein» oder: «Gotts Gnad und sein Barmherzigkeit», das man nach der Weise des St. Beatenlieds singt, oder «Dein, dein soll sein das Herze mein». Er konnte das Hackbrett schlagen und die Laute ein wenig. *Die genannten Lieder stehen tatsächlich alle seit der 2. Ausgabe (um 1537) im Konstanzer Gesangbuch, dazu noch die vorliegende, von Johannes Jud nicht erwähnte Bearbeitung des 9. Psalms. Die beiden Psalmen Juds stehen dem Stil von Zwinglis 69. Psalm sehr nahe: Barform, kurze Zeilen, sehr wenige Verstöße gegen die «Jambenglätte» (hier in 9 Strophen zu 12 Versen = 108 Versen nur 8 Verstöße). Man dürfte kaum fehlgehen in der Annahme, daß es Zwingli war, der Jud zum Psalmendichten angeregt hat. Auffallend ist nun, daß die beiden Psalmbereimungen stilistisch sehr stark eigengeprägte Melodien haben, denen in diesem Gesangbuch nichts Vergleichbares an die Seite zu stellen ist – außer den um 1552 dann hinzukommenden Hoflied-Melodien Zwinglis. Da nichts bekannt ist von einer kompositorischen Tätigkeit Leo Juds, haben wir mit der Möglichkeit zu rechnen, daß Zwingli die Texte seines Freundes vertont hat.*

Der 72. Psalm
Deus iudicium tuum regi da etc.
Leo Jud

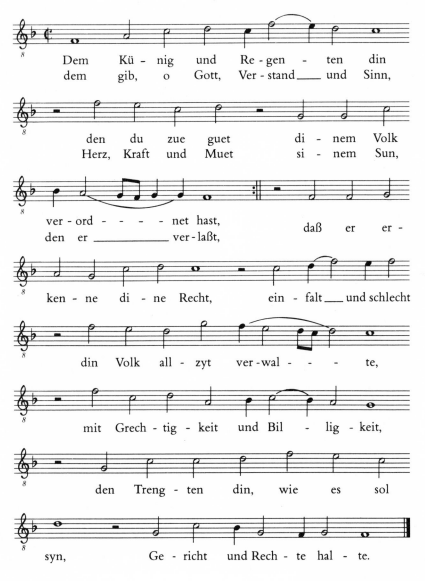

Dem Kü - nig und Re - gen - ten din
dem gib, o Gott, Ver - stand___ und Sinn,

den du zue guet di - nem Volk
Herz, Kraft und Muet si - nem Sun,

ver - ord - - - - - net hast,
den er _____ ver - laßt, daß er er -

ken - ne di - ne Recht, ein - falt___ und schlecht

din Volk all - zyt ver - wal - - - te,

mit Grech - tig - keit und Bil - lig - keit,

den Treng - ten din, wie es sol

syn, Ge - richt und Rech - te hal - te.

(weitere 7 Strophen)

Von dieser zweiten Psalmbereimung Juds gilt dasselbe wie von der vorangehenden (4). Der Text umfaßt 8 Strophen zu 12 Zeilen = 96 Verse; darin kommen nur 6 Verstöße gegen die «Jambenglätte» vor. (In den beiden andern bei Nr. 4 genannten Texten Juds, beides Kontrafakturen, sind es im einen Fall auf 36 Verse zwei Verstöße, im andern auf 42 Verse ein Verstoß). In dieser Melodie ist die zweite Abgesangszeile mit der dritten und vierten Abgesangszeile in Zwinglis Psalmlied (1) zu vergleichen, und die folgende Zeile ist ein wörtliches Zitat der inhaltlich entscheidenden Stelle Din Haf bin ich, mach ganz ald brich im Pestlied (2). Dennoch machen diese beiden Melodien nicht den Eindruck von Nachahmungen, sondern sind genauso überlegen geformt wie die erwiesenermaßen echten Zwingli-Melodien, so daß die Vermutung, Zwingli sei ihr Schöpfer, starkes Gewicht bekommt.

6

Der 37. Psalm

Noli aemulari in malignantibus, etc.

Ludwig Hätzer

dem   Gras   uf   grüe - ner   Ou - en.

(weitere 22 Strophen)

Eine dritte Melodie im Konstanzer Gesangbuch (seit 1537), die genau denselben Stil aufweist, steht bei der 23strophigen Bereimung des 37. Psalms durch den 1529 in Konstanz hingerichteten Spiritualisten Ludwig Hätzer. Die erste Abgesangszeile stimmt genau mit der entsprechenden des Pestliedes (2) überein. Im übrigen muß man mit diesen Melodien zu knapperen Strophenformen (4, 5, 6) immer auch die ältere Melodie des Kappeler Liedes (3 A) vergleichen. Es wäre doch recht verwunderlich, wenn drei Textdichter (Zwingli, Jud und Hätzer) ihre Lieder in genau demselben unverwechselbaren Stil vertont hätten, den wir in den Quellen dieses Umkreises sonst nirgends antreffen. Viel näher liegt die Annahme, daß diese Melodien aus einer und derselben Feder stammen.

JOHANNES CALVIN

Der weite Anmarschweg

Calvin ist fast eine Generation jünger als Luther und Zwingli. Als Zwingli am 11. Oktober 1531 auf dem Schlachtfeld von Kappel fiel, war Calvin ein 22jähriger Jüngling. Emanuel Stickelberger läßt ihn in seinem Zwingli-Roman in jener Nacht, in der Zwingli starb, als nach Italien wandernden Studenten im Kloster Kappel Herberge nehmen und von denen, die eben den Tod des Zürcher Erzketzers feierten, seinen Geleitbrief für die Weiterreise empfangen. Vier Jahre später weilt Calvin, nun bereits ein Gelehrter und zum reformatorischen Glauben Bekehrter, in Basel, wo die erste Ausgabe seines Hauptwerkes, der «Institutio Christianae Religionis» – Unterweisung im christlichen Glauben – geschrieben und dann gedruckt wird. Obwohl der deutschen Sprache nicht mächtig, wird er in Basel – etwa bei Oswald Myconius im Münster – den Gottesdienst besucht haben. Dort lernte er etwas kennen, was ihm unbekannt war: Die Gemeinde sang Lied-Psalmen. Und wenn Calvin gefragt hätte, wo die herkommen, so hätte man ihm ein in Straßburg gedrucktes Büchlein gezeigt und ihm die Namen Martin Butzer, Wolfgang Fabricius Capito, Matthäus Greiter, Wolfgang Dachstein, Ludwig Oeler, aber auch den großen Namen Martin Luther genannt. Bei der Behandlung des Abendmahls im vierten Kapitel seines eben genannten Werkes skizziert Calvin einen Abendmahlsgottesdienst, wie er sich aus der Heiligen Schrift ergeben müßte, und erwähnt dabei den Psalmengesang während der Austeilung und zum Abschluß des Gottesdienstes.

Anfang September 1536 hält Guillaume Farel, mit der Durchführung der Reformation in der Stadt Genf beschäftigt, den auf der Durchreise abgestiegenen jungen und schüchternen Gelehrten dort fest – eine der ergreifendsten Szenen aus der Reformationsgeschichte, aus Calvins eigener Feder überliefert. Calvin kann diesem Ruf, in welchem er Gottes Stimme erkennt, nicht widerstehen. Er tritt in die Arbeit mit ein, zunächst als schlecht besoldeter Bibellehrer und theologischer Berater Farels. In dieser Eigenschaft verfaßt er für Farel die erste Genfer Kirchenordnung, die am 16. Januar 1537 dem Rat der Stadt zur Beschlußfassung vorlag. Auch darin wird der Psalmengesang der Gemeinde erwähnt, allerdings erst als Forderung. Aber Calvin hält programmatisch fest: So wie wir es jetzt machen, sind die Gebete der Gläubigen so kalt, daß es uns zur großen Schande gereicht und Verwirrung stiftet. Die Psalmen könnten uns anreizen, unsere Herzen zu Gott zu erheben, und uns bewegen zum Eifer, ihn an-

zurufen und die Ehre seines Namens mit Lobgesängen zu erhöhen. *Und dann wird praktisch angeordnet, daß die Kinder als Vorsänger-gruppe fungieren sollen; sie sollen die Gemeinde vertreten, bis diese die Gesänge selbst auch im Ohr hat.*

Bald danach erhielt Calvin eine Pfarrstelle in Genf. Ohne die Prie-sterweihe erhalten zu haben und ohne ein ordentliches Theologie-studium absolviert zu haben, wurde der Verfasser der «Institutio» zum Verbi Divini Minister – eines der Ämter, das diese Kirchenord-nung vorsieht. Doch der Aufbau eines schriftgemäßen Gemeinwe-sens will nicht gelingen. Zu viele auseinanderstrebende Kräfte ma-chen in der Stadt ihren Einfluß geltend, die mehr und mehr zum brodelnden Kessel wird. Die beiden Reformatoren sehen sich außer-stande, unter diesen Umständen das nach Berner Muster vorge-schriebene Oster-Abendmahl auszuteilen. Diese Weigerung führt zum Bruch mit dem Rat, und mit Beschluß vom Osterdienstag wer-den die beiden mit einem blinden Amtsbruder zusammen aus der Stadt verwiesen. Am 25. April 1537 verlassen sie Genf. Calvin und Farel erreichen über Bern und Zürich erneut Basel. Farel läßt sich von dort nach Neuenburg rufen. Calvin bleibt. Er will in kein kirchliches Amt mehr eintreten. Doch Straßburg hält um ihn an. Ähnlich wie Fa-rel ziemlich genau zwei Jahre zuvor gelingt es den Straßburgern, Calvin zwingend klarzumachen, daß die Kirche Christi dort seiner dringend bedarf. Wirtschaftliche Überlegungen – Calvin ist mittel- und stellenlos! – tun das Ihre dazu, und der heimatlos Gewordene verläßt Anfang September 1538 Basel in Richtung Straßburg.

Wir mußten diesen Abschnitt der Biographie Calvins in knappen Zügen schildern, weil wir es als ein Stück göttlicher Vorsehung be-trachten, daß Calvin diesen Weg geführt wurde. Das, was er für die Geschichte des Kirchengesangs zu leisten berufen war, wäre sonst schwerlich in dieser Weise zustande gekommen, wie wir es im fol-genden zu schildern haben.

Das erste Kirchengesangbuch in französischer Sprache

In Straßburg trifft Calvin ähnliche liturgische Gebräuche an, wie er sie in Basel kennengelernt hatte. Die Melodie des einen oder ande-ren der Psalmlieder mochte er noch im Ohr haben. Seine Aufgabe war, neben der Durchführung theologischer Vorlesungen am Sturm-schen Gymnasium, die Betreuung der evangelischen Christen fran-zösischer Zunge, die aus Frankreich hatten fliehen müssen und nun

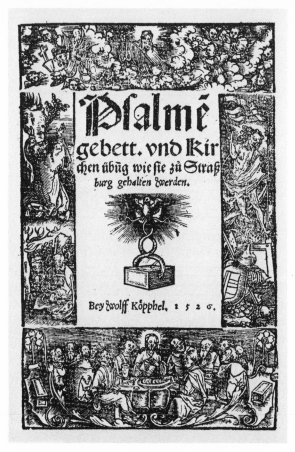

Abb. 8a. Titelblatt des Straßburger Gesangbuches von *1526*, aus dem die folgenden
beiden Abbildungen mit Greiters Lied zum *119.* Psalm entnommen sind.

in der deutschen Stadt an der Sprachgrenze Zuflucht gefunden hatten. Er wurde in seiner Funktion als französischer Pfarrer den deutschen Pfarrern der Stadt gleichgestellt und bekam das Recht, mit seiner Gemeinde Abendmahl zu feiern. Und da schlägt – irgendwann
um die Jahreswende *1538/39* – die Geburtsstunde des späteren Hu-
genotten-Psalters. Auf seinen Reisen durch sein Heimatland im Jahre
1535 mag Calvin dem begabten Hofdichter Franz I., Clément Marot,
begegnet sein. Er zählte zu denen, die dem neuen Glauben anhingen.
Und dieser Marot war (spätestens *1533*) auf den Gedanken gekommen, biblische Psalmen auf Melodien von Pariser Chansons in
Reime zu bringen. Als echter Humanist ließ er dem Aufsetzen einer

219

Abb. 8b. Lied über den Anfang des 119. Psalms vom Straßburger Münsterkantor Matthäus Greiter aus dem Straßburger Liturgie- und Gesangbuch von 1526. Text und Melodie stammen von Greiter. Die gotischen Choralnoten, die für diese Art von Musik eigentlich ungeeignet sind, sollen die liturgische Bedeutung des neuen

Psalmdichtung tiefgründige Textstudien vorausgehen, für die er die neuesten Kommentare, vor allem die von Lefèvre d'Estaples und Martin Butzer, beizog. Das Singen solcher Psalmen muß in den Kreisen des Hofes wie eine Art Singbewegung um sich gegriffen haben. Wenn Calvin damals Marot nicht persönlich begegnet sein sollte, dann hat er spätestens durch das eine oder andere seiner Straßburger Gemeindeglieder solche Texte in die Hand bekommen. Und damit hatte er das, was er brauchte, um seine Gottesdienste analog denen der deutschsprachigen Straßburger Gemeinden einrichten zu können.

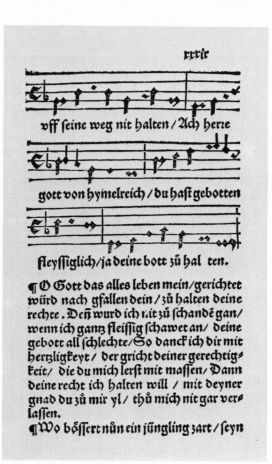

xxxij

vff feine weg nit halten / Ach herre

gott von hymelreich / du haſt gebotten

fleyſſiglich / ja deine bott zů hal ten.

¶ O Gott das alles leben mein / gerichtet
würd nach gfallen dein / zů halten deine
rechte. Deñ wurd ich nit zů ſchandē gan /
wenn ich gantz fleiſſig ſchawet an / deine
gebott all ſchlechte / So danck ich dir mit
hertzligkeyt / der gricht deiner gerechtigkeit / die du mich lerſt mit maſſen / Dann
deine recht ich halten will / mit deyner
gnad du zů mir yl / thů mich nit gar ver-
laſſen.
¶ Wo böſſert nůn ein jüngling zart / ſeyn

Kirchenliedes zeigen: Es tritt an die Stelle des gregorianischen Chorals, der so aufgezeichnet wurde. Die senkrechten Striche an den Zeilenenden sind die Pausenzeichen dieser Notation. Diese Melodie Greiters verwendete Calvin für sein Lied
über den 36. Psalm (Abb. 9). Zürich, Zentralbibliothek.

Er brauchte nur die Musiker, die für die deutschen Straßburger Psalmen die Melodien gemacht hatten, um entsprechende Singweisen
für die Texte Marots zu bitten.

Die Auswahl der Psalmen, von denen er eine Bearbeitung Marots
zur Hand hatte, war zufällig. Er wollte sie ergänzen. Und dafür be-
schritt er – diese Tatsache ist durch eine briefliche Äußerung an Farel
in Neuenburg belegt – den umgekehrten Weg: Er nahm einzelne der
in den deutschen Gottesdiensten der Stadt gesungenen Melodien
und schrieb dazu in der Art Marots selbst die Texte. Es ist anzuneh-

221

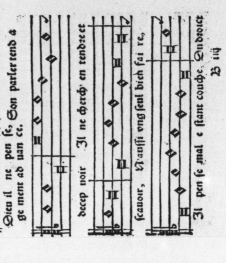

Abb. 9. Vier Seiten aus Calvins Straßburger Gesangbüchlein von 1539, dem ersten evangelischen Kirchengesangbuch in französischer Sprache, mit Calvins Bereimung des 36. Psalms (Nr. 2) auf die ganz wenig veränderte Melodie Greiters zum 119. Psalm (Abb. 8). Von der Choralnotation sind nur die Pausenzeichen übriggeblieben, die nun aussehen wie Taktstriche, die Noten hingegen sind Mensuralnoten.

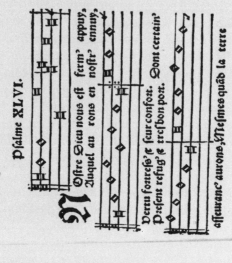

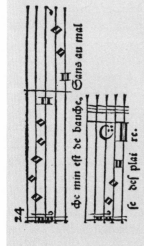

25

Et le droict de celuy maintient
Qui deuant toy chemine
Affin que sur moy l'inhumain
Son pied n'aduance et que la main
Du meschant ne me greue
L'hôme iniqu'est la trebuche
Et estant par terre couche
Jamais ne se releue.
fin.

Psalme XLVI.

Nostre Dieu nous est ferm' appuy,
Auquel au rons en nostr' ennuy,
Vertu seurese' & seur confort.
Present refug' & tresbon port. Dont certain'
asseurance aurons, Mesmes quãd la terre

B v

24

Oc min est de bauche, Sans au mal

se des plai rc.

Sire es cieulx attaint ta bonte
Et es nües ta verite
Tant hault quon les regarde
Ta iustice sembl' es haultz montz
Tes iugemens es lieur profondz
L'hôm' & beste tu garde
Seigour' est ta benignite
Les humains auront seurete
Soubz lombre de tes aelles
De tes biens se ressasiront
Et du fleuu' abreuuez seront
De tes delices belles.

Car source de vie en toy as
Et ta clarte se fuiras
Qui noz yeulx illumine
Pourfuys ta bonte vere les tiens

men, daß sich die so entstehenden Lieder nur allmählich zusammenfanden. Als es deren 22 waren, entschloß Calvin sich, sie drucken zu lassen. Ein einziges Exemplar dieses ersten französischen Kirchengesangbuches hat sich in München erhalten. Es ist in Straßburg bei Johannes Knobloch 1539 gedruckt worden und enthält neben 13 Texten Marots (mit ziemlich vielen Abweichungen vom Urtext des Dichters und mit vorher unbekannten, offenbar jetzt neu geschaffenen Melodien) auch neun Texte, von denen zwei nachweislich, die andern so gut wie sicher von Calvin selbst stammen. Sie sind bis auf einen auf bereits vorhandene Straßburger Melodien gedichtet. Unter ihnen ist auch der 46. Psalm (3). Ob es Calvin bewußt war, daß Luther diesen Psalm zum Ausgangspunkt für eines seiner schon damals berühmtesten Lieder gewählt hatte? Zu fünf weiteren Psalmliedern (1, 2, 4, 5, 6) kommen ein Lied über die Zehn Gebote (7) und eines über den Lobgesang Simeons (8) hinzu. Diese beiden biblischen Stücke gehörten für Calvin später zu den festen Teilen der Abendmahlsliturgie. Wahrscheinlich hat er sie schon in Straßburg so verwendet. Dasselbe wird vom Apostolischen Glaubensbekenntnis gelten, das er (in Prosa) der Straßburger Credo-Melodie unterlegte (9); in seiner späteren Genfer Liturgie hat er dann auf dieses Stück ganz verzichtet.

Im Gegensatz zu Luther und Zwingli hat also Calvin seine Liedtexte nicht selbst vertont. Daß er der musikalischen Seite des Gemeindegesangs gleichgültig oder gar verständnislos gegenübergestanden hätte, kann man dennoch nicht sagen. Wie wäre es sonst möglich, daß er an einem Teil der von ihm aus der Straßburger Tradition übernommenen Melodien gezielte Änderungen vornahm, die deutlich auf die später für den Genfer Melodie-Stil maßgebenden Regeln hinzielen, so die Ausmerzung von Punktierungen und Ligaturen (1, 2, 4, 6), aber auch andere Eingriffe (3, 4, 6).

Daß und wie das Straßburger Gesangbuch Calvins im Gottesdienst verwendet wurde, dafür ist uns ein Zeugnis erhalten geblieben, das eine Eigenheit des reformierten Kirchengesangs schon für diese frühe Zeit belegt: Die Gemeinde singt im Gottesdienst nicht auswendig – wie das weithin für die lutherischen Gebiete gilt –, sondern jedermann hat das Gesangbuch in der Hand. 1545 schreibt ein wallonischer Student aus Straßburg an seinen Freund: Sie werden nie ermessen können, wie lieblich es ist und wie ruhig das Gewissen wird, wenn man da weilt, wo Gottes Wort rein verkündigt und die Sakramente unverfälscht ausgeteilt werden; ebenso, wenn man die

schönen Psalmen und Wundertaten des Herrn singen hört... Anfänglich konnte ich die Freudentränen nicht zurückhalten, wenn ich singen hörte. Sie würden keine Stimme vernehmen, die die andern übertönt. Jedermann hält ein Gesangbuch in seiner Hand. Männer wie Frauen, alle preisen den Herrn.

Calvin hat dieses Büchlein nicht als Ziel, sondern als Anfang betrachtet, wenn er auch im Augenblick seiner Veröffentlichung noch nicht wissen konnte, welches die weiteren Geschicke dieses Gesangbuchs sein sollten. Aber er hätte bestimmt in jedem Fall Mittel und Wege gesucht, um zum vollständigen Liedpsalter zu kommen. Die Gelegenheit zur Fortsetzung ergab sich wohl früher, als er sich das dachte.

Calvins Genfer Psalter

1541 trat die Stadt Genf mit der Bitte an Calvin heran, er möchte zurückkehren. Es spricht für die große Noblesse dieses ganz und gar nicht kämpferisch veranlagten Mannes und widerspricht dem Bild eines Finsterlings, das manche von ihm haben, daß er die Größe hatte, ohne Stolz und ohne Rachsucht auf diese Bitte einzugehen, nach Genf zurückzukehren und dort, ohne großes Aufheben zu machen, mit seiner Predigt an der Stelle weiterzufahren, wo er vor vier Jahren hatte aufhören müssen. Die einzige Bedingung, die er gestellt hatte, war, daß eine verpflichtende Kirchenordnung geschaffen werden müsse. Das geschah denn auch. Systematisch legte Calvin den Grund zu einem wohlgeordneten evangelischen Kirchenwesen.

Dazu gehörte eine Gottesdienstordnung und ein Psalmen-Gesangbuch. Gleich Luther und Zwingli war Calvin liturgiegestalterisch tätig. Und gleich Luther fühlte er sich verpflichtet, seiner Gemeinde ein Rollenbuch für ihre aktive Beteiligung am Gottesdienst in die Hand zu geben. Calvin besorgte sich weitere 17 Psalm-Übertragungen Marots. Von Psalm 1 bis 15 war die Reihe nun schon vollständig. Für einen der von ihm bereimten Psalmen (5) hatte er jetzt einen Text Marots; er ließ den seinen fallen. Die übrigen behielt er, mit kleinen Retuschen an Text und Melodie, einstweilen bei. Für die neuen Texte ließ er (wohl vom Kantor an St. Pierre, Guillaume Franc) die Melodien bereitstellen. Den Liedern fügte er die Liturgie für den Predigt- und Abendmahlsgottesdienst, die Taufe, die Trauung und den Krankenbesuch bei, versah das Ganze mit einer Vorrede und ließ es 1542 bei Jean Gérard in Genf drucken – ohne irgendwo seinen Namen zu nennen. Im Jahr darauf kommt Clément Marot, der be-

reits zweimal seiner evangelischen Gesinnung wegen in Haft gewesen war, als Flüchtling nach Genf. Calvin beauftragt ihn, die Bereimung des gesamten Psalters an die Hand zu nehmen. Ehe Marot im gleichen Jahr Genf wieder verläßt, sind immerhin 19 weitere Psal-

Tout le plaifir d'vn captif deliuré.

O toy chafcun,ie te veulx fair‿entendre,
Et remonſtrer la voy‿,ou tu dois tendre,
En ayant l'oeil droit deſſus toy planté,
Pour t'addreſſer,comm‿experimenté.

Ne reſemblez le cheual & la mule,
Qui n'ont en eulx intelligence nulle:
De mors & frain,leur bouche vas domptant,
Que contre toy,ne viennent refiſtant.

L'homm‿endurcy fera dompté de mefmes,
Par maulx fans fin,& par douleurs extremes:
Mais,qui en Dieu fon efpoir afferra,
Enuironné de mercy fe verra.

Or, prenez donc en Dieu refiouiſſance
luftes efleuz,qui auez congnoiſſance
De verité:menez ioy‿or'endroit,
Chafcun de vous,qui auez le coeur droit.

PSALME XXXVI.

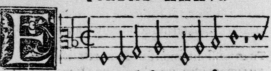

N moy le fe cret penfement,
Car, il fe complaift en fes faictz,

Abb. 10. Der Anfang von Psalm 36 (Nr. 2) aus Calvins erstem Genfer Gesangbuch von 1542. Die Notenwerte der Melodie sind gegenüber der Notierung von 1539

men übertragen und ist ein knappes Drittel des Psalters singbar. Calvin läßt das Gesangbuch in dieser Form neu drucken, erweitert dabei seine Vorrede und nennt nun auch in der Anrede an die Leser zu Beginn seinen Namen. Seine eigenen Texte läßt er zugunsten solcher

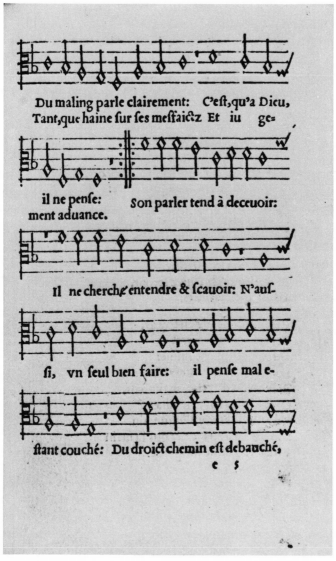

um die Hälfte verkürzt und die zu dieser Notenschrift gehörenden Pausenzeichen eingesetzt. Stuttgart, Württembergische Landesbibliothek.

Marots fallen. Damit verschwinden auch die deutschen Straßburger Melodien – bis auf eine: Matthäus Greiters Melodie Es sind doch selig alle, die bleibt als Weise für den 36. Psalm stehen. Hier hat also Marot Calvins Metrum übernommen. Dies ist auch der Fall beim Lobgesang Simeons. Die Annahme liegt nahe, daß Calvin dem Dichter gegenüber einen entsprechenden Wunsch ausgesprochen hat. Auf jeden Fall ist die Verbindung der Melodie Greiters mit dem 36. Psalm und das Metrum des Canticum Simeonis das einzige, was von Calvin im Kirchengesang bis heute geblieben ist. (Dieses zweite Genfer Gesangbuch von 1543 ist zwar verloren, aber rekonstruierbar.)

Es ist hier nicht der Ort, die weitere Entwicklung des Genfer Psalters im einzelnen zu verfolgen. Zu diesem grundlegenden reformatorischen Gesangbuch sind nur drei Feststellungen, die im besonderen mit Calvin zu tun haben, noch anzufügen:

Einmal ist darauf hinzuweisen, daß es nachweislich Calvin war, der die Fertigstellung des Genfer Psalters in der Folge vorangetrieben hat. Als Marot 1543 Genf verließ und 1544 in Turin starb, ohne sein Psalmenwerk vollendet zu haben, hat Calvin dafür gesorgt, daß dieses Werk nicht Torso blieb; er berief Theodor Beza in diese Aufgabe. 1551 erschien eine wesentlich erweiterte Ausgabe mit 34 neuen Bereimungen Bezas und neuen Melodien von Francs Nachfolger Loys Bourgeois. 1562 erschien die erste vollständige Ausgabe mit allen 150 Psalmen nebst dem Zehn-Gebote-Lied und dem Canticum Simeonis mit 125 Melodien; die noch fehlenden hatte nachweislich der dritte evangelische Genfer Kantor, Pierre Dagues, geschaffen. In 20 Jahren (wenn man die Straßburger Anfänge dazunimmt, sind es 23) war dieses Gesangbuch zu seiner endgültigen Gestalt herangewachsen. Seine Texte stammen von nur zwei, die Melodien von nur drei Händen. Eine solche Geschlossenheit weisen nur ganz wenige Werke in der Gesangbuchgeschichte auf, unter den stark verbreiteten keines. Diese Geschlossenheit gehört wohl mit zu dem, was diesem Gesangbuch seine enorme Durchschlagskraft gab, und es kann kein Zweifel daran bestehen, daß Calvin es war, der für seine Vollendung sorgte. Calvin war nicht der Erfinder des Psalmliedes – dieser Ruhm gehört Luther –, auch nicht der erste, der einen vollständigen Liedpsalter schuf – hier sind ihm die Augsburger Täufer 1537 vorangegangen, und die Straßburger haben diese Arbeit ein Jahr später erstmals mit Noten nachgedruckt –, aber er war unter all jenen, die in der Reformationszeit kirchlich anerkannte Gesangbücher schufen, der erste, der konsequent und ausschließlich und mit bleibendem Er-

folg das Gesangbuch des Alten Bundes in Form von Liedern zum
Gesangbuch der Kirche des Neuen Bundes gemacht hat.

Zum zweiten ist festzuhalten – was oft übersehen wird –, daß die-
ses maßgebende Gesangbuch der Reformierten französischer Zunge
(und dann bald halb Europas) seinen Ursprung im deutschen Kir-
chengesang hat und somit letztlich dem Anstoß, der von Luther her
kam, sein Dasein verdankt. Im besonderen ist sein Melodie-Stil ein-
deutig von demjenigen Straßburgs geprägt. Die starke Betonung der
Zeilenstruktur, welche durch die Grundschlagpausen zwischen den
Zeilen und durch den Beginn und Schluß jeder Zeile mit einer
Grundschlagnote erreicht wird, ist Straßburger Erbe. Calvin war es,
der dieses Erbe nach Genf vermittelte. Er muß es auch gewesen sein,
der dem Straßburger Melodie-Stil ein noch eindeutigeres Gepräge
gab. Die Änderungen, die er an den Weisen Matthäus Greiters vor-
nahm, als er sie für seine eigenen Psalmlieder verwendete (1, 2, 4, 6),
werden später zu Regeln, die von allen drei Melodieschöpfern des
Genfer Psalters mit überraschender Einmütigkeit angewandt werden:
In den 125 Melodien des Genfer Psalters kommt nicht eine einzige
Punktierung vor und gibt es nur ganz wenige Stellen mit Ligaturen.
Der Dreiertakt kommt ebenfalls nicht vor. Wenn man in Calvins
Vorrede liest, der Psalmengesang dürfe nicht leichtfüßig und be-
schwingt (léger et volage) sein, sondern müsse Gewicht und Würde
(poids et majesté) haben, dann weiß man, woher diese strengen Vor-
schriften kommen. Wie sollten drei Melodienschöpfer einen so ein-
heitlichen Stil geschrieben haben, wenn nicht ein Gestaltungsprinzip
von einer maßgebenden Stelle aus durchgehalten wurde? Das muß
Calvin selbst gewesen sein. Und wenn es schließlich unter den 125
Melodien Beispiele für sämtliche zwölf Kirchentöne des Glarean-
schen Systems gibt, dann kann das gleichfalls nicht Zufall sein, son-
dern zeugt von einem übergeordneten Plan, den wir wohl nur bei
Calvin suchen können.

Zum dritten: Eine weitere Quelle des Genfer Melodiestils ist die
humanistische Odenkomposition: So wie man die Versmaße der
klassischen Antike damals im Lateinunterricht mit Melodien in nur
zwei Notenwerten, entsprechend den langen und kurzen Silben,
sang, in der Meinung, damit der antiken Prosodie gerecht zu werden,
so läßt der christliche Humanist Calvin die heiligen Gesänge des
christlichen Altertums wieder auferstehen, indem er sie nach einer
ähnlichen Methode für das ganze Christenvolk singbar machen läßt.
Und wenn dann Loys Bourgeois, Claude Goudimel und viele andere

diese Psalmlieder mehrstimmig vertonen, so wählen sie in erster Linie denselben homophonen Satzstil, der bei den Odenkompositionen angewandt wurde.

Der Genfer Psalter fing schon im Jahre seiner Fertigstellung an, in sein Ursprungsgebiet zurückzuwirken: 1562 taucht zum erstenmal eine Genfer Psalmweise im deutschen Kirchengesang auf, und zwar in Straßburg. In der deutschen Fassung Ambrosius Lobwassers wurde diesem Buch im deutschen Sprachgebiet seit 1573 ein beispielloser Erfolg zuteil. Der römisch-katholische Liedpsalter Caspar Ulenbergs (1582) wie der lutherische Cornelius Beckers (1602), den dann Heinrich Schütz vertont hat (1628/61), sind geschaffen worden, um dem Siegeszug des calvinistischen Psalters Einhalt zu gebieten, und zeugen somit indirekt ebenfalls von der gewaltigen Breitenwirkung dieses auf Calvin zurückgehenden Werks. Wenn auch Calvins Name heute aus den Gesangbüchern verschwunden ist, so bleibt doch der Erfolg der Beharrlichkeit, mit welcher er die einheitliche Bereimung und Vertonung des gesamten Psalters durchgesetzt hat, stets lebendig. Und seine Maßnahme, dieses Gesangbuch zum reformierten Normal-Gesangbuch gemacht zu haben, wird stets beispielgebend bleiben.

AVLCVNS
pſcaulmes et cantiques
mys en chant.

A Straſburg.

1539.

Abb. 11. Der schlichte Titel von Calvins erstem Gesangbuch, dem die Abb. 9 entnommen ist und in dem die hier folgenden Psalmlieder und Gesänge stehen.

Psaume 25

1 A toi Seig - neur je lè - ve - rai
ne per - mets que, comme é - ga - ré,

mon â - me pour ai - de a - voir;
je sois con - fus de mon es - poir.

Ne souff - re que mes en - ne - mis

pren - nent é - bat - te - ment en moi,[1]

me voy - ant en ex - trê - - me é-moi

par la trop longue op - pres - se mis.[2]

2 Ainsi sera en sûreté
de toi jamais n'avoir refus
quiconque atteint ta vérité,
mais l'inique sera confus.
Fais-moi, Seigneur, considérer
le chemin que je dois tenir,
la voie pour bien parvenir
à te droitement honorer.

3 Dirige-moi en la clarté
de ta très sainte instruction.
Mon cœur en toi s'est arrêté,
O Dieu de ma salvation.
De tous tes bienfaits anciens
ne mets en oubli le long cours;

Psalm 25

1 *Zu dir, Herr, will ich emporheben*
meine Seele, um Hilfe zu bekommen;
laß nicht zu, daß als Verirrter
ich an meiner Hoffnung irre werde.
   Dulde nicht, daß meine Feinde
   sich über mich lustig machen,
   wenn sie mich in äußerste Aufregung versetzt sehen
   durch allzu langes Leiden.

2 *So wird gewiß sein können,*
von dir niemals zurückgewiesen zu werden,
wer immer deine Wahrheit ergreift;
der Übeltäter jedoch wird beschämt werden.
   Laß mich, Herr, bedenken,
   welchen Weg ich einschlagen muß,
   den Pfad, auf welchem ich wirklich dazu gelange,
   dich richtig zu ehren.

3 *Führe mich in die Klarheit*
deiner heiligsten Unterweisung.
Mein Herz hat sich für dich entschlossen,
o Gott meines Heils.
   Laß die lange Reihe deiner früheren Wohltaten
   nicht in Vergessenheit geraten;

comme as fait sur les tiens toujours,
envers moi ta grâce entretiens.

4 Les fautes qu'ai faites contre toi
et tant d'offences effaçant,
O Dieu, pour ta bonté, de moi
te souvienne en me bienfaisant.
En justice et droit le Seigneur
est du tout pur et impollu:
pourtant le chemin de salut [3]
il démontrera au pécheur.

5 L'esprit bénin il conduira
pour à bonne fin l'amener.
Comme bon maître enseignera
l'humble où il lui faut cheminer.
Miséricorde et vérité
notre Dieu garde entièrement
à tous ceux qui en loyauté
gardent sa loi et testament.

6 Las en mon forfait n'a sinon [4]
extrême horreur, o Seigneur Dieu;
mais par la grandeur de ton nom
à ta bonté donne en moi lieu.
Où est celui qui son désir
appliqué à Dieu craindre aura?
Et l'Eternel lui montrera
le droit chemin qu'il doit choisir.

7 Son âme au milieu de tous biens
sera mise pour s'éjouir,
et après lui les enfants siens
de la terre pourront jouir.
Tous craignant Dieu sont introduits
au grand trésor de ses secrets
et aux salutaires décrets
sont de son alliance instruits.

8 J'ai les yeux sans cesse éveillés
vers Dieu, son secours attendant:
c'est lui qui d'embûches mes pieds
délivrera en les guidant.
A moi, Seigneur, tant malmené,
ta face bénigne réduis, [5]
car d'angoisse pressé je suis
étant de tous abandonné.

234

wie du den Deinen gegenüber stets getan hast,
so laß deine Gnade über mich walten.

4 Indem du die Fehler, die ich dir gegenüber gemacht habe,
und so viele Versündigungen tilgst,
o Gott, gedenke meiner um deiner Güte willen,
und laß mir Gutes widerfahren.
In Gerechtigkeit und Recht ist der Herr
vollkommen rein und unbefleckt;
darum wird er dem Sünder
den Heilsweg zeigen.

5 Den gutherzigen Geist wird er führen,
um ihn an ein gutes Ziel zu bringen.
Als guter Lehrer wird er dem Demütigen zeigen,
auf welchem Pfad er gehen muß.
Erbarmen und Wahrheit
hält unser Gott vollkommen
all jenen gegenüber, die in Aufrichtigkeit
sein Gesetz und Vermächtnis bewahren.

6 Ach, in meiner Missetat ist nur
äußerstes Entsetzen, o mein Herr Gott;
doch durch die Größe deines Namens
gib deiner Güte Raum in mir.
Wo ist der, welcher, wenn er sein Verlangen
auf Gott richtet, sich fürchten muß?
Und Gott wird ihm zeigen,
den rechten Weg, den er zu wählen hat.

7 Seine Seele wird mitten in alle Güter
gestellt werden, um sich zu erfreuen,
und nach ihm werden seine Kinder
aus der Erde Nutzen ziehen.
Alle, die Gott fürchten, werden eingeführt
in den großen Schatz seiner Geheimnisse
und werden in den heilbringenden Gesetzen
seines Bundes unterrichtet.

8 Meine Augen sind ständig wach
zu Gott hin und erwarten seine Hilfe;
er wird meine Füße vom Fall
befreien und sie führen.
Herr, bringe mir, der ich so übel dran bin,
dein gütiges Antlitz näher,
denn ich bin von Angst bedrückt,
weil ich von allen verlassen bin.

9 De mon cœur les afflictions
se dilatent pour l'enserrer;
pourtant tes consolations [3]
dilate pour le desserrer.
   A la grande détresse où je suis
plaise à toi, Sire, avoir égard,
ainsi détournant le regard
de mes péchés que tu poursuis.

10 Que ton œil considère aussi
mes adversaires d'autre part:
car le nombre en est engrossi,
et leur rage comme flamme ard. [6]
   Pour ne me laisser donc choir,
me gardant, sois-moi protecteur,
et me délivrant, rédempteur,
puisqu'en toi j'ai eu mon espoir.

11 Fais que droiture et équité
me soient en soulagement,
car en toi et ta vérité
mon attente a contentement.
   Dieu, de ton salut la douceur
fais à ton peuple élu sentir,
le faisant à la fin sortir
de toute misère et langueur.

---

[1] *ébattement = distraction, jouissance.* [2] *oppresse = souffrance, malheur.*
[3] *pourtant = c'est pourquoi, voilà pourquoi.* [4] *las = hélas.* [5] *réduire = rappro-cher.* [6] *ardre = brûler.*

9 Die Leiden meines Herzens
breiten sich aus und engen es ein;
darum weite deinen Trost aus
und mach es frei.
Auf die große Not, in der ich bin,
wollest du, Herr, achthaben,
und dafür den Blick wegwenden
von meinen Sünden, die du verfolgst.

10 Daß dein Auge doch andererseits
auch meine Gegner ansehe,
denn ihre Zahl ist groß geworden
und ihre Wut brennt wie die Flamme.
Um mich also nicht fallen zu lassen,
bewahre mich, und sei mir ein Beschützer,
befreie mich und sei mir ein Erlöser,
denn auf dich habe ich meine Hoffnung gesetzt.

11 Laß Aufrichtigkeit und Redlichkeit
mir zur Linderung dienen,
denn in dir und in deiner Wahrheit
findet meine Erwartung Genüge.
Gott, laß dein auserwähltes Volk
die Milde deines Heiles spüren,
und laß es endlich herausgehen
aus aller Not und Verzagtheit.

*Die Melodie steht im Straßburger Gesangbuch seit 1525. Sie gehört
zu Matthäus Greiters Bereimung des 125. Psalms* (Nur welche hie
ihr Hoffnung gar). *Calvin hat die punktierten Rhythmen in der ersten und in der vorletzten Zeile ausgeglichen und die Endung der
Zeilen 2, 4, 5 und 8 durch Auflösung der Kadenz-Ligatur bzw. durch
Spaltung des vorletzten Tons männlich gemacht. Wie Luther und
Zwingli bei ihren ersten Psalmdichtungen, wählt auch Calvin hier einen Klagepsalm. In Strophe 4,4 – 8 ist die Reimordnung c d d c verlassen zugunsten c d c d (wie in der ersten Strophenhälfte). In der ersten Genfer Ausgabe von Calvins Psalter (1542) steht diese Psalmbearbeitung (mit Varianten) noch, später wird sie durch jene Marots mit
neuer Melodie ersetzt.*

Psaume 36

1 En moi le se - cret pen - se - ment
car il se com - plaît en ses faits

du ma - lin par - le clai - re - ment,
tant, que hai - ne sur ses mé - faits

c'est qu'à Dieu il ne pen - se,
et ju - ge - ment a - van - ce.

Son par - ler tend à dé - ce - voir,

il ne cherche en - ten - dre et sa - voir,

n' aus - si un seul bien fai - re;

il pen - se mal é - tant cou - ché,

du droit che - min est dé - bau - ché

sans au mal se dé - plai - re.

Psalm 36

1 *In mir spricht der geheime Gedanke*
des Bösen deutlich,
daß er nämlich nicht an Gott denkt,
denn er gefällt sich in seinen Taten
so sehr, daß der Unwille über seine Missetaten
und das Gericht sich mehrt.
Sein Sprechen zielt darauf ab, zu täuschen,
er sucht weder Verstehen noch Wissen,
auch keine einzige gute Tat.
Er denkt böse, (selbst) wenn er schläft;
er ist vom rechten Weg abgekommen,
ohne am Bösen Mißfallen zu finden.

2 Sire, aux cieux atteint ta bonté
   et aux nues ta vérité
   tant haut qu'on les regarde.
   Ta justice semble aux hauts monts, [1]
   tes jugements aux lieux profonds.
   L'homme et bête tu gardes.
   Notoire est ta bénignité,
   les humains sauront sûreté
   sous l'ombre de tes ailes;
   de tes biens se rassasiont
   et du fleuve abreuvés seront
   de tes délices belles.

3 Car source de vie en toi as
   et ta clarté luire feras,
   qui nos yeux illumine.
   Poursuis ta bonté vers les tiens,
   et le droit de celui maintiens
   qui devant toi chemine,
   afin que sur moi l'inhumain
   son pied n'avance et que la main
   du méchant ne me grève.
   L'homme inique est là trébuché,
   et étant par terre couché
   jamais ne se relève.

[1] semble = *ressemble.*

2 Herr, deine Güte reicht bis zum Himmel,
bis zu den Wolken deine Wahrheit,
wie hoch hinauf man ihnen auch zuschaue.
Deine Gerechtigkeit ist wie die hohen Berge,
deine Urteile sind wie die Abgründe.
Mensch und Tier behütest du.
Offenbar ist deine Güte.
Die Menschen werden Geborgenheit finden
im Schatten deiner Flügel;
an deinen Gütern werden sie sich satt essen,
und am Fluß werden sie getränkt
von deinen herrlichen Wonnen.

3 Denn du hast in dir die Quelle des Lebens,
und du wirst deine Klarheit leuchten lassen,
die unsere Augen erhellt.
Laß deine Güte den Deinen weiterhin zugute kommen,
und erhalte das Recht dessen aufrecht,
der vor dir wandelt,
damit der Unmenschliche seinen Fuß
nicht auf mich zu in Bewegung setzt,
und daß des Bösen Hand mich nicht verletzt.
Sieh, der ungerechte Mensch ist gestrauchelt;
er liegt auf dem Boden
und steht nie mehr auf.

Dies ist der einzige Fall, in welchem Calvins Melodiewahl auch für
den endgültigen Genfer Psalter maßgebend bleibt. Matthäus Greiters
Melodie zur Bereimung der ersten 16 Verse aus Psalm 119 von 1525
(Es sind doch selig alle, die) wird zu einer der wichtigsten Melodien
des späteren Hugenottenpsalters, namentlich in Verbindung mit dem
dazu geschriebenen Text Bezas nach Psalm 68 (Que Dieu se montre
seulement). Calvin hat schon 1539 die ursprünglichen Punktierungen in den Zeilen 10 und 11 und die Ligatur in Zeile 9 eliminiert. In
der Genfer Ausgabe von 1542 wurden dann in Zeile 7 und 9 noch
zwei weitere melodische Korrekturen vorgenommen. Seit 1543 ersetzt Marots Text denjenigen Calvins, aber die Melodie bleibt.

3

Psaume 46

A

1 No - tre Dieu nous est fer - me ap-pui,
au - quel au - rons en no - tre en-nui

ver - tu, for - tres-se et sûr con - fort,
pré - sent re - fu-ge et très bon port,

dont cer - tai - ne as - su - rance au - rons,

mê - me quand la ter - re ver - rons

par tremb - le - ment se dé - ro - cher

et monts dans la mer se ca - cher,

B

1 No - tre Dieu nous est fer - me ap-pui,
au - quel au - rons en no - tre en-nui

ver - tu, for - tres - se et sûr con - fort,
pré - sent re - fu - ge et très bon port,

dont cer - tai - ne as - su - rance au - rons,

242

Psalm 46

1 *Unser Gott ist uns fester Halt,*
  Stärke, Zuflucht und sicherer Trost;
  bei ihm werden wir in unserem Verdruß
  bereitstehende Zuflucht und sehr guten Hafen finden,
  womit wir gewisse Zuversicht haben,
  auch wenn wir sehen, wie die Erde
  sich im Beben herabläßt
  und wie sich Berge im Meer verbergen,

mê - me quand la ter - re ver - rons

par tremb - le - ment se dé - ro - cher

et monts dans la mer se ca - cher,

2 quand la mer, bruyant et tonnant,
comme par courroux s'enflera
et, les grands rochers étonnant, [1]
de vagues les ébranlera.
Car la cité qu'a Dieu élue,
qui pour sa maison lui a plue,
son ruisseau doux et clair aura
qui toujours la réjouira.

3 Le Seigneur y est au milieu,
pourtant ferme elle se tiendra; [2]
pour l'aider en temps et en lieu
de grand matin il veillera.
Les peuples se sont tempêtés,
royaumes en trouble ont étés,
mais Dieu les tençant de sa voix [3]
les rend en un moment tous cois.

4 Dieu des armées conducteur,
le Dieu de Jacob est pour nous,
pourtant nous sera protecteur [2]
contre nos adversaires tous.
Pourtant venez apercevoir, [2]
chacun de vous s'applique à voir
les merveilles que Dieu a faites
quand ses ennemis a défait.

5 C'est lui qui par son seul édit
peut toute la terre apaiser,
et au monde sans contredit
toute bataille fait cesser.
C'est lui qui peut les arcs briser,
lances en pièces menuiser,

2 wenn das Meer lärmend und donnernd
wie in Wut sich aufbläht,
die großen Felsen erschüttert und
sie mit den Wellen in Bewegung setzt.
Denn die Stadt, die Gott erwählt hat,
welche ihm als sein Haus gefallen hat,
wird ihren sanften und lauteren Bach besitzen,
welcher sie stets erfreuen wird.

3 Der Herr ist dort in der Mitte,
daher wird sie festbleiben;
um ihr jederzeit zu helfen,
wird er vom frühen Morgen über ihr wachen.
Die Völker sind in Aufruhr geraten,
Königreiche sind in Unruhe gekommen,
aber wenn Gott sie mit seiner Stimme schilt,
werden sie augenblicklich alle ruhig.

4 Gott, der Führer der (himmlischen) Heerscharen,
der Gott Jakobs, ist mit uns;
so wird er unser Beschützer sein
gegen alle unsere Feinde.
So kommt und schauet,
jeder von euch befleißige sich zu sehen
die Wundertaten, die Gott vollbracht hat,
als er seine Feinde besiegte.

5 Er ist es, der allein durch seinen Befehl
die ganze Erde zur Ruhe bringen kann
und auf der Welt alle Schlachten
ohne Widerspruch beendigen kann.
Er ist es, der die Wogen brechen,
Lanzen zersplittern kann;

de la flamme va consumant [4]
les charriots, les abîmant. [5]

6 Pourtant fait à tous à savoir [6]
qu'il est celui qui redouté
doit être pour son grand pouvoir,
et en tout le monde exalté.
Dieu, des armées le recteur,
nous sera toujours pour tuteur,
le Dieu de Jacob nous sera
pour refuge et nous gardera.

[1] *étonner = ébranler.*   [2] *pourtant = c'est pourquoi, voilà pourquoi.*   [3] *tencer = gronder.*   [4] *de la flamme: instrumental.*   [5] *abîmer = faire disparaître, anéantir, effacer.*   [6] *C'est pourquoi il fait savoir à tous.*

4
Psaume 91

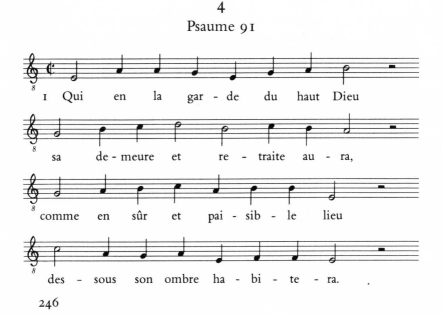

1 Qui en la gar - de du haut Dieu
sa de - meure et re - traite au - ra,
comme en sûr et pai - sib - le lieu
des - sous son ombre ha - bi - te - ra.

mit Feuer verbrennt er
die Kampfwagen und vernichtet sie.

6 *Darum läßt er alle wissen,*
daß er es ist, der
um seiner großen Macht willen gefürchtet
und auf der ganzen Welt gepriesen werden muß.
Gott, der Lenker der (himmlischen) Heere,
wird uns immer als Beistand dienen,
der Gott Jakobs wird uns
als Zuflucht dienen
und uns behüten.

Für diesen Trostpsalm wählt Calvin die Straßburger Weise Wolfgang
Dachsteins zu Psalm 15 (O Herr, wer wird sein Wohnung han) *von*
1526. Am Ende der Stollen wie des Abgesangs verwandelt er durch
Auflösung der Kadenz-Ligaturen die weiblichen in männliche En-
dungen. Ferner wird das Metrum durch Wiederholung der ersten
Abgesangszeile von 7 auf 8 Zeilen erweitert. Die Ligatur in der
1. Zeile bleibt bestehen. Aber schon in der Genfer Ausgabe des Psal-
ters von 1542 wird die durch den Oktavsprung sehr charakteristische
Stollenmelodie völlig neu konzipiert (B). Die Melodie ist nun rein
syllabisch. Später wird der Text durch einen von Marot ersetzt. Die-
ser bekommt erst 1551 durch Loys Bourgeois eine endgültige Melo-
die.

Psalm 91

1 *Wer in der Obhut des hohen Gottes*
seine Wohnung und seinen Ruhesitz hat,
wird wie an einem sicheren und friedlichen Ort
unter seinem Schatten wohnen.
Ich werde kühn zu Gott sagen:
«Du bist meine Burg und Hoffnung;
darum werde ich es wagen, mein Vertrauen
unablässig auf dich zu setzen.»

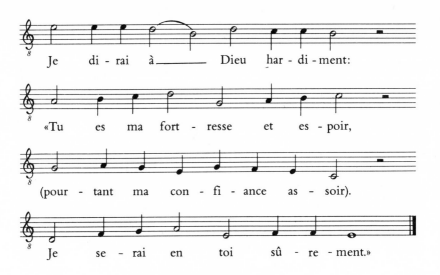

Je di - rai à Dieu har - di - ment:

«Tu es ma fort - resse et es - poir,

(pour - tant ma con - fi - ance as - soir).

Je se - rai en toi sû - re - ment.»

2 Puis en moi-même revenant
je dis: Dieu te délivrera
de tout encombrier survenant
et des lacs te dépêtrera.[1]
    Sous ses plumes étant en paix,
    et sous son aile à sûreté,
    auras toujours sa vérité
    pour targe et bouclier bien épais.

3 Par quoi ne craindras point d'avoir
mauvaise rencontre de nuit,
ni coup de flèche recevoir
tiré à toi quand le jour luit.
    Soit en ténèbres ou clarté
    que ruine passe en nuisant
    et tout çà et là détruisant:
    tu seras en tranquillité.

4 Quand mille à une main verras,
dix mille à l'autre trébucher,[2]
tout le malheur échapperas,
sans que de toi puisse approcher.
    Ton œil verra évidemment
    que la mortelle affliction
    tombera en confusion
    sus l'inique, pour son paiement.

5 En Dieu chercheras ton confort,
pourtant de lui seras aidé;[3]

2 *Wenn ich dann an mich selbst denke,*
sage ich: Gott wird dich befreien
von jedem Hindernis
und von den Fallstricken.
  Unter seinen Schwingen bist du im Frieden
  und unter seinem Flügel in Sicherheit;
  du wirst seine Wahrheit immer
  als Tartsche und als sehr starken Schild haben.

3 *Daher wirst du dich nicht zu fürchten haben,*
  weder vor einer bösen Begegnung in der Nacht,
  noch vor einem Pfeil,
  der auf dich geschossen wird, wenn der Tag leuchtet.
  Ob in Finsternis oder bei Tageslicht
  das Verderben schädigend
  und alles hier und dort zerstörend vorbeikommt,
  du wirst in Ruhe sein.

4 *Wenn du zur einen Hand tausend,*
  zur anderen zehntausend fallen siehst,
  wirst du dem Unheil entgehen,
  ohne daß es sich dir nähern kann.
  Dein Auge wird mit Gewißheit sehen,
  daß das tödliche Leid
  zu seiner Beschämung
  auf den Schnöden fallen wird, ihm zur Strafe.

5 *Wenn du in Gott Trost suchst,*
  dann wird er dir helfen;

comme dessus un rocher fort
sus lui ton refuge as fondé.
 Malheur aucun ne t'adviendra,
 plaie aucune pour te blesser,
 ne pour tous les tiens oppresser
 ton tabernacle n'atteindra.

6 Car pour ton salut maintenir
à ses anges il a mandé
qu'ès voies qu'auras à tenir
par eux tu sois toujours gardé.
 En leurs mains ils te porteront,
 te faisant tel soulagement
 qu'à rencontre ou empêchement
 jamais tes pieds ne heurteront.

7 Sus l'aspic, serpent venimeux,
et le lion tu marcheras;
lionceau et dragon hideux
sans dommage au pied fouleras.
 Dieu dit de toi: «Je l'aiderai,
 puisqu'en estime il m'a tenu;
 puisqu'il a mon nom reconnu,
 en tout bien je l'exalterai.

8 M'invocant, il sera ouï,
prochain m'aura en tout émoi,
pour être en la fin réjoui
et mis en honneur de par moi.
 Sa vie aura heureusement,
 par ma grâce, bon et long cours,
 et de ma vertu le secours
 le conduira en sauvement.»

---

[1] *lacs (n. m.) = noeud coulant pour capturer le gibier ou certains animaux nuisibles; fig.: piège.* [2] *Quand tu verras trébucher mille à une main, dix mille à l'autre.* [3] *pourtant = c'est pourquoi.*

wie auf einem festen Felsen
hast du auf ihm deinen Zufluchtsort gegründet.
  Kein Leid wird dir widerfahren,
  keine Plage wird, dich zu verletzen
  noch die Deinen zu bedrängen,
  dein Zelt treffen.

6 *Denn, um dein Heil zu bewahren,*
  hat er seinen Engeln befohlen,
  daß du auf den Wegen, die du zu gehen hast,
  von ihnen stets beschützt seiest.
    Sie werden dich auf ihren Händen tragen
    und bringen dir solchen Beistand,
    daß bei einem Zusammentreffen oder Hindernis
    deine Füße niemals anstoßen werden.

7 *Du wirst über die Viper, die giftige Schlange,*
  und über den Löwen schreiten,
  du wirst den jungen Löwen und den garstigen Drachen
  ohne Schaden unter die Füße treten können.
    Gott sagt von dir: «Ich werde ihm helfen,
    weil er mich in Ehren gehalten hat;
    weil er meinen Namen anerkannt hat,
    werde ich ihn herrlich erhöhen.

8 *Wenn er mich anruft, wird er erhört werden,*
  er wird mich nahe haben in aller Not
  und am Ende erfreut
  und durch mich zu Ehren gebracht werden.
    Sein Leben wird in Glück
    durch meine Gnade gut sein und lange währen,
    und die Hilfe meiner Kraft
    wird ihn in die Erlösung führen.»

*Wenn man Calvins Melodie-Ideal kennengelernt hat, versteht man,
daß er die Konstanzer Melodie zu Psalm 91 von Wolfgang Mösel
nicht übernehmen konnte und zu Greiters Melodie des Psalms 51
von 1525 griff* (O Herre Gott, begnade mich), *in welcher er die Wiederholung des vierzeiligen Stollens und die vorletzte Zeile wegließ.
Ferner hat er in Zeile 5 die Ligatur durch Weglassung der punktierten
Durchgangsnote vereinfacht. So ist eine zweiteilige, achtzeilige Melodie entstanden, wobei die 3., 4. und letzte Zeile durch Spaltung der
vorletzten Note statt einer weiblichen eine männliche Endung erhielten. Die ohnehin nicht sehr überzeugende Melodie ist dadurch
allerdings nicht besser geworden. Sie wurde deshalb für die Genfer*

Ausgabe von *1542 (wohl durch Guillaume Franc) einschneidend bearbeitet, indem sie aus dem phrygischen in den dorischen Modus versetzt wurde (B). Die endgültige Melodie zu diesem Psalm (Text von Marot) zeigt nur noch wenige Anklänge an diese Genfer Fassung der Straßburger Weise.*

5

Psaume 113

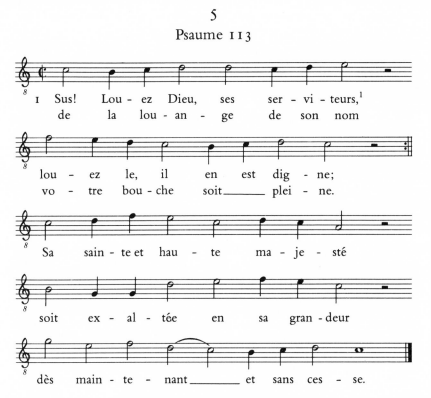

1 Sus! Lou - ez Dieu, ses ser - vi - teurs,[1]
de la lou - an - ge de son nom

lou - ez le, il en est dig - ne;
vo - tre bou - che soit_____ plei - ne.

Sa sain - te et hau - te ma - je - sté

soit ex - al - tée en sa gran - deur

dès main - te - nant_____ et sans ces - se.

2 Tant qu'étend le soleil son cours
dessus toute la terre,
le nom de Dieu partout reluit
plein de magnificence.
    Sus tous peuples et nations[1]
    le seigneur Dieu est élevé,
    même tous les cieux surmonte.

3 Où a notre Dieu son pareil
qui lui ressemble en gloire?
Lequel a si haut élevé
son trône et habitacle,

Psalm 113

1 *Auf, lobet Gott, ihr, seine Diener;*
 lobt ihn, er ist dessen würdig;
 des Lobes seines Namens
 sei euer Mund voll.
  Seine heilige und hohe Majestät
  sei gepriesen in ihrer Größe
  von nun an und ohne Unterlaß.

2 *Soweit die Sonne ihren Lauf erstreckt*
 über die ganze Erde,
 erstrahlt der Name Gottes überall
 voller Herrlichkeit.
  Über alle Völker und Nationen
  ist der Herr Gott erhaben;
  auch alle Himmel überragt er.

3 *Wo hat unser Gott seinesgleichen,*
 der ihm an Ruhm gleichkommt?
 Der so hoch droben
 seinen Thron und Wohnsitz hat,

dont il se baisse à contempler
les créatures qu'il maintient
tant au ciel comme en la terre;

4 qui le pauvre, en terre abattu,
fait sortir et élève,
qui l'homme nu et anéanti
suscite de la fiente,[2]
pour les hautement colloquer,[3]
les ayant de misère ôtés,
entre les princes du peuple;

5 qui bénit en fécondité
les femmes infertiles,
celle qui ne pouvait porter
multiplie en semence.
Sus! Louez donques le Seigneur,[4]
rendez la louange à son nom,
telle que ses faits méritent.

---

[1] sus *(ici)* = *au-dessus de.*   [2] *fiente* = *excréments de certains animaux.*   [3] *colloquer* = *placer.*   [4] *donques* = *donc.*

6

Psaume 138

1 Lou - an - ge et grâ - ce   je   te   ren - drai,
En   ton   saint temp - le   j'a - do - re - rai,

de   tout mon cœur   te   mag - ni - fie - rai
la   gran - deur de   ton   nom chan - te - rai

von wo er sich niederbeugt, um anzusehen
die Geschöpfe, die er am Leben erhält,
im Himmel wie auf Erden;

4 der den Armen, der zu Boden geworfen wurde,
gehen läßt und erhebt;
der den nackten und zunichte gewordenen Menschen
aus dem Kot aufstehen läßt,
um ihnen hoch oben einen Platz zu geben
– nachdem er sie aus dem Elend befreit hat –
unter den Fürsten des Volkes;

5 der mit Fruchtbarkeit segnet
die unfruchtbaren Frauen,
die, welche keine Kinder tragen konnte,
mit Nachkommen vermehrt.
Auf, darum lobet den Herrn,
bringt seinem Namen Lob,
so wie es seinen Taten gebührt.

Unter Luthers Psalmliedern findet man kein Loblied. Calvin jedoch
hat in seine kleine Auswahl neben Marots 103. Psalm auch noch diesen Lobpsalm aufgenommen und ihm die fröhliche Straßburger Melodie von Luthers Aus tiefer Not von 1524 beigegeben; sie stammt
sehr wahrscheinlich von Wolfgang Dachstein. Calvins Fassung
stimmt mit der des Konstanzer Gesangbuchs, die etwas anders lautet
als die der frühen Straßburger Quellen, überein; nur die Textvertei-
lung ist in der Schlußzeile anders geregelt, wohl deshalb, weil Calvin
hier das Metrum um eine Silbe erweitert hat. Genf 1542 bringt bereits die neue Bereimung Marots mit neuer Melodie.

Psalm 138

1 Lob und Dank will ich dir erweisen,
von ganzem Herzen will ich dich verherrlichen,
vor allen Fürsten.
In deinem heiligen Tempel will ich anbeten,
die Größe deines Namens will ich besingen
um deiner Milde und Wahrheit willen.

de - vant tou - te prin - ci - pau - té.
pour ta clé - men - ce et vé - ri - té.

Com - me sus tout ta ma - je - sté[1]

par ta pa - role as ex - al - tée,[1]

quand j'ai à toi ma voix haus - sée,

in - con - ti - nent m'as ex - au - cé,

de ta ver - tu me sou - te - nant,

mon âme en é - tat main - te - nant. Al -

lé - lu - ia, al - lé - - - lu - ia.

2 Tous rois de la terre te loueront,
à ta grandeur se soumettront,
étant en ta parole appris,
de tes faits chantant la dignité;
car à ta grand' gloire as limité[2]
ciel et terre pour ton pourpris.[3]

En hautesse, pour commander
le Seigneur est assis ès cieux;
néanmoins incline les yeux
pour l'humble et petit regarder;

256

So wie du deine Majestät über alles
durch dein Wort erhöht hast,
hast du, als ich meine Stimme zu dir erhoben habe,
mich sogleich erhört
und mich mit deiner Kraft gestützt,
meine Seele wohl bewahrt.
Halleluja, Halleluja.

2 *Alle Könige der Erde werden dich loben,*
   werden sich deiner Größe unterwerfen;
   in deinem Wort unterwiesen,
   werden sie die Würde deiner Taten besingen,
   denn zu deiner großen Ehre hast du
   Himmel und Erde zu deinem Wohnsitz bestimmt.
      In Erhabenheit, um zu gebieten,
      thront der Herr in den Himmeln;
      dennoch neigt er seine Augen nieder,
      um den Demütigen und Kleinen anzusehen.

le superbe en son jugement
de loin voit par contemnement.[4]
Alléluia, alléluia.

3 D'affliction si je suis grevé,
en vigueur et vie relevé
serai par ton soulagement;
sus mes ennemis se dressera
ta main, et leur fureur rompra,
et en elle aurai sauvement.
Le Seigneur en moi poursuivra
sa bénignité à toujours.
O Dieu, du monde outre le cours,[5]
ta clémence persistera:
l'œuvre de ta main commencé
tu n'oublieras pour délaissé.
Alléluia, alléluia.

[1] *exalter = élever.*   [2] *limiter = fixer.*   [3] *pourpris = habitation, séjour.*   [4] *contemnement = mépris, dédain.*   [5] *outre le cours du monde (outre: préposition).*

7

Cantique de Siméon
au chap. 2 de Saint Luc

1 Main - te- nant, Seig-neur Dieu, as don- né en moi lieu à ta sain - te pro - mes - se,

Den Hochmütigen sieht er in seinem Urteil
von weitem mit Verachtung an.
Halleluja, Halleluja.

3   Wenn ich von Trübsal geplagt bin,
werde ich zu Kraft und Leben erweckt
durch deine Hilfe;
gegen meine Feinde wird sich deine Hand erheben
und ihre Wut zerschlagen,
und in ihr werde ich Heil finden.
Der Herr wird mir seine Güte
auf immer erhalten.
O Gott, über den Lauf der Welt hinaus
wird deine Gnade bestehen.
Das Werk deiner Hand, das du begonnen hast,
wirst du nicht als etwas Liegengelassenes vergessen.
Hallelujua, Halleluja.

Dies ist ein weiterer Lobpsalm; er beginnt und schließt im Bibeltext
mit Halleluja. Als Refrain gehört dieser Lobruf zu der gewählten
Melodie Matthäus Greiters. Es ist die seines 114. Psalms (Da Israel
aus Ägypten zog) von 1526. In der 3. Stollenzeile ist wohl irrtümlich
die erste statt der vorletzten Note gespalten. Wir haben diesen Irrtum
richtiggestellt, womit klar wird, daß Calvin auch hier eine weibliche
durch eine männliche Zeilenschlußbildung ersetzt hat. In der Genfer
Ausgabe von 1542 hat Calvin den Text überarbeitet (z. B. Beginn von
der Einzahl in die Mehrzahl versetzt); auch an der Melodie sind Ver-
änderungen vorgenommen worden. Seit 1543 tritt die Übertragung
Marots mit einer neuen Melodie von Guillaume Franc an die Stelle
derjenigen Calvins.

Der Lobgesang Simeons
im 2. Kapitel des Lukas

1   Nun, Herr Gott,
hast du in mir Raum gegeben
deinem heiligen Versprechen,

puis - que ton ser - vi - teur   sor - tir   de tout mal -

heur   en   bon re - pos tu lais - ses.

2 Car mes yeux clairement
   ont vu le sauvement[1]
   auquel gît pleine joie,[2]
   que par ta bonté voir
   et de toi recevoir
   attendu tant j'avoie.[3]

3 Tu l'as haut élevé,
   comme un but approuvé,
   auquel chacun doit tendre,
   car envers tous humains
   ta grâce par ses mains
   tu as voulu étendre,

4 afin qu'aux ignorants
   et aux peuples errants
   soit lumière et adresse,[4]
   aussi que le bonheur
   et la gloire et honneur
   d'Israël il redresse.

[1] *sauvement = sauvetage, salut.*   [2] *auquel gît = dans lequel est placé.*   [3] *j'avoie = j'avais.*   [4] *adresse = guide.*

260

indem du deinen Diener
aus allem Unglück
in gute Ruhe hingehen läßt.

2 Denn meine Augen haben
in Klarheit das Heil gesehen,
in welchem volle Freude liegt,
welches durch deine Güte zu sehen
und von dir zu erhalten,
ich so sehr erwartet hatte.

3 Du hast es hoch erhoben,
wie ein erprobtes Ziel,
nach welchem jeder streben muß,
denn über alle Menschen
wolltest du durch seine Hände
deine Gnade ausbreiten,

4 damit es den Unwissenden
und den irrenden Völkern
Licht und Führer sei,
auch damit es das Glück
und den Ruhm und die Ehre
Israels wieder aufrichte.

Die vorliegende Liedbearbeitung des Lobgesanges Simeons (Lukas
2,29–32) ist der Beweis dafür, daß Calvins Straßburger Psalmen-
Sammlung nach und nach zusammengekommen ist: Calvin dichtet
hier nicht auf eine der deutschen Straßburger Melodien, sondern auf
eine der Melodien, die er von Greiter und Dachstein für die Texte
Marots schreiben ließ: Er wählte das Metrum von Psalm 3, ließ aber
auch diesen Text dann mit einer eigenen, neuen Weise (wahrscheinlich von Wolfgang Dachstein) versehen. Calvin will jedem Text sein
eigenes Melodiegewand geben, wie das auch im späteren Genfer
Psalter weitgehend verwirklicht ist (151 Texte und 125 Melodien).
    In der ersten Genfer Ausgabe von 1542 steht das Lied noch mit
Calvins Text und der Straßburger Melodie, allerdings mit rhythmischen und melodischen Varianten. Seit 1543 wird Calvins Text dann
durch jenen Marots ersetzt. Marot hat immerhin auch hier das von
Calvin gewählte Versmaß beibehalten.

8
Les dix commandements
pris du XXᵉ d'Exode

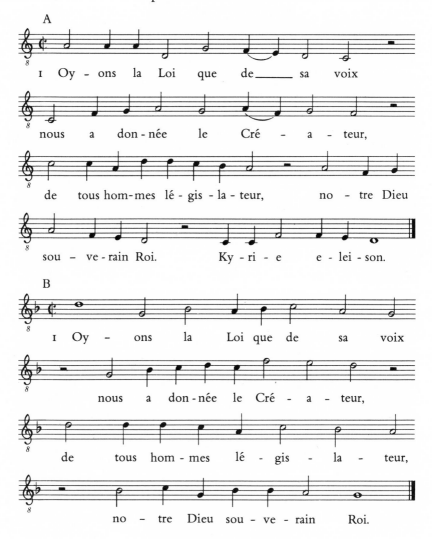

A

1 Oy - ons la Loi que de____ sa voix
nous a don - née le Cré - a - teur,
de tous hom-mes lé - gis - la - teur, no - tre Dieu
sou - ve - rain Roi. Ky - ri - e e - lei - son.

B

1 Oy - ons la Loi que de sa voix
nous a don - née le Cré - a - teur,
de tous hom - mes lé - gis - la - teur,
no - tre Dieu sou - ve - rain Roi.

2 Je suis le Seigneur que tu dois
seul pour Dieu servir et aimer:
autre Dieu faire ou renommer[1]
n'entreprendras devant moi.
Kyrie eleison.

Die Zehn Gebote
aus dem 20. Kapitel des Buches Exodus

1 *Laßt uns das Gesetz hören, das mit seiner Stimme*
der Schöpfer uns gegeben hat,
der Gesetzgeber aller Menschen,
unser Gott, höchster König.
Kyrie eleison.

2 *Ich bin der Herr, den allein du*
als Gott fürchten und lieben sollst:
Einen anderen Gott zu machen oder zu verehren,
sollst du mir gegenüber nicht unternehmen.
Kyrie eleison.

3 Image point ne forgeras
  pour mon essence figurer,
  pour invoquer ou honorer,
  ma gloire leur assignant.
  Kyrie eleison.

4 Le nom de Dieu ne pollueras
  mais saint et sacré te sera;
  car Dieu pour innocent n'aura[2]
  tout homme en vain le prenant.
  Kyrie eleison.

5 Le sabbat tu sanctifieras,
  en Dieu toujours te reposant,
  et l'ordre et police observant
  qu'a mis Dieu entre les jours.
  Kyrie eleison.

6 Honneur et crainte porteras
  à père et mère, les servant,
  afin que sur terre vivant
  en paix achèves ton cours.
  Kyrie eleison.

7 Homicide point ne seras
  tant de fait comme de vouloir;
  à haine et courroux nul pouvoir
  ne donneras en ton cœur.
  Kyrie eleison.

8 En chasteté tu viveras
  ton cœur purement contenant,
  de ton corps ne contaminant,
  par paillardise, l'honneur.
  Kyrie eleison.

9 Le bien d'autrui injustement
  à toi tirer ne tâcheras,
  rapine ou fraude ne feras
  afin d'accroître le tien.
  Kyrie eleison.

10 Contre ton prochain faussement
  de ta langue ne mentiras;
  mais en vérité serviras
  à son honneur et son bien.
  Kyrie eleison.

11 Ton cœur d'aucun désir tenté
  ne soit du bien de tes prochains,

3 Du sollst kein Bild machen,
mein Wesen darzustellen,
um es anzurufen oder zu verehren
und meine Ehre darauf zu übertragen.
Kyrie eleison.

4 Du sollst den Namen Gottes nicht entweihen,
sondern er soll dir heilig und geweiht sein;
denn Gott wird den nicht für unschuldig halten,
der ihn unnütz braucht.
Kyrie eleison.

5 Den Sabbat sollst du heilig halten,
indem du stets in Gott ausruhst
und die Abfolge und Ordnung beachtest,
die Gott unter den Tagen festgelegt hat.
Kyrie eleison.

6 Ehre und Furcht sollst du
Vater und Mutter erweisen, indem du ihnen dienst,
damit du in einem ruhigen Leben
auf Erden deinen Lauf vollendest.
Kyrie eleison.

7 Du sollst kein Mörder sein,
weder in Tat noch in Absicht;
du sollst Haß und Zorn keine Macht
geben in deinem Herzen.
Kyrie eleison.

8 Du sollst in Keuschheit leben,
dein Herz rein halten,
und die Ehre deines Leibes
nicht durch Ausschweifung verunreinigen.
Kyrie eleison.

9 Den Besitz des Andern auf unrechte Weise
an dich zu bringen, sollst du nicht versuchen.
Raub oder Veruntreuung sollst du nicht begehen,
um das Deine zu vermehren.
Kyrie eleison.

10 Gegen deinen Nächsten sollst du
mit deiner Zunge nicht fälschlich lügen,
vielmehr in Wahrhaftigkeit dienen
seiner Ehre und seinem Gut.
Kyrie eleison.

11 Dein Herz soll von keinem Wunsch
nach Hab und Gut deiner Nächsten in Versuchung geführt werden,

mais ton amour vers tous humains
s'encline au lieu de t'aimer.
Kyrie eleison.

12 Dieu, qui de toute sainteté
contiens seul la vertu en toi,
à la justice de ta loi
veuille nos mœurs conformer.
Kyrie eleison.

[1] *renommer: nommer souvent et avec éloges, célébrer.*   [2] *avoir pour: tenir pour.*

9
Crédo

Je crois en Dieu, le Pè - re tout-puis-sant,

cré - a - teur du ciel et de ter - re,

et en Jé-sus Christ, son fils u - ni-que,

no - tre Seig-neur, qui a é - té con - çu

deine Liebe aber soll sich auf alle Menschen
richten, anstatt dich selbst zu lieben.
Kyrie eleison.

12 Gott, der du aus ganzer Heiligkeit
allein die Tugend in dir besitzt:
an das Recht deines Gesetzes
wollest du unser Tun und Lassen anpassen.
Kyrie eleison.

Für sein Zehn Gebote-Lied wählt Calvin die Straßburger Melodie zu
Luthers längerem Zehn Gebote-Lied vn 1525 (Dies sind die heilgen
Zehn Gebot). Mit der Melodie hat Calvin den Kyrie-Refrain übernommen. Mit dem Halleluja bei Nr. 6 verschwindet auch dieser liturgische Ruf im Genfer Psalter schon seit 1542 vollständig. Dort
steht nämlich zwar noch Calvins Text, aber mit einer neuen Melodie
ohne Kyrie-Refrain (B). In der Ausgabe von 1543 stand dann sehr
wahrscheinlich bereits Marots Übertragung mit jener neuen Melodie
Guillaume Francs, die dann schon 1567 in der Bearbeitung Johann
Baptist Seegers zu Wenn wir in höchsten Nöten sein in den deutschen Kirchengesang gelangt ist.

Credo

Ich glaube an Gott, den allmächtigen Vater, Schöpfer des Himmels und der
Erde, und an Jesus Christus, seinen einzigen Sohn, unseren Herrn, der empfangen wurde vom Heiligen Geist, geboren von der Jungfrau Maria; er hat
gelitten unter Pontius Pilatus, ist gekreuzigt worden, ist gestorben und begraben worden und ist hinabgestiegen in die Hölle; am dritten Tag ist er
von den Toten auferstanden und dann aufgestiegen in die Himmel, wo er
sitzt zur Rechten Gottes, des allmächtigen Vaters; von dort wird er kommen, zu richten über die Lebenden und die Toten. Ich glaube auch an den
Heiligen Geist, an die heilige katholische Kirche, die Gemeinschaft der
Heiligen, die Vergebung der Sünden, die Auferstehung des Fleisches, das
ewige Leben. Amen.

du Saint Es - prit, né de la Vier - ge

Ma - ri - e; a souf-fert sous Pon - ce

Pi - la - te, cru - ci - fi - é, mort et

en - sé - ve - li, et est des - cen - du aux[1]

en - fers; le troi - siè - me jour est res -

su - sci - té des morts, et puis est

mon - té aux[1] cieux, où il est as - sis

à la dex - tre de Dieu le Pè - re

tout pu - is - sant; de là vien - dra

ju - ger les vifs et les morts. Je crois aus - si

au Saint Es - prit, la sainte E - gli - se

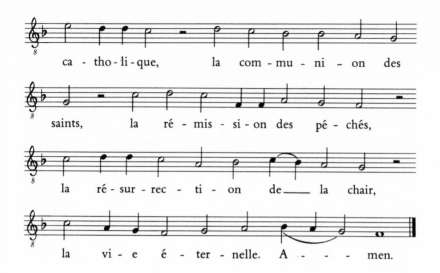

ca - tho - li - que, la com - mu - ni - on des saints, la ré - mis - si - on des pé - chés, la ré - sur - rec - ti - on de___ la chair, la vi - e é - ter - nelle. A - - - men.

Calvin unterlegt der Straßburger Credo-Melodie von *1524* nicht ohne Geschick den französischen Prosatext des Apostolicums. Der Melodieverlauf wird nicht verändert, aber es waren für die Unterlegung des französischen Textes mannigfache Tonspaltungen und Tonwiederholungen nötig. Dabei hat Calvin die Zahl der Ligaturen von *14* auf *6* verringert. In der ersten Ausgabe des Genfer Psalters von *1542* finden wir eine gereimte Fassung des Credo von Marot mit neuer Melodie. Später verschwindet das Credo ganz aus dem Genfer Psalter und damit aus der Genfer Liturgie.

Psaume et chanson je chanterai
à un seul Dieu, tant que serai.

A Dieu seul soit honneur
et gloire.

*

Psalm und Gesang werde ich singen
einem einzigen Gott, solange ich lebe.

Gott allein sei Ehre
und Ruhm.

La Préface du Psautier Genevois de 1542/1543

A tous chrétiens et amateurs de la Parole de Dieu, salut.

Comme c'est une chose bien requise en la Chrétienté, et des plus nécessaires, que chaque fidèle observe et entretienne la communion de l'Eglise en son endroit, fréquentant les assemblées qui se font tant le dimanche que les autres jours pour honorer et servir Dieu, aussi est-il expédient et raisonnable que tous connaissent et entendent ce qui se dit et fait au temple, pour en recevoir fruit et édification. Car notre Seigneur n'a pas institué l'ordre que nous devons tenir quand nous nous réunissons en son nom seulement pour amuser le monde à voir et regarder, mais plutôt il a voulu qu'il en revînt profit à tout son peuple, comme saint Paul témoigne, commandant que tout ce qui se fait en l'Eglise soit rapporté à l'édification commune de tous; ce que le serviteur ne commanderait pas, que telle ne fût l'intention du Maître. Or cela ne se peut faire, que nous ne soyons instruits pour avoir intelligence de tout ce qui a été ordonné pour notre utilité. Car de dire que nous puissions avoir dévotion, soit à prières, soit à cérémonies, sans y rien entendre, c'est une grande moquerie, quoiqu'il se dise communément. Ce n'est pas une chose morte ni brutale que bonne affection envers Dieu, mais c'est un mouvement vif, procédant du Saint-Esprit, quand le cœur est droitement touché et l'entendement illuminé. Et de fait, si on pouvait être édifié des choses qu'on voit, sans connaître ce qu'elles signifient, saint Paul ne défendrait pas si rigoureusement de parler en langue inconnue, et n'userait de cette raison, qu'il n'y a nulle édification sinon où il y a doctrine. C'est pourquoi, si nous voulons bien honorer les saintes ordonnances de notre Seigneur, desquelles nous usons en l'Eglise, le principal est de savoir ce qu'elles contiennent, ce qu'elles veulent dire, et à quelle fin elles tendent, afin que l'usage en soit utile et salutaire, et par conséquent droitement réglé. Or il y a en somme trois choses que notre Seigneur nous a commandées d'observer en nos assemblées spirituelles, à savoir, la prédication de sa parole, les oraisons publiques et solennelles, et l'administration de ses Sacrements. Je renonce à parler

Die Gesangbuchvorrede von 1542/1543

Johannes Calvin wünscht allen Christen und denen, die Gottes Wort lieb haben, Heil.

In der Christenheit ist es wichtig und etwas vom Nötigsten, daß jeder Gläubige die Gemeinschaft mit der Kirche an seinem Ort pflegt, indem er die Versammlungen besucht, die am Sonntag wie an den anderen Tagen stattfinden, um Gott die Ehre zu geben und ihm zu dienen. Und so ist es auch zweckmäßig und vernünftig, daß alle wissen und verstehen, was im Gotteshaus gesagt und getan wird; nur so können sie daraus Frucht und Erbauung gewinnen. Denn unser Herr hat die Ordnung, die wir einhalten, wenn wir uns in seinem Namen versammeln, nicht eingesetzt, um der Welt Unterhaltung zum Anschauen und Zuschauen zu bieten, sondern er hat vielmehr gewollt, daß seinem ganzen Volk daraus ein Gewinn entstehe, wie der heilige Paulus das bezeugt, wenn er anordnet, daß alles, was in der Kirche geschieht, auf die gemeinsame Erbauung aller gerichtet sein soll (1.Korinther 14,1–5); und das würde der Diener nicht anordnen, wenn es nicht die Absicht des Meisters wäre.

Nun darf es nicht vorkommen, daß wir der Unterweisung mangeln, all das zu verstehen, was zu unserem Nutzen eingerichtet worden ist. Denn es wäre ja aufs Höchste lächerlich, zu meinen, wir könnten andächtig sein, sei es zum Gebet, sei es zu den heiligen Handlungen, ohne etwas zu verstehen – obwohl das immer wieder behauptet wird. Die wirkliche Zuneigung zu Gott ist nichts Totes oder Plumpes, sondern es ist eine lebendige Bewegung aus dem Heiligen Geist, wenn das Herz unmittelbar berührt und der Verstand erleuchtet wird. Und in der Tat, wenn man erbaut werden könnte durch Dinge, die man sieht, ohne zu wissen, was sie bedeuten, würde der heilige Paulus das Zungenreden nicht so streng verbieten und würde nicht behaupten, es gäbe keine Erbauung, wo es keine Lehre gibt (1.Korinther 14,6–19). Darum, wenn wir die heiligen Ordnungen unseres Herrn, an die wir uns in der Kirche halten, recht in Ehren halten wollen, dann haben wir in erster Linie zu wissen, was sie enthalten, was sie bedeuten und wohin sie zielen, damit ihr Gebrauch nützlich und heilsam und somit auch richtig geregelt sei.

Nun ist es im Ganzen dreierlei, was unser Herr uns bei unseren geistlichen Versammlungen zu halten befohlen hat, nämlich die Predigt seines Wortes, die öffentlichen und feierlichen Gebete und die Verwaltung der Sakramente. Ich sehe für diesmal davon ab, über die

des prédications pour cette heure, d'autant qu'il n'en est pas question. Touchant les deux autres parties qui restent, nous avons le commandement exprès du Saint-Esprit que les oraisons se fassent en langue commune et connue au peuple; et dit l'apôtre que le peuple ne peut répondre «amen» à la prière qui a été faite en langue étrange. Or est-il ainsi, que puisqu'on la fait au nom et en la personne de tous, que chacun en doit être participant. Pour cette raison cela a été une trop grande impudence à ceux qui ont introduit la langue latine par les Eglises, où elle n'était communément entendue. Et il n'y a subtilité ni ruse qui les puisse excuser, que cette façon ne soit perverse et déplaisante à Dieu. Car il ne faut présumer qu'il ait agréable ce qui se fait directement contre son vouloir, et comme par dépit de lui. Or on ne le saurait plus dépiter que d'aller ainsi à l'encontre de sa défense, et se glorifier en cette rébellion, comme si c'était une chose sainte et fort louable. Quant aux Sacrements, si nous regardons bien leur nature, nous connaîtrons que c'est une coutume perverse de les célébrer en telle sorte que le peuple n'en ait sinon la vue, sans exposition des mystères qui y sont contenus. Car si ce sont paroles visibles (comme saint Augustin les nomme), il ne faut pas qu'il y ait seulement un spectacle extérieur, mais que la doctrine soit conjointe avec, pour en donner intelligence. Et aussi notre Seigneur, en les instituant, a bien démontré cela, car il dit que ce sont témoignages de l'alliance qu'il a faite avec nous, et qu'il a affermie par sa mort. Il faut bien donc, pour leur donner lieu, que nous sachions et connaissions ce qui s'y dit; autrement ce serait en vain que notre Seigneur ouvrirait la bouche pour parler, s'il n'y avait oreilles pour écouter. Quoiqu'il ne soit point nécessaire d'en faire longue dispute. Car quand la chose sera jugée de sens rassis, il n'y aura celui qui ne confesse que c'est pure sottise d'amuser le peuple en des signes dont la signification ne lui soit point exposée. Pour cette raison il est facile de voir qu'on profane les Sacrements de Jésus Christ, les administrant de telle manière que le peuple ne comprenne point les paroles qui y sont dites. Et de fait, on voit les superstitions qui en sont sorties. Car on estime communément que la

Predigt zu sprechen, weil es sich hier nicht darum handelt. Was die beiden anderen Elemente angeht, haben wir den ausdrücklichen Auftrag des Heiligen Geistes, daß die Gebete in der allgemeinen Volkssprache gehalten werden. Und der Apostel sagt, daß das Volk nicht mit «Amen» antworten kann, wenn das Gebet in einer fremden Sprache gesprochen worden ist (1. Korinther 14,16). So ist es, weil jeder muß teilnehmen können, wenn einer im Namen und an Stelle von allen spricht. Deshalb war es eine zu große Unverschämtheit von jenen, welche die lateinische Sprache in den Kirchen eingeführt haben, wo man sie nicht allgemein verstand. Und es gibt keine Spitzfindigkeit noch Sophisterei, die sie von dem Vorwurf befreien könnte, daß dies eine verkehrte und Gott mißfällige Art sei. Denn man darf doch nicht annehmen, es gefalle ihm, was seinem Willen unmittelbar zuwider läuft und gewissermaßen ihm zum Trotz geschieht. Man könnte ihn nicht mehr verachten, als indem man solcherart seinem Verbot zuwiderhandelt und sich mit dieser Auflehnung sich erst noch brüstet, als ob das eine heilige und wohllöbliche Sache wäre.

Was die Sakramente angeht: Wenn wir ihr Wesen genau betrachten, werden wir erkennen, daß es ein verkehrter Brauch ist, sie so zu feiern, daß das Volk davon nichts als den Anblick hat, ohne Erläuterung der darin enthaltenen Geheimnisse. Wenn dies doch sichtbare Worte sind (wie Augustin die Sakramente bezeichnet), dann darf es dabei nicht nur ein äußerliches Schauspiel geben, sondern die Lehre muß damit verbunden sein, um ihnen Sinn zu geben. Unser Herr hat dies auch, als er sie einsetzte, deutlich gezeigt, denn er sagt, daß dies Zeugnisse des Bundes seien, den er mit uns geschlossen und mit seinem Tode besiegelt hat (1. Korinther 11,25). Es ist daher nötig, daß wir, um ihnen Raum zu geben, wissen und verstehen, was dabei gesprochen wird; andernfalls würde unser Herr vergeblich seinen Mund öffnen, um zu reden, wenn keine Ohren da wären, welche hören. Aber es ist nicht nötig, dies weiter zu erörtern. Denn, wenn man die Sache mit ruhiger Überlegung beurteilt, wird es keinen geben, der nicht eingestünde, daß es reine Taschenspielerei ist, das Volk mit Zeichenhandlungen zu unterhalten, deren Bedeutung ihm überhaupt nicht erklärt wird. So ist es leicht einzusehen, daß man die Sakramente Jesu Christi entweiht, wenn man sie so verwaltet, daß das Volk von den Worten, die dabei gesprochen werden, rein nichts versteht. Und man sieht ja tatsächlich den Aberglauben, der daraus erwachsen ist. Denn man meint allgemein, die Konsekration sowohl

consécration tant de l'eau du Baptême que du pain et du vin en la Cène de notre Seigneur soit comme une espèce d'enchantement; c'est-à-dire, quand on a soufflé et prononcé de bouche les paroles, que les créatures insensibles en sentent la vertu, encore que les hommes n'y entendent rien. Or la vraie consécration est celle qui se fait par la parole de foi, quand elle est déclarée et reçue, comme dit saint Augustin: ce qui est expressément compris aux paroles de Jésus Christ. Car il ne dit pas au pain qu'il soit fait son corps, mais il adresse la parole à la compagnie des fidèles, disant: «Prenez, mangez, etc.» Si nous voulons donc bien célébrer le Sacrement, il nous faut avoir la doctrine par laquelle ce qui y est signifié nous soit déclaré. Je sais bien que cela semble fort étrange à ceux qui ne l'ont pas accoutumé, comme il advient en toutes choses nouvelles, mais c'est bien raison, si nous sommes disciples de Jésus Christ, que nous préférions son institution à notre coutume. Et ne nous doit pas sembler nouveau ce qu'il a institué dès le commencement.

Si cela ne peut encore entrer en l'entendement d'un chacun, il nous faut prier Dieu qu'il lui plaise illuminer les ignorants, pour leur faire entendre combien il est plus sage que tous les hommes de la terre, afin qu'ils apprennent de ne s'arrêter plus à leur propre sens, ni à la sagesse folle et enragée de leurs conducteurs qui sont aveugles. Cependant pour l'usage de notre Eglise, il nous a semblé bon de faire publier comme un formulaire des prières et des Sacrements, afin que chacun reconnaisse ce qu'il oït dire et faire en l'assemblée chrétienne. Combien que ce livre ne profitera pas seulement au peuple de cette Eglise, mais aussi à tous ceux qui désireront savoir quelle forme doivent tenir et suivre les fidèles, quand ils se réunissent au nom de Jésus Christ.

Nous avons donc recueilli en un sommaire la façon de célébrer les Sacrements et sanctifier le mariage; semblablement des prières et louanges desquelles nous usons. Nous parlerons puis après des Sacrements. Quant aux prières publiques, il y en a deux espèces. Les unes se font par simple parole, les autres avec chant. Et ce n'est pas chose inventée depuis peu de temps. Car dès la première origine de l'Eglise cela a été, comme il appert par les histoires. Et même saint Paul ne

des Taufwassers, als auch von Brot und Wein beim Abendmahl unseres Herrn sei eine Art Verwandlung. Das heißt, man meint, wenn man mit dem Munde die Worte geflüstert und ausgesprochen habe, spürten die fühllosen Elemente die Kraft, auch wenn die Menschen dabei nichts vernehmen. Aber die wahre Konsekration ist die, welche durch das Wort des Glaubens geschieht, wenn es verkündet und angenommen wird, wie der heilige Augustinus sagt (80. Predigt zu Johannes): das, was ausdrücklich enthalten ist in den Worten Jesu Christi. Denn er sagt nicht zum Brot, es solle sein Leib werden, sondern er richtet das Wort an die Versammlung der Gläubigen und sagt: «Nehmet, esset, usw.» (Matthäus 26,26). Wenn wir demnach das Sakrament richtig feiern wollen, müssen wir die Lehre haben, durch welche uns das, was damit gemeint ist, erklärt wird. Ich weiß wohl, daß das jenen recht fremd erscheint, die sich noch nicht daran gewöhnt haben, wie es mit allen neuen Dingen geht. Aber es ist ganz in Ordnung, daß wir, wenn wir Jesu Christi Jünger sein wollen, seine Anordnung unserer Gewohnheit vorziehen. Und es darf uns nicht als neu erscheinen, was er von Anfang an eingesetzt hat.

Wenn das noch nicht ins Verständnis eines jeden eindringen kann, dann müssen wir Gott bitten, daß er die Unwissenden erleuchten wolle, sodaß sie verstehen, wieviel weiser er ist als alle Menschen auf der Welt, und lernen, nicht länger bei ihrem eigenen Verstand stehen zu bleiben, auch nicht bei der törichten und tollen Weisheit ihrer blinden Führer.

Was nun den Gebrauch in unserer Kirche angeht, schien es uns richtig, eine Art Formular der Gebete und Sakramente erscheinen zu lassen, damit jeder nachlesen kann, was er in der Christenversammlung sprechen und handeln hört. Umso mehr als dieses Buch nicht nur dem Volk dieser Kirche von Nutzen ist, sondern auch allen andern, die wissen wollen, welche Ordnung die Gläubigen befolgen sollen, wenn sie im Namen Jesu Christi zusammenkommen.

So haben wir in einem Handbüchlein gesammelt: die Ordnung für die Feier der Sakramente und für die Eheeinsegnung, ferner die Bitten und Lobpreisungen, die wir in Gebrauch haben. Von den Sakramenten wird ein ander Mal die Rede sein. Was nun die gemeinsamen Gebete angeht, so gibt es deren zweierlei: Die einen werden mit schlichten Worten vorgetragen, die andern mit Gesang. Und das ist keine Erfindung aus allerjüngster Zeit. Denn seit den ersten Anfängen der Kirche gab es das, wie aus der Geschichte klar hervorgeht. Und selbst der heilige Paulus spricht nicht nur vom Beten mit dem

parle pas seulement de prier de bouche, mais aussi de chanter. Et à la vérité, nous connaissons par expérience que le chant a grande force et vigueur d'émouvoir et enflamber le cœur des hommes, pour invoquer et louer Dieu d'un zèle plus véhément et ardent. Il y a toujours à faire en sorte que le chant ne soit léger ni volage, mais qu'il y ait poids et majesté (comme dit saint Augustin) et ainsi, qu'il y ait grande différence entre la musique qu'on fait pour réjouir les hommes à table et en leur maison, et entre les Psaumes qui se chantent en l'Eglise, en la présence de Dieu et de ses anges. Or quand on voudra droitement juger de la forme qui est ici exposée, nous espérons qu'on la trouvera sainte et pure, vu qu'elle est simplement réglée à l'édification dont nous avons parlé.

Combien que l'usage de la chanterie s'extende plus loin, c'est que même par les maisons et par les champs ce nous soit une incitation et comme un organe à louer Dieu, et élever nos cœurs à lui, pour nous consoler en méditant sa vertu, bonté, sagesse et justice, ce qui est plus nécessaire qu'on ne saurait dire.

Pour le premier, ce n'est pas sans cause que le Saint-Esprit nous exhorte si soigneusement par les saintes Ecritures de nous réjouir en Dieu, et que toute notre joie soit là réduite, comme à sa vraie fin; car il connaît combien nous sommes enclins à nous réjouir en vanité. Tout ainsi donc que notre nature nous tire et induit à chercher tous moyens de réjouissance folle et vicieuse; aussi au contraire, notre Seigneur, pour nous distraire et retirer des allèchements de la chair et du monde, nous présente tous moyens qu'il est possible, afin de nous occuper en cette joie spirituelle, laquelle il nous recommande tant. Or entre les autres choses qui sont propres pour récréer l'homme et lui donner volupté, la musique est ou la première, ou l'une des principales, et nous faut estimer que c'est un don de Dieu destiné à cet usage. Parquoi d'autant plus devons-nous regarder de n'en point abuser, de peur de la souiller et contaminer, la convertissant en notre condamnation, où elle était dédiée à notre profit et salut. Quand il n'y aurait autre considération que cette seule, si nous doit-elle bien émouvoir à modérer l'usage de la musique, pour la faire servir à toute honnêteté; et qu'elle ne soit point occasion de nous lâcher la bride à

Mund, sondern auch vom Singen (*1. Korinther 14,15*). Und wahrhaftig, wir wissen aus Erfahrung, daß das Singen große Kraft und Wirkung hat, die Herzen der Menschen zu bewegen und zu entflammen, so daß sie Gott mit heiligerem und glühenderem Eifer anrufen und loben. Man sollte stets darauf achten, daß das Singen nicht oberflächlich und flatterhaft sei, sondern Gewicht und Würde habe (wie der heilige Augustinus sagt), und daß man sorgfältig unterscheide zwischen der Musik, die gemacht wird, um die Menschen bei Tisch und zu Hause zu erfreuen, und den Psalmen, die in der Kirche gesungen werden, in der Gegenwart Gottes und seiner Engel. Wir hoffen nun, daß, wenn man die hier vorgelegte Gesangsform gerecht beurteilen will, man sie für heilig und rein befinden wird, denn sie ist ausgerichtet auf die Erbauung, von der die Rede war.

Wie weit auch immer sich der Brauch des Singens ausbreitet, auch in den Häusern und auf dem Feld, so soll uns das ein Aufruf und wie ein Organ sein, um Gott zu loben und unsere Herzen zu ihm zu erheben, um uns zu trösten, indem wir sein Vermögen, seine Güte, Weisheit und Gerechtigkeit bedenken; und das ist viel notwendiger, als man sagen kann.

Zum ersten ermahnt uns der Heilige Geist durch die Heilige Schrift nicht ohne Grund so nachdrücklich, uns in Gott zu freuen und daß all unsere Freude dahin ausgerichtet sein soll als auf ihr wahres Ziel. Denn er weiß, wie sehr wir geneigt sind, uns an Nichtigem zu freuen. Ganz so nun, wie unsere Natur uns hinzieht und verführt, alle Mittel zu törichter und lasterhafter Belustigung zu suchen, so reicht uns unser Herr im Gegenteil, um uns von den Verlockungen des Fleisches und der Welt abzuziehen und zurückzuhalten, alle nur möglichen Mittel, um uns mit der geistlichen Freude zu beschäftigen, die er uns so sehr ans Herz legt.

Unter den anderen Dingen nun, die geeignet sind, den Menschen Wohnung und Genuß zu verschaffen, ist die Musik das erste oder doch eines der wichtigsten, und wir haben es als eine für diesen Gebrauch bestimmte Gottesgabe einzuschätzen. Umso mehr sollen wir deshalb darauf achten, daß wir sie nicht mißbrauchen, aus Furcht, sie zu besudeln und zu verseuchen, indem wir sie zu unserer Verdammnis verdrehen, wo sie von Gott zu unserem Nutzen und Heil bestimmt ist. Auch wenn es keine andere Überlegung als nur diese eine gäbe, so müßte schon sie allein uns dazu veranlassen, den Gebrauch der Musik zu mäßigen, um sie der Sittsamkeit dienstbar zu machen und damit sie in keiner Weise Gelegenheit gäbe, die Zügel schießen

dissolution, ou de nous effeminer en délices désordonnées, et qu'elle ne soit point instrument de paillardise, ni d'aucune impudicité. Mais encore y a-t-il davantage, car à grand'peine y a-t-il en ce monde chose qui puisse plus tourner ou fléchir çà et là les mœurs des hommes, comme Platon l'a prudemment considéré. Et de fait, nous expérimentons qu'elle a une vertu secrète et quasi incroyable à émouvoir les cœurs en une sorte ou en l'autre. C'est pourquoi nous devons être d'autant plus diligents à la réglér en telle sorte qu'elle nous soit utile, et nullement pernicieuse. Pour cette cause les docteurs anciens de l'Eglise se complaignent souvent de ce que le peuple de leur temps était adonné à chansons déshonnêtes et impudiques, lesquelles non sans cause ils estiment et appellent poison mortel et satanique, pour corrompre le monde. Or en parlant maintenant de la musique, je comprends deux parties, à savoir la lettre, ou sujet et matière, secondement, le chant ou la mélodie. Il est vrai que toute parole mauvaise (comme dit saint Paul) pervertit les bonnes mœurs, mais quand la mélodie est avec, cela transperce beaucoup plus fort le cœur, et entre au-dedans, de telle manière que comme par un entonnoir le vin est jeté dedans le vaisseau; ainsi le venin et la corruption est distillée jusqu'au profond du cœur, par la mélodie. Qu'est-il donc question de faire? C'est d'avoir chansons non seulement honnêtes, mais aussi saintes, lesquelles nous soient comme aiguillons pour nous inciter à prier et louer Dieu, à méditer ses œuvres, afin de l'aimer, craindre, honorer et glorifier. Or ce que dit saint Augustin est vrai, que nul ne peut chanter choses dignes de Dieu sinon qu'il ait reçu d'icelui. Pour cette raison, quand nous aurons bien rôdé partout pour chercher çà et là, nous ne trouverons meilleures chansons ni plus propres pour ce faire que les Psaumes de David, lesquels le Saint-Esprit lui a dictés et faits. Et c'est pourquoi, quand nous les chantons, nous sommes certains que Dieu nous met en la bouche les paroles, comme si luimême chantait en nous, pour exalter sa gloire. Pour cette raison Chrysostome exhorte tant hommes que femmes et petits enfants de s'accoutumer à les chanter, afin que cela soit comme une méditation pour s'associer à la compagnie des Anges. Au reste, il nous faut souvenir de ce que dit saint Paul, que les chansons spirituelles ne se peuvent bien chanter que de cœur. Or le cœur requiert l'intelligence. Et en

zu lassen zu Sittenlosigkeit oder uns zu verweichlichen in ungeordneten Vergnügungen, und in keiner Weise zur Sittenlosigkeit oder irgendeiner Unzucht werde.

Aber es gibt noch weitere Überlegungen: Es gibt ja in dieser Welt kaum etwas, das auf die Sitten der Menschen so oder so einen größeren Einfluß hätte, wie Plato das mit Recht darlegt. Und in der Tat, wir erfahren es, daß die Musik eine verborgene und fast unglaubliche Kraft hat, die Herzen in der einen oder anderen Weise zu bewegen. Darum müssen wir um so sorgfältiger sein, sie so zu handhaben, daß sie uns zum Nutzen ist und auf keine Weise zum Schaden. Aus diesem Grunde beklagen sich die alten Kirchenlehrer des öfteren darüber, daß das Volk ihrer Zeit sich unanständigen und unkeuschen Liedern hingibt, die sie nicht ohne Grund als tödliches und satanisches Gift bezeichnen, das die Welt zugrunde richtet.

Wenn ich hier nun von der Musik spreche, so meine ich ihre beiden Bestandteile, nämlich das Wort oder den Gegenstand und Inhalt und andererseits den Gesang oder die Melodie. Es stimmt, daß alle schlechte Rede, wie der heilige Paulus sagt (1. Korinther 15,33), die guten Sitten verdirbt, aber wenn die Melodie dabei ist, trifft dies das Herz sehr viel stärker und dringt darin ein; wie wenn der Wein durch einen Trichter ins Faß gegossen wird, so wird das Gift und die Verderbnis durch die Melodie bis auf den Grund des Herzens gebracht.

Was ist nun da zu machen? Wir brauchen Lieder, die nicht nur anständig, sondern auch heilig sind, Lieder, die uns gleich Stacheln zum Bitten, zum Lob Gottes reizen, zum Nachdenken über seine Werke, damit wir ihn lieben, fürchten, ehren und preisen. Dabei trifft zu, was der heilige Augustinus sagt: daß niemand etwas singen kann, was Gottes würdig ist, wenn er es nicht von ihm empfangen hat. Darum, wir mögen suchen, wo wir wollen, wir werden keine besseren und dazu geeigneteren Lieder finden als die Psalmen Davids, die der Heilige Geist ihm eingegeben und gemacht hat. Und so sind wir, wenn wir sie singen, gewiß, daß Gott uns die Worte in den Mund legt, als ob er selbst in uns sänge, um seine Ehre zu erhöhen. Deshalb ermahnt Chrysostomus sowohl Männer wie Frauen und kleine Kinder, sich anzugewöhnen sie zu singen, damit dies gleichsam eine Versenkung sei, um sich der Gesellschaft der Engel beizugesellen.

Im Übrigen haben wir uns zu erinnern an das, was der heilige Paulus sagt, daß die geistlichen Lieder richtig nur mit dem Herzen gesungen werden können (Epheser 5,19; Kolosser 3,16). Das Herz aber

279

cela (dit saint Augustin) gît la différence entre le chant des hommes, et celui des oiseaux. Car une linotte, un rossignol, un perroquet chanteront bien, mais ce sera sans entendre. Or le propre don de l'homme est de chanter en sachant ce qu'il dit. Après l'intelligence doit suivre le cœur et l'affection, ce qui ne peut être que nous n'ayons le Cantique imprimé en notre mémoire, pour jamais ne cesser de chanter. Pour ces raisons ce présent livre même à cette cause, outre le reste qui a été dit, doit être en singulière recommandation à chacun qui désire se réjouir honnêtement et selon Dieu, voir à son salut, au profit de ses prochains; et ainsi il n'est point nécessaire d'être beaucoup recommandé de par moi, vu qu'en soi-même il porte son prix et sa réputation. Seulement que le monde soit si bien avisé, qu'au lieu de chansons en partie vaines et frivoles, en partie sottes et lourdes, en partie sales et vilaines, et par conséquent mauvaises et nuisibles, dont il a usé par ci-devant, il s'accoutume ci-après à chanter ces divins et célestes Cantiques avec le bon Roi David. Touchant la mélodie, il a semblé le meilleur qu'elle fût modérée en la sorte que nous l'avons mise, pour emporter poids et majesté convenable au sujet, et même pour être propre à chanter en l'Eglise, selon qu'il a été dit.

De Genève ce 10 de juin, 1543.

beansprucht den Verstand. Und darin (sagt der heilige Augustinus) liegt der Unterschied zwischen dem Singen der Menschen und dem der Vögel. Denn ein Sperling, eine Nachtigall, ein Papagei singen schön, aber ohne Verstehen. Das besondere Geschenk an den Menschen ist jedoch, daß er singen kann im Wissen, was er sagt. Herz und Gefühl sollen dem Verstand nachfolgen, was aber nicht möglich ist, wenn wir das Lied nicht in unser Gedächtnis eingeprägt haben, um niemals mit dem Singen aufhören zu müssen.

Aus diesen Gründen – ja aus dem eben genannten Grund schon allein, ohne alles Übrige, was gesagt wurde – soll dieses Buch jedem, der sich ehrbar und im Sinne Gottes erfreuen will, besonders empfohlen sein, im Blick auf sein Heil und zum Nutzen seiner Nächsten. So muß es auch von mir nicht besonders empfohlen werden, denn es trägt seinen Wert und sein Lob in sich. Nur daß die Welt richtig informiert ist, daß sie anstelle der zum Teil eitlen und lästerlichen, zum Teil albernen und plumpen, zum Teil schmutzigen und häßlichen und damit schlechten und schädlichen Lieder, die man vordem gebraucht hat, sich von nun an daran gewöhnt, mit dem guten König David diese göttlichen und himmlischen Lieder zu singen.

Was die Melodien angeht, so schien es das Beste, daß sie gemäßigt würden so wie wir sie jetzt wiedergegeben haben, damit sie Gewicht und Würde bekommen, wie es dem Gegenstand angemessen ist, und auch, damit sie geeignet sind, in der Kirche gesungen zu werden, wie es dargelegt worden ist.

Genf, den 10. Juni 1543.

Erläuterung hymnologischer Fachausdrücke

Die Absicht, dieses Buch auch für Nicht-Fachleute lesbar zu machen, stößt da und dort an Grenzen: Das konsequente Vermeiden von Fachausdrücken würde mitunter den Text so umständlich machen, daß das Gegenteil des Gewollten erreicht würde. Wir geben deshalb hier knappe Erläuterungen derjenigen Fachausdrücke, die wir für unvermeidbar hielten. Dabei wurde nur gerade so viel gesagt, als für diesen Zusammenhang nötig schien, weshalb die Erläuterungen ungleichmäßig ausführlich und häufig lückenhaft sind und auf jeden Fall für ein hymnologisches Lexikon nicht immer maßgeblich sein können.

Abgesang *nennt man den auf die beiden Stollen folgenden dritten Teil der als «Barform» bezeichneten Strophenform.*

Agnus Dei *heißt mit den Anfangsworten seines lateinischen Textes der letzte der fünf feststehenden Gesänge des Meß-Formulars, ursprünglich während der Brotbrechung vor der Kommunion, bei Luther während der Kommunion gesungen.*

Antiphon *nennt man den Vers, der in der Psalmodie-Praxis einem Psalm vorausgeschickt wird und der jeweils auch den Psalm beschließt und nach dem Gloria Patri wiederholt wird. Ihre Melodie hebt sich ihrer Art nach vom Sprechgesang des Psalms meist deutlich ab.*

Apostolicum: *Das sogenannte «apostolische Glaubensbekenntnis» (in der heutigen Formulierung seit dem 9. Jahrhundert verwendet) ist im Mittelalter das Taufbekenntnis und wird deshalb vor allem im Katechismus-Unterricht gebraucht. Es hat seinen liturgischen Ort vor allem im Predigt-Gottesdienst.*

Barform *nennt man jene Strophenformen, die aus zwei gleichgebauten Stollen und dem sie in der Regel an Länge übertreffenden Abgesang bestehen. Die Melodie weist darum das Formschema A A B auf.*

Benedictus *heißt nach dem Anfang seines lateinischen Textes der in der Mette (Laudes) gesungene Lobgesang des Zacharias (Lukas 1,68–79).*

«Auf Bergreihenweise» *meint eine im 16. Jahrhundert offenbar bei Bergleuten übliche Singpraxis, bei der an einzelnen Zeilenenden lange Melismen angehängt werden.*

Binnenreim *ist ein Reim zwischen der Mitte und dem Ende einer Zeile oder zwischen der Mitte zweier Zeilen, z.B.*
Bald abseit geht sonst die Fahrt;
das brächt Freud dem Widerpart, ... (Zwingli Nr. 3).

Als Cantica *(Einzahl: Canticum) bezeichnet man die psalmähnlichen poetischen Stücke der Bibel außerhalb des Psalters, die liturgisch ähnlich wie die Psalmen verwendet werden. Die Zahl der alttestamentlichen Cantica*

steht nicht fest. Aus dem Neuen Testament sind es die Lobgesänge des Zacharias, der Gottesmutter Maria und des greisen Simeon aus Lukas 1 und 2, zu denen bei Luther der kurze Lobgesang der Engel aus Lukas 2,14 hinzukommt.

Cantio bedeutet soviel wie Lied. Man bezeichnet mit diesem Fachausdruck jene lateinischen, oft schon vor der Reformation auch in deutscher Fassung auftretenden Lieder mit volkstümlicher, häufig auf dem Dur-Dreiklang aufgebauten Melodik und vorwiegend dreizeitigem Rhythmus, die zu den hohen Festtagen von Schülern und vom Volk am Rande der Liturgie gesungen wurden und zum Teil im reformatorischen und nachreformatorischen Kirchenlied fortleben.

Cantus firmus nennt man die melodietragende Stimme eines Liedsatzes.

Als Choral bezeichnet man die einstimmige liturgische Musik des Mittelalters (sogenannter Gregorianischer Choral). Ihre besondere Notation, die Choralnotation, gibt seit etwa 1050 wohl die Tonhöhen und ungefähre Werte für die Tondauer an, doch ist diese Musik rhythmisch nicht genau festgelegt und bedarf der rhythmischen Interpretation vom Wort her. Die lutherische Reformation hat (im Gegensatz zu derjenigen Zwinglis und Calvins) die chorale liturgische Musik nicht völlig verworfen und sogar einige Neuschöpfungen in diesem Stil hervorgebracht. Für die Notierung choraler Melodien bediente man sich verschiedener Notenformen. In der heutigen Übertragung verwendet man für den Grundwert (Punctum) halslose Notenköpfe, die im Falle von Neumen (mehrere Töne auf einer Silbe) unmittelbar aneinandergerückt werden. Eine Eigenheit der Reformationszeit ist die Mischnotation, in welcher Elemente der Mensuralnotation mit solchen der Choralnotation verbunden sind, vor allem, um das Punctum rhythmisch unterteilen zu können (s. Luther Nr. 39). In Straßburg hat man mensurale Melodien in Choralnotation aufgezeichnet, um deutlich zu machen, daß das neue evangelische Kirchenlied nun die liturgische Funktion und Würde des gregorianischen Chorals hat. Zu beachten ist dabei, daß die Grundschlag-Pause in der Choralnotation die Gestalt eines modernen Taktstriches hat.

Als Credo bezeichnet man im engeren Sinne das in der Messe seit 1014 regelmäßig verwendete Nizänokonstantinopolitanum, im weiteren Sinne jedes Glaubensbekenntnis, vor allem wenn es in der Liturgie verwendet wird.

Diskant heißt die oberste Stimme eines Vokal- oder Instrumentalsatzes zu Luthers, Zwinglis und Calvins Zeit. Sie wurde meist von ungebrochenen Knabenstimmen, selten von sehr hohen Männerstimmen gesungen und war nur in Ausnahmefällen die melodietragende Stimme.

Als Doxologie kann man jeden liturgischen Lobpreis Gottes bezeichnen. Kleine Doxologie heißt gewöhnlich das Gloria Patri; die große Doxologie ist das Gloria der Messe. Auch den Schlußlobpreis des Vaterunsers bezeichnet man so.

Epiklese *ist die Anrufung des Heiligen Geistes über den Abendmahlsgaben im eucharistischen Gottesdienst. In Analogie dazu spricht man bei einer Anrufung des Geistes im Zusammenhang mit der Wortverkündigung von einer Wort-Epiklese.*

Epiphanias-Zeit *nennt man in der lutherischen Liturgik die Nach-Weihnachtszeit von Epiphanias (6. Januar) bis zum Beginn der Vorfastenzeit; sie kann je nachdem, ob Ostern früh oder spät liegt, kürzer oder länger sein.*

Als Eucharistie *bezeichnet man nach altkirchlichem Vorbild heute den Gottesdienst mit dem Mahl des Herrn immer dann, wenn man stärker konfessionell geprägte Ausdrücke wie Abendmahl oder Messe vermeiden will.*

Figural *heißt in der Reformationszeit die (meist polyphone) Mensuralmusik im Gottesdienst im Gegensatz zur choralen.*

Formular *nennt man einen schriftlich festgelegten liturgischen Wortlaut.*

Glareansches System der Kirchentöne: *Der mit Zwingli befreundete Glarner Humanist Heinrich Loriti (genannt Glareanus) hat 1548 unter dem Titel «Dodekachordon» ein musiktheoretisches Werk herausgegeben, in welchem er das mittelalterliche System der acht Kirchentöne um vier (äolisch, hypo-äolisch, ionisch, hypo-ionisch) auf zwölf erweiterte. Im Musikunterricht galt in der zweiten Hälfte des 16. Jahrhunderts dieses System.*

Gloria *heißt nach dem Anfang des lateinischen Textes der zweite unter den feststehenden Gesängen der Meß-Ordnung, beginnend mit dem Lobgesang der Engel aus Lukas 2,14* (Ehre sei Gott in der Höhe ...).

Gloria patri: *Die sogenannte kleine Doxologie (Ehre sei dem Vater und dem Sohn und dem Heiligen Geist wie im Anfang, so auch jetzt und alle Zeit und in Ewigkeit. Amen), die im lateinischen Text mit diesen beiden Worten beginnt, beschließt in der liturgischen Tradition der mittelalterlichen Kirche den Gesang der Psalmen und Cantica. Bei der Übertragung der Psalmen in die Liedform haben Luther, Zwingli und Calvin auf dieses liturgische Element verzichtet, auch dann, wenn diese Lieder für den gottesdienstlichen Gebrauch bestimmt waren. Die Straßburger und später auch andere Gesangbuch-Redaktoren haben dann jedoch den Liedern Luthers solche Gloria-patri-Strophen angefügt. In seinen für die Gemeindepsalmodie eingerichteten Psalmen und Cantica (Nr. 39–41) hingegen hat Luther das Gloria patri beibehalten.*

Graduale: *Psalmgesang zwischen den beiden Lesungen der Meßordnung, von Luther in seiner Deutschen Messe durch ein (Psalm-)Lied ersetzt.*

Hofweise *ist die Bezeichnung für einen zwischen 1450 und 1550 belegten Stil bürgerlicher Liedkomposition: Solistische Tenor-Lieder mit Begleitung eines vierstimmigen Instrumentalsatzes, mit rhythmisch reichen, mehr oder weniger melismatischen Melodien, in denen meist mehrmals wiederkehrende Formeln verwendet werden. Die Texte sind in der Regel*

weltlich und häufig von einer kühlen Distanziertheit geprägt; auch sie verwenden gern formelhaftes Gut. Luther und Zwingli sind die ersten, die diesen Liedtypus geistlich verwenden.

Homophon *nennt man einen Tonsatz, in welchem alle Stimmen stets gleichzeitig fortschreiten und also der Melodienrhythmus auch derjenige der Begleitstimmen ist. Gegensatz: polyphon.*

Hymnus *heißt die älteste Gattung des Kirchenliedes, erstmals bezeugt bei Ambrosius von Mailand im letzten Viertel des 4. Jahrhunderts und wahrscheinlich auch von ihm erfunden. Der klassische ambrosianische Hymnus besteht aus 8 Strophen mit 4 Zeilen zu 4 Jamben, wobei die letzte Strophe eine Doxologie enthält. Bald kommen auch andere Strophenformen auf. Seinen liturgischen Ort hat der Hymnus von Anfang an im Stundengebet. Seit dem 9. Jahrhundert kennt man Versuche deutscher Hymnenübersetzungen.*

Als isometrisch *bezeichnet man eine Melodie mit festgelegtem Takt, deren Töne alle (oder fast alle) von gleicher Dauer sind.*

Jambenglätte *hat man gelegentlich das Zusammenfallen von Versakzent und Wortbetonung in einem Liedtext, wie es beim Hoflied zu den Merkmalen gehört, genannt. Im 16. Jahrhundert ist dies noch durchaus nicht für den ganzen Bereich der Dichtung die Regel, wie dann seit dem frühen Barock.*

Ein Kadenz-Melisma *ist eine aus mehreren Tönen bestehende Figur über der drittletzten, vorletzten oder letzten Silbe einer Liedzeile*

Kanon *nennt man in der liturgischen Fachsprache das eucharistische Hochgebet mit den Einsetzungsworten oder dessen nach dem Sanctus mit «Te igitur» beginnenden Teil.*

Katechismus *nennt man ein meist für die Schüler bestimmtes, knappes Lehrbuch des christlichen Glaubens. Seit dem Frühmittelalter gelten als Grundlage der Glaubensunterweisung die Zehn Gebote, das Vaterunser und das Apostolische Glaubensbekenntnis (nebst einer wechselnden Zahl weiterer Stücke). Die Reformatoren haben ihren Unterweisungsbüchern in erster Linie diese drei Stücke (dazu Taufe und Abendmahl) zugrunde gelegt. Diese drei Texte bezeichnet man daher als Katechismus-Stücke, die längeren oder kürzeren Auslegungen derselben für die Unterweisung der Jugend als Katechismus.*

Kirchentöne: *Anstelle unserer beiden Tongeschlechter (Dur, Moll) kannte man im Mittelalter (bis zum Beginn des Barocks) deren acht, die man als Kirchentöne bezeichnet. Sie sind durch die verschiedene Lage der Dominante und der Halbtonschritte im Verhältnis zum Grundton und durch die Lage des Grundtons im Verhältnis zum melodischen Raum gekennzeichnet (dorisch, hypodorisch, phygisch, hypophygisch, lydisch, hypolydisch, mixolydisch, hypomixolydisch, häufig einfach in dieser Reihenfolge durchgezählt: 1. Ton, 2. Ton usw.).*

286

Kommunion *nennt man in ganz unterschiedlichen konfessionellen Traditionen die Austeilung des Herrenmahles.*

Komplet: *Den kurzen Nachtgottesdienst vor dem Schlafengehen aus der klösterlichen Tradition des Mittelalters hat die Reformation als Gemeindegottesdienst nicht übernommen, weshalb das ihm zugeordnete Canticum, der Lobgesang Simeons* (Nunc dimittis), *neue Funktionen bekam.*

Konsekration *(Weihung) nennt sowohl die römisch-katholische Kirche als auch Calvin das Aussprechen der Einsetzungsworte Christi über den Elementen der Eucharistie.*

Von Kontrafakt(ur) *spricht man dann, wenn ein Lied nachweislich auf Grund eines anderen geschaffen ist, von welchem nicht nur die Melodie und das Metrum übernommen sind, sondern dessen Text auch in dem des neuen Liedes in irgendeiner Weise anklingt, so daß der Bezug zum zugrundeliegenden Lied mit ein Teil der Aussage des neuen Liedes ist. Es gibt Kontrafakturen von weltlich zu geistlich, von geistlich zu weltlich und von geistlich zu geistlich.*

Das Kyrie *ist der erste der fünf feststehenden Gesänge des Meß-Formulars, eine griechische Anrufung Christi, im Mittelalter schon auf die drei Personen der göttlichen Dreieinigkeit bezogen. Luther hat in der Deutschen Messe den meist neunteiligen Ruf auf drei Rufe reduziert. Mit «Kyrie eleison» oder verdeutscht «Kyrieleis» werden auch die Leisen jeweils beschlossen.*

Leise *nennt man eine mit dem Ruf «Kyrie eleison» oder «Kyrieleis» endende volkssprachliche Strophe aus dem deutschen Mittelalter (seit dem 12. Jahrhundert), die in eine Festtags-Sequenz eingeschoben wurde. Von ihr ist sie meist auch melodisch (oder doch in ihrer Tonalität) abhängig. Manche Leisen wurden auch bei anderen Gelegenheiten als geistliche Volkslieder gern gesungen. So bildeten sie einen kleinen Grundstock an bekanntem Liedgut, bei welchem die Reformation mit dem Gemeindegesang anknüpfen konnte.*

Ligatur *nennt man in der Mensuralnotation die Verbindung mehrerer Töne über einer Silbe: was man heute mit einem Bindebogen bezeichnet, wurde damals durch das platzsparende Aneinanderschreiben der Noten bezeichnet, das bestimmten Regeln unterlag.*

Als Lutherstrophe *wird die Strophenform bezeichnet, die 7 Zeilen mit 8, 7, 8, 7, 8, 8, 7 Silben, Barform und das Reimschema a b a b c c x aufweist (x ist eine Waise, d. h. eine Zeile, die reimlos ist). Luther hat fünf seiner Lieder in diesem Metrum geschrieben (18, 24, 25, 28, 30); sie ist jedoch nicht erst bei ihm, sondern schon im Minnesang anzutreffen.*

Magnificat *heißt nach dem Anfang seines lateinischen Textes das in der Vesper gesungene erste Canticum aus dem Neuen Testament, der Lobgesang Marias aus Lukas 1,46–55.*

Melisma *(mit Betonung auf dem e) nennt man eine Folge von mehreren Tönen über einer Textsilbe; eine melismatische Melodie ist somit eine, in der zahlreiche Melismen vorkommen.*

Als Mensuralnotation *bezeichnet man die zur Reformationszeit für die rhythmisch festgelegte, namentlich auch für die mehrstimmige Musik verwendete Notenschrift, die in vielem unserer heutigen Notenschrift gleichkommt.*

Messe, Meß-Formular: *Der abendländische eucharistische Gottesdienst heißt seit dem 6. Jahrhundert nach seinem letzten Stück, der Entlassung, Missa. Diese Bezeichnung wurde, in der deutschen Form «Messe», von der Reformation überall dort übernommen, wo man an der liturgischen Grundstruktur und an wichtigen Teilen dieses Formulars festhielt.*

Metrum *ist im Lied die festgeformte Zeilen- und Versstruktur der Strophe. Ein* metrischer *Text ist im Gegensatz zu einem freien einer, der einer bestimmten rhythmischen Regel folgt.*

Mette *heißt der tägliche Morgengottesdienst nach mittelalterlicher Tradition, im Luthertum als (vor allem sonn- und festtäglicher) Frühgottesdienst übernommen.*

Modell *nennt man das Grundschema, nach welchem alle Verse eines Psalms oder Canticums in der Psalmodie vorgetragen werden.*

Modus *bedeutet soviel wie Kirchenton (s. dort).*

Eine Motette *ist die mehrstimmige Vertonung eines Prosatextes, in welcher keine Stimme eine führende Rolle im Sinne eines cantus firmus hat.*

Neume *nennt man eine Folge mehrerer Töne über einer Silbe im gregorianischen Choral.*

Nizänokonstantinopolitanum *nennt man das Glaubensbekenntnis, welches auf den ökumenischen Konzilen von Nizäa (325) und Konstantinopel (381) festgelegt wurde. Es gehört seit 1014 zu den festen Stücken der Meß-Ordnung des Abendlandes.*

Nunc dimittis *heißt nach dem Anfang seines lateinischen Textes der in der Komplet gesungene Lobgesang Simeons aus Lukas 2, 29–32. Luther hat ihn als Lied zu Lichtmeß (2. Februar) bearbeitet (Nr. 7), während Calvin ihn nach Straßburger Vorbild als Dankgesang nach der Kommunion verwendete (Nr. 7).*

Odenkomposition: *Die Strophenformen der Oden des Horaz und anderer antiker Gedichte prägte man im ausgehenden Mittelalter den Schülern bisweilen damit ein, daß man diese Gedichte auf dafür geschaffene Melodien singen ließ, in denen die langen Silben durch lange, die kurzen durch kurze Töne wiedergegeben waren. Diese Melodien wurden dann auch vierstimmig homophon vertont, eine Singpraxis, die sich auf die Entwicklung des Kirchengesanges ausgewirkt hat.*

Präfation *nennt man den ersten, lobpreisenden Teil des großen Abendmahlsgebetes (Hochgebet), auf welchen mit dem Sanctus-Gesang geantwortet wird.*

Prosodie *nennt man in der antiken Verslehre die Behandlung der Silben nach ihrer Länge und Kürze und damit die Lehre vom Vortrag eines Gedichts.*

Psalmodie *nennt man den Vollzug des liturgischen Psalmgebets im Sprechgesang der Gemeinde, des liturgischen Chores oder des Kantors, der nach bestimmten Regeln geordnet ist. Normalerweise liegt ihm ein Grundschema (Modell) zugrunde, das auf die verschieden langen Verse des biblischen Textes von Psalmen und Cantica angewendet wird. Man zählt acht sogenannte* Psalmtöne, *deren Modelle von den acht Kirchentönen bestimmt sind; ein neunter, unregelmäßiger mit zwei verschiedenen Rezitationstönen für die beiden Vershälften, der sogenannte tonus peregrinus (= Wanderton), wurde von Luther dem Magnificat und dem Auszugspsalm 114 zugewiesen, doch ist seine psalmodische Bearbeitung dieses Canticums nicht erhalten geblieben.*

Punctum *heißt die Einzelnote (Grundwert) der Choralnotation.*

Als Quellen *bezeichnet man die handschriftlichen und gedruckten Wiedergaben von Texten, Melodien und Sätzen aus deren Entstehungs- und ersten Verbreitungszeit, im vorliegenden Falle bei Luther bis 1546, bei Zwingli bis zum Ende des 16.Jahrhunderts, während bei Calvin im vorliegenden Zusammenhang ohnehin nur die beiden Drucke von 1539 und 1542 in Betracht kommen.*

Sanctus *heißt nach dem Anfang des lateinischen Textes der feststehende Gesang, mit welchem auf den ersten, lobpreisenden Teil des großen Abendmahlsgebetes (Hochgebet) geantwortet wird. Seinem vollen Wortlaut nach ist das Sanctus aus Jesaja 6,3 und Matthäus 21,9b zusammengesetzt.*

Schlagreim *ist ein Reim zwischen dem Ende einer Zeile und dem Beginn der nächsten, z.B.:*
Herr, nun selbst den Wagen halt.
Bald abseit sonst geht die Fahrt: ... (Zwingli Nr. 3)

Sequenz: *Nach dem Halleluja-Psalm und vor dem Evangelium wird in die Meß-Ordnung seit dem 9.Jahrhundert (vor allem an Festtagen) ein Wechselgesang des Chores eingefügt. Hauptmerkmal dieser Gesangsform ist die Gliederung in Strophen-Paare, von denen jedes seine eigene Melodie hat. Zwischen die Strophen-Paare wurden seit dem 12.Jahrhundert dann und wann die vom Volk gesungenen volkssprachlichen Leisen eingefügt. Sie stehen darum häufig melodisch im Zusammenhang mit der betreffenden Sequenz.*

Stollen *heißen die melodisch gleichlautenden beiden ersten Teile der als «Barform» bezeichneten Strophenform.*

Syllabisch *nennt man eine Singweise, die jede Silbe (griech./lat. syllaba) mit einem Ton versieht und somit keine Ligaturen oder Melismen enthält.*

Tenor *(auf der erste Silbe betont) heißt zur Zeit der Reformation jene Stimme eines mehrstimmigen Satzes, welche in der Regel die Melodie*

trägt. *Daher kann man Liedmelodien dieser Zeit, vor allem, wenn sie Liedsätzen entnommen sind, überhaupt als Tenores bezeichnen.*

Tricinium *ist ein dreistimmiges Stück, in der Regel für Singstimmen.*

Trinitatis: *Fest der göttlichen Dreieinigkeit am Sonntag nach Pfingsten.*

Ton *bedeutet in der hymnologischen Fachsprache nicht nur das, was man auch heute so bezeichnet, sondern außerdem 1. die (meist nach ihrem ursprünglichen Text benannte) Melodie eines Liedes, nach welcher ein anderes gesungen werden soll (z. B.* im Ton ‹A solis ortus cardine› *oder:* im Ton als man um die Kränze singet), *und 2. das Tongeschlecht (z. B.* im ersten Ton = *dorisch).*

Variante: *Fast jedes mehrfach und über einen längeren Zeitraum hin überlieferte Kirchenlied zeigt mit der Zeit (bisweilen sogar von Anfang an) in Text und Melodie Abweichungen, die entweder auf bewußte redaktionelle Maßnahmen von Herausgebern zurückgehen, auf Druckfehlern beruhen oder auch bisweilen den von der Volksliedforschung als «umsingen» oder «zersingen» bezeichneten Vorgang belegen können.*

Vesper *heißt der tägliche Abendgottesdienst nach mittelalterlicher Tradition, im Luthertum als (vor allem sonn- und festtäglicher) Nachmittagsgottesdienst übernommen.*

Literatur

Es soll hier nicht ein vollständiges Verzeichnis der Luther, Zwingli und Calvin betreffenden hymnologischen Literatur geboten werden. Es sollen vielmehr nur einige wenige Werke genannt werden, die demjenigen Leser, der mehr wissen und die Belege für das hier Ausgeführte kennenlernen möchte, den Weg in die Fachliteratur öffnen.

Allgemein

Das deutsche Kirchenlied *(DKL). Kritische Gesamtausgabe der Melodien. Herausgegeben von Konrad Ameln, Markus Jenny und Walther Lipphardt. Band I/1: Verzeichnis der Drucke von den Anfängen bis 1800. Kassel usw. 1975. Band I/2: Register dazu. Kassel usw. 1980.*

Walter Blankenburg: *Die Entwicklung der Hymnologie seit etwa 1950. In: Theologische Rundschau 42 (1977), S. 131–170 und 360–405; 44 (1979), S. 36–69, 239–279 und 319–349.*

Markus Jenny: *Geschichte des deutschschweizerischen evangelischen Gesangbuches im 16. Jahrhundert. Basel 1962.*

Markus Jenny: *The Hymns of Zwingli and Luther – a Comparison. In: Cantors at the Crossroads. Essays on Church Music in honour of Walter E. Buszin. St. Louis, Missouri, 1967, S. 45–63.*

Markus Jenny: *Die Herkunftsangaben im Kirchengesangbuch. In: Zwingliana 14 (1978), S. 493–525, und in: Jahrbuch für Liturgik und Hymnologie 24, Kassel 1980, S. 53–68.*

Luther

Martin Luther: *Sämtliche Werke (Weimarer Ausgabe), Band 35, Weimar 1923 (enthält die Lieder und Gesangbuchvorreden, bearbeitet von Wilhelm Lucke, Hans Joachim Moser, Otto Albrecht).*

Wilhelm Stapel: *Luthers Lieder und Gedichte. Stuttgart 1950.*

Martin Luther: *Geistliche Lieder (bearbeitet von Otto Dietz). München 1950 (Sonderdruck aus Band 3 der Münchener Luther-Ausgabe).*

Kurt Aland: *Luther deutsch. Die Werke Martin Luthers in neuer Auswahl für die Gegenwart. Band 6: Kirche und Gemeinde. Stuttgart und Göttingen 1966.*

Martin Luther: *Die deutschen geistlichen Lieder. Herausgegeben von Gerhard Hahn. Tübingen 1967 (die neuste Urtext-Ausgabe).*

Markus Jenny: *Luthers geistliche Lieder und Kirchengesänge. Vollständige Neuedition in Ergänzung zu Band 35 der Weimarer Ausgabe. Archiv zur Weimarer Ausgabe der Werke Martin Luthers, Band 3 (in Vorbereitung).*

Otto Schließke: *Handbuch der Lutherlieder. Göttingen 1948.*

Gerhard Hahn: *Evangelium als literarische Anweisung. Zu Luthers Stellung in der Geschichte des deutschen kirchlichen Liedes. München 1981.*

Zwingli

Markus Jenny: *Zwinglis Lieder. In: Jahrbuch für Liturgik und Hymnologie 14 (1969), S. 63–102 (enthält den Urtext der drei Lieder Zwinglis).*
Markus Jenny: *Des Reformators Kampf und Sieg. Zur Datierung und Deutung von Zwinglis Pestlied. In: Neue Zürcher Zeitung 6. November 1966, Blatt 5.*
Markus Jenny: *Ergänzungen zur Liste der Zürcher Gesangbuchdrucke im Reformationsjahrhundert. In: Zwingliana 13 (1969), S. 132–143.*

Calvin

Pierre Pidoux: *Le Psautier Huguenot du XVIe Siècle. Mélodies et Documents. Bâle 1962.*
Sir Richard R. Terry: *Calvin's First Psalter (1539). London 1932.*
Emanuel Stickelberger: *Calvin. Eine Darstellung. Gotha 1931.*
Jean Cadier: *Calvin. Der Mann, den Gott bezwungen hat. Zollikon 1959.*
Markus Jenny: *Der Genfer Psalter. In: Musik und Altar 18 (1966) S. 157–167.*

Bildnachweis

Abb. 11: Lichtbildwerkstätte «Alpenland», Viktor Harrandt und Günther Leipelt, Nagelgasse 1, A-1010 Wien.
Abb. 4 und 6: Ton + Bild Schmidt, Bahnhofstraße 39, CH-2501 Biel, nach Vorlagen aus dem Besitz des Verfassers.
Alle übrigen Abbildungen: Aufnahmen der angegebenen Bibliotheken.

Nachwort

Was hier vorliegt, ist keine philologische Urtext-Ausgabe. Es wurde nicht nur die Orthographie modernisiert und die Interpunktion heutigen Gepflogenheiten angepaßt, sondern es wurde auch, wo es sich machen ließ, der Text unserem Sprachgebrauch angenähert. Diesem letztgenannten Bemühen waren in den poetischen Texten naturgemäß sehr enge Grenzen gesetzt, wollte man nicht an vielen Stellen Reim und Metrum stören und damit das Kunstwerk entstellen. So mußte häufig zum Hilfsmittel der Fußnote gegriffen werden. Im Falle der Lieder Zwinglis wären diese so zahlreich geworden, daß sich hier die zeilenweise wörtliche Übersetzung empfahl, das Verfahren, das bei Calvin ohnehin angewendet werden mußte.

Metrische Unebenheiten (Verstöße gegen das Prinzip des Zusammenfallens von Wortbetonung und Versakzent) wurden absichtlich nirgends behoben. Hierin gehen wir absichtlich viel weniger weit als die heutigen Kirchengesangbücher, während sich im übrigen einige Textretouchen finden, die bei der Übernahme der betreffenden Texte in heutige Gesangbücher erwogen werden sollten.

Bei den Prosatexten Luthers (Vorreden, Einleitungen, Überschriften) wurde mit dem überlieferten Text freier verfahren; hier liegt eine eigentliche Übertragung ins heutige Hochdeutsch vor, die allerdings soweit als möglich Luthers Sprechweise noch hörbar sein läßt.

Das Französisch Calvins steht dem heutigen Französisch um einiges näher als Luthers Sprache dem heutigen Deutsch. Um so eher konnte dort das gleiche Verfahren angewendet werden wie in den Texten Luthers, wobei die Vorrede nicht anders behandelt zu werden brauchte als die Lieder.

Bibelstellen werden in den Fußnoten gelegentlich angegeben, wenn es dem Verständnis dient; doch hätte es zu weit geführt, hätte man systematisch den biblischen Hintergrund der Liedtexte mit Stellenangaben belegen wollen. Es war deshalb auch nicht sinnvoll, ein Bibelstellenregister anzulegen.

Im Sinne eines Nachtrags sei darauf hingewiesen, daß die eigenhändige Niederschrift von Luthers Vaterunser-Lied (vgl. S. 89 oben) vor kurzem wieder aufgetaucht ist und heute in der Staatsbibliothek, Preußischer Kulturbesitz, in Berlin liegt.

Bei Calvins Psaltervorrede unterblieb die Angabe, bis zu welcher Stelle die Fassung von 1542 reicht. Sie endet mit S. 276, Zeile 12. Im letzten Satz der Fortsetzung von 1543 versucht Calvin offensichtlich

zu begründen, wieso in mehreren Fällen die Straßburger Melodien durch andere ersetzt wurden (hier z.B. Nr. 1 und 7).

Schließlich ist ein Wort des Dankes fällig. Es gilt einmal Prof. Dr. Gerhard Ebeling, Zürich, der durch seinen Auftrag der Revision von Band 35 der Weimarer Luther-Ausgabe den entscheidenden Anstoß auch zu diesem für eine breitere Öffentlichkeit bestimmten und daher einerseits enger gefaßten, andererseits aber auch erweiterten Ausgabe gegeben hat. Dann ist cand. phil. Philippe Maurer, Zürich, zu danken für seine Umschrift der Texte Calvins in heutiges Französisch und für die Mithilfe bei der Herstellung der Prosa-Übersetzung der Liedtexte Calvins. Neben ihm hat auch Dr. h. c. Pierre Pidoux, Montreux, meine Übersetzung von Calvins Psalter-Vorrede geprüft und bei der Klärung zweier durch Druckfehler entstellter Stellen in Calvins Liedern entscheidend geholfen; auch ihm sei bestens gedankt. Nicht vergessen sei meine Sekretärin, Frau Margrit Loosli-Roth, Port, und der treffliche Notengraphiker Heinz Zumbrunn, Aegerten. Ganz besonderer Dank aber gebührt Herrn Werner Blum im Theologischen Verlag Zürich, der in einem ungewöhnlichen Ausmaß positiv auf die Gestalt dieses Buches eingewirkt hat. Am allerwärmsten aber danke ich dem Typographen Max Caflisch, Schwerzenbach, der das Werden dieses Buches in einer Weise mitgetragen hat, die weit über das hinausgeht, was ein Buchhersteller normalerweise an ein solches Werk wendet. M. J.

Verzeichnis der Liedanfänge
und Textanfänge bzw. Bezeichnungen liturgischer
Gesänge und Texte

*Durch Antiquaschrift sind herausgehoben die Anfänge der Lieder und Gesänge von Luther, Zwingli und Calvin. An erster Stelle steht dort, mit den Buchstaben L, Z oder C davor, die Nummer des betreffenden Stücks und die Seite, auf der es abgedruckt ist (mit nachfolgendem Kommentar). Dahinter folgen, wie bei allen übrigen Liedanfängen, die Seiten, auf denen das betreffende Stück erwähnt wird.
M = Melodie*

Ach du arger Heinze, was hast du getan *(M. Luther)* 27
Ach du armer Judas, was hast du getan 27, 168 f.
Ach Gott, vom Himmel sieh darein *(L 24)* 102
    17, 19, 28, 29 f., 30, 35, 96, 112, 116 (bis), 144, 177; M: 30 (bis)
Ach hilf mich Leid und sehnlich Klag (Adam von Fulda) 149
Agnus Dei 15, 28, 154, 168
All Ehr und Lob soll Gottes sein (nicht von Luther) 28
Allerheiligen-Litanei 24
Apostolicum 25, 224
A solis ortus cardine (Sedulius) 22, 33, 43, 55
A toi Seigneur je lèverai (C 1) 232
    224 (bis)
Aus fremden Landen komm ich her 50
Aus tiefer Not schrei ich zu dir *(4 Str.) (L 30a)* 119
    17 (bis), 19, 28, 29 f., 96, 105, 112, 116, 144, 177; M: 30 (ter), 146, 255
Aus tiefer Not schrei ich zu dir *(5 Str.) (L 30b)* 122
    35, 105, 163 (Anm.), 171

Benedictus 29, 37, 151, 155

Cantica 36, 37, 57, 151
Canticum Mariae s. Magnificat
Canticum Simeonis 26, 228, 258; s. auch Nunc dimittis
Canticum Zachariae s. Benedictus
Capitan, Herr Gott, Vater mein (Albrecht von Preußen) 150
Christe, der du bist Tag und Licht 149
Christe, du Lamm Gottes *(L 44)* 167
    28, 37 f., 154; M: 30
Christe qui lux es et dies 149
Christ ist erstanden *(L 38)* 149
    15, 23 (bis), 36, 58, 60, 63, 149; M: 30

Verzeichnis der Namen

von Personen und Orten, jedoch ohne Calvin, Luther, Zwingli und Genf, Wittenberg, Zürich sowie bloße Druckortsangaben.

Ich danke meiner Gattin Marguerite
für die intensive und kundige Mitarbeit,
ohne welche dieses Buch nicht zur rechten Zeit
fertiggeworden wäre
Wir widmen es gemeinsam unseren Kindern
Titus Andreas
Joel Matthias
Hanna Ruth
Mirjam Elisabeth
Simon Markus
Daniel Stefan
Thomas Samuel
und ihren Ehegatten

CIP-Kurztitelaufnahme der Deutschen Bibliothek

Jenny, Markus:
Luther, Zwingli, Calvin in ihren Liedern / Markus Jenny. – Zürich: Theologischer
Verlag, 1983.
ISBN 3-290-11530-5

Gesamtgestaltung: Max Caflisch, Schwerzenbach
Musiknotensatz: Musiknotenatelier Heinz Zumbrunn, Aegerten/Biel
Satz und Druck: Druckerei Meier & Cie AG, Schaffhausen
Buchbindearbeiten: Buchbinderei Weber, Winterthur
© 1983 by Theologischer Verlag Zürich

Markus Jenny

LUTHER · ZWINGLI · CALVIN
IN IHREN LIEDERN

Theologischer Verlag Zürich

Contents

Acknowledgments

I want to express my heartfelt thanks to friends and colleagues who aided me in the development of this book. My gratitude goes to my editors at Praeger, Alison Bricken and Katie Chase, for their help, encouragement, and belief in this book. Nancy Humphreys was enormously helpful with her insightful comments on the manuscript, new ideas, information about additional resources, and her support. Jan Hagan contributed sound advice and useful comments on the manuscript. Special thanks go to Mimi Abramovitz for her particularly thorough reading of the manuscript and extensive commentary, as well as stimulating conversations on the topic over the years. Insofar as clarity and insight are achieved in this book, much credit goes to these colleagues. We did not always agree, however. I take full responsibility for the final product.

I would like to thank the following persons for answering my questions and providing me with current information with speed and goodwill: Patricia Cole from the General Accounting Office; Ann Kolker from the National Women's Law Center; Ann Moss from the Pension Rights Center; Laura Loeb from the Older Women's League; Vicky Gottlich from the National Senior Citizen's Law Center; Tom Cerino from the Employee Benefit Research Institute; Marjorie Kopp of the Social Legislation Information Service of the Child Welfare League of America. I also received timely help from the Center for Women Policy Studies, the American Association of Retired Persons, the Institute for Research on Poverty at the University of Wisconsin-Madison, the NOW Legal Defense and Education Fund, the Children's Defense Fund, and the Child Care Employee Project.

Finally, I would like to thank all the friends who provided encouragement, moral support, and "survival skills training" during this lengthy process. Special thanks go to Judy Reed, Dolores Smith, Elizabeth Lytle, Jennie Hanson, Walt Marz, Pam Freeman, Effie Bastas, and Polly Armstrong.

1

Introduction

Analysis of why something happens sometimes gets short circuited by the temptation to ascribe everything to one single factor, such as capitalism or motherhood.... Above all, we need not feel that we must answer the "why" of everything all at once with a single explanation.[1]

The development and use of theory are crucial to feminist scholarship. It is not enough to see the world through a "gender lens," documenting what previously escaped our notice. We must also take responsibility to name what we see and try to make sense out of it. The process is fraught with many dangers. There is the danger of unknowingly reconstituting traditional masculinist and white supremacist notions, pouring old wine into new bottles.[2] There is danger in promoting notions that are so appealing that they become too soon solidified and blind us to realities that contradict our prettier and perhaps neater theories. There is danger in too much simplicity—and too much complexity. And there is fear—fear of conflict as passionate theorists disagree. But we must press on because naming what we see is too important. Barbara DuBois emphasizes the importance with the following:

In science as in society, the power of naming is at least twofold: naming defines the quality and value of that which is named—and it also denies reality and value to that which is never named, never uttered. That which has no name, that for which we have no words or concepts, is rendered mute and invisible: powerless to inform or transform our consciousness of our experience, our understanding, our vision; powerless to claim its own existence.[3]

This book is an attempt to name what has heretofore been unnamed and invisible, to use feminist theory to try to define the function of gender in the social welfare system. It is done with the understanding that complex political realities have complex and multiple determinants. It is also undertaken with the assumption that political, economic, and sociological theory to date have made important contributions to our understanding of various aspects of the system. Thus, my standpoint is not to suggest that we reject everything that has gone before but instead to seek to explain the existence of phenomena and problems that seem unexplainable in the context of analyses to date.

STATEMENT OF THE PROBLEM

The social welfare system in the United States today can be viewed as a vast network of public policies and programs designed to provide goods and services to individuals, families, groups, and organizations. This provision presumably serves the greater good of society by promoting the general welfare as well as maintaining and promoting social institutions and behaviors thought to be beneficial to social systems. Yet a quick perusal of the major social welfare systems in the United States reveals the existence of what seem to be anachronistic rules.

Many social welfare policies were developed within social systems in which traditional one-earner nuclear families were the norm, and divorce and single parenthood the exceptions. Gender roles in American society have changed considerably and rapidly in the past 50 years. In 1935, when the Social Security Act was passed, only 15 percent of married women were in the labor force. Families were larger, divorce was uncommon, and women were not expected even to help support their families, let alone themselves. Thus, welfare laws have excluded men lest they shirk from their duty to work to support their families. Social Security laws have provided best for men workers and their dependents. Child welfare policies assume that most women are mothers, that children need their mothers' exclusive care, and that fathers should support both.

At first glance, it would seem that policy makers simply need to respond to the demographic changes that have occurred in the twentieth century by constructing new policies that mitigate against the economic disadvantages of divorce and single parenthood. But policy makers have been explicitly reluctant to do this. The social welfare system has been slow in responding to changing gender roles and the different experiences of men and women in the family, labor force, and society. Proposed changes and additions to current policies and programs that would reflect the current life situations of families and individuals have been actively opposed as being "antifamily," too costly, not realistic, and what not. Few changes have been made and those that have been implemented, as we shall see, may be called into question as to the extent to which they actually serve to meet social needs.

To understand the cause of this reluctance to change policies tied to outdated norms it is necessary to interpret the function of the social welfare system in its treatment of women. In fact, the social welfare system has been designed to perpetuate a system in which women's place is in the nuclear family. The divorce rate, women's emergence in great numbers into the labor force, and the growth in out-of-wedlock births has challenged the status quo, in spite of incentives to the contrary. Yet policy makers hesitate to make changes that would have implications for fundamental notions of gender roles that remain strong in American culture.

Perhaps the most noteworthy example of what is happening is the reaction to women's poverty. With the popularization of the term "feminization of poverty,"[4] many social welfare researchers and analysts have documented and discussed widespread poverty among women, generally concentrating on the rise of single-parent families. Circumstances contributing to this problem have been identified as women's low pay in the labor market, low welfare payments, lack of child support enforcement, and the welfare state itself. Yet many scholars blame women's poverty on the very existence of single-parent families and see society's goal as the restoration of the traditional family—that is, preventing teenage out-of-wedlock pregnancy and divorce, and/or strengthening poor Black and white men's financial ability to support families. While many liberal and conservative analysts may differ with regard to the treatment of poor women (whether to use coercion or persuasion or incentives) they clearly wish to see these women return to (or find) husbands. Some purport to the desire to see women in the labor force supporting themselves and their children, but I will argue that these stated intentions, because they conflict with the marriage goal, tend to remain rhetorical or otherwise unattainable in practice.

Accepted leftist analyses of the social welfare system in the United States usually include the assertion that it is driven by the demands of the capitalist economy. Frances Fox Piven and Richard Cloward's *Regulating the Poor* is the classic work that explicates this hypothesis.[5] Thus, welfare benefits are said to be set "low enough" so as not to hamper incentives to work and to ensure that a pool of low-wage labor is available when needed. Social welfare policies represent the state's attempt to mediate the demands of the economic system and the state's need to keep social peace. Thus, while social control is exerted, independence and self-support are the basic principles that are commonly assumed to be at least the mainstream value base to our policies and programs.

In fact, the treatment of women in the social welfare system does not always provide work incentives or encourage self-support. While women on welfare are ostensibly pressured to work, programs to get them into the work force usually exclude, by design, large numbers of them. Some wives who have never been attached to the labor force are richly rewarded by the Social Security system as dependents of high-wage workers. Programs function so that men and women are differently rewarded or punished for different circumstances and behaviors.[6]

Some of the gender differences in social welfare can be traced to the responsibilities that women take on as mothers, by which men are not similarly burdened. But this distinction is not sufficient to explain the treatment of different categories of women from program to program. Widows with small children covered by Social Security Survivor's Insurance, for example, are treated quite differently (more generously and with less stigma) from women receiving Aid to Families with Dependent Children.

PURPOSE AND OUTLINE OF THE BOOK

This book examines the function of gender assumptions in the social welfare system and places it in a feminist theoretical framework. My thesis is that women's relationships to men as well as their motherhood status are variables that are stronger than work ethic principles in shaping social welfare policies. Thus married women with their husbands are rewarded better than women without men, whether they be divorced, widowed, or never married, not only in poverty-related policies, but those related to the middle class as well. Women are expected to be dependent upon men and when they are not, they are significantly disadvantaged. Because the expectation of dependency is different for men and women, the work ethic is differently applied to men and women. Women are not expected to be able to support themselves and there are barriers to their doing so. Economic dependency, even if partial, on individual men or on the state, is the most acceptable and rewarded status for women in the United States today. As we shall see, this pattern of incentives to marriage is repeated from program to program.

Recognizing that a woman's attachment to a man and the nature of that attachment is key to her (and her children's) treatment in the social welfare system changes the ways in which that system can be rationally analyzed and evaluated. It is important to understanding the underlying values that inform policy development and implementation. Only with this new understanding can fundamental reform be effected.

This book's feminist analysis clarifies the seeming incoherence in the treatment of women in the U.S. social welfare system. It identifies gender as a key variable in the current controversy about the future of social welfare and clarifies analyses about "family structure," which are frequently based on assumptions about appropriate gender roles. It will use feminist theory as a basis for deriving a common thread of gender assumptions throughout a variety of social welfare policies and programs. It will draw primarily on the work of Nancy Hartsock, who, in *Money, Sex, and Power*, describes the development of a masculinist world view that creates a community in which it is imperative to separate the sexes and dominate women.[7] This theoretical framework will be used to clarify the current status of welfare, work experience, and training programs; the custody and care of children; Social Security and pension programs.

It is important to note that the use herein of the gender designations of man and woman refers to a conceptualization of two very different ways of thinking and perceiving the world. The masculine is the dominant form, constitutes the infrastructure of Western thought, and is considered by most to be superior and of most value. The feminine is at best relegated to particular spheres of society (the home and the nursery) and although romanticized, in fact is considered inferior and part of a lower domain. The terms do not refer to individual men and women, or even groups of men and women. It is probably true that most people incorporate some of both ways of thinking some or all of the time, although women are more likely to incorporate and adopt the masculine forms, since these provide the rules for getting about in the world. However, many men incorporate feminine forms. The point here is that in our culture one way of thinking, a way that derives from masculine traditions, is considered superior by most people and essentially determines how social policy is formulated and implemented and how the country is run.

Chapter 2 includes a brief review of some feminist theories that seek to explain the differential treatment of gender in Western society. This discussion provides a background to the explication of the theoretical perspective that I have chosen to apply to the social welfare system. Conceptualized by Hartsock, it is a theory of the "genderedness of power." She posits the existence of a white masculine world view that explains the need of the "collectivity" of men to create a community in which women must be dominated and controlled. I have conceptualized this need as "patriarchal necessity." In the rest of the book I will apply this theory in attempting to explain why certain social welfare policies—institutional products derived from the polity, as it were, of men—function the way that they do. I will also suggest ways that the outcomes of social welfare policies concerning women are functional not only to patriarchy but to capitalism and white supremacy.

In Chapter 2 I have also included a discussion of the important work of Mimi Abramovitz, *Regulating the Lives of Women*, a history of the treatment of women in the social welfare system.[8] Abramovitz suggests that the "family ethic" has constituted the ideological basis of women's treatment over time. Her work is discussed here because we are both trying to understand why as well as how gender is regarded differentially in social welfare. Our work is often theoretically congruent, yet at some points we differ. To advance scholarship in this area, and at the risk of making us seem to differ more than we do, I have attempted to explicate our differences from my point of view.

In Chapter 3 the major government program for poor women and children in the United States, Aid to Families with Dependent Children, is described and analyzed with respect to gender and patriarchal necessity. The program functions to stigmatize women, keep them poor, and blame them for their condition. The work of several prominent theorists with regard to welfare reform is also discussed from a feminist theoretical perspective.

Chapter 4 is devoted to a description and analysis of work and work training programs for poor women, including the provisions of the Family Support Act, a major "reform" passed recently by the Congress. It is a paradox that the

prototype programs for this legislation, ostensibly created to make women independent, perpetuate their dependency and can be expected to continue to do
so.

Chapter 5 focuses on child support and child custody issues and how the care
of children as an issue of public policy limits women's choices while expanding
men's. Chapter 6 deals with the daytime care of children, a major issue for
employed mothers, and examines how public policy wavers between the demands
of patriarchy and the demands of capitalism, with the lives of children in the
balance. Other child welfare issues, adoption and foster care, are also discussed
briefly.

Chapters 7 and 8 shift the perspective to the plight of older women in patriarchal
society. In Chapter 7 the Social Security system, designed to fulfill the needs
of traditional families, is discussed. Chapter 8 describes the treatment of women
under the Employee Retirement Income Security Act, major legislation that has
revolutionized private pensions in the United States in the past decade.

Chapter 9, the final chapter, includes an overview of the former analyses and
some overall suggestions for reform. I also discuss how one might use the concept
of patriarchal necessity to analyze other programs and to predict the acceptability
of reform legislation affecting women. Finally, new models of policy analysis
and perspectives on social science research are introduced.

NOTES

1. Charlotte Bunch, "Not by Degrees: Feminist Theory and Education," in her
Passionate Politics: Feminist Theory in Action (New York: St. Martin's Press, 1987),
244.

2. Hartsock uses the terms masculine and "masculinist" rather than "male" to denote
a socially constructed as opposed to a biologically determined sexuality. I think that this
distinction is important and will use it too. See Nancy C. M. Hartsock, *Money, Sex,
and Power; Toward a Feminist Historical Materialism* (New York: Longman, 1983),
14, n. 13.

3. Barbara DuBois, "Passionate Scholarship: Notes on Values, Knowing and Method
in Feminist Social Science," in *Theories of Women's Studies*, eds. Gloria Bowles and
Renate Duelli-Klein (London: Routledge and Kegan Paul, 1983), 108.

4. This term was first coined by Diana Pearce, "The Feminization of Poverty: Women,
Work and Welfare," *Urban and Social Change Review*, February 1978: 28–36.

5. Frances Fox Piven and Richard A. Cloward, *Regulating the Poor: The Functions
of Public Welfare* (New York: Vintage Books, 1971).

6. It should be acknowledged that many social welfare policies are technically "gender neutral." For example, a single male parent is eligible for welfare payments. Likewise,
Social Security dependents' benefits for spouses may be awarded to husbands or wives.
Nevertheless, social welfare policies are designed with particular gender-driven situations
in mind. Except in rare cases, dependent spouses are wives and single parents on welfare
are women.

7. Hartsock, *Money, Sex, and Power*.

8. Mimi Abramovitz, *Regulating the Lives of Women: Social Welfare Policy from
Colonial Times to the Present* (Boston: South End Press, 1988).

2

Theory

To address women's lives and experience in their own terms, to create theory grounded in the actual experience and language of women, is the central agenda for feminist social science and scholarship.[1]

Theories of feminism have developed rapidly over the past two decades and constitute some of the most exciting scholarship in academia today. Some of this scholarship has focused on the origins of patriarchy—that is, how and why masculinist dominance came to be as well as how and why it is perpetuated. My interest is in the application of such theory to the way in which women are treated in the social welfare system. Taken alone, the questions posed are complex. Added to the complexity is the question of how class dominance and white supremacy have come about and interact with gender dominance.

Nancy Hartsock's conceptualization of the genderedness of power in *Money, Sex, and Power: Toward a Feminist Historical Materialism*, is a feminist perspective of the masculinist development of community. From this community societal institutions such as the social welfare system are derived. It is Hartsock's view that informs my conception of how social welfare institutions function with regard to gender. In this chapter I will discuss some of the major themes and debates regarding the origins of women's oppression and then describe Hartsock's view in more detail.

From Hartsock's theoretical perspective I have formulated the concept of "patriarchal necessity," which informs the social welfare system's treatment of women. It will be contrasted with the concept of the "family ethic," a newly

popularized notion of the guiding ideology of gender in social welfare conceptualized by Mimi Abramovitz in her ground-breaking book, *Regulating the Lives
of Women*.[2] Her historical work demonstrates how the social welfare system has
over time upheld the family ethic in mediating between the demands of patriarchy
and the demands of capitalism. My approach and that of Abramovitz coincide
to a great extent, but to some degree we differ. At the conclusion of this chapter
I compare our work and attempt to elucidate our differences.

PATRIARCHY

The theorists I discuss have defined patriarchy variously. For those unfamiliar
with the term I present my definition of patriarchy as an introduction to the
theoretical discussion. Patriarchy is a system of sexual hierarchical relations,
supported by law, culture, and societal norms, wherein masculine dominance is
maintained. "Patriarchal necessity," which will be further delineated at the end
of the chapter, is defined as the need among the "collectivity" of men to separate
the sexes and devalue and control women.

THEORETICAL CONSTRUCTS

In the recent new wave of the feminist movement, two early and identifiable
strains of feminist theory—radical feminism and socialist feminism—began with
perspectives rather distant from each other. Radical feminists tended to concentrate on the everyday life experiences of women with men, and blamed patriarchy,
a system of male domination, for the oppression of women. The oppression,
they said, was based on the biological differences between the sexes. Shulamith
Firestone, in her well-known radical feminist work, *The Dialectic of Sex*, was
a major proponent of this view.[3] What made her radical was that she identified
women as a "sex class" equivalent to an economic class of persons. Her solution
to women's oppression was to eliminate biological differences through techno-
logical advances such as in vitro fertilization and the like. She was criticized for
having an ahistorical perspective and ignoring economic concerns. She tended
to see all oppression as rooted in gender domination and although she envisioned
a socialist utopia, the connections in her work between class and gender issues
were at best vague. She also assumed that women could obtain control of birth
technology.

Reading Firestone's work in the context of today's sophisticated birth technology gives emphasis to the limitations of her approach. It is not at all clear
that separating the birth-giving function from women will serve to liberate them.
On the contrary, new birth technologies have the potential of robbing women
of a positive, uniquely female, and deeply meaningful experience. Since Firestone's work was first published, feminists have come not only to acknowledge
but to appreciate and applaud the characteristics that make women different from
men.

Early Marxist feminists, on the other hand, focused almost exclusively on capitalism as the source of patriarchy and thus the oppression of women. They agreed with the assertion of Marx and Engels that patriarchy arose with the development of private property; that women are the property of men (their husbands) just as capital is the property of the ruling class.[4] They overlooked the fact that Marx and Engels, in spite of their prescription that women should enter the labor force, perceived women's work in the home as natural to their gender and promoted the sexual division of labor. The ultimate conclusion was that if private property were to be destroyed, so would patriarchy.[5] There were several theoretical contradictions to this view, however, soon identified by what Natalie Sokoloff refers to as "Later Marxist Feminists."

These later theorists further isolated gender as a distinct category and found the earlier analysis wanting. As Sokoloff states: "The fact that it is women who are recruited into low-status, low-waged, female-dominated occupations in industries with low capital, poor job mobility, limited job security, and little decision-making power is intimately connected to patriarchal capitalism, not capital alone.[6] Thus it was patriarchy, not capitalism, that relegated women to the home and men to the marketplace and later divided the sexes in the marketplace.[7] The question remained, however, as to the basis of patriarchy and how it operates in conjunction with capitalism. Heidi Hartmann answered this question by recognizing a materialist base for patriarchy. In her now classic article, "The Unhappy Marriage of Marxism and Feminism," Hartmann discusses this materialist base. She points out that Firestone recognized the materialism inherent in "the work women do reproducing the species."[8] She faults Firestone only in that she limits her notion of this material base to reproduction alone. Hartmann states:

Hierarchies "work" at least in part because they create vested interests in the status quo. Those at the higher levels can "buy off" those at the lower levels by offering them power over those still lower. In the hierarchy of patriarchy, all men, whatever their rank in the patriarchy, are bought off by being able to control at least some women. . . . Men are dependent on one another (despite their hierarchical ordering) to maintain their control over women. The material base upon which patriarchy rests lies most fundamentally in men's control over women's labor power. Men maintain this control by excluding women from access to some essential productive resources (in capitalist societies, for example, jobs that pay living wages) and by restricting women's sexuality. Monogamous heterosexual marriage is one relatively recent and efficient form that seems to allow men to control both these areas. . . . The services women render men, and which exonerate men from having to perform many unpleasant tasks (like cleaning toilets) occur outside as well as inside the family setting.[9]

Hartmann's perspective led many theorists to the recognition that men benefit materially from patriarchal control regardless of how it reinforces or contradicts capitalism. Whether this materialist base is somehow a key to the understanding of patriarchy is still open to question.

According to socialist feminist theory, the sexual division of labor in both the home and marketplace is an essential component of the support of both capitalism and patriarchy. Women are socialized to have their first allegiance to the home and children and thus only a secondary commitment to the workplace, justifying their channeling into low-paid, dead-end positions that capitalize on their "natural" caretaking abilities. Likewise, their inability to command high wages in the labor force reinforces their secondary position in the home, where their unpaid labor is trivialized.[10] Thus, their subordination in each place reinforces their subordination in the other.

For Black women, white supremacy deepens their subordination in the workplace, relegating them into more odious and lower paying jobs than those available to white women. This also helps support patriarchy because it minimizes the significance of Black women's historical presence in great numbers in the labor force.

The congruence of patriarchy and capitalism should not mask the contradictions that must continually be mediated. Wage-earning women are more likely to demand authority in the home, and, indeed, white women's increasing opportunities in the labor force have been associated with a rise in marital disruption.[11] Despite their definition as secondary wage earners, women have a history of demanding better wages and working conditions in the labor force.[12] Indeed, competition with women in the labor force, the fact that women's labor cheapens men's labor, and the desire to continue to enjoy women's labor in the home have motivated men to block women's economic advancement. Women can look to labor unions and other groups of men determined to maintain the privileges of patriarchy, as well as the demands of capital, for sources of their labor market troubles.[13]

These contradictions have led Zillah Eisenstein to predict that women's emergence into the labor force in large numbers will force liberal feminists to more radical analyses of the oppression of women. She states: "The reality of the married woman wage earner becomes a contradiction in terms. Is she dependent as a woman or independent as a worker?"[14] Women's consciousness of the "double day" of employed work and housework and the realities of the marketplace will lead them to give credence to the belief that women are treated as a "sex class" and will radicalize them.

Some maintain that the forces of patriarchy are independent of capitalism, while others insist that they are integrally related with each other and with white supremacy as systems of dominance. Patriarchy, capitalism, and white supremacy simultaneously reinforce and contradict each other in a dynamic that is not always balanced and not completely understood.

In my view many theories of feminism can no longer be categorized easily into "radical" or "socialist" slots.[15] Feminist theorists are examining specific aspects of women's oppression, such as violence against women and pornography; the meanings and origins of gender roles, particularly the meaning of motherhood to both men and women; and the nature of women and men. Radical feminists have moved from focusing on only the biological differences between the sexes to other gender differences. "Women's nature," heretofore denigrated, is celebrated as a positive phenomenon. As Hester Eisenstein has commented, "From an attempt to minimize differences between men and women, feminist theory moved to a celebration of female differences, and a woman-centered perspective."[16] But the origin of women's and men's "natures" is also a matter of debate. Some celebrants see women's nature as innate and espouse the "intrinsic superiority of women."[17] Others see it as socially constructed and thus, with masculine nature, as subject to change. Hester Eisenstein has criticized theorists who have abandoned economic concerns in favor of a woman-centered retreat from everyday political struggle.[18]

There does seem to be a continuing "split" between theorists who focus exclusively on economic forces and those who look either to areas of oppression not immediately related to economics or to theories that root oppression not in class systems but in psychology. Part of this split is due to the felt need to reduce all oppressions to a single kind of "umbrella" oppression, from which all other oppressions derive and, if eliminated, would "right" everything else. For example, if only we got rid of sexism, racism would disappear, or vice versa. Those who feel that they have *the* answer, however, sometimes reason that the logical political response is to concentrate on the struggle to overcome just one "ism." The idea that an encompassing theoretical notion could explain all is compelling, but the political extension of the tentative beginnings of such ideas is nonsense. For one thing, it may be that domination can and has been caused by multiple forces. Second, new forces may be perpetuating some oppressions, so that elimination of the "original" cause may be irrelevant to their eradication. Third, it is in the nature of domination to divide and scatter the dominated and such arguments serve, rather than oppose, oppressive mechanisms.

Notwithstanding feminist theories that examine the relationship between patriarchy and capitalism, I find that economic analyses fall short of explaining the ferociousness with which patriarchy is enforced through hatred, violence, and murder of the spirit. Likewise, white supremacy operates in a manner contrary to pure market reasoning and thus cannot satisfactorily be explained solely in economic terms. Moreover, white supremacy and patriarchy predated capitalism and are currently practiced in socialist countries.

Acknowledging the powerful force of capitalism in shaping our lives, I look to feminist theorists who have chosen to probe further the nature of patriarchy as it combines with capitalism and white supremacy to enforce masculine social and economic domination. Compulsory heterosexuality and the intensity and scope of masculine violence against women are two important themes in this work.

COMPULSORY HETEROSEXUALITY

The concept of compulsory heterosexuality was first suggested by Adrienne Rich as a powerful mechanism for maintaining women's subordination and controlling their behavior. She states:

[W]hen we look hard and clearly at the extent and elaboration of measures designed to keep women within a male sexual purlieu, it becomes an inescapable question whether the issue we have to address as feminists is, not simple "gender inequality," nor the domination of culture by males, nor mere "taboos against homosexuality," but the enforcement of heterosexuality for women as a means of assuring male right of physical, economical, and emotional access. One of many means of enforcement is, of course, the rendering invisible of the lesbian possibility, an engulfed continent which rises fragmentedly to view from time to time only to become submerged again. Feminist research and theory that contributes to lesbian invisibility or marginality is actually working against the liberation and empowerment of women as a group.[19]

Independent women must not be tolerated; if there is no way to ensure their dependency, making them invisible and/or unacceptable may do just as well. Rich notes that "women identified women," whom she puts on a continuum of lesbianism that is broader than proclivities in sexual relations, have indeed been either rendered invisible or devalued. She discusses Zora Neale Hurston and Emily Dickenson in this way:

[L]ives such as these are seen as deviant, as pathological, or as emotionally and sensually deprived. . . . And the work of such women—whether merely the daily work of individual or collective survival and resistance, or the work of the writer, the activist, the reformer, the anthropologist, or the artist—the work of self-creation—is undervalued, or seen as the bitter fruit of "penis envy," or the sublimation of repressed eroticism, or the meaningless rant of a "manhater."[20]

When they are visible, however, as Rich suggests, it becomes necessary to make lesbians seem to be substitutes for men. She states: "I would suggest that lesbian existence has been most recognized and tolerated where it has resembled a "deviant" version of heterosexuality; e.g., where lesbians have, like Stein and Toklas, played heterosexual roles (or seemed to in public) and have been chiefly identified with male culture."[21]

Rich suggests that the experiences of homosexual men are quite different from those of lesbian women.[22] Indeed, many white homosexual men share white male privilege and wish only to be fully included (that is, given their rightful place) in the capitalist, white supremacist, patriarchal hierarchy. Notwithstanding the political viewpoints of homosexual men, however, feminist analysis suggests that the violent oppression of homosexual men is due to their seeming preference to be "woman-like," that is, their rejection of male prerogatives and their lowering themselves to a female realm. Luce Irigary suggests, for example, that homosexual men are considered deviant because they use the penis as a source of pleasure rather than power.[23] Betty Powell has suggested that gay men are oppressed for acting as if they were women; lesbians for acting as if they were free.[24] Thus, compulsory heterosexuality imposes itself on women and men for the same reason: the maintenance of women's subordination and control of their behavior.

WOMAN HATRED AND VIOLENCE AGAINST WOMEN

Mary Daly has documented massive hatred and violence toward women exemplified by widow-burning (*suttee*) in India, the Chinese ritual of footbinding, the genital mutilation of young girls in Africa, the massacre of women as witches in Europe, and American gynecology and psychotherapy.[25] In her book, *Gyn/ecology*, she not only exposes the brutal historical and contemporary realities of masculine violence but documents the obscene indifference of generations of masculine "scholars" to these atrocities.

Far from being "history," violence against women continues every day around the world. In Nicaragua, 44 percent of men admit to beating their wives or girlfriends. In India, "bride-burning" is commonplace.[26] In the United States in 1987, 1,500 women were killed by husbands or boyfriends. Most of these women were killed after they left their male partners.[27] This shocking statistic refutes the myth that women would be safe if only they would leave their abusers.

Another recurring type of violence against women, rape, was traced in history by Susan Brownmiller in *Against Our Will: Men, Women and Rape*. Brownmiller argued that the threat of rape as much as the act itself is functional to patriarchy as a way of inhibiting women's freedom of action and perpetuating the notion of women as the property of men.[28] Since Brownmiller and Daly published these classic works in the 1970s a large literature, which both documents antiwoman violence and tries to understand it, has developed. Both Andrea Dworkin and Susan Griffin have argued pornography's function as dominating and silencing women.[29] The perpetuation of woman-hatred and violence, past and present, is persuasive evidence for patriarchy's profound need not only to control women but to maintain their "otherness" in an almost subhuman category.

GENDER AND OPPRESSION: FEMINIST PSYCHOANALYTIC THEORY

Feminist psychoanalytic theory attempts to explain women's oppression and gender differences in a psychological framework. With the rejection of Freud's notion of penis envy to explain all sex differences, psychoanalytic constructs, especially the development of object relations, are employed. One theorist, Nancy Chodorow, suggests that boys, because they are mothered by women and not men, grow up with the need to strive for individuation and separation in order to maintain gender identity.[30] In contrast, girls grow up with a sense of relatedness to others, without as strong a need to set up rigid boundaries between themselves and others. She states:

From the retention of preoedipal attachments to their mother, growing girls come to define and experience themselves as continuous with others; their experience of self contains more flexible or permeable ego boundaries. Boys come to define themselves as more separate and distinct, with a greater sense of rigid ego boundaries and differentiation. The basic feminine sense of self is connected to the world, the basic masculine sense of self is separate.[31]

Chodorow's purpose was to seek to explain why women and not men perform mothering functions. Her work, however, has implications for the broader question of the gendered division of labor and the oppression of women. According to her theory, girls' identification with their mothers brings with it a sense of continuity with others. In contrast, boys, in order to attain gender identity, must reject identification with their mothers. Boys not only grow up to see girls and women as "other," but have a strong need to do so in order to maintain their own gender identity. Because fathers do not "mother" infants, boys' identification with their fathers is in a sense an identification with an idealized masculinity, and thus rigid and stereotypical.[32]

In this way boys construct their masculinity "largely in negative terms."[33] This construction is more precarious than gender construction in girls and is harder to maintain. Indeed, it must be maintained through a lifelong rather rigid differentiation from women as "other" and a basic contempt for women.[34] Chodorow contends that both sexes develop hostility toward their mothers during the oedipal period, but that this hostility in girls is focused specifically on their mothers. In boys it is generalized to all women. "A boy's contempt serves to free him not only from his mother but also from the femininity within himself."[35]

It is important to note that Chodorow rejects the idea that psychoanalytic theory can provide sufficient explanation for an understanding of civilization and culture. She looks to its clinical evidence to develop theoretical notions of human behavior.[36] Nevertheless, I believe that Chodorow has contributed greatly to at least a partial explanation of the "rootedness" of the sexual division of labor and the devaluation of women in Western society. That the solution to the problem can be found in men's taking up the task of mothering is less evident. We need to know more about the development of object relations and the impact of "learning" one's gender, through subtle cues, from the moment of birth.

Chodorow contends that "good enough" mothering, because of its affectional quality, cannot be "learned by behavioral imitation," and therefore she implies that it is not the product of sex role socialization.[37] I question this conclusion. Sex role socialization need not be simply task-oriented. If one assumes that the affectional capacity exists in both sexes (which she does), then it could be that the socialization of girls helps to develop that capacity while boys are socialized to repress these feelings. Boys, moreover, are socialized to feel shame when they feel (and act on) maternal affections and are rewarded greatly for their oppression of women and rejection of all things feminine, especially including feminine sentiments.[38] Besides, there is no evidence that inequality of the sexes would be eradicated even if men took on the tasks of mothering. Research indicates that boys and girls are perceived differently and treated differently in the first few hours of life. Does a mother, because of her socialization, perceive her son as somehow better than herself and not as good as her daughter? Does a baby get to "know" this? And would a man doing the "mothering" feel and communicate similar values?

With men taking on more parenting tasks, gender roles may evolve differently, but this will not necessarily lead to equal valuation of men and women. Boys may still be rewarded for their oppression of women and rejection of all things feminine. Dworkin suggests, for example, that "boys become men to escape becoming victims by definition."[39] By the time they are adolescents, boys are not expected to see their mothers as authorities. Social critics lament the existence of so many teen boys without fathers at the same time sending a strong message to these boys that they are not expected to listen to their mothers. This creates a self-fulfilling prophecy as we observe boys in fatherless homes become unmanageable. It is more important to society to maintain the devaluation of women as a component of masculinity than it is to create lawful citizens.

Chodorow's theory has been criticized for neglecting to take into account differences in relationships among Black mothers and daughters and Black families.[40] This criticism is valid and is an example of the importance of one's standpoint in one's analysis of a problem. Privileged white feminist analysts have tended to ignore racial differences and to place more emphasis on men as "other" than have women of color or working-class women.[41] Likewise, recent studies of precolonial African society challenge the notion that women universally have always been in a subordinate position.[42] This type of evidence considerably weakens psychoanalytic notions that presumably should hold across cultures. It does not preclude, however, the existence of differential influences within cultures.

FEMINIST HISTORICAL MATERIALISM

In her important work, *Money, Sex, and Power*, Hartsock seeks to discover the epistomological roots of white masculine domination and postulates a gendered theory of power.[43] Her work is a brilliant integration of radical and socialist feminist thought, bringing together heretofore disparate observations of economic oppression, psychological theory, and masculine violence. Hartsock analyzes the Marxist failure to take the "genderedness of power" into account. Building on Marxist theory she expands its meaning to develop a feminist standpoint.[44]

Hartsock uses the concept of a feminist standpoint to compare the positions of the proletariat and of women in capitalist and patriarchal society. It is based on the premise that the visions of material life of a ruling class and a subordinate class will be inversions of the other. However, the vision of the ruling class is "partial and perverse." Thus men, because they are members of the dominant group, can have only a partial view of knowledge and reality. Yet the ruling class structures the material conditions under which all are forced to live. The ruled or subordinate class, in contrast, has the potential of developing, through struggle, a vision of the underlying nature of material reality, a more "complete," as it were, vision of social relations, and a notion of a liberatory end to oppression.[45]

From her feminist standpoint, Hartsock has built upon Chodorow's work to posit a masculine world view that is based on the concept of the dichotomous nature of things and the concomitant perception of the world as a series of dualisms. Boys look beyond the material "female" life of the home to the outside world to identify with an "abstract masculinity."[46] She states:

The boy's construction of self in opposition to unity with the mother, his construction of identity as differentiation from the mother, sets a hostile and combative dualism at the heart of both the community men construct and the masculinist world view by means of which they understand their lives.[47]

In other words, men need to maintain the differentiation of self from "the other," or risk fusion with the mother. The construction of dualisms is in service to this need, extending beyond the relationship between men and women to men's relationships to the material world.[48] Hartsock explains:

Masculinity must be attained by means of opposition to the concrete world of daily life, by escaping from contact with the female world of the household into the masculine world of politics or public life. This experience of two worlds, one valuable, if abstract and deeply unattainable, the other useless and demeaning, if concrete and necessary, lies at the heart of a series of dualisms—abstract/concrete, mind/body, culture/nature, ideal/real, stasis/change. And these dualisms are overlaid by gender; only the first of each pair is associated with the male.[49]

Of the dualistic framework described by Hartsock, the mind/body dualism, with the former masculine and the latter feminine, is central to this masculine world view. The body is seen as inferior to the mind, the abstract (masculine) on a higher plane than the concrete (feminine), and "man's" most noble aspirations are linked to overcoming or conquering the natural world, even death, for a higher purpose. In this construct women represent the inferior realm of material need. A woman-mother represents nature, the temptations of the flesh, the earth. She also represents the mundane necessities of life, filth, and death.[50]

In contrast to this masculine world view, women's life experience leads them to a different view:

Women's construction of self in relation to others leads in an opposite direction—toward opposition to dualisms of any sort; valuation of concrete, everyday life; a sense of variety of connectednesses and continuities both with other persons and with the natural world. If material life structures consciousness, women's relationally defined existence, bodily experience of boundary challenges, and activity of transforming both physical objects and human beings must be expected to result in a world view to which dichotomies are foreign.[51]

Thus Hartsock extends the notion of the materialist base to patriarchy. Hartsock suggests that the "masculinist" world view incorporates the necessity of masculine domination of women. Man's conquest of nature includes the conquest of women as part of the materialistic side of the dualistic framework. Men must not only control women's labor but women in general for their base in the material world. Moreover, the separation of gender roles can be accomplished only through domination and control because women's holistic world view seeks connections and relationships that threaten the dualistic structure of society that men have created. "Dualism," Hartsock notes, "along with the dominance of one side of the dichotomy over the other, marks phallocentric society and social theory."[52]

In her book Hartsock demonstrated the existence of this dualistic perspective in market and exchange theories of power in capitalistic society and in ancient Greece, chosen because it was a society not based on market relations.[53] She also discussed the theoretical and empirical evidence for the relationship of violent domination and sexuality pervasive in society and congruently the gendered nature of domination, violence, and control. In so doing she provides a theoretical basis for masculinist domination outside of market demands.

Hartsock implies that the feminist standpoint places women in a position not only to obtain a vision of reality that is whole, but also to develop a vision of how things could be.

The articulation of a feminist standpoint based on women's relational self-definition and activity exposes the world men have constructed and the self-understanding that manifests these social relations as both partial and perverse. More important, by drawing out the potentiality available in the actuality and thereby exposing the inhumanity of human relations, it embodies a distress that requires a solution. The experience of continuity and relation—with others, with the natural world, of mind with body—provide [sic] an ontological base for developing a nonproblematic social synthesis, a social synthesis that need not operate through the denial of the body, the attack on nature, or the death struggle between the self and other, a social synthesis that does not depend on any of the forms taken by abstract masculinity.[54]

This "social synthesis" has, she implies, the potential of leading to the transformation of society into a life-affirming community of persons free of the sexual division of labor. How this will come about is not clear. She rejects Chodorow's notion that shared parenting, taken alone, will achieve this.[55]

In her analysis of the gendered nature of power, Hartsock is discussing a particular type of power: power as masculine domination. She states that women's conceptions of power are different from men's and generally do not include the concept of domination.[56] She does not deal with the issue of whether and to what degree women exercise power as domination. In a sense she constructs her own dualism simply by stating the perceived differences without addressing women's domination over others. Neither does she deal with the issue of white supremacy and its relationship to the class and gender dominance that she describes. These issues are related.

BLACK FEMINIST THEORY

Bell Hooks, in her second volume of Black feminist theory, expresses sharp disagreement with the perspective that men are the sole source of domination and violence.

Much has been made of the idea that women are nurturers who affirm life whereas men are the killers, the warriors who negate life. Yet women act in nurturing roles even as they socialize young children as parents or educators to believe "might makes right," even as they exercise abusive domination and control over children, even as they physically abuse children in increasing numbers.... The responsibility for female commitment to domination and control over others can [sic] be simply placed on men. If women active in feminist movement had a different value system from that of men, they would not endorse domination and control over others under any circumstances. . .[57]

Hooks is a keen observer of the domination of white women over men and women of color as well as their own children. She cautions that one cannot excuse women their domination and violence with the reasoning that they are simply "carrying out the orders of men, that they are male-identified."[58]

Indeed, in a later work Hooks suggests that the parent-child relationship may have been a "site for the construction of a paradigm of domination."[59] Although such a relationship does not necessarily lead to domination, "it lends itself to the enactment of a social drama wherein domination could easily occur as a means of exercising and maintaining control."[60] In this view women are not always victims and men are not always oppressors. This example speaks to the potential and actual practice of domination and oppression on the part of women and both women and men as a source of domination.

I would agree that women who initiate and participate in domination and control are certainly not simply cringing subordinates carrying out commands. This does not mean, however, that they are not "male-identified," a term that Hooks does not define. In fact, persons who are dominated and controlled often "identify with the aggressor." Examples are common of persons who act against the interests of their selves or their group or mimic the behavior of a dominant group. This does not absolve groups or individuals of the responsibility for their behavior but neither does it contradict the idea that domination and control may spring from a gendered source. The existence of murderers, for example, does not negate the possibility that human beings are basically good, nor prove that they are basically bad; it does force an examination of the complexity of human behavior and causality and the development of theoretical accounts that can explain, rather than ignore, contradictions.

On the other hand, since domination is experienced in families on an everyday basis, it may be that men and women learn forms of domination that are gender and race "appropriate." This view would suggest that the gender distinctions made by Chodorow and Hartsock are not as dichotomous as they are drawn, particularly when it comes to actual domination and violence on the part of women. Whereas both men and women have the capacity for affectional ties as well as violent opposition, both are socialized to repress and express these in different ways.

White supremacist society in fact encourages white women to behave oppressively toward minority men and women and white women oblige. Discussing "men's" oppression of "women," without racial designation, ignores the relative positions of Black men and women vis-a-vis white women. Gloria Joseph rightfully argues that Black men never have had and have no real power over white women.[61] In contrast, white women have power over Black men.

I would suggest that when it exists, white women's liberty to dominate Black men derives from the women's class positions and/or the degree to which they are in favorable positions within patriarchy. (Insofar as women's economic position derives from patriarchy, the two may amount to the same thing.) Otherwise it would be too threatening to patriarchy because of what it would symbolize about gender relations. This is not to absolve white women of responsibility or to trivialize the effects of their domination of Black men. Nor does it mean that white women lack the capacity to resist or to bring about important change.

White women have consistently conspired with white men to oppress Black men. Indeed, an important source of the persecution of Black men has been the myth that they are drawn to rape white women and white women must be "protected" from them. White women have encouraged this view, simultaneously supporting white supremacy and their own positions as the "property" of white men who will not tolerate any competition from Black men. Yet the power white women exercise over Black men is at the largesse of white men. In contrast, their ability to dominate Black women is fundamentally different because it is not threatening to masculinist prerogatives. Thus white women's oppression of Black women can be more blatant and absolute. Moreover, from a gendered perspective, it may derive partially from a projection of self-hatred on the part of white women.

In spite of these distinctions, however, Black men do share, or have learned, the dominant white masculine view of women as inferior to men and behave accordingly in Black communities.[62] White supremacist society has encouraged the idea that Black women are an important source of Black men's troubles. Because Black women have experienced greater labor force participation than white women, this wage-earning behavior has been viewed as a negative by Black men and the wider society. It is cited as a source of Black men's emasculation and their children's delinquency.[63] It is ironic that Black women on welfare who stay home with their children are also blamed for their children's delinquency because of their welfare dependency. Thus, Black women are faced with the racism and sexism of the wider society as well as sexism from Black men, who hold a patriarchal alliance with white men.[64]

Hooks expresses ideas similar to Hartsock's views regarding both Black and white men and violence. Hooks states: "As the psychology of masculinity in sexist societies teaches men that to acknowledge and express pain negates masculinity and is a symbolic castration, causing pain rather than expressing it restores men's sense of completeness, of wholeness, of masculinity."[65] Hartsock and Hooks agree, then, that masculinity is socially constructed. Neither asserts that it is biologically inherent, nor that one gender is superior to another. Thus, while there may be a socially constructed relationship between masculinity and violence, that is not to deny women's capacity for or history of violence. The capacity for domination and violence in women and men, however, does not preclude the vision of alternative notions of gender, motivation, and behavior, "a nonproblematic social synthesis," to use Hartsock's words.

CHODOROW AND HARTSOCK REVISITED

Notwithstanding its shortcomings, Chodorow's contribution lends weight to an explanation of the power and persistence of masculine domination over time. By defining the urge to dominate as coming from a need to differentiate the self from the other, she makes sense out of the masculinist resistance to change. It is not only the enjoyment of power and privilege that moves men to cling to the status quo, she says, but the need to define one's self, begun almost from the moment of birth.

Hartsock takes Chodorow's theory of gender differences to posit a theory of power and political structure, but she too hesitates to claim that psychoanalytic theory can explain all. Her intent is to demonstrate how masculine and not feminine experience is replicated in societal institutions, the cultural construction of sexuality and Western thought.[66] To Hartsock, the shared psychological experiences of the collectivity of men results in a dualistic world view that has a profound impact on gender relations and the exercise of political power.

An analysis of patriarchy's relationship to white supremacy from the perspective of the oppressed groups might have changed Hartsock's analysis. It may not have, however, since Hartsock is, after all, striving to describe the origins and outcomes of a white masculine ruling class world view. It is from the white masculine ruling class that societal institutions, including the social welfare system, derive. Notwithstanding the limitations of her work, it is Hartsock's perspective that informs my analysis of the social welfare system.

SOCIAL WELFARE SYSTEM ANALYSES

In her book, *Regulating the Lives of Women*, Mimi Abramovitz has made an important advance to our understanding of how gender has influenced development of the social welfare system.[67] She applies the concept of the "family ethic" in her history of the social welfare system's treatment of women. Both Abramovitz and I attempt to examine women's relationship to the welfare state with the use of conceptual frameworks. We both struggle with how patriarchy expresses itself through the social welfare system. In this book I will use the concept of "patriarchal necessity" in examining current social welfare policies, but with the same aim of trying to get at the essence of the meaning of gender in the system. Our approaches coincide to a great extent but to some degree we differ.

Abramovitz draws from a socialist-feminist tradition in her conceptualization of the "family ethic." She uses the concept of the "family ethic" to explain how the dual functions of capitalism and patriarchy are encoded in the social welfare system and operate to keep women subordinate at home and in the workplace. The ideology of the family ethic tells women that their proper role is "marry and have children while being supported by and subordinate to a male breadwinner."[68] The family ethic is an ideology that attempts to solidify the congruence between individual behavior and institutional demands. Thus the family ethic helps to maintain the gendered division of labor at home and in the marketplace. This serves patriarchy by keeping women subservient in both places. It helps capitalism by preserving a pool of cheap labor and by reproducing the labor force at home. Furthermore, in the social welfare system the family ethic helps to mediate the demands for women's labor in the market and in the home.

Abramovitz distinguishes between a colonial family ethic, which stressed women's place in the home but as a productive laborer, and an "industrial family ethic."[69] The industrial family ethic served to expand women's reproductive activities at home and stigmatized women who entered the labor force. It maintained patriarchal control through the sexual division of labor both at home and in the marketplace and the depression of women's wages. With the rise of industrial capitalism, patriarchy adapted with gender arrangements that preserved woman's subordinate status by replicating her subordination at home into the marketplace. Over time, as capitalism advanced, patriarchal authority was shifted from the family to the state. She states: "As market relations slowly lessened men's ability to control the labor of family members and increased their wives' and children's access to economic resources, familial patriarchy alone no longer sufficed to maintain male domination and the gender division of labor."[70] Thus, "familial patriarchy gave way to social or public patriarchy." As women emerged in the labor market it became necessary for the state to take over many patriarchal prerogatives previously in the realm of individual men.[71]

According to Abramovitz the family ethic has been differentially applied to minority, working class, poor, and husbandless women. She asserts that privileged white women, and not Black and poor white women, have been given the "rights of womanhood," that is, "claims to femininity, protection, economic

support, and respectability.''[72] Black, white working class, poor, and husbandless women are deprived of these ''rights'' and so are welfare mothers because
their life circumstances often ''force'' them to divert from the family ethic. In
the capitalist patriarchal system a few women are channeled into full-time work
in the home where they maintain a devalued private sphere and reproduce the
work force. Other women are kept in reserve, as it were, as a cheap pool of
labor. These women, Black and white poor and working class women, are often
forced to enter the labor force out of economic necessity but when they do they
are punished for being ''out of role''—that is, violating the family ethic.

There is no doubt that the family ethic has been and continues to be an important
ideological force that influences behavior and is applied by societal institutions
to control women and justify institutional demands. Yet I have problems with
it as an explanatory concept for several reasons.

First, historians and feminist theorists have conceptualized the institution of
the family as the primary mechanism for the oppression of women in Western
civilization. Therefore, using the family as an analytical concept for understanding the oppression of women is, I think, problematic and confusing. Second,
while the family ethic is important to society, it is merely a popular ideology
that influences institutions and individuals. Used as an explanatory concept it
does not explicate adequately its function to its underlying source, the patriarchal
system. Third, Abramovitz's use of the family ethic places a great deal of
emphasis on the demands of capitalism for the control of women's labor. In my
view she deemphasizes the influence of patriarchy to the way social systems
treat women. I conclude that social welfare's treatment of men primarily functions
to uphold and serve the economy and its treatment of women is primarily, albeit
not exclusively, in service to patriarchy.

The concept I use is ''patriarchal necessity,'' which is simply a convenient
label for the force that drives the social welfare system in its treatment of women.
Patriarchal necessity is defined as the need among the collectivity of men to
separate the sexes and devalue and control women. This results in the perpetuation
of women's dependency with the simultaneous espousal of its inevitability. The
foundation of patriarchal necessity derives from Hartsock who draws from socialist feminism, radical feminism, and feminist psychoanalytical concepts to
understand the underpinnings of patriarchy. It assumes that male violence and
the persistence of misogynistic practices in societal institutions are based on more
than economic arrangements. It also assumes that patriarchy is driven not only
to control women's labor and their reproductive capacities, but as a social system
to construct and maintain separation and fundamental differences between women
and men.

Patriarchal necessity gives rise to and is maintained by the sexual assignment
of private and public life, which has been described as ''continuous in Western
history.''[73] In modern times it is accomplished through the following: compulsory
heterosexuality; the threat of rape; the institution of marriage; the sexual division
of labor, with women in the ''private'' realm of the home and men in the ''public''

sphere; occupational and task segregation in the labor force; economic control through lower pay; and through the punishment and control of "manlessness."

Since the institution of marriage is the major way in which women are controlled socially and economically, marriage for women must not only be promoted, but there must be punishment of those women who lack men and thereby (if only by implication) spurn the control of men. Accordingly, women must never appear to be capable of enjoying or sustaining a comfortable, secure independence, emotionally, socially, or economically. Thus, unmarried women, welfare mothers, divorced women, widows, and lesbians must be punished for their condition of manlessness through stigma, humiliation, sexual innuendo, and meager benefits. While many of these women wish to marry and have children and be supported by their husbands, thus conforming with the family ethic, many others do not. They are not forced by life circumstances to divert from this common ideology, as Abramovitz asserts. Most women are eager to be in the labor force. Many women wish to live alone, remain childless and/or care for other's children, live with their women lovers, or live with friends or relatives, and do so as best they can. Patriarchal institutions work against their being able to live as they wish successfully and comfortably. Punishing these women for their manlessness is a major patriarchal function of the social welfare system.

Some socialist feminists maintain that capitalism and patriarchy are autonomous but inseparable, that "capitalist production is shaped by the forces of male dominance and that male dominance is organized by capitalist class relations."[74] This is true but it is important to remember that capitalism and patriarchy are inseparable only insofar as patriarchy has the capacity to infiltrate, as it were, whatever political economy prevails.[75] Thus, socialist countries and precapitalist societies have also dominated and controlled women's lives.

In my view, women's condition of independence, or its symbol, manlessness, is the underlying threat to patriarchy that informs patriarchal social norms. Thus, a woman alone is at risk of rape regardless of whether she has a husband and children; rape and violence are also patriarchal functions that serve to control women. Likewise, the social welfare system punishes and controls women without men.

Both Abramovitz and I often examine the same phenomena and use the same gender lens to analyze what is occurring. It is the way we interpret the occurrence that differs. For example, widows who have complied all their lives with the family ethic in the Social Security system do not always fare better than divorced or never married women. Applying patriarchal necessity, I conclude that these women, having become manless, must be treated less well than they would if they were still with their husbands; they become no different than never married women. It seems that if a family ethic were actually encoded in the social welfare system, these women would be rewarded for their lifelong allegiance to it. Abramovitz explains this "paradox" by saying that widows are punished because they are no longer carrying out the family ethic; their "reproductive and home-

making responsibilities decline.'' They have "no reproductive tasks to perform."[76] Clearly, these interpretations are close and some readers may conclude
that they amount to the same thing. The family ethic punishes husbandless
women; patriarchal necessity punishes manless women. What is the difference?
The difference to me hinges on the purpose and scope of patriarchy.

Some feel that patriarchy requires women to be with men for purposes of
control and domination. Family life is the most favored way for this to happen,
particularly since then men are afforded the fruits of women's labor and capitalism
also benefits. Therefore, the social welfare system uses the family ethic to mystify
its basic patriarchal function, which is the domination and control of women
who are not attached to individual men. In service to this overriding function
the social welfare system sometimes contradicts the family ethic. As in the case
of widows, the family ethic is not always directly related to the actual benefits
of the social welfare system.

The traditional family form is primarily needed by patriarchy for the subordination of women. The reproduction of labor exists in other family forms.
Single mothers can and do bring up children who join the labor force. In fact,
the increase in divorce leads to the establishment of multiple dwellings for persons
who previously would have lived together. This is beneficial to various industries,
such as housing, furniture, household appliances, and thus helpful to the capitalist
economy. Different family forms that have sprung up in recent years all have
the capacity to provide respite from the demands of the work world and reproduce
and maintain able willing workers. It is not capitalism but patriarchy that has a
stake in opposing families without men.

I agree with the assertion that the social welfare system mediates the demands
of capitalism and patriarchy and that the ways it does this are different for men
and women. However, I would maintain that its treatment of men is more
important to the capitalist economy than its treatment of women. The family
ethic did not lock women into a subordinate family role; patriarchy did.[77] Over
the centuries patriarchy has continually intervened to preserve masculine domination. Women's treatment in the economy is in some ways convenient to
capitalism but not particularly necessary to it. As Hartmann asserts:

If for purposes of social control, capitalists organize work in a particular way, nothing
about capital itself determines who (that is, which individuals with which ascriptive
characteristics) shall occupy the higher, and who the lower rungs of the wage labor force.
It helps, of course, that capitalists themselves are likely to be the dominant social group
and hence racist (and sexist). Capitalism inherits the ascribed characteristics of the dominant groups as well as of the subordinate ones.[78]

Thus capitalism inherited the subordinate position of women and patriarchy
maintains it. The social welfare system is reflective of both institutions as well
as white supremacy. To the extent that the social welfare system operates to
support the economy and function as a mechanism of social control, social welfare

policy and programs have institutionalized ways for both to happen. Nevertheless, the social control of women has been influenced particularly by the institution of patriarchy.

From this perspective the "rights of womanhood" are denied poor and working class women, particularly those who are Black, not so much because of the family ethic, but because of the intervention of white supremacist and capitalist forces. When these protections are bestowed on white women it is not in response to claims, but at the largesse of individual white men who have historically preferred their women "feminine" (read: weak) and have afforded their women the protections and status suitable to all things under the men's control. Women without men, and women who are with men in low positions in class and racial hierarchies, have no access to these things. White supremacy and class relations interact with patriarchy to provide differential treatment to racial minorities and low-income persons.

In this vein, it must be understood that not all men dominate all women, just as not all individual capitalists dominate all workers. However, all men are advantaged by patriarchy, just as all capitalists profit from workers' labor and all whites profit from white supremacy, however individuals divert from the norm. Also, these hierarchies interact with and variously supercede each other, so that many men, particularly minority group men and working class men in general, are dominated by white men in a clear hierarchy. Also, women of color are oppressed by white women. Patriarchy, capitalism, and white supremacy are hierarchical systems; patriarchy is not the only hierarchy and may or may not be the most salient in an individual circumstance.

The following chapters use this theoretical base to analyze various aspects of the social welfare system.

NOTES

1. Barbara DuBois, "Passionate Scholarship: Notes on Values, Knowing and Method in Feminist Social Science," in *Theories of Women's Studies*, eds. Gloria Bowles and Renate Duelli-Klein (London: Routledge and Kegan Paul, 1983), 108.

2. Mimi Abramovitz, *Regulating the Lives of Women* (Boston: South End Press, 1988).

3. Shulamith Firestone, *The Dialectic of Sex* (New York: Wm. Morrow, 1970).

4. Natalie J. Sokoloff, *Between Money and Love: The Dialectic of Women's Home and Market Work* (New York: Praeger Publishers, 1980), 116.

5. Ibid., 119.

6. Ibid., 143. The same thing, of course, can be said of the recruitment of Black women and men into particular jobs, the current practice of which goes beyond the demands of capitalism. Notwithstanding the fact that this practice began in this country with the free labor mechanism of slavery, capitalism is no longer well served by racial discrimination. In exchange for a ready pool of cheap labor, capitalism must forgo hiring Black women and men with superior skills and talents in favor of mediocre and incompetent white men and women.

7. Ibid., 151.

8. Heidi Hartmann, "The Unhappy Marriage of Marxism and Feminism," in *Women and Revolution*, ed. Lydia Sargeant (Boston: South End Press, 1981), 12.

9. Ibid., 15.

10. Hilary Land, "Who Cares for the Family?" *Journal of Social Policy* 7, no. 3 (1978): 282; also Mary McIntosh, "The State and the Oppression of Women," in *Feminism and Materialism: Women and Modes of Production*, eds. Annette Kuhn and Ann Marie Wolpe (London: Routledge and Kegan Paul, 1978), 255; also Zillah Eisenstein, *The Radical Future of Liberal Feminism* (Boston: Northeastern University Press, 1986), 202–3.

11. Irwin Garfinkel and Sara S. McLanahan, *Single Mothers and Their Children: A New American Dilemma* (Washington, D.C.: The Urban Institute Press, 1986), 67.

12. Alice Kessler-Harris, *Out to Work: A History of Wage-Earning Women in the United States*, (Oxford: Oxford University Press, 1982), 38–44.

13. Land, 283; Maureen Power, "Agenda for Conflict: Pitting Capital Against Patriarchy," presented at the 1983 conference of the Mid-Atlantic Women's Studies Association, Middletown, PA, October 1983.

14. Eisenstein, 202–3.

15. A third "slot," liberal feminism, is often included with the other two. For the most part it eschews an ideological base beyond the liberal philosophy of Western democracies. Briefly stated, it is based on the view that women simply need equal opportunity to fit into the existing social and economic system and men need the opportunity to be free to participate in child care and the joys and comforts of the home. See Betty Friedan, *The Second Stage* (New York: Summit Books, 1981).

16. Hester Eisenstein, *Contemporary Feminist Thought* (Boston: G. K. Hall, 1983), 140.

17. Ibid., 141.

18. Ibid., 125.

19. Adrienne Rich, "Compulsory Heterosexuality and Lesbian Existence," *Signs* 5, no. 4 (Summer 1980): 647–48.

20. Ibid., 652. See also Joanna Russ, *How to Suppress Women's Writing* (Austin: University of Texas Press, 1983). The author discusses how women's work is devalued or ignored or attributed to men.

21. Ibid., 648n.

22. Ibid., 649.

23. Luce Irigary, "When the Goods Get Together," in *New French Feminisms: An Anthology*, eds. Elaine Marks and Isabelle de Courtrivon (Amherst: University of Massachusetts Press, 1980), 107–10.

24. Betty Powell, speech delivered to the Sexuality Task Force conference of D.C. NOW, Washington, D.C., 1978.

25. Mary Daly, *Gyn/ecology* (Boston: Beacon Press, 1978).

26. Lori Heise, "The Global War Against Women," *The Washington Post*, April 9, 1989.

27. Dick Polman, "In the Shadow of Violence," *The Philadelphia Inquirer*, April 9, 1989.

28. Susan Brownmiller, *Against Our Will: Men, Women and Rape* (New York: Simon and Schuster, 1975).

29. See Andrea Dworkin, *Pornography: Men Possessing Women* (New York: Perigee/

G. P. Putnam's Sons, 1981); and Susan Griffin, *Pornography and Silence: Culture's Revenge Against Nature* (New York: Harper and Row, 1981).

30. Nancy Chodorow, *The Reproduction of Mothering: Psychoanalysis and the Sociology of Gender* (Berkeley: University of California Press, 1978), ch. 10, 159–70.

31. Ibid., 169. Carol Gilligan's study of gender differences in the development of moral values supports Chodorow's theory. She found that women's moral considerations tend to center on relational systems, that is, how one's actions will help or harm people, with an emphasis on caring, nurturing, and mutual responsibility for each other. In contrast, men's moral values uphold the ideal of morality as adherence to abstract principles that transcend situational concerns. See Carol Gilligan, *In a Different Voice: Psychological Theory and Women's Development* (Cambridge, MA: Harvard University Press, 1982).

32. Ibid., 181.

33. Ibid., 182.

34. See also Jane Flax, "Contemporary American Families: Decline or Transformation?" in *Families, Politics and Public Policy: A Feminist Dialogue on Women and the State*, ed. Irene Diamond (New York: Longman, 1983), 32.

35. Chodorow, 182.

36. Ibid., 53.

37. Ibid., 32–34.

38. For evidence of boys' learned rejection of women, one need only spend some time observing little boys. I have seen, for example, a four-year-old boy jeering at a grown woman as she jogged down the street.

39. Dworkin, 51.

40. Gloria I. Joseph and Jill Lewis, *Common Differences: Conflicts in Black and White Feminist Perspectives* (Boston: South End Press, 1981), 9.

41. Linda Alcoff, "Cultural Feminism versus Post-Structuralism: The Identity Crisis in Feminist Theory," *Signs* 13, no. 3 (Spring 1988): 405–36.

42. See Gloria Joseph, "The Incomplete Menage a Trois: Marxism, Feminism, and Racism," in *Women and Revolution*, ed. Sargeant, 98; and Ifi Amadiume, *Male Daughters, Female Husbands: Gender and Sex in an African Society* (New York: Zed Books, 1987).

43. Nancy C. M. Hartsock, *Money, Sex, and Power: Toward A Feminist Historical Materialism* (New York: Longman, 1983). Hartsock's analysis is lengthy and complex and cannot be summarized here. I urge the reader to read this work in its entirety.

44. Ibid., 138–39. To explore further the concept of a feminist standpoint, see Dorothy Smith, *The Everyday World as Problematic: A Feminist Sociology* (Boston: Northeastern University Press, 1987).

45. Hartsock, 118.

46. Ibid., 241.

47. Ibid., 240.

48. Ibid.

49. Ibid., 241.

50. Ibid., 240–47, 253.

51. Ibid., 242.

52. Ibid., 241.

53. Ibid., 187.

54. Ibid., 246.

55. Ibid., 247.

56. Ibid., 253.

57. Bell Hooks, *Feminist Theory: From Margin to Center* (Boston: South End Press, 1984), 86.

58. Ibid., 86.

59. Bell Hooks, *Talking Back: Thinking Feminist, Thinking Black* (Boston: South End Press, 1989), 20.

60. Ibid., 20.

61. Joseph, 100.

62. Ibid. See also Bell Hooks, *Ain't I a Woman: Black Women and Feminism* (Boston: South End Press, 1981), ch. 3.

63. Hooks, *Ain't I a Woman*, 79, 93.

64. Ibid., 99, 117.

65. Hooks, *Feminist Theory*, 122. Hooks points out that this "socially constructed fantasy of masculinity" can be lethal to Black men, who often kill each other off in the process of achieving it.

66. Hartsock, 240.

67. Abramovitz. My discussion here cannot capture the richness of this book, which will undoubtedly become a classic. For a comprehensive view of Abramovitz's perspective and where we agree and disagree, it will be necessary for the reader to read both books.

68. Ibid., 3.

69. Ibid., 52, 111.

70. Ibid., 32, citing Carol Brown, "Mothers, Fathers and Children: From Private to Public Patriarchy," in Sargeant, 239–67; and Jane Ursel, "The State and the Maintenance of Patriarchy: A Case Study of Family, Labour and Welfare Legislation in Canada," in *Family, Economy and State*, eds. James Dickinson and Bob Russell (New York: St. Martin's Press, 1986), 150–92.

71. For discussions of how and why patriarchy was partially shifted to the state, see Eileen Boris and Peter Bardaglio, "The Transformation of Patriarchy: The Historic Role of the State," in *Families, Politics*, Diamond, 70–93; and Brown, ibid.

72. Abramovitz, 38.

73. Z. Eisenstein, 22. See also Kathleen Gough, "The Origin of the Family," in *Women: A Feminist Perspective* 3rd ed., ed. Jo Freeman (Palo Alto: CA: Mayfield, 1984), 83–99.

74. Abramovitz, 25.

75. See Marilyn French, *Beyond Power: On Women, Men and Morals* (New York: Ballantine Books, 1985); Z. Eisenstein, 26; Hartmann, 17; Audre Lorde, "Sexism: An American Disease in Blackface," in *Sister Outsider* (Trumansburg, NY: The Crossing Press, 1984), 64.

76. Abramovitz, 203.

77. Ibid., 39.

78. Hartmann, 24.

3

Aid to Families with Dependent Children

There is a one-and-a-half-hour set of questions to ask before someone can get on welfare, and these kinds of questions would take the Virgin Mary to make people not feel badly.[1]

The public policy issue of poverty among woman-headed families is difficult to solve because it goes to the heart of the conflict between patriarchal requirements and the demands of capital. It is almost impossible to relieve women's poverty through public policy without either providing welfare benefits at levels unacceptable to the capitalist economy or providing opportunities for women's independence unacceptable to patriarchy. Yet their poverty cannot be ignored. Children are involved and society is not prepared to abandon them altogether. Moreover, ignoring the situation would constitute an admission that women could be expected to support themselves and their children, just as the paucity of welfare benefits for able-bodied men projects the message that they could and should be supporting themselves. So the alternative of doing nothing is also threatening to patriarchy. It is quite a dilemma.

While women's poverty is not a new phenomenon, it has come to national attention in recent years, partly as a result of the women's movement and partly because of the growth in woman-headed families. Although over the past 30 years the poverty rate for woman-headed families has gone down,[2] such families previously were few in number and constituted a smaller proportion of the total poverty population. In 1959, woman-headed families accounted for 9.8 percent of all families[3] and 23 percent of families in poverty.[4] In 1986 families headed by women made up 16 percent of all families and 51 percent of families in poverty.[5] Almost 40 percent of white families headed by women and with related children under 18 years of age were in poverty; for Black families the figure was 58 percent.[6] Until this critical mass of sorts began to become more visible, poverty, when it was viewed at all, was family poverty, or elderly poverty. Now the nation recognizes the "feminization of poverty."[7]

This chapter will address the major U.S. income support strategy for poor women with children and related poverty issues, programs, and strategies directed at women raising children single-handedly. Poverty among other categories of women will be addressed in subsequent chapters.

AID TO FAMILIES WITH DEPENDENT CHILDREN

Aid to Families with Dependent Children (AFDC) is the major welfare program that provides for poor woman-headed families. A means-tested program for single parents and their children, the national AFDC caseload includes 3.7 million families with 6.5 million children and 3.1 million mothers.[8] This includes more than 11 percent of the total child population and 44.7 percent of the population in poverty.[9] The average AFDC recipient family size in 1987 was three, usually including a mother and two children.[10] The average monthly AFDC payment per family in 1988 was $370 nationwide; average payments ranged from $114 in Alabama to $594 in Alaska.[11] Program benefits, combined with Food Stamps, the other major source of income for public assistance recipients, have eroded over the years. In real dollars, the combined AFDC and Food Stamp benefits declined by more than 20 percent between 1972 and 1988.[12] Almost all AFDC recipients fall below the government's designated poverty threshold, which was approximately $9,056 for a family of three in 1988.[13]

AFDC is a program for children deprived of parental care and support due to parental death, continued absence from the home, incapacity, or unemployment. Until recently, two parent families were ineligible for benefits in most states. The caseload consists mainly of women and their children. In 1987, about half of the women were unmarried and 35 percent divorced or separated; 52.6 percent were between the ages of 20 and 29; 3.3 percent of AFDC mothers were under the age of 20.[14] Most welfare "spells"—that is, periods of welfare receipt— last for less than four years, and about one third last less than two years. But a majority of persons enrolled in AFDC at any one time are usually in a spell that will last eight or more years. These persons are considered long-term recipients and are the source of most of the expense and most of the concern about welfare.[15] Never-married women under age 25 who begin receiving AFDC when their youngest child is less than three years old are considered most at risk of long-term receipt.[16] Yet the common picture of generations of persons repeating a cycle of welfare receipt is a myth. Studies indicate that most daughters growing up in welfare-dependent families do not become welfare dependent as young adults. Only 19 percent of Black daughters and 26 percent of white daughters were found to be relying heavily on welfare as adults.[17] Moreover, research on the effects of parental welfare receipt on the work efforts of sons found no consistent effects.[18]

There is a great deal of controversy as well over the issue of how women become dependent upon welfare. Many believe that because two-parent families have been ineligible, husbands have left their families to enable their wives and children to receive assistance. Others believe that the existence of AFDC provides an incentive for young women to give birth out of wedlock. In fact there is some evidence that AFDC has a minor influence on the rate of divorce and separation. The amount of the grant also affects living arrangements. If financially feasible, AFDC mothers are likely to set up their own households rather than live with other relatives. However, AFDC has no impact upon the incidence of child-bearing among unmarried women.[19]

Longitudinal studies have shown that most spells of welfare receipt have begun with a relationship change, either the departure of the husband (45 percent) or the birth of a child (30 percent). Likewise, women have been most likely to get off welfare by becoming wives (35 percent). Increases in their earnings accounted for just 21 percent of spell endings.[20]

While literally all means-tested programs bear some stigma, the controversy around AFDC is vehement. The program is expensive and both the left and the right repeatedly have referred to it as a mess. The design and implementation of this program, as well as its recent overhaul, exemplify problems of gender assumptions that plague all who encounter the program.

The forerunners to AFDC in the United States were the Mothers' Pensions or Widows' Pensions programs, established in the states shortly after the turn of the century. It was not until the implementation of Mothers' Pensions' benefits that welfare programs were specifically designed to aid single mothers and their children.[21] The enthusiasm for a Mothers' Pension provision was spearheaded by the child advocates who ran the White House Conference on Children in 1909. One of the most significant pronouncements to come out of that conference was the statement that children should not be removed from their homes for reasons of poverty alone. By 1926 almost all of the states had welfare programs, called Widows' Pensions or Mothers' Pensions, to help widowed mothers care for their children at home.[22]

The state programs were, from the beginning, paternalistic and highly selective about who received benefits.[23] Investigators visited the households of recipients to determine whether the children were being raised in a "suitable home."[24] The investigation was based on the sexist assumption that unmarried women with children were probably sexually promiscuous. That such practices consti-tuted harassment and not child protection was clear when the grant was denied but the children were left in the home. But the threat of loss of her children was ever present for women who applied for aid. If a home was found unsuitable, aid could be denied and the mother might have no choice but to place her children in the care of the state. Moreover, even though the payments were frequently less than any reasonable estimation of subsistence level, the recipients were distrusted and sometimes referred to in the press as "gilt-edged widows."[25]

The recipients of Mothers' Pensions were, due to discrimination in eligibility determination, primarily white widows.[26] Financial aid was dependent not only upon need, but on the woman's link to the father of her children: death and imprisonment of the husband were acceptable, divorce or desertion less acceptable, and out-of-wedlock parenthood completely unacceptable.[27] The issue focused on the reluctance of the state to encourage men to abandon their families. But the women and children and not the men were punished for these circumstances. White widows and their children were the most likely to receive help, but even after meeting the stringent eligibility requirements, the mothers were subject to constant monitoring of their child care and moral behavior. A woman without a man was sexually suspect and had to be careful to be above suspicion lest her character be impugned.[28] The sexist assumption was that the woman either could not hold on to her man or was up to no good. Her lack of attachment to a man was quite threatening to patriarchy and evoked punishment and control of her sexual behavior.

This historically documented harassment of white widowed mothers on welfare has often been overlooked. At a recent conference, for example, one discussant cited U.S. attitudes toward the poor as especially negative due to the current perception of the poor as an "under-class" of "Blacks or Hispanics, of sexually loose welfare mothers, drug addicts, criminals, and lazy dropouts."[29] It is true that much of today's stigmatization and harassment of welfare mothers is worsened by white supremacist brutality. But it is well to remember that in the early days of these programs, racism kept some women from getting benefits at all, and misogyny guided the program rules for the chosen few. In fact the stigma related to welfare has been imposed on women throughout this country's history of imparting such benefits, regardless of the race of the women, the legitimacy of their children, or their chaste and law-abiding behavior. This is another indication that the oppression of women in the "care" of the social welfare system was a functional part of its design.

The Social Security Act, with the establishment in 1935 of Aid to Dependent Children (ADC, renamed Aid to Families with Dependent Children in 1962) and Survivor's Insurance (SI) in 1939, made two provisions for single mothers and their children. The latter program, part of the social insurance portion of the act, provided benefits for widows and children of covered men workers. ADC was considered a temporary stopgap program that would provide for families ineligible for SI. At the inception of SI, 43 percent of the 254,000 ADC families were transferred to the Old Age and Survivors Insurance rolls.[30] It was assumed that the population in need consisted solely of widows and their children and thus SI would eventually take over the preponderance of the caseload. Indeed, the Advisory Council on Social Security recognized the inferior nature of ADC as compared with SI, noting that "relief [ADC] is not the most desirable way of meeting childhood dependency."[31] Yet they ignored the fact that even in

1939 the majority of the recipients were children of divorced, separated, and unmarried mothers.[32] What happened, in fact, was the evolution of two programs, separate and unequal, each serving mothers alone with children, but the insurance program was more adequate and without stigma, the welfare program less adequate and fraught with punitive measures.[33] Since 1970 the real benefits for children under SI have increased by 53 percent, while those for children under AFDC have been cut by 13 percent. Children receiving SI receive almost three times what is provided children under AFDC. The former group of children is primarily white and in the latter group the children are mostly Black or Hispanic.[34] Thus a white supremacist and patriarchal system has operated to divide women racially and with regard to the "acceptability" of one's marital status.

Few analysts discuss AFDC policy in relationship to the more adequate SI, and the major population benefiting, namely children, is not considered a reasonable beneficiary category to combine the programs. Consider the words of Robert M. Ball, Social Security Commissioner from 1962 to 1973 and respected advocate for the system:

Social security would be able to reduce somewhat the 8 percent of the AFDC load that arises from the disability of a parent if disability insurance were liberalized . . . , but it seems to me that it is impossible to insure against the risks of desertion, divorce, or illegitimacy. The occurrence of these events is *too much within the control of those affected* to make it reasonable to use an insurance technique (emphasis added).[35]

He is raising, of course, the possibility of fault, when he speaks of "control." Unfortunately, children are never in control of the events mentioned, and women often aren't either.

ADC replaced state Widows' and Mothers' Pension programs but perpetuated their meager benefits, the stigma, and the restrictive requirements. From the beginning, federal funds for the other Social Security Act public assistance titles—Aid to the Blind and Old Age Assistance—were more generous.[36] Moreover, ADC originally provided only children's benefits, and was thereby designed as though a mother would not have to use a portion of the benefit for her own upkeep. A payment for the child's caretaker was not added until 1950. In some places, ADC was not available during harvest time, when such families were expected to work in the fields.

The "suitable home" rules, used in Mothers' Pension programs, were incorporated into the ADC program in most states. Mothers considered immoral or unfit could lose their children or, more likely, be denied ADC and awarded the lower state General Assistance grant instead.[37] As with Mothers' Pensions, it was not the children's protection but the patriarchal control of the women's sexual behavior that was the issue. Later, as the rolls increased and women with illegitimate children were included, "man in the house" or "substitute parent" rules were established. Any man with whom a recipient had a relationship was expected to support her and her children. The discovery of such a man constituted the discovery of a "substitute parent" and would result in a cutoff of the family's grant. "Refusal to cooperate," including refusal to admit unannounced investigators into one's home at any hour of the day or night (called "midnight raids"), could also result in the cessation of the grant.[38] Both the suitable home rules and the farm work provisions were disproportionately applied to Black families.[39] Once again racism compounded the sexism in the system.

These diligent efforts were ostensibly undertaken to rule out fraud and cheating. However, they were not being applied with equal vigor to detect fraud among aged, blind, and disabled recipients of welfare grants. Their imposition on AFDC recipients functioned to humiliate and control them. The state was enabled thereby to assume the masculine function of subjugating women. Even today, stigma and humiliation are the price of applying for aid. Although the harassing techniques associated with "suitable home" and "substitute parent" rules have been eliminated, women are still subject to many personal questions about their sexual behavior, justified by a need to establish the children's paternity.

In 1962, Congress passed the public welfare amendments to the Social Security Act that provided federal matching funds to help the states give services to the current, former, and potential recipients of welfare. The social welfare lobby, comprised primarily of social workers, convinced the legislature that services would somehow get the welfare recipients off the rolls.[40] Since counseling was the service that predominated in the service plans, this push for services to eliminate dependency was related to the notion that people are poor because of some psychological flaw. With treatment, the dependent could become independent. The services not only did not serve to decrease the rolls but shortly thereafter the AFDC rolls started rising.

Between 1965 and 1976 the number of families served by AFDC increased more than threefold.[41] A variety of circumstances contributed to this phenomenon. In the 1960s the welfare program became better known than ever before. The National Welfare Rights Organization and its local branches worked to educate people about their eligibility and their right to welfare and, with the help of legal advocates, held the agencies to enforcing their own regulations regarding eligibility. As a result more eligible people applied and were accepted by the program. Welfare departments were forced to become much less blatantly punitive toward recipients.[42] Midnight raids were discontinued.[43] At the same time there was an increase in the illegitimacy rate,[44] with larger numbers of unmarried women applying for and obtaining aid,[45] and the divorce rate was also going up.[46] The advocacy strategies of the War on Poverty may also have spurred this rise in the welfare rolls.

It appears that the job-related poverty strategies of the War on Poverty in the 1960s focused on male-headed families. The poverty strategy for single women with children was to secure their right to welfare, not to get them into the labor force. In 1959 the poverty rate for female-headed families was 42.6 percent; it went down to 32.5 percent in 1970. In contrast the rate for "all other families" went from 15.8 percent to 7.2 percent in the same years.[47] Whether it was the War on Poverty or the war in Viet Nam that brought a greater proportion of male-headed families out of poverty is a matter for debate. We know that women on welfare stayed below or near poverty level. Notwithstanding this evidence, however, a thorough gender-sensitive history of the War on Poverty has not been done.

By 1967 Congress grew disillusioned with the unfulfilled promises of the 1962 service provisions and added new amendments tied to employment-related activities. In 1969, work incentives were built into the AFDC program. Previous to this time, a recipient's grant was reduced, dollar for dollar, by any amount earned. The new legislation provided for deductibles for child care and work expenses, and earnings disregards of 100 percent on the first $30 and 33 percent of additional earnings (known as the "30 and one-third" provision). Furthermore, in the early 1970s, income maintenance was separated from the provision of social services, jettisoning the long-lived notion that relief without counsel doomed clients to dependency and degradation. The notion of welfare as an entitlement was strengthened. Meanwhile, advocates pushed for the federalization of welfare, hoping to make the program uniform across states and bring an end to the punitive discretionary practices that still operated in local areas.

Nixon's Family Assistance Plan (FAP) would have provided a guaranteed national minimum income. But conservatives, maintaining that welfare should remain a local matter, opposed it. Many liberals also opposed it on the grounds that the minimum was too low. After a period of struggle and compromise, only part of FAP, the adult provisions, was enacted, leaving AFDC as it was. Women and children were to be left out.

The establishment of the Supplemental Security Income (SSI) program in 1973 increased the disparity between the adult welfare programs and the treatment of women with children on welfare. SSI combined the previous Aid to the Blind, Aid to the Disabled, and Old Age Assistance programs into one federal means-tested program. SSI pays, on the average, more than AFDC. The average monthly payment amount per person on AFDC in April 1988 was $126.52,[48] while for an SSI individual in the same month the benefit was $259.43.[49] SSI is more equitable from state to state, and since 1975 it has had an automatic adjustment of benefits tied to yearly increases in the cost of living. Although means-tested it is much less stigmatized and some writers no longer refer to it as "welfare." It was designed to resemble Social Security retirement insurance in order to reduce the stigma the elderly might feel in applying for it. Indeed, the Social Security Administration was given administrative jurisdiction over the program. With the adoption of SSI, AFDC remained as the "welfare mess," and its recipients even more stigmatized. Welfare reform for women and children, attempted unsuccessfully by the Carter administration, remained an unachieved goal until Ronald Reagan became president.

OMNIBUS BUDGET RECONCILIATION ACT

Created and strong-armed through Congress by the Reagan administration, the Omnibus Budget Reconciliation Act (OBRA) of 1981 changed the AFDC program in several ways. One of the most devastating changes was a diminution of the work-incentive provisions. Limits of $75 per month for work expenses and $160 per month for child care were imposed. Also the $30 and one-third disregard of earnings was limited to the first four months of employment. The Earned Income Tax Credit (EITC), a tax refund for low income workers with children, was to be counted as income whether or not an eligible family was actually receiving it. Other changes included limiting a family's allowable resources to $1,000 and the assumption, in determining a family's eligibility and grant level, that a stepparent contributes to a child's support, whether or not he or she has any legal liability to do so. Eligibility was restricted to families with incomes below 150 percent of the state standard of need and denied to a pregnant woman with no children until the third trimester of pregnancy. OBRA also changed the rules of the AFDC-Unemployed Parent (AFDC-UP) program, a program for two-parent families with children operated at state option. (In 1988, 23 states operated such programs, but the total AFDC-UP recipients constituted less than 9 percent of the national caseload.[50]) The new rule specified that the qualifying unemployed parent must be the family's principal earner. OBRA also instituted various work training and workfare provisions that allowed the states some leeway to redesign their Work Incentive Programs and develop work-related demonstration projects. These will be discussed in Chapter 4.

In 1984, in the Deficit Reduction Act, Congress modified some of the OBRA rules to make them less severe. The gross income eligibility limit was increased to 185 percent of the state need standard. The work expense disregard of $75 was applied to part-time as well as full-time work, and the $30 disregard was extended to the first 12 months of employment. The EITC could be counted only when it is received. The act determined that families losing AFDC eligibility due to the four-month limit on the earnings disregard are eligible for nine months of Medicaid coverage, and an additional six months at state option. The 1984 provisions also established a monthly disregard of $50 of child support received by a family.[51]

The 1984 amendments also added a new eligibility restriction. Now parents and all minor siblings must be included in the AFDC unit for purposes of determining eligibility. This means, for example, that half-siblings' income, from sources such as Social Security or child support, must be counted as income available to the family "filing unit."

AFTERMATH OF OBRA

In 1981 AFDC families with average earnings were, on the average, at 101 percent of the poverty standard. OBRA reduced that average to 81 percent in 1982.[52] The situation is still bad; now AFDC families in every state except

Alaska and Hawaii live below the poverty level. Thirty states provide benefits that are less than 50 percent of poverty level.[53] But it is not just the Reagan changes that make life hard for women and children on AFDC. Benefit levels, which have not kept up with inflation, have been dropping since 1970. In 1983 the average monthly benefit to each recipient of AFDC was $107.20, less than the $112.41 it had been in 1967 (in constant 1983 dollars).[54] Also, benefit cuts and restrictions have reduced the numbers of poor families who are even covered by AFDC provisions. During the 1970s, 83 percent of all poor families and more than 75 percent of poor children received AFDC benefits. By 1983, the percentage of poor families with children receiving AFDC was down to 62.9 percent and just 53.3 percent of poor children received such benefits.[55]

FAMILY SUPPORT ACT

On October 13, 1988, President Reagan signed into law the Family Support Act (PL 100-485), a welfare "reform" bill that ties the obligation to participate in job search, job training, or work experience to the receipt of AFDC benefits. A more thorough analysis of the work provisions of the bill will be taken up in Chapter 4. Its other provisions include the requirement that states provide AFDC-UP for at least six months out of the year. At state option, unmarried minor parents may be eligible for AFDC only if they live with their parents or adult guardians and the benefit can be paid to such adults on their behalf. The bill also includes various provisions to help strengthen and streamline child support enforcement activities.[56] Child support enforcement will be discussed in detail in Chapter 5.

Various versions of this legislation went by the boards as the lawmakers struggled to achieve something that could be passed. The Reagan administration was not active in pushing this bill and threatened to veto it at various points in the deliberations. Conservative forces axed versions that included provisions for benefit levels up to the poverty level for recipient families and in general opposed increasing generosity. Thus, only minor changes that would increase benefits were made: upping the child care expense disregard from $160 to $175 a month (and to $200 for children under age two), increasing the standard work expense deduction from $75 to $90, and disregarding the EITC entirely for the purpose of determining the benefit amount.

WHAT HAS HAPPENED

Literally all of the changes in the AFDC program brought about by OBRA were based on patriarchal assumptions and made life worse for welfare mothers and their children. The provision to limit AFDC-UP eligibility to families in which only the "principal" earner is unemployed was a way of limiting eligibility for families with unemployed wives and reestablishing the patriarchal standard of men as breadwinners. Likewise, restricting eligibility to the third trimester of pregnancy is a punitive measure directed toward single mothers, and is ironic in view of the Reagan administrations's position that a fetus is a person from the moment of conception. Furthermore, the stepparent rule reactivates the ''substitute parent'' assumptions of the early program, since it assumes that a man married to a woman should also be supporting her children. Thus patriarchy ''assigns'' this responsibility; men are free to disregard it, but the women suffer if it is not assumed.

In the struggle that ensued after OBRA's passage, Congress was perceived as pulling in the reins on the conservative agenda of the Reagan administration. Indeed, it restored some OBRA cuts and held the line on even more punitive measures. If permitted by Congress, Reagan would have gone farther and relegated the AFDC program to the states, which historically have administered welfare programs from a punitive white supremacist patriarchal standpoint. Yet the meliorative adjustments made by the Congress in 1984 were also brushed by gender assumptions. Congress let stand the most severe reduction in work incentives. Instead it implemented or restored support incentives, thereby increasing the women's dependency. The $50 child support disregard, however beneficial to women and children, also bears the implication that fathers deserve an incentive to support their children.[57] Yet women do not deserve an incentive to join the labor market.

Extending AFDC-UP to all the states, even for six months, was a measure that will serve to bring some equity to the treatment of two-parent versus one-parent families. It represents an attempt, however, to restore and uphold the patriarchal institution of marriage. In spite of evidence to the contrary,[58] there remains the belief that couples break up so the wife can become eligible for welfare; this is a way to try to prevent that breakup. Although the men in these families have a more stringent work requirement, the extension weakens somewhat the economy's ability to control the labor force participation of able-bodied men.

Insofar as the men have a ''choice'' of AFDC or working, they will have an alternative to taking the lower paying jobs. Most men do not have this alternative; they are expected to work under any conditions and welfare is not an option. The lack of welfare for the majority of able-bodied men serves capitalism in that it provides a pool of cheap labor. In this instance, providing welfare for able-bodied men, the needs of patriarchy have imposed upon the demands of capital. Nevertheless, the six-month proviso will keep the benefit time-limited for any family and the eligibility requirements may well keep the AFDC-UP rolls relatively low.

WORK AND WORK INCENTIVES

When OBRA was passed, many welfare recipients who were employed but receiving partial AFDC grants were completely dropped from the rolls. Many predicted that these recipients would realize that welfare alone would pay more (not to mention providing Medicaid coverage) than employment and would quit their jobs and reapply for assistance, this time for full grants. This did not happen, even though for many it would have been an economically sound decision.[59] Yet the question remains as to why the Reagan administration chose to risk an increase in the cost of AFDC. The elimination of monetary work incentives seemed to contradict the Reagan philosophy of getting welfare recipients to work and its goal of reducing welfare costs.

Applying the concept of patriarchal necessity leads to the conclusion that the cuts were made to reduce the federal budget marginally, punish the women by reducing their incomes, and make it appear once again that the people on assistance consist of a lazy underclass who have to be forced to work. The newly created work programs, codified in the 1988 Family Support Act (see Chapter 4) were set up to replace the monetary work incentives in order to maintain more control over the women's work search and work activities and more efficiently channel them into low-paying service sector jobs. Women are indeed being forced into dead-end jobs with unsafe or distasteful working conditions. But the striking thing about the new work programs is not what they are doing but what they are not doing. They are marginally effective at best, do not get people out of poverty, and are vastly underfunded. This is functional to patriarchy and capitalism because it makes AFDC even more stigmatized and certainly will make bad jobs more attractive to some. Women will remain poor, however, either dependent on welfare or marginally subsisting on their wages. In either case, their best route out of poverty will continue to be marriage.

REFORMERS AND RHETORIC

Social science interpretations of the data about women's poverty and welfare reform have reflected the concept of "patriarchal necessity" and thereby given great credence to the rationales of policy makers. The common emphasis on family structure in research experiments and analyses, for example, has served to generate and/or inhibit policy initiatives. Interpretations of data generally consider barriers to marriage or incentives to marital breakup as inherently undesirable. The conditions within the marriage, however impoverished, are of considerably less concern.

In the late 1960s and early 1970s, income maintenance experiments were conducted in Seattle and Denver (the experiments are often referred to as "SIME-DIME"). Persons in various family "types" were guaranteed income over a period of time, regardless of work effort and regardless of family structure. Thus, husbands and wives who separated or divorced were guaranteed continued income from the state. The outcomes of these experiments suggested that providing welfare benefits to married couples increased divorce rates by as much as 50 percent.[60] These results spawned numerous interpretations of the negative impact of men's loss of the role of "breadwinner," and were a major inhibiting effect on even the mention of a guaranteed income for two-parent families. It was thought that depriving men of the breadwinner role had the strong potential of destroying marriages.[61] The results of the experiments also discouraged those who thought that restricting welfare to single parents led to marital breakups because it forced men to abandon their families so they could receive needed welfare support. Now it appears that the data were misinterpreted.

A recent and convincing reexamination of the SIME-DIME experimental design and data has led to the conclusion that the experiments did not show an increased tendency to divorce among those in the experimental group.[62] This new conclusion may have helped the inclusion of the AFDC-UP measure in the Family Support Act. An interesting by-product of this new revelation is the question of what analysts are going to do with their "male role performance" interpretations of the challenged conclusions.[63]

Reagan administration officials have tended to focus on family structure as the "cause" of female poverty, citing the high divorce rate, the increase in out-of-wedlock births, and AFDC itself as promoting and encouraging the formulation of female-headed households. This is a view shared by a variety of analysts and scholars across the political spectrum.

Irwin Garfinkel and Sara S. McLanahan, from the prestigious Institute for Research on Poverty at the University of Wisconsin-Madison, for example, have amassed evidence that single parenthood is bad for children. In their book, *Single Mothers and Their Children: A New American Dilemma*, Garfinkel and McLanahan posit a "new American dilemma." The dilemma, as the authors see it, is whether policy makers should "give priority to reducing the economic insecurity of mother-only families or to reducing their prevalence and dependence."[64] This issue, and the stated bias that "two parents can do a better job of raising children than one parent,"[65] set the parameters that shape the rest of the volume. The authors build a case that mother-only families are detrimental to children. These families are poorer than two-parent families and experience more residential moves, changes in employment and work hours (for mothers, compared to *fathers* in two-parent families), and changes in household composition, all of which can be stressful to children. The authors assert as well that after divorce families lose "social networks and social support systems," ignoring evidence that it is women who build and sustain these systems for themselves and their families. They cite higher mental health utilization rates for these families and neglect to mention women's greater propensity to seek formal help for their problems.[66] The data they cite are far from conclusive.

Garfinkel and McLanahan identify the increase in mother-only families as primarily due to the likelihood of white women to divorce and Black women not to marry. They submit that increasing opportunities in the labor force for white women have made their economic independence more viable and increased the likelihood of marital disruption. They point to Black men's decreasing economic opportunities as the main cause of Black women's not marrying, because the gains of marriage are reduced and "the role of the husband as breadwinner" is undermined.[67]

Garfinkel and McLanahan try to solve the "new American dilemma" by proposing benefits they believe will relieve the economic insecurity of these families without increasing their numbers. Their recommendations, while they would go far in alleviating women's poverty, are primarily based on patriarchal income support measures, better child support supplemented by the state, and a form of a national minimum income.[68] These things would be very helpful to woman-headed families but they amount to continued dependency.

A less bold approach is their proposal for AFDC work relief, including guaranteed jobs at minimum wage or education and training for women without preschool children. This proposal avoids the costs of preschool child care, but would exclude the majority of the current AFDC caseload, 60 percent of which consists of women with children under six. New recipients could be ineligible for as long as six years. Yet they also propose guaranteed jobs or work relief for noncustodial fathers, who would not have to wait six years to get it.[69] These analysts are herein promoting the twentieth-century version of U.S. middle-class marriage and family. While some of their remedies are new and have the potential of being especially helpful to children, they perpetuate patriarchal gender arrangements.

In contrast, in the well-touted and influential book, *Losing Ground: American Social Policy 1950–1980*, conservative Charles Murray is more explicit in his assertion that the welfare system has been a disincentive to marriage and family self-support.[70] His hypothetical couple, Harold and Phyllis, have, in his estimation, no choice but to marry in 1960 when they discover that Phyllis is pregnant; in 1970 there are financial incentives to avoid marriage and live together.[71] Putting aside the flaws in his assumptions, and there are several, his main concern appears to be that men and women should marry, regardless of their financial circumstances within the marriage. It is instructive to note that he does not recommend that Phyllis get a job to support her child; he is more concerned that the couple get married.[72] Christopher Jencks summarizes Murray's case succinctly: "Shorn of rhetoric, then, the 'empirical' case against the welfare system comes to this. First, high AFDC benefits allow single mothers to set up their own households. Second, high AFDC benefits allow mothers to end bad marriages. Third, high benefits may make divorced mothers more cautious about remarrying."[73] Note that these choices constitute for women a separate financial existence apart from their relationship with men, which gives them a certain autonomy. But, as Jencks points out, dependence on AFDC or dependence on a husband's paycheck is still dependence for women.[74] Murray never makes this distinction.

Jencks suggests that the difference for Murray may be that when Harold and Phyllis are married, their problems are their own, but when Phyllis is alone with her children the society feels some "collective responsibility" for her and the care of her children.[75] He cautions against the impulse to "drive her back into Harold's arms so that we no longer have to think about her."[76] This "collective responsibility" is, of course, patriarchal control by the state. Personal patriarchal control is preferred; the solution for Murray and others like him is for women to have no choice in this regard. Murray's perspective clearly views the institution of marriage as the proper locus of responsibility for the financial care and control of women and children. This is a central, primary patriarchal assumption. Other alternatives are unacceptable and thus, in his book, minimized or ignored.

Murray presents a very conservative perspective, but even liberals have concentrated on the "family structure" cause of women's poverty. William Julius Wilson, sociologist from the University of Chicago and self-proclaimed "social democrat," also focuses on this issue. Wilson recommends a host of macro-economic solutions to the problems of inner-city poverty congruent with a liberal agenda and anathema to the conservative point of view. However, his focus on single parenthood is as intense as Murray's. He differs from Murray in his argument for the cause of single-parent families among Blacks. Murray blames it on the incentives of the welfare system and Wilson blames it on unemployment among Black men, which diminishes the "pool" of marriageable Black men.

Wilson points out that Black women face a diminishing pool of "marriage-able" (i.e., "economically stable") men. The labor force participation rate of Black male teenagers (aged 16 to 19) was 36.5 percent in 1980, having fallen from 59.5 percent in 1940. For white male teens, the rate went up from 46.4 to 55.5 in the same time span.[77] Wilson and Kathryn Neckerman devised an index of the ratio of employed young men to women of the same race and age group, which they call the "male marriageable pool," and found a "sharp decline" in the nonwhite ratios from the 1960s compared with rising ratios for whites.[78] With Neckerman, Wilson concludes that fewer Black men than white men are economically in a position to marry and therefore suggests that "the increasing rate of joblessness among Black men merits serious consideration as a major underlying factor in the rise of Black single mothers and female-headed households."[79] Wilson expounded on this theme in his book, *The Truly Disadvantaged*, and while he does recommend that employment opportunities be available for both men and women of the "underclass,"[80] he concentrates almost exclusively on the unemployment problems of men and defines female-headed families as a social problem akin to crime and drug addiction.[81] Both Wilson and Murray wish to see these women marry.

Like Wilson, many researchers and analysts give lip service to the employment problems of both young men and young women, but their analyses often concentrate exclusively on young men. David Ellwood and Lawrence Summers, for example, reviewed the problem of unemployment among Black and white youth aged 16 to 19, citing a large increase for Blacks of both sexes and not for whites between 1954 and 1980. In their related discussion of welfare policy, however, they concentrate on Black male youth "to avoid problems associated with the child bearing decisions of young women."[82] While the Ellwood and Summers analysis is important, it addresses only one-half of the problem of Black youth unemployment, and in this sense it is typical of work on this topic.[83] Since the significant financial contribution of wives to the family is a growing trend, it is important to pay attention at the outset to female as well as male youth unemployment rates. Attention to female youth unemployment also may help to shed some light on the problem of teenage pregnancy. One could hypothesize, for example, that young women who are unemployed and who see no other lives ahead of them beyond motherhood, see no reason to delay the onset of motherhood. They exercise the only choice they see.

Concentration on marriage and male wage earners often ignores the evidence that for Black families poverty status doesn't change with the transition to or from marriage. Mary Jo Bane cites the Michigan Panel Study of Income Dynamics in examining the income status of individuals who moved into single-parent female-headed households. Among those who were poor in the first year after the transition, three-quarters of the whites became poor when that transition took place while two-thirds of the Blacks were already poor before the transition.[84] She states: "Though there has been a dramatic, and shocking, increase in female-headed households among Blacks, and an equally dramatic "feminization" of Black poverty, one cannot conclude that much of the poverty could have been avoided had families only stayed together."[85] This finding highlights the fact that two adults are increasingly needed to support families and that increasing the proportion of married couple families among Blacks may not alleviate poverty among them.

Again, the concern here is not with poverty per se, but with women subsisting without men. Undoubtedly many Black women would wish not only to be married but to be married to Black men with stable incomes and good financial futures. These women, like their unemployed men counterparts, have few viable choices under current societal conditions. But the women are blamed for the perpetuation of these societal conditions in the way they raise their sons! No less an authority than Dr. Alvin F. Poussaint, prominent Black psychiatrist, Associate Professor of Psychiatry and Associate Dean for Student Affairs at the Harvard Medical School, said the following in a letter to the *New York Times*.

One problem, which deserves further study, is that many single black mothers are angry with black men, sometimes with justification. When they talk among themselves, these women commonly disparage men. Their conversations symbolize the negative atmosphere in which many black boys are being raised. . . . These boys often grow up feeling ill equipped to become competent members of society. . . . A significant number of black men in prison have themselves been victims of neglect and child abuse and, in turn, they assault and murder one another at alarming rates.[86]

Statements like these recur throughout discussions about Black families today. Black women, already faced with impoverishment, are thus faced with sexist accusations, even within their own communities, about their ultimate responsibility for their sons' deaths. I would suggest that Black men who buy into this patriarchal thinking are helping to enable the forces of white supremacy and capitalism to maintain the status quo. Black women are easy targets for the ruling class.

TEENAGE PREGNANCY

Teenage pregnancy is a subset of the feminization of poverty issue because the two are so closely associated. Women who were teenagers when their first child was born account for more than half the total of the AFDC budget and 71 percent of all recipient mothers under 30.[87] Teen childbearing is associated with high medical risks for mother and child and mother's low educational attainment, and teen marriages are generally unstable.[88]

Teen childbearing is of particular concern for patriarchy because of the autonomy of unwed teen mothers and the likelihood that even married ones will end up unmarried and on welfare. This is a threat to the patriarchal family.

In contrast, to women's advocates teen pregnancy is also considered a problem because having a child at such a young age robs a young girl of the pleasures of youth and limits her opportunities and choices for years to come. Notwithstanding these serious effects, however, it is important to be realistic about the problem and define it accordingly.

Age alone, for teens over 15, need not be a medical risk for childbearing, and their health problems are related to lack of access or use of medical care.[89] There is some evidence that most teen mothers, even if they rely on welfare for a time, do not rely on it indefinitely.[90] Furthermore, teen parents are no more prone to child abuse than older parents.[91] These factors are often ignored amid the current hysteria over teen motherhood.

It is instructive to note that teen childbearing has declined over the past 30 years for both Black and white women aged 15 and over. For younger teens there have not been declines, but increases have been minimal. What has increased are the rates and numbers of out-of-wedlock births, especially among white teen women.[92] In the 1950s teen pregnancy was likely to be an occasion for marriage or adoption. Now this is no longer the case.[93] It is the increase in teen single parents that has led to the current concern, not teen parenthood per se.

In examining this phenomenon and proposing solutions, a great deal of attention has been paid to teen girls' decisions about sexual relations, contraception, and childbearing, and much less to their personal development. In their comprehensive review of studies of teen pregnancy, Kristin Moore and Martha Burt could only suggest that early pregnancy is related to a lack of alternatives for teen women; there had been almost no studies on this. Nevertheless they make the point that

teenagers, especially poor and minority teenagers, may perceive less incentive to avoid early childbearing because discrimination limits their future opportunities. . . . If [research] support is found for our hypothesis that poor opportunities cause low motivation, then there is an additional reason to encourage efforts to eradicate discrimination on the basis of race and sex.[94]

In sum, concerns about the overall problem of teen pregnancy mask more focused concerns about single parenthood, symbolic of independence for women and inimical to patriarchy, and welfare dependency. Proposed solutions often concentrate on controlling young women's sexual behavior (saying "no" to sex and/or using contraception) or disincentives for independence, such as the new welfare rule that *unmarried* mothers who are minors must live with their parents to be eligible for AFDC. This conveys the clear patriarchal message that young mothers should live only with parents or husbands. In fact there is some evidence that marriage may make a young mother's situation worse, by increasing her chance of having more closely spaced children, decreasing the likelihood of her returning to school (except when her husband is a high school graduate), and lessening child care help from her family.[95] While there has been emphasis on comprehensive services for teen parents and their children,[96] an insufficient connection has been made, notwithstanding Moore and Burt's comments, between the girls' real vocational opportunities and expectations and their decisions about sex and parenthood. For the most part, the definition of the problem and its proposed solutions constitute a patriarchal construct only peripherally related to the overall well-being of the young women affected.[97]

ANALYSIS

According to patriarchal necessity, women's dependency is necessary to the differentiation of gender roles and the perpetuation of the patriarchal system. This dependency is maintained as a legitimate function of the welfare system in the absence of support by individual men, which is the preferred mode of dependency. But women must also be punished for their manlessness. Women and children have received and continue to receive less aid than the poor aged or handicapped, and they have been subject to much more stigmatization. This differential treatment serves as an incentive to marriage and a punishment for the unmarried.

Under patriarchy, women who are divorced or separated are blamed for the marital split regardless of which spouse initiated it. Furthermore, single women, particularly those with illegitimate children, are dangerously independent of men. Women are in great danger of becoming poor upon divorce, and even the nonpoor suffer substantial drops in income. One study showed that after divorce, the incomes of single mother-headed households dropped in every income category, by as much as one-half for the highest income category to one quarter for the lowest income level. These declines persisted as long as the family was headed by a woman.[98] All of these women are subject to potential punishment or control. Those who manage to stay off welfare are controlled by low wages, discrimination in the housing market, and opprobrium for their supposed incompetence to raise children without men. For women on welfare, and many single mothers must resort to it, punishment and control has permeated the administration of the AFDC program from its inception.

This is the hidden American dilemma. Society is presumably concerned with the dependence of mother-only families, but the concern is only with state-related dependence. Murray says that welfare breaks up marriages; others say that it does not. Neither side questions the solution of marriage as the answer to women's poverty, even when there is evidence that marriage will not always alleviate this poverty, especially among Black women and children, who are the most impoverished. Dependence on individual men is not only acceptable but preferred to economic independence in the work world. Garfinkel and McLanahan, for example, state as a given that most welfare women working full-time year-round would not be able to pull their families out of poverty.[99] They admit that "over half of the gender gap is due to something other than differences in productivity, *presumably* discrimination" (emphasis added).[100] Yet they do not mention or advocate pay equity or the elimination of sex role segregation and sex discrimination in the labor force. These solutions are not acceptable to patriarchal society.

Chapter 4 will address social welfare policies and programs designed to have an impact on poor women's labor force participation.

NOTES

1. Ruth Sidel, *Women and Children Last: The Plight of Poor Women in Affluent America* (New York: Penguin Books, 1986), 94, quoting Dorothy Johnson, Atlanta social worker.

2. It was 43 percent in 1959 compared with 34.5 percent in 1984, for example. See Bureau of the Census, Current Population Reports, Series P-60, No. 152, *Characteristics of the Population Below the Poverty Level: 1984* (Washington, D. C.: U.S. Government Printing Office, 1986), T.4., 20.

3. Bureau of the Census, *Statistical Abstract of the United States: 1960* (Washington, D. C.: U.S. Government Printing Office, 1960), 41.

4. *Population Below the Poverty Level: 1984*, T.4., 20. My calculations.

5. Bureau of the Census, Current Population Reports, Series P-60, No. 160, *Poverty in the United States: 1986* (Washington, D. C.: U.S. Government Printing Office, 1988), T. 13, 64. Moreover, in 1986, 63 percent of all poor unrelated individuals were females. Were it not for male children in female-headed households, the proportion of the poor who are female would be even higher. See T. 8, 32–5.

6. Ibid., T. 14, 65.

7. See note 4, Chapter 1.

8. Department of Health and Human Services, Social Security Administration, Office of Policy, Family Support Administration, Office of Family Assistance, *Quarterly Public Assistance Statistics: April-June, 1985*, SSA Publication No. 13-11705, December, 1986, 1.

9. House of Representatives, Committee on Ways and Means, *Background Material and Data on Programs within the Jurisdiction of the Committee on Ways and Means*, 1989 Edition (Washington, D. C.: U.S. Government Printing Office, 1989), 560.

10. Ibid., 561.

11. Ibid., 558.

12. *Background Material*, T. 35, 881.

13. Ibid., T. 1, 941.

14. Ibid., T.22, 563.

15. Ibid., 582.

16. David T. Ellwood, "Targeting 'Would-Be' Long-Term Recipients of AFDC" (Princeton, NJ: Mathematica Policy Research, 1986).

17. *Background Material*, 585.

18. Greg J. Duncan and Saul D. Hoffman, "The Use and Effects of Welfare: A Survey of Recent Evidence," *Social Service Review*, June 1988:253.

19. David T. Ellwood and Mary Jo Bane, "The Impact of AFDC on Family Structure and Living Arrangements" (Boston: Harvard University, 1985), 5, 6-7. See also Duncan and Hoffman.

20. *Background Material*, 586.

21. I include only recent history in this section, as this book is not intended to be an historical account. An excellent history of welfare benefits for women paupers in the United States since the colonial era can be found in Mimi Abramovitz, *Regulating the Lives of Women: Social Welfare Policy from Colonial Times to the Present* (Boston: South End Press, 1988).

22. Blanche D. Coll, *Perspectives in Public Welfare* (Washington, D. C.: U.S. Government Printing Office, 1973), 78.

23. Ibid., 79.

24. Winifred Bell, *Aid to Dependent Children* (New York: Columbia University Press, 1965), 5, 8.

25. Coll, 79.

26. Bell, 9, 10.

27. Ibid., 8–9.

28. Ibid., 8–9, 14.

29. James Patterson, "Reflections on Papers by Hugh Heclo and Gary Burtless, for Conference Sponsored by Institute for Research on Poverty," appended to Hugh Heclo, "The Political Foundations of Antipoverty Policy," IRP Conference Paper, "Poverty and Policy: Retrospect and Prospects," Williamsburg, VA, December 6–8, 1984. (Madison: Institute for Research on Poverty, University of Wisconsin-Madison, 1985), 4.

30. Abramovitz, 265.

31. Ibid., quoting U.S. Advisory Council on Social Security, *Final Report, December 10, 1938*, Senate Doc. 4, 76th Congress, Session 2 (1939), 17.

32. Ibid. This is a little known fact. It is commonly believed that widows and their children were in the majority.

33. There were 326,183 widowed mothers and fathers and 1.8 million children awarded SI benefits in January 1988. The average benefit amount for mothers and fathers was $349.81 and the average benefit for children was $352.87. In the same month the average welfare payment per AFDC *family* was $367.01. See Department of Health and Human Services, Social Security Administration, Office of Policy, Office of Research and Statistics, *Monthly Benefit Statistics: Summary Program Data*, August 1988, T.1, 1; T.12, 10.

34. Daniel Patrick Moynihan, "Our Poorest Citizens—Children," *Focus*, Institute for Research on Poverty (University of Wisconsin-Madison), 11, no. 1 (Spring 1988): 5.

35. Robert M. Ball, *Social Security: Today and Tomorrow* (New York: Columbia University Press, 1978), 360.

36. Bell, 22–23.

37. Ibid., 32–42.

38. Ibid., 76–79, 184–89.

39. Ibid., 32, 34, 57, 58.

40. June Axinn and Herman Levin, *Social Welfare: A History of the American Response to Need* (New York: Harper and Row, 1982), 250–52.

41. Department of Health and Human Services, Social Security Administration, *Social Security Bulletin* 45 (October 1982): 54.

42. Frances Fox Piven and Richard A. Cloward, *Poor People's Movements: Why They Succeed: How They Fail* (New York: Pantheon Books, 1977), 266–75, 294, 297–305.

43. Axinn and Levin, 246.

44. In 1965 the ratio of births to unmarried women per 1,000 total live births was 77.4; in 1976 it was 147.8. See Department of Health and Human Services, National Center for Health Statistics, *Vital Statistics of the United States 1978* (Washington, D. C.: U.S. Government Printing Office, 1978), 1:1–53.

45. According to Bell (p. 226), about 13 percent of the children on AFDC in 1958 were illegitimate. By 1977 the percentage had gone up to 33.8; also see Bureau of the Census, *Statistical Abstracts of the United States: 1982–83*, 103rd edition (Washington, D. C.: U.S. Government Printing Office, 1982), 343. I am assuming that many, if not most, of the mothers gave birth out of wedlock before going on the rolls rather than after.

46. The divorce rate per 1,000 total population rose from 2.5 in 1965 to 5.0 in 1976. See *Vital Statistics of the United States 1978* 3:2-5.

47. *Population Below the Poverty Level: 1984*, T. 4, 20.

48. *Monthly Benefit Statistics*, T. 12. This excludes AFDC-UP families.

49. Ibid., T. 4.

50. Ibid., T. 12, 10.

51. However, child support payments are not disregarded in the calculation of food stamp benefits, so the marginal increase for AFDC families is actually less than $50.

52. Tom Joe, *Profiles of Families in Poverty: Effects of the FY 1983 Budget Proposals on the Poor* (Washington, D. C.: Center for the Study of Social Policy, 1982), 3.

53. Harrell R. Rodgers, Jr., *Poor Women, Poor Families: The Economic Plight of America's Female-Headed Households* (Armonk, NY: M. E. Sharpe, 1986), 74–75. He is citing House of Representatives, Committee on Ways and Means, *Children in Poverty*, 99th Congress, 1st Session (Washington, D. C.: U.S. Government Printing Office, 1985), 197. For data and analysis of the effects of OBRA, see also Rosemary C. Sarri, "Federal Policy Changes and the Feminization of Poverty," *Child Welfare* 64, no. 3 (May–June 1985): 235–47.

54. Rodgers, 71.

55. Ibid., 75.

56. House of Representatives, 100th Congress, *Family Support Act of 1988: Conference Report*, Report 100–998.

57. I consider the $50 child support disregard a good measure because it benefits the women and children and because it serves to help poor fathers actually give something to their children rather than feeling they are exchanging funds with the government. The beneficial nature of the provision in the short run, however, does not eliminate, and should not mystify, its patriarchal basis.

58. Irwin Garfinkel and Sara S. McLanahan, *Single Mothers and Their Children: A New American Dilemma* (Washington, D. C.: The Urban Institute Press, 1986), 58. See also Duncan and Hoffman.

59. The prospect of total dependency on welfare rather than a supplement to working was apparently unbearable to the women who chose employment. This outcome surprised many social welfare advocates who had predicted a rise in the welfare rolls due to women quitting their jobs and going back on welfare. This stand contradicted their long history of presenting the world with the solid accumulated evidence that welfare recipients really want to work. This turnabout was, in my view, indicative of widespread ambivalence over women's labor force participation. Even for social welfare advocates who know differently, it is easier to see it as economic coercion than the women's choice.

60. See Lyle P. Groeneveld, Michael T. Hannan, and Nancy B. Tuma, "Marital Stability," in *Final Report of the Seattle-Denver Income Maintenance Experiment, Volume I. Design and Results* (Menlo Park, CA: SRI International, May 1983). Also "Independence Effects on Marital Dissolution: Results from the Seattle and Denver Income Maintenance Experiments," *American Journal of Sociology* 84 (1987): 611–33.

61. Garfinkel and McLanahan, 60–61.

62. See Glen G. Cain and Douglas A. Wissoker, "Do Income Maintenance Programs Break Up Marriages? A Reevaluation of SIME-DIME," *Focus*, Institute for Research on Poverty (University of Wisconsin-Madison), 10, no. 4 (Winter 1987–88): 1–14.

63. See Garfinkel and McLanahan, 60–62.

64. Ibid., 2.

65. Ibid., 5.

66. Ibid., 11, 16–17.

67. Ibid., 167.

68. Ibid., 153, 183–184.

69. Ibid., 188.

70. Charles Murray, *Losing Ground: American Social Policy 1950–1980* (New York: Basic Books, 1984).

71. Ibid., 157–64.

72. Murray does advocate further on that former AFDC mothers (after he has hypothetically abolished the AFDC system) get jobs (p. 231), but this is not an integral part of his argument throughout the book. In the last chapter his statement, "Welfare mothers who want to get into the labor force are likely to find a wide range of help," is not followed up with any explanation as to why they are not getting that help now.

73. Christopher Jencks, "How Poor Are the Poor?" *The New York Review of Books*, May 9, 1985, 45.

74. Ibid., 46.

75. Ibid., 45–46.

76. Ibid., 46.

77. William Julius Wilson and Kathryn M. Neckerman, "Poverty and Family Structure: The Widening Gap Between Evidence and Public Policy Issues," in *Fighting Poverty: What Works and What Doesn't*, eds. Sheldon H. Danziger and Daniel H. Weinberg (Cambridge, MA: Harvard University Press, 1986), 246.

78. Ibid., 253.

79. Ibid.

80. William Julius Wilson, *The Truly Disadvantaged* (Chicago: University of Chicago Press, 1987), 106, 150.

81. Ibid., 20, 154.

82. David Ellwood and Lawrence Summers, "Poverty in America: Is Welfare the Answer or the Problem?," in Danziger and Weinberg, 100.

83. See also Richard B. Freeman and Harry J. Holzer (eds.), *The Black Youth Employment Crisis* (Chicago: The University of Chicago Press, 1986). Belying its title, this book is a report of a survey of Black male youth, aged 16 to 24, in Boston, Chicago, and Philadelphia. They explain that the sample was limited to men because "the employment and social problems facing Black women are quite different" (p. 4). They neglect to mention how and why they think the women's problems are different. This study concludes that, among other things, rising female labor force participation (Black and white) has "seriously hurt the job opportunities of young [male] blacks" (p. 11).

84. Mary Jo Bane, "Household Composition and Poverty," in Danziger and Weinberg, 227.

85. Ibid., 231.

86. Letter to the Editor, *New York Times*, April 19, 1989.

87. Kristin A. Moore and Martha A. Burt, *Private Crisis, Public Cost: Policy Perspectives on Teenage Childbearing* (Washington, D. C.: The Urban Institute Press, 1982), 1.

88. Ibid., 18–19, 21.

89. Ibid., 19–20.

90. Ibid., 23.

91. Richard A. Weatherley, "Teenage Parenthood and Poverty," in *Beyond Welfare*, ed. Harrell R. Rodgers, Jr. (Armonk, NY: M. E. Sharpe, 1988), 121.

92. Moore and Burt, 8–15. See also Department of Health and Human Services, National Center for Health Statistics, *Vital Statistics of the United States, 1985*, Vol. 1, Natality, DHHS Publication No. (PHS) 88–1113, 6.

93. Moore and Burt, 82.

94. Ibid., 143.

95. Catherine S. Chilman, "Feminist Issues in Teenage Parenting," *Child Welfare* 64, no. 3 (May–June 1985): 232.

96. See, for example, *A Call to Action: Final Report of the Governor's Task Force on Teen Pregnancy* (Baltimore: State of Maryland, 1985). This report recommends a comprehensive approach ranging from family responsibility to the role of the media, educational reform, employment opportunities, and improved and accessible health care. Sex and race discrimination in the work world and women's differential wage compensation are not addressed. Moreover, comprehensive recommendations rarely lead to comprehensive policy initiatives.

97. The Family Support Act of 1988 includes an authorization for demonstration projects in four states to provide "counseling and service to high-risk teenagers." Nonacademic services and self-image counseling are to be provided "in order to reduce the rates of pregnancy, suicide, substance abuse, and school dropout among such teenagers" (*Conference Report*, 65). These projects should be monitored not only for their effectiveness but also for their differential treatment of girls and boys. Their potential is limited, however, by their focus on the individual and not the social structure.

98. Elizabeth A. Mulroy, "Who Are Single-Parent Families and Where Do They Live?" in *Women as Single Parents*, ed. Elizabeth A. Mulroy (Dover, MA: Auburn House Publishing Company, 1988), 20, citing Robert Weiss, "The Impact of Marital

Dissolution on Income and Consumption in Single-Parent Households,'' *Journal of Marriage and the Family*, February 1984:117.

   99. Garfinkel and McLanahan, 172.

100. Ibid., 23

4

Poor Women and Work Training: Back to the Future

A woman will come to me all starry-eyed, "Guess what, I have a job."
Then we sit down and go over her expenses, and she realizes, "Oh well,
I can't afford that."[1]

At this writing the United States is awash with a renewed emphasis on getting "welfare mothers" into the work force. Work demonstration projects throughout the 1980s have led to a new "welfare to work" reform bill, the Family Support Act (PL 100-485), signed by President Reagan on October 13, 1988. Billed as the expression of a "new consensus" in the *New York Times*, it adds significantly more work-related requirements to the AFDC program[2] While there is much optimism about this new direction, few know what the demonstration programs have accomplished or what the federal law promises to achieve. This chapter will review the recent history and current status of public policy efforts to promote the employment of welfare mothers as well as the provisions of the new law. The review will be followed by an analysis of the programs to date and a theoretical interpretation of why these programs are quite functional to patriarchal demands.

PREVIOUS FEDERAL EFFORTS

Incentives for AFDC recipients to work were first introduced in the 1960s, reversing earlier rules that allowed recipients to stay at home to care for their children. The change came about as a result of a change in attitudes toward the recipient population. Increasing proportions of Black women and never-married women with children were coming on the rolls and overall increases in numbers were a cause for alarm. Between 1965 and 1976 the number of families served by AFDC increased more than threefold.[3] Meanwhile large numbers of middle- and upper-income women were entering the labor force. Thus, in 1967 Congress introduced AFDC work incentives and work programs to lower the welfare roles and to soft pedal the incongruence of public policies encouraging poor women to stay home with their children while middle-class women commonly left their children to enter the labor force. AFDC rules were changed to encourage working. In addition, the Work Incentive Program (WIN) was established to provide job training, job referrals, and supportive social services such as child care to AFDC recipients.

From the beginning, WIN program policies were gender-driven, as priority was given to fathers. It was assumed that a work program, like AFDC itself, was a less acceptable substitute for women's economic dependency within the family. The policy set the tone for the program and also diverted scarce resources from women AFDC recipients.

In fact very few people were served by the WIN program and most participants obtained jobs on their own without benefit of the program.[4] Moreover, the jobs didn't pay well; as a result, many registrants remained economically dependent on AFDC.[5] Mildred Rein indicates that many registrants received services and training that were not immediately work-related,[6] and that available funds for child care were minimally allocated for WIN registrants.[7] The WIN program was so poorly funded and insufficiently supported that for most women it was simply a "work registration" program.

In the 1960s, within and without the War on Poverty programs, Congress also established various other work programs to aid different population groups. In 1973 the Comprehensive Employment and Training Act (CETA) consolidated many of these programs. CETA originally stressed training over employment, but partly as a result of the 1974–75 recession, it later began to emphasize public service employment (PSE). However, CETA tended to shun welfare mothers. Consequently, women on AFDC, if they were served at all, were served by the less effective and poorly funded WIN program.

CURRENT PROGRAMS

In 1981 the Omnibus Budget Reconciliation Act gave various options to the states regarding new work experience and training programs for AFDC recipients. The Community Work Experience Program (CWEP) placed AFDC recipients in jobs to "work off" their welfare benefits at minimum wage rates. This is what is commonly known as "workfare." "Grant Diversion" allowed states to use welfare grant monies to provide a source of wage subsidies for recipients working in on-the-job training (OJT) positions, usually in the private sector. Under the Work Incentive Demonstration Program states were also given the option to replace their WIN programs with tailor-made employment and training programs. WIN funding provided the most monies for these new work programs. Yet total WIN funding declined by 70 percent between 1981 and 1987, giving some indication of the federal commitment to helping women on welfare obtain employment.[8]

The Job Training Partnership Act (JTPA) of 1982 replaced CETA and effectively shifted major job training program responsibilities from the federal government to the states. Unlike CETA, JTPA requires concrete evidence of reduced welfare dependency, which means targeting of AFDC (and General Assistance) welfare recipients. However, it also requires that most funds be spent on training rather than administration and support services, which is detrimental to women needing child care, and is going to make it difficult for programs to reduce welfare dependency not to mention poverty. Moreover, its meager funding allows it to serve even fewer participants than the WIN demonstrations, which served only a fraction of the adult AFDC caseload.[9]

PAUCITY OF INFORMATION

Because there are few federal reporting requirements, uniform data on AFDC work programs are lacking, making it extremely difficult to examine and compare programs. A 1985 study by the General Accounting Office (GAO) of 61 AFDC work-related programs in 38 states documented the problem of insufficient data:

Three-quarters or fewer of the programs collected data on age (72 percent), gender (75 percent), race (62 percent), or number of children (61 percent). Less than 60 percent of the programs collected data on education level (57 percent), work history (36 percent), length of time on welfare (51 percent), or age of the youngest child (56 percent).[10]

A subsequent 1987 GAO study of WIN Demonstration projects in four states also could not with any accuracy compare participation rates, caseload characteristics, number of participants in various activities, and program accomplishments.[11] (Likewise, JTPA does not require programs to aggregate data by sex, except for total numbers served.)[12]

The federal government does require programs to report the amount of "savings" incurred by comparing program costs with the reduction or elimination of the welfare grants of those program participants who find jobs. This calculation does not account for recidivism or those who have gotten jobs on their own without the program.[13] Thus the "savings" are likely to be highly exaggerated.

EVALUATION STUDIES

Most of the information about recent welfare-to-work efforts has come from major evaluation studies carried out by the GAO and the Manpower Demonstration Research Corporation (MDRC). The GAO studies included 61 AFDC-related work programs that operated in federal fiscal year 1985 in 38 states[14] and an in-depth look at AFDC employment programs in Massachusetts, Michigan, Oregon, and Texas.[15] MDRC's ongoing experimental design studies have included Arkansas, San Diego, Chicago, Maine, Baltimore, New Jersey, Virginia, and West Virginia.[16]

A look at MDRC and GAO study findings sheds some light on pertinent questions about these programs. The questions asked in the research and the interpretations of the results are quite as important as the answers obtained. To a considerable extent the questions chosen to be asked reflected patriarchal and capitalistic bias. MDRC in particular tended to concentrate on the extent of potential state savings, managerial effectiveness, and the feasibility of coercive administrative mechanisms. Although the GAO seemed more client centered in its investigations, neither organization concentrated on the antipoverty effects of the program or the subjective experiences of the participants who went through them. Nevertheless one can summarize common themes in the state programs studied by examining the evaluation reports.

A close examination of these reports reveals that the programs tend to manipulate eligibility standards according to market demand and available resources rather than client need; provide job search activities rather than meaningful work training or education; ignore child care, transportation, and other predictable needs of participants; focus training and education on skills associated with "women's" low-paying jobs. Some programs have flagrantly applied unfair sanctions for supposed noncompliance, particularly in workfare programs. Perhaps most important, those women who have obtained jobs through the programs usually have not been able to escape poverty status.

Administrative Feasibility

MDRC focused the feasibility issue around two basic questions. The first is whether people can be made to work for their welfare. The second is whether the state can make good on the threat—that is, monitor participant activities accurately. Simply keeping track of welfare clients under ordinary circumstances is difficult. In their studies MDRC found that the majority of participants were indeed accounted for and referred to this "success" as a "major management achievement" when compared with the WIN program, which was a model of inefficiency. However, the achievement may have been accomplished because the programs were brief and easy to monitor. Researchers point out that the average work requirement lasted 13 weeks and the data might be quite different in a more widespread program without a time limit.[17] Moreover, the *need* for mandatory workfare—that is, the question of whether people would work voluntarily if given the chance—was not addressed. In fact, there is ample evidence that, given the resources and opportunity, people on welfare will enter the labor force voluntarily.[18]

Cost-Benefit Analyses

Work programs are expected to save money or at least pay for themselves. Comparing state findings with a glass that can be seen as half full or half empty, Judith Gueron emphasizes positive results: "First, the results dispel the notion that employment and training interventions do not work. In light of the findings for these work/welfare initiatives, it is no longer defensible to argue that welfare employment initiatives have no value."[19] In fact, the participants earned more than those in the control groups who did not participate and in fact there were welfare savings. But MDRC's definition of success is weighted toward state savings rather than escape from impoverishment. The empty half of the glass represents the modesty of the employment gains. Gueron states: "Thus, while it is worthwhile to operate these programs, they will not move substantial numbers of people out of poverty.[20] Indeed, large numbers remained on welfare during the duration of the program, and the amounts of total income received by the experimentals over the controls averaged very little.[21] GAO's data agree with this finding; half of the programs reported that more than 48 percent of the participants remained on welfare after they found employment.[22]

Even the limited success cited by MDRC could possibly be wiped out in a full-blown program that had to face problems that were avoided in the demonstrations. Gueron states:

It is important to note that *child care was not a major issue* in these programs, since their requirements were mostly short-term and limited mainly to women with school-age children. However, the availability and quality of child care would be much more important if either of these conditions changed, or if the programs made even larger differences in the rate at which women moved out of the home and into permanent jobs. . . . It is not clear . . . whether work programs can be extended to an even greater share of the AFDC caseload . . . without compromising quality, encountering political or administrative resistance, or raising broader issues such as *whether welfare recipients would displace regular workers either during or after the program.* (emphasis added).[23]

In addition to this light treatment of fundamental problems, MDRC has persisted in presenting state and participant cost-benefit analyses as if they were comparable. For example, an MDRC report had the following to say about the San Diego job search-CWEP sequence: "both AFDC women and the taxpayers came out ahead by a substantial margin. For the average AFDC experimental, net benefits were projected to be about $800 for the five years after random assignment; savings for taxpayers were over $1,000 per experimental during the same period."[24] The benefit for the average participant, $800 over five years, comes to $13.33 per month, which is what the average experimental "made" over and above what she might have "made" had she been in the control rather than the experimental group. Surely the cost to the women was more than monetary, and should be compared with that $13.33 a month! This trivialization of costs to participants is common to evaluation studies in this area.

Project Goals

The GAO describes the WIN program as caught between two rather conflicting goals: "immediately reducing welfare expenditures through quick job placements" and "helping individuals increase their abilities to achieve long-term self-sufficiency by improving their education and skills prior to placement in unsubsidized jobs, which may or may not reduce expenditures more in the long run."[25] For most programs, there is no conflict: a successful project increases the hours worked, the amount earned, and decreases the amounts of welfare support received. If a woman remains poor, that is her problem. Self-sufficiency is a relative term denoting a continuum of less welfare receipt to self-support through employment and is not related to poverty status.

Eligibility Requirements

Eligibility rules are often manipulated to exclude as well as include potential participants. Good programs that require greater resources per participant often include only a chosen few. Participation can be mandatory or target particular groups for services. In West Virginia, for example, traditional views about mothers in the labor force resulted in a program concentrated on the AFDC-Unemployed Parent program (available for two-parent families in about half the states) recipients, primarily men.[26] The 1985 GAO study found that most programs were mandatory for some people.[27]

Most programs automatically excluded women with children under the age of six, even on a voluntary basis. If applied nationally this practice would exclude 60 percent of the AFDC caseload.[28] Excluding them leaves out young, new beneficiaries and can result in an overrepresentation of men in the program. The GAO found that AFDC-UP recipients, mostly men, made up about 21 percent of the work program participants whose status was known.[29] Giving priority to male participants not only eliminates the problem of child care, the GAO report suggests, but is easier because men have more work experience and are easier to place in jobs.[30] Michigan's local administrators indicated to GAO researchers that they give high priority to applicants most likely to get jobs since "numbers of job placements determine local office funding."[31] On the other hand, Massachusetts' Employment and Training Choices (ET) program cited priority groups that were "so broad that they cover almost the entire AFDC caseload."[32]

The need for child care and transportation was a cause of exclusion in some programs. Fifty-two percent of the program administrators in the GAO survey identified lack of transportation as applying to their participants to a very great, great, or moderate extent.[33] Other barriers to employment that could result in exclusion were illiteracy, attitudinal problems, medical problems, and low educational attainment.[34] It appears that programs opted to exclude anyone with problems that the program wished to avoid.

A typical quotation from one of the MDRC studies indicates that programs took little responsibility for changing the environment sufficiently to increase the project's success.

[F]actors external to the WORK program shaped its scope and scale. Public transportation exists in only two of the nine operating areas, and substantial numbers of program eligibles were *de facto* exempted from participation because they had no way of getting to program activities. In some areas, convenient, accessible day care was not available. In the more rural counties, the number of participants was constrained by the need to keep on good terms with the small number of area employers.[35]

This last remark refers to the fact that employers often have predetermined notions about hiring welfare recipients and the work program staff hesitated to force these recipients on the employers. Programs that are unwilling to tackle transportation, child care needs, and employer bias accordingly narrow their focus considerably.

Considering the exclusions, it is not surprising that few persons have been served. Accurate numbers are difficult to obtain since federal reporting requirements vary for different programs. The people who are counted can include those who are simply registered for service, those awaiting job slots, or those who only received an orientation.[36] Thus the GAO finding of program service to just 22 percent of all adult AFDC recipients is a generous figure.[37]

Type of Work/Training

Welfare-to-work programs do nothing to change societal patterns of women's employment. Women are prepared for low-paying, dead-end "women's" jobs. In 1987, 77 percent of women worked in clerical, sales, service, and factory jobs, earning 65 cents for every dollar earned by men.[38] A ranking of 52 industries in 1982 found that apparel and textile products industries, fiftieth in hourly wages, ranked first in terms of female employment. Eighty-two percent of this industry's workers are women.[39] Welfare-to-work programs correspond with this reality and do nothing to try to expand the women's opportunities. The jobs targeted are entry-level positions, such as clerical, maintenance, parks, and human services, that do not develop skills.[40]

The GAO found that job *search* activities rather than education and training formed the bulk of programs. Only about 10 percent of participants received any type of education or training and 4.5 percent received work experience.[41] "Job readiness" is often determined by the job market; if one can get a job, any job, then one is "job ready." Good diagnostics are not done on participants and thus actual needs are not determined.[42]

Support Services Provided

Incredibly, the use of and the need for support services have not been quantified.[43] In the GAO survey the median program spent $24.41 per participant or about 7 percent of its total budget on transportation.[44] The median amount spent for child care was $34 per participant, which accounted for 6.4 percent of the median program's total budget.[45] Few programs provided funds or services for after-school care. One way of solving the problem of child care was to schedule activities during school hours.[46] Program officials were more likely to identify lack of transportation as a barrier to participation than lack of child care.[47]

Duration of Employment

The duration of employment is another, often overlooked, measure of a program's success. In Baltimore a small study of barriers to employment among WIN mandatory welfare recipients indicated that participants are very aware of this issue. Half of the 115 clients surveyed selected permanence as the most important factor in job selection. The other choices—wages, advancement chances, and medical benefits—were each chosen as most important by less than 20 percent of the respondents. Only 11 percent cited job permanence as the least important factor.[48]

Since few programs do any postprogram follow-up, it is difficult to discover how long jobs were held. GAO reports:

At 90 days after employment, the five programs collecting the data reported between 56 and 72 percent still employed, with a median of 65 percent. At 180 days after employment, the seven programs that collected data reported from 22 to 78 percent still employed, with a median of 62 percent.[49]

The most optimistic interpretation of this finding is that perhaps three out of five participants will keep their jobs for up to six months. But the reality is that solid data on job duration after welfare-to-work programs does not exist.

Abuses and Mandatory Participation

Mandatory rules foster oppression of women and minimize choice. They subject participants to harassment and abuse. A study of New York City's mandatory program found that it relies on recipients to obtain not only their own child care but their training as well.[50] Only new applicants had their training needs assessed; ongoing clients were immediately given workfare assignments, which were poorly monitored.[51] The study found inadequate communication with clients; poor assessment and assignment procedures; insufficient and ineffective training opportunities; insufficient services; inadequate remedial education; and overuse of sanctions. One-third of recipients, including 8,000 families in one six-month period, were sanctioned. Sanctions were withdrawn or reversed in 98 percent of the appeals.[52] This high proportion of reversals is indicative of intentionally unfair sanctioning.

Another example of workfare abuse was described in the MDRC study of the

WIN Demonstration program in Cook County, Illinois, that ran from 1981 to 1985. Program staff had average caseloads of around 300 and were evaluated according to how much welfare savings they achieved through case closings and grant reductions. With this encouragement, the degree of sanctioning was quite high.[53] Each had a quota of "positive terminations."[54] There were no statistically significant effects on employment or earnings for the experimental group, and they were projected to be even worse off than controls after five years, due to loss of Medicaid and other benefits.[55] This program was replaced in late 1985 by the statewide Project Chance, which reportedly is more service oriented and includes protections for clients against unfair sanctioning.[56]

Notwithstanding these examples, the GAO found that across the nation, "officials tended to view the participation requirements as, not a hurdle AFDC applicants and recipients must surmount to receive benefits, but a way to 'get people through the door'—people who might not voluntarily participate because of fear, distrust, or lack of self-confidence."[57] Also, sanctioning seemed to be more concentrated in certain programs and states rather than widespread.[58] They found that CWEPs (workfare) tended to sanction more frequently and speculated that this may be because these programs are more often implemented as a deterrent to welfare receipt rather than a service to AFDC recipients.[59] Yet it is important to understand that regardless of whether intentions are benign or malevolent, mandatory participation requirements are oppressive and unnecessary.

The Women Themselves

To their credit, MDRC asked mandatory program participants their opinion of the fairness of the work requirements. While answers differed somewhat among states, for the most part participants thought that the work requirement was fair. However, they were also clear that the employer was benefitting more than they were and that they would prefer paid jobs.[60] While these answers are instructive, there is much more that needs to be known about participants' views of these programs. More research effort must be placed on asking the women themselves about their experiences in these work programs and the impact on their daily lives.

JOB TRAINING PARTNERSHIP ACT

JTPA is a much smaller program than even the WIN Demonstrations. However, a recent study of JTPA's treatment of women is worthy of mention. The study found inadequate support services for women participants and a preponderance of training and placement in low paying, traditionally female jobs.[61] Training contractors are only partially reimbursed for their work if they do not meet cost and placement rate standards. They thus have reason to emphasize short-term, clerical training, with which many women have some familiarity, and avoid more expensive nontraditional training.[62] Researchers found that women were given little or no orientation to nontraditional job possibilities and wage issues were often not discussed.[63] Even when given wage information, many of the participants denied grim predictions of low wages, thinking that they would somehow make more than the norm. One woman asserted that if one can get $4.50 per hour *without* skills, surely one must be able to get more with skills.[64] Nevertheless there was widespread agreement among program administrators that the jobs obtained do not even pay enough for subsistence. The women judged most likely to make it had free child care or rent from relatives or other sources of outside help.

FAMILY SUPPORT ACT

The Family Support Act was a direct outgrowth of the results of the state OBRA demonstration project evaluations. The negatives were ignored and MDRC's judgment of modest success and workable programs won the day for proponents of this legislation. Title II of the act, the Job Opportunities and Basic Skills (JOBS) Training Program, consolidates the WIN program, WIN Demonstrations, CWEP, Work Supplementation, and job search activities into a new Title IV-F of the Social Security Act. There are no provisions for nonpoverty wages, nontraditional job training, and only a weakly worded provision for "reasonable" expectations of the participants. Since it encompasses most of what the OBRA programs have been doing, it will allow most state programs to continue under the new rubric with minor modifications and expansion. The state welfare agency may choose to administer the JOBS program directly or by contracts or agreements with the JTPA. The provisions of the act that are not related to work issues were described in Chapter 3. The work-related provisions will be discussed here.

Each state must establish a "job opportunities and basic skills training" program operational statewide by October 1, 1992. An "employability plan," based on participants' needs assessments and the available resources and services, will spell out the participants' obligations and the state service and program provision. However, the law specifically states that such plan shall not be construed to be a "contract."[65] In other words, although participation is mandatory for the welfare client, concomitant state services are not guaranteed.

States are given some leeway as to what elements to include in their programs, but they must include: educational activities including high school equivalency, achievement of literacy, and English proficiency; job skills training; job readiness activities; job development and job placement; and at least two of the following: group and individual job search, on-the-job training, work supplementation (Grant Diversion) programs, and community work experience programs. The law requires providing high school equivalency education to persons under age 20, and encourages it for persons over that age unless the employability plan does not require a high school diploma. Postsecondary education may be offered "in appropriate cases."[66]

The separate funding for the JOBS program was established as a capped entitlement program, which is a firmer promise of actual funding than a simple authorization of funds, which requires yearly specific appropriations from Congress. States will be required to spend some of their own funds in order to match federal monies by specific percentages for different activities. Federal matching for this program begins at $600 million for fiscal year 1989, goes up to $1.1 billion in FY 1995, then is reduced to $1 billion for FY 1996 and beyond. States will be funded according to their proportion of adult AFDC recipients nationwide.[67] The federal expectation of participation rates of eligible participants begins at 7 percent in fiscal year 1990 and goes up to 20 percent in fiscal year 1995.[68] For AFDC-UP, required participation is much higher, beginning at 40 percent and going up to 75 percent in 1998.[69]

The new law states that mothers on AFDC with children over age three (or age one at state option) must participate in job training, education, job search, or be placed in a job. Registration for a program cannot be interpreted as "participation," which happened in the WIN program. The state must guarantee child care "to the extent that it is determined by the agency to be necessary" for an individual's employment, training, or education activities, and if the state determines that the individual is "participating satisfactorily." Within these caveats, if child care is not available, participation is not required. Parents responsible for the care of children under the age of six may not be required to participate for more than 20 hours per week, except for educational activities such as high school equivalency, remedial help, or English as a second language. Sanctions for nonparticipation consist of eliminating the parent or parents from the AFDC "eligibility unit" in calculating the grant. Thus, funds will be available for the children but not their caretaker.

As mentioned in Chapter 3, the Family Support Act requires states to include financially eligible two-parent families in which the principal earner is unemployed into their AFDC program for at least six months per year. This essentially expands the previously optional AFDC-UP program to all states for at least half a year. The Family Support Act includes special provisions for these families. In two-parent families, only one parent is required to participate, but both may be required at state option if child care is available. In addition, the law states that at least one parent must participate in a work program for at least 16 hours a week, and both parents may be required to participate in JOBS program activities up to 40 hours per person per week.

On the plus side, no net loss of cash income can result for any participant from taking a job through the JOBS program—that is, income must be at least what it was when the family was totally on welfare. Volunteers for the programs, even if officially exempt from participation, are to be given priority. Funds for child care are to be a state/federal "match."[70] Moreover, like Medicaid, child care provisions will be an "open-ended" entitlement. That is, as long as the state can demonstrate the need for the funds and can put up the matching funds, there is no set limit on the spending amount that the federal government will match. Other support services, however, such as transportation, are to be funded under the capped amount allocated for the JOBS program.

There are transition provisions extending child care benefits on a sliding fee scale for 12 months beyond welfare receipt and extending Medicaid eligibility for 12 months with the possibility of charging a premium after 6 months. It is notable that the transition provisions have a "sunset" clause; that is, they are due to be repealed after 1998 in the absence of congressional action. In the interim these provisions are to be studied to determine whether AFDC recipients go back on welfare in order to qualify once again for child care and medical benefits.[71] This is a tacit acknowledgement that it will be extremely difficult for women to afford medical insurance and child care on their own even after they obtain employment.

The law targets certain groups of AFDC recipients by penalizing states that spend less than 55 percent of their budgets on them. The targeted groups are long-term recipients, defined as those who have received welfare for three out of the last five years;[72] custodial parents under age 24 who have not completed high school; and recipients who will become ineligible for AFDC within two years when the youngest child comes of age.

At this writing the Department of Health and Human Services has issued proposed rules for these programs, offering flexibility to the states that would seriously pare down program expectations and service delivery. The Bush administration proposes that programs need not be statewide or, alternatively, that up to 95 percent of participants could simply be asked to fulfill "minimal" requirements of "high school classes, job searches and employment referrals." The proposed rules state that "informal" child care arrangements at "little or no cost" are to be encouraged, with the caveat that "the child care guarantee does not mean that paid child care must be available for every participant." Moreover, college courses would only be allowed if directly related to "useful employment in a recognized occupation."[73] The rather grandiose JOBS program, then, is being eroded even before implementation.

ANALYSIS

Lessons Learned

Work programs for women on welfare continue to be geared to low-paying, dead-end jobs that do not get them off welfare, let alone out of poverty. They ignore evidence that education and training are better than job experience for participant self-sufficiency in the long run.[74] They are also fraught with contradictions regarding eligibility, services, and funding.

In this review, I have cited only two instances of punitive requirements and harassment of workfare participants. While it is important to expose and eliminate abuses, it is perhaps even more important to expose the inherent flaws and inconsistencies that exist even in programs that bear a semblance of benevolent intentions and reasonable expectations. As programs expand and multiply under the new legislation, however, abuses are likely to increase with them.

It is noteworthy that the women's educational and training needs were generally not assessed by these programs. Thus, actual needs and potential for long-term successful economic independence remain unknown. Furthermore, the lack of uniform reporting requirements served to limit the breadth of data for analysis, thereby making it impossible for advocates to find and use data to press for change. With the advent of the JOBS program, while advocates are organizing in the states to monitor programs and press for fair and adequate state provisions, it may still be difficult to obtain a national picture of program results.

It is also remarkable that no efforts were made to distinguish between internal barriers to participation, intrinsic to the individual, such as illness, and external barriers, such as a lack of child care or transportation. One is led to wonder what state administrators think are the reasons that women go on welfare to begin with. If the women *had* child care or transportation, many of them would not have needed welfare. It seems bizarre that programs designed to serve mothers bar some of them on the basis of their motherhood.

Likewise, providing programs during school hours to avoid having to provide child care represents a complete departure from any conceivable attempt to serve the goal of job attainment and maintenance. Surely most of the women participating during school hours will not be able to find real jobs that only require their presence during that time. Ignoring the eventual problem of the need for child care reduces the job-related activity to a meaningless exercise.

The new law contains some safeguards that the demonstration programs did not, such as assessing a participant's skills and needs and prohibiting work for wages lower than welfare. Yet the lack of safeguards against nonpoverty wages and absence of requirements for significant job training render skills assessment rather meaningless. The allowance for higher education may make it possible for a lucky few to achieve real advancement, but the proposed rules reduce even this marginal bright spot. In any case the participation rates required for full federal reimbursement provide an incentive for the states to spend the least amount possible per participant; as much "creaming" (choosing the most "job ready" participants) as possible is likely. Giving priority status to volunteers to the program may also increase creaming, since persons motivated to volunteer may be easier to work with. Ironically, those mandated to participate may, because of this priority rule, be given poorer quality service. Finally, although the length of time participants may engage in job search is limited by the law, and job search must be combined with some other educational or work activity, this inexpensive program is likely to continue to be the common denominator of most state programs. The proposed rules are paving the way for this eventuality.

The mandatory nature of the new law will eliminate one important source of quality control. Participants will not be allowed to "vote with their feet" into quality programs and out of poor ones.[75] Unfortunately the media are more apt to address client fraud than program abuses. In the states, advocates' work will be cut out for them.

Finally, the enthusiastic response to the flawed demonstration projects that led up to this legislation can only be cause for pessimism. The demonstration projects often worked *around* the major needs of the participants, such as child care and transportation. They did not address or solve them. Thus their evaluations offer no suggestions, creative or otherwise, on how to provide for them. The data we have, as well as the experience of women in JTPA, suggest that we can expect that large numbers of women will remain unserved, excluded, given short-term training or meaningless experience in low-paying jobs, provided with few or no auxiliary services, and remain poor.

The assumptions that are being made about women on welfare are covert, buried in cultural meanings that are not addressed, so that these logical contradictions are not apparent to the administrators or the evaluators. The following theoretical analysis attempts to clarify the origins of the inherent problems mystified by these programs.

Theoretical Analysis

The "issue" of "welfare mothers" in the workplace can be seen as a subset of the overall issue of women in the labor force. Many feminist theorists see it as intrinsic to the conflictual relationship between capitalism and patriarchy. For example, Zillah Eisenstein points out that

the unprecedented number of married women in the labor force *potentially* undermines the patriarchal controls on women as dependents in marriage and begins to undermine the patriarchal structure of male and female hierarchical relations rooted in the division of the home and the market. . . . The reality of the married woman wage earner becomes a contradiction in terms. Is she dependent as a woman or independent as a worker?[76]

Thus it is in the interests of patriarchy to emphasize a woman's role as mother and to restrict her opportunities in the labor market. As Eisenstein puts it,

the sexual hierarchy used within the labor force is maintained through the definition of woman as primarily a mother. The sexual job ghetto within the labor force maintains this definition of woman as mother in that it places her in a secondary position within the labor force, reinforcing her primary position within the home. If a woman has limited alternatives for jobs in the world of paid work, and her wages are low, her dependence on a man has not fundamentally changed, particularly if she is married with children. Only 46 percent of all jobs in the economy pay enough to sustain a family at a "reasonable" level.[77]

Without a male provider a woman wage earner is generally economically uncomfortable and in a position to seek relief from an alternative source, namely marriage. In marriage she can continue her labor force participation, but this participation can then be labeled auxiliary to her husband's primary paycheck, and she is once again safely ensconced in the patriarchal institution of matrimony. Furthermore, "the reinforcement of the sexual division of labor in the labor force protects its operation in the family."[78] Women's jobs, besides being low-paid, are often characterized as ladylike, expressive, caretaking positions, often reproducing their role at home in the workplace.

Capitalism is served by these restrictions on married women's opportunities in the labor force because they preserve a cheap available pool of labor, just as racial restrictions operate to reserve Black women and men for the lowest-paying and most undesirable jobs. Black and white women are controlled not only by low pay but also by the extension of the stigma on women's work at home into the workplace. Thus the contradiction between women's dependence and women's labor force participation is mediated by the sexual division of labor in the labor force.

It is important to acknowledge that for the patriarchal status quo to be maintained it is not necessary for *all* women to be restricted in the labor market and kept in low-paying jobs. Examples of rich, successful career women are frequently mentioned in the press and seem to give the lie to the above analysis. These examples serve to mystify the reality of the majority of women, leading many to think that women are doing better than they are and others to aspire to goals that are achievable only for the very few. Thus, when a woman does not achieve the status and success she seeks, she can be led to believe that it was due to an insufficiency within herself rather than external restrictions. For those who persist, the media frequently depict successful career women as unhappy, unfulfilled, and conflicted over their participation in the "rat race" of the labor market when they would prefer to go home and raise families. Those women who do make the choice to give it all up and devote themselves to their homes and families receive a great deal of publicity. However, all of the well-paid women executives make up a very small percentage of women in the paid labor force. Most women are not even close to having high-paying executive careers. Many who do are "safely" within marriages that provide a patriarchal context to their lives. Others have reached achievement in women's job areas, segregated from men's labor market endeavors, and of course are compensated less well than men in similar jobs.

Seven million welfare mothers are another story. They are not safely within the bonds of matrimony. A woman receiving AFDC who gets a paid job performs all the duties of the double day—even more if we assume that if she had a husband at home he would perform at least some household tasks—but she is one step outside of the patriarchal system that is institutionalized in marriage. If she can get ahead in the work world she can seriously threaten the assumptions and bonds of patriarchy. Single mothers seek work to support themselves and their children. Allowing them to do so with adequate wages and in great numbers would indeed have the potential to change the face of how society sees women's potential in the labor force. Because in their case the answer to Eisenstein's question, "Is she dependent as a woman or independent as a worker?" would squarely fall on the side of independence.

The OBRA programs mediated this conflict by excluding many women who are mothers of young children and, for those they did serve, by concentrating efforts on jobs that will not provide a comfortable living or opportunity for advancement. The new JOBS program will be somewhat less exclusionary with regard to children's ages, but will be no different with regard to job training or placement. Furthermore, child care is far from guaranteed. The law specifically states that participation may not be required if child care is not available. The required participation rate of 20 percent after five years reveals the expectation that many women will not be participating.

The success of the program will have much to do with states' willingness to pay for child care under the open-ended federal match. However, a lack of resources for transportation and other support services will continue to be one of the major barriers to full participation in the program. For individual women this will be a mixed blessing. Among the few programs that will provide some real opportunities for education, training, or advancement, the excluded women will lose out. For those who would otherwise be subjected to degrading work or activities that get them nowhere, the exclusion will be fortuitous. Women will undoubtedly continue to look for work on their own.

Clearly, it is much harder for poor women to handle the demands of child-rearing and paid employment because they do not have the resources to make their tasks easier. This fact has not been confronted by welfare officials, however. Instead there is a question about whether welfare mothers are "psychologically equipped" to handle things.[79] This subtle form of blaming the victim plays into patriarchal prejudices about welfare mothers—that there is something wrong with them. It asserts that we should spare them these demands because there is something about *them* that makes them unable to handle them. Certainly, some AFDC recipients are mentally and/or physically impaired but this is not the majority. If the resources are lacking to serve these women and their children, it would be a simple matter to state this and avoid blaming the women. But such a statement would contradict the stigmatizing and controlling function of these programs.

The demonstration programs to date have contained their own mechanisms of failure and were designed in such a way that the failure seems inevitable because of the shortcomings of participants. The public relations for these programs imply that most women are required to participate in them. Thus, when only a few actually achieve self-sufficiency, the rest can be blamed for lack of skills, enthusiasm, intelligence, or initiative. The new federal program can be expected to follow suit.

Patriarchy would be weakened if provisions were made to make it easier to be an employed mother, because this would be an acknowledgment that the work done at home is work that requires time and effort. Capitalism would be affected because provisions such as child care, flextime, and so forth would also make it more likely that more women would strive to advance in the work world, making it harder to maintain and justify the wage differential between men and women, which can be accounted for partially by some women's need for jobs that allow them to attend to household responsibilities, picking children up at exact times, and so on. However, the demands of the economy are not always congruent with those of patriarchy. The rapidly shrinking supply of labor may force some companies to compete for employees with promises of higher wages and better fringe benefits. When women are targeted these inducements will undoubtedly include such things as on-site child care and the like. One can predict nevertheless that patriarchal mechanisms will make these benefits more accessible to married women. Providing large numbers of low-income women with decent wages in the absence of social agitation is highly unlikely.

It is a patriarchal necessity to control and inhibit women who are ostensibly not controlled by men within matrimony. They continue to be punished for their manlessness and incentives to marriage are maintained. The women's status as mothers is emphasized but not attended to. Instead of accommodating to the needs related to child care and child rearing through child care programs and other services, the programs will use the child care problem as a way of controlling this population.

Short of a social revolution, then, work programs for women on AFDC must fail. Patriarchy requires women's dependency. Capitalism is served with the availability of a low-wage pool of labor. In any case, there are not enough jobs per se, and certainly not enough jobs that pay sufficiently to effect a massive move from welfare rolls to work rolls. Therefore, the only alternative for the state, in mediating between the conflicts encountered and the clamor to decrease this dependent population and save taxpayer dollars, is to construct policies and programs that are marginally successful. Programs should be successful enough to help some women achieve financial independence, and to lower the cost of welfare (and the latter can be done very well without the former). But they should not be successful enough to threaten the social order.

Conclusion

The recent well-publicized and massive work projects begun in the states are hardly new and do not bode well for the welfare recipients in the long run. One can predict from them marginal welfare savings, strong incentives for marriage, perpetuation of women's dependency, and continued denigration of welfare mothers. For when the programs fail to meet expectations, administrators and politicians will blame the participants themselves, and not the design of the programs (the real culprit) for the marginal results. This failure will serve capitalism, patriarchy, and white supremacy by once again preserving a cheap labor pool and by once again proving that women, especially Black and Hispanic women, cannot make it on their own. Women's dependency will be maintained, yet described as inevitable. Black and Hispanic women will be hardest hit, since the media have made them the prototype of welfare recipients. It will be implied that they are more interested in having babies than working, thus inverting the imposition of motherhood on women by making it seem, in this case, an unfortunate personal choice for which they must pay the consequences of poverty and stigma. Of course the "choice" for which they are bearing the consequences is their unmarried status and thus their existence, symbolically, outside of patriarchal control.

Considered together, the elimination of the AFDC work incentive provisions in 1981 and the imposition of Family Support Act work requirements in 1988 represent an increase in the state's control over women's lives and a lessening of their chances of having incomes above the poverty level. Under the dictates of patriarchal necessity, poor women and their children will continue to live in uncomfortable and precarious financial conditions.

Chapter 5 will address child support and child custody policies and how they too impose patriarchal controls on women's lives.

NOTES

1. Joan Walsh, "Take this Job or Shove It," *Mother Jones* 13, no. 7 (September 1988): 52. The quotation is from a case manager of California's welfare-to-work GAIN program in Santa Clara County.

2. W. K. Stevens, "The Welfare Consensus," *New York Times*, June 22, 1988.

3. Department of Health and Human Services, Social Security Administration, *Social Security Bulletin* 45 (October 1982): 54.

4. General Accounting Office, *An Overview of the WIN Program: Its Objectives, Accomplishments, and Problems* (Washington, D. C.: U.S. General Accounting Office, 1982), 16.

5. Ibid., 21.

6. Mildred Rein, *Dilemmas of Welfare Policy: Why Work Strategies Haven't Worked* (New York: Praeger Publishers, 1982), 66.

7. Mildred Rein, "Work in Welfare: Past Failures and Future Strategies," *Social Service Review* 56 (June 1982): 214.

8. General Accounting Office, *Work and Welfare: Current AFDC Work Programs and Implications for Federal Policy* (Washington, D. C.: U.S. General Accounting Office, 1987) (GAO/HRD-87-34), 45.

9. Ibid., 75.

10. Ibid., 59.

11. General Accounting Office, *Work and Welfare: Analysis of AFDC Employment Programs in Four States* (Washington, D. C.: General Accounting Office, 1988) (GAO/HRD-88-33FS), 10–11.

12. Jo Sanders, *Staying Poor: How the Job Training Partnership Act Fails Women* (Metuchen, NJ: The Scarecrow Press, 1988), 90–91.

13. *Current AFDC Work Programs*, 114–15.

14. Ibid., 32-33.

15. *Analysis of AFDC Employment Programs*.

16. Judith B. Gueron, *Reforming Welfare with Work: Occasional Paper Number Two*,

Ford Foundation Project on Social Welfare and the American Future (New York: Ford Foundation, 1987), 14.

17. Ibid., 19.

18. Leonard Goodwin, *Do the Poor Want to Work?* (Washington, D. C.: The Brookings Institution, 1972). See also Greg J. Duncan, *Years of Poverty: Years of Plenty* (Ann Arbor: University of Michigan, 1984), 78. Also, current programs that are voluntary, such as the Massachusetts ET program and Baltimore's programs, invariably have waiting lists of welfare mothers who wish to participate.

19. Gueron, 22.

20. Ibid., 29.

21. Ibid., 24–27.

22. *Current AFDC Work Programs*, 104–5.

23. Gueron, 34.

24. Judith B. Gueron, *Work Initiatives for Welfare Recipients* (New York: Manpower Demonstration Research Corporation, 1986), 19.

25. *Current AFDC Work Programs*, 29. Another goal, often articulated in the states, has been to discourage cheaters (applicants for AFDC who presumably already have hidden jobs or income and are expected to withdraw their applications for welfare when faced with a work requirement). In fact MDRC found no evidence that the work requirement deterred people from applying for welfare (Gueron, *Reforming Welfare*, 30–31).

26. Daniel Friedlander, Marjorie Erickson, Gayle Hamilton, and Virginia Knox, *West Virginia: The Demonstration of State Work/Welfare Initiatives* (New York: Manpower Demonstration Research Corporation, 1986), 6–10.

27. *Current AFDC Work Programs*, 50.

28. Ibid., 55.

29. Ibid., 58.

30. Ibid.

31. *Analysis of AFDC Employment Programs*, 26.

32. Ibid.

33. *Current AFDC Work Programs*, 61.

34. Ibid., 50.

35. Janet C. Quint, Barbara S. Goldman, and Judith B. Gueron, *Arkansas: Interim Findings from the Arkansas WIN Demonstration Program* (New York: Manpower Demonstration Research Corporation, 1984), xvi.

36. *Current AFDC Work Programs*, 49.

37. Ibid., 52.

38. National Commission on Working Women of Wider Opportunities for Women, "Women and the Vote—1988, A Fact Sheet" (Washington, D. C.: Wider Opportunities for Women, 1988), 1.

39. Janet L. Norwood, *The Male-Female Earnings Gap: A Review of the Employment and Earnings Issue* (Washington, D. C.: U.S. Department of Labor, Bureau of Labor Statistics, Report 673, 1982).

40. Gueron, *Work Initiatives*, 13. For an excellent presentation and discussion of women's labor market history and current status, see Barbara Bergmann, *The Economic Emergence of Women* (New York: Basic Books, 1986).

41. *Current AFDC Work Programs*, 69.

42. Ibid., 73.

43. Ibid., 81.

44. Ibid., 90.

45. Ibid., 83.

46. Ibid., 88.

47. Ibid., 92.

48. M. Boeckmann, *Study of Barriers to Employment for WIN Mandatory Welfare Recipients* (Baltimore: Maryland Department of Human Resources, Office of Welfare Employment Policy, 1984), 4.

49. *Current AFDC Work Programs*, 107.

50. Fred Sebesta and Morton Sklar, *Hope or Hassle: A Study of New York City's Welfare-to-Work Initiatives for AFDC Recipients* (Rochester, NY: Statewide Youth Advocacy Inc., 1987), 1.

51. Ibid., 20.

52. Ibid., 2–3.

53. Daniel Friedlander, Stephen Freedman, Gayle Hamilton, and Janet Quint, *Illinois: Final Report on Job Search and Work Experience in Cook County: Executive Summary* (New York: Manpower Demonstration Research Corporation, 1987), 2–3.

54. Ibid., 14.

55. Ibid., 18.

56. Ibid., 1.

57. *Current AFDC Work Programs*, 50.

58. Ibid., 62.

59. Ibid., 63.

60. Gueron, *Reforming Welfare*, 20.

61. Sanders, v–ix. The study surveyed women's centers with JTPA experience, visited ten of them, and collected data from five JTPA offices serving a total of 14,912 women and men.

62. Ibid., 36–37.

63. Ibid., 41–42.

64. Ibid., 53. This is, of course, a logical assumption, but untrue for many jobs that employ women.

65. House of Representatives, 100th Congress, *Family Support Act of 1988: Conference Report*, Report 100–998, 20.

66. Ibid., 21–22.

67. Ibid., 32.

68. Ibid., 34.

69. Ibid., 36.

70. The match is to be the same as that for Medicaid, in which, depending upon the degree of poverty in the state, the federal government pays between 50 and 80 percent of the cost and the state pays the rest.

71. *Conference Report*, 44.

72. Most AFDC families leave the rolls on their own in less than three years. See Department of Health and Human Services, Family Support Administration, *Characteristics and Financial Circumstances of AFDC Recipients: 1986* (Washington, D. C.: DHHS), 1.

73. Kenneth J. Cooper, "Bush to Propose Leeway for States in Crafting Welfare Work Programs," *The Philadelphia Inquirer*, April 19, 1989.

74. Laurie J. Bassi and Orley Ashenfelter, "The Effect of Direct Job Creation and

Training Programs on Low-Skilled Workers,'' in *Fighting Poverty: What Works and What Doesn't*, eds. Sheldon H. Danziger and Daniel H. Weinberg (Cambridge, MA: Harvard University Press, 1986), 140.

75. However, women with children under age six will be able to opt for just 20 hours of participation if programs do not meet their needs.

76. Zillah Eisenstein, *The Radical Future of Liberal Feminism* (Boston: Northeastern University Press, 1986), 202–3.

77. Ibid., 210.

78. Ibid.

79. *Current AFDC Work Programs*, 57.

5

Motherhood and Public Policy I: Child Custody and Child Support

... [I]t is illusory to believe that writing something down in a statute book always makes it happen in real life.[1]

Public policies for or about children inevitably have a great impact upon women because women are their primary caretakers. Few public policies concerning children reach fruition without mothers in mind. Indeed, most adult women are mothers. The definition of mother implied in public policy, however, is often a traditional patriarchal one: an image of mommy at home involved exclusively with housework and child care. Few women fit this picture.

This chapter will address the public policy issues of child support and child custody. Both are regulated by the courts and in practice are predicated on particular and sometimes seemingly inconsistent notions of the proper role of motherhood and the proper obligations of fatherhood. Yet they serve patriarchy by perpetuating women's devalued, albeit traditional, role as mothers. Women are defined as mothers first regardless of the other circumstances of their lives, but given little or no help with carrying out this assigned role.[2] Women are often placed in a situation of having to choose between their own needs and those of their children. This mechanism can be very effective in inhibiting and controlling women's behavior, in effect holding children hostage to the cause of patriarchal necessity. In contrast, men are granted a great deal of control as well as a range of choices with regard to their family roles and fatherhood status.

MOTHERHOOD

Motherhood as we know it is a phenomenon that emerged in the nineteenth century. Prior to that time, women were engaged in economically productive work at home, among other things making clothes and food for the family as well as doing household chores. Child care was one of women's many tasks. Older siblings were substantially involved with caring for younger children. In a typical mother's day her children were not the center of her attention.[3] Moreover, under English common law fathers were the natural guardians, indeed the "owners" of their children, entitled to their services and having a natural right to their custody if the parents separated.[4]

In the nineteenth century the movement of paid labor from the home to the workplace led to the explicit promotion of the "separate spheres" ideology that placed men in the public arena and left women in the home. Women's role at home became more exclusively focused on providing services for the family, such as cooking, cleaning, laundering, and caring for children. Likewise, the "tender years" legal presumption, which assumed that young children (generally under seven years of age) were better off with their mothers, was established. Older children, however, were often still thought to be more in need of their fathers.[5] Also, a mother determined unfit, commonly because of adultery, could be denied custody of young children.[6]

The shift to the tender years presumption can be seen as a response to the emerging economic and patriarchal arrangements that excluded women and children from wage labor. As Hartmann suggests:

As children's ability to earn money declined, their legal relationship to their parents changed. At the beginning of the industrial era in the United States, fulfilling children's need for their fathers was thought to be crucial, even primary, to their happy development; fathers had legal priority in cases of contested custody. As children's ability to contribute to the economic well-being of the family declined, mothers came increasingly to be viewed as crucial to the happy development of their children, and gained legal priority in cases of contested custody. Here patriarchy adapted to the changing economic role of children; when children were productive, men claimed them; as children became unproductive, they were given to women.[7]

Thus, child custody was no longer useful to men when economic gain was no longer involved. For the most part the separate spheres ideology allowed men to continue to control, through economic dominance and patriarchal marriage, the scope of their wives' and children's behavior. Furthermore, tying women even more closely to their motherhood roles provided an additional way of keeping them in the home and out of the labor market.

In present times, it is less acceptable to view women as keepers of the hearth, but we still harbor the belief that children need their mothers in a rather exclusive relationship confined to the home. Women who divert from this standard, and most women today do in one way or another, must bear the dual burdens of guilt and subtle social disapproval. Since women have been entering the labor force in increasing numbers, it is remarkable that society can continue to cling to a value that is not congruent with most people's overt behavior.[8] In my view the value that mothers should bear sole responsibility for their children exists because it has turned out to be exceedingly useful to patriarchy and to the capitalist system as well.

In contrast to the norm that defines women by their motherhood status, men have a separate identity apart from their fatherhood. Fatherhood for men who have sired children is not something assigned as much as chosen. Their major societal obligation is to support their children monetarily. Unlike mothers, however, society is sympathetic to men's setting the conditions under which their obligations as fathers will be undertaken.

CHILD CUSTODY

Into the 1970s in the United States the legal presumption in favor of the mother's superior suitability for custody of the children in the case of divorce was widespread. A national consensus, backed up by a variety of experts in child development, prevailed.[9] Studies of state and local records dating from the 1870s indicate on average about 85 percent of custody awards were to mothers, 10 percent to fathers, and the rest to relatives or for shared custody.[10] In the 1970s changes in the maternal preference standard began to emerge and were rapidly adopted by most states. Since that time, however, the living arrangements for most children after divorce have not changed. About 90 percent of children today remain in their mother's custody after divorce.[11] A glance at this proportion might lead to the conclusion that maternal preference is still the norm, but evidence indicates that this is not the case. Fathers are simply not requesting custody. However, when they do they often get it.

Recent research data from California sheds light on the custody issue. In her ground-breaking work, *The Divorce Revolution*, Lenore Weitzman presents the results of extensive research undertaken between 1968 and 1981 of the effects of California's no-fault divorce law (passed in 1970).[12] Under this law custody was the only area in which fault could continue to be a factor.[13] This put a chink in the armor of maternal presumption and was followed in 1973 by a change that instructed judges to award custody based on the best interests of the child, totally eliminating mother preference.[14] Yet neither of these changes had an impact upon the patterns of custody requests or awards.[15] Weitzman found that most men did not request custody; even when they told interviewers that they would like to have it, they did little or nothing to pursue it. Research elsewhere also indicates that fewer than 15 percent of divorce cases will include a fully contested custody battle.[16] Weitzman concluded that "the major reason for the low rate of father custody awards lies in the preferences of divorcing men and women: most divorcing fathers are not seriously interested in having custody while most divorcing mothers are."[17]

Among men in Weitzman's study petitioning for custody, two-thirds obtained
it through negotiations or private agreements. In addition one-third of those
contesting it were awarded it by judges.[18] There is some question about how
voluntary the private agreements were, since some women reported being threatened with expensive legal battles that they could not afford.[19] One-third of the
women interviewed indicated that their husbands had threatened to ask for custody as a bargaining chip in the negotiations. Weitzman concluded: "Men see
custody as part of a total package of divorce issues that are, to some extent, 'all
up for grabs.' Women, by contrast, draw a line when it comes to custody."[20]
So notwithstanding the fact that most children live with their mothers, a large
percentage of men who want custody get it.

According to her analysis of case law, Nancy Polikoff contends that judges
in custody cases tend to be biased against employed mothers. She sees a trend
of fathers agreeing to maternal custody at the time of divorce only to request a
change later, after remarriage.[21] Fathers with female relatives or new wives at
home have been favored over employed mothers with full-time housekeepers.[22]
But of course child support awards are never sufficient to allow the mother to
stay home fulltime to care for her children. When she is condemned for her
employment, she can never win. Yet she can also be condemned for her *unemployment*. In 1983 the District of Columbia Court of Appeals ruled that the
fact that a woman is on AFDC can be taken into account in awarding custody.[23]
Remarrying doesn't help women either. Having a new husband does not have
the edge for women that having a new wife does for men; stepfathers are not
expected to aid in child care.[24]

Lynn Schafran also reports the difficulties custodial mothers have in obtaining
permission to move for career reasons, while noncustodial fathers are never
prevented from moving away from their children. She cites a 1983 case in
Louisiana, in which a mother requested permission to move to the District of
Columbia to take a job with the National Labor Relations Board. The judge
labeled her a "careerist" and granted custody to the father.[25]

The degree of nurturance provided to the children by each parent during the
marriage is often disregarded because it is associated with maternal preference.
Indeed, it would probably result in more mothers winning custody battles, since
most men are still relatively uninvolved with basic child care.[26] Yet if both
parents work outside the home, it is sometimes assumed that they share child
care equally.[27] And if a man engages in *any* child care activities, he is given a
great deal of credit. In contrast, an employed mother is suspect. Polikoff contends
that this is because paternal contributions are "still so noticeable" whereas
society continues to require total devotion from mothers. She states: "By this
standard, men will always look good for doing more than nothing, and women
will always look bad for doing less than everything."[28]

Weitzman reports that by 1985 as many as 30 states had passed joint custody
laws. Joint custody can be custodial, legal (pertaining to important decisions
regarding the child), or both. Joint custody is intended to ensure children's

continued relationships with both parents after divorce. Indeed, research has shown that children's distress after divorce can be reduced by fathers' continued involvement with them and an ongoing cooperative coparental relationship.[29] But the positive potential of joint custody as an arrangement that encourages coparenting has not always been fulfilled. Weitzman indicates that many joint custody arrangements are what would previously have been called "liberal visitation."[30] Mothers continue to provide most of the day to day care of their children.[31] In some cases the mothers who are providing custodial care are simply hamstrung by the complications of joint decision making that joint legal custody imposes; "fathers get equal rights without equal responsibility."[32] Joint custody can also mean a lower support award for the mother, even when she provides physical care on a full-time basis.[33]

Joint custody can likewise affect the AFDC eligibility requirement that a child be lacking parental support or care. In situations in which children spend even part of the time in their fathers' homes, AFDC is denied in some states. AFDC is a program for children deprived of parental support or care due to parental death, continued absence, incapacity, or unemployment. In joint custody cases, states differ as to whether or when one parent is considered "absent" and whether the absence is "continuous."[34] Other states examine the child's relationship with the "absent" parent to determine whether the child is indeed deprived of parental care. Families in which children spend time in their father's home have been denied AFDC in some states. Many states are making determinations on a case-by-case basis. Without attention to this matter, discretion, variability, and confusion can result in forcing parents to turn to the much less adequate state General Assistance programs for financial support.[35]

Among men who do not, for whatever reason, obtain physical custody of their children, a great many seem to drift away from the relationship, even when joint custody has been arranged. In fact, almost one in four California fathers ceased to see their children at all after divorce, while 30 percent saw them at least once a week, 33 percent saw them once or twice a month, and 14 percent saw them less than once a month.[36] National figures are even more dismal; one study of children between the ages of eleven and sixteen found that 52 percent of the children had not seen or heard from their fathers at all after divorce.[37] When the noncustodial parent was a mother, however, 86 percent of the children had seen their mothers within the past year and 31 percent saw them on the average of once a week.[38]

CHILD SUPPORT

In addition to abandoning their relationships with their children, many men also neglect to provide child support. For the majority of women and children who remain together after divorce, the enforcement of men's child support obligations has become a social problem of considerable proportions. In the spring of 1986, of the 8.8 million women living with children under age 21 whose fathers were absent, only about 5.4 million had been awarded child support payments. Of these, just 4.4 million had been due to receive payments in the previous year. Half of these women received the full amount, one quarter received partial payments, and one quarter did not receive any payments at all.[39] A recent report from the state of Wisconsin indicated that 70 percent of absent parents became delinquent in their payments within three years.[40] Nationally, the average payment each family received in 1985 was $2,200, down 12 percent from the 1983 average.[41]

Lack of child support payments from their fathers means poverty status for many children. Approximately one-third of the women with children from an absent father had poverty incomes in 1983.[42] One study indicated that, in 1981, about one-third of the divorced and separated women who did not receive child support were below poverty level compared with 12 percent of the women who received such support.[43] Furthermore poverty status is related to receipt of public assistance; a 1979 study found 38 percent of women not receiving child support receiving public assistance, compared with 13 percent of women who had support income.[44]

Contrary to popular opinion, noncustodial fathers have not always been required to support their children. Even after the tender years presumption began to favor maternal custody, fathers were still entitled to whatever earnings their children might have. Later, when fathers were no longer entitled to these earnings, they were not obliged to render support because they did not have access to their children's services. The practice of requiring noncustodial fathers to pay for their children's upkeep did not become widespread until the 1920s.[45]

Congressional concern over child support increased in the 1950s and 1960s mainly because of the growing numbers of women and children on welfare. Between 1950 and 1975 various federal child support laws were passed. They were brought together in the more comprehensive Child Support Enforcement (CSE) Act, signed by President Ford in 1975. It became a new Part D of Title IV of the Social Security Act. Commonly called IV-D, it created a program to be administered by the states and funded jointly by the state and federal governments that would serve to locate absent parents and obtain support payments from them. The program was amended by the Child Support Enforcement Amendments of 1984 and again by the Family Support Act of 1988.

The program requires the states to provide the following services: assistance in the location of absent parents, establishment of paternity, establishment and enforcement of child support obligations, and collection of support payments. The law originally emphasized support payments from fathers of AFDC children by providing an incentive payment to states of a percentage of collections made on behalf of AFDC families. In 1984 the incentive payments were extended to collections made for non-AFDC families as well. The federal government also pays a percentage of the state and local administrative costs for both AFDC and non-AFDC families. A $50 per month child support disregard for the determination of AFDC benefit levels was added in 1984.[46] Also added in the 1984 amendments were the following actions to enforce compliance after certain arrearages occurred: mandatory wage withholding, withholding of state income tax funds, and placing liens on real and personal property.

The Family Support Act strengthened several of the requirements of the 1984 amendments. Whereas states had been required to establish guidelines for child support awards, the new law mandates their use by judges and other officials unless there is a written finding that application of the guidelines would be unjust or inappropriate in a particular case. The law also provides for immediate wage withholding even in the absence of arrearage unless the court finds there is good cause not to require it or if the two parties agree in writing on an alternative arrangement.[47] States must also increase the percentage of AFDC cases for which paternity is established. The federal government will pay 90 percent matching funds for the relevant laboratory tests to establish paternity. Finally, the $50 disregard of child support payments for AFDC cases will apply only to payments that were made on time.

Public Policy in Action

Awards. In spite of the popular belief that court child support awards are exorbitant, there is a great deal of research evidence that most men can comfortably afford to pay the child support awards to which they have become obligated. Ron Haskins reports that "nearly all America's absent fathers, even those whose children are on welfare, earn enough to be capable of contributing a significant amount toward supporting their children."[48] Weitzman points out that the average award is less than the level of welfare, and that except for the lowest income levels it is unusual for a court to order more than one-quarter of a man's income in child support or more than one-third for child support and alimony combined.[49] Furthermore, negligence in paying child support spans all income levels.[50]

Child support awards tend not to cover expenses adequately, and are particularly deficient in taking into account expenses for child care, special medical care, or savings for college.[51] Most states have lowered the age of majority from 21 to 18. Since courts rarely award support into adulthood, young adults are not only often deprived of college tuition, but also the financial upkeep necessary for school attendance. This poses a particular burden for midlife middle-class divorcing women.[52]

Interestingly, the California judges interviewed in Weitzman's study commonly referred to an award limit of 50 percent of a payor's salary, yet the statistics showed that these same judges rarely awarded more than one-third of a husband's net income. Moreover, the awards made were usually lower than those in suggested judicial guidelines.[53]

Visitation. It is commonly said that men withhold support payments because their ex-wives interfere with their right to visit their children. Notwithstanding the moral ambiguity of withholding food from one's children in order to coerce their mother into behaving differently, this reason for nonpayment is a myth. In fact there is no correlation between support award compliance and complaints about visitation. Men who pay regularly and those who don't are equally as likely or unlikely to complain about visitation problems.[54] Even men who share joint legal custody of their children with the children's mothers are just as likely to be delinquent in support payments than those who don't.[55] In fact women appear to be as upset about the fathers' lack of parenting as they are about their failure to pay support.[56] Yet the common association between lack of support and problems of visitation is so pervasive that Congress included in the 1988 Family Support Act funds for demonstration projects to address "child access problems" for the purpose of improving collection of child support orders.[57]

The fact of visitation, however, has been linked to the continuance of support payments, if not the amount of the support payment paid.[58] Thus, while the connection between problems with visitation and delinquency in payments is weak, delinquent parents tend not to visit. It may be that fathers who see their children regularly are more likely to be conscientious about their financial upkeep. Alternatively, the opposite may apply. That is, fathers who are not motivated to pay child support may also lack interest in seeing their children. Or, given the potential of conflict in visits from nonpaying fathers, these fathers may accept the lack of contact with their children as the price of noncompliance with support orders. In any case links between support payments, degree of visitation, familial relationships, and child support enforcement are the subject of ongoing study.

IV-D Agency Enforcement. Many social welfare advocates opposed the passage of IV-D because it seemed that its only purpose was to harass women on welfare and their poor ex-husbands who couldn't afford to pay child support anyway. This opposition has subsided as society has become more concerned about the increase in single-parent families, the large numbers of out-of-wedlock births, and the continued burden of the state in paying AFDC benefits. Moreover, research has indicated that most fathers can afford to pay at least some child support. Finally, the experience of collection efforts demonstrates that child support enforcement is cost-effective. That is, the total costs of administering CSE programs have been consistently less than the aggregate amounts collected. This is something that program opponents didn't believe was possible.

Notwithstanding its current cost-effectiveness, the proportional results of collection efforts in the CSE program to date have been mixed. Between 1976 and 1981, annual collections increased from $512 million to $1.6 billion. Yet in 1983, unpaid child support totaled $3 billion.[59] In 1985 only 7.3 percent of AFDC payments were recovered through the program and about 10 percent of the absent parents paid support. Collections did exceed administrative costs, but by just $1.38 to the dollar.[60] The General Accounting Office also reports lower average child support payments for interstate cases, which need better tracking and monitoring in the states.[61]

States were required to have the provisions of the 1984 amendments in place by October 1, 1985, except in cases in which state law had to be changed in order to implement a component of the program or when a state could demonstrate that a provision was not necessary for its effective or efficient enforcement. In these cases the secretary of the Department of Health and Human Services could grant an implementation delay or exemption. The GAO surveyed state implementation of 14 provisions of the 1984 amendments. They reported that as of March 31, 1986, "only Oregon had fully implemented all 14 provisions, and only 1 provision (appointing state commissions on child support) had been fully implemented by all states." Only three states (Minnesota, Oregon, and Utah) had implemented all 39 procedures necessary for wage withholding. Ten states had implemented the 10 procedures necessary to put in place state tax refund withholding.[62] The implementation of procedures for liens on personal property was more readily achieved; 34 states had the 6 required procedures in place as of March 31.[63] The GAO was critical of federal efforts in monitoring state compliance. Some regional offices did not have accurate information about states' delayed implementation dates and no penalties for noncompliance had been imposed.[64]

The states have also been slow in establishing paternity and obtaining support orders for AFDC cases. A 1984 GAO study of a sample of AFDC cases in eight locations found that 40 percent of the AFDC children needing paternity determinations and/or support orders did not receive them because "their cases (1) were never opened, (2) were closed prematurely, or (3) remained open but unattended."[65] They refer to inadequate case management on the state level made worse by a lack of federal standards for these activities. Furthermore, they found unreliable and inadequate state reporting on accomplishments.[66] Federal and state efforts appear to be focused on collections rather than support orders. Even in the collections area, though, they are far from achieving full implementation.

If and when IV-D ever becomes fully implemented, it is possible that the program will no longer be cost-effective. If, for example, most attention to date has been focused on men who are known to be gainfully employed and/or easily reachable, it may be that the expansion of the program will produce diminishing returns. A larger proportion of the fathers yet to be located may be unemployed or have such low incomes as to lower even further the direct cost/benefit ratio. If that occurs then the advisability of continuing the program will hinge on other issues, such as a father's moral obligation to support his children. There may be another monetary benefit to the state, however, in the form of a deterrence effect. It has been suggested that the certainty of having to support their offspring may become an incentive for young men to take more responsibility for pregnancy prevention.[67] This might have a palpable impact on the AFDC rolls.

Court Enforcement. Even when the IV-D agency tracks down an absent father, his fate regarding support awards and their enforcement resides in the courts. The courts have not been helpful to women and children in this regard. Weitzman places blame on two specific judicial practices: the failure to order wage assignments and the waiving of arrearage. She states: "The California judges we interviewed were well informed and were aware that the law required wage assignments when support was two months overdue. But they chose not to follow the law."[68] Moreover, judges frequently waived arrearage for men brought to court because they owed back payments. Weitzman cites numerous instances of fathers excused from their legal obligations by sympathetic judges. Judges also tended to avoid other remedies, such as having payments sent to the court, because they didn't want to embarrass the men.[69] A similar problem was identified in New York State by the Child Support Commission, which reported that in 1985 most of the complaints it received involved judges' "unwillingness to demand compliance or impose penalties for noncompliance."[70] Divorced women also experienced a great deal of difficulty, at considerable expense, locating ex-husbands who moved out of state.

Court problems do not only involve judges, but other actors as well, even those who are supposed to be working in a woman's behalf. Weitzman reports that the women's lawyers often did not take them seriously or relied on threatening letters rather than pushing for the strongest remedies, such as wage attachment. District attorneys were not much help either. Many women give up pursuing the matter because of the aggravation and the expense.[71] The aggravation involved cannot be overstated. The chair of the Coalition of Women for Child Support in New York State testified: "Individually we have been told that our unsuccessful attempts to collect uncollected child support build character. . . . We have also been told that we are vindictive, money-grubbing, that we made our beds and now we must lie in them."[72] Members spent an average of seven years trying to get their court-ordered support enforced. Schafran presents the following case as an example of judicial bias:

A Rochester attorney described being at a conference in the judge's chambers on behalf of a woman who had been attempting to enforce a child support order for 14 years. The father's attorney said to the judge, "It's been 14 years, why doesn't she leave him alone?" and the judge said to the mother's attorney, "Yes, why doesn't she leave him alone?"[73]

Few women, of course, have the financial resources to pursue the matter for 14 years. Moreover, some see giving in as the price of keeping their children.

As mentioned above, many women hesitate to press for child support for fear of their husband's pressing for custody. Women also tend to focus on the interpersonal aspects of the divorce negotiation. Thus, many women conceded to low child support amounts either for fear of losing custody or because they wished to preserve a positive relationship for themselves and their children with their ex-spouses. As Weitzman observed:

It often seemed as if both partners were focused on the husband and what he wanted or offered: while he worried about his checkbook, she worried about how he was feeling, how he would react, and how she might find a solution that would please, or at least satisfy him. Because of their greater tendency to empathize, then, women may well agree to solutions that compromise their own interests.[74]

In this vein Schafran, attorney for the NOW Legal Defense and Education Fund, reports that divorce mediation, a popular alternative to litigation, can work against many women, who are much more likely than their husbands to agree to a compromise in order to satisfy the mediator.[75] Thus women's tendency to form connections and avoid conflict can work against their self-interest and that of their children.

Wisconsin Experiment

In Wisconsin a statewide standard for child support payments coupled with automatic wage withholding became law in 1987. Under this program, the Child Support Assurance System (CSAS), noncustodial parents are required to pay a set percentage of gross income varied only by the number of children involved: 17 percent for one child, and 25, 29, 31, and 34 percent for two, three, four, and five or more children, respectively.[76] In addition, in four pilot counties, a demonstration program, which became operational in 1988, will be ongoing through 1993. In these counties all children legally entitled to child support will be guaranteed an assured benefit, either paid entirely or partially by the absent parent's support requirement. Those support payments that fall below the assured benefit will be supplemented by the state. A single child living with one parent will receive an annual benefit of $1,000. The benefits for two, three, four, and five children are $3,528, $4,222, $4,828, and $5,224, respectively. The benefit will be taxed with a progressive tax rate, but will not change at all in relation to the custodial parent's other income. In fact low-income custodial parents who are employed will receive a work expense subsidy of $1 per hour worked for one child and $1.75 for two or more children.[77]

The CSAS program in Wisconsin is based on the premise that it is fairer to have a system in which the child support award amount will be standardized. Noncustodial parents can be assured of equity from case to case. The demonstration program attached to this is a kind of children's allowance for single-parent families. Custodial parents can be sure of a set amount of child support regardless of changes in the noncustodial parent's income. Moreover, earned income does not reduce the payment, as in the AFDC program.

Applying the Wisconsin support standards nationwide (and presuming a tax on only the first $50,000 of income for child support purposes), Garfinkel and McLanahan estimated the impact upon woman-headed single-parent families. They found that the income of these families would increase by more than $10 billion and the poverty gap would be reduced by nearly $2 billion. Likewise, Garfinkel and Oellerich estimate that the assurance program, including government subsidies, could reduce the poverty gap for families with eligible children by almost 40 percent and the AFDC caseloads by almost 50 percent. The government could save about $2.3 billion if it achieved 100 percent compliance in payments; it would break even if 70 percent of the standard were paid.[78]

Returns are not yet in on the new Wisconsin law and child support experiment.

Preliminary reports indicated that judges in pilot counties were not uniformly ordering immediate wage withholding and that court clerks were tending to represent the support orders in dollar amounts instead of proportions of gross income.[79] Although the new law was not fully in effect when the data were obtained, the former practice may indicate judges' reluctance to enforce the law and the latter tendency may make it difficult to assign the required payment amount as fathers' incomes increase.

ANALYSIS

"It is a traditional liberty for Americans to pull up stakes, leave and start a new life elsewhere, free of earlier responsibilities." This comment was made by a successful California attorney in regard to child support. Harry Krause, a strong proponent of parental responsibility, refers to this remark as "perhaps a quaint misapplication of pioneer philosophy."[80] It is not clear whether Krause noticed that the statement refers only to American men. Nowhere is it a traditional liberty for American *women* to eschew responsibilities and start a new life elsewhere, especially if the responsibilities involve the care and upkeep of children. The man's statement is a gross illustration of an attitude that allows men the range of choices available to fathers in the United States today.

Social welfare policies with regard to children allow men maximum control and minimum responsibility. The patriarchal system has a stake in maintaining the primacy of a woman's role as a mother and her inability to perform this role well without depending financially on men or on the state. While it is true that in our liberalized society some men have gladly taken on a greater role in child care and housework, their numbers are very small. While men who do take more child caring responsibilities pay a price for doing so, the price mainly comes from job changes or decreased labor force participation. The legal system favors most men's choices with regard to both custody and child support, notwithstanding the politics of the "fathers' rights" movement. The issue of fathers' rights mystifies the patriarchal necessity for the legal system to maintain men's control of women, children, and how their money is spent. Polikoff notes, for example, that the fathers' rights movement focuses on fathers' rights as parents at the time of divorce rather than "social change facilitating co-parenting during marriage."[81] This is so because the fathers' rights movement is not about parenting but about control. It is about maintaining masculine prerogatives.

The slow implementation of the Child Support Enforcement laws suggests a reluctance in the states to impose such a sweeping change in social policy. Yet even under full implementation, the ultimate awards and enforcement of support will continue to rest in the courts, with attorneys and judges who uphold patriarchal norms. The behavior of the courts illustrates how patriarchy can operate in spite of official legislative mandate that seems to be favorable to women and children. Judges carry out the dictates of patriarchal necessity by treating women as supplicants for money that should be their children's right. With a great deal of consistency these courts punish women without men. They control women and help individual men to do so. Men are allowed to go free or pay, as they wish. In child support cases, women are pictured as parasites wanting something for nothing, or nagging shrews with unreasonable demands. Always there is the implication that women are not competent or responsible enough to spend the money wisely. They are not good mothers and nothing they can do or say is convincing enough. Moreover, the money, time, and energy required for women to obtain their children's rights in the courts are frequently so great that it is saner to give up. Upon giving up, a woman can resign herself to life as a struggle or, preferably, remarry.

In view of the central power of the courts in setting awards and enforcement, the new child support enforcement provisions of the Family Support Act of 1988 are not likely to be any more effective in increasing child support obligation payments than was the 1984 law. In Weitzman's study judges consistently over-estimated the actual amounts of their orders, awarded amounts lower than the suggested guidelines, and disregarded the requirement that wage withholding be imposed. In the new law the courts will have the option of disregarding the award guidelines and finding a good cause not to impose wage withholding. In this circumstance one can anticipate divorce lawyers pressing for settlements in which judges exercise their options in favor of noncustodial parents. Moreover, women will continue to have limited financial resources for lengthy court battles. The legal system is perhaps "closing in" a bit on the process by requiring explicit reasons for judicial behavior outside of Congress' recommendations. This may improve the situation marginally and give the illusion of great progress. Nevertheless, most judges are well aware of their prerogatives and are not likely to eschew their powers of discretion. There has been nothing in their decisions regarding child support up to now to suggest otherwise.

In custody cases women can lose their children if they are on welfare because they are too poor, or they can lose their children if they go out to work since that means they are not completely devoted to their children. Devotion to children above all is a convenient patriarchal norm because it assures that in the majority of cases women will assume custody when men don't want it. But when men want their children, the criteria for custody can easily shift to favor fathers.

The system functions to discourage single parenthood and to maintain mas-culinist dominance over the private sphere. Single parenthood is at odds with the patriarchal notion of motherhood because there is no man to mediate between the family, the economy, and the state, no man to be in control over the mothering that takes place. In the absence of such a man, a woman must remain uncom-fortable and seemingly incompetent.

The discouragement of single parenthood, however, can be seen as only one function of the intransigence of the systems related to child custody and support. Women's independence as single parents is not the only threat. If that were the case, then women who had remarried would be advantaged in custody cases. The additional element is the relationship of men to the private sphere, over which they must maintain dominance.

A man, in relation to "his woman," must always appear to be dominant in both the public and private spheres and thus able to choose his place and participation in the home. The home is by definition a place that man dominates; thus "a man's home is his castle." At the same time, men are not supposed to need homes and families in the same way that women do. Cultural notions that men are chased by women and roped in or somehow tricked into marriage and domesticity reflect this view. Even then, while men are understood to be won over to the domestic life, they must maintain a degree of control or put themselves in danger of being henpecked. Thus, when judges hesitate to order wage assignment, it is well to contemplate what sort of embarrassment they are sparing these fathers. Is it embarrassment because of the public revelation of the father's delinquency? Or is it embarrassment over his ex-wife getting something over on him, a woman besting him, as it were, or the private sphere triumphing over the public? Women deserve nothing. Their demands are to be resisted as unfeminine nagging. This was the overwhelming experience of women in New York who testified regarding their difficulties in obtaining child support. Individual masculine dominance of women and the home has thus consistently been upheld by the state.

It is important to recognize that for men who are with their wives and children the norm of support is quite different. Both men and women tend to see men in the role of breadwinner, even when wives contribute substantially to the family's economic upkeep.[82] In this situation men are expected to provide support, but patriarchy also affords them control and dominance. In contrast, the expectation of support for women and children by an absent father is asking him to assume responsibility without concomitant control, simply because his wife and children have the right to his support.

In custody cases, the patriarchal system lends individual men distinct patriarchal privileges. Thus, in spite of the fact that single parenthood is threatening to patriarchy, women who have remarried cannot be given preference in custody disputes over single fathers because it would be a humiliating violation of the individual father's domination and control. In contrast, men with new wives are at an advantage. Mothers are interchangeable. Fathers are not. It is almost shocking how easily the cultural message that children require mothers bound to them in devotion and sacrifice can be discarded in service to the patriarchal privileges of individual men.

The lack of progress in the CSE program may reflect another dilemma of patriarchy and class. As the program progresses in its implementation it will increasingly go after both higher income fathers and a larger proportion of fathers whose children are in the AFDC population. While these two groups are not mutually exclusive, one may assume that many if not most fathers of children on AFDC are for the most part poor or near poor themselves. Also large numbers of them are Black. Lumping together these two groups presents conflicts for patriarchy and capitalism and white supremacy.

Patriarchy calls for control of women under masculine domination. Child support from fathers is patriarchal insofar as it is preferred to women breadwinners adequately supporting themselves and their children. On the other hand, a strong tenet of patriarchy is masculine autonomy and optimal choice. Men are not supposed to be tied to their women and children. Thus child support enforcement is threatening to this principle, especially as it applies to the white masculine ruling class.

For low-income white men and Black men it is another matter. Race and class relations intervene to give these men fewer patriarchal prerogatives than those for higher status men. The IV-D program was originally focused exclusively on these men. It is functional to class interests as well as white supremacy to have a cultural image of these men as the real culprits, shirking their manly duties by not supporting their families. However, pursuing them led to the discovery that men at all income levels neglect to support their children and resultant pressure to expand the program. Further pursuit may result in increased public knowledge of the stark reality of the significant proportion of men, particularly Black men, who lack jobs and income. This may lead to public pressure for training and job development for inner city Black men. Such reforms, however, threaten capitalism's need for a readily available pool of cheap labor. White supremacy would also challenged by such programs, Wilson's protestations to the contrary.

The Wisconsin Child Support Assurance Program bears watching as it combines a strong parental support obligation with a governmental commitment to children's well being. It also is supportive of women's labor force participation. However, for middle-income families divorce settlements for wives may be adapted to reflect this guarantee of future support. The program's success may also result in more men fighting for custody in order to maintain control over their economic prerogatives.[83] If the initial finding of judges' reluctance to order immediate withholding and the assignment of total amounts rather than a percentage of income is sustained, the Wisconsin program may be waylaid by patriarchal necessity at the judicial level. In any case, success in Wisconsin does not guarantee national adoption of such a program.

Chapter 6 will continue the theme of public policy, motherhood, and children, focusing on the influence of patriarchy on day care and other child welfare service programs.

NOTES

1. Lynn Hecht Schafran, "Gender Bias in the Courts," in *Women As Single Parents: Confronting the Institutional Barriers in the Courts, the Workplace, and the Housing Market*, ed. Elizabeth A. Mulroy (Dover, MA: Auburn House Publishing Company, 1988), 70.

2. In my view, all public policies and practices, from abortion laws to childbirth technology to public school hours, serve to perpetuate women's maximum childbearing and child rearing responsibilities while leaving most of the control and regulation of these activities in the hands of men policy makers, administrators, and fathers. Abortion, childbearing, and reproductive technology will not be discussed here. See Zillah R. Eisenstein, *The Radical Future of Liberal Feminism* (Boston: Northeastern University Press, 1986), 236–44; and Gena Corea, *The Mother Machine: Reproductive Technologies From Artificial Insemination to Artificial Wombs* (New York: Harper and Row, 1985).

3. Michelle Hoffnung, "Motherhood: Contemporary Conflict for Women," in *Women: A Feminist Perspective*, ed. Jo Freeman (New York: Mayfield Publishing Company, 1984), 125.

4. Lenore J. Weitzman, *The Divorce Revolution: The Unexpected Social and Economic Consequences for Women and Children in America* (New York: The Free Press, 1985), 219.

5. Ibid.

6. Nancy D. Polikoff, "Gender and Child-Custody Determinations: Exploding the Myths," in *Politics and Public Policy: A Feminist Dialogue on Women and the State*, ed. Irene Diamond (New York: Longman, 1983), 186.

7. Heidi Hartmann, "The Unhappy Marriage of Marxism and Feminism," in *Women and Revolution*, ed. Lydia Sargeant (Boston: South End Press, 1981), 23.

8. Bergmann maintains that women's increasing labor force participation can be attributed to the fact that "higher wages . . . have made women's time too valuable to be devoted entirely to homemaking." See Barbara Bergmann, *The Economic Emergence of Women* (New York: Basic Books, 1986), 6. An additional factor may be their historical pattern of economically productive work. It has only been a short time that women's work in the home has been so narrowly restricted to housework and child care. While women's work within the family did not afford them their own earnings, they have for most of history engaged in work in the home that was more varied and had a direct impact on the family's economic well-being. Entering the labor force is the only route to a return to this type of work.

9. Weitzman, 220–21.

10. Ibid., 222.

11. Polikoff, 184.

12. Weitzman. Her research included examinations of random samples of 2,500 court dockets and in-depth interviews with family law attorneys, family law judges, English legal experts, and divorced men and women.

13. Ibid., 223.

14. Ibid., 231.

15. Ibid., 225–32.

16. Ross A. Thompson, "The Father's Case in Child Custody Disputes: The Contributions of Psychological Research," in *Fatherhood and Family Policy*, eds. Michael E. Lamb and Abraham Sagi (Hillsdale, NJ: Lawrence Erlbaum, 1983), 55.

17. Weitzman, 244.

18. Ibid., 236, 233, 233 n66. They were most interested in older children, especially boys. In fact there were no cases in which a father contested custody in families in which there were only girl children.

19. Ibid., 234–35.

20. Ibid., 311.

21. Polikoff, 190.

22. Ibid. See also Schafran, 57.

23. Schafran, 58.

24. Polikoff, 190.

25. Schafran, 56.

26. Thompson, 65. Research indicates, however, that fathers who do involve themselves in child care are quite competent to do so (p. 66).

27. Polikoff, 188. However, one state, West Virginia, has a "primary caretaker" presumption (see pp. 195–96).

28. Ibid., 191.

29. Joyce Everett, "Patterns and Implications of Child Support and Enforcement Practices for Children's Well-Being," Working Paper No. 128 (Wellesley, MA: Wellesley College Center for Research on Women, 1984).

30. Weitzman, 250.

31. Ibid., 258.

32. Polikoff, 192.

33. Schafran, 59.

34. Jan L. Hagan and George Hoshino, "Joint Custody of Children and AFDC Eligibility," *Social Service Review*, December 1985:640.

35. Ibid., 641, 644.

36. Weitzman, 258.

37. Frank F. Furstenberg, Christine W. Nord, James L. Peterson, and Nicholas Zill, "The Life Course of Children of Divorce: Marital Disruption and Parental Contact," *American Sociological Review* 48 (October 1983):656–68.

38. Ibid., T. 6, 663.

39. Bureau of the Census, Current Population Reports, Series P-23, No. 154, *Child Support and Alimony: 1985 (Supplemental Report)* (Washington, D. C.: U. S. Government Printing Office, 1989): 1.

40. Irwin Garfinkel, "The Evolution of Child Support Policy," *Focus* (Institute for Research on Poverty, University of Wisconsin-Madison) 11, no. 1 (Spring 1988): 14.

41. Schafran, 47.

42. Lowell H. Lima and Robert C. Harris, "The Child Support Enforcement Program in the United States," in *Child Support: From Debt Collection to Social Policy*, eds. Alfred J. Kahn and Sheila B. Kamerman (Newberry Park, CA: Sage Publications, 1988), 22.

43. Lenore J. Weitzman, "Child Support: Myths and Reality," in Kahn and Kamerman, 252.

44. Ibid., 252.

45. Polikoff, p. 186.

46. With this provision, low-income fathers could feel that they were really aiding their children rather than just simply reimbursing the state to save tax dollars.

47. Immediate wage withholding must be in place within two years for IV-D Child Support Enforcement cases and for all support orders issued after December 31, 1993.

48. Ron Haskins, "Child Support: A Father's View," in Kahn and Kamerman, 306–27.

49. Weitzman, "Child Support," 258, 254–55. Most women, of course, do not receive alimony awards. Note that just 19 percent of women divorced before 1970 and 13 percent

of women divorced after 1980 had agreements or awards to receive alimony, and their record of actually receiving the amounts due is about the same as for child support. See Schafran, 47.

50. Weitzman, "Child Support," 259.

51. Schafran, 47. See also Weitzman, *The Divorce Revolution*, 270–71.

52. Frances Leonard, *Divorce and Older Women* (Washington, D.C.: Older Women's League, 1987), 3.

53. Weitzman, *The Divorce Revolution*, 266–68.

54. Weitzman, "Child Support," 260. See also Schafran, 55.

55. Weitzman, *The Divorce Revolution*, 255.

56. Weitzman, "Child Support," 261. See also Dorothy C. Miller, *Helping the Strong: An Exploration of the Needs of Families Headed by Women* (Silver Spring, MD: National Association of Social Workers, 1987), 23–25.

57. House of Representatives, 100th Congress, *Family Support Act of 1988: Conference Report*, Report 100-998, 63.

58. Everett. See also Furstenberg et al.; J. Wallerstein and D. Huntington, "Bread and Roses: Nonfinancial Issues Related to Fathers' Economic Support for Their Children Following Divorce," in *The Parental Child Support Obligation*, ed. Judith Cassetty (Lexington, MA: Lexington Books, 1983).

59. General Accounting Office, *Child Support: States' Progress in Implementing the 1984 Amendments* (Washington, D.C.: GAO, 1986) (GAO/HRD-87-11), 10.

60. Alfred J. Kahn and Sheila B. Kamerman, "Child Support in the United States: The Problem," in Kahn and Kamerman, 13.

61. "Problems GAO Identified in Work on Child Support Enforcement Program," Statement of Joseph F. Delfico, Senior Associate Director, Human Resources Division, General Accounting Office, Before the Subcommittee on Public Assistance and Unemployment Compensation, Committee on Ways and Means, House of Representatives, February 23, 1988, 1, 4, 6. See also General Accounting Office, *Interstate Child Support: Case Data Limitations, Enforcement Problems, Views on Improvements Needed* (Washington, D.C.: GAO, January, 1989) (GAO/HRD-89-25). One barrier to efficiency noted is that many states do not yet have automated systems for tracking out-of-state cases. See General Accounting Office, *Child Support: State Progress in Developing Automated Enforcement Systems* (Washington, D.C.: February, 1989) (GAO/HRD-89-10FS).

62. *States' Progress in Implementing the 1984 Amendments*, 19, 22. Ten states were exempted from this provision because they do not have a state income tax.

63. Ibid., 28.

64. Ibid., 36. Comments from the Department of Health and Human Services were included in Appendix V of the report. The comments objected to some of the GAO's criticisms and reported the following compliance numbers as of August 15, 1986: mandatory wage withholding fully implemented: 11 states; state tax offset fully implemented: 18 states; liens on personal property fully implemented: 39 states (pp. 60–64).

65. General Accounting Office, *Child Support: Need to Improve Efforts to Identify Fathers and Obtain Support Orders* (Washington, D.C.: GAO, April, 1987) (GAO/HRD-87-37), 3.

66. Ibid., 4.

67. Irwin Garfinkel and Sara S. McLanahan, *Single Mothers and Their Children: A New American Dilemma* (Washington, D.C.: The Urban Institute Press, 1986), 154. They add that increased enforcement may deter some men from divorcing. It may also inhibit men's tendency to have more children with new wives.

68. Weitzman, "Child Support," 267.

69. Weitzman, *The Divorce Revolution*, 285.

70. Schafran, 53.

71. Weitzman, *The Divorce Revolution*, 288.

72. Schafran, 54.

73. Ibid.

74. Weitzman, *The Divorce Revolution*, 315.

75. Schafran, 45.

76. Garfinkel and McLanahan, 137.

77. "Child Support Assurance System: An Update," *Focus* (Institute for Research on Poverty, University of Wisconsin-Madison) 10, no. 3 (Fall 1987): 17. See also Tom Corbett, "Child Support Assurance: Wisconsin Demonstration," *Focus* 9, no. 1 (Spring 1986): 1–5.

78. Garfinkel and McLanahan, 152–53.

79. "Child Support Assurance System: An Update," 16–17.

80. Harry D. Krause, "Reflections on Child Support," in Kahn and Kamerman, 228.

81. Polikoff, 185.

82. Jean L. Potuchek, "Who's Responsible for Supporting the Family? Employed Wives and the Breadwinner Role," Working Paper No. 186. (Wellesley, MA: Wellesley College Center for Research on Women, 1988).

83. Garfinkel and McLanahan, 154.

6

Motherhood and Public Policy II: Social Welfare Services for Children

Children are only as well off as their mothers.[1]

Traditionally social welfare services for children, or child welfare services, have upheld a patriarchal notion of motherhood. Women are expected to be the sole caretakers of their children, and they are expected to carry out their child caring tasks without help from anyone. Thus most services for children were conceptualized as "substitute care." The services were substituting for a mother's care. Day care, foster family care, and institutional care for children as well as adoption were all classified under the rubric of substitute care.[2]

Another important child welfare service, protective services for children, developed as a mechanism for the state to detect instances in which parents were not carrying out their duties. The state was then charged with helping the parents achieve a minimal level of parenting while their children were safely in substitute care. With the exception of day care for children, this system is essentially still in place today. This chapter will address briefly the general realm of child welfare services and their patriarchal basis. Then day care policies will be addressed in more depth.

CHILD WELFARE

Prevention

While the concept of prevention is often given lip service in child welfare literature, few resources have been allocated to it. Thus, services for families tend to be relatively unavailable until the family has become so dysfunctional as to be no longer able to cope. Usually services are offered only at the point at which abuse, neglect, or abandonment have come to public attention. At this point sometimes services are offered to counsel or educate the parents, for the most part the mother, about child rearing. Sometimes day care is provided in order to give her a respite from the burdens of child care. As Carol Meyer notes, prevention is normally confined to that which is done to avoid placement, rather than addressed to provision of services to families to prevent dysfunction.[3]

In fact, very little is available to prevent placement. If services to prevent family dysfunction were offered, responsibility for child caring would partially shift from the family to the society at large. The restrictive socially constructed definition of the role of motherhood might change. This in turn would lessen the burden of mothers for the care of their children, eliminating a major patriarchal tool for the manipulation of women. Women are expected to be good mothers without any outside help, and they are not given any special credit when they are (mother's day cards notwithstanding). When they fail, however, they are subject to reprobation. If society offered help to prevent dysfunction, many more mothers would avoid the shame of having failed as mothers, and the fear of such shame might lose its social control function.

Foster Care

Instead of prevention, "foster care persists as a central solution to family problems." This solution simply substitutes one mother for another, preserving women's prescribed societal role.[4] Moreover, foster mothers, as all child care workers, receive little compensation for providing such care, devaluing the work and preserving the notion that mothering should come from the heart, embracing self-sacrifice and eschewing monetary reward. Historically foster mothers were considered clients of child welfare agencies. Their status has changed to one closer to an employee, but they generally do not receive employee benefits. They are closer to being volunteers who are reimbursed for their expenses. Except in cases of specialized foster care for children with special needs, board rates for foster care are calculated to cover only the costs of the child(ren)'s upkeep. Remuneration for the parents is not included.

The foster care population nationally has been growing in absolute size and contains a higher proportion of older and special needs children.[5] Foster family care rates in 1985 ranged from a low of $121.30 per month in West Virginia to a top rate of $547.50 in Alaska and Oregon. The average rate in 1985 was $255.95 (having risen 27 percent from 1982). The median rate for 1985 was $242.98 paid by Rhode Island. The standard rate includes the basic monthly rate plus, where applicable, special clothing allowances and personal and incidental allowances. However, it does not include additional payments for special needs children or any other extraordinary payments, which are sometimes issued.

Not does it include county maintenance payment supplements, which can raise the amount.[6]

A 1980 survey examined a random sample of foster families in eight states (Alabama, Arkansas, North Dakota, Rhode Island, Texas, Utah, Virginia, and Wisconsin). Over two-thirds of the families in the sample were below the national median income. They were asked whether the payments and reimbursements were enough to pay for the actual expenses—65 percent said no. Items they have to contribute regularly included: clothing, entertainment, food, vacations, travel to visit biological parents, medical, insurance, and dental.[7]

Sometimes children are placed in institutional care rather than foster families. This is likely to occur more often with children who are unmanageable or with adolescents who might experience difficulty adjusting to a new family at a time when they are beginning to focus on breaking away from family life to assert their individual selves. Yet institutional care for children is also reflective of the cultural definition of motherhood in that service provision is related to gender. As Martin Wolins observes:

As early as the 19th century, institutional care of *deprived* children seems to have been primarily the task of females, but males staffed programs for the *depraved*. . . . As it evolved. . . into a nurturing system, paternal roles became deemphasized. . . . Substitute care-taking structures that are intimate, governed by affective relationships, possessing few formal rules and a high order of voluntary reciprocity. . . tend to have female caretakers. . . . Large settings, organized hierarchically, governed by numerous rules, will have proportionately more male caretakers.[8]

Masculine settings were constructed to instill discipline for delinquent populations. Foster family care and institutional care in smaller settings such as group homes have been constructed to provide mother substitutes.

Thus, except for delinquents, the foster care system relies on women's labor. In foster family care, where most foster children reside, this labor takes place at home. Previously foster mothers were required to be full-time homemakers, but the need for foster homes has forced the system to accept women who are in the labor force. The family is seen as the best place for children, but the system has increasingly been unable to recruit new foster parents because the demands are quite high and the financial remuneration often isn't even enough to pay for the children's upkeep. The care of children is women's work and there is still the notion that it should be done on a voluntary basis, out of mother love, even for other people's children.

Financial help for child care, whether it be subsidies for families or payment for services rendered, is always low. Thus day care mothers, day care workers in centers, child care workers in institutions, foster parents, and AFDC mothers are expected to care for children with minimal financial help or remuneration. As a result, the child welfare system is faced with a situation of continual crisis.

Meyer recommends an overhaul of the foster care system that recognizes that children can be cared for and influenced positively by a variety of persons in many roles. She visualizes a transformation of the foster care system that turns it into "an efficient social service rather than a 'pretend' natural family home."[9] Foster parents need not be mothers, but can be staff members. And placements can be in the neighborhoods where the children live, allowing free visiting with their mothers, family, and friends, and avoiding traumatic separations from home, school, and all things familiar. This would replace the common practice of removing children from their poor urban neighborhoods and placing them in middle-class suburban homes, a classist rescue operation that makes it even harder to return the children to their families.[10]

What Meyer is suggesting is revolutionary in its challenge to patriarchal notions of motherhood. It belies the sacredness of motherhood in its suggestion that mothers can really be aided in their parenting tasks, not by getting them to conform better to an idealized notion of motherhood, but by relieving them of some of the tasks heretofore exclusively assigned to mothers. It suggests that a variety of persons can perform parenting and that children will be better off for it. This plan would enhance the quality of life for children and tend to preclude the need for the ultimate form of substitute care, adoption.

Adoption

Adoption services have changed considerably in the twentieth century, mainly because of a scarcity of white babies. Since the 1950s, young pregnant white girls have been more likely either to have abortions or to keep their babies than to give them up for adoption. This circumstance has led to marked changes in the adoption business in the United States and a great increase in international adoptions.[11]

Another reason for the change in adoption services was the change in the professional community's opinion of foster care. The publication in 1973 of *Beyond the Best Interests of the Child*[12] criticized the temporary arrangements of most children in foster care as extremely detrimental to children. Written by two psychoanalysts and a lawyer, the book caused a stir among child welfare policy makers and academics. Another book, *Children of the Storm: Black Children and American Child Welfare*, had already outlined the white supremacist neglectful history of the child welfare system's treatment of Black children.[13] As these books began to influence the child welfare field, a 1978 report from the Children's Defense Fund, *Children Without Homes*, presented the results of a national survey of foster children that indicated official neglect and shocking conditions throughout the country.[14] These books greatly influenced the attitudes and activities of policy makers, administrators, and advocates. Efforts began to get more foster children returned home or adopted.

As a result of changes in the system, previously "unadoptable" children became "hard to place" or "special needs" children and a variety of mechanisms and incentives were built into state systems to try to improve adoption services for these previously forgotten children. Multistate adoption exchanges were established so that the pool of potential parents for any one child could be expanded. Moreover, the concept of "permanency planning" was developed to sensitize persons at all levels of the child welfare system that the achievement of a safe and loving and permanent situation for children should be given high priority.

As a result of these changes today, many traditional adoption agencies have extended themselves beyond previous expectations, working hard to place children with emotional and physical limitations, interracial children, sibling groups together, and older children. Agencies' recruitment efforts have been extended to institutions in Black communities, such as churches and fraternal organizations, and agencies have changed their economic requirements to include rather than exclude potential adoptive parents in limited financial circumstances. Laws have been passed to subsidize adoption in some cases, particularly to allow (and help) foster parents to adopt, and to extend medical coverage for handicapped children who would not be able to be covered by their adoptive parents' policies. No child is considered too old or too handicapped to be adopted by someone. Yet with all these noticeable improvements in the system, a look at how these children are placed indicates the influence of patriarchy.

Young, white, married couples with good incomes have the best opportunity to adopt the few healthy white babies that are available. They tend to adopt younger, healthier children. It was an innovation to allow single adults to adopt children at all, and this has been a boon to those who wish to care for and nurture children. But these persons can adopt only the most needy children (read: those children that couples don't want)—that is, children over the age of two and those of mixed race or with handicapping conditions.[15] While there is still an assumption that the best placement is with two-parent families with the wife a full-time mother, these couples generally get the children who are least in need. The children most in need go to single adults who must be mother and father to the children and are in the labor force most of the week. The system perpetuates the elitist notion that normal American families are middle-class, two-parent families with healthy children raised from birth. It is certainly helpful to the individual children that the pool of potential foster and adoptive parents has been broadened, but it has typically been done in such a way as to preserve the social order.

If the adoption system were really devoted solely to helping the children, surely the children most in need would go to the families considered best equipped to help them, families with resources such as a full-time mother and a comfortable income. Paradoxically, patriarchy is upheld through the reward system of giving infants only to families with acceptable structures.[16] Another issue with patriarchal implications is the issue of "closed" versus "open" adoptions. Until quite recently all adoptions were "closed," that is, the identity of the birth mother was kept secret from all but the placement agency. Adopted children were not allowed information about their birth parents, and birth and adoptive parents were kept ignorant of all but the most superficial facts about each other. Indeed, it has been common practice to alter birth certificates so that the earliest official record lists the adoptive parents as the real parents. There even were cases in which hospital officials incorrectly informed the birth parent of the sex of her child in order to throw her off the track in case she was tempted to search for her child.[17]

This secrecy was maintained ostensibly to protect both parties (adoptive and birth parents) from disruption by the other, and to provide maximum security for the child. However, the illegitimacy of the child and the conviction that it would be difficult if not impossible for a single woman to raise that child pervaded these activities. The stigma of being a bastard, the shame of having no father, or a father with a different name than the mother on the birth certificate, was spared the child.

At present adoptions are more nearly open than previously, for a variety of reasons. Many older children, who already know their parents and/or other relatives, are adopted, and they continue to see these blood relations from time to time. Advances in genetic research lend weight to the need for adoptees to have access to their biological families' medical histories. A great number of adult adoptees have undertaken searches for their birth parents and have also lobbied for changes in the laws that will make searches easier. Finally, so few young women are relinquishing their newborn babies for adoption and so many independent adoptions take place that agencies have added inducements to adoption for the birth mothers. It is now common, for example, for birth mothers to be given profiles of adoptive couples and to be allowed to choose among them. Nevertheless, the system still clings to the notion that bearing a child out of wedlock should be stigmatized and that child rearing by two parents is vastly superior to single parenthood.

The child welfare system, then, from preventive services to adoption services, revolves around a woman's primary role as mother and mothering as central to children's care. It also perpetuates race and class designations, favoring white middle-class families and providing differential benefits and services to nontraditional and poor families. This orientation has prevented it from developing and implementing quality services for children.

CHILD CARE

The saga of the rise and fall of day care provision in this country is a perfect illustration of how women's needs are attended to only within the restrictive contexts of patriarchy and capitalism. The need for good and affordable care for children of employed mothers is at an all time high, yet public policy has radically changed and reduced its provision in just a few short years.

Demand and Supply

The number of women in the paid labor force has been growing beyond previous predictions, especially among married women with very young children.

Labor force participation rates for women increased from 43 percent in 1970 to 55 percent in 1986. The paid labor force now includes more than 70 percent of the mothers of school-aged children. The rates for married mothers with children under age three jumped 25 percent, from 41 to 51 percent, in the six years between 1980 and 1986. As a result, married women with children under three are more likely to be in the labor force than their unmarried counterparts. It is now predicted that two-thirds of women with preschool-aged children and three-quarters of mothers with school-aged children will be in the labor force by the mid-1990s.[18]

As for the current supply of child care, it is difficult to obtain a national picture of its availability, partially because there is no official federal data collection. In addition, much care that is provided is "underground," that is, not licensed or registered, and therefore not part of any state's official records. Notwithstanding these restrictions, Alfred J. Kahn and Sheila B. Kamerman pieced together the best available information to arrive at an estimate of what exists today. They found that day care for three- to five-year olds was quantitatively adequate, but officially licensed or registered care for infants and toddlers is "in short supply." Family day care—child care in the provider's or consumer's home—is the most widely available form of care. In the past, this was often carried out by relatives, and still is to some degree, but care by relatives is declining. The supply of after-school care is also deficient in many places.[19] They estimate that more than 2 million children aged five through thirteen remain unsupervised by an adult after school.[20]

The average annual cost per family for child care is reputed to be $3,000 per child, but costs can be as much as $10,000 a year and higher.[21] A Census Bureau survey of child care use during the winter of 1984–85 cited a median weekly payment of $38, but this included payments to relatives, who generally receive less than the going rate. The Census Bureau estimated that child care costs averaged $45 to $75 per week for preschoolers and over $100 per week for center care or care by in-home housekeepers.[22] The overall estimated amount spent by employed women for child care arrangements was $11.1 billion. Child care constitutes 21–25 percent of poor families' income and 17 percent of single parents' income.[23]

Federal Child Care Policy: Pre-Reagan

Profound changes took place within the child care field during the Reagan administration. To assess the scope and impact of these changes, it is necessary to review the history of day care in the United States and picture child care before and after Reagan.

Day nurseries for working mothers were first established in the United States by wealthy women for the benefit of poor mothers who needed to be in the labor force. The first center was opened in 1838. Centers expanded after the Civil War to provide for children of war widows.[24] Social reformers during the Progressive Era at the turn of the century also established nurseries in poor neighborhoods for employed mothers. Day care was seen primarily as a social service for poor and troubled families and was primarily funded through private dona-tion.[25] Kindergarten, in contrast, begun in this country in the second half of the nineteenth century, stressed the social and educational needs of young children and operated on a part-day basis for the children of middle- and upper-income parents who could afford it.[26]

It was not until the Depression that the federal government began to subsidize day care, and then it was for the purpose of employing school personnel who were out of work. Later, during World War II the Lanham Act provided for day care centers to be established near industrial centers that needed to employ women in the defense industry. It was assumed, however, even among advocates for these centers, that day care should be used only in extenuating circumstances. Federal Children's Bureau staff even fought against making the centers too convenient because women might be tempted to keep their children in care after the war.[27]

After the war federal support was withdrawn and publicly supported day care remained in the few states and localities that chose to subsidized them. Women were encouraged to leave their jobs and return home to their rightful place. Many women did not make this retreat, however, and Congress finally acknowledged their need for child care by passing a tax deduction for child care expenses in 1954.[28] Since then there have been three types of federal subsidies for child care: tax-related provisions, subsidies for direct provision, and Head Start.

In the 1960s, Head Start, a developmental program for poor children, was launched. It was based on the belief that poor children started school already behind their middle-class counterparts and needed enrichment programs to bring them up to par before they began. Head Start was created in the tradition of developmental preschool kindergartens and adapted for disadvantaged children. However, it was never intended to serve the function of child care for employed mothers. Indeed, only 10 percent of children in Head Start today are in full-day programs.[29]

Simultaneous with their concern about bringing poor children up to par with their middle-class counterparts, Congress was faced with increasing welfare rolls and seemingly became desirous of getting welfare mothers into the labor force. Day care for poor mothers had to be a component of any such project. Thus the Public Welfare Amendments of 1962 included an authorization of day care funds to facilitate the employment of welfare mothers, and day care was included as a support service when the WIN program was established in 1967.[30]

It is noteworthy that Head Start followed the kindergarten model and did not incorporate the day nursery model as well. It was designed in such a way that parental involvement in center activities was integral to the program and timed in such a way that employed parents could not participate and in many cases could not enroll their children. It's as if the policy makers and planners thought of the Head Start population and the children of those welfare mothers who were to be prodded into working as *different* people. To this day, Head Start remains a very popular, but limited program for some lucky poor children,[31] some of whose mothers are presented with a kind of catch-22: go to work and better your family and settle for what day care you can get, or remain on welfare and let your children reap the benefits of Head Start.

As more women joined the labor force in the 1960s, federal officials, congressional leaders, and child advocates saw the need for a comprehensive bill providing funds and guidelines for the provision of quality child care throughout the county. Such a bill was hammered out and passed by the Congress in 1971, only to be vetoed by President Nixon, who suggested that "communal care" for children was un-American.[32] Similar bills were also defeated (before passage) in 1975 and 1979.[33] In 1975, well-organized smear tactics of right-wing forces resulted in thousands of letters sent to Congress protesting child care legislation that the writers felt would somehow exert "government control over the American family."[34] The opposition was so great that in 1979, when Senator Cranston tried again to get a child care bill through the Congress, even the Carter administration opposed it. President Carter had campaigned on family issues and Vice-President Mondale had been a leading advocate for child care in the Senate. Yet the administration's statement on the issue included the following:

there are those who believe that we are helping families with the funds we have committed to the care of children whose parents must work. But there are others who would argue just the reverse. They believe that providing public support for child care places government in the role of supplanting an important parental responsibility, namely the care of young children. On even so basic a question as that, there are differences; in the face of such wide divergence it is understandable that there is still no single national policy with regard to child care.[35]

Thus, in spite of the need and in spite of a variety of advocates, strong and organized opposition to comprehensive federal leadership in child care succeeded in blocking its development.[36] It is important to recognize that this opposition was soundly in force for at least ten years before Ronald Reagan became president.

Changes in the Reagan Administration

Provision. Kahn and Kamerman note that "decentralization, privatization, and deregulation became the guiding principles in federal child care policy in the 1980s."[37] The Reagan administration's child care emphasis was on what Kahn and Kamerman term "demand" subsidies, or funds made available to the consumer of services through tax breaks.[38] These policies ostensibly were calculated to encourage development of private proprietary market expansion to meet the (subsidized) demand. Cuts were made in social services funds, or direct subsidies to providers, reducing child care provision in the public and nonprofit sectors. As with other "market mechanisms," the end result was to put into place policies that would benefit higher income persons and shut out the poor and the less well off.

Tax Mechanisms. The only child care provision that actually expanded under Reagan is the Dependent Care Tax Credit (sometimes called the Child Care Tax Credit), which was increased slightly in 1981. Families can deduct from their federal income taxes between 20 and 30 percent of their costs of child care up to $2,400 for one child and $4,800 for two or more children. The maximum tax credit is 30 percent of $4,800 in expenses, or $1,440, for taxpayers with two or more children and adjusted gross incomes below $10,000 or 20 percent of $4,800, or $960, for taxpayers with two or more dependents and incomes over $28,000. In 1987 about $3.5 billion was assigned to this provision, and the cost was expected to rise to $4 billion in 1988.[39] It is now the largest single federal source of financial support for child care.[40]

The Dependent Care Tax Credit is not refundable and is most helpful to higher income families. In 1981, 4.6 million families claimed the Tax Credit; the majority (64 percent) were above the median income level and just 7 percent had incomes below $10,000.[41] Child care advocates in 1983 were successful in getting the credit added to the short income tax form (1040A) to facilitate its use by those who don't itemize. This seems to have helped to some degree, since 22 percent of the tax benefits in 1983 went to those with adjusted gross incomes under $15,000 and 62 percent went to taxpayers with annual gross incomes under $30,000.[42] Nevertheless, many families with very low incomes and low tax liabilities find it impossible to take full advantage of the credit.

The Urban Institute used microsimulation techniques to look at the distributional characteristics of the current Child Care Tax Credit and found it to be highly regressive. Just 3 percent of the total credit awarded goes to families in the lowest 30 percent of income distribution. One-quarter goes to families in the bottom half. A full 75 percent goes to families in the top half of income distribution.[43] Two-thirds of the total amount assigned for the credit goes to two-parent families. Among single-parent families, half of the credit amounts are assigned to those in the bottom half of income distribution. Yet just 10 percent of the credits go to families in the lowest third.[44]

Another child care tax benefit is employer-provided Dependent Care Assistance Plans (DCAPs). It allows employers to deduct from a worker's wages up to $5,000 that is set aside for child care and is excluded from federal income tax liabilities. Voluntary salary reduction by employees as part of a "cafeteria plan" of employee benefits is the most popular form of this benefit. However, most employees, particularly those with low incomes, are not covered by these plans, and those who are often cannot afford to put aside money for child care.[45] The estimated cost for this, and plans in which employers provide more direct assistance, is about $110 million in forgone revenues.[46]

The DCAP provisions also allow employers to provide vouchers for services, on-site care, or information and referral services; most employers have not engaged in these activities and those that do are generally minimally involved. Nationwide only about 3,000 employers (0.5 percent of all employers) provide any kind of child care assistance; of these, few provide on-site care or vouchers.[47] A 1985 survey of medium and large firms found that only 1 percent of the workers were entitled to some form of child care subsidy as a fringe benefit. The bottom line is that employers do not see a need for child care provision or subsidies, since they have a ready supply of labor without them; only 20 percent of the current work force consists of parents with young children.[48]

Recent changes in the tax law, effective in 1989, will make child care tax benefits somewhat less beneficial and harder to obtain. Henceforth a taxpayer who excludes dependent care expenses under a DCAP must offset, dollar for dollar, the amount that has been excluded under the DCAP from the amount that can be claimed under the credit. Previously a taxpayer with two children and a year's bill of $6,000 of child care expenses could have $5,000 of tax free dollars withheld from her salary for child care *and* claim the tax credit for the other $1,000 of expenses. Since the maximum that can be claimed under the credit is $4,800, and more than this amount has been used for the DCAP, the taxpayer may no longer claim the credit for the remaining $1,000.[49] This new change will affect higher income parents who have access to a DCAP and spend more than $5,000 per year on child care.

Another change includes lowering the age limit for children for whom dependent care expenses can be claimed, from 15 down to 13. Also, taxpayers who claim the credit or participate in a DCAP will be required to furnish the name, address, and taxpayer identification number of the person providing the dependent care service. This will severely restrict the use of family day care providers who are unwilling to operate unless they can avoid reporting their income to the Internal Revenue Service. If one assumes that these providers charge less than licensed providers, it may also increase the cost of care for some parents.

AFDC Disregard. Another "tax" measure that was changed by the Reagan administration was the amount of child care expenses that could be disregarded in calculating the AFDC benefits of employed AFDC recipients. Before the Omnibus Budget Reconciliation Act of 1981, designed by the Reagan administration, child care costs were included in "work expenses" and the amount that could be disregarded was to be "reasonably attributable to the earning of income."[50] In 1981 OBRA separated the child care expense allowance and capped it at a maximum allowable amount of $160 per month per child.[51] The change has been noticeable. In 1980 the AFDC child care disregard paid for $120 million in child care costs; by 1986 child care payments under this provision were down to $35 million.[52] A Massachusetts study attributed changes among AFDC mothers to less formal care or even leaving children alone due to the increased out-of-pocket costs that resulted from this change.[53]

The Family Support Act of 1988 increased the AFDC child care disregard from $160 to $175 per child per month and to $200 for children under age two.

This is an improvement only if one can imagine that adequate child care can be provided for as little as $8.75 to $10 per day.

Direct Subsidies. OBRA cut by 20 percent the social services funds of Title XX of the Social Security Act, the major source of federal services funds to the states. It also eliminated the obligation for states to match federal Title XX dollars in a 25-75 ratio.[54] In response, many states severely restricted or eliminated their child care programs in favor of more urgently needed services such as protective services for abused and neglected children, already operating at minimum levels—32 states cut child care staffs, 33 lowered their standards, and 24 decreased training programs in order to save money.[55]

The AFDC disregard became more important because of the cut in Title XX funds. Many mothers lost their Title XX funded day care and were forced to try to find care under the $160 limit. Forcing the children of AFDC mothers out of Title XX-provided day care was expedient for the states, which could then divert the "saved" Title XX monies into other social services. Evelyn Moore reports that a study of the problem found that for working families forced on to the disregard, continuing Title XX-type care would amount to individual income losses as high as $125 a month, "obviously an impossible sum for poor families."[56] AFDC families were placed in the untenable position of either trying to pay for child care out of their other benefits or trying to find child care priced at $8 per day! Ironically, the federal government, which funds most of the AFDC benefit, also incurs some cost at the state's Title XX savings.[57]

Standards. Standards for out-of-home day care for children began in the late nineteenth and early twentieth centuries and were slow in developing.[58] Initial regulations focused on health and safety features and were poorly administered. Standards were developed by the Children's Bureau in 1942 that included suggested adult-child ratios and provisions for affectionate care and appropriate play activities and supplies. Concern among child advocates and government officials about the regulation of day care culminated in the development of the Federal Interagency Day Care Requirements (FIDCR) in 1968. These standards were to apply to all day care agencies receiving federal monies. After they were developed, the FIDCR were a constant source of controversy, primarily owing to their low staff-child ratio requirements. Since child care services are labor-intensive, staff-child ratios have a great impact on the cost of providing service. Child development advocates pushed for FIDCR's enforcement while providers, threatening that they would have to close their doors if they were enforced, enlisted the aid of some parents in protesting their enforcement. Between 1968 and 1980, the FIDCR were periodically suspended by Congress as the controversy wore on and studies were made to test the importance of their provisions. Finally, a compromise was struck that set standards that were acceptable to all.

A study of the FIDCR policy process in children's issues, published in 1982, stated: "Presumably by 1982, the Federal Interagency Day Care Requirements will, 14 years after the first set was promulgated, be enforced for the first time."[59] Unfortunately, this statement proved to be too optimistic. For with the election of Ronald Reagan as president, almost overnight all of the arguments, meetings, and memos ground to a halt.

The Omnibus Budget Reconciliation Act of 1981, strong-armed through the Congress by the Reagan administration, eliminated federal day care standards in a single stroke.[60] The FIDCR were dead and with their demise federal concern over the issue of standards for day care ceased. Currently, no federal agency is even officially concerned with such standards. As Kahn and Kamerman note: "A federal 'presence' in child care has disappeared. Except for the Head Start program, there is no federal agency with child care responsibility and no child care staff."[61]

The rationale for eliminating the FIDCR was adherence to a philosophy of decentralization—that is, the conviction that such responsibility should rest in the states. However, states had followed the federal lead over the years and, in spite of the fact that the FIDCR weren't enforced, had improved their services in anticipation of the imposition of higher standards. Kahn and Kamerman report that with the withdrawal of federal concern, some states have cut back on their monitoring activities and, in the family day care field, some states have eased requirements in order to encourage the development of an increased supply.[62]

Current Situation

The Reagan administration and the Congress did not abandon child care in the 1980s. It simply shifted benefits to middle- and upper-income families. In so doing, it helped further its goal of privatization and market mechanisms for the provision of child care. As Kahn and Kamerman report:

The heads of several proprietary chains have indicated that the child care tax credit was a special boon to their companies since it provided an indirect public subsidy to providers who were largely unable or unwilling to serve children from low-income families and who would never have qualified for Title XX funds under proposed standards or been eligible under policies in many states.[63]

As a result of this mechanism, the availability of child care has increased. This has little meaning, however, for low-income parents who cannot afford the fees. Large commercial chains have reported as much as 20 percent vacancy rates attributable to fees that exceed what some parents can afford to pay. What we have now is less choice and less diversity for the poor, while proprietary chains, which focus their locations and marketing plans on two-earner, middle-class families, have grown tremendously.[64]

The 1988 Family Support Act does increase federal involvement in child day care provision from the zero involvement it arrived at in 1981, but by no means restores or implies a return to federal leadership. The most important child care provision is the open-ended funding for child care for children of JOBS program participants. Since child care may be extended to participants beyond their time in the program, this may prove to be very helpful to them and also serve as an incentive for increased supplies of this care.

As for quality, the Family Support Act also requires states to establish procedures to assure that center-based care meet health and safety standards and to "endeavor to develop guidelines" for family day care. The bill authorizes $13 million in FY 1990 and 1991 for grants to states to improve child care licensing and registration requirements and to monitor care provided to AFDC children. Nevertheless, child care standards remain a local matter. Moreover, proposed regulations recently released by the Bush administration's Department of Health and Human Services stress the use of free "informal" sources of child care.[65]

Current Proposals

At this writing, there are two child care bills floating in Congress. They attempt to combine features from two approaches. The Bush administration proposed a modification of the dependent care tax credit. It would provide a refundable credit of up to $1,000 for each child under the age of four in families in which at least one parent was in the labor force with incomes up to $13,000 per year. It does not directly subsidize child care, would include families in which the mother stayed home, and would apply to child care provided by relatives or friends. The president has referred to it as a plan based on "parental choice," ironically reminiscent of the abortion choice movement.[66] The bill has been criticized as very inadequate. It is estimated that it would cover less than 2 percent of the population.[67]

In contrast to the Bush proposal, the Act for Better Child Care Services (ABC bill) would provide direct child care subsidies to families with children up to the age of 15 whose income did not exceed the median in the state. It would also set minimum federal standards for day care providers, giving them six years to comply.[68] This bill has wide acceptance among child advocates and a fair amount of bipartisan support.

It is believed that with such interest in child care among legislators in both parties and the administration new legislation will come out by the end of the congressional session in the fall of 1989. Yet President Bush is already threatening to veto it. Child care continues to be a volatile issue and, judging from past experience, no child care bill is a sure thing.

Costs for Women

It is noteworthy that solving some women's child care problems has exacerbated the problems of low wages for women's work. Most of the approximately 2.03 million child care workers in the United States, 96 percent of whom are women, make less than $10,000 a year.[69] In family day care, the most frequently used type of care, the providers make even less. Providers work below minimum wage and often put in 12-hour work days. Even when they get paid "under the table" to avoid taxes, their income remains below market wages.[70] Although much of this care is informal, that is, unlicensed and unrecognized, experts estimate that there are 1.5 million providers caring for 5 million children, "mostly in unregulated care," and constituting about 60 to 90 percent of the supply of all child care.[71] Purportedly only about 40 percent of this care is provided by relatives.[72]

Family day care promises to provide motherly care in a home atmosphere, although there is evidence of frequent turnover of providers and some parental dissatisfaction.[73] Also, Black parents tend to prefer center care or home care by relatives.[74] Yet family day care is convenient and, perhaps above all, cheap. Women fighting for fair and equitable wages in the workplace often do not feel the same way about the wages they pay to their family day care providers.

The new tax law will likely serve to speed the process of professionalization, licensure, and registration of family day care. Once they are prevented from earning money "under the table," providers will have less reason to avoid state registration or licensure and are also likely to raise their prices. Those who do not wish to be more established in the business of child care may cease to provide service except to the few parents who are willing to forgo the tax break (and some may, if the price is cheap enough).[75]

ANALYSIS

Adequate affordable child care for all parents who want it would remove a crucial barrier to women's employment and women's independence. Such provision, however, would be very threatening to patriarchy and also to capitalism. Day care is a threat to patriarchy in that it is a threat to male control—it promotes women's independence. It strikes at the heart of the patriarchal definition of mothering as the only acceptable source of child care. It is a threat to conventional marriage, since it aids women's advancement in the world of work. It is a threat to capitalism, in that it removes one additional excuse to keep women in low-paying positions. Insofar as it might allow women to work longer hours with less worry, it is a threat to male supremacy in the work force.

Notwithstanding these threats, day care is becoming more widely available as women demand it. Yet it is consistent with patriarchal necessity that the greatest growth in the availability and affordability of day care in recent years has been most helpful to married, middle- and upper-income women, who are within the bounds of patriarchal marriage. At a time when the entire nation seems very concerned, even frenzied, about poor single parents and the need to get them into the labor force and off the welfare rolls, the federal government has reduced one of the major means of achieving this goal. The women who need subsidies the most, single mothers, have seen a diminution of their access to day care. Patriarchal necessity demands that they not be afforded a comfortable existence outside masculinist control, and day care would aid this endeavor.

The elimination of federal involvement in day care standards is also functional to patriarchy in that the entire burden of choosing adequate care, not to mention figuring out what adequacy is, is placed on individual women.[76] The state provides little to enhance or ensure her piece of mind. Her worthiness as a mother then is judged in her choice of child care. There is no official help with this private decision.[77]

Day care's impact on children is also a threat to traditional notions of family and motherhood. Meyer suggests that day care introduces to children a more expanded sense of socialization and sharing, acceptance of the "population mix of their society," and a different understanding of care and protection. She states: "It is the feminist perspective that allows for a different kind of understanding of day care through its redefinition of the rigid and stereotyped boundaries of the idea of parenting or mothering."[78] Children growing up in day care might indeed come to accept as commonplace the notion that a variety of persons can offer love and protection and educational experiences to children. This is not a brand new idea. Up to the nineteenth century this is how children grew up and, indeed, many wealthy children still grow up in the care of persons in addition to their parents. If one considers that day care might usher in a new (or renewed) conception of what it means to be a mother, it is not surprising that a great deal of the research on day care has focused on whether it causes damage to the mother-child bond.[79]

The new interest in child care in Washington is in response to a crescendo of demand throughout the country. Yet the Bush administration's proposal clings to the preservation of the patriarchal family and the sacred bond of motherhood, citing choice and informal care. The provision of adequate well-regulated child care would not only be expensive but would threaten the social construction of motherhood as women's central responsibility.

The child care debate is also a class issue for feminist women. If we increase the availability of child care for white middle class children by providing poorly paying jobs for poor women of color and white women, we have achieved a degree of equality for some women at the expense of other women, playing out the notion that feminism is about white women's sharing in the privileges of white men. Making this point, Bell Hooks quotes Toni Morrison:

(It is a source of amusement even now to black women to listen to feminist talk of liberation while somebody's nice black grandmother shoulders the daily responsibility of child rearing and floor mopping, and the liberated one comes home to examine the housekeeping, correct it, and be entertained by the children.) If Women's Lib needs those grandmothers to thrive, it has a serious flaw.[80]

If the white women's movement fails to fight for adequate pay for child care workers it will be echoing the moral failure to which some white feminist leaders were prone in the debates about suffrage for Black men versus Black and white women. Compromising in this way would be economical and convenient for many middle- and upper-income women but would not only be morally reprehensible but also play into the hands of patriarchy. Patriarchy has a stake, after all, in perpetuating its brand of motherhood, all the while devaluing the work that it involves. That is the reason that child carers get paid so little in the first place. Paying women who care for other people's children adequate wages would not only be helpful to the child carers but would change the value and nature of motherhood altogether.

Sheila Kamerman has noted that until recently feminists have avoided taking on the issue of child care for fear that their doing so would reinforce the notion of women's role as sole child carers.[81] She accurately suggests that the child care issue is a catch-22 for women. If women want change, they are going to have to arrange it. Children are hostages between women's aspirations to change and expand their roles and patriarchy's refusal to help them do it, even if it means inadequate care for children. If women turn their backs on the issue they may, in a sense, be relinquishing the qualities of care and relatedness that theorists recognize as more characteristic of women's development. On the other hand, if they wholeheartedly take on the issue of child care as their own, they are reinforcing traditional notions of the responsibilities of motherhood and letting society, as it were, off the hook, with regard to broader change.

One could argue, though, that however increased child care provisions are obtained, both women and children will benefit. Having removed this basic barrier to social change, women would be free to move on to advocate other changes. Perhaps children would grow up with new notions of motherhood and parenting. But it is these new notions that underlie the reluctance of the patriarchal state to embrace wholeheartedly public child care provisions.

Chapter 7 will address the influence of patriarchy in the treatment of older women in the Social Security system.

NOTES

1. Carol H. Meyer, "A Feminist Perspective on Foster Family Care: A Redefinition of the Categories," *Child Welfare* 64, no. 3 (May–June 1985): 250.

2. See Alfred Kadushin, "Child Welfare Services," in *Encyclopedia of Social Work*, 18th edition (Silver Spring, MD: National Association of Social Workers, 1987), 268. Day care is no longer classified under the substitute care category.

3. Meyer, 251.

4. Ibid.

5. Dr. Raymond C. Collins, "Foster Care Rates: Trends and Implications," *Washington Social Legislation Bulletin* 30, Issue 16 (August 1987): 61.

6. Ibid., 61–62.

7. Ibid., 64.

8. Martin Wolins, "The Gender Dilemma in Social Welfare: Who Cares for the Children?" in *Fatherhood and Family Policy*, eds. Michael E. Lamb and Abraham Sagi (Hillsdale, NJ: Lawrence Erlbaum, 1983), 124.

9. Meyer, 257.

10. Ibid., 256.

11. It has also led to a greater emphasis on research in birth technology that will produce, in one way or another, white babies for childless white couples.

12. Joseph Goldstein, Anna Freud, and Albert J. Solnit, *Beyond the Best Interests of the Child* (New York: The Free Press, 1973).

13. Andrew Billingsley and Jeanne M. Giovannoni, *Children of the Storm: Black Children and American Child Welfare* (New York: Harcourt Brace Jovanovich, 1972).

14. Jane Knitzer and Mary Lee Allen, *Children Without Homes* (Washington, D.C.: Children's Defense Fund, 1978).

15. Wolins, 116.

16. However, for many couples none of the children available in the United States fill the bill; they want infants and infants can be obtained from other countries (for a fee).

17. Personal communication with a woman to whom this happened.

18. Alfred J. Kahn and Sheila B. Kamerman, *Child Care: Facing the Hard Choices* (Dover, MA: Auburn House Publishing Company, 1987), 11–12, 95.

19. Ibid., 13–14.

20. NOW Legal Defense and Education Fund, "Facts on Child Care," (Washington, D.C.: NOW Legal Defense and Education Fund, 1988), 2.

21. Ibid.

22. "Census Bureau Reports on Child Care Arrangements, Winter 1984–85," *Washington Social Legislation Bulletin*, 30, Issue 12 (June 1987): 47.

23. "Facts on Child Care," 2.

24. Jill Norgren, "Child Care," in *Women: A Feminist Perspective*, 3rd edition, ed. Jo Freeman (Palo Alto, CA: Mayfield, 1984), 142.

25. See Anna Mayer, *Day Care as a Social Instrument* (New York: Columbia University School of Social Work, 1965).

26. Norgren, 142.

27. Ibid., 142–43.

28. John R. Nelson, "The Politics of Federal Day Care Regulations," in *Day Care: Scientific and Social Policy Issues*, eds. Edward F. Zigler and Edmund W. Gordon (Dover, MA: Auburn House Publishing Company, 1982), 269.

29. Kahn and Kamerman, 21.

30. Nelson, 270–73.

31. Head Start serves about 16 percent of eligible children. See "Facts on Child Care," 1.

32. For a thorough discussion of the development of this bill and its defeat see Gilbert Y. Steiner, *The Children's Cause* (Washington, D.C.: The Brookings Institution, 1976), Chapter 5, "The Politics of Comprehensive Legislation," 90–117.

33. Rochelle Beck, "Beyond the Stalemate in Child Care Public Policy," in Zigler and Gordon, 308.

34. Gilbert Y. Steiner, *The Futility of Family Policy* (Washington, D.C.: The Brookings Institution, 1981), 91.

35. Ibid., 94, quoting Arabella Martinez [HEW assistant secretary for Human Development Services], "Statement before the Senate Subcommittee on Child and Human Development," February 21, 1979, 8.

36. Beck, 309.

37. Kahn and Kamerman, 3.

38. Ibid., 94.

39. Roberta Otts Barnes, *The Distributional Effects of Alternative Child Care Proposals* (Washington, D.C.: The Urban Institute, 1988), 2.

40. Kahn and Kamerman, 21, 95–96.

41. Ibid.

42. Ibid., 97.

43. Barnes, 4.

44. Ibid., 5.

45. Kahn and Kamerman, 197–98.

46. Ibid., 21, 97.

47. "Facts on Child Care," 1.

48. Kahn and Kamerman, 198–99.

49. "Changes in the Dependent Care Tax Programs," *Washington Social Legislation Bulletin* 30, Issue 47 (December 1988): 187. This article was prepared by the National Women's Law Center for the *Bulletin*. The article also points out that under the new law, the credit will likely become more attractive to taxpayers in the 15 percent (low income) tax bracket because of the higher tax (20–30 percent) tax savings. For higher earners in the 28 percent bracket, the opposite will probably be true. See also Kahn and Kamerman, 197–98.

50. House of Representatives, Committee on Ways and Means, *Background Material and Data on Programs Within the Jurisdiction of the Committee on Ways and Means* (Washington, D. C.: U.S. Government Printing Office, 1984), 308.

51. Other work expenses were also capped, at $75 per month.

52. Kahn and Kamerman, 97. This drop can also be partially attributed to the fact that many working mothers on AFDC were dropped from the rolls entirely as a result of OBRA.

53. Ibid., 105.

54. "October 1 Block Grant Rules Define Federal-State Transaction," *Washington Social Legislation Bulletin*, 27, Issue 20 (October 1981): 78. See also Kahn and Kamerman, 20, who also point out that the child care food program, since restored, was also cut drastically by OBRA. Furthermore the elimination of public service employment under the Comprehensive Employment and Training Act ended CETA subsidized staffing for day care.

55. Kahn and Kamerman, 22, citing Helen Blank, *Children and Federal Child Care Cuts* (Washington, D.C.: Children's Defense Fund, 1983), 5–7.

56. Evelyn Moore, "Day Care: A Black Perspective," in Zigler and Gordon, 430.

57. Ibid.

58. For a thorough history of day care standards and regulations up to 1980 see Nelson. For recent history of day care regulations, Kahn and Kamerman pick up where Nelson leaves off.

59. Cheryl D. Hayes (ed.), *Making Policies for Children: A Study of the Federal Process* (Washington, D.C.: National Academy Press, 1982), 27.

60. Kahn and Kamerman, 106.

61. Ibid., 23.

62. Ibid., 259.

63. Ibid., 99.

64. Ibid., 100–1, 105. They note that for lower income families school systems are slowly taking up some of the slack, especially for three-five year olds and school-aged

children, but not for infants. See Chapter 5, in which they discuss school sponsored child care.

65. Kenneth J. Cooper, "Bush to Propose Leeway for States in Crafting Welfare Work Programs," *The Philadelphia Inquirer*, April 1989.

66. Bernard Weintraub, "Bush Proposes Tax Credits to Aid Child Care," *New York Times*, March 16, 1989.

67. Jerry Estill, "Bush and Senators Offer Child-Care Plans," *The Philadelphia Inquirer*, March 16, 1989.

68. Ibid.

69. "Facts on Child Care," 2. Other estimates of the number of child care workers range between 1 million and 3.4 million. See: "In Whose Hands?" (Hand-out No. 760) (Washington, D. C.: National Association for the Care of Young Children, 1985): 1.

70. Kahn and Kamerman, 222.

71. Ibid., 204.

72. "Facts on Child Care," 2.

73. Kahn and Kamerman, 209.

74. Moore, 417.

75. I have heard of parents who will forgo this benefit in order to keep their chosen situation, either because of quality or convenience or both. In some cases it is also possible that the care is already so economical that switching to a higher priced provider would cancel out the tax benefit.

76. Even in two-parent families, it is the wife who is responsible for the child care arrangements. See Sheila B. Kamerman, *Parenting in an Unresponsive Society* (New York: The Free Press, 1980), 63–64.

77. Child advocacy and parent groups have issued a variety of local and state publications to help parents make this choice. Nevertheless, ensuring quality of care is not a matter of public policy.

78. Meyer, 253–54.

79. Michael Rutter, "Social-Emotional Consequences of Day Care for Preschool Children," in Zigler and Gordon, 4. In fact, research has shown that children's bonds with their parents are not disturbed by day care and day care need not be deleterious to children's growth and development (p. 22). Outcomes may depend, of course, on the quality of the day care provided as well as the emotional maturity of the parents and their relationship with the child. See also Kahn and Kamerman, 16–17. Their review of the literature agrees with this assessment, with the possible exception of infant care. They cite one expert who doubts the advisability of center care for infants under one year of age.

80. Bell Hooks, *Feminist Theory: From Margin to Center* (Boston: South End Press, 1984) quoting Toni Morrison, "What the Black Woman Thinks about Women's Lib," *New York Times Magazine*, August 22, 1971, 50.

81. Sheila B. Kamerman, "Child Care Services: An Issue for Gender Equity and Women's Solidarity," *Child Welfare* 64, no. 3 (May–June 1985):261. See also Steiner, 1976.

7

Social Security and Women's Lives

Not until the relationship is broken by death, desertion, or divorce do [women] find that their relationship with the male world was not all that good after all.[1]

Older women in society are not free from the dictates of patriarchy. Patriarchal necessity operates through public policies to disadvantage the large numbers of older women who are unmarried. Older women are more likely to be poor than older men and are more likely to rely on public programs as a source of their subsistence. Yet the major public program that provides income to the elderly, Social Security, is constructed in such a way that men are more apt to benefit from it.

This chapter will address the gender-related dysfunctions and inequities of the Social Security system, notably Old Age, Survivor's, and Disability Insurance (OASDI), to the circumstances of women's lives. Various suggestions for reforming the system will be reviewed as well as policy makers' responses to these potential reforms. The Medicare program, the major publicly provided health insurance program for the older population, will not be included in the discussion.

OLDER WOMEN AND POVERTY

Older women outnumber men in total numbers (six out of ten elderly are women)[2] and numbers in poverty. Currently 72 percent of our elderly poor are women.[3] The poverty rate for women over 65, 15.2 percent, is 80 percent higher than for men of the same age.[4] Married couples are best off financially, followed by unmarried men and unmarried women. The poverty rate for married couples aged 65 or older in 1986 was 6 percent, compared with 16 percent for unmarried men and 22 percent for unmarried women. Among the Black elderly the poverty rate for married couples was 18 percent, for unmarried men 35 percent, and 43 percent for unmarried women. The comparable figures for persons of Spanish origin were 14 percent, 28, percent and 32 percent.[5] The median retirement income for married couples over 65 in 1986 was $15,240, compared with $7,870 for unmarried men and $6,500 for unmarried women.[6]

Unmarried older women, because of women's greater life expectancy, far outnumber unmarried men. More than half of women between the ages of 65 and 74 are unmarried (widowed, divorced, separated, or never married) while almost 80 percent of men of the same age are married and living with their spouses.[7] Chances are that a woman will be a widow before age 65 and live alone for 10 to 20 more years. The older women get, the more likely they are to live alone. Of those over 75, 51 percent of women live alone compared with 19 percent of men.[8]

Older women tend to have fewer sources of income than men do. About 70 percent of older single women rely on Social Security as their main source of income.[9] Men's private pensions sometimes have no provision for survivor's benefits, or the couple may opt out of them in favor of higher benefits during the husband's lifetime. On their own, women are less likely to work in jobs that carry pension benefits. In 1982 private pensions went to 33 percent of older married couples, 24 percent of nonmarried men, and just 13 percent of non-married women.[10] However, even women who do have several sources of income, including such things as Social Security, pensions, and assets, generally have less income from each source than men do. Moreover, since women live longer than men, they have more years over which to stretch any savings they may have.

Among Social Security beneficiaries, single women receive the lowest benefits. Table 1 shows the median benefits for white, Black, and Spanish origin couples and unmarried persons (widowed, divorced, separated, and never married) in 1986.

It is noteworthy that the lowest median yearly benefit income went to Black women, who tend to be in the labor force full time and more consistently than white women, and are more likely to collect their own benefits as workers rather than as spouses.[11] Although the Social Security system is tied to labor force participation, for women this participation may not result in better benefits. Black women's lower benefits are the result of more frequent employment in occupations not covered by Social Security, their low compensation in the covered jobs that they do obtain, and their husbands' low benefit amounts.[12] The system tends to work better for some populations than others; low-income persons of color and single white women fare much less well than white males and their

Table 1
Median Income from Social Security Benefits for Beneficiaries Aged 65 or Older by Race and Spanish Origin, 1986

	Married Couples	Nonmarried Men	Nonmarried Women
White	9260.	5850.	5250.
Black	6700.	5330.	3690.
Spanish Origin	7440.	4880.	3860.

Source: U.S. Department of Health and Human Services, Social Security Administration, Office of Policy, Office of Research and Statistics, by Susan Grad, *Income of the Population 55 and Older*, SSA Publication No. 13-11871, 1988, T. 26, p. 64.
Note: Amounts are rounded to the nearest $10.

live-in spouses. Thus, a system intended to compensate to some degree for societal financial disadvantages tends to perpetuate them.

BACKGROUND

The Social Security insurance program is the most generous and the most expensive social program in the United States today.[13] Funded through payroll taxes paid by workers and employers, it provides protection against the risks of loss of income due to death, disability, or retirement.[14] Benefits are related to the past earnings of covered workers and are adjusted for increases in the cost of living. Families of workers as well as workers themselves are afforded protections.

Signed into law by President Franklin D. Roosevelt in 1935, the original plan for the Social Security system tied retirement benefits to a worker's participation in the labor force. It was designed to be an old age annuity, funded by payroll taxes paid by employees and employers. The longer a worker was employed (in jobs covered by Social Security) and paid Social Security taxes and the more money he or she earned, the larger the benefit. However, the element of adequacy, the principle of providing a benefit that bears some relationship to potential or probable need, was also part of the original design.

To make the benefit more adequate for lower income workers, the benefit formula was weighted to return a larger proportion of previous income (a higher replacement rate) to lower wage earners.[15] Notwithstanding this provision, however, at the beginning most low-wage workers were not included in the program at all. Covered workers, representing about 58 percent of all paid employment at the time, included those in commerce or industry, excepting railroad employees.[16] Occupations excluded were disproportionately made up of minority men and women and white women workers.[17] It was not until 1950 and afterward that additional occupations were gradually included in the system.[18]

The Social Security system was changed significantly before any benefits were paid. In 1939 dependents and survivors' provisions became part of the system, extending benefits to include coverage for the worker's dependents, another bow to the adequacy principle. Thus, protection against the risk of loss of earned income due to retirement was provided not only for workers but also for families, through their breadwinners, generally the husband and father. A worker's benefit, or Primary Insurance Amount (PIA), was to be paid in full at age 65. A wife was entitled to one half of her husband's benefit, so the couple could receive a maximum of 150 percent of the PIA.[19] If she had worked in covered employment she could get her own PIA or the spousal benefit, whichever was greater. A protection against the risk of the death of the breadwinner was also provided for families.[20] This extension of benefits was based on the accurate view of most women, albeit middle-class white women, as wives and homemakers, economically dependent on their husbands.

In 1940, only one in four women, and just 17 percent of married women,[21] were in the labor force. Only 3 out of 20 households in that year had both the husband and wife in the labor force at the same time.[22] It was generally expected that husbands would provide financial support for their wives and children. A logical extension of this expectation was to design the Social Security system to extend this support to survivors and retiring spouses through their husbands' and fathers' Social Security earnings credits. It is significant, however, that the framers were more concerned with the well-being of wives of mostly white male covered workers than they were with women workers and men and women minority workers, most of whom were left uncovered altogether.

With regard to wives, it was expected that they would join the paid labor force in increasing numbers, earning their own credits rather than having to rely on their husbands' credits for coverage.[23] A simple transition would take place.[24] Little thought was given to the fact that women's participation in the labor force does not resemble men's. In fact the transition to women earning their own credits as workers did not result in benefits for women as adequate as that provided for men.

First, women are concentrated in low-paying occupations with median earnings approximately 65 percent of men's median earnings. Benefits are thus lower for women workers, even though weighting gives them, as low earners, a higher proportion of preretirement earnings than higher wage earners. Second, women's labor force participation is broken up by the responsibility of rearing children. Women's years of employment average 23 years compared to 40 years for men.[25] Dropping out of the labor force for intermittent periods of time deprives women of continuous earnings records resulting in lower benefits. The dichotomy of the career woman versus the housewife and mother is a myth. Women take on one or both roles at different times according to their individual and family circumstances. A third unforseen factor affecting women's coverage is the rising divorce rate. Framers of the act assumed that most couples would remain together through retirement, and considered married persons' benefits supplementing their spouses' benefits. Finally, women live longer than men and are likely to be alone in old age and have more years over which to stretch any retirement savings.

These differences between men's and women's lives form the basis of why today the system does not work as well for women as it does for men. Men's experiences of labor force participation are assumed to be the norm, and the system has been designed to accommodate them.

PROBLEMS AND SOLUTIONS

Some of the specific areas of the system that have been found to be dysfunctional, along with some incremental changes that would alleviate existing problems, will be described in this section.[26]

Homemakers/Mothers

Social Security benefits are based on a worker's average adult lifetime earnings beginning when one is 21, or after 1951, whichever was later, and the year before one reaches age 62. Years out of the labor force during one's adult years count as zero in the averaging, with the exception of the five years of lowest (or no) earnings. The computation period will be 35 years (40 years minus 5) for those reaching age 62 in 1991 or later. Thus, one will have had to have 35 years of covered employment to avoid any "zero" years averaged in.

For a woman, the five drop-out years are frequently the times she left work to have children and care for them. She is disadvantaged immediately because taking five years out of the labor force uses up, as it were, the opportunity that she might have had of discounting the five years of beginning salary in a career. The situation is often worse than this, however, since a woman often has more than five years out of the labor force for caretaking responsibilities; these additional years add zero years to her record.

An intermittent labor force work pattern for women has persisted in spite of women's increased labor force participation. In 1980, 43 percent of women between the ages of 21 and 29 who had ever been employed took at least six months off from work for family reasons. This time out accounted for, on average, 21 percent of the women's potential work years out of the work force; while the comparable figure for men was 4.5 percent.[27] An Urban Institute simulation predicts that only 39 percent of women between 62 and 69 in the year 2030 will have averaged 35 or more years in covered employment. Today most men are in the labor force for more than 35 years.[28]

One incremental measure that would have an immediate impact upon this problem would be to allow additional "drop-out years" for child caring and dependent care for other relatives. This could easily be calculated and could be used by either wife, husband, or in some combination. "Homemaker credits" for both homemaking and child care, funded by general revenues or paid by the homemaker at the self-employed rate, have also been suggested. This proposal is problematic because of the difficulty of defining who would qualify as a homemaker, however, and self-employed contributions would make the plan prohibitive to those who might need it the most. A more comprehensive solution, simply providing for a shorter averaging period, 10 to 20 years, would have the advantage of helping all persons who are likely to be unemployed frequently during adulthood. This includes minority men as well as minority women and white women. It would make the system conform to the way people live rather than to the employment histories of an elite group.

Another dysfunction of the system for married women workers who take time out of the labor force is the "recency of work" test for disability benefits. Under current law, workers must have worked five of the previous ten years to qualify for disability benefits. A woman could work in covered employment for as many as ten years, take ten years to bear and raise children, and be unable to receive disability benefits. Homemakers who have not worked in paid employment covered by the system are not eligible for disability benefits at all. Extending disability benefits to homemakers would solve the problem; liberalizing the recency of work test would be a helpful incremental measure.

Homemakers are also left out of the system's survivor provisions, in spite of the fact that the costs of replacing housework and child care are considerable. Some survivor provision for homemakers would help remedy this serious gap.

Divorced Women

Divorced women are the worst off among Social Security beneficiaries and their numbers are growing. Computer simulations indicate that by the year 2030 one-third of women over age 65 (compared with 10 percent today) will be divorced.[29]

Divorced women whose ex-husbands are alive are entitled to the same 50 percent of the worker's retirement benefit that is accorded wives.[30] However, spouses' benefits for divorced persons are not payable unless the marriage lasted at least ten years. About eight in ten women meet this requirement.[31] When their ex-husbands are deceased, they receive the same amount as widows, 100 percent of the worker's benefit. One problem is that the 50 percent spouse's benefit, intended as a supplement, is generally insufficient for a divorced or separated spouse living apart from the worker spouse. However, the problem of low benefits for divorced women is also related to their wages and work records.

Few divorced women actually receive only a spouse's benefit. In 1980–81, only 0.05 percent received just these benefits. Of divorced women retiring in 1980–81, the majority, 66 percent, received benefits based solely on their own earnings credits."[32] However, the rest were "dually entitled" to their own benefits plus the difference between the worker's benefit and half of the spouse benefit. Thus, 34 percent of divorced women received the same benefit they would have received if they had just been entitled to a spouse's benefit.

To help those women who are disadvantaged by virtue of their divorced status, a limited solution would be to reduce the ten-year duration of marriage requirement. Another remedy would be to increase the retired spouse's benefits just for divorced spouses, perhaps paying 75 or 100 percent of the worker's PIA. Another remedy would be to allow divorced women to collect their own worker's retirement benefit as well as the spouse's benefit, with the spouse's benefit reduced somewhat if the worker's benefit reaches maximum levels.

Young Widows

Benefits are not provided for nondisabled surviving spouses under age 60 unless they are caring for children. Since the average age of widowhood in the United States is 56 years, this creates the widow's gap, the time between the death of the spouse and the age at which survivor's benefits can be collected. In 1983 there were 2 million widows under the age of 60; 1.25 million of them could not qualify for Social Security benefits because they were not caring for a child under age 16.[33] Also, benefits begun at age 60 are permanently reduced by 71.5 percent from what they would be if the beneficiaries waited until age 65 to collect.[34]

Two remedies for the widow's gap would be to pay widow's benefits before age 60 (perhaps age 50), or pay a spouse's adjustment benefit for one or two years, providing some income while the widow finds employment. It could be subject to an earnings test, which would confine the benefit to persons with little or no previous earnings.

Aged Widows

Aged widows depend primarily on Social Security for support, tend to have little earning capacity because of advanced age, and their chances of being poor increase with advancing age.[35] A great deal of concern has been focused on this population, sometimes called the "old old," and considered among the most worthy of help. Options for helping them include: increase benefits for the very aged beneficiaries; provide full, unreduced benefits for survivors at age 60 or 62 instead of the current age of 65; permit the surviving spouse to inherit the earnings credits of the deceased spouse; or pay unreduced widow's benefits at age 50.

One proposal, made by former Commissioner of Social Security Robert Ball, would be to reduce the amount of the spouse's benefit from 50 percent to 33.3 percent of the worker's PIA and then increase the PIAs of all workers by 12.5 percent. Retired couples would receive the same amount as they do under current law, but widow(er)s would receive higher benefits since they would get 100 percent of the deceased worker's increased PIA. This would improve adequacy

Table 2
Average Annual Lifetime Earnings and Monthly 1987 Social Security Retirement and Survivor Benefits

	Allens	Boyles	Cohens	Dominicks
Earnings				
Husband	$24,000	$12,000	$16,000	$24,000
Wife	0	12,000	8,000	8,000
Total	24,000	24,000	24,000	32,000
Retirement Benefits				
Husband	797	499	606	797
Wife	398	499	393	398
Total	1,195	988	999	1,195
Survivor Benefits	797	499	606	797

Source: Edith U. Fierst and Nancy Duff Campbell (eds.), *Earnings Sharing in Social Security: A Model for Reform: Report of the Technical Committee on Earnings Sharing* (Washington, D.C.: Center for Women Policy Studies, 1988), Table A-1.3.1.2.3 and Table A-1.2.2.3, pp. 18, 19.

for single aged persons and surviving spouses who have low or no earnings credits. However, it would be detrimental to retired divorced homemakers since their current benefit of 50 percent is already considered inadequate. They would gain only after the death of the worker.

Employed Women and System Inequities

Inequities related to women workers have taken on increasing significance as the numbers of married women workers have increased. The retirement benefits of married women as paid workers largely duplicate their benefits as dependent spouses. An employed wife receives her own benefit and in addition, if her spouse's benefit is in excess of her own, she receives the difference between the two. For practical purposes she receives either her own retirement benefit or half her husband's benefit, whichever is greater. She doesn't get both, and thus her benefit may be the same as if she had never paid Social Security taxes on her earnings.[36]

The upshot of this inequity is that different benefit amounts may be paid to married couples with the same total average earnings. Under the present system, a couple composed of two retired workers can receive lower total benefits than a couple with the same lifetime earnings credits all earned by one spouse. Consider the hypothetical couples represented in Table 2. Clearly the Allens are much better off than the Boyles, who nevertheless had the same combined earnings. Moreover, the Dominicks, who in fact had higher earnings than the

Allens, make out no better than the Allens, since wife Allen was entitled to a full spouse's benefit and wife Dominick was not entitled to *both* her own benefit as a worker and the spouse's benefit; her employment did not add to the couple's Social Security retirement income, even though the couple technically has accrued more earnings credits and paid more Social Security taxes.

The same inequity occurs with survivor's benefits. Different benefit amounts may be paid to the survivors of married couples with the same total average earnings. Assuming the same average lifetime earnings credits, the survivor's benefit is highest when one spouse had all the earnings and lowest when a couple's earnings were divided equally. For retirees and survivors, the traditional couple, with housewife at home, is favored.

Some persons see this inequity as unimportant. Sylvester Schieber states, for example, that "it is only relative to non-wage-earning spouses that wage-earning women are disadvantaged." He points out that only 8.2 percent of all benefits paid to retired workers and dependents in 1970 were spouse benefits.[37] Moreover, it has been estimated that by the year 2030 most women will be entitled to their own benefits as workers and just 5 percent of women will be totally dependent on their spouses' benefits for retirement income.[38] Admittedly the problems of women in the system have more to do with their average labor force wages and their patterns of employment than the inequities related to spousal and worker's benefits. The fact remains, however, that the system is designed to reward economic dependency of one spouse upon another and in effect to disregard certain women's earnings in the calculation of retirement and survivor benefits. For men's low wages, the system compensates with a weighting factor. Instead of compensating for women's low wages, the system is set up to disregard them.

Single versus Married Workers

There are inequities as well between single and married wage earners. A single deceased worker without children or dependent parents leaves no benefits to be passed on after her or his death. Nor can the single retired worker receive an additional 50 percent of her or his retirement benefit toward the support of a partner or relative other than an elderly parent or a minor child.[39] Thus the institutions of marriage and parenthood are the only officially recognized familial support mechanisms. The requirement that single persons subsidize the married was purposeful. Abramovitz quotes the Advisory Council on Social Security as redesigning the benefit formula so as to "reduce the eventual benefits, but not the taxes payable, to individuals as single annuitants."[40] (Not surprisingly, most women workers at the time were single.) The inclusion of other relatives as eligible dependents was dismissed as administratively unfeasible.[41]

The debate on this issue has not been great, probably because most people marry and few quarrel with provisions that benefit children. Many of those left out, however, are also in need. It is not uncommon for persons to support dependents other than spouses and children, especially in low-income communities. In addition single gay men and lesbians have no mechanism for using dependent and survivor benefits for lovers and friends. Single wage earners significantly subsidize the retirement and survivor's benefits of all married persons and their families, including generous benefits for nonemployed spouses as well as children.[42] The needs of nontraditional family groups have purposely been excluded.

Recent Changes in the Law

The Omnibus Budget Reconciliation Act (OBRA) of 1981 made several changes in OASDI, two of which made the system even less responsive to women. The first involved the minimum benefit, which was an amount paid to covered workers, dependents, and survivors when the benefit formula would otherwise indicate a lower amount based on the worker's wages and employment history. In other words, there was a floor in the system. In 1977, Congress froze the minimum benefit at $122. This essentially introduced a phaseout, as earnings and benefits would rise over time. The Reagan administration proposed eliminating the minimum benefit entirely for current and future beneficiaries. Congress passed these changes but later restored the minimum benefit to current beneficiaries in response to a storm of protest. The decision to eliminate this benefit for new beneficiaries will affect 100,000 persons who would have been eligible in 1982, and presumably thousands of others since then.[43]

Those most affected by this change are those whom the minimum benefit was intended to help, persons in long-term, low-paying employment or intermittent or part-time employment who rely on Social Security as their major source of retirement income. Because women are much more likely to have had this experience, the sex-blind system has been altered in a way that is especially harmful to women.[44]

Another important change made through OBRA discontinued benefits for caretakers of child beneficiaries when the child reaches age 16, rather than 18, as in the previous law. For widows this in essence lengthens the widow's gap for two additional years. By 1984, approximately 200,000 previously entitled persons were deprived of this benefit.

Also under OBRA, benefits for children between 18 and 22 who are full-time students in postsecondary school were eliminated through a rapid phasing out, as were benefits for elementary or secondary students beyond age 19. This imposed an additional burden on families. Thirty-two percent of these benefits previously went to families with incomes under $5,000, and almost two-thirds to children whose families' incomes were less than $15,000. About 800,000 students received these benefits in 1979; about 62 percent of these were children of deceased workers, and 22 percent were from minority families.[45] Thus, female-headed households were greatly impacted by this change. Widowed mothers are undoubtedly finding it harder if not impossible to send their children to college.

One change made in 1983 that will be particularly detrimental to women is the change in the retirement age, which is gradually being raised (two months a year) from 65; it will go to 66 in 2009, and will reach 67 by 2027. A worker's benefit will not be 100 percent of his or her maximum allowable benefit (PIA) unless he or she works until the full retirement age. Although persons will still be allowed to retire at age 62 (and benefit computations will still be averaged for earnings up to age 62), the actuarial benefit reduction for early retirement will be greater. Under the previous system a retiree at age 62 received a benefit approximately 80 percent of what she or he would have received at 65 (80 percent of the PIA); likewise the spouse's benefit was 37.5 percent (of the PIA) at 62 and 50 percent at 65. Under the new law the percentage of the full benefit that will be paid to retiring workers at age 62 will drop gradually to 70 percent in 2022. Workers retiring at age 65 in that year and thereafter will receive only 86.66 percent of their PIA.[46] This change is expected to affect many people. Currently 63 percent of all benefits paid to men and 72 percent to women have been actuarially reduced.[47] Since a higher proportion of women workers retire before age 65 (half of all women compared with one-third of all men), this change will affect proportionately more women than men. Furthermore, it may be difficult for women to modify their retirement decision to accommodate to the law, since 75 percent of early retirees retire early due to health or employment problems. Displaced homemakers in particular, who are often just getting by while waiting for their eligibility to begin, will face even lower benefits than before.[48]

Two other important changes that were made in 1983 to bolster the financial health of the system were a one-time delay in the cost-of-living adjustment for six months and the taxing of 50 percent of benefits if the adjusted gross income is $25,000 or more for single individuals or $32,000 or more for couples. As benefits rise, more and more persons will be taxed on half their benefits. Sheila Zedlewski has pointed out that the long-run financial burden of these changes and the rise in the retirement age will fall for the most part on the elderly population. The long-run projected distributional effects of all of the 1983 amendments for beneficiaries aged 62–69 in 2030, the first cohort experiencing the full effects of the changes, are calculated to mean an 8 to 9 percent drop in income for low-income persons. The hardest hit are unmarried women, followed by unmarried men; the least affected are married couples.[49] Changes made in 1983 to benefit women included indexing (updating) the calculation of wages of workers who died leaving young widows. This corrected an inequity whereby widows who became eligible for benefits years after their husbands' deaths were awarded benefits based on outdated wages. The new law also permitted divorced spouses to receive spouses' retirement benefits whether or not the spouse has actually retired; previously she had to wait until her ex-husband actually retired, even if he had reached retirement age. The law also continued benefits to disabled and divorced widow(er)s who have remarried, a provision already available to widow(er)s.[50]

STRUCTURAL REFORM

A proposal that would restructure the system in the direction of alleviating the problems for women is called earnings-sharing. It is based on the premise that both partners in a marriage form an economic as well as a social unit, with each contributing equally. Under the simplest plan, each partner would accrue earnings credits based on one-half of the combined earnings of the couple, and the credits could be divided yearly, at divorce, when one spouse becomes disabled, or when either spouse reaches age 62. It would give women a "portable earnings record" as homemakers and paid workers and offer better protection to divorced and widowed spouses. Several versions of earnings-sharing have been proposed, with transitional provisions to protect persons who would otherwise be greatly disadvantaged during the phase-in of the new plan, plus some suggested incremental measures to assure adequacy for the majority.[51]

A "Modified Earnings Sharing Plan" was devised by the Technical Committee on Earnings Sharing, a Washington-based group of women's advocates with considerable expertise in Social Security and pension issues. Their comprehensive reform package includes a transition plan from the current system, a basic earnings sharing model, and several other rule changes. The plan includes a 24-month survivor's adjustment benefit for widow(er)s; provisions for adequate disability benefits for both spouses; caretaker benefits not only for survivors caring for children but for spouses caring for their disabled spouses; and child caring credits for very low earners.[52]

The Technical Committee plan was tested in a simulation model by the Urban Institute. Their plan would increase adequacy for women and men at the lowest income levels, including increasing benefits for more than one-third of minority women.[53] One-earner couples, declining in numbers, would receive lower benefits than under current law. Likewise, divorced men would experience average decreases in benefits of about 9 percent. Some women, including about one-fourth of widows, for example, would also experience decreases in benefits in comparison with present law. For the most part, however, decreases would mainly fall on those with the highest income levels and increases would primarily benefit those at the lowest income levels.[54]

Another plan, combined with earnings-sharing, has been proposed by Dr. Martha Ozawa. Her plan focuses on the fact that under current conditions a retiree's benefit consists of much more than past contributions plus interest.[55] For the most part, future beneficiaries will also receive more in benefits than they could reasonably expect if they had the money for personal investment, although the rate of return will not be as high as for those who are retiring today.[56] The additional amount results from the benefit formulae that take adequacy into account, such as indexing wages and raising benefits according to the consumer price index. Ozawa refers to this addition as a subsidy. Since the subsidy is a transfer presumably in the service of adequacy, she asks why these subsidies should be proportionate to prior earnings. This, she says, is like giving the highest scholarships to children of families with the highest income.[57] For example, for workers retiring at age 65 in 1982, a maximum earner, married male worker with a dependent spouse, received a subsidy of $828 per month. A minimum earner, also married with a dependent spouse, received a subsidy of only $472 per month. These amounts are over and above what they received as a benefit based on past contributions plus interest.[58]

To remedy the anomaly of giving the highest benefits to those least in need, Ozawa proposes a double-decker plan. The first deck would consist of a flat amount to all elderly at the level of the poverty line and funded through general revenues. This would provide the same subsidy to everyone at age 65, achieving real equity regarding subsidies. The second-deck benefit would be directly tied to Social Security taxes plus interest with an earnings sharing component.

Ozawa's plan is very persuasive because it would provide both adequacy and equity in one stroke and also incorporate the goals of earnings sharing. Double-decker plans, however, are very unpopular. Many believe that funding any part of the system through general revenues will destroy the sense people have that they have earned their benefits. There is also the fear that the minimum benefit would eventually be means-tested, further destroying the universality and concomitant acceptance of the system as something for everyone. Double-decker plans have been proposed and rejected for as long as the system has been in operation.[59]

POLICY MAKERS AND WOMEN'S ISSUES

The 1979 Advisory Council on Social Security took up the issue of women for the first time, and endorsed a modified earnings-sharing plan that would include the division of earnings credits at divorce, inheritance of earnings credits by a surviving spouse, and a phase-out of dependents' and survivors' benefits for aged and disabled widows, widowers, and divorced spouses.[60] Nothing came of this endorsement. Since that time official interest in even a modified version has waned.

The 1981 report of the National Commission on Social Security included women's concerns but rejected earnings-sharing as a solution since it refused to support any plan that would reduce some person's benefits even while increasing them for others.[61] The Commission report highlighted the advantages Social Security has provided to women as spouses and low-wage workers and rather defensively mentioned that actuarial adjustments had never been made to reflect the fact that women live longer than men, an adjustment that would result in lower benefits for women.[62] Nevertheless the Commission recommended some incremental changes that would benefit women.

The National Commission on Social Security Reform, a bipartisan group convened in 1981 in order to recommend solutions to the deteriorating financial condition of the system, issued its final report in January 1983.[63] It recommended just a few incremental changes that would be of particular benefit to women, some of which were subsequently passed by the Congress, along with several changes geared to shoring up the financial solidity of the system and restoring the public's confidence in its survival. It was not primarily concerned with women's issues, however.

Since the late 1970s and early 1980s earnings-sharing has not been a hot issue in Congress. Representative Oakar and Senator Cranston generally introduce earnings-sharing bills each year, often included in a legislative package labeled the Economic Equity Act, an omnibus package of bills affecting women's economic well-being. However, Congress is lukewarm on the issue and women's advocacy organizations, while supporting the concept, are not concentrating on specific earnings-sharing proposals.

ANALYSIS

It should be evident that the Social Security system is quite complex and impossible to encompass in a few pages. Any and all reforms must be studied carefully for unexpected as well as intended consequences. The issue of cost is also of great concern, particularly as the size of the covered work force shrinks and the benefit population increases. However, commitment to change generally precedes serious efforts to deal with the barriers to change. This chapter has featured a variety of remedies available to deal with some of the issues involved, many of them incremental. These potential remedies are well known to persons who labor to improve the system. Notwithstanding this knowledge, there is a strong tendency to ignore women's issues and to continue to favor white men.

One might argue that the Social Security system should not be made to compensate for labor market practices that depress women's salaries, keep them in low-paying jobs, and deny them pensions. In the best of all possible worlds these inequitable practices will not exist. Certainly women's rights advocates must not stop pushing for reforms in the marketplace. We cannot expect, however, that reforms will happen overnight. The overall differential between men's and women's wages has held alarmingly constant over the years, in spite of new opportunities and the gains of individual women that are frequently cited in the press. Besides, two other considerations give credence to changing the system to accommodate to women's lives.

First, the system has from its beginning been designed to provide some compensation for differential treatment in the workplace. Weighted benefits are based on the fact that some people get paid less than others. To compensate, lower income people receive a benefit that represents a higher proportion of preretirement earnings than that received by those with higher incomes. Dependents' and survivors' benefits are another compensation for differences in market practices. Persons with dependent spouses or several children do not get paid more than single or childless persons. However, it is assumed that at the time of death, disability, or retirement, a larger total amount will be needed to provide for the worker's dependents, so such a provision has been made.

A second consideration giving credence to change the system is women's work at home as homemakers and mothers. Supposedly lauded in our society, women who stay home to care for the children and keep the houses of male breadwinners are not recognized as contributors to the family unit and workers in their own right, despite our capacity to estimate in economic terms what their labor is worth. They become eligible for dependent's benefits, a derogatory and misleading label for an adult benefit. Women's labor force participation does not bring them much more respect, and the Social Security system is reflective of society's estimation. Moreover, it is likely that women's work lives will continue to include homemaking and work force participation, and thus will not come to resemble men's work patterns. Recognizing women's work instead of their dependency would change the system considerably.

The treatment of older women in the social welfare system lends clarity to a feminist analysis because it is so clearly a continuation of the treatment they received in their younger years. With men, they are better off. Without them, they have few options. It matters little whether they were single parents or lifetime homemakers. Most older women are single, whether they be widowed, divorced, separated, or never married. In society they are not defined as mothers except in sentimental or derogatory ways. Under the Social Security system, married elderly couples fare best; and most older men are a part of these couples. In the final analysis, women without men are left with less than adequate incomes and supports, whether or not they have been married and raised children. Single elderly women face increasing poverty as they get older, and they have lower incomes and are at greater risk of impoverishment than single men.

Older women are controlled through meager incomes and oppressive societal images of aging women as unattractive and ineffectual except for such things as making pies and doting on grandchildren. They are often depicted as silly or petty people. Their work, undertaken at home or in the marketplace, is not publicly recognized. What they have accomplished in their lives, whether they have married and had children or not, is of little consequence in the structure of the system.

Shulamit Reinharz has noted that "the older, divorced, separated or widowed homemaker has no counterpart in the male world."[64] This is indeed true, but it is also true of women workers. In fact few, if any, women's work lives find counterparts in the male world, because women labor force workers are also homemakers and caretakers. Even never married women who have spent all their adult lives in the work world have had to do housework and compete with men who either had wives to do it for them or the money to purchase it. Until *men* change and do housework and child care, women's work lives will *never* resemble men's. If work force discrimination against women were to disappear tomorrow, and everything else stayed the same, many women would still be disadvantaged by having a double day of work. The ultimate reform would be to change the work world and men's work lives. If men were required to do the enormity of work expected of women, for example, the nation would have gone to a four-day work week long ago.

Short of revolutionizing the work world, an important reform would be simply to acknowledge and reward women's work lives as they are. Social Security denies them this dignity. The duplication of dependent's benefits and worker's benefits for married women with the restriction that they cannot collect both simultaneously denies the economic worth of the homemaker and trivializes the labor force participation of married women workers. But because women's work must seem trivial or nonexistent and their dependency emphasized, even naming women's work, particularly work at home, as labor worthy of note is profoundly threatening to patriarchy. The Social Security system functions to uphold patriarchal necessity in that women's work—that is, women's independent behavior—doesn't fit as well as their dependency on individual men. The best way to be economically comfortable is, as always, to be with a man. Since women outlive men, however, the outcome is especially cruel. Women who would never have chosen freely to be alone must live without their husbands and without adequate incomes; and remarriage is not an option for most.

Reforms of Social Security, particularly earnings-sharing, damage the image of the man provider and the woman dependent in the family. Earnings-sharing would confine the concept of dependency to children and would change the image of men's dominance. Being the higher earner in a couple would have little or no meaning for benefit purposes.[65] Women's work at home would be recognized as real work with economic worth to the household.

Two other potential effects of earnings-sharing are worthy of mention. In fact, divorced men would potentially lose money under earnings-sharing, particularly those whose spouses had no earnings. Like child support laws, this change would weaken men's control over their money and their autonomy of choice in leaving their wives. Men who had more control in marriage by virtue of their being the sole earners would lose the most. Conversely, the change would actually constitute an incentive for men to support women's increased earnings, since husbands would either benefit from their wives' earnings credits or stand to lose less the more their wives earned. Ironically, there would be an incentive for married couples to stay together. But the marriage from this perspective would not follow a patriarchal model. The trade-off for men would be a big price in patriarchal terms, including less opportunity for domination and control, and a blurring of sex roles.

Chapter 8 will address the impact of patriarchy on laws governing private pensions.

NOTES

1. Jessie Bernard, *The Female World* (New York: The Free Press, 1981), 151.

2. Sara E. Rix, *Older Women, The Economics of Aging* (Washington, D.C.: Women's Research and Education Institute, 1984), 2.

3. Bureau of the Census, *Poverty in the United States: 1986*, Current Population Reports, Consumer Income, Series P-60, No. 160 (Washington, D.C.: U.S. Government Printing Office, 1988), T. 11, 55–60.

4. The poverty rate for the general population in 1986 was 13.6 percent. For women over 65 it was 15.2 percent compared with 8.4 percent for men. For Black women over 65 it was 35.5 percent and for Black men it was 24.2 percent. See ibid.

5. Department of Health and Human Services, Social Security Administration, Office of Policy, Office of Research and Statistics, by Susan Grad. *Income of the Population 55 or Older, 1986* (Washington, D.C.: 1988) (SSA Publication No. 13-11871), T. 51, 97–98.

6. Ibid., 57, 59, 60.

7. Rix, 4.

8. Older Women's League, "Selected Data on Persons 65 and Over" (Washington, D. C.:Older Women's League, 1988.

9. *Income of the Population 55 or Older, 1986*, 84.

10. Rix, 9.

11. Mimi Abramovitz, *Regulating the Lives of Women: Social Welfare Policy from Colonial Times to the Present* (Boston: South End Press, 1988), 255.

12. Contrary to popular opinion, domestic service work, even when performed only weekly or biweekly, is not an excluded occupation if it pays more than a minimum amount per quarter. Employers and employees tend to avoid the payment of the Social Security tax for a variety of reasons, but in the long run it is quite detrimental to the worker. She not only loses out on retirement and survivor's benefits, but disability coverage as well.

13. This chapter refers to historical precedents and changes only insofar as they are related to present-day circumstances. Various changes in the Social Security system related to gender have been made over the years. Originally the system had several gender-specific rules, such as requiring husband survivors to prove their prior financial dependence on their deceased wage-earning wives. For a history of women's provisions in the system see Abramovitz, Chapter 8, "Old Age Insurance," 241–71. For more general historical summaries see Sylvester J. Schieber, *Social Security: Perspectives on Preserving the System* (Washington, D. C.: Employee Benefit Research Institute, 1982), Chapter I, "The Evolution of the Social Security Program," 7–44, and Robert M. Ball, "Social Security Across the Generations," in *Social Security and Economic Well-Being Across Generations*, ed. John R. Gist (Washington, D. C.: American Association of Retired Persons, 1988).

14. The payroll tax rate for employees and employers was 7.51 percent of wages up to $48,000 in 1989. This includes the tax for health insurance provisions as well as retirement, disability, and survivor's insurance. See House of Representatives, Committee on Ways and Means, *Background Material and Data on Programs within the Jurisdiction of the Committee on Ways and Means* , 1989 Edition (Washington, D.C.: U.S. Government Printing Office, 1989), T. 1, 67.

15. Today a worker who has worked his or her life at the minimum wage can expect a wage replacement from Social Security of a little more than 77 percent; for a couple it may be higher. For average earners the replacement rate is almost 43 percent and for high earners 24.4 percent. See *Background Material*, 14.

16. Schieber, 17.

17. Ibid., 18.

18. Ibid.

19. This rule is actually gender neutral in that it applies to higher and lower earner

spouses. To simplify matters and to indicate which spouse is affected in the preponderance of cases, I use the gendered terms husband and wife.

20. Protection against the loss of income due to the disability of the breadwinner was added in 1956. Health insurance for the elderly was added in 1965.

21. Department of Health, Education, and Welfare, *Report of the HEW Task Force on the Treatment of Women Under Social Security* (Washington, D.C.: DHEW, 1978), 5.

22. Martha N. Ozawa, *Income Maintenance and Work Incentives: Toward a Synthesis* (New York: Praeger Publishers, 1982), 141, citing Richard V. Burkhauser, "Earnings Sharing: Incremental and Fundamental Reform," paper delivered to the Conference on Social Security and the Changing Roles of Women, cosponsored by the Institute for Research on Poverty and the Women's Studies Research Center, University of Wisconsin, April 11–12, 1980.

23. House of Representatives, Committee on Ways and Means, Subcommittee on Social Security, *Report on Earnings Sharing Implementation Study*, 99th Congress, 1st Session WMCP: 99-4, (Washington, D.C.: U.S. Government Printing Office, 1985), 1.

24. It is estimated that this transition will have almost been completed by the year 2030, at which time most women will be entitled to their own Social Security benefit as workers. Just 5 percent will be solely dependent on their spouses' benefits for retirement income. See "Women's Equity Issues: Is Earnings Sharing the Answer?" in *Social Security: The Long View: Proceedings of a Conference Held June 20–21, 1983*, ed. Mary Gardiner Jones (College Park: Center for Business and Public Policy, College of Business and Management, University of Maryland, 1983), 115. However, because of their lower wages, many women will continue to be eligible for a partial spouses' benefit, or "dual entitlement." See Edith U. Fierst and Nancy Duff Campbell (eds.), *Earnings Sharing in Social Security: A Model for Reform: Report of the Technical Committee on Earnings Sharing* (Washington, D. C.: Center for Women Policy Studies, 1988), 21.

25. Marilyn R. Block, "Working Paper 3: Income Maintenance Concerns of Older Women" (College Park: National Policy Center on Women and Aging, University of Maryland, 1983), 21.

26. For a more complete discussion of the major issues regarding women's status and benefits in the Social Security system, see Fierst and Campbell; *Report on Earnings Sharing Implementation Study*; Dorothy C. Miller, "Social Security and the Changing Roles of Men and Women," *Washington Social Legislation Bulletin* 26, Issue 14 (July 1979); Richard V. Burkhauser and Karen C. Holden (eds), *A Challenge to Social Security: The Changing Roles of Women and Men in American Society* (New York: Academic Press, 1982); Department of Health, Education, and Welfare, *Social Security and the Changing Roles of Men and Women* (Washington, D. C.: DHEW, 1979); and *Report of the HEW Task Force*.

27. Rix, 26.

28. Fierst and Campbell, 21, 17.

29. Jones, 114–15.

30. More than one woman, therefore, may be entitled to retirement benefits based on one man's earnings record. For example, both the ex-wife and current wife of a man who divorced and remarried may each be entitled to 50 percent of his retirement benefit.

31. *Report on Earnings Sharing Implementation Study*, 8.

32. Ibid., 9.

33. Ibid., xi.

34. Fierst and Campbell, 19.

35. *Income of the Population 55 or Older, 1986*, T. 55, 105.

36. It should be noted, however, that married women workers earn disability coverage on their records as workers, something not available to them as homemakers.

37. Schieber, 253–54.

38. Jones, 115.

39. The elderly parent must have been financially dependent on the worker, however.

40. Abramovitz, 261, quoting Advisory Council on Social Security, *Final Report 1937–1938*, in *The Report of the Committee on Economic Security of 1935 and Other Basic Documents Relating to the Social Security Act*, 50th Anniversary Edition (Washington, D.C.: National Council on Social Welfare, 1985), 195.

41. Abramovitz, 262.

42. See Schieber, 251–52.

43. Estimate of the Social Security Administration (SSA), obtained through a conversation with an SSA official.

44. There remains a "special minimum benefit," which is not based on the worker's average earnings but instead on years of covered employment. This is designed to help those who have worked in covered employment over many years with especially low earnings. See *Background Material*, 5–6.

45. Abramovitz, p. 265.

46. *Background Material*, 12.

47. Ibid., 15.

48. See Dorothy C. Miller, "The 'Feminization' of Poverty: Women and Proposed Social Security Cuts," *Washington Social Legislation Bulletin* 27, Issue 16 (August 1981).

49. Sheila R. Zedlewski, "The Increasing Fiscal Burden on the Elderly," in Gist, *Social Security and Economic Well-Being*, 146–49.

50. Jules Berman, "The Social Security Act Amendments of 1983," *Washington Social Legislation Bulletin* 28, Issue 8 (April 1983).

51. The most comprehensive proposal and analysis of earnings sharing to date can be found in Fierst and Campbell. See also *Report on Earnings Sharing Implementation Study*. This study was actually carried out by staff of the Department of Health and Human Services. An analysis of this report was done by the Congressional Budget Office (CBO) and published as *Earnings Sharing Options for the Social Security System* (Washington, D.C.: Congressional Budget Office, January 1986). A summary and discussion of the HHS and CBO analyses can be found in Dorothy C. Miller, "Update on Earnings Sharing: Winners and Losers," *Washington Social Legislation Bulletin* 29, Issue 44 (October 1986).

52. Fierst and Campbell, 1–11.

53. Ibid., 49.

54. Ibid., 48.

55. Martha Ozawa, "Who Receives Subsidies through Social Security, and How Much?" *Social Work* 27, no. 2 (March 1982):129–34.

56. See Schieber, 28–32; and Robert M. Ball, "Social Security Across Generations," in Gist, 27. Schieber includes calculations made by Robert J. Myers that indicate that by the year 2000 for men and 2020 for women, single workers who are maximum earners will on average receive less than the total of their lifetime contributions plus interest. Ball observes, however, that such calculations are based on persons who always earn the maximum, are never unemployed, never marry or have children, do not die leaving

survivors, and never become disabled. Not only does this description refer to few persons, but the calculation contradicts the basic assumption of any insurance program, namely that it is impossible to know beforehand what one's life circumstances will be. Thus, social insurance provides against the *risk* of great hardship; the fortuitous avoidance of such hardship does not negate the *potential* worth of the protection. I agree with Ball.

57. Ozawa, "Who Receives Subsidies," 132.

58. Ibid., 131.

59. Schieber, 25.

60. *Report of the 1979 Advisory Council on Social Security*, reprinted by the Committee on Ways and Means, WMCP: 96–45, 96th Congress, 1st Session, 1980, 85.

61. *Social Security in America's Future: Final Report of the National Commission on Social Security, March, 1981* (Washington, D.C.: National Commission on Social Security, 1981), 230–31.

62. Ibid., 227. Neither, of course, has any adjustment ever been made to reflect the fact that whites live longer than Blacks do; this would result in lower benefits for whites or higher ones for Blacks.

63. *Report of the National Commission on Social Security Reform* (Washington, D.C.: U.S. Government Printing Office, 1983), 2–5. For a summary of this report, see Jules H. Berman, "The Report of the President's Commission on Social Security Reform," *Washington Social Legislation Bulletin* 28, Issue 3 (February 1983).

64. Shulamit Reinharz, "Friends or Foes: Gerontological and Feminist Theory," *Women's Studies International Forum* 9, no. 5 (1986):511.

65. The Technical Committee's Modified Earnings Sharing Plan does retain the concept of higher and lower earners for the purpose of ensuring adequate disability benefits. See Fierst and Campbell, 35.

8

Pensions

For men, they created retirement plans, medical benefits, profit sharing and gold watches. For women, they created Mother's Day.[1]

In 1987 tax breaks for employer-sponsored private pension plans cost the American taxpayer about $37 billion. The federal government has intervened significantly into a system that was originally designed to ensure employee loyalty to particular companies through deferred compensation. Created by and for the patriarchy, however, federal private pension regulations serve best the white masculine ruling class.

Private benefit systems and tax benefits are categories of benefits not usually ascribed to the social welfare system, yet they constitute an important contribution to the population's well-being at government expense. Richard Titmuss divided social welfare functions into three areas: fiscal welfare, occupational welfare, and social welfare.[2] The third, the social welfare system of direct transfers and social programs, has been the focus of most of this book. The government has increasingly become involved, however, with impacting the other systems to achieve broad social welfare goals. The occupational welfare system is the private system of employee benefits associated with one's employment. The use of the tax system, or fiscal welfare, has been a convenient way for the state to influence the occupational welfare system of employee benefits.

Private pensions were originally a mechanism by which an employer could obtain employee loyalty through deferred compensation paid at or after retirement. Now they are also driven by federal rules that help ensure fairness and adequacy of benefits for employees at all income levels and job tenure. This chapter will address the impact upon women of federal policy regarding private pensions.[3]

WOMEN AND PRIVATE PENSIONS

Women are less likely to receive private pensions and when they do, they receive lower benefits than men do. In 1986, 22.2 percent of white women received pension income, compared with 47 percent of white men. Among Blacks, 15.4 percent of the women received pensions compared with 28.2 percent of men. For Hispanic persons, the comparable figures were 7.1 percent of women and 28.1 percent for men. Average pension incomes for white men and women were, respectively, $7,506 and $4,390; for Black men and women, $5,102 and $4,496; and for Hispanic men and women, $5,594 and $2,925.[4]

In 1982 private pensions went to 33 percent of older married couples, 24 percent of nonmarried men, and just 13 percent of nonmarried women.[5] In 1983, 67 percent of two-earner couples were entitled to future private pension benefits, compared with 65 percent of one-earner couples in which the husband is employed. Two-earner couples are more likely to have this entitlement because they can be covered by one or two plans or both plans.[6] Among unmarried persons, 44 percent of men and women were entitled to future benefits from their own employers' plans.

Gender differences in pension coverage and provisions are related to several factors. Women predominate among low-wage workers who are less likely to be in jobs that provide pension coverage. Just 32 percent of workers earning less than $10,000 were covered by an employer-sponsored plan in 1983, compared with 82 percent of workers with incomes over $25,000.[7] When women are covered their pensions are lower. Also, a widow receiving pension benefits based on her husband's pension usually receives only one-half of the benefit the couple received when her husband was alive.[8] In addition to these factors, federal rules governing private pensions tend to favor men's work patterns.

U.S. PENSION POLICY

The Employee Retirement Income Security Act (ERISA) was passed in 1974 to set standards for the "qualification" of private pension plans. A "qualified plan" is one that adheres to all of the regulations of ERISA and the relevant tax code and therefore obtains numerous tax benefits for employers. ERISA includes parameters for literally all aspects of private pension plans, from funding to benefit distribution, providing needed protections for covered workers. Public policy has by no means been set on the many issues involved, however, and the public has a financial stake in an acceptable policy. Private pension plans represent a considerable tax shelter for employers; the cost to the American taxpayer was estimated at $37 billion in 1987.[9]

ERISA, like the retirement provisions of the Social Security Act, was designed to be most helpful to a white male work pattern: long-term employment in one job with little or no time out of the work force. Nevertheless, because ERISA came about after the new wave of the Women's Movement was under way, feminists were quick to examine it with a gender lens. Early in ERISA's inception, advocates for older women identified various ERISA provisions that left loopholes or caused disadvantages for women and they were successful in having several of them changed in the 1980s. Among the laws that have significantly changed ERISA's treatment of women are: the Tax Equity and Fiscal Responsibility Act (TEFRA) of 1982; the Retirement Equity Act (REA) of 1984; the Tax Reform Act (TRA) of 1986; and the Omnibus Budget Reconciliation Act of 1986.

A variety of types of pensions plans, sometimes differing for different types of employers or groups of employers, are allowable under ERISA. Plans can be "defined contribution plans," which guarantee a set contribution by the employer with a subsequent benefit based on the investment proceeds of the contributions; they do not guarantee a specific retirement benefit. Alternatively, "defined benefit plans" guarantee a specific pension amount determined by a formula and usually related to earnings. Some employers provide a combination of both defined contribution and defined benefit plans. Most plans are defined benefit plans.[10] In 1980, 60 percent of persons covered by pension plans (about 30 million) were in defined benefit plans; 26 percent (13 million) were in a defined benefit plan with at least one supplemental defined contribution plan; and 14 percent (7 million) were covered by defined contribution plans.[11]

ERISA RULES AND WOMEN

ERISA rules are extremely complex.[12] This chapter will discuss some of the major rules that affect women workers and proposed changes that are calculated to be helpful to women.

Minimum Participation and Vesting

Vesting is a nonforfeitable right to an accrued pension benefit achieved by putting in a requisite number of years of service (i.e., years on the job). If a worker leaves before becoming vested she or he is not entitled to a pension. Vesting is very important because it is possible to be covered by pension plans in all of one's jobs and still not be entitled to a pension upon retirement. In 1983, 59 percent of men were covered by a pension plan compared to almost 53 percent of women. Yet close to 50 percent of men were entitled to receive benefits at retirement compared with just 38 percent of women.[13] The difference between coverage and entitlement is vesting. Under a law just passed, plans may require gradual vesting over three to seven years of employment or a full five years of employment (called "cliff vesting") before one is fully vested.[14]

Since before this change, most employer-sponsored plans used ten-year cliff vesting, the likelihood is that five-year cliff vesting, rather than graduated vesting, will be adopted by most plans.[15]

There are two exceptions to the vesting rule. "Top-heavy plans," in which high wage earners predominate, are required to have minimum vesting schedules of two to six years or three-year cliff vesting. Small offices with one or two highly paid professionals and several clerical staff are most likely to have such plans.[16] Since women are highly likely to constitute the low-paid workers in establishments with top-heavy plans, they should benefit from this change in the law. The other exception to the vesting rule is for "multiemployer" plans, those negotiated by a union of workers in the same industry but with unrelated employers. They may require ten years of employment before one is completely vested.

"Participation" constitutes the number of years of one's employment for which pension benefit contributions have been made; this is called plan "enrollment." Under the law employers need not count the first year of service toward participation. The age of the employee may be considered, although the minimum ages were changed recently. Current law requires that years counted toward vesting begin at age 18 and participation years begin at age 21. An employee can take a job at age 18, become vested at age 23, and have two years of accrued benefits (the years between 21 and 23).

Before the Retirement Equity Act, employers could discount altogether the years before the age of 25. Since women have their highest labor market participation rate between the ages of 20 and 24, women's advocates urged the lowering of the age limits. The Employee Benefit Research Institute (EBRI) simulation model indicated that with the advent of REA, 583,000 more workers would be plan participants in 1985 and 295,000 would have met vesting standards. The coverage increase represents only 5.6 percent of the estimated 10.4 million private-sector workers aged 21 to 24 and the vesting increase constitutes just 3.1 percent of all young workers. The change did not affect the 10.5 percent of young workers who work less than half time or the 32.3 percent who are employed for less than a year. Notwithstanding these small proportions, however, most of those newly covered and/or vested are probably women.[17]

Breaks-in-Service

The "rule of parity" has held that "breaks-in-service" (interruptions to employment by participating nonvested workers) can incur a penalty. If the number of consecutive one-year breaks in service equals or exceeds five years, a plan will be allowed to discount years of service before the break in calculating participation and vesting. This provision was liberalized under REA to accommodate women, who are more likely to take consecutive years out of the labor force to care for children.

Another change made by REA allows unpaid absences related to pregnancy, birth, adoptive placement, or child care immediately after a birth or placement to be credited with up to 501 hours for purposes of determining whether a one-year break-in-service has occurred in computing participation and vesting. Benefits need not be accrued, however, for this unpaid time out.

Spouses and Widows

ERISA originally provided that pension plans that provide an annuity as the normal form of benefit must provide a Joint Survivor Annuity to married participants who reach normal retirement age under the plan. However, the participant, generally the husband, was allowed to waive the benefit without his spouse's knowledge. REA stipulated that the participant cannot waive the survivor benefit without the spouse's written consent, and broadened the definition of the types of plans that must provide a Joint and Survivor Annuity.

The General Accounting Office estimates that a maximum of 17 percent of widows of men workers who retired in 1982 could have benefited from the new provision, assuming of course that all of the couples in which the husband waived the survivor annuity would choose it under the new conditions.[18] Furthermore, those widows who would gain would not gain much; at the lowest income level the gain could be expected to increase retirement income by about 12 percent, less than $100 per month.[19] The GAO makes the additional point that men who have private pensions generally have higher incomes. As a result, even when they do not opt for the survivor annuity, their widows generally receive Social Security benefits that keep them above the poverty line.[20]

As a result of REA the law also provides that in the case of a vested participant who dies before the annuity starting date and who has a surviving spouse, a qualified Pre-Retirement Survivor Annuity (PSA) shall be provided to the surviving spouse. This provision as well cannot be waived by the participant without his spouse's written consent. EBRI predicts that the impact of this provision for widows will be "substantial."[21]

Divorce Proceedings

As a result of REA, the ERISA law provides for payment of benefits in accordance with the requirements of any qualified court order providing for child support, alimony payments, or marital property rights to a spouse, former spouse, child, or other dependent of a participant. Thus, the pension benefit is subject to court decisions regarding the division of property at the time of divorce as well as court-ordered personal support obligations of the participant.[22] This provision may be helpful to divorcing women.

Age

The OBRA of 1986 prohibited plans from excluding workers who start a job after age 60 and requires plans to continue giving pension credits to individuals working past age 65. These provisions will presumably be particularly helpful to displaced homemakers who are returning to the labor force and all low-wage workers who continue working past the usual retirement age. However, the provision will affect just a small proportion of the labor force.[23]

PROBLEMS OF CONCERN TO WOMEN

There is no question that ERISA has been helpful to workers in general, but there are significant gaps in the provisions that are specifically disadvantageous to women.

Integration

The law allows private pension plans to integrate with Social Security. A plan that is integrated with Social Security allows an employer to consider his contributions to the private pension plan and his Social Security taxes together in calculating the percentage of his employee's salary or wages that he contributes toward the employee's retirement. Thus if his contribution rate is at the Social Security tax rate the pension plan could accrue nothing for employees whose incomes are below the maximum taxable income for Social Security. The majority of women have earned incomes below this level. Likewise, the integrated plan calculates the employee's Social Security benefit as part of the total defined retirement and survivor's benefit. That is, a percentage of the employee's Social Security retirement benefit is subtracted from her or his private pension benefit. When a retiree's Social Security benefit is raised in response to an increase in the cost of living, her or his pension benefit is reduced. In this way, lower paid workers can be "integrated out" of a plan. About 55 percent of participants in large- and medium-sized firms are included in plans that are integrated. About 32 percent of production workers and 72 percent of white-collar workers are included in integrated plans.[24]

The reasoning behind integration is that employers are already paying Social Security taxes and the worker's benefit package derives from both Social Security and the employer's contributions to the worker's pension. Since lower paid workers receive a higher proportion of their preretirement earnings (a higher replacement rate) in Social Security benefits, the employer is compensating higher earners for this by providing similar replacement rates for all employees.[25] In this way no worker ends up receiving more in monthly retirement benefits than she or he did in wages. The reasoning is faulty, however.

Employers do not pay higher Social Security taxes for lower income employees. In fact employers pay higher taxes for the higher paid workers up to the taxable limit. It thus seems unfair for them to count Social Security benefits toward the pension benefit. Moreover, the weighting of benefit calculations for lower paid workers under Social Security is based on *need*. They receive benefits at a higher earnings replacement rate because it is estimated that they will need a higher proportion of previous income during retirement in order to meet expenses. Persons in the highest earner category still receive higher benefits and they have the opportunity to have more disposable income beyond basic subsistence. Private pension plans are not and have never been based on need and, indeed, integration works against the adequacy measure built into Social Security.

Integrating private plans with Social Security deprives lower wage workers of one of the commonly accepted private benefits of working and asks the American taxpayer to subsidize pensions for higher wage workers. Companies save money and can concentrate pension benefits on higher paid workers. Integration is a way to reward higher income employees without having to do likewise for lower paid workers.

Two changes have mitigated somewhat the effects of integration. TEFRA disallowed the use of integration in top-heavy plans. Likewise, the Tax Reform Act of 1986 limited the effects of integration by stipulating that no employee's pension benefit can be reduced by more than 50 percent because of receipt of Social Security benefits. This will be very helpful to women, who predominate among low-income wage earners, particularly in small offices, but integration will still impinge upon their pension benefits.

Survivor Annuities

Under Joint and Survivor Annuity plans, the retirement benefit may be halved when the participant dies but the amount cannot be changed if the spouse dies, a practice that disadvantages widows. Thus couples that opt for survivor benefits for widows can generally not expect the same survivor provision for wives as husbands.

Vesting Revisited

Women workers and men low-wage workers are likely to change jobs more frequently than higher wage workers and therefore are more likely to benefit from shorter vesting rules. Indeed, the change from ten-year to five-year vesting has been especially helpful to women workers.[26] Ironically, however, women who enter nontraditional employment, such as construction and trucking, are likely to be covered under union negotiated multiemployer plans and thus may be required to wait ten years before vesting.[27] Furthermore, even five-year vesting presents problems for some women, since half of women workers have less than four years on the job.[28] A study done by the Urban Institute for the National Senior Citizens Law Center indicates that three-year vesting would allow over 1 million more women to be collecting pension benefits by the year 2020.[29]

Job Tenure

Some firms have practices that reward employees increasingly according to their years of employment. ''Backloading'' is the practice of building into a pension plan a higher benefit accrual rate in an employee's later years in a company. While the degree to which a plan may provide for backloading is limited by ERISA, it is still considered a problem. This practice works against women and all those who do not stay in one job for a long time. It rewards those with a steady, noninterrupted, longevous work pattern, a decreasing phenomenon in the United States.

Another factor related to longevity on the job is the "fractional rule," which allows employers to reduce the pension benefits of workers who do not remain with the organization until retirement age. The formula rewards years worked closer to retirement age more favorably than years worked at younger ages. The rule reduces the monthly pension benefit by a worker's years of service divided by the number of years the worker would have worked if she or he stayed until the stipulated retirement age. For example, suppose the benefit formula is 1 percent per year of service. Jane Smith begins employment at age 25 and leaves for another job at age 40, with a salary of $30,000. She would expect to get a pension worth $30,000 $\times$ .01 $\times$ 15 = $4,500. Under the fractional rule, she will get $4,500 $\times$ 15/40 = $1,687.50. (Her years of service, 15, are divided by the years she would have worked if she had stayed to the retirement age of 65, 40 years.) Compare Suzanne Smith, who begins employment at age 40 and leaves the company at age 55. For comparison purposes, let us say that her salary upon leaving is the same as Jane Smith's, $30,000, and the benefit formula is the same. Suzanne doesn't get the full $4,500 either, but she does get $4,500 $\times$ 15/25 = $2,700. Even though she worked the same number of years and is subject to the same benefit formula, she is favored because the years counted are closer to the retirement age. The fractional rule applies not only when a worker leaves of her own accord, but also when the company's pension plan is terminated, or when a worker is terminated.[30] It could provide an incentive for employers to find ways to get their employees to leave before retirement age. The rule has been dubbed "outdated and unfair" for penalizing workers who leave before retirement age.[31]

Portability

Pension "portability" is the ability to carry over one's vested benefits from one job to another. Men and women are estimated to hold an average of ten to eleven jobs in a lifetime, having held four jobs already by age 24 and four more jobs over the following 15 years, with less "job hopping" with age. In their later years the pattern changes; many workers will attain as many as 19 years with one employer.[32]

With a few exceptions, portability does not exist for private pensions.[33] Finding a way to facilitate portability is important to the adequacy of retirement income for two reasons. First, left to their own devices, workers often spend their lump-sum pension disbursement when they leave a job. The development of Individual Retirement Accounts (IRAs) was supposed to facilitate portability, since there are tax advantages for rolling over these sums into IRA accounts. However, few have taken advantage of this. Second, pension plans favor those who stay with the same job over a long period of time. Two persons with the same salary or wage histories will have very different pension benefits when one stays covered by the same plan for her work life and the other vests with several pension plans. One study indicated that a worker who had four jobs, each lasting ten years and under different pension plans, would get about half the pension of another worker with the same wages who works at the same job under the same plan for 40 years.[34] This is sometimes called "job mobility loss." Since, when one leaves a job, the benefit is frozen, inflation erodes the purchasing power of the benefit amount. Women, whose life expectancy is about five years longer than men's, are more prone to this effect over time.[35] Also, one's benefit does not take into account future salary increases.[36] This loss is particularly detrimental to workers covered by defined benefit plans.[37]

REA changed the amount that defined benefit plans could provide as lump-sum payments to departing workers, from \$1,750 to \$3,500. For most young workers aged 21 to 24 the sums will be under this amount. Since more than 70 percent of all recipients of preretirement lump-sum distributions use these funds for consumption purposes, there was some question whether the effects of REA in strengthening retirement provisions, however small, would be eroded by this other change.[38] However, the Tax Reform Act changed the equation again by making it less desirable for individuals to cash out their lump-sum payments. TRA eliminated the ten-year income averaging option for personal income taxes and imposed a 10 percent penalty for lump sum payments that are *not* rolled over into an IRA. This is the same as the penalty for early withdrawals from an IRA.[39] This provision may provide an important incentive to private retirement savings.

Under defined contribution plans the impact of limited portability is less because one's final benefit is based on the market performance of an investment plan (rather than final earnings and years of service, for example). Thus, the funds invested continue to grow after the worker leaves and the benefit at retirement is less susceptible to the impact of inflation.[40] Encouraging the establishment of more defined contribution plans would allow for more convenience in any portability notion, but it would involve risk because the final benefit is not guaranteed and retirement planning would be hampered. Allowing beneficiaries to control the investment after leaving an employer, another option, would increase risk by placing the burden of investment judgment on the individual worker rather than the employer.[41] Those with the least knowledge or inclination could lose substantially and not realize it until the damage was done.

Coverage

Perhaps the most important issue involving women and private pensions is the issue of coverage. All other things being equal, women who are not covered by a pension plan cannot receive benefits. Women tend to be concentrated in jobs that do not provide pension benefits, in service industries and in small organizations and offices in which the employers are less likely to provide them. Small businesses, which have a pension coverage rate of 25 percent, employ 45 percent of all women.[42] Almost 46 percent of women work in low coverage industries compared with 34 percent of men.[43]

EBRI reports that 52 percent of the variation in coverage among workers can be explained by the degree of unionization at different firms and firm size. For example, fewer than 10 percent of workers in small firms (with fewer than 100 employees) are unionized. Yet among these unionized firms, 73 percent of the workers are covered by a pension plan, compared with 28 percent in nonunionized small firms.[44] Compared with men, women tend not to be in unions; 26 percent of women work under union contracts compared with 35 percent of men.[45]

The percentage of employed workers covered by pension plans is not expected to expand much in the future, particularly since the industries that tend to have higher coverage are declining and those with the lowest coverage are expanding. Thus, manufacturing employs a declining share of workers compared with retail and service industries.[46] The Department of Labor estimates that almost all of the net increase of 21 million jobs expected by the year 2000 will be in the service-producing sector. The occupation group with the greatest increase (5.4 million jobs) will be service workers, dominated by women employees and least likely to have pension plans.[47]

There are also ways in which women are excluded from pension plans even when they work for organizations that provide them. Although the TRA increased the percentage of firm employees that must be covered in qualified plans, from 56 percent to 70 percent, employers may exclude some employees by categories, such as "all secretaries" or "all casual workers," as long as enough workers at different salary levels are in the excluded group. (That is, the excluded category cannot simply consist of lower paid employees.)[48] In 1985, the coverage rate in nondurable goods manufacturing, for example, was 49 percent for women compared with 65 percent for men. A survey of industries showed that men had higher coverage in all of them with the exception of construction.[49]

Since spouses can be entitled to benefits under private pension plans, married couples have higher coverage rates than single persons. Two-earner couples, whose combined pension benefits can be derived from one or two sources, have a pension coverage rate of 68 percent, compared with 59 percent for one-earner couples in which the husband is the wage earner. Among unmarried persons, employed women's coverage is 53 percent compared with 47 percent for employed men.[50]

Another issue affecting women's coverage is the rule that a worker must put in 1,000 hours of service, or roughly half time work, per year in order for that year to count toward pension participation and vesting. There is some evidence that employers in the retail and service industries have been deliberately scheduling employees to work just under the 1,000-hour limit, so they can automatically be excluded from pension coverage.[51] Furthermore, persons who by intention work less than half time can be excluded regardless of other factors such as tenure with the company. In 1985, 16.7 million women workers aged 18 and over worked part-time, compared with 7.6 million men.[52] Since women are much more likely to work part-time than men, this restriction falls more heavily on them.

A very popular reform among advocates is the idea of reducing the hours of work requirement from 1,000 to 500 per year in order to help part-time workers, who are primarily women. A study by Sheila Zedlewski of the Urban Institute, however, indicated that this would not help many part-time workers. The reasons are that (1) only 18 percent of women workers are in this category; (2) only 39 percent of these workers are in jobs with pension coverage; (3) of those workers in jobs with pension coverage, 44 percent are already participating in their plans; (4) part-time work tends to be temporary for women, who later move into full-time jobs; and (5) some women who work 500-1,000 hours do not meet the other ERISA requirements, such as tenure and service requirements.[53] Nevertheless, this change could make a great deal of difference to some women's retirement resources.

A final issue regarding coverage is the fact that the decision to offer pensions to employees is a voluntary decision made by employers. Most small firms with fewer than 100 employees do not opt to provide pensions to their employees. If these small firms were to begin to offer pensions, great numbers of workers could receive coverage. Consider the following estimates from EBRI:

If firms with fewer than 100 workers were as likely to have a pension plan as firms with 100 to 500 workers, 7.6 million more employees would be covered; of these, 3.6 million would be vested....If firms with 100 to 500 employees were as likely to have a plan as firms with over 500 workers, there would be 2.2 million more covered workers and 837,000 more vested workers.[54]

ANALYSIS

The laws governing private pensions in the United States today are congruent with the concept of patriarchal necessity. Women have easily been excluded and the benefits of those included kept to a minimum. The types of occupations in which women workers find themselves are less likely to have pension plans. Furthermore, pension plan formulas are most likely to provide larger guaranteed benefits to highly compensated white male workers. The functional result of these outcomes is to ensure that women will receive less adequate pension income than that of men and to perpetuate the notion that women cannot make it on their own. Married women, safely within patriarchal control, have more access to pension coverage and entitlement. Married women are financially better off than all single women, whether they be divorced, widowed, or never married. Unmarried women as a specific group, however, do not seem to be quite as disadvantaged as they are in other areas of public policy. All Black and white women workers as well as men workers in low-paying occupations are disadvantaged. Yet the pay scales for women and occupational segregation by gender combine with the pension system to disadvantage women.

The recent positive changes for women in ERISA can lead one to conclude that the theoretical notion of patriarchal necessity is too pessimistic for what is happening in public policy in the real world. On the other hand, one can argue that it is possible to change and modify patriarchal institutions for women's benefit. ERISA is a new law and policy groups already concerned with the needs of the elderly and of women were in place when the law was passed. Because of the complex technical nature of the law, a variety of changes in it have been considered necessary, lending a window of opportunity for women's advocates to press for their particular interests. Nevertheless, the work world in general continues to restrict women's opportunities and wage levels and is hostile to women's needs. This circumstance limits the possibilities of pension reform for benefiting women. The assault on women workers is strong enough elsewhere to compensate for whatever gains women are making in the area of private pensions.

Hamstrung by the regressive tax base of the Social Security system, public policy encouragement of private pension systems has been another way to aid income adequacy for the elderly. But private pension benefits are even more tied to labor force compensation than Social Security and thus have been of limited help to women. Nevertheless, basic changes in ERISA as well as Social Security, notably attention to women's work and employment patterns, are an alternative to a comprehensive restructuring of the labor market and may be more obtainable in the short run.[55] Some recent changes in the law have been beneficial to women. A study by ICF Inc., commissioned by the American Association of Retired Persons, indicated that by 2020 the changes brought about by the Tax Reform Act will increase the number of women receiving pensions by 22 percent and their average pension payments by 33 percent. The number of persons receiving pensions will have increased by 16 percent and their pension benefits by 21 percent.[56] Yet more needs to be done.

Two basic changes that would help women considerably would be to disallow integration entirely and to require vesting after three years. Finding a way to make pensions more portable would also be of considerable help.

There is no lack of suggestions for increasing portability. ERISA could require "portability of service" (which exists in the Social Security system) by requiring final employers to consider years of service with other employers in determining pension benefits. It would be very costly.[57] Another idea is the "portability of pension credits" before vesting, also similar to Social Security.[58] A "portability of assets" reform would allow people to reinvest deferred vested benefits upon leaving a job. The Pension Rights Center estimates that such a change would result in women's collecting benefits over 18 percent higher in 2020.[59] Similar to allowing workers to roll over assets to their IRAs, this would "shift the investment risk from the plan to the individual.''[60] This is risky because not everyone is capable of making wise investment decisions. An alternative would be a federally operated "central clearing house" for cashed-out pension assets. This would transfer the responsibility to the federal government and lead to the political question of how to invest these funds (a debate currently going on with regard to Social Security trust funds).[61]

One of the biggest drawbacks of private pensions for all low-income workers is the fact that, unlike Social Security, they are generally not indexed, so that after retirement their value erodes over time. Some pension plans do provide some cost-of-living adjustments, but even when they do, they do not keep up with inflation.[62] Indexing could be required; the British pension system, for example, includes a type of indexing.[63] Requiring employers to index vested pension benefits with an average earnings index would reduce but not eliminate job mobility loss. The Congressional Budget Office estimates that such indexing would increase the liabilities of a typical plan by 10 to 20 percent.[64]

Suggestions for reforming the system are quite ambitious and tend not to make explicit the inherent assumption that employers will voluntarily continue to make the changes required to be qualified under ERISA. Currently pension plans are not increasing in the United States. As long as they are voluntary, one can assume that even fewer employers will opt to provide pension coverage (or, at least, ERISA plan coverage) if the cost of doing so is perceived as too much of a burden. Employers always have the option of constructing "unqualified" pension plans based on idiosyncratic formulae for some or all of their employees. This is a basic barrier to fundamental reform.

Portability of service and indexing would also result in employers' loss of influence over job turnover. Moreover, they would be unable to recoup investments in recruiting and training workers.[65] Keep in mind too that none of these reforms will help the majority of low-income workers, who are not covered by pension plans and cannot hope to be under a voluntary system.

Leaving pension saving up to the individual worker with federal tax help, which Individual Retirement Accounts do, is not realistic for low-income taxpayers either. A survey by the Investment Company Institute found that among persons without IRAs, 72 percent could not afford the contributions and only 22 percent already had pension coverage that they considered adequate.[66]

Private pensions are not going to help low-income persons without indexing and universal coverage, provisions against which one can predict employers would organize successfully. Some analysts have referred to a basic conflict between pensions as a mechanism of personnel management and pensions as a mechanism of social welfare policy.[67] They are both of course and will continue to be, but where the balance should be struck is crucial. As long as any plans are subsidized by tax revenues, the public has a right and responsibility to set fair standards for them.

Some analysts have proposed a "mandatory universal pension system."[68] It could be possible to require all firms to have qualified pension plans, in which all employees must be included, as a cost of doing business. Plans could vary in provisions from minimal coverage to very elaborate compensation so that businesses could still use their plans to compete for employees. Policy makers could remodel Social Security as well so that the provisions of both systems would be coordinated without canceling each other out. Short of this comprehensive reform, only small improvements for women can be expected.

Social Security and private pension systems together fail to serve women adequately because they are based on white masculine work patterns and tend to favor higher wage workers. In both systems, reforms that would be helpful to women have been dismissed as too costly and unrealistic. Having been marginalized in the marketplace, women are concomitantly marginalized in programs designed to help marketplace workers. Taken together, the two programs tend to reinforce the definition of women as marginal workers in the labor force, denying sex discrimination and the gendered division of labor that keep women in their place and prevent them from reaping the rewards of employment-related public policies. In this instance the demands of patriarchy, capitalism, and white supremacy coincide very well and serve as formidable barriers to change.

NOTES

1. Older Women's League, "The OWL Observer" (Washington, D.C.: OWL, 1985).

2. Richard Titmuss, "The Role of Redistribution in Social Policy," *Social Security Bulletin* 28 (June 1965): 14–20.

3. There are reportedly more than 30 federal retirement programs, plus various state and local public pension programs. These will not be addressed here. For information about women and public pensions, see Marilyn R. Block, "Working Paper 3: Income Maintenance Concerns of Older Women" (College Park: National Policy Center on Women and Aging, University of Maryland, 1983) 28–31.

4. Older Women's League, "Pension Data for Persons Age 65 and Over" (Washington, D.C.: Older Women's League, 1988).

5. Sara E. Rix, *Older Women: The Economics of Aging* (Washington, D.C.: Women's Research and Education Institute, 1984), 9.

6. Emily S. Andrews, *The Changing Profile of Pensions in America* (Washington, D.C.: Employee Benefit Research Institute, 1985), 68.

7. Ibid., 48.

8. National Senior Citizens Law Center, "Fact Sheet: Why Women Do Not Receive Pension Benefits" (Washington, D.C.: National Senior Citizens Law Center, 1988).

9. Anne Moss, "A Prospectus on Working Women's Concerns, H.R. 2577—The Economic Equity Act," Statement of the Pension Rights Center Before the Subcommittee on Employment Opportunities, House Committee on Education and Labor, July 22, 1987 (Washington, D.C.: Pension Rights Center, 1987).

10. Andrews, 9.

11. "Pension Portability and Preservation: Issues and Proposals," Statement of Joseph F. Delfico, Senior Associate Director, Human Resources Division, United States General Accounting Office, Before the Subcommittee on Oversight, Committee on Ways and

Means, House of Representatives, July 12, 1988, (Washington, D. C.: General Accounting Office, 1988), 5. (Hereafter cited as "Delfico.")

12. For more comprehensive information about ERISA, see Employee Benefit Research Institute, *Fundamentals of Employee Benefit Programs*, 3rd Edition (Washington, D.C.: EBRI, 1987); and Andrews.

13. Andrews, 62. These figures are for nonagricultural wage and salary workers.

14. "Partial vesting" means that one may be entitled to a reduced benefit at retirement.

15. Andrews, 58.

16. However, small offices tend not to have ERISA-qualified pensions plans for their employees at all.

17. Andrews, 74, 134–35. The simulation was for nonagricultural wage and salary workers and assumed that young workers would not change their employment patterns, such as seeking jobs with pension coverage, as a result of the law.

18. General Accounting Office, *Retirement Income: 1984 Pension Law Will Help Some Widows but Not the Poorest* (Washington, D.C.: General Accounting Office, 1988) (GAO/HRD-88-77), 26. See also Andrews, 139–41.

19. *1984 Pension Law*, 27.

20. Ibid., 27, 32.

21. Andrews, 143.

22. Noting that few women receive alimony but many more receive some property settlement, EBRI suggests that this provision will have greatest impact if pension benefits are treated as property rather than alimony. See Andrews, 146.

23. Ibid., 150–51.

24. Ibid., 43.

25. Ibid., 10.

26. Ibid., 156.

27. Anne Moss, "Statement of the Pension Rights Center before the House Ways and Means Committee Subcommittee on Oversight, on Pension Portability," July 12, 1988 (Washington, D.C.: Pension Rights Center, 1988), 3.

28. Ibid., 4. The median number of years on a job for men is 5.1 years, for women 3.7 years, (p. 2).

29. Ibid., 4.

30. Ruth Simon, "Look Before You Leave," *Forbes*, November 14, 1988. See also American Association of Retired Persons, *A Guide to Understanding Your Pension Plan* (Washington, D.C.: AARP, 1989).

31. Moss, "Statement," 5.

32. Andrews, 161, citing Robert E. Hall, "The Importance of Lifetime Jobs in the U.S. Economy," *American Economic Review*, September 1982: 716–24.

33. In 1985 about 6.3 million workers, 16 percent of private pension plan participants, were covered by multiemployer plans that provided some portability from job to job. There are also some "single employer" plans with reciprocity agreements, accounting for about 8 percent of all private single employer plans. See Delfico, 15.

34. Moss "Statement," 6.

35. Block, 26.

36. Delfico, 8–12.

37. Ibid., 8–14.

38. Andrews, 58, 138, 162–63.

39. Delfico, 17.

40. Ibid., 12.

41. Andrews, 164–65.

42. Vicki Gottlich, "Fact Sheet: Why Women Do Not Receive Pension Benefits" (Washington, D. C.: National Senior Citizens Law Center, 1988): 3n, quoting Census Bureau, *Pensions: Worker Coverage and Retirement Income, 1984* (Washington, D. C.: U. S. Government Printing Office, 1984): 5.

43. Andrews, 64.

44. Ibid., 50.

45. Ibid., 64.

46. Alicia H. Munnell, "The Private Pension System and its Role in Providing Economic Security," Statement before the National Commission on Social Security Reform, May 10, 1982, 4.

47. Women's Bureau, "Women and Workforce 2000," *Facts on U.S. Working Women* (Washington, D.C.: U. S. Department of Labor, 1988), Fact Sheet No. 88-1.

48. Moss, "Prospectus."

49. National Senior Citizens Law Center, "Coverage Issues in Women's Industries" (Washington, D.C.: National Senior Citizens Law Center, 1988), 2, citing Richard A. Ippolito and Walter W. Koldrubetz, *The Handbook of Pension Statistics* (Chicago: Commerce Clearing House, 1986): 95.

50. Andrews, 66–67.

51. Moss, "Prospectus."

52. Bureau of the Census, *Poverty in the United States: 1986*, Current Population Reports, Series P-60, No. 160 (Washington, D. C.: U.S. Government Printing Office, 1988), T. 10, 41–42.

53. Sheila Zedlewski, "Effects of a Reduction in the Hours of Work Pension Participation Requirement," paper prepared by the Urban Institute for the National Senior Citizens Law Center, 1988. This finding highlights the fact that pension legislation has often been debated and even changed in the absence of firm data indicating how many persons a change would affect.

54. Andrews, 166.

55. See Greg J. Duncan, *Years of Poverty: Years of Plenty: The Changing Economic Fortunes of American Workers and Their Families*. (Ann Arbor: University of Michigan, Institute for Social Research, 1984), 63.

56. C. A. Beier, Nancy Duff Campbell, and Ann Kolker, *The Tax Reform Act of 1986: The Return for Women* (Washington, D.C.: National Women's Law Center, 1988), 35.

57. Delfico, 20.

58. Block, 24.

59. Moss, "Statement," 8.

60. Delfico, 24.

61. Ibid., 26.

62. Munnell, 7.

63. Moss, "Prospectus."

64. Delfico, 21.

65. Ibid.

66. Beier, Campbell, and Kolker, 36.

67. Delfico, 27.

68. Munnell, 11–12.

9

Conclusion

There is nothing natural about the way life is structured sexually; it is a historical and political phenomenon. It reflects conscious organization and protection.[1]

Books on social welfare topics commonly conclude with a list of recommendations to remedy the ills and gaps in the system. Indeed, various suggestions for reform have been suggested in this book. There is no lack of suggestions as to how to change the social welfare system to better benefit women, children, and families. There are existing reform proposals that, if achieved, would alleviate poverty for all poor persons, regardless of family composition. Many have advocated a noncategorical guaranteed minimum income, a national health program for everyone, better housing, and universal social services including comprehensive child care.[2] Well-known proposals for Social Security and private pension reform were outlined in Chapters 7 and 8.

As proposals are developed beyond the suggestion state, however, and are prepared for legislative enactment, often their original goals become obscured. It is within the specific areas of design that biased assumptions and distortions in thinking tend to appear. The Work Incentive Program, for example, was a liberal program that failed through its design as well as from a lack of resources. Indeed, as proposals for reform get closer to the corridors of power and thus become more likely to be considered, policy analysts tend to make them more categorical, more specific, more punitive, less comprehensive, more cynical, more traditional. They become more functional to patriarchy, capitalism, and white supremacy.

The problem with the system is not that policy analysts and politicians don't know what to try next. Nor is it really the difficulty of reconciling competing conservative versus liberal ideologies. The problem is that the current system is for the most part functional for patriarchy, capitalism, and white supremacy. Thus there is no real incentive for the ruling class to change. Attempts to achieve change are blocked because of inherent cultural and institutional biases that often go unnoticed by many of the individuals who shape policies. Given this analysis, the best hope of achieving real change lies in changing the biases that block progress. Without examining these fundamental barriers to change and developing ways to break down these barriers, limited progress can be expected.

THE FUNCTIONAL STATUS QUO

Patriarchal necessity is the need among the collectivity of men to dominate and control women. It permeates all aspects of the state's relationship to the people, including the design and administration of its social welfare institutions. Women's place in society has been defined as under the control of men, preferably through the institution of marriage. The social welfare system, which has been constructed by the state to provide for citizen needs that cannot (or will not) be met by the marketplace, tends to serve a great number of women who are not attached to men. Social welfare policies that concern women express the dictates of patriarchal necessity, albeit sometimes superceded by the institutional influences of capitalism and white supremacy.

Under the dictates of patriarchal necessity, the only acceptable solution to most women's poverty is the "Cinderella Solution." Either the prince comes or Cinderella continues being Cinderella—poor, downtrodden, in a menial job, or dependent on the state. And often this works. In fact, the principal way that women escape from poverty is through marriage. The solution works best for white women, however, since Black women are less likely to remarry. But if the prince shows up and the family is still poor, the situation is ignored or the husband is blamed, since the financial status of the family becomes his problem and the woman is safely dependent upon a man.

Patriarchal necessity provides a conceptual explanation for the weakness in the welfare-to-work programs that are currently gearing up in the states. They are not really about achieving financial independence for women. They are about marginal welfare savings, an increase in the low-wage labor pool, and the public image of doing something about welfare.

Children have suffered greatly because of social welfare's treatment of women. Dependent by definition, they are no threat to patriarchy. Yet few ways have been found to support children without favoring their caretakers and contributing to the caretaker's independence. Patriarchy demands that women be defined as mothers and those who reject motherhood be at best considered unnatural.

Women are thus assigned motherhood but refused the resources to carry out its tasks unless they are within patriarchal control. Ironically this withholding of resources is fed by the romantic notion of mothers caring for children against all odds. We believe that mothers can do anything and mothers themselves come to expect that of themselves. When they can't they blame themselves and society does too.

Patriarchal necessity also explains why older women find themselves less protected by social welfare programs than men are. When the prince is gone, they are out of luck. Their poverty is minimized or ignored. Patriarchy expects older women to be taken care of, physically by female relatives and financially by male relatives. They are not afforded the same level of universally accepted support from the Social Security system that men can rely on. They are less likely than men to be able to look to the private pension system for additional resources in old age. Older women are to be either trivialized as little old ladies or romanticized as long-suffering mothers. Above all they should be quiet. Independent assertive older women are rendered invisible or a joke. A few older women have positions of class that enable them to demand respect. For most, the perpetuation of their dependency status and the disrespect and even contempt directed at them can be seen as a continuation of the treatment of women in youth and middle-age.[3]

CHANGES NEEDED

Fundamental change in the social welfare system with regard to women will not occur without basic changes in patriarchal institutional arrangements. It must first be recognized that the dualistic view of home versus marketplace is a false dichotomy. Both spheres are interdependent. Yet patriarchal institutions consistently create and promote a dichotomous view of the two. This socially constructed dichotomy must be demystified and eliminated. This would strike at the patriarchal system because it would reveal the real dependence men have on women and would elevate the status of the home as equally important and sometimes interrelated with the public sphere. It is a cliché to say that we fear the intrusion of the government and the marketplace into the sanctity of the home. In fact we fear the *opposite*. Because of the masculinist need for separation and control, much more profound is the fear of the intrusion of the home into the public arena.[4]

Recognizing the interdependence of home and workplace could lead to modifications in each that make it easier for people to exist and coordinate activities in both. A shorter work week, flextime hours, child care at the workplace, and liberal dependent-care-leave policies would be an acknowledgment that the workplace is dependent on home-like functions. Modifying home design and community resources would recognize that most adults are employed and away from home part of the day. Community and home design could be changed to meet the changing needs of families. Such things as adequate housing for persons in all income levels; inexpensive and convenient transportation to work, child care, and school; convenient opportunities for food buying and preparation; and convenient laundry facilities would help facilitate the integration of home and workplace. These changes would enable people to lead lives holistically instead of being forced to compartmentalize and distort one realm to meet the demands of the other.

Changes in Social Security could also help break down the conceptual barrier between marketplace and home. Social Security credits for adults providing dependent care at home—including care of partners, friends, and relatives outside of the traditional nuclear family—would affirm housekeeping and dependent care as the work that it is. It would also expand the notion of family beyond the patriarchal framework. Moreover, older women would have the opportunity to be as economically secure and independent as their men counterparts.

This fading of public and private distinctions must include the emergence of women as equal participants in the marketplace. They must not be relegated to a separate and inferior domain. Pay equity and new conceptions of motherhood and child caring would be the result of this change. For men the change would entail men's full participation in the home as well as ownership of the problems of both home and workplace. Until child care, for example, is seen as a societal rather than a woman's issue, it will not be fully recognized as a need.

According to Chodorow, this breakdown of barriers can be achieved through a change of socialization of girls and boys from birth. This can be accomplished if men begin to ''mother'' infants (See Chapter 1). While this solution is a partial one and somewhat problematic, its end—a breakdown in sex role stereotyping and masculinist dominance from early ages—is greatly needed. All people who raise children can help this cause, even if men cannot be persuaded to ''mother'' infants. It is not sufficient to raise girls to be more secure within themselves and more expansive about what they can accomplish in their lives. We must also raise our boys to be whole human beings. Boys must be encouraged to play with dolls—to exercise the nurturing part of themselves. They must also learn to share fundamental responsibility for household functions. We cannot expect men to be taught for their whole lives that it is unmanly for them to be involved with housework and child care and then expect them to turn around and do it willingly as an adult.

PRACTICAL IMMEDIATE SOLUTIONS

In the short run, the recognition of patriarchal barriers to reform can aid in understanding the most and least threatening of proposals to relieve poverty among woman-headed households. Joyce Gelb and Marian Lief Palley use the yard-stick of ''role change'' versus ''role equity'' for the measurement of how successful a particular public policy agenda will be in the legislative arena.[5] Role equity issues are proposals that extend to women rights that are enjoyed by other groups. They are narrow in their implications. Role change issues, in contrast, "appear to produce change in the dependent female role of wife, mother, and homemaker, holding out the potential of greater sexual freedom and independence in a variety of contexts."[6] This distinction is persuasive. A perception that a particular policy will change gender roles is certainly more threatening to the patriarchal system than one that seemingly follows the liberal tradition of giving everyone the same break. In reality, however, there are few policy changes that would effect role equity without having a profound influence on role change.

As Eisenstein demonstrates in her book, *The Radical Future of Liberal Feminism*, liberal reforms that seem to give women greater opportunities for equity simply make more obvious the larger barriers to change.[7] Women who have become employed and have ended up with the double day of employed work and housework have learned the hard way that without significant changes in men's and women's role behaviors and expectations it is impossible to achieve real equity. Legislators have also come to recognize the implications of seemingly innocuous liberal reform and have become suspicious of legislative proposals that purport only to promote role equity and eschew role change. An alternative yardstick for measuring the acceptability of proposed social legislation is the degree to which it threatens to oppose patriarchal necessity.

Income Support Measures

Income maintenance solutions to women's poverty are, in general, congruent with patriarchy, because they do not disrupt the status of women's economic dependency. However, the closer they get to providing adequate support with concomitant freedom for the women to spend the money as they see fit, the more threatening they are. Economic security, however obtained, affords an opportunity for comfortable living and autonomous action.

Child support enforcement measures present a catch-22 for patriarchal society. They promote the patriarchal family by obligating men to support their children. On the other hand, they interfere with men's economic autonomy and provide women with financial help without corresponding controls. In contrast, means-tested programs, such as AFDC, are laced with restrictive controls, demeaning requirements, and inadequate funds. It is not surprising that AFDC is the major income maintenance program for poor women in need.

Some analysts have called for higher welfare benefits for single-parent families. In the short run this would of course be helpful to their economic upkeep. However, it does not get them out of the trap of dependency and underclass status. Objecting broadly to any type of centralized social welfare program, Steven Wineman speaks of AFDC recipients as an example:

At best, raising benefit levels and eliminating the degradations of recipient status would elevate economically dependent mothers to the social situation of financially supported (middle-class) housewives, with the State playing the role of husband. Welfare mothers would still be dependent, economically and psychologically; would still lack options for paying jobs; would still be trapped at home, performing a package of socially devalued tasks. Of course, insisting that only work performed outside the home can be meaningful or dignified is yet another way of devaluing childrearing and house-work. What mothers (and fathers) need is a range of options which create possibilities for varying combinations of work performed in and out of the home, with both kinds of work valued as socially contributive. This requires social and economic arrangements which are beyond the reach of any version of welfare.[8]

Wineman recognizes that however beneficial raises in welfare payments may be to women and children in the short run, such payments are intrinsically demeaning. AFDC recipients are kept a dependent underclass, without power or status. Wineman's solution also goes to breaking down the artificial barriers between home and marketplace.

Family or children's allowances, provided in all industrialized countries except the United States, are frequently proposed as an income measure that would help families with children. Family allowances are universal payments made to families with children as part of the state's contribution to the well-being of the next generation. They differ from welfare because they are provided regardless of income and thus their receipt does not carry stigma. Payments are made per child and a progressive income tax mitigates against the expense of providing these payments without a means test. They have the function of reconciling family size and wage rates, and they recognize the state's responsibility to support the nation's future through its children.

The fact that arch conservative George Gilder approves of children's allowances is sufficient to make all feminists suspicious of such a measure. In his book, *Wealth and Poverty*, Gilder states that children's allowances have allowed France "to avoid the blight of dependency that afflicts the United States."[9] He ignores the fact that establishing children's allowances would simply shift women's dependency status to a less degrading form. In the short run, however, children's allowances would help single-parent families as well as all families with children. They would also be congruent with patriarchy and thus perhaps easier to get past the legislative process. Yet one would not expect high levels of support through this mechanism lest the benefit provide a disincentive for parents to labor force participation or a comfortable independence for single women parents.

Labor Force Participation Measures

It is important to recognize that most women seek ties to the labor force and that women's employment makes a difference in all families. Studies of AFDC recipients before 1981 (when employed women were essentially dropped from the welfare rolls) indicated that while on welfare, 40 percent of family heads had earnings and an additional 27 percent of others in the household (usually older children) also had income from work. Black women showed greater and longer labor force attachment than white women.[10] The problem is not labor force participation but the kind and duration of the jobs obtained.

An important social welfare provision, the Earned Income Tax Credit, is already in place and has been expanded recently. The EITC, like Social Security, represents an income support measure that is related to labor force participation. Calculated as a percentage of earned income, it is a refundable tax credit available to low-income workers with children. It is intended to encourage work force participation and offset the Social Security tax for low-income families. The provision was liberalized by the Tax Reform Act of 1986, which indexed the credit for inflation and extended the income limits. The maximum credit in 1989 was $910 for annual income levels between $6,810 and $10,240. The credit is phased out as income rises. In 1989 the credit was available to families with earned income up to $19,340. The income must be earned and the credit is available only to individuals or couples who maintain a household for a child. The number of children in the household is unrelated to the credit.[11]

The EITC is a good example of a type of beneficial legislation that is congruent with patriarchal and capitalist institutional arrangements. It supports the work ethic and is phased out gradually so as to retain an incentive for higher earnings. It essentially subsidizes employers. It is directed at better financial provision for children and since it is available to all families with children it does not favor one family form over another. This does not promote patriarchy but does not oppose it either. It promotes women's labor force participation but upholds their lower pay status by providing for their children in an alternative manner. Thus, further expansion of the EITC to alleviate poverty in woman-headed families would not face the patriarchal barriers that other reforms, such as pay equity, might.

Pay equity for women would ensure them equal pay for equal work and equal pay for work of comparable worth. Pay equity statutes would help to make sure that "women's jobs" paid as well as "men's jobs" that require similar skills. Nurses could be compensated as well as truck drivers. Pay equity legislation that assures pay equity in government jobs has been passed in some states. Pay equity for women and subsidized child care, both of which would promote women's independence and blur gender roles, are very threatening to patriarchy. There is no way to make them less threatening. Thus one might predict that pay equity and child care will be harder to obtain than income support provisions that at least maintain women's economic dependency.

It is not surprising that workfare and work training programs are the major labor force participation measures in place to aid women's poverty. As discussed in Chapter 4, the programs currently developing in this area are unlikely to help more than a few women. Pay equity, in contrast, is often ignored in official circles.

The social control factor in workfare should not be lost in the rhetoric about gainful employment. The case for social control of welfare recipients has best been made recently in the widely praised book, *Beyond Entitlement: The Social*

Obligations of Citizenship, by Lawrence M. Mead.[12] Mead criticizes the welfare system for providing benefits without expecting anything in return and thus, in his opinion, fostering the development of a population that rejects the social norm of gainful employment. Mead singles out just one population that receives social benefits (persons on welfare, particularly AFDC recipients), ignores all of this populations's work efforts as well as the barriers to job attainment, and assumes that job turnover is always the fault of the employees. He claims simply to favor work in exchange for wages or benefits, but he reveals himself in his preference for workfare, working off a welfare grant, to Public Service Employment, which is a real job in the public sector that pays real wages.[13] (The latter was a program eliminated when the Comprehensive Employment and Training Act was converted to the Job Training Partnership Act.) Mead's ode to work mystifies the patriarchal control functions of his proposals.

ISSUES OF RACE, ETHNICITY AND POVERTY

While both minority and white women are forced to cope with patriarchal institutions, Black, Hispanic, and other minority women are also oppressed by white supremacist mechanisms in social welfare institutions. When reforms are suggested, minority women's circumstances tend to be ignored or minimized, even when they are most in need. An example of this can be seen in recent discussions about the AFDC population.

Differences in the AFDC population are beginning to be distinguished along racial lines. There is a significant proportion of the AFDC population that can and is beginning to be termed "temporarily" poor, made up mainly of white women who became poor as a result of divorce. Because of inadequate or absent child support and their inability to support themselves, these women are plunged into poverty and go on welfare. They are likely to remarry or, because of their educational levels, to obtain jobs that are adequate enough to allow them to get off welfare. In contrast is a population of poor women on welfare, disproportionately Black, who became pregnant as teenagers and who have few skills and no high school diplomas. These women are least likely to remarry or to get off welfare as a result of jobs, although many do. They are sometimes referred to as the "underclass."

It has been proposed that a new form of social insurance should be introduced to tide over recently divorced persons with children (mostly women), while they set up new households and obtain jobs. It would institutionalize the need among the recently divorced for short-term financial help. The new benefit would eliminate their need to go on welfare and thus reduce stigma. This solution would serve to help those least in need. It would mainly help white women and could function to isolate Black women on welfare even further as an underclass of persons, the welfare mothers of stereotype. Such a solution should be avoided because of its potential to magnify and increase the opportunities for racial oppression, just as the establishment of the Supplemental Security Income program created social insurance for the poor elderly, blind, and disabled and left poor woman-headed families as the only recipients in the oppressive AFDC program.

In seeking solutions to the problems of poverty among women, one must also keep in mind that pay equity and child support would best help the most advantaged women. Child support from poor men will yield some, but in many cases insufficient, benefits. Pay equity will be helpful but will not achieve non-poverty status in all one-earner households. Many poor women, and particularly poor Black, Hispanic, and Native American women, will require additional strategies for the alleviation of poverty in their households. A feminist movement to end economic oppression of women must include all women.

EUROPEAN SOLUTIONS

Many European countries have established family policies that have increasingly focused on provisions that have as their goal societal equality for women and help for single-parent families.[14] These activities stand as a challenge to my theoretical premise that patriarchal necessity is a driving force in the social welfare system. Why would such resistance to reform exist in the United States and not in Europe? Are we not dealing simply with economic forces or cultural notions that will take a while to change but will evolve as they have in Europe? To answer these questions, it is well to examine why and how such policies have been promoted and implemented in Europe, and what has been their result.

Family policies related to women's labor force participation in Europe, particularly Sweden, France, and East Germany, were prompted by a declining birth rate and a desire to maximize the size of the current work force. The needs of the economy have driven these gender-related policies. European countries have therefore devised policies that make it "easier for women to have children and still be employed, or to withdraw from the labor force for as short a time as possible."[15] The policies have been helpful to women's dual roles as mothers and as workers and have eased women's double day, but they have not ushered in equality for women. Thus, while they are more progressive than U.S. policies they were not constructed primarily to achieve equality for women and indeed have not done so.

Even Sweden, a radical contrast to the United States, has not yet achieved equal status for women or paternal involvement in the home, in spite of public policies that have explicitly attempted to effect these changes. Women in Sweden, as elsewhere on the globe, earn less than men and are more likely to be in lower paying occupations. They are also more likely than men to work part time.[16] Few men have taken advantage of Sweden's liberal paid parental leave policy which requires employers to grant parental leave to fathers and mothers without penalty.[17] Michael Lamb and James Levine report that fewer than 10 percent of the eligible fathers took one day or more of parental leave in 1977. Those who took any time took very little. This was true across all income categories.[18]

It would seem, then, that the economic need for women workers in the labor force has overcome some patriarchal biases in Europe insofar as family policies are concerned. European countries also appear to have a stronger commitment to the care of children, as evidenced by their children's allowance provisions. However, women continue to earn less than men do, they are denied significant advancement in the work world, and they continue to be faced with the double day. Thus, patriarchal control is still existent. Europe's example indicates that patriarchy can be forced to adapt to opposing cultural and economic circumstances.

NEW MODELS OF POLICY ANALYSIS

New models of policy analysis and research would also help in changing social welfare policies that impact upon women's lives. Because of the development of very large data bases, social science methods in social policy have tended to concentrate on quantitative techniques in recent years. While analyses of nationally generated data over time have contributed greatly to our knowledge of the impact of social policies and programs on specific populations, these analyses are not sufficient for discovering all that needs to be known about people's experience with these programs. People's lives become obscured by the statistical data. Furthermore, the standpoint from which the data are gathered and analyzed tends to be dominated by a white masculinist ruling class perspective. This affects the questions asked and the interpretations of the answers.

Qualitative methods that include interviews of social welfare program participants will add depth and a different perspective to information gained from quantitative techniques. It may also help to inform social scientists of additional questions to be asked in construction of large data sets. Ways of using qualitative as well as quantitative methods in tandem need development and application. Not only survey data and conversations with women, but simulations of women's real life experiences should be systematically built into social research and policy analysis.[19] Simulated experiences of social welfare clients incorporated seriously and systematically into the process of policy analysis would broaden the scope of reality for policy analysts, providing help in conceptualizing problems from a client's perspective and facilitating creative and relevant policy alternatives. From these it is likely that previously unrecognized needs and solutions will emerge.

These new models of social research and policy analysis combine masculine and feminine world orientations. Incorporating qualitative processes of data collection would have the goal of grounding policy analysis to material reality. Together they should move policy analysts toward androgynous thinking by attempting to break down the false dichotomies of abstract principles and material life. The new models would reject the false assumption that there is any such thing as pure objectivity and would accept the inevitability of subjectivity. They would reject the dualistic notion of the private realm versus the public, recognizing the needs, demands, and importance to the individual of both realms, and their interdependence. They would begin and end with the individual and the family, relating analyses of larger systemic forces to the experiences of people affected by them.

Another avenue that must be pursued is the acknowledgment of the common experiences that women share in their relationship to the social welfare system throughout the life span. While it is important to recognize diversity among women and attend to differential perspectives and needs along race, class, and ethnic lines, in social welfare there is sometimes danger in conceptualizing policy that one designs for the ''other.'' Social welfare policy analysts have traditionally separated themselves categorically from the populations they purport to serve. Neither are feminists immune to convenient categorizations. Hence white middle-class women do not find a contradiction between their feminist pursuits and their exploitation of the women who clean their houses or take care of their children. Likewise, childless women unconsciously buy into stereotypes of motherhood. Differently abled women are categorized by their ''disability'' and their identities as women disregarded. Feminist younger women also have tended to objectify older women as role models without also seeing them as women like themselves. Vigorously seeking to know what diversity among women really means in terms of everyday experiences and needs, we must also seek and share with each other the experiences we have in common. We all have been social welfare clients or know personally women who are. Let us speak about our experiences. We must come to grips with the fact that in very important ways, ''they'' are ''us.''

NOTES

1. Zillah Eisenstein, *The Radical Future of Liberal Feminism* (Boston: Northeastern University Press, 1986), 224.

2. For example, see Winifred Bell, *Contemporary Social Welfare* (New York: Macmillan, 1983); and Harrell Rodgers, *The Cost of Social Neglect* (Armonk, NY: M. E. Sharpe, 1982).

3. For a discussion of the parallels between society's treatment of younger and older women, see Shulamit Reinharz, ''Friends or Foes: Gerontological and Feminist Theory,'' *Women's Studies International Forum* 9, no. 5 (1986): 503–14.

4. Evidence of this can be elicited at any time by taking children to a work setting and observing the reactions their presence evokes.

5. Joyce Gelb and Marian Lief Palley, *Women and Public Policies* (Princeton, NJ: Princeton University Press, 1982), 7.

6. Ibid., 8.

7. Eisenstein, 201–19.

8. Steven Wineman, *The Politics of Human Services: Radical Alternatives to the Welfare State* (Boston: South End Press, 1984), 42.

9. George Gilder, *Wealth and Poverty* (New York: Bantam Books, 1981), 153.

10. Mildred Rein, *Dilemmas of Welfare Policy: Why Work Strategies Haven't Worked* (New York: Praeger Publishers, 1982), 123–25.

11. House of Representatives, Committee on Ways and Means, *Background Material and Data on Programs within the Jurisdiction of the Committee on Ways and Means*, 1989 Edition (Washington, D.C.: U.S. Government Printing Office, 1989), 791.

12. Lawrence M. Mead, *Beyond Entitlement: The Social Obligations of Citizenship* (New York: The Free Press, 1986).

13. Ibid., 146.

14. See Sheila B. Kamerman and Alfred J. Kahn (eds.), *Family Policy: Government and Families in Fourteen Countries* (New York: Columbia University Press, 1978), 480; and Gilbert Y. Steiner, *The Futility of Family Policy* (Washington, D.C.: The Brookings Institution, 1981), 177–92.

15. Michael E. Lamb and James A. Levine, "The Swedish Parental Insurance Policy: An Experiment in Social Engineering," in *Fatherhood and Family Policy*, eds. Michael E. Lamb and Abraham Sagi (Hillsdale, NJ: Lawrence Erlbaum, 1983), 40.

16. Ibid., 48.

17. Ibid., 39.

18. Ibid., 45.

19. For a discussion of simulation in a feminist context, see Thelma McCormack, "Good Theory or Just Theory? Toward a Feminist Philosophy of Social Science," *Women's Studies International Quarterly* 4 (1981):4.

Selected Bibliography

Abramovitz, Mimi. *Regulating the Lives of Women: Social Welfare Policy from Colonial Times to the Present*. Boston: South End Press, 1988.

Alcoff, Linda. "Cultural Feminism versus Post-Structuralism: The Identity Crisis in Feminist Theory," *Signs* 13, no. 3 (Spring 1988): 405–36.

Amadiume, Ifi. *Male Daughters, Female Husbands: Gender and Sex in an African Society*. New York: Zed Books, 1987.

American Association of Retired Persons. *A Guide to Understanding Your Pension Plan*. Washington, D. C.: AARP, 1989.

Andrews, Emily S. *The Changing Profile of Pensions in America*. Washington, D. C.: Employee Benefit Research Institute, 1985.

Auspos, Patricia, George Cave, and David Long. *Maine: Final Report on the Training Opportunities in the Private Sector Program*. New York: Manpower Demonstration Research Corporation, 1988.

Axinn, June and Herman Levin. *Social Welfare: A History of the American Response to Need*. New York: Harper and Row, 1982.

Ball, Robert M. "Social Security Across the Generations." In *Social Security and Economic Well-Being Across Generations*, edited by John R. Gist. Washington, D. C.: American Association of Retired Persons, 1988.

———. *Social Security: Today and Tomorrow*. New York: Columbia University Press, 1978.

Bane, Mary Jo. "Household Composition and Poverty." In *Fighting Poverty: What Works and What Doesn't*, edited by Sheldon H. Danziger and Daniel H. Weinberg, 209–31. Cambridge, MA: Harvard University Press, 1986.

——— and David T. Ellwood. *The Dynamics of Dependence: The Routes to Self-Sufficiency*. Cambridge, MA: Urban Systems Research and Engineering, 1983.

Barnes, Roberta Otts. *The Distributional Effects of Alternative Child Care Proposals.* Washington, D. C.: The Urban Institute, 1988.

Bassi, Laurie J. and Orley Ashenfelter, "The Effect of Direct Job Creation and Training Programs on Low-Skilled Workers." In *Fighting Poverty: What Works and What Doesn't*, edited by Sheldon H. Danziger and Daniel H. Weinberg, 133–51. Cambridge, MA: Harvard University Press, 1986.

Beck, Rochelle. "Beyond the Stalemate in Child Care Public Policy." In *Day Care: Scientific and Social Policy Issues*, edited by Edward F. Zigler and Edmund W. Gordon, 307–37. Dover, MA: Auburn House Publishing Company, 1982.

Beier, C. A., Nancy Duff Campbell, and Ann Kolker. *The Tax Reform Act of 1986: The Return for Women.* Washington, D. C.: National Women's Law Center, 1988.

Bell, Winifred. *Aid to Dependent Children.* New York: Columbia University Press, 1965.

———. *Contemporary Social Welfare.* New York: Macmillan, 1983.

Bergmann, Barbara. *The Economic Emergence of Women.* New York: Basic Books, 1986.

Berman, Jules H. "The Report of the President's Commission on Social Security Reform." *Washington Social Legislation Bulletin* 28, Issue 3 (February 1983).

———. "The Social Security Act Amendments of 1983." *Washington Social Legislation Bulletin* 28, Issue 8 (April 1983).

Billingsley, Andrew and Jeanne M. Giovannoni. *Children of the Storm: Black Children and American Child Welfare.* New York: Harcourt Brace Jovanovich, 1972.

Block, Marilyn R. "Working Paper 3: Income Maintenance Concerns of Older Women." College Park: National Policy Center on Women and Aging, University of Maryland, 1983.

Boeckmann, Margaret. *Study of Barriers to Employment for WIN Mandatory Welfare Recipients.* Baltimore, Maryland Department of Human Resources, Office of Welfare Employment Policy, 1984.

Boris, Eileen and Peter Bardaglio. "The Transformation of Patriarchy: The Historic Role of the State." In *Families, Politics and Public Policy*, edited by Irene Diamond, 70–93. New York: Longman, 1983.

Brown, Carol. "Mothers, Fathers and Children: From Private to Public Patriarchy." In *Women and Revolution*, edited by Lydia Sargeant, 239–67. Boston: South End Press, 1981.

Brownmiller, Susan. *Against Our Will: Men, Women and Rape.* New York: Simon & Schuster, 1975.

Bunch, Charlotte. *Passionate Politics: Feminist Theory in Action.* (New York: St. Martin's Press, 1987).

Burkhauser, Richard V. and Karen C. Holden (eds.). *A Challenge to Social Security: The Changing Roles of Women and Men in American Society.* New York: Academic Press, 1982.

Cain, Glen G. and Douglas A. Wissoker. "Do Income Maintenance Programs Break Up Marriages? A Reevaluation of SIME-DIME." *Focus* (Institute for Research on Poverty, University of Wisconsin-Madison) 10, no. 4 (Winter 1987–88): 1–14.

Cassetty, Judith (ed.). *The Parental Child Support Obligation.* Lexington, MA: Lexington Books, 1983.

"Census Bureau Reports on Child Care Arrangements, Winter 1984–85." *Washington Social Legislation Bulletin* 30, Issue 12 (June 1987): 45–48.

Center for the Study of Social Policy. *The "Flip-Side" of Black Families Headed by*

Women: The Economic Status of Black Men. Washington, D. C.: The Center for the Study of Social Policy, 1984.

————. *Working Female-Headed Families in Poverty: Three Studies of Low-Income Families Affected by the AFDC Policy Changes of 1981*. Washington, D. C.: The Center for the Study of Social Policy, 1984.

"Changes in the Dependent Care Tax Programs." *Washington Social Legislation Bulletin* 30, Issue 47 (December 1988): 187.

"Child Support Assurance System: An Update." *Focus* (Institute for Research on Poverty, University of Wisconsin-Madison) 10, no. 3 (Fall 1987): 16–18.

Chilman, Catherine S. "Feminist Issues in Teenage Parenting." *Child Welfare* 64, no. 3 (May–June 1985): 225–34.

Chodorow, Nancy. *The Reproduction of Mothering: Psychoanalysis and the Sociology of Gender*. Berkeley: University of California Press, 1978.

Coll, Blanche D. *Perspectives in Public Welfare*. Washington, D. C.: U. S. Government Printing Office, 1973.

Collins, Raymond C. "Foster Care Rates: Trends and Implications." *Washington Social Legislation Bulletin* 30, Issue 16 (August 1987): 61–64.

Corbett, Tom. "Child Support Assurance: Wisconsin Demonstration." *Focus* (Institute for Research on Poverty, University of Wisconsin-Madison) 9, no. 1 (Spring 1986): 1–5.

Daly, Mary. *Gyn/ecology*. Boston: Beacon Press, 1978.

Danziger, Sheldon H. and Daniel H. Weinberg, eds. *Fighting Poverty: What Works and What Doesn't*. Cambridge, MA: Harvard University Press, 1986.

Diamond, Irene, ed. *Families, Politics, and Public Policy*. New York: Longman, 1983.

DuBois, Barbara. "Passionate Scholarship: Notes on Values, Knowing and Method in Feminist Social Science." In *Theories of Women's Studies*, edited by Gloria Bowles and Renate Duelli-Klein, 105–13. London: Routledge and Kegan Paul, 1983.

Duncan, Greg J. *Years of Poverty: Years of Plenty: The Changing Economic Fortunes of American Workers and Their Families*. Ann Arbor: University of Michigan, Institute for Social Research, 1984.

———— and Saul D. Hoffman. "The Use and Effects of Welfare: A Survey of Recent Evidence." *Social Service Review*, June 1988: 238–57.

Dworkin, Andrea. *Pornography: Men Possessing Women*. New York: Perigee/G. P. Putnam's Sons, 1981.

Eisenstein, Hester. *Contemporary Feminist Thought*. Boston: G. K. Hall, 1983.

Eisenstein, Zillah. *The Radical Future of Liberal Feminism*. Boston: Northeastern University Press, 1986.

Ellwood, David T. "Targeting 'Would-Be' Long-Term Recipients of AFDC." Princeton, NJ: Mathematica Policy Research, 1986.

———— and Mary Jo Bane. "The Impact of AFDC on Family Structure and Living Arrangements." Boston: Harvard University, 1985.

———— and Lawrence Summers. "Poverty in America: Is Welfare the Answer or the Problem?" In *Fighting Poverty: What Works and What Doesn't*, edited by Sheldon H. Danzinger and Daniel H. Weinberg. Cambridge, MA: Harvard University Press, 1986.

Employee Benefit Research Institute. *Fundamentals of Employee Benefit Programs*, 3rd edition. Washington, D. C.: EBRI, 1987.

Everett, Joyce. "Patterns and Implications of Child Support and Enforcement Practices for Children's Well-Being." Working Paper No. 128. Wellesley, MA: Wellesley College Center for Research on Women, 1984.

Fierst, Edith U. and Nancy Duff Campbell (eds.). *Earnings Sharing in Social Security: A Model for Reform: Report of the Technical Committee on Earnings Sharing.* Washington, D. C.: Center for Women Policy Studies, 1988.

Firestone, Shulamith. *The Dialectic of Sex.* New York: Wm. Morrow, 1970.

Flax, Jane. "Contemporary American Families: Decline or Transformation?" In *Families, Politics and Public Policy: A Feminist Dialogue on Women and the State,* edited by Irene Diamond, 21–40. New York: Longman, 1983.

Freeman, Richard B. and Harry J. Holzer (eds.). *The Black Youth Employment Crisis.* Chicago: The University of Chicago Press, 1986.

French, Marilyn. *Beyond Power: On Women, Men and Morals.* New York: Ballantine Books, 1985.

Friedan, Betty. *The Second Stage.* New York: Summit Books, 1981.

Friedlander, Daniel, Marjorie Erickson, Gayle Hamilton, and Virginia Knox. *West Virginia: The Demonstration of State Work/Welfare Initiatives: Final Report on the Community Work Experience Demonstrations.* New York: Manpower Demonstration Research Corporation, 1986.

―――, Stephen Freedman, Gayle Hamilton, and Janet Quint. *Illinois: Final Report on Job Search and Work Experience in Cook County.* New York: Manpower Demonstration Research Corporation, 1987.

―――, Gregory Hoerz, David Long, and Janet Quint. *Maryland: Final Report on the Employment Initiatives Evaluation.* New York: Manpower Demonstration Research Corporation, 1985.

Furstenberg, Frank F. et al. "The Life Course of Children of Divorce: Marital Disruption and Parental Contact." *American Sociological Review* 48 (October 1983): 656–68.

Garfinkel, Irwin. "The Evolution of Child Support Policy." *Focus* (Institute for Research on Poverty, University of Wisconsin-Madison) 11, no. 1 (Spring 1988): 11–16.

―――― and Sara S. McLanahan. *Single Mothers and Their Children: A New American Dilemma.* Washington, D. C.: The Urban Institute Press, 1986.

Gelb, Joyce and Marian Lief Palley. *Women and Public Policies.* Princeton, NJ: Princeton University Press, 1982.

Gilder, George. *Wealth and Poverty.* New York: Bantam Books, 1981.

Gilligan, Carol. *In a Different Voice: Psychological Theory and Women's Development.* Cambridge, MA: Harvard University Press, 1982.

Gist, John R. (ed.). *Social Security and Economic Well-Being Across Generations.* Washington, D. C.: American Association of Retired Persons, 1988.

Goldman, Barbara, Daniel Friedlander, and David Long. *California: Final Report on the San Diego Job Search and Work Experience Demonstration.* New York: Manpower Demonstration Research Corporation, 1986.

Goldstein, Joseph, Anna Freud and Albert J. Solnit. *Before the Best Interests of the Child.* New York: The Free Press, 1979.

――. *Beyond the Best Interests of the Child.* New York: The Free Press, 1973.

Goodwin, Leonard. *Do the Poor Want to Work?* Washington, D.C: The Brookings Institution, 1972.

Gough, Kathleen. "The Origin of the Family." In *Women: A Feminist Perspective*, 3rd edition, edited by Jo Freeman, 83–99. Palo Alto, CA: Mayfield, 1984.

Gould, Ketayun H. "A Minority-Feminist Perspective on Child Welfare Issues." *Child Welfare* 64, no. 3 (May–June 1985): 291–305.

Griffin, Susan. *Pornography and Silence: Culture's Revenge Against Nature*. New York: Harper and Row, 1981.

Groeneveld, Lyle P., Michael T. Hannan, and Nancy B. Tuma. "Marital Stability." In *Final Report of the Seattle-Denver Income Maintenance Experiment, Volume 1. Design and Results*. Menlo Park, CA: SRI International, May 1983.

Gueron, Judith. *Reforming Welfare with Work. Occasional Paper Number Two*, Ford Foundation Project on Social Welfare and the American Future. New York: Ford Foundation, 1987.

————. *Work Initiatives for Welfare Recipients*. New York: Manpower Demonstration Research Corporation, 1986.

Hagan, Jan L. and George Hoshino. "Joint Custody of Children and AFDC Eligibility." *Social Service Review*, December 1985: 636–46.

Hartmann, Heidi. "The Unhappy Marriage of Marxism and Feminism." In *Women and Revolution*, edited by Lydia Sargeant, 1–41. Boston: South End Press, 1981.

Hartsock, Nancy C. M. *Money, Sex, and Power: Toward a Feminist Historical Materialism*. New York: Longman, 1983.

Haskins, Ron. "Child Support: A Father's View." In *Child Support: From Debt Collection to Social Policy*, edited by Alfred J. Kahn and Sheila B. Kamerman, 306–27. Newberry Park, CA: Sage Publications, 1988.

Hayes, Cheryl D. (ed.). *Making Policies for Children: A Study of the Federal Process*. Washington, D. C.: National Academy Press, 1982.

Hoffnung, Michelle. "Motherhood: Contemporary Conflict for Women." In *Women: A Feminist Perspective*, 3rd edition, edited by Jo Freeman, 124–38. Palo Alto, CA: Mayfield, 1984.

Hooks, Bell. *Ain't I a Woman: Black Women and Feminism*. Boston: South End Press, 1981.

————. *Feminist Theory: From Margin to Center*. Boston: South End Press, 1984.

————. *Talking Back: Thinking Feminist, Thinking Black*. Boston: South End Press, 1989.

Irigary, Luce. "When the Goods Get Together." In *New French Feminisms: An Anthology*, edited by Elaine Marks and Isabellede Courtrivon, 107–10. Amherst: University of Massachusetts Press, 1980.

Jencks, Christopher. "How Poor Are the Poor?" *The New York Review of Books*, May 9, 1985.

Joe, Tom. *Profiles of Families in Poverty: Effects of the FY 1983 Budget Proposals on the Poor*. Washington, D. C.: Center for the Study of Social Policy, 1982.

Jones, Mary Gardiner (ed.). *Social Security: The Long View: Proceedings of a Conference Held June 20–21, 1983*. College Park: Center for Business and Public Policy, College of Business and Management, University of Maryland, 1983.

Joseph, Gloria I. "The Incomplete Menage à Trois: Marxism, Feminism, and Racism." In *Women and Revolution*, edited by Lydia Sargeant, 91–107. Boston: South End Press, 1981.

———— and Jill Lewis. *Common Differences: Conflicts in Black and White Feminist Perspectives*. Boston: South End Press, 1981.

Kahn, Alfred J. and Sheila B. Kamerman. *Child Care: Facing the Hard Choices*. Dover, MA: Auburn House Publishing Company, 1987.

———. (eds.). *Child Support: From Debt Collection to Social Policy*. Newberry Park, CA: Sage Publications, 1988.

Kamerman, Sheila B. "Child Care Services: An Issue for Gender Equity and Women's Solidarity." *Child Welfare* 64, no. 3 (May–June 1985): 259–71.

———. *Parenting in an Unresponsive Society*. New York: The Free Press, 1980.

Kessler-Harris, Alice. *Out to Work: A History of Wage-Earning Women in the United States*. Oxford: Oxford University Press, 1982.

Knitzer, Jane and Mary Lee Allen. *Children Without Homes*. Washington, D. C.: Children's Defense Fund, 1978.

Krause, Harry D. "Reflections on Child Support." In *Child Support: From Debt Collection to Social Policy*, edited by Alfred J. Kahn and Sheila B. Kamerman, 227–50. Newberry Park, CA: Sage Publications, 1988.

Lamb, Michael E. and Abraham Sagi (eds.). *Fatherhood and Family Policy*. Hillsdale, NJ: Lawrence Erlbaum, 1983.

Land, Hilary. "Who Cares for the Family?" *Journal of Social Policy* 7, no. 3 (1978): 257–84.

Law, Sylvia. "Women, Work, Welfare, and the Preservation of Patriarchy," *University of Pennsylvania Law Review* 131, no. 6 (May 1983):1249–1339.

Leonard, Frances. *Divorce and Older Women*. Washington, D. C.: Older Women's League, 1987.

Lima, Lowell H. and Robert C. Harris. "The Child Support Enforcement Program in the United States." In *Child Support: From Debt Collection to Social Policy* edited by Alfred J. Kahn and Sheila B. Kamerman, 20–44. Newberry Park, CA: Sage Publications, 1988.

Linden, Barbara H. and Deborah C. Vincent. *Workfare in Theory and Practice*. Washington, D. C.: National Social Science and Law Center, 1982.

Lorde, Audre. *Sister Outsider*. Trumansburg, NY: The Crossing Press, 1984.

Mayer, Anna. *Day Care as a Social Instrument*. New York: Columbia University School of Social Work, 1965.

McCormack, Thelma. "Good Theory or Just Theory? Toward A Feminist Philosophy of Social Science." *Women's Studies International Quarterly* 4 (1981).

McIntosh, Mary. "The State and the Oppression of Women." In *Feminism and Materialism: Women and Modes of Production*, edited by Annette Kuhn and Ann Marie Wolpe, 254–90. London: Routledge and Kegan Paul, 1978.

Mead, Lawrence M. *Beyond Entitlement: The Social Obligations of Citizenship*. New York: The Free Press, 1986.

Meyer, Carol H. "A Feminist Perspective on Foster Family Care: A Redefinition of the Categories," *Child Welfare* 64, no. 3 (May–June 1985): 249–58.

Miller, Dorothy C. "The 'Feminization' of Poverty: Women and Proposed Social Security Cuts." *Washington Social Legislation Bulletin* 27, Issue 16 (August 1981).

———. *Helping the Strong: An Exploration of the Needs of Families Headed by Women*. Silver Spring, MD: National Association of Social Workers, 1987.

———. "Social Security and the Changing Roles of Men and Women." *Washington Social Legislation Bulletin* 26, Issue 14 (July 1979).

———. "Update on Earnings Sharing: Winners and Losers." *Washington Social Legislation Bulletin* 29, Issue 44 (October 1986).

Moore, Kristin A. and Martha A. Burt. *Private Crisis, Public Cost: Policy Perspectives on Teenage Childbearing*. Washington, D. C.: The Urban Institute Press, 1982.

Moss, Anne. "A Prospectus on Working Women's Concerns, H.R. 2577—The Economic Equity Act." Statement of the Pension Rights Center Before the Subcommittee on Employment Opportunities, House Committee on Education and Labor, July 22, 1987. Washington, D. C.: Pension Rights Center, 1987.

———. "Statement of the Pension Rights Center before the House Ways and Means Committee Subcommittee on Oversight, on Pension Portability," July 12, 1988. Washington, D. C.: Pension Rights Center, 1988.

Mulroy, Elizabeth A. (ed.). *Women as Single Parents: Confronting the Institutional Barriers in the Courts, the Workplace, and the Housing Market*. Dover, MA: Auburn House Publishing Company, 1988.

Munnell, Alicia H. "The Private Pension System and Its Role in Providing Economic Security." Statement before the National Commission on Social Security Reform, May 10, 1982.

Murray, Charles. *Losing Ground: American Social Policy 1950–1980*. New York: Basic Books, 1984.

National Commission on Social Security. *Social Security in America's Future: Final Report of the National Commission on Social Security, March, 1981*. Washington, D. C.: National Commission on Social Security, 1981.

National Commission on Social Security Reform. *Report of the National Commission on Social Security Reform*. Washington, D. C.: U. S. Government Printing Office, 1983.

National Commission on Working Women of Wider Opportunities for Women. "Women and the Vote—1988, A Fact Sheet." Washington, D. C.: Wider Opportunities for Women, 1988.

National Senior Citizens Law Center. "Coverage Issues in Women's Industries." Washington, D. C.: National Senior Citizens Law Center, 1988.

———. "Fact Sheet: Why Women Do Not Receive Pension Benefits." Washington, D. C.: National Senior Citizens Law Center, 1988.

Nelson, John R. "The Politics of Federal Day Care Regulations." In *Day Care: Scientific and Social Policy Issues*, edited by Edward F. Zigler and Edmund W. Gordon, 267–306. Dover, MA: Auburn House Publishing Company, 1982.

Newton, Margaret W. "Women and Pension Coverage." In *The American Woman 1988–89: A Status Report* edited by Sara E. Rix, 264–70. New York: W. W. Norton, 1988.

Norgren, Jill. "Child Care." In *Women: A Feminist Perspective*, 3rd edition, edited by Jo Freeman, 139–53. Palo Alto, CA: Mayfield, 1984.

Norwood, Janet L. *The Male-Female Earnings Gap: A Review of the Employment and Earnings Issue*. Report 673. Washington, D. C.: Bureau of Labor Statistics, 1982.

NOW Legal Defense and Education Fund. "Facts on Child Care." Washington, D. C.: NOW Legal Defense and Education Fund, 1988.

"October 1 Block Grant Rules Define Federal-State Transaction." *Washington Social Legislation Bulletin* 27, Issue 20 (October 1981): 77–78.

Older Women's League. "Pension Data for Persons Age 65 and Over." Washington, D. C.: Older Women's League, 1988.

———. "Selected Data on Persons 65 and Over." Washington, D. C.: Older Women's League, 1988.

Ozawa, Martha N. *Income Maintenance and Work Incentives: Toward a Synthesis.* New York: Praeger Publishers, 1982.

———. "Who Receives Subsidies through Social Security, and How Much?" *Social Work* 27, no. 2 (March 1982): 129–34.

Pearce, Diana. "The Feminization of Poverty: Women, Work and Welfare," *Urban and Social Change Review*, February 1978:28–36.

Piven, Frances Fox and Richard A. Cloward. *Poor People's Movements: Why They Succeed: How They Fail.* New York: Pantheon Books, 1977.

———. *Regulating the Poor: The Functions of Public Welfare.* (New York: Vintage Books, 1971).

Polikoff, Nancy D. "Gender and Child-Custody Determinations: Exploding the Myths." In *Politics and Public Policy: A Feminist Dialogue on Women and the State*, edited by Irene Diamond, 183–202. New York: Longman, 1983.

Potuchek, Jean L. "Who's Responsible for Supporting the Family? Employed Wives and the Breadwinner Role." Working Paper No. 186. Wellesley, MA: Wellesley College Center for Research on Women, 1988.

Quint, Janet C., Barbara S. Goldman, and Judith B. Gueron. *Arkansas: Interim Findings from the Arkansas WIN Demonstration Program.* New York: Manpower Demonstration Research Corporation, 1984.

Rein, Mildred. *Dilemmas of Welfare Policy: Why Work Strategies Haven't Worked.* New York: Praeger Publishers, 1982.

———. "Work in Welfare: Past Failures and Future Strategies." *Social Service Review* 56 (June 1982).

Reinharz, Shulamit. "Friends or Foes: Gerontological and Feminist Theory." *Women's Studies International Forum* 9, no. 5 (1986): 503–14.

Rich, Adrienne. "Compulsory Heterosexuality and Lesbian Existence." *Signs* 5, no. 4 (Summer, 1980): 631–60.

Rix, Sara E. *Older Women: The Economics of Aging.* Washington, D. C.: Women's Research and Education Institute, 1984.

——— (ed.). *The American Woman: 1988-89: A Status Report.* New York: W. W. Norton, 1988.

Rodgers, Harrell R., Jr. *The Cost of Social Neglect.* Armonk, NY: M. E. Sharpe, 1982.

———. *Poor Women, Poor Families: The Economic Plight of America's Female-Headed Households.* Armonk, NY: M. E. Sharpe, 1986.

Russ, Joanna. *How to Suppress Women's Writing.* Austin: University of Texas Press, 1983.

Rutter, Michael. "Social-Emotional Consequences of Day Care for Preschool Children." In *Day Care: Scientific and Social Policy Issues*, edited by Edward F. Zigler and Edmund W. Gordon, 3–32. Dover, MA: Auburn House Publishing Company, 1982.

Sanders, Jo. *Staying Poor: How the Job Training Partnership Act Fails Women.* Metuchen, NJ: The Scarecrow Press, 1988.

Sargeant, Lydia, ed. *Women and Revolution.* Boston: South End Press, 1981.

Sarri, Rosemary C. "Federal Policy Changes and the Feminization of Poverty." *Child Welfare* 64, no. 3 (May–June 1985):235–47.

Schafran, Lynn Hecht. "Gender Bias in the Courts." In *Women as Single Parents: Confronting the Institutional Barriers in the Courts, the Workplace, and the*

Housing Market, edited by Elizabeth A. Mulroy, 39–72. Dover, MA: Auburn House Publishing Company, 1988.

Schieber, Sylvester J. *Social Security: Perspectives on Preserving the System*. Washington, D. C.: Employee Benefit Research Institute, 1982.

Sebesta, Fred and Morton Sklar. *Hope or Hassle: A Study of New York City's Welfare-to-Work Initiatives for AFDC Recipients*. Rochester, NY: Statewide Youth Advocacy Inc., 1987.

Sidel, Ruth. *Women and Children Last: The Plight of Poor Women in Affluent America*. New York: Penguin Books, 1986.

Simon, Ruth. "Look Before You Leave." *Forbes*, November 14, 1988.

Smith, Dorothy. *The Everyday World as Problematic: A Feminist Sociology*. Boston: Northeastern University Press, 1987.

Sokoloff, Natalie J. *Between Money and Love: The Dialectic of Women's Home and Market Work*. New York: Praeger Publishers, 1980.

Steiner, Gilbert. *The Children's Cause*. Washington, D. C.: The Brookings Institution, 1976.

———. *The Futility of Family Policy*. Washington, D. C.: The Brookings Institution, 1981.

Thompson, Ross A. "The Father's Case in Child Custody Disputes: The Contributions of Psychological Research." In *Fatherhood and Family Policy*, edited by Michael E. Lamb and Abraham Sagi, 53–100. Hillsdale, NJ: Lawrence Erlbaum, 1983.

Titmuss, Richard. "The Role of Redistribution in Social Policy." *Social Security Bulletin* 28 (June 1965): 14–20.

U. S. Bureau of the Census. *Poverty in the United States:1986*. Current Population Reports, Series P-60, no. 160. Washington, D. C.: U. S. Government Printing Office, 1988.

U. S. Congress. Congressional Budget Office. *Earnings Sharing Options for the Social Security System*. Washington, D. C.: Congressional Budget Office, 1986.

———. House. 100th Congress. *Family Support Act of 1988: Conference Report*. Report 100-998.

———. House. Committee on Ways and Means. *Background Material and Data on Programs within the Jurisdiction of the Committee on Ways and Means*, 1989 Edition. Washington, D. C.: U. S. Government Printing Office, 1989.

———. House. Committee on Ways and Means. *Report of the 1979 Advisory Council on Social Security*. 96th Congress, 1st session WMCP: 96-45. Washington, D. C.: U. S. Government Printing Office, 1980.

———. House. Committee on Ways and Means, Subcommittee on Social Security. *Report on Earnings Sharing Implementation Study*. 99th Congress, 1st session WMCP: 99-4. Washington, D. C.: U. S. Government Printing Office, 1985.

U. S. Department of Health and Human Services. Family Support Administration, Office of Family Assistance, Division of Research, Evaluation and Statistics, State Data and Program Characteristics Branch. *Characteristics and Financial Circumstances of AFDC Recipients: 1986*. Washington, D. C.: DHHS.

———. Social Security Administration, Office of Policy, Office of Research and Statistics, by Susan Grad. *Income of the Population 55 or Older, 1986*. Washington, D. C.: 1988. SSA Publication no. 13-11871.

U. S. Department of Health, Education, and Welfare. *Report of the HEW Task Force on the Treatment of Women Under Social Security.* Washington, D. C.: DHEW, 1978.

————. *Social Security and the Changing Roles of Men and Women.* Washington, D. C.: DHEW, 1979.

U. S. Department of Labor. Women's Bureau. "Women and Workforce 2000: Facts on U. S. Working Women." Fact Sheet No. 88-1. Washington, D. C.: Women's Bureau, 1988.

U. S. General Accounting Office. *An Overview of the WIN Program: Its Objectives, Accomplishments, and Problems.* Washington, D. C.: GAO, 1982.

————. *Child Support: Need to Improve Efforts to Identify Fathers and Obtain Support Orders.* Washington, D. C.: GAO, 1987. GAO/HRD-87-37.

————. *Child Support: State Progress in Developing Automated Enforcement Systems.* Washington, D. C.: GAO, 1989. GAO/HRD-89-10FS.

————. *Child Support: States' Progress in Implementing the 1984 Amendments.* Washington, D. C.: GAO, 1986. GAO/HRD-87-11.

————. *Interstate Child Support: Case Data Limitations, Enforcement Problems, Views on Improvements Needed.* Washington, D. C.: GAO, 1989. GAO/HRD-89-25.

————. "Pension Portability and Preservation: Issues and Proposals." Statement of Joseph F. Delfico, Senior Associate Director, Human Resources Division, before the Subcommittee on Oversight, Committee on Ways and Means, House of Representatives, July 12, 1988. Washington, D. C.: GAO, 1988.

————. *Private Pensions: Portability and Preservation of Vested Pension Benefits.* Washington, D. C.: GAO, 1989. GAO/HRD-89-15BR.

————. "Problems GAO Identified in Work on Child Support Enforcement Program." Statement of Joseph F. Delfico, Senior Associate Director, Human Resources Division, before the Subcommittee on Public Assistance and Unemployment Compensation, Committee on Ways and Means, House of Representatives, February 23, 1988.

————. *Retirement Income: 1984 Pension Law Will Help Some Widows but Not the Poorest.* Washington, D. C.: GAO, 1988.

————. *Work and Welfare: Analysis of AFDC Employment Programs in Four States.* Washington, D. C.: GAO, 1988.

————. *Work and Welfare: Current AFDC Work Programs and Implications for Federal Policy.* Washington, D. C.: GAO, 1987.

Wallace, John and David Long. *GAIN: Planning and Early Implementation: California's Greater Avenues for Independence Program.* New York: Manpower Demonstration Research Corporation, 1987.

Walsh, Joan. "Take This Job or Shove It." *Mother Jones* 13, no. 7 (September 1988).

Weatherley, Richard A. "Teenage Parenthood and Poverty." In *Beyond Welfare*, edited by Harrell Rodgers, 114–34. Armonk, NY: M. E. Sharpe, 1988.

Weitzman, Lenore J. "Child Support: Myths and Reality." In *Child Support: From Debt Collection to Social Policy*, edited by Alfred J. Kahn and Sheila B. Kamerman, 251–76. Newberry Park, CA: Sage Publications, 1988.

————. *The Divorce Revolution: The Unexpected Social and Economic Consequences for Women and Children in America.* New York: The Free Press, 1985.

Wilson, William Julius. *The Truly Disadvantaged: The Inner City, the Underclass, and Public Policy.* Chicago: University of Chicago Press, 1987.

———— and Kathryn Neckerman. "Poverty and Family Structure: The Widening Gap

Between Evidence and Public Policy Issues." In *Fighting Poverty: What Works and What Doesn't*, edited by Sheldon H. Danziger and Daniel H. Weinberg. Cambridge, MA: Harvard University Press, 1986.

Wineman, Steven. *The Politics of Human Services: Radical Alternatives to the Welfare State*. Boston: South End Press, 1984.

Wolins, Martin. "The Gender Dilemma in Social Welfare: Who Cares for the Children?" In *Fatherhood and Family Policy*, edited by Michael E. Lamb and Abraham Sagi, 113–28. Hillsdale, NJ: Lawrence Erlbaum, 1983.

Zedlewski, Sheila. "Effects of a Reduction in the Hours of Work Pension Participation Requirement." Paper prepared by the Urban Institute for the National Senior Citizens Law Center. Washington, D. C.: National Senior Citizens Law Center, 1988.

———. "The Increasing Fiscal Burden on the Elderly." In *Security and Economic Well-Being Across Generations*, edited by John R. Gist, 137–65. Washington, D. C.: AARP, 1988.

Index

ABOUT THE AUTHOR

DOROTHY C. MILLER is Assistant Professor in the Center for Women's Studies, Wichita State University. She has spoken and written extensively on public policy issues concerning women, with articles published in such journals as *Affilia*, *Social Work*, *Social Service Review*, and the *Journal of Sociology and Social Welfare*. Her last major work was *Helping the Strong: An Exploration of the Needs of Families Headed by Women*, a national study sponsored and published by the National Association of Social Workers. Before entering academia she was a consultant for the Child Welfare League of America, where she served a year as Director of the Hecht Institute for State Child Welfare Planning. She has doctoral and master's degrees in Social Welfare from Columbia University and a bachelor's degree in English Literature from the University of Pennsylvania.